D1507659

Mixed Heritage

Also by Catherine Blakemore

Faraway Places: Your Source for Picture Books That Fly Children to 82 Countries
How Big is Your Class? Practical Tips for Teaching Small and Large Primary Grade Classes
A Public School of Your Own: Your Guide to Creating and Running a Charter School

Mixed Heritage

**Your Source for Books
for Children and Teens about
Persons and Families of Mixed Racial,
Ethnic, and/or Religious Heritage**

Catherine Blakemore

**Adams-Pomeroy Press
Albany, Wisconsin**

Published by: Adams-Pomeroy Press
P.O. Box 189
Albany, Wisconsin 53502

Printed in the United States of America
First Printing 2012

Cover by Robert Howard

Publisher's Cataloging-in-Publication
(Provided by Quality Books, Inc.)

Blakemore, Catherine.
   Mixed heritage : your source for books for children
and teens about persons and families of mixed racial,
ethnic, and/or religious heritage / Catherine Blakemore.
   p. cm.
   Includes bibliographical references and index.
   LCCN 2011916883
   ISBN-13: 978-0-9661009-9-0
   ISBN-10: 0-9661009-9-9

   1. Racially mixed people--Juvenile literature--
Bibliography. 2. Racially mixed children--Ethnic
identity--Juvenile literature--Bibliography.
3. Ethnicity in literature--Bibliography. 4. Religion--
Juvenile literature--Bibliography.   I. Title.

Z5118.E84B53 2012   016.3058
                           QBI11-600194

Contents

Acknowledgments

While attending the 2003 Reading the World Conference at the University of San Francisco, I realized the importance of juvenile books that present persons and families of mixed heritage. It was there that I decided to write this bibliography. I take full responsibility for its contents.

When I started to write *Mixed Heritage*, I had no idea of the magnitude of the undertaking. It was only with the assistance of the supportive and efficient staff of the Albertson Memorial Library in Albany, Wisconsin, that I was able to secure the many books that are included. My special thanks to Laurie Thill, Librarian Assistant, who throughout the years handled so many of my almost weekly interlibrary loan requests. I am also greatly indebted to Library Directors Jacci Baker, Hilary Bauman, and Ann Trow as well as to Library Assistants Tracy Anderson, Kara Blue, Adam Brunner, Trina Manthei, Chris Mauerman, Karla Neild, and Jennifer Riemer and to Library Pages Clare Koopmans and Jason Moore for their work in fulfilling my requests.

After the first draft of *Mixed Heritage* was completed, I submitted individual sections to Hilary Bauman, Elizabeth Blakemore, Nancy Blakslee, Gay Cuthill, Sharon Cybart, Sharon MacLaren, Carrie Marlette, Andrew Oliver, Laurie Thill, and Gail Van Hove. My thanks to each of them for volunteering their time to read through their sections, to note editorial errors, and to provide helpful comments and suggestions.

It is to Mary Brinkopf that I give my highest thanks. She spent hours accomplishing the prodigious task of twice reviewing the long manuscript. Once more, she provided exceptional editing, offered invaluable insights, and served as my sounding board.

I am also greatly indebted to cover designer Robert Howard and his expertise. Thank you.

Finally, I would like to express my thanks to the authors, including those covered here, who have written juvenile books about persons and families of mixed heritage. It through their writings that many children and teens find affirmation.

Introduction

Mixed Heritage is a guide to children's literature about persons and families of mixed racial, ethnic, and/or religious heritage. It is unique in that it identifies, classifies, and summarizes or describes more than 1,000 books, including those that present biographical information on some 250 individuals. The book's format and indexes facilitate book selection. Its intended audience is librarians, teachers, parents, and other adults who are in a position to help young people discover relevant books.

Goals

The primary goal of *Mixed Heritage* is to enable children and teenagers of mixed heritage or members of families of mixed heritage to find affirmation in literature which introduces them to persons like themselves, real and fictional, who experience or have experienced a wide variety of challenges, to the coping strategies they have used, and to the decisions they have made (or in some cases society has made) to identify with one or all of their heritages. Hopefully, these books will boost their readers' pride in themselves and provide them with useful insights as they shape their own paths.

It is also the purpose of *Mixed Heritage* to introduce young readers to books that promote their understanding and acceptance of those whose heritage differs from their own.

Coverage

Mixed Heritage differs from bibliographies covering children's books about individuals and families of dual culture or heritage in that it embraces only those persons and families whose heritage is also mixed. Many people of dual heritage are not of mixed heritage.

To clarify, with the exception of Native Americans, all citizens of the United States have come from other cultures, for either they or their ancestors have emigrated from another country. For example, children of immigrants from Japan live within both the Japanese and American cultures and Italian-Americans whose families have been in the United States for generations may still celebrate their Italian heritage. They live in two cultures and have two heritages (Japanese and American; Italian and American), but their heritages are not mixed. They are Americans whose ancestors all come from Japan or all come from Italy.

It is when those of different heritages marry, e.g., a Japanese-American marries an Italian-American, that they create a family of mixed heritage. If these couples have children, their children will be persons of mixed heritage. Likewise, families of mixed heritage are formed when a Native American marries an African-American, a Cherokee marries a Seminole, a Brazilian marries a Canadian, or a Catholic marries a Baptist.

Families that are of mixed heritage also occur when adults are responsible for the care of a child whose heritage differs from their own.

In some cases, the books focus on the effects of societal attitudes or actions on persons or families of mixed heritage or on the struggles to find one's identity. In other books the character's mixed heritage is merely mentioned, but is not discussed further. These books are also covered in this guide as children need to see themselves reflected in books.

Annotations

Each book's entry contains a bibliographic reference, a description or synopsis of the book, a designation of the age level of its intended audience, and a notation as to whether it is fiction or nonfiction. With the exception of books in the "General" chapter, it also includes information on the heritages of the families or persons it covers.

Age Levels

The bibliographical description or summary of each book includes one or more of the following designations: Pre-K, Primary, Intermediate, and Older. The ages and grade levels covered by each designation are listed below.

Pre-K:	Ages 2-6	Preschool-Kindergarten
Primary:	Ages 6-8	Grades 1-3
Intermediate:	Ages 8-12	Grades 3-6
Older:	Ages 12 & up	Grades 7-12

These categories provide general guidelines. The ages at which children will enjoy particular books depends on a number of factors, including their experience with books, whether they are reading or listening to the books, their vocabulary levels, their reading levels, their familiarity with the subject area, and their interest in the subject.

There are especially wide differences in the maturity and interests of readers in the Older category. In some cases the book annotations note that a book is appropriate for the oldest readers in this category and in other cases the content descriptions will provide guidance.

Fiction or Nonfiction

The annotated reference for each book notes whether it is fiction or nonfiction. For some books, and especially biographies written for younger children, the line between fiction and nonfiction may not be clearly defined and has been determined subjectively. Also, in *Mixed Heritage* poetry has usually been designated as fiction.

Heritages

In *Mixed Heritage* a person's identity is dependent on his/her country of birth. In some cases this may not correspond to the individual's citizenship as each country has its own citizenship laws regarding persons born within its boundaries.

Information on the heritage designations in each chapter is included in each chapter's introduction.

Organization

Mixed Heritage is organized into seven chapters: "General;" "Persons of Mixed Racial and/or Ethnic Heritage;" "Persons of Mixed Religious Heritage;" "Couples of Mixed Heritage;" "Families Including a Child of the Same Nationality, But a Different Heritage;" "Families Including a Child of a Different Nationality;" and "Biographies." Within each chapter categories are organized alphabetically, and within each category books are listed alphabetically by author. The easiest way to locate books that are about persons of specific heritages is to use the "Subject Index." The "Contents" is also helpful.

The content of each chapter is summarized below as well as in each chapter's introduction.

General

This chapter covers books that provide an overall look at individuals and families of mixed racial, ethnic, and/or religious heritage. It includes books that present the history of interracial marriage and adoption, governmental policies, societal attitudes, racial classification, and international adoption. Other books in this chapter are based on interviews of persons of mixed heritage or from families of mixed heritage, who present their own experiences and perspectives on such subjects as the stereotypical attitudes they have encountered from strangers, classmates, relatives, and/or members of their own ethnic groups; the dilemma of finding their own identity; and the advantages and disadvantages of being "mixed." Some books include coping strategies and resource sections.

This chapter also includes books that provide biographical information on many individuals of mixed heritage, that depict numerous children of mixed heritage, and that celebrate individual and familial diversity.

Persons of Mixed Racial and/or Ethnic Heritage

This chapter covers books about specific individuals of mixed race and/or ethnicity. Books about persons who are Jewish are included here as well as in the chapter "Individuals of Mixed Religious Heritage." The chapter categorizes the names of persons covered in the "Biography" chapter and cross-references these names to that chapter.

Persons of Mixed Religious Heritage

Books about individual persons of mixed religious heritage are covered in this chapter. Books about persons who are Jewish are included here as well as in the chapter "Individuals of Mixed Racial and/or Ethnic Heritage." This chapter includes books involving organized religions, but not all differing religious beliefs. For instance, the mixed religious heritage of a person whose Navajo father holds beliefs different from those of his/her Hopi mother is not included.

The names of persons covered in the "Biography" chapter are categorized and cross-referenced to that chapter.

Couples of Mixed Heritage

This chapter covers books presenting specific couples. It first provides an informational listing of persons covered in the "Biography" chapter and cross-references these persons to that chapter. The next part of this chapter presents references of books which include couples of mixed heritage who do not have children of mixed heritage or whose children of mixed heritage are adopted.

Families Including a Child of the Same Nationality, But a Different Heritage

The great majority of the books in this chapter cover families of mixed heritage created when children are adopted domestically, a parent remarries, or, due to parental death or other circumstances, new caregiver situations (including orphanages) occur. In some instances, the books tell of slave or abducted children who must live with adults of a different heritage. The chapter does not include books in which children go to live with a grandparent.

Each category in this chapter first lists the names of actual persons covered in the "Biography" chapter and cross-references these names to that chapter. Other books follow these name listings.

Families Including a Child of a Different Nationality

Most of the books included in this chapter cover specific families of mixed heritage created when children are adopted or cared for by those from another country. In some instances, the books tell of slave or abducted children or of children cared for in orphanages.

The names of persons covered in the "Biography" chapter are listed first in each category and cross-referenced to that chapter. Book listings follow these listings.

Biographies

This chapter covers books about actual persons, both living and dead. Each person in this chapter has been cross-referenced from one or more of the previous five chapters: "Persons of Mixed Racial and/or Ethnic Heritage;" "Persons of Mixed Religious Heritage;" "Couples of Mixed Heritage;" "Families Including a Child of the Same Nationality, But a Different Heritage;" and "Families Including a Child of a Different Nationality."

The term biography is used broadly to include not only nonfictional accounts of a person's life, but also fictional life stories and books of nonfiction and fiction in which the person appears. Further, the books do not have to mention the mixed heritage of the person or his/her family.

I. General

Introduction

This chapter covers books that provide an overall look at individuals and families of mixed racial, ethnic, and/or religious heritage. It includes books that present the history of interracial marriage and adoption, governmental policies, societal attitudes, racial classification, and international adoption. Other books in this chapter are based on interviews of persons of mixed heritage or from families of mixed heritage, who present their own experiences and perspectives on such subjects as the stereotypical attitudes they have encountered from strangers, classmates, relatives, and/or members of their own ethnic groups; the dilemma of finding their own identity; and the advantages and disadvantages of being "mixed." Some books include coping strategies and resource sections.

This chapter also includes books that provide biographical information on many individuals of mixed heritage, that depict numerous children of mixed heritage, and that celebrate individual and familial diversity.

Books about specific individuals are covered in the next six chapters.

References

Agard, John. *Half-caste and Other Poems*. London: Hodder Children's Books, 2005. 80 p.

This book of poetry for high schoolers includes poems about interracial individuals and relationships. Among them are: "Half-caste," "My Move Your Move," "Coal's Son and Diamond's Daughter," "Twins," "Cowtalk," "The Giant with a Taste of Mongrel Blood," "Behind the Menu," and "Marriage of Opposites."
Older; Fiction

Alderman, Bruce, ed. *Interracial Relationships*. Farmington Hills, Mich.: Greenhaven Press, 2007. 112 p. (Social Issues Firsthand)

The introduction in this book discusses interracial relationships, four of the narratives present personal experiences and insights about persons of mixed race, and a fifth tells of an interracial marriage. Listings of resources and organizations to contact are appended.
Older; Nonfiction

Avery, Susan, and Linda Skinner. *Extraordinary American Indians*. Chicago: Children's Press, 1992. 272 p.

This resource presents biographical information on more than fifty Native Americans, including some of mixed heritage.
Older; Nonfiction

Becker, John T., and Stanli K. Becker, eds. *All Blood Is Red . . . All Shadows Are Dark!* Illustrated by J. Howard Noel. Cleveland: Seven Shadows Press, 1984. 168 p.

John T. (Tom) Becker, who is Irish-German-American, and his wife, Stanli K. Becker, who is African-American, have five young children. One of the four who are adopted is biracial. All seven family members are responsible for individual sections of this book, which recounts their personal and family experiences as a multiracial family. Teaching their children to be aware of and proud of their individual differences, the editors present information on the history of racial classification in the United States and advocate their belief that race is and should be regarded as an "absurdity."
Intermediate, Older; Nonfiction

Bode, Janet. *Different Worlds: Interracial and Cross-Cultural Dating*. New York: Franklin Watts, 1989. 128 p.

Based primarily on interviews with six teenage couples who are dating interracially and/or cross-culturally, this book is written for and about teens. It looks at the history of prejudice and racism; discusses negative reactions of parents, relatives, and classmates; examines why adolescents make their dating choices; and mentions some positive aspects of interracial dating. Although it does not cover the topics of interracial marriage and families, four of the twelve teens interviewed are of mixed heritage: African-American/European-American; Protestant English-American/Catholic Irish-American; Cuban/Puerto Rican; and Mexican-Spanish-American. A bibliography, a listing of resource organizations, and an index are included.
Older; Nonfiction

Boyd, Brian. *When You Were Born in Korea: A Memory Book for Children Adopted from Korea*. Photographs by Stephen Wunrow. St. Paul: Yeong & Yeong Book Company, 1993. 48 p.

Text and photographs show the process that brings Korean children to their adoptive American parents. It tells of birthmothers, birthmother's homes, baby's homes, foster homes, and adoption agencies and emphasizes the many people who care for and about the children: birthparents, nurses, social workers, foster parents, doctors, trip escorts, and Traveler's Aid Society volunteers.
Primary, Intermediate; Nonfiction

Bradman, Tony, ed. *Give Me Shelter: Stories about Children Who Seek Asylum*. London: Frances Lincoln Children's Books (Distributed by Publishers Group West), 2007. 224 p.

This book includes several stories about children who go without their families to seek asylum in other countries.
Older; Fiction

Cruz, Bárbara C. *Multiethnic Teens and Cultural Identity: A Hot Issue*. Berkeley Heights, N.J.: Enslow Publishers, 2001. 64 p.
This informative book looks at interracial marriages and children of mixed race in the United States. It traces the history of the categorization of persons of mixed race, tells of the terms which have been used by and for them, and points out the pros and cons of including a multiracial or multi-ethnic category on governmental and school forms. The book presents the diversified experiences of a number of individuals of mixed race as well as information on well-known persons of mixed heritage. It delves into the issue of choosing to identify with one or many cultures and contains references to organizations and periodicals for interracial families. Notes and an index are included.
Older; Nonfiction

Curie, Stephan. *Adoption*. San Diego: Lucent Books, 1996. 96 p. (Lucent Overview Series)
In a chapter on transracial adoption this book examines its history, government policies, and arguments pro and con. A chapter on international adoption discusses its increase in recent years, the contrasting and changing policies of sending countries, and opposing views on its effects on sending countries and on the adopted children.
Older; Nonfiction

de Guzman, Michael. *The Bamboozlers*. New York: Farrar Straus Giroux, 2005. 176 p.
When twelve-year-old Albert spends three days with Wendell, the bamboozling grandfather he'd never met, they travel from Albert's small Idaho town to Seattle. There, with the help of his friends and of Albert, Wendell succeeds in conning a much-disliked con man, and Albert's life changes for the better. Wendell and Albert are of mixed race, but as the elderly con man describes his heritage as comprising a large variety of ethnic groups, it is difficult to determine what his—and Albert's—are meant to be.
Intermediate, Older; Fiction

Dramer, Kim. *Native Americans and Black Americans*. Philadelphia: Chelsea House Publishers, 1997. 96 p. (Indians of North America)
This book provides a detailed history of Native Americans and black Americans and of the relationships between them, including their intermarriage. It covers, among other topics, the early mingling of Indian and slave populations on West Indies sugar plantations; efforts to create antagonism between the two populations during the Revolutionary War; Cherokee and Seminole slave owners; the black Seminoles; the roles of York and Sacajawea on the Lewis and Clark expedition; the importance of African-Americans in the fur trade; the fighting of Native Americans on sides in the Civil War; the westward migration and later the Great Migration of African-Americans; the Harlem Renaissance; the changing policies of the Federal government towards Native Americans, including removal, allotment,

termination, relocation, and self-determination; and the racial identification of persons of mixed heritage.
Older; Nonfiction

DuPrau, Jeanne. *Adoption: The Facts, Feelings, and Issues of a Double Heritage*. New York: Julian Messner, 1990. 140 p.

This book on adoption includes a discussion of transracial adoption. It describes how adoption of minority children by white parents became more common in the 1960s because of the civil rights movement, but then declined as it faced opposition, particularly by black organizations. The book also provides information on international adoptions, especially of children from Vietnam, South Korea, and Latin America.
Intermediate, Older; Nonfiction

Erlbach, Arlene. *The Families Book: True Stories about Real Kids and the People They Live With and Love*. Photographs by Stephen J. Carrera. Illustrated by Lisa Wagner. Minneapolis: Free Spirit Publishing, 1996. 120 p.

In a section of this book, children tell about their families, that include a family in which the father is Lutheran and the mother Jewish; a family in which the father is African-American and the mother Caucasian; a family with four children in which Caucasian parents have adopted a biracial American girl and a boy from Romania; and a family with Caucasian parents and eleven children, six of whom were adopted from Korea.
Intermediate; Nonfiction

Fassler, C. Richard. *Rainbow Kids: Hawaii's Gift to America*. Photographs by author. Honolulu: White Tiger Press, 1998. 96 p.

Pointing out that the 1990 census showed that more than one-third of Hawaii's population was mixed race and that there is a multiracial harmony in that state, this book presents color photographs of 108 children of mixed race. They include the author's daughter who is Chinese-Swiss-French-English-Welsh-American. The ethnicities represented by these Hawaiian "Rainbow Kids" are African-American, Algonquin, Cherokee, Chinese, Cook Islands Maori, Czech, Danish, Dutch, English, Filipino, French, German, Hawaiian, Hungarian, Irish, Italian, Japanese, Jewish, Korean, Mongolian, Nipmuck, Norwegian, Ojibwa, Okinawan, Pohnpeian, Polish, Portuguese, Russian, Samoan, Scottish, Slovak, Spanish, Swedish, Swiss, Tahitian, Tongan, Ukrainian, Vietnamese, and Welsh.
Primary, Intermediate, Older; Nonfiction

Fry, Annette R. *The Orphan Trains*. New York: New Discovery Books, 1994. 96 p. (American Events)

This book provides a detailed description of the sending of children who were mostly from the streets, orphanages, and impoverished families of New York City and Boston to foster parents in rural New York State and westward farming communities. These "orphan trains" were originated by those who felt children would flourish within families as opposed to living as street children or in institutions. The trains started in the mid-nineteenth century, with the last orphan train leaving New York City in 1929. In 1875, the peak year for children sent by the New York City Children's Aid Society,

4,026 children were sent on orphan trains. The sending organizations were Protestant and Catholic, serving very few African-American children, but with Jewish children transferred to them and sometimes being baptized as Catholics. The book mentions one Irish immigrant boy who was taken in by an Iowa German couple and a woman raised in Colorado by a Catholic couple, who discovered as an adult that she was born Jewish, with a Jewish father from New York City and a Jewish mother from Russia. Older; Nonfiction

Gaskins, Pearl Fuyo. *What Are You? Voices of Mixed-Race Young People*. New York: Henry Holt and Company, 1999. 288 p.

This book presents edited excerpts from taped interviews of more than forty persons of mixed race aged fourteen to twenty-eight, as well as interspersed commentaries. The interviewees present their views, based on their personal experiences, on a wide range of subjects, including their reactions to questions about their heritage, discrimination and harassment they have encountered, racial categories, the one drop rule for blacks, the use of blood quantum for Native Americans, the ways they are viewed in different situations, the impact of race within their families, the role of race within American society, dating, finding one's identity, and the negatives and positives of being mixed. An extensive resource section is included. Older; Nonfiction

Gay, Kathlyn. *"I Am Who I Am": Speaking Out about Multiracial Identity*. New York: Franklin Watts, 1995. 144 p.

Drawing on interviews, periodical articles, and books, this study provides a comprehensive look at persons and families of mixed race. It discusses such topics as the history of racial labeling, ethnocentrism, racial mixing, and anti-miscegenation laws; classification and myths about persons of mixed race; parenting and coping strategies; discrimination; nonacceptance by one's own racial groups; pressure to choose one racial identity; antagonism towards mixed families; transracial adoptions; categorization on census and other forms; and efforts to educate people about interracial families through organizations, media, and college classes. The appendix includes an extensive list of interracial support groups, chapter source notes, a bibliography, and an index. Older; Nonfiction

Gay, Kathlyn. *The Rainbow Effect: Interracial Families*. New York: Franklin Watts, 1987. 144 p.

Written in the mid-1980s, this book provides a detailed examination of interracial experiences and issues by presenting the views of numerous interracial family members and of professionals in the field. Stereotypical attitudes; name-calling; acceptance by relatives; dating; interracial families formed by remarriage, adoption, and foster care; special insights gained by mixed race children; parenting strategies; and support groups are among the subjects discussed. A reading list, chapter notes, a list of resource organizations, and an index are included. Older; Nonfiction

Grimes, Nikki. *Aneesa Lee and the Weaver's Gift*. Illustrated by Ashley Bryan. New York: Lothrop, Lee and Shepard Books, 1999. 32 p.

Aneesa Lee, who is black, white, and Japanese, weaves a distinctive tapestry of different colors that reveals different emotions. Written in verse, this picture book celebrates the universal art of weaving and includes a glossary of weaving terms accompanied by a labeled illustration of a loom.
Primary, Intermediate; Fiction

Hamanaka, Sheila. *All the Colors of the Earth*. Illustrated by author. New York: Morrow Junior Books, 1994. 32 p.

Through verse and illustrations, this book displays children with different skin colors and kinds of hair that reflect nature and the colors of love. Several of the children pictured are biracial.
Pre-K, Primary; Fiction

Haugen, David M., ed. *Interracial Relationships*. Farmington Hills, Mich.: Greenhaven Press, 2006. 104 p. (At Issue)

One article in this book discusses the experiences of a child of mixed race, while others focus on interracial marriage. They cover such topics as the reasons for the increase in interracial relationships, the conflicting opinions of blacks towards relationships with whites, the opposition of some parents to their children's interracial marriages, and Biblical passages on marriage between persons of different races.
Older; Nonfiction

Haugen, David M., and Matthew J. Box, eds. *Adoption*. Detroit: Greenhaven Press, 2006. 112 p. (Social Issues Firsthand)

In this book one narrative by Laurie Landry tells of the process she and her husband followed to adopt a baby from China and another gives an account by seventeen-year-old Thai Tanawan Free explaining how it was not until high school that he came to accept his looking different from his Caucasian adoptive parents and classmates.
Older; Nonfiction

Isadora, Rachel. *What a Family! A Fresh Look at Family Trees*. Illustrated by author. New York: G. P. Putnam's Sons, 2006. 36 p.

This picture book shows that members of an extended family often have similar characteristics, such as dimples, ears that wiggle, and freckles. The illustrations show that persons of mixed race are among the four generations of descendents of John (born in 1890) and Hildegard (born in 1901).
Pre-K, Primary; Fiction

Jenness, Aylette. *Families: A Celebration of Diversity, Commitment, and Love*. Photographs by author. Boston: Houghton Mifflin Company, 1990. 48 p.

In this book, which emphasizes the diversity of American families, seventeen children describe their families. In addition to the family of a boy who was adopted from Cambodia, several families depicted in the photographs appear to contain members of different ethnicities.
Intermediate, Older; Nonfiction

Katz, William Loren. *Black Indians: A Hidden Heritage*. New York: Atheneum, 1986. 208 p.

This book presents a detailed account of the common interests—and often marriages of African-Americans and Native Americans—and the roles of black Indians in the nation's history up to the twentieth century. It includes coverage of the black Seminoles, black Indian fur trappers, the Five Civilized Nations, and the transition of Oklahoma from Indian Territory to statehood. It also provides biographical information on a number of black Indians.
Intermediate, Older; Nonfiction

Katz, William Loren. *Black Women of the Old West*. New York: Atheneum Books for Young Readers, 1995. 96 p.

Illustrated with numerous photographs, this book provides a detailed look at the lives and roles of African-American frontier women and tells of the intermarriage of many African-Americans and Native Americans.
Intermediate, Older; Nonfiction

Keller, Holly. *Horace*. Illustrated by author. New York: Greenwillow, 1991. 32 p.

In this picture book Horace, a leopard, hates having spots instead of the stripes of his adoptive tiger parents and his cousins. Running away to a park, he has fun playing with the children of a leopard family, but when evening comes, Horace is happy to be reunited with his tiger parents.
Pre-K, Primary; Fiction

Krementz, Jill. *How It Feels To Be Adopted*. Photographs by author. New York: Alfred A. Knopf, 1982. 120 p.

Black-and-white photographs accompany the author's interviews with nineteen children who talk about being adopted: how they feel about it, their knowledge of and feelings about their birthparents and whether they want to meet them, their experiences as adopted children, and, for five of them, what it is like to be part of a mixed race family. One of these children, who is African-American, has been adopted by an African-American father, but has adopted brothers of different ethnicities.
Intermediate, Older; Nonfiction

Kuklin, Susan. *Families*. Photographs by author. New York: Hyperion Books for Children, 2006. 40 p.

Text and color photographs present interviews with American children, who talk about their families. Their families include seven families with children of mixed race, ethnicity, or religion, with one also including a child adopted from Sierra Leone. In an eighth family a child has been adopted from China. In a ninth family an adopted American child is of a race different from that of one of her fathers.
Primary, Intermediate; Nonfiction

Landau, Elaine. *Interracial Dating and Marriage*. New York: Julian Messner, 1993. 112 p.

This book's introduction presents two detailed histories of interracial marriage: the first of African-American intermarriage with Caucasians and the second of intermarriages involving Japan-

ese-Americans. In both cases the introduction describes factors, including governmental actions and societal attitudes, which affected the frequency of these marriages. The bulk of the book presents interviews with ten teenagers and five adults or adult couples who describe their views of and/or experiences with interracial dating and marriage. Seven of the teens interviewed came to the United States from other countries; two of the teens are interracial. Two of the adult interviews are with interracial couples; another contains advice from a minister. A resource list and an index are included.
Older; Nonfiction

Lanier, Shannon, and Jane Feldman. *Jefferson's Children: The Story of One American Family*. Photographs by Jane Feldman. Introduction by Lucian K. Truscott IV. Historical Essays by Annette Gordon-Reed and Beverley Gray. New York: Random House, 2000. 144 p.
After attending the May 1999 Monticello reunion of descendants of Thomas Jefferson, Sidney Lanier, who is a descendant of Madison Hemings, teamed up with photographer Jane Feldman to interview descendants of Thomas Jefferson and his wife Martha Wayles Jefferson and of Thomas Woodson, Madison Hemings, and Eston Hemings, those three of Jefferson and Sally Hemings' children whose lines can be traced. The resulting book contains a variety of individual and family interviews and photographs that reveal the family histories of the interviewees as well as their personal experiences and opinions. There is talk about whether the Hemings family members are indeed descendants of Jefferson's and should be allowed in the family graveyard, which is controlled by the Monticello Association. The bulk of the book consists of Hemings family interviews that tell what it means to be of mixed race; how some family members have passed as white; of some not being personally accepted because they look black or, on the other hand, look white; and of the Hemings' many achievements throughout the generations. Both Jeffersons and Hemings talk of family, of the importance of learning of their past, and of the hope for many that members of this family can eventually become one.
Older; Nonfiction

Layne, Steven L. *Over Land and Sea: A Story of International Adoption*. Illustrated by Jan Bower. Gretna, La.: Pelican Publishing Company, 2005. 32 p.
Paintings of babies and young children of different ethnicities distinguish this picture book on international adoption. It does not mention the birthparents of the adopted children, the cultures from which they have come, nor the locations of their adoptive families, but states that they have come home.
Pre-K; Fiction

Liptak, Karen. *Adoption Controversies*. New York: Franklin Watts, 1993. 160 p. (The Changing Family)
A chapter in this book covers transracial adoptions. It provides background information, presents the pros and cons of interracial adoptions within the United States and from abroad, and examines the special issues raised by the adoption of Native American children.
Older; Nonfiction

Nash, Gary B. *Forbidden Love: The Secret History of Mixed-Race America*. Illustrated by author. New York: Henry Holt and Company, 1999. 224 p.

This book presents a comprehensive history of interracial marriages in the United States from the marriage of Pocahontas and John Rolfe to the marriage of Tiger Woods' parents. In addition to providing biographical information on a number of persons of mixed race, it presents and analyzes the changing perceptions of interracial marriage by covering such topics as the differing attitudes of Spanish/Portuguese and English colonists, polygenesis, Darwin, Chinese laborers in California, Greenwich Village, the Harlem Renaissance, World War II, and immigration. The book includes photographs, chapter notes, and an index.
Older; Nonfiction

Nash, Renea D. *Coping as a Biracial/Biethnic Teen*. New York: The Rosen Publishing Group, 1995. 128 p.

Citing earlier findings and using individual examples, this book provides many suggestions for biracial teens. Stressing the overriding need to establish a racial identity, it tells of the importance of communicating with parents and others, of getting support, of learning how to deal with racism, and of recognizing the positives of a diverse heritage. One chapter covers the problems of racial identity boxes, and another gives advice to teens who have been adopted transracially. A list of support groups, a glossary, a reading list, and an index are appended.
Older; Nonfiction

O'Hearn, Claudine Chiawei, ed. *Half and Half: Writers on Growing Up Biracial and Bicultural*. New York: Pantheon Books, 1998. 288 p.

A number of authors, journalists, and poets write about being of mixed heritage, marrying those of another culture, and/or raising a biracial child.
Older; Nonfiction

Packard, Gwen K. *Coping in an Interfaith Family*. New York: The Rosen Publishing Group, 1993. 192 p. (Coping)

Filled with numerous examples of different interfaith families and directed primarily to interfaith couples, this book covers such topics as choosing a religious identity for the family, religious education, celebrating holidays and rituals, relationships with other family members and friends, and selecting a house of worship. It includes comments from children in interfaith families and discusses the choices teens make. A glossary, listings of resource organizations and reading material, and an index are included.
Older; Nonfiction

Rosenberg, Maxine B. *Being Adopted*. Photographs by George Ancona. New York: Lothrop, Lee & Shepard Books, 1984. 48 p.

Illustrated with black-and-white photographs, this book features three children. Seven-year-old Rebecca, whose birthfather is African-American and birthmother European-American and Cheyenne, is the adopted daughter of an African-American father and a European-American mother. Ten-year-old

Andrei was adopted from India by European-American parents, and eight-year-old Karin, the author's daughter, was adopted from Korea by her European-American parents. The book covers some of the questions and fears of younger adopted children: being afraid when they come to their adoptive families, wondering whether they caused their parents to give them up, fearing their adoptive parents will give them up, dreaming and wondering about their birthparents, and not looking like other members of their families. It also affirms that adopted children are just as much family members as are biological children.
Primary, Intermediate; Nonfiction

Rosenberg, Maxine B. *Growing Up Adopted*. Afterword by Lois Ruskai Melina. New York: Bradbury Press, 1989. 128 p.
In this book eight children and six adults relate their experiences and thoughts about growing up as adopted children. The four children who were adopted by parents of a different race, in each case European-American, are Josh, adopted as was a little sister from Colombia; Amy, who was adopted from Ecuador; Mark, who was adopted from Korea; and Shakine, an African-American boy who was born with spinal bifida in the United States and lives in a family of seven children, four of whom are adopted and of ethnicities other than their adoptive parents. Three of the adults are of a different race than their European-American parents. Chris was adopted from France as was her brother, Sam was adopted from Korea and has an adopted sister of mixed race and two non-adopted brothers, and Jamie, an African-European-American, has two sisters who are not adopted and four adopted siblings of mixed race.
Intermediate, Older; Nonfiction

Rosenberg, Maxine B. *Living in Two Worlds*. Photographs by George Ancona. New York: Lothrop, Lee & Shepard Books, 1986. 48 p.
This book explains how races evolved and how many children have a greater resemblance to one of their parents. It discusses the teasing and unwanted questions biracial children face and points to the benefits of living in two cultures. The book's text and black-and-white photographs focus on five children: Toah, who is African-European-American; Megan, who is African-European-American and Cherokee; Jesse, who is Chinese-European-American; and Shashi and Anil, who are Indian-European-American.
Intermediate; Nonfiction

Schlissel, Lillian. *Black Frontiers: A History of African American Heroes in the Old West*. New York: Simon & Schuster Books for Young Readers, 1995. 80 p.
This book, which is illustrated with photographs, includes a section titled "Black Indians" and biographical information on several African-Americans of mixed race.
Intermediate, Older; Nonfiction

Slade, Suzanne Buckingham. *Adopted: The Ultimate Teen Guide*. Illustrated by Christopher Papile, Mary Sandage, and Odelia Witt. Photographs by Chris Washburn. Lanham, Md.: The Scarecrow Press, 2007. 272 p. (It Happened to Me, No. 20)

This book includes chapters on international adoption and on transracial adoption (including international adoption). It provides teens who live in families of mixed race with a multitude of suggestions and resources. For instance, the book discusses how to handle questions they are asked and how to seek their birthparents. For those teenagers adopted from other countries it presents ways of learning about their countries of birth, both to discover their cultural heritage and the conditions which may have caused them to be available for adoption. It includes descriptions of the experiences of individual adoptees, informational inserts, photographs, and chapter notes.
Older; Nonfiction

Stanford, Eleanor, ed. *Interracial America: Opposing Viewpoints*. Farmington Hills, Mich.: Greenhaven Press, 2006. 208 p. (Opposing Viewpoints)
Essays presenting the pros and cons of multiracial classification, interracial relationships, transracial adoption, and being biracial are included in this book for teenagers.
Older; Nonfiction

Szumski, Bonnie, ed. *Interracial America: Opposing Viewpoints*. San Diego: Greenhaven Press, 1996. 240 p. (Opposing Viewpoints)
In this book for high school students, six of the opinion pieces focus on interracial families by advocating the pros and cons of racial matching in adoptions, of biracial raising of children of mixed race, and of interracial marriage differing from marriage of persons of the same race.
Older; Nonfiction

Wilkinson, Sook, and Nancy Fox, eds. *After the Morning Calm: Reflections of Korean Adoptees*. Bloomfield Hills, Mich.: Sunrise Ventures, 2002. 192 p.
In this book nine men and seventeen women present their experiences and feelings about being adopted from South Korea. One went to live with a Dutch family, another was adopted by Norwegians, and the remainder became the children of American parents. Their ages at adoption ranged from infancy to teenager. One suffered in Korea because he was the son of a Korean woman and a white American soldier. Another was the subject of her mother Marjorie Ann Waybill's fictional book. They all were succeeding as adults. Their writings describe the impact of looking different from their peers, the difficulties of reconciling two cultures, and the effects of visiting South Korea. The book contains photographs and an appended resource section.
Older; Nonfiction

Williams, Garth. *The Rabbits' Wedding*. Illustrated by author. New York: Harper & Brothers, 1958. 36 p.
Featuring large illustrations, this picture book tells how the little black rabbit's wish that he could always be with the little white rabbit comes true when they are wed. Published in 1958, this book created controversy because of its depiction of a black-white marriage.
Pre-K; Fiction

Williams, Mary E., ed. *Adoption*. Farmington Hills, Mich.: Greenhaven Press, 2006. 232 p.

Opinion pieces in this book support and oppose transracial adoption and international adoption. Older; Nonfiction

II. Persons of Mixed Racial and/or Ethnic Heritage

Introduction

This chapter covers books about specific individuals of mixed race and/or ethnicity. Books about persons who are Jewish are included here as well as in the chapter "Individuals of Mixed Religious Heritage." The "General" chapter includes books that discuss the topic of mixed heritage.

With the exception of North America, the chapter is organized alphabetically by continent or region of heritage: African, Asian, European, Oceanian (including Australian), and South American. For individuals of North American heritage, the major sections are listed by country or geographical region: American (of the United States), Canadian, Central American, Mexican, and West Indian. Within the major sections there are subsections, which in many cases include secondary and even tertiary subsections:

Asian—

Indonesian—

Japanese-Indonesian—

The listings are categorized according to the individual's nation of birth. For instance, if a girl's parents emigrated from India and England to Australia where she was born, she is listed according to her country of birth, Australian, as English-Australian and Indian-Australian, but not under English or Indian. With the exception of persons born in land ceded to the United States under the treaty ending the Mexican-American War, persons born within the boundaries of the current United States are classified American, regardless of whether the area was at that time under the United States government.

If a person in a book is identified only as an American who is white and American Indian, the book would be listed under the more general categories, European-American and Native American:

American—

European-American—

(book listing)

American—

Native American—

(book listing)

On the other hand, if there is a book about an American whose heritage is Scottish and Cherokee, it would be categorized as follows:

American—
    European-American—
        Scottish-American—
        (book listing)
American—
    Native American—
        Cherokee—
        (book listing)

Each category in this chapter first lists the names of persons covered in the "Biography" chapter and cross-references these names to that chapter. Book references follow these name listings.

The heritage designation for each book reads:

Heritage from father/Heritage from mother

e.g., Nigerian/Irish or

    Irish and Nigerian (if the side of the family is not known)

The order in which the heritages are listed is immaterial.

References

A. Unspecified Nationality

Spiegler, Louise. *The Amethyst Road*. New York: Clarion Books, 2005. 336 p.

Sixteen-year-old Serena's gypsy tribe has declared her an outcast by association because her older sister is an unwed mother. When she unsuccessfully tries to keep her baby niece Zara from being taken away by non-gypsy officials, one of them falls and Serena must escape. She meets Shem, who is leaving his musician uncles, and they journey together seeking to find Serena's mother, to get Zara back, to have Serena's outcast status overturned, and to enable Shem to be accepted by a merchant gypsy tribe. The book tells of Serena's impetuous spirit, of the animosity she encounters, of her conflicting Romani and non-Romani sides, and of her changing feelings towards Shem. By the end of the story Serena not only has found her mother, become Zara's guardian, and married Shem, but also has used her talents to help the Romanies.

Non-Romani/Romani

Older; Fiction

B. African

Cape Verdean

African-Cape Verdean

Lyons, Mary E. *Letters from a Slave Boy: The Story of Joseph Jacobs*. New York: Atheneum Books for Young Readers, 2007. 208 p.

This book of historical fiction is a companion book to *Letters from a Slave Girl*, which tells the story of Harriet Jacobs. It presents her son Joseph's narrative of his life from the age of nine until his departure to mine gold in Australia in about 1852. Growing up in Edenton, North Carolina, with his great-grandmother and sister, he is unaware that his mother, who is an escaped slave, is hiding in the house and that he is the son of a white neighbor, Samuel Sawyer. In 1843 Joseph leaves for Boston where he briefly attends the abusive Smith School and then becomes a printer's apprentice. Running away to New Bedford, he works on the docks and goes off for almost three years on a whaling ship. On board the ship he encounters a sailor from the Cape Verde Islands who has been looked after since boyhood by the ship's Quaker captain. Joseph next goes to California to mine for gold with his Uncle John, until the two set off for Australia where they will be free. Joseph struggles with the treatment he receives as a slave, his feelings about the Irish boy who works on the ship with him and dies, the decision as to whether he should pass as white, and the terrible worry that he and his mother will be captured by slave hunters. The book includes some information on Joseph's later life.
Portuguese/African-Cape Verdean
Older; Fiction

Portuguese-Cape Verdean

Lyons, Mary E. *Letters from a Slave Boy: The Story of Joseph Jacobs*. New York: Atheneum Books for Young Readers, 2007. 208 p.

This book of historical fiction is a companion book to *Letters from a Slave Girl*, which tells the story of Harriet Jacobs. It presents her son Joseph's narrative of his life from the age of nine until his departure to mine gold in Australia in about 1852. Growing up in Edenton, North Carolina, with his great-grandmother and sister, he is unaware that his mother, who is an escaped slave, is hiding in the house and that he is the son of a white neighbor, Samuel Sawyer. In 1843 Joseph leaves for Boston where he briefly attends the abusive Smith School and then becomes a printer's apprentice. Running away to New Bedford, he works on the docks and goes off for almost three years on a whaling ship. On board the ship he encounters a sailor from the Cape Verde Islands who has been looked after since boyhood by the ship's Quaker captain. Joseph next goes to California to mine for gold with his Uncle John, until the two set off for Australia where they will be free. Joseph struggles with the treatment he receives as a slave, his feelings about the Irish boy who works on the ship with him and dies, the decision as to whether he should pass as white, and the terrible worry that he and his mother will be captured by slave hunters. The book includes some information on Joseph's later life.

Portuguese/African-Cape Verdean
Older; Fiction

Eritrean

Zephaniah, Benjamin. *Refugee Boy*. New York: Bloomsbury Children's Books, 2001. 304 p.

Alem was born in the town of Badme, which was claimed by both Eritrea and Ethiopia. When Alem and his parents lived in Ethiopia, soldiers forced them to leave because Alem's mother was Eritrean and when they moved to Eritrea, soldiers demanded that they leave because of his Ethiopian father. Fourteen-year-old Alem and his father go to England, supposedly on holiday, but when Alem wakes up in their hotel he discovers that his father has left him so that he can grow up in safety. The Refugee Council places Alem in a children's home, but he runs away after one night because of the intolerable environment. He is then placed with Irish foster parents, the Fitzgeralds. Alem likes the kind and supportive Fitzgerald family, his English school, and his new friends. This story details the process which Alem must follow to gain political asylum, the murder of his mother near the Eritrean-Ethiopian border, his father's arriving in England, the denial of their asylum request which means that they will have to return to life-threatening Ethiopia, the campaign waged by Alem's schoolmates on their behalf, and finally the killing of Alem's father outside the London headquarters of the East African Solidarity Trust, an organization advocating unity and peace which his parents had helped found.
Ethiopian/Eritrean
Older; Fiction

Ethiopian-Eritrean

Zephaniah, Benjamin. *Refugee Boy*. New York: Bloomsbury Children's Books, 2001. 304 p.

Alem was born in the town of Badme, which was claimed by both Eritrea and Ethiopia. When Alem and his parents lived in Ethiopia, soldiers forced them to leave because Alem's mother was Eritrean and when they moved to Eritrea, soldiers demanded that they leave because of his Ethiopian father. Fourteen-year-old Alem and his father go to England, supposedly on holiday, but when Alem wakes up in their hotel he discovers that his father has left him so that he can grow up in safety. The Refugee Council places Alem in a children's home, but he runs away after one night because of the intolerable environment. He is then placed with Irish foster parents, the Fitzgeralds. Alem likes the kind and supportive Fitzgerald family, his English school, and his new friends. This story details the process which Alem must follow to gain political asylum, the murder of his mother near the Eritrean-Ethiopian border, his father's arriving in England, the denial of their asylum request which means that they will have to return to life-threatening Ethiopia, the campaign waged by Alem's schoolmates on their behalf, and finally the killing of Alem's father outside the London headquarters of the East African Solidarity Trust, an organization advocating unity and peace which his parents had helped found.
Ethiopian/Eritrean
Older; Fiction

Ethiopian

Zephaniah, Benjamin. *Refugee Boy*. New York: Bloomsbury Children's Books, 2001. 304 p.

Alem was born in the town of Badme, which was claimed by both Eritrea and Ethiopia. When Alem and his parents lived in Ethiopia, soldiers forced them to leave because Alem's mother was Eritrean and when they moved to Eritrea, soldiers demanded that they leave because of his Ethiopian father. Fourteen-year-old Alem and his father go to England, supposedly on holiday, but when Alem wakes up in their hotel he discovers that his father has left him so that he can grow up in safety. The Refugee Council places Alem in a children's home, but he runs away after one night because of the intolerable environment. He is then placed with Irish foster parents, the Fitzgeralds. Alem likes the kind and supportive Fitzgerald family, his English school, and his new friends. This story details the process which Alem must follow to gain political asylum, the murder of his mother near the Eritrean-Ethiopian border, his father's arriving in England, the denial of their asylum request which means that they will have to return to life-threatening Ethiopia, the campaign waged by Alem's schoolmates on their behalf, and finally the killing of Alem's father outside the London headquarters of the East African Solidarity Trust, an organization advocating unity and peace which his parents had helped found.
Ethiopian/Eritrean
Older; Fiction

Eritrean-Ethiopian

Zephaniah, Benjamin. *Refugee Boy*. New York: Bloomsbury Children's Books, 2001. 304 p.

Alem was born in the town of Badme, which was claimed by both Eritrea and Ethiopia. When Alem and his parents lived in Ethiopia, soldiers forced them to leave because Alem's mother was Eritrean and when they moved to Eritrea, soldiers demanded that they leave because of his Ethiopian father. Fourteen-year-old Alem and his father go to England, supposedly on holiday, but when Alem wakes up in their hotel he discovers that his father has left him so that he can grow up in safety. The Refugee Council places Alem in a children's home, but he runs away after one night because of the intolerable environment. He is then placed with Irish foster parents, the Fitzgeralds. Alem likes the kind and supportive Fitzgerald family, his English school, and his new friends. This story details the process which Alem must follow to gain political asylum, the murder of his mother near the Eritrean-Ethiopian border, his father's arriving in England, the denial of their asylum request which means that they will have to return to life-threatening Ethiopia, the campaign waged by Alem's schoolmates on their behalf, and finally the killing of Alem's father outside the London headquarters of the East African Solidarity Trust, an organization advocating unity and peace which his parents had helped found.
Ethiopian/Eritrean
Older; Fiction

Kenyan

Kikuyu Kenyan

Quintana, Anton. *The Bamboo King*. Translated from Dutch by John Nieuwenhuizen. New York: Walker and Company, 1999. 192 p.

Set in East Africa, this book relates the story of Morengáru. Growing up in his father's land of the Masai, he is poorly treated because he is half-Kikuyu. Going to his mother's Kikuyu village, he is a reminder to his grandfather of his own earlier transgression and is unfairly banished. The story describes the differing Masai and Kikuyu cultures and how Morengáru, removed from both, came to live with and be king of a troop of baboons. And, it tells how Morengáru caused the death of two leopards, the first at the request of the Kikuyu and the last to avenge the death of Gray, the real leader of the baboons. Masai Kenyan/Kikuyu Kenyan
Older; Fiction

Masai Kenyan

Quintana, Anton. *The Bamboo King*. Translated from Dutch by John Nieuwenhuizen. New York: Walker and Company, 1999. 192 p.

Set in East Africa, this book relates the story of Morengáru. Growing up in his father's land of the Masai, he is poorly treated because he is half-Kikuyu. Going to his mother's Kikuyu village, he is a reminder to his grandfather of his own earlier transgression and is unfairly banished. The story describes the differing Masai and Kikuyu cultures and how Morengáru, removed from both, came to live with and be king of a troop of baboons. And, it tells how Morengáru caused the death of two leopards, the first at the request of the Kikuyu and the last to avenge the death of Gray, the real leader of the baboons. Masai Kenyan/Kikuyu Kenyan
Older; Fiction

Malagasy

McCaughrean, Geraldine. *The Pirate's Son*. New York: Scholastic Press, 1998. 304 p.

In 1719 fourteen-year-old Nathan is expelled from his English school when the school discovers that he is a pauper. The newly-orphaned Nathan, who has long been fascinated with pirates, and his "mousy" thirteen-year-old sister Maud go off to Madagascar with Nathan's older schoolmate Tamo, whose late father was a notorious pirate. There Tamo, who despised his father, learns that his Malagasy mother has married another pirate and feels compelled to take up piracy. Nathan, steeped in his parson father's Christianity, cannot accept the lifestyle and beliefs of the Malagasies. It is Maud who releases Tamo from his pirate fate, expels the pirates from the village, and thrives in her new environment. English and Christian/Malagasy and non-Christian
Older; Fiction

English-Malagasy

McCaughrean, Geraldine. *The Pirate's Son*. New York: Scholastic Press, 1998. 304 p.

In 1719 fourteen-year-old Nathan is expelled from his English school when the school discovers that he is a pauper. The newly-orphaned Nathan, who has long been fascinated with pirates, and his "mousy" thirteen-year-old sister Maud go off to Madagascar with Nathan's older schoolmate Tamo, whose late father was a notorious pirate. There Tamo, who despised his father, learns that his Malagasy mother has married another pirate and feels compelled to take up piracy. Nathan, steeped in his parson father's Christianity, cannot accept the lifestyle and beliefs of the Malagasies. It is Maud who releases Tamo from his pirate fate, expels the pirates from the village, and thrives in her new environment.
English and Christian/Malagasy and non-Christian
Older; Fiction

Mozambican

Farmer, Nancy. *A Girl Named Disaster*. New York: Orchard Books, 1996. 320 p. (A Richard Jackson Book)

Set in about 1981 in Mozambique and Zimbabwe, this is the story of the girl Nhamo, whose mother had been killed by a leopard and whose father had fled from Mozambique after he killed a man. Despite the efforts of her beloved grandmother and of a Portuguese-Mozambican couple, a spirit medium commands that Nhamo be married as payment to the cruel brother of the man her father had killed. Escaping, Nhamo undertakes the lonely journey from Mozambique to Zimbabwe to find her father. Resourceful and imaginative, Nhamo spends countless hours rowing a small boat against the current; encounters Shona spirits; takes comfort in talking to her "mother," the woman depicted in a magazine margarine advertisement; stays among baboons; and reaches a Zimbabwean scientific research center where she comes to feel at home and is exorcised from a curse by Vapostori Christians. She discovers her father is dead, lives as an unwelcome guest with his wealthy relatives, learns from her sympathetic great-grandfather about her parents, and is able to spend summers working at the research center. Throughout the book Nhamo is a teller of southeastern African stories.
Zimbabwean/Mozambican
Older; Fiction

Zimbabwean-Mozambican

Farmer, Nancy. *A Girl Named Disaster*. New York: Orchard Books, 1996. 320 p. (A Richard Jackson Book)

Set in about 1981 in Mozambique and Zimbabwe, this is the story of the girl Nhamo, whose mother had been killed by a leopard and whose father had fled from Mozambique after he killed a man. Despite the efforts of her beloved grandmother and of a Portuguese-Mozambican couple, a spirit medium commands that Nhamo be married as payment to the cruel brother of the man her father had killed. Escaping, Nhamo undertakes the lonely journey from Mozambique to Zimbabwe to find her father. Resourceful and imaginative, Nhamo spends countless hours rowing a small boat against the current;

encounters Shona spirits; takes comfort in talking to her "mother," the woman depicted in a magazine margarine advertisement; stays among baboons; and reaches a Zimbabwean scientific research center where she comes to feel at home and is exorcised from a curse by Vapostori Christians. She discovers her father is dead, lives as an unwelcome guest with his wealthy relatives, learns from her sympathetic great-grandfather about her parents, and is able to spend summers working at the research center. Throughout the book Nhamo is a teller of southeastern African stories.
Zimbabwean/Mozambican
Older; Fiction

South African

Afrikaner-South African

Rochman, Hazel, selector. *Somehow Tenderness Survives: Stories of Southern Africa*. New York: Harper & Row, 1988. 160 p.
  "Country Lovers" by Nadine Gordimer and "When the Train Comes" by Zoë Wicomb are among the ten stories and autobiographical accounts in this book. "Country Lovers" tells of a white boy, Paulus Eysendyck, and Thebedi, a black girl, who grow up as playmates and then lovers. After Paulus visits Thebedi's hut, her baby, who has his father's features, is dead. At a trial Paulus is judged not guilty of murder. In "When the Train Comes" a coloured girl waits with feelings of trepidation and self-degradation for the train that will carry her to the previously all-white St. Mary's School.
Afrikaner/Black-South African
Older; Fiction

Black-South African

Rochman, Hazel, selector. *Somehow Tenderness Survives: Stories of Southern Africa*. New York: Harper & Row, 1988. 160 p.
  "Country Lovers" by Nadine Gordimer and "When the Train Comes" by Zoë Wicomb are among the ten stories and autobiographical accounts in this book. "Country Lovers" tells of a white boy, Paulus Eysendyck, and Thebedi, a black girl, who grow up as playmates and then lovers. After Paulus visits Thebedi's hut, her baby, who has his father's features, is dead. At a trial Paulus is judged not guilty of murder. In "When the Train Comes" a coloured girl waits with feelings of trepidation and self-degradation for the train that will carry her to the previously all-white St. Mary's School.
Afrikaner/Black-South African
Older; Fiction

Coloured-South African

Jones, Toecky. *Skindeep*. New York: Harper & Row Publishers, 1986. 256 p.
  Set in apartheid South Africa, this novel for older teenagers tells of the love affair of blond eighteen-year-old Rhonda and nineteen-year-old Dave, who is coloured, but passing for white. Their dating

has its ups and downs as Dave is afraid of its long-term consequences. When by chance he encounters his birthmother, who had given him to a Jewish family to raise when he was seven, he finally reveals his identity to Rhonda. Initially shocked, she then tries, despite her family's objections, to get back together with Dave, but he refuses. Rhonda, who had wanted to go to England, decides to remain in South Africa and work against apartheid.
Coloured-South African
Older; Fiction

Naidoo, Beverly. *Out of Bounds: Seven Stories of Conflict and Hope*. New York: HarperCollins Publishers, 2003. 192 p.

"The Noose," one of this book's stories about South Africa, is set in 1955 after the 1950 enactments of the Population Registration Act and the Group Areas Act. A young boy is upset because his family will have to move to a township just for Coloureds and he will not only leave the neighborhood he loves but also be separated from one of his buddies who is Indian. The boy and his friends enjoy Lone Ranger comics and movies and he hopes that his seamstress mother will make him a Lone Ranger suit. However, receiving the suit for his tenth birthday loses its importance when his father, who is Coloured, is classified as African and may not be able to remain with the family.
Coloured-South African
Intermediate, Older; Fiction

Rochman, Hazel, selector. *Somehow Tenderness Survives: Stories of Southern Africa*. New York: Harper & Row, 1988. 160 p.

"Country Lovers" by Nadine Gordimer and "When the Train Comes" by Zoë Wicomb are among the ten stories and autobiographical accounts in this book. "Country Lovers" tells of a white boy, Paulus Eysendyck, and Thebedi, a black girl, who grow up as playmates and then lovers. After Paulus visits Thebedi's hut, her baby, who has his father's features, is dead. At a trial Paulus is judged not guilty of murder. In "When the Train comes" a coloured girl waits with feelings of trepidation and self-degradation for the train that will carry her to the previously all-white St. Mary's School.
Coloured-South African
Older; Fiction

Silver, Norman. *An Eye for Color*. New York: Dutton Children's Books, 1993. 192 p.

This book tells of Basil's experiences watching persons of different colors as he grows up in Cape Town. He observes the rich white children whose mother commits suicide; the Afrikaner father who points a gun at him when he finds out it is an English-South African who is dating his daughter; the priest with whom he, a Jew, shares a pleasant conversation; his family's coloured servant who is given twenty rands when she finds and returns to a white woman her handbag containing more than 4,000 rands worth of jewelry; the white man who fires a Xhosa man from his gardening job because he has completed night school; the Indian-Malay man who deceives the municipality in order to secure funds to support his developmentally-disabled daughter and her five children; the coloured tramp he befriends whose shack is destroyed by his friend's father; the police who tail him and his mother because they help coloured persons who are severely handicapped; and his dream girl who, darker than

her parents and siblings, is reclassified as coloured, is forced to leave her white boarding school, and is killed during a boycott. When he is eighteen, Basil avoids being recruited into the army by pretending to be schizophrenic, to see different things with each eye. In truth, he does see contradictory sides of South African life.
Coloured-South African
Older; Fiction

Indian-South African

Silver, Norman. *An Eye for Color*. New York: Dutton Children's Books, 1993. 192 p.
   This book tells of Basil's experiences watching persons of different colors as he grows up in Cape Town. He observes the rich white children whose mother commits suicide; the Afrikaner father who points a gun at him when he finds out it is an English-South African who is dating his daughter; the priest with whom he, a Jew, shares a pleasant conversation; his family's coloured servant who is given twenty rands when she finds and returns to a white woman her handbag containing more than 4,000 rands worth of jewelry; the white man who fires a Xhosa man from his gardening job because he has completed night school; the Indian-Malay man who deceives the municipality in order to secure funds to support his developmentally-disabled daughter and her five children; the coloured tramp he befriends whose shack is destroyed by his friend's father; the police who tail him and his mother because they help coloured persons who are severely handicapped; and his dream girl who, darker than her parents and siblings, is reclassified as coloured, is forced to leave her white boarding school, and is killed during a boycott. When he is eighteen, Basil avoids being recruited into the army by pretending to be schizophrenic, to see different things with each eye. In truth, he does see contradictory sides of South African life.
Indian-Malay-South African
Older; Fiction

Malay-South African

Silver, Norman. *An Eye for Color*. New York: Dutton Children's Books, 1993. 192 p.
   This book tells of Basil's experiences watching persons of different colors as he grows up in Cape Town. He observes the rich white children whose mother commits suicide; the Afrikaner father who points a gun at him when he finds out it is an English-South African who is dating his daughter; the priest with whom he, a Jew, shares a pleasant conversation; his family's coloured servant who is given twenty rands when she finds and returns to a white woman her handbag containing more than 4,000 rands worth of jewelry; the white man who fires a Xhosa man from his gardening job because he has completed night school; the Indian-Malay man who deceives the municipality in order to secure funds to support his developmentally-disabled daughter and her five children; the coloured tramp he befriends whose shack is destroyed by his friend's father; the police who tail him and his mother because they help coloured persons who are severely handicapped; and his dream girl who, darker than her parents and siblings, is reclassified as coloured, is forced to leave her white boarding school, and is killed during a boycott. When he is eighteen, Basil avoids being recruited into the army by pretending

to be schizophrenic, to see different things with each eye. In truth, he does see contradictory sides of South African life.
Indian-Malay-South African
Older; Fiction

Sudanese

African (Dinka or Nuba)-Sudanese

Levitin, Sonia. *Dream Freedom*. San Diego: Silver Whistle, 2000. 192 p.

This book is based on the campaign of schoolchildren to free Dinka and Nuba slaves taken by Arabs from the northern part of Sudan during that country's civil war. The book presents the fictional stories of an American boy's collecting newspapers to raise money to buy slaves' freedom and of Sudanese affected in different ways by the slavery. It includes a story of Fatima, a girl of mixed Arab and African race who, born a slave, knows of nothing but obeying one's master and is not interested in freedom, and of a Sudanese bishop of African and Arab heritage who brings gifts to a refugee camp. A bibliography and a resource section are included.
Arab-Sudanese and African (Dinka or Nuba)-Sudanese
Intermediate, Older; Fiction

Arab-Sudanese

Levitin, Sonia. *Dream Freedom*. San Diego: Silver Whistle, 2000. 192 p.

This book is based on the campaign of schoolchildren to free Dinka and Nuba slaves taken by Arabs from the northern part of Sudan during that country's civil war. The book presents the fictional stories of an American boy's collecting newspapers to raise money to buy slaves' freedom and of Sudanese affected in different ways by the slavery. It includes a story of Fatima, a girl of mixed Arab and African race who, born a slave, knows of nothing but obeying one's master and is not interested in freedom, and of a Sudanese bishop of African and Arab heritage who brings gifts to a refugee camp. A bibliography and a resource section are included.
Arab-Sudanese and African (Dinka or Nuba)-Sudanese
Intermediate, Older; Fiction

Tanzanian

African-Tanzanian

Doherty, Berlie. *The Girl Who Saw Lions*. New York: Roaring Brook Press, 2008. 256 p. (A Neal Porter Book)

In alternating chapters this book relates the stories of Rosa, the thirteen-year-old daughter of a Tanzanian father and an English mother, who lives with her mother in Sheffield, England, and Abela, a nine-year-old Tanzanian whose parents both die of AIDS. Rosa, who loves taking ice skating lessons

with her mother, initially feels rejected when her mum wants to adopt a little girl and then hurt when the four-year-old Tanzanian boy whom she comes to love cannot be adopted because his father shows up. Abela is sent for sale to London by her unscrupulous uncle, is kept captive in the apartment of his naïve white bride, runs away to a nearby school, and goes to live with a Nigerian foster family. When Abela is given resident status, she becomes Rosa's little sister.
African-Tanzanian/English; European-Tanzanian/African-Tanzanian
Intermediate, Older; Fiction

European-Tanzanian

Doherty, Berlie. *The Girl Who Saw Lions*. New York: Roaring Brook Press, 2008. 256 p. (A Neal Porter Book)

In alternating chapters this book relates the stories of Rosa, the thirteen-year-old daughter of a Tanzanian father and an English mother, who lives with her mother in Sheffield, England, and Abela, a nine-year-old Tanzanian whose parents both die of AIDS. Rosa, who loves taking ice skating lessons with her mother, initially feels rejected when her mum wants to adopt a little girl and then hurt when the four-year-old Tanzanian boy whom she comes to love cannot be adopted because his father shows up. Abela is sent for sale to London by her unscrupulous uncle, is kept captive in the apartment of his naïve white bride, runs away to a nearby school, and goes to live with a Nigerian foster family. When Abela is given resident status, she becomes Rosa's little sister.
European-Tanzanian/African-Tanzanian
Intermediate, Older; Fiction

English-Tanzanian

Doherty, Berlie. *The Girl Who Saw Lions*. New York: Roaring Brook Press, 2008. 256 p. (A Neal Porter Book)

In alternating chapters this book relates the stories of Rosa, the thirteen-year-old daughter of a Tanzanian father and an English mother, who lives with her mother in Sheffield, England, and Abela, a nine-year-old Tanzanian whose parents both die of AIDS. Rosa, who loves taking ice skating lessons with her mother, initially feels rejected when her mum wants to adopt a little girl and then hurt when the four-year-old Tanzanian boy whom she comes to love cannot be adopted because his father shows up. Abela is sent for sale to London by her unscrupulous uncle, is kept captive in the apartment of his naïve white bride, runs away to a nearby school, and goes to live with a Nigerian foster family. When Abela is given resident status, she becomes Rosa's little sister.
African-Tanzanian/English
Intermediate, Older; Fiction

C. American

African-American

See   Attucks, Crispus
Beckwourth, James (Jim) Pierson
Berry, Halle Maria
Beyoncé
Bibb, Henry
Bonga, George
Brown, Anne Wiggins
Brown, Eve
Cardozo, Francis Lewis
Carey, Mariah
Cary, Mary Ann Shadd
Coker, Daniel
Coleman, Elizabeth (Bessie)
Crawford, Goldsby
Dandridge, Dorothy
Douglass, Frederick
Du Bois, William Edward Burghardt (W. E. B.)
Early, Sarah Jane Woodson
Haley, Alexander (Alex) Murray Palmer
Hamilton, Virginia Esther
Haynes, Lemuel
Healy, James Augustine
Healy, Michael
Healy, Patrick Francis
Hemings, Beverly
Hemings, Harriet
Hemings, John
Hemings, Sally
Hodges, Ben
Hope, John
Horne, Lena
Horse, John
Hughes, James Mercer Langston
Jacobs, Harriet Ann
Jacobs, Joseph
Jeter, Derek Sanderson
Johnson, Dwayne Douglass

Jones, John
Keys, Alicia
Kidd, Jason Frederick
Langston, John Mercer
Lewis, Mary Edmonia
Limber, Jim
Loving, Mildred Delores Jeter
Malcolm X
Mason, Bridget (Biddy)
McBride, James
Morgan, Garrett Augustus
O'Brien, Daniel (Dan) Dion
O'Brien, Maria de la Soledad Teresa (Soledad)
Parks, Rosa Louise McCauley
Parsons, Lucia (Lucy) Gonzàles
Peake, Mary Smith Kelsey
Pickett, Bill
Rillieux, Norbert
Rose, Edward
Schomburg, Arthur Alfonso
Senna, Danzy
Smalls, Robert
Smith, Nolle
Stewart, John
Te Ata
Turner, Tina
Walker, Alice Malsenior
Walker, Maggie Dalena (Lena) Mitchell
Wamba, Philippe
Washington, Booker Taliaferro
Washington, Fannie Norton Smith
Washington, Margaret James Murray
Washington, Olivia A. Davidson
White, George Henry
White, Walter Frances
Williams, Daniel Hale
Williams, Mary Harris
Woods, Tiger
Woodson, Lewis

Adoff, Arnold. *All the Colors of the Race*. Illustrated by John Steptoe. New York: Lothrop, Lee & Shepard Books, 1982. 56 p.

Poems celebrate a girl who is Polish, German, Russian, and Jewish on her father's side and African-American and Protestant on her mother's. She looks forward to the time when we will cease *looking* at colors and *love* all colors of the human race.
Polish-German-Russian-American Jewish/African-American Protestant
Intermediate, Older; Fiction

Adoff, Arnold. *black is brown is tan*. Illustrated by Emily Arnold McCully. New York: Harper & Row, 1973. 32 p. Reissued with updated illustrations. HarperCollins/Amistad, 2002.

Adoff's poem and McCully's accompanying illustrations celebrate black, white, and shades in-between as they present the daily life of a close-knit family: two small children, their black mom, grandma, and uncle and their white daddy, granny, and aunt.
European-American/African-American
Pre-K, Primary; Fiction

Adoff, Arnold. *Hard to Be Six*. Illustrated by Cheryl Hanna. New York: Lothrop, Lee & Shepard Books, 1991. 32 p.

A six-year-old boy, who longs to be as big as his ten-year-old sister, is reassured by his family that he is indeed growing bigger. However, it is the words on his grandfather's gravestone that encourage him to slow down and live in the present. The illustrations depict a father who is white and a mother and grandparents who are African-American.
African-American/European-American
Pre-K, Primary; Fiction

Adoff, Jaime. *The Death of Jayson Porter*. New York: Jump at the Sun/Hyperion, 2008. 272 p.

This book for a high school audience tells of the depressing life of sixteen-year-old Jayson Porter, who throughout the story contemplates the day when he will jump off the eighteenth floor of his apartment building. Jayson's father, who has left the family, is a crackhead. Jayson's mother is an alcoholic, who delights in physically abusing Jayson. Jayson narrowly escapes being shot, smokes pot with his best friend Trax, is one of only two non-white students in his private school, has sex with his girlfriend, suffers the death of Trax when a meth lab explodes, and learns that his parents are not his real parents. Jayson does jump, but from the seventh floor where Trax lived. He miraculously escapes death, but is gravely injured. The story ends hopefully as Jayson is finally united with his real mother, who has turned her life around and always loved him.
African-American/European-American
Older; Fiction

Adoff, Jaime. *Jimi & Me*. New York: Jump at the Sun, 2005. 336 p.

This novel in verse is filled with despair as thirteen-year-old Keith experiences the shooting death of his father, moving from Brooklyn to a small Ohio town, taunting at his new school, his mother's slide into depression, the hatred both of them feel when they find out that his father was giving their money to another woman and the son they had, and learning that this sixteen-year-old half brother is named Jimi, the name of his idol Jimi Hendrix. When Keith meets his half brother, he discovers the

truth and begins to go on with his life.
African-American and Cherokee/European-American
Older; Fiction

Angel, Ann. *Real for Sure Sister*. Illustrated by Joanne Bowring. Fort Wayne, Ind.: Perspectives Press, 1988. 72 p.

Nine-year-old Amanda is adopted as are her brothers Nicky and Joey, who is Mexican Indian. Although she adores her little brothers, she has conflicting feelings about Stevi, the biracial (black/white) baby her family is planning to adopt. Amanda initially wants another brother, not a sister, and then tries to ignore Stevi in case the adoption doesn't go through. She shares her concern with her parents, who are white, and with her best friend, who has been adopted from Korea. It is a happy day when Amanda's entire family goes to court and Stevi becomes her real sister.
African-European-American
Primary; Fiction

Becker, John T., and Stanli K. Becker, eds. *All Blood Is Red . . . All Shadows Are Dark!* Illustrated by J. Howard Noel. Cleveland: Seven Shadows Press, 1984. 168 p.

John T. (Tom) Becker, who is Irish-German-American, and his wife, Stanli K. Becker, who is African-American, have five young children. One of the four who are adopted is biracial. All seven family members are responsible for individual sections of this book, which recounts their personal and family experiences as a multiracial family. Teaching their children to be aware of and proud of their individual differences, the editors present information on the history of racial classification in the United States and advocate their belief that race is and should be regarded as an "absurdity."
Irish-German-American/African-American; African-European-American
Intermediate, Older; Nonfiction

Binch, Caroline. *Silver Shoes*. Illustrated by author. New York: DK Publishing, 2001. 28 p.

Loving her grandmother's silver dancing shoes, Molly wants a pair of her own when she starts dance lessons. She unhappily discovers that the adult ones she gets her mother to buy at the thrift store cannot be used at her dance class, but decides to dance without them. Then finally, on her birthday, Molly's wish for silver shoes comes true. The illustrations in this picture book show that Molly's mother is African-American and her father and grandparents are Caucasian.
European-American/African-American
Pre-K, Primary; Fiction

Bode, Janet. *Different Worlds: Interracial and Cross-Cultural Dating*. New York: Franklin Watts, 1989. 128 p.

Based primarily on interviews with six teenage couples who are dating interracially and/or cross-culturally, this book is written for and about teens. It looks at the history of prejudice and racism; discusses negative reactions of parents, relatives, and classmates; examines why adolescents make their dating choices; and mentions some positive aspects of interracial dating. Although it does not cover the topics of interracial marriage and families, four of the twelve teens interviewed are of mixed race or

heritage: African-American/European-American; Protestant English-American/Catholic Irish-American; Cuban/Puerto Rican; and Mexican-Spanish-American. A bibliography, a listing of resource organizations, and an index are included.
African-American/European-American
Older; Nonfiction

Bradman, Tony, and Eileen Browne. *Through My Window*. Morristown, N.J.: Silver Burdett Company, 1986. 28 p.

A little girl, who must stay inside her apartment because she is ill, keeps looking out the window for her mother, who is going to bring her a surprise after work. She sees the mail carrier, the milk delivery lady, the window cleaner, her next door neighbor, the neighbor's dog—and finally her mother, who has the surprise: a toy doctor kit. The pictures show that the girl's father, who is home with her, is Caucasian and her mother is African-American.
European-American/African-American
Pre-K, Primary; Fiction

Brashares, Ann. *Forever in Blue: The Fourth Summer of the Sisterhood*. New York: Delacorte Press, 2007. 400 p. (Sisterhood of the Traveling Pants)

This fourth book of the series takes place after Carmen, Lena, Tibby, and Bridget's freshman year in college. Carmen's year at Williams College has been a disaster. She finds herself ungrounded with her mother, stepfather, and baby brother moving into a new house, discovers that she has no idea how to make friends, and feels invisible. Her only college friend, aspiring actress Julia, has persuaded Carmen to spend the summer with her at a theater festival in Vermont where Carmen will be on a stage crew. When the casting director persuades Carmen to audition, Carmen, who has never acted, is amazed to discover that she is the only apprentice chosen for a role in the theater's major production. Julia becomes hostile to Carmen and, then, pretending to be helpful, teaches Carmen how to read her role in meter. The professional actors are dismayed that Carmen now sounds like a robot. Carmen finally realizes that Julia takes pleasure in her failures, and she once again immerses herself in her role. Lena, who had been crushed when her Greek boyfriend Kostas married a Greek woman whom he had impregnated, is enrolled in a painting class in Providence, Rhode Island. There she is impressed with classmate Leo, an outstanding artist who is equally engrossed in painting. Getting to know him and his artistic African-American mother, Lena has her first sexual experience with him. Tibby, who has been going with Bailey's friend Brian, also loses her virginity. However, she becomes distressed that she may be pregnant and, after discovering that she isn't, breaks up with Brian. She then gives Lena's younger sister Effie an okay to go out with him. With Bridget's boyfriend Eric away for the summer in Mexico, she goes to Turkey for an archaeological dig. There she discovers that she loves digging and falls for an archaeology professor until she sees his wife and children. At the book's conclusion Tibby is reunited with Brian, Bridget is reunited with Eric, and Lena, Tibby, and Bridget go to Vermont to attend Carmen's successful opening night. Then the four friends fly to Greece to search for the Traveling Pants, which Effie has accidentally lost, Lena and Kostas meet, and the four friends realize that they have moved beyond the Pants. The mixed heritages of Carmen, Bridget, and

Eric should be familiar to readers of *The Sisterhood of the Traveling Pants*.
European-American/African-American
Older; Fiction

Brooks, Bruce. *Prince*. New York: Harper Trophy, 1998. 144 p. (A Laura Geringer Book) (The Wolfbay Wings #5)

Middle-schooler Prince, who is black and French Canadian, loves to play ice hockey and sing swing songs. Not surprisingly, he finds it difficult to fit in with his Maryland black classmates who want him to join the basketball team and mock his "white" sport. In this story, which is filled with hockey action, Prince, remaining true to himself, finally gains his classmates' support.
African-American and French Canadian
Intermediate, Older; Fiction

Carbone, Elisa. *Last Dance on Holladay Street*. New York: Alfred A. Knopf, 2005. 208 p.

In this story, which is set in the 1870s in Colorado, thirteen-year-old Eva leaves her prairie homestead when her adoptive African-American parents die. She travels to Denver in hopes that the mother who gave her away as an infant will let her stay. Shocked when she discovers that her mother is white and a prostitute, Eva must live in the brothel, dancing in its dance hall and becoming increasingly indebted to its madam. When it appears that she will have to work "upstairs," Eva escapes. With the help of an elderly black man Eva travels to Georgetown, is attacked by a mountain lion, and sent back to Denver to live in an orphanage. Then, through her ingenuity, Eva manages to set up a small successful eating house with her mother and half sister.
African-American/European-American
Older; Fiction

Chocolate, Debbi. *Elizabeth's Wish*. Orange, N.J.:Just Us Books, 1994. 120 p. (NEATE)

Naimah, **E**lizabeth, **A**nthony, **T**ayesha, and **E**ddie are eighth-grade friends who call themselves NEATE. Together they work towards having rap and not heavy-metal music at their school dance, Tayesha struggles with her biracial identity, and Elizabeth wants to win the grand prize in a talent search. NEATE's efforts make it possible to have both a rap and a heavy-metal band at the dance. Tayesha stands up for herself, declaring to tormentors that she is just as black as they are, and Elizabeth, overcoming a sore throat and a sprained ankle, wins the contest and donates her prize money to a campaign to save a homeless shelter. This book is a sequel to *NEATE to the Rescue*.
African-American/German
Intermediate, Older; Fiction

Chocolate, Debbi. *NEATE to the Rescue*. Orange, N.J.: Just Us Books, 1992. 104 p. (NEATE)

When eighth-grader Naimah and her friends secretly try to help her mother be reelected to her newly re-districted city council seat, they unintentionally cause a disturbance at her opponent's rally. Grounded, Naimah concentrates on her own campaign for student council president, which she wins. She then comes up with an idea that, with the support of her friends, is a major factor in her mother's

come-from-behind victory. One of Naimah's four friends is Tayesha, whose African-American father married her German mother when he was in the army in Germany.
African-American/German
Intermediate, Older; Fiction

Crutcher, Chris. *Whale Talk*. New York: Dell Laurel-Leaf, 2002. 224 p.

This novel tells of T. J. Jones, an adopted seventeen-year-old of mixed race, who in his senior year of high school organizes a swimming team of boys regarded as misfits by their classmates and the school and who are, except for T. J., mediocre swimmers. The story focuses on T. J.'s efforts to have his teammates rewarded for their Herculean efforts by receiving athletic letters. The book shows how the boys come to share their backgrounds and feelings and to become part of a cohesive group in which each feels valued and accepted. Thanks primarily to his father, T. J. learns to control his own rage.
African-Japanese-American/Swiss-Norwegian-American
Older; Fiction

Curry, Jane Louise. *The Black Canary*. New York: Margaret K. McElderry Books, 2005. 288 p.

When almost-thirteen-year-old James visits London with his parents, he passes into the London of 1600 where he is snatched off the street to become a member of the Children of the Chapel Royal, who are actors and members of the queen's chapel choir. Since he was small, James has resented music since he blames the musical careers of his parents for their absences. Always feeling invisible, including when his relatives, both black and Caucasian, assume he is like them, James as one of the Children discovers that he loves to sing, for in singing he recognizes who he can be. James must decide whether he wishes to perform as a singer before Queen Elizabeth I or return to his family—if he can get back.
English-American/African-American
Intermediate, Older; Fiction

Danziger, Paula. *It's an Aardvark-Eat-Turtle World*. New York: Delacorte Press, 1985. 144 p.

When fourteen-year-old Rosie's mother and Rosie's best friend Phoebe's father move in together, Rosie is pleased that the four of them will form a family. However, when Phoebe gets upset with Rosie's mother and also with Rosie because she spends time with Jason, her first boyfriend, and when Phoebe decides to move out and live with her mother, Rosie discovers that family relationships are not easy. She also suffers from the hateful remark of a man who objects to mixed race Rosie and Canadian Jason being together. At the story's end Phoebe decides to work things out and come back and Rosie spends a happy Christmas Eve with both Jason and Phoebe.
African-American Protestant/European-American Jewish
Intermediate, Older; Fiction

Davol, Marguerite W. *Black, White, Just Right!* Illustrated by Irene Trivas. Morton Grove, Ill.: Albert Whitman & Company. 1993. 32 p.

Relating ways her African-American mother and her Caucasian father differ in how they look and what they like, a little girl tells of her own looks and preferences which are "just right."
European-American/African-American
Pre-K, Primary; Fiction

De la Peña, Matt. *Mexican Whiteboy.* New York: Delacorte Press, 2008. 256 p.

Sixteen-year-old Danny chooses to spend his summer vacation with his Mexican-American father's family in National City, California, so that he can then fly to Ensenada, Mexico, and find his father. Since his father left his San Diego family three years earlier, Danny has been heartbroken to the extent that he seldom speaks, not wanting to use his mother's English. His goal is to please his father by becoming a great pitcher. He has exceptional talent, but is plagued by his lack of control. During the eventful summer Danny makes an unlikely best friend, Uno, who initially punched Danny. Uno needs to make money so that he can move away from his Mexican-American mother and step-father and live with his black father. Through hours of practice with Uno, Danny works on his pitching skills and discovers how to keep the ball in the strike zone when people are watching. Together Uno and Danny successfully hustle the area's best hitters, thereby earning money for Uno. Although he cannot speak Spanish and she cannot speak English, Danny falls in love with Liberty, who is newly arrived from Mexico and has a white father. Further, Danny finally finds out the truth about his father and comes to accept himself.
African-American/Mexican-American
Older; Fiction

Dorris, Michael. *The Window.* New York: Hyperion Paperbacks for Children, 1999. 112 p.

When eleven-year-old Rayona's mother is ordered into an alcohol rehabilitation program, two efforts at finding Rayona a foster home fail and her father decides he can't care for her. It is then that Rayona learns that her African-American father is half Irish-American. He takes her from Seattle to Louisville where she enjoys her temporary stay with her Irish-American grandmother, great-aunt, and great-grandmother and meets an older African-American cousin. It is with regret that Rayona leaves her newfound relatives, but with happiness that she is reunited with her much-missed Native American mother—and with gratitude that a window on her life has been opened.
African-Irish-American/Native American
Intermediate, Older; Fiction

Erlbach, Arlene. *The Families Book: True Stories about Real Kids and the People They Live With and Love.* Photographs by Stephen J. Carrera. Illustrated by Lisa Wagner. Minneapolis: Free Spirit Publishing, 1996. 120 p.

In a section of this book, children tell about their families, that include a family in which the father is Lutheran and the mother Jewish; a family in which the father is African-American and the mother Caucasian; a family with four children in which Caucasian parents have adopted a biracial American girl and a boy from Romania; and a family with Caucasian parents and eleven children, six of whom were adopted from Korea.

African-American/European-American
Intermediate; Nonfiction

Flake, Sharon G. *Begging for Change*. New York: Jump at the Sun, 2007. 256 p.

This sequel to *Money Hungry* again focuses on the girl Raspberry Hill, now fourteen. It begins with Raspberry's mother going to the hospital after being severely beaten by a neighbor girl whom she had reported to the authorities. Consumed as usual by the desire for money to help keep her mother and herself solvent, Raspberry steals from her friend Zora's purse and also takes change from an elderly neighborhood friend. Throughout the story Raspberry is afraid that Zora will tell her father, Dr. Mitchell, who is dating Raspberry's mother and who is like a father to Raspberry. She is also afraid that she is turning into her own father, who, homeless and high on drugs, comes to the Hills' apartment and steals Raspberry's money. Although not telling her father (Dr. Mitchell) about the theft from her purse, Zora stops being Raspberry's friend. In this story Mai, another of Raspberry's friends, continues to be so upset at being taunted because of her mixed racial appearance that she has her arm tattooed "100% black" and is mean to her visiting Korean-American cousins. By the book's conclusion Raspberry gets her first boyfriend, confesses to Dr. Mitchell, and plans to return the money to her neighbor. Also, she and her mother move out of the projects into a nicer and safer apartment, Zora makes up with Raspberry, and Mai grudgingly comes to accept her cousins.
South Korean/African-American
Intermediate, Older; Fiction

Flake, Sharon G. *Money Hungry*. New York: Jump at the Sun, 2001. 192 p.

This is the story of thirteen-year-old African-American Raspberry and her friends: Zora, Mai, and Ja'nae. Raspberry, who lives with her mother in the projects, is determined that they will never again live on the streets. She spends her time, sometimes with her friends' help, making money: selling items at school, cleaning houses of the elderly, and helping at a car wash. Zora resents her physician father's being close to Raspberry's mother. The daughter of a Korean father and a black mother, Mae is constantly the target of racial insults because she is part Korean. She takes it out on her Korean father and wishes her mother had married a black man. Ja'nae doesn't pay her debt to Raspberry and steals from her grandfather to pay bus fare for her irresponsible mother to come and take her away. All Raspberry's efforts to have money come to nothing when her mother, mistakenly thinking Raspberry has stolen her earned money, throws some of it out the window and then their apartment is robbed. The book concludes with Raspberry and her mother's efforts to stay off the streets. The story is continued in the sequel, *Begging for Change*.
South Korean/African-American
Intermediate, Older; Fiction

Flood, Pansie Hart. *It's a Test Day, Tiger Turcotte*. Illustrated by Amy Wummer. Minneapolis: Carolrhoda Books, 2004. 72 p.

In this chapter book seven-year-old Tiger, who is of mixed race, is worried when it is time to take a big practice test, but becomes really upset when he has to fill in the race bubble. The African-American volunteer tells him to fill in Black and his teacher concludes he should fill in Other, but Tiger decides to

leave that question blank because he isn't a weird or different "other." Tiger feels better when his father explains that just as ice cream can have mixed flavors, so people can be of mixed race. He feels even better when the next day there is an answer sheet that includes a Multiracial bubble and he discovers that a classmate is both black and Japanese.
African-American and Meherrin/Costa Rican; African-American and Japanese
Primary; Fiction

Flood, Pansie Hart. *Tiger Turcotte Takes on the Know-It-All*. Illustrated by Amy Wummer. Minneapolis: Carolrhoda Books, 2005. 72 p.

Second-grader Tiger doesn't like "germy" girls and especially Donna Overton, who is a know-it-all. When Tiger and Donna call each other names in art class, they have to go to after-school detention. It is there that Tiger discovers he sort of likes Donna. There is no mention of Tiger's identity in this chapter book, but readers of *It's a Test Day, Tiger Turcotte* will know he is of mixed race.
African-American and Meherrin/Costa Rican; African-American and Japanese
Primary; Fiction

Forrester, Sandra. *Dust from Old Bones*. New York: Morrow Junior Books, 1999. 176 p.

This story is set in the stratified society of the New Orleans of 1838. Thirteen-year-old Simone, who is a person of color, struggles with the probability that her pretty cousin Claire-Marie will go to quadroon balls and be chosen by a Creole "protector" [as his mistress]. She envies the life of Madelon, her aunt who lives in France where she is not faced with racial discrimination. Nevertheless, Simone comes to realize that her restricted life as a person of color is much better than that of black slaves, who if lucky enough to be freed had to leave New Orleans. Simone's admiration for Madelon, who comes to visit, disappears when she betrays not only Simone, but also the two slaves she was committed to free. It is Simone who leads the slaves through a swamp to a safe house.
African-Creole-American/African-Creole-Haitian; Creole-American/African-Creole-
  Haitian
Older; Fiction

Frazier, Sundee T. *Brendan Buckley's Universe and Everything in It*. New York: Delacorte Press, 2007. 208 p.

Ten-year-old Brendan's time is spent working on his Tae Kwon Do and trying to figure out the answers to the many questions which face him. A budding scientist, Brendan by chance meets the grandfather who is never spoken of at a mineral exhibit. Secretly visiting his newly-discovered grandfather and even sneaking off on a thunder-egg hunting expedition with him, Brendan finally discovers the disturbing truth that his grandfather had opposed his mother's marriage to his black father and cut off contact. Through Brandon's efforts the family learns the importance of forgiveness and Brandon not only learns about telling the truth, but also comes to appreciate that he, like rocks with their mixed minerals, is both black and white.
African-American/European-American
Intermediate; Fiction

Gallo, Donald R., editor. *Join In: Multiethnic Short Stories by Outstanding Writers for Young Adults*. New York: Delacorte Press, 1993. 272 p.

One of the seventeen short stories in this book is "Next Month . . . Hollywood" by Jean Davies Okimoto. Rodney, who is Japanese-Polish American, wants to be an Asian rapper. With the support of his good friend Ivy, who is Filipino-African-American, he plans for the two of them to appear in their high school talent show. When they preview their act before a different audience, the results are unexpectedly uproarious. Ivy realizes that their performance should be a comedy act and, at last, becomes Rodney's girlfriend.

Filipino-American/African-American

Older; Fiction

Graham, Bob. *Oscar's Half Birthday*. Illustrated by author. Cambridge, Mass.: Candlewick Press, 2005. 32 p.

Three-year-old Millie, her European-American father, her African-American mother, and their dog take Millie's brother Oscar to Bellevue Hill for his six-month-old birthday. Picnickers on the hill join them in the joyous celebration. No specific setting is noted in the book so it is assumed that the family is American although, as the author-illustrator lives in Australia, it may be an Australian family.

European-American/African-American

Preschool, Primary; Fiction

Grimes, Nikki. *Oh, Brother!* Illustrated by Mike Benny. New York: Greenwillow Books, 2008. 32 p.

In this picture book story narrated through twenty poems, Xavier resents the intrusion of his new stepbrother. As the boys get to know each other's feelings they become closer and, with the birth of their baby sister, make a pact of brotherhood.

African-American/Latin-American

Pre-K, Primary; Fiction

Hahn, Mary Downing. *Promises to the Dead*. New York: Clarion Books, 2000. 202 p.

It is Maryland in 1861 when the Civil War is just beginning and many in the state support the South. Jesse, a twelve-year-old white boy who is looking for turtles, encounters an escaped slave, who, before dying, makes Jesse promise that he will deliver her young boy, Perry, the son of her deceased owner, to the owner's sister in Baltimore. The book recounts the boys' numerous adventures as they encounter rioting in Baltimore; discover that Perry's aunt has gone to Virginia; find out, upon arriving there, that the white aunt does not want Perry; escape with a group of slaves; and throughout are pursued by the cruel slave catcher, Abednego Botfield, who, when dying, also extracts a promise from Jesse.

European-American/African-European-American

Intermediate, Older; Fiction

Hamanaka, Sheila. *Grandparents Song*. Illustrated by author. New York: HarperCollins Publishers, 2003. 32 p.

In this picture book, which is written in verse, a girl tells how her grandparents came from four directions—her maternal grandmother from the West, her maternal grandfather from Europe, her paternal grandmother from Mexico, and her paternal grandfather from Africa—and how they are all part of her.

African-Mexican-American/European-American and Native American
Pre-K, Primary, Intermediate; Fiction

Hamilton, Virginia. *Arilla Sun Down*. New York: Scholastic, 1976. 304 p.

This novel tells of twelve-year-old Arilla whose mother is sure of her identity as an African-American woman, whose Native American father alternates between his work at an Ohio college and leaving for his boyhood home, and whose older brother, Jack Sun Run, delights in parading his Native American heritage. Always in her brother's shadow, certain that he hates her, and terribly jealous, Arilla treasures the times that he treats her nicely. The book tells of Arilla's writing her autobiography; of old James False Face, her only friend when she was little; of Susanne Shy Woman who is Sioux and Cheyenne; of sneaking out at night with Sun Run and his girlfriend to go roller skating; of sledding with her father on an exciting, but dangerous hill; of saving Sun Run's life and discovering he had saved hers; and, throughout the book, of her struggle to find her own identity.

Native American/African-American
Older; Fiction

Hamilton, Virginia. *Junius Over Far*. New York: Harper & Row Publishers, 1985. 288 p.

Fourteen-year-old American, Junius Rawlings, has grown up very close to his grandfather Jackabo and speaks with a Caribbean accent and lilt. When Jackabo, feeling that he is a burden, returns to his tiny island, he lives on the old rundown Rawlings plantation with Burtie Rawlings, its elderly white owner with whom Jackabo has a contentious relationship. When Burtie disappears, Jackabo, who is forgetful and disoriented, writes Junius' family that Burtie was taken by pirates and he himself was accosted by them. Junius and his father Damius, who has rejected his island past, fly down to check on Jackabo. The mystery is solved, Jackabo agrees to go back to the States, Damius comes to enjoy the island, and the black Rawlings finally are accorded their due.

African-St. Kitts and Nevisian/African-American
Older; Fiction

Hamilton, Virginia. *Plain City*. New York: The Blue Sky Press, 1993. 208 p

With a father she mistakenly believes is missing in action in Vietnam, an African-American mother who is a singer-stripteaser and seldom at home, and classmates who ostracize her, twelve-year-old Buhlaire feels sad, alone, and confused. It is when she learns that her father is alive and living in her town that her life changes. She finds her father, a mixed race drifter with mental illness who loves her, considers going to live with him, and, in the process of discovering the truth about her family members, comes to accept them—and to have her first friend.

African-European-American/African-American
Older; Fiction

Hausherr, Rosmarie. *Celebrating Families*. New York: Scholastic Press, 1997. 32 p.

Among the families celebrated in this book are Jahsee's, whose father is from the Virgin Islands and whose mother is Norwegian-American, and Alexandra's, who was adopted from Brazil by two European-American mothers. The book is illustrated with photographs.

African-Virgin Islander/Norwegian-American

Primary, Intermediate; Nonfiction

Heath, Amy. *Sofie's Role*. Illustrated by Sheila Hamanaka. New York: Four Winds Press, 1992. 32 p.

On the day before Christmas, young Sofie is told that she can finally tend the counter at her parents' bakery. However, the customers don't notice her so she helps in the back—until a schoolmate comes in and it is Sofie who fills her order. In the illustrations, Sofie's mother is shown as African-American and her father as European-American.

European-American/African-American

Pre-K, Primary; Fiction

Highwater, Jamake. *The Ceremony of Innocence*. New York: Harper & Row, Publishers, 1985. 192 p. (The Ghost Horse Cycle)

The Ceremony of Innocence is the second book in *The Ghost Horse Cycle*, a series for teenagers. It is the sequel to *Legend Days*, which describes Amana's childhood experiences as a Blood (Blackfoot). In this book Amana, whose family has died, has left her people and is destitute. She comes to live with an immature French Canadian, who deserts her before the birth of their daughter Jemina. Although sustained by her friendship with a French-Cree woman who runs a brothel, Amana suffers when Jemina grows up obsessed with finery and is married to the drunkard Jamie Ghost Horse and when her older grandson is only interested in things "American." Amana's hope lies in Sitko, her younger grandson, who treasures his Native American heritage.

African-American and Cherokee/French Canadian-American and Blackfoot (Blood)

Older; Fiction

Highwater, Jamake. *I Wear the Morning Star*. New York: Harper & Row, Publishers, 1986. 160 p. (The Ghost Horse Cycle)

This third book in *The Ghost Horse Cycle* for the oldest readers tells the story of Sitko and his miserable boyhood. Sitko is placed in a boarding school where he is mistreated by the adults and scorned by the other children. His alcoholic father, Jamie Ghost Horse, realizing that Sitko deserves a better life, allows Alexander, his former friend and now the lover of his ex-wife Jemina, to adopt Sitko, and Sitko goes to live with Alexander, Jemina, and his grandmother Amana in the San Fernando Valley. Not able to figure out his past and deeply confused about his identity, Sitko continues a life filled with unhappiness, mitigated only by his friendship with a farm boy, his school's art club, and his painting. At the end of the book, Jamie shoots Jemina and Alexander, killing her and wounding Alexander. Jamie perishes in a truck crash, Sitko's older brother loses his life in a plane crash, the elderly Amana dies, and Sitko, the only one remaining, preserves his Blood (Blackfoot) past through his paintings.

African-American and Cherokee/French Canadian-American and Blackfoot (Blood)

Older; Fiction

Hooks, William H. *The Ballad of Belle Dorcas*. Illustrated by Brian Pinkney. New York: Dragonfly Books, 1990. 40 p.

Belle, whose father is a slave owner and mother a slave, is freed at birth and, thereby, a free-issue person. However, instead of marrying a free-issue man, she marries Joshua, a slave. When a new master takes over the plantation, he wants to sell Joshua. Belle seeks help from a conjure woman, who casts spells. First, she shows Belle how to save Joshua from being sent south by turning him into a cedar tree, and then how to transform him into a man each night. When the master makes the tree into a smokehouse roof and then moves the smokehouse into the woods, Belle is desolate. However, once again the conjure woman comes to the rescue. This tale is illustrated in a scratchboard style that enhances the atmosphere.
European-American/African-American
Primary, Intermediate; Fiction

Hurmence, Belinda. *Tancy*. New York: Clarion Books, 1984. 216 p.

Set in North Carolina at the end of the Civil War, this book tells of just-freed eighteen-year-old Tancy, who discovers that the deceased master of the plantation was her father. Tancy sets out to find her mother, who had been sold from the plantation when Tancy was very young. As she cares for a little boy who accompanies her, gives him up to his mother, works at a Freedmen's Bureau where she befriends a white woman, and gets a rude surprise when she meets her own mother, Tancy learns what it means to be free. At the book's conclusion Tancy must decide whether to return to the plantation, live with her mother in Shantytown, or chart her own course.
European-American/African-American
Older; Fiction

Hutchins, Pat. *There's Only One of Me!* Illustrated by author. New York: Greenwillow Books, 2003. 24 p.

In a cumulative text a five-year-old girl recognizes that she is her mother's daughter, her sister's sister, her half brother's half sister . . . and a birthday girl. The book's illustrations show that her uncle is African-American, her aunt is European-American, and her cousin is both.
African-American/European-American
Pre-K, Primary; Fiction

Igus, Toyomi. *Two Mrs. Gibsons*. Illustrated by Daryl Wells. San Francisco: Children's Book Press, 1996. 32 p.

In this picture book a little girl tells of the two Mrs. Gibsons who love her: the Japanese Mrs. Gibson who is her mother and the African-American Mrs. Gibson who is her grandmother.
African-American/Japanese
Pre-K, Primary; Fiction

Jones, Adrienne. *So, Nothing Is Forever*. Illustrated by Richard Cuffari. Boston: Houghton Mifflin Company, 1974. 256 p.

After her parents are killed in an automobile accident, fifteen-year-old Talene is determined to keep herself, her thirteen-year-old brother Joey, and her two-year-old brother Adam together during the year before their soldier uncle can care for them. When a social worker intends to place them in foster homes, with Adam possibly put up for adoption, the three children run away from New York to northern California in hopes that they can stay with their grandmother Anna, who had rejected their mother when she married a black man. Unhappy to see them, hostile Anna says they can stay for only a couple of weeks, but as their stay extends, the children are kept wondering as to how long it will last. During their time with Anna, Joey briefly runs away, an acquaintance from their bus trip joins them at Anna's, Adam almost drowns, the boy-crazy abused neighbor girl commits suicide, and the children come to understand their grandmother.
African-American/European-American
Older; Fiction

Kidd, Ronald. *On Beale Street*. New York: Simon & Schuster Books for Young Readers, 2008. 256 p.

It is 1954 in segregated Memphis, Tennessee. When fifteen-year-old Johnny goes to hear the music on Beale Street in the Negro section, his life changes. Caught up in the blues music, he meets young Elvis Presley, who also frequents Beale Street, volunteers and then works for Sam Phillips who launches Presley's career, and learns about the inequities of Negro life from Lamont, the son of Will Turner who is a Negro chauffeur and gardener. Johnny also wonders about the father he never knew and why his mother wants him to keep away from Will and Lamont. It is not until the end of the story that Johnny learns that he is Will's son and must make a decision that affects his own life and the lives of Lamont, his mother, and Will.
African-American/European-American
Older; Fiction

Koller, Jackie French. *A Place to Call Home*. New York: Atheneum Books for Young Readers, 1995. 208 p.

Fifteen-year-old Anna struggles to take care of her five-year-old sister and baby brother when their alcoholic abusive mother abandons them. Soon Anna discovers that their mother has committed suicide. Realizing that no one will want to adopt all three of them since the little ones are Caucasian and she is much older and of mixed race, Anna keeps her mother's disappearance a secret. Then, disguised as a boy, Anna takes the bus from Connecticut to Mississippi in hopes that her mother's parents will look after them. There she learns why her mother left. Her grandparents disapproved of her mother's relationship with a black man, and, after Anna was born, her police chief grandfather probably murdered her father. Anna finally realizes that she cannot care for her siblings and, with the help of a wise boyfriend, agrees to the adoption. Surprisingly Anna too will be adopted: by the older couple who runs the neighborhood convenience store.
African-American/European-American
Older; Fiction

Kuklin, Susan. Families. Photographs by author. New York: Hyperion Books for Children, 2006. 40 p.

Text and color photographs present interviews with American children, who talk about their families. Their families include seven families with children of mixed race, ethnicity, or religion, with one also including a child adopted from Sierra Leone. In an eighth family a child has been adopted from China. In a ninth family an adopted American child is of a race different from that of one of her fathers.
German-Jewish-American and Mescalero Apache/African-American; African-American/German
Primary, Intermediate; Nonfiction

Kuklin, Susan. *How My Family Lives in America*. Photographs by author. New York: Bradbury Press, 1992. 32 p.
One of this book's photo-essays presents the New York City family of five-year-old Sanu whose father was born in Senegal and mother in Baltimore. Sanu has visited her father's homeland and enjoys the way her family's activities incorporate its culture.
Senegalese/African-American
Pre-K, Primary; Nonfiction

Kurtz, Jane. *Faraway Home*. Illustrated by E. B. Lewis. San Diego: Gulliver Books, 2000. 32 p.
Desta is reluctant to have her father leave for Ethiopia to be with his ill mother. It is so far away and perhaps he won't come back. Reassured by her father's descriptions of Ethiopia and his boyhood there, Desta comes to accept that he misses Ethiopia, her grandmother misses him, and he will return.
Ethiopian/African-American
Pre-K, Primary; Fiction

Landau, Elaine. *Interracial Dating and Marriage*. New York: Julian Messner, 1993. 112 p.
This book's introduction presents two detailed histories of interracial marriage: the first of African-American intermarriage with Caucasians and the second of intermarriages involving Japanese-Americans. In both cases the introduction describes factors, including governmental actions and societal attitudes, which affected the frequency of these marriages. The bulk of the book presents interviews with ten teenagers and five adults or adult couples who describe their views of and/or experiences with interracial dating and marriage. Seven of the teens interviewed came to the United States from other countries; two of the teens are interracial. Two of the adult interviews are with interracial couples; another contains advice from a minister. A resource list and an index are included.
African-English-Indian-Italian-Dominican
Older; Nonfiction

Lester, Julius. *To Be a Slave*. 30th anniversary ed. Illustrated by Tom Feelings. New York: Dial Books, 1998. 168 p.
Among the slave narratives in this book is one by Doc Daniel Dowdy, which was recorded by the Federal Writers' Project in the 1930s and included in a 1945 book, *Lay My Burden Down*, edited by B.A. Botkin. This account of Dowdy's seeing his half white cousin Eliza bought and freed at a slave auction by an abolitionist from New York is expanded upon in Virginia Frances Schwartz' novel *Send One Angel Down*.

European-American/African-American
Older; Nonfiction

Levin, Beatrice. *John Hawk: White Man, Black Man, Indian Chief.* Austin: Eakin Press, 1988. 192 p.

This is the fictional story of John White, the son of a Georgia plantation owner and a slave mother, who becomes the lifelong friend of Osceola. The two meet as boys and, at Osceola's urging, John runs away to live with the Seminoles. He takes a new name, John Hawk, marries a Seminole woman, befriends a man who is Spanish-American and African-American, and becomes a Seminole chief. With Osceola he experiences the betrayals and tragedies preceding and during the Second Seminole War. A bibliography is included.

European-American/African-American; Spanish/African-American
Older; Fiction

Lewin, Michael Z. *Cutting Loose.* New York: Henry Holt and Company, 1999. 528 p.

Set in the nineteenth century, this is the story of Jackie's search for Teddy Zeph, who has murdered Jackie's best friend, Nance. The text alternates between the present and the past, starting with the story of Jackie's grandmother Claudette at the time she was orphaned. There are parallels among the characters' lives. Claudette is sold at a pauper auction, Jackie's father Matthew is sold by his New York City baseball team to a team in St. Louis, and Jackie goes to live with a new family that chooses her when she is displayed by the Children's Aid Society. Claudette murders her lover's father, and Matthew and Nance are murdered. Claudette disguises herself as a man to escape capture, and Jackie disguises herself as a man to pursue a baseball career. Both Jackie and her father play baseball in England as well as in the United States. Nance performs for Buffalo Bill's Wild West Show, and Jackie and Teddy Zeph perform on the stage in London. Further, Claudette's father is French, Teddy's mother is Spanish, and Nance, whose mother is African-American, passes as white.

European-American/African-American
Older; Fiction

MacGregor, Rob. *Hawk Moon.* New York: Simon & Schuster Books for Young Readers, 1996. 192 p.

Hawk Moon is the sequel to *Prophecy Rock.* When Will returns to Aspen, Colorado, from the Hopi Reservation where he has spent the summer, he tells his girlfriend Myra that he thinks they should break up, but does not give her the chance to tell him what is bothering her. She disappears from the ghost town where he had left her, and Will becomes the prime target of the investigation into her kidnapping. This mystery has many twists and turns as Will comes to suspect classmates, his mother's boyfriend, and members of the sheriff's department. He is helped by Corey, a girl of mixed race who is a computer geek, and he experiences visions of Masau, the Hopi's kachina ruler.

European-American/African-American
Older; Fiction

McClain, Lee. *My Alternate Life.* New York: Smooch, 2004. 188 p.

At age fifteen Trinity B. Jones is sent from foster care in Pittsburgh to live with a well-off rural family. Trinity wants instead to be reunited with her birthmother who had left her at Saint Helen's

Home for Girls when she was eight. Thanks to the amazing computer game her social worker gives her, Trinity is able to observe and hear her mother, who has married a wealthy man and craves media attention. Trinity focuses her efforts on becoming reunited with her mother. To that end, she tries to get the cruel sex-crazy boy, who will probably become the Fall King, to invite her to the Fall Dance so that she will become the Fall Queen and win her mother's acclaim. However, that project ends when he almost rapes her. Trinity also gets her foster mother to let the Fall Dance be a benefit for Saint Helen's and, using a classmate's name, invites her birthmother to be dance sponsor. At the dance, Trinity realizes which family is best for her.
African-American/European-American
Older; Fiction

McDonald, Janet. *Off-Color*. New York: Frances Foster Books, 2007. 176 p.
    Fifteen-year-old Cameron, who believes that her father is Italian, loves hanging out with her three best friends and doesn't take school seriously. Then her mother loses her job in a nail salon and gets one at lower wages in the owner's other salon in an African-American section of Brooklyn. Cameron and her mother must move into the projects, but, thanks to the school guidance counselor Mr. Siciliano, she is able to remain at her old high school. When Cameron discovers from an old photo that her father is black, she is shocked and blames her mother for not having told her about him and for his not being there for her. Cameron, her mother, her friends, her mother's coworkers, her multi-cultures class, and Mr. Siciliano spend time talking about race, about being biracial, about Mariah Carey, and about Malcolm X who Cameron hears in class was propelled to become a black national-ist because of his white-appearing mother. Cameron learns that one of her mother's coworkers is Korean and Irish, that Mr. Siciliano is half black, and that many celebrities are of mixed race. At her Sweet Sixteen party, Cameron enjoys her old best friends and new friends from the projects and even meets the boy who becomes her boyfriend.
African-American/Norwegian-American; Italian/African-American
Older; Fiction

McKissack, Patricia C. *Run Away Home*. New York: Scholastic Press, 1997. 176 p.
    In 1888 Sky, a fifteen-year-old Chiricahua Apache boy, escapes from a train of Apache prisoners and hides on the farm of twelve-year-old Sarah Jane Crossman, her African-American father, and her mother, who is of African-Scottish-Irish and Seminole heritage. George Wrattan, an Army scout and interpreter, allows the Crossmans to keep Sky with them until he recovers from his swamp fever. In the meantime boll weevils destroy the family's cotton crop, night riders come to their farm, and Sarah Jane's father, who is skilled as a carpenter, gets an order from Booker T. Washington to build desks for nearby Tuskegee Institute. Sky becomes healthy, but Wrattan, whose wife is Apache, gives per-mission for him to remain on the farm.
African-American/African-Scottish-Irish-American and Seminole
Intermediate, Older; Fiction

Meyer, Carolyn. *Denny's Tapes*. New York: Margaret K. McElderry Books, 1987. 224 p.
    Almost eighteen-year old Denny, the son of an African-American father and a white mother, and

sixteen-year-old Stephanie, the daughter of his white stepfather, fall in love. When his stepfather discovers them together, he orders Denny to leave the house. This story for high school readers is about Denny's journey from Pennsylvania to San Francisco to find his father and on the way to meet his two grandmothers. Although Denny doesn't get together with his musician father who has left for a couple months for a gig in Houston, his trip turns out to be a memorable one. In Chicago he meets his African-American grandmother, who is highly cultivated and had objected to his parents' marriage because of his mother's lower social status. In Nebraska, he meets his mother's mother, who had objected to the marriage because of his father's race and believes Africans-Americans have lower intelligence. However, Denny comes to care for both his grandmothers. His Chicago grandmother spends time teaching him about black history, including about her friend Langston Hughes, and shows him how to develop his natural talent on the piano. Denny discovers that his Nebraska grandmother is largely imprisoned in bed by her cruel daughter-in-law, is full of love for him, and greatly appreciates his organ playing. In Chicago Denny also has a romantic relationship with a beautiful twenty-four-year-old African-American woman, and in Colorado he is rescued by a cowgirl from a pair of tourists who object to what they wrongly assume is an interracial relationship. When he gets to San Francisco, Denny realizes that he has learned a lot about himself, that he wants to become a musician, and that he is going to wait for his father.
African-American/Swedish-American
Older; Fiction

Meyer, Carolyn. *Jubilee Journey*. San Diego: Gulliver Books, 1997. 288 p.

In this sequel to *White Lilacs*, it is 1996 and eighty-seven-year-old Rose Lee has invited her thirteen-year-old great-granddaughter Emily Rose and her family to attend the Freedomtown Juneteenth Diamond Jubilee. Growing up in Connecticut, Emily Rose has always regarded herself as a "double" as her father is French-American and her mother is African-American. However, she and her brothers Steven and Robbie have no idea what it means to be black in Dillon, Texas. They quickly learn of the attitudes of some whites when Steven is set up and abused and of the closeness and pride of the African-American community. In this story Rose Lee reveals what has happened to her and her family during the past seventy-five years. Emily Rose gets a new friend who thinks she should be just black and decides to remain in Denton to learn more about being black so she can better understand herself. Alicia, Rose Lee's best friend in Connecticut, has a Nigerian father and an English mother.
French-American and Catholic/African-European-American, Seminole, and Baptist
Intermediate, Older; Fiction

Meyer, Carolyn. *White Lilacs*. San Diego: Gulliver Books, 1993. 256 p.

Set in 1921 this is the story of Freedomtown, the section of Dillon, Texas, where African-Americans have lived since 1870 and of twelve-year-old Rose Lee, who experiences its sorrow when the whites force the residents to leave and move to the Flats, an undesirable part of town, so that the whites can build a city park and be further away from the blacks. It tells of Rose Lee's family and neighbors who are powerless to prevent Freedomtown's removal, of the thoughtlessness of the white women, of the Klan, of Rose's brother Henry being tarred and feathered, of the "colored school" being burned down, of Rose's Aunt Susannah who leaves her teaching job in St. Louis to teach the children

of the Flats, of the Quaker white lady Emily Firth who loses her job because she stands up for the blacks, of the white girl Catherine Jane who saves Henry, and of Rose Lee, who preserves Freedomtown in her drawings. Although Rose Lee and Susannah are mostly African-American, Rose Lee's paternal grandfather is part Seminole and her maternal great-grandfather was white. Susannah's paternal grandfather was white.
African-American and Seminole/African-European-American; African-European-American/African-American
Intermediate, Older; Fiction

Miles, Betty. *All It Takes Is Practice*. New York: Bullseye Books, 1989. 112 p.
Fifth grader Stuart wishes he had a best friend in addition to his neighborhood friend Alison. His wish comes true when Peter enters his Kansas classroom. Stuart is surprised when he discovers that Peter's mother is black. That doesn't matter to Stuart, his parents, or Alison, but raises the ire of Alison's father, who is also unappreciative of his daughter's interest in sports. When Stuart and Peter go downtown, they are attacked by three bigoted teenagers, and Stuart learns what it means to be a best friend.
European-American/African-American
Intermediate; Fiction

Monk, Isabell. *Family*. Illustrated by Janice Lee Porter. Minneapolis: Carolrhoda Books, 2001. 32 p.
In this sequel to *Hope*, Hope and her parents visit her mother's Aunt Poogee for a dinner with her African-American extended family. Hope brings a surprise dish to the gathering: pickles with peppermint sticks inside. The recipe from a cousin on her father's side is a big hit and Aunt Poogee tells Hope that it is now part of her family's recipes. The book includes four of the recipes from the dinner.
European-American/African-American
Pre-K, Primary; Fiction

Monk, Isabell. *Hope*. Illustrated by Janice Lee Porter. Minneapolis: Carolrhoda Books, 1999. 32 p.
In this picture book biracial Hope is upset when an acquaintance of her great-aunt Poogee thoughtlessly asks if Hope is mixed. Aunt Poogee explains to Hope that she is indeed mixed. She is Hope, mixed with love and the faith of her ancestors.
European-American/African-American
Pre-K, Primary; Fiction

Moses, Sheila P. *The Baptism*. New York: Margaret K. McElderry Books, 2007. 144 p.
Set in Northampton County, North Carolina, probably in the late 1940s, identical twins Leon and Luke, who have just turned twelve, are supposed to behave so they can go to their church's mornin' bench and be saved. Then on the coming Sunday they are be baptized in the Roanoke River so that lying and sinning are behind them. Unlike Luke, who is the "good" twin, the narrator Leon figures that he has only six more days to enjoy sinning. The story reveals that their father had probably been murdered, but the white perpetrator was not arrested and that their mother is married to "Filthy Frank"

whom Leon cannot stand. Leon rubs "White Cousin" with poison ivy and gets Luke to leave with him from a neighbor's house during a tornado that blows off their grandmother's roof. Angry that the grandmother will stay in their house, Filthy Frank runs off with their mother's money. Luke behaves well enough to go to the mornin' bench on Thursday. Surprisingly, on Friday Leon goes to the mornin' bench and both boys are baptized on Sunday. But the big surprise is that their mother's white half brother hugs her after the robbery, arranges for Filthy Frank's arrest, and with his wife, mother, and son attends the baptism.
African-European-American/African-European-American
Intermediate; Fiction

Murphy, Rita. *Black Angels*. New York: Delacorte Press, 2001. 176 p.

It is 1961 and Freedom Riders are on the way to a small Georgia town. Sophie, the Jenkins family's maid whom eleven-year-old Celli adores, is an outspoken African-American in the conservative Southern town. Celli finds it difficult to grasp the meaning of the civil rights movement and to cope with the sudden discovery that the grandmother she had never met is black. During the summer Celli becomes less concerned with the negative effects Sophie's actions have on her life and helps free Sophie from jail and save a friend who is Jewish and African-American.
African-European-American/European-American; European-American and Jewish/African-American
Intermediate, Older; Fiction

Nichols, Joan Kane. *All But the Right Folks*. Owings Mills, Md.: Stemmer House Publishers, 1985. 112 p.

Danny doesn't realize he is half white until he meets his grandmother Helga and goes to spend the summer with her in New York City. Suffering from asthma, bed-wetting, and teasing at his San Francisco school, Danny enjoys New York as he bikes with his grandmother; befriends Thelma Jean, her little brother Willy, and Charlayne; and starts learning karate from Charlayne's older sister. However, his new friends, two of whom are of mixed heritage, reject him because he lied that Helga was his nanny. Further, he worries that his deceased mother was a druggie like his Uncle Billy; his father insists that Danny is black and is not proud of him; and he discovers that Helga has lied to him. Everything improves when Danny uses his karate mental and kicking skills to escape kidnappers, and he decides that he is a bridge between black and white.
African-American/European-American; Panamanian-Chinese-American/African-American; African-American/African-American Choctaw
Intermediate; Fiction

O'Connor, Barbara. *Me and Rupert Goody*. New York: Frances Foster Books, 1999. 112 p.

Although unrelated, Uncle Beau is like a surrogate father to eleven-year-old Jennalee. Except for school hours, she spends her days at his general store. When African-American Rupert Goody comes to the store claiming that Uncle Beau is his father, Jennalee is consumed by jealousy and treats him terribly. It is not until the end of the story that she comes to accept the slow, but sweet Rupert and to realize that they are both part of Uncle Beau's family.

European-American/African-American
Intermediate, Older; Fiction

Okimoto, Jean Davies. *Talent Night*. New York: Scholastic, 1995. 176 p.

When seventeen-year-old Rodney and his nineteen-year-old sister Suzanne learn that their great-uncle Hideki, whom they have never met, might give them each $10,000 if they have kept their mother's Japanese heritage, Rodney works on mastering karate kicks, Suzanne tries out Japanese flower arranging, and they both learn about haiku poetry and Japanese cooking. They discover when Uncle Hideki visits that he is not worth impressing since he is unbearably traditional and insults Rodney's half African-American girlfriend. However, they become closer to their Japanese heritage by learning from their mother about the prejudice she endured as a Japanese-American during the 1940s. Molly from *Molly by Any Other Name* appears very briefly in this book.

Filipino-American/African American
Older; Fiction

Park, Hee Jung, creator. *Hotel Africa Volume 1*. Translated from Korean by Jihae Hong. Los Angeles: Tokyopop, 2007. 256 p.

This graphic novel is the first book about Elvis, Ed, and July, friends trying to make it in the film industry. Their story is interlaced with that of Hotel Africa, the subject of a screenplay they are trying to produce. Hotel Africa tells of the guesthouse in Utah which Elvis's mother and grandmother open when he is four. It is then that Elvis learns that his father was a black singer and died in a nightclub of an electric shock. Elvis meets the hotel's guests: Geo, the Indian who remains with them and adores his mother; two tough-appearing motorcyclists, one of whom sings him a bedtime lullaby; a stepfather and his little stepson who learn of their love for each other; two teenage girls whose double suicide attempt is thwarted; and a woman who receives the letters a man who loved her had written her for more than thirty years. Little Elvis is disappointed when he learns that he is a flower boy and not the groom of his first love, and he is the only one who knows that, when his elderly friend Oliver dies, he has gone to meet the beautiful actress of his dreams.

African-American/European-American
Older; Fiction

Park, Hee Jung, creator. *Hotel Africa Volume 2*. Translated from Korean by Jihae Hong. Los Angeles: Tokyopop, 2008. 264 p.

In this continuation of volume one, little Elvis meets more hotel guests: Dominique, his mother's inconsiderate and demanding high school classmate who returns from the city and gets together with a classmate who has long loved her; a seventeen-year-old boy and a fifteen-year-old girl who say they are siblings, but are really lovers; Hillie, an old dog who dies after his master dies, but not before Elvis has come to love him; and an African-American friend of his mother who confesses she had loved Tran before he became Elvis' father. She was devastated after he died until she found Lionel, a blind white boy whom she cares for. The book also tells how Elvis ironed his hair to make it straight and it ended up in an Afro. As adults, Elvis' friend Ed tells how he discovered he was gay when he fell in love with Ian, who died of a drug overdose, and Elvis gets a puppy, whom he names Hillie.

African-American/European-American
Older; Fiction

Patrick, Denise Lewis. *The Longest Ride*. New York: Henry Holt and Company, 1999. 176 p.

It is 1865 and fourteen-year-old Midnight Son, an escaped slave who is accompanied by his white friend Lou Boy, decides that he must return from Colorado to Texas to rescue his mother and two younger sisters and to find his older sister who had been sold years earlier. Injured in a blizzard, Midnight Son is taken to an Arapaho camp. After it is destroyed by American soldiers, Winter Mary and Eagle Eye, Arapaho siblings whose mother is African-American, join Midnight Son and Lou Boy to fulfill their dying mother's wish to find her sister. In the ensuing story, the four of them travel to Texas and Louisiana in search of Midnight Son's family. This book is the sequel to *The Adventures of Midnight Son*.
Arapaho/African-American
Intermediate, Older; Fiction

Peck, Richard. *The River Between Us*. New York: Dial Books, 2003. 176 p.

Set at the beginning of the Civil War, this book tells how the life of fifteen-year-old Tilly and her family changes when two mysterious strangers, Delphine and her apparent servant Calinda, arrive via steamboat at Grand Tower, Illinois. Coming from New Orleans, Delphine with her elegant clothes and fancy ways is like no one the town has ever seen. The two stay with Tilly's family, and Tilly's twin brother Noah falls in love with Delphine. When now-sixteen Noah goes off to join the Yankee army, their mother is so upset, since her husband had earlier left her, that she sends Tilly and Delphine off to Cairo, Illinois, to bring Noah home. The book tells of the horrible living conditions in Cairo and especially of the unsanitary hospital tents. Noah, who suffers from dysentery, recovers enough that he is sent off to fight in the nearby battle of Belmont, Missouri, in which he is wounded and has to have his left arm amputated. The two girls stay in Cairo tending to Noah and other soldiers, and upon their return home with Noah learn that Tilly's distraught mother, seeing the coffin of her husband which she mistook for Noah's, drowned herself in the river. The story also reveals that to Tilly's surprise Delphine and Calinda are sisters and that Delphine's father is indeed the wealthy Jules Duval, but that he is her mother's protector, not her husband as in New Orleans whites cannot marry Creoles. Following the war Calinda, a conjure woman, leaves Grand Tower so that she will not raise suspicion that Delphine has African blood. Although Delphine refuses to marry a white man, she and Noah live as husband and wife, but their son is passed off as the son of Tilly and her husband.
Creole (African-French-Spanish)-Haitian-American
Older; Nonfiction

Reynolds, Marilyn. *If You Loved Me*. Buena Park, Calif.: Morning Glory Press, 1999. 224 p. (True-to-Life-Series from Hamilton High)

In this book for older teenagers, high school senior Lauren lives with her grandmother, the one supportive constant throughout her life, is in love with her caring boyfriend Tyler, and is close to her best friend Amber. Lauren hates her parents, who abandoned her, and especially her mother, who caused her to be born drug-addicted and was blown up when a makeshift methamphetamine

lab exploded. All changes when Lauren is betrayed by Tyler, betrays Amber, and discovers the identity of her "stalker." Terribly upset, she withdraws from life until she begins to realize the complexity of love and the need for forgiveness.
African-Chinese-American/European-American
Older; Fiction

Rinaldi, Ann. *Come Juneteenth*. New York: Harcourt, 2007. 256 p.

Although President Lincoln delivered his Emancipation Proclamation in January 1863, Texas plantation owners kept their slaves unaware of their freedom until General Gordon Granger issued the Emancipation Proclamation for Texas on June 19, 1865, a day later celebrated as Juneteenth. This historical novel relates the effects of the owners' secret on one Texas family and of the secret which young teenager Luli has promised to keep. It tells of the relationship between Luli and her almost-sister Sis Goose, who is half white and half black and is very much a part of the plantation family, of the bond between Luli and her adult brother Gabe, and of Gabe's love for Sis Goose. The story ends tragically when, in an attempt to take Sis Goose away from a Yankee colonel, Luli shoots her. Other characters in the novel are a little African-American boy who has nowhere to go and a Kickapoo boy whose mother Gabe has killed during the war.
European-American/African-American
Older; Fiction

Rodowsky, Colby. *That Fernhill Summer*. New York: Farrar Straus Giroux, 2006. 176 p.

When an unknown aunt calls thirteen-year-old Kiara's apartment to say that the grandmother she never heard of is ill, Kiara discovers that she has a whole new extended family: two aunts, two uncles, twin nine-year-old boy cousins, two girl cousins her own age, and Zenobia, her incredibly difficult grandmother. When Zenobia balks at going to a nursing home, it is decided that she can return to Fernhill, her unusual house, with two home health aides to care for her and the three girl cousins to keep her company. During the summer the girls try in vain to make Zenobia happy and Kiara discovers that her mother was banished from Zenobia's family, not because she married a black man, but because she quit art school and "wasted" her artistic talent.
African-American/European-American
Intermediate, Older; Fiction

Rosenberg, Maxine B. *Being Adopted*. Photographs by George Ancona. New York: Lothrop, Lee & Shepard Books, 1984. 48 p.

Illustrated with black-and-white photographs, this book features three children. Seven-year-old Rebecca, whose birthfather is African-American and birthmother European-American and Cheyenne, is the adopted daughter of an African-American father and a European-American mother. Ten-year-old Andrei was adopted from India by European-American parents, and Karin, the author's eight-year-old daughter, was adopted from Korea by her European-American parents. The book covers some of the questions and fears of younger adopted children: being afraid when they come to their adoptive families, wondering whether they caused their parents to give them up, fearing their adoptive parents will give them up, dreaming and wondering about their birthparents, and not looking like other members of their families. It also affirms that adopted children are just as much family members as are biological children.

African-American/European-American and Cheyenne

Primary, Intermediate; Nonfiction

Rosenberg, Maxine B. *Growing Up Adopted*. Afterword by Lois Ruskai Melina. New York: Bradbury Press, 1989. 128 p.

In this book eight children and six adults relate their experiences and thoughts about growing up as adopted children. The four children who were adopted by parents of a different race, in each case European-American, are Josh, adopted as was a little sister from Colombia; Amy, who was adopted from Ecuador; Mark, who was adopted from Korea; and Shakine, an African-American boy who was born with spinal bifida in the United States and lives in a family of seven children, four of whom are adopted and of ethnicities other than their adoptive parents. Three of the adults are of a different race than their European-American parents. Chris was adopted from France as was her brother, Sam was adopted from Korea and has an adopted sister of mixed race and two non-adopted brothers, and Jamie, an African-European-American, has two sisters who are not adopted and four adopted siblings of mixed race.

African-European-American

Intermediate, Older; Nonfiction

Rosenberg, Maxine B. *Living in Two Worlds*. Photographs by George Ancona. New York: Lothrop, Lee & Shepard Books, 1986. 48 p.

This book explains how races evolved and how many children have a greater resemblance to one of their parents. It discusses the teasing and unwanted questions biracial children face and points to the benefits of living in two cultures. The book's text and black-and-white photographs focus on five children: Toah, who is African-European-American; Megan, who is African-European-American and Cherokee; Jesse, who is Chinese-European-American; and Shashi and Anil, who are Indian-European-American.

African-American/European-American; African-American and Cherokee/European-American

Intermediate; Nonfiction

Schwartz, Ellen. *Stealing Home*. Plattsburgh, N.Y.: Tundra Books of Northern New York, 2006. 224 p.

When ten-year-old Joey's mother dies, he is sent to live with her estranged family: his disapproving grandfather, his loving aunt, and his cousin, a girl who loves baseball as much as he does. Set in 1947, this is a story about the racial prejudice facing biracial Joey, first in his native Bronx by African-American boys who won't let him play baseball and then in Brooklyn where white boys won't let him play ball and where a woman insults him and his deceased mother. It relates how Joey's new friends and his aunt finally stand up for him against the bigots, how Joey and his grandfather come to understand and accept each other, and how, home at last, Joey changes his allegiance from the Bronx Bombers to Jackie Robinson and the Brooklyn Dodgers.

African-American and non-Jewish/European-American and Jewish

Intermediate; Fiction

Schwartz, Virginia Frances. *Send One Angel Down*. New York: Holiday House, 2000. 176 p.

This novel is based upon a true story recorded in *To Be a Slave* by Julius Lester, with Doc Daniel Dowdy's name changed to Abram. At age six Abram sees his newborn cousin Eliza and knows immediately that she will encounter trouble because of her blue eyes. Abram helps raise Eliza and watches as she grows from a toddler into a young girl who plays with and is bossed by the plantation owner's older daughter and into a responsible nine-year-old who tends the slave breeder and field workers' babies. It is Abram who reluctantly tells Eliza that she is the daughter of the plantation owner. In this story, which reveals the horrors of slavery, Eliza at age fifteen is bought at the auction block by a man from New York, who not only frees her, but rescues her from Alabama by providing her with a job as his family's nanny.
European-American/African-American
Older; Fiction

Seabrooke, Brenda. *The Bridges of Summer*. New York: Cobblehill Books, 1992. 160 p.

When she visits her Gullah grandmother Quanamina, fourteen-year-old Zarah, who lives in New York City, finds the life of South Carolina Gullahs distressingly backward. Quanamina's isolated house has no electricity or running water and she can't read. Zarah discovers that not only is Quanamina easily scandalized by her modern ways, but so too is her new white friend's grandmother, who still acts like a slave owner with servants. When Quanamina dies, Zarah cleverly manages to sell her land, thereby securing the future for her five-year-old cousin and herself.
African-Arab-American Gullah/African-American
Older; Fiction

Senisi, Ellen B. *For My Family, Love Allie*. Photographs by author. Morton Grove, Ill.: Albert Whitman & Company, 1998. 32 p.

In this picture book Allie wants to make a present for the large family party to be held at her house. All by herself she makes peanut-butter treats. Then, after her African-American and European-American relatives cook together, play games together, and eat together, they all enjoy Allie's dessert.
African-Jamaican-American/European-American
Pre-K, Primary; Fiction

Shusterman, Neal. *Red Rider's Hood*. New York: Dutton Children's Books, 2004. 192 p. (Dark Fusion)

Sixteen-year-old Red, who is of mixed race, is shocked when he discovers that dogs, cats, and teenagers in his neighborhood are the victims of werewolves and that thirty years ago his grandparents had been werewolf hunters who got rid of the wolves existing then. However, there are now new werewolves under the control of the earlier leader's grandson, Cedric. In this suspenseful tale Red teams up with his grandmother and Marissa (whose brother may be a werewolf) to destroy the twenty-two wolves of Cedric's gang. However, when Red joins the gang to spy on them, he finds himself attracted to the wolves and their powers. It is not until Grandma and Marissa battle the wolves that Red decides which side he is on.
South Korean-American/African-European-American
Older; Fiction

Singer, Marilyn, ed. *Face Relations: 11 Stories About Seeing Beyond Color*. New York: Simon & Schuster Books for Young Readers, 2004. 240 p.

In "Gold" by Marina Budhos, fifteen-year-old Jemma, who has moved from Trinidad to New Jersey, goes out with Jared and comes to realize that they are going too far in their relationship. Then, when Jared apologizes to her mother, Jemma recognizes how good he is and that for them, as for her parents, differences in heritage do not matter.
African-Irish-American and Cherokee
Older; Fiction

Singer, Marilyn, ed. *Face Relations: 11 Stories About Seeing Beyond Color*. New York: Simon & Schuster Books for Young Readers, 2004. 240 p.

In "Mr. Ruben" by Rita Williams-Garcia, Dee wants her friends Myra and Shaheed, who is African-Arab-American, to go out together, but Myra won't go unless she finds out whether their ninth grade math teacher is at least part black so that she can have a crush on him. Dee says they can figure it out by looking at his visiting brother, but the brother turns out to be an identical twin.
African-Arab-American
Older; Fiction

Singer, Marilyn, ed. *Face Relations: 11 Stories About Seeing Beyond Color*. New York: Simon & Schuster Books for Young Readers, 2004. 240 p.

In the story "Skins" by Joseph Bruchac, Mitchell, who is half Abenaki, provides needed support to the high school star quarterback, whom everyone assumes is Indian, but is really Hungarian. Mitchell also becomes close friends with Randolph, who is African-American and Native American.
African-American, Cherokee, and Choctaw/African-American, Cherokee, and Choctaw
Older; Fiction

Smith, Cynthia Leitich. *Rain Is Not My Indian Name*. New York: HarperCollins Publishers, 2001. 144 p.

Since her best friend Galen was killed in a traffic accident on New Year's Day (her birthday), fourteen-year-old Rain, who is of mixed race, has withdrawn from her friends and from going out into her small Kansas town. However, despite refusing to become a participant, she agrees early in the summer to take photographs of her aunt's Native American camp. Rain is upset with Galen's mother and her opposition to the camp and with her former second best friend African-American Queenie, who attends the camp although it is not discovered until later that she has a Seminole ancestor. Then, on the Fourth of July (Galen's birthday), Rain is ready to move beyond his death.
African-American and Seminole
Intermediate, Older; Fiction

Smith, Sherri L. *Hot, Sour, Salty, Sweet*. New York: Delacorte Press, 2008. 176 p.

This is the story of the day fourteen-year-old Ana Shen graduates from junior high school. Just as she begins her speech as salutatorian, the school's water main breaks, drenching the attendees and canceling her speech. Then her best friend invites Japanese-American Jamie Tabata, the boy she has long

had a crush on, to come with his family to Ana's house for dinner that evening. This sends Ana's extended family into a tizzy as they prepare a feast combining the favorite dishes of her Chinese grandmother and her African-American grandparents. The process is complicated by the animosity of the grandmothers, who even compete in promising Ana gifts, including a college education and a house. Just when Ana has had enough, Jamie's family and then, unexpectedly, the class flirt arrive at her house. The dinner is a disaster, largely because Jamie's father looks down upon Ana and her family and compares the dinner to a food court meal. Ana explodes. Standing up for all the grievances her minority family members have suffered, she orders Mr. Tabata to leave. Jamie sides with Ana and the two discover they like each other.
Chinese-American/African-American
Older; Fiction

Steptoe, John. *Creativity*. Illustrated by E. B. Lewis. New York: Clarion Books, 1997. 32 p.
  When Hector, a Spanish-speaking boy from Puerto Rico, joins his class, Charles, who is African-American, wonders why they have the same skin color. While making friends with Hector, he learns about the mixing of races and how doing something differently can be creative.
African-Cuban-American/African-American
Intermediate; Fiction

Straight, Susan. *Bear E. Bear*. Illustrated by Marisabina Russo. New York: Hyperion Books for Children, 1995. 32 p.
  After Gaila's baby sister drops Bear E. Bear into a gutter, Gaila keeps careful watch over the special stuffed bear as he is cleaned in the washing machine and then dried in the dryer. The illustrations in this picture book reveal that Gaila's mother is white, her father is brown-skinned, and both Gaila and Bear E. Bear are light brown.
African-American/European-American
Pre-K, Primary; Fiction

Tate, Eleanora E. *Just an Overnight Guest*. New York: The Dial Press, 1980. 192 p.
  Everything seems to go wrong for nine-year-old African-American Margie when her mother brings four-year-old Ethel to stay as an overnight guest with the two of them and Margie's thirteen-year-old sister Alberta. Ethel, a half white girl who lives with her mother in the white trash part of town, is a disruptive and destructive terror. She wets Margie's bed, breaks her treasured shell collection, and creates such havoc at a movie theater that the family must leave. Margie and Alberta are embarrassed to be seen with her, their mother endures criticism from the town's gossips, and when Margie is mean to Ethel, her mother always seems to takes Ethel's side. When, to Margie's dismay, Ethel's mother postpones her return, Ethel's stay is extended. However, thanks to her mother's kind treatment, Ethel's behavior improves and Margie, learning that Ethel has been abused and has no toys, manages to play with her. However, when Margie's father returns home from his road trip and Ethel cottons up to him, Margie's jealousy returns. It is only when her father tells her that Ethel is her cousin and that she hasn't taken away his love, that Margie accepts Ethel as a family member.

African-American/European-American
Intermediate; Fiction

Taylor, Mildred D. *The Land*. New York: Phyllis Fogelman Books, 2001. 392 p.

This prequel to the earlier-published books about the Logan family presents the story of Cassie's grandfather Paul-Edward Logan during the years following the Civil War. The son of a white farm owner and a former slave, Paul-Edward is treated as a son by his father, who has him sit with his siblings at the family table and provides him with an education. Paul-Edward loves the family's Georgia land and dreams of becoming a landowner when he grows up. However, despite his father's advice and warnings, he only realizes the difficulties his mixed race will cause when he is betrayed by the brother to whom he is closest. Forced to flee with his best friend Mitchell when Mitchell's life is in danger, Paul-Edward works in a lumber camp and uses his skills with horses and as a carpenter to save some money and enter into contracts to secure the Mississippi land which he has set his heart on. This is a story of the terrible treatment which Negroes received in the South, of the kindnesses of a few white people, of Mitchell's marrying Caroline whom Paul-Edward had fancied, of the friendship of the three of them, of Mitchell's being killed, and of the realization of Paul-Edward's dreams.
European-American/African American and Native American
Older; Fiction

Taylor, Mildred D. *Let the Circle Be Unbroken*. New York: Puffin Books, 1991. 400 p.

Narrated by young Cassie, who is part of the third generation of the Logan family, this book relates the experiences of her colored family during the terrible financial hardships of the 1930s Depression. She relates how she witnesses the murder trial and the predetermined guilty verdict of the family's innocent friend T.J.; sees how efforts to create a biracial Farm Workers' Union are thwarted; learns of the fraud used by plantation owners to deprive small cotton farmers of government money; accompanies an older black woman who has extensively studied the Mississippi Constitution, but is refused voter registration and ordered off her land; and worries with her family when her fourteen year-old older brother runs off to save their property by working in the cane fields of Louisiana where he is subjected to unthinkable treatment. In this story Cassie's father David tells of his mixed heritage, and there is hostility from both blacks and whites towards one of Cassie's uncles who has married a white woman. The couple's fifteen-year-old daughter Suzella finds it difficult to be biracial and decides that she will pass as a white. In other books about this generation of Logans—*Mississippi Bridge*; *Song of the Trees*; *The Friendship*; *Roll of Thunder, Hear My Cry*; and *The Road to Memphis*—the family is identified for readers as colored, not as mixed race.
African-European-American and Native American/African-American; African-American/European-American
Older; Fiction

Taylor, Mildred D. *The Well: David's Story*. New York: Dial Books for Young Readers, 1995. 96 p.

Set in the early 1900s, this book tells of an episode in the life of David Logan, Paul-Edward's son and Cassie's father. When David is ten-years-old, there is a severe drought, and both white and colored neighbors come to the Logan farm to get water from their well. David and his thirteen-year-old

hotheaded brother Hammer are treated abysmally by the mean Simms boys, who are white. When Hammer hits one of them after he has hit David, the sheriff is summoned as it is a serious crime for a black to hit a white. Caroline, David and Hammer's mother, has to whip both of her sons in front of the Simms and they have to do work for Mr. Simms. The Simms boys continue to harass David and Hammer, but when they pollute the water in the Logan's well, both they and their father get their comeuppance. Paul-Edward plays a role in this book and it is mentioned that he is half white.
African-European-American and Native American/African-American
Intermediate; Fiction

Thomas, Joyce Carol. *The Blacker the Berry*. Illustrated by Floyd Cooper. New York: Joanna Cotler Books, 2008. 32 p.

In this picture book thirteen poems and accompanying paintings present the beauty of varied black skin shades, including the raspberry black of an African-American and Seminole boy, the cranberry red of an African-Irish-American girl, and the snowberry color of an African-European-American girl.
African-American and Seminole; African-Irish-American; African-European-American
Primary, Intermediate; Fiction

Thomas, Joyce Carol. *The Golden Pasture*. New York: Scholastic, 1986. 144 p.

Since his infancy when he was snatched from his Cherokee mother by his father, Carl Lee and his grandfather have had a special bond. He enjoys spending summers on his grandfather's Oklahoma farm, a welcome respite from being with his father who pays him no attention except for criticism. Alerted by distressful wails, Carl Lee finds the wild appaloosa whom his grandfather had kept hidden and who has pulled a muscle. After nursing the horse back to health, Carl Lee rides him in a rodeo where he learns the truth about the legendary wild horse Thunderfoot and comes to appreciate his father's heroism.
African-American/Cherokee
Intermediate, Older; Fiction

Tocher, Timothy. *Chief Sunrise, John McGraw, and Me*. Illustrated by Greg Copeland. Chicago: Cricket Books, 2004. 160 p.

When baseball-loving fifteen-year-old Hank escapes from his mean alcoholic father by jumping into a train boxcar, he discovers that it is already occupied by Chief Sunrise, who says he is a Seminole and wants to pitch for the New York Giants. As the two travel in 1919 from Georgia to New York, Hank, disguised as a girl, plays a game as shortstop for a female baseball team, Chief Sunrise earns money by pitching to carnival goers, and the two share a boxcar with a horse. The Giant's manager John McGraw hires Chief Sunrise as a pitcher and Hank as a batboy. Chief Sunrise becomes an immediate pitching star, but everything changes when Hank meets his father at Sing Sing prison and learns that Chief Sunrise is not Indian, but half colored.
European-American/African-American
Intermediate, Older; Fiction

Updike, John. *A Child's Calendar*. Rev. ed. Illustrated by Trina Schart Hyman. New York: Holiday House, 1999. 32 p.

Featuring Updike's poems and Hyman's paintings, this picture book presents a year in the life of a Vermont family: an African-American husband, a Caucasian mother, and their two small sons.
African-American/European-American
Pre-K, Primary; Fiction

Viglucci, Pat Costa. *Cassandra Robbins, Esq.* Madison: Square One Publishers, 1987. 190 p.

Adopted as a baby by white parents, seventeen-year-old Cassandra, who is of mixed race, feels that being the family's only girl is of more significance than being its only brown member. However, when her brother brings Josh, his African-American college roommate, home for the summer, Cassandra experiences mixed feelings about her identity. She is especially jealous when Josh is with a white girl. She finds that the white boy with whom she goes to a concert is surprisingly nice, but that his mother is a bigot, and she encounters hostility from two black girls. By the end of the summer Cassandra has learned a lot about herself and the complexities of love.
African-American/European-American
Older; Fiction

Viglucci, Patricia Costa. *Sun Dance at Turtle Rock*. Rochester, N.Y.: Stone Pine Books, 1996. 136 p.

Twelve-year-old Cody, whose white father had died in a car accident six years earlier, goes to spend the summer with his paternal grandfather Zachariah, who had objected to the marriage of his father to his African-American mother. Cody is treated lovingly by his aunt, uncle, and their toddler son and spends much of the time exploring the town and the surrounding Allegheny Mountains with their daughter Jem. However, although his grandfather shows warmth towards Cody's cousins, he treats Cody coldly because of his race and is especially upset that Cody may be adopted by his black stepfather and take his stepfather's name. The last straw for Cody comes when Zachariah takes the side of a bigoted neighbor boy instead of his. Cody realizes that he is like the Plains Indians who in a Sun Dance had tortured themselves to prove themselves worthy, in Cody's case of his father's father. Cody plans to leave until he saves Jem from a bear. Then Zachariah expresses his love for Cody, and Cody decides that, although it will take time for his grandfather to change, he will stay for the rest of the summer.
European-American Catholic/African-American Baptist
Intermediate; Fiction

Wayans, Kim, and Kevin Knotts. *All Mixed Up!* Illustrated by Soo Jeong. New York: Grosset & Dunlap, 2008. 112 p. (Amy Hodgepodge)

Amy Hodges is introduced in this first book of the *Amy Hodgepodge* series, which features pictures posted in Amy's scrapbook. Moving to a new town after having experienced only home schooling, Amy is excited to be starting fourth grade at Emerson Charter School. However, her first day starts out disastrously. She wears the wrong clothes, tears her dress when she removes its flower, sings too loudly in music class, is laughed at by classmates Liza and Jennifer, and discovers that a paper saying "Stupid new girl" has been taped to her back by Rory. However, her day improves when she is befriended in the cafeteria by Maya, Jesse, Rusty, Pia, and twins Lola and Cole. Upset by a racial insult from Jennifer, she discovers that the twins are black and white, Jesse is black and Puerto Rican, Pia is Chinese-American and white, and Rusty is Latino, Native American, and white. Learning that Amy's father is black and white and her mother Japanese and South Korean-American, they affectionately nickname her Amy Hodgepodge. The story continues with the group entering a school talent show where Amy, inspired by Rusty who has to earn money to buy his costume, overcomes her stage fright and becomes the group's lead singer.

African-European-American/Japanese-South Korean-American; European-American/African-American; African-Puerto Rican-American

Primary, Intermediate; Fiction

Wayans, Kim, and Kevin Knotts. *Digging Up Trouble*. Illustrated by Soo Jeong. New York: Grosset & Dunlap, 2010. 112 p. (Amy Hodgepodge)

After foolishly letting her dog Giggles off his leash to play with another dog at the Farmer's Market, Amy is unable to find him. She spends a stressful night until in the morning the family receives a call from an older man, Irving Coleman, who reports that Giggles has come to his home with his dog. Then, after being reunited with Giggles, Amy realizes that helping Irving restore his community garden would make a perfect green project for the school class assignment. The two fourth grade classes adopt Amy's idea and decide to raise money for the needed tools and supplies by having a bake sale and a car wash. Amy is worried when she is placed in charge of the bake sale team, but because of the help of her visiting community-organizer grandmother and team members, including Lola, Pia, and Rusty, there are many baked goods for sale. However, things turn contentious when the bake sale team and the car wash team, including Jesse and Maya, become overly competitive. After teachers intervene, the teams decide to refer customers to each other. With the proceeds earned and the work of Amy's gardener grandmother and the fourth graders, Irving's garden again becomes a neighborhood asset. Referring to the mixed racial identity of some of Amy's friends, this sixth book in the series specifically identifies the heritages of Lola and Cole as well as of Amy.

African-European-American/Japanese-South Korean-American; European-American/African-American; African-Puerto Rican-American

Primary, Intermediate; Fiction

Wayans, Kim, and Kevin Knotts. *Happy Birthday to Me*. Illustrated by Soo Jeong. New York: Grosset & Dunlap, 2008. 112 p. (Amy Hodgepodge)

In this sequel to *All Mixed Up!* Amy looks forward to celebrating her birthday with her new friends as well as with her family. Maya, Jesse, Pia, and Lola accept her invitation to her tenth birthday sleepover where Amy plans to have a Japanese tea ceremony and do origami. Amy's spirits wane when she fears her family is planning to move to California. She is really upset when her four friends decide to go to an Amber Skye concert instead of her party. When Lola's brother Cole discovers that Amy has not invited other guests, he texts the concertgoers, and the four girls leave the concert to go to Amy's house. It is then that Amy discovers what true friends they are and the advisability of telling her problems and her fears to her family. This book points out the mixed heritages of Amy and most of her friends.

African-European-American/Japanese-South Korean-American; European-American/African-American; African-Puerto Rican-American
Primary, Intermediate; Fiction

Wayans, Kim, and Kevin Knotts. *Lost and Found*. Illustrated by Soo Jeong. New York: Grosset & Dunlap, 2008. 112 p. (Amy Hodgepodge)

Amy Hodgepodge persuades her parents to let her go on the fourth grade two-and-a-half day wilderness trip. However, she doesn't feel as pleased about it when she is placed in a group without her friends, but with Jennifer and Rory who don't like her. Further, she falls in the mud during the obstacle course, goes overboard with Jennifer in their canoe, and is embarrassed that she doesn't know what s'mores are. However, Amy is supported by Lola, Jesse, Maya, and Pia with whom she shares a tent. Together they enjoy tricking Cole, Rusty, and two other boys. Then when she, Jennifer, Rory, and two others get lost in the woods, Amy uses her compass to lead them back to camp—and receives the Best Camper award. In this third book in the series, Amy's mixed heritage is noted. Readers of the first book, *All Mixed Up!*, will be aware of the mixed heritages of five of her friends.
African-European-American/Japanese-South Korean-American; European-American/African-American; African-Puerto Rican-American
Primary, Intermediate; Fiction

Wayans, Kim, and Kevin Knotts. *Playing Games*. Illustrated by Soo Jeong. New York: Grosset & Dunlap, 2008. 112 p. (Amy Hodgepodge)

When Evelyn, the star player of the Comets girls' basketball team, injures her arm, Amy Hodgepodge reluctantly agrees to take her place so that the team will have the required eight players. Amy has neither played basketball nor is she familiar with the game. She is a terrible player, and her mistake causes the team to lose to the worst team in the league. Amy tries to fake a twisted ankle so she can be on the bench, but even that fails and she decides to quit. However, after confessing her problem to Rusty, he offers to coach her, with Amy, in return, helping him sing harmony in the friends' fourth grade music class performance. Unaware of the fact that Amy has improved, her teammates don't pass her the ball. It is not until the end of an important game that Amy demonstrates her secret talent as a three-point shooter. Amy's mixed heritage is noted in this fourth book in the series. Readers of the first book, *All Mixed Up!*, will be familiar with the mixed heritages of most of her friends.
African-European-American/Japanese-South Korean-American; European-American/African-American; African-Puerto Rican-American
Primary, Intermediate; Fiction

Wayans, Kim, and Kevin Knotts. *The Secret's Out*. Illustrated by Soo Jeong. New York: Grosset & Dunlap, 2009. 112 p. (Amy Hodgepodge)

Amy, Lola, Jesse, Pia, and Maya decide to enter as a group in their school's competitive annual spring art show. Amy comes up with the idea of tracing their body outlines on a large poster board and then painting and decorating them. The girls would stand behind holes that would show their faces. With the exception of Pia, the others are enthused about Amy's plan. Indeed, Pia's personality seems to have changed. She has become distracted, negative, and rude. Finally, she confides to Amy, with Amy's promise not to tell, that she fears that, since her father and stepmother are going to have a baby, her father won't pay attention to her. When Amy accidentally reveals Pia's secret to Lola, there are unforeseen consequences. Lola tells Jesse, and Jesse lets the secret out to classmates. The friends become so angry at each other that their Best Friends art display is jeopardized. It is not until they practice forgiveness that they restore their friendship—and their project ties for fourth grade first place. In this fifth book in the series, Amy's mixed heritage is noted, and series readers will be aware of the mixed heritages of most of her friends.

African-European-American/Japanese-South Korean-American; European-American/African-American; African-Puerto Rica-American
Primary, Intermediate; Fiction

Whitmore, Arvella. *Trapped Between the Lash and the Gun: A Boy's Journey*. New York: Dial Books, 1999. 192 p.

Upset because his dad has left, twelve-year-old Jordan wants to remain behind when his mother and sister move to the suburbs so as part of a gang he can earn the airfare to go live with his father. He even steals his grandfather's prized ancestral watch to pawn to get money for a gun. However, when Jordan approaches the pawnshop, he loses the watch and is transported to the 1800s where he meets the young slave boy Uriah, who is his great-great-great-great grandfather. The bulk of this book relates the story of Jordan's horrible experiences when he is mistaken for a runaway slave: picking cotton for hours, being beaten, not having enough to eat, hiding from paddyrollers (poor whites who look for runaway slaves), becoming part of a chain gang, and being sold at a slave auction. Fortunately, Jordan is bought by a worker with the Underground Railroad and, after discovering that the plantation master is Uriah's father, finally secures the watch, which brings him back to the present. There he rejects his gang membership, is shot and wounded by its leader, learns that his father is in prison, and treasures life with his family.

European-American/African-American
Intermediate, Older; Fiction

Williams, Mary E., ed. *Adoption*. Farmington Hills, Mich.: Greenhaven Press, 2006. 232 p.

In a chapter "Transracial Adoption Should Be Encouraged," Arlene Istar Lev, who is Jewish, tells how she and her lesbian partner adopted their African-American and biracial sons.

African-Irish-American
Older; Nonfiction

Wilson, Diane Lee. *Black Storm Comin'*. New York: Margaret K. McElderry Books, 2005. 304 p.

It is September 1860 and twelve-year-old Colton Wescott, his part African-American mother, his white father, his ten- and four-year-old sisters, and a newborn brother are in Utah Territory as they travel to Sacramento where his mother's half sister lives. Others in the wagon train treat them poorly because of his mother's blackness and, when Colton's father accidentally shoots Colton, he abandons the family. With Colton's mother very ill, it is up to the young boy and his little sisters to bury the baby and, with two of the oxen team killed for food by some wagoneers, to get to Dayton where there

is a doctor. Colton needs to earn money for the doctor and personally to deliver freedom papers to his aunt in California. The story describes Colton's buying a pitiful-looking horse, Badger, to prove that he can be a Pony Express rider and his making the perilous trip from Carson City across the Sierra Nevada to Sportsman Hall and back as far as Genoa where he has an accident. Then, after being fired, Colton steals a Pony Express packet containing urgent news from Washington and, with it, rides Badger through a snowstorm to Sacramento where he delivers it and the freedom papers. On the way he saves the life of a man who has guessed the secret that he is colored and, by the story's conclusion, realizes that he should both be himself and not judge others by their appearance.
European-American/African-European-American
Older; Fiction

Wolf, Allan. *Zane's Trace.* Cambridge, Mass.: Candlewick Press, 2007. 208 p.

In this book for high schoolers, teenager Zane, who suffers grand mal seizures and constantly writes his thoughts on his bedroom walls, feels that he is responsible for the deaths of his schizophrenic mother (because he was at school) and his grandfather (because he crossed off his name from the family tree he had drawn). Zane drives from Baltimore to Zanesville, Ohio, to commit suicide on his mother's grave. On the way he has supernatural encounters with his dead parents, his grandfather, and several of his ancestors. Finally reaching the Zanesville cemetery, Zane understands that he has a caring brother and friends and that it is he who must keep his deceased family's souls alive.
Wyandot/African-European-American
Older; Fiction

Woodson, Jacqueline. *Behind You.* New York: G. P. Putnam's Sons, 2004. 128 p.

This sequel to *If You Come Softly* follows the months after fifteen-year-old Miah's mistaken-identity killing by New York City police. His African-American parents Nelia and Norman, his school basketball teammate Kennedy, his best friend Carlton, and his white girlfriend Ellie suffer in their grief. Finally they begin to heal: Nelia starts writing another novel; Carlton, who is of mixed race, finally admits he is gay; Norman begins talking with his former wife Nelia; Nelia, Ellie, and Carlton have a closer relationship; and Ellie, Carlton, and Kennedy become friends. Ignoring the advice of his deceased grandmother, Miah continues to look down upon them until he realizes that they all know they are loved.
African-American/European-American
Older; Fiction

Woodson, Jacqueline. *The House You Pass on the Way.* New York: Delacorte Press, 1997. 112 p.

Fourteen-year-old Staggerlee has an atypical family. Her father's parents, noted entertainers who had appeared on *The Ed Sullivan Show*, had been killed in a bombing when they chose to go to a Civil Rights demonstration. There is now a statue of them in her town, and her family has shunned publicity. Further, her family has been estranged from its relatives for the past twenty years because, after her grandparents' deaths, her black father and white mother got married. Lonely Staggerlee is delighted that her cousin Trout, a girl her own age, is coming to spend the summer. Fast becoming friends, Staggerlee discovers that she, like Trout, is attracted to girls. When high school begins, Staggerlee, with

a new assurance, starts to make friends and become involved in school activities. However, she is thrown for a loop when Trout writes that she has a boyfriend. Staggerlee finally decides that she'll just have to wait and see how her life turns out.
African-American/European-American
Older; Fiction

Woodson, Jacqueline. *If You Come Softly*. New York: G. P. Putnam's Sons, 1998. 192 p.

This is the tragic love story of two high school sophomores who fall in love when Ellie (Elisha), carrying her textbooks, crashes into Miah (Jeremiah) on their first day at a private New York City school. African-American Miah's mother is a noted novelist and his father is a famous film producer who has left Miah's mother for another woman. Ellie is a Jewish girl whose much older siblings left home some time earlier. Her mother had twice deserted and then returned to the family. Miah and Ellie sense something familiar about each other, for they both suffer from loss and fear of abandonment. Their romance progresses slowly as they are shy with each other, but then acknowledge their feelings. They encounter stares and verbal abuse from strangers who don't like interracial couples, and Ellie's favorite sister doesn't approve. When Ellie finally meets Miah's mother, she is warmly accepted. However, on the evening that Ellie is going to tell her parents about her boyfriend, police, who are looking for a tall dark man, shoot and kill Miah, as, dribbling his basketball in Central Park, he dreams about scoring for Ellie and his team. Carleton, Miah's best friend in this book, has a black father and a white mother. The story continues in *Behind You*.
African-American/European-American
Older; Fiction

Woodson, Jacqueline. *Miracle's Boys*. New York: G. P. Putnam's Sons, 2000. 144 p.

This story, which occurs during one weekend, tells of three orphaned brothers who still suffer from deaths they feel they could have prevented. Twenty-two-year-old Ty´ree, who has given up a college opportunity to be his brothers' legal guardian, wishes that twelve years ago he had not alerted his father to a drowning woman and dog so that his father would not have died a hero's death from hypothermia. Twelve-year-old Lafayette, the book's narrator, agonizes that when he was nine he could have saved his mother Milagro by getting help earlier when she was in insulin shock. Fifteen-year-old Charlie regrets that he wasn't there when his parents died and that an injured dog he helped did not live. Ty´ree and Lafayette are very close, but Charlie, who seems to have changed into a different person, is headed for trouble. At the story's conclusion all three of Milagro's boys stand together as a family.
African-American/Puerto Rican
Older; Fiction

Wyeth, Sharon Dennis. *Orphea Proud*. New York: Delacorte Press, 2004. 208 p.

In this novel, which is for older teens, sixteen-year-old Orphea presents the story of her life to the audience at a show at the Club Nirvana in Queens, New York. Growing up in Pennsylvania, Orphea suffers the death of her father when she is seven and the death of her beloved mother when she is eight. Going to live with her much older half brother Rupert and his wife, Orphea meets Lissa when they are both ten and they immediately become best friends. Orphea writes poetry, and Lissa paints pictures. As the two grow older, Orphea fears she is gay because of her feelings toward Lissa. On an eventful day when they are sixteen, Orphea and Lissa make out in Orphea's bedroom, but are caught by homophobic Rupert. Rupert beats up Orphea and says something to Lissa as she escapes in her car. Before she reaches home, Lissa is killed when skidding in the snow. Orphea is devastated. Unable to cope with her distress and behavior, Rupert sends Orphea to live with her two great-aunts in mountainous Virginia. There Orphea recovers; befriends her fourteen-year-old white neighbor Raynor, who cannot read, but paints psychedelic pictures of horses; and finally admits to her understanding great-aunts that she is gay. It is also in Virginia that African-American Orphea learns that her great-great-grandfather Babe was white and that she and Raynor are cousins. Babe's sister stole Babe's body out of the black cemetery and reburied him in the white cemetery which blacks could not enter. It is Orphea and Raynor who enable the great-aunts to visit their grandfather's grave. Orphea and Raynor then go to Queens for the summer to perform and live with the couple who had befriended Orphea in Pennsylvania and now own the casino.

African-American/African-European-American; African-European-American/European-American
Older; Fiction

Wyeth, Sharon Dennis. *The World of Daughter McGuire*. New York: Delacorte Press, 1994. 176 p.

Eleven-year-old Daughter's parents have separated, and she, her two younger brothers, and her mother have moved into a house next to her mother's parents. Daughter, whose deceased grandfather was Irish-American Catholic and whose other grandparents are Russian Jewish, African-American, and Italian-American, is called a "zebra" by a schoolmate and wishes that she was not all mixed-up. She is further concerned that the differences between her mother and father in careers and lifestyles will result in divorce. In this story Daughter learns to be proud of her heritages and is relieved when her parents decide to try to stay together despite their differences.

Irish-American Catholic and Russian-American Jewish/African-Italian-American
Intermediate; Fiction

Angolan-American

Rinaldi, Ann. *Cast Two Shadows: The American Revolution in the South*. San Diego: Gulliver Books, 1998. 288 p. (Great Episodes)

Set in 1780 in South Carolina, this story is narrated by fourteen-year-old Caroline, the daughter of a white father and a mixed race slave. Looking white, Caroline is raised by her white family: her Loyalist stepmother, her imprisoned rebel father, her older half brother Johnny who is fighting with the Loyalists, and her older half sister Georgia Ann who is dining with Lord Rawdon, the British colonel who has commandeered their plantation and confines Caroline, Georgia Ann, and her step-mother in an upstairs chamber. Because of the extreme cruelty of the British, Caroline decides to be a rebel. She cleverly convinces Rawdon to let her go with her Negro grandmother Miz Melindy to bring home Johnny, who is injured and, unbeknownst to Rawdon, has become a rebel. On the journey, Caroline bonds with Miz Melindy and learns the truth about her mother. Upon her return, she and her stepmother escape from Rawdon and his British troops.

European-American/Angolan-European-American
Older; Fiction

Ashanti-American. See also West African-American

See   Cuffe, Paul

Creole-American. See also individual heritages

See   Beyoncé

Forrester, Sandra. *Dust from Old Bones*. New York: Morrow Junior Books, 1999. 176 p.

This story is set in the stratified society of the New Orleans of 1838. Thirteen-year-old Simone, who is a person of color, struggles with the probability that her pretty cousin Claire-Marie will go to quadroon balls and be chosen by a Creole "protector" [as his mistress]. She envies the life of Madelon, her aunt who lives in France where she is not faced with racial discrimination. Nevertheless, Simone comes to realize that her restricted life as a person of color is much better than that of black slaves, who if lucky enough to be freed had to leave New Orleans. Simone's admiration for Madelon, who comes to visit, disappears when she betrays not only Simone, but also the two slaves she was committed to free. It is Simone who leads the slaves through a swamp to a safe house.
African-Creole-American/African-Creole-Haitian; Creole-American/African-Creole-Haitian
Older; Fiction

Peck, Richard. *The River Between Us*. New York: Dial Books, 2003. 176 p.

Set at the beginning of the Civil War, this book tells how the life of fifteen-year-old Tilly and her family changes when two mysterious strangers, Delphine and her apparent servant Calinda, arrive via steamboat at Grand Tower, Illinois. Coming from New Orleans, Delphine with her elegant clothes and fancy ways is like no one the town has ever seen. The two stay with Tilly's family where Tilly's twin brother Noah falls in love with Delphine. When now-sixteen Noah goes off to join the Yankee army, their mother is so upset, since her husband had earlier left her, that she sends Tilly and Delphine off to Cairo, Illinois, to bring Noah home. The book tells of the horrible living conditions in Cairo and especially of the unsanitary hospital tents. Noah, who suffers from dysentery, recovers enough that he is sent off to fight in the nearby battle of Belmont, Missouri, in which he is wounded and has to have his left arm amputated. The two girls stay in Cairo tending to Noah and other soldiers, and upon their return home with Noah learn that Tilly's distraught mother, seeing the coffin of her husband which she mistook for Noah's, drowned herself in the river. The story also reveals that to Tilly's surprise Delphine and Calinda are sisters and that Delphine's father is indeed the wealthy Jules Duval, but that he is her mother's protector, not her husband as in New Orleans whites cannot marry Creoles. Following the war Calinda, a conjure woman, leaves Grand Tower so that she will not raise suspicion that Delphine has African blood. Although Delphine refuses to marry a white man, she and Noah live as husband and wife, but their son is passed off as the son of Tilly and her husband.

Creole (African-French-Spanish)-Haitian-American
Older; Nonfiction

Walter, Mildred Pitts. *Ray and the Best Family Reunion Ever*. New York: HarperCollins Publishers, 2002. 128 p.

Eleven-year-old Ray is the only member of his Creole family with ebony skin. When he goes to a large family reunion in Natchitoches, Louisiana, Ray discovers that he and Gran-papa Philippe are the only ones there with dark skin. To make matter worse, Ray looks like his grandfather whom his father and almost all his relatives despise. This is the story of Ray's secret bonding with Gran-papa Philippe, his appreciation of his grandfather's talent, and his effecting a reconciliation between his father and Philippe.
Creole (Nigerian-French-Spanish-Native American)-Haitian-American/Creole (French-Spanish-West African-Native American)-American
Intermediate; Fiction

Ethiopian-American

Kurtz, Jane. *Faraway Home*. Illustrated by E. B. Lewis. San Diego: Gulliver Books, 2000. 32 p.

Desta is reluctant to have her father leave for Ethiopia to be with his ill mother. It is so far away and perhaps he won't come back. Reassured by her father's descriptions of Ethiopia and his boyhood there, Desta comes to accept that he misses Ethiopia, her grandmother misses him, and he will return.
Ethiopian/African-American
Pre-K, Primary; Fiction

Guinean-American. See also West African-American

See   Banneker, Benjamin

Gullah-American

Herron, Carolivia. *Always an Olivia: A Remarkable Family History*. Illustrated by Jeremy Tugeau. Minneapolis: Kar-Ben Publishing, 2007. 32 p.

In this picture book Carol Olivia's great-grandmother tells her about her Jewish ancestors, who were banished from Spain and Portugal and finally moved to Italy. One of their descendents and her future husband escaped from pirates and traveled by ship to Georgia. Their descendents intermarried with the Geechees (Gullahs) of Sea Island.
Gullah-Italian-Spanish-American Jewish
Primary, Intermediate; Fiction

Seabrooke, Brenda. *The Bridges of Summer*. New York: Cobblehill Books, 1992. 160 p.

When she visits her Gullah grandmother Quanamina, fourteen-year-old Zarah, who lives in New York City, finds the life of South Carolina Gullahs distressingly backward. Quanamina's isolated house

has no electricity or running water and she can't read. Zarah discovers that not only is Quanamina easily scandalized by her modern ways, but so too is her new white friend's grandmother, who still acts like a slave owner with servants. When Quanamina dies, Zarah cleverly manages to sell her land, thereby securing the future for her five-year-old cousin and herself.
African-Arab-American Gullah/African-American
Older; Fiction

Kenyan-American

See   Harris, Betty Wright
       Obama, Barack

Melungeon-American

Naylor, Phyllis Reynolds. *Sang Spell*. New York: Aladdin Paperbacks, 2000. 224 p.

Hitchhiking from Massachusetts to Dallas to live with his aunt because his mother has died, teenager Josh is mugged and left on a road in Appalachia where he is picked up by a Melungeon, who takes him to Canara, an isolated primitive community. Everything is strange and illogical there, and Josh becomes increasingly frustrated in his efforts to escape. The road he takes ends up at the exact place he started. Trying to swim towards a river's opposite shore takes him only a short distance, and a roadside restaurant and a school appear and disappear at regular intervals. Josh discovers that his father was probably Melungeon and befriends a girl whose father was stoned to death when his efforts to escape accidentally caused fatalities. Finally, with new insights and the realization that he must keep Canara's secrets, Josh is able to get away. [The Melungeon people are of mixed race living primarily in the central Appalachians. There is controversy as to their origin and their heritage, but they are often regarded as tri-racial: European-American, African-American, and Native American. In this novel they are identified as Portuguese who, over time, became mixed with a number of other peoples.]
Portuguese (Melungeon)-American/Irish-American; Celtic-American/Portuguese (Melungeon)-American
Older; Fiction

Nigerian-American. See also West African-American

Meyer, Carolyn. *Jubilee Journey*. San Diego: Gulliver Books, 1997. 288 p.

In this sequel to *White Lilacs*, it is 1996 and eighty-seven-year-old Rose Lee has invited her thirteen-year-old great-granddaughter Emily Rose and her family to attend the Freedomtown Juneteenth Diamond Jubilee. Growing up in Connecticut, Emily Rose has always regarded herself as a "double" as her father is French-American and her mother is African-American. However, she and her brothers Steven and Robbie have no idea what it means to be black in Dillon, Texas. They quickly learn of the attitudes of some whites when Steven is set up and abused and of the closeness and pride of the African-American community. In this story Rose Lee reveals what has happened to her and her family during the past seventy-five years. Emily Rose gets a new friend who thinks she should be just black

and decides to remain in Denton to learn more about being black so she can better understand herself. Alicia, Rose Lee's best friend in Connecticut, has a Nigerian father and an English mother.
Nigerian/English
Intermediate, Older; Fiction

Walter, Mildred Pitts. *Ray and the Best Family Reunion Ever*. New York: HarperCollins Publishers, 2002. 128 p.

Eleven-year-old Ray is the only member of his Creole family with ebony skin. When he goes to a large family reunion in Natchitoches, Louisiana, Ray discovers that he and Gran-papa Philippe are the only ones there with dark skin. To make matter worse, Ray looks like his grandfather whom his father and almost all his relatives despise. This is the story of Ray's secret bonding with Gran-papa Philippe, his appreciation of his grandfather's talent, and his effecting a reconciliation between his father and Philippe.
Creole (Nigerian-French-Spanish-Native American)-Haitian-American/Creole (French-Spanish-West African-Native American)-American
Intermediate; Fiction

North African-American

Pearce, Jonathan. *John-Browne's Body & Sole: A Semester of Life*. Stockton, Calif.: Balona Books, 2005. 168 p.

This book is presented as a journal written by thirteen-year-old Jack for a language arts assignment. It tells how he and the two other boys who are involved in an altercation learn how aikido (a martial art) and scripting can be used to prevent fighting and teach respect. In writing of his experiences, Jack expresses his feelings about his family, his friends, racism (his grandmother is Japanese), his piano recital, and his mother's terminal cancer.
Japanese-English-French-North African-Russian-European-American/European-American
Older; Fiction

Senegalese-American. See also West African-American

See   Banneker, Benjamin?

Kuklin, Susan. *How My Family Lives in America*. Photographs by author. New York: Bradbury Press, 1992. 32 p.

One of this book's photo-essays presents the New York City family of five-year-old Sanu whose father was born in Senegal and mother in Baltimore. Sanu has visited her father's homeland and enjoys the way her family's activities incorporate its culture.
Senegalese/African-American
Pre-K, Primary; Nonfiction

Sierra Leonean-American. See also West African-American

See   Culberson, Sarah

West African-American. See also Ashanti-American, Guinean-American, Nigerian-American, Senegalese-American, Sierra Leonean-American

Adoff, Jaime. *Names Will Never Hurt Me*. New York: Dutton Children's Books, 2004. 192 p.
This story takes place on the first anniversary of the killing of a student in a suburban high school. It focuses on four students: Kurt, a "freak" who is subjected to constant student harassment; Mark, who gains power over other students and is the school snitch; Ryan, the popular star quarterback, who is abused by his father; and Tisha, the unpopular biracial girl. In a setting where adults are for the most part oblivious to the potentially explosive feelings of the first three, it is Ryan's father who provides the explosives, Ryan who confronts his father with a gun, Mark whose scheming fails, Tisha who displays her bravery, and Kurt who may have been ready to unleash his hatred, but instead becomes a hero.
Eastern European-American/West African-American
Older; Fiction

Walter, Mildred Pitts. *Ray and the Best Family Reunion Ever*. New York: HarperCollins Publishers, 2002. 128 p.
Eleven-year-old Ray is the only member of his Creole family with ebony skin. When he goes to a large family reunion in Natchitoches, Louisiana, Ray discovers that he and Gran-papa Philippe are the only ones there with dark skin. To make matter worse, Ray looks like his grandfather whom his father and almost all his relatives despise. This is the story of Ray's secret bonding with Gran-papa Philippe, his appreciation of his grandfather's talent, and his effecting a reconciliation between his father and Philippe.
Creole (Nigerian-French-Spanish-Native American)-Haitian-American/Creole (French-Spanish-West African-Native American)-American
Intermediate; Fiction

Young, Karen Romano. *Cobwebs*. New York: Greenwillow Books, 2004. 400 p.
In this unusual story Nancy, a high school sophomore who as yet has no spider traits, is the daughter of part spider parents. Her father is a roofer who prefers living up high; her mother is a weaver who has to remain low; her Granny is a knitter and potter; and her Grandpa Joke is a doctor. Nancy's family becomes involved with Nico, a Greek-American journalist who blackmails Grandpa Joke into bringing Granny to heal his wife. In the process, Granny lose her life. The story focuses on the identities of the rumored Angel of Brooklyn and the Wound Healer, the growing attraction between Nancy and Niko's son Dion, and Nancy's concerns about whether she is or is not part spider.
Jamaican-West African-American/Italian-Scottish-American
Older; Fiction

Zairian-American

See   Wamba, Philippe

Asian-American

Arab-American

Seabrooke, Brenda. *The Bridges of Summer*. New York: Cobblehill Books, 1992. 160 p.

When she visits her Gullah grandmother Quanamina, fourteen-year-old Zarah, who lives in New York City, finds the life of South Carolina Gullahs distressingly backward. Quanamina's isolated house has no electricity or running water and she can't read. Zarah discovers that not only is Quanamina easily scandalized by her modern ways, but so too is her new white friend's grandmother, who still acts like a slave owner with servants. When Quanamina dies, Zarah cleverly manages to sell her land, thereby securing the future for her five-year-old cousin and herself.
African-Arab-American Gullah/African-American
Older; Fiction

Singer, Marilyn, ed. *Face Relations: 11 Stories About Seeing Beyond Color*. New York: Simon & Schuster Books for Young Readers, 2004. 240 p.

In "Mr. Ruben" by Rita Williams-Garcia, Dee wants her friends Myra and Shaheed, who is African-Arab-American, to go out together, but Myra won't go unless she finds out whether their ninth grade math teacher is at least part black so that she can have a crush on him. Dee says they can figure it out by looking at his visiting brother, but the brother turns out to be an identical twin.
African-Arab-American
Older; Fiction

Armenian-American

Bruchac, Joseph. *The Dark Pond*. Illustrated by Sally Wern Comport. New York: HarperCollins Publishers, 2004. 160 p.

Armie, who has a gift for communing with birds and animals, is continually drawn to the dangerous dark pond near his boarding school dorm. He is twice kept from approaching it, first by a fox and then by Mitch, a zoology graduate student who realizes from Abenaki stories that the creature that dwells in the pond has a very long life cycle and for some reason has awoken. Armie saves Mitch's life when Mitch attempts to kill the giant wormlike creature—and comes to realize that his schoolmates actually like him.
Armenian-American/Shawnee
Intermediate, Older; Fiction

Chinese-American

See   Chau, Jen
       See, Lisa
       Thompson, Beverly Yuen
       Tsang, Lori

Wong, Janet S.
Woods, Tiger

Callan, Annie. *Taf.* Chicago: Cricket Books, 2001. 256 p. (A Marcato Book)

In 1915, thinking that she has accidentally killed her toddler brother, twelve-year-old Taf runs away from home in search of her father who had gone West years earlier. On her four year journey to Wallowa County, Oregon, she meets a boy who lets her sleep in his tree hideout, stays with a farm couple, and receives a coin from a visionary Basque woman. In Pendleton, Oregon, she falls in love with a young man who is Chinese-Nez Perce, is courted by a policeman, becomes part of a musical trio, and cares for two neglected little girls. When she finally reaches Wallowa, she realizes that the search for her father is futile and that it is her lot to continue her journey. Written for young adults, this book presents Taf's growing up: her loneliness, her dauntless spirit, her yearning for love, the sorrows she encounters, the friends who care for her, and her discovery of her true self.
Chinese/Nez Perce
Older; Fiction

Cheng, Andrea. *Grandfather Counts*. Illustrated by Ange Zhang. New York: Lee & Low Books, 2000. 32 p.

When Helen's maternal grandfather comes from China, she must give up her bedroom and is unable to communicate with him. It is when they count the train cars passing their house that Helen's grandfather begins to learn English and she starts learning Chinese. The illustrations in this story of the initial bonding of grandfather and granddaughter show Helen's father as European-American.
European-American/Chinese
Pre-K, Primary; Fiction

Cheng, Andrea. *Shanghai Messenger*. Illustrated by Ed Young. New York: Lee & Low Books, 2005. 40 p.

Eleven-year-old May, who is part Chinese, travels by herself from Ohio to Shanghai to visit her grandmother's family and report everything back to her grandmother. Initially homesick, May comes to love Shanghai: the food, the life, and her Chinese relatives. Returning, she brings back the message that theirs is one family that embraces both those born in China and in America. The illustrations, the free-verse text, and the use of Mandarin words add to the story.
European-American/Chinese-American
Intermediate; Fiction

Freeman, Martha. *The Trouble with Babies*. Illustrated by Cat Bowman Smith. New York: Holiday House, 2002. 128 p.

When nine-year-old Holly moves into her new house, she meets her interesting neighbors, including Annie, who thinks her month-old sister is yucky, and Xavier, who has invented a de-yuckification device. The de-yuckification box produces surprising results, Annie realizes she likes her sister, and Holly discovers that she too is going to become a big sister. Annie and her baby sister have a Chinese father and a mother who is Polish-American and Jewish.

Chinese/Polish American and Jewish
Intermediate; Fiction

Hollyer, Belinda, selector. *The Kingfisher Book of Family Poems*. Illustrated by Holly Swain. New York: Kingfisher, 2003. 224 p.

This collection of poems about families includes the short poem "Face It" by Janet S. Wong about a girl who has features of her Chinese and French ancestors—and of herself.
Chinese and French
Primary, Intermediate; Fiction

Kadohata, Cynthia. *Outside Beauty*. New York: Atheneum Books for Young Readers, 2008. 272 p.

It is 1983 and twelve-year-old Shelby lives with her three sisters and their Japanese-American mother Helen in Chicago. Helen is obsessed with her beauty and using it to attract rich men. She spends time conveying her lifestyle to her daughters, all of whom have different fathers and who are very close to each other. When Helen is severely injured in an automobile accident, including damage to her face, the sisters are sent to live temporarily with their respective fathers whom they barely know. Shelby, the narrator, comes to like life in Arkansas with her Japanese father, whose only apparent fault is that he dresses poorly, but worries about her six-year-old sister Maddie, who has gone to live with her domineering, cruel father. Realizing the terrible effect he is having on Maddie, Shelby unsuccessfully tries running away to rescue her. The sisters and their fathers get together in Chicago when for a time Helen seems near death, and, for Maddie's sake, the sixteen year old sister secretly drives with the other sisters to a Colorado cabin. After the girls are caught, it is agreed that Shelby's father will look after all of them in Chicago until Helen is well. Helen ends up with her physician as a boyfriend, but Shelby realizes that it is not exterior beauty which counts.
Chinese-American/Japanese-American
Older; Fiction

Namioka, Lensey. *Half and Half*. New York: Delacorte Press, 2003. 144 p.

Eleven-year-old Fiona Cheng faces a dilemma when she must fill in the race box on her folk dancing class application as she is both white and Asian. She then faces another difficult choice. After agreeing to perform in her grandfather's Scottish dance group's performance at Seattle's Folk Fest, she discovers that at the same time she is supposed to appear, dressed in the elegant costume her Chinese grandmother has made, at her father's presentation of his children's book in which she is the model for the Chinese heroine. This problem seems to be resolved when Fiona's brother Ron agrees to wear a kilt and take her place in the Scottish dancing. Then when Ron injures his ankle, it is Fiona who not only solves the conflicting schedule problem, but learns that it doesn't matter which of your cultures you most outwardly resemble, they are of equal value.
Chinese/Scottish
Intermediate; Fiction

Nichols, Joan Kane. *All But the Right Folks*. Owings Mills, Md.: Stemmer House Publishers, 1985. 112 p.

Danny doesn't realize he is half white until he meets his grandmother Helga and goes to spend the summer with her in New York City. Suffering from asthma, bed-wetting, and teasing at his San Francisco school, Danny enjoys New York as he bikes with his grandmother; befriends Thelma Jean, her little brother Willy, and Charlayne; and starts learning karate from Charlayne's older sister. However, his new friends, two of whom are of mixed heritage, reject him because he lied that Helga was his nanny. Further, he worries that his deceased mother was a druggie like his Uncle Billy; his father insists that Danny is black and is not proud of him; and he discovers that Helga has lied to him. Everything improves when Danny uses his karate mental and kicking skills to escape kidnappers, and he decides that he is a bridge between black and white.
Panamanian-Chinese-American/African-American
Intermediate; Fiction

Platt, Randall Beth. *The Likes of Me*. New York: Delacorte Press, 2000. 256 p.

This is the story of the amazing year, 1918, in the life of fourteen-year-old Cordelia, an albino who is half white and half Chinese. With her mother dead and her stepmother Babe a giant, Cordelia is completely innocent of the ways of the world and fears she is dying when she has her first period. Cordelia falls in love with the half Indian Squirl and with him breaks the rules by riding the flume of the lumber camp where her father is superintendent. Thinking she has become pregnant by kissing Squirl, Cordelia runs away to Seattle. She does not realize that she has gone to live in a brothel, earns money as a freak with her "lucky" hair, and finally comes to her senses about Squirl and Babe.
European-American/Chinese
Older; Fiction

Reynolds, Marilyn. *If You Loved Me*. Buena Park, Calif.: Morning Glory Press, 1999. 224 p. (True-to-Life-Series from Hamilton High)

In this book for older teenagers, high school senior Lauren lives with her grandmother, the one supportive constant throughout her life, is in love with her caring boyfriend Tyler, and is close to her best friend Amber. Lauren hates her parents, who abandoned her, and especially her mother who caused her to be born drug-addicted and was blown up when a makeshift methamphetamine lab exploded. All changes when Lauren is betrayed by Tyler, betrays Amber, and discovers the identity of her "stalker." Terribly upset, she withdraws from life until she begins to realize the complexity of love and the need for forgiveness.
African-Chinese-American/European-American
Older; Fiction

Rosenberg, Maxine B. *Living in Two Worlds*. Photographs by George Ancona. New York: Lothrop, Lee & Shepard Books, 1986. 48 p.

This book explains how races evolved and how many children have a greater resemblance to one of their parents. It discusses the teasing and unwanted questions biracial children face and points to the benefits of living in two cultures. The book's text and black-and-white photographs focus on five children: Toah, who is African-European-American; Megan, who is African-European-American and Cherokee; Jesse, who is Chinese-European American; and Shashi and Anil, who are Indian-European-American.

European-American and Jewish/Chinese-American and Christian
Intermediate; Nonfiction

Smith, Sherri L. *Hot, Sour, Salty, Sweet*. New York: Delacorte Press, 2008. 176 p.

This is the story of the day fourteen-year-old Ana Shen graduates from junior high school. Just as she begins her speech as salutatorian, the school's water main breaks, drenching the attendees and canceling her speech. Then her best friend invites Japanese-American Jamie Tabata, the boy she has long had a crush on, to come with his family to Ana's house for dinner that evening. This sends Ana's extended family into a tizzy as they prepare a feast combining the favorite dishes of her Chinese grandmother and her African-American grandparents. The process is complicated by the animosity of the grandmothers, who even compete in promising Ana gifts, including a college education and a house. Just when Ana has had enough, Jamie's family and then, unexpectedly, the class flirt arrive at her house. The dinner is a disaster, largely because Jamie's father looks down upon Ana and her family and compares the dinner to a food court meal. Ana explodes. Standing up for all the grievances her minority family members have suffered, she orders Mr. Tabata to leave. Jamie sides with Ana and the two discover they like each other.
Chinese-American/African-American
Older; Fiction

Wayans, Kim, and Kevin Knotts. *All Mixed Up!* Illustrated by Soo Jeong. New York: Grosset & Dunlap, 2008. 112 p. (Amy Hodgepodge)

Amy Hodges is introduced in this first book of the *Amy Hodgepodge* series, which features pictures posted in Amy's scrapbook. Moving to a new town after having experienced only home schooling, Amy is excited to be starting fourth grade at Emerson Charter School. However, her first day starts out disastrously. She wears the wrong clothes, tears her dress when she removes its flower, sings too loudly in music class, is laughed at by classmates Liza and Jennifer, and discovers that a paper saying "Stupid new girl" has been taped to her back by Rory. However, her day improves when she is befriended in the cafeteria by Maya, Jesse, Rusty, Pia, and twins Lola and Cole. Upset by a racial insult from Jennifer, she discovers that the twins are black and white, Jesse is black and Puerto Rican, Pia is Chinese-American and white, and Rusty is Latino, Native American, and white. Learning that Amy's father is black and white and her mother Japanese and South Korean-American, they affectionately nickname her Amy Hodgepodge. The story continues with the group entering a school talent show where Amy, inspired by Rusty who has to earn money to buy his costume, overcomes her stage fright and becomes the group's lead singer.
Chinese-American/European-American
Primary, Intermediate; Fiction

Wayans, Kim, and Kevin Knotts. *Digging Up Trouble*. Illustrated by Soo Jeong. New York: Grosset & Dunlap, 2010. 112 p. (Amy Hodgepodge)

After foolishly letting her dog Giggles off his leash to play with another dog at the Farmer's Market, Amy is unable to find him. She spends a stressful night until in the morning the family receives a call from an older man, Irving Coleman, who reports that Giggles has come to his home with his dog. Then, after being reunited with Giggles, Amy realizes that helping Irving restore his community garden would make a perfect green project for the school class assignment. The two fourth grade classes adopt Amy's idea and decide to raise money for the needed tools and supplies by having a bake sale and a car wash. Amy is worried when she is placed in charge of the bake sale team, but because of the help of her visiting community-organizer grandmother and team members, including Lola, Pia, and Rusty, there are many baked goods for sale. However, things turn contentious when the bake sale team and the car wash team, including Jesse and Maya, become overly competitive. After teachers intervene, the teams decide to refer customers to each other. With the proceeds earned and the work of Amy's gardener grandmother and the fourth graders, Irving's garden again becomes a neighborhood asset. Referring to the mixed racial identity of some of Amy's friends, this sixth book in the series specifically identifies the heritages of Lola and Cole as well as of Amy.

Chinese-American/European-American

Primary, Intermediate; Fiction

Wayans, Kim, and Kevin Knotts. *Happy Birthday to Me*. Illustrated by Soo Jeong. New York: Grosset & Dunlap, 2008. 112 p. (Amy Hodgepodge)

In this sequel to *All Mixed Up!* Amy looks forward to celebrating her birthday with her new friends as well as with her family. Maya, Jesse, Pia, and Lola accept her invitation to her tenth birthday sleepover where Amy plans to have a Japanese tea ceremony and do origami. Amy's spirits wane when she fears her family is planning to move to California. She is really upset when her four friends decide to go to an Amber Skye concert instead of her party. When Lola's brother Cole discovers that Amy has not invited other guests, he texts the concertgoers, and the four girls leave the concert to go to Amy's house. It is then that Amy discovers what true friends they are and the advisability of telling her problems and her fears to her family. This book points out the mixed heritages of Amy and most of her friends.

Chinese-American/European-American

Primary, Intermediate; Fiction

Wayans, Kim, and Kevin Knotts. *Lost and Found*. Illustrated by Soo Jeong. New York: Grosset & Dunlap, 2008. 112 p. (Amy Hodgepodge)

Amy Hodgepodge persuades her parents to let her go on the fourth grade two-and-a-half day wilderness trip. However, she doesn't feel as pleased about it when she is placed in a group without her friends, but with Jennifer and Rory who don't like her. Further, she falls in the mud during the obstacle course, goes overboard with Jennifer in their canoe, and is embarrassed that she doesn't know what s'mores are. However, Amy is supported by Lola, Jesse, Maya, and Pia with whom she shares a tent. Together they enjoy tricking Cole, Rusty, and two other boys. Then when she, Jennifer, Rory, and two others get lost in the woods, Amy uses her compass to lead them back to camp—and receives the Best Camper award. In this third book in the series, Amy's mixed heritage is noted. Readers of the first book, *All Mixed Up!*, will be aware of the mixed heritages of five of her friends.

Chinese-American/European-American

Primary, Intermediate; Fiction

Wayans, Kim, and Kevin Knotts. *Playing Games*. Illustrated by Soo Jeong. New York: Grosset & Dunlap, 2008. 112 p. (Amy Hodgepodge)

When Evelyn, the star player of the Comets girls' basketball team, injures her arm, Amy Hodgepodge reluctantly agrees to take her place so that the team will have the required eight players. Amy has neither played basketball nor is she familiar with the game. She is a terrible player, and her mistake causes the team to lose to the worst team in the league. Amy tries to fake a twisted ankle so she can be on the bench, but even that fails and she decides to quit. However, after confessing her problem to Rusty, he offers to coach her, with Amy, in return, helping him sing harmony in the friends' fourth grade music class performance. Unaware of the fact that Amy has improved, her teammates don't pass her the ball. It is not until the end of an important game that Amy demonstrates her secret talent as a three-point shooter. Amy's mixed heritage is noted in this fourth book in the series. Readers of the first book, *All Mixed Up!*, will be familiar with the mixed heritages of most of her friends.
Chinese-American/European-American
Primary, Intermediate; Fiction

Wayans, Kim, and Kevin Knotts. *The Secret's Out*. Illustrated by Soo Jeong. New York: Grosset & Dunlap, 2009. 112 p. (Amy Hodgepodge)

Amy, Lola, Jesse, Pia, and Maya decide to enter as a group in their school's competitive annual spring art show. Amy comes up with the idea of tracing their body outlines on a large poster board and then painting and decorating them. The girls would stand behind holes that would show their faces. With the exception of Pia, the others are enthused about Amy's plan. Indeed, Pia's personality seems to have changed. She has become distracted, negative, and rude. Finally, she confides to Amy, with Amy's promise not to tell, that she fears that, since her father and stepmother are going to have a baby, her father won't pay attention to her. When Amy accidentally reveals Pia's secret to Lola, there are unforeseen consequences. Lola tells Jesse, and Jesse lets the secret out to classmates. The friends become so angry at each other that their Best Friends art display is jeopardized. It is not until they practice forgiveness that they restore their friendship—and their project ties for fourth grade first place. In this fifth book in the series, Amy's mixed heritage is noted, and series readers will be aware of the mixed heritages of most of her friends.
Chinese-American/European-American
Primary, Intermediate; Fiction

Wong, Janet S. *The Next New Year*. Illustrated by Yangsook Choi. New York: Frances Foster Books/Farrar Straus and Giroux, 2000. 32 p.

In this picture book a young American boy, who has a Chinese father and a Korean mother, prepares for Chinese New Year. His two best friends, who, like him, are of mixed heritage, will also celebrate the holiday.
Chinese/South Korean
Pre-K, Primary; Fiction

Yep, Laurence. *The Cook's Family*. New York: G. P. Putnam's Sons, 1998. 192 p.

In this sequel to *Ribbons*, twelve-year-old Robin and her younger brother are upset by their parents'

quarreling about whether their family should sacrifice to support their uncle's store. Robin's grandmother is upset by the quarreling about the store among her three grown children. By chance, Robin and Grandmother become pretend daughter and wife, respectively, of a distraught Chinese cook whose family has presumably died of starvation. As members of this fantasy family, Robin learns about being a Chinese daughter, Grandmother enjoys talking with the cook about old-time China, and they both escape from the stresses of their own family. When the cook's real daughter turns up, the fantasy family disappears, but, with new insights, Robin and Grandmother ease Robin's parents' dissension.
European-American/Chinese
Intermediate, Older; Fiction

Yep, Laurence. *Ribbons*. New York: The Putnam & Gossett Group. 1997. 192 p.

Eleven-year-old Robin, who excels at and loves dancing, is devastated when her parents say she must give up her ballet lessons to help finance bringing her Chinese grandmother to San Francisco. Determined to be a dancer, Robin practices constantly on the concrete garage floor in her pointe shoes even after she has outgrown them and her feet hurt. She is especially riled when Grandmother blatantly favors her five-year-old brother, causes conflict between her parents, and says that Robin must give up ballet. It is only after Robin accidentally views her grandmother's hideously deformed feet, which had been bound in China, that she understands her grandmother and the two become friends. Then, when Robin is diagnosed with hammer toes, it is Grandmother who supports Robin's decision to dance with pain rather than undergo surgery and, when Grandmother discovers that Robin's parents have borne the entire expense of bringing her to the United States, it is Grandmother who makes Robin's uncles help shoulder the costs. Robin's story is continued in *The Cook's Family*.
European-American/Chinese
Intermediate, Older; Fiction

Yep, Laurence. *Thief of Hearts*. New York: HarperCollins Publishers, 1995. 208 p.

Everything changes for thirteen-year-old Stacy when she is asked to help Hong Ch'un, a girl who has just moved to her town from China and will be in her class. Stacy doesn't like Hong Ch'un, who is rude and calls her a t'ung chng (mixed seed) because of her white father and Chinese-American mother. When Stacy says that Hong Ch'un should be treated fairly after stolen items are found in her backpack, a schoolmate also calls her a half-breed. Stacy, her mother, and great-grandmother drive to San Francisco's Chinatown to find Hong Ch'un, who has run away after being accused of stealing. It is then that Stacy gains a greater appreciation of her mother and her Chinese heritage, discovers how to see with her heart, and, with the help of her great-grandmother and her father, lays a trap that catches the real thief. This book is a sequel to *Child of the Owl*, which is about Stacy's mother.
European-American/Chinese-American
Intermediate, Older; Fiction

Filipino-American

Gallo, Donald R., editor. *Join In: Multiethnic Short Stories by Outstanding Writers for Young Adults*. New York: Delacorte Press, 1993. 272 p.

One of the seventeen short stories in this book is "Next Month . . . Hollywood" by Jean Davies Okimoto. Rodney, who is Japanese-Polish American, wants to be an Asian rapper. With the support of his good friend Ivy, who is Filipino-African-American, he plans for the two of them to appear in their high school talent show. When they preview their act before a different audience, the results are unexpectedly uproarious. Ivy realizes that their performance should be a comedy act and, at last, becomes Rodney's girlfriend.
Filipino-American/African-American
Older; Fiction

Okimoto, Jean Davies. *Talent Night*. New York: Scholastic, 1995. 176 p.

When seventeen-year-old Rodney and his nineteen-year-old sister Suzanne learn that their great-uncle Hideki, whom they have never met, might give them each $10,000 if they have have kept their mother's Japanese heritage, Rodney works on mastering karate kicks, Suzanne tries out Japanese flower arranging, and they both learn about haiku poetry and Japanese cooking. They discover when Uncle Hideki visits that he is not worth impressing since he is unbearably traditional and insults Rodney's half African-American girlfriend. However, they become closer to their Japanese heritage by learning from their mother about the prejudice she endured as a Japanese-American during the 1940s. Molly from *Molly by Any Other Name* appears very briefly in this book.
Filipino-American/African-American
Older; Fiction

Indian-American

See   Mehta, Nina

Iyengar, Malathi Michelle. *Romina's Rangoli*. Illustrated by Jennifer Wanardi. Fremont, Calif.: Shen's Books, 2007. 32 p.

When Romina's teacher asks her students to make something representing their individual heritages, Romina doesn't know how to present two cultures since her father is from India and her mother is from Mexico. She finally solves the dilemma by creating an Indian rangoli pattern with Mexican papel picado, cut paper, as the design material.
Indian/Mexican
Primary; Fiction

Krishnaswami, Uma. *Bringing Asha Home*. Illustrated by Jamel Akib. New York: Lee & Low Books, 2006. 32 p.

As Arun endures a seemingly endless wait for his new baby sister Asha to come from India, he continues to fold paper airplanes, using some of them as a mobile for her room, others to demonstrate his father flying to India and returning home with Asha, and a special decorated one to be given to Asha in India. When Asha arrives at the airport, thanks to her caregivers in India, she gives Arun a rakhi bracelet, the bracelet given by sisters to brothers on the Rakhi Indian holiday.

Indian/European-American
Pre-K, Primary; Fiction

Lamba, Marie. *What I Meant*. New York: Random House, 2007. 320 p.

Ever since her father's sister-in law has moved in, there has been a change in fifteen-year-old Sang's family. Her widowed Indian aunt Chachi is a complaining, critical kleptomaniac who steals food and money and blames the thefts on Sang. In the meantime Sang is head over heels in love with her classmate Jason and is upset that her parents will not allow her to date until she is sixteen. When her mother catches Sang in the lie that she was at an ice skating rink with her best friend Gina, her parents don't believe her allegations about Chachi. Her mother even takes her to a doctor since she believes Sang is bulimic. To make matters worse, for an unknown reason Gina turns against Sang. The situation comes to a climax when Sang sneaks off to Philadelphia to see a concert with Jason and his friend Gary. She sees Gina alone in another train car, and, when Gina leaves the train toting a large backpack, Sang realizes that she is running away. Getting off the train Sang follows Gina through the dark city streets and then calls Gina's mother as to her whereabouts. Robbed of her money and return ticket, Sang goes back to the train station where Gary is searching for her. Sang comes to realize that Gina and Jason are no longer her friends, but that she has other supportive classmates. Further, when Sang stands up to Chachi, who is about to reveal a damaging secret about her mother, Sang's parents and her visiting Indian uncle believe her and Chachi is made to leave.
Indian and Sikh/Italian-American and Catholic
Older; Fiction

Landau, Elaine. *Interracial Dating and Marriage*. New York: Julian Messner, 1993. 112 p.

This book's introduction presents two detailed histories of interracial marriage: the first of African-American intermarriage with Caucasians and the second of intermarriages involving Japanese-Americans. In both cases the introduction describes factors, including governmental actions and societal attitudes, which affected the frequency of these marriages. The bulk of the book presents interviews with ten teenagers and five adults or adult couples who describe their views of and/or experiences with interracial dating and marriage. Seven of the teens interviewed came to the United States from other countries; two of the teens are interracial. Two of the adult interviews are with interracial couples; another contains advice from a minister. A resource list and an index are included.
African-English-Indian-Italian-Dominican
Older; Nonfiction

Perkins, Mitali. *Monsoon Summer*. New York: Laurel-Leaf Books, 2004. 272 p.

Fifteen-year-old Jazz and her family go to Pune, India, for the summer so that her Indian mother can set up a clinic for pregnant women at the orphanage from which she was adopted. Jazz hates to leave Steve, her best friend and business partner whom she secretly loves. She also feels that because of a disastrous earlier experience she is unable to help others and should not volunteer at the orphanage. During the summer things change. Jazz's introverted father finds he enjoys teaching computer skills to the orphanage's nuns, her ten-year-old brother temporarily gives up being a "bug" guy to become a "soccer" guy, and Jazz comes to realize that she is not only big, but beautiful, that she has a

unique way of helping one of the orphans, and that she should tell Steve of her true feelings.
Nordic-American/Indian
Older; Fiction

Rosenberg, Maxine B. *Living in Two Worlds*. Photographs by George Ancona. New York: Lothrop, Lee & Shepard Books, 1986. 48 p.

This book explains how races evolved and how many children have a greater resemblance to one of their parents. It discusses the teasing and unwanted questions biracial children face and points to the benefits of living in two cultures. The book's text and black-and-white photographs focus on five children: Toah, who is African-European-American; Megan, who is African-European-American and Cherokee; Jesse, who is Chinese-European-American; and Shashi and Anil, who are Indian-European-American.
Indian/European-American
Intermediate; Nonfiction

Iranian-American

See   Farmanfarmaian, Roxane

Israeli-American

Elkeles, Simone. *How to Ruin a Summer Vacation*. Woodbury, Minn.: Flux, 2006. 240 p.

Sixteen-year-old Amy's parents never married, and her Israeli father, now an American resident, has been largely absent from her life. When Amy has to go with him to Israel to meet his family, that knows nothing about her existence, she is angry with her father, resentful about changing her summer vacation plans, and fearful about the safety of being in Israel. Overreactive Amy immediately likes her Israeli grandmother and her little Israeli cousin, but has to endure the hostility of the cousin with whom she rooms and eighteen-year-old Avi. She is constantly doing something wrong in their presence. It is not until the last part of her trip that Amy comes to appreciate her Israeli heritage, learns that her father had been rebuffed in his efforts to be with her, and falls in love with Avi.
German-Israeli Jewish/European-American non-Jewish
Older; Fiction

Japanese-American

See   Ikeda, Stewart David
        Noguchi, Isamu
        Ohno, Apolo Anton

Carey, Janet Lee. *Molly's Fire*. New York: Atheneum Books for Young Readers, 2000. 208 p.

Set in Maine during World War II, this is the story of the friendship of three young teens who miss their fathers: Peter, whose rich father pays him no attention; Jane, who has never seen her Japanese father

and is the target of anti-Japanese hatred; and Molly, who refuses to believe that her Army Air Corps father has died in an airplane crash in Holland.
Japanese/ European-American
Intermediate, Older; Fiction

Crutcher, Chris. *Whale Talk*. New York: Dell Laurel-Leaf, 2002. 224 p.

This novel tells of T. J. Jones, an adopted seventeen-year-old of mixed race, who in his senior year of high school organizes a swimming team of boys regarded as misfits by their classmates and the school and who are, except for T. J., mediocre swimmers. The story focuses on T. J.'s efforts to have his teammates rewarded for their Herculean efforts by receiving athletic letters. The book shows how the boys come to share their backgrounds and feelings and to become part of a cohesive group in which each feels valued and accepted. Thanks primarily to his father, T. J. learns to control his own rage.
African-Japanese-American/Swiss-Norwegian-American
Older; Fiction

Easton, Kelly. *Hiroshima Dreams*. New York: Dutton Children's Books, 2007. 208 p.

When Lin's Japanese grandmother comes to visit, she immediately recognizes five-year-old Lin as a kindred spirit. Lin is so shy that she barely speaks, but is able to sense what is about to happen. Lin becomes very close to her Obaachan, who teaches her about Japan, shows how her how to meditate, imparts wisdom, and tells Lin that she too has precognition. As the years pass and with Obaachan's support, Lin plays her cello in an orchestra, makes a best friend in her new school, and uses her vision to help police locate a missing boy. When Obaachan dies from leukemia, the result of being a fifteen-year-old in Hiroshima when the atomic bomb was dropped, Lin is devastated. Then, the boy she has been attracted to since kindergarten becomes her boyfriend and Lin accepts her gift of vision.
Irish-American Catholic/Japanese Buddhist, Shinto, and Catholic
Older; Fiction

Flood, Pansie Hart. *It's a Test Day, Tiger Turcotte*. Illustrated by Amy Wummer. Minneapolis: Carolrhoda Books, 2004. 72 p.

In this chapter book seven-year-old Tiger, who is of mixed race, is worried when it is time to take a big practice test, but becomes really upset when he has to fill in the race bubble. The African-American volunteer tells him to fill in Black and his teacher concludes he should fill in Other, but Tiger decides to leave that question blank because he isn't a weird or different "other." Tiger feels better when his father explains that just as ice cream can have mixed flavors, so people can be of mixed race. He feels even better when the next day there is an answer sheet that includes a Multiracial bubble and he discovers that a classmate is both black and Japanese.
African-American and Japanese
Primary; Fiction

Flood, Pansie Hart. *Tiger Turcotte Takes on the Know-It-All*. Illustrated by Amy Wummer. Minneapolis: Carolrhoda Books, 2005. 72 p.

Second-grader Tiger doesn't like "germy" girls and especially Donna Overton, who is a know-it-all. When Tiger and Donna call each other names in art class, they have to go to after-school detention. It is there that Tiger discovers he sort of likes Donna. There is no mention of Tiger's identity in this chapter book, but readers of *It's a Test Day, Tiger Turcotte* will know he is of mixed race.
African-American and Japanese
Primary; Fiction

Friedman, Ina R. *How My Parents Learned to Eat*. Illustrated by Allen Say. Boston: Houghton Mifflin Company, 1984. 32 p.

A young girl reports how, when they were courting, her American sailor father learned how to eat with chopsticks and her Japanese mother learned how to eat with a knife, fork, and spoon before they ate together. Their daughter can eat either way.
European-American/Japanese
Pre-K, Primary; Fiction

Gallo, Donald R., editor. *Join In: Multiethnic Short Stories by Outstanding Writers for Young Adults*. New York: Delacorte Press, 1993. 272 p.

One of the seventeen short stories in this book is "Next Month . . . Hollywood" by Jean Davies Okimoto. Rodney, who is Japanese-Polish American, wants to be an Asian rapper. With the support of his good friend Ivy, who is Filipino-African-American, he plans for the two of them to appear in their high school talent show. When they preview their act before a different audience, the results are unexpectedly uproarious. Ivy realizes that their performance should be a comedy act and, at last, becomes Rodney's girlfriend.
Polish-American/Japanese-American
Older; Fiction

García, Cristina. *I Wanna Be Your Shoebox*. New York: Simon & Schuster Books for Young Readers, 2008. 208 p.

Eighth-grader Zumi loves surfing, her baby cousin adopted from Guatemala, and playing clarinet in her middle school orchestra—and even spearheads the orchestra's money-raising punk-reggae concert to save it from being eliminated. However, most of all she treasures her cancer-ridden grandfather and the story of his life which he tells her before dying.
Japanese-Russian-American Jewish/Guatemalan-Cuban
Older; Fiction

Igus, Toyomi. *Two Mrs. Gibsons*. Illustrated by Daryl Wells. San Francisco: Children's Book Press, 1996. 32 p.

In this picture book a little girl tells of the two Mrs. Gibsons who love her: the Japanese Mrs. Gibson who is her mother and the African-American Mrs. Gibson who is her grandmother.
African-American/Japanese
Pre-K, Primary; Fiction

Iijima, Geneva Cobb. *The Way We Do It in Japan*. Illustrated by Paige Billin-Frye. Morton Grove, Ill.: Albert Whitman & Company, 2002. 32 p.

When Gregory and his parents move to his father's native Japan, Gregory notes many differences and happily does things as the Japanese do. However, on his first day at school, he feels out of place eating his peanut butter sandwich, but doesn't like the fish which the other children are served. Resolving to eat fish as the Japanese do, on his second day Gregory is pleasantly surprised when the class also gets peanut butter and jelly sandwiches as the Americans do. The text includes Japanese words accompanied with notes as to their meaning and pronunciation.
Japanese/European-American
Pre-K, Primary; Fiction

Irwin, Hadley. *Kim/Kimi*. New York: Margaret K. McElderry Books, 1987. 208 p.

Sixteen-year-old Kim's Japanese-American father died before her birth and she enjoys living with her European-American mother and stepfather in Iowa. However, she is upset about others regarding her as Japanese and associating her with World War II Japan. Into teen romance novels which always have perfect endings for their heroines and in the habit of running away from problems, Kim "runs" off to Sacramento to try to find her father's family, which had disowned him. There she learns of the terrible Japanese-American concentration camps of World War II and of their effects on those imprisoned—and she meets her grandmother and her aunt.
Japanese-American/Irish-American
Older; Fiction

Kadohata, Cynthia. *Outside Beauty*. New York: Atheneum Books for Young Readers, 2008. 272 p.

It is 1983 and twelve-year-old Shelby lives with her three sisters and their Japanese-American mother Helen in Chicago. Helen is obsessed with her beauty and using it to attract rich men. She spends time conveying her lifestyle to her daughters, all of whom have different fathers and who are very close to each other. When Helen is severely injured in an automobile accident, including damage to her face, the sisters are sent to live temporarily with their respective fathers whom they barely know. Shelby, the narrator, comes to like life in Arkansas with her Japanese father, whose only apparent fault is that he dresses poorly, but worries about her six-year-old sister Maddie, who has gone to live with her domineering, cruel father. Realizing the terrible effect he is having on Maddie, Shelby unsuccessfully tries running away to rescue her. The sisters and their fathers get together in Chicago when for a time Helen seems near death, and, for Maddie's sake, the sixteen year old sister secretly drives with the other sisters to a Colorado cabin. After the girls are caught, it is agreed that Shelby's father will look after all of them in Chicago until Helen is well. Helen ends up with her physician as a boyfriend, but Shelby realizes that it is not exterior beauty which counts.
European-American/Japanese-American; Italian-American/Japanese-American, Chinese-American/Japanese-American
Older; Ficton

Kuklin, Susan. *Families*. Photographs by author. New York: Hyperion Books for Children, 2006. 40 p.

Text and color photographs present interviews with American children, who talk about their families. Their families include seven families with children of mixed race, ethnicity, or religion, with one also including a child adopted from Sierra Leone. In an eighth family a child has been adopted from China. In a ninth family an adopted American child is of a race different from that of one of her fathers.
European-American/Japanese-American
Primary, Intermediate; Nonfiction

Lisle, Janet Taylor. *The Crying Rocks*. New York: Atheneum Books for Young Readers, 2003. 208 p. (A Richard Jackson Book)

Thirteen-year-old Joelle, who was adopted at the age of five by Vern and Aunt Mary Louise, does not look like anyone she knows in Rhode Island. She is upset by what she is told of her past: of being thrown out of a Chicago apartment window by her mother, being put in an orphanage there, traveling by freight train to Connecticut, and then being cared for by an old woman while living in a wooden crate near a railway depot. Joelle is befriended by an adoring eight-year-old girl who is European- and Japanese-American and by a classmate Carlos, who is of mixed heritage. Together Joelle and Carlos learn of the early Narragansett Indians and explore the wooded area, including the Crying Rocks, where they lived. Carlos learns the truth about the accident at the Crying Rocks where his older brother died and Joelle learns the truth about her background. Vern is her real father, her mother was Narragansett, and both her mother and twin sister died in Chicago.
European-American/Japanese
Intermediate, Older; Fiction

Okimoto, Jean Davies. *Molly by Any Other Name*. New York: Scholastic, 1990. 288 p.

When she is seventeen years old, Molly, who knows only that she is Asian-American, learns at school about an adoptee search organization. Excited, but scared, she agonizes over whether to learn more about her birthmother and perhaps meet her. As her search proceeds, the novel explores the reactions of Molly, her father, her mother, her birthmother, and her birthmother's husband and young son.
Japanese/Japanese-Canadian
Older; Fiction

Okimoto, Jean Davies. *Talent Night*. New York: Scholastic, 1995. 176 p.

When seventeen-year-old Rodney and his nineteen-year-old sister Suzanne learn that their great-uncle Hideki, whom they have never met, might give them each $10,000 if they have kept their mother's Japanese heritage, Rodney works on mastering karate kicks, Suzanne tries out Japanese flower arranging, and they both learn about haiku poetry and Japanese cooking. They discover when Uncle Hideki visits that he is not worth impressing since he is unbearably traditional and insults Rodney's half African-American girlfriend. However, they become closer to their Japanese heritage by learning from their mother about the prejudice she endured as a Japanese-American during the 1940s. Molly from *Molly by Any Other Name* appears very briefly in this book.
Polish-American/Japanese-American; Japanese/Japanese-Canadian
Older; Fiction

Pearce, Jonathan. *John-Browne's Body & Sole: A Semester of Life*. Stockton, Calif.: Balona Books, 2005. 168 p.

This book is presented as a journal written by thirteen-year-old Jack for a language arts assignment. It tells how he and the two other boys who are involved in an altercation learn how aikido (a martial art) and scripting can be used to prevent fighting and teach respect. In writing of his experiences, Jack expresses his feelings about his family, his friends, racism (his grandmother is Japanese), his piano recital, and his mother's terminal cancer.

Japanese-English-French-North African-Russian-European-American/European-American

Older; Fiction

Strasser, Todd. *Battle Drift*. Illustrated by Craig Phillips. New York: Simon Pulse, 2006. 224 p. (DriftX)

This second book of the *DriftX* trilogy focuses on Kennin's two drifting competitions with Ian, who continually taunts him because of his mixed race. In both cases Kennin realizes that it is foolish to race because of the road conditions, but his younger friend Tito has bet all his money on him. After beating Ian in the first race of a nighttime tsuiso, the tsuiso is called off because of the unusual Las Vegas rain and Ian claims his loss doesn't count since Kennin wasn't skidding enough. The second race occurs on a new dangerously narrow steep course. Kennin beats Ian in the first round and another driver in the second, but when he goes into the finals, his car loses a wheel, and the book ends with his crash. This story also tells of the affection which Kennin's friend Angelita feels for him, of her jealousy when the sexy Mariel butts in, of Kennin's sister's indebtedness to the gangster Jack for the $5,000 cost of her breast enlargement surgery, and of Jack's threat to Kennin that he must throw the second tsuiso.

European-American/Japanese

Older; Fiction

Strasser, Todd. *Sideways Glory*. Illustrated by Craig Phillips. New York: Simon Pulse, 2006. 208 p. (DriftX)

The final book in this trilogy starts with Kennin in the hospital with his leg broken in two places from his drift racing crash. His friend Angelita's car, which he was driving and which she hoped to sell for her college tuition, is totaled thanks to her younger brother Tito. He loosened the lug nuts because of a threat from the gangster Jack. Kennin's sister is not only in debt to Jack, her boyfriend and boss, but is also the victim of his physical abuse. He has caused her to become a prostitute, and she has become a meth user. When Kennin is sufficiently healed to return to work washing cars at the Babylon Casino, he borrows a BMW parked there and rescues his sister, whom he hides in a rehab center. In this story Kennin again helps Angelita's cousin Raoul elude the police when he has stolen a car and Angelita suffers from the attention Kennin pays to the flirtatious Mariel. Kennin is saved from some of his problems by the owner of the Babylon, who gives Kennin $5,000 to have his sister's Corolla worked on so he can drive it as a tandem drifter at the casino's new track. A dramatic ending concludes the series.

European-American/Japanese

Older; Fiction

Strasser, Todd. *Slide or Die*. Illustrated by Craig Phillips. New York: Simon Pulse, 2006. 224 p. (DriftX)

This is the first book in the *DriftX* trilogy, which centers its stories around drifting, downhill car racing in which the cars skid around turns. Teenager Kennin, who has moved to Las Vegas, seems mysterious to his schoolmates since he is tight-lipped about his personal life: his white father is in prison, his Japanese mother died three months earlier, his older sister has to earn money to support herself and Kennin, the two live in a trailer in an unsavory part of town, and Kennin's best friend died in California while drifting. In this story, Kennin, his friend Tito, Tito's sister Angelita, and their older cousin Raoul attend an illegal nighttime tsuiso, a two car drifting competition. The three teenagers discover that Raoul is driving a stolen car, Kennin rescues a tsuiso racer from a burning car, and, in order to save the drunken Raoul from arrest, manages to elude chasing police cars in a daring drive down a mountain. At the story's conclusion Kennin decides to race the bigot Ian in a tsuioso.
European-American/Japanese
Older; Fiction

Wayans, Kim, and Kevin Knotts. *All Mixed Up!* Illustrated by Soo Jeong. New York: Grosset & Dunlap, 2008. 112 p. (Amy Hodgepodge)

Amy Hodges is introduced in this first book of the *Amy Hodgepodge* series, which features pictures posted in Amy's scrapbook. Moving to a new town after having experienced only home schooling, Amy is excited to be starting fourth grade at Emerson Charter School. However, her first day starts out disastrously. She wears the wrong clothes, tears her dress when she removes its flower, sings too loudly in music class, is laughed at by classmates Liza and Jennifer, and discovers that a paper saying "Stupid new girl" has been taped to her back by Rory. However, her day improves when she is befriended in the cafeteria by Maya, Jesse, Rusty, Pia, and twins Lola and Cole. Upset by a racial insult from Jennifer, she discovers that the twins are black and white, Jesse is black and Puerto Rican, Pia is Chinese-American and white, and Rusty is Latino, Native American, and white. Learning that Amy's father is black and white and her mother Japanese and South Korean-American, they affectionately nickname her Amy Hodgepodge. The story continues with the group entering a school talent show where Amy, inspired by Rusty who has to earn money to buy his costume, overcomes her stage fright and becomes the group's lead singer.
African-European-American/Japanese-South Korean-American
Primary, Intermediate; Fiction

Wayans, Kim, and Kevin Knotts. *Digging Up Trouble*. Illustrated by Soo Jeong. New York: Grosset & Dunlap, 2010. 112 p. (Amy Hodgepodge)

After foolishly letting her dog Giggles off his leash to play with another dog at the Farmer's Market, Amy is unable to find him. She spends a stressful night until in the morning the family receives a call from an older man, Irving Coleman, who reports that Giggles has come to his home with his dog. Then, after being reunited with Giggles, Amy realizes that helping Irving restore his community garden would make a perfect green project for the school class assignment. The two fourth grade classes adopt Amy's idea and decide to raise money for the needed tools and supplies by having a bake sale and a car wash. Amy is worried when she is placed in charge of the bake sale team,

but because of the help of her visiting community-organizer grandmother and team members, including Lola, Pia, and Rusty, there are many baked goods for sale. However, things turn contentious when the bake sale team and the car wash team, including Jesse and Maya, become overly competitive. After teachers intervene, the teams decide to refer customers to each other. With the proceeds earned and the work of Amy's gardener grandmother and the fourth graders, Irving's garden again becomes a neighborhood asset. Referring to the mixed racial identity of some of Amy's friends, this sixth book in the series specifically identifies the heritages of Lola and Cole as well as of Amy.
African-European-American/Japanese-South Korean-American
Primary, Intermediate; Fiction

Wayans, Kim, and Kevin Knotts. *Happy Birthday to Me*. Illustrated by Soo Jeong. New York: Grosset & Dunlap, 2008. 112 p. (Amy Hodgepodge)

In this sequel to *All Mixed Up!* Amy looks forward to celebrating her birthday with her new friends as well as with her family. Maya, Jesse, Pia, and Lola accept her invitation to her tenth birthday sleepover where Amy plans to have a Japanese tea ceremony and do origami. Amy's spirits wane when she fears her family is planning to move to California. She is really upset when her four friends decide to go to an Amber Skye concert instead of her party. When Lola's brother Cole discovers that Amy has not invited other guests, he texts the concertgoers, and the four girls leave the concert to go to Amy's house. It is then that Amy discovers what true friends they are and the advisability of telling her problems and her fears to her family. This book points out the mixed heritages of Amy and most of her friends.
African-European-American/Japanese-South Korean-American
Primary, Intermediate; Fiction

Wayans, Kim, and Kevin Knotts. *Lost and Found*. Illustrated by Soo Jeong. New York: Grosset & Dunlap, 2008. 112 p. (Amy Hodgepodge)

Amy Hodgepodge persuades her parents to let her go on the fourth grade two-and-a-half day wilderness trip. However, she doesn't feel as pleased about it when she is placed in a group without her friends, but with Jennifer and Rory who don't like her. Further, she falls in the mud during the obstacle course, goes overboard with Jennifer in their canoe, and is embarrassed that she doesn't know what s'mores are. However, Amy is supported by Lola, Jesse, Maya, and Pia with whom she shares a tent. Together they enjoy tricking Cole, Rusty, and two other boys. Then when she, Jennifer, Rory, and two others get lost in the woods, Amy uses her compass to lead them back to camp—and receives the Best Camper award. In this third book in the series, Amy's mixed heritage is noted. Readers of the first book, *All Mixed Up!*, will be aware of the mixed heritages of five of her friends.
African-European-American/Japanese-South Korean-American
Primary, Intermediate; Fiction

Wayans, Kim, and Kevin Knotts. *Playing Games*. Illustrated by Soo Jeong. New York: Grosset & Dunlap, 2008. 112 p. (Amy Hodgepodge)

When Evelyn, the star player of the Comets girls' basketball team, injures her arm, Amy Hodgepodge reluctantly agrees to take her place so that the team will have the required eight players.

Amy has neither played basketball nor is she familiar with the game. She is a terrible player, and her mistake causes the team to lose to the worst team in the league. Amy tries to fake a twisted ankle so she can be on the bench, but even that fails and she decides to quit. However, after confessing her problem to Rusty, he offers to coach her, with Amy, in return, helping him sing harmony in the friends' fourth grade music class performance. Unaware of the fact that Amy has improved, her teammates don't pass her the ball. It is not until the end of an important game that Amy demonstrates her secret talent as a three-point shooter. Amy's mixed heritage is noted in this fourth book in the series. Readers of the first book, *All Mixed Up!*, will be familiar with the mixed heritages of most of her friends.
African-European-American/Japanese-South Korean-American
Primary, Intermediate; Fiction

Wayans, Kim, and Kevin Knotts. *The Secret's Out*. Illustrated by Soo Jeong. New York: Grosset & Dunlap, 2009. 112 p. (Amy Hodgepodge)
Amy, Lola, Jesse, Pia, and Maya decide to enter as a group in their school's competitive annual spring art show. Amy comes up with the idea of tracing their body outlines on a large poster board and then painting and decorating them. The girls would stand behind holes that would show their faces. With the exception of Pia, the others are enthused about Amy's plan. Indeed, Pia's personality seems to have changed. She has become distracted, negative, and rude. Finally, she confides to Amy, with Amy's promise not to tell, that she fears that, since her father and stepmother are going to have a baby, her father won't pay attention to her. When Amy accidentally reveals Pia's secret to Lola, there are unforeseen consequences. Lola tells Jesse, and Jesse lets the secret out to classmates. The friends become so angry at each other that their Best Friends art display is jeopardized. It is not until they practice forgiveness that they restore their friendship—and their project ties for fourth grade first place. In this fifth book in the series, Amy's mixed heritage is noted, and series readers will be aware of the mixed heritages of most of her friends.
African-European-American/Japanese-South Korean-American
Primary, Intermediate; Fiction

Werlin, Nancy. *Black Mirror: A Novel*. New York: Dial Books, 2001. 256 p.
In this book for older teenagers sixteen-year-old Frances is a loner and so upset by her mixed race appearance that for years she has not been able to look at herself in the mirror. When her brother Daniel commits suicide by an overdose of heroin, Frances is shocked and feels guilty that she had no longer been close to him. When she considers joining Unity Service, the preparatory school charitable institution in which Daniel was so active, she experiences conflicting emotions and encounters negative reactions from its members. Discovering that something strange is going on at Unity, Frances, with the help of a man who is mildly retarded, finds out the terrible truth about Unity and the death of her brother.
European-American and Jewish/Japanese-American and Buddhist
Older; Fiction

Lebanese-American

See   Hayek-Jiménez, Salma Valgarma

Nye, Naomi Shihab. *Going Going*. New York: Greenwillow Books, 2005. 240 p.

Since early childhood Florrie has treasured old things, especially old buildings and businesses, and wanted to protect them. She had loved walking about San Antonio with her late Lebanese grand-father and sharing his love and knowledge of San Antonio. Now sixteen, Florrie launches a campaign to stop people from shopping at franchise businesses, which are destroying the unique character of the city. Enlisting classmates and neighbors to support independent businesses, she receives positive input and publicity, but is discouraged when her project to canoe along the River Walk is aborted. However, Florrie's fervor returns when the family learns that a Taco Bell is to be built next to her mother's Mexican restaurant.

Mexican-American/Lebanese-Mexican-American

Older; Fiction

Palestinian-American

See   Nye, Naomi Shihab

Nye, Naomi Shihab. *Habibi*. New York: Simon Pulse, 1999. 288 p.

Fourteen-year-old Liyana, her younger brother Rafik, and her parents move from St. Louis to her Palestinian father's homeland. There the children meet their Arab grandmother and relatives and become friends with a brother and sister who are growing up in a Palestinian refugee camp. Liyana attends an Armenian school in Jerusalem, a Jewish boy becomes her boyfriend, and her father is put in jail. Within the tensions of the region, the family embraces those of all faiths and strives to promote peace.

Palestinian/European-American

Intermediate, Older; Fiction

South Korean-American

See   Wong, Janet S.

Flake, Sharon G. *Begging for Change*. New York: Jump at the Sun, 2007. 256 p.

This sequel to *Money Hungry* again focuses on the girl Raspberry Hill, now fourteen. It begins with Raspberry's mother going to the hospital after being severely beaten by a neighbor girl whom she had reported to the authorities. Consumed as usual by the desire for money to help keep her mother and herself solvent, Raspberry steals from her friend Zora's purse and also takes change from an eld-erly neighborhood friend. Throughout the story Raspberry is afraid that Zora will tell her father, Dr. Mitchell, who is dating Raspberry's mother and who is like a father to Raspberry. She is also afraid that she is turning into her own father, who, homeless and high on drugs, comes to the Hills' apartment

and steals Raspberry's money. Although not telling her father (Dr. Mitchell) about the theft from her purse, Zora stops being Raspberry's friend. In this story Mai, another of Raspberry's friends, continues to be so upset at being taunted because of her mixed racial appearance that she has her arm tattooed "100% black" and is mean to her visiting Korean-American cousins. By the book's conclusion Raspberry gets her first boyfriend, confesses to Dr. Mitchell, and plans to return the money to her neighbor. Also, she and her mother move out of the projects into a nicer and safer apartment, Zora makes up with Raspberry, and Mai grudgingly comes to accept her cousins.
South Korean/African-American
Intermediate, Older; Fiction

Flake, Sharon G. *Money Hungry*. New York: Jump at the Sun, 2001. 192 p.
    This is the story of thirteen-year-old African-American Raspberry and her friends: Zora, Mai, and Ja'nae. Raspberry, who lives with her mother in the projects, is determined that they will never again live on the streets. She spends her time, sometimes with her friends' help, making money: selling items at school, cleaning houses of the elderly, and helping at a car wash. Zora resents her physician father's being close to Raspberry's mother. The daughter of a Korean father and a black mother, Mae is constantly the target of racial insults because she is part Korean. She takes it out on her Korean father and wishes her mother had married a black man. Ja'nae doesn't pay her debt to Raspberry and steals from her grandfather to pay bus fare for her irresponsible mother to come and take her away. All Raspberry's efforts to have money come to nothing when her mother, mistakenly thinking Raspberry has stolen her earned money, throws some of it out the window and then their apartment is robbed. The book concludes with Raspberry and her mother's efforts to stay off the streets. The story is continued in the sequel, *Begging for Change*.
South Korean/African-American
Intermediate, Older; Fiction

McDonald, Janet. *Off-Color*. New York: Frances Foster Books, 2007. 176 p.
    Fifteen-year-old Cameron, who believes that her father is Italian, loves hanging out with her three best friends and doesn't take school seriously. Then her mother loses her job in a nail salon and gets one at lower wages in the owner's other salon in an African-American section of Brooklyn. Cameron and her mother must move into the projects, but, thanks to the school guidance counselor Mr. Siciliano, she is able to remain at her old high school. When Cameron discovers from an old photo that her father is black, she is shocked and blames her mother for not having told her about him and for his not being there for her. Cameron, her mother, her friends, her mother's coworkers, her multicultures class, and Mr. Siciliano spend time talking about race, about being biracial, about Mariah Carey, and about Malcolm X who Cameron hears in class was propelled to become a black nationalist because of his white-appearing mother. Cameron learns that one of her mother's coworkers is Korean and Irish, that Mr. Siciliano is half black, and that many celebrities are of mixed race. At her Sweet Sixteen party, Cameron enjoys her old best friends and new friends from the projects and even meets the boy who becomes her boyfriend.
South Korean/Irish
Older; Fiction

Shin, Sun Yung. *Cooper's Lesson*. Translated by Min Paek. Illustrated by Kim Cogan. San Francisco: Children's Book Press, 2004. 32 p.

In this bilingual English and Korean picture book, young Cooper, whose mother is Korean, feels out of place in Mr. Lee's grocery store since he can't speak Korean. Angry because Mr. Lee won't speak English to him, Cooper tries to steal a brush for his mother, but is caught by the grocer. Then, as Kim performs chores for Mr. Lee, he learns to speak Korean and to appreciate his mixed heritage.
European-American/South Korean
Primary, Intermediate; Fiction

Shusterman, Neal. *Red Rider's Hood*. New York: Dutton Children's Books, 2004. 192 p. (Dark Fusion)

Sixteen-year-old Red, who is of mixed race, is shocked when he discovers that dogs, cats, and teenagers in his neighborhood are the victims of werewolves and that thirty years ago his grandparents had been werewolf hunters who got rid of the wolves existing then. However, there are now new werewolves under the control of the earlier leader's grandson, Cedric. In this suspenseful tale Red teams up with his grandmother and Marissa (whose brother may be a werewolf) to destroy the twenty-two wolves of Cedric's gang. However, when Red joins the gang to spy on them, he finds himself attracted to the wolves and their powers. It is not until Grandma and Marissa battle the wolves that Red decides which side he is on.
South Korean-American/African-European-American
Older; Fiction

Wayans, Kim, and Kevin Knotts. *All Mixed Up!* Illustrated by Soo Jeong. New York: Grosset & Dunlap, 2008. 112 p. (Amy Hodgepodge)

Amy Hodges is introduced in this first book of the *Amy Hodgepodge* series, which features pictures posted in Amy's scrapbook. Moving to a new town after having experienced only home schooling, Amy is excited to be starting fourth grade at Emerson Charter School. However, her first day starts out disastrously. She wears the wrong clothes, tears her dress when she removes its flower, sings too loudly in music class, is laughed at by classmates Liza and Jennifer, and discovers that a paper saying "Stupid new girl" has been taped to her back by Rory. However, her day improves when she is befriended in the cafeteria by Maya, Jesse, Rusty, Pia, and twins Lola and Cole. Upset by a racial insult from Jennifer, she discovers that the twins are black and white, Jesse is black and Puerto Rican, Pia is Chinese-American and white, and Rusty is Latino, Native American, and white. Learning that Amy's father is black and white and her mother Japanese and South Korean-American, they affectionately nickname her Amy Hodgepodge. The story continues with the group entering a school talent show where Amy, inspired by Rusty who has to earn money to buy his costume, overcomes her stage fright and becomes the group's lead singer.
African-European-American/Japanese-South Korean-American
Primary, Intermediate; Fiction

Wayans, Kim, and Kevin Knotts. *Digging Up Trouble*. Illustrated by Soo Jeong. New York: Grosset & Dunlap, 2010. 112 p. (Amy Hodgepodge)

After foolishly letting her dog Giggles off his leash to play with another dog at the Farmer's Market, Amy is unable to find him. She spends a stressful night until in the morning the family receives a call from an older man, Irving Coleman, who reports that Giggles has come to his home with his dog. Then, after being reunited with Giggles, Amy realizes that helping Irving restore his community garden would make a perfect green project for the school class assignment. The two fourth grade classes adopt Amy's idea and decide to raise money for the needed tools and supplies by having a bake sale and a car wash. Amy is worried when she is placed in charge of the bake sale team, but because of the help of her visiting community-organizer grandmother and team members, including Lola, Pia, and Rusty, there are many baked goods for sale. However, things turn contentious when the bake sale team and the car wash team, including Jesse and Maya, become overly competitive. After teachers intervene, the teams decide to refer customers to each other. With the proceeds earned and the work of Amy's gardener grandmother and the fourth graders, Irving's garden again becomes a neighborhood asset. Referring to the mixed racial identity of some of Amy's friends, this sixth book in the series specifically identifies the heritages of Lola and Cole as well as of Amy.
African-European-American/Japanese-South Korean-American
Primary, Intermediate; Fiction

Wayans, Kim, and Kevin Knotts. *Happy Birthday to Me*. Illustrated by Soo Jeong. New York: Grosset & Dunlap, 2008. 112 p. (Amy Hodgepodge)
In this sequel to *All Mixed Up!* Amy looks forward to celebrating her birthday with her new friends as well as with her family. Maya, Jesse, Pia, and Lola accept her invitation to her tenth birthday sleepover where Amy plans to have a Japanese tea ceremony and do origami. Amy's spirits wane when she fears her family is planning to move to California. She is really upset when her four friends decide to go to an Amber Skye concert instead of her party. When Lola's brother Cole discovers that Amy has not invited other guests, he texts the concertgoers, and the four girls leave the concert to go to Amy's house. It is then that Amy discovers what true friends they are and the advisability of telling her problems and her fears to her family. This book points out the mixed heritages of Amy and most of her friends.
African-European-American/Japanese-South Korean-American
Primary, Intermediate; Fiction

Wayans, Kim, and Kevin Knotts. *Lost and Found*. Illustrated by Soo Jeong. New York: Grosset & Dunlap, 2008. 112 p. (Amy Hodgepodge)
Amy Hodgepodge persuades her parents to let her go on the fourth grade two-and-a-half day wilderness trip. However, she doesn't feel as pleased about it when she is placed in a group without her friends, but with Jennifer and Rory who don't like her. Further, she falls in the mud during the obstacle course, goes overboard with Jennifer in their canoe, and is embarrassed that she doesn't know what s'mores are. However, Amy is supported by Lola, Jesse, Maya, and Pia with whom she shares a tent. Together they enjoy tricking Cole, Rusty, and two other boys. Then when she, Jennifer, Rory, and two others get lost in the woods, Amy uses her compass to lead them back to camp—and receives the Best Camper award. In this third book in the series, Amy's mixed heritage is noted. Readers of the first book, *All Mixed Up!*, will be aware of the mixed heritages of five of her friends.

African-European-American/Japanese-South Korean-American
Primary, Intermediate; Fiction

Wayans, Kim, and Kevin Knotts. *Playing Games*. Illustrated by Soo Jeong. New York: Grosset & Dunlap, 2008. 112 p. (Amy Hodgepodge)

When Evelyn, the star player of the Comets girls' basketball team, injures her arm, Amy Hodgepodge reluctantly agrees to take her place so that the team will have the required eight players. Amy has neither played basketball nor is she familiar with the game. She is a terrible player, and her mistake causes the team to lose to the worst team in the league. Amy tries to fake a twisted ankle so she can be on the bench, but even that fails and she decides to quit. However, after confessing her problem to Rusty, he offers to coach her, with Amy, in return, helping him sing harmony in the friends' fourth grade music class performance. Unaware of the fact that Amy has improved, her team-mates don't pass her the ball. It is not until the end of an important game that Amy demonstrates her secret talent as a three-point shooter. Amy's mixed heritage is noted in this fourth book in the series. Readers of the first book, *All Mixed Up!*, will be familiar with the mixed heritages of most of her friends.

African-European-American/Japanese-South Korean-American
Primary, Intermediate; Fiction

Wayans, Kim, and Kevin Knotts. *The Secret's Out*. Illustrated by Soo Jeong. New York: Grosset & Dunlap, 2009. 112 p. (Amy Hodgepodge)

Amy, Lola, Jesse, Pia, and Maya decide to enter as a group in their school's competitive annual spring art show. Amy comes up with the idea of tracing their body outlines on a large poster board and then painting and decorating them. The girls would stand behind holes that would show their faces. With the exception of Pia, the others are enthused about Amy's plan. Indeed, Pia's personality seems to have changed. She has become distracted, negative, and rude. Finally, she confides to Amy, with Amy's promise not to tell, that she fears that, since her father and stepmother are going to have a baby, her father won't pay attention to her. When Amy accidentally reveals Pia's secret to Lola, there are unforeseen consequences. Lola tells Jesse, and Jesse lets the secret out to classmates. The friends become so angry at each other that their Best Friends art display is jeopardized. It is not until they practice forgiveness that they restore their friendship—and their project ties for fourth grade first place. In this fifth book in the series, Amy's mixed heritage is noted, and series readers will be aware of the mixed heritages of most of her friends.

African-European-American/Japanese-South Korean-American
Primary, Intermediate; Fiction

Wong, Janet S. *Minn and Jake's Almost Terrible Summer*. Illustrated by Geneviève Côté. New York: Frances Foster Books. 2008. 112 p.

It is in this sequel to *Minn and Jake* that Jake's mixed heritage is revealed. Ten-year-old Jake, his Korean grandmother, his mother, and his little brother spend the summer in Los Angeles, his old hometown. Deliberately choosing to avoid planned activities, Jake discovers that his former friends want nothing to do with him after learning that his best friend in his new town is a lizard-catching girl,

Minn. Further, he is embarrassed when Haylee, the girl he used to like, sees him coming out of the ladies' room in his mother's pink shirt and then later as he is attempting to get rid of ants in his clothes. When Minn visits Los Angeles, she is surprised to learn he is part Korean, is amused when tanning lotion makes him looks like a spotted hyena, is jealous of Haylee, and disapproves of his getting ahead of others at Disneyland by putting his grandmother in a wheelchair. It is only when he apologizes that his summer vacation improves.

French-German-American/South Korean-Norwegian-American

Intermediate; Fiction

Wong, Janet S. *The Next New Year*. Illustrated by Yangsook Choi. New York: Frances Foster Books/Farrar Straus and Giroux, 2000. 32 p.

In this picture book a young American boy, who has a Chinese father and a Korean mother, prepares for Chinese New Year. His two best friends, who, like him, are of mixed heritage, will also celebrate the holiday.

Chinese/South Korean

Pre-K, Primary; Fiction

Syrian-American

See   Abdul, Paula
      Halaby, Najeeb Elias
      Noor Al Hussein, Queen of Jordan

Taiwanese-American

Headley, Justina Chen. *Nothing but the Truth (and a few white lies)*. Boston: Little, Brown and Company, 2006. 256 p.

Fifteen-year-old Patty Ho is tormented by a schoolmate, is lectured to and overprotected by her Taiwanese mother, and believes she is a misfit. When her mother sends her to California to spend a month attending Stanford University's math camp, she experiences a new world: a daring roommate who shows her how to climb buildings, an understanding camp teaching assistant, and her first kiss, from a boy who subsequently breaks her heart. She also meets Auntie Lu and Uncle Vic, her aunt's African-American significant other; learns the truth about her father; and comes to appreciate both her mother and her own hapa (half Asian, half white) self.

European-American/Taiwanese

Older; Fiction

Thai-American

See   Woods, Tiger

Canadian-American

See   Abdul, Paula

Aboriginal Canadian-American. See Native Canadian-American

African-Canadian-American

See   Johnson, Dwayne Douglass (The Rock)

Asian-Canadian-American

Japanese-Canadian-American

Okimoto, Jean Davies. *Molly by Any Other Name*. New York: Scholastic, 1990. 288 p.

When she is seventeen years old, Molly, who knows only that she is Asian-American, learns at school about an adoptee search organization. Excited, but scared, she agonizes over whether to learn more about her birthmother and perhaps meet her. As her search proceeds, the novel explores the reactions of Molly, her father, her mother, her birthmother, and her birthmother's husband and young son.
Japanese/Japanese-Canadian
Older; Fiction

Okimoto, Jean Davies. *Talent Night*. New York: Scholastic, 1995. 176 p.

When seventeen-year-old Rodney and his nineteen-year-old sister Suzanne learn that their great-uncle Hideki, whom they have never met, might give them each $10,000 if they have kept their Japanese heritage, Rodney works on mastering karate kicks, Suzanne tries out Japanese flower arranging, and they both learn about haiku poetry and Japanese cooking. They discover when Uncle Hideki visits that he is not worth impressing since he is unbearably traditional and insults Rodney's half African-American girlfriend. However, they become closer to their Japanese heritage by learning from their mother about the prejudice she endured as a Japanese-American during the 1940s. Molly from *Molly by Any Other Name* appears very briefly in this book.
Japanese/Japanese-Canadian
Older; Fiction

European-Canadian-American

Frost, Helen. *Diamond Willow*. New York: Frances Foster Books, 2008. 128 p.

In this story, which is set in the interior of Alaska, twelve-year-old Diamond Willow, called Willow, returns solo with three sled dogs from a visit with her grandparents. Speeding on a blind curve, they crash into a fallen tree, thereby causing the treasured dog Roxy to lose her sight. When Willow's parents decide to euthanize Roxy, Willow and a friend secretly set out to take the injured dog to her grandparents, but become lost overnight in a blizzard. Throughout these experiences Willow's an-

cestors, reincarnated as a red fox, a spruce hen, a mouse, and one of the sled dogs, try to help Willow. The story then presents the surprising revelation that Willow had a twin sister, Diamond, who died shortly after birth and has become Roxy. The book is largely written in verse with a distinctive text design that complements the story.
European-Canadian-American/Athabascan
Intermediate, Older; Fiction

Stauffacher, Sue. *S'gana: The Black Whale.* Anchorage: Alaska Northwest Books, 1992. 224 p.
When Derek, who is one quarter Haida, visits his grandparents in Wisconsin, he goes to Ocean Park where the black whale S'gana performs. In touch with her spirit, which appears as a Haida girl, Derek realizes that S'gana is dying because she has been taken from her ocean home. Through the insights gained from a small Haida whale carving and with the help of his grandparents and the whale's trainer, twelve-year-old Derek initiates a campaign to free S'gana. His efforts are too late, but when he visits S'gana's pod off the coast of British Columbia, her legend is fulfilled.
European-American/European-Canadian and Canadian Haida
Intermediate, Older; Fiction

Stucky, Naomi R. *Sara's Summer.* Scottsdale, Pa.: Herald Press, 1990. 144 p.
Recently orphaned, fifteen-year-old Sara goes to spend the summer in Manitoba with her father's Hutterite family whom she has never met. There she is fondly welcomed and fully participates in the life of the contained community. Sara experiences both the Hutterite traditions, rituals, and rules which govern even the most minute aspects of their lives and the isolation of the community's residents, both physically and because of the absence of telephones, radio, and television. Sara learns that her musician father left the Hutterites because they did not permit musical instruments. Faced with the difficult decision as to whether to leave her new family at the end of the summer, Sara chooses to return to Toronto to pursue her education and have the options to determine her own future.
European-Canadian Hutterite/European-American non-Hutterite
Intermediate, Older; Fiction

French Canadian-American

See   Alba, Jessica Marie
        Charbonneau, Jean-Baptiste (Pomp)
        Drouillard, George
        Erdrich, Louise
        Pelotte, Donald
        Thorpe, James (Jim) Francis

Brooks, Bruce. *Prince.* New York: Harper Trophy, 1998. 144 p. (A Laura Geringer Book) (The Wolfbay Wings #5)
Middle-schooler Prince, who is black and French Canadian, loves to play ice hockey and sing swing songs. Not surprisingly, he finds it difficult to fit in with his Maryland black classmates who want him

to join the basketball team and mock his "white" sport. In this story, which is filled with hockey action, Prince, remaining true to himself, finally gains his classmates' support.
African-American and French Canadian
Intermediate, Older; Fiction

Bruchac, Joseph. *Hidden Roots*. New York: Scholastic Press, 2004. 144 p.

It is 1954 and eleven-year-old Sonny lives with his mother and his father, who is often angry and physically abusive. Sonny enjoys the company of an older friend, "Uncle" Louie, a man who had worked for his mother's parents when she was a child and from whom he learns much about the Adirondack area of New York State where they live. Sonny wonders about the many subjects he is not allowed to discuss and questions that remain unanswered: why he should be afraid of being "crept up on," what bad things happened in Vermont, and why his father doesn't want Uncle Louis around. It is only after he and Uncle Louis learn from the Jewish school librarian that her parents had sent her as a child from Germany to England for safety, that Uncle Louis tells Sonny the truth. Uncle Louis is his grandfather, who, like his late wife, had been sterilized during the Vermont Eugenics Project because they were Indians and who had fled Vermont so that Sonny's mother would not be taken away. It was because Sonny's family wanted to protect him from being treated like an Indian that they had kept his identity a secret, but it is when the secret is revealed to Sonny that his father, who is also part Indian, is released from his anger and shame.
European-American and Native American/French Canadian-American, Abenaki and Mohican
Intermediate, Older; Fiction

Carvell, Marlene. *Who Will Tell My Brother?* New York: Hyperion Books for Children, 2002. 160 p.

Written in free verse, this fictionalized story is based on a true experience. High school senior Evan, who looks like his English-American mother, has come to value the Mohawk part of his family. Upset by his school's tasteless Indian mascot, he pursues his older brother's earlier effort to have it changed. Persistent, Evan goes to the principal, to the school newspaper office, and repeatedly to the school board to stress the injustice it does to Native Americans. As a result he is cruelly taunted, his brother's dog is killed, and the school board passes a resolution proclaiming the Indian as a permanent mascot. However, in the process Evan gains a group of supportive friends who express their disapproval of the intolerance.
Mohawk and French Canadian-American/English-American
Older; Fiction

Ernst, Kathleen. *Trouble at Fort La Pointe*. Illustrated by Jean-Paul Tibbles and Greg Dearth. Middleton, Wis: Pleasant Company Publications, 2000. 176 p. (American Girl History Mysteries)

In 1732 when her family goes with other Ojibwa to spend the summer on La Pointe Island (now Madeline Island, Wisconsin), Suzette's father is accused of stealing furs from the adjacent Fort La Pointe. Twelve-year-old Suzette, who is Métis, with a French-Ojibwa mother and a French Canadian father, is determined to find the stolen furs and clear her father's name. She and her Métis friend Gabrielle discover the cave where the furs are stored and manage to escape when they are trapped there. Suzette then proves the identity of the real thief. Feeling that with her blue eyes, she is neither

French nor Ojibwa, Suzette realizes that it was through the skills she learned from being both that she secured her father's release. A minor character in the book has an Ojibwa father and a Dakota mother.
French Canadian/Métis (French-Ojibwa); Métis
Intermediate, Older; Fiction

Highwater, Jamake. *The Ceremony of Innocence*. New York: Harper & Row, Publishers, 1985. 192 p. (The Ghost Horse Cycle)

The *Ceremony of Innocence* is the second book in *The Ghost Horse Cycle*, a series for teenagers. It is the sequel to *Legend Days*, which describes Amana's childhood experiences as a Blood (Blackfoot). In this book Amana, whose family has died, has left her people and is destitute. She comes to live with an immature French Canadian, who deserts her before the birth of their daughter Jemina. Although sustained by her friendship with a French-Cree woman who runs a brothel, Amana suffers when Jemina grows up obsessed with finery and is married to the drunkard Jamie Ghost Horse and when her older grandson is only interested in things "American." Amana's hope lies in Sitko, her younger grandson, who treasures his Native American heritage.
French Canadian/Blackfoot (Blood); African-American and Cherokee/French Canadian-American and Blackfoot (Blood)
Older; Fiction

Highwater, Jamake. *I Wear the Morning Star*. New York: Harper & Row, Publishers, 1986. 160 p. (The Ghost Horse Cycle)

This third book in *The Ghost Horse Cycle* for the oldest readers tells the story of Sitko and his miserable boyhood. Sitko is placed in a boarding school where he is mistreated by the adults and scorned by the other children. His alcoholic father, Jamie Ghost Horse, realizing that Sitko deserves a better life, allows Alexander, his former friend and now the lover of his ex-wife Jemina, to adopt Sitko, and Sitko goes to live with Alexander, Jemina, and his grandmother Amana in the San Fernando Valley. Not able to figure out his past and deeply confused about his identity, Sitko continues a life filled with unhappiness, mitigated only by his friendship with a farm boy, his school's art club, and his painting. At the end of the book, Jamie shoots Jemina and Alexander, killing her and wounding Alexander. Jamie perishes in a truck crash, Sitko's older brother loses his life in a plane crash, the elderly Amana dies, and Sitko, the only one remaining, preserves his Blood (Blackfoot) past through his paintings.
French Canadian/Blackfoot (Blood); African-American and Cherokee/French Canadian-American and Blackfoot (Blood)
Older; Fiction

Native Canadian-American

Carter, Alden R. *Dogwolf*. New York: Scholastic, 1994. 240 p.

This is a novel of a hot summer when tower sitters spot fires in the Federal forest of northern Wisconsin and fire crews fight them. It is also the summer when Pete, aged fifteen, struggles to find

who he is. Half white and half Native American, he is haunted by the persistent howling of the some-how-kindred creature who is a dogwolf. Knowing that it cannot stand being penned in a cage, Pete determines to free it, either by shooting it or by letting it out. Loose, the dogwolf terrorizes the countryside and the Chippewa reservation—killing animals and then Pete's friend—until finally Pete confronts and shoots it.
Métis Canadian/Chippewa and Swedish-American
Older; Nonfiction

Frost, Helen. *Diamond Willow*. New York: Frances Foster Books, 2008. 128 p.

In this story, which is set in the interior of Alaska, twelve-year-old Diamond Willow, called Willow, returns solo with three sled dogs from a visit with her grandparents. Speeding on a blind curve, they crash into a fallen tree, thereby causing the treasured dog Roxy to lose her sight. When Willow's parents decide to euthanize Roxy, Willow and a friend secretly set out to take the injured dog to her grandparents, but become lost overnight in a blizzard. Throughout these experiences Willow's ancestors, reincarnated as a red fox, a spruce hen, a mouse, and one of the sled dogs, try to help Willow. The story then presents the surprising revelation that Willow had a twin sister, Diamond, who died shortly after birth and has become Roxy. The book is largely written in verse with a distinctive text design that complements the story.
European-Canadian-American/Athabascan
Intermediate, Older; Fiction

Stauffacher, Sue. *S'gana: The Black Whale*. Anchorage: Alaska Northwest Books, 1992. 224 p.

When Derek, who is one quarter Haida, visits his grandparents in Wisconsin, he goes to Ocean Park where the black whale S'gana performs. In touch with her spirit, which appears as a Haida girl, Derek realizes that S'gana is dying because she has been taken from her ocean home. Through the insights gained from a small Haida whale carving and with the help of his grandparents and the whale's trainer, twelve-year-old Derek initiates a campaign to free S'gana. His efforts are too late, but when he visits S'gana's pod off the coast of British Columbia, her legend is fulfilled.
European-American/European-Canadian and Canadian Haida
Intermediate, Older; Fiction

Central American-American— See also Latin American-American

Costa Rican-American

Flood, Pansie Hart. *It's a Test Day, Tiger Turcotte*. Illustrated by Amy Wummer. Minneapolis: Carolrhoda Books, 2004. 72 p.

In this chapter book seven-year-old Tiger, who is of mixed race, is worried when it is time to take a big practice test, but becomes really upset when he has to fill in the race bubble. The African-American volunteer tells him to fill in Black and his teacher concludes he should fill in Other, but Tiger decides to leave that question blank because he isn't a weird or different "other." Tiger feels better when his father explains that just as ice cream can have mixed flavors, so people can be of mixed race. He feels even better when the next day there is an answer sheet that includes a Multiracial bubble and he discovers that a classmate is both black and Japanese.
African-American and Meherrin/Costa Rican
Primary; Fiction

Flood, Pansie Hart. *Tiger Turcotte Takes on the Know-It-All*. Illustrated by Amy Wummer. Minneapolis: Carolrhoda Books, 2005. 72 p.

Second-grader Tiger doesn't like "germy" girls and especially Donna Overton, who is a know-it-all. When Tiger and Donna call each other names in art class, they have to go to after-school detention. It is there that Tiger discovers he sort of likes Donna. There is no mention of Tiger's identity in this chapter book, but readers of *It's a Test Day Tiger Turcotte* will know he is of mixed race.
African-American and Meherrin/Costa Rican
Primary; Fiction

Guatemalan-American

See   Goldman, Francisco

García, Cristina. *I Wanna Be Your Shoebox*. New York: Simon & Schuster Books for Young Readers, 2008. 208 p.

Eighth-grader Zumi loves surfing, her baby cousin adopted from Guatemala, and playing clarinet in her middle school orchestra—and even spearheads the orchestra's money-raising punk-reggae concert to save it from being eliminated. However, most of all she treasures her cancer-ridden grandfather and the story of his life which he tells her before dying.
Japanese-Russian-American Jewish/Guatemalan-Cuban
Older; Fiction

Nicaraguan-American

See   Richardson, William (Bill) Blaine III

Panamanian-American

Nichols, Joan Kane. *All But the Right Folks*. Owings Mills, Md.: Stemmer House Publishers, 1985. 112 p.

Danny doesn't realize he is half white until he meets his grandmother Helga and goes to spend the summer with her in New York City. Suffering from asthma, bed-wetting, and teasing at his San Francisco school, Danny enjoys New York as he bikes with his grandmother; befriends Thelma Jean, her little brother Willy, and Charlayne; and starts learning karate from Charlayne's older sister. However, his new friends, two of whom are of mixed heritage, reject him because he lied that Helga was his nanny. Further, he worries that his deceased mother was a druggie like his Uncle Billy; his father insists that Danny is black and is not proud of him; and he discovers that Helga has lied to him. Everything improves when Danny uses his karate mental and kicking skills to escape kidnappers, and he decides that he is a bridge between black and white.
Panamanian-Chinese-American/African-American
Intermediate; Fiction

Salvadoran-American

See   Martínez, Rubén

European-American

See   Ahyoka
Beckwourth, James (Jim) Pierson
Bibb, Henry
Bonnin, Gertrude Simmons
Cardozo, Francis Lewis
Carson, Adaline
Chau, Jen
Coker, Daniel
Cole, Lynette
Crawford, Goldsby
Culberson, Sarah
Douglass, Frederick
Early, Sarah Jane Woodson
Espinel, Luisa
Estévez, Emilio
Farmanfarmaian, Roxane
Farragut, David Glasgow
Goldman, Francisco
Halaby, Najeeb Elias
Haynes, Lemuel
Healy, James Augustine
Healy, Michael
Healy, Patrick Francis
Hinojosa-Smith, Rolando
Horne, Lena
Ikeda, Stewart David
Jacobs, Harriet Ann
Jacobs, Joseph
LaFlesche, Francis (Frank)
Langston, John Mercer
Little, Frank
Lynn, Loretta Webb
Momoday, Navarre Scott
Morgan, Garrett Augustus
Noor Al Hussein, Queen of Jordan
Nye, Naomi Shihab
Ohno, Apolo Anton

Osceola
Parks, Rosa Louise McCauley
Parton, Dolly Rebecca
Payne, Andrew Hartley
Peake, Mary Smith Kelsey
Pickett, Bill
Picotte, Susan LaFlesche
Prinze, Freddie James, Jr.
Richardson, William (Bill) Blaine III
Rillieux, Norbert
Rogers, Will, Jr.
Ronstadt, Linda
Rose, Edward
See, Lisa
Sequoyah
Sheen, Charlie
Smalls, Robert
Smith, Nolle
Te Ata
Thompson, Beverly Yuen
Tibbles, Susette LaFlesche
Tinker, Clarence Leonard
Washington, Booker Taliaferro
Washington, Olivia A. Davidson
Watie, Stand
West, W. Richard, Jr.
White, Walter Francis
Williams, Daniel Hale
Williams, Mary Harris
Woodson, Lewis

Ada, Alma Flor. *I Love Saturday y domingos*. Illustrated by Elivia Savadier. New York: Atheneum Books for Young Readers, 2002. 32 p.

A little girl enjoys spending Saturdays with her paternal grandfather, who is the son of European immigrants, and her paternal grandmother, who is a descendant of settlers. She enjoys Sundays with her maternal grandfather, who is Mexican-American, and her maternal grandmother, who is Mexican-American and Native American. On her sixth birthday all four grandparents come to her house for the celebration. The text is similar for each weekend's activities, thereby making it possible to repeat some of the words in Spanish in describing the Sunday visits.

European-American /Mexican-American and Native American
Pre-K, Primary; Fiction

Adoff, Arnold. *black is brown is tan*. Illustrated by Emily Arnold McCully. New York: Harper & Row, 1973. 32 p. Reissued with updated illustrations. HarperCollins/Amistad, 2002.

Adoff's poem and McCully's accompanying illustrations celebrate black, white, and shades in-between as they present the daily life of a close-knit family: two small children, their black mom, grandma, and uncle and their white daddy, granny, and aunt.
European-American/African-American
Pre-K, Primary; Fiction

Adoff, Arnold. *Hard to Be Six*. Illustrated by Cheryl Hanna. New York: Lothrop, Lee & Shepard Books, 1991. 32 p.

A six-year-old boy, who longs to be as big as his ten-year-old sister, is reassured by his family that he is indeed growing bigger. However, it is the words on his grandfather's gravestone that encourage him to slow down and live in the present. The illustrations depict a father who is white and a mother and grandparents who are African-American.
African-American/European-American
Pre-K, Primary; Fiction

Adoff, Jaime. *The Death of Jayson Porter*. New York: Jump at the Sun/Hyperion, 2008. 272 p.

This book for a high school audience tells of the depressing life of sixteen-year-old Jayson Porter, who throughout the story contemplates the day when he will jump off the eighteenth floor of his apartment building. Jayson's father, who has left the family, is a crackhead. Jayson's mother is an alcoholic, who delights in physically abusing Jayson. Jayson narrowly escapes being shot, smokes pot with his best friend Trax, is one of only two non-white students in his private school, has sex with his girlfriend, suffers the death of Trax when a meth lab explodes, and learns that his parents are not his real parents. Jayson does jump, but from the seventh floor where Trax lived. He miraculously escapes death, but is gravely injured. The story ends hopefully as Jayson is finally united with his real mother, who has turned her life around and always loved him.
African-American/European-American
Older; Fiction

Adoff, Jaime. *Jimi & Me*. New York: Jump at the Sun, 2005. 336 p.

This novel in verse is filled with despair as thirteen-year-old Keith experiences the shooting death of his father, moving from Brooklyn to a small Ohio town, taunting at his new school, his mother's slide into depression, the hatred both of them feel when they find out that his father was giving their money to another woman and the son they had, and learning that this sixteen-year-old half brother is named Jimi, the name of his idol Jimi Hendrix. When Keith meets his half brother, he discovers the truth and begins to go on with his life.
African-American and Cherokee/European-American
Older, Fiction

Alder, Elizabeth. *Crossing the Panther's Path*. New York: Farrar Straus Giroux, 2002. 240 p.

This book is based on the life of Billy Caldwell and his close relationship with Tecumseh, the Shawnee chief. Tecumseh, as leader of warriors from a number of Indian nations and in alliance with the British army in Canada, sought to reclaim the lands which the Americans took from the Indians. Billy, who is Irish-Mohawk, serves as soldier, interpreter, and then captain in the British Indian Department in the War of 1812. This story tells of the battles of Tippecanoe, Chicago, Detroit, the River Raisin, and the Thames River; of Billy's courageous actions; of his love of a European-American and Ojibwa woman; and of his decision to forgo fighting and help the Indians through peaceful means.
European-American/Chippewa
Older; Fiction

Amado, Elisa. *Cousins*. Illustrated by Luis Garay. Toronto: Groundwood Books, 2004. 32 p.

A little girl, who lives with her Latin-American father and her maternal grandmother, is jealous of her Catholic cousin, who will celebrate her first communion and carry the pretty rosary that is at her paternal grandmother's house. Stealing the rosary, she feels terribly guilty and on her own goes to the Catholic church to confess.
Latin-American and Catholic/European-American and non-Catholic
Pre-K, Primary; Fiction

Angel, Ann. *Real for Sure Sister*. Illustrated by Joanne Bowring. Fort Wayne, Ind.: Perspectives Press, 1988. 72 p.

Nine-year-old Amanda is adopted as are her brothers Nicky and Joey, who is Mexican Indian. Although she adores her little brothers, she has conflicting feelings about Stevi, the biracial (black/white) baby her family is planning to adopt. Amanda initially wants another brother, not a sister, and then tries to ignore Stevi in case the adoption doesn't go through. She shares her concern with her parents, who are white, and with her best friend, who has been adopted from Korea. It is a happy day when Amanda's entire family goes to court and Stevi becomes her real sister.
African-European-American
Primary; Fiction

Applegate, Stan. *The Devil's Highway*. Illustrated by James Watling. Atlanta: Peachtree, 1998. 160 p.

Just after leaving his family farm in Franklin, Tennessee, to search for his grandfather and escape from the men who are after him, Zeb comes upon ten-year-old Hannah. Half Choctaw and half Caucasian, Hannah has gotten away from outlaws who had kidnapped her six months earlier. Together they travel southward on the Natchez Trace, a highly dangerous road in 1811. Hannah finally is reunited with her parents in Washington, Mississippi, but Zeb, who becomes an honorary Choctaw on the way, must continue looking for his grandfather in nearby Natchez. An author's note provides information about the Natchez Trace.
European-American/Choctaw
Intermediate, Older; Fiction

Applegate, Stan. *Natchez Under-the-Hill*. Illustrated by James Watling. Atlanta: Peachtree, 1999. 192 p.

In this sequel to *The Devil's Highway*, fourteen-year-old Zeb succeeds in finding his grandfather in Natchez and in returning with him to their Tennessee home. Zeb's adventures in the book include winning a horse race, escaping from jail and from being pressed into the British navy, rescuing stolen horses, experiencing the comet and the earthquake of 1811, and revisiting the Choctaw's Yowani Village. Zeb's friend Hannah, who is Caucasian-Choctaw, plays a prominent role in the story.
European-American/Choctaw
Intermediate; Fiction

Baskin, Nora Raleigh. *The Truth about My Bat Mitzvah*. New York: Simon & Schuster Books for Young Readers, 2008. 144 p.

Twelve-year-old Caroline's father is Christian and her mother is non-practicing Jewish. Caroline has never thought about being Jewish until her grandmother's death and receiving the Star of David necklace her grandmother had wanted her to have. She keeps the necklace a secret, learns about being Jewish from her best friend Rachel who is about to have a bat mitzvah celebration, and discovers that her great-grandparents, who came from a non-practicing Jewish German-American family, had objected to her grandfather's marriage to her Russian Jewish immigrant grandmother. Also, initially her grandparents had not been happy about her mother's marrying a non-Jew. Caroline comes to realize that she wants to be Jewish and that she doesn't need a bat mitzvah party to be a bat mitzvah.
European-American Christian/German-Russian-American Jewish
Intermediate; Fiction

Becker, John T., and Stanli K. Becker, eds. *All Blood Is Red . . . All Shadows Are Dark!* Illustrated by J. Howard Noel. Cleveland: Seven Shadows Press, 1984. 168 p.

John T. (Tom) Becker, who is Irish-German-American, and his wife, Stanli K. Becker, who is African-American, have five young children. One of the four who are adopted is biracial. All seven family members are responsible for individual sections of this book, which recounts their personal and family experiences as a multiracial family. Teaching their children to be aware of and proud of their individual differences, the editors present information on the history of racial classification in the United States and advocate their belief that race is and should be regarded as an "absurdity."
African-European-American
Intermediate, Older; Nonfiction

Binch, Caroline. *Silver Shoes*. Illustrated by author. New York: DK Publishing, 2001. 28 p.

Loving her grandmother's silver dancing shoes, Molly wants a pair of her own when she starts dance lessons. She unhappily discovers that the adult ones she gets her mother to buy at the thrift store cannot be used at her dance class, but decides to dance without them. Then finally, on her birthday, Molly's wish for silver shoes comes true. The illustrations in this picture book show that Molly's mother is African-American and her father and grandparents are Caucasian.
European-American/African-American
Pre-K, Primary; Fiction

Bode, Janet. *Different Worlds: Interracial and Cross-Cultural Dating*. New York: Franklin Watts, 1989. 128 p.

Based primarily on interviews with six teenage couples who are dating interracially and/or cross-culturally, this book is written for and about teens. It looks at the history of prejudice and racism; discusses negative reactions of parents, relatives, and classmates; examines why adolescents make their dating choices; and mentions some positive aspects of interracial dating. Although it does not cover the topics of interracial marriage and families, four of the twelve teens interviewed are of mixed race or heritage: African-American/European-American; Protestant English-American/Catholic Irish-American; Cuban/Puerto Rican; and Mexican-Spanish-American. A bibliography, a listing of resource organizations, and an index are included.

African-American/European-American

Older; Nonfiction

Bradman, Tony, and Eileen Browne. *Through My Window*. Morristown, N.J.: Silver Burdett Company, 1986. 28 p.

A little girl, who must stay inside her apartment because she is ill, keeps looking out the window for her mother, who is going to bring her a surprise after work. She sees the mail carrier, the milk delivery lady, the window cleaner, her next door neighbor, the neighbor's dog—and finally her mother, who has the surprise: a toy doctor kit. The pictures show that the girl's father, who is home with her, is Caucasian and her mother is African-American.

European-American/African-American

Pre-K, Primary; Fiction

Brashares, Ann. *Forever in Blue: The Fourth Summer of the Sisterhood*. New York: Delacorte Press, 2007. 400 p. (Sisterhood of the Traveling Pants)

This fourth book of the series takes place after Carmen, Lena, Tibby, and Bridget's freshman year in college. Carmen's year at Williams College has been a disaster. She finds herself ungrounded with her mother, stepfather, and baby brother moving into a new house, discovers that she has no idea how to make friends, and feels invisible. Her only college friend, aspiring actress Julia, has persuaded Carmen to spend the summer with her at a theater festival in Vermont where Carmen will be on a stage crew. When the casting director persuades Carmen to audition, Carmen, who has never acted, is amazed to discover that she is the only apprentice chosen for a role in the theater's major production. Julia becomes hostile to Carmen and, then, pretending to be helpful, teaches Carmen how to read her role in meter. The professional actors are dismayed that Carmen now sounds like a robot. Carmen finally realizes that Julia takes pleasure in her failures, and she once again immerses herself in her role. Lena, who had been crushed when her Greek boyfriend Kostas married a Greek woman whom he had impregnated, is enrolled in a painting class in Providence, Rhode Island. There she is impressed with classmate Leo, an outstanding artist who is equally engrossed in painting. Getting to know him and his artistic African-American mother, Lena has her first sexual experience with him. Tibby, who has been going with Bailey's friend Brian, also loses her virginity. However, she becomes distressed that she may be pregnant and, after discovering that she isn't, breaks up with Brian. She then gives Lena's younger sister Effie an okay to go out with him. With Bridget's boyfriend Eric away

for the summer in Mexico, she goes to Turkey for an archaeological dig. There she discovers that she loves digging and falls for an archaeology professor until she sees his wife and children. At the book's conclusion Tibby is reunited with Brian, Bridget is reunited with Eric, and Lena, Tibby, and Bridget go to Vermont to attend Carmen's successful opening night. Then the four friends fly to Greece to search for the Traveling Pants, which Effie has accidentally lost, Lena and Kostas meet, and the four friends realize that they have moved beyond the Pants. The mixed heritages of Carmen, Bridget, and Eric should be familiar to readers of *The Sisterhood of the Traveling Pants*.
European-American/African-American; European-American/Puerto Rican-American; Dutch/European-American; European-American/Mexican
Older; Fiction

Brashares, Ann. *Girls in Pants: The Third Summer of the Sisterhood*. New York: Delacorte Press, 2005. 352 p. (Sisterhood of the Traveling Pants)
Bridget, Lena, Tibby, and Carmen graduate from high school at the beginning of this third book in the series, which details the four seventeen-year-olds' lives during the summer before college. Lena, who is still getting over Kostas, enjoys her summer drawing class. Defying and lying to her father, she continues to attend after he has forbidden her to continue because of the nude models. When he discovers her deceit, he announces that he will not pay for her going to the Rhode Island School of Design. Heeding the suggestion of the class teacher, Lena embarks on an art portfolio project that just may win her a scholarship to the RISD. Tibby has conflicting feelings when Brian asks her to the senior party, but is devastated when, because she has left her window open, her three-year-old sister tries to climb the nearby apple tree and, falling, has a fractured skull and broken bones. Finding it difficult to have her new stepfather David living in her house and upset by the news that she will become a sister, Carmen considers going to the nearby University of Maryland rather than Williams College so that she can be closer to home. She hates her job taking care of Valia, Lena's grandmother, who has become very disagreeable because she is homesick for her native Greece. Carmen also worries that Win, the boy she likes, has the false impression that she is a good person. Bridget spends her summer coaching at a soccer camp in Pennsylvania where she is surprised to discover that one of the coaches is Eric with whom she had a relationship two summers earlier in California. Still strongly drawn to him, but trying to be more sensible, she and Eric become friends and he nurses her through an illness. It is an eventful summer as Carmen and Win frantically drive to Downington, Pennsylvania, to bring David back to Bethesda for his son's early birth and Carmen discovers that she loves her baby brother and wants to go to Williams. Valia is happy that she can return to Greece, and Lena receives the RSID scholarship and her father's approval. Tibby overcomes her feelings of unworthiness by climbing out of her window and down the apple tree and being Carmen's mother's successful, albeit unorthodox, birth coach. It is then that she is able to get back together with Brian. And, Eric tells Bridget that he has broken up with his girlfriend, and they profess how much they care for each other. Readers of the initial book in this series will be aware of the mixed heritages of Carmen, Bridget, and Eric.
European-American/Puerto Rican-American; Dutch/European-American; European-American/Mexican
Older; Fiction

Brashares, Ann. *The Second Summer of the Sisterhood.* New York: Delacorte Press, 2003. 384 p. (Sisterhood of the Traveling Pants)

This second book of the series describes Carmen, Lena, Bridget, and Tibby's experiences during the summer before their seventeenth birthdays. Once again, the pants are passed among them, but they no longer fit Bridget, who has been so down because of her earlier sexual relationship with Eric, that she has gained weight, given up soccer, and dyed her pretty blonde hair. Using a fake name, Bridget travels to Alabama where she gets a job cleaning her grandmother Greta's attic and finds mementos of her deceased mother. As the summer progresses Bridget gets back in shape, is able to wear the pants, confesses her identity to Greta and to her long ago best friend Billy, coaches and then stars for Billy's soccer team, and realizes that Greta is like a mother to her. Tibby goes to a film program at a college in Virginia. Befriending two shallow classmates, she produces a highly embarrassing film about her mother and is excruciated when her mother comes to the viewing. Upset by the damage she has done to her relationships with her mother and Brian, a friend of hers and Bailey's, she redeems herself by making a moving film about Bailey, who died from cancer. Both Carmen and Lena also experience strained relationships with their mothers. Carmen is jealous of her mother's romance with David, sabotages it, and then manages to restore it. Lena pesters her mother about the man Eugene in her mother's past and regrets that she has broken off with Kostas. When Kostas visits her, she discovers that he really is in love with her. However, going to Greece for her beloved grandfather's funeral, Lena finds out that Kostas has had to marry a Greek woman whom he impregnated. Fortunately, she learns about Eugene from her mother and is attracted to Carmen's stepbrother Paul. The story ends when the girls' mothers, who had not been close since Bridget's mother's death, resume their friendship. The mixed heritages of Carmen, Bridget, and Eric were revealed in *The Sisterhood of the Traveling Pants.* European-American/Puerto Rican-American; Dutch/European-American; European-American/Mexican Older; Fiction

Brashares, Ann. *The Sisterhood of the Traveling Pants.* New York: Delacorte Press, 2001. 304 p. (Sisterhood of the Traveling Pants)

In this initial book of the series, four girls who are almost sixteen discover that a pair of blue jeans that Carmen had purchased at a thrift shop somehow fits all of them. Close friends their entire lives, the girls establish a Sisterhood in which they will pass the pants among each other as they separate during their summer vacation. Bridget, an athlete whose father is Dutch and whose mother had committed suicide, goes to a soccer camp in Baja, California, where she shines as a player. She is strongly attracted to camp coach Eric, whose mother is Mexican, loses her virginity to him, and then becomes confused and upset. Carmen, who had been looking forward to a vacation with her divorced father in South Carolina, is shocked to learn that he is engaged and is living with his fiancée and her two children. Ignored and treated like an outsider because of her Puerto Rican appearance, Carmen finally becomes so frustrated and angry that she throws a rock through the house window and runs away back to Bethesda, Maryland. Lena, a beautiful introverted girl, goes with her sister to stay in Greece with her grandparents. Enjoying painting the lovely scenery, she inadvertently leads her grandparents to believe she has been raped by Kostas, a family friend, and causes a fight between their grandfathers. Tibby, who remains at home, gets a tedious job at a drugstore and becomes friends with Bailey, a twelve-year-old girl who has leukemia and with whom she films a movie. The pants seem to

have no positive effect on the girls' experiences until the end of the summer. Then Lena gets the courage to apologize to Kostas and tell him she loves him; Carmen gets the courage to go to her father's wedding after telling him that she is mad at him; Tibby gets the courage to visit Bailey in the hospital when she is dying; and Bridget receives the support she needs from the pants (and Lena who brings them to her).
European-American/Puerto Rican-American; Dutch/European-American; European-American/Mexican
Older; Fiction

Bruchac, Joseph. *Hidden Roots*. New York: Scholastic Press, 2004. 144 p.
It is 1954 and eleven-year-old Sonny lives with his mother and his father, who is often angry and physically abusive. Sonny enjoys the company of an older friend, "Uncle" Louie, a man who had worked for his mother's parents when she was a child and from whom he learns much about the Adirondack area of New York State where they live. Sonny wonders about the many subjects he is not allowed to discuss and questions that remain unanswered: why he should be afraid of being "crept up on," what bad things happened in Vermont, and why his father doesn't want Uncle Louis around. It is only after he and Uncle Louis learn from the Jewish school librarian that she had been sent as a child from Germany to England for safety, that Uncle Louis tells Sonny the truth. Uncle Louis is his grandfather, who, like his late wife, had been sterilized during the Vermont Eugenics Project because they were Indians and who had fled Vermont so that Sonny's mother would not be taken away. It was because Sonny's family wanted to protect him from being treated like an Indian that they had kept his identity a secret, but it is when the secret is revealed to Sonny that his father, who is also part Indian, is released from his anger and shame.
European-American and Native American/French Canadian-American, Abenaki and Mohican
Intermediate, Older; Fiction

Carbone, Elisa. *Last Dance on Holladay Street*. New York: Alfred A. Knopf, 2005. 208 p.
In this story, which is set in the 1870s in Colorado, thirteen-year-old Eva leaves her prairie homestead when her adoptive African-American parents die. She travels to Denver in hopes that the mother who gave her away as an infant will let her stay. Shocked when she discovers that her mother is white and a prostitute, Eva must live in the brothel, dancing in its dance hall and becoming increasingly indebted to its madam. When it appears that she will have to work "upstairs," Eva escapes. With the help of an elderly black man Eva travels to Georgetown, is attacked by a mountain lion, and sent back to Denver to live in an orphanage. Then, through her ingenuity, Eva manages to set up a small successful eating house with her mother and half sister.
African-American/European-American
Older; Fiction.

Carey, Janet Lee. *Molly's Fire*. New York: Atheneum Books for Young Readers, 2000. 208 p.
Set in Maine during World War II, this is the story of the friendship of three young teens who miss their fathers: Peter, whose rich father pays him no attention; Jane, who has never seen her Japanese father and is the target of anti-Japanese hatred; and Molly, who refuses to believe that her Army Air Corps father has died in an airplane crash in Holland.

Japanese/ European-American
Intermediate, Older; Fiction

Charbonneau, Eileen. *The Ghosts of Stony Clove*. New York: Orchard Books, 1988. 160 p.

Building upon a ghost story of the Catskill Mountains and set in the early 1800s, this book tells of four years in the lives of Ginny Rockwell, who is Dutch-English-American, and Asher Woods, who is of mixed Native American and European-American heritage. When Ginny is almost twelve and Asher is fifteen, they go at night to the supposedly haunted Squire Sutherland's house where they encounter the squire, the servant girl he was said to have murdered fifty years earlier, a white dog, and a riderless horse. In this story of dreams, ghosts, cruelty, and goodness, Ginny comes to take care of the squire and inherit his property, while Asher, abused and persecuted because he is Indian, travels out west to find his family and then returns to marry Ginny. Their story is continued in the book, *In the Time of the Wolves*.

French-American and Wiechquaesgeck (Wiekagjock)/ European-American and Mohican
Older; Fiction

Charbonneau, Eileen. *In the Time of the Wolves*. New York: Tor-Doherty Associates, 1994. 192 p.

This story focuses on Josh Woods, the teenaged son of Asher Woods and Ginny Rockwell whose story began in the book *The Ghosts of Stony Clove*. It is now 1824 and Josh is greatly upset by his father who is part Indian and whose strange ways he finds disturbing. Josh wants to get away from the Catskills where he feels like an outsider, but his father opposes his going to Harvard. Josh is then befriended by Rebecca Elliott, who is a daughter of the Chase family which abused Asher when he was its bound servant. She supports Josh's getting a higher education and encourages his animosity towards his father. When Asher accepts the prediction of his Catholic friend Quinn and urges others to prepare for a year without summer, the neighbors at first reject his advice and, then, when there are summer frosts and snowstorms, blame him for their misfortunes. They also suspend Josh's mother from attending Congregational church services because she danced with her husband at a wake for Quinn. Josh accepts Rebecca's negative view of his parents and runs away with her. However, when he discovers that Rebecca and her relatives are seeking to take away his mother's inheritance and place his siblings in their custody, he realizes that he has been played for a dupe. Returning home he saves his father from a rabid gray wolf.

European-French-American, Mohican, and Wiechquaesgeck (Wiekagjock)/Dutch-English-American
Older; Fiction

Cheng, Andrea. *Grandfather Counts*. Illustrated by Ange Zhang. New York: Lee & Low Books, 2000. 32 p.

When Helen's maternal grandfather comes from China, she must give up her bedroom and is unable to communicate with him. It is when they count the train cars passing their house that Helen's grandfather begins to learn English and she starts learning Chinese. The illustrations in this story of the initial bonding of grandfather and granddaughter show Helen's father as European-American.

European-American/Chinese
Pre-K, Primary; Fiction

Cheng, Andrea. *Shanghai Messenger*. Illustrated by Ed Young. New York: Lee & Low Books, 2005. 40 p.

Eleven-year-old May, who is part Chinese, travels by herself from Ohio to Shanghai to visit her grandmother's family and report everything back to her grandmother. Initially homesick, May comes to love Shanghai: the food, the life, and her Chinese relatives. Returning, she brings back the message that theirs is one family that embraces both those born in China and in America. The illustrations, the free-verse text, and the use of Mandarin words add to the story.
European-American/Chinese-American
Intermediate; Fiction

Creel, Ann Howard. *Call Me the Canyon: A Love Story*. Weston, Conn.: Brown Barn Books, 2006. 224 p.

This novel takes place during the turn of the twentieth century in the Glen Canyon area of Utah and Arizona. Fifteen-year-old Madolen, whose Navajo mother had died years before, leaves her father to live with a Mormon family from whom she can learn to read. She becomes close to the family, especially to its daughter Claire, who becomes her steadfast friend, but is forced by the mother to leave after Claire's little brother Gabriel dies accidentally while under the girls' care. Madolen lives alone in a cabin as she supports herself by gathering gold dust and searches in vain for a gold-filled canyon she remembers from her childhood. Madolen then guides Wallis, a wealthy and educated young man, to places where he can pursue his interests in the area's ancient history. Madolen's love for Wallis is not returned until almost the end of the story when they decide to get married. However, realizing his reluctance to introduce a woman of Navajo blood to his Eastern family, Madolen leaves him and later marries Yiska, the Navajo whom she had previously disliked.
European-American/Navajo
Older; Fiction

Curry, Jane Louise. *Dark Shade*. New York: Margaret K. McElderry Books, 1998. 176 p.

Independently Kip and Maggie are able to climb through a newly-formed spring to enter the world of the 1758 French and Indian War where British forces are cutting a road through the Pennsylvania forest to reach the French-controlled Fort Dusquesne and where the Lenape (Delaware) have a village near the road. Maggie saves the life of Robert Mackenzie, a lost Scottish Redcoat, and Kip is going to be adopted into a Lenape family until Maggie finds him. Afraid that their actions are changing the course of history, Kip and Maggie learn that they have altered and then restored it and that they are distant cousins, both descendents of Robert Mackenzie and his Lenape wife, Shawanaken. Corn Tassel, a minor character in this novel, is a British woman who has been adopted by the Lenape.
Scottish-European-American and Lenape/European-American; European-American/Scottish-European-American and Lenape
Older; Fiction

Danziger, Paula. *It's an Aardvark-Eat-Turtle World*. New York: Delacorte Press, 1985. 144 p.

When fourteen-year-old Rosie's mother and Rosie's best friend Phoebe's father move in together,

Rosie is pleased that the four of them will form a family. However, when Phoebe gets upset with Rosie's mother and also with Rosie because she spends time with Jason, her first boyfriend, and when Phoebe decides to move out and live with her mother, Rosie discovers that family relationships are not easy. She also suffers from the hateful remark of a man who objects to mixed race Rosie and Canadian Jason being together. At the story's end Phoebe decides to work things out and come back and Rosie spends a happy Christmas Eve with both Jason and Phoebe.

African-American Protestant/European-American Jewish

Intermediate, Older; Fiction

Davol, Marguerite W. *Black, White, Just Right!* Illustrated by Irene Trivas. Morton Grove, Ill.: Albert Whitman & Company. 1993. 32 p.

Relating ways her African-American mother and her Caucasian father differ in how they look and what they like, a little girl tells of her own looks and preferences which are "just right."

European-American/African-American

Pre-K, Primary; Fiction

de Jenkins, Lyll Becerra. *Celebrating the Hero*. New York: Puffin Books, 1995. 192 p.

After her mother dies, seventeen-year-old Camila travels to her mother's hometown in Colombia to attend a ceremony honoring her late grandfather, whom she has regarded as a hero, and to learn about her mother's past. She discovers that although her grandfather was the town's benefactor, he was a cruel man who destroyed her grandmother. Camila's trip brings some closure to her grief and the realization that perhaps someday she, like her mother, will be able to forgive her grandfather.

European-American/Colombian

Older; Fiction

De la Peña, Matt. *Mexican Whiteboy*. New York: Delacorte Press, 2008. 256 p.

Sixteen-year-old Danny chooses to spend his summer vacation with his Mexican-American father's family in National City, California, so that he can then fly to Ensenada, Mexico, and find his father. Since his father left his San Diego family three years earlier, Danny has been heartbroken to the extent that he seldom speaks, not wanting to use his mother's English. His goal is to please his father by becoming a great pitcher. He has exceptional talent, but is plagued by his lack of control. During the eventful summer Danny makes an unlikely best friend, Uno, who initially punched Danny. Uno needs to make money so that he can move away from his Mexican-American mother and step-father and live with his black father. Through hours of practice with Uno, Danny works on his pitching skills and discovers how to keep the ball in the strike zone when people are watching. Together Uno and Danny successfully hustle the area's best hitters, thereby earning money for Uno. Although he cannot speak Spanish and she cannot speak English, Danny falls in love with Liberty, who is newly arrived from Mexico and has a white father. Further, Danny finally finds out the truth about his father and comes to accept himself.

Mexican-American/European-American

Older; Fiction

Elkeles, Simone. *How to Ruin a Summer Vacation*. Woodbury, Minn.: Flux, 2006. 240 p.

Sixteen-year-old Amy's parents never married, and her Israeli father, now an American resident, has been largely absent from her life. When Amy has to go with him to Israel to meet his family, that knows nothing about her existence, she is angry with her father, resentful about changing her summer vacation plans, and fearful about the safety of being in Israel. Overreactive Amy immediately likes her Israeli grandmother and her little Israeli cousin, but has to endure the hostility of the cousin with whom she rooms and eighteen-year-old Avi. She is constantly doing something wrong in their presence. It is not until the last part of her trip that Amy comes to appreciate her Israeli heritage, learns that her father had been rebuffed in his efforts to be with her, and falls in love with Avi.
German-Israeli Jewish/European-American non-Jewish
Older; Fiction

Erlbach, Arlene. *The Families Book: True Stories about Real Kids and the People They Live With and Love*. Photographs by Stephen J. Carrera. Illustrated by Lisa Wagner. Minneapolis: Free Spirit Publishing, 1996. 120 p.

In a section of this book, children tell about their families, that include a family in which the father is Lutheran and the mother Jewish; a family in which the father is African-American and the mother Caucasian; a family with four children in which Caucasian parents have adopted a biracial American girl and a boy from Romania; and a family with Caucasian parents and eleven children, six of whom were adopted from Korea.
African-American/European-American
Intermediate; Nonfiction

Ernst, Kathleen. *Highland Fling*. Chicago: Cricket Books, 2006. 224 p.

Exceedingly upset by her Polish-American father who had an extramarital affair, by moving from Wisconsin to North Carolina with her divorced mother and younger sister, and by the immersion of her mother and sister in everything to do with the Scottish MacDonald clan, fifteen-year-old Tanya reluctantly goes with them to the Highland Games. Longing to become an independent filmmaker, Tanya decides to make a documentary revealing the nostalgic pretense of the Highland Games. However, after meeting a young bagpiper from Puerto Rico who has Scottish heritage, his grandmother, and a Highland Games woman athlete whose mixed heritage does not include Scottish forebears, Tanya decides to make a different documentary and to have a talk with her father.
Puerto-Rican/European-Scottish-American
Older; Fiction

Fitch, Janet. *Kicks*. New York: Fawcett Juniper, 1995. 224 p

With a father who is brain-damaged from an accident, an overly-strict Russian mother, and a studious older brother who receives most of her mother's attention, fifteen-year-old Laurie feels that life is like being on a driverless bus. For years she has tried to be like her fearless friend Carla, who is becoming increasingly wild and even promiscuous. Thoughtful, timid Laurie, who wants to become a movie director, shoplifts and hitchhikes with Carla and then goes with Carla and her boyfriend to what turns out to be a remote drug hangout where she has beer and drugs and almost loses her virginity.

Managing to escape, she is called that night by Carla, who needs help. It is then that Laurie finally appreciates her mother, who goes with Laurie to the house and bravely rescues the critically ill Carla. Finally recognizing Carla's falseness and her own worth, Laurie teams up with the boy who has always been her friend to shoot a movie.
European-American/Russian
Older; Fiction

Frazier, Sundee T. *Brendan Buckley's Universe and Everything in It*. New York: Delacorte Press, 2007. 208 p.

Ten-year-old Brendan's time is spent working on his Tae Kwon Do and trying to figure out the answers to the many questions which face him. A budding scientist, Brendan by chance meets the grandfather who is never spoken of at a mineral exhibit. Secretly visiting his newly-discovered grandfather and even sneaking off on a thunder-egg hunting expedition with him, Brendan finally discovers the disturbing truth that his grandfather had opposed his mother's marriage to his black father and cut off contact. Through Brandon's efforts the family learns the importance of forgiveness and Brandon not only learns about telling the truth, but also comes to appreciate that he, like rocks with their mixed minerals, is both black and white.
African-American/European-American
Intermediate; Fiction

Friedman, Ina R. *How My Parents Learned to Eat*. Illustrated by Allen Say. Boston: Houghton Mifflin Company, 1984. 32 p.

A young girl reports how, when they were courting, her American sailor father learned how to eat with chopsticks and her Japanese mother learned how to eat with a knife, fork, and spoon before they ate together. Their daughter can eat either way.
European-American/Japanese
Pre-K, Primary; Fiction

Frost, Helen. *Diamond Willow*. New York: Frances Foster Books, 2008. 128 p.

In this story, which is set in the interior of Alaska, twelve-year-old Diamond Willow, called Willow, returns solo with three sled dogs from a visit with her grandparents. Speeding on a blind curve, they crash into a fallen tree, thereby causing the treasured dog Roxy to lose her sight. When Willow's parents decide to euthanize Roxy, Willow and a friend secretly set out to take the injured dog to her grandparents, but become lost overnight in a blizzard. Throughout these experiences Willow's ancestors, reincarnated as a red fox, a spruce hen, a mouse, and one of the sled dogs, try to help Willow. The story then presents the surprising revelation that Willow had a twin sister, Diamond, who died shortly after birth and has become Roxy. The book is largely written in verse with a distinctive text design that complements the story.
European-Canadian-American/Athabascan
Intermediate, Older; Fiction

Garland, Sherry. *The Last Rainmaker*. San Diego: Harcourt, Brace & Company, 1997. 336 p.

It is 1900 and thirteen-year-old Caroline, mourning the death of her beloved European-American grandmother, is living with her cruel great-aunt. Her rejoicing when her father comes, presumably to have her join him, turns to anger when he sells her horse, ships her off to a stepcousin, and plans to sell her adoption rights to her great-aunt. Caroline, who has discovered that her deceased mother was Native American and not of royal Italian blood as she had been told, runs away to the Wild West show where her mother had performed. There she meets her grandfather and learns to appreciate Native Americans. When her grandfather dies, Caroline decides not to choose between her two heritages, but to determine her own path.
European-American/Wichita
Older; Fiction

George, Jean Craighead. *Julie*. Illustrated by Wendell Minor. New York: HarperCollins Publishers, 1994. 240 p.

In this sequel to *Julie of the Wolves*, Julie, who is now fourteen, is living in Kangik with her father Kapugen and his new wife Ellen. Trapped with Ellen in a blizzard, Julie comes to accept her white stepmother. However, Julie knows that Kapugen was the one who killed her adoptive wolf father Amaroq and will kill his son Kapu and the new wolf pack in order to protect his herd of musk ox that sustains the Alaskan village's economy. Journeying to find the wolf pack, Julie manages to lead it away from the village to a place where the wolves can feed on moose. Kapugen and Ellen name their new baby boy Amaroq; Julie falls in love with Peter, an Eskimo from Siberia; and when the wolves come back, Kapugen finally returns to his Eskimo ways and spares them.
Eskimo/European-American
Intermediate, Older; Fiction

George, Jean Craighead. *Julie's Wolf Pack*. Illustrated by Wendell Minor. New York: HarperCollins Publishers, 1997. 208 p.

This sequel to *Julie* is devoted almost entirely to the story of Julie's Avalik River wolf pack. It traces its activities through four years during which Kapu asserts himself as its Alpha (leader); the wolf Ice Blink spreads rabies on the tundra; Silver has two more puppies; Kapu is trapped for a medical study; Silver dies; Kapu's daughter Sweet Fur Amy becomes the new Alpha; and, released, Kapu joins his mate Aaka. There is little about Julie and her human family. However, her little half brother Amaroq bonds with one of Silver's wolf pups which becomes a sled dog leader for Kapugen. At the book's end Julie and Peter marry and are hired to live on the tundra and study the wolves.
Eskimo/European-American
Intermediate, Older; Fiction

George, Jean Craighead. *Water Sky*. New York: Harper & Row, 1987. 220 p.

Teenage Lincoln travels to Barrow, Alaska, to stay with his father's elderly Eskimo friend Vincent Ologak and to find his Uncle Jack, who had taught Lincoln how to sail. Uncle Jack had not been heard from in the two years since he left for Barrow to stop the Eskimo from killing the endangered bowhead whale. When Lincoln arrives in Alaska, he discovers that one of his great-great-grandmothers was

an Eskimo and that the whales killed by the Eskimo are not causing the bowhead whale to become extinct, but are essential for their survival. Lincoln spends his time at Vincent's whale camp looking for the whale Nukik, which Vincent believes is to come to Lincoln to be killed. Lincoln learns that the man called Musk Ox is really Uncle Jack, who has changed his belief about the whales and married an Eskimo. The whale does come to Lincoln, but he cannot make himself kill it. It is killed by another boy on the umiaq; Vincent dies happily after learning Nukik has been killed; and the grateful people of Barrow are filled with the spirit of tolerance and sharing. Filled with information about the Eskimo culture and whaling, this story describes the hostility some Eskimos showed towards whites, Lincoln's wanting to be accepted as an Eskimo, the recognition he is given, and his realization that he will always be an outsider.
European-American and Iñupiat Eskimo/European-American
Older; Fiction

Graham, Bob. *Oscar's Half Birthday*. Illustrated by author. Cambridge, Mass.: Candlewick Press, 2005. 32 p.

Three-year-old Millie, her European-American father, her African-American mother, and their dog take Millie's brother Oscar to Bellevue Hill for his six-month-old birthday. Picnickers on the hill join them in the joyous celebration. No specific setting is noted in the book so it is assumed that the family is American although, as the author-illustrator lives in Australia, it may be an Australian family.
European-American/African-American
Preschool, Primary; Fiction

Gregory, Kristiana. *Orphan Runaways*. New York: Scholastic Press, 1998. 160 p.

In 1878, having recently been orphaned by an influenza epidemic, twelve-year-old Danny and his six-year-old brother Judd escape from an abusive orphanage and travel from San Francisco to find their uncle in a rowdy California mining town. They are looked after by a hotel owner who cares for orphan children until, after several months, the boys' uncle locates them. However, Danny, influenced by the prejudice of his new friends and the community, rejects his kind uncle because of his Chinese-American girlfriend whom he later marries. Danny finally overcomes his prejudice and with Judd becomes part of his uncle's family.
Irish/European-American
Intermediate; Fiction

Hahn, Mary Downing. *Promises to the Dead*. New York: Clarion Books, 2000. 202 p.

It is Maryland in 1861 when the Civil War is just beginning and many in the state support the South. Jesse, a twelve-year-old white boy who is looking for turtles, encounters an escaped slave, who, before dying, makes Jesse promise that he will deliver her young boy, Perry, the son of her deceased owner, to the owner's sister in Baltimore. The book recounts the boys' numerous adventures as they encounter rioting in Baltimore; discover that Perry's aunt has gone to Virginia; find out, upon arriving there, that the white aunt does not want Perry; escape with a group of slaves; and throughout are pursued by the cruel slave catcher, Abednego Botfield, who, when dying, also extracts a promise from Jesse.

European-American/African-European-American
Intermediate, Older; Fiction

Hamanaka, Sheila. *Grandparents Song*. Illustrated by author. New York: HarperCollins Publishers, 2003. 32 p.

In this picture book, which is written in verse, a girl tells how her grandparents came from four directions—her maternal grandmother from the West, her maternal grandfather from Europe, her paternal grandmother from Mexico, and her paternal grandfather from Africa—and how they are all part of her.
African-Mexican-American/European-American and Native American
Pre-K, Primary, Intermediate; Fiction

Hamilton, Virginia. *Plain City*. New York: The Blue Sky Press, 1993. 208 p

With a father she mistakenly believes is missing in action in Vietnam, an African-American mother who is a singer-stripteaser and seldom at home, and classmates who ostracize her, twelve-year-old Buhlaire feels sad, alone, and confused. It is when she learns that her father is alive and living in her town that her life changes. She finds her father, a mixed race drifter with mental illness who loves her, considers going to live with him, and, in the process of discovering the truth about her family members, comes to accept them—and to have her first friend.
African-European-American/African-American
Older; Fiction

Headley, Justina Chen. *Nothing but the Truth (and a few white lies)*. Boston: Little, Brown and Company, 2006. 256 p.

Fifteen-year-old Patty Ho is tormented by a schoolmate, is lectured to and overprotected by her Taiwanese mother, and believes she is a misfit. When her mother sends her to California to spend a month attending Stanford University's math camp, she experiences a new world: a daring roommate who shows her how to climb buildings, an understanding camp teaching assistant, and her first kiss, from a boy who subsequently breaks her heart. She also meets Auntie Lu and Uncle Vic, her aunt's African-American significant other; learns the truth about her father; and comes to appreciate both her mother and her own hapa (half Asian, half white) self.
European-American/Taiwanese
Older; Fiction

Heath, Amy. *Sofie's Role*. Illustrated by Sheila Hamanaka. New York: Four Winds Press, 1992. 32 p.

On the day before Christmas, young Sofie is told that she can finally tend the counter at her parents' bakery. However, the customers don't notice her so she helps in the back—until a schoolmate comes in and it is Sofie who fills her order. In the illustrations, Sofie's mother is shown as African-American and her father as European-American.
European-American/African-American
Pre-K, Primary; Fiction

Hesse, Karen. *Aleutian Sparrow*. New York: Margaret K. McElderry Books, 2003. 160 p.

In this historical novel, which is written in unrhymed verses, a young girl tells how in June 1942 the Aleuts were evacuated from their villages for protection from the Japanese. She describes the poor and unhealthy conditions they endured in internment camps in Wrangell and then near Ketchikan, Alaska, their longing for their Aleutian life and homes, their retention in exile even after the Japanese posed no threat to the Aleutians, the deaths of the girl's best friend and others, and the devastation, caused by Japanese bombs and American servicemen, which they discovered when they were finally allowed to return home in April 1945.
European-American/Aleut
Older; Fiction

Holm, Jennifer L. *Penny from Heaven*. New York: Random House, 2006. 288 p.

During the eventful summer of 1953 Penny spends time with both sides of her divided family: her mother and maternal grandparents and her late Italian father's mother, siblings, and relatives. Abetted by her cousin Freddie, Penny sneaks into her Italian grandmother's room to find out the color of her underwear, digs in the yard for treasure, and disobeys her mother by going to the beach. She gets a black eye, goes to a Dodgers game for her twelfth birthday, misbehaves to discourage her mother's Irish-American suitor, and, when her arm is caught in a clothes wringer, spends weeks in the hospital. It is there that she comes to accept her soon-to-be stepfather and discovers that her father had been imprisoned during World War II, because as an Italian "enemy alien," he had a radio. Penny also manages to ease the hostilities between the two branches of her family.
Italian and Catholic/European-American and Methodist
Intermediate, Older; Fiction

Hooks, William H. *The Ballad of Belle Dorcas*. Illustrated by Brian Pinkney. New York: Dragonfly Books, 1990. 40 p.

Belle, whose father is a slave owner and mother a slave, is freed at birth and, thereby, a free-issue person. However, instead of marrying a free-issue man, she marries Joshua, a slave. When a new master takes over the plantation, he wants to sell Joshua. Belle seeks help from a conjure woman, who casts spells. First, she shows Belle how to save Joshua from being sent south by turning him into a cedar tree, and then how to transform him into a man each night. When the master makes the tree into a smokehouse roof and then moves the smokehouse into the woods, Belle is desolate. However, once again the conjure woman comes to the rescue. This tale is illustrated in a scratchboard style that enhances the atmosphere.
European-American/African-American
Primary, Intermediate; Fiction

Hoyt-Goldsmith, Diane. *Totem Pole*. Photographs by Lawrence Migdale. Illustrated by David Boxley. New York: Holiday House, 1990. 32 p.

This book's color photographs and text show the wolf mask and halibut hook made by David's father, a Tsimshian woodcarver, and the cedar box made by his great-great-grandfather. It describes how young David assists his father in making a totem pole for the Klallam Indians who live near their

Kingston, Washington home, and then performs two dances with him at the totem pole-raising ceremony. A glossary is included.
Tsimshian/European-American
Intermediate; Nonfiction

Hurmence, Belinda. *Tancy*. New York: Clarion Books, 1984. 216 p.

Set in North Carolina at the end of the Civil War, this book tells of just-freed eighteen-year-old Tancy, who discovers that the deceased master of the plantation was her father. Tancy sets out to find her mother, who had been sold from the plantation when Tancy was very young. As she cares for a little boy who accompanies her, gives him up to his mother, works at a Freedmen's Bureau where she befriends a white woman, and gets a rude surprise when she meets her own mother, Tancy learns what it means to be free. At the book's conclusion Tancy must decide whether to return to the plantation, live with her mother in Shantytown, or chart her own course.
European-American/African-American
Older; Fiction

Hutchins, Pat. *There's Only One of Me!* Illustrated by author. New York: Greenwillow Books, 2003. 24 p.

In a cumulative text a five-year-old girl recognizes that she is her mother's daughter, her sister's sister, her half brother's half sister . . . and a birthday girl. The book's illustrations show that her uncle is African-American, her aunt is European-American, and her cousin is both.
African-American/European-American
Pre-K, Primary; Fiction

Iijima, Geneva Cobb. *The Way We Do It in Japan*. Illustrated by Paige Billin-Frye. Morton Grove, Ill.: Albert Whitman & Company, 2002. 32 p.

When Gregory and his parents move to his father's native Japan, Gregory notes many differences and happily does things as the Japanese do. However, on his first day at school, he feels out of place eating his peanut butter sandwich, but doesn't like the fish which the other children are served. Resolving to eat fish as the Japanese do, on his second day Gregory is pleasantly surprised when the class also gets peanut butter and jelly sandwiches as the Americans do. The text includes Japanese words accompanied with notes as to their meaning and pronunciation.
Japanese/European-American
Pre-K, Primary; Fiction

James, J. Alison. *Sing for a Gentle Rain*. New York: Atheneum, 1990. 228 p.

Teenagers James and Sweet Rain are alike in many ways. Their mothers have either left or died, their fathers have abandoned them, and they are being raised by their loving grandfathers. However, James is an American boy of the twentieth century and Spring Rain is an Anasazi girl of the thirteenth century. The book uses alternating chapters to tell how James is drawn to exploring the Anasazi culture and Spring Rain realizes that she must find the right man to give her a son who will lead her people from their land of drought to a more fertile one. Then, drawn by Spring Rain's song, James encounters her on a Southwestern mesa, stays as a stranger in her Anasazi village, falls in love with her, fathers her son, and is sent back by her song to his own home.

Pueblo Indian/European-American

Older; Fiction

Jones, Adrienne. *So, Nothing Is Forever*. Illustrated by Richard Cuffari. Boston: Houghton Mifflin Company, 1974. 256 p.

After her parents are killed in an automobile accident, fifteen-year-old Talene is determined to keep herself, her thirteen-year-old brother Joey, and her two-year-old brother Adam together during the year before their soldier uncle can care for them. When a social worker intends to place them in foster homes, with Adam possibly put up for adoption, the three children run away from New York to northern California in hopes that they can stay with their grandmother Anna, who had rejected their mother when she married a black man. Unhappy to see them, hostile Anna says they can stay for only a couple of weeks, but as their stay extends, the children are kept wondering as to how long it will last. During their time with Anna, Joey briefly runs away, an acquaintance from their bus trip joins them at Anna's, Adam almost drowns, the boy-crazy abused neighbor girl commits suicide, and the children come to understand their grandmother.

African-American/European-American

Older; Fiction

Kadohata, Cynthia. *Outside Beauty*. New York: Atheneum Books for Young Readers, 2008. 272 p.

It is 1983 and twelve-year-old Shelby lives with her three sisters and their Japanese-American mother Helen in Chicago. Helen is obsessed with her beauty and using it to attract rich men. She spends time conveying her lifestyle to her daughters, all of whom have different fathers and who are very close to each other. When Helen is severely injured in an automobile accident, including damage to her face, the sisters are sent to live temporarily with their respective fathers whom they barely know. Shelby, the narrator, comes to like life in Arkansas with her Japanese father, whose only apparent fault is that he dresses poorly, but worries about her six-year-old sister Maddie, who has gone to live with her domineering, cruel father. Realizing the terrible effect he is having on Maddie, Shelby unsuccessfully tries running away to rescue her. The sisters and their fathers get together in Chicago when for a time Helen seems near death, and, for Maddie's sake, the sixteen year old sister secretly drives with the other sisters to a Colorado cabin. After the girls are caught, it is agreed that Shelby's father will look after all of them in Chicago until Helen is well. Helen ends up with her physician as a boyfriend, but Shelby realizes that it is not exterior beauty which counts.

European-American/Japanese-American

Older; Fiction

Kidd, Ronald. *On Beale Street*. New York: Simon & Schuster Books for Young Readers, 2008. 256 p.

It is 1954 in segregated Memphis, Tennessee. When fifteen-year-old Johnny goes to hear the music on Beale Street in the Negro section, his life changes. Caught up in the blues music, he meets young Elvis Presley, who also frequents Beale Street, volunteers and then works for Sam Phillips who launches Presley's career, and learns about the inequities of Negro life from Lamont, the son of Will

Turner who is a Negro chauffeur and gardener. Johnny also wonders about the father he never knew and why his mother wants him to keep away from Will and Lamont. It is not until the end of the story that Johnny learns that he is Will's son and must make a decision that affects his own life and the lives of Lamont, his mother, and Will.
African-American/European-American
Older; Fiction

Kimmell, Elizabeth Cody. *In the Stone Circle*. New York: Scholastic, 1998. 240 p.
When fourteen-year-old Cristyn and her father go to Wales so he can spend two months doing research for a book on medieval Wales, they share a rental house with another author, her daughter, and her son. The children discover that Carwen, a ghost from the thirteenth century, lives in the room of a very old house that is beneath theirs. Carwen seems to want something from Cristyn. It is not until the end of the book that Cristyn discovers what it is and thereby enables Carwen to join her long-deceased father. In the process Cristyn learns about her own Welsh mother, who had died when she was three, and to know that her mother is always with her.
European-American/Welsh
Intermediate, Older; Fiction

Koller, Jackie French. *A Place to Call Home*. New York: Atheneum Books for Young Readers, 1995. 208 p.
Fifteen-year-old Anna struggles to take care of her five-year-old sister and baby brother when their alcoholic abusive mother abandons them. Soon Anna discovers that their mother has committed suicide. Realizing that no one will want to adopt all three of them since the little ones are Caucasian and she is much older and of mixed race, Anna keeps her mother's disappearance a secret. Then, disguised as a boy, Anna takes the bus from Connecticut to Mississippi in hopes that her mother's parents will look after them. There she learns why her mother left. Her grandparents disapproved of her mother's relationship with a black man, and, after Anna was born, her police chief grandfather probably murdered her father. Anna finally realizes that she cannot care for her siblings and, with the help of a wise boyfriend, agrees to the adoption. Surprisingly Anna too will be adopted: by the older couple who runs the neighborhood convenience store.
African-American/European-American
Older; Fiction

Kretzer-Malvehy, Terry. *Passage to Little Bighorn*. Flagstaff, Ariz.: Rising Moon, 1999. 232 p.
In this novel fifteen-year-old Dakota is discouraged because his Irish-American father has remarried and left the family, his Lakota mother has just returned from a two year treatment of depression, and he has been living with his father's father. When he visits the Little Bighorn Battlefield, Dakota finds himself swept back to 1876 where he becomes the "chosen relative" of wise and kind Sitting Bull. He experiences Lakota life: going on a buffalo hunt, counting coup by capturing two Crow horses, surviving a grizzly bear attack, receiving a Lakota name, becoming friends with a boy who is European-American and Lakota, falling for a daughter of Sitting Bull, meeting his great-great-great grandmother and great-great grandfather, and witnessing the terrible battles of the Rosebud and the Little

Bighorn. It is with the Lakota that Dakota learns how he should live, and he decides to return to his real family.
European-American/Lakota
Older; Fiction

Krishnaswami, Uma. *Bringing Asha Home*. Illustrated by Jamel Akib. New York: Lee & Low Books, 2006. 32 p.

As Arun endures a seemingly endless wait for his new baby sister Asha to come from India, he continues to fold paper airplanes, using some of them as a mobile for her room, others to demonstrate his father flying to India and returning home with Asha, and a special decorated one to be given to Asha in India. When Asha arrives at the airport, thanks to her caregivers in India, she gives Arun a rakhi bracelet, the bracelet given by sisters to brothers on the Rakhi Indian holiday.
Indian/European-American
Pre-K, Primary; Fiction

Kuklin, Susan. *Families*. Photographs by author. New York: Hyperion Books for Children, 2006. 40 p.

Text and color photographs present interviews with American children, who talk about their families. Their families include seven families with children of mixed race, ethnicity, or religion, with one also including a child adopted from Sierra Leone. In an eighth family a child has been adopted from China. In a ninth family an adopted American child is of a race different from that of one of her fathers.
Greek-American/European-American; European-American/Japanese-American
Primary, Intermediate; Nonfiction

Lachtman, Ofelia Dumas. *Call Me Consuelo*. Houston: Arte Público Press, 1997. 152 p.

After her parents are killed in an automobile accident, Consuelo goes to live with her Mexican-American aunt and uncle and then leaves her small California town to live with her father's mother in Los Angeles. Although very homesick, she makes friends and with them becomes involved in mysterious events occurring in an old movie lot near her grandmother's gated community. When Consuelo has the opportunity to return to her aunt and uncle, she realizes that she doesn't want to abandon her caring grandmother.
European-American/Mexican-American
Intermediate; Fiction

Lampman, Evelyn Sibley. *Half-Breed*. Illustrated by Ann Grifalconi. Garden City, N.Y.: Doubleday & Company, 1967. 264 p.

Twelve-year-old Hardy leaves his Crow mother because she is marrying a man of the same clan and travels by himself to Oregon to find the white father who had left when he was six. Reaching his father's cabin with the help of Dr. John McLoughlin [later known as "Father of Oregon"] and his half Chippewa wife Marguerite and marshal Joe Meeks and his Cheyenne wife Virginia, Hardy discovers that his father has left to go to California to mine gold. Hardy decides to wait for his father and is aided during his stay by Old Ironsides veteran Bill Johnson and his Cheyenne wife Nancy on whose

land the cabin is located. To Hardy's surprise his father's sister Rhody arrives from the East and stays with Hardy. Hardy is very upset by her white ways, especially her making him perform squaw's chores and burning his medicine bag. He also suffers from the poor treatment he receives in Portland because he is part Indian. After Hardy's father returns and then leaves, Hardy decides to go back to live with the Crow. However, after his father again returns and then decides to leave, Hardy realizes that the responsible thing is to do is to remain with Aunt Rhody who is his family.
European-American/Crow
Intermediate, Older; Fiction

Lester, Julius. *To Be a Slave*. 30th anniversary ed. Illustrated by Tom Feelings. New York: Dial Books, 1998. 168 p.

Among the slave narratives in this book is one by Doc Daniel Dowdy, which was recorded by the Federal Writers' Project in the 1930s and included in a 1945 book, *Lay My Burden Down*, edited by B.A. Botkin. This account of Dowdy's seeing his half white cousin Eliza bought and freed at a slave auction by an abolitionist from New York is expanded upon in Virginia Frances Schwartz' novel *Send One Angel Down*.
European-American/African-American
Older; Nonfiction

Levin, Beatrice. *John Hawk: White Man, Black Man, Indian Chief*. Austin: Eakin Press, 1988. 192 p.

This is the fictional story of John White, the son of a Georgia plantation owner and a slave mother, who becomes the lifelong friend of Osceola. The two meet as boys and, at Osceola's urging, John runs away to live with the Seminoles. He takes a new name, John Hawk, marries a Seminole woman, befriends a man who is Spanish and African-American, and becomes a Seminole chief. With Osceola he experiences the betrayals and tragedies preceding and during the Second Seminole War. A bibliography is included.
European-American/African-American
Older; Fiction

Levin, Betty. *Brother Moose*. New York: Greenwillow Books, 1990. 224 p.

When Nell, an orphan from England, is sent in the 1870s to live with a couple in Canada's Maritime Provinces, she discovers that her prospective mother, Mrs. Fowler, has moved to Maine to have a baby. Next Nell is kidnapped by robbers, escapes, and travels with her fellow orphan Louisa, an Indian named Joe Pennowit, and his twelve year old grandson to Maine. However, because Joe mistakenly thinks he has killed one of the men who kidnapped Nell, the four leave the road to escape the robbers and the police. On their difficult journey they go by wagon, by sleigh, and by an abandoned train car, which is pulled by their horse and a moose they have tamed. Nell finally reaches Mrs. Fowler, but her adoption hopes take a surprising turn.
European-Canadian or European-American/Canadian Micmac or American Passamaquoddy or Penobscot
Older; Fiction

Lewin, Michael Z. *Cutting Loose*. New York: Henry Holt and Company, 1999. 528 p.

Set in the nineteenth century, this is the story of Jackie's search for Teddy Zeph, who has murdered Jackie's best friend, Nance. The text alternates between the present and the past, starting with the story of Jackie's grandmother Claudette at the time she was orphaned. There are parallels among the characters' lives. Claudette is sold at a pauper auction, Jackie's father Matthew is sold by his New York City baseball team to a team in St. Louis, and Jackie goes to live with a new family that chooses her when she is displayed by the Children's Aid Society. Claudette murders her lover's father, and Matthew and Nance are murdered. Claudette disguises herself as a man to escape capture, and Jackie disguises herself as a man to pursue a baseball career. Both Jackie and her father play baseball in England as well as in the United States. Nance performs for Buffalo Bill's Wild West Show, and Jackie and Teddy Zeph perform on the stage in London. Further, Claudette's father is French, Teddy's mother is Spanish, and Nance, whose mother is African-American, passes as white.
European-American/African-American; French/European-American; European-American/Spanish
Older; Fiction

Lipsyte, Robert. *The Brave*. New York: HarperCollins Publishers, 1991. 208 p. (A Charlotte Zolotow Book)

This book is the sequel to *The Contender*. Unhappy with his life on the Moscondaga Reservation and resentful about the unfair treatment he has received in a boxing match, seventeen-year-old Sonny Bear, who is of mixed race, takes off for New York City. He no sooner arrives than he is picked up by two hustlers, becomes their decoy in carrying a bag of crack, and ends up in a juvenile correction facility. It is the police officer, Sergeant Alfred Brooks, the protagonist of *The Contender*, who recognizes Sonny's potential as a boxer if he can control his rage. Sonny returns to the reservation to be trained by his great-uncle Jake and then comes back to New York City to Donatelli's Gym where Brooks had trained. Finally learning to harness the fire within him, Sonny advances in amateur fights until he is disqualified because of his earlier fighting for pay. However, with the help of his new friend, Martin Witherspoon, he embarks on a professional boxing career.
European-American/Native American
Older; Fiction

Lipsyte, Robert. *The Chief*. New York: HarperTrophy, 1995. 240 p.

This second book about the half Moscondaga boxer Sonny Bear is narrated by Martin Witherspoon, who is writing a book about Sonny. It is the sequel to *The Brave*. At the beginning of this story, frustrated Sonny Bear is about to quit boxing. Then, spurred on by the example of Muhammad Ali who used publicity to advance his career, Sonny Bear and Martin head to Las Vegas where television reports Martin's public challenge of the boxer Elston Hubbard, Jr. Sonny Bear is taken under the wing of has-been champion John L. Sullivan, who is scheduled to fight Hubbard. The older Sullivan and nineteen-year-old Sonny become friends, bonding because of the shared prejudice directed towards their people, the Jews and the Indians. Sonny gains notoriety by winning a preliminary match and forcing an end to the Hubbard-Sullivan fight when Sullivan is being critically injured. Sullivan subsequently dies, and Sonny Bear loses a close fight with Hubbard. However, when Sonny draws upon his heritage to save the

Moscondaga Nation from an internal dispute over a gambling casino, he achieves a greater victory.
European-American/Native American
Older; Fiction

Lipsyte, Robert. *Warrior Angel*. New York: HarperCollins Publishers, 2003. 192 p.

Warrior Angel is the sequel to *The Chief* and the third book about the mixed race boxer Sonny Bear, who was introduced in *The Brave*. Now under contract to the promoter Elston Howard, Sonny Bear has defeated the heavyweight champion Floyd (The Wall) Hall and as the book begins is about to fight a challenger. However, Sonny feels strangely out of it and fights listlessly. He only retains the title because of a split decision. Sonny is contacted by e-mail by a delusional teenager Starkey, who having become immersed in the book about Sonny which Martin Witherspoon has written, feels that he is Warrior Angel sent on a mission by the Creator to save Sonny. Sonny leaves Hubbard to meet Starkey at Donatelli's Gym where he had once trained. Although Sonny loses a fight with Hall, he follows Starkey's advice to find the answer he is seeking and then saves Starkey from heeding the voices he hears and committing suicide.
European-American/Native American
Older; Fiction

Lisle, Janet Taylor. *The Crying Rocks*. New York: Atheneum Books for Young Readers, 2003. 208 p. (A Richard Jackson Book)

Thirteen-year-old Joelle, who was adopted at the age of five by Vern and Aunt Mary Louise, does not look like anyone she knows in Rhode Island. She is upset by what she is told of her past: of being thrown out of a Chicago apartment window by her mother, being put in an orphanage there, traveling by freight train to Connecticut, and then being cared for by an old woman while living in a wooden crate near a railway depot. Joelle is befriended by an adoring eight-year-old girl who is European- and Japanese-American and by a classmate Carlos, who is of mixed heritage. Together Joelle and Carlos learn of the early Narragansett Indians and explore the wooded area, including the Crying Rocks, where they lived. Carlos learns the truth about the accident at the Crying Rocks where his older brother died and Joelle learns the truth about her background. Vern is her real father, her mother was Narragansett, and both her mother and twin sister died in Chicago.
European-American/Japanese; Colombian-English-Spanish-American and Sioux/European-American
Intermediate, Older; Fiction

Little, Kimberley Griffiths. *Enchanted Runner*. New York: Avon Books, 1999. 160 p.

Twelve-year-old Kendall has an almost magical urge to run. After his mother's death, he is invited to visit his great-grandfather in the Acoma Pueblo in New Mexico. There Kendall finds himself in a very unfamiliar environment, becomes acutely aware that he is only half Acoman, and learns that his great-grandfather was one of a group of Acoma Runners. Kendall feels compelled to run each day to the Enchanted Mesa, which he hopes will reveal his destiny. When Kendall's great-grandfather fails to return from a visit to a sacred shrine, it is Kendall who finds him and gets help. At the end of the story, Kendall is accepted by the Acoma as the last of the Snake Clan.

European-American/Acoman
Intermediate, Older; Fiction

Little, Kimberley Griffiths. *The Last Snake Runner*. New York: Alfred A. Knopf, 2002. 208 p.

In this sequel to *Enchanted Runner*, Kendall, now fourteen, has just returned from the Acoma Pueblo where he has become a full member of the Acoma, his late mother's people. Very upset when he learns that his father has married a woman descended from the Spanish conquistadors who in 1599 destroyed the Acoma Pueblo, Kendall has his brother take him back to Acoma. There, in a mesa near the pueblo, he is transported back to the sixteenth century where he experiences life in the ancient Snake Clan and participates in the last Acoma Snake dance. Although Kendall is unable to save the pueblo from the conquistadors, he brings hope that the Acoma will survive.

European-American/Acoman
Older; Fiction

MacGregor, Rob. *Hawk Moon*. New York: Simon & Schuster Books for Young Readers, 1996. 192 p.

Hawk Moon is the sequel to *Prophecy Rock*. When Will returns to Aspen, Colorado, from the Hopi Reservation where he has spent the summer, he tells his girlfriend Myra that he thinks they should break up, but does not give her the chance to tell him what is bothering her. She disappears from the ghost town where he had left her, and Will becomes the prime target of the investigation into her kidnapping. This mystery has many twists and turns as Will comes to suspect classmates, his mother's boyfriend, and members of the sheriff's department. He is helped by Corey, a girl of mixed race who is a computer geek, and he experiences visions of Masau, the Hopi's kachina ruler.

European-American/African-American
Older; Fiction

MacGregor, Rob. *Prophecy Rock*. New York: Laurel-Leaf Books, 1995. 208 p.

When teenager Will goes to spend the summer with his father, who is chief of police on the Hopi reservation, he becomes involved in the investigation of two murders. It first appears that the murderer is a preacher, a Hopi who now condemns the Hopis and their prophecies. Suspicion then turns to whoever believes himself to be Pahana, the Elder White Brother, who is the expected Hopi savior. However, who is that person: the mixed race hospital worker, the white doctor, or the ethnologist, who is also white? As Will helps in solving this mystery, he falls for a Hopi girl, travels about the Arizona reservation, and learns of the Hopi culture.

European and Hopi
Older; Fiction

Mason, Cherie. *Everybody's Somebody's Lunch*. Illustrated by Gustav Moore. Gardiner, Maine: Tilbury House, Publishers, 1998. 40 p.

After her cat is killed in the woods next to her farm, a young girl learns about predators and their prey from her teacher, her grandmother, and her own observations—and comes to a fuller understanding of nature. The book's paintings complement the story.

European-American and Passamaquoddy
Intermediate; Fiction

McClain, Lee. *My Alternate Life*. New York: Smooch, 2004. 188 p.

At age fifteen Trinity B. Jones is sent from foster care in Pittsburgh to live with a well-off rural family. Trinity wants instead to be reunited with her birthmother who had left her at Saint Helen's Home for Girls when she was eight. Thanks to the amazing computer game her social worker gives her, Trinity is able to observe and hear her mother, who has married a wealthy man and craves media attention. Trinity focuses her efforts on becoming reunited with her mother. To that end, she tries to get the cruel sex-crazy boy, who will probably become the Fall King, to invite her to the Fall Dance so that she will become the Fall Queen and win her mother's acclaim. However, that project ends when he almost rapes her. Trinity also gets her foster mother to let the Fall Dance be a benefit for Saint Helen's and, using a classmate's name, invites her birthmother to be dance sponsor. At the dance, Trinity realizes which family is best for her.
African-American/European-American
Older; Fiction

McLaren, Clemence. *Dance for the Land*. New York: Atheneum Books for Young Readers, 1999. 160 p.

Twelve-year-old Kate is unhappy and homesick when she leaves her California home for Hawaii, not only because she misses her dog and ballet troupe, but also because, with her Caucasian looks, she doesn't fit in. She is tormented at school and, unlike her Hawaiian-looking older brother, is not accepted by her uncle. As the story progresses, Kate comes to love dancing hulas, learns about her Hawaiian heritage, helps bring harmony between her always-arguing father and uncle, and, thanks to her uncle, is reunited with her dog. The book presents the conflict between her uncle's wanting Hawaii to become an independent country and her father's advocacy of establishing a Native Hawaiian nation within the state of Hawaii.
Native Hawaiian/European-American
Intermediate, Older; Fiction

Meyer, Carolyn. *Jubilee Journey*. San Diego: Gulliver Books, 1997. 288 p.

In this sequel to *White Lilacs*, it is 1996 and eighty-seven-year-old Rose Lee has invited her thirteen-year-old great-granddaughter Emily Rose and her family to attend the Freedomtown Juneteenth Diamond Jubilee. Growing up in Connecticut, Emily Rose has always regarded herself as a "double" as her father is French-American and her mother is African-American. However, she and her brothers Steven and Robbie have no idea what it means to be black in Dillon, Texas. They quickly learn of the attitudes of some whites when Steven is set up and abused and of the closeness and pride of the African-American community. In this story Rose Lee reveals what has happened to her and her family during the past seventy-five years. Emily Rose gets a new friend who thinks she should be just black and decides to remain in Denton to learn more about being black so she can better understand herself. Alicia, Rose Lee's best friend in Connecticut, has a Nigerian father and an English mother.
French-American and Catholic/African-European-American, Seminole, and Baptist
Intermediate, Older; Fiction

Meyer, Carolyn. *White Lilacs*. San Diego: Gulliver Books, 1993. 256 p.

Set in 1921 this is the story of Freedomtown, the section of Dillon, Texas, where African-Americans have lived since 1870 and of twelve-year-old Rose Lee, who experiences its sorrow when the whites force the residents to leave and move to the Flats, an undesirable part of town, so that the whites can build a city park and be further away from the blacks. It tells of Rose Lee's family and neighbors who are powerless to prevent Freedomtown's removal, of the thoughtlessness of the white women, of the Klan, of Rose's brother Henry being tarred and feathered, of the "colored school" being burned down, of Rose's Aunt Susannah who leaves her teaching job in St. Louis to teach the children of the Flats, of the Quaker white lady Emily Firth who loses her job because she stands up for the blacks, of the white girl Catherine Jane who saves Henry, and of Rose Lee, who preserves Freedomtown in her drawings. Although Rose Lee and Susannah are mostly African-American, Rose Lee's paternal grandfather is part Seminole and her maternal great-grandfather was white. Susannah's paternal grandfather was white.

African-American and Seminole/African-European-American; African-European-American/African-American

Intermediate, Older; Fiction

Miles, Betty. *All It Takes Is Practice*. New York: Bullseye Books, 1989. 112 p.

Fifth grader Stuart wishes he had a best friend in addition to his neighborhood friend Alison. His wish comes true when Peter enters his Kansas classroom. Stuart is surprised when he discovers that Peter's mother is black. That doesn't matter to Stuart, his parents, or Alison, but raises the ire of Alison's father, who is also unappreciative of his daughter's interest in sports. When Stuart and Peter go downtown, they are attacked by three bigoted teenagers, and Stuart learns what it means to be a best friend.

European-American/African-American

Intermediate; Fiction

Miner, Chalise. *Rain Forest Girl: More Than an Adoption Story*. Photographs by Phil Miner. Childs, Md.: Mitchell Lane Publishers, 1998. 48 p.

Photographs and text describe Diana's adoption as she experienced it. Seven-year-old Diana and her newborn sister were removed from their home in the Brazilian jungle as their grandmother and mother were not able to care for them. Diana lived in a Brazilian convent before she was adopted by American parents and went with them to her new home in Kansas City. At first everything was strange to Diana, but she felt better when she became friends with a Portuguese-speaking girl, whose parents were American and Brazilian. Now as a teenager, Diana still keeps in touch with her Brazilian friends.

European-American/Brazilian

Intermediate; Nonfiction

Monk, Isabell. *Family*. Illustrated by Janice Lee Porter. Minneapolis: Carolrhoda Books, 2001. 32 p.

In this sequel to *Hope*, Hope and her parents visit her mother's Aunt Poogee's for a dinner with her African-American extended family. Hope brings a surprise dish to the gathering: pickles with peppermint sticks inside. The recipe from a cousin on her father's side is a big hit and Aunt Poogee tells

Hope that it is now a part of her family's recipes. The book includes four of the recipes from the dinner.
European-American/African-American
Pre-K, Primary; Fiction

Monk, Isabell. *Hope*. Illustrated by Janice Lee Porter. Minneapolis: Carolrhoda Books, 1999. 32 p.

In this picture book biracial Hope is upset when an acquaintance of her great-aunt Poogee thoughtlessly asks if Hope is mixed. Aunt Poogee explains to Hope that she is indeed mixed. She is Hope, mixed with love and the faith of her ancestors.
European-American/African-American
Pre-K, Primary; Fiction

Moonshower, Candie. *The Legend of Zoey: A Novel*. New York: Delacorte Press, 2006. 224 p.

This story is based on the legend of the 1811 and 1812 New Madrid Earthquakes that alleges they resulted from the curse placed by a Choctaw chief on the Chickasaw chief Reelfoot who defied him by marrying his daughter Laughing Eyes. When thirteen-year-old Zoey goes on a school field trip to Reelfoot Lake in western Tennessee, she is swept away in a drainage ditch during an electrical storm and finds herself back in 1811 with a thirteen-year-old girl Prudence and her mother. Journals written by Zoey and Prudence tell of their difficult journey as they try to reach safety from the earthquakes. They learn of each other's lives, hopes, and worries; become friends; and spend time with Reelfoot and Laughing Eyes, whom Zoey discovers are her ancestors. There are surprises awaiting Zoey when she returns to the present day.
European-American/European-American, Chickasaw, and Choctaw
Intermediate, Older; Fiction

Moses, Sheila P. *The Baptism*. New York: Margaret K. McElderry Books, 2007. 144 p.

Set in Northampton County, North Carolina, probably in the late 1940s, identical twins Leon and Luke, who have just turned twelve, are supposed to behave so they can go to their church's mornin' bench and be saved. Then on the coming Sunday they are be baptized in the Roanoke River so that lying and sinning are behind them. Unlike Luke, who is the "good" twin, the narrator Leon figures that he has only six more days to enjoy sinning. The story reveals that their father had probably been murdered, but the white perpetrator was not arrested and that their mother is married to "Filthy Frank" whom Leon cannot stand. Leon rubs "White Cousin" with poison ivy and gets Luke to leave with him from a neighbor's house during a tornado that blows off their grandmother's roof. Angry that the grandmother will stay in their house, Filthy Frank runs off with their mother's money. Luke behaves well enough to go to the mornin' bench on Thursday. Surprisingly, on Friday Leon goes to the mornin' bench and both boys are baptized on Sunday. But the big surprise is that their mother's white half brother hugs her after the robbery, arranges for Filthy Frank's arrest, and with his wife, mother, and son attends the baptism.
African-European-American/African-European-American
Intermediate; Fiction

Mower, Nancy Alpert. *I Visit My Tutu and Grandma*. Illustrated by Patricia A. Wozniak. Kailua, Hawaii: Press Pacifica, 1984. 24 p. (Treasury of Children's Hawaiian Stories)

In this picture book set in Hawaii, a little girl enjoys a visit with her two grandmothers: one Hawaiian-American and the other European-American. Her Hawaiian-American grandmother uses many Hawaiian words.

Hawaiian-American/European-American

Pre-K; Fiction

Murphy, Rita. *Black Angels*. New York: Delacorte Press, 2001. 176 p.

It is 1961 and Freedom Riders are on the way to a small Georgia town. Sophie, the Jenkins family's maid whom eleven-year-old Celli adores, is an outspoken African-American in the conservative Southern town. Celli finds it difficult to grasp the meaning of the civil rights movement and to cope with the sudden discovery that the grandmother she had never met is black. During the summer Celli becomes less concerned with the negative effects Sophie's actions have on her life and helps free Sophie from jail and save a friend who is Jewish and African-American.

African-European-American/European-American; European-American and Jewish/African-American

Intermediate, Older; Fiction

Nelson, Suzanne. *The Sound of Munich*. New York: Speak, 2006. 224 p. (S.A.S.S.: Students Across the Seven Seas)

Californian Siena, who is into yoga and astrology, spends the spring semester of her junior year in Munich, Germany, as part of a study-abroad program. She is eager to learn about Germany, the homeland of her father who died when she was a baby, and to fulfill the last item on his carpe diem list: thank Peter Schwalm, the man who had enabled him and his parents to escape from East Berlin. The experience exceeds Siena's expectations as she makes two best friends, has a romance with her resident adviser, becomes immersed in German life, works hard to do well in her classes, and locates and meets Peter.

German/European-American

Older; Fiction

Nichols, Joan Kane. *All But the Right Folks*. Owings Mills, Md.: Stemmer House Publishers, 1985. 112 p.

Danny doesn't realize he is half white until he meets his grandmother Helga and goes to spend the summer with her in New York City. Suffering from asthma, bed-wetting, and teasing at his San Francisco school, Danny enjoys New York as he bikes with his grandmother; befriends Thelma Jean, her little brother Willy, and Charlayne; and starts learning karate from Charlayne's older sister. However, his new friends, two of whom are of mixed heritage, reject him because he lied that Helga was his nanny. Further, he worries that his deceased mother was a druggie like his Uncle Billy; his father insists that Danny is black and is not proud of him; and he discovers that Helga has lied to him. Everything improves when Danny uses his karate mental and kicking skills to escape kidnappers, and he decides that he is a bridge between black and white.

African-American/European-American
Intermediate; Fiction

Nye, Naomi Shihab. *Habibi*. New York: Simon Pulse, 1999. 288 p.

Fourteen-year-old Liyana, her younger brother Rafik, and her parents move from St. Louis to her Palestinian father's homeland. There the children meet their Arab grandmother and relatives and become friends with a brother and sister who are growing up in a Palestinian refugee camp. Liyana attends an Armenian school in Jerusalem, a Jewish boy becomes her boyfriend, and her father is put in jail. Within the tensions of the region, the family embraces those of all faiths and strives to promote peace.
Palestinian/European-American
Intermediate, Older; Fiction

O'Connor, Barbara. *Me and Rupert Goody*. New York: Frances Foster Books, 1999. 112 p.

Although unrelated, Uncle Beau is like a surrogate father to eleven-year-old Jennalee. Except for school hours, she spends her days at his general store. When African-American Rupert Goody comes to the store claiming that Uncle Beau is his father, Jennalee is consumed by jealousy and treats him terribly. It is not until the end of the story that she comes to accept the slow, but sweet Rupert and to realize that they are both part of Uncle Beau's family.
European-American/African-American
Intermediate, Older; Fiction

Okimoto, Jean Davies. *The Eclipse of Moonbeam Dawson*. New York: Tom Doherty Associates, 1998. 192 p.

Fifteen-year-old Moonbeam knows that he no longer wants to live with his hippie-activist mother. Taking a job at a nearby resort in British Columbia, he befriends Gloria, who is of European-Japanese-Canadian heritage, and falls for Michelle, a rich pretty hotel guest. By the end of the story, Moonbeam has recognized Michelle's falseness and decided both to change his name to Reid, the last name of a half Haida sculptor, and to look up his late Haida father's family.
Haida/European-American
Older; Fiction

Ostow, Micol. *Emily Goldberg Learns to Salsa*. New York: Razorbill, 2006. 212 p.

Emily with her family flies from New York to Puerto Rico for the funeral of the grandmother she had never met. As Emily's mother is stressed out by returning to her Puerto Rican family, Emily stays behind in Puerto Rico to help her. Emily has trouble adjusting to her newfound family and especially to Lucy, a cousin who dislikes her. By the end of the stay Emily has come to appreciate Puerto Rico, she and Lucy are friends, and the two discover that Emily's mother had not returned to Puerto Rico by choice, but, because, by marrying a Jewish man, she was cut off by the grandmother.
European-Jewish-American/Puerto Rican and Catholic
Older; Fiction

Oughton, Jerrie. *Music from a Place Called Half Moon*. Boston: Houghton Mifflin Company, 1995. 176 p.

In this novel which is set in 1956 in a mountainous North Carolina town, thirteen-year-old Edie Jo's father stirs up a hornet's nest when he proposes that the church's vacation bible school be open to the entire community, including Indians and "half-breeds." There is a terrible rift in Edie Jo's family as her mother opposes her husband's action. At first Edie Jo isn't sure where she stands, but after she and her brother barely escape from threatening teenage Indian boys, she decides she is against integration. Then she gets to know the half Cherokee Clarence Fish, who plays beautiful harmonica music and likes her poems. Just after Edie Jo realizes that she is in love with Clarence, she witnesses his murder by his older brother. In the midst of her grief and as her mother struggles to be more tolerant, Edie Jo takes a first step towards reducing her town's prejudice.
European-American and Cherokee
Intermediate, Older; Fiction

Park, Hee Jung, creator. *Hotel Africa Volume 1*. Translated from Korean by Jihae Hong. Illustrated by author. Los Angeles: Tokyopop, 2007. 256 p.

This graphic novel is the first in a series about Elvis, Ed, and July, friends trying to make it in the film industry. Their story is interlaced with that of Hotel Africa, the subject of a screenplay they are trying to produce. Hotel Africa tells of the guesthouse in Utah which Elvis's mother and grandmother open when he is four. It is then that Elvis learns that his father was a black singer and died in a nightclub of an electric shock. Elvis meets the hotel's guests: Geo, the Indian who remains with them and adores his mother; two tough-appearing motorcyclists, one of whom sings him a bedtime lullaby; a stepfather and his little stepson who learn of their love for each other; two teenage girls whose double suicide attempt is thwarted; and a woman who receives the letters a man who loved her had written her for more than thirty years. Little Elvis is disappointed when he learns that he is a flower boy and not the groom of his first love, and he is the only one who knows that, when his elderly friend Oliver dies, he has gone to meet the beautiful actress of his dreams.
African-American/European-American
Older; Fiction

Park, Hee Jung, creator. *Hotel Africa Volume 2*. Translated from Korean by Jihae Hong. Los Angeles: Tokyopop, 2008. 264 p.

In this continuation of volume one, little Elvis meets more hotel guests: Dominique, his mother's inconsiderate and demanding high school classmate who returns from the city and gets together with a classmate who has long loved her; a seventeen-year-old boy and a fifteen-year-old girl who say they are siblings, but are really lovers; Hillie, an old dog who dies after his master dies, but not before Elvis has come to love him; and an African-American friend of his mother who confesses she had loved Tran, before he became Elvis' father. She was devastated after he died until she found Lionel, a blind white boy whom she cares for. The book also tells how Elvis ironed his hair to make it straight and it ended up in an Afro. As adults, Elvis' friend Ed tells how he discovered he was gay when he fell in love with Ian, who died of a drug overdose, and Elvis gets a puppy, whom he names Hillie.

African-American/European-American
Older; Fiction

Pearce, Jonathan. *John-Browne's Body & Sole:A Semester of Life*. Stockton, Calif.: Balona Books, 2005. 168 p.

This book is presented as a journal written by thirteen-year-old Jack for a language arts assignment. It tells how he and the two other boys who are involved in an altercation learn how aikido (a martial art) and scripting can be used to prevent fighting and teach respect. In writing of his experiences, Jack expresses his feelings about his family, his friends, racism (his grandmother is Japanese), his piano recital, and his mother's terminal cancer.
Japanese-English-French-North African-Russian-European-American/European-American
Older; Fiction

Peck, Robert Newton. *Jo Silver*. Englewood, Fla: Pineapple Press, 1985. 144 p.

Sixteen-year-old Kenny plays hooky from school to try to find Jo Silver, the reclusive half Mohawk author whom he and his teacher, Dr. Gray, greatly admire. The story details Kenny's hike through the Adirondacks where he is pursued by would-be robbers and climbs a steep granite rock. Kenny is rewarded when he meets and gains insights from the elderly Jo Silver, who, although now blind, is self-sufficient. On the way back Kenny is surprised to meet Dr. Gray, who reveals his long-kept secret.
Mohawk/European-American
Older; Fiction

Platt, Randall Beth. *The Likes of Me*. New York: Delacorte Press, 2000. 256 p.

This is the story of the amazing year, 1918, in the life of fourteen-year-old Cordelia, an albino who is half white and half Chinese. With her mother dead and her stepmother Babe a giant, Cordelia is completely innocent of the ways of the world and fears she is dying when she has her first period. Cordelia falls in love with the half Indian Squirl and with him breaks the rules by riding the flume of the lumber camp where her father is superintendent. Thinking she has become pregnant by kissing Squirl, Cordelia runs away to Seattle. She does not realize that she has gone to live in a brothel, earns money as a freak with her "lucky" hair, and finally comes to her senses about Squirl and Babe.
European-American/Chinese; European-American and Native American
Older; Fiction

Porte, Barbara Ann. *Something Terrible Happened: A Novel*. New York: Orchard Books, 1994. 224 p.

When Gillian is ten, her mother, who is black, gets AIDS, and nothing is ever the same for Gillian and her family. Affected in both body and mind, her mother takes Gillian from New York City to Florida where they end up homeless. The two return to New York City where Gillian's grandmother tends to her daughter and sends Gillian to live with her late white father's brother and his family in Oak Ridge, Tennessee. Filled with resentment, worry, and loneliness, Gillian hates her life in that white community and, after her mother's death, runs wild. Things improve both for Gillian's grandmother as she takes up running and graduate work and for Gillian when she learns of the difficult pasts of a "cousin" who had been adopted from the Philippines and of her Uncle Henry.

European-American/St. Lucian-Trinidadian-American
Older; Fiction

Powell, Neva. *The Long Crossing*. Illustrated by Eugene Powell. New York: Avocet Press, 1998. 128 p.

Leading a horse-drawn sleigh carrying logs from a lumber camp, young Johnny makes a perilous trip through a blizzard and cracking ice across Lake Michigan to a railroad siding. As he travels, he recalls his life from the time his mother died and he went to live with an old man and his cruel wife, who refused to let his Indian father see him. As a nine-year-old Johnny began doing a man's farm work and he continued to do so when, after the old couple died, he went to live in the house of the old woman's kind niece and her husband. While living there, he experienced his first automobile ride, saw an aeroplane, and was given a bike. As Johnny safely completes his dangerous journey, he proudly acclaims his Indian heritage.
European-American and Native American/European-American
Intermediate, Older; Fiction

Resau, Laura. *Red Glass*. New York: Delacorte Press, 2007. 304 p.

This novel details the transformation of Sophie from Sophie la Delicada (the Delicate whose life is restricted by allergies, worries, and fears) into Sophie la Fuerte (the Strong, who undertakes and completes a very dangerous journey). Sixteen-year-old Sophie lives in Tucson with her English mother, her Mexican stepfather, and her great-aunt Dika, a Bosnian refugee. Then the family takes in five-year-old Pablo whose parents have died as his family tried to escape from Mexico. A year later, so that Pablo can see his relatives and decide where he wants to live, Sophie, Pablo, and Dika join Dika's boyfriend, Mr. Lorenzo, and his son Ángel, who are bound, via Mexico, for Guatemala to see whether Flor Blanca, their wife and mother, respectively, is alive and to find her jewels. The group spends a week in Pablo's Oaxaca village where Sophie and Ángel express their feelings for each other. Mr. Lorenzo and Ángel then go on to Guatemala, but are unable to return as Ángel is savagely attacked and their passports and money stolen. With Dika injured from a fall, Sophie travels by herself to Guatemala, a trip which is not at all safe, especially for a white girl. In Guatemala Ángel shares a hospital room with one of his attackers, Flor Blanca's fate is revealed, and Ángel decides whether to remain in Guatemala. Likewise, in Mexico Pablo decides whether he will stay there.
European-American/English
Older; Fiction

Reynolds, Marilyn. *If You Loved Me*. Buena Park, Calif.: Morning Glory Press, 1999. 224 p. (True-to-Life-Series from Hamilton High)

In this book for older teenagers, high school senior Lauren lives with her grandmother, the one supportive constant throughout her life, is in love with her caring boyfriend Tyler, and is close to her best friend Amber. Lauren hates her parents, who abandoned her, and especially her mother who caused her to be born drug-addicted and was blown up when a makeshift methamphetamine lab exploded. All changes when Lauren is betrayed by Tyler, betrays Amber, and discovers the identity of her "stalker." Terribly upset, she withdraws from life until she begins to realize the complexity of love

and the need for forgiveness.
African-Chinese-American/European-American
Older; Fiction

Rinaldi, Ann. *The Blue Door*. New York: Scholastic, 1996. 288 p. (The Quilt Trilogy)

The Blue Door concludes the Chelmsford family trilogy begun in *A Stitch in Time* and continued in *Broken Days*. In 1840 Nathaniel Chelmsford is still alive, but all of his children with the exception of Abby have died. Abby, who had left her Massachusetts home when she was fifteen, has never returned from the South. In this book her fourteen-year-old granddaughter Amanda, who is the narrator, is sent back to Massachusetts to save her father's cotton plantation and to fulfill her grandmother's wishes that she gain the power to help others and return Abby's part of the family quilt. On her journey Amanda is threatened with death by the man who causes a steamboat explosion and steals her grandmother's quilt piece. As a result, Amanda must assume a different identity and pretend to be mute, her family thinks she has died, her great-grandfather rejects her as an imposter, and she has to work in her great-grandfather's cotton mill where labor conditions are unsafe and insufferable. It is only as she gains power by aiding her fellow mill workers and is helped by Nancy, her half Shawnee cousin earlier known as Walking Breeze, that Amanda is accepted by her great-grandfather and that Abby's quilt piece is returned.
Shawnee/European-American
Older; Fiction

Rinaldi, Ann. *Broken Days*. New York: Scholastic, 1995. 288 p. (The Quilt Trilogy)

This sequel to *A Stitch in Time* is set immediately preceding and during the War of 1812. Fourteen-year-old Ebie Chelmsford is the narrator of this book which continues the story of the Chelmsford family. The daughter of Cabot, who is often away at sea, and of a mother who deserted them, Ebie lives with her Aunt Hannah, who is loved by both Richard Lander, a sea captain, and Louis Gaudineer, an Indian agent. Ebie's Aunt Thankful, who has lived with the Shawnee, dies and at her request, her half Shawnee daughter, fourteen-year-old Walking Breeze, comes to Salem to live with her Aunt Hannah. Resentful of her intrusion, Ebie steals Thankful's family quilt, the only proof of Walking Breeze's identity. She places it in a bundle for Georgie, the half Shawnee woman earlier known as Night Song, who, filled with anger at the whites, has become a disturbed recluse. As the story evolves, Louis is killed in the massacre at Fort Dearborn, Georgie becomes a Quaker, Hannah and Richard marry, and Ebie finally comes to her senses and helps restore her family by getting Thankful's quilt to Hannah.
European-American/Shawnee; Shawnee/European-American
Older; Fiction

Rinaldi, Ann. *Cast Two Shadows: The American Revolution in the South*. San Diego: Gulliver Books, 1998. 288 p. (Great Episodes)

Set in 1780 in South Carolina, this story is narrated by fourteen-year-old Caroline, the daughter of a white father and a mixed race slave. Looking white, Caroline is raised by her white family: her Loyalist stepmother, her imprisoned rebel father, her older half brother Johnny who is fighting with the Loyalists, and her older half sister Georgia Ann who is dining with Lord Rawdon, the British colonel

who has commandeered their plantation and confines Caroline, Georgia Ann, and her stepmother in an upstairs chamber. Because of the extreme cruelty of the British, Caroline decides to be a rebel. She cleverly convinces Rawdon to let her go with her Negro grandmother Miz Melindy to bring home Johnny, who is injured and, unbeknownst to Rawdon, has become a rebel. On the journey, Caroline bonds with Miz Melindy and learns the truth about her mother. Upon her return, she and her stepmother escape from Rawdon and his British troops.
European-American/Angolan-European-American
Older; Fiction

Rinaldi, Ann. *Come Juneteenth*. New York: Harcourt, 2007. 256 p.

Although President Lincoln delivered his Emancipation Proclamation in January 1863, Texas plantation owners kept their slaves unaware of their freedom until General Gordon Granger issued the Emancipation Proclamation for Texas on June 19, 1865, a day later celebrated as Juneteenth. This historical novel relates the effects of the owners' secret on one Texas family and of the secret which young teenager Luli has promised to keep. It tells of the relationship between Luli and her almost-sister Sis Goose, who is half white and half black and is very much a part of the plantation family, of the bond between Luli and her adult brother Gabe, and of Gabe's love for Sis Goose. The story ends tragically when, in an attempt to take Sis Goose away from a Yankee colonel, Luli shoots her. Other characters in the novel are a little African-American boy who has nowhere to go and a Kickapoo boy whose mother Gabe has killed during the war.
European-American/African-American
Older; Fiction

Rinaldi, Ann. *A Stitch in Time*. New York: Scholastic, 1994. 320 p. (The Quilt Trilogy)

In this first book of a trilogy about the Chelmsford family of Salem, Massachusetts, the narrator is Hannah, the oldest sister who strives to keep her family together as symbolized by the quilt she and her sisters are making that includes fabric from those whom the family trusts. In the eventful period from 1788 to 1791, Nathaniel Chelmsford, their cruel father, goes on to a trip to Ohio Territory. He is accompanied by his elder son Lawrence and his headstrong youngest daughter Thankful. Thankful is kidnapped by the Shawnee and decides to remain with them. Abby, the fifteen-year-old sister, elopes with Nate Videau, a Southern ship captain, and together they survive a shipwreck in the Caribbean. Cabot, the youngest sibling whose mother died during his childbirth, discovers that Nathaniel is not his father. Hannah, who with Cabot remains at their Salem home, saves her father's cotton mill, becomes betrothed to Richard Lander, who takes his ship on a secret trade route to Sumatra, and agrees to raise Night Song, the half Shawnee baby of Louis Gaudineer, the man to whom she was earlier betrothed. Sequels to this book are *Broken Days* and *The Blue Door*.
European-American/Shawnee
Older; Fiction

Rodowsky, Colby. *That Fernhill Summer*. New York: Farrar Straus Giroux, 2006. 176 p.

When an unknown aunt calls thirteen-year-old Kiara's apartment to say that the grandmother she never heard of is ill, Kiara discovers that she has a whole new extended family: two aunts, two uncles,

twin nine-year-old boy cousins, two girl cousins her own age, and Zenobia, her incredibly difficult grandmother. When Zenobia balks at going to a nursing home, it is decided that she can return to Fernhill, her unusual house, with two home health aides to care for her and the three girl cousins to keep her company. During the summer the girls try in vain to make Zenobia happy and Kiara discovers that her mother was banished from Zenobia's family, not because she married a black man, but because she quit art school and "wasted" her artistic talent.
African-American/European-American
Intermediate, Older; Fiction

Rosenberg, Maxine B. *Being Adopted*. Photographs by George Ancona. New York: Lothrop, Lee & Shepard Books, 1984. 48 p.

Illustrated with black-and-white photographs, this book features three children. Seven-year-old Rebecca, whose birthfather is African-American and birthmother European-American and Cheyenne, is the adopted daughter of an African-American father and a European-American mother. Ten-year-old Andrei was adopted from India by European-American parents, and Karin, the author's eight-year-old daughter, was adopted from Korea by her European-American parents. The book covers some of the questions and fears of younger adopted children: being afraid when they come to their adoptive families, wondering whether they caused their parents to give them up, fearing their adoptive parents will give them up, dreaming and wondering about their birthparents, and not looking like other members of their families. It also affirms that adopted children are just as much family members as are biological children.
African-American/European-American and Cheyenne
Primary, Intermediate; Nonfiction

Rosenberg, Maxine B. *Growing Up Adopted*. Afterword by Lois Ruskai Melina. New York: Bradbury Press, 1989. 128 p.

In this book eight children and six adults relate their experiences and thoughts about growing up as adopted children. The four children who were adopted by parents of a different race, in each case European-American, are Josh, adopted as was a little sister from Colombia; Amy, who was adopted from Ecuador; Mark, who was adopted from Korea; and Shakine, an African-American boy who was born with spinal bifida in the United States and lives in a family of seven children, four of whom are adopted and of ethnicities other than their adoptive parents. Three of the adults are of a different race than their European-American parents. Chris was adopted from France as was her brother, Sam was adopted from Korea and has an adopted sister of mixed race and two non-adopted brothers, and Jamie, an African-European-American, has two sisters who are not adopted and four adopted siblings of mixed race.
African-European-American
Intermediate, Older; Nonfiction

Rosenberg, Maxine B. *Living in Two Worlds*. Photographs by George Ancona. New York: Lothrop, Lee & Shepard Books, 1986. 48 p.

This book explains how races evolved and how many children have a greater resemblance to one of their parents. It discusses the teasing and unwanted questions biracial children face and points to the benefits of living in two cultures. The book's text and black-and-white photographs focus on five children: Toah, who is African-European-American; Megan, who is African-European-American and Cherokee; Jesse, who is Chinese-European-American; and Shashi and Anil, who are Indian-European-American.

African-American/European-American; Indian/European-American; European-American and Jewish/Chinese-American and Christian; African-American and Cherokee/European-American

Intermediate; Nonfiction

Ryan, Pam Munoz. *Becoming Naomi León*. New York: Scholastic, 2005. 272 p.

Fifth-grader Naomi and her younger brother Owen live happily with their great-grandmother Gram in a large trailer in California. Seven years earlier their irresponsible mother had left them there. At that time Owen was covered with infected insect bites and Naomi was suffering from selective muteness. When their alcoholic and abusive mother and her boyfriend come to reclaim Naomi and move her to Las Vegas to be their babysitter, Gram, Naomi, and Owen go to Oaxaca, Mexico, to search for Santiago León, the children's father who had earlier wanted them. As they had hoped, Santiago comes to the annual La Noche de los Rábanos (Night of the Radishes), the children are reunited with him, and he writes a letter to the California court urging that Naomi be allowed to remain with Gram. However, it is only when the judge discovers that their mother does not want Owen because he is physically disabled and when Naomi finds the courage of a lion (león) to speak up that Gram is awarded Naomi's custody.

Mexican/European-American

Intermediate; Fiction

Sauerwein, Leigh. *The Way Home*. Illustrated by Miles Hyman. New York: Farrar, Straus & Giroux, 1994. 128 p.

This book contains six stories, including "Storm Warning" and "The Dress." "Storm Warning" is set in Nebraska in 1989. When Jonathan, the Indian who is Joe's best friend, saves the twelve-year-old boy during a tornado, Joe realizes that Jonathan is his father. "The Dress," which is set in 1876, tells of Laura's first visit to her Aunt Ella. Laura learns that when Ella was young, she was captured by Cheyenne. She married a Cheyenne warrior and they had three children. However, Ella was the only survivor when soldiers attacked the Cheyenne village, and she was returned to her white family, who continue to ostracize her.

European-American and Lakota Sioux/European-American

Intermediate; Fiction

Schultz, Jan Neubert. *Battle Cry*. Minneapolis: Carolrhoda Books, 2006. 240 p

This book of historical fiction is set in southern Minnesota where Dakota Indians who had been mistreated rose up in the bloody Dakota Conflict of 1862. It tells of the bond between the fictional teenagers, Chaska, son of the Dakota Indian John Other Day (who really existed) and a white mother, and Johnny, who is white. Vivid descriptions detail the fighting as Johnny and Chaska participate in the Battles of Fort Ridgley and Birch Coolee. A man who is Dakota and white is involved in the fighting; Johnny's twelve-year-old sister is kidnapped by Dakota; Chaska is unjustly ordered to be executed; Johnny manages to secure his release; and the two of them witness the hanging of innocent Dakota.

Dakota/European-American; European-American and Dakota

Older; Fiction

Schwartz, Ellen. *Stealing Home*. Plattsburgh, N.Y.: Tundra Books of Northern New York, 2006. 224 p.

When ten-year-old Joey's mother dies, he is sent to live with her estranged family: his disapproving grandfather, his loving aunt, and his cousin, a girl who loves baseball as much as he does. Set in 1947, this is a story about the racial prejudice facing biracial Joey, first in his native Bronx by African-American boys who won't let him play baseball and then in Brooklyn where white boys won't let him play ball and where a woman insults him and his deceased mother. It relates how Joey's new friends and his aunt finally stand up for him against the bigots, how Joey and his grandfather come to understand and accept each other, and how, home at last, Joey changes his allegiance from the Bronx Bombers to Jackie Robinson and the Brooklyn Dodgers.

African-American and non-Jewish/European-American and Jewish

Intermediate; Fiction

Schwartz, Virginia Frances. *Send One Angel Down*. New York: Holiday House, 2000. 176 p.

This novel is based upon a true story recorded in *To Be a Slave* by Julius Lester, with Doc Daniel Dowdy's name changed to Abram. At age six Abram sees his newborn cousin Eliza and knows immediately that she will encounter trouble because of her blue eyes. Abram helps raise Eliza and watches as she grows from a toddler into a young girl who plays with and is bossed by the plantation owner's older daughter and into a responsible nine-year-old who tends the slave breeder and field workers' babies. It is Abram who reluctantly tells Eliza that she is the daughter of the plantation owner. In this story, which reveals the horrors of slavery, Eliza at age fifteen is bought at the auction block by a man from New York, who not only frees her, but rescues her from Alabama by providing her with a job as his family's nanny.

European-American/African-American

Older; Fiction

Senisi, Ellen B. *For My Family, Love Allie*. Photographs by author. Morton Grove, Ill.: Albert Whitman & Company, 1998. 32 p.

In this picture book Allie wants to make a present for the large family party to be held at her house. All by herself she makes peanut-butter treats. Then, after her African-American and European-American relatives cook together, play games together, and eat together, they all enjoy Allie's dessert.

African-Jamaican-American/European-American

Pre-K, Primary; Fiction

Shin, Sun Yung. *Cooper's Lesson*. Translated by Min Paek. Illustrated by Kim Cogan. San Francisco: Children's Book Press, 2004. 32 p.

In this bilingual English and Korean picture book, young Cooper, whose mother is Korean, feels out of place in Mr. Lee's grocery store since he can't speak Korean. Angry because Mr. Lee won't speak English to him, Cooper tries to steal a brush for his mother, but is caught by the grocer. Then, as Kim performs chores for Mr. Lee, he learns to speak Korean and to appreciate his mixed heritage.
European-American/South Korean
Primary, Intermediate; Fiction

Shusterman, Neal. *Red Rider's Hood*. New York: Dutton Children's Books, 2004. 192 p. (Dark Fusion)

Sixteen-year-old Red, who is of mixed race, is shocked when he discovers that dogs, cats, and teenagers in his neighborhood are the victims of werewolves and that thirty years ago his grandparents had been werewolf hunters who got rid of the wolves existing then. However, there are now new werewolves under the control of the earlier leader's grandson, Cedric. In this suspenseful tale Red teams up with his grandmother and Marissa (whose brother may be a werewolf) to destroy the twenty-two wolves of Cedric's gang. However, when Red joins the gang to spy on them, he finds himself attracted to the wolves and their powers. It is not until Grandma and Marissa battle the wolves that Red decides which side he is on.
South Korean-American/African-European-American
Older; Fiction

Skurzynski, Gloria, and Alane Ferguson. *Escape from Fear*. Washington, D.C.: National Geographic Society, 2002. 160 p. (Mysteries in Our National Parks)

When the Landon family visits St. John Island in the Virgin Islands, they meet thirteen-year-old Forrest, the adopted son of a wealthy American diplomat and his wife. Forrest has run away from his Denver home to find his birthmother and to save her from danger. He manages to locate her and, with the Landon children, watches as she aids illegal aliens who have fled from poverty-stricken Haiti on a boat involved in poaching endangered hawksbill turtles.
European-American/African-Virgin Islander of the United States
Intermediate, Older; Fiction

Smith, Doris Buchanan. *Remember the Red-Shouldered Hawk*. New York: G. P. Putnam's Sons, 1994. 160 p.

When he is twelve, John-too has a lot to deal with. Nanna, his Czech grandmother whom he adores, comes to live with his family, but her Alzheimer's with its forgetfulness and bizarre talk and behavior distresses and embarrasses him. John-too is also upset by his best friend's sudden display of bigotry. When Ku Klux Klan members burn a cross at the home of his nephew Adam, whose mother is John-too's sister and whose father is Puerto Rican, it is Nanna who stands up to them.
Puerto Rican/Czech-European-American
Intermediate, Older; Fiction

Springer, Nancy. *The Boy on a Black Horse*. New York: Atheneum, 1994. 176 p.

Gray, whose parents and brother have died in a boating accident, lives with her Aunt Liana, who

is depressed after the death of her husband and two children in the same accident. Gray befriends a new classmate, a fifteen-year-old gypsy boy Chav, who rides a black stallion, takes care of his younger brother and sister, and lives in a silo. Chav feels worthless and is filled with anger at himself and non-gypsies. When his sister becomes ill with chicken pox, Gray takes Chav and his siblings to her house where Liana finds purpose in caring for them. However, hating to be penned up in the house, falsely accused of vandalism, and about to lose his beloved stallion, Chav sets off with a gun to kill himself and those attending a homecoming game. Thanks to Gray, disaster is averted. Chav and his brother, who witnessed their father murdering their mother, receive the support they need, and Gray is finally able to speak about her family's accident.
European-American/Romani-American
Older; Fiction

Stauffacher, Sue. *S'gana: The Black Whale*. Anchorage: Alaska Northwest Books, 1992. 224 p.

When Derek, who is one quarter Haida, visits his grandparents in Wisconsin, he goes to Ocean Park where the black whale S'gana performs. In touch with her spirit, which appears as a Haida girl, Derek realizes that S'gana is dying because she has been taken from her ocean home. Through the insights gained from a small Haida whale carving and with the help of his grandparents and the whale's trainer, twelve-year-old Derek initiates a campaign to free S'gana. His efforts are too late, but when he visits S'gana's pod off the coast of British Columbia, her legend is fulfilled.
European-American/European-Canadian and Canadian Haida
Intermediate, Older; Fiction

Straight, Susan. *Bear E. Bear*. Illustrated by Marisabina Russo. New York: Hyperion Books for Children, 1995. 32 p.

After Gaila's baby sister drops Bear E. Bear into a gutter, Gaila keeps careful watch over the special stuffed bear as he is cleaned in the washing machine and then dried in the dryer. The illustrations in this picture book reveal that Gaila's mother is white, her father is brown-skinned, and both Gaila and Bear E. Bear are light brown.
African-American/European-American
Pre-K, Primary; Fiction

Strasser, Todd. *Battle Drift*. Illustrated by Craig Phillips. New York: Simon Pulse, 2006. 224 p. (DriftX)

This second book of the *DriftX* trilogy focuses on Kennin's two drifting competitions with Ian, who continually taunts him because of his mixed race. In both cases Kennin realizes that it is foolish to race because of the road conditions, but his younger friend Tito has bet all his money on him. After beating Ian in the first race of a nighttime tsuiso, the tsuiso is called off because of the unusual Las Vegas rain and Ian claims his loss doesn't count since Kennin wasn't skidding enough. The second race occurs on a new dangerously narrow steep course. Kennin beats Ian in the first round and another driver in the second, but when he goes into the finals, his car loses a wheel, and the book ends with his crash. This story also tells of the affection which Kennin's friend Angelita feels for him, of her jealousy when the sexy Mariel butts in, of Kennin's sister's indebtedness to the gangster Jack for the

$5,000 cost of her breast enlargement surgery, and of Jack's threat to Kennin that he must throw the second tsuiso.
European-American/Japanese
Older; Fiction

Strasser, Todd. *Sideways Glory*. Illustrated by Craig Phillips. New York: Simon Pulse, 2006. 208 p. (DriftX)

The final book in this trilogy starts with Kennin in the hospital with his leg broken in two places from his drift racing crash. His friend Angelita's car, which he was driving and which she hoped to sell for her college tuition, is totaled thanks to her younger brother Tito. He loosened the lug nuts because of a threat from the gangster Jack. Kennin's sister is not only in debt to Jack, her boyfriend and boss, but is also the victim of his physical abuse. He has caused her to become a prostitute, and she has become a meth user. When Kennin is sufficiently healed to return to work washing cars at the Babylon Casino, he borrows a BMW parked there and rescues his sister, whom he hides in a rehab center. In this story Kennin again helps Angelita's cousin Raoul elude the police when he has stolen a car and Angelita suffers from the attention Kennin pays to the flirtatious Mariel. Kennin is saved from some of his problems by the owner of the Babylon, who gives Kennin $5,000 to have his sister's Corolla worked on so he can drive it as a tandem drifter at the casino's new track. A dramatic ending concludes the series.
European-American/Japanese
Older; Fiction

Strasser, Todd. *Slide or Die*. Illustrated by Craig Phillips. New York: Simon Pulse, 2006. 224 p. (DriftX)

This is the first book in the *DriftX* trilogy, which centers its stories around drifting, downhill car racing in which the cars skid around turns. Teenager Kennin, who has moved to Las Vegas, seems mysterious to his schoolmates since he is tight-lipped about his personal life: his white father is in prison, his Japanese mother died three months earlier, his older sister has to earn money to support herself and Kennin, the two live in a trailer in an unsavory part of town, and Kennin's best friend died in California while drifting. In this story, Kennin, his friend Tito, Tito's sister Angelita, and their older cousin Raoul attend an illegal nighttime tsuiso, a two car drifting competition. The three teenagers discover that Raoul is driving a stolen car, Kennin rescues a tsuiso racer from a burning car, and, in order to save the drunken Raoul from arrest, manages to elude chasing police cars in a daring drive down a mountain. At the story's conclusion Kennin decides to race the bigot Ian in a tsuiso.
European-American/Japanese
Older; Fiction

Strauss, Victoria. *Guardian of the Hills*. New York: Morrow Junior Books, 1995. 240 p.

During the Great Depression, sixteen-year-old Pamela moves with her mother to her mother's childhood home in Arkansas. There Pamela meets her grandfather for the first time and learns about her deceased Quapaw grandmother, who abandoned her Quapaw family and responsibilities. Pamela is little prepared for what transpires. Her grandfather finances an archaeological excavation on a nearby hill built by Mound People, and Pamela learns from her great-aunt that humans were once sacrificed on this hill and that evil may again arise from the Stern Dreamer who is buried there. It is up to Pamela to make the crucial choice that will determine others' fate and that results in her becoming the new Quapaw Guardian.

European-American/European-American and Quapaw

Older; Fiction

Stucky, Naomi R. *Sara's Summer*. Scottsdale, Pa.: Herald Press, 1990. 144 p.

Recently orphaned, fifteen-year-old Sara goes to spend the summer in Manitoba with her father's Hutterite family whom she has never met. There she is fondly welcomed and fully participates in the life of the contained community. Sara experiences both the Hutterite traditions, rituals, and rules which govern even the most minute aspects of their lives and the isolation of the community's residents, both physically and because of the absence of telephones, radio, and television. Sara learns that her musician father left the Hutterites because they did not permit musical instruments. Faced with the difficult decision as to whether to leave her new family at the end of the summer, Sara chooses to return to Toronto to pursue her education and have the options to determine her own future.

European-Canadian Hutterite/European-American non-Hutterite

Intermediate, Older; Fiction

Tate, Eleanora E. *Just an Overnight Guest*. New York: The Dial Press, 1980. 192 p.

Everything seems to go wrong for nine-year-old African-American Margie when her mother brings four-year-old Ethel to stay as an overnight guest with the two of them and Margie's thirteen-year-old sister Alberta. Ethel, a half white girl who lives with her mother in the white trash part of town, is a disruptive and destructive terror. She wets Margie's bed, breaks her treasured shell collection, and creates such havoc at a movie theater that the family must leave. Margie and Alberta are embarrassed to be seen with her, their mother endures criticism from the town's gossips, and when Margie is mean to Ethel, her mother always seems to takes Ethel's side. When, to Margie's dismay, Ethel's mother postpones her return, Ethel's stay is extended. However, thanks to her mother's kind treatment, Ethel's behavior improves and Margie, learning that Ethel has been abused and has no toys, manages to play with her. However, when Margie's father returns home from his road trip and Ethel cottons up to him, Margie's jealousy returns. It is only when her father tells her that Ethel is her cousin and that she hasn't taken away his love, that Margie accepts Ethel as a family member.

African-American/European-American

Intermediate; Fiction

Taylor, Mildred D. *The Land*. New York: Phyllis Fogelman Books, 2001. 392 p.

This prequel to the earlier-published books about the Logan family presents the story of Cassie's grandfather Paul-Edward Logan during the years following the Civil War. The son of a white farm owner and a former slave, Paul-Edward is treated as a son by his father, who has him sit with his siblings at the family table and provides him with an education. Paul-Edward loves the family's Georgia land and dreams of becoming a landowner when he grows up. However, despite his father's advice and warnings, he only realizes the difficulties his mixed race will cause when he is betrayed by the

brother to whom he is closest. Forced to flee with his best friend Mitchell when Mitchell's life is in danger, Paul-Edward works in a lumber camp and uses his skills with horses and as a carpenter to save some money and enter into contracts to secure the Mississippi land which he has set his heart on. This is a story of the terrible treatment which Negroes received in the South, of the kindnesses of a few white people, of Mitchell's marrying Caroline whom Paul-Edward had fancied, of the friendship of the three of them, of Mitchell's being killed, and of the realization of Paul-Edward's dreams.
European-American/African-American and Native American
Older; Fiction

Taylor, Mildred D. *Let the Circle Be Unbroken*. New York: Puffin Books, 1991. 400 p.
    Narrated by young Cassie, who is part of the third generation of the Logan family, this book relates the experiences of her colored family during the terrible financial hardships of the 1930s Depression. She relates how she witnesses the murder trial and the predetermined guilty verdict of the family's innocent friend T.J.; sees how efforts to create a biracial Farm Workers' Union are thwarted; learns of the fraud used by plantation owners to deprive small cotton farmers of government money; accompanies an older black woman who has extensively studied the Mississippi Constitution, but is refused voter registration and ordered off her land; and worries with her family when her fourteen year-old older brother runs off to save their property by working in the cane fields of Louisiana where he is subjected to unthinkable treatment. In this story Cassie's father David tells of his mixed heritage, and there is hostility from both blacks and whites towards one of Cassie's uncles who has married a white woman. The couple's fifteen-year-old daughter Suzella finds it difficult to be biracial and decides that she will pass as a white. In other books about this generation of Logans—*Mississippi Bridge*; *Song of the Trees*; *The Friendship*; *Roll of Thunder, Hear My Cry*; and *The Road to Memphis*—the family is identified for readers as colored, not as mixed race.
African-European-American and Native American/African-American; African-American/European-American
Older; Fiction

Taylor, Mildred D. *The Well: David's Story*. New York: Dial Books for Young Readers, 1995. 96 p.
    Set in the early 1900s, this book tells of an episode in the life of David Logan, Paul-Edward's son and Cassie's father. When David is ten-years-old, there is a severe drought, and both white and colored neighbors come to the Logan farm to get water from their well. David and his thirteen-year-old hotheaded brother Hammer are treated abysmally by the mean Simms boys, who are white. When Hammer hits one of them after he has hit David, the sheriff is summoned as it is a serious crime for a black to hit a white. Caroline, David and Hammer's mother, has to whip both of her sons in front of the Simms and they have to do work for Mr. Simms. The Simms boys continue to harass David and Hammer, but when they pollute the water in the Logan's well, both they and their father get their comeuppance. Paul-Edward plays a role in this book and it is mentioned that he is half white.
African-European-American and Native American/African-American
Intermediate; Fiction

Tenny, Dixie. *Call the Darkness Down*. New York: Atheneum, 1984. 204 p. (A Margaret K. McElderry Book)

Although for years Morfa has heard tales of Wales from Gwenfair, her Welsh mother, Gwenfair has refused to say anything about her parents and why she left her beloved Wales. When Morfa spends her freshman year at a Welsh college, she immediately becomes immersed in Welsh life: having Welsh friends, learning the Welsh language, and experiencing Welsh culture. She also has scary moments with a strange man in a dark coat and, pushed off a castle wall, narrowly escapes death. In this suspenseful story of the forces of light and dark, of mystical powers, and of spells, Morfa finally discovers the terrible truth about her family and must save her life from her murderous grandmother.

English-European-American/Welsh

Older; Fiction

Thomas, Joyce Carol. *The Blacker the Berry*. Illustrated by Floyd Cooper. New York: Joanna Cotler Books, 2008. 32 p.

In this picture book thirteen poems and accompanying paintings present the beauty of varied black skin shades, including the raspberry black of an African-American and Seminole boy, the cranberry red of an African-Irish-American girl, and the snowberry color of an African-European-American girl.

African-European-American

Primary, Intermediate; Fiction

Tocher, Timothy. *Chief Sunrise, John McGraw, and Me*. Illustrated by Greg Copeland. Chicago: Cricket Books, 2004. 160 p.

When baseball-loving fifteen-year-old Hank escapes from his mean alcoholic father by jumping into a train boxcar, he discovers that it is already occupied by Chief Sunrise, who says he is a Seminole and wants to pitch for the New York Giants. As the two travel in 1919 from Georgia to New York, Hank, disguised as a girl, plays a game as shortstop for a female baseball team, Chief Sunrise earns money by pitching to carnival goers, and the two share a boxcar with a horse. The Giant's manager John McGraw hires Chief Sunrise as a pitcher and Hank as a batboy. Chief Sunrise becomes an immediate pitching star, but everything changes when Hank meets his father at Sing Sing prison and learns that Chief Sunrise is not Indian, but half colored.

European-American/African-American

Intermediate, Older; Fiction

Torres, Leyla. *Liliana's Grandmothers*. Illustrated by author. New York: Farrar Straus Giroux, 1998. 32 p.

In this picture book Liliana loves visiting both her grandmother who lives on her street and her grandmother who lives in an unspecified South American country.

European-South American-American

Pre-K, Primary; Fiction

Updike, John. *A Child's Calendar*. Rev. ed. Illustrated by Trina Schart Hyman. New York: Holiday House, 1999. 32 p.

Featuring Updike's poems and Hyman's paintings, this picture book presents a year in the life of a Vermont family: an African-American husband, a Caucasian mother, and their two small sons.
African-American/European-American
Pre-K, Primary; Fiction

Vanasse, Deb. *A Distant Enemy*. New York: Puffin Books, 1999. 192 p.

Fourteen-year-old Joseph, whose white father has abandoned his family, hates everyone white. When officials of the Alaska Department of Fish and Game come to his Yupik Eskimo village to speak about an emergency fishing closure, he slashes the tires of their Cessna plane. Upset that his new white teacher Mr. Townsend has come into his duck blind, Joseph spreads the rumor that Mr. Townsend has wasted birds while hunting. When Joseph is falsely accused of stealing, he realizes that the girl he likes doesn't believe in his innocence because of his earlier lying. Consumed with anger, frustration, and guilt, Joseph runs off. He is saved from severe hypothermia by Mr. Townsend and comes to realize the importance of forgiveness.
European-American/Eskimo
Intermediate, Older; Fiction

Viglucci, Pat Costa. *Cassandra Robbins, Esq.* Madison: Square One Publishers, 1987. 190 p.

Adopted as a baby by white parents, seventeen-year-old Cassandra, who is of mixed race, feels that being the family's only girl is of more significance than being its only brown member. However, when her brother brings Josh, his African-American college roommate, home for the summer, Cassandra experiences mixed feelings about her identity. She is especially jealous when Josh is with a white girl. She finds that the white boy with whom she goes to a concert is surprisingly nice, but that his mother is a bigot, and she encounters hostility from two black girls. By the end of the summer Cassandra has learned a lot about herself and the complexities of love.
African-American/European-American
Older; Fiction

Viglucci, Patricia Costa. *Sun Dance at Turtle Rock*. Rochester, N.Y.: Stone Pine Books, 1996. 136 p.

Twelve-year-old Cody, whose white father had died in a car accident six years earlier, goes to spend the summer with his paternal grandfather Zachariah, who had objected to the marriage of his father to his African-American mother. Cody is treated lovingly by his aunt, uncle, and their toddler son and spends much of the time exploring the town and the surrounding Allegheny Mountains with their daughter Jem. However, although his grandfather shows warmth towards Cody's cousins, he treats Cody coldly because of his race and is especially upset that Cody may be adopted by his black stepfather and take his stepfather's name. The last straw for Cody comes when Zachariah takes the side of a bigoted neighbor boy instead of his. Cody realizes that he is like the Plains Indians who in a Sun Dance had tortured themselves to prove themselves worthy, in Cody's case of his father's father. Cody plans to leave until he saves Jem from a bear. Then Zachariah expresses his love for Cody, and Cody decides that, although it will take time for his grandfather to change, he will stay for the rest of the summer.

European-American Catholic/African-American Baptist
Intermediate; Fiction

Wallace, Bill. *Buffalo Gal.* New York: Pocket Books, 1993. 192 p. (A Minstrel Book)

It is 1904 and fifteen-year-old Amanda is on a trip from San Francisco to Oklahoma Territory and Texas with her mother who wants to save buffalo from extinction by getting some of them to a ranch. Amanda is unhappy about everything: the trains, the trip, and especially David, the half Comanche boy she meets at Fort Sills who insults her and, with two others, will accompany them into Texas in search of a buffalo herd. David is especially annoying after she almost beats him in a horse race and the two continually spat. On the journey Amanda is saved from an alligator and a rattlesnake; the group survives a severe thunderstorm; a Texas rancher, his Mexican wife, and their two children provide welcome hospitality; Amanda and David fight off a buffalo; Amanda is given the buffalo's calf as a birthday present; and the buffalo herd is captured. Amanda finally realizes that David cares for her and as she leaves for San Francisco, she agrees to marry him.
European-American/Comanche; European-American/Mexican
Older; Fiction

Wayans, Kim, and Kevin Knotts. *All Mixed Up!* Illustrated by Soo Jeong. New York: Grosset & Dunlap, 2008. 112 p. (Amy Hodgepodge)

Amy Hodges is introduced in this first book of the *Amy Hodgepodge* series, which features pictures posted in Amy's scrapbook. Moving to a new town after having experienced only home schooling, Amy is excited to be starting fourth grade at Emerson Charter School. However, her first day starts out disastrously. She wears the wrong clothes, tears her dress when she removes its flower, sings too loudly in music class, is laughed at by classmates Liza and Jennifer, and discovers that a paper saying "Stupid new girl" has been taped to her back by Rory. However, her day improves when she is befriended in the cafeteria by Maya, Jesse, Rusty, Pia, and twins Lola and Cole. Upset by a racial insult from Jennifer, she discovers that the twins are black and white, Jesse is black and Puerto Rican, Pia is Chinese-American and white, and Rusty is Latino, Native American, and white. Learning that Amy's father is black and white and her mother Japanese and South Korean-American, they affectionately nickname her Amy Hodgepodge. The story continues with the group entering a school talent show where Amy, inspired by Rusty who has to earn money to buy his costume, overcomes her stage fright and becomes the group's lead singer.
African-European-American/Japanese-South Korean-American; European-American/African-American; Chinese-American/European-American; European-Latin American-American and Native American
Primary, Intermediate; Fiction

Wayans, Kim, and Kevin Knotts. *Digging Up Trouble.* Illustrated by Soo Jeong. New York: Grosset & Dunlap, 2010. 112 p. (Amy Hodgepodge)

After foolishly letting her dog Giggles off his leash to play with another dog at the Farmer's Market, Amy is unable to find him. She spends a stressful night until in the morning the family receives a call from an older man, Irving Coleman, who reports that Giggles has come to his home with his dog. Then, after being reunited with Giggles, Amy realizes that helping Irving restore his community garden would make a perfect green project for the school class assignment. The two fourth grade classes adopt Amy's idea and decide to raise money for the needed tools and supplies by having a bake sale and a car wash. Amy is worried when she is placed in charge of the bake sale team, but because of the help of her visiting community-organizer grandmother and team members, including Lola, Pia, and Rusty, there are many baked goods for sale. However, things turn contentious when the bake sale team and the car wash team, including Jesse and Maya, become overly competitive. After teachers intervene, the teams decide to refer customers to each other. With the proceeds earned and the work of Amy's gardener grandmother and the fourth graders, Irving's garden again becomes a neighborhood asset. Referring to the mixed racial identity of some of Amy's friends, this sixth book in the series specifically identifies the heritages of Lola and Cole as well as of Amy.

African-European-American/Japanese-South Korean-American; European-American/African-American; Chinese American/ European-American; European-Latin American-American and Native American
Primary, Intermediate; Fiction

Wayans, Kim, and Kevin Knotts. *Happy Birthday to Me*. Illustrated by Soo Jeong. New York: Grosset & Dunlap, 2008. 112 p. (Amy Hodgepodge)

In this sequel to *All Mixed Up!* Amy looks forward to celebrating her birthday with her new friends as well as with her family. Maya, Jesse, Pia, and Lola accept her invitation to her tenth birthday sleepover where Amy plans to have a Japanese tea ceremony and do origami. Amy's spirits wane when she fears her family is planning to move to California. She is really upset when her four friends decide to go to an Amber Skye concert instead of her party. When Lola's brother Cole discovers that Amy has not invited other guests, he texts the concertgoers, and the four girls leave the concert to go to Amy's house. It is then that Amy discovers what true friends they are and the advisability of telling her problems and her fears to her family. This book points out the mixed heritages of Amy and most of her friends.

African-European-American/Japanese-South Korean-American; European-American/African-American; Chinese-American/European American; European-Latin American-American and Native American
Primary, Intermediate; Fiction

Wayans, Kim, and Kevin Knotts. *Lost and Found*. Illustrated by Soo Jeong. New York: Grosset & Dunlap, 2008. 112 p. (Amy Hodgepodge)

Amy Hodgepodge persuades her parents to let her go on the fourth grade two-and-a-half day wilderness trip. However, she doesn't feel as pleased about it when she is placed in a group without her friends, but with Jennifer and Rory who don't like her. Further, she falls in the mud during the obstacle course, goes overboard with Jennifer in their canoe, and is embarrassed that she doesn't know what s'mores are. However, Amy is supported by Lola, Jesse, Maya, and Pia with whom she shares a tent. Together they enjoy tricking Cole, Rusty, and two other boys. Then when she, Jennifer, Rory, and two others get lost in the woods, Amy uses her compass to lead them back to camp—and receives the Best Camper award. In this third book in the series, Amy's mixed heritage is noted. Readers of the first book, *All Mixed Up!*, will be aware of the mixed heritages of five of her friends.

African-European-American/Japanese-South Korean-American; European-American/African-American; Chinese-American/European-American; European-Latin American-American and Native American
Primary, Intermediate; Fiction

Wayans, Kim, and Kevin Knotts. *Playing Games*. Illustrated by Soo Jeong. New York: Grosset & Dunlap, 2008. 112 p. (Amy Hodgepodge)

When Evelyn, the star player of the Comets girls' basketball team, injures her arm, Amy Hodgepodge reluctantly agrees to take her place so that the team will have the required eight players. Amy has neither played basketball nor is she familiar with the game. She is a terrible player, and her mistake causes the team to lose to the worst team in the league. Amy tries to fake a twisted ankle so she can be on the bench, but even that fails and she decides to quit. However, after confessing her problem to Rusty, he offers to coach her, with Amy, in return, helping him sing harmony in the friends' fourth grade music class performance. Unaware of the fact that Amy has improved, her teammates don't pass her the ball. It is not until the end of an important game that Amy demonstrates her secret talent as a three-point shooter. Amy's mixed heritage is noted in this fourth book in the series. Readers of the first book, *All Mixed Up!*, will be familiar with the mixed heritages of most of her friends.
African-European-American/Japanese-South Korean-American; European-American/African-American; Chinese-American/European-American; European-Latin American-American and Native American
Primary, Intermediate; Fiction

Wayans, Kim, and Kevin Knotts. *The Secret's Out*. Illustrated by Soo Jeong. New York: Grosset & Dunlap, 2009. 112 p. (Amy Hodgepodge)

Amy, Lola, Jesse, Pia, and Maya decide to enter as a group in their school's competitive annual spring art show. Amy comes up with the idea of tracing their body outlines on a large poster board and then painting and decorating them. The girls would stand behind holes that would show their faces. With the exception of Pia, the others are enthused about Amy's plan. Indeed, Pia's personality seems to have changed. She has become distracted, negative, and rude. Finally, she confides to Amy, with Amy's promise not to tell, that she fears that, since her father and stepmother are going to have a baby, her father won't pay attention to her. When Amy accidentally reveals Pia's secret to Lola, there are unforeseen consequences. Lola tells Jesse, and Jesse lets the secret out to classmates. The friends become so angry at each other that their Best Friends art display is jeopardized. It is not until they practice forgiveness that they restore their friendship—and their project ties for fourth grade first place. In this fifth book in the series, Amy's mixed heritage is noted, and series readers will be aware of the mixed heritages of most of her friends.
African-European-American/Japanese-South Korean-American; European-American/African-American; Chinese-American/European-American; European-Latin American-American and Native American
Primary, Intermediate; Fiction

Werlin, Nancy. *Black Mirror: A Novel*. New York: Dial Books, 2001. 256 p.

In this book for older teenagers sixteen-year-old Frances is a loner and so upset by her mixed race appearance that for years she has not been able to look at herself in the mirror. When her brother Daniel commits suicide by an overdose of heroin, Frances is shocked and feels guilty that she had no

longer been close to him. When she considers joining Unity Service, the preparatory school charitable institution in which Daniel was so active, she experiences conflicting emotions and encounters negative reactions from its members. Discovering that something strange is going on at Unity, Frances, with the help of a man who is mildly retarded, finds out the terrible truth about Unity and the death of her brother.
European-American and Jewish/Japanese-American and Buddhist
Older; Fiction

Whitmore, Arvella. *Trapped Between the Lash and the Gun: A Boy's Journey*. New York: Dial Books, 1999. 192 p.

Upset because his dad has left, twelve-year-old Jordan wants to remain behind when his mother and sister move to the suburbs so as part of a gang he can earn the airfare to go live with his father. He even steals his grandfather's prized ancestral watch to pawn to get money for a gun. However, when Jordan approaches the pawnshop, he loses the watch and is transported to the 1800s where he meets the young slave boy Uriah, who is his great-great-great-great-grandfather. The bulk of this book relates the story of Jordan's horrible experiences when he is mistaken for a runaway slave: picking cotton for hours, being beaten, not having enough to eat, hiding from paddyrollers (poor whites who look for runaway slaves), becoming part of a chain gang, and being sold at a slave auction. Fortunately, Jordan is bought by a worker with the Underground Railroad and, after discovering that the plantation master is Uriah's father, finally secures the watch, which brings him back to the present. There he rejects his gang membership, is shot and wounded by its leader, learns that his father is in prison, and treasures life with his family.
European-American/African-American
Intermediate, Older; Fiction

Wilson, Diane Lee. *Black Storm Comin'*. New York: Margaret K. McElderry Books, 2005. 304 p.

It is September 1860 and twelve-year-old Colton Wescott, his part African-American mother, his white father, his ten- and four-year-old sisters, and a newborn brother are in Utah Territory as they travel to Sacramento where his mother's half sister lives. Others in the wagon train treat them poorly because of his mother's blackness and, when Colton's father accidentally shoots Colton, he abandons the family. With Colton's mother very ill, it is up to the young boy and his little sisters to bury the baby and, with two of the oxen team killed for food by some wagoneers, to get to Dayton where there is a doctor. Colton needs to earn money for the doctor and personally to deliver freedom papers to his aunt in California. The story describes Colton's buying a pitiful-looking horse, Badger, to prove that he can be a Pony Express rider and his making the perilous trip from Carson City across the Sierra Nevada to Sportsman Hall and back as far as Genoa where he has an accident. Then, after being fired, Colton steals a Pony Express packet containing urgent news from Washington and, with it, rides Badger through a snowstorm to Sacramento where he delivers it and the freedom papers. On the way he saves the life of a man who has guessed the secret that he is colored and, by the story's conclusion, realizes that he should both be himself and not judge others by their appearance.
European-American/African-European-American
Older; Fiction

Wing, Natasha. *Jalapeño Bagels.* Illustrated by Robert Casilla. New York: Atheneum Books for Young Readers, 1996. 24 p.

Pablo helps his parents at their Mexican-Jewish-American bakery and decides that he will take jalapeño bagels to his class International Day as they, like him, are a mixture of two cultures. This picture book includes recipes for chango bars and jalapeño bagels as well as a glossary of Spanish and Yiddish words.
European-American and Jewish/Mexican-American
Pre-K, Primary; Fiction

Wolf, Allan. *Zane's Trace.* Cambridge, Mass.: Candlewick Press, 2007. 208 p.

In this book for high schoolers, teenager Zane, who suffers grand mal seizures and constantly writes his thoughts on his bedroom walls, feels that he is responsible for the deaths of his schizophrenic mother (because he was at school) and his grandfather (because he crossed off his name from the family tree he had drawn). Zane drives from Baltimore to Zanesville, Ohio, to commit suicide on his mother's grave. On the way he has supernatural encounters with his dead parents, his grandfather, and several of his ancestors. Finally reaching the Zanesville cemetery, Zane understands that he has a caring brother and friends and that it is he who must keep his deceased family's souls alive.
Wyandot/African-European-American
Older; Fiction

Woodson, Jacqueline. *Behind You.* New York: G. P. Putnam's Sons, 2004. 128 p.

This sequel to *If You Come Softly* follows the months after fifteen-year-old Miah's mistaken-identity killing by New York City police. His African-American parents Nelia and Norman, his school basketball teammate Kennedy, his best friend Carlton, and his white girlfriend Ellie suffer in their grief. Finally they begin to heal: Nelia starts writing another novel; Carlton, who is of mixed race, finally admits he is gay; Norman begins talking with his former wife Nelia; Nelia, Ellie, and Carlton have a closer relationship; and Ellie, Carlton, and Kennedy become friends. Ignoring the advice of his deceased grandmother, Miah continues to look down upon them until he realizes that they all know they are loved.
African-American/European-American
Older; Fiction

Woodson, Jacqueline. *The House You Pass on the Way.* New York: Delacorte Press, 1997. 112 p.

Fourteen-year-old Staggerlee has an atypical family. Her father's parents, noted entertainers who had appeared on *The Ed Sullivan Show*, had been killed in a bombing when they chose to go to a Civil Rights demonstration. There is now a statue of them in her town, and her family has shunned publicity. Further, her family has been estranged from its relatives for the past twenty years because, after her grandparents' deaths, her black father and white mother got married. Lonely Staggerlee is delighted that her cousin Trout, a girl her own age, is coming to spend the summer. Fast becoming friends, Staggerlee discovers that she, like Trout, is attracted to girls. When high school begins, Staggerlee, with a new assurance, starts to make friends and become involved in school activities. However, she is thrown for a loop when Trout writes that she has a boyfriend. Staggerlee finally decides that she'll

just have to wait and see how her life turns out.
African-American/European-American
Older; Fiction

Woodson, Jacqueline. *If You Come Softly*. New York: G. P. Putnam's Sons, 1998. 192 p.

This is the tragic love story of two high school sophomores who fall in love when Ellie (Elisha), carrying her textbooks, crashes into Miah (Jeremiah) on their first day at a private New York City school. African-American Miah's mother is a noted novelist and his father is a famous film producer who has left Miah's mother for another woman. Ellie is a Jewish girl whose much older siblings left home some time earlier. Her mother had twice deserted and then returned to the family. Miah and Ellie sense something familiar about each other, for they both suffer from loss and fear of abandonment. Their romance progresses slowly as they are shy with each other, but then acknowledge their feelings. They encounter stares and verbal abuse from strangers who don't like interracial couples, and Ellie's favorite sister doesn't approve. When Ellie finally meets Miah's mother, she is warmly accepted. However, on the evening that Ellie is going to tell her parents about her boyfriend, police, who are looking for a tall dark man, shoot and kill Miah, as, dribbling his basketball in Central Park, he dreams about scoring for Ellie and his team. Carleton, Miah's best friend in this book, has a black father and a white mother. The story continues in *Behind You*.
African-American/European-American
Older; Fiction

Wyeth, Sharon Dennis. *Orphea Proud*. New York: Delacorte Press, 2004. 208 p.

In this novel, which is for older teens, sixteen-year-old Orphea presents the story of her life to the audience at a show at the Club Nirvana in Queens, New York. Growing up in Pennsylvania, Orphea suffers the death of her father when she is seven and the death of her beloved mother when she is eight. Going to live with her much older half brother Rupert and his wife, Orphea meets Lissa when they are both ten and they immediately become best friends. Orphea writes poetry, and Lissa paints pictures. As the two grow older, Orphea fears she is gay because of her feelings toward Lissa. On an eventful day when they are sixteen, Orphea and Lissa make out in Orphea's bedroom, but are caught by homophobic Rupert. Rupert beats up Orphea and says something to Lissa as she escapes in her car. Before she reaches home, Lissa is killed when skidding in the snow. Orphea is devastated. Unable to cope with her distress and behavior, Rupert sends Orphea to live with her two great-aunts in mountainous Virginia. There Orphea recovers; befriends her fourteen-year-old white neighbor Raynor, who cannot read, but paints psychedelic pictures of horses; and finally admits to her understanding great-aunts that she is gay. It is also in Virginia that African-American Orphea learns that her great-great-grandfather Babe was white and that she and Raynor are cousins. Babe's sister stole Babe's body out of the black cemetery and reburied him in the white cemetery which blacks could not enter. It is Orphea and Raynor who enable the great-aunts to visit their grandfather's grave. Orphea and Raynor then go to Queens for the summer to perform and live with the couple who had befriended Orphea in Pennsylvania and now own the casino.
African-American/African-European-American; African-European-American/European-American
Older; Fiction

Yep, Laurence. *The Cook's Family*. New York: G. P. Putnam's Sons, 1998. 192 p.

In this sequel to *Ribbons*, twelve-year-old Robin and her younger brother are upset by their parents' quarreling about whether their family should sacrifice to support their uncle's store. Robin's grandmother is upset by the quarreling about the store among her three grown children. By chance, Robin and Grandmother become pretend daughter and wife, respectively, of a distraught Chinese cook whose family has presumably died of starvation. As members of this fantasy family, Robin learns about being a Chinese daughter, Grandmother enjoys talking with the cook about old-time China, and they both escape from the stresses of their own family. When the cook's real daughter turns up, the fantasy family disappears, but, with new insights, Robin and Grandmother ease Robin's parents' dissension.
European-American/Chinese
Intermediate, Older; Fiction

Yep, Laurence. *Ribbons*. New York: The Putnam & Gossett Group. 1997. 192 p.

Eleven-year-old Robin, who excels at and loves dancing, is devastated when her parents say she must give up her ballet lessons to help finance bringing her Chinese grandmother to San Francisco. Determined to be a dancer, Robin practices constantly on the concrete garage floor in her pointe shoes even after she has outgrown them and her feet hurt. She is especially riled when Grandmother blatantly favors her five-year-old brother, causes conflict between her parents, and says that Robin must give up ballet. It is only after Robin accidentally views her grandmother's hideously deformed feet, which had been bound in China, that she understands her grandmother and the two become friends. Then, when Robin is diagnosed with hammer toes, it is Grandmother who supports Robin's decision to dance with pain rather than undergo surgery and, when Grandmother discovers that Robin's parents have borne the entire expense of bringing her to the United States, it is Grandmother who makes Robin's uncles help shoulder the costs. Robin's story is continued in *The Cook's Family*.
European-American/Chinese
Intermediate, Older; Fiction

Yep, Laurence. *Thief of Hearts*. New York: HarperCollins Publishers, 1995. 208 p.

Everything changes for thirteen-year-old Stacy when she is asked to help Hong Ch'un, a girl who has just moved to her town from China and will be in her class. Stacy doesn't like Hong Ch'un, who is rude and calls her a t'ung chng (mixed seed) because of her white father and Chinese-American mother. When Stacy says that Hong Ch'un should be treated fairly after stolen items are found in her backpack, a schoolmate also calls her a half-breed. Stacy, her mother, and great-grandmother drive to San Francisco's Chinatown to find Hong Ch'un, who has run away after being accused of stealing. It is then that Stacy gains a greater appreciation of her mother and her Chinese heritage, discovers how to see with her heart, and, with the help of her great-grandmother and her father, lays a trap that catches the real thief. This book is a sequel to *Child of the Owl*, which is about Stacy's mother.
European-American/Chinese-American
Intermediate, Older; Fiction

Zindel, Paul. *The Gadget*. New York: Laurel-Leaf Books, 2003. 192 p.

In 1944 when twelve-year-old Stephen is living in London with his English mother, he watches with horror as his cousin dies on a rooftop during a German air raid. The next March Stephen is sent to stay with his American father physicist at the secret town of Los Alamos. Upset that his father is consumed with developing a "gadget" and largely ignores him, Stephen spends time with a new older friend, Alexei Nagavatsky, and his family. Alexei and Stephen try to discover what is going on at Los Alamos. Stephen escapes an apparent attempted kidnapping while on a school trip to Santa Fe, and he and Alexei travel to Alamogordo where they witness the explosion of the first atomic bomb. It is after this that Stephen discovers that the Nagavatskys are spies and he is almost murdered. The story raises ethical questions about the dropping of the atomic bomb on Japan and includes both a chronology of World War II and the development of the bomb and a descriptive listing of those involved with the bomb's development and use.
European-American/English
Older; Fiction

Acadian-French-American

See   Tinker, Clarence Leonard

Austrian-American

See   Mehta, Nina

Wosmek, Frances. *A Brown Bird Singing*. Illustrated by Ted Lewin. New York: Beech Tree Paperback Books, 1986. 128 p.

Years ago, after her mother had died from a fever, Anego's Chippewa father Hamigeesek had left her to stay with the Veselka family. The only Indian in her northern Minnesota community, Anego sometimes thinks about the brown bird she once held and gets a warm supportive feeling. Anego passes fourth grade, raises an orphaned fawn and grieves when a hunter shoots it, joins in the excitement of the family's getting a car, and, after thinking she is not needed when a baby brother is born, helps save his life and realizes how much she cares for him. Anego is very close to her Irish Ma, sister Sheila, and Austrian-American Pa, who is her best friend, and she dreads the time that the hardly-remembered Hamigeesek will take her from them. However, when he does come, Hamigeesek kindly assures Anego that she can remain with the Veselkas and, by having her hold a brown bird, brings back her memories of her Chippewa mother.
Austrian-American/Irish
Intermediate; Fiction

Celtic-American

Naylor, Phyllis Reynolds. *Sang Spell*. New York: Aladdin Paperbacks, 2000. 224 p.

Hitchhiking from Massachusetts to Dallas to live with his aunt because his mother has died, teen-

ager Josh is mugged and left on a road in Appalachia where he is picked up by a Melungeon, who takes him to Canara, an isolated primitive community. Everything is strange and illogical there, and Josh becomes increasingly frustrated in his efforts to escape. The road he takes ends up at the exact place he started. Trying to swim towards a river's opposite shore takes him only a short distance, and a roadside restaurant and a school appear and disappear at regular intervals. Josh discovers that his father was probably Melungeon and befriends a girl whose father was stoned to death when his efforts to escape accidentally caused fatalities. Finally, with new insights and the realization that he must keep Canara's secrets, Josh is able to get away. [The Melungeon people are of mixed race living primarily in the central Appalachians. There is controversy as to their origin and their heritage, but they are often regarded as tri-racial: European-American, African-American, and Native American. In this novel they are identified as Portuguese who, over time, became mixed with a number of other peoples.]
Celtic-American/Portuguese (Melungeon)-American
Older; Fiction

Creole-American. See also individual heritages

See   Beyoncé

Forrester, Sandra. *Dust from Old Bones*. New York: Morrow Junior Books, 1999. 176 p.

This story is set in the stratified society of the New Orleans of 1838. Thirteen-year-old Simone, who is a person of color, struggles with the probability that her pretty cousin Claire-Marie will go to quadroon balls and be chosen by a Creole "protector" [as his mistress]. She envies the life of Madelon, her aunt who lives in France where she is not faced with racial discrimination. Nevertheless, Simone comes to realize that her restricted life as a person of color is much better than that of black slaves, who if lucky enough to be freed had to leave New Orleans. Simone's admiration for Madelon, who comes to visit, disappears when she betrays not only Simone, but also the two slaves she was committed to free. It is Simone who leads the slaves through a swamp to a safe house.
African-Creole-American/African-Creole-Haitian; Creole-American/African-Creole-Haitian
Older; Fiction

Peck, Richard. *The River Between Us*. New York: Dial Books, 2003. 176 p.

Set at the beginning of the Civil War, this book tells how the life of fifteen-year-old Tilly and her family changes when two mysterious strangers, Delphine and her apparent servant Calinda, arrive via steamboat at Grand Tower, Illinois. Coming from New Orleans, Delphine with her elegant clothes and fancy ways is like no one the town has ever seen. The two stay with Tilly's family, and Tilly's twin brother Noah falls in love with Delphine. When now-sixteen Noah goes off to join the Yankee army, their mother is so upset, since her husband had earlier left her, that she sends Tilly and Delphine off to Cairo, Illinois, to bring Noah home. The book tells of the horrible living conditions in Cairo and especially of the unsanitary hospital tents. Noah, who suffers from dysentery, recovers enough that he is sent off to fight in the nearby battle of Belmont, Missouri, in which he is wounded and has to have his left arm amputated. The two girls stay in Cairo tending to Noah and other soldiers, and upon their

return home with Noah learn that Tilly's distraught mother, seeing the coffin of her husband which she mistook for Noah's, drowned herself in the river. The story also reveals that to Tilly's surprise Delphine and Calinda are sisters and that Delphine's father is indeed the wealthy Jules Duval, but that he is her mother's protector, not her husband as in New Orleans whites cannot marry Creoles. Following the war Calinda, a conjure woman, leaves Grand Tower so that she will not raise suspicion that Delphine has African blood. Although Delphine refuses to marry a white man, she and Noah live as husband and wife, but their son is passed off as the son of Tilly and her husband.
Creole (African-French-Spanish)-Haitian-American
Older; Nonfiction

Walter, Mildred Pitts. *Ray and the Best Family Reunion Ever*. New York: HarperCollins Publishers, 2002. 128 p.

   Eleven-year-old Ray is the only member of his Creole family with ebony skin. When he goes to a large family reunion in Natchitoches, Louisiana, Ray discovers that he and Gran-papa Philippe are the only ones there with dark skin. To make matter worse, Ray looks like his grandfather whom his father and almost all his relatives despise. This is the story of Ray's secret bonding with Gran-papa Philippe, his appreciation of his grandfather's talent, and his effecting a reconciliation between his father and Philippe.
Creole (Nigerian-French-Spanish-Native American)-Haitian-American/Creole (French-Spanish-West African-Native American)-American
Intermediate; Fiction

Czech-American

Smith, Doris Buchanan. *Remember the Red-Shouldered Hawk*. New York: G. P. Putnam's Sons, 1994. 160 p.

   When he is twelve, John-too has a lot to deal with. Nanna, his Czech grandmother whom he adores, comes to live with his family, but her Alzheimer's with its forgetfulness and bizarre talk and behavior distresses and embarrasses him. John-too is also upset by his best friend's sudden display of bigotry. When Ku Klux Klan members burn a cross at the home of his nephew Adam, whose mother is John-too's sister and whose father is Puerto Rican, it is Nanna who stands up to them.
Puerto Rican/Czech-European-American
Intermediate, Older; Fiction

Danish-American

See   Alba, Jessica Marie

Dutch-American

See   Mankiller, Wilma Pearl
       Rogers, Will, Jr.

Rogers, William (Will) Penn Adair
Ronstadt, Linda
Williams, William Carlos
Woods, Tiger

Brashares, Ann. *Forever in Blue: The Fourth Summer of the Sisterhood*. New York: Delacorte Press, 2007. 400 p. (Sisterhood of the Traveling Pants)

This fourth book of the series takes place after Carmen, Lena, Tibby, and Bridget's freshman year in college. Carmen's year at Williams College has been a disaster. She finds herself ungrounded with her mother, stepfather, and baby brother moving into a new house, discovers that she has no idea how to make friends, and feels invisible. Her only college friend, aspiring actress Julia, has persuaded Carmen to spend the summer with her at a theater festival in Vermont where Carmen will be on a stage crew. When the casting director persuades Carmen to audition, Carmen, who has never acted, is amazed to discover that she is the only apprentice chosen for a role in the theater's major production. Julia becomes hostile to Carmen and, then, pretending to be helpful, teaches Carmen how to read her role in meter. The professional actors are dismayed that Carmen now sounds like a robot. Carmen finally realizes that Julia takes pleasure in her failures, and she once again immerses herself in her role. Lena, who had been crushed when her Greek boyfriend Kostas married a Greek woman whom he had impregnated, is enrolled in a painting class in Providence, Rhode Island. There she is impressed with classmate Leo, an outstanding artist who is equally engrossed in painting. Getting to know him and his artistic African-American mother, Lena has her first sexual experience with him. Tibby, who has been going with Bailey's friend Brian, also loses her virginity. However, she becomes distressed that she may be pregnant and, after discovering that she isn't, breaks up with Brian. She then gives Lena's younger sister Effie an okay to go out with him. With Bridget's boyfriend Eric away for the summer in Mexico, she goes to Turkey for an archaeological dig. There she discovers that she loves digging and falls for an archaeology professor until she sees his wife and children. At the book's conclusion Tibby is reunited with Brian, Bridget is reunited with Eric, and Lena, Tibby, and Bridget go to Vermont to attend Carmen's successful opening night. Then the four friends fly to Greece to search for the Traveling Pants, which Effie has accidentally lost, Lena and Kostas meet, and the four friends realize that they have moved beyond the Pants. The mixed heritages of Carmen, Bridget, and Eric should be familiar to readers of *The Sisterhood of the Traveling Pants*.
Dutch/European-American
Older; Fiction

Brashares, Ann. *Girls in Pants: The Third Summer of the Sisterhood*. New York: Delacorte Press, 2005. 352 p. (Sisterhood of the Traveling Pants)

Bridget, Lena, Tibby, and Carmen graduate from high school at the beginning of this third book in the series, which details the four seventeen-year-olds' lives during the summer before college. Lena, who is still getting over Kostas, enjoys her summer drawing class. Defying and lying to her father, she continues to attend after he has forbidden her to continue because of the nude models. When he discovers her deceit, he announces that he will not pay for her going to the Rhode Island School

of Design. Heeding the suggestion of the class teacher, Lena embarks on an art portfolio project that just may win her a scholarship to the RISD. Tibby has conflicting feelings when Brian asks her to the senior party, but is devastated when, because she has left her window open, her three-year-old sister tries to climb the nearby apple tree and, falling, has a fractured skull and broken bones. Finding it difficult to have her new stepfather David living in her house and upset by the news that she will become a sister, Carmen considers going to the nearby University of Maryland rather than Williams College so that she can be closer to home. She hates her job taking care of Valia, Lena's grandmother, who has become very disagreeable because she is homesick for her native Greece. Carmen also worries that Win, the boy she likes, has the false impression that she is a good person. Bridget spends her summer coaching at a soccer camp in Pennsylvania where she is surprised to discover that one of the coaches is Eric with whom she had a relationship two summers earlier in California. Still strongly drawn to him, but trying to be more sensible, she and Eric become friends and he nurses her through an illness. It is an eventful summer as Carmen and Win frantically drive to Downington, Pennsylvania, to bring David back to Bethesda for his son's early birth and Carmen discovers that she loves her baby brother and want to go to Williams. Valia is happy that she can return to Greece, and Lena receives the RSID scholarship and her father's approval. Tibby overcomes her feelings of unworthiness by climbing out of her window and down the apple tree and being Carmen's mother's successful, albeit unorthodox, birth coach. It is then that she is able to get back together with Brian. And, Eric tells Bridget that he has broken up with his girlfriend, and they profess how much they care for each other. Readers of the initial book in this series will be aware of the mixed heritages of Carmen, Bridget, and Eric.
Dutch/European-American
Older; Fiction

Brashares, Ann. *The Second Summer of the Sisterhood*. New York: Delacorte Press, 2003. 384 p. (Sisterhood of the Traveling Pants)

This second book of the series describes Carmen, Lena, Bridget, and Tibby's experiences during the summer before their seventeenth birthdays. Once again, the pants are passed among them, but they no longer fit Bridget, who has been so down because of her earlier sexual relationship with Eric, that she has gained weight, given up soccer, and dyed her pretty blonde hair. Using a fake name, Bridget travels to Alabama where she gets a job cleaning her grandmother Greta's attic and finds mementos of her deceased mother. As the summer progresses Bridget gets back in shape, is able to wear the pants, confesses her identity to Greta and to her long ago best friend Billy, coaches and then stars for Billy's soccer team, and realizes that Greta is like a mother to her. Tibby goes to a film program at a college in Virginia. Befriending two shallow classmates, she produces a highly embarrassing film about her mother and is excruciated when her mother comes to the viewing. Upset by the damage she has done to her relationships with her mother and Brian, a friend of hers and Bailey's, she redeems herself by making a moving film about Bailey, who died from cancer. Both Carmen and Lena also experience strained relationships with their mothers. Carmen is jealous of her mother's romance with David, sabotages it, and then manages to restore it. Lena pesters her mother about the man Eugene in her mother's past and regrets that she has broken off with Kostas. When Kostas visits her, she discovers that he

really is in love with her. However, going to Greece for her beloved grandfather's funeral, Lena finds out that Kostas has had to marry a Greek woman whom he impregnated. Fortunately, she learns about Eugene from her mother and is attracted to Carmen's stepbrother Paul. The story ends when the girls' mothers, who had not been close since Bridget's mother's death, resume their friendship. The mixed heritages of Carmen, Bridget, and Eric were revealed in *The Sisterhood of the Traveling Pants*.
Dutch/European-American
Older; Fiction

Brashares, Ann. *The Sisterhood of the Traveling Pants*. New York: Delacorte Press, 2001. 304 p. (Sisterhood of the Traveling Pants)

In this initial book of the series, four girls who are almost sixteen discover that a pair of blue jeans that Carmen had purchased at a thrift shop somehow fits all of them. Close friends their entire lives, the girls establish a Sisterhood in which they will pass the pants among each other as they separate during their summer vacation. Bridget, an athlete whose father is Dutch and whose mother had committed suicide, goes to a soccer camp in Baja, California, where she shines as a player. She is strongly attracted to camp coach Eric whose mother is Mexican, loses her virginity to him, and then becomes confused and upset. Carmen, who had been looking forward to a vacation with her divorced father in South Carolina, is shocked to learn that he is engaged and is living with his fiancée and her two children. Ignored and treated like an outsider because of her Puerto Rican appearance, Carmen finally becomes so frustrated and angry that she throws a rock through the house window and runs away back to Bethesda, Maryland. Lena, a beautiful introverted girl, goes with her sister to stay in Greece with her grandparents. Enjoying painting the lovely scenery, she inadvertently leads her grandparents to believe she has been raped by Kostas, a family friend, and causes a fight between their grandfathers. Tibby, who remains at home, gets a tedious job at a drugstore and becomes friends with Bailey, a twelve-year-old girl who has leukemia and with whom she films a movie. The pants seem to have no positive effect on the girls' experiences until the end of the summer. Then Lena gets the courage to apologize to Kostas and tell him she loves him; Carmen gets the courage to go to her father's wedding after telling him that she is mad at him; Tibby gets the courage to visit Bailey in the hospital when she is dying; and Bridget receives the support she needs from the pants (and Lena who brings them to her).
Dutch/European-American
Older; Fiction

Charbonneau, Eileen. *In the Time of the Wolves*. New York: Tor-Doherty Associates, 1994. 192 p.

This story focuses on Josh Woods, the teenaged son of Asher Woods and Ginny Rockwell whose story began in the book *The Ghosts of Stony Clove*. It is now 1824 and Josh is greatly upset by his father who is part Indian and whose strange ways he finds disturbing. Josh wants to get away from the Catskills where he feels like an outsider, but his father opposes his going to Harvard. Josh is then befriended by Rebecca Elliott, who is a daughter of the Chase family which abused Asher when he was its bound servant. She supports Josh's getting a higher education and encourages his animosity towards his father. When Asher accepts the prediction of his Catholic friend Quinn and urges others to prepare for a year without summer, the neighbors at first reject his advice and, then, when there are summer frosts and snowstorms, blame him for their misfortunes. They also suspend Josh's mother from attending Congregational church services because she danced with her husband at a wake for Quinn. Josh accepts Rebecca's negative view of his parents and runs away with her. However, when he discovers that Rebecca and her relatives are seeking to take away his mother's inheritance and place his siblings in their custody, he realizes that he has been played for a dupe. Returning home he saves his father from a rabid gray wolf.

European-French-American, Mohican, and Wiechquaesgeck (Wiekagjock)/Dutch-English-American
Older; Fiction

Hausman, Gerald. *Night Flight*. New York: Philomel Books, 1996. 144 p.

Set in the summer of 1957, this is the story of two twelve-year-old boys: Max, who is incredibly cruel and controlling, and Jeff, who always tries to please him. When the boys' dogs as well as many others are poisoned, Max, whose father had been a Nazi, decides that Jews, whom he hates, are the culprits. Jeff, who had previously ignored his own Jewish heritage, struggles with Max's extreme views and actions, but, egged on by Max, shoots a dart into a Jewish family's front door. Jeff finally comes to realize what Max is—and what he himself can be.

Hungarian-Jewish/Dutch-English-Scottish-American and Iroquois and Methodist
Older; Fiction

Eastern European-American. See also Russian-American

Adoff, Jaime. *Names Will Never Hurt Me*. New York: Dutton Children's Books, 2004. 192 p.

This story takes place on the first anniversary of the killing of a student in a suburban high school. It focuses on four students: Kurt, a "freak" who is subjected to constant student harassment; Mark, who gains power over other students and is the school snitch; Ryan, the popular star quarterback, who is abused by his father; and Tisha, the unpopular biracial girl. In a setting where adults are for the most part oblivious to the potentially explosive feelings of the first three, it is Ryan's father who provides the explosives, Ryan who confronts his father with a gun, Mark whose scheming fails, Tisha who displays her bravery, and Kurt who may have been ready to unleash his hatred, but instead becomes a hero.

Eastern European-American/West African-American
Older; Fiction

English-American

See   Banneker, Benjamin
       Beckwourth, James (Jim) Pierson
       Berry, Halle Maria
       Bosomworth, Mary Musgrove Matthews?
       Bruchac, Joseph
       Dandridge, Dorothy
       Dorris, Michael

Early, Sarah Jane Woodson
Hughes, James Mercer Langston
Hemings, Beverly
Hemings, Harriet
Hemings, John
Hemings, Sally
Jefferson. Thomas
Mehta, Nina
Obama, Barack
Rogers, Will, Jr.?
Rogers, William (Will) Penn Adair?
Rolfe, Thomas
Ronstadt, Linda
Tinker, Clarence Leonard
Williams, William Carlos
Woodson, Lewis?

Benedict, Helen. *The Opposite of Love*. New York: Viking, 2007. 304 p.

In this novel for older teenagers, seventeen-year-old Madge lives with her English mother, an illegal immigrant who has been imprisoned and disappears for stretches at a time. Half white and half black, Madge feels like an outcast in her Pennsylvania town where she encounters blatant racism, but is supported by her aunt and a core of friends, including Kishna, her Indian best friend with whom she has her first love affair. On visits to her cousin in New York City, Madge encounters a neglected four-year-old black boy, who doesn't want to return to the apartment where he lives. Aware of the terrible mistreatment of some children in foster care, compassionate Madge takes him home with her. The story presents the complex consequences of Madge's action and the legal and ethical questions which she faces.
Jamaican/English
Older; Fiction

Bode, Janet. *Different Worlds: Interracial and Cross-Cultural Dating*. New York: Franklin Watts, 1989. 128 p.

Based primarily on interviews with six teenage couples who are dating interracially and/or cross-culturally, this book is written for and about teens. It looks at the history of prejudice and racism; discusses negative reactions of parents, relatives, and classmates; examines why adolescents make their dating choices; and mentions some positive aspects of interracial dating. Although it does not cover the topics of interracial marriage and families, four of the twelve teens interviewed are of mixed race or heritage: African-American/European-American; Protestant English-American/Catholic Irish-American; Cuban/Puerto Rican; and Mexican-Spanish-American. A bibliography, a listing of resource organizations, and an index are included.
English-American Protestant/Irish-American Catholic
Older; Nonfiction

Carvell, Marlene. *Who Will Tell My Brother?* New York: Hyperion Books for Children, 2002. 160 p.

Written in free verse, this fictionalized story is based on a true experience. High school senior Evan, who looks like his English-American mother, has come to value the Mohawk part of his family. Upset by his school's tasteless Indian mascot, he pursues his older brother's earlier effort to have it changed. Persistent, Evan goes to the principal, to the school newspaper office, and repeatedly to the school board to stress the injustice it does to Native Americans. As a result he is cruelly taunted, his brother's dog is killed, and the school board passes a resolution proclaiming the Indian as a permanent mascot. However, in the process Evan gains a group of supportive friends who express their disapproval of the intolerance.
Mohawk and French Canadian-American/English-American
Older; Fiction

Charbonneau, Eileen. *In the Time of the Wolves.* New York: Tor-Doherty Associates, 1994. 192 p.

This story focuses on Josh Woods, the teenaged son of Asher Woods and Ginny Rockwell whose story began in the book *The Ghosts of Stony Clove.* It is now 1824 and Josh is greatly upset by his father who is part Indian and whose strange ways he finds disturbing. Josh wants to get away from the Catskills where he feels like an outsider, but his father opposes his going to Harvard. Josh is then befriended by Rebecca Elliott, who is a daughter of the Chase family which abused Asher when he was its bound servant. She supports Josh's getting a higher education and encourages his animosity towards his father. When Asher accepts the prediction of his Catholic friend Quinn and urges others to prepare for a year without summer, the neighbors at first reject his advice and, then, when there are summer frosts and snowstorms, blame him for their misfortunes. They also suspend Josh's mother from attending Congregational church services because she danced with her husband at a wake for Quinn. Josh accepts Rebecca's negative view of his parents and runs away with her. However, when he discovers that Rebecca and her relatives are seeking to take away his mother's inheritance and place his siblings in their custody, he realizes that he has been played for a dupe. Returning home he saves his father from a rabid gray wolf.
European-French-American, Mohican, and Wiechquaesgeck (Wiekagjock)/Dutch-English-American
Older; Fiction

Curry, Jane Louise. *The Black Canary.* New York: Margaret K. McElderry Books, 2005. 288 p.

When almost-thirteen-year-old James visits London with his parents, he passes into the London of 1600 where he is snatched off the street to become a member of the Children of the Chapel Royal, who are actors and members of the queen's chapel choir. Since he was small, James has resented music since he blames the musical careers of his parents for their absences. Always feeling invisible, including when his relatives, both black and Caucasian, assume he is like them, James as one of the Children discovers that he loves to sing, for in singing he recognizes who he can be. James must decide whether he wishes to perform as a singer before Queen Elizabeth I or return to his family—if he can get back.
English-American/African-American
Intermediate, Older; Fiction

Hausman, Gerald. *Night Flight*. New York: Philomel Books, 1996. 144 p.

Set in the summer of 1957, this is the story of two twelve-year-old boys: Max, who is incredibly cruel and controlling, and Jeff, who always tries to please him. When the boys' dogs as well as many others are poisoned, Max, whose father had been a Nazi, decides that Jews, whom he hates, are the culprits. Jeff, who had previously ignored his own Jewish heritage, struggles with Max's extreme views and actions, but, egged on by Max, shoots a dart into a Jewish family's front door. Jeff finally comes to realize what Max is—and what he himself can be.
Hungarian-Jewish/Dutch-English-Scottish-American and Iroquois and Methodist
Older; Fiction

Ketchum, Liza. *Where the Great Hawk Flies*. New York: Clarion Books, 2005. 272 p.

In 1780 during the Revolutionary War the British brought Caughnawaga Indians from Canada to raid the colonists living in Vermont. During the raid Daniel, his little sister, and their mother, a Pequot-Mohegan, hid in a cave while his English father served in the militia called up to chase the raiders. During the same raid Hiram was snatched by the Indians and then released and his Uncle Abner was captured and imprisoned in Canada. This story starts two years later when eleven-year-old Hiram and his family move to the property near thirteen-year-old Daniel's. Hiram is both scared of and antagonistic to Daniel and his family, and Daniel resents Hiram's derogatory remarks about Indians. The situation is compounded when Daniel's medicine man grandfather moves in with Daniel's family and builds a wigwam on the property and when Uncle Abner returns to Hiram's family. After some harrowing events Daniel and Hiram become friends. Mr. Sikes, one of the neighbors in this book, is Abenaki and French-American.
English/Pequot and Mohegan
Intermediate, Older; Fiction

Kuklin, Susan. *Families*. Photographs by author. New York: Hyperion Books for Children, 2006. 40 p.

Text and color photographs present interviews with American children, who talk about their families. Their families include seven families with children of mixed race, ethnicity, or religion, with one also including a child adopted from Sierra Leone. In an eighth family a child has been adopted from China. In a ninth family an adopted American child is of a race different from that of one of her fathers.
English-German-American/Ecuadorian
Primary, Intermediate; Nonfiction

Lacapa, Kathleen, and Michael Lacapa. *Less than Half, More than Whole*. Illustrated by Michael Lacapa. Flagstaff, Ariz.: Northland Publishing, 1994. 40 p.

This picture book is based on the author's family. Tony, who does not look like either his Caucasian or his Indian friend, is bothered about being called less than half and seeks understanding from his maternal grandmother, his older siblings, his uncle, and his paternal grandfather. It is when he realizes the meaning of an ear of corn that Tony knows that in truth he is more than whole. Designs from different Native American cultures complement the book's paintings.

Apache, Hopi, and Tewa/English-Irish-American and Mohawk
Primary, Intermediate; Fiction

Landau, Elaine. *Interracial Dating and Marriage*. New York: Julian Messner, 1993. 112 p.

This book's introduction presents two detailed histories of interracial marriage: the first of African-American intermarriage with Caucasians and the second of intermarriages involving Japanese-Americans. In both cases the introduction describes factors, including governmental actions and societal attitudes, which affected the frequency of these marriages. The bulk of the book presents interviews with ten teenagers and five adults or adult couples who describe their views of and/or experiences with interracial dating and marriage. Seven of the teens interviewed came to the United States from other countries; two of the teens are interracial. Two of the adult interviews are with interracial couples; another contains advice from a minister. A resource list and an index are included.
African-English-Indian-Italian-Dominican
Older; Nonfiction

Lisle, Janet Taylor. *The Crying Rocks*. New York: Atheneum Books for Young Readers, 2003. 208 p. (A Richard Jackson Book)

Thirteen-year-old Joelle, who was adopted at the age of five by Vern and Aunt Mary Louise, does not look like anyone she knows in Rhode Island. She is upset by what she is told of her past: of being thrown out of a Chicago apartment window by her mother, being put in an orphanage there, traveling by freight train to Connecticut, and then being cared for by an old woman while living in a wooden crate near a railway depot. Joelle is befriended by an adoring eight-year-old girl who is European- and Japanese-American and by a classmate Carlos, who is of mixed heritage. Together Joelle and Carlos learn of the early Narragansett Indians and explore the wooded area, including the Crying Rocks, where they lived. Carlos learns the truth about the accident at the Crying Rocks where his older brother died and Joelle learns the truth about her background. Vern is her real father, her mother was Narragansett, and both her mother and twin sister died in Chicago.
Colombian-English-Spanish-American and Sioux/European-American
Intermediate, Older; Fiction

McKissack. Patricia C. *Run Away Home*. New York: Scholastic Press, 1997. 176 p.

In 1888 Sky, a fifteen-year-old Chiricahua Apache boy, escapes from a train of Apache prisoners and hides on the farm of twelve-year-old Sarah Jane Crossman, her African-American father, and her mother, who is of African-Scottish-Irish and Seminole heritage. George Wrattan, an Army scout and interpreter, allows the Crossmans to keep Sky with them until he recovers from his swamp fever. In the meantime boll weevils destroy the family's cotton crop, night riders come to their farm, and Sarah Jane's father, who is skilled as a carpenter, gets an order from Booker T. Washington to build desks for nearby Tuskegee Institute. Sky becomes healthy, but Wrattan, whose wife is Apache, gives permission for him to remain on the farm.
English-French-Swedish-American
Intermediate, Older; Fiction

Meyer, Carolyn. *Jubilee Journey*. San Diego: Gulliver Books, 1997. 288 p.

In this sequel to *White Lilacs*, it is 1996 and eighty-seven-year-old Rose Lee has invited her thirteen-year-old great-granddaughter Emily Rose and her family to attend the Freedomtown Juneteenth Diamond Jubilee. Growing up in Connecticut, Emily Rose has always regarded herself as a "double" as her father is French-American and her mother is African-American. However, she and her brothers Steven and Robbie have no idea what it means to be black in Dillon, Texas. They quickly learn of the attitudes of some whites when Steven is set up and abused and of the closeness and pride of the African-American community. In this story Rose Lee reveals what has happened to her and her family during the past seventy-five years. Emily Rose gets a new friend who thinks she should be just black and decides to remain in Denton to learn more about being black so she can better understand herself. Alicia, Rose Lee's best friend in Connecticut, has a Nigerian father and an English mother.
Nigerian/English
Intermediate, Older; Fiction

Moore, Robin. *Maggie among the Seneca*. New York: J. B. Lippincott, 1990. 112 p.

Sixteen-year-old Maggie, who is Irish, is kidnapped in 1778 by the Seneca and taken from central Pennsylvania to the Senecan village on the Genesee River. Staying at first with two Senecan women, Maggie then goes to live with Frenchgirl, who, kidnapped at an early age, is French and English, but now regards herself as Senecan. Maggie agrees to marry Frenchgirl's brother so she can go on a hunting trip to the Allegheny River and escape from there to her aunt's. However, when Maggie's husband dies, she stays to tend his burial scaffold. Maggie has a baby, survives the destruction of the village by the colonial army, and then goes to live with her aunt. The book is the sequel to *The Bread Sister of Sinking Creek*.
French-English-American and Senecan/Irish-American
Intermediate, Older; Fiction

Pearce, Jonathan. *John-Browne's Body & Sole: A Semester of Life*. Stockton, Calif.: Balona Books, 2005. 168 p.

This book is presented as a journal written by thirteen-year-old Jack for a language arts assignment. It tells how he and the two other boys who are involved in an altercation learn how aikido (a martial art) and scripting can be used to prevent fighting and teach respect. In writing of his experiences, Jack expresses his feelings about his family, his friends, racism (his grandmother is Japanese), his piano recital, and his mother's terminal cancer.
Japanese-English-French-North African-Russian-European-American/European-American
Older; Fiction

Rees, Celia. *Sorceress*. Cambridge, Mass.: Candlewick Press, 2003. 352 p.

Agnes, an eighteen-year-old Mohawk college student, decides to help a researcher who is trying to learn the fate of Mary Newbury, an English girl forced to flee from her Puritan settlement because she was accused of practicing witchcraft. Agnes feels a strange connection to Mary, who may be the medicine woman whose story has been carried down in her family. Visiting her aunt on her Mohawk reservation, Agnes is transported back to the 1600s where she experiences Mary's life. Mary marries

Jaybird, a Pennacook Indian, and bears two children: a daughter, who is murdered as a child by the English, and a son, Black Fox, who becomes a warrior. Mary saves Ephraim, an eleven-year-old white boy injured in an Indian attack, and raises him as her son. When she, Black Fox, and Ephraim visit Mount Royale to trade furs, Mary is captured by a Frenchman and then rescued by her two sons. Fleeing from their pursuers, they end up living in a Mohawk village where Mary is able to stem a smallpox epidemic. The author relates Mary's earlier story in the book *Witch Child*.
Pennacook (Pentucket)/English; Mohawk/Mohawk, Pennacook (Pentucket) and English-American
Older; Fiction

Resau, Laura. *Red Glass*. New York: Delacorte Press, 2007. 304 p.

This novel details the transformation of Sophie from Sophie la Delicada (the Delicate whose life is restricted by allergies, worries, and fears) into Sophie la Fuerte (the Strong, who undertakes and completes a very dangerous journey). Sixteen-year-old Sophie lives in Tucson with her English mother, her Mexican stepfather, and her great-aunt Dika, a Bosnian refugee. Then the family takes in five-year-old Pablo whose parents have died as his family tried to escape from Mexico. A year later, so that Pablo can see his relatives and decide where he wants to live, Sophie, Pablo, and Dika join Dika's boyfriend, Mr. Lorenzo, and his son Ángel, who are bound, via Mexico, for Guatemala to see whether Flor Blanca, their wife and mother, respectively, is alive and to find her jewels. The group spends a week in Pablo's Oaxaca village where Sophie and Ángel express their feelings for each other. Mr. Lorenzo and Ángel then go on to Guatemala, but are unable to return as Ángel is savagely attacked and their passports and money stolen. With Dika injured from a fall, Sophie travels by herself to Guatemala, a trip which is not at all safe, especially for a white girl. In Guatemala Ángel shares a hospital room with one of his attackers, Flor Blanca's fate is revealed, and Ángel decides whether to remain in Guatemala. Likewise, in Mexico Pablo decides whether he will stay there.
European-American/English
Older; Fiction

Stainer, M. L. *The Lyon's Crown*. Illustrated by James Melvin. Circleville, N.Y.: Chicken Soup Press, 2004. 176 p. (The Lyon Saga)

In this final book of *The Lyon Saga*, smallpox has come to Croatan Island and killed many residents, including Jess's Croatan husband Akaiyan and her English mother. Jess sends her three children away to Jamestown as Robert Ashbury, who has long loved her, has offered to provide sanctuary for them. Now in their early twenties and of mixed Croatan-English blood, the three must pretend to be English, adapt to English ways, and endure hostility towards "savages" from Virginian residents who have suffered Indian attacks. Suzanne/Oohah-ne falls in love with and marries Robert Ashbury's stepson, and William/Caun-reha adapts to life in Jamestown and Henrico, where they move. However, George/Wauh-kuaene suffers in the English environment until Jess comes to take him back to Croatan Island. This book tells of John Rolfe's work in cultivating tobacco for the English market and of his love for Pocahontas, who comes to Henrico, and accepts Christianity.
Croatan/English
Older; Fiction

Stainer, M. L. *The Lyon's Pride*. Illustrated by James Melvin. Circleville, N.Y.: Chicken Soup Press, 1998. 176 p. (The Lyon Saga)

The sequel to *The Lyon's Roar* and *The Lyon's Cub*, this book is part of *The Lyon Saga*, which relates a story of Jess Archarde and some of the other English settlers of the Lost Colony, who believing to be abandoned by their governor John White, move from Roanoke Island to live with the nearby Croatan Indians. In this book Jess helps lead some of the colonists who are leaving Croatan Island; marries Akaiyan, a Croatan; helps raise wolf cubs; has a baby, Oohahn-ne/Suzanne; mourns the death of her father; celebrates the marriage of Enrique, a former Spanish soldier, to a Croatan woman; and, again pregnant, hides when a pirate ship lands at Croatan Island.
Croatan/English
Older; Fiction

Stainer, M. L. *The Lyon's Throne*. Illustrated by James Melvin. Circleville, N.Y.: Chicken Soup Press, 1999. 168 p. (The Lyon Saga)

In this sequel to *The Lyon's Pride*, English Jess, her Croatan husband Akaiyan, their baby Oohahn-ne/Suzanne, Spanish Enrique, his Croatan wife Te-lah-tai, and other Croatan Indians are captured by pirates. When the pirate ship is sunk by an English vessel, they are all taken to England where their freedom is bought by John White, who had been the governor of the Lost Colony. This book tells of Jess's successful efforts to have Queen Elizabeth I free Enrique, who is imprisoned in the Tower of London, and send the group back to Croatan Island. During the story Jess gives birth to a baby Caun-reha/William when she is in the Queen's quarters, Te-lah-tai has a baby, Jess rejects an Englishman Robert Ashbury who falls in love with her, Robert gives her a magnificent white mare, and, upon their return, Jess has a third baby, Wauh-kuaene/George.
Croatan/English
Older; Fiction

Tenny, Dixie. *Call the Darkness Down*. New York: Atheneum, 1984. 204 p. (A Margaret K. McElderry Book)

Although for years Morfa has heard tales of Wales from Gwenfair, her Welsh mother, Gwenfair has refused to say anything about her parents and why she left her beloved Wales. When Morfa spends her freshman year at a Welsh college, she immediately becomes immersed in Welsh life: having Welsh friends, learning the Welsh language, and experiencing Welsh culture. She also has scary moments with a strange man in a dark coat and, pushed off a castle wall, narrowly escapes death. In this suspenseful story of the forces of light and dark, of mystical powers, and of spells, Morfa finally discovers the terrible truth about her family and must save her life from her murderous grandmother.
English-European-American/Welsh
Older; Fiction

Wright, Susan Kimmel. *The Secret of the Old Graveyard*. Scottdale, Pa.: Herald Press, 1993. 184 p.

At the same time that thirteen-year-old Nellie's parents are notified they are to go to Colombia to adopt the baby they've wanted, strange things start to happen at her family farm's old graveyard. This story tells of Nellie's worry about her parents traveling to Colombia, of her concerns as to how a baby

will affect her already offbeat family, of her exciting detective work with her friend Peggy to find whoever has vandalized the cemetery, and of her discoveries that the boy she has a crush on is adopted, is of mixed heritage—and likes her.
English-French-Irish-American
Intermediate, Older; Fiction

Zindel, Paul. *The Gadget*. New York: Laurel-Leaf Books, 2003. 192 p.

In 1944 when twelve-year-old Stephen is living in London with his English mother, he watches with horror as his cousin dies on a rooftop during a German air raid. The next March Stephen is sent to stay with his American father physicist at the secret town of Los Alamos. Upset that his father is consumed with developing a "gadget" and largely ignores him, Stephen spends time with a new older friend, Alexei Nagavatsky, and his family. Alexei and Stephen try to discover what is going on at Los Alamos. Stephen escapes an apparent attempted kidnapping while on a school trip to Santa Fe, and he and Alexei travel to Alamogordo where they witness the explosion of the first atomic bomb. It is after this that Stephen discovers that the Nagavatskys are spies and he is almost murdered. The story raises ethical questions about the dropping of the atomic bomb on Japan and includes both a chronology of World War II and the development of the bomb and a descriptive listing of those involved with the bomb's development and use.
European-American/English
Older; Fiction

Finnish-American

See   O'Brien, Daniel (Dan) Dion

French-American

See   Brown, Eve
Cruzatte, Pierre
Deloria, Ella Cara
Deloria, Phillip Samuel (Sam)
Deloria, Vine, Jr.
Deloria, Vine, Sr.
Dorris, Michael
Du Bois, William Edward Burghardt (W. E. B.)
Garreau, Antoine
Harjo, Joy
Hughes, James Mercer Langston
LaBiche, François
LaFlesche, Francis (Frank)
Picotte, Susan LaFlesche
Rillieux, Norbert

Tibbles, Susette LaFlesche
Williams, William Carlos

Bruchac, Joseph. *Fox Song*. Illustrated by Paul Morin. New York: Philomel Books, 1993, 32 p.

Missing her Abenaki great-grandmother who has just died, Jamie remembers their special times together in the nearby woods. Then, when Jamie sings the greeting song that her great-grandmother taught her, her great-grandmother's best friend, a fox, appears and Jamie understands that she will never be alone.
French-American/ Abenaki and French-American
Primary, Intermediate; Fiction

Charbonneau, Eileen. *The Ghosts of Stony Clove*. New York: Orchard Books, 1988. 160 p.

Building upon a ghost story of the Catskill Mountains and set in the early 1800s, this book tells of four years in the lives of Ginny Rockwell, who is Dutch-English-American, and Asher Woods, who is of mixed Native American and European-American heritage. When Ginny is almost twelve and Asher is fifteen, they go at night to the supposedly haunted Squire Sutherland's house where they encounter the squire, the servant girl he was said to have murdered fifty years earlier, a white dog, and a riderless horse. In this story of dreams, ghosts, cruelty, and goodness, Ginny comes to take care of the squire and inherit his property, while Asher, abused and persecuted because he is Indian, travels out west to find his family and then returns to marry Ginny. Their story is continued in the book, *In the Time of the Wolves*.
French-American and Wiechquaesgeck (Wiekagjock)/ European-American and Mohican
Older; Fiction

Charbonneau, Eileen. *In the Time of the Wolves*. New York: Tor-Doherty Associates, 1994. 192 p.

This story focuses on Josh Woods, the teenaged son of Asher Woods and Ginny Rockwell whose story began in the book *The Ghosts of Stony Clove*. It is now 1824 and Josh is greatly upset by his father who is part Indian and whose strange ways he finds disturbing. Josh wants to get away from the Catskills where he feels like an outsider, but his father opposes his going to Harvard. Josh is then befriended by Rebecca Elliott, who is a daughter of the Chase family which abused Asher when he was its bound servant. She supports Josh's getting a higher education and encourages his animosity towards his father. When Asher accepts the prediction of his Catholic friend Quinn and urges others to prepare for a year without summer, the neighbors at first reject his advice and, then, when there are summer frosts and snowstorms, blame him for their misfortunes. They also suspend Josh's mother from attending Congregational church services because she danced with her husband at a wake for Quinn. Josh accepts Rebecca's negative view of his parents and runs away with her. However, when he discovers that Rebecca and her relatives are seeking to take away his mother's inheritance and place his siblings in their custody, he realizes that he has been played for a dupe. Returning home he saves his father from a rabid gray wolf.
European-French-American, Mohican, and Wiechquaesgeck (Wiekagjock)/Dutch-English-American
Older; Fiction

Duey, Kathleen. *Celou Sudden Shout, Wind River, 1826*. New York: Aladdin Paperbacks, 1998. 160 p. (American Diaries)

With a French fur trapper father and a Shoshone mother, twelve-year-old Celou is well aware of the differing beliefs and customs of the two cultures. When her father is away for a rendevous, Crows kidnap her mother and two younger brothers. Celou rides for help to the Shoshone big camp, only to discover that it has been attacked by Blackfoot. Drawing upon what she has learned from both parents, she then stealthily follows the Crows and, with bravery and ingenuity, rescues her family and saves herself.
French-American/Shoshone
Intermediate, Older; Fiction

Highwater, Jamake. *The Ceremony of Innocence*. New York: Harper & Row, Publishers, 1985. 192 p. (The Ghost Horse Cycle)

The Ceremony of Innocence is the second book in *The Ghost Horse Cycle*, a series for teenagers. It is the sequel to *Legend Days*, which describes Amana's childhood experiences as a Blood (Blackfoot). In this book Amana, whose family has died, has left her people and is destitute. She comes to live with an immature French Canadian, who deserts her before the birth of their daughter Jemina. Although sustained by her friendship with a French-Cree woman who runs a brothel, Amana suffers when Jemina grows up obsessed with finery and is married to the drunkard Jamie Ghost Horse and when her older grandson is only interested in things "American." Amana's hope lies in Sitko, her younger grandson, who treasures his Native American heritage.
French/Cree
Older; Fiction

Hollyer, Belinda, selector. *The Kingfisher Book of Family Poems*. Illustrated by Holly Swain. New York: Kingfisher, 2003. 224 p.

This collection of poems about families includes the short poem "Face It" by Janet S. Wong about a girl who has features of her Chinese and French ancestors—and of herself.
Chinese and French
Primary, Intermediate; Fiction

Ketchum, Liza. *Where the Great Hawk Flies*. New York: Clarion Books, 2005. 272 p.

In 1780 during the Revolutionary War the British brought Caughnawaga Indians from Canada to raid the colonists living in Vermont. During the raid Daniel, his little sister, and their mother, a Pequot-Mohegan, hid in a cave while his English father served in the militia called up to chase the raiders. During the same raid Hiram was snatched by the Indians and then released and his Uncle Abner was captured and imprisoned in Canada. This story starts two years later when eleven-year-old Hiram and his family move to the property near thirteen-year-old Daniel's. Hiram is both scared of and antagonistic to Daniel and his family, and Daniel resents Hiram's derogatory remarks about Indians. The situation is compounded when Daniel's medicine man grandfather moves in with Daniel's family and builds a wigwam on the property and when Uncle Abner returns to Hiram's family. After some harrowing events Daniel and Hiram become friends. Mr. Sikes, one of the neighbors in this book, is Abenaki and French-American.

French-American and Abenaki
Intermediate, Older; Fiction

Lewin, Michael Z. *Cutting Loose*. New York: Henry Holt and Company, 1999. 528 p.

Set in the nineteenth century, this is the story of Jackie's search for Teddy Zeph, who has murdered Jackie's best friend, Nance. The text alternates betweem the present and the past, starting with the story of Jackie's grandmother Claudette at the time she was orphaned. There are parallels among the characters' lives. Claudette is sold at a pauper auction, Jackie's father Matthew is sold by his New York City baseball team to a team in St. Louis, and Jackie goes to live with a new family that chooses her when she is displayed by the Children's Aid Society. Claudette murders her lover's father, and Matthew and Nance are murdered. Claudette disguises herself as a man to escape capture, and Jackie disguises herself as a man to pursue a baseball career. Both Jackie and her father play baseball in England as well as in the United States. Nance performs for Buffalo Bill's Wild West Show, and Jackie and Teddy Zeph perform on the stage in London. Further, Claudette's father is French, Teddy's mother is Spanish, and Nance, whose mother is African-American, passes as white.

French/European-American
Older; Fiction

McKissack, Patricia C. *Run Away Home*. New York: Scholastic Press, 1997. 176 p.

In 1888 Sky, a fifteen-year-old Chiricahua Apache boy, escapes from a train of Apache prisoners and hides on the farm of twelve-year-old Sarah Jane Crossman, her African-American father, and her mother, who is of African-Scottish-Irish and Seminole heritage. George Wrattan, an Army scout and interpreter, allows the Crossmans to keep Sky with them until he recovers from his swamp fever. In the meantime boll weevils destroy the family's cotton crop, night riders come to their farm, and Sarah Jane's father, who is skilled as a carpenter, gets an order from Booker T. Washington to build desks for nearby Tuskegee Institute. Sky becomes healthy, but Wrattan, whose wife is Apache, gives permission for him to remain on the farm.

English-French-Swedish-American
Intermediate, Older; Fiction

Meyer, Carolyn. *Jubilee Journey*. San Diego: Gulliver Books, 1997. 288 p.

In this sequel to *White Lilacs*, it is 1996 and eighty-seven-year-old Rose Lee has invited her thirteen-year-old great-granddaughter Emily Rose and her family to attend the Freedomtown Juneteenth Diamond Jubilee. Growing up in Connecticut, Emily Rose has always regarded herself as a "double" as her father is French-American and her mother is African-American. However, she and her brothers Steven and Robbie have no idea what it means to be black in Dillon, Texas. They quickly learn of the attitudes of some whites when Steven is set up and abused and of the closeness and pride of the African-American community. In this story Rose Lee reveals what has happened to her and her family during the past seventy-five years. Emily Rose gets a new friend who thinks she should be just black and decides to remain in Denton to learn more about being black so she can better understand herself. Alicia, Rose Lee's best friend in Connecticut, has a Nigerian father and an English mother.

French-American and Catholic/African-European-American, Seminole, and Baptist
Intermediate, Older; Fiction

Moore, Robin. *Maggie among the Seneca*. New York: J. B. Lippincott, 1990. 112 p.

Sixteen-year-old Maggie, who is Irish, is kidnapped in 1778 by the Seneca and taken from central Pennsylvania to the Senecan village on the Genesee River. Staying at first with two Senecan women, Maggie then goes to live with Frenchgirl, who, kidnapped at an early age, is French and English, but now regards herself as Senecan. Maggie agrees to marry Frenchgirl's brother so she can go on a hunting trip to the Allegheny River and escape from there to her aunt's. However, when Maggie's husband dies, she stays to tend his burial scaffold. Maggie has a baby, survives the destruction of the village by the colonial army, and then goes to live with her aunt. The book is the sequel to *The Bread Sister of Sinking Creek.*
French-English-American and Senecan/Irish-American
Intermediate, Older; Fiction

Pearce, Jonathan. *John-Browne's Body & Sole: A Semester of Life*. Stockton, Calif.: Balona Books, 2005. 168 p.

This book is presented as a journal written by thirteen-year-old Jack for a language arts assignment. It tells how he and the two other boys who are involved in an altercation learn how aikido (a martial art) and scripting can be used to prevent fighting and teach respect. In writing of his experiences, Jack expresses his feelings about his family, his friends, racism (his grandmother is Japanese), his piano recital, and his mother's terminal cancer.
Japanese-English-French-North African-Russian-European-American/European-American
Older; Fiction

Peck, Richard. *The River Between Us*. New York: Dial Books, 2003. 176 p.

Set at the beginning of the Civil War, this book tells how the life of fifteen-year-old Tilly and her family changes when two mysterious strangers, Delphine and her apparent servant Calinda, arrive via steamboat at Grand Tower, Illinois. Coming from New Orleans, Delphine with her elegant clothes and fancy ways is like no one the town has ever seen. The two stay with Tilly's family, and Tilly's twin brother Noah falls in love with Delphine. When now-sixteen Noah goes off to join the Yankee army, their mother is so upset, since her husband had earlier left her, that she sends Tilly and Delphine off to Cairo, Illinois, to bring Noah home. The book tells of the horrible living conditions in Cairo and especially of the unsanitary hospital tents. Noah, who suffers from dysentery, recovers enough that he is sent off to fight in the nearby battle of Belmont, Missouri, in which he is wounded and has to have his left arm amputated. The two girls stay in Cairo tending to Noah and other soldiers, and upon their return home with Noah learn that Tilly's distraught mother, seeing the coffin of her husband which she mistook for Noah's, drowned herself in the river. The story also reveals that to Tilly's surprise Delphine and Calinda are sisters and that Delphine's father is indeed the wealthy Jules Duval, but that he is her mother's protector, not her husband as in New Orleans whites cannot marry Creoles. Following the war Calinda, a conjure woman, leaves Grand Tower so that she will not raise suspicion that Delphine has African blood. Although Delphine refuses to marry a white man, she and Noah live

as husband and wife, but their son is passed off as the son of Tilly and her husband.
Creole (African-French-Spanish)-Haitian-American
Older; Nonfiction

Raphael, Marie. *Streets of Gold: A Novel*. New York: Persea Books, 2001. 224 p.

Set at the turn of the twentieth century and illustrated with period photographs, this is the story of almost fourteen-year-old Marisia, who with her parents, two brothers and little sister must flee their Polish home because her older brother Stefan, who was conscripted into the Russian army, deserted and is in danger. The book tells of the family's escape from Poland, their arrival in Hamburg, and their transatlantic boat ride to New York City where they endure the discomforts of steerage and Marisia befriends Sofia, a beautiful Polish girl. Upon arrival at Ellis Island, immigrant authorities refuse to admit Marisia's little sister Katrina, who is showing signs of tuberculosis. Faced with the decision of staying, as Stefan must, in New York, Marisia chooses to remain and not return to Hamburg with her parents and her younger siblings. The book tells of Marisia's experiences as she serves as a maid in Sofia's family house, watches as Sofia's cruel father locks her in her room for refusing a prosperous suitor, rescues Sofia from a fire that injures her and disfigures Sofia, is depressed by Katrina's death, encounters a woman who sponsors her artistic pursuits, and produces posters that depict the assailants who attacked Stefan because of his union association. In the end, Sofia becomes engaged to Dr. Heinrich, a man of German and French heritage who had tended to the girls' burns, and Marisia's parents and younger brother arrive in New York.
German/French
Older; Fiction

Resau, Laura. *What the Moon Saw: A Novel*. New York: Delacorte Press, 2006. 272 p.

Fourteen-year-old Clara's life turns upside down when she leaves her suburban Maryland home to visit her grandparents in a remote village in Oaxaca, Mexico. There she stays in a cluster of huts without a telephone, TV, or computer, and it is there that she comes to love exploring the mountains, being with Pedro the neighbor boy, and with him finding the secret waterfall. It is also there that Clara hears the story of her grandmother's life and learns that, like her grandmother, she has a spirit animal (a heron) and is a healer.
Mixtec Mexican/French-Norwegian-Welsh-American
Older; Fiction

Sanders, Scott Russell. *Bad Man Ballad*. New ed. Bloomington, Ind.: Indiana University Press, 2004. 264 p. (The Library of Indiana Classics)

Set during the War of 1812, this story traces the involvement of three very different individuals, who become responsible for an incredibly strong and frightening giant known as Bear Walks. Ely discovers the body of an unscrupulous dwarf who has presumably been murdered by the giant outside the hut of Rain Hawk, who is French and Shawnee and, like Ely, an older teenager and an orphan. Ely and Owen, a lawyer who has come to the community from Philadelphia, are deputized by the town of Roma to hunt down the giant and return him for trial. They travel through Ohio and into Indiana where they discover the giant in an old Indian cave on the banks of the Ohio River. Bear Walks regards Ely

as his brother and follows him wherever he goes. Joined on the way back by Rain Hawk, the three realize that the dimwitted Bear Walks should not be prosecuted for murder. Upon their return to Roma where, as elsewhere, the giant is regarded as a terrifying freak, Owen is unable to convince the jury that Bear Walks murdered the dwarf in defense of Rain Hawk.
French/Shawnee
Older; Fiction

Savageau, Cheryl. *Muskrat Will Be Swimming*. Illustrated by Robert Hynes. Flagstaff, Ariz.: Northland Publishing, 1996. 32 p.
   Jeannie, who is of French and Indian heritage, loves the lake where she lives, but doesn't like the children at school calling her a Lake Rat. Her grandfather relates how he used to be called a Frog, but points out that being called an animal relative, a frog or a lake rat (a muskrat) shouldn't hurt one's feelings. He tells Jeanne the Seneca story of how Muskrat helped create the world, and Jeannie, like Muskrat, dives to the bottom of the lake to bring up some earth.
French-American and Native American
Primary, Intermediate; Fiction

Urban, Betsy. *Waiting for Deliverance*. New York: Orchard Books, 2000. 192 p.
   This book is set in 1793 in western New York where there is tension between the Americans and the Seneca, who supported the British during the Revolutionary War. Fourteen-year-old orphan Livy, who is terrified of Indians, is sold at a pauper's auction to Gideon, who was raised by Senecas and educated by Anglican Canadians, and whose Senecan brother Rising Hawk often stays with him and his wife. When Livy is sent to a Senecan village to help its women learn how to spin, she is suddenly accused of being a witch. After escaping with Rising Hawk, with whom she is often at odds, Livy discovers that she is in love with him. In this story Rising Hawk has a French ancestor.
Senecan/French and Senecan
Older; Fiction

Walter, Mildred Pitts. *Ray and the Best Family Reunion Ever*. New York: HarperCollins Publishers, 2002. 128 p.
   Eleven-year-old Ray is the only member of his Creole family with ebony skin. When he goes to a large family reunion in Natchitoches, Louisiana, Ray discovers that he and Gran-papa Philippe are the only ones there with dark skin. To make matter worse, Ray looks like his grandfather whom his father and almost all his relatives despise. This is the story of Ray's secret bonding with Gran-papa Philippe, his appreciation of his grandfather's talent, and his effecting a reconciliation between his father and Philippe.
Creole (Nigerian-French-Spanish-Native American)-Haitian-American/Creole (French-Spanish-West African-Native American)-American
Intermediate; Fiction

Williams, Laura E. *Slant*. Minneapolis: Milkweed Editions, 2008. 168 p.
   Thirteen-year-old Lauren and her five-year old Chinese sister live with their adoptive English

professor father in Connecticut. Their mother had died three years earlier, Lauren hates being called derogatory names by two classmates and even called "Slant" by Sean, the boy she has a crush on. She feels she can stop the abuse and be much happier by having surgery to change the shape of her Korean eyes. When Lauren discovers that her mother had committed suicide and that corrective surgery on her nose when she was thirteen had not stopped her depression, she decides against the surgery. Lauren discovers that she can stand up for herself, and she even gets Sean as a boyfriend.
French-German-Irish-American
Intermediate, Older; Fiction

Wong, Janet S. *Minn and Jake's Almost Terrible Summer*. Illustrated by Geneviève Côté. New York: Frances Foster Books. 2008. 112 p.

It is in this sequel to *Minn and Jake* that Jake's mixed heritage is revealed. Ten-year-old Jake, his Korean grandmother, his mother, and his little brother spend the summer in Los Angeles, his old hometown. Deliberately choosing to avoid planned activities, Jake discovers that his former friends want nothing to do with him after learning that his best friend in his new town is a lizard-catching girl, Minn. Further, he is embarrassed when Haylee, the girl he used to like, sees him coming out of the ladies' room in his mother's pink shirt and then later as he is attempting to get rid of ants in his clothes. When Minn visits Los Angeles, she is surprised to learn he is part Korean, is amused when tanning lotion makes him looks like a spotted hyena, is jealous of Haylee, and disapproves of his getting ahead of others at Disneyland by putting his grandmother in a wheelchair. It is only when he apologizes that his summer vacation improves.
French-German-American/South Korean-Norwegian-American
Intermediate; Fiction

Wong, Janet S. *The Next New Year*. Illustrated by Yangsook Choi. New York: Frances Foster Books/Farrar Straus and Giroux, 2000. 32 p

In this picture book a young American boy, who has a Chinese father and a Korean mother, prepares for Chinese New Year. His two best friends, who, like him, are of mixed heritage, will also celebrate the holiday.
French and German
Pre-K, Primary; Fiction

Wright, Susan Kimmel. *The Secret of the Old Graveyard*. Scottdale, Pa.: Herald Press, 1993. 184 p.

At the same time that thirteen-year-old Nellie's parents are notified they are to go to Colombia to adopt the baby they've wanted, strange things start to happen at her family farm's old graveyard. This story tells of Nellie's worry about her parents traveling to Colombia, of her concerns as to how a baby will affect her already offbeat family, of her exciting detective work with her friend Peggy to find whoever has vandalized the cemetery, and of her discoveries that the boy she has a crush on is adopted, is of mixed heritage—and likes her.
English-French-Irish-American
Intermediate, Older; Fiction

German-American

See   Cary, Mary Ann Shadd
       Depp, John (Johnny) Christopher II
       Erdrich, Louise
       Espinel, Luisa
       Grace, Princess of Monaco
       Jones, John
       Ronstadt, Linda
       Schomburg, Arthur Alfonso
       Shriver, Maria
       Tinker, Clarence Leonard

Adoff, Arnold. *All the Colors of the Race*. Illustrated by John Steptoe. New York: Lothrop, Lee & Shepard Books, 1982. 56 p.

Poems celebrate a girl who is Polish, German, Russian, and Jewish on her father's side and African-American and Protestant on her mother's. She looks forward to the time when we will cease *looking* at colors and *love* all colors of the human race.
Polish-German-Russian-American Jewish/African-American Protestant
Intermediate, Older; Fiction

Baskin, Nora Raleigh. *The Truth about My Bat Mitzvah*. New York: Simon & Schuster Books for Young Readers, 2008. 144 p.

Twelve-year-old Caroline's father is Christian and her mother is non-practicing Jewish. Caroline has never thought about being Jewish until her grandmother's death and receiving the Star of David necklace her grandmother had wanted her to have. She keeps the necklace a secret, learns about being Jewish from her best friend Rachel who is about to have a bat mitzvah celebration, and discovers that her great-grandparents, who came from a non-practicing Jewish German-American family, had objected to her grandfather's marriage to her Russian Jewish immigrant grandmother. Also, initially her grandparents had not been happy about her mother's marrying a non-Jew. Caroline comes to realize that she wants to be Jewish and that she doesn't need a bat mitzvah party to be a bat mitzvah.
European-American Christian/German-Russian-American Jewish
Intermediate; Fiction

Becker, John T., and Stanli K. Becker, eds. *All Blood Is Red . . . All Shadows Are Dark!* Illustrated by J. Howard Noel. Cleveland: Seven Shadows Press, 1984. 168 p.

John T. (Tom) Becker, who is Irish-German-American, and his wife, Stanli K. Becker, who is African-American, have five young children. Of the four who are adopted one is biracial. All seven family members are responsible for individual sections of this book, which recounts their personal and family experiences as a multiracial family. Teaching their children to be aware of and proud of their individual differences, the editors present information on the history of racial classification in the United States and advocate their belief that race is and should be regarded as an "absurdity."

Irish-German-American/African-American
Intermediate, Older; Nonfiction

Chocolate, Debbi. *Elizabeth's Wish*. Orange, N.J.: Just Us Books, 1994. 120 p. (NEATE)

Naimah, **E**lizabeth, **A**nthony, **T**ayesha, and **E**ddie are eighth-grade friends who call themselves NEATE. Together they work towards having rap and not heavy-metal music at their school dance, Tayesha struggles with her biracial identity, and Elizabeth wants to win the grand prize in a talent search. NEATE's efforts make it possible to have both a rap and a heavy-metal band at the dance. Tayesha stands up for herself, declaring to tormentors that she is just as black as they are, and Elizabeth, overcoming a sore throat and a sprained ankle, wins the contest and donates her prize money to a campaign to save a homeless shelter. This book is a sequel to *NEATE to the Rescue*.
African-American/German
Intermediate, Older; Fiction

Chocolate, Debbi. *NEATE to the Rescue*. Orange, N.J.: Just Us Books, 1992. 104 p. (NEATE)

When eighth-grader Naimah and her friends secretly try to help her mother be reelected to her newly re-districted city council seat, they unintentionally cause a disturbance at her opponent's rally. Grounded, Naimah concentrates on her own campaign for student council president, which she wins. She then comes up with an idea that, with the support of her friends, is a major factor in her mother's come-from-behind victory. One of Naimah's four friends is Tayesha, whose African-American father married her German mother when he was in the army in Germany.
African-American/German
Intermediate, Older; Fiction

Elkeles, Simone. *How to Ruin a Summer Vacation*. Woodbury, Minn.: Flux, 2006. 240 p.

Sixteen-year-old Amy's parents never married, and her Israeli father, now an American resident, has been largely absent from her life. When Amy has to go with him to Israel to meet his family, that know nothing about her existence, she is angry with her father, resentful about changing her summer vacation plans, and fearful about the safety of being in Israel. Overreactive Amy immediately likes her Israeli grandmother and her little Israeli cousin, but has to endure the hostility of the cousin with whom she rooms and eighteen-year-old Avi. She is constantly doing something wrong in their presence. It is not until the last part of her trip that Amy comes to appreciate her Israeli heritage, learns that her father had been rebuffed in his efforts to be with her, and falls in love with Avi.
German-Israeli Jewish/European-American non-Jewish
Older; Fiction

Ernst, Kathleen. *Highland Fling*. Chicago: Cricket Books, 2006. 224 p.

Exceedingly upset by her Polish-American father who had an extramarital affair, by moving from Wisconsin to North Carolina with her divorced mother and younger sister, and by the immersion of her mother and sister in everything to do with the Scottish MacDonald clan, fifteen-year-old Tanya reluctantly goes with them to the Highland Games. Longing to become an independent filmmaker, Tanya decides to make a documentary revealing the nostalgic pretense of the Highland Games. However, after

meeting a young bagpiper from Puerto Rico who has Scottish heritage, his grandmother, and a Highland Games woman athlete whose mixed heritage does not include Scottish forebears, Tanya decides to make a different documentary and to have a talk with her father.
German-Irish-Italian-Swedish-American
Older; Fiction

Jennings, Patrick. *Faith and the Electric Dogs*. Decorations by author. New York: Scholastic, 1996. 144 p.

The narrator—and author—of this fanciful tale is Edison, a mutt from San Cristóbal de las Casas, Mexico, who asserts that it is true. He is taken in by Faith, a ten-year-old homesick American girl, whose mother has married a Mexican and who hates Mexico because she can't speak Spanish and is teased. With help from a craftsman, Faith builds a rocket powered by pig fat and jalapeño peppers and sets off with Edison for San Francisco. Unfortunately, the rocket goes down in a storm. The two of them end up on an island in the Pacific Ocean, which is deserted except for four mutts and a seventy-year-old man who had come down on the island when he was ten after the balloon he was taking to return from Mexico to England was pierced by a seagull. The story concludes with Faith and Edison's return to Mexico, her happiness there, and an explanation of how Edison become a writer. Definitions of the many Spanish and Bowwow (canine) words used in the text are provided in the margins and also in a glossary.
Italian-American/German-Scottish-Irish-American
Intermediate; Fiction

Jennings, Patrick. *Faith and the Rocket Cat*. Decorations by author. New York: Scholastic Press, 1998. 240 p.

In this sequel to *Faith and the Electric Dogs*, Edison the mutt relates another fantastic story. When Faith, her mother, and her stepfather move to San Francisco, Faith wants to impress classmate Alex and Edison wishes to befriend Daphne, a whippet show dog, by taking them for a ride in Faith's rocket. Faith, Edison, Alex, Daphne—and Faith's mother—crash-land in Death Valley where they encounter coyotes and find Faith's late father's cat. All ends well in this story in which words presented in Bowwow and Arf (dog languages), Mew (cat language), Spanish, French, Italian, Chinese, Latin, and Turkish are defined both in the margins and in a glossary.
Italian-American/German-Scottish-Irish-American
Intermediate; Fiction

Kuklin, Susan. *Families*. Photographs by author. New York: Hyperion Books for Children, 2006. 40 p.

Text and color photographs present interviews with American children, who talk about their families. Their families include seven families with children of mixed race, ethnicity, or religion, with one also including a child adopted from Sierra Leone. In an eighth family a child has been adopted from China. In a ninth family an adopted American child is of a race different from that of one of her fathers.
German-Jewish-American and Mescalero Apache/African-American; English-German-American/

Ecuadorian; African-American/German
Primary, Intermediate; Nonfiction

MacGregor, Rob. *Hawk Moon*. New York: Simon & Schuster Books for Young Readers, 1996. 192 p.
    Hawk Moon is the sequel to *Prophecy Rock*. When Will returns to Aspen, Colorado, from the Hopi Reservation where he has spent the summer, he tells his girlfriend Myra that he thinks they should break up, but does not give her the chance to tell him what is bothering her. She disappears from the ghost town where he had left her, and Will becomes the prime target of the investigation into her kidnapping. This mystery has many twists and turns as Will comes to suspect classmates, his mother's boyfriend, and members of the sheriff's department. He is helped by Corey, a girl of mixed race who is a computer geek, and he experiences visions of Masau, the Hopi's kachina ruler.
Hopi/German-American
Older; Fiction

MacGregor, Rob. *Prophecy Rock*. New York: Laurel-Leaf Books, 1995. 208 p.
    When teenager Will goes to spend the summer with his father, who is chief of police on the Hopi reservation, he becomes involved in the investigation of two murders. It first appears that the murderer is a preacher, a Hopi who now condemns the Hopis and their prophecies. Suspicion then turns to whoever believes himself to be Pahana, the Elder White Brother, who is the expected Hopi savior. However, who is that person: the mixed race hospital worker, the white doctor, or the ethnologist, who is also white? As Will helps in solving this mystery, he falls for a Hopi girl, travels about the Arizona reservation, and learns of the Hopi culture.
Hopi/German-American
Older; Fiction

Nelson, Suzanne. *The Sound of Munich*. New York: Speak, 2006. 224 p. (S.A.S.S.: Students Across the Seven Seas)
    Californian Siena, who is into yoga and astrology, spends the spring semester of her junior year in Munich, Germany, as part of a study-abroad program. She is eager to learn about Germany, the homeland of her father who died when she was a baby, and to fulfill the last item on his carpe diem list: thank Peter Schwalm, the man who had enabled him and his parents to escape from East Berlin. The experience exceeds Siena's expectations as she makes two best friends, has a romance with her resident adviser, becomes immersed in German life, works hard to do well in her classes, and locates and meets Peter.
German/European-American
Older; Fiction

Raphael, Marie. *Streets of Gold: A Novel*. New York: Persea Books, 2001. 224 p.
    Set at the turn of the twentieth century and illustrated with period photographs, this is the story of almost fourteen-year-old Marisia, who with her parents, two brothers and little sister must flee their Polish home because her older brother Stefan, who was conscripted into the Russian army, deserted and is in danger. The book tells of the family's escape from Poland, their arrival in Hamburg, and their

transatlantic boat ride to New York City where they endure the discomforts of steerage and Marisia befriends Sofia, a beautiful Polish girl. Upon arrival at Ellis Island, immigrant authorities refuse to admit Marisia's little sister Katrina, who is showing signs of tuberculosis. Faced with the decision of staying, as Stefan must, in New York, Marisia chooses to remain and not return to Hamburg with her parents and her younger siblings. The book tells of Marisia's experiences as she serves as a maid in Sofia's family house, watches as Sofia's cruel father locks her in her room for refusing a prosperous suitor, rescues Sofia from a fire that injures her and disfigures Sofia, is depressed by Katrina's death, encounters a woman who sponsors her artistic pursuits, and produces posters that depict the assailants who attacked Stefan because of his union association. In the end, Sofia becomes engaged to Dr. Heinrich, a man of German and French heritage who had tended to the girls' burns, and Marisia's parents and younger brother arrive in New York.
German/French
Older; Fiction

Smith, Cynthia Leitich. *Rain Is Not My Indian Name*. New York: HarperCollins Publishers, 2001. 144 p.

Since her best friend Galen was killed in a traffic accident on New Year's Day (her birthday), fourteen-year-old Rain, who is of mixed race, has withdrawn from her friends and from going out into her small Kansas town. However, despite refusing to become a participant, she agrees early in the summer to take photographs of her aunt's Native American camp. Rain is upset with Galen's mother and her opposition to the camp and with her former second best friend African-American Queenie, who attends the camp although it is not discovered until later that she has a Seminole ancestor. Then, on the Fourth of July (Galen's birthday), Rain is ready to move beyond his death.
Irish-German-American and Ojibwa/Scottish-Irish-American, Cherokee, and Muskogee
Intermediate, Older; Fiction

Williams, Laura E. *Slant*. Minneapolis: Milkweed Editions, 2008. 168 p.

Thirteen-year-old Lauren and her five-year old Chinese sister live with their adoptive English professor father in Connecticut. Their mother had died three years earlier, Lauren hates being called derogatory names by two classmates and even called "Slant" by Sean, the boy she has a crush on. She feels she can stop the abuse and be much happier by having surgery to change the shape of her Korean eyes. When Lauren discovers that her mother had committed suicide and that corrective surgery on her nose when she was thirteen had not stopped her depression, she decides against the surgery. Lauren discovers that she can stand up for herself, and she even gets Sean as a boyfriend.
French-German-Irish-American
Intermediate, Older; Fiction

Wong, Janet S. *Minn and Jake's Almost Terrible Summer*. Illustrated by Geneviève Côté. New York: Frances Foster Books. 2008. 112 p.

It is in this sequel to *Minn and Jake* that Jake's mixed-heritage is revealed. Ten-year-old Jake, his Korean grandmother, his mother, and his little brother spend the summer in Los Angeles, his old hometown. Deliberately choosing to avoid planned activities, Jake discovers that his former friends

want nothing to do with him after learning that his best friend in his new town is a lizard-catching girl, Minn. Further, he is embarrassed when Haylee, the girl he used to like, sees him coming out of the ladies' room in his mother's pink shirt and then later as he is attempting to get rid of ants in his clothes. When Minn visits Los Angeles, she is surprised to learn he is part Korean, is amused when tanning lotion makes him looks like a spotted hyena, is jealous of Haylee, and disapproves of his getting ahead of others at Disneyland by putting his grandmother in a wheelchair. It is only when he apologizes that his summer vacation improves.
French-German-American/South Korean-Norwegian-American
Intermediate; Fiction

Wong, Janet S. *The Next New Year*. Illustrated by Yangsook Choi. New York: Frances Foster Books/Farrar Straus and Giroux, 2000. 32 p

In this picture book a young American boy, who has a Chinese father and a Korean mother, prepares for Chinese New Year. His two best friends, who, like him, are of mixed heritage, will also celebrate the holiday.
French and German
Pre-K, Primary; Fiction

Greek-American

Kuklin, Susan. *Families*. Photographs by author. New York: Hyperion Books for Children, 2006. 40 p.

Text and color photographs present interviews with American children, who talk about their families. Their families include seven families with children of mixed race, ethnicity, or religion, with one also including a child adopted from Sierra Leone. In an eighth family a child has been adopted from China. In a ninth family an adpted American child is of a race different from that of one of her fathers.
Greek-American/European-American
Primary, Intermediate; Nonfiction

Young, Karen Romano. *Cobwebs*. New York: Greenwillow Books, 2004. 400 p.

In this unusual story Nancy, a high school sophomore who as yet has no spider traits, is the daughter of part spider parents. Her father is a roofer who prefers living up high; her mother is a weaver who has to remain low; her Granny is a knitter and potter; and her Grandpa Joke is a doctor. Nancy's family becomes involved with Nico, a Greek-American journalist who blackmails Grandpa Joke into bringing Granny to heal his wife. In the process, Granny loses her life. The story focuses on the identities of the rumored Angel of Brooklyn and the Wound Healer, the growing attraction between Nancy and Niko's son Dion, and Nancy's concerns about whether she is or is not part spider.
Greek-American/Navajo
Older; Fiction

Hungarian-American

See   Prinze, Freddie James, Jr.

Hausman, Gerald. *Night Flight*. New York: Philomel Books, 1996. 144 p.

   Set in the summer of 1957, this is the story of two twelve-year-old boys: Max, who is incredibly cruel and controlling, and Jeff, who always tries to please him. When the boys' dogs as well as many others are poisoned, Max, whose father had been a Nazi, decides that Jews, whom he hates, are the culprits. Jeff, who had previously ignored his own Jewish heritage, struggles with Max's extreme views and actions, but, egged on by Max, shoots a dart into a Jewish family's front door. Jeff finally comes to realize what Max is—and what he himself can be.
Hungarian-Jewish/Dutch-English-Scottish-American and Iroquois and Methodist
Older; Fiction

Irish-American

See   Aguilera, Christina
      Carey, Mariah
      Deloria, Ella Cara
      Deloria, Phillip Samuel (Sam)
      Deloria, Vine, Jr.
      Deloria, Vine, Sr.
      dePaola, Tomie
      Depp, John (Johnny) Christopher II
      Dorris, Michael
      Estévez, Emilio
      Grace, Princess of Monaco
      Haley, Alexander (Alex) Murray Palmer
      Healy, James Augustine
      Healy, Michael
      Healy, Patrick Francis
      Hemings, John?
      Jeter, Derek Sanderson
      Keys, Alicia
      Kidd, Jason Frederick
      Lynn, Loretta Webb
      Mankiller, Wilma Pearl
      Noguchi, Isamu
      Obama, Barack
      O'Brien, Maria de la Soledad Teresa (Soledad)
      O'Hearn, Claudine Chiawei
      Rogers, Will, Jr.
      Rogers, William (Will) Penn Adair
      Senna, Danzy
      Sheen, Charlie
      Sheen, Martin

Shriver, Maria
Thorpe, James (Jim) Francis
Walker, Maggie Dalena (Lena) Mitchell
Washington, Margaret James Murray
White, George Henry

Becker, John T., and Stanli K. Becker, eds. *All Blood Is Red . . . All Shadows Are Dark!* Illustrated by J. Howard Noel. Cleveland: Seven Shadows Press, 1984. 168 p.

John T. (Tom) Becker, who is Irish-German-American, and his wife, Stanli K. Becker, who is African-American, have five young children. One of the four who are adopted is biracial. All seven family members are responsible for individual sections of this book, which recounts their personal and family experiences as a multiracial family. Teaching their children to be aware of and proud of their individual differences, the editors present information on the history of racial classification in the United States and advocate their belief that race is and should be regarded as an "absurdity."
Irish-German-American/African-American
Intermediate, Older; Nonfiction

Bode, Janet. *Different Worlds: Interracial and Cross-Cultural Dating*. New York: Franklin Watts, 1989. 128 p.

Based primarily on interviews with six teenage couples who are dating interracially and/or cross-culturally, this book is written for and about teens. It looks at the history of prejudice and racism; discusses negative reactions of parents, relatives, and classmates; examines why adolescents make their dating choices; and mentions some positive aspects of interracial dating. Although it does not cover the topics of interracial marriage and families, four of the twelve teens interviewed are of mixed race or heritage: African-American/European-American; Protestant English-American/Catholic Irish-American; Cuban/Puerto Rican; and Mexican-Spanish-American. A bibliography, a listing of resource organizations, and an index are included.
English-American Protestant/Irish-American Catholic
Older; Nonfiction

Brown, Don. *The Notorious Izzy Fink*. New Milford, Conn.: Roaring Brook Press, 2006. 160 p. (A Deborah Brodie Book)

New York City's Lower East Side of the 1890s comes alive in this book about the thirteen-year-olds Sam Glodsky, who is Irish-Russian-American, and Izzy Fink, who twice double-crosses Sam. It is a story of boys eeking out a living—hawking newspapers, cleaning a stable, grabbing coal that has fallen off a coal wagon—; of the teenage gangs of Irish, Jewish, Italians, and pickpockets; of a gangster; of corrupt police; of Tammany; and of the threat of cholera. Amazingly, in the end it is Sam's father who emerges from his depression and comes to Sam's rescue.
Russian and Jewish/Irish and Catholic
Intermediate, Older; Fiction

Cruz, Maria Colleen. *Border Crossing: A Novel*. Houston: Piñata Books, 2003. 128 p.

Cesi, who is twelve-years-old and of mixed race, feels she can discover who she is by finding out more about the Mexican heritage which her father doesn't discuss. When questions to her mother, both grandmothers, her brother, and her father don't satisfy her, she takes off by herself to cross the border from California to Tijuana. With the help of a Mexican-American boy she meets and of his aunt, Cesi learns about Mexicans, the prejudice her father faced as a boy, and who she really is. In the process her father comes to realize that by protecting his children he has unintentionally made their lives more difficult.
Mexican-American/Irish-American and Cherokee
Intermediate, Older; Fiction

Dorris, Michael. *The Window*. New York: Hyperion Paperbacks for Children, 1999. 112 p.

When eleven-year-old Rayona's mother is ordered into an alcohol rehabilitation program, two efforts at finding Rayona a foster home fail and her father decides he can't care for her. It is then that Rayona learns that her African-American father is half-Irish-American. He takes her from Seattle to Louisville where she enjoys her temporary stay with her Irish-American grandmother, great-aunt, and great-grandmother and meets an older African-American cousin. It is with regret that Rayona leaves her newfound relatives, but with happiness that she is reunited with her much-missed Native American mother—and with gratitude that a window on her life has been opened.
African-Irish-American/Native American
Intermediate, Older; Fiction

Easton, Kelly. *Hiroshima Dreams*. New York: Dutton Children's Books, 2007. 208 p.

When Lin's Japanese grandmother comes to visit, she immediately recognizes five-year-old Lin as a kindred spirit. Lin is so shy that she barely speaks, but is able to sense what is about to happen. Lin becomes very close to her Obaachan, who teaches her about Japan, shows how her how to meditate, imparts wisdom, and tells Lin that she too has precognition. As the years pass and with Obaachan's support, Lin plays her cello in an orchestra, makes a best friend in her new school, and uses her vision to help police locate a missing boy. When Obaachan dies from leukemia, the result of being a fifteen-year-old in Hiroshima when the atomic bomb was dropped, Lin is devastated. Then, the boy she has been attracted to since kindergarten becomes her boyfriend and Lin accepts her gift of vision.
Irish-American Catholic/Japanese Buddhist, Shinto, and Catholic
Older; Fiction

Ernst, Kathleen. *Highland Fling*. Chicago: Cricket Books, 2006. 224 p.

Exceedingly upset by her Polish-American father who had an extramarital affair, by moving from Wisconsin to North Carolina with her divorced mother and younger sister, and by the immersion of her mother and sister in everything to do with the Scottish MacDonald clan, fifteen-year-old Tanya reluctantly goes with them to the Highland Games. Longing to become an independent filmmaker, Tanya decides to make a documentary revealing the nostalgic pretense of the Highland Games. However, after meeting a young bagpiper from Puerto Rico who has Scottish heritage, his grandmother, and a Highland Games woman athlete whose mixed heritage does not include Scottish forebears, Tanya decides to make a different documentary and to have a talk with her father.

German-Irish-Italian-Swedish-American
Older; Fiction

Grattan-Domínguez, Alejandro. *Breaking Even*. Houston: Arte Público Press, 1997. 256 p.

Now eighteen and a high school graduate, Val is determined to leave his small Texas town and travel to California. However, his plans are interrupted when he discovers that his girlfriend is pregnant and that his father, whom he had been told was dead, had abandoned him and his mother and is still alive. Val travels to El Paso to find him and joins his father and his father's new girlfriend in trying to raise money through crooked gambling tactics. Val earns his father's admiration, but finally understands that his father is a compulsive gambler, who cares more for money than family. Val also comes to realize the goodness of his stepfather and makes a responsible decision about his future life.
Irish/Mexican
Older; Fiction

Gregory, Kristiana. *Orphan Runaways*. New York: Scholastic Press, 1998. 160 p.

In 1878, having recently been orphaned by an influenza epidemic, twelve-year-old Danny and his six-year-old brother Judd escape from an abusive orphanage and travel from San Francisco to find their uncle in a rowdy California mining town. They are looked after by a hotel owner who cares for orphan children until, after several months, the boys' uncle locates them. However, Danny, influenced by the prejudice of his new friends and the community, rejects his kind uncle because of his Chinese-American girlfriend whom he later marries. Danny finally overcomes his prejudice and with Judd becomes part of his uncle's family.
Irish/European-American
Intermediate; Fiction

Hassler, Jon. *Jemmy*. New York: Atheneum, 1981. 180 p. (A Margaret K. McElderry Book)

Seventeen-year-old Jemmy Stott, whose mother is dead, lives in rural Minnesota with her alcoholic father and her younger brother and sister. When Jemmy's father requires her to quit school to take care of her younger siblings, Jemmy's future looks bleak. Caught in a blizzard, she takes refuge in the house of the Chapmans, an artist and his wife. During the six months the Chapmans live in the area, they have a tremendous impact on the Stotts. Mr. Chapman's portrayal of Jenny as the Maiden of Eagle Rock becomes the focal point of a large mural in Minneapolis, she learns to paint, and she discovers that it is all right to be both Indian and white.
Irish-American/Chippewa
Older; Fiction

Irwin, Hadley. *Kim/Kimi*. New York: Margaret K. McElderry Books, 1987. 208 p.

Sixteen-year-old Kim's Japanese-American father died before her birth and she enjoys living with her European-American mother and stepfather in Iowa. However, she is upset about others regarding her as Japanese and associating her with World War II Japan. Into teen romance novels which always have perfect endings for their heroines and in the habit of running away from problems, Kim "runs" off to Sacramento to try to find her father's family, which had disowned him. There she learns of the

terrible Japanese-American concentration camps of World War II and of their effects on those imprisoned—and she meets her grandmother and her aunt.
Japanese-American/Irish-American
Older; Fiction

Kretzer-Malvehy, Terry. *Passage to Little Bighorn*. Flagstaff, Ariz.: Rising Moon, 1999. 232 p.

In this novel fifteen-year-old Dakota is discouraged because his Irish-American father has remarried and left the family, his Lakota mother has just returned from a two year treatment of depression, and he has been living with his father's father. When he visits the Little Bighorn Battlefield, Dakota finds himself swept back to 1876 where he becomes the "chosen relative" of wise and kind Sitting Bull. He experiences Lakota life: going on a buffalo hunt, counting coup by capturing two Crow horses, surviving a grizzly bear attack, receiving a Lakota name, becoming friends with a boy who is European-American and Lakota, falling for a daughter of Sitting Bull, meeting his great-great-great grandmother and great-great grandfather, and witnessing the terrible battles of the Rosebud and the Little Bighorn. It is with the Lakota that Dakota learns how he should live, and he decides to return to his real family.
Irish-American/Lakota (Hunkpapa)
Older; Fiction

Lacapa, Kathleen, and Michael Lacapa. *Less than Half, More than Whole*. Illustrated by Michael Lacapa. Flagstaff, Ariz.: Northland Publishing, 1994. 40 p.

This picture book is based on the author's family. Tony, who does not look like either his Caucasian or his Indian friend, is bothered about being called less than half and seeks understanding from his maternal grandmother, his older siblings, his uncle, and his paternal grandfather. It is when he realizes the meaning of an ear of corn that Tony knows that in truth he is more than whole. Designs from different Native American cultures complement the book's paintings.
Apache, Hopi, and Tewa/English-Irish-American and Mohawk
Primary, Intermediate; Fiction

Lisle, Janet Taylor. *The Crying Rocks*. New York: Atheneum Books for Young Readers, 2003. 208 p. (A Richard Jackson Book)

Thirteen-year-old Joelle, who was adopted at the age of five by Vern and Aunt Mary Louise, does not look like anyone she knows in Rhode Island. She is upset by what she is told of her past: of being thrown out of a Chicago apartment window by her mother, being put in an orphanage there, traveling by freight train to Connecticut, and then being cared for by an old woman while living in a wooden crate near a railway depot. Joelle is befriended by an adoring eight-year-old girl who is European- and Japanese-American and by a classmate Carlos, who is of mixed heritage. Together Joelle and Carlos learn of the early Narragansett Indians and explore the wooded area, including the Crying Rocks, where they lived. Carlos learns the truth about the accident at the Crying Rocks where his older brother died and Joelle learns the truth about her background. Vern is her real father, her mother was Narragansett, and both her mother and twin sister died in Chicago.
Irish-American/Narragansett
Intermediate, Older; Fiction

Martin, Nora. *The Eagle's Shadow*. New York: Scholastic Press, 1997. 176 p.

In 1946 when twelve-year-old Clearie's father is assigned to spend a year in Japan, Clearie is sent to live in a remote Alaskan village with her mother's Tlingit relatives whom she has never met. Clearie feels unaccepted by them because of her mother's bad reputation. She is also saddled by the sense of incompetence with which her father regards her. However, as Clearie makes friends, learns to paddle a canoe, fish, spin yarn, and do carpentry, and receives praise from her critical aunt, she realizes that for the first time she belongs and is part of a family.

Irish-American/Tlingit

Intermediate, Older; Fiction

McDonald, Janet. *Off-Color*. New York: Frances Foster Books, 2007. 176 p.

Fifteen-year-old Cameron, who believes that her father is Italian, loves hanging out with her three best friends and doesn't take school seriously. Then her mother loses her job in a nail salon and gets one at lower wages in the owner's other salon in an African-American section of Brooklyn. Cameron and her mother must move into the projects, but, thanks to the school guidance counselor Mr. Siciliano, she is able to remain at her old high school. When Cameron discovers from an old photo that her father is black, she is shocked and blames her mother for not having told her about him and for his not being there for her. Cameron, her mother, her friends, her mother's coworkers, her multi-cultures class, and Mr. Siciliano spend time talking about race, about being biracial, about Mariah Carey, and about Malcolm X who Cameron hears in class was propelled to become a black nationalist because of his white-appearing mother. Cameron learns that one of her mother's coworkers is Korean and Irish, that Mr. Siciliano is half black, and that many celebrities are of mixed race. At her Sweet Sixteen party, Cameron enjoys her old best friends and new friends from the projects and even meets the boy who becomes her boyfriend.

South Korean/Irish

Older; Fiction

Moore, Robin. *Maggie among the Seneca*. New York: J. B. Lippincott, 1990. 112 p.

Sixteen-year-old Maggie, who is Irish, is kidnapped in 1778 by the Seneca and taken from central Pennsylvania to the Senecan village on the Genesee River. Staying at first with two Senecan women, Maggie then goes to live with Frenchgirl, who, kidnapped at an early age, is French and English, but now regards herself as Senecan. Maggie agrees to marry Frenchgirl's brother so she can go on a hunting trip to the Allegheny River and escape from there to her aunt's. However, when Maggie's husband dies, she stays to tend his burial scaffold. Maggie has a baby, survives the destruction of the village by the colonial army, and then goes to live with her aunt. The book is the sequel to *The Bread Sister of Sinking Creek*.

French-English-American and Senecan/Irish-American

Intermediate, Older; Fiction

Naylor, Phyllis Reynolds. *Sang Spell*. New York: Aladdin Paperbacks, 2000. 224 p.

Hitchhiking from Massachusetts to Dallas to live with his aunt because his mother has died, teenager Josh is mugged and left on a road in Appalachia where he is picked up by a Melungeon, who

takes him to Canara, an isolated primitive community. Everything is strange and illogical there, and Josh becomes increasingly frustrated in his efforts to escape. The road he takes ends up at the exact place he started. Trying to swim towards a river's opposite shore takes him only a short distance, and a roadside restaurant and a school appear and disappear at regular intervals. Josh discovers that his father was probably Melungeon and befriends a girl whose father was stoned to death when his efforts to escape accidentally caused fatalities. Finally, with new insights and the realization that he must keep Canara's secrets, Josh is able to get away. [The Melungeon people are of mixed race living primarily in the central Appalachians. There is controversy as to their origin and their heritage, but they are often regarded as tri-racial [European-American, African-American, and Native American]. In this novel they are identified as Portuguese who, over time, became mixed with a number of other peoples.]
Portuguese (Melongeon)-American/Irish-American
Older; Fiction

Singer, Marilyn, ed. *Face Relations: 11 Stories About Seeing Beyond Color*. New York: Simon & Schuster Books for Young Readers, 2004. 240 p.

In "Gold" by Marina Budhos, fifteen-year-old Jemma, who has moved from Trinidad to New Jersey, goes out with Jared and comes to realize that they are going too far in their relationship. Then, when Jared apologizes to her mother, Jemma recognizes how good he is and that for them, as for her parents, differences in heritage do not matter.
African-Irish-American and Cherokee
Older; Fiction

Smith, Cynthia Leitich. *Rain Is Not My Indian Name*. New York: HarperCollins Publishers, 2001. 144 p.

Since her best friend Galen was killed in a traffic accident on New Year's Day (her birthday), fourteen-year-old Rain, who is of mixed race, has withdrawn from her friends and from going out into her small Kansas town. However, despite refusing to become a participant, she agrees early in the summer to take photographs of her aunt's Native American camp. Rain is upset with Galen's mother and her opposition to the camp and with her former second best friend African-American Queenie, who attends the camp although it is not discovered until later that she has a Seminole ancestor. Then, on the Fourth of July (Galen's birthday), Rain is ready to move beyond his death.
Irish-German-American and Ojibwa/Scottish-Irish-American, Cherokee, and Muskogee
Intermediate, Older; Fiction

Thomas, Joyce Carol. *The Blacker the Berry*. Illustrated by Floyd Cooper. New York: Joanna Cotler Books, 2008. 32 p.

In this picture book thirteen poems and accompanying paintings present the beauty of varied black skin shades, including the raspberry black of an African-American and Seminole boy, the cranberry red of an African-Irish-American girl, and the snowberry color of an African-European-American girl.
African-Irish-American
Primary, Intermediate; Fiction

Williams, Laura E. *Slant*. Minneapolis: Milkweed Editions, 2008. 168 p.

Thirteen-year-old Lauren and her five-year old Chinese sister live with their adoptive English professor father in Connecticut. Their mother had died three years earlier, Lauren hates being called derogatory names by two classmates and even called "Slant" by Sean, the boy she has a crush on. She feels she can stop the abuse and be much happier by having surgery to change the shape of her Korean eyes. When Lauren discovers that her mother had committed suicide and that corrective surgery on her nose when she was thirteen had not stopped her depression, she decides against the surgery. Lauren discovers that she can stand up for herself, and she even gets Sean as a boyfriend.
French-German-Irish-American
Intermediate, Older; Fiction

Williams, Mary E., ed. *Adoption*. Farmington Hills, Mich.: Greenhaven Press, 2006. 232 p.

In a chapter "Transracial Adoption Should Be Encouraged," Arlene Istar Lev, who is Jewish, tells how she and her lesbian partner adopted their African-American and biracial sons.
African-Irish-American
Older; Nonfiction

Wosmek, Frances. *A Brown Bird Singing*. Illustrated by Ted Lewin. New York: Beech Tree Paperback Books, 1986. 128 p.

Years ago, after her mother had died from a fever, Anego's Chippewa father Hamigeesek had left her to stay with the Veselka family. The only Indian in her northern Minnesota community, Anego sometimes thinks about the brown bird she once held and gets a warm supportive feeling. Anego passes fourth grade, raises an orphaned fawn and grieves when a hunter shoots it, joins in the excitement of the family's getting a car, and, after thinking she is not needed when a baby brother is born, helps save his life and realizes how much she cares for him. Anego is very close to her Irish Ma, sister Sheila, and Austrian-American Pa, who is her best friend, and she dreads the time that the hardly-remembered Hamigeesek will take her from them. However, when he does come, Hamigeesek kindly assures Anego that she can remain with the Veselkas and, by having her hold a brown bird, brings back her memories of her Chippewa mother.
Austrian-American/Irish
Intermediate; Fiction

Wright, Susan Kimmel. *The Secret of the Old Graveyard*. Scottdale, Pa.: Herald Press, 1993. 184 p.

At the same time that thirteen-year-old Nellie's parents are notified they are to go to Colombia to adopt the baby they've wanted, strange things start to happen at her family farm's old graveyard. This story tells of Nellie's worry about her parents traveling to Colombia, of her concerns as to how a baby will affect her already offbeat family, of her exciting detective work with her friend Peggy to find whoever has vandalized the cemetery, and of her discoveries that the boy she has a crush on is adopted, is of mixed heritage—and likes her.
English-French-Irish-American
Intermediate, Older; Fiction

Wyeth, Sharon Dennis. *The World of Daughter McGuire*. New York: Delacorte Press, 1994. 176 p.

Eleven-year-old Daughter's parents have separated, and she, her two younger brothers, and her mother have moved into a house next to her mother's parents. Daughter, whose deceased grandfather was Irish-American Catholic and whose other grandparents are Russian Jewish, African-American, and Italian-American, is called a "zebra" by a schoolmate and wishes that she was not all mixed-up. She is further concerned that the differences between her mother and father in careers and lifestyles will result in divorce. In this story Daughter learns to be proud of her heritages and is relieved when her parents decide to try to stay together despite their differences.

Irish-American Catholic and Russian-American Jewish/African-Italian-American

Intermediate; Fiction

Italian-American

See   dePaola, Tomie

       Keys, Alicia

Ernst, Kathleen. *Highland Fling*. Chicago: Cricket Books, 2006. 224 p.

Exceedingly upset by her Polish-American father who had an extramarital affair, by moving from Wisconsin to North Carolina with her divorced mother and younger sister, and by the immersion of her mother and sister in everything to do with the Scottish MacDonald clan, fifteen-year-old Tanya reluctantly goes with them to the Highland Games. Longing to become an independent filmmaker, Tanya decides to make a documentary revealing the nostalgic pretense of the Highland Games. However, after meeting a young bagpiper from Puerto Rico who has Scottish heritage, his grandmother, and a Highland Games woman athlete whose mixed heritage does not include Scottish forebears, Tanya decides to make a different documentary and to have a talk with her father.

German-Irish-Italian-Swedish-American

Older; Fiction

Herron, Carolivia. *Always an Olivia: A Remarkable Family History*. Illustrated by Jeremy Tugeau. Minneapolis: Kar-Ben Publishing, 2007. 32 p.

In this picture book Carol Olivia's great-grandmother tells her about her Jewish ancestors, who were banished from Spain and Portugal and finally moved to Italy. One of their descendents and her future husband escaped from pirates and traveled by ship to Georgia. Their descendents intermarried with the Geechees (Gullahs) of Sea Island.

Gullah-Italian-Spanish-American Jewish

Primary, Intermediate; Fiction

Holm, Jennifer L. *Penny from Heaven*. New York: Random House, 2006. 288 p.

During the eventful summer of 1953 Penny spends time with both sides of her divided family: her mother and maternal grandparents and her late Italian father's mother, siblings, and relatives. Abetted by her cousin Freddie, Penny sneaks into her Italian grandmother's room to find out the color of her

underwear, digs in the yard for treasure, and disobeys her mother by going to the beach. She gets a black eye, goes to a Dodgers game for her twelfth birthday, misbehaves to discourage her mother's Irish-American suitor, and, when her arm is caught in a clothes wringer, spends weeks in the hospital. It is there that she comes to accept her soon-to-be stepfather and discovers that her father had been imprisoned during World War II because, as an Italian "enemy alien," he had a radio. Penny also manages to ease the hostilities between the two branches of her family.
Italian and Catholic/European-American and Methodist
Intermediate, Older; Fiction

Jennings, Patrick. *Faith and the Electric Dogs*. Decorations by author. New York: Scholastic, 1996. 144 p.

The narrator—and author— of this fanciful tale is Edison, a mutt from San Cristóbal de las Casas, Mexico, who asserts that it is true. He is taken in by Faith, a ten-year-old homesick American girl, whose mother has married a Mexican and who hates Mexico because she can't speak Spanish and is teased. With help from a craftsman, Faith builds a rocket powered by pig fat and jalapeño peppers and sets off with Edison for San Francisco. Unfortunately, the rocket goes down in a storm. The two of them end up on an island in the Pacific Ocean, which is deserted except for four mutts and a seventy-year-old man who had come down on the island when he was ten after the balloon he was taking to return from Mexico to England was pierced by a seagull. The story concludes with Faith and Edison's return to Mexico, her happiness there, and an explanation of how Edison become a writer. Definitions of the many Spanish and Bowwow (canine) words used in the text are provided in the margins and also in a glossary.
Italian-American/German-Scottish-Irish-American
Intermediate; Fiction

Jennings, Patrick. *Faith and the Rocket Cat*. Decorations by author. New York: Scholastic Press, 1998. 240 p.

In this sequel to *Faith and the Electric Dogs*, Edison the mutt relates another fantastic story. When Faith, her mother, and her stepfather move to San Francisco, Faith wants to impress classmate Alex and Edison wishes to befriend Daphne, a whippet show dog, by taking them for a ride in Faith's rocket. Faith, Edison, Alex, Daphne—and Faith's mother—crash-land in Death Valley where they encounter coyotes and find Faith's late father's cat. All ends well in this story in which words presented in Bowwow and Arf (dog languages), Mew (cat language), Spanish, French, Italian, Chinese, Latin, and Turkish are defined both in the margins and in a glossary.
Italian-American/German-Scottish-Irish-American
Intermediate; Fiction

Kadohata, Cynthia. *Outside Beauty*. New York: Atheneum Books for Young Readers, 2008. 272 p.

It is 1983 and twelve-year-old Shelby lives with her three sisters and their Japanese-American mother Helen in Chicago. Helen is obsessed with her beauty and using it to attract rich men. She spends time conveying her lifestyle to her daughters, all of whom have different fathers and who are very close to each other. When Helen is severely injured in an automobile accident, including damage

to her face, the sisters are sent to live temporarily with their respective fathers whom they barely know. Shelby, the narrator, comes to like life in Arkansas with her Japanese father, whose only apparent fault is that he dresses poorly, but worries about her six-year-old sister Maddie, who has gone to live with her domineering, cruel father. Realizing the terrible effect he is having on Maddie, Shelby unsuccessfully tries running away to rescue her. The sisters and their fathers get together in Chicago when for a time Helen seems near death, and, for Maddie's sake, the sixteen year old sister secretly drives with the other sisters to a Colorado cabin. After the girls are caught, it is agreed that Shelby's father will look after all of them in Chicago until Helen is well. Helen ends up with her physician as a boyfriend, but Shelby realizes that it is not exterior beauty which counts.
Italian-American/Japanese-American
Older; Fiction

Lamba, Marie. *What I Meant*. New York: Random House, 2007. 320 p.
Ever since her father's sister-in law has moved in, there has been a change in fifteen-year-old Sang's family. Her widowed Indian aunt Chachi is a complaining, critical kleptomaniac who steals food and money and blames the thefts on Sang. In the meantime Sang is head over heels in love with her classmate Jason and is upset that her parents will not allow her to date until she is sixteen. When her mother catches Sang in the lie that she was at an ice skating rink with her best friend Gina, her parents don't believe her allegations about Chachi. Her mother even takes her to a doctor since she believes Sang is bulimic. To make matters worse, for an unknown reason Gina turns against Sang. The situation comes to a climax when Sang sneaks off to Philadelphia to see a concert with Jason and his friend Gary. She sees Gina alone in another train car, and, when Gina leaves the train toting a large backpack, Sang realizes that she is running away. Getting off the train Sang follows Gina through the dark city streets and then calls Gina's mother as to her whereabouts. Robbed of her money and return ticket, Sang goes back to the train station where Gary is searching for her. Sang comes to realize that Gina and Jason are no longer her friends, but that she has other supportive classmates. Further, when Sang stands up to Chachi, who is about to reveal a damaging secret about her mother, Sang's parents and her visiting Indian uncle believe her and Chachi is made to leave.
Indian and Sikh/Italian-American and Catholic
Older; Fiction

Landau, Elaine. *Interracial Dating and Marriage*. New York: Julian Messner, 1993. 112 p.
This book's introduction presents two detailed histories of interracial marriage: the first of African-American intermarriage with Caucasians and the second of intermarriages involving Japanese-Americans. In both cases the introduction describes factors, including governmental actions and societal attitudes, which affected the frequency of these marriages. The bulk of the book presents interviews with ten teenagers and five adults or adult couples who describe their views of and/or experiences with interracial dating and marriage. Seven of the teens interviewed came to the United States from other countries; two of the teens are interracial. Two of the adult interviews are with interracial couples; another contains advice from a minister. A resource list and an index are included.
African-English-Indian-Italian-Dominican
Older; Nonfiction

McDonald, Janet. *Off-Color*. New York: Frances Foster Books, 2007. 176 p.

Fifteen-year-old Cameron, who believes that her father is Italian, loves hanging out with her three best friends and doesn't take school seriously. Then her mother loses her job in a nail salon and gets one at lower wages in the owner's other salon in an African-American section of Brooklyn. Cameron and her mother must move into the projects, but, thanks to the school guidance counselor Mr. Siciliano, she is able to remain at her old high school. When Cameron discovers from an old photo that her father is black, she is shocked and blames her mother for not having told her about him and for his not being there for her. Cameron, her mother, her friends, her mother's coworkers, her multicultures class, and Mr. Siciliano spend time talking about race, about being biracial, about Mariah Carey, and about Malcolm X who Cameron hears in class was propelled to become a black nationalist because of his white-appearing mother. Cameron learns that one of her mother's coworkers is Korean and Irish, that Mr. Siciliano is half black, and that many celebrities are of mixed race. At her Sweet Sixteen party, Cameron enjoys her old best friends and new friends from the projects and even meets the boy who becomes her boyfriend.
Italian/African-American
Older; Fiction

Skurzynski, Gloria, and Alane Ferguson. *Ghost Horses*. Washington, D.C.: National Geographic Society, 2000. 160 p. (Mysteries in Our National Parks)

When Jack and Ashley Landon's parents take in a Shoshone brother and sister, Ethan, twelve, and Summer, ten, as emergency foster care children, blond Jack immediately senses the dislike which Ethan has for whites. Traveling together to visit Zion National Park and the nearby area, Jack unfairly blames Ethan for the rocks which fall down the canyon walls towards them and for Ashley's almost being trampled by a wild white mustang, "a ghost horse." Ethan is pleased with the bad luck that the Landons are experiencing which he attributes to the Ghost Dance that Jack and Ashley danced. Steven, the Landon's father, takes Jack and Ethan for a hike in the Zion Narrows to help them work out their enmity, while Olivia, the Landon's mother, takes Ashley and Summer to revisit the mustangs. In an eventful finish Ethan saves Jack during a flash flood, Jack suffers hypothermia during which he may have seen Ethan and Summer's deceased parents, and Summer gives Olivia the clue that solves the problem of the ghost horses' strange behavior. In this book the Landons' heritage is identified, a factor which is relevant as Ethan's animosity is directed towards Jack who looks like his Norwegian-American father, whereas Ashley resembles her Italian-American mother.
Norwegian-American and ?/Italian-American
Intermediate, Older; Fiction

Smith, Roland. *Thunder Cave*. New York: Hyperion Paperbacks for Children, 1997. 256 p.

When he is fourteen-years-old, Jake's mother dies in a New York City traffic accident and his stepfather decides to send him to live with an aunt and uncle whom he dislikes. Jake sets off on his own to find his Hopi father who, somewhere in a remote area of Kenya, is studying elephant behavior and is worried about poachers who are killing elephants for their ivory. This book recounts Jake's adventures in Nairobi where his bike is stolen and he manages to steal it back and in the bush where he encounters a lion, becomes very ill, escapes from a brush fire, and, floating in a river along with

dead and dying animals, is rescued by the Masai, Supeet. Supeet, who is looking for the renowned witch doctor who might help him bring rain to the drought-stricken land, joins Jake on his journey. Subsequently, they meet the witch doctor, Jake is captured by poachers and again rescued by Supeet, Supeet is temporarily blinded by a cobra, but "apparently" manages to bring rain, and Jake, recaptured by the poachers, is reunited with his father, but as a hostage. Thanks to the cleverness of Jake, his father, and Supeet, all ends well.
Hopi/Italian-American
Older; Fiction

Wyeth, Sharon Dennis. *The World of Daughter McGuire*. New York: Delacorte Press, 1994. 176 p.
Eleven-year-old Daughter's parents have separated, and she, her two younger brothers, and her mother have moved into a house next to her mother's parents. Daughter, whose deceased grandfather was Irish-American Catholic and whose other grandparents are Russian Jewish, African-American, and Italian-American, is called a "zebra" by a schoolmate and wishes that she was not all mixed-up. She is further concerned that the differences between her mother and father in careers and lifestyles will result in divorce. In this story Daughter learns to be proud of her heritages and is relieved when her parents decide to try to stay together despite their differences.
Irish-American Catholic and Russian-American Jewish/African-Italian-American
Intermediate; Fiction

Young, Karen Romano. *Cobwebs*. New York: Greenwillow Books, 2004. 400 p.
In this unusual story Nancy, a high school sophomore who as yet has no spider traits, is the daughter of part spider parents. Her father is a roofer who prefers living up high; her mother is a weaver who has to remain low; her Granny is a knitter and potter; and her Grandpa Joke is a doctor. Nancy's family becomes involved with Nico, a Greek-American journalist who blackmails Grandpa Joke into bringing Granny to heal his wife. In the process, Granny loses her life. The story focuses on the identities of the rumored Angel of Brooklyn and the Wound Healer, the growing attraction between Nancy and Niko's son Dion, and Nancy's concerns about whether she is or is not part spider.
Jamaican-West African-American/Italian-Scottish-American
Older; Fiction

Melungeon-American

Naylor, Phyllis Reynolds. *Sang Spell*. New York: Aladdin Paperbacks, 2000. 224 p.
Hitchhiking from Massachusetts to Dallas to live with his aunt because his mother has died, teenager Josh is mugged and left on a road in Appalachia where he is picked up by a Melungeon, who takes him to Canara, an isolated primitive community. Everything is strange and illogical there, and Josh becomes increasingly frustrated in his efforts to escape. The road he takes ends up at the exact place he started. Trying to swim towards a river's opposite shore takes him only a short distance, and a roadside restaurant and a school appear and disappear at regular intervals. Josh discovers that his father was probably Melungeon and befriends a girl whose father was stoned to death when his efforts to escape accidentally caused fatalities. Finally, with new insights and the realization that he must keep

Canara's secrets, Josh is able to get away. [The Melungeon people are of mixed race living primarily in the central Appalachians. There is controversy as to their origin and their heritage, but they are often regarded as tri-racial: European-American, African-American, and Native American. In this novel they are identified as Portuguese who, over time, became mixed with a number of other peoples.]
Portuguese (Melungeon)-American/Irish-American; Celtic-American/Portuguese (Melungeon)-American
Older; Fiction

Nordic-American. See also Norwegian-American, Swedish-American

Perkins, Mitali. *Monsoon Summer*. New York: Laurel-Leaf Books, 2004. 272 p.
Fifteen-year-old Jazz and her family go to Pune, India, for the summer so that her Indian mother can set up a clinic for pregnant women at the orphanage from which she was adopted. Jazz hates to leave Steve, her best friend and business partner whom she secretly loves. She also feels that because of a disastrous earlier experience she is unable to help others and should not volunteer at the orphanage. During the summer things change. Jazz's introverted father finds he enjoys teaching computer skills to the orphanage's nuns, her ten-year-old brother temporarily gives up being a "bug" guy to become a "soccer" guy, and Jazz comes to realize that she is not only big, but beautiful, that she has a unique way of helping one of the orphans, and that she should tell Steve of her true feelings.
Nordic-American/Indian
Older; Fiction

Norwegian-American. See also Nordic-American

Crutcher, Chris. *Whale Talk*. New York: Dell Laurel-Leaf, 2002. 224 p.
This novel tells of T. J. Jones, an adopted seventeen-year-old of mixed race, who in his senior year of high school organizes a swimming team of boys regarded as misfits by their classmates and the school and who are, except for T. J., mediocre swimmers. The story focuses on T. J.'s efforts to have his teammates rewarded for their Herculean efforts by receiving athletic letters. The book shows how the boys come to share their backgrounds and feelings and to become part of a cohesive group in which each feels valued and accepted. Thanks primarily to his father, T. J. learns to control his own rage.
African-Japanese-American/Swiss-Norwegian-American
Older; Fiction

Hausherr, Rosmarie. *Celebrating Families*. New York: Scholastic Press, 1997. 32 p.
Among the families celebrated in this book are Jahsee's, whose father is from the Virgin Islands and whose mother is Norwegian-American, and Alexandra's, who was adopted from Brazil by two European-American mothers. The book is illustrated with photographs.
African-Virgin Islander/Norwegian-American
Primary, Intermediate; Nonfiction

McDonald, Janet. *Off-Color*. New York: Frances Foster Books, 2007. 176 p.

Fifteen-year-old Cameron, who believes that her father is Italian, loves hanging out with her three best friends and doesn't take school seriously. Then her mother loses her job in a nail salon and gets one at lower wages in the owner's other salon in an African-American section of Brooklyn. Cameron and her mother must move into the projects, but, thanks to the school guidance counselor Mr. Siciliano, she is able to remain at her old high school. When Cameron discovers from an old photo that her father is black, she is shocked and blames her mother for not having told her about him and for his not being there for her. Cameron, her mother, her friends, her mother's coworkers, her multicultures class, and Mr. Siciliano spend time talking about race, about being biracial, about Mariah Carey, and about Malcolm X who Cameron hears in class was propelled to become a black nationalist because of his white-appearing mother. Cameron learns that one of her mother's coworkers is Korean and Irish, that Mr. Siciliano is half black, and that many celebrities are of mixed race. At her Sweet Sixteen party, Cameron enjoys her old best friends and new friends from the projects and even meets the boy who becomes her boyfriend.
African-American/Norwegian-American
Older; Fiction

Resau, Laura. *What the Moon Saw: A Novel*. New York: Delacorte Press, 2006. 272 p.

Fourteen-year-old Clara's life turns upside down when she leaves her suburban Maryland home to visit her grandparents in a remote village in Oaxaca, Mexico. There she stays in a cluster of huts without a telephone, TV, or computer, and it is there that she comes to love exploring the mountains, being with Pedro the neighbor boy, and with him finding the secret waterfall. It is also there that Clara hears the story of her grandmother's life and learns that, like her grandmother, she has a spirit animal (a heron) and is a healer.
Mixtec Mexican/French-Norwegian-Welsh-American
Older; Fiction

Skurzynski, Gloria, and Alane Ferguson. *Ghost Horses*. Washington, D.C.: National Geographic Society, 2000. 160 p. (Mysteries in Our National Parks)

When Jack and Ashley Landon's parents take in a Shoshone brother and sister, Ethan, twelve, and Summer, ten, as emergency foster care children, blond Jack immediately senses the dislike which Ethan has for whites. Traveling together to visit Zion National Park and the nearby area, Jack unfairly blames Ethan for the rocks which fall down the canyon walls towards them and for Ashley's almost being trampled by a wild white mustang, "a ghost horse." Ethan is pleased with the bad luck that the Landons are experiencing which he attributes to the Ghost Dance that Jack and Ashley danced. Steven, the Landon's father, takes Jack and Ethan for a hike in the Zion Narrows to help them work out their enmity, while Olivia, the Landon's mother, takes Ashley and Summer to revisit the mustangs. In an eventful finish Ethan saves Jack during a flash flood, Jack suffers hypothermia during which he may have seen Ethan and Summer's deceased parents, and Summer gives Olivia the clue that solves the problem of the ghost horses' strange behavior. In this book the Landons' heritage is identified, a factor which is relevant as Ethan's animosity is directed towards Jack who looks like his Norwegian-American father, whereas Ashley resembles her Italian-American mother.

Norwegian-American and ?/Italian-American
Intermediate, Older; Fiction

Wong, Janet S. *Minn and Jake's Almost Terrible Summer*. Illustrated by Geneviève Côté. New York: Frances Foster Books. 2008. 112 p.

It is in this sequel to *Minn and Jake* that Jake's mixed heritage is revealed. Ten-year-old Jake, his Korean grandmother, his mother, and his little brother spend the summer in Los Angeles, his old hometown. Deliberately choosing to avoid planned activities, Jake discovers that his former friends want nothing to do with him after learning that his best friend in his new town is a lizard-catching girl, Minn. Further, he is embarrassed when Haylee, the girl he used to like, sees him coming out of the ladies' room in his mother's pink shirt and then later as he is attempting to get rid of ants in his clothes. When Minn visits Los Angeles, she is surprised to learn he is part Korean, is amused when tanning lotion makes him looks like a spotted hyena, is jealous of Haylee, and disapproves of his getting ahead of others at Disneyland by putting his grandmother in a wheelchair. It is only when he apologizes that his summer vacation improves.
French-German-American/South Korean-Norwegian-American
Intermediate; Fiction

Polish-American

See   McBride, James

Adoff, Arnold. *All the Colors of the Race*. Illustrated by John Steptoe. New York: Lothrop, Lee & Shepard Books, 1982. 56 p.

Poems celebrate a girl who is Polish, German, Russian, and Jewish on her father's side and African-American and Protestant on her mother's. She looks forward to the time when we will cease *looking* at colors and *love* all colors of the human race.
Polish-German-Russian-American Jewish/African-American Protestant
Intermediate, Older; Fiction

Ernst, Kathleen. *Highland Fling*. Chicago: Cricket Books, 2006. 224 p.

Exceedingly upset by her Polish-American father who had an extramarital affair, by moving from Wisconsin to North Carolina with her divorced mother and younger sister, and by the immersion of her mother and sister in everything to do with the Scottish MacDonald clan, fifteen-year-old Tanya reluctantly goes with them to the Highland Games. Longing to become an independent filmmaker, Tanya decides to make a documentary revealing the nostalgic pretense of the Highland Games. However, after meeting a young bagpiper from Puerto Rico who has Scottish heritage, his grandmother, and a Highland Games woman athlete whose mixed heritage does not include Scottish forebears, Tanya decides to make a different documentary and to have a talk with her father.
Polish-American and Catholic/Scottish-American and Presbyterian
Older; Fiction

Freeman, Martha. *The Trouble with Babies*. Illustrated by Cat Bowman Smith. New York: Holiday House, 2002. 128 p.

When nine-year-old Holly moves into her new house, she meets her interesting neighbors, including Annie, who thinks her month-old sister is yucky, and Xavier, who has invented a de-yuckification device. The de-yuckification box produces surprising results, Annie realizes she likes her sister, and Holly discovers that she too is going to become a big sister. Annie and her baby sister have a Chinese father and a mother who is Polish-American and Jewish.
Chinese/Polish American and Jewish
Intermediate; Fiction

Gallo, Donald R., editor. *Join In: Multiethnic Short Stories by Outstanding Writers for Young Adults*. New York: Delacorte Press, 1993. 272 p.

One of the seventeen short stories in this book is "Next Month . . . Hollywood" by Jean Davies Okimoto. Rodney, who is Japanese-Polish American, wants to be an Asian rapper. With the support of his good friend Ivy, who is Filipino-African-American, he plans for the two of them to appear in their high school talent show. When they preview their act before a different audience, the results are unexpectedly uproarious. Ivy realizes that their performance should be a comedy act and, at last, becomes Rodney's girlfriend.
Polish-American/Japanese-American
Older; Fiction

Okimoto, Jean Davies. *Talent Night*. New York: Scholastic, 1995. 176 p.

When seventeen-year-old Rodney and his nineteen-year-old sister Suzanne learn that their great-uncle Hideki, whom they have never met, might give them each $10,000 if they have kept their mother's Japanese heritage, Rodney works on mastering karate kicks, Suzanne tries out Japanese flower arranging, and they both learn about haiku poetry and Japanese cooking. They discover when Uncle Hideki visits that he is not worth impressing since he is unbearably traditional and insults Rodney's half African-American girlfriend. However, they become closer to their Japanese heritage by learning from their mother about the prejudice she endured as a Japanese-American during the 1940s. Molly from *Molly by Any Other Name* appears very briefly in this book.
Polish-American/Japanese-American
Older; Fiction

Osa, Nancy. *Cuba 15*. New York: Delacorte Press, 2003. 304 p.

In September Violet's Cuban grandmother proposes she be given a quinceañero, an elaborate ceremony celebrating a girl's being fifteen and becoming a woman. Violet dreads the occasion, which is set for the following May. However, during the intervening months she finds out more about the quinceañero, lends her own touch to the party, and learns about her Cuban heritage and the controversial issue of the United States' embargo of Cuba. Violet also matures as she becomes a contributing member of her school's speech team and has her first boyfriend. The party is a great success—and Violet's father finally agrees to discuss Cuba with her and her brother.

Cuban/Polish-American
Older; Fiction

Smith, Cynthia Leitich. *Indian Shoes*. Illustrated by Jim Madsen. New York: HarperCollins Publishers, 2002. 80 p.

This book tells of the close relationship between Ray and his Grampa Halfmoon, who live together in Chicago. For instance, Ray cleverly bargains to get a pair of Seminole moccasins for his homesick grandfather and together they attend a Cubs game, celebrate Christmas with the neighborhood pets, solve the problem of missing pants when Ray serves as wedding ring bearer for their Choctaw friend and her Polish-Menominee groom, and, visiting their relatives in Oklahoma, go fishing and catch more than fish.

Polish-American and Menominee
Primary, Intermediate; Fiction

Terris, Susan. *Whirling Rainbows*. Garden City, N.Y.: Doubleday & Company, 1974. 168 p.

Thirteen-year-old Leah, who was adopted in infancy by a Jewish couple, wants to find her Indian roots when she goes to a Wisconsin summer camp. One disaster seems to follow another as she is mocked for being "Indian" and blamed, often unjustly, for misdeeds. However, although she does not find the Indian relics she is seeking, Leah learns much during the summer: that she has been trying to be close to the wrong cousin, that she has become an accomplished canoeist, that she has displayed leadership on a hazardous camping trip, and that she is no longer concerned about being adopted.

Polish-American/Chippewa
Older; Fiction

Portuguese-American

See   Campbell, Ben Nighthorse

Naylor, Phyllis Reynolds. *Sang Spell*. New York: Aladdin Paperbacks, 2000. 224 p.

Hitchhiking from Massachusetts to Dallas to live with his aunt because his mother has died, teenager Josh is mugged and left on a road in Appalachia where he is picked up by a Melungeon, who takes him to Canara, an isolated primitive community. Everything is strange and illogical there, and Josh becomes increasingly frustrated in his efforts to escape. The road he takes ends up at the exact place he started. Trying to swim towards a river's opposite shore takes him only a short distance, and a roadside restaurant and a school appear and disappear at regular intervals. Josh discovers that his father was probably Melungeon and befriends a girl whose father was stoned to death when his efforts to escape accidentally caused fatalities. Finally, with new insights and the realization that he must keep Canara's secrets, Josh is able to get away. [The Melungeon people are of mixed race living primarily in the central Appalachians. There is controversy as to their origin and their heritage, but they are often regarded as tri-racial: European-American, African-American, and Native American. In this novel they are identified as Portuguese who, over time, became mixed with a number of other peoples.]

Portuguese (Melungeon)-American/Irish-American; Celtic-American/Portuguese (Melungeon)-American
Older; Fiction

Romani-American

Springer, Nancy. *The Boy on a Black Horse*. New York: Atheneum, 1994. 176 p.

Gray, whose parents and brother have died in a boating accident, lives with her Aunt Liana, who is depressed after the death of her husband and two children in the same accident. Gray befriends a new classmate, a fifteen-year-old gypsy boy Chav, who rides a black stallion, takes care of his younger brother and sister, and lives in a silo. Chav feels worthless and is filled with anger at himself and non-gypsies. When his sister becomes ill with chicken pox, Gray takes Chav and his siblings to her house where Liana finds purpose in caring for them. However, hating to be penned up in the house, falsely accused of vandalism, and about to lose his beloved stallion, Chav sets off with a gun to kill himself and those attending a homecoming game. Thanks to Gray, disaster is averted. Chav and his brother, who witnessed their father murdering their mother, receive the support they need, and Gray is finally able to speak about her family's accident.
European-American/Romani-American
Older; Fiction

Russian-American. See also Eastern European-American

See   McBride, James
       Mehta, Nina

Adoff, Arnold. *All the Colors of the Race*. Illustrated by John Steptoe. New York: Lothrop, Lee & Shepard Books, 1982. 56 p.

Poems celebrate a girl who is Polish, German, Russian, and Jewish on her father's side and African-American and Protestant on her mother's. She looks forward to the time when we will cease *looking* at colors and *love* all colors of the human race.
Polish-German-Russian-American Jewish/African-American Protestant
Intermediate, Older; Fiction

Baskin, Nora Raleigh. *The Truth about My Bat Mitzvah*. New York: Simon & Schuster Books for Young Readers, 2008. 144 p.

Twelve-year-old Caroline's father is Christian and her mother is non-practicing Jewish. Caroline has never thought about being Jewish until her grandmother's death and receiving the Star of David necklace her grandmother had wanted her to have. She keeps the necklace a secret, learns about being Jewish from her best friend Rachel who is about to have a bat mitzvah celebration, and discovers that her great-grandparents, who came from a non-practicing Jewish German-American family, had objected to her grandfather's marriage to her Russian Jewish immigrant grandmother. Also, initially her grandparents had not been happy about her mother's marrying a non-Jew. Caroline comes to realize

that she wants to be Jewish and that she doesn't need a bat mitzvah party to be a bat mitzvah.
European-American Christian/German-Russian-American Jewish
Intermediate; Fiction

Brown, Don. *The Notorious Izzy Fink*. New Milford, Conn.: Roaring Brook Press, 2006. 160 p. (A Deborah Brodie Book)

New York City's Lower East Side of the 1890s comes alive in this book about the thirteen-year-olds Sam Glodsky, who is Irish-Russian-American, and Izzy Fink, who twice double-crosses Sam. It is a story of boys eeking out a living—hawking newspapers, cleaning a stable, grabbing coal that has fallen off a coal wagon—; of the teenage gangs of Irish, Jewish, Italians, and pickpockets; of a gangster; of corrupt police; of Tammany; and of the threat of cholera. Amazingly, in the end it is Sam's father who emerges from his depression and comes to Sam's rescue.
Russian and Jewish/Irish and Catholic
Intermediate, Older; Fiction

Fitch, Janet. *Kicks*. New York: Fawcett Juniper, 1995. 224 p

With a father who is brain-damaged from an accident, an overly-strict Russian mother, and a studious older brother who receives most of her mother's attention, fifteen-year-old Laurie feels that life is like being on a driverless bus. For years she has tried to be like her fearless friend Carla, who is becoming increasingly wild and even promiscuous. Thoughtful, timid Laurie, who wants to become a movie director, shoplifts and hitchhikes with Carla and then goes with Carla and her boyfriend to what turns out to be a remote drug hangout where she has beer and drugs and almost loses her virginity. Managing to escape, she is called that night by Carla, who needs help. It is then that Laurie finally appreciates her mother, who goes with Laurie to the house and bravely rescues the critically ill Carla. Finally recognizing Carla's falseness and her own worth, Laurie teams up with the boy who has always been her friend to shoot a movie.
European-American/Russian
Older; Fiction

García, Cristina. *I Wanna Be Your Shoebox*. New York: Simon & Schuster Books for Young Readers, 2008. 208 p.

Eighth-grader Zumi loves surfing, her baby cousin adopted from Guatemala, and playing clarinet in her middle school orchestra—and even spearheads the orchestra's money-raising punk-reggae concert to save it from being eliminated. However, most of all she treasures her cancer-ridden grandfather and the story of his life which he tells her before dying.
Japanese-Russian-American Jewish/Guatemalan-Cuban
Older; Fiction

Olivas, Daniel A. *Benjamin and the Word/Benjamín y la palabra*. Illustrated by Don Dyen. Spanish translation by Gabriele Baeze Ventura. Houston: Piñata Books, 2005. 32 p.

In this bilingual picture book, Benjamin is terribly upset when his friend James calls him a derogatory word. Benjamin's Mexican-American father points out that Benjamin looks like him and his Russian-American mother and that people sometimes use mean words to hurt the feelings of those who are different. Benjamin's father also helps Benjamin see that James was angry because Benjamin had beaten him at handball. When Benjamin gets to school, James apologizes and agrees never again to use mean words, and the boys resume their friendship.

Mexican-American/Russian-American and Jewish

Primary; Fiction

Pearce, Jonathan. *John-Browne's Body & Sole: A Semester of Life*. Stockton, Calif.: Balona Books, 2005. 168 p.

This book is presented as a journal written by thirteen-year-old Jack for a language arts assignment. It tells how he and the two other boys who are involved in an altercation learn how aikido (a martial art) and scripting can be used to prevent fighting and teach respect. In writing of his experiences, Jack expresses his feelings about his family, his friends, racism (his grandmother is Japanese), his piano recital, and his mother's terminal cancer.

Japanese-English-French-North African-Russian-European-American/European-American

Older; Fiction

Wyeth, Sharon Dennis. *The World of Daughter McGuire*. New York: Delacorte Press, 1994. 176 p.

Eleven-year-old Daughter's parents have separated, and she, her two younger brothers, and her mother have moved into a house next to her mother's parents. Daughter, whose deceased grandfather was Irish-American Catholic and whose other grandparents are Russian Jewish, African-American, and Italian-American, is called a "zebra" by a schoolmate and wishes that she was not all mixed-up. She is further concerned that the differences between her mother and father in careers and lifestyles will result in divorce. In this story Daughter learns to be proud of her heritages and is relieved when her parents decide to try to stay together despite their differences.

Irish-American Catholic and Russian-American Jewish/African-Italian-American

Intermediate; Fiction

Scottish-American

See   Baez, Joan Chandos
Chisholm, Jesse
Duwali
Hope, John
Hughes, James Mercer Langston
Malcolm X
Obama, Barack
Ross, John
Weatherford, William

Banks, Sara H. *Remember My Name*. Illustrated by Birgitta Saflund. Niwot, Colo.: Roberts Rinehart Publishers, 1993. 128 p.

When her parents die, eleven-year-old Annie, who is half Cherokee and half Scottish-American, leaves her Cherokee grandmother to live with her Cherokee uncle and his wife in New Echota. She attends school and becomes best friends with Righteous Cry, a black girl about her age who is a slave. When in 1838 the Cherokees are forced to leave to travel westward in the Trail of Tears, Annie's uncle sends her and Righteous (now freed) to travel, almost all the way by themselves, back to Annie's mountain home.
Scottish/Cherokee
Intermediate; Fiction

Carter, Forrest. *The Education of Little Tree*. 25th anniversity ed. Albuquerque: University of New Mexico Press, 2001. 238 p.
Set during the Great Depression in the Appalachian Mountains, this book tells the story of Little Tree during the years when he was five-, six-, and seven-years-old. With both his parents dead, Little Tree went to live with his half Cherokee grandfather, his Cherokee grandmother, and their hounds. There he received unconditional love and came to practice the Cherokee way of listening to and respecting all of nature. Little Tree accepted his grandfather's unique views of George Washington, politicians, and preachers and concluded from his own experience that he should never trade with a Christian. He twice kept men from discovering his grandfather's secret whiskey still, was saved from a rattlesnake by his grandfather, and learned figuring from a Jewish peddler, vocabulary words from the dictionary, and swear words from his grandfather. Little Tree spent time enduring harsh treatment in an orphanage before happily returning to the family and the land he loved.
Scottish-American and Cherokee
Older; Fiction

Curry, Jane Louise. *Dark Shade*. New York: Margaret K. McElderry Books, 1998. 176 p.
Independently Kip and Maggie are able to climb through a newly-formed spring to enter the world of the 1758 French and Indian War where British forces are cutting a road through the Pennsylvania forest to reach the French-controlled Fort Dusquesne and where the Lenape have a village near the road. Maggie saves the life of Robert Mackenzie, a lost Scottish Redcoat, and Kip is going to be adopted into a Lenape family until Maggie finds him. Afraid that their actions are changing the course of history, Kip and Maggie learn that they have altered and then restored it and that they are distant cousins, both descendents of Robert Mackenzie and his Lenape wife, Shawanaken. Corn Tassel, a minor character in this novel, is a British woman who has been adopted by the Lenape.
Scottish-European-American and Lenape/European-American; European-American/Scottish-European-American and Lenape
Older; Fiction

Ernst, Kathleen. *Highland Fling*. Chicago: Cricket Books, 2006. 224 p.
Exceedingly upset by her Polish-American father who had an extramarital affair, by moving from Wisconsin to North Carolina with her divorced mother and younger sister, and by the immersion of her mother and sister in everything to do with the Scottish MacDonald clan, fifteen-year-old Tanya reluctantly goes with them to the Highland Games. Longing to become an independent film-

maker, Tanya decides to make a documentary revealing the nostalgic pretense of the Highland Games. However, after meeting a young bagpiper from Puerto Rico who has Scottish heritage, his grandmother, and a Highland Games woman athlete whose mixed heritage does not include Scottish forebears, Tanya decides to make a different documentary and to have a talk with her father.
Polish-American and Catholic/Scottish-American and Presbyterian; Puerto-Rican/European-Scottish-American
Older; Fiction

Hausman, Gerald. *Night Flight*. New York: Philomel Books, 1996. 144 p.

Set in the summer of 1957, this is the story of two twelve-year-old boys: Max, who is incredibly cruel and controlling, and Jeff, who always tries to please him. When the boys' dogs as well as many others are poisoned, Max, whose father had been a Nazi, decides that Jews, whom he hates, are the culprits. Jeff, who had previously ignored his own Jewish heritage, struggles with Max's extreme views and actions, but, egged on by Max, shoots a dart into a Jewish family's front door. Jeff finally comes to realize what Max is—and what he himself can be.
Hungarian-Jewish/Dutch-English-Scottish-American and Iroquois and Methodist
Older; Fiction

Namioka, Lensey. *Half and Half*. New York: Delacorte Press, 2003. 144 p.

Eleven-year-old Fiona Cheng faces a dilemma when she must fill in the race box on her folk dancing class application as she is both white and Asian. She then faces another difficult choice. After agreeing to perform in her grandfather's Scottish dance group's performance at Seattle's Folk Fest, she discovers that at the same time she is supposed to appear, dressed in the elegant costume her Chinese grandmother has made, at her father's presentation of his children's book in which she is the model for the Chinese heroine. This problem seems to be resolved when Fiona's brother Ron agrees to wear a kilt and take her place in the Scottish dancing. Then when Ron injures his ankle, it is Fiona who not only solves the conflicting schedule problem, but learns that it doesn't matter which of your cultures you most outwardly resemble, they are of equal value.
Chinese/Scottish
Intermediate; Fiction

Spooner, Michael. *Last Child*. New York: Henry Holt and Company, 2005. 240 p.

Set in 1837 in the midst of a smallpox epidemic in what is now North Dakota, Rosalie is more comfortable helping her Scottish father, who is the bookkeeper at Fort Clark, than in being with her Mandan mother. Because of her superior attitude, she has only her father and her grandmother Muskrat Woman as friends. When Rosalie goes with her father to keep a log of the buffalo robes which have fallen from the capsized boat of the French trapper Bedeaux, they are attacked by Dakota and she is kidnapped by those responsible for the attack: a Mandan who is under the influence of whiskey and a scoundrel who has deliberately brought smallpox to the area and wants revenge on her father. Rosalie manages to escape and to make a bull boat with which she saves Bedeaux and returns to the Mandan village. There, with the assistance of her former husband Bedeaux, Muskrat Woman isolates Rosalie, inoculates her with the virus of a Mandan recovering from smallpox, holds the ceremony which makes

her a woman, and helps her in resolving the conflict between her Mandan and Scottish identities. Antoine Garreau, who served as interpreter for Fort Clark's managing officer, is a minor character in this novel.
Scottish/Mandan
Older; Fiction

Young, Karen Romano. *Cobwebs*. New York: Greenwillow Books, 2004. 400 p.
In this unusual story Nancy, a high school sophomore who as yet has no spider traits, is the daughter of part spider parents. Her father is a roofer who prefers living up high; her mother is a weaver who has to remain low; her Granny is a knitter and potter; and her Grandpa Joke is a doctor. Nancy's family becomes involved with Nico, a Greek-American journalist who blackmails Grandpa Joke into bringing Granny to heal his wife. In the process, Granny loses her life. The story focuses on the identities of the rumored Angel of Brooklyn and the Wound Healer, the growing attraction between Nancy and Niko's son Dion, and Nancy's concerns about whether she is or is not part spider.
Jamaican-West African-American/Italian-Scottish-American
Older; Fiction

Scottish-Irish-American

See   Bosomworth, Mary Musgrove Matthews?
Brown, Anne Wiggins
Parker, Quanah
Parks, Rosa Louise McCauley
Parton, Dolly Rebecca
Rogers, William (Will) Penn Adair?
Rogers, Will, Jr.?
Tallchief, Maria
Tallchief, Marjorie Louise

Jennings, Patrick. *Faith and the Electric Dogs*. Decorations by author. New York: Scholastic, 1996. 144 p.
The narrator—and author—of this fanciful tale is Edison, a mutt from San Cristóbal de las Casas, Mexico, who asserts that it is true. He is taken in by Faith, a ten-year-old homesick American girl, whose mother has married a Mexican and who hates Mexico because she can't speak Spanish and is teased. With help from a craftsman, Faith builds a rocket powered by pig fat and jalapeño peppers and sets off with Edison for San Francisco. Unfortunately, the rocket goes down in a storm. The two of them end up on an island in the Pacific Ocean, which is deserted except for four mutts and a seventy-year-old man who had come down on the island when he was ten after the balloon he was taking to return from Mexico to England was pierced by a seagull. The story concludes with Faith and Edison's return to Mexico, her happiness there, and an explanation of how Edison become a writer. Definitions of the many Spanish and Bowwow (canine) words used in the text are provided in the margins and also in a glossary.

Italian-American/German-Scottish-Irish-American
Intermediate; Fiction

Jennings, Patrick. *Faith and the Rocket Cat*. Decorations by author. New York: Scholastic Press, 1998. 240 p.

In this sequel to *Faith and the Electric Dogs*, Edison the mutt relates another fantastic story. When Faith, her mother, and her stepfather move to San Francisco, Faith wants to impress classmate Alex and Edison wishes to befriend Daphne, a whippet show dog, by taking them for a ride in Faith's rocket. Faith, Edison, Alex, Daphne—and Faith's mother—crash-land in Death Valley where they encounter coyotes and find Faith's late father's cat. All ends well in this story in which words presented in Bowwow and Arf (dog languages), Mew (cat language), Spanish, French, Italian, Chinese, Latin, and Turkish are defined both in the margins and in a glossary.
Italian-American/German-Scottish-Irish-American
Intermediate; Fiction

McKissack, Patricia C. *Run Away Home*. New York: Scholastic Press, 1997. 176 p.

In 1888 Sky, a fifteen-year-old Chiricahua Apache boy, escapes from a train of Apache prisoners and hides on the farm of twelve-year-old Sarah Jane Crossman, her African-American father, and her mother, who is of African-Scottish-Irish and Seminole heritage. George Wrattan, an Army scout and interpreter, allows the Crossmans to keep Sky with them until he recovers from his swamp fever. In the meantime boll weevils destroy the family's cotton crop, night riders come to their farm, and Sarah Jane's father, who is skilled as a carpenter, gets an order from Booker T. Washington to build desks for nearby Tuskegee Institute. Sky becomes healthy, but Wrattan, whose wife is Apache, gives permission for him to remain on the farm.
African-American/African-Scottish-Irish-American and Seminole
Intermediate, Older; Fiction

Smith, Cynthia Leitich. *Rain Is Not My Indian Name*. New York: HarperCollins Publishers, 2001. 144 p.

Since her best friend Galen was killed in a traffic accident on New Year's Day (her birthday), fourteen-year-old Rain, who is of mixed race, has withdrawn from her friends and from going out into her small Kansas town. However, despite refusing to become a participant, she agrees early in the summer to take photographs of her aunt's Native American camp. Rain is upset with Galen's mother and her opposition to the camp and with her former second best friend African-American Queenie, who attends the camp although it is not discovered until later that she has a Seminole ancestor. Then, on the Fourth of July (Galen's birthday), Rain is ready to move beyond his death.
Irish-German-American and Ojibwa/Scottish-Irish-American, Cherokee, and Muskogee
Intermediate, Older; Fiction

Slovak-American

See   Bruchac, Joseph

Spanish-American

See   Dandridge, Dorothy
        Estévez, Emilio
        Farragut, David Glasgow
        Goldman, Francisco
        Hayek-Jiménez, Salma Valgarma
        Martínez, Rubén
        Richardson, William (Bill) Blaine III
        Sheen, Charlie
        Sheen, Martin
        Williams, William Carlos

Bode, Janet. *Different Worlds: Interracial and Cross-Cultural Dating.* New York: Franklin Watts, 1989. 128 p.
    Based primarily on interviews with six teenage couples who are dating interracially and/or cross-culturally, this book is written for and about teens. It looks at the history of prejudice and racism; discusses negative reactions of parents, relatives, and classmates; examines why adolescents make their dating choices; and mentions some positive aspects of interracial dating. Although it does not cover the topics of interracial marriage and families, four of the twelve teens interviewed are of mixed race or heritage: African-American/European-American; Protestant English-American/Catholic Irish-American; Cuban/Puerto Rican; and Mexican-Spanish-American. A bibliography, a listing of resource organizations, and an index are included.
Mexican-Spanish-American
Older; Nonfiction

Herron, Carolivia. *Always an Olivia: A Remarkable Family History.* Illustrated by Jeremy Tugeau. Minneapolis: Kar-Ben Publishing, 2007. 32 p.
    In this picture book Carol Olivia's great-grandmother tells her about her Jewish ancestors, who were banished from Spain and Portugal and finally moved to Italy. One of their descendents and her future husband escaped from pirates and traveled by ship to Georgia. Their descendents intermarried with the Geechees (Gullahs) of Sea Island.
Gullah-Italian-Spanish-American Jewish
Primary, Intermediate; Fiction

Levin, Beatrice. *John Hawk: White Man, Black Man, Indian Chief.* Austin: Eakin Press, 1988. 192 p.
    This is the fictional story of John White, the son of a Georgia plantation owner and a slave mother, who becomes the lifelong friend of Osceola. The two meet as boys and, at Osceola's urging, John runs away to live with the Seminoles. He takes a new name, John Hawk, marries a Seminole woman, befriends a man who is Spanish-American and African-American, and becomes a Seminole chief. With Osceola he experiences the betrayals and tragedies preceding and during the Second Seminole War. A bibliography is included.

Spanish/African-American
Older; Fiction

Lewin, Michael Z. *Cutting Loose*. New York: Henry Holt and Company, 1999. 528 p.

Set in the nineteenth century, this is the story of Jackie's search for Teddy Zeph, who has murdered Jackie's best friend, Nance. The text alternates between the present and the past, starting with the story of Jackie's grandmother Claudette at the time she was orphaned. There are parallels among the characters' lives. Claudette is sold at a pauper auction, Jackie's father Mathew is sold by his New York City baseball team to a team in St. Louis, and Jackie goes to live with a new family that chooses her when she is displayed by the Children's Aid Society. Claudette murders her lover's father, and Matthew and Nance are murdered. Claudette disguises herself as a man to escape capture, and Jackie disguises herself as a man to pursue a baseball career. Both Jackie and her father play baseball in England as well as in the United States. Nance performs for Buffalo Bill's Wild West Show, and Jackie and Teddy Zeph perform on the stage in London. Further, Claudette's father is French, Teddy's mother is Spanish, and Nance, whose mother is African-American, passes as white.

European-American/Spanish
Older; Fiction

Lisle, Janet Taylor. *The Crying Rocks*. New York: Atheneum Books for Young Readers, 2003. 208 p. (A Richard Jackson Book)

Thirteen-year-old Joelle, who was adopted at the age of five by Vern and Aunt Mary Louise, does not look like anyone she knows in Rhode Island. She is upset by what she is told of her past: of being thrown out of a Chicago apartment window by her mother, being put in an orphanage there, traveling by freight train to Connecticut, and then being cared for by an old woman while living in a wooden crate near a railway depot. Joelle is befriended by an adoring eight-year-old girl who is European- and Japanese-American and by a classmate Carlos, who is of mixed heritage. Together Joelle and Carlos learn of the early Narragansett Indians and explore the wooded area, including the Crying Rocks, where they lived. Carlos learns the truth about the accident at the Crying Rocks where his older brother died and Joelle learns the truth about her background. Vern is her real father, her mother was Narragansett, and both her mother and twin sister died in Chicago.

Colombian-English-Spanish-American and Sioux/European-American
Intermediate, Older; Fiction

Peck, Richard. *The River Between Us*. New York: Dial Books, 2003. 176 p.

Set at the beginning of the Civil War, this book tells how the life of fifteen-year-old Tilly and her family changes when two mysterious strangers, Delphine and her apparent servant Calinda, arrive via steamboat at Grand Tower, Illinois. Coming from New Orleans, Delphine with her elegant clothes and fancy ways is like no one the town has ever seen. The two stay with Tilly's family, and Tilly's twin brother Noah falls in love with Delphine. When now-sixteen Noah goes off to join the Yankee army, their mother is so upset, since her husband had earlier left her, that she sends Tilly and Delphine off to Cairo, Illinois, to bring Noah home. The book tells of the horrible living conditions in Cairo and especially of the unsanitary hospital tents. Noah, who suffers from dysentery, recovers enough that he is sent

off to fight in the nearby battle of Belmont, Missouri, in which he is wounded and has to have his left arm amputated. The two girls stay in Cairo tending to Noah and other soldiers, and upon their return home with Noah learn that Tilly's distraught mother, seeing the coffin of her husband which she mistook for Noah's, drowned herself in the river. The story also reveals that to Tilly's surprise Delphine and Calinda are sisters and that Delphine's father is indeed the wealthy Jules Duval, but that he is her mother's protector, not her husband as in New Orleans whites cannot marry Creoles. Following the war Calinda, a conjure woman, leaves Grand Tower so that she will not raise suspicion that Delphine has African blood. Although Delphine refuses to marry a white man, she and Noah live as husband and wife, but their son is passed off as the son of Tilly and her husband.
Creole (African-French-Spanish)-Haitian-American
Older; Nonfiction

Walter, Mildred Pitts. *Ray and the Best Family Reunion Ever*. New York: HarperCollins Publishers, 2002. 128 p.

Eleven-year-old Ray is the only member of his Creole family with ebony skin. When he goes to a large family reunion in Natchitoches, Louisiana, Ray discovers that he and Gran-papa Philippe are the only ones there with dark skin. To make matter worse, Ray looks like his grandfather whom his father and almost all his relatives despise. This is the story of Ray's secret bonding with Gran-papa Philippe, his appreciation of his grandfather's talent, and his effecting a reconciliation between his father and Philippe.
Creole (Nigerian-French-Spanish-Native American)-Haitian-American/Creole (French-Spanish-West African-Native American)-American
Intermediate; Fiction

Swedish-American. See also Nordic-American

See   Noor Al Hussein, Queen of Jordan

Carter, Alden R. *Dogwolf*. New York: Scholastic, 1994. 240 p.

This is a novel of a hot summer when tower sitters spot fires in the Federal forest of northern Wisconsin and fire crews fight them. It is also the summer when Pete, aged fifteen, struggles to find who he is. Half white and half Native American, he is haunted by the persistent howling of the somehow-kindred creature who is a dogwolf. Knowing that it cannot stand being penned in a cage, Pete determines to free it, either by shooting it or by letting it out. Loose, the dogwolf terrorizes the countryside and the Chippewa reservation—killing animals and then Pete's friend—until finally Pete confronts and shoots it.
Métis-Canadian/Chippewa and Swedish-American
Older; Nonfiction

Ernst, Kathleen. *Highland Fling*. Chicago: Cricket Books, 2006. 224 p.

Exceedingly upset by her Polish-American father who had an extramarital affair, by moving from Wisconsin to North Carolina with her divorced mother and younger sister, and by the immersion of

her mother and sister in everything to do with the Scottish MacDonald clan, fifteen-year-old Tanya reluctantly goes with them to the Highland Games. Longing to become an independent filmmaker, Tanya decides to make a documentary revealing the nostalgic pretense of the Highland Games. However, after meeting a young bagpiper from Puerto Rico who has Scottish heritage, his grandmother, and a Highland Games woman athlete whose mixed heritage does not include Scottish forebears, Tanya decides to make a different documentary and to have a talk with her father.
German-Irish-Italian-Swedish-American
Older; Fiction

McKissack. Patricia C. *Run Away Home*. New York: Scholastic Press, 1997. 176 p.
    In 1888 Sky, a fifteen-year-old Chiricahua Apache boy, escapes from a train of Apache prisoners and hides on the farm of twelve-year-old Sarah Jane Crossman, her African-American father, and her mother, who is of African-Scottish-Irish and Seminole heritage. George Wrattan, an Army scout and interpreter, allows the Crossmans to keep Sky with them until he recovers from his swamp fever. In the meantime boll weevils destroy the family's cotton crop, night riders come to their farm, and Sarah Jane's father, who is skilled as a carpenter, gets an order from Booker T. Washington to build desks for nearby Tuskegee Institute. Sky becomes healthy, but Wrattan, whose wife is Apache, gives permission for him to remain on the farm.
English-French-Swedish-American
Intermediate, Older; Fiction

Meyer, Carolyn. *Denny's Tapes*. New York: Margaret K. McElderry Books, 1987. 224 p.
    Almost eighteen-year old Denny, the son of an African-American father and a white mother, and sixteen-year-old Stephanie, the daughter of his white stepfather, fall in love. When his stepfather discovers them together, he orders Denny to leave the house. This story for high school readers is about Denny's journey from Pennsylvania to San Francisco to find his father and on the way to meet his two grandmothers. Although Denny doesn't get together with his musician father who has left for a couple months for a gig in Houston, his trip turns out to be a memorable one. In Chicago he meets his African-American grandmother, who is highly cultivated and had objected to his parents' marriage because of his mother's lower social status. In Nebraska, he meets his mother's mother, who had objected to the marriage because of his father's race and believes Africans-Americans have lower intelligence. However, Denny comes to care for both his grandmothers. His Chicago grandmother spends time teaching him about black history, including about her friend Langston Hughes, and shows him how to develop his natural talent on the piano. Denny discovers that his Nebraska grandmother is largely imprisoned in bed by her cruel daughter-in-law, is full of love for him, and greatly appreciates his organ playing. In Chicago Denny also has a romantic relationship with a beautiful twenty-four-year-old African-American woman and in Colorado is rescued by a cowgirl from a pair of tourists who object to what they wrongly assume is an interracial relationship. When he gets to San Francisco, Denny realizes that he has learned a lot about himself, that he wants to become a musician, and that he is going to wait for his father.
African-American/Swedish-American
Older; Fiction

Singer, Marilyn, ed. *Face Relations: 11 Stories About Seeing Beyond Color*. New York: Simon & Schuster Books for Young Readers, 2004. 240 p.

In the story "Skins" by Joseph Bruchac, Mitchell, who is half Abenaki, provides needed support to the high school star quarterback, whom everyone assumes is Indian, but is really Hungarian. Mitchell also becomes close friends with Randolph, who is African-American and Native American.
Abenaki/Swedish
Older; Fiction

Swiss-American

See   Dorris, Michael

Crutcher, Chris. *Whale Talk*. New York: Dell Laurel-Leaf, 2002. 224 p.

This novel tells of T. J. Jones, an adopted seventeen-year-old of mixed race, who in his senior year of high school organizes a swimming team of boys regarded as misfits by their classmates and the school and who are, except for T. J., mediocre swimmers. The story focuses on T. J.'s efforts to have his teammates rewarded for their Herculean efforts by receiving athletic letters. The book shows how the boys come to share their backgrounds and feelings and to become part of a cohesive group in which each feels valued and accepted. Thanks primarily to his father, T. J. learns to control his own rage.
African-Japanese-American/Swiss-Norwegian-American
Older; Fiction

Welsh-American

See   Early, Sarah Jane Woodson?
         Hemings, Beverly?
         Hemings, Harriet?
         Jefferson, Thomas
         Rogers, Will, Jr.
         Woodson, Lewis?

Kimmell, Elizabeth Cody. *In the Stone Circle*. New York: Scholastic, 1998. 240 p.

When fourteen-year-old Cristyn and her father go to Wales so he can spend two months doing research for a book on medieval Wales, they share a rental house with another author, her daughter, and her son. The children discover that Carwen, a ghost from the thirteenth century, lives in the room of a very old house that is beneath theirs. Carwen seems to want something from Cristyn. It is not until the end of the book that Cristyn discovers what it is and thereby enables Carwen to join her long-deceased father. In the process Cristyn learns about her own Welsh mother, who had died when she was three, and to know that her mother is always with her.
European-American/Welsh
Intermediate, Older; Fiction

Resau, Laura. *What the Moon Saw: A Novel*. New York: Delacorte Press, 2006. 272 p.

Fourteen-year-old Clara's life turns upside down when she leaves her suburban Maryland home to visit her grandparents in a remote village in Oaxaca, Mexico. There she stays in a cluster of huts without a telephone, TV, or computer, and it is there that she comes to love exploring the mountains, being with Pedro the neighbor boy, and with him finding the secret waterfall. It is also there that Clara hears the story of her grandmother's life and learns that, like her grandmother, she has a spirit animal (a heron) and is a healer.
Mixtec Mexican/French-Norwegian-Welsh-American
Older; Fiction

Tenny, Dixie. *Call the Darkness Down*. New York: Atheneum, 1984. 204 p. (A Margaret K. McElderry Book)

Although for years Morfa has heard tales of Wales from Gwenfair, her Welsh mother, Gwenfair has refused to say anything about her parents and why she left her beloved Wales. When Morfa spends her freshman year at a Welsh college, she immediately becomes immersed in Welsh life: having Welsh friends, learning the Welsh language, and experiencing Welsh culture. She also has scary moments with a strange man in a dark coat and, pushed off a castle wall, narrowly escapes death. In this suspenseful story of the forces of light and dark, of mystical powers, and of spells, Morfa finally discovers the terrible truth about her family and must save her life from her murderous grandmother.
English-European-American/Welsh
Older; Fiction

Jewish-American

See   Cardozo, Francis Lewis
       Goldman, Francisco
       Hughes, James Mercer Langston
       McBride, James
       Mehta, Nina
       Smalls, Robert

Adoff, Arnold. *All the Colors of the Race*. Illustrated by John Steptoe. New York: Lothrop, Lee & Shepard Books, 1982. 56 p.

Poems celebrate a girl who is Polish, German, Russian, and Jewish on her father's side and African-American and Protestant on her mother's. She looks forward to the time when we will cease *looking* at colors and *love* all colors of the human race.
Polish-German-Russian-American Jewish/African-American Protestant
Intermediate, Older; Fiction

Baskin, Nora Raleigh. *The Truth about My Bat Mitzvah*. New York: Simon & Schuster Books for Young Readers, 2008. 144 p.

Twelve-year-old Caroline's father is Christian and her mother is non-practicing Jewish. Caroline has never thought about being Jewish until her grandmother's death and receiving the Star of David necklace her grandmother had wanted her to have. She keeps the necklace a secret, learns about being Jewish from her best friend Rachel who is about to have a bat mitzvah celebration, and discovers that her great-grandparents, who came from a non-practicing Jewish German-American family, had objected to her grandfather's marriage to her Russian Jewish immigrant grandmother. Also, initially her grandparents had not been happy about her mother's marrying a non-Jew. Caroline comes to realize that she wants to be Jewish and that she doesn't need a bat mitzvah party to be a bat mitzvah.
European-American Christian/German-Russian-American Jewish
Intermediate; Fiction

Blume, Judy. *Are You There God? It's Me, Margaret*. Scarsdale, N.Y.: Bradbury Press, 1970. 156 p.

When eleven-year-old Margaret moves to New Jersey, she joins a club with three other girls and together they puzzle about growing up: bras, menstruation, and kissing boys. Margaret, whose Jewish father and Christian mother don't practice any religion, also spends time on her school project to determine which religion she should be. After attending Jewish and Protestant services, briefly visiting a Catholic confessional, and being with her Jewish grandmother and Christian grandparents, Margaret concludes that she is not ready to decide, but she does learn that you shouldn't always believe what people tell you.
Jewish/Christian
Intermediate; Fiction

Brown, Don. *The Notorious Izzy Fink*. New Milford, Conn.: Roaring Brook Press, 2006. 160 p. (A Deborah Brodie Book)

New York City's Lower East Side of the 1890s comes alive in this book about the thirteen-year-olds Sam Glodsky, who is Irish-Russian-American, and Izzy Fink, who twice double-crosses Sam. It is a story of boys eeking out a living—hawking newspapers, cleaning a stable, grabbing coal that has fallen off a coal wagon—; of the teenage gangs of Irish, Jewish, Italians, and pickpockets; of a gangster; of corrupt police; of Tammany; and of the threat of cholera. Amazingly, in the end it is Sam's father who emerges from his depression and comes to Sam's rescue.
Russian and Jewish/Irish and Catholic
Intermediate, Older; Fiction

Cohen, Deborah Bodin. *Papa Jethro*. Illustrated by Jane Dippold. Minneapolis: Kar-Ben Publishing, 2007. 32 p.

When Rachel wonders why her grandfather is Christian and she is Jewish, he tells her a story about Moses' son Gershom, who was Jewish, and his Midianite grandfather Jethro whose daughter Zipporah was Moses' wife.
Christian and Jewish
Pre-K, Primary; Fiction

Cooper, Ilene. *Sam I Am*. New York: Scholastic Press, 2004. 256 p.

The celebration of Hanukkah-Christmas at Sam's house is a disaster with bad feelings between Sam's Jewish father and Episcopal mother that are exacerbated by the arguing of their grandmothers. Because of this bad experience and studying the Holocaust as a school assignment, twelve-year-old Sam questions who he is, why there are so many religions, why religions fight, and why God allows bad things to occur. Finally, with the help of his family and through recognizing that his first "crush" is not what she seems, Sam begins to find answers to his questions. Both he and his family come to recognize that they can be Jewish and Christian.
Jewish and European-American/Episcopal and European-American
Intermediate, Older; Fiction

Danziger, Paula. *It's an Aardvark-Eat-Turtle World*. New York: Delacorte Press, 1985. 144 p.

When fourteen-year-old Rosie's mother and Rosie's best friend Phoebe's father move in together, Rosie is pleased that the four of them will form a family. However, when Phoebe gets upset with Rosie's mother and also with Rosie because she spends time with Jason, her first boyfriend, and when Phoebe decides to move out and live with her mother, Rosie discovers that family relationships are not easy. She also suffers from the hateful remark of a man who objects to mixed race Rosie and Canadian Jason being together. At the story's end Phoebe decides to work things out and come back and Rosie spends a happy Christmas Eve with both Jason and Phoebe.
African-American Protestant/European-American Jewish
Intermediate, Older; Fiction

Elkeles, Simone. *How to Ruin a Summer Vacation*. Woodbury, Minn.: Flux, 2006. 240 p.

Sixteen-year-old Amy's parents never married, and her Israeli father, now an American resident, has been largely absent from her life. When Amy has to go with him to Israel to meet his family, that knows nothing about her existence, she is angry with her father, resentful about changing her summer vacation plans, and fearful about the safety of being in Israel. Overreactive Amy immediately likes her Israeli grandmother and her little Israeli cousin, but has to endure the hostility of the cousin with whom she rooms and eighteen-year-old Avi. She is constantly doing something wrong in their presence. It is not until the last part of her trip that Amy comes to appreciate her Israeli heritage, learns that her father had been rebuffed in his efforts to be with her, and falls in love with Avi.
German-Israeli Jewish/European-American non-Jewish
Older; Fiction

Erlbach, Arlene. *The Families Book: True Stories about Real Kids and the People They Live With and Love*. Photographs by Stephen J. Carrera. Illustrated by Lisa Wagner. Minneapolis: Free Spirit Publishing, 1996. 120 p.

This book contains a section in which children tell about their families, which include a family in which the father is Lutheran and the mother Jewish; a family in which the father is African-American and the mother Caucasian; a family with four children in which Caucasian parents have adopted a biracial American girl and a boy from Romania; and a family with Caucasian parents and eleven children, six of whom were adopted from Korea.
Lutheran/Jewish
Intermediate; Nonfiction

Freeman, Martha. *The Trouble with Babies*. Illustrated by Cat Bowman Smith. New York: Holiday House, 2002. 128 p.

When nine-year-old Holly moves into her new house, she meets her interesting neighbors, including Annie, who thinks her month-old sister is yucky, and Xavier, who has invented a de-yuckification device. The de-yuckification box produces surprising results, Annie realizes she likes her sister, and Holly discovers that she too is going to become a big sister. Annie and her baby sister have a Chinese father and a mother who is Polish-American and Jewish.
Chinese/Polish American and Jewish
Intermediate; Fiction

García, Cristina. *I Wanna Be Your Shoebox*. New York: Simon & Schuster Books for Young Readers, 2008. 208 p.

Eighth-grader Zumi loves surfing, her baby cousin adopted from Guatemala, and playing clarinet in her middle school orchestra—and even spearheads the orchestra's money-raising punk-reggae concert to save it from being eliminated. However, most of all she treasures her cancer-ridden grandfather and the story of his life which he tells her before dying.
Japanese-Russian-American Jewish/Guatemalan-Cuban
Older; Fiction

Hausman, Gerald. *Night Flight*. New York: Philomel Books, 1996. 144 p.

Set in the summer of 1957, this is the story of two twelve-year-old boys: Max, who is incredibly cruel and controlling, and Jeff, who always tries to please him. When the boys' dogs as well as many others are poisoned, Max, whose father had been a Nazi, decides that Jews, whom he hates, are the culprits. Jeff, who had previously ignored his own Jewish heritage, struggles with Max's extreme views and actions, but, egged on by Max, shoots a dart into a Jewish family's front door. Jeff finally comes to realize what Max is—and what he himself can be.
Hungarian-Jewish/Dutch-English-Scottish-American and Iroquois and Methodist
Older; Fiction

Herron, Carolivia. *Always an Olivia: A Remarkable Family History*. Illustrated by Jeremy Tugeau. Minneapolis: Kar-Ben Publishing, 2007. 32 p.

In this picture book Carol Olivia's great-grandmother tells her about her Jewish ancestors, who were banished from Spain and Portugal and finally moved to Italy. One of their descendents and her future husband escaped from pirates and traveled by ship to Georgia. Their descendents intermarried with the Geechees (Gullahs) of Sea Island.
Gullah-Italian-Spanish-American Jewish
Primary, Intermediate; Fiction

Howe, James. *Kaddish for Grandpa in Jesus' Name Amen*. Illustrated by Catherine Stock. New York: Atheneum Books for Young Readers, 2004. 32 p.

When her much loved Christian grandfather dies, five-year-old Emily, who is Jewish, remembers him at a Christian funeral, at a Jewish ceremony in her home, and, in her own way, by touching his glasses case each night at bedtime.
Christian and Jewish/Jewish
Pre-K, Primary; Fiction

Kuklin, Susan. *Families*. Photographs by author. New York: Hyperion Books for Children, 2006. 40 p.

Text and color photographs present interviews with American children, who talk about their families. Their families include seven families with children of mixed race, ethnicity, or religion, with one also including a child adopted from Sierra Leone. In an eighth family a child has been adopted from China. In a ninth family an adopted American child is of a race different from that of one of her fathers.
German-Jewish-American and Mescalero Apache/African-American; Christian/Jewish
Primary, Intermediate; Nonfiction

Murphy, Rita. *Black Angels*. New York: Delacorte Press, 2001. 176 p.

It is 1961 and Freedom Riders are on the way to a small Georgia town. Sophie, the Jenkins family's maid whom eleven-year-old Celli adores, is an outspoken African-American in the conservative Southern town. Celli finds it difficult to grasp the meaning of the civil rights movement and to cope

with the sudden discovery that the grandmother she had never met is black. During the summer Celli becomes less concerned with the negative effects Sophie's actions have on her life and helps free Sophie from jail and save a friend who is Jewish and African-American.
European-American and Jewish/African-American
Intermediate, Older; Fiction

Older, Effin. *My Two Grandmothers*. Illustrated by Nancy Hayashi. San Diego: Harcourt, 2000. 32 p.
    In this picture book Lily loves visiting her two grandmothers and enjoys each of their traditions, including Hanukkah and Christmas. Deciding that they should be able to try each other's special food and activities, she invites them to her first traditional grandmothers' party.
Jewish and Christian
Pre-K, Primary; Fiction

Olivas, Daniel A. *Benjamin and the Word/Benjamín y la palabra*. Illustrated by Don Dyen. Spanish translation by Gabriele Baeze Ventura. Houston: Piñata Books, 2005. 32 p.
    In this bilingual picture book, Benjamin is terribly upset when his friend James calls him a derogatory word. Benjamin's Mexican-American father points out that Benjamin looks like him and his Russian-American mother and that people sometimes use mean words to hurt the feelings of those who are different. Benjamin's father also helps Benjamin see that James was angry because Benjamin had beaten him at handball. When Benjamin gets to school, James apologizes and agrees never again to use mean words, and the boys resume their friendship.
Mexican-American/Russian-American and Jewish
Primary; Fiction

Ostow, Micol. *Emily Goldberg Learns to Salsa*. New York: Razorbill, 2006. 212 p.
    Emily with her family flies from New York to Puerto Rico for the funeral of the grandmother she had never met. As Emily's mother is stressed out by returning to her Puerto Rican family, Emily stays behind in Puerto Rico to help her. Emily has trouble adjusting to her newfound family and especially to Lucy, a cousin who dislikes her. By the end of the stay Emily has come to appreciate Puerto Rico, she and Lucy are friends, and the two discover that Emily's mother had not returned to Puerto Rico by choice, but because by marrying a Jewish man she was cut off by the grandmother.
European-Jewish-American/ Puerto Rican and Catholic
Older; Fiction

Rosenberg, Maxine B. *Living in Two Worlds*. Photographs by George Ancona. New York: Lothrop, Lee & Shepard Books, 1986. 48 p.
    This book explains how races evolved and how many children have a greater resemblance to one of their parents. It discusses the teasing and unwanted questions biracial children face and points to the benefits of living in two cultures. The book's text and black-and-white photographs focus on five children: Toah, who is African-European-American; Megan, who is African-European-American and Cherokee; Jesse, who is Chinese-European-American; and Shashi and Anil, who are Indian-European-American.

European-American and Jewish/Chinese-American and Christian
Intermediate; Nonfiction

Schwartz, Ellen. *Stealing Home*. Plattsburgh, N.Y.: Tundra Books of Northern New York, 2006. 224 p.

When ten-year-old Joey's mother dies, he is sent to live with her estranged family: his disapproving grandfather, his loving aunt, and his cousin, a girl who loves baseball as much as he does. Set in 1947, this is a story about the racial prejudice facing biracial Joey, first in his native Bronx by African-American boys who won't let him play baseball and then in Brooklyn where white boys won't let him play ball and where a woman insults him and his deceased mother. It relates how Joey's new friends and his aunt finally stand up for him against the bigots, how Joey and his grandfather come to understand and accept each other, and how, home at last, Joey changes his allegiance from the Bronx Bombers to Jackie Robinson and the Brooklyn Dodgers.
African-American and non-Jewish/European-American and Jewish
Intermediate; Fiction

Werlin, Nancy. *Black Mirror: A Novel*. New York: Dial Books, 2001. 256 p.

In this book for older teenagers sixteen-year-old Frances is a loner and so upset by her mixed race appearance that for years she has not been able to look at herself in the mirror. When her brother Daniel commits suicide by an overdose of heroin, Frances is shocked and feels guilty that she had no longer been close to him. When she considers joining Unity Service, the preparatory school charitable institution in which Daniel was so active, she experiences conflicting emotions and encounters negative reactions from its members. Discovering that something strange is going on at Unity, Frances, with the help of a man who is mildly retarded, finds out the terrible truth about Unity and the death of her brother.
European-American and Jewish/Japanese-American and Buddhist
Older; Fiction

Wing, Natasha. *Jalapeño Bagels*. Illustrated by Robert Casilla. New York: Atheneum Books for Young Readers, 1996. 24 p.

Pablo helps his parents at their Mexican-Jewish-American bakery and decides that he will take jalapeño bagels to his class International Day as they, like him, are a mixture of two cultures. This picture book includes recipes for chango bars and jalapeño bagels as well as a glossary of Spanish and Yiddish words.
European-American and Jewish/Mexican-American
Pre-K, Primary; Fiction

Wyeth, Sharon Dennis. *The World of Daughter McGuire*. New York: Delacorte Press, 1994. 176 p.

Eleven-year-old Daughter's parents have separated, and she, her two younger brothers, and her mother have moved into a house next to her mother's parents. Daughter, whose deceased grandfather was Irish-American Catholic and whose other grandparents are Russian Jewish, African-American, and Italian-American, is called a "zebra" by a schoolmate and wishes that she was not all mixed-up.

She is further concerned that the differences between her mother and father in careers and lifestyles will result in divorce. In this story Daughter learns to be proud of her heritages and is relieved when her parents decide to try to stay together despite their differences.

Irish-American Catholic and Russian-American Jewish/African-Italian-American

Intermediate; Fiction

Latin American-American. See also Central American-American, Mexican-American, South American-American, West Indian-American

Amado, Elisa. *Cousins*. Illustrated by Luis Garay. Toronto: Groundwood Books, 2004. 32 p.

A little girl, who lives with her Latin-American father and her maternal grandmother, is jealous of her Catholic cousin, who will celebrate her first communion and carry the pretty rosary that is at her paternal grandmother's house. Stealing the rosary, she feels terribly guilty and on her own goes to the Catholic church to confess.

Latin-American and Catholic/European-American and non-Catholic

Pre-K, Primary; Fiction

Grimes, Nikki. *Oh, Brother!* Illustrated by Mike Benny. New York: Greenwillow Books, 2008. 32 p.

In this picture book story narrated through twenty poems Xavier resents the intrusion of his new stepbrother. As the boys get to know each other's feelings they become closer and, with the birth of their baby sister, make a pact of brotherhood.

African-American/Latin-American

Pre-K, Primary; Fiction

Wayans, Kim, and Kevin Knotts. *All Mixed Up!* Illustrated by Soo Jeong. New York: Grosset & Dunlap, 2008. 112 p. (Amy Hodgepodge)

Amy Hodges is introduced in this first book of the *Amy Hodgepodge* series, which features pictures posted in Amy's scrapbook. Moving to a new town after having experienced only home schooling, Amy is excited to be starting fourth grade at Emerson Charter School. However, her first day starts out disastrously. She wears the wrong clothes, tears her dress when she removes its flower, sings too loudly in music class, is laughed at by classmates Liza and Jennifer, and discovers that a paper saying "Stupid new girl" has been taped to her back by Rory. However, her day improves when she is befriended in the cafeteria by Maya, Jesse, Rusty, Pia, and twins Lola and Cole. Upset by a racial insult from Jennifer, she discovers that the twins are black and white, Jesse is black and Puerto Rican, Pia is Chinese-American and white, and Rusty is Latino, Native American, and white. Learning that Amy's father is black and white and her mother Japanese and South Korean-American, they affectionately nickname her Amy Hodgepodge. The story continues with the group entering a school talent show where Amy, inspired by Rusty who has to earn money to buy his costume, overcomes her stage fright and becomes the group's lead singer.

European-Latin American-American and Native American

Primary, Intermediate; Fiction

Wayans, Kim, and Kevin Knotts. *Digging Up Trouble*. Illustrated by Soo Jeong. New York: Grosset & Dunlap, 2010. 112 p. (Amy Hodgepodge)

After foolishly letting her dog Giggles off his leash to play with another dog at the Farmer's Market, Amy is unable to find him. She spends a stressful night until in the morning the family receives a call from an older man, Irving Coleman, who reports that Giggles has come to his home

with his dog. Then, after being reunited with Giggles, Amy realizes that helping Irving restore his community garden would make a perfect green project for the school class assignment. The two fourth grade classes adopt Amy's idea and decide to raise money for the needed tools and supplies by having a bake sale and a car wash. Amy is worried when she is placed in charge of the bake sale team, but because of the help of her visiting community-organizer grandmother and team members, including Lola, Pia, and Rusty, there are many baked goods for sale. However, things turn contentious when the bake sale team and the car wash team, including Jesse and Maya, become overly competitive. After teachers intervene, the teams decide to refer customers to each other. With the proceeds earned and the work of Amy's gardener grandmother and the fourth graders, Irving's garden again becomes a neighborhood asset. Referring to the mixed racial identity of some of Amy's friends, this sixth book in the series specifically identifies the heritages of Lola and Cole as well as of Amy.
European-Latin American-American and Native American
Primary, Intermediate; Fiction

Wayans, Kim, and Kevin Knotts. *Happy Birthday to Me*. Illustrated by Soo Jeong. New York: Grosset & Dunlap, 2008. 112 p. (Amy Hodgepodge)

In this sequel to *All Mixed Up!* Amy looks forward to celebrating her birthday with her new friends as well as with her family. Maya, Jesse, Pia, and Lola accept her invitation to her tenth birthday sleepover where Amy plans to have a Japanese tea ceremony and do origami. Amy's spirits wane when she fears her family is planning to move to California. She is really upset when her four friends decide to go to an Amber Skye concert instead of her party. When Lola's brother Cole discovers that Amy has not invited other guests, he texts the concertgoers, and the four girls leave the concert to go to Amy's house. It is then that Amy discovers what true friends they are and the advisability of telling her problems and her fears to her family. This book points out the mixed heritages of Amy and most of her friends.
European-Latin American-American and Native American
Primary, Intermediate: Fiction

Wayans, Kim, and Kevin Knotts. *Lost and Found*. Illustrated by Soo Jeong. New York: Grosset & Dunlap, 2008. 112 p. (Amy Hodgepodge)

Amy Hodgepodge persuades her parents to let her go on the fourth grade two-and-a-half day wilderness trip. However, she doesn't feel as pleased about it when she is placed in a group without her friends, but with Jennifer and Rory who don't like her. Further, she falls in the mud during the obstacle course, goes overboard with Jennifer in their canoe, and is embarrassed that she doesn't know what s'mores are. However, Amy is supported by Lola, Jesse, Maya, and Pia with whom she shares a tent. Together they enjoy tricking Cole, Rusty, and two other boys. Then when she, Jennifer, Rory, and two others get lost in the woods, Amy uses her compass to lead them back to camp—and receives the Best Camper award. In this third book in the series, Amy's mixed heritage is noted. Readers of the first book, *All Mixed Up!*, will be aware of the mixed heritages of five of her friends.
European-Latin American-American and Native American
Primary, Intermediate; Fiction

Wayans, Kim, and Kevin Knotts. *Playing Games*. Illustrated by Soo Jeong. New York: Grosset & Dunlap, 2008. 112 p. (Amy Hodgepodge)

When Evelyn, the star player of the Comets girls' basketball team, injures her arm, Amy Hodgepodge reluctantly agrees to take her place so that the team will have the required eight players. Amy has neither played basketball nor is she familiar with the game. She is a terrible player, and her mistake causes the team to lose to the worst team in the league. Amy tries to fake a twisted ankle so she can be on the bench, but even that fails and she decides to quit. However, after confessing her problem to Rusty, he offers to coach her, with Amy, in return, helping him sing harmony in the friends' fourth grade music class performance. Unaware of the fact that Amy has improved, her team-mates don't pass her the ball. It is not until the end of an important game that Amy demonstrates her secret talent as a three-point shooter. Amy's mixed heritage is noted in this fourth book in the series. Readers of the first book, *All Mixed Up!*, will be familiar with the mixed heritages of most of her friends.
European-Latin American-American and Native American
Primary, Intermediate; Fiction

Wayans, Kim, and Kevin Knotts. *The Secret's Out*. Illustrated by Soo Jeong. New York: Grosset & Dunlap, 2009. 112 p. (Amy Hodgepodge)

Amy, Lola, Jesse, Pia, and Maya decide to enter as a group in their school's competitive annual spring art show. Amy comes up with the idea of tracing their body outlines on a large poster board and then painting and decorating them. The girls would stand behind holes that would show their faces. With the exception of Pia, the others are enthused about Amy's plan. Indeed, Pia's personality seems to have changed. She has become distracted, negative, and rude. Finally, she confides to Amy, with Amy's promise not to tell, that she fears that, since her father and stepmother are going to have a baby, her father won't pay attention to her. When Amy accidentally reveals Pia's secret to Lola, there are unforeseen consequences. Lola tells Jesse, and Jesse lets the secret out to classmates. The friends become so angry at each other that their Best Friends art display is jeopardized. It is not until they practice forgiveness that they restore their friendship—and their project ties for fourth grade first place. In this fifth book in the series, Amy's mixed heritage is noted, and series readers will be aware of the mixed heritages of most of her friends.
European-Latin American-American and Native American
Primary, Intermediate; Fiction

Mexican-American. See also Latin American-American

See   Alba, Jessica
         Baez, Joan Chandos
         Crawford, Goldsby (Cherokee Bill)?
         Dandridge, Dorothy
         Espinel, Luisa
         Hinojosa-Smith, Rolando
         Hodges, Ben
         Martínez, Rubén
         Olmos, Edward James
         Parsons, Lucia (Lucy) Gonzàles
         Pickett, Bill
         Richardson, William (Bill) Blaine III
         Ronstadt, Linda
         Senna, Danzy

Ada, Alma Flor. *I Love Saturday y domingos*. Illustrated by Elivia Savadier. New York: Atheneum Books for Young Readers, 2002. 32 p.

A little girl enjoys spending Saturdays with her paternal grandfather, who is the son of European immigrants, and her paternal grandmother, who is a descendant of settlers. She enjoys Sundays with her maternal grandfather, who is Mexican-American, and her maternal grandmother, who is Mexican-American and Native American. On her sixth birthday all four grandparents come to her house for the celebration. The text is similar for each weekend's activities, thereby making it possible to repeat some of the words in Spanish in describing the Sunday visits.
European-American/Mexican-American and Native American
Pre-K, Primary; Fiction

Bode, Janet. *Different Worlds: Interracial and Cross-Cultural Dating*. New York: Franklin Watts, 1989. 128 p.

Based primarily on interviews with six teenage couples who are dating interracially and/or cross-culturally, this book is written for and about teens. It looks at the history of prejudice and racism; discusses negative reactions of parents, relatives, and classmates; examines why adolescents make their dating choices; and mentions some positive aspects of interracial dating. Although it does not cover the topics of interracial marriage and families, four of the twelve teens interviewed are of mixed race or heritage: African-American/European-American; Protestant English-American/Catholic Irish-American; Cuban/Puerto Rican; and Mexican-Spanish-American. A bibliography, a listing of resource organizations, and an index are included.
Mexican-Spanish-American
Older; Nonfiction

Brashares, Ann. *Forever in Blue: The Fourth Summer of the Sisterhood.* New York: Delacorte Press, 2007. 400 p. (Sisterhood of the Traveling Pants)

This fourth book of the series takes place after Carmen, Lena, Tibby, and Bridget's freshman year in college. Carmen's year at Williams College has been a disaster. She finds herself ungrounded with her mother, stepfather, and baby brother moving into a new house, discovers that she has no idea how to make friends, and feels invisible. Her only college friend, aspiring actress Julia, has persuaded Carmen to spend the summer with her at a theater festival in Vermont where Carmen will be on a stage crew. When the casting director persuades Carmen to audition, Carmen, who has never acted, is amazed to discover that she is the only apprentice chosen for a role in the theater's major production. Julia becomes hostile to Carmen and, then, pretending to be helpful, teaches Carmen how to read her role in meter. The professional actors are dismayed that Carmen now sounds like a robot. Carmen finally realizes that Julia takes pleasure in her failures, and she once again immerses herself in her role. Lena, who had been crushed when her Greek boyfriend Kostas married a Greek woman whom he had impregnated, is enrolled in a painting class in Providence, Rhode Island. There she is impressed with classmate Leo, an outstanding artist who is equally engrossed in painting. Getting to know him and his artistic African-American mother, Lena has her first sexual experience with him. Tibby, who has been going with Bailey's friend Brian, also loses her virginity. However, she becomes distressed that she may be pregnant and, after discovering that she isn't, breaks up with Brian. She then gives Lena's younger sister Effie an okay to go out with him. With Bridget's boyfriend Eric away for the summer in Mexico, she goes to Turkey for an archaeological dig. There she discovers that she loves digging and falls for an archaeology professor until she sees his wife and children. At the book's conclusion Tibby is reunited with Brian, Bridget is reunited with Eric, and Lena, Tibby, and Bridget go to Vermont to attend Carmen's successful opening night. Then the four friends fly to Greece to search for the Traveling Pants, which Effie has accidentally lost, Lena and Kostas meet, and the four friends realize that they have moved beyond the Pants. The mixed heritages of Carmen, Bridget, and Eric should be familiar to readers of *The Sisterhood of the Traveling Pants.*
European-American/Mexican
Older; Fiction

Brashares, Ann. *Girls in Pants: The Third Summer of the Sisterhood.* New York: Delacorte Press, 2005. 352 p. (Sisterhood of the Traveling Pants)

Bridget, Lena, Tibby, and Carmen graduate from high school at the beginning of this third book in the series, which details the four seventeen-year-olds' lives during the summer before college. Lena, who is still getting over Kostas, enjoys her summer drawing class. Defying and lying to her father, she continues to attend after he has forbidden her to continue because of the nude models. When he discovers her deceit, he announces that he will not pay for her going to the Rhode Island School of Design. Heeding the suggestion of the class teacher, Lena embarks on an art portfolio project that just may win her a scholarship to the RISD. Tibby has conflicting feelings when Brian asks her to the senior party, but is devastated when, because she has left her window open, her three-year-old sister tries to climb the nearby apple tree and, falling, has a fractured skull and broken bones. Finding it difficult

to have her new stepfather David living in her house and upset by the news that she will become a sister, Carmen considers going to the nearby University of Maryland rather than Williams College so that she can be closer to home. She hates her job taking care of Valia, Lena's grandmother, who has become very disagreeable because she is homesick for her native Greece. Carmen also worries that Win, the boy she likes, has the false impression that she is a good person. Bridget spends her summer coaching at a soccer camp in Pennsylvania where she is surprised to discover that one of the coaches is Eric with whom she had a relationship two summers earlier in California. Still strongly drawn to him, but trying to be more sensible, she and Eric become friends and he nurses her through an illness. It is an eventful summer as Carmen and Win frantically drive to Downington, Pennsylvania, to bring David back to Bethesda for his son's early birth and Carmen discovers that she loves her baby brother and wants to go to Williams. Valia is happy that she can return to Greece, and Lena receives the RSID scholarship and her father's approval. Tibby overcomes her feelings of unworthiness by climbing out of her window and down the apple tree and being Carmen's mother's successful, albeit unorthodox, birth coach. It is then that she is able to get back together with Brian. And, Eric tells Bridget that he has broken up with his girlfriend, and they profess how much they care for each other. Readers of the initial book in this series will be aware of the mixed heritages of Carmen, Bridget, and Eric.
European-American/Mexican
Older; Fiction

Brashares, Ann. *The Second Summer of the Sisterhood*. New York: Delacorte Press, 2003. 384 p. (Sisterhood of the Traveling Pants)

This second book of the series describes Carmen, Lena, Bridget, and Tibby's experiences during the summer before their seventeenth birthdays. Once again, the pants are passed among them, but they no longer fit Bridget, who has been so down because of her earlier sexual relationship with Eric, that she has gained weight, given up soccer, and dyed her pretty blonde hair. Using a fake name, Bridget travels to Alabama where she gets a job cleaning her grandmother Greta's attic and finds mementos of her deceased mother. As the summer progresses Bridget gets back in shape, is able to wear the pants, confesses her identity to Greta and to her long ago best friend Billy, coaches and then stars for Billy's soccer team, and realizes that Greta is like a mother to her. Tibby goes to a film program at a college in Virginia. Befriending two shallow classmates, she produces a highly embarrassing film about her mother and is excruciated when her mother comes to the viewing. Upset by the damage she has done to her relationships with her mother and Brian, a friend of hers and Bailey's, she redeems herself by making a moving film about Bailey, who died from cancer. Both Carmen and Lena also experience strained relationships with their mothers. Carmen is jealous of her mother's romance with David, sabotages it, and then manages to restore it. Lena pesters her mother about the man Eugene in her mother's past and regrets that she has broken off with Kostas. When Kostas visits her, she discovers that he really is in love with her. However, going to Greece for her beloved grandfather's funeral, Lena finds out that Kostas has had to marry a Greek woman whom he impregnated. Fortunately, she learns about Eugene from her mother and is attracted to Carmen's stepbrother Paul. The story ends when the girls' mothers, who had not been close since Bridget's mother's death, resume their friendship. The mixed heritages of Carmen, Bridget, and Eric were revealed in *The Sisterhood of the Traveling Pants*.

European-American/Mexican
Older; Fiction

Brashares, Ann. *The Sisterhood of the Traveling Pants*. New York: Delacorte Press, 2001. 304 p. (Sisterhood of the Traveling Pants)

In this initial book of the series, four girls who are almost sixteen discover that a pair of blue jeans that Carmen had purchased at a thrift shop somehow fits all of them. Close friends their entire lives, the girls establish a Sisterhood in which they will pass the pants among each other as they separate during their summer vacation. Bridget, an athlete whose father is Dutch and whose mother had committed suicide, goes to a soccer camp in Baja, California, where she shines as a player. She is strongly attracted to camp coach Eric whose mother is Mexican, loses her virginity to him, and then becomes confused and upset. Carmen, who had been looking forward to a vacation with her divorced father in South Carolina, is shocked to learn that he is engaged and is living with his fiancée and her two children. Ignored and treated like an outsider because of her Puerto Rican appearance, Carmen finally becomes so frustrated and angry that she throws a rock through the house window and runs away back to Bethesda, Maryland. Lena, a beautiful introverted girl, goes with her sister to stay in Greece with her grandparents. Enjoying painting the lovely scenery, she inadvertently leads her grandparents to believe she has been raped by Kostas, a family friend, and causes a fight between their grandfathers. Tibby, who remains at home, gets a tedious job at a drugstore and becomes friends with Bailey, a twelve-year-old girl who has leukemia and with whom she films a movie. The pants seem to have no positive effect on the girls' experiences until the end of the summer. Then Lena gets the courage to apologize to Kostas and tell him she loves him; Carmen gets the courage to go to her father's wedding after telling him that she is mad at him; Tibby gets the courage to visit Bailey in the hospital when she is dying; and Bridget receives the support she needs from the pants (and Lena who brings them to her). European-American/Mexican
Older; Fiction

Cruz, Maria Colleen. *Border Crossing: A Novel*. Houston: Piñata Books, 2003. 128 p.

Cesi, who is twelve-years-old and of mixed race, feels she can discover who she is by finding out more about the Mexican heritage which her father doesn't discuss. When questions to her mother, both grandmothers, her brother, and her father don't satisfy her, she takes off by herself to cross the border from California to Tijuana. With the help of a Mexican-American boy she meets and of his aunt, Cesi learns about Mexicans, the prejudice her father faced as a boy, and who she really is. In the process her father comes to realize that by protecting his children he has unintentionally made their lives more difficult.
Mexican-American/Irish-American and Cherokee
Intermediate, Older; Fiction

De la Peña, Matt. *Mexican Whiteboy*. New York: Delacorte Press, 2008. 256 p.

Sixteen-year-old Danny chooses to spend his summer vacation with his Mexican-American father's family in National City, California, so that he can then fly to Ensenada, Mexico, and find his father. Since his father left his San Diego family three years earlier, Danny has been heartbroken to the

extent that he seldom speaks, not wanting to use his mother's English. His goal is to please his father by becoming a great pitcher. He has exceptional talent, but is plagued by his lack of control. During the eventful summer Danny makes an unlikely best friend, Uno, who initially punched Danny. Uno needs to make money so that he can move away from his Mexican-American mother and stepfather and live with his black father. Through hours of practice with Uno, Danny works on his pitching skills and discovers how to keep the ball in the strike zone when people are watching. Together Uno and Danny successfully hustle the area's best hitters, thereby earning money for Uno. Although he cannot speak Spanish and she cannot speak English, Danny falls in love with Liberty, who is newly arrived from Mexico and has a white father. Further, Danny finally finds out the truth about his father and comes to accept himself.
Mexican-American/European-American; African-American/Mexican-American
Older; Fiction

Grattan-Domínguez, Alejandro. *Breaking Even*. Houston: Arte Público Press, 1997. 256 p.
    Now eighteen and a high school graduate, Val is determined to leave his small Texas town and travel to California. However, his plans are interrupted when he discovers that his girlfriend is pregnant and that his father, whom he had been told was dead, had abandoned him and his mother and is still alive. Val travels to El Paso to find him and joins his father and his father's new girlfriend in trying to raise money through crooked gambling tactics. Val earns his father's admiration, but finally understands that his father is a compulsive gambler, who cares more for money than family. Val also comes to realize the goodness of his stepfather and makes a responsible decision about his future life.
Irish/Mexican
Older; Fiction

Hamanaka, Sheila. *Grandparents Song*. Illustrated by author. New York: HarperCollins Publishers, 2003. 32 p.
    In this picture book, which is written in verse, a girl tells how her grandparents came from four directions—her maternal grandmother from the West, her maternal grandfather from Europe, her paternal grandmother from Mexico, and her paternal grandfather from Africa—and how they are all part of her.
African-Mexican-American/European-American and Native American
Pre-K, Primary, Intermediate; Fiction

Hernández, Irene Beltrán. *Heartbeat Drumbeat*. Houston: Arte Público Press, 1992. 136 p.
    This is a novel about Morgana, a young woman who lives with her Mexican-American father and her Navajo mother near the Sandia Mountains of New Mexico. It presents the beliefs and rituals of both cultures as it tells of the death of Morgana's elderly Navajo mentor, of her bout with Rocky Mountain fever, of her rescue of a Seminole neighbor, of the attack by a bear which nearly killed her father, of her mother's sudden death, and of her tumultuous relationship with Eagle Eyes, whom she finally marries.

Mexican-American/Navajo
Older; Fiction

Iyengar, Malathi Michelle. *Romina's Rangoli*. Illustrated by Jennifer Wanardi. Fremont, Calif.: Shen's Books, 2007. 32 p.

When Romina's teacher asks her students to make something representing their individual heritages, Romina doesn't know how to present two cultures since her father is from India and her mother is from Mexico. She finally solves the dilemma by creating an Indian rangoli pattern with Mexican papel picado, cut paper, as the design material.
Indian/Mexican
Primary; Fiction

Lachtman, Ofelia Dumas. *Call Me Consuelo*. Houston: Arte Público Press, 1997. 152 p.

After her parents are killed in an automobile accident, Consuelo goes to live with her Mexican-American aunt and uncle and then leaves her small California town to live with her father's mother in Los Angeles. Although very homesick, she makes friends and with them becomes involved in mysterious events occurring in an old movie lot near her grandmother's gated community. When Consuelo has the opportunity to return to her aunt and uncle, she realizes that she doesn't want to abandon her caring grandmother.
European-American/Mexican-American
Intermediate; Fiction

Nye, Naomi Shihab. *Going Going*. New York: Greenwillow Books, 2005. 240 p.

Since early childhood Florrie has treasured old things, especially old buildings and businesses, and wanted to protect them. She had loved walking about San Antonio with her late Lebanese grandfather and sharing his love and knowledge of San Antonio. Now sixteen, Florrie launches a campaign to stop people from shopping at franchise businesses, which are destroying the unique character of the city. Enlisting classmates and neighbors to support independent businesses, she receives positive input and publicity, but is discouraged when her project to canoe along the River Walk is aborted. However, Florrie's fervor returns when the family learns that a Taco Bell is to be built next to her mother's Mexican restaurant.
Mexican-American/Lebanese-Mexican-American
Older; Fiction

Olivas, Daniel A. *Benjamin and the Word/Benjamín y la palabra*. Illustrated by Don Dyen. Spanish translation by Gabriele Baeze Ventura. Houston: Piñata Books, 2005. 32 p.

In this bilingual picture book, Benjamin is terribly upset when his friend James calls him a derogatory word. Benjamin's Mexican-American father points out that Benjamin looks like him and his Russian-American mother and that people sometimes use mean words to hurt the feelings of those who are different. Benjamin's father also helps Benjamin see that James was angry because Benjamin had beaten him at handball. When Benjamin gets to school, James apologizes and agrees never again to use mean words, and the boys resume their friendship.

Mexican-American/Russian-American and Jewish
Primary; Fiction

Ryan, Pam Munoz. *Becoming Naomi León*. New York: Scholastic, 2005. 272 p.

Fifth-grader Naomi and her younger brother Owen live happily with their great-grandmother Gram in a large trailer in California. Seven years earlier their irresponsible mother had left them there. At that time Owen was covered with infected insect bites and Naomi was suffering from selective muteness. When their alcoholic and abusive mother and her boyfriend come to reclaim Naomi and move her to Las Vegas to be their babysitter, Gram, Naomi, and Owen go to Oaxaca, Mexico, to search for Santiago León, the children's father who had earlier wanted them. As they had hoped, Santiago comes to the annual La Noche de los Rábanos (Night of the Radishes), the children are reunited with him, and he writes a letter to the California court urging that Naomi be allowed to remain with Gram. However, it is only when the judge discovers that their mother does not want Owen because he is physically disabled and when Naomi finds the courage of a lion (león) to speak up that Gram is awarded Naomi's custody.
Mexican/European-American
Intermediate; Fiction

Wallace, Bill. *Buffalo Gal*. New York: Pocket Books, 1993. 192 p. (A Minstrel Book)

It is 1904 and fifteen-year-old Amanda is on a trip from San Francisco to Oklahoma Territory and Texas with her mother who wants to save buffalo from extinction by getting some of them to a ranch. Amanda is unhappy about everything: the trains, the trip, and especially David, the half Comanche boy she meets at Fort Sills who insults her and, with two others, will accompany them into Texas in search of a buffalo herd. David is especially annoying after she almost beats him in a horse race and the two continually spat. On the journey Amanda is saved from an alligator and a rattlesnake; the group survives a severe thunderstorm; a Texas rancher, his Mexican wife, and their two children provide welcome hospitality; Amanda and David fight off a buffalo; Amanda is given the buffalo's calf as a birthday present; and the buffalo herd is captured. Amanda finally realizes that David cares for her and as she leaves for San Francisco, she agrees to marry him.
European-American/Mexican
Older; Fiction

Wing, Natasha. *Jalapeño Bagels*. Illustrated by Robert Casilla. New York: Atheneum Books for Young Readers, 1996. 24 p.

Pablo helps his parents at their Mexican-Jewish-American bakery and decides that he will take jalapeño bagels to his class International Day as they, like him, are a mixture of two cultures. This picture book includes recipes for chango bars and jalapeño bagels as well as a glossary of Spanish and Yiddish words.
European-American and Jewish/Mexican-American
Pre-K, Primary; Fiction

Wong, Janet S. *The Next New Year.* Illustrated by Yangsook Choi. New York: Frances Foster Books/Farrar Straus and Giroux, 2000. 32 p

In this picture book a young American boy, who has a Chinese father and a Korean mother, prepares for Chinese New Year. His two best friends, who, like him, are of mixed heritage, will also celebrate the holiday.
Hopi and Mexican
Pre-K, Primary; Fiction

Mixtec-American

Resau, Laura. *What the Moon Saw: A Novel.* New York: Delacorte Press, 2006. 272 p.

Fourteen-year-old Clara's life turns upside down when she leaves her suburban Maryland home to visit her grandparents in a remote village in Oaxaca, Mexico. There she stays in a cluster of huts without a telephone, TV, or computer, and it is there that she comes to love exploring the mountains, being with Pedro the neighbor boy, and with him finding the secret waterfall. It is also there that Clara hears the story of her grandmother's life and learns that, like her grandmother, she has a spirit animal (a heron) and is a healer.
Mixtec Mexican/French-Norwegian-Welsh-American
Older; Fiction

Native American

See   Brown, Eve
        Cardozo, Francis Lewis
        Horne, Lena
        Hughes, James Langston
        Langston, John Mercer
        Morgan, Garrett Augustus
        Olmos, Edward James
        Parks, Rosa Louisa McCauley
        Pickett, Bill
        Richardson, William (Bill) Blaise III
        Stewart, John
        White, George Henry
        Williams, Daniel Hale
        Woods, Tiger

Ada, Alma Flor. *I Love Saturday y domingos*. Illustrated by Elivia Savadier. New York: Atheneum Books for Young Readers, 2002. 32 p.

A little girl enjoys spending Saturdays with her paternal grandfather, who is the son of European immigrants, and her paternal grandmother, who is a descendant of settlers. She enjoys Sundays with her maternal grandfather, who is Mexican-American, and her maternal grandmother, who is Mexican-American and Native American. On her sixth birthday all four grandparents come to her house for the celebration. The text is similar for each weekend's activities, thereby making it possible to repeat some of the words in Spanish in describing the Sunday visits.

European-American/Mexican-American and Native American

Pre-K, Primary; Fiction

Bruchac, Joseph. *Hidden Roots*. New York: Scholastic Press, 2004, 144 p.

It is 1954 and eleven-year-old Sonny lives with his mother and his father, who is often angry and physically abusive. Sonny enjoys the company of an older friend, "Uncle" Louie, a man who had worked for his mother's parents when she was a child and from whom he learns much about the Adirondack area of New York State where they live. Sonny wonders about the many subjects he is not allowed to discuss and questions that remain unanswered: why he should be afraid of being "crept up on," what bad things happened in Vermont, and why his father doesn't want Uncle Louis around. It is only after he and Uncle Louis learn from the Jewish school librarian that her parents had sent her as a child from Germany to England for safety, that Uncle Louis tells Sonny the truth. Uncle Louis is his grandfather, who, like his late wife, had been sterilized during the Vermont Eugenics Project because they were Indians and who had fled Vermont so that Sonny's mother would not be taken away. It was because Sonny's family wanted to protect him from being treated like an Indian that they had kept his identity a secret, but it is when the secret is revealed to Sonny that his father, who is also part Indian, is released from his anger and shame.

European-American and Native American/French Canadian-American, Abenaki and Mohican
Intermediate, Older; Fiction

Dorris, Michael. *The Window*. New York: Hyperion Paperbacks for Children, 1999. 112 p.

When eleven-year-old Rayona's mother is ordered into an alcohol rehabilitation program, two efforts at finding Rayona a foster home fail and her father decides he can't care for her. It is then that Rayona learns that her African-American father is half Irish-American. He takes her from Seattle to Louisville where she enjoys her temporary stay with her Irish-American grandmother, great-aunt, and great-grandmother and meets an older African-American cousin. It is with regret that Rayona leaves her newfound relatives, but with happiness that she is reunited with her much-missed Native American mother—and with gratitude that a window on her life has been opened.
African-Irish-American/Native American
Intermediate, Older; Fiction

Hamanaka, Sheila. *Grandparents Song*. Illustrated by author. New York: HarperCollins Publishers, 2003. 32 p.

In this picture book, which is written in verse, a girl tells how her grandparents came from four directions—her maternal grandmother from the West, her maternal grandfather from Europe, her paternal grandmother from Mexico, and her paternal grandfather from Africa—and how they are all part of her.
African-Mexican-American/European-American and Native American
Pre-K, Primary, Intermediate; Fiction

Hamilton, Virginia. *Arilla Sun Down*. New York: Scholastic, 1976. 304 p.

This novel tells of twelve-year-old Arilla whose mother is sure of her identity as an African-American woman, whose Native American father alternates between his work at an Ohio college and leaving for his boyhood home, and whose older brother, Jack Sun Run, delights in parading his Native American heritage. Always in her brother's shadow, certain that he hates her, and terribly jealous, Arilla treasures the times that he treats her nicely. The book tells of Arilla's writing her autobiography; of old James False Face, her only friend when she was little; of Susanne Shy Woman who is Sioux and Cheyenne; of sneaking out at night with Sun Run and his girlfriend to go roller skating; of sledding with her father on an exciting, but dangerous hill; of saving Sun Run's life and discovering he had saved hers; and, throughout the book, of her struggle to find her own identity.
Native American/African-American
Older; Fiction

Lipsyte, Robert. *The Brave*. New York: HarperCollins Publishers, 1991. 208 p. (A Charlotte Zolotow Book)

This book is the sequel to *The Contender*. Unhappy with his life on the Moscondaga Reservation and resentful about the unfair treatment he has received in a boxing match, seventeen-year-old Sonny Bear, who is of mixed race, takes off for New York City. He no sooner arrives than he is picked up by two hustlers, becomes their decoy in carrying a bag of crack, and ends up in a juvenile correction

facility. It is the police officer, Sergeant Alfred Brooks, the protagonist of *The Contender*, who recognizes Sonny's potential as a boxer if he can control his rage. Sonny returns to the reservation to be trained by his great-uncle Jake and then comes back to New York City to Donatelli's Gym where Brooks had trained. Finally learning to harness the fire within him, Sonny advances in amateur fights until he is disqualified because of his earlier fighting for pay. However, with the help of his new friend, Martin Witherspoon, he embarks on a professional boxing career.
European-American/Native American
Older; Fiction

Lipsyte, Robert. *The Chief*. New York: HarperTrophy, 1995. 240 p.
This second book about the half Moscondaga boxer Sonny Bear is narrated by Martin Witherspoon, who is writing a book about Sonny. It is the sequel to *The Brave*. At the beginning of this story, frustrated Sonny Bear is about to quit boxing. Then, spurred on by the example of Muhammad Ali who used publicity to advance his career, Sonny Bear and Martin head to Las Vegas where television reports Martin's public challenge of the boxer Elston Hubbard, Jr. Sonny Bear is taken under the wing of has-been champion John L. Sullivan, who is scheduled to fight Hubbard. The older Sullivan and nineteen-year-old Sonny become friends, bonding because of the shared prejudice directed towards their people, the Jews and the Indians. Sonny gains notoriety by winning a preliminary match and forcing an end to the Hubbard-Sullivan fight when Sullivan is being critically injured. Sullivan subsequently dies, and Sonny Bear loses a close fight with Hubbard. However, when Sonny draws upon his heritage to save the Moscondaga Nation from an internal dispute over a gambling casino, he achieves a greater victory.
European-American/Native American
Older; Fiction

Lipsyte, Robert. *Warrior Angel*. New York: HarperCollins Publishers, 2003. 192 p.
Warrior Angel is the sequel to *The Chief* and the third book about the mixed race boxer Sonny Bear, who was introduced in *The Brave*. Now under contract to the promoter Elston Howard, Sonny Bear has defeated the heavyweight champion Floyd (The Wall) Hall and as the book begins is about to fight a challenger. However, Sonny feels strangely out of it and fights listlessly. He only retains the title because of a split decision. Sonny is contacted by e-mail by a delusional teenager Starkey, who having become immersed in the book about Sonny which Martin Witherspoon has written, feels that he is Warrior Angel sent on a mission by the Creator to save Sonny. Sonny leaves Hubbard to meet Starkey at Donatelli's Gym where he had once trained. Although Sonny loses a fight with Hall, he follows Starkey's advice to find the answer he is seeking and then saves Starkey from heeding the voices he hears and committing suicide.
European-American/Native American
Older; Fiction

Platt, Randall Beth. *The Likes of Me*. New York: Delacorte Press, 2000. 256 p.
This is the story of the amazing year, 1918, in the life of fourteen-year-old Cordelia, an albino who is half white and half Chinese. With her mother dead and her stepmother Babe a giant, Cordelia

is completely innocent of the ways of the world and fears she is dying when she has her first period. Cordelia falls in love with the half-Indian Squirl and with him breaks the rules by riding the flume of the lumber camp where her father is superintendent. Thinking she has become pregnant by kissing Squirl, Cordelia runs away to Seattle. She does not realize that she has gone to live in a brothel, earns money as a freak with her "lucky" hair, and finally comes to her senses about Squirl and Babe.
European-American and Native American
Older; Fiction

Powell, Neva. *The Long Crossing*. Illustrated by Eugene Powell. New York: Avocet Press, 1998. 128 p.

Leading a horse-drawn sleigh carrying logs from a lumber camp, young Johnny makes a perilous trip through a blizzard and cracking ice across Lake Michigan to a railroad siding. As he travels, he recalls his life from the time his mother died and he went to live with an old man and his cruel wife, who refused to let his Indian father see him. As a nine-year-old Johnny began doing a man's farm work and he continued to do so when, after the old couple died, he went to live in the house of the old woman's kind niece and her husband. While living there, he experienced his first automobile ride, saw an aeroplane, and was given a bike. As Johnny safely completes his dangerous journey, he proudly acclaims his Indian heritage.
European-American and Native American/European-American
Intermediate, Older; Fiction

Savageau, Cheryl. *Muskrat Will Be Swimming*. Illustrated by Robert Hynes. Flagstaff, Ariz.: Northland Publishing, 1996. 32 p.

Jeannie, who is of French and Indian heritage, loves the lake where she lives, but doesn't like the children at school calling her a Lake Rat. Her grandfather relates how he used to be called a Frog, but points out that being called an animal relative, a frog or a lake rat (a muskrat) shouldn't hurt one's feelings. He tells Jeanne the Seneca story of how Muskrat helped create the world, and Jeannie, like Muskrat, dives to the bottom of the lake to bring up some earth.
French-American and Native American
Primary, Intermediate; Fiction

Taylor, Mildred D. *The Land*. New York: Phyllis Fogelman Books, 2001. 392 p.

This prequel to the earlier-published books about the Logan family presents the story of Cassie's grandfather Paul-Edward Logan during the years following the Civil War. The son of a white farm owner and a former slave, Paul-Edward is treated as a son by his father, who has him sit with his siblings at the family table and provides him with an education. Paul-Edward loves the family's Georgia land and dreams of becoming a landowner when he grows up. However, despite his father's advice and warnings, he only realizes the difficulties his mixed race will cause when he is betrayed by the brother to whom he is closest. Forced to flee with his best friend Mitchell when Mitchell's life is in danger, Paul-Edward works in a lumber camp and uses his skills with horses and as a carpenter to save some money and enter into contracts to secure the Mississippi land which he has set his heart on. This is a story of the terrible treatment which Negroes received in the South, of the kindnesses of a few white

people, of Mitchell's marrying Caroline whom Paul-Edward had fancied, of the friendship of the three of them, of Mitchell's being killed, and of the realization of Paul-Edward's dreams.
European-American/African-American and Native American
Older; Fiction

Taylor, Mildred D. *Let the Circle Be Unbroken*. New York: Puffin Books, 1991. 400 p.
Narrated by young Cassie, who is part of the third generation of the Logan family, this book relates the experiences of her colored family during the terrible financial hardships of the 1930s Depression. She relates how she witnesses the murder trial and the predetermined guilty verdict of the family's innocent friend T.J.; sees how efforts to create a biracial Farm Workers' Union are thwarted; learns of the fraud used by plantation owners to deprive small cotton farmers of government money; accompanies an older black woman who has extensively studied the Mississippi Constitution, but is refused voter registration and ordered off her land; and worries with her family when her fourteen year-old older brother runs off to save their property by working in the cane fields of Louisiana where he is subjected to unthinkable treatment. In this story Cassie's father David tells of his mixed heritage, and there is hostility from both blacks and whites towards one of Cassie's uncles who has married a white woman. The couple's fifteen-year-old daughter Suzella finds it difficult to be biracial and decides that she will pass as a white. In other books about this generation of Logans—*Mississippi Bridge*; *Song of the Trees*; *The Friendship*; *Roll of Thunder, Hear My Cry*; and *The Road to Memphis*—the family is identified for readers as colored, not as mixed race.
African-European-American and Native American/African-American
Older; Fiction

Taylor, Mildred D. *The Well: David's Story*. New York: Dial Books for Young Readers, 1995. 96 p.
Set in the early 1900s, this book tells of an episode in the life of David Logan, Paul-Edward's son and Cassie's father. When David is ten-years-old, there is a severe drought, and both white and colored neighbors come to the Logan farm to get water from their well. David and his thirteen-year-old hotheaded brother Hammer are treated abysmally by the mean Simms boys, who are white. When Hammer hits one of them after he has hit David, the sheriff is summoned as it is a serious crime for a black to hit a white. Caroline, David and Hammer's mother, has to whip both of her sons in front of the Simms and they have to do work for Mr. Simms. The Simms boys continue to harass David and Hammer, but when they pollute the water in the Logan's well, both they and their father get their comeuppance. Paul-Edward plays a role in this book and it is mentioned that he is half white.
African-European-American and Native American/African-American
Intermediate; Fiction

Walter, Mildred Pitts. *Ray and the Best Family Reunion Ever*. New York: HarperCollins Publishers, 2002. 128 p.
Eleven-year-old Ray is the only member of his Creole family with ebony skin. When he goes to a large family reunion in Natchitoches, Louisiana, Ray discovers that he and Gran-papa Philippe are the only ones there with dark skin. To make matter worse, Ray looks like his grandfather whom his father and almost all his relatives despise. This is the story of Ray's secret bonding with Gran-papa

Philippe, his appreciation of his grandfather's talent, and his effecting a reconciliation between his father and Philippe.

Creole (Nigerian-French-Spanish-Native American)-Haitian-American/Creole (French-Spanish-West African-Native American)-American

Intermediate; Fiction

Wayans, Kim, and Kevin Knotts. *All Mixed Up!* Illustrated by Soo Jeong. New York: Grosset & Dunlap, 2008. 112 p. (Amy Hodgepodge)

Amy Hodges is introduced in this first book of the *Amy Hodgepodge* series, which features pictures posted in Amy's scrapbook. Moving to a new town after having experienced only home schooling, Amy is excited to be starting fourth grade at Emerson Charter School. However, her first day starts out disastrously. She wears the wrong clothes, tears her dress when she removes its flower, sings too loudly in music class, is laughed at by classmates Liza and Jennifer, and discovers that a paper saying "Stupid new girl" has been taped to her back by Rory. However, her day improves when she is befriended in the cafeteria by Maya, Jesse, Rusty, Pia, and twins Lola and Cole. Upset by a racial insult from Jennifer, she discovers that the twins are black and white, Jesse is black and Puerto Rican, Pia is Chinese-American and white, and Rusty is Latino, Native American, and white. Learning that Amy's father is black and white and her mother Japanese and South Korean-American, they affectionately nickname her Amy Hodgepodge. The story continues with the group entering a school talent show where Amy, inspired by Rusty who has to earn money to buy his costume, overcomes her stage fright and becomes the group's lead singer.

European-Latin American-American and Native American

Primary, Intermediate; Fiction

Wayans, Kim, and Kevin Knotts. *Digging Up Trouble*. Illustrated by Soo Jeong. New York: Grosset & Dunlap, 2010. 112 p. (Amy Hodgepodge)

After foolishly letting her dog Giggles off his leash to play with another dog at the Farmer's Market, Amy is unable to find him. She spends a stressful night until in the morning the family receives a call from an older man, Irving Coleman, who reports that Giggles has come to his home with his dog. Then, after being reunited with Giggles, Amy realizes that helping Irving restore his community garden would make a perfect green project for the school class assignment. The two fourth grade classes adopt Amy's idea and decide to raise money for the needed tools and supplies by having a bake sale and a car wash. Amy is worried when she is placed in charge of the bake sale team, but because of the help of her visiting community-organizer grandmother and team members, including Lola, Pia, and Rusty, there are many baked goods for sale. However, things turn contentious when the bake sale team and the car wash team, including Jesse and Maya, become overly competitive. After teachers intervene, the teams decide to refer customers to each other. With the proceeds earned and the work of Amy's gardener grandmother and the fourth graders, Irving's garden again becomes a neighborhood asset. Referring to the mixed racial identity of some of Amy's friends, this sixth book in the series specifically identifies the heritages of Lola and Cole as well as of Amy.

European-Latin American-American and Native American

Primary, Intermediate; Fiction

Wayans, Kim, and Kevin Knotts. *Happy Birthday to Me*. Illustrated by Soo Jeong. New York: Grosset & Dunlap, 2008. 112 p. (Amy Hodgepodge)

In this sequel to *All Mixed Up!* Amy looks forward to celebrating her birthday with her new friends as well as with her family. Maya, Jesse, Pia, and Lola accept her invitation to her tenth birthday sleepover where Amy plans to have a Japanese tea ceremony and do origami. Amy's spirits wane when she fears her family is planning to move to California. She is really upset when her four friends decide to go to an Amber Skye concert instead of her party. When Lola's brother Cole discovers that Amy has not invited other guests, he texts the concertgoers, and the four girls leave the concert to go to Amy's house. It is then that Amy discovers what true friends they are and the advisability of telling her problems and her fears to her family. This book points out the mixed heritages of Amy and most of her friends.
European-Latin American-American and Native American
Primary, Intermediate; Fiction

Wayans, Kim, and Kevin Knotts. *Lost and Found*. Illustrated by Soo Jeong. New York: Grosset & Dunlap, 2008. 112 p. (Amy Hodgepodge)

Amy Hodgepodge persuades her parents to let her go on the fourth grade two-and-a-half day wilderness trip. However, she doesn't feel as pleased about it when she is placed in a group without her friends, but with Jennifer and Rory who don't like her. Further, she falls in the mud during the obstacle course, goes overboard with Jennifer in their canoe, and is embarrassed that she doesn't know what s'mores are. However, Amy is supported by Lola, Jesse, Maya, and Pia with whom she shares a tent. Together they enjoy tricking Cole, Rusty, and two other boys. Then when she, Jennifer, Rory, and two others get lost in the woods, Amy uses her compass to lead them back to camp—and receives the Best Camper award. In this third book in the series, Amy's mixed heritage is noted. Readers of the first book, *All Mixed Up!*, will be aware of the mixed heritages of five of her friends.
European-Latin American-American and Native American
Primary, Intermediate; Fiction

Wayans, Kim, and Kevin Knotts. *Playing Games*. Illustrated by Soo Jeong. New York: Grosset & Dunlap, 2008. 112 p. (Amy Hodgepodge)

When Evelyn, the star player of the Comets girls' basketball team, injures her arm, Amy Hodgepodge reluctantly agrees to take her place so that the team will have the required eight players. Amy has neither played basketball nor is she familiar with the game. She is a terrible player, and her mistake causes the team to lose to the worst team in the league. Amy tries to fake a twisted ankle so she can be on the bench, but even that fails and she decides to quit. However, after confessing her problem to Rusty, he offers to coach her, with Amy, in return, helping him sing harmony in the friends' fourth grade music class performance. Unaware of the fact that Amy has improved, her teammates don't pass her the ball. It is not until the end of an important game that Amy demonstrates her secret talent as a three-point shooter. Amy's mixed heritage is noted in this fourth book in the series. Readers of the first book, *All Mixed Up!*, will be familiar with the mixed heritages of most of her friends.
European-Latin American-American and Native American
Primary, Intermediate; Fiction

Wayans, Kim, and Kevin Knotts. *The Secret's Out*. Illustrated by Soo Jeong. New York: Grosset & Dunlap, 2009. 112 p. (Amy Hodgepodge)

Amy, Lola, Jesse, Pia, and Maya decide to enter as a group in their school's competitive annual spring art show. Amy comes up with the idea of tracing their body outlines on a large poster board and then painting and decorating them. The girls would stand behind holes that would show their faces. With the exception of Pia, the others are enthused about Amy's plan. Indeed, Pia's personality seems to have changed. She has become distracted, negative, and rude. Finally, she confides to Amy, with Amy's promise not to tell, that she fears that, since her father and stepmother are going to have a baby, her father won't pay attention to her. When Amy accidentally reveals Pia's secret to Lola, there are unforeseen consequences. Lola tells Jesse, and Jesse lets the secret out to classmates. The friends become so angry at each other that their Best Friends art display is jeopardized. It is not until they practice forgiveness that they restore their friendship—and their project ties for fourth grade first place. In this fifth book in the series, Amy's mixed heritage is noted, and series readers will be aware of the mixed heritages of most of her friends.
European-Latin American-American and Native American
Primary, Intermediate; Fiction

Abenaki

See   Bruchac, Joseph
         Pelotte, Donald

Bruchac, Joseph. *Fox Song*. Illustrated by Paul Morin. New York: Philomel Books, 1993, 32 p.

Missing her Abenaki great-grandmother who has just died, Jamie remembers their special times together in the nearby woods. Then, when Jamie sings the greeting song that her great-grandmother taught her, her great-grandmother's best friend, a fox, appears and Jamie understands that she will never be alone.
French-American/ Abenaki and French-American
Primary, Intermediate; Fiction

Bruchac, Joseph. *Hidden Roots*. New York: Scholastic Press, 2004. 144 p.

It is 1954 and eleven-year-old Sonny lives with his mother and his father, who is often angry and physically abusive. Sonny enjoys the company of an older friend, "Uncle" Louie, a man who had worked for his mother's parents when she was a child and from whom he learns much about the Adirondack area of New York State where they live. Sonny wonders about the many subjects he is not allowed to discuss and questions that remain unanswered: why he should be afraid of being "crept up on," what bad things happened in Vermont, and why his father doesn't want Uncle Louis around. It is only after he and Uncle Louis learn from the Jewish school librarian that her parents had sent her as a child from Germany to England for safety, that Uncle Louis tells Sonny the truth. Uncle Louis is his grandfather, who, like his late wife, had been sterilized during the Vermont Eugenics Project because they were Indians and who had fled Vermont so that Sonny's mother would not be taken away. It was because Sonny's family wanted to protect him from being treated like an Indian that they had kept his identity a secret, but it is when the secret is revealed to Sonny that his father, who is also part Indian, is released from his anger and shame.

European-American and Native American/French Canadian-American, Abenaki and Mohican

Intermediate, Older; Fiction

Ketchum, Liza. *Where the Great Hawk Flies*. New York: Clarion Books, 2005. 272 p.

In 1780 during the Revolutionary War the British brought Caughnawaga Indians from Canada to raid the colonists living in Vermont. During the raid Daniel, his little sister, and their mother, a Pequot-Mohegan, hid in a cave while his English father served in the militia called up to chase the raiders. During the same raid Hiram was snatched by the Indians and then released and his Uncle Abner was captured and imprisoned in Canada. This story starts two years later when eleven-year-old Hiram and his family move to the property near thirteen-year-old Daniel's. Hiram is both scared of and antagonistic to Daniel and his family, and Daniel resents Hiram's derogatory remarks about Indians. The situation is compounded when Daniel's medicine man grandfather moves in with Daniel's family and builds a wigwam on the property and when Uncle Abner returns to Hiram's family. After some harrowing events Daniel and Hiram become friends. Mr. Sikes, one of the neighbors in this book, is Abenaki and French-American.

French-American and Abenaki

Intermediate, Older; Fiction

Singer, Marilyn, ed. *Face Relations: 11 Stories About Seeing Beyond Color*. New York: Simon & Schuster Books for Young Readers, 2004. 240 p.

In the story "Skins" by Joseph Bruchac, Mitchell, who is half Abenaki, provides needed support to the high school star quarterback, whom everyone assumes is Indian, but is really Hungarian. Mitchell also becomes close friends with Randolph, who is African-American and Native American.

Abenaki/Swedish

Older; Fiction

Acoman

Little, Kimberley Griffiths. *Enchanted Runner*. New York: Avon Books, 1999. 160 p.

Twelve-year-old Kendall has an almost magical urge to run. After his mother's death, he is invited to visit his great-grandfather in the Acoma Pueblo in New Mexico. There Kendall finds himself in a very unfamiliar environment, becomes acutely aware that he is only half Acoman, and learns that his great-grandfather was one of a group of Acoma Runners. Kendall feels compelled to run each day to the Enchanted Mesa, which he hopes will reveal his destiny. When Kendall's great-grandfather fails to return from a visit to a sacred shrine, it is Kendall who finds him and gets help. At the end of the story, Kendall is accepted by the Acoma as the last of the Snake Clan.

European-American/Acoman

Intermediate, Older; Fiction

Little, Kimberley Griffiths. *The Last Snake Runner*. New York: Alfred A. Knopf, 2002. 208 p.

In this sequel to *Enchanted Runner*, Kendall, now fourteen, has just returned from the Acoma Pueblo where he has become a full member of the Acoma, his late mother's people. Very upset when he learns that his father has married a woman descended from the Spanish conquistadors who in 1599 destroyed the Acoma Pueblo, Kendall has his brother take him back to Acoma. There, in a mesa near the pueblo, he is transported back to the sixteenth century where he experiences life in the ancient Snake Clan and participates in the last Acoma Snake dance. Although Kendall is unable to save the pueblo from the conquistadors, he brings hope that the Acoma will survive.
European-American/Acoman
Older; Fiction

Aleut

Hesse, Karen. *Aleutian Sparrow*. New York: Margaret K. McElderry Books, 2003. 160 p.

In this historical novel, which is written in unrhymed verses, a young girl tells how in June 1942 the Aleuts were evacuated from their villages for protection from the Japanese. She describes the poor and unhealthy conditions they endured in internment camps in Wrangell and then near Ketchikan, Alaska, their longing for their Aleutian life and homes, their retention in exile even after the Japanese posed no threat to the Aleutians, the deaths of the girl's best friend and others, and the devastation, caused by Japanese bombs and American servicemen, which they discovered when they were finally allowed to return home in April 1945.
European-American/Aleut
Older; Fiction

Apache

Lacapa, Kathleen, and Michael Lacapa. *Less than Half, More than Whole*. Illustrated by Michael Lacapa. Flagstaff, Ariz.: Northland Publishing, 1994. 40 p.

This picture book is based on the author's family. Tony, who does not look like either his Caucasian or his Indian friend, is bothered about being called less than half and seeks understanding from his maternal grandmother, his older siblings, his uncle, and his paternal grandfather. It is when he realizes the meaning of an ear of corn that Tony knows that in truth he is more than whole. Designs from different Native American cultures complement the book's paintings.
Apache, Hopi, and Tewa/English-Irish-American and Mohawk
Primary, Intermediate; Fiction

Mescalero Apache

See   Anderson, Ross

Kuklin, Susan. *Families*. Photographs by author. New York: Hyperion Books for Children, 2006. 40 p.

Text and color photographs present interviews with American children, who talk about their families. Their families include seven families with children of mixed race, ethnicity, or religion, with one also including a child adopted from Sierra Leone. In an eighth family a child has been adopted from China. In a ninth family an adopted American child is of a race different from that of one of her fathers. German-Jewish-American and Mescalero Apache/African-American
Primary, Intermediate; Nonfiction

Arapaho

See   Anderson, Ross
       Carson, Adaline

Patrick, Denise Lewis. *The Longest Ride*. New York: Henry Holt and Company, 1999. 176 p.

It is 1865 and fourteen-year-old Midnight Son, an escaped slave who is accompanied by his white friend Lou Boy, decides that he must return from Colorado to Texas to rescue his mother and two younger sisters and to find his older sister who had been sold years earlier. Injured in a blizzard, Midnight Son is taken to an Arapaho camp. After it is destroyed by American soldiers, Winter Mary and Eagle Eye, Arapaho siblings whose mother is African-American, join Midnight Son and Lou Boy to fulfill their dying mother's wish to find her sister. In the ensuing story, the four of them travel to Texas and Louisiana in search of Midnight Son's family. This book is the sequel to *The Adventures of Midnight Son*.
Arapaho/African-American
Intermediate, Older; Fiction

Arikara

See   Garreau, Antoine

Athabascan

Frost, Helen. *Diamond Willow*. New York: Frances Foster Books, 2008. 128 p.

In this story, which is set in the interior of Alaska, twelve-year-old Diamond Willow, called Willow, returns solo with three sled dogs from a visit with her grandparents. Speeding on a blind curve, they crash into a fallen tree, thereby causing the treasured dog Roxy to lose her sight. When Willow's parents decide to euthanize Roxy, Willow and a friend secretly set out to take the injured dog to her grandparents, but become lost overnight in a blizzard. Throughout these experiences Willow's ancestors, reincarnated as a red fox, a spruce hen, a mouse, and one of the sled dogs, try to help Willow. The story then presents the surprising revelation that Willow had a twin sister, Diamond, who died shortly after birth and has become Roxy. The book is largely written in verse with a distinctive text design that complements the story.

European-Canadian-American/Athabascan
Intermediate, Older; Fiction

Blackfoot

Highwater, Jamake. *The Ceremony of Innocence*. New York: Harper & Row, Publishers, 1985. 192 p. (The Ghost Horse Cycle)

   The Ceremony of Innocence is the second book in *The Ghost Horse Cycle*, a series for teenagers. It is the sequel to *Legend Days*, which describes Amana's childhood experiences as a Blood (Blackfoot). In this book Amana, whose family has died, has left her people and is destitute. She comes to live with an immature French Canadian, who deserts her before the birth of their daughter Jemina. Although sustained by her friendship with a French-Cree woman who runs a brothel, Amana suffers when Jemina grows up obsessed with finery and is married to the drunkard Jamie Ghost Horse and when her older grandson is only interested in things "American." Amana's hope lies in Sitko, her younger grandson, who treasures his Native American heritage.
French Canadian/Blackfoot (Blood); African-American and Cherokee/French Canadian-American and Blackfoot (Blood)
Older; Fiction

Highwater, Jamake. *I Wear the Morning Star*. New York: Harper & Row, Publishers, 1986. 160 p. (The Ghost Horse Cycle)

   This third book in *The Ghost Horse Cycle* for the oldest readers tells the story of Sitko and his miserable boyhood. Sitko is placed in a boarding school where he is mistreated by the adults and scorned by the other children. His alcoholic father, Jamie Ghost Horse, realizing that Sitko deserves a better life, allows Alexander, his former friend and now the lover of his ex-wife Jemina, to adopt Sitko, and Sitko goes to live with Alexander, Jemina, and his grandmother Amana in the San Fernando Valley. Not able to figure out his past and deeply confused about his identity, Sitko continues a life filled with unhappiness, mitigated only by his friendship with a farm boy, his school's art club, and his painting. At the end of the book, Jamie shoots Jemina and Alexander, killing her and wounding Alexander. Jamie perishes in a truck crash, Sitko's older brother loses his life in a plane crash, the elderly Amana dies, and Sitko, the only one remaining, preserves his Blood (Blackfoot) past through his paintings.
French Canadian/Blackfoot (Blood); African-American and Cherokee/French Canadian-American and Blackfoot (Blood)
Older; Fiction

Cherokee

See   Ahyoka
      Ballard, Louis
      Brown, Anne Wiggins

Chisholm, Jesse
Coleman, Elizabeth (Bessie)?
Crawford, Goldsby (Cherokee Bill)
Depp, John (Johnny) Christopher II
Duwali
Hamilton, Virginia
Harjo, Joy
Harris, Betty Wright
Hughes, James Mercer Langston
Little, Frank
Lynn, Loretta Webb
Mankiller, Wilma
Momaday, Navarre Scott
Obama, Barack?
Parton, Dolly Rebecca
Payne, Andrew Hartley
Pickett, Bill
Rogers, Will, Jr.
Rogers, William (Will) Penn Adair
Rose, Edward
Ross, John
Sequoyah
Turner, Tina
Walker, Alice Malsenior
Watie, Stand

Adoff, Jaime. *Jimi & Me*. New York: Jump at the Sun, 2005. 336 p.

This novel in verse is filled with despair as thirteen-year-old Keith experiences the shooting death of his father, moving from Brooklyn to a small Ohio town, taunting at his new school, his mother's slide into depression, the hatred both of them feel when they find out that his father was giving their money to another woman and the son they had, and learning that this sixteen-year-old half brother is named Jimi, the name of his idol Jimi Hendrix. When Keith meets his half brother, he discovers the truth and begins to go on with his life.

African-American and Cherokee/European-American
Older, Fiction

Banks, Sara H. *Remember My Name*. Illustrated by Birgitta Saflund. Niwot, Colo.: Roberts Rinehart Publishers, 1993. 128 p.

When her parents die, eleven-year-old Annie, who is half Cherokee and half Scottish-American, leaves her Cherokee grandmother to live with her Cherokee uncle and his wife in New Echota. She attends school and becomes best friends with Righteous Cry, a black girl about her age who is a slave. When in 1838 the Cherokees are forced to leave to travel westward in the Trail of Tears, Annie's uncle

sends her and Righteous (now freed) to travel, almost all the way by themselves, back to Annie's mountain home.
Scottish/Cherokee
Intermediate; Fiction

Carter, Forrest. *The Education of Little Tree.* 25th anniversity ed. Albuquerque: University of New Mexico Press, 2001. 238 p.

Set during the Great Depression in the Appalachian Mountains, this book tells the story of Little Tree during the years when he was five-, six-, and seven-years-old. With both his parents dead, Little Tree went to live with his half Cherokee grandfather, his Cherokee grandmother, and their hounds. There he received unconditional love and came to practice the Cherokee way of listening to and respecting all of nature. Little Tree accepted his grandfather's unique views of George Washington, politicians, and preachers and concluded from his own experience that he should never trade with a Christian. He twice kept men from discovering his grandfather's secret whiskey still, was saved from a rattlesnake by his grandfather, and learned figuring from a Jewish peddler, vocabulary words from the dictionary, and swear words from his grandfather. Little Tree spent time enduring harsh treatment in an orphanage before happily returning to the family and the land he loved.
Scottish-American and Cherokee
Older; Fiction

Cruz, Maria Colleen. *Border Crossing: A Novel.* Houston: Piñata Books, 2003. 128 p.

Cesi, who is twelve-years-old and of mixed race, feels she can discover who she is by finding out more about the Mexican heritage which her father doesn't discuss. When questions to her mother, both grandmothers, her brother, and her father don't satisfy her, she takes off by herself to cross the border from California to Tijuana. With the help of a Mexican-American boy she meets and of his aunt, Cesi learns about Mexicans, the prejudice her father faced as a boy, and who she really is. In the process her father comes to realize that by protecting his children he has unintentionally made their lives more difficult.
Mexican-American/Irish-American and Cherokee
Intermediate, Older; Fiction

Highwater, Jamake. *The Ceremony of Innocence.* New York: Harper & Row, Publishers, 1985. 192 p. (The Ghost Horse Cycle)

The Ceremony of Innocence is the second book in *The Ghost Horse Cycle*, a series for teenagers. It is the sequel to *Legend Days*, which describes Amana's childhood experiences as a Blood (Blackfoot). In this book Amana, whose family has died, has left her people and is destitute. She comes to live with an immature French Canadian, who deserts her before the birth of their daughter Jemina. Although sustained by her friendship with a French-Cree woman who runs a brothel, Amana suffers when Jemina grows up obsessed with finery and is married to the drunkard Jamie Ghost Horse and when her older grandson is only interested in things "American." Amana's hope lies in Sitko, her younger grandson, who treasures his Native American heritage.

African-American and Cherokee/French Canadian-American and Blackfoot (Blood)
Older; Fiction

Highwater, Jamake. *I Wear the Morning Star*. New York: Harper & Row, Publishers, 1986. 160 p. (The Ghost Horse Cycle)

This third book in *The Ghost Horse Cycle* for the oldest readers tells the story of Sitko and his miserable boyhood. Sitko is placed in a boarding school where he is mistreated by the adults and scorned by the other children. His alcoholic father, Jamie Ghost Horse, realizing that Sitko deserves a better life, allows Alexander, his former friend and now the lover of his ex-wife Jemina, to adopt Sitko, and Sitko goes to live with Alexander, Jemina, and his grandmother Amana in the San Fernando Valley. Not able to figure out his past and deeply confused about his identity, Sitko continues a life filled with unhappiness, mitigated only by his friendship with a farm boy, his school's art club, and his painting. At the end of the book, Jamie shoots Jemina and Alexander, killing her and wounding Alexander. Jamie perishes in a truck crash, Sitko's older brother loses his life in a plane crash, the elderly Amana dies, and Sitko, the only one remaining, preserves his Blood (Blackfoot) past through his paintings.
African-American and Cherokee/French Canadian-American and Blackfoot (Blood)
Older; Fiction

Oughton, Jerrie. *Music from a Place Called Half Moon*. Boston: Houghton Mifflin Company, 1995. 176 p.

In this novel which is set in 1956 in a mountainous North Carolina town, thirteen-year-old Edie Jo's father stirs up a hornet's nest when he proposes that the church's vacation bible school be open to the entire community, including Indians and "half-breeds." There is a terrible rift in Edie Jo's family as her mother opposes her husband's action. At first Edie Jo isn't sure where she stands, but after she and her brother barely escape from threatening teenage Indian boys, she decides she is against integration. Then she gets to know the half Cherokee Clarence Fish, who plays beautiful harmonica music and likes her poems. Just after Edie Jo realizes that she is in love with Clarence, she witnesses his murder by his older brother. In the midst of her grief and as her mother struggles to be more tolerant, Edie Jo takes a first step towards reducing her town's prejudice.
European-American and Cherokee
Intermediate, Older; Fiction

Rosenberg, Maxine B. *Living in Two Worlds*. Photographs by George Ancona. New York: Lothrop, Lee & Shepard Books, 1986. 48 p.

This book explains how races evolved and how many children have a greater resemblance to one of their parents. It discusses the teasing and unwanted questions biracial children face and points to the benefits of living in two cultures. The book's text and black-and-white photographs focus on five children: Toah, who is African-European-American; Megan, who is African-European-American and Cherokee; Jesse, who is Chinese-European-American; and Shashi and Anil, who are Indian-European-American.
African-American and Cherokee/European-American
Intermediate; Nonfiction

Singer, Marilyn, ed. *Face Relations: 11 Stories About Seeing Beyond Color*. New York: Simon & Schuster Books for Young Readers, 2004. 240 p.

In "Gold" by Marina Budhos, fifteen-year-old Jemma, who has moved from Trinidad to New Jersey, goes out with Jared and comes to realize that they are going too far in their relationship. Then, when Jared apologizes to her mother, Jemma recognizes how good he is and that for them, as for her parents, differences in heritage do not matter.
African-Irish-American and Cherokee
Older; Fiction

Singer, Marilyn, ed. *Face Relations: 11 Stories About Seeing Beyond Color*. New York: Simon & Schuster Books for Young Readers, 2004. 240 p.

In the story "Skins" by Joseph Bruchac, Mitchell, who is half Abenaki, provides needed support to the high school star quarterback, whom everyone assumes is Indian, but is really Hungarian. Mitchell also becomes close friends with Randolph, who is African-American and Native American.
African-American, Cherokee, and Choctaw/African-American, Cherokee, and Choctaw
Older; Fiction

Smith, Cynthia Leitich. *Indian Shoes*. Illustrated by Jim Madsen. New York: HarperCollins Publishers, 2002. 80 p.

This book tells of the close relationship between Ray and his Grampa Halfmoon, who live together in Chicago. For instance, Ray cleverly bargains to get a pair of Seminole moccasins for his homesick grandfather and together they attend a Cubs game, celebrate Christmas with the neighborhood pets, solve the problem of missing pants when Ray serves as wedding ring bearer for his Choctaw friend and her Polish-Menominee groom, and, visiting their relatives in Oklahoma, go fishing and catch more than fish.
Cherokee and Seminole
Primary, Intermediate; Fiction

Smith, Cynthia Leitich. *Rain Is Not My Indian Name*. New York: HarperCollins Publishers, 2001. 144 p.

Since her best friend Galen was killed in a traffic accident on New Year's Day (her birthday), fourteen-year-old Rain, who is of mixed race, has withdrawn from her friends and from going out into her small Kansas town. However, despite refusing to become a participant, she agrees early in the summer to take photographs of her aunt's Native American camp. Rain is upset with Galen's mother and her opposition to the camp and with her former second best friend African-American Queenie, who attends the camp although it is not discovered until later that she has a Seminole ancestor. Then, on the Fourth of July (Galen's birthday), Rain is ready to move beyond his death.
Irish-German-American and Ojibwa/Scottish-Irish-American, Cherokee, and Muskogee
Intermediate, Older; Fiction

Thomas, Joyce Carol. *The Golden Pasture*. New York: Scholastic, 1986. 144 p.

Since his infancy when he was snatched from his Cherokee mother by his father, Carl Lee and his

grandfather have had a special bond. He enjoys spending summers on his grandfather's Oklahoma farm, a welcome respite from being with his father who pays him no attention except for criticism. Alerted by distressful wails, Carl Lee finds the wild appaloosa whom his grandfather had kept hidden and who has pulled a muscle. After nursing the horse back to health, Carl Lee rides him in a rodeo where he learns the truth about the legendary wild horse Thunderfoot and comes to appreciate his father's heroism.
African-American/Cherokee
Intermediate, Older; Fiction

Cheyenne

See   West, W. Richard, Jr.

Hamilton, Virginia. *Arilla Sun Down*. New York: Scholastic, 1976. 304 p.
   This novel tells of twelve-year-old Arilla whose mother is sure of her identity as an African-American woman, whose Native American father alternates between his work at an Ohio college and leaving for his boyhood home, and whose older brother, Jack Sun Run, delights in parading his Native American heritage. Always in her brother's shadow, certain that he hates her, and terribly jealous, Arilla treasures the times that he treats her nicely. The book tells of Arilla's writing her autobiography; of old James False Face, her only friend when she was little; of Susanne Shy Woman who is Sioux and Cheyenne; of sneaking out at night with Sun Run and his girlfriend to go roller skating; of sledding with her father on an exciting, but dangerous hill; of saving Sun Run's life and discovering he had saved hers; and, throughout the book, of her struggle to find her own identity.
Sioux and Cheyenne
Older; Fiction

Rosenberg, Maxine B. *Being Adopted*. Photographs by George Ancona. New York: Lothrop, Lee & Shepard Books, 1984. 48 p.
   Illustrated with black-and-white photographs, this book features three children. Seven-year-old Rebecca, whose birthfather is African-American and birthmother European-American and Cheyenne, is the adopted daughter of an African-American father and a European-American mother. Ten-year-old Andrei was adopted from India by European-American parents, and Karin, the author's eight-year-old daughter, was adopted from Korea by her European-American parents. The book covers some of the questions and fears of younger adopted children: being afraid when they come to their adoptive families, wondering whether they caused their parents to give them up, fearing their adoptive parents will give them up, dreaming and wondering about their birthparents, and not looking like other members of their families. It also affirms that adopted children are just as much family members as are biological children.
African-American/European-American and Cheyenne
Primary, Intermediate; Nonfiction

Northern Cheyenne

See   Campbell, Ben Nighthorse

Southern Cheyenne

See   Anderson, Ross

Chickasaw

See   Te Ata

Krementz, Jill. *How It Feels To Be Adopted*. Photographs by author. New York: Alfred A. Knopf, 1982. 120 p.

    Black-and-white photographs accompany the author's interviews with nineteen children who talk about being adopted: how they feel about it, their knowledge of and feelings about their birthparents and whether they want to meet them, their experiences as adopted children, and, for five of them, what it is like to be part of a mixed race family. One of these children, who is African-American, has been adopted by an African-American father, but has adopted brothers who are Hispanic, Korean, and biracial.
Seminole, Choctaw, and Chickasaw
Intermediate, Older; Nonfiction

Moonshower, Candie. *The Legend of Zoey: A Novel*. New York: Delacorte Press, 2006. 224 p.

    This story is based on the legend of the 1811 and 1812 New Madrid Earthquakes that alleges they resulted from the curse placed by a Choctaw chief on the Chickasaw chief Reelfoot who defied him by marrying his daughter Laughing Eyes. When thirteen-year-old Zoey goes on a school field trip to Reelfoot Lake in western Tennessee, she is swept away in a drainage ditch during an electrical storm and finds herself back in 1811 with a thirteen-year-old girl Prudence and her mother. Journals written by Zoey and Prudence tell of their difficult journey as they try to reach safety from the earthquakes. They learn of each other's lives, hopes, and worries; become friends; and spend time with Reelfoot and Laughing Eyes, whom Zoey discovers are her ancestors. There are surprises awaiting Zoey when she returns to the present day.
European-American/European-American, Chickasaw, and Choctaw
Intermediate, Older; Fiction

Chippewa

See   Bonga, George
         Lewis, Mary Edmonia
         Pontiac

Alder, Elizabeth. *Crossing the Panther's Path*. New York: Farrar Straus Giroux, 2002. 240 p.

This book is based on the life of Billy Caldwell and his close relationship with Tecumseh, the Shawnee chief. Tecumseh, as leader of warriors from a number of Indian nations and in alliance with the British army in Canada, sought to reclaim the lands which the Americans took from the Indians. Billy, who is Irish-Mohawk, serves as soldier, interpreter, and then captain in the British Indian Department in the War of 1812. This story tells of the battles of Tippecanoe, Chicago, Detroit, the River Raisin, and the Thames River; of Billy's courageous actions; of his love of a European-American and Ojibwa woman; and of his decision to forgo fighting and help the Indians through peaceful means.
European-American/Chippewa
Older; Fiction

Carter, Alden R. *Dogwolf*. New York: Scholastic, 1994. 240 p.

This is a novel of a hot summer when tower sitters spot fires in the Federal forest of northern Wisconsin and fire crews fight them. It is also the summer when Pete, aged fifteen, struggles to find who he is. Half white and half Native American, he is haunted by the persistent howling of the some-how-kindred creature who is a dogwolf. Knowing that it cannot stand being penned in a cage, Pete determines to free it, either by shooting it or by letting it out. Loose, the dogwolf terrorizes the countryside and the Chippewa reservation—killing animals and then Pete's friend—until finally Pete confronts and shoots it.
Métis-Canadian/Chippewa and Swedish-American
Older; Nonfiction

Ernst, Kathleen. *Trouble at Fort La Pointe*. Illustrated by Jean-Paul Tibbles and Greg Dearth. Middleton, Wis.: Pleasant Company Publications, 2000. 176 p. (American Girl History Mysteries)

In 1732 when her family goes with other Ojibwa to spend the summer on La Pointe Island (now Madeline Island, Wisconsin), Suzette's father is accused of stealing furs from the adjacent Fort La Pointe. Twelve-year-old Suzette, who is Métis, with a French-Ojibwa mother and a French Canadian father, is determined to find the stolen furs and clear her father's name. She and her Métis friend Gabrielle discover the cave where the furs are stored and manage to escape when they are trapped there. Suzette then proves the identity of the real thief. Feeling that with her blue eyes, she is neither French nor Ojibwa, Suzette realizes that it was through the skills she learned from being both that she secured her father's release. A minor character in the book has an Ojibwa father and a Dakota mother.
French Canadian/Métis (French-Ojibwa); Métis; Ojibwa/Dakota
Intermediate, Older; Fiction

Hassler, Jon. *Jemmy*. New York: Atheneum, 1981. 180 p. (A Margaret K. McElderry Book)

Seventeen-year-old Jemmy Stott, whose mother is dead, lives in rural Minnesota with her alcoholic father and her younger brother and sister. When Jemmy's father requires her to quit school to take care of her younger siblings, Jemmy's future looks bleak. Caught in a blizzard, she takes refuge in the house of the Chapmans, an artist and his wife. During the six months the Chapmans live in the area, they have a tremendous impact on the Stotts. Mr. Chapman's portrayal of Jemmy as the Maiden

of Eagle Rock becomes the focal point of a large mural in Minneapolis, she learns to paint, and she discovers that it is all right to be both Indian and white.
Irish-American/Chippewa
Older; Fiction

Smith, Cynthia Leitich. *Jingle Dancer*. Illustrated by Cornelius Van Wright and Ying-Hwa Hu. New York: Morrow Junior Books, 2000. 32 p.

In this picture book Jenna wants to jingle dance in the next powwow, but doesn't have the four rows of jingles which her dress needs. However, she manages to borrow rows of jingles from three relatives and a neighbor and then dances for the four of them. The author's note identifies Jenna as Muskogee and Ojibwa.
Chippewa and Muskogee
Pre-K, Primary; Fiction

Smith, Cynthia Leitich. *Rain Is Not My Indian Name*. New York: HarperCollins Publishers, 2001. 144 p.

Since her best friend Galen was killed in a traffic accident on New Year's Day (her birthday), fourteen-year-old Rain, who is of mixed race, has withdrawn from her friends and from going out into her small Kansas town. However, despite refusing to become a participant, she agrees early in the summer to take photographs of her aunt's Native American camp. Rain is upset with Galen's mother and her opposition to the camp and with her former second best friend African-American Queenie, who attends the camp although it is not discovered until later that she has a Seminole ancestor. Then, on the Fourth of July (Galen's birthday), Rain is ready to move beyond his death.
Irish-German-American and Ojibwa/Scottish-Irish-American, Cherokee, and Muskogee
Intermediate, Older; Fiction

Terris, Susan. *Whirling Rainbows*. Garden City, N.Y.: Doubleday & Company, 1974. 168 p.

Thirteen-year-old Leah, who was adopted in infancy by a Jewish couple, wants to find her Indian roots when she goes to a Wisconsin summer camp. One disaster seems to follow another as she is mocked for being "Indian" and blamed, often unjustly, for misdeeds. However, although she does not find the Indian relics she is seeking, Leah learns much during the summer: that she has been trying to be close to the wrong cousin, that she has become an accomplished canoeist, that she has displayed leadership on a hazardous camping trip, and that she is no longer concerned about being adopted.
Polish-American/Chippewa
Older; Fiction

Turtle Mountain Chippewa

See   Erdrich, Louise

Choctaw

See   Coleman, Elizabeth (Bessie)?

Mason, Bridget (Biddy)
Smith, Nolle

Applegate, Stan. *The Devil's Highway*. Illustrated by James Watling. Atlanta: Peachtree, 1998. 160 p.

Just after leaving his family farm in Franklin, Tennessee, to search for his grandfather and escape from the men who are after him, Zeb comes upon ten-year-old Hannah. Half Choctaw and half Caucasian, Hannah has gotten away from outlaws who kidnapped her six months earlier. Together they travel southward on the Natchez Trace, a highly dangerous road in 1811. Hannah finally is reunited with her parents in Washington, Mississippi, but Zeb, who becomes an honorary Choctaw on the way, must continue looking for his grandfather in nearby Natchez. An author's note provides information about the Natchez Trace.
European-American/Choctaw
Intermediate, Older; Fiction

Applegate, Stan. *Natchez Under-the-Hill*. Illustrated by James Watling. Atlanta: Peachtree, 1999. 192 p.

In this sequel to *The Devil's Highway*, fourteen-year-old Zeb succeeds in finding his grandfather in Natchez and in returning with him to their Tennessee home. Zeb's adventures in the book include winning a horse race, escaping from jail and from being pressed into the British navy, rescuing stolen horses, experiencing the comet and the earthquake of 1811, and revisiting the Choctaw's Yowani Village. Zeb's friend Hannah, who is Caucasian-Choctaw, plays a prominent role in the story.
European-American/Choctaw
Intermediate, Older; Fiction

Krementz, Jill. *How It Feels To Be Adopted*. Photographs by author. New York: Alfred A. Knopf, 1982. 120 p.

Black-and-white photographs accompany the author's interviews with nineteen children who talk about being adopted: how they feel about it, their knowledge of and feelings about their birthparents and whether they want to meet them, their experiences as adopted children, and, for five of them, what it is like to be part of a mixed race family. One of these children, who is African-American, has been adopted by an African-American father, but has adopted brothers who are Hispanic, Korean, and biracial.
Seminole, Choctaw, and Chickasaw
Intermediate, Older; Nonfiction

Moonshower, Candie. *The Legend of Zoey: A Novel*. New York: Delacorte Press, 2006. 224 p.

This story is based on the legend of the 1811 and 1812 New Madrid Earthquakes that alleges they resulted from the curse placed by a Choctaw chief on the Chickasaw chief Reelfoot who defied him by marrying his daughter Laughing Eyes. When thirteen-year-old Zoey goes on a school field trip to Reelfoot Lake in western Tennessee, she is swept away in a drainage ditch during an electrical storm and finds herself back in 1811 with a thirteen-year-old girl Prudence and her mother. Journals written by Zoey and Prudence tell of their difficult journey as they try to reach safety from the earthquakes.

They learn of each other's lives, hopes, and worries; become friends; and spend time with Reelfoot and Laughing Eyes, whom Zoey discovers are her ancestors. There are surprises awaiting Zoey when she returns to the present day.
European-American/European-American, Chickasaw, and Choctaw
Intermediate, Older; Fiction

Nichols, Joan Kane. *All But the Right Folks*. Owings Mills, Md.: Stemmer House Publishers, 1985. 112 p.

Danny doesn't realize he is half white until he meets his grandmother Helga and goes to spend the summer with her in New York City. Suffering from asthma, bed-wetting, and teasing at his San Francisco school, Danny enjoys New York as he bikes with his grandmother; befriends Thelma Jean, her little brother Willy, and Charlayne; and starts learning karate from Charlayne's older sister. However, his new friends, two of whom are of mixed heritage, reject him because he lied that Helga was his nanny. Further, he worries that his deceased mother was a druggie like his Uncle Billy; his father insists that Danny is black and is not proud of him; and he discovers that Helga has lied to him. Everything improves when Danny uses his karate mental and kicking skills to escape kidnappers, and he decides that he is a bridge between black and white.
African-American/African-American Choctaw
Intermediate; Fiction

Singer, Marilyn, ed. *Face Relations: 11 Stories About Seeing Beyond Color*. New York: Simon & Schuster Books for Young Readers, 2004. 240 p.

In the story "Skins" by Joseph Bruchac, Mitchell, who is half Abenaki, provides needed support to the high school star quarterback, whom everyone assumes is Indian, but is really Hungarian. Mitchell also becomes close friends with Randolph, who is African-American and Native American.
African-American, Cherokee, and Choctaw/African-American, Cherokee, and Choctaw
Older; Fiction

Coeur d'Alene

See   Alexie, Sherman J., Jr.

Comanche

See   Parker, Quanah

Wallace, Bill. *Buffalo Gal*. New York: Pocket Books, 1993. 192 p. (A Minstrel Book)

It is 1904 and fifteen-year-old Amanda is on a trip from San Francisco to Oklahoma Territory and Texas with her mother who wants to save buffalo from extinction by getting some of them to a ranch. Amanda is unhappy about everything: the trains, the trip, and especially David, the half Comanche boy she meets at Fort Sills who insults her and, with two others, will accompany them into Texas in search of a buffalo herd. David is especially annoying after she almost beats him in a horse race and the two continually spat. On the journey Amanda is saved from an alligator and a rattlesnake; the group survives a severe thunderstorm; a Texas rancher, his Mexican wife, and their two children provide welcome hospitality; Amanda and David fight off a buffalo; Amanda is given the buffalo's calf as a birthday present; and the buffalo herd is captured. Amanda finally realizes that David cares for her and as she leaves for San Francisco, she agrees to marry him.

European-American/Comanche

Older; Fiction

Cree

Highwater, Jamake. *The Ceremony of Innocence*. New York: Harper & Row, Publishers, 1985. 192 p. (The Ghost Horse Cycle)

The Ceremony of Innocence is the second book in *The Ghost Horse Cycle*, a series for teenagers. It is the sequel to *Legend Days*, which describes Amana's childhood experiences as a Blood (Blackfoot). In this book Amana, whose family has died, has left her people and is destitute. She comes to live with an immature French Canadian, who deserts her before the birth of their daughter Jemina. Although sustained by her friendship with a French-Cree woman who runs a brothel, Amana suffers when Jemina grows up obsessed with finery and is married to the drunkard Jamie Ghost Horse and when her older grandson is only interested in things "American." Amana's hope lies in Sitko, her younger grandson, who treasures his Native American heritage.

French/Cree

Older; Fiction

Creek. See Muskogee

Croatan

Stainer, M. L. *The Lyon's Crown*. Illustrated by James Melvin. Circleville, N.Y.: Chicken Soup Press, 2004. 176 p. (The Lyon Saga)

In this final book of *The Lyon Saga*, smallpox has come to Croatan Island and killed many residents, including Jess's Croatan husband Akaiyan and her English mother. Jess sends her three children away to Jamestown as Robert Ashbury, who has long loved her, has offered to provide sanctuary for them. Now in their early twenties and of mixed Croatan-English blood, the three must pretend to be English, adapt to English ways, and endure hostility towards "savages" from Virginian residents who have suffered Indian attacks. Suzanne/Oohah-ne falls in love with and marries Robert Ashbury's stepson, and William/Caun-reha adapts to life in Jamestown and Henrico, where they move. However, George/Wauh-kuaene suffers in the English environment until Jess comes to take him back to Croatan Island. This book tells of John Rolfe's work in cultivating tobacco for the English market and of his love for Pocahontas, who comes to Henrico and accepts Christianity.

Croatan/English

Older; Fiction

Stainer, M. L. *The Lyon's Pride*. Illustrated by James Melvin. Circleville, N.Y.: Chicken Soup Press, 1998. 176 p. (The Lyon Saga)

The sequel to *The Lyon's Roar* and *The Lyon's Cub*, this book is part of *The Lyon Saga*, which relates a story of Jess Archarde and some of the other English settlers of the Lost Colony, who believing to be abandoned by their governor John White, move from Roanoke Island to live with the nearby Croatan Indians. In this book Jess helps lead some of the colonists who are leaving Croatan Island; marries Akaiyan, a Croatan; helps raise wolf cubs; has a baby, Oohahn-ne/Suzanne; mourns the death of her father; celebrates the marriage of Enrique, a former Spanish soldier, to a Croatan woman; and, again pregnant, hides when a pirate ship lands at Croatan Island.
Croatan/English
Older; Fiction

Stainer, M. L. *The Lyon's Throne*. Illustrated by James Melvin. Circleville, N.Y.: Chicken Soup Press, 1999. 168 p. (The Lyon Saga)

In this sequel to *The Lyon's Pride*, English Jess, her Croatan husband Akaiyan, their baby Oohahn-ne/Suzanne, Spanish Enrique, his Croatan wife Te-lah-tai, and other Croatan Indians are captured by pirates. When the pirate ship is sunk by an English vessel, they are all taken to England where their freedom is bought by John White, who had been the governor of the Lost Colony. This book tells of Jess's successful efforts to have Queen Elizabeth I free Enrique, who is imprisoned in the Tower of London, and send the group back to Croatan Island. During the story Jess gives birth to a baby Caun-reha/William when she is in the Queen's quarters, Te-lah-tai has a baby, Jess rejects an Englishman Robert Ashbury who falls in love with her, Robert gives her a magnificent white mare, and, upon their return, Jess has a third baby, Wauh-kuaene/George.
Croatan/English
Older; Fiction

Crow

Lampman, Evelyn Sibley. *Half-Breed*. Illustrated by Ann Grifalconi. Garden City, N.Y.: Doubleday & Company, 1967. 264 p.

Twelve-year-old Hardy leaves his Crow mother because she is marrying a man of the same clan and travels by himself to Oregon to find the white father who had left when he was six. Reaching his father's cabin with the help of Dr. John McLoughlin [later known as "Father of Oregon"] and his half Chippewa wife Marguerite and marshal Joe Meeks and his Cheyenne wife Virginia, Hardy discovers that his father has left to go to California to mine gold. Hardy decides to wait for his father and is aided during his stay by *Old Ironsides* veteran Bill Johnson and his Cheyenne wife Nancy on whose land the cabin is located. To Hardy's surprise his father's sister Rhody arrives from the East and stays with Hardy. Hardy is very upset by her white ways, especially her making him perform squaw's chores and burning his medicine bag. He also suffers from the poor treatment he receives in Portland because he is part Indian. After Hardy's father returns and then leaves, Hardy decides to go back to

live with the Crow. However, after his father again returns and then decides to leave, Hardy realizes that the responsible thing is to do is to remain with Aunt Rhody who is his family.
European-American/Crow
Intermediate, Older; Fiction

Dakota. See Sioux

Delaware

Curry, Jane Louise. *Dark Shade*. New York: Margaret K. McElderry Books, 1998. 176 p.

Independently Kip and Maggie are able to climb through a newly-formed spring to enter the world of the 1758 French and Indian War where British forces are cutting a road through the Pennsylvania forest to reach the French-controlled Fort Dusquesne and where the Lenape have a village near the road. Maggie saves the life of Robert Mackenzie, a lost Scottish Redcoat, and Kip is going to be adopted into a Lenape family until Maggie finds him. Afraid that their actions are changing the course of history, Kip and Maggie learn that they have altered and then restored it and that they are distant cousins, both descendents of Robert Mackenzie and his Lenape wife, Shawanaken. Corn Tassel, a minor character in this novel, is a British woman who has been adopted by the Lenape.
Scottish-European-American and Lenape/European-American; European-American/Scottish-European-American and Lenape
Older; Fiction

Duwamish

See   Seattle

Eskimo

George, Jean Craighead. *Julie*. Illustrated by Wendell Minor. New York: HarperCollins Publishers, 1994. 240 p.

In this sequel to *Julie of the Wolves*, Julie, who is now fourteen, is living in Kangik with her father Kapugen and his new wife Ellen. Trapped with Ellen in a blizzard, Julie comes to accept her white stepmother. However, Julie knows that Kapugen was the one who killed her adoptive wolf father Amaroq and will kill his son Kapu and the new wolf pack in order to protect his herd of musk ox that sustains the Alaskan village's economy. Journeying to find the wolf pack, Julie manages to lead it away from the village to a place where the wolves can feed on moose. Kapugen and Ellen name their new baby boy Amaroq; Julie falls in love with Peter, an Eskimo from Siberia; and when the wolves come back, Kapugen finally returns to his Eskimo ways and spares them.
Eskimo/European-American
Intermediate, Older; Fiction

George, Jean Craighead. *Julie's Wolf Pack*. Illustrated by Wendell Minor. New York: HarperCollins Publishers, 1997. 208 p.

This sequel to *Julie* is devoted almost entirely to the story of Julie's Avalik River wolf pack. It traces its activities through four years during which Kapu asserts himself as its Alpha (leader); the wolf Ice Blink spreads rabies on the tundra; Silver has two more puppies; Kapu is trapped for a medical study; Silver dies; Kapu's daughter Sweet Fur Amy becomes the new Alpha; and, released, Kapu joins his mate Aaka. There is little about Julie and her human family. However, her little half brother Amaroq bonds with one of Silver's wolf pups, which becomes a sled dog leader for Kapugen. At the book's end Julie and Peter marry and are hired to live on the tundra and study the wolves.
Eskimo/European-American
Intermediate, Older; Fiction

Vanasse, Deb. *A Distant Enemy*. New York: Puffin Books, 1999. 192 p.

Fourteen-year-old Joseph, whose white father has abandoned his family, hates everyone white. When officials of the Alaska Department of Fish and Game come to his Yupik Eskimo village to speak about an emergency fishing closure, he slashes the tires of their Cessna plane. Upset that his new white teacher Mr. Townsend has come into his duck blind, Joseph spreads the rumor that Mr. Townsend has wasted birds while hunting. When Joseph is falsely accused of stealing, he realizes that the girl he likes doesn't believe in his innocence because of his earlier lying. Consumed with anger, frustration, and guilt, Joseph runs off. He is saved from severe hypothermia by Mr. Townsend and comes to realize the importance of forgiveness.
European-American/Eskimo
Intermediate, Older; Fiction

Iñupiat Eskimo

George, Jean Craighead. *Water Sky*. New York: Harper & Row, 1987. 220 p.

Teenage Lincoln travels to Barrow, Alaska, to stay with his father's elderly Eskimo friend Vincent Ologak and to find his Uncle Jack, who had taught Lincoln how to sail. Uncle Jack had not been heard from in the two years since he left for Barrow to stop the Eskimo from killing the endangered bowhead whale. When Lincoln arrives in Alaska, he discovers that one of his great-great-grandmothers was an Eskimo and that the whales killed by the Eskimo are not causing the bowhead whale to become extinct, but are essential for their survival. Lincoln spends his time at Vincent's whale camp looking for the whale Nukik, which Vincent believes is to come to Lincoln to be killed. Lincoln learns that the man called Musk Ox is really Uncle Jack, who has changed his belief about the whales and married an Eskimo. The whale does come to Lincoln, but he cannot make himself kill it. It is killed by another boy on the umiaq; Vincent dies happily after learning Nukik has been killed; and the grateful people of Barrow are filled with the spirit of tolerance and sharing. Filled with information about the Eskimo culture and whaling, this story describes the hostility some Eskimos showed towards whites, Lincoln's wanting to be accepted as an Eskimo, the recognition he is given, and his realization that he will always be an outsider.

European-American and Iñupiat Eskimo/European-American
Older; Fiction

Flathead

See   Washakie

Haida

Okimoto, Jean Davies. *The Eclipse of Moonbeam Dawson*. New York: Tom Doherty Associates, 1998. 192 p.

Fifteen-year-old Moonbeam knows that he no longer wants to live with his hippie-activist mother. Taking a job at a nearby resort in British Columbia, he befriends Gloria, who is of European-Japanese-Canadian heritage, and falls for Michelle, a rich pretty hotel guest. By the end of the story, Moonbeam has recognized Michelle's falseness and decided both to change his name to Reid, the last name of a half Haida sculptor, and to look up his late Haida father's family.
Haida/European-American
Older; Fiction

Smith, Sherri L. *Lucy the Giant*. New York: Delacorte Press, 2002. 224 p.

Fifteen-year-old Lucy lives with her alcoholic father and encounters constant harassment at school because of her large size. When her beloved dog dies, Lucy leaves her Sitka home and goes to Kodiak where she pretends to be an adult named Barbara and gets a job on a crabbing boat. Despite the hard work, she finally feels accepted and part of a family. When her true identity is revealed, Lucy, now wiser and more mature, returns to her home.
Non-Haida/Haida
Older; Fiction

Hopi

Lacapa, Kathleen, and Michael Lacapa. *Less than Half, More than Whole*. Illustrated by Michael Lacapa. Flagstaff, Ariz.: Northland Publishing, 1994. 40 p.

This picture book is based on the author's family. Tony, who does not look like either his Caucasian or his Indian friend, is bothered about being called less than half and seeks understanding from his maternal grandmother, his older siblings, his uncle, and his paternal grandfather. It is when he realizes the meaning of an ear of corn that Tony knows that in truth he is more than whole. Designs from different Native American cultures complement the book's paintings.
Apache, Hopi, and Tewa/English-Irish-American and Mohawk
Primary, Intermediate; Fiction

MacGregor, Rob. *Hawk Moon*. New York: Simon & Schuster Books for Young Readers, 1996. 192 p.

Hawk Moon is the sequel to *Prophecy Rock*. When Will returns to Aspen, Colorado, from the Hopi

Reservation where he has spent the summer, he tells his girlfriend Myra that he thinks they should break up, but does not give her the chance to tell him what is bothering her. She disappears from the ghost town where he had left her, and Will becomes the prime target of the investigation into her kidnapping. This mystery has many twists and turns as Will comes to suspect classmates, his mother's boyfriend, and members of the sheriff's department. He is helped by Corey, a girl of mixed race who is a computer geek, and he experiences visions of Masau, the Hopi's kachina ruler.
Hopi/German-American
Older; Fiction

MacGregor, Rob. *Prophecy Rock*. New York: Laurel-Leaf Books, 1995. 208 p.

When teenager Will goes to spend the summer with his father, who is chief of police on the Hopi reservation, he becomes involved in the investigation of two murders. It first appears that the murderer is a preacher, a Hopi who now condemns the Hopis and their prophecies. Suspicion then turns to whoever believes himself to be Pahana, the Elder White Brother, who is the expected Hopi savior. However, who is that person: the mixed race hospital worker, the white doctor, or the ethnologist, who is also white? As Will helps in solving this mystery, he falls for a Hopi girl, travels about the Arizona reservation, and learns of the Hopi culture.
Hopi/German-American; European and Hopi
Older; Fiction

Smith, Roland. *Thunder Cave*. New York: Hyperion Paperbacks for Children, 1997. 256 p.

When he is fourteen-years-old, Jake's mother dies in a New York City traffic accident and his stepfather decides to send him to live with an aunt and uncle whom he dislikes. Jake sets off on his own to find his Hopi father who, somewhere in a remote area of Kenya, is studying elephant behavior and is worried about poachers who are killing elephants for their ivory. This book recounts Jake's adventures in Nairobi where his bike is stolen and he manages to steal it back and in the bush where he encounters a lion, becomes very ill, escapes from a brush fire, and, floating in a river along with dead and dying animals, is rescued by the Masai, Supeet. Supeet, who is looking for the renowned witch doctor who might help him bring rain to the drought-stricken land, joins Jake on his journey. Subsequently, they meet the witch doctor, Jake is captured by poachers and again rescued by Supeet, Supeet is temporarily blinded by a cobra, but "apparently" manages to bring rain, and Jake, recaptured by the poachers, is reunited with his father, but as a hostage. Thanks to the cleverness of Jake, his father, and Supeet, all ends well.
Hopi/Italian-American
Older; Fiction

Wong, Janet S. *The Next New Year*. Illustrated by Yangsook Choi. New York: Frances Foster Books/Farrar Straus and Giroux, 2000. 32 p

In this picture book a young American boy, who has a Chinese father and a Korean mother, prepares for Chinese New Year. His two best friends, who, like him, are of mixed heritage, will also celebrate the holiday.

Hopi and Mexican
Pre-K, Primary; Fiction

Hunkpapa. See Sioux

Iñupait. See Eskimo

Iowa

See: LaFlesche, Francis (Frank)
      Picotte, Susan LaFlesche
      Tibbles, Susette LaFlesche

Iroquois. See also Mohawk, Oneida, Senecan

Hausman, Gerald. *Night Flight*. New York: Philomel Books, 1996. 144 p.

Set in the summer of 1957, this is the story of two twelve-year-old boys: Max, who is incredibly cruel and controlling, and Jeff, who always tries to please him. When the boys' dogs as well as many others are poisoned, Max, whose father had been a Nazi, decides that Jews, whom he hates, are the culprits. Jeff, who had previously ignored his own Jewish heritage, struggles with Max's extreme views and actions, but, egged on by Max, shoots a dart into a Jewish family's front door. Jeff finally comes to realize what Max is—and what he himself can be.
Hungarian-Jewish/Dutch-English-Scottish-American and Iroquois and Methodist
Older; Fiction

Kickapoo

See Thorpe, James (Jim) Francis

Kiowa

See Momaday, Navarre Scott

Lakota. See Sioux

Lenape. See Delaware

Mandan

Spooner, Michael. *Last Child*. New York: Henry Holt and Company, 2005. 240 p.

Set in 1837 in the midst of a smallpox epidemic in what is now North Dakota, Rosalie is more comfortable helping her Scottish father, who is the bookkeeper at Fort Clark, than in being with her

Mandan mother. Because of her superior attitude, she has only her father and her grandmother Muskrat Woman as friends. When Rosalie goes with her father to keep a log of the buffalo robes which have fallen from the capsized boat of the French trapper Bedeaux, they are attacked by Dakota and she is kidnapped by those responsible for the attack: a Mandan who is under the influence of whiskey and a scoundrel who has deliberately brought smallpox to the area and wants revenge on her father. Rosalie manages to escape and to make a bull boat with which she saves Bedeaux and returns to the Mandan village. There, with the assistance of her former husband Bedeaux, Muskrat Woman isolates Rosalie, inoculates her with the virus of a Mandan recovering from smallpox, holds the ceremony which makes her a woman, and helps her in resolving the conflict between her Mandan and Scottish identities. Antoine Garreau, who served as interpreter for Fort Clark's managing officer, is a minor character in this novel.
Scottish/Mandan
Older; Fiction

Meherrin

Flood, Pansie Hart. *It's a Test Day, Tiger Turcotte*. Illustrated by Amy Wummer. Minneapolis: Carolrhoda Books, 2004. 72 p.

In this chapter book seven-year-old Tiger, who is of mixed race, is worried when it is time to take a big practice test, but becomes really upset when he has to fill in the race bubble. The African-American volunteer tells him to fill in Black and his teacher concludes he should fill in Other, but Tiger decides to leave that question blank because he isn't a weird or different "other." Tiger feels better when his father explains that just as ice cream can have mixed flavors, so people can be of mixed race. He feels even better when the next day there is an answer sheet that includes a Multiracial bubble and he discovers that a classmate is both black and Japanese.
African-American and Meherrin/Costa Rican
Primary; Fiction

Flood, Pansie Hart. *Tiger Turcotte Takes on the Know-It-All*. Illustrated by Amy Wummer. Minneapolis: Carolrhoda Books, 2005. 72 p.

Second-grader Tiger doesn't like "germy" girls and especially Donna Overton, who is a know-it-all. When Tiger and Donna call each other names in art class, they have to go to after-school detention. It is there that Tiger discovers he sort of likes Donna. There is no mention of Tiger's identity in this chapter book, but readers of *It's a Test Day, Tiger Turcotte* will know he is of mixed race.
African-American and Meherrin/Costa Rican
Primary; Fiction

Melungeon

Naylor, Phyllis Reynolds. *Sang Spell*. New York: Aladdin Paperbacks, 2000. 224 p.

Hitchhiking from Massachusetts to Dallas to live with his aunt because his mother has died, teenager Josh is mugged and left on a road in Appalachia where he is picked up by a Melungeon, who takes him to Canara, an isolated primitive community. Everything is strange and illogical there, and Josh becomes increasingly frustrated in his efforts to escape. The road he takes ends up at the exact place he started. Trying to swim towards a river's opposite shore takes him only a short distance, and a roadside restaurant and a school appear and disappear at regular intervals. Josh discovers that his father was probably Melungeon and befriends a girl whose father was stoned to death when his efforts to escape accidentally caused fatalities. Finally, with new insights and the realization that he must keep Canara's secrets, Josh is able to get away. [The Melungeon people are of mixed race living primarily in the central Appalachians. There is controversy as to their origin and their heritage, but they are often regarded as tri-racial: European-American, African-American, and Native American. In this novel they are identified as Portuguese who, over time, became mixed with a number of other peoples.]

Portuguese (Melungeon)-American/Irish-American; Celtic-American/Portuguese (Melungeon)-American

Older, Fiction

Menominee

Smith, Cynthia Leitich. *Indian Shoes*. Illustrated by Jim Madsen. New York: HarperCollins Publishers, 2002. 80 p.

This book tells of the close relationship between Ray and his Grampa Halfmoon, who live together in Chicago. For instance, Ray cleverly bargains to get a pair of Seminole moccasins for his homesick grandfather and together they attend a Cubs game, celebrate Christmas with the neighborhood pets, solve the problem of missing pants when Ray serves as wedding ring bearer for their Choctaw friend and her Polish-Menominee groom, and, visiting their relatives in Oklahoma, go fishing and catch more than fish.

Polish-American and Menominee

Primary, Intermediate; Fiction

Métis. See also individual heritages

Ernst, Kathleen. *Trouble at Fort La Pointe*. Illustrated by Jean-Paul Tibbles and Greg Dearth. Middleton, Wis.: Pleasant Company Publications, 2000. 176 p. (American Girl History Mysteries)

In 1732 when her family goes with other Ojibwa to spend the summer on La Pointe Island (now Madeline Island, Wisconsin), Suzette's father is accused of stealing furs from the adjacent Fort La Pointe. Twelve-year-old Suzette, who is Métis, with a French-Ojibwa mother and a French Canadian father, is determined to find the stolen furs and clear her father's name. She and her Métis friend Gabrielle discover the cave where the furs are stored and manage to escape when they are trapped there. Suzette then proves the identity of the real thief. Feeling that with her blue eyes, she is neither French nor Ojibwa, Suzette realizes that it was through the skills she learned from being both that she secured her father's release. A minor character in the book has an Ojibwa father and a Dakota mother.

French Canadian/Métis (French-Ojibwa); Métis

Intermediate, Older; Fiction

Modoc

See   Dorris, Michael

Mohawk

Carvell, Marlene. *Who Will Tell My Brother?* New York: Hyperion Books for Children, 2002. 160 p.

Written in free verse, this fictionalized story is based on a true experience. High school senior Evan, who looks like his English-American mother, has come to value the Mohawk part of his family. Upset by his school's tasteless Indian mascot, he pursues his older brother's earlier effort to have it changed. Persistent, Evan goes to the principal, to the school newspaper office, and repeatedly to the school board to stress the injustice it does to Native Americans. As a result he is cruelly taunted, his brother's dog is killed, and the school board passes a resolution proclaiming the Indian as a permanent mascot. However, in the process Evan gains a group of supportive friends who express their disapproval of the intolerance.
Mohawk and French Canadian-American/English-American
Older; Fiction

Lacapa, Kathleen, and Michael Lacapa. *Less than Half, More than Whole*. Illustrated by Michael Lacapa. Flagstaff, Ariz.: Northland Publishing, 1994. 40 p.

This picture book is based on the author's family. Tony, who does not look like either his Caucasian or his Indian friend, is bothered about being called less than half and seeks understanding from his maternal grandmother, his older siblings, his uncle, and his paternal grandfather. It is when he realizes the meaning of an ear of corn that Tony knows that in truth he is more than whole. Designs from different Native American cultures complement the book's paintings.
Apache, Hopi, and Tewa/English-Irish-American and Mohawk
Primary, Intermediate; Fiction

Peck, Robert Newton. *Jo Silver*. Englewood, Fla.: Pineapple Press, 1985. 144 p.

Sixteen-year-old Kenny plays hooky from school to try to find Jo Silver, the reclusive half Mohawk author whom he and his teacher, Dr. Gray, greatly admire. The story details Kenny's hike through the Adirondacks where he is pursued by would-be robbers and climbs a steep granite rock. Kenny is rewarded when he meets and gains insights from the elderly Jo Silver, who, although now blind, is self-sufficient. On the way back Kenny is surprised to meet Dr. Gray, who reveals his long-kept secret.
Mohawk/European-American
Older; Fiction

Rees, Celia. *Sorceress*. Cambridge, Mass.: Candlewick Press, 2003. 352 p.

Agnes, an eighteen-year-old Mohawk college student, decides to help a researcher who is trying to learn the fate of an English girl Mary Newbury, who was forced to flee from her Puritan settlement because she was accused of practicing witchcraft. Agnes feels a strange connection to Mary, who may

be the medicine woman whose story has been carried down in her family. Visiting her aunt on her Mohawk reservation, Agnes is transported back to the 1600s where she experiences Mary's life. Mary marries Jaybird, a Pennacook Indian, and bears two children: a daughter, who is murdered as a child by the English, and a son, Black Fox, who becomes a warrior. Mary saves Ephraim, an eleven-year-old white boy injured in an Indian attack, and raises him as her son. When she, Black Fox, and Ephraim visit Mount Royale to trade furs, Mary is captured by a Frenchman and then rescued by her two sons. Fleeing from their pursuers, they end up living in a Mohawk village where Mary is able to stem a smallpox epidemic. The author relates Mary's earlier story in the book *Witch Child*.
Mohawk/Mohawk, Pennacook (Pentucket) and English-American
Older; Fiction

Mohegan

Ketchum, Liza. *Where the Great Hawk Flies*. New York: Clarion Books, 2005. 272 p.

In 1780 during the Revolutionary War the British brought Caughnawaga Indians from Canada to raid the colonists living in Vermont. During the raid Daniel, his little sister, and their mother, a Pequot-Mohegan, hid in a cave while his English father served in the militia called up to chase the raiders. During the same raid Hiram was snatched by the Indians and then released and his Uncle Abner was captured and imprisoned in Canada. This story starts two years later when eleven-year-old Hiram and his family move to the property near thirteen-year-old Daniel's. Hiram is both scared of and antagonistic to Daniel and his family, and Daniel resents Hiram's derogatory remarks about Indians. The situation is compounded when Daniel's medicine man grandfather moves in with Daniel's family and builds a wigwam on the property and when Uncle Abner returns to Hiram's family. After some harrowing events Daniel and Hiram become friends. Mr. Sikes, one of the neighbors in this book, is Abenaki and French-American.
English/Pequot and Mohegan
Intermediate, Older; Fiction

Mohican

Bruchac, Joseph. *Hidden Roots*. New York: Scholastic Press, 2004. 144 p.

It is 1954 and eleven-year-old Sonny lives with his mother and his father, who is often angry and physically abusive. Sonny enjoys the company of an older friend, "Uncle" Louie, a man who had worked for his mother's parents when she was a child and from whom he learns much about the Adirondack area of New York State where they live. Sonny wonders about the many subjects he is not allowed to discuss and questions that remain unanswered: why he should be afraid of being "crept up on," what bad things happened in Vermont, and why his father doesn't want Uncle Louis around. It is only after he and Uncle Louis learn from the Jewish school librarian that her parents had sent her as a child from Germany to England for safety, that Uncle Louis tells Sonny the truth. Uncle Louis is his grandfather, who, like his late wife, had been sterilized during the Vermont Eugenics Project because they were Indians and who had fled Vermont so that Sonny's mother would not be taken away. It was because Sonny's family wanted to protect him from being treated like an Indian that they

had kept his identity a secret, but it is when the secret is revealed to Sonny that his father, who is also part Indian, is released from his anger and shame.
European-American and Native American/French Canadian American, Abenaki and Mohican
Intermediate, Older; Fiction

Charbonneau, Eileen. *The Ghosts of Stony Clove*. New York: Orchard Books, 1988. 160 p.

Building upon a ghost story of the Catskill Mountains and set in the early 1800s, this book tells of four years in the lives of Ginny Rockwell, who is Dutch-English-American, and Asher Woods, who is of mixed Native American and European-American heritage. When Ginny is almost twelve and Asher is fifteen, they go at night to the supposedly haunted Squire Sutherland's house where they encounter the squire, the servant girl he was said to have murdered fifty years earlier, a white dog, and a riderless horse. In this story of dreams, ghosts, cruelty, and goodness, Ginny comes to take care of the squire and inherit his property, while Asher, abused and persecuted because he is Indian, travels out west to find his family and then returns to marry Ginny. Their story is continued in the book, *In the Time of the Wolves*.
French-American and Wiechquaesgeck (Wiekagjock)/ European-American and Mohican
Older; Fiction

Charbonneau, Eileen. *In the Time of the Wolves*. New York: Tor-Doherty Associates, 1994. 192 p.

This story focuses on Josh Woods, the teenaged son of Asher Woods and Ginny Rockwell whose story began in the book *The Ghosts of Stony Clove*. It is now 1824 and Josh is greatly upset by his father who is part Indian and whose strange ways he finds disturbing. Josh wants to get away from the Catskills where he feels like an outsider, but his father opposes his going to Harvard. Josh is then befriended by Rebecca Elliott, who is a daughter of the Chase family which abused Asher when he was its bound servant. She supports Josh's getting a higher education and encourages his animosity towards his father. When Asher accepts the prediction of his Catholic friend Quinn and urges others to prepare for a year without summer, the neighbors at first reject his advice and, then, when there are summer frosts and snowstorms, blame him for their misfortunes. They also suspend Josh's mother from attending Congregational church services because she danced with her husband at a wake for Quinn. Josh accepts Rebecca's negative view of his parents and runs away with her. However, when he discovers that Rebecca and her relatives are seeking to take away his mother's inheritance and place his siblings in their custody, he realizes that he has been played for a dupe. Returning home he saves his father from a rabid gray wolf.
European-French-American, Mohican, and Wiechquaesgeck (Wiekagjock)/Dutch-English-American
Older; Fiction

Muskogee

See   Bosomworth, Mary Musgrove Matthews
       Harjo, Joy
       Osceola

Parsons, Lucia (Lucy) Gonzàles
Weatherford, William

Smith, Cynthia Leitich. *Jingle Dancer.* Illustrated by Cornelius Van Wright and Ying-Hwa Hu. New York: Morrow Junior Books, 2000. 32 p.

In this picture book Jenna wants to jingle dance in the next powwow, but doesn't have the four rows of jingles which her dress needs. However, she manages to borrow rows of jingles from three relatives and a neighbor and then dances for the four of them. The author's note identifies Jenna as Muskogee and Ojibwa.
Chippewa and Muskogee
Pre-K, Primary; Fiction

Smith, Cynthia Leitich. *Rain Is Not My Indian Name.* New York: HarperCollins Publishers, 2001. 144 p.

Since her best friend Galen was killed in a traffic accident on New Year's Day (her birthday), fourteen-year-old Rain, who is of mixed race, has withdrawn from her friends and from going out into her small Kansas town. However, despite refusing to become a participant, she agrees early in the summer to take photographs of her aunt's Native American camp. Rain is upset with Galen's mother and her opposition to the camp and with her former second best friend African-American Queenie, who attends the camp although it is not discovered until later that she has a Seminole ancestor. Then, on the Fourth of July (Galen's birthday), Rain is ready to move beyond his death.
Irish-German-American and Ojibwa/Scottish-Irish-American, Cherokee, and Muskogee
Intermediate, Older; Fiction

Narragansett

Lisle, Janet Taylor. *The Crying Rocks.* New York: Atheneum Books for Young Readers, 2003. 208 p. (A Richard Jackson Book)

Thirteen-year-old Joelle, who was adopted at the age of five by Vern and Aunt Mary Louise, does not look like anyone she knows in Rhode Island. She is upset by what she is told of her past: of being thrown out of a Chicago apartment window by her mother, being put in an orphanage there, traveling by freight train to Connecticut, and then being cared for by an old woman while living in a wooden crate near a railway depot. Joelle is befriended by an adoring eight-year-old girl who is European- and Japanese-American and by a classmate Carlos, who is of mixed heritage. Together Joelle and Carlos learn of the early Narragansett Indians and explore the wooded area, including the Crying Rocks, where they lived. Carlos learns the truth about the accident at the Crying Rocks where his older brother died and Joelle learns the truth about her background. Vern is her real father, her mother was Narragansett, and both her mother and twin sister died in Chicago.
Irish-American/Narragansett
Intermediate, Older; Fiction

Natick

See   Attucks, Crispus?

Navajo

See   Dockstader, Frederick J.
       Turner, Tina

Creel, Ann Howard. *Call Me the Canyon: A Love Story*. Weston, Conn.: Brown Barn Books, 2006. 224 p.

This novel takes place during the turn of the twentieth century in the Glen Canyon area of Utah and Arizona. Fifteen-year-old Madolen, whose Navajo mother had died years before, leaves her father to live with a Mormon family from whom she can learn to read. She becomes close to the family, especially to its daughter Claire, who becomes her steadfast friend, but is forced by the mother to leave after Claire's little brother Gabriel dies accidentally while under the girls' care. Madolen lives alone in a cabin as she supports herself by gathering gold dust and searches in vain for a gold-filled canyon she remembers from her childhood. Madolen then guides Wallis, a wealthy and educated young man, to places where he can pursue his interests in the area's ancient history. Madolen's love for Wallis is not returned until almost the end of the story when they decide to get married. However, realizing his reluctance to introduce a woman of Navajo blood to his Eastern family, Madolen leaves him and later marries Yiska, the Navajo whom she had previously disliked.
European-American/Navajo
Older; Fiction

Hernández, Irene Beltrán. *Heartbeat Drumbeat*. Houston: Arte Público Press, 1992. 136 p.

This is a novel about Morgana, a young woman who lives with her Mexican-American father and her Navajo mother near the Sandia Mountains of New Mexico. It presents the beliefs and rituals of both cultures as it tells of the death of Morgana's elderly Navajo mentor, of her bout with Rocky Mountain fever, of her rescue of a Seminole neighbor, of the attack by a bear which nearly killed her father, of her mother's sudden death, and of her tumultuous relationship with Eagle Eyes, whom she finally marries.
Mexican-American/Navajo
Older; Fiction

Young, Karen Romano. *Cobwebs*. New York: Greenwillow Books, 2004. 400 p.

In this unusual story Nancy, a high school sophomore who as yet has no spider traits, is the daughter of part spider parents. Her father is a roofer who prefers living up high; her mother is a weaver who has to remain low; her Granny is a knitter and potter; and her Grandpa Joke is a doctor. Nancy's family becomes involved with Nico, a Greek-American journalist who blackmails Grandpa Joke into

bringing Granny to heal his wife. In the process, Granny loses her life. The story focuses on the identities of the rumored Angel of Brooklyn and the Wound Healer, the growing attraction between Nancy and Niko's son Dion, and Nancy's concerns about whether she is or is not part spider.
Greek-American/Navajo
Older; Fiction

Nez Perce

Callan, Annie. *Taf.* Chicago: Cricket Books, 2001. 256 p. (A Marcato Book)
   In 1915, thinking that she has accidentally killed her toddler brother, twelve-year-old Taf runs away from home in search of her father who had gone West years earlier. On her four year journey to Wallowa County, Oregon, she meets a boy who lets her sleep in his tree hideout, stays with a farm couple, and receives a coin from a visionary Basque woman. In Pendleton, Oregon, she falls in love with a young man who is Chinese-Nez Perce, is courted by a policeman, becomes part of a musical trio, and cares for two neglected little girls. When she finally reaches Wallowa, she realizes that the search for her father is futile and that it is her lot to continue her journey. Written for young adults, this book presents Taf's growing up: her loneliness, her dauntless spirit, her yearning for love, the sorrows she encounters, the friends who care for her, and her discovery of her true self.
Chinese/Nez Perce
Older; Fiction

Ojibwa. See Chippewa

Odawa. See Ottawa

Omaha

See   Cruzatte, Pierre
      Labiche, François
      LaFlecsche, Francis (Frank)?
      Picotte, Susan LaFlesche?
      Tibbles, Susette LaFlesche?

Oneida

See   Dockstader, Frederick, J.

Osage

See   Tallchief, Maria
      Tallchief, Marjorie

Te Alta
Tinker, Clarence Leonard

Oto

See: LaFleseche, Francis (Frank)?
Picotte, Susan LaFlesche?
Tibbles, Susette LaFlesche?

Ottawa

See   Pontiac

Passamaquoddy

Levin, Betty. *Brother Moose*. New York: Greenwillow Books, 1990. 224 p.

When Nell, an orphan from England, is sent in the 1870s to live with a couple in Canada's Maritime Provinces, she discovers that her prospective mother, Mrs. Fowler, has moved to Maine to have a baby. Next Nell is kidnapped by robbers, escapes, and travels with her fellow orphan Louisa, an Indian named Joe Pennowit, and his twelve year old grandson to Maine. However, because Joe mistakenly thinks he has killed one of the men who kidnapped Nell, the four leave the road to escape the robbers and the police. On their difficult journey they go by wagon, by sleigh, and by an abandoned train car, which is pulled by their horse and a moose they have tamed. Nell finally reaches Mrs. Fowler, but her adoption hopes take a surprising turn.
European-Canadian or European-American/Canadian Micmac or American Passamaquoddy or Penobscot
Older; Fiction

Mason, Cherie. *Everybody's Somebody's Lunch*. Illustrated by Gustav Moore. Gardiner, Maine: Tilbury House, Publishers, 1998. 40 p.

After her cat is killed in the woods next to her farm, a young girl learns about predators and their prey from her teacher, her grandmother, and her own observations—and comes to a fuller understanding of nature. The book's paintings complement the story.
European-American and Passamaquoddy
Intermediate; Fiction

Pennacook (Pentucket)

Rees, Celia. *Sorceress*. Cambridge, Mass.: Candlewick Press, 2003. 352 p.

Agnes, an eighteen-year-old Mohawk college student, decides to help a researcher who is trying to learn the fate of Mary Newbury, an English girl who was forced to flee from her Puritan settlement because she was accused of practicing witchcraft. Agnes feels a strange connection to Mary, who may

be the medicine woman whose story has been carried down in her family. Visiting her aunt on her Mohawk reservation, Agnes is transported back to the 1600s where she experiences Mary's life. Mary marries Jaybird, a Pennacook Indian, and bears two children: a daughter, who is murdered as a child by the English, and a son, Black Fox, who becomes a warrior. Mary saves Ephraim, an eleven-year-old white boy injured in an Indian attack, and raises him as her son. When she, Black Fox, and Ephraim visit Mount Royale to trade furs, Mary is captured by a Frenchman and then rescued by her two sons. Fleeing from their pursuers, they end up living in a Mohawk village where Mary is able to stem a smallpox epidemic. The author relates Mary's earlier story in the book *Witch Child*.
Pennacook (Pentucket)/English; Mohawk/Mohawk, Pennacook (Pentucket) and English-American
Older; Fiction

Penobscot

Levin, Betty. *Brother Moose*. New York: Greenwillow Books, 1990. 224 p.
    When Nell, an orphan from England, is sent in the 1870s to live with a couple in Canada's Maritime Provinces, she discovers that her prospective mother, Mrs. Fowler, has moved to Maine to have a baby. Next Nell is kidnapped by robbers, escapes, and travels with her fellow orphan Louisa, an Indian named Joe Pennowit, and his twelve year old grandson to Maine. However, because Joe mistakenly thinks he has killed one of the men who kidnapped Nell, the four leave the road to escape the robbers and the police. On their difficult journey they go by wagon, by sleigh, and by an abandoned train car, which is pulled by their horse and a moose they have tamed. Nell finally reaches Mrs. Fowler, but her adoption hopes take a surprising turn.
European-Canadian or European-American/Canadian Micmac or American Passamaquoddy or Penobscot
Older; Fiction

Pequot

See   Cuffe, Paul?

Ketchum, Liza. *Where the Great Hawk Flies*. New York: Clarion Books, 2005. 272 p.
    In 1780 during the Revolutionary War the British brought Caughnawaga Indians from Canada to raid the colonists living in Vermont. During the raid Daniel, his little sister, and their mother, a Pequot-Mohegan, hid in a cave while his English father served in the militia called up to chase the raiders. During the same raid Hiram was snatched by the Indians and then released and his Uncle Abner was captured and imprisoned in Canada. This story starts two years later when eleven-year-old Hiram and his family move to the property near thirteen-year-old Daniel's. Hiram is both scared of and antagonistic to Daniel and his family, and Daniel resents Hiram's derogatory remarks about Indians. The situation is compounded when Daniel's medicine man grandfather moves in with Daniel's family and builds a wigwam on the property and when Uncle Abner returns to Hiram's family. After some harrowing events Daniel and Hiram become friends. Mr. Sikes, one of the neighbors in this book, is Abenaki and French-American.

English/Pequot and Mohegan
Intermediate, Older; Fiction

Ponca

See   LaFlesche, Francis (Frank)?
       Picotte, Susan LaFlesche?
       Tibbles, Susette LaFlesche?

Potawatomi

See   Hamilton, Virginia
       Thorpe, James (Jim) Francis

Powhatan

See   Rolfe, Thomas

Pueblo

James, J. Alison. *Sing for a Gentle Rain*. New York: Atheneum, 1990. 228 p.

Teenagers James and Sweet Rain are alike in many ways. Their mothers have either left or died, their fathers have abandoned them, and they are being raised by their loving grandfathers. However, James is an American boy of the twentieth century and Spring Rain is an Anasazi girl of the thirteenth century. The book uses alternating chapters to tell how James is drawn to exploring the Anasazi culture and Spring Rain realizes that she must find the right man to give her a son who will lead her people from their land of drought to a more fertile one. Then, drawn by Spring Rain's song, James encounters her on a Southwestern mesa, stays as a stranger in her Anasazi village, falls in love with her, fathers her son, and is sent back by her song to his own home.
Pueblo Indian/European-American
Older; Fiction

Quapaw

See   Ballard, Louis

Strauss, Victoria. *Guardian of the Hills*. New York: Morrow Junior Books, 1995. 240 p.

During the Great Depression, sixteen-year-old Pamela moves with her mother to her mother's childhood home in Arkansas. There Pamela meets her grandfather for the first time and learns about her deceased Quapaw grandmother, who abandoned her Quapaw family and responsibilities. Pamela is little prepared for what transpires. Her grandfather finances an archaeological excavation on a nearby hill

built by Mound People, and Pamela learns from her great-aunt that humans were once sacrificed on this hill and that evil may again arise from the Stern Dreamer who is buried there. It is up to Pamela to make the crucial choice that will determine others' fate and that results in her becoming the new Quapaw Guardian.
European-American/European-American and Quapaw
Older; Fiction

Rappahannock

See   Loving, Mildred Delores Jeter

Sac and Fox

See   Thorpe, James (Jim) Francis

Seminole

See   Horse, John
       Mason, Bridget (Biddy)

Krementz, Jill. *How It Feels To Be Adopted*. Photographs by author. New York: Alfred A. Knopf, 1982. 120 p.

Black-and-white photographs accompany the author's interviews with nineteen children who talk about being adopted: how they feel about it, their knowledge of and feelings about their birthparents and whether they want to meet them, their experiences as adopted children, and, for five of them, what it is like to be part of a mixed race family. One of these children, who is African-American, has been adopted by an African-American father, but has adopted brothers who are Hispanic, Korean, and biracial.
Seminole, Choctaw, and Chickasaw
Intermediate, Older; Nonfiction

McKissack, Patricia C. *Run Away Home*. New York: Scholastic Press, 1997. 176 p.

In 1888 Sky, a fifteen-year-old Chiricahua Apache boy, escapes from a train of Apache prisoners and hides on the farm of twelve-year-old Sarah Jane Crossman, her African-American father, and her mother, who is of African-Scottish-Irish and Seminole heritage. George Wrattan, an Army scout and interpreter, allows the Crossmans to keep Sky with them until he recovers from his swamp fever. In the meantime boll weevils destroy the family's cotton crop, night riders come to their farm, and Sarah Jane's father, who is skilled as a carpenter, gets an order from Booker T. Washington to build desks for nearby Tuskegee Institute. Sky becomes healthy, but Wrattan, whose wife is Apache, gives permission for him to remain on the farm.
African-American/African-Scottish-Irish-American and Seminole
Intermediate, Older; Fiction

Meyer, Carolyn. *Jubilee Journey*. San Diego: Gulliver Books, 1997. 288 p.

In this sequel to *White Lilacs*, it is 1996 and eighty-seven-year-old Rose Lee has invited her thirteen-year-old great-granddaughter Emily Rose and her family to attend the Freedomtown Juneteenth Diamond Jubilee. Growing up in Connecticut, Emily Rose has always regarded herself as a "double" as her father is French-American and her mother is African-American. However, she and her brothers Steven and Robbie have no idea what it means to be black in Dillon, Texas. They quickly learn of the attitudes of some whites when Steven is set up and abused and of the closeness and pride of the African-American community. In this story Rose Lee reveals what has happened to her and her family during the past seventy-five years. Emily Rose gets a new friend who thinks she should be just black and decides to remain in Denton to learn more about being black so she can better understand herself. Alicia, Rose Lee's best friend in Connecticut, has a Nigerian father and an English mother.
French-American and Catholic/African-European-American, Seminole, and Baptist
Intermediate, Older; Fiction

Meyer, Carolyn. *White Lilacs*. San Diego: Gulliver Books, 1993. 256 p.

Set in 1921 this is the story of Freedomtown, the section of Dillon, Texas, where African-Americans have lived since 1870 and of twelve-year-old Rose Lee, who experiences its sorrow when the whites force the residents to leave and move to the Flats, an undesirable part of town, so that the whites can build a city park and be further away from the blacks. It tells of Rose Lee's family and neighbors who are powerless to prevent Freedomtown's removal, of the thoughtlessness of the white women, of the Klan, of Rose's brother Henry being tarred and feathered, of the "colored school" being burned down, of Rose's Aunt Susannah who leaves her teaching job in St. Louis to teach the children of the Flats, of the Quaker white lady Emily Firth who loses her job because she stands up for the blacks, of the white girl Catherine Jane who saves Henry, and of Rose Lee, who preserves Freedomtown in her drawings. Although Rose Lee and Susannah are mostly African-American, Rose Lee's paternal grandfather is part Seminole and her maternal great-grandfather was white. Susannah's paternal grandfather was white.
African-American and Seminole/African-European-American
Intermediate, Older; Fiction

Smith, Cynthia Leitich. *Indian Shoes*. Illustrated by Jim Madsen. New York: HarperCollins Publishers, 2002. 80 p.

This book tells of the close relationship between Ray and his Grampa Halfmoon, who live together in Chicago. For instance, Ray cleverly bargains to get a pair of Seminole moccasins for his homesick grandfather and together they attend a Cubs game, celebrate Christmas with the neighborhood pets, solve the problem of missing pants when Ray serves as wedding ring bearer for their Choctaw friend and her Polish-Menominee groom, and, visiting their relatives in Oklahoma, go fishing and catch more than fish.
Cherokee and Seminole
Primary, Intermediate; Fiction

Smith, Cynthia Leitich. *Rain Is Not My Indian Name*. New York: HarperCollins Publishers, 2001. 144 p.

Since her best friend Galen was killed in a traffic accident on New Year's Day (her birthday), fourteen-year-old Rain, who is of mixed race, has withdrawn from her friends and from going out into her small Kansas town. However, despite refusing to become a participant, she agrees early in the summer to take photographs of her aunt's Native American camp. Rain is upset with Galen's mother and her opposition to the camp and with her former second best friend African-American Queenie, who attends the camp although it is not discovered until later that she has a Seminole ancestor. Then, on the Fourth of July (Galen's birthday), Rain is ready to move beyond his death.
African-American and Seminole
Intermediate, Older; Fiction

Thomas, Joyce Carol. *The Blacker the Berry*. Illustrated by Floyd Cooper. New York: Joanna Cotler Books, 2008. 32 p.

In this picture book thirteen poems and accompanying paintings present the beauty of varied black skin shades, including the raspberry black of an African-American and Seminole boy, the cranberry red of an African-Irish-American girl, and the snowberry color of an African-European-American girl.
African-American and Seminole
Primary, Intermediate; Fiction

Seneca

Moore, Robin. *Maggie among the Seneca*. New York: J. B. Lippincott, 1990. 112 p.

Sixteen-year-old Maggie, who is Irish, is kidnapped in 1778 by the Seneca and taken from central Pennsylvania to the Seneca village on the Genesee River. Staying at first with two Seneca women, Maggie then goes to live with Frenchgirl, who, kidnapped at an early age, is French and English, but now regards herself as Seneca. Maggie agrees to marry Frenchgirl's brother so she can go on a hunting trip to the Allegheny River and escape from there to her aunt's. However, when Maggie's husband dies, she stays to tend his burial scaffold. Maggie has a baby, survives the destruction of the village by the colonial army, and then goes to live with her aunt. The book is the sequel to *The Bread Sister of Sinking Creek*.
French-English-American and Seneca/Irish-American
Intermediate, Older; Fiction

Urban, Betsy. *Waiting for Deliverance*. New York: Orchard Books, 2000. 192 p.

This book is set in 1793 in western New York where there is tension between the Americans and the Seneca, who supported the British during the Revolutionary War. Fourteen-year-old orphan Livy, who is terrified of Indians, is sold at a pauper's auction to Gideon, who was raised by Senecas and educated by Anglican Canadians, and whose Seneca brother Rising Hawk often stays with him and his wife. When Livy is sent to a Seneca village to help its women learn how to spin, she is suddenly accused of being a witch. After escaping with Rising Hawk, with whom she is often at odds, Livy discovers that she is in love with him. In this story Rising Hawk has a French ancestor.

Seneca/French and Seneca
Older; Fiction

Shawnee

See   Drouillard, George
       Washington, Fannie Norton Smith

Bruchac, Joseph. *The Dark Pond*. Illustrated by Sally Wern Comport. New York: HarperCollins Publishers, 2004. 160 p.

   Armie, who has a gift for communing with birds and animals, is continually drawn to the dangerous dark pond near his boarding school dorm. He is twice kept from approaching it, first by a fox and then by Mitch, a zoology graduate student who realizes from Abenaki stories that the creature that dwells in the pond has a very long life cycle and for some reason has awoken. Armie saves Mitch's life when Mitch attempts to kill the giant wormlike creature—and comes to realize that his schoolmates actually like him.

Armenian-American/Shawnee
Intermediate, Older; Fiction

Rinaldi, Ann. *The Blue Door*. New York: Scholastic, 1996. 288 p. (The Quilt Trilogy)

   The Blue Door concludes the Chelmsford family trilogy begun in *A Stitch in Time* and continued in *Broken Days*. In 1840 Nathaniel Chelmsford is still alive, but all of his children with the exception of Abby have died. Abby, who had left her Massachusetts home when she was fifteen, has never returned from the South. In this book her fourteen-year-old granddaughter Amanda, who is the narrator, is sent back to Massachusetts to save her father's cotton plantation and to fulfill her grandmother's wishes that she gain the power to help others and return Abby's part of the family quilt. On her journey Amanda is threatened with death by the man who causes a steamboat explosion and steals her grandmother's quilt piece. As a result, Amanda must assume a different identity and pretend to be mute, her family thinks she has died, her great-grandfather rejects her as an imposter, and she has to work in her great-grandfather's cotton mill where labor conditions are unsafe and insufferable. It is only as she gains power by aiding her fellow mill workers and is helped by Nancy, her half Shawnee cousin earlier known as Walking Breeze, that Amanda is accepted by her great-grandfather and that Abby's quilt piece is returned.

Shawnee/European-American
Older; Fiction

Rinaldi, Ann. *Broken Days*. New York: Scholastic, 1995. 288 p. (The Quilt Trilogy)

   This sequel to *A Stitch in Time* is set immediately preceding and during the War of 1812. Fourteen-year-old Ebie Chelmsford is the narrator of this book which continues the story of the Chelmsford family. The daughter of Cabot, who is often away at sea, and of a mother who deserted them, Ebie lives with her Aunt Hannah, who is loved by both Richard Lander, a sea captain, and Louis Gaudineer, an Indian agent. Ebie's Aunt Thankful, who has lived with the Shawnee, dies and at her

request, her half Shawnee daughter, fourteen-year-old Walking Breeze, comes to Salem to live with her Aunt Hannah. Resentful of her intrusion, Ebie steals Thankful's family quilt, the only proof of Walking Breeze's identity. She places it in a bundle for Georgie, the half Shawnee woman earlier known as Night Song, who, filled with anger at the whites, has become a disturbed recluse. As the story evolves, Louis is killed in the massacre at Fort Dearborn, Georgie becomes a Quaker, Hannah and Richard marry, and Ebie finally comes to her senses and helps restore her family by getting Thankful's quilt to Hannah.
European-American/Shawnee; Shawnee/European-American
Older; Fiction

Rinaldi, Ann. *A Stitch in Time*. New York: Scholastic, 1994. 320 p. (The Quilt Trilogy)
In this first book of a trilogy about the Chelmsford family of Salem, Massachusetts, the narrator is Hannah, the oldest sister who strives to keep her family together as symbolized by the quilt she and her sisters are making that includes fabric from those whom the family trusts. In the eventful period from 1788 to 1791, Nathaniel Chelmsford, their cruel father, goes on to a trip to Ohio Territory. He is accompanied by his elder son Lawrence and his headstrong youngest daughter Thankful. Thankful is kidnapped by the Shawnee and decides to remain with them. Abby, the fifteen-year-old sister, elopes with Nate Videau, a Southern ship captain, and together they survive a shipwreck in the Caribbean. Cabot, the youngest sibling whose mother died during his childbirth, discovers that Nathaniel is not his father. Hannah, who with Cabot remains at their Salem home, saves her father's cotton mill, becomes betrothed to Richard Lander, who takes his ship on a secret trade route to Sumatra, and agrees to raise Night Song, the half Shawnee baby of Louis Gaudineer, the man to whom she was earlier betrothed. Sequels to this book are *Broken Days* and *The Blue Door*.
European-American/Shawnee
Older; Fiction

Sanders, Scott Russell. *Bad Man Ballad*. New ed. Bloomington, Ind.: Indiana University Press, 2004. 264 p. (The Library of Indiana Classics)
Set during the War of 1812, this story traces the involvement of three very different individuals, who become responsible for an incredibly strong and frightening giant known as Bear Walks. Ely discovers the body of an unscrupulous dwarf who has presumably been murdered by the giant outside the hut of Rain Hawk, who is French and Shawnee and, like Ely, an older teenager and an orphan. Ely and Owen, a lawyer who has come to the community from Philadelphia, are deputized by the town of Roma to hunt down the giant and return him for trial. They travel through Ohio and into Indiana where they discover the giant in an old Indian cave on the banks of the Ohio River. Bear Walks regards Ely as his brother and follows him wherever he goes. Joined on the way back by Rain Hawk, the three realize that the dimwitted Bear Walks should not be prosecuted for murder. Upon their return to Roma where, as elsewhere, the giant is regarded as a terrifying freak, Owen is unable to convince the jury that Bear Walks murdered the dwarf in defense of Rain Hawk.
French/Shawnee
Older; Fiction

Shoshone

See   Charbonneau, Jean Baptiste (Pomp)
        Washakie

Duey, Kathleen. *Celou Sudden Shout, Wind River, 1826*. New York: Aladdin Paperbacks, 1998. 160 p. (American Diaries)

With a French fur trapper father and a Shoshone mother, twelve-year-old Celou is well aware of the differing beliefs and customs of the two cultures. When her father is away for a rendevous, Crows kidnap her mother and two younger brothers. Celou rides for help to the Shoshone big camp, only to discover that it has been attacked by Blackfoot. Drawing upon what she has learned from both parents, she then stealthily follows the Crows and, with bravery and ingenuity, rescues her family and saves herself.

French-American/Shoshone
Intermediate, Older; Fiction

Sioux

See   Crawford, Goldsby (Cherokee Bill)?

Hamilton, Virginia. *Arilla Sun Down*. New York: Scholastic, 1976. 304 p.

This novel tells of twelve-year-old Arilla whose mother is sure of her identity as an African-American woman, whose Native American father alternates between his work at an Ohio college and leaving for his boyhood home, and whose older brother, Jack Sun Run, delights in parading his Native American heritage. Always in her brother's shadow, certain that he hates her, and terribly jealous, Arilla treasures the times that he treats her nicely. The book tells of Arilla's writing her autobiography; of old James False Face, her only friend when she was little; of Susanne Shy Woman who is Sioux and Cheyenne; of sneaking out at night with Sun Run and his girlfriend to go roller skating; of sledding with her father on an exciting, but dangerous hill; of saving Sun Run's life and discovering he had saved hers; and, throughout the book, of her struggle to find her own identity.

Sioux and Cheyenne
Older; Fiction

Lisle, Janet Taylor. *The Crying Rocks*. New York: Atheneum Books for Young Readers, 2003. 208 p. (A Richard Jackson Book)

Thirteen-year-old Joelle, who was adopted at the age of five by Vern and Aunt Mary Louise, does not look like anyone she knows in Rhode Island. She is upset by what she is told of her past: of being thrown out of a Chicago apartment window by her mother, being put in an orphanage there, traveling by freight train to Connecticut, and then being cared for by an old woman while living in a wooden crate near a railway depot. Joelle is befriended by an adoring eight-year-old girl who is European- and Japanese-American and by a classmate Carlos, who is of mixed heritage. Together Joelle and Carlos learn of the early Narragansett Indians and explore the wooded area, including the Crying Rocks, where they lived. Carlos learns the truth about the accident at the Crying Rocks where his older brother died and Joelle learns the truth about her background. Vern is her real father, her mother was Narragansett, and both her mother and twin sister died in Chicago.

Colombian-English-Spanish-American and Sioux/European-American

Intermediate, Older; Fiction

Dakota

See   Deloria, Ella Cara
        Deloria, Phillip Samuel (Sam)
        Deloria, Vine, Jr.
        Deloria, Vine, Sr.

Ernst, Kathleen. *Trouble at Fort La Pointe*. Illustrated by Jean-Paul Tibbles and Greg Dearth. Middleton, Wis. Pleasant Company Publications, 2000. 176 p. (American Girl History Mysteries)

In 1732 when her family goes with other Ojibwa to spend the summer on La Pointe Island (now Madeline Island, Wisconsin), Suzette's father is accused of stealing furs from the adjacent Fort La Pointe. Twelve-year-old Suzette, who is Métis, with a French-Ojibwa mother and a French Canadian father, is determined to find the stolen furs and clear her father's name. She and her Métis friend Gabrielle discover the cave where the furs are stored and manage to escape when they are trapped there. Suzette then proves the identity of the real thief. Feeling that with her blue eyes, she is neither French nor Ojibwa, Suzette realizes that it was through the skills she learned from being both that she secured her father's release. A minor character in the book has an Ojibwa father and a Dakota mother.

Ojibwa/Dakota

Intermediate, Older; Fiction

Schultz, Jan Neubert. *Battle Cry*. Minneapolis: Carolrhoda Books, 2006. 240 p

This book of historical fiction is set in southern Minnesota where Dakota Indians who had been mistreated rose up in the bloody Dakota Conflict of 1862. It tells of the bond between the fictional teenagers, Chaska, son of the Dakota Indian John Other Day [who really existed] and a white mother, and Johnny, who is white. Vivid descriptions detail the fighting as Johnny and Chaska participate in the Battles of Fort Ridgley and Birch Coolee. A man who is Dakota and white is involved in the fighting; Johnny's twelve-year-old sister is kidnapped by Dakota; Chaska is unjustly ordered to be executed; Johnny manages to secure his release; and the two of them witness the hanging of innocent Dakota.

Dakota/European-American; European-American and Dakota

Older; Fiction

Yankton Dakota

See   Bonnin, Gertrude Simmons

Lakota

Kretzer-Malvehy, Terry. *Passage to Little Bighorn*. Flagstaff, Ariz.: Rising Moon, 1999. 232 p.

In this novel fifteen-year-old Dakota is discouraged because his Irish-American father has remarried and left the family, his Lakota mother has just returned from a two year treatment of depression, and he has been living with his father's father. When he visits the Little Bighorn Battlefield, Dakota finds himself swept back to 1876 where he becomes the "chosen relative" of wise and kind Sitting Bull. He experiences Lakota life: going on a buffalo hunt, counting coup by capturing two Crow horses, surviving a grizzly bear attack, receiving a Lakota name, becoming friends with a boy who is European-American and Lakota, falling for a daughter of Sitting Bull, meeting his great-great-great grandmother and great-great grandfather, and witnessing the terrible battles of the Rosebud and the Little Bighorn. It is with the Lakota that Dakota learns how he should live, and he decides to return to his real family.
European-American/Lakota
Older; Fiction

Sauerwein, Leigh. *The Way Home*. Illustrated by Miles Hyman. New York: Farrar, Straus & Giroux, 1994. 128 p.

This book contains six stories, including "Storm Warning" and "The Dress." "Storm Warning" is set in Nebraska in 1989. When Jonathan, the Indian who is Joe's best friend, saves the twelve-year-old boy during a tornado, Joe realizes that Jonathan is his father. "The Dress," which is set in 1876, tells of Laura's first visit to her Aunt Ella. Laura learns that when Ella was young, she was captured by Cheyenne. She married a Cheyenne warrior and they had three children. However, Ella was the only survivor when soldiers attacked the Cheyenne village, and she was returned to her white family, who continue to ostracize her.
European-American and Lakota Sioux/European-American
Intermediate; Fiction

Hunkpapa

Kretzer-Malvehy, Terry. *Passage to Little Bighorn*. Flagstaff, Ariz.: Rising Moon, 1999. 232 p.

In this novel fifteen-year-old Dakota is discouraged because his Irish-American father has remarried and left the family, his Lakota mother has just returned from a two year treatment of depression, and he has been living with his father's father. When he visits the Little Bighorn Battlefield, Dakota finds himself swept back to 1876 where he becomes the "chosen relative" of wise and kind Sitting Bull. He experiences Lakota life: going on a buffalo hunt, counting coup by capturing two Crow horses, surviving a grizzly bear attack, receiving a Lakota name, becoming friends with a boy who is European-American and Lakota, falling for a daughter of Sitting Bull, meeting his great-great-great grandmother and great-great grandfather, and witnessing the terrible battles of the Rosebud and the Little Bighorn. It is with the Lakota that Dakota learns how he should live, and he decides to return to his real family.

Irish-American/Lakota (Hunkpapa)
Older; Fiction

Spokane

See   Alexie, Sherman J., Jr.

Suquamish

See   Seattle

Tewa

Lacapa, Kathleen, and Michael Lacapa. *Less than Half, More than Whole*. Illustrated by Michael Lacapa. Flagstaff, Ariz.: Northland Publishing, 1994. 40 p.

This picture book is based on the author's family. Tony, who does not look like either his Caucasian or his Indian friend, is bothered about being called less than half and seeks understanding from his maternal grandmother, his older siblings, his uncle, and his paternal grandfather. It is when he realizes the meaning of an ear of corn that Tony knows that in truth he is more than whole. Designs from different Native American cultures complement the book's paintings.

Apache, Hopi, and Tewa/English-Irish-American and Mohawk
Primary, Intermediate; Fiction

Tlingit

Martin, Nora. *The Eagle's Shadow*. New York: Scholastic Press, 1997. 176 p.

In 1946 when twelve-year-old Clearie's father is assigned to spend a year in Japan, Clearie is sent to live in a remote Alaskan village with her mother's Tlingit relatives whom she has never met. Clearie feels unaccepted by them because of her mother's bad reputation. She is also saddled by the sense of incompetence with which her father regards her. However, as Clearie makes friends, learns to paddle a canoe, fish, spin yarn, and do carpentry, and receives praise from her critical aunt, she realizes that for the first time she belongs and is part of a family.

Irish-American/Tlingit
Intermediate, Older; Fiction

Tsimshian

Hoyt-Goldsmith, Diane. *Totem Pole*. Photographs by Lawrence Migdale. Illustrated by David Boxley. New York: Holiday House, 1990. 32 p.

This book's color photographs and text show the wolf mask and halibut hook made by David's father, a Tsimshian woodcarver, and the cedar box made by his great-great-grandfather. It describes how young David assists his father in making a totem pole for the Klallam Indians who live near their

Kingston, Washington home, and then performs two dances with him at the totem pole-raising cere-mony, A glossary is included.
Tsimshian/European-American
Intermediate; Nonfiction

Wampanoag

Gay Head Wampanoag

See   Cuffe, Paul?

Wichita

Garland, Sherry. *The Last Rainmaker*. San Diego: Harcourt, Brace & Company, 1997. 336 p.

It is 1900 and thirteen-year-old Caroline, mourning the death of her beloved European-American grandmother, is living with her cruel great-aunt. Her rejoicing when her father comes, presumably to have her join him, turns to anger when he sells her horse, ships her off to a stepcousin, and plans to sell her adoption rights to her great-aunt. Caroline, who has discovered that her deceased mother was Native American and not of royal Italian blood as she had been told, runs away to the Wild West show where her mother had performed. There she meets her grandfather and learns to appreciate Native Americans. When her grandfather dies, Caroline decides not to choose between her two heritages, but to determine her own path.
European-American/Wichita
Older; Fiction

Wiechquaesgeck (Wiekagjock)

Charbonneau, Eileen. *The Ghosts of Stony Clove*. New York: Orchard Books, 1988. 160 p.

Building upon a ghost story of the Catskill Mountains and set in the early 1800s, this book tells of four years in the lives of Ginny Rockwell, who is Dutch-English-American, and Asher Woods, who is of mixed Native American and European-American heritage. When Ginny is almost twelve and Asher is fifteen, they go at night to the supposedly haunted Squire Sutherland's house where they encounter the squire, the servant girl he was said to have murdered fifty years earlier, a white dog, and a riderless horse. In this story of dreams, ghosts, cruelty, and goodness, Ginny comes to take care of the squire and inherit his property, while Asher, abused and persecuted because he is Indian, travels out west to find his family and then returns to marry Ginny. Their story is continued in the book, *In the Time of the Wolves*.
French-American and Wiechquaesgeck (Wiekagjock)/ European-American and Mohican
Older; Fiction

Charbonneau, Eileen. *In the Time of the Wolves*. New York: Tor-Doherty Associates, 1994. 192 p.

This story focuses on Josh Woods, the teenaged son of Asher Woods and Ginny Rockwell whose

story began in the book *The Ghosts of Stony Clove*. It is now 1824 and Josh is greatly upset by his father who is part Indian and whose strange ways he finds disturbing. Josh wants to get away from the Catskills where he feels like an outsider, but his father opposes his going to Harvard. Josh is then befriended by Rebecca Elliott, who is a daughter of the Chase family which abused Asher when he was its bound servant. She supports Josh's getting a higher education and encourages his animosity towards his father. When Asher accepts the prediction of his Catholic friend Quinn and urges others to prepare for a year without summer, the neighbors at first reject his advice and, then, when there are summer frosts and snowstorms, blame him for their misfortunes. They also suspend Josh's mother from attending Congregational church services because she danced with her husband at a wake for Quinn. Josh accepts Rebecca's negative view of his parents and runs away with her. However, when he discovers that Rebecca and her relatives are seeking to take away his mother's inheritance and place his siblings in their custody, he realizes that he has been played for a dupe. Returning home he saves his father from a rabid gray wolf.
European-French-American, Mohican, and Wiechquaesgeck (Wiekagjock)/Dutch-English-American
Older; Fiction

Wyandot

Wolf, Allan. *Zane's Trace*. Cambridge, Mass.: Candlewick Press, 2007. 208 p.

In this book for high schoolers, teenager Zane, who suffers grand mal seizures and constantly writes his thoughts on his bedroom walls, feels that he is responsible for the deaths of his schizophrenic mother (because he was at school) and his grandfather (because he crossed off his name from the family tree he had drawn). Zane drives from Baltimore to Zanesville, Ohio, to commit suicide on his mother's grave. On the way he has supernatural encounters with his dead parents, his grandfather, and several of his ancestors. Finally reaching the Zanesville cemetery, Zane understands that he has a caring brother and friends and that it is he who must keep his deceased family's souls alive.
Wyandot/African-European-American
Older; Fiction

Yankton Dakota. See Sioux

Oceanian-American

Australian-American

See   O'Brien, Maria de la Soledad Teresa (Soledad)

Hawaiian-American

McLaren, Clemence. *Dance for the Land*. New York: Atheneum Books for Young Readers, 1999. 160 p.

Twelve-year-old Kate is unhappy and homesick when she leaves her California home for Hawaii, not only because she misses her dog and ballet troupe, but also because, with her Caucasian looks, she doesn't fit in. She is tormented at school and, unlike her Hawaiian-looking older brother, is not accepted by her uncle. As the story progresses, Kate comes to love dancing hulas, learns about her Hawaiian heritage, helps bring harmony between her always-arguing father and uncle, and, thanks to her uncle, is reunited with her dog. The book presents the conflict between her uncle's wanting Hawaii to become an independent country and her father's advocacy of establishing a Native Hawaiian nation within the state of Hawaii.
Native Hawaiian/European-American
Intermediate, Older; Fiction

Mower, Nancy Alpert. *I Visit My Tutu and Grandma*. Illustrated by Patricia A. Wozniak. Kailua, Hawaii: Press Pacifica, 1984. 24 p. (Treasury of Children's Hawaiian Stories)

In this picture book set in Hawaii, a little girl enjoys a visit with her two grandmothers: one Hawaiian-American and the other European-American. Her Hawaiian-American grandmother uses many Hawaiian words.
Hawaiian-American/European-American
Pre-K; Fiction

Samoan-American

See   Johnson, Dwayne Douglass (The Rock)

South American-American. See also Latin American-American

Torres, Leyla. *Liliana's Grandmothers*. Illustrated by author. New York: Farrar Straus Giroux, 1998. 32 p.

In this picture book Liliana loves visiting both her grandmother who lives on her street and her grandmother who lives in an unspecified South American country.
European-South American-American
Pre-K, Primary; Fiction

Argentine-American

Delacre, Lulu. *Salsa Stories*. Illustrated by author. New York: Scholastic Press, 2000. 112 p.

At a New Year's Day celebration in Carmen Teresa's home, some of her relatives, a family friend, and the housekeeper tell stories of their childhoods which she might include in the new notebook she has received. The stories are about their childhoods in Cuba, Puerto Rico, Argentina, Mexico, Peru, and Guatemala. Carmen Teresa surprises those present when she decides instead to write down the recipes for foods mentioned in the stories and served at the celebration. This book includes both the stories and the recipes.
Puerto-Rican and Cuban-American/Argentine-American
Intermediate; Fiction

Brazilian-American

Miner, Chalise. *Rain Forest Girl: More Than an Adoption Story*. Photographs by Phil Miner. Childs, Md.: Mitchell Lane Publishers, 1998. 48 p.

Photographs and text describe Diana's adoption as she experienced it. Seven-year-old Diana and her newborn sister were removed from their home in the Brazilian jungle as their grandmother and mother were not able to care for them. Diana lived in a Brazilian convent before she was adopted by American parents and went with them to her new home in Kansas City. At first everything was strange to Diana, but she felt better when she became friends with a Portuguese-speaking girl, whose parents were American and Brazilian. Now as a teenager, Diana still keeps in touch with her Brazilian friends.
European-American/Brazilian
Intermediate; Nonfiction

Colombian-American

de Jenkins, Lyll Becerra. *Celebrating the Hero*. New York: Puffin Books, 1995. 192 p.

After her mother dies, seventeen-year-old Camila travels to her mother's hometown in Colombia to attend a ceremony honoring her late grandfather, whom she has regarded as a hero, and to learn about her mother's past. She discovers that although her grandfather was the town's benefactor, he was a cruel man who destroyed her grandmother. Camila's trip brings some closure to her grief and the realization that perhaps someday she, like her mother, will be able to forgive her grandfather.

European-American/Colombian
Older; Fiction

Lisle, Janet Taylor. *The Crying Rocks*. New York: Atheneum Books for Young Readers, 2003. 208 p. (A Richard Jackson Book)

Thirteen-year-old Joelle, who was adopted at the age of five by Vern and Aunt Mary Louise, does not look like anyone she knows in Rhode Island. She is upset by what she is told of her past: of being thrown out of a Chicago apartment window by her mother, being put in an orphanage there, traveling by freight train to Connecticut, and then being cared for by an old woman while living in a wooden crate near a railway depot. Joelle is befriended by an adoring eight-year-old girl who is European- and Japanese-American and by a classmate Carlos, who is of mixed heritage. Together Joelle and Carlos learn of the early Narragansett Indians and explore the wooded area, including the Crying Rocks, where they lived. Carlos learns the truth about the accident at the Crying Rocks where his older brother died and Joelle learns the truth about her background. Vern is her real father, her mother was Narragansett, and both her mother and twin sister died in Chicago.

Colombian-English-Spanish-American and Sioux/European-American
Intermediate, Older; Fiction

Ecuadorian-American

See   Aguilera, Christina

Hoyt-Goldsmith, Diane. *Three Kings Day: A Celebration at Christmastime*. Photographs by Lawrence Migdale. New York: Holiday House, 2004. 32 p.

Through numerous color photographs and text this book describes the history and celebration of Three Kings Day. It relates the legend of the three kings and follows ten-year-old Veronica and her family as they celebrate the holiday in New York City. Veronica makes a king mask, attends a paranda (spontaneous concert), eats a special meal, walks in the El Musee del Barrio's Three Kings Day Parade, and receives gifts. The book includes a glossary.

Puerto-Rican-American/Ecuadorian-American
Primary, Intermediate; Nonfiction

Kuklin, Susan. *Families*. Photographs by author. New York: Hyperion Books for Children, 2006. 40 p.

Text and color photographs present interviews with American children, who talk about their families. Their families include seven families with children of mixed race, ethnicity, or religion, with one also including a child adopted from Sierra Leone. In an eighth family a child has been adopted from China. In a ninth family an adopted American child is of a race different from that of one of her fathers.

English-German-American/Ecuadorian
Primary, Intermediate; Nonfiction

Venezuelan-American

See   Carey, Mariah

West Indian-American. See also Latin American-American

See   Williams, Mary Harris

Bahamian-American

See   Du Bois, William Edward Burghardt (W. E. B.)

Creole-American. See also individual heritages

See   Knowles, Beyoncé Giselle

Forrester, Sandra. *Dust from Old Bones*. New York: Morrow Junior Books, 1999. 176 p.
    This story is set in the stratified society of the New Orleans of 1838. Thirteen-year-old Simone, who is a person of color, struggles with the probability that her pretty cousin Claire-Marie will go to quadroon balls and be chosen by a Creole "protector" [as his mistress]. She envies the life of Madelon, her aunt who lives in France where she is not faced with racial discrimination. Nevertheless, Simone comes to realize that her restricted life as a person of color is much better than that of black slaves, who if lucky enough to be freed had to leave New Orleans. Simone's admiration for Madelon, who comes to visit, disappears when she betrays not only Simone, but also the two slaves she was committed to free. It is Simone who leads the slaves through a swamp to a safe house.
African-Creole-American/African-Creole-Haitian; Creole-American/African-Creole-Haitian
Older; Fiction

Peck, Richard. *The River Between Us*. New York: Dial Books, 2003. 176 p.
    Set at the beginning of the Civil War, this book tells how the life of fifteen-year-old Tilly and her family changes when two mysterious strangers, Delphine and her apparent servant Calinda, arrive via steamboat at Grand Tower, Illinois. Coming from New Orleans, Delphine with her elegant clothes and fancy ways is like no one the town has ever seen. The two stay with Tilly's family, and Tilly's twin brother Noah falls in love with Delphine. When now-sixteen Noah goes off to join the Yankee army, their mother is so upset, since her husband had earlier left her, that she sends Tilly and Delphine off to Cairo, Illinois, to bring Noah home. The book tells of the horrible living conditions in Cairo and especially of the unsanitary hospital tents. Noah, who suffers from dysentery, recovers enough that he is sent off to fight in the nearby battle of Belmont, Missouri in which he is wounded and has to have his left arm amputated. The two girls stay in Cairo tending to Noah and other soldiers, and upon their return home with Noah learn that Tilly's distraught mother, seeing the coffin of her husband which she mistook for Noah's, drowned herself in the river. The story also reveals that to Tilly's surprise Delphine and Calinda are sisters and that Delphine's father is indeed the wealthy Jules Duval, but that he is her mother's protector, not her husband as in New Orleans whites cannot marry Creoles. Following the war Calinda, a conjure woman, leaves Grand Tower so that she will not raise suspicion that Delphine has African blood. Although Delphine refuses to marry a white man, she and Noah live as husband and wife, but their son is passed off as the son of Tilly and her husband.

Creole (African-French-Spanish)-Haitian-American
Older; Nonfiction

Walter, Mildred Pitts. *Ray and the Best Family Reunion Ever*. New York: HarperCollins Publishers, 2002. 128 p.

Eleven-year-old Ray is the only member of his Creole family with ebony skin. When he goes to a large family reunion in Natchitoches, Louisiana, Ray discovers that he and Gran-papa Philippe are the only ones there with dark skin. To make matter worse, Ray looks like his grandfather whom his father and almost all his relatives despise. This is the story of Ray's secret bonding with Gran-papa Philippe, his appreciation of his grandfather's talent, and his effecting a reconciliation between his father and Philippe.

Creole (Nigerian-French-Spanish-Native American)-Haitian-American/Creole (French-Spanish-West African-Native American)-American
Intermediate; Fiction

Cuban-American

See   O'Brien, Maria de la Soledad Teresa (Soledad)

Bode, Janet. *Different Worlds: Interracial and Cross-Cultural Dating*. New York: Franklin Watts, 1989. 128 p.

Based primarily on interviews with six teenage couples who are dating interracially and/or cross-culturally, this book is written for and about teens. It looks at the history of prejudice and racism; discusses negative reactions of parents, relatives, and classmates; examines why adolescents make their dating choices; and mentions some positive aspects of interracial dating. Although it does not cover the topics of interracial marriage and families, four of the twelve teens interviewed are of mixed race or heritage: African-American/European-American; Protestant English-American/Catholic Irish-American; Cuban/Puerto Rican; and Mexican-Spanish-American. A bibliography, a listing of resource organizations, and an index are included.

Cuban/Puerto Rican
Older; Nonfiction

Delacre, Lulu. *Salsa Stories*. Illustrated by author. New York: Scholastic Press, 2000. 112 p.

At a New Year's Day celebration in Carmen Teresa's home, some of her relatives, a family friend, and the housekeeper tell stories of their childhoods which she might include in the new notebook she has received. The stories are about their childhoods in Cuba, Puerto Rico, Argentina, Mexico, Peru, and Guatemala. Carmen Teresa surprises those present when she decides instead to write down the recipes for foods mentioned in the stories and served at the celebration. This book includes both the stories and the recipes.

Puerto-Rican and Cuban-American/Argentine-American
Intermediate; Fiction

García, Cristina. *I Wanna Be Your Shoebox*. New York: Simon & Schuster Books for Young Readers, 2008. 208 p.

Eighth-grader Zumi loves surfing, her baby cousin adopted from Guatemala, and playing clarinet in her middle school orchestra—and even spearheads the orchestra's money-raising punk-reggae concert to save it from being eliminated. However, most of all she treasures her cancer-ridden grandfather and the story of his life which he tells her before dying.
Japanese-Russian-American Jewish/Guatemalan-Cuban
Older; Fiction

Osa, Nancy. *Cuba 15*. New York: Delacorte Press, 2003. 304 p.

In September Violet's Cuban grandmother proposes she be given a quinceañero, an elaborate ceremony celebrating a girl's being fifteen and becoming a woman. Violet dreads the occasion, which is set for the following May. However, during the intervening months she finds out more about the quinceañero, lends her own touch to the party, and learns about her Cuban heritage and the controversial issue of the United States' embargo of Cuba. Violet also matures as she becomes a contributing member of her school's speech team and has her first boyfriend. The party is a great success—and Violet's father finally agrees to discuss Cuba with her and her brother.
Cuban/Polish-American
Older; Fiction

Steptoe, John. *Creativity*. Illustrated by E. B. Lewis. New York: Clarion Books, 1997. 32 p.

When Hector, a Spanish-speaking boy from Puerto Rico, joins his class, Charles, who is African-American, wonders why they have the same skin color. While making friends with Hector, he learns about the mixing of races and how doing something differently can be creative.
African-Cuban-American/African-American
Intermediate; Fiction

Dominican-American

See   Cary, Mary Ann Shadd

Kuklin, Susan. *Families*. Photographs by author. New York: Hyperion Books for Children, 2006. 40 p.

Text and color photographs present interviews with American children, who talk about their families. Their families include seven families with children of mixed race, ethnicity, or religion, with one also including a child adopted from Sierra Leone. In an eighth family a child has been adopted from China. In a ninth family an adopted American child is of a race different from that of one of her fathers.
Puerto-Rican-American/Dominican
Primary, Intermediate; Nonfiction

Landau, Elaine. *Interracial Dating and Marriage*. New York: Julian Messner, 1993. 112 p.

This book's introduction presents two detailed histories of interracial marriage: the first of African-

American intermarriage with Caucasians and the second of intermarriages involving Japanese-Americans. In both cases the introduction describes factors, including governmental actions and societal attitudes, which affected the frequency of these marriages. The bulk of the book presents interviews with ten teenagers and five adults or adult couples who describe their views of and/or experiences with interracial dating and marriage. Seven of the teens interviewed came to the United States from other countries; two of the teens are interracial. Two of the adult interviews are with interracial couples; another contains advice from a minister. A resource list and an index are included.
African-English-Indian-Italian-Dominican
Older; Nonfiction

Grenadian-American

See   Malcolm X

Haitian-American

See   Du Bois, William Edward Burghardt (W. E. B.)

Forrester, Sandra. *Dust from Old Bones*. New York: Morrow Junior Books, 1999. 176 p.
   This story is set in the stratified society of the New Orleans of 1838. Thirteen-year-old Simone, who is a person of color, struggles with the probability that her pretty cousin Claire-Marie will go to quadroon balls and be chosen by a Creole "protector" [as his mistress]. She envies the life of Madelon, her aunt who lives in France where she is not faced with racial discrimination. Nevertheless, Simone comes to realize that her restricted life as a person of color is much better than that of black slaves, who if lucky enough to be freed had to leave New Orleans. Simone's admiration for Madelon, who comes to visit, disappears when she betrays not only Simone, but also the two slaves she was committed to free. It is Simone who leads the slaves through a swamp to a safe house.
African-Creole-American/African-Creole-Haitian; Creole-American/African-Creole-Haitian
Older; Fiction

Peck, Richard. *The River Between Us*. New York: Dial Books, 2003. 176 p.
   Set at the beginning of the Civil War, this book tells how the life of fifteen-year-old Tilly and her family changes when two mysterious strangers, Delphine and her apparent servant Calinda, arrive via steamboat at Grand Tower, Illinois. Coming from New Orleans, Delphine with her elegant clothes and fancy ways is like no one the town has ever seen. The two stay with Tilly's family, and Tilly's twin brother Noah falls in love with Delphine. When now-sixteen Noah goes off to join the Yankee army, their mother is so upset, since her husband had earlier left her, that she sends Tilly and Delphine off to Cairo, Illinois, to bring Noah home. The book tells of the horrible living conditions in Cairo and especially of the unsanitary hospital tents. Noah, who suffers from dysentery, recovers enough that he is sent off to fight in the nearby battle of Belmont, Missouri, in which he is wounded and has to have his left arm amputated. The two girls stay in Cairo tending to Noah and other soldiers, and upon their return home with Noah learn that Tilly's distraught mother, seeing the coffin of her husband which she

mistook for Noah's, drowned herself in the river. The story also reveals that to Tilly's surprise Delphine and Calinda are sisters and that Delphine's father is indeed the wealthy Jules Duval, but that he is her mother's protector, not her husband as in New Orleans whites cannot marry Creoles. Following the war Calinda, a conjure woman, leaves Grand Tower so that she will not raise suspicion that Delphine has African blood. Although Delphine refuses to marry a white man, she and Noah live as husband and wife, but their son is passed off as the son of Tilly and her husband.
Creole (African-French-Spanish)-Haitian-American
Older; Nonfiction

Walter, Mildred Pitts. *Ray and the Best Family Reunion Ever*. New York: HarperCollins Publishers, 2002. 128 p.

Eleven-year-old Ray is the only member of his Creole family with ebony skin. When he goes to a large family reunion in Natchitoches, Louisiana, Ray discovers that he and Gran-papa Philippe are the only ones there with dark skin. To make matter worse, Ray looks like his grandfather whom his father and almost all his relatives despise. This is the story of Ray's secret bonding with Gran-papa Philippe, his appreciation of his grandfather's talent, and his effecting a reconciliation between his father and Philippe.
Creole (Nigerian-French-Spanish-Native American)-Haitian-American/Creole (French-Spanish-West African-Native American)-American
Intermediate; Fiction

Jamaican-American

See   Dandridge, Dorothy
        Tsang, Lori

Benedict, Helen. *The Opposite of Love*. New York: Viking, 2007. 304 p.

In this novel for older teenagers, seventeen-year-old Madge lives with her English mother, an illegal immigrant who has been imprisoned and disappears for stretches at a time. Half white and half black, Madge feels like an outcast in her Pennsylvania town where she encounters blatant racism, but is supported by her aunt and a core of friends, including Kishna, her Indian best friend with whom she has her first love affair. On visits to her cousin in New York City, Madge encounters a neglected four-year-old black boy, who doesn't want to return to the apartment where he lives. Aware of the terrible mistreatment of some children in foster care, compassionate Madge takes him home with her. The story presents the complex consequences of Madge's action and the legal and ethical questions which she faces.
Jamaican/English
Older; Fiction

Senisi, Ellen B. *For My Family, Love Allie*. Photographs by author. Morton Grove, Ill.: Albert Whitman & Company, 1998. 32 p.

In this picture book Allie wants to make a present for the large family party to be held at her house.

All by herself she makes peanut-butter treats. Then, after her African-American and European-American relatives cook together, play games together, and eat together, they all enjoy Allie's dessert.
African-Jamaican-American/European-American
Pre-K, Primary; Fiction

Young, Karen Romano. *Cobwebs*. New York: Greenwillow Books, 2004. 400 p.

In this unusual story Nancy, a high school sophomore who as yet has no spider traits, is the daughter of part spider parents. Her father is a roofer who prefers living up high; her mother is a weaver who has to remain low; her Granny is a knitter and potter; and her Grandpa Joke is a doctor. Nancy's family becomes involved with Nico, a Greek-American journalist who blackmails Grandpa Joke into bringing Granny to heal his wife. In the process, Granny loses her life. The story focuses on the identities of the rumored Angel of Brooklyn and the Wound Healer, the growing attraction between Nancy and Niko's son Dion, and Nancy's concerns about whether she is or is not part spider.
Jamaican-West African-American/Italian-Scottish-American
Older; Fiction

Puerto Rican-American

See   Campeche, José
         Cole, Lynette
         Prinze, Freddie James, Jr.
         Williams, William Carlos

Bode, Janet. *Different Worlds: Interracial and Cross-Cultural Dating*. New York: Franklin Watts, 1989. 128 p.

Based primarily on interviews with six teenage couples who are dating interracially and/or cross-culturally, this book is written for and about teens. It looks at the history of prejudice and racism; discusses negative reactions of parents, relatives, and classmates; examines why adolescents make their dating choices; and mentions some positive aspects of interracial dating. Although it does not cover the topics of interracial marriage and families, four of the twelve teens interviewed are of mixed race or heritage: African-American/European-American; Protestant English-American/Catholic Irish-American; Cuban/Puerto Rican; and Mexican-Spanish-American. A bibliography, a listing of resource organizations, and an index are included.
Cuban/Puerto Rican
Older; Nonfiction

Brashares, Ann. *Forever in Blue: The Fourth Summer of the Sisterhood*. New York: Delacorte Press, 2007. 400 p. (Sisterhood of the Traveling Pants)

This fourth book of the series takes place after Carmen, Lena, Tibby, and Bridget's freshman year in college. Carmen's year at Williams College has been a disaster. She finds herself ungrounded with her mother, stepfather, and baby brother moving into a new house, discovers that she has no idea how to make friends, and feels invisible. Her only college friend, aspiring actress Julia, has persuaded Carmen

to spend the summer with her at a theater festival in Vermont where Carmen will be on a stage crew. When the casting director persuades Carmen to audition, Carmen, who has never acted, is amazed to discover that she is the only apprentice chosen for a role in the theater's major production. Julia becomes hostile to Carmen and, then, pretending to be helpful, teaches Carmen how to read her role in meter. The professional actors are dismayed that Carmen now sounds like a robot. Carmen finally realizes that Julia takes pleasure in her failures, and she once again immerses herself in her role. Lena, who had been crushed when her Greek boyfriend Kostas married a Greek woman whom he had impregnated, is enrolled in a painting class in Providence, Rhode Island. There she is impressed with classmate Leo, an outstanding artist who is equally engrossed in painting. Getting to know him and his artistic African-American mother, Lena has her first sexual experience with him. Tibby, who has been going with Bailey's friend Brian, also loses her virginity. However, she becomes distressed that she may be pregnant and, after discovering that she isn't, breaks up with Brian. She then gives Lena's younger sister Effie an okay to go out with him. With Bridget's boyfriend Eric away for the summer in Mexico, she goes to Turkey for an archaeological dig. There she discovers that she loves digging and falls for an archaeology professor until she sees his wife and children. At the book's conclusion Tibby is reunited with Brian, Bridget is reunited with Eric, and Lena, Tibby, and Bridget go to Vermont to attend Carmen's successful opening night. Then the four friends fly to Greece to search for the Traveling Pants, which Effie has accidentally lost, Lena and Kostas meet, and the four friends realize that they have moved beyond the Pants. The mixed heritages of Carmen, Bridget, and Eric should be familiar to readers of *The Sisterhood of the Traveling Pants*.
European-American/Puerto Rican-American
Older; Fiction

Brashares, Ann. *Girls in Pants: The Third Summer of the Sisterhood*. New York: Delacorte Press, 2005. 352 p. (Sisterhood of the Traveling Pants)

Bridget, Lena, Tibby, and Carmen graduate from high school at the beginning of this third book in the series, which details the four seventeen-year-olds' lives during the summer before college. Lena, who is still getting over Kostas, enjoys her summer drawing class. Defying and lying to her father, she continues to attend after he has forbidden her to continue because of the nude models. When he discovers her deceit, he announces that he will not pay for her going to the Rhode Island School of Design. Heeding the suggestion of the class teacher, Lena embarks on an art portfolio project that just may win her a scholarship to the RISD. Tibby has conflicting feelings when Brian asks her to the senior party, but is devastated when, because she has left her window open, her three-year-old sister tries to climb the nearby apple tree and, falling, has a fractured skull and broken bones. Finding it difficult to have her new stepfather David living in her house and upset by the news that she will become a sister, Carmen considers going to the nearby University of Maryland rather than Williams College so that she can be closer to home. She hates her job taking care of Valia, Lena's grandmother, who has become very disagreeable because she is homesick for her native Greece. Carmen also worries that Win, the boy she likes, has the false impression that she is a good person. Bridget spends her summer coaching at a soccer camp in Pennsylvania where she is surprised to discover that one of the coaches is Eric with whom she had a relationship two summers earlier in California. Still strongly drawn to him, but trying to be more sensible, she and Eric become friends and he nurses her through an illness. It is an eventful summer as Carmen and Win frantically drive to Downington, Pennsylvania, to bring David back to Bethesda for his son's early birth and Carmen discovers that she loves her baby brother and wants to go to Williams. Valia is happy that she can return to Greece, and Lena receives the RSID scholarship and her father's approval. Tibby overcomes her feelings of unworthiness by climbing out of her window and down the apple tree and being Carmen's mother's successful, albeit unorthodox, birth coach. It is then that she is able to get back together with Brian. And, Eric tells Bridget that he has broken up with his girlfriend, and they profess how much they care for each other. Readers of the initial book in this series will be aware of the mixed heritages of Carmen, Bridget, and Eric.

European-American/Puerto Rican-American
Older; Fiction

Brashares, Ann. *The Second Summer of the Sisterhood*. New York: Delacorte Press, 2003. 384 p. (Sisterhood of the Traveling Pants)

This second book of the series describes Carmen, Lena, Bridget, and Tibby's experiences during the summer before their seventeenth birthdays. Once again, the pants are passed among them, but they no longer fit Bridget, who has been so down because of her earlier sexual relationship with Eric, that she has gained weight, given up soccer, and dyed her pretty blonde hair. Using a fake name, Bridget travels to Alabama where she gets a job cleaning her grandmother Greta's attic and finds mementos of her deceased mother. As the summer progresses Bridget gets back in shape, is able to wear the pants, confesses her identity to Greta and to her long ago best friend Billy, coaches and then stars for Billy's soccer team, and realizes that Greta is like a mother to her. Tibby goes to a film program at a college in Virginia. Befriending two shallow classmates, she produces a highly embarrassing film about her mother and is excruciated when her mother comes to the viewing. Upset by the damage she has done to her relationships with her mother and Brian, a friend of hers and Bailey's, she redeems herself by making a moving film about Bailey, who died from cancer. Both Carmen and Lena also experience strained relationships with their mothers. Carmen is jealous of her mother's romance with David, sabotages it, and then manages to restore it. Lena pesters her mother about the man Eugene in her mother's past and regrets that she has broken off with Kostas. When Kostas visits her, she discovers that he really is in love with her. However, going to Greece for her beloved grandfather's funeral, Lena finds out that Kostas has had to marry a Greek woman whom he impregnated. Fortunately, she learns about Eugene from her mother and is attracted to Carmen's stepbrother Paul. The story ends when the girls' mothers, who had not been close since Bridget's mother's death, resume their friendship. The mixed heritages of Carmen, Bridget, and Eric were revealed in *The Sisterhood of the Traveling Pants*.

European-American/Puerto Rican-American
Older; Fiction

Brashares, Ann. *The Sisterhood of the Traveling Pants*. New York: Delacorte Press, 2001. 304 p. (Sisterhood of the Traveling Pants)

In this initial book of the series, four girls who are almost sixteen discover that a pair of blue jeans that Carmen had purchased at a thrift shop somehow fits all of them. Close friends their entire lives, the girls establish a Sisterhood in which they will pass the pants among each other as they separate during their summer vacation. Bridget, an athlete whose father is Dutch and whose mother had committed suicide, goes to a soccer camp in Baja, California, where she shines as a player. She is strongly attracted to camp coach Eric whose mother is Mexican, loses her virginity to him, and then becomes confused and upset. Carmen, who had been looking forward to a vacation with her divorced father in South Carolina, is shocked to learn that he is engaged and is living with his fiancée and her two children. Ignored and treated like an outsider because of her Puerto Rican appearance, Carmen finally becomes so frustrated and angry that she throws a rock through the house window and runs away back to Bethesda, Maryland. Lena, a beautiful introverted girl, goes with her sister to stay in Greece with her grandparents. Enjoying painting the lovely scenery, she inadvertently leads her grandparents to believe she has been raped by Kostas, a family friend, and causes a fight between their grandfathers. Tibby, who remains at home, gets a tedious job at a drugstore and becomes friends with Bailey, a twelve-year-old girl who has leukemia and with whom she films a movie. The pants seem to have no positive effect on the girls' experiences until the end of the summer. Then Lena gets the courage to apologize to Kostas and tell him she loves him; Carmen gets the courage to go to her father's wedding after telling him that she is mad at him; Tibby gets the courage to visit Bailey in the hospital when she is dying; and Bridget receives the support she needs from the pants (and Lena who brings them to her).

European-American/Puerto Rican-American
Older; Fiction

Delacre, Lulu. *Salsa Stories*. Illustrated by author. New York: Scholastic Press, 2000. 112 p.

At a New Year's Day celebration in Carmen Teresa's home, some of her relatives, a family friend, and the housekeeper tell stories of their childhoods which she might include in the new notebook she has received. The stories are about their childhoods in Cuba, Puerto Rico, Argentina, Mexico, Peru, and Guatemala. Carmen Teresa surprises those present when she decides instead to write down the recipes for foods mentioned in the stories and served at the celebration. This book includes both the stories and the recipes.

Puerto-Rican and Cuban-American/Argentine-American
Intermediate; Fiction

Ernst, Kathleen. *Highland Fling*. Chicago: Cricket Books, 2006. 224 p.

Exceedingly upset by her Polish-American father who had an extramarital affair, by moving from Wisconsin to North Carolina with her divorced mother and younger sister, and by the immersion of her mother and sister in everything to do with the Scottish MacDonald clan, fifteen-year-old Tanya reluctantly goes with them to the Highland Games. Longing to become an independent filmmaker, Tanya decides to make a documentary revealing the nostalgic pretense of the Highland Games. However, after meeting a young bagpiper from Puerto Rico who has Scottish heritage, his grandmother, and a Highland Games woman athlete whose mixed heritage does not include Scottish forebears, Tanya decides to make a different documentary and to have a talk with her father.

Puerto-Rican/European-Scottish-American
Older; Fiction

Hoyt-Goldsmith, Diane. *Three Kings Day: A Celebration at Christmastime*. Photographs by Lawrence Migdale. New York: Holiday House, 2004. 32 p.

Through numerous color photographs and text this book describes the history and celebration of Three Kings Day. It relates the legend of the three kings and follows ten-year-old Veronica and her family as they celebrate the holiday in New York City. Veronica makes a king mask, attends a paranda (spontaneous concert), eats a special meal, walks in the El Musee del Barrio's Three Kings Day Parade, and receives gifts. The book includes a glossary.
Puerto-Rican-American/Ecuadorian-American
Primary, Intermediate; Nonfiction

Kuklin, Susan. *Families*. Photographs by author. New York: Hyperion Books for Children, 2006. 40 p.

Text and color photographs present interviews with American children, who talk about their families. Their families include seven families with children of mixed race, ethnicity, or religion, with one also including a child adopted from Sierra Leone. In an eighth family a child has been adopted from China. In a ninth family an adopted American child is of a race different from that of one of her fathers.
Puerto-Rican-American/Dominican
Primary, Intermediate; Nonfiction

Ostow, Micol. *Emily Goldberg Learns to Salsa*. New York: Razorbill, 2006. 212 p.

Emily with her family flies from New York to Puerto Rico for the funeral of the grandmother she had never met. As Emily's mother is stressed out by returning to her Puerto Rican family, Emily stays behind in Puerto Rico to help her. Emily has trouble adjusting to her newfound family and especially to Lucy, a cousin who dislikes her. By the end of the stay Emily has come to appreciate Puerto Rico, she and Lucy are friends, and the two discover that Emily's mother had not returned to Puerto Rico by choice, but because, by marrying a Jewish man, she was cut off by the grandmother.
European-Jewish-American/Puerto Rican and Catholic
Older; Fiction

Smith, Doris Buchanan. *Remember the Red-Shouldered Hawk*. New York: G. P. Putnam's Sons, 1994. 160 p.

When he is twelve, John-too has a lot to deal with. Nanna, his Czech grandmother whom he adores, comes to live with his family, but her Alzheimer's with its forgetfulness and bizarre talk and behavior distresses and embarrasses him. John-too is also upset by his best friend's sudden display of bigotry. When Ku Klux Klan members burn a cross at the home of his nephew Adam, whose mother is John-too's sister and whose father is Puerto Rican, it is Nanna who stands up to them.
Puerto Rican/Czech-European-American
Intermediate, Older; Fiction

Steptoe, John. *Creativity*. Illustrated by E. B. Lewis. New York: Clarion Books, 1997. 32 p.

When Hector, a Spanish-speaking boy from Puerto Rico, joins his class, Charles, who is African-American, wonders why they have the same skin color. While making friends with Hector, he learns about the mixing of races and how doing something differently can be creative.

African-Spanish-Puerto Rican and Native Puerto Rican
Intermediate; Fiction

Wayans, Kim, and Kevin Knotts. *All Mixed Up!* Illustrated by Soo Jeong. New York: Grosset & Dunlap, 2008. 112 p. (Amy Hodgepodge)

Amy Hodges is introduced in this first book of the *Amy Hodgepodge* series, which features pictures posted in Amy's scrapbook. Moving to a new town after having experienced only home schooling, Amy is excited to be starting fourth grade at Emerson Charter School. However, her first day starts out disastrously. She wears the wrong clothes, tears her dress when she removes its flower, sings too loudly in music class, is laughed at by classmates Liza and Jennifer, and discovers that a paper saying "Stupid new girl" has been taped to her back by Rory. However, her day improves when she is befriended in the cafeteria by Maya, Jesse, Rusty, Pia, and twins Lola and Cole. Upset by a racial insult from Jennifer, she discovers that the twins are black and white, Jesse is black and Puerto Rican, Pia is Chinese-American and white, and Rusty is Latino, Native American, and white. Learning that Amy's father is black and white and her mother Japanese and South Korean-American, they affectionately nickname her Amy Hodgepodge. The story continues with the group entering a school talent show where Amy, inspired by Rusty who has to earn money to buy his costume, overcomes her stage fright and becomes the group's lead singer.
African-Puerto Rican-American
Primary, Intermediate; Fiction

Wayans, Kim, and Kevin Knotts. *Digging Up Trouble*. Illustrated by Soo Jeong. New York: Grosset & Dunlap, 2010. 112 p. (Amy Hodgepodge)

After foolishly letting her dog Giggles off his leash to play with another dog at the Farmer's Market, Amy is unable to find him. She spends a stressful night until in the morning the family receives a call from an older man, Irving Coleman, who reports that Giggles has come to his home with his dog. Then, after being reunited with Giggles, Amy realizes that helping Irving restore his community garden would make a perfect green project for the school class assignment. The two fourth grade classes adopt Amy's idea and decide to raise money for the needed tools and supplies by having a bake sale and a car wash. Amy is worried when she is placed in charge of the bake sale team, but because of the help of her visiting community-organizer grandmother and team members, including Lola, Pia, and Rusty, there are many baked goods for sale. However, things turn contentious when the bake sale team and the car wash team, including Jesse and Maya, become overly competitive. After teachers intervene, the teams decide to refer customers to each other. With the proceeds earned and the work of Amy's gardener grandmother and the fourth graders, Irving's garden again becomes a neighborhood asset. Referring to the mixed racial identity of some of Amy's friends, this sixth book in the series specifically identifies the heritages of Lola and Cole as well as of Amy.
African-Puerto Rican-American
Primary, Intermediate; Fiction

Wayans, Kim, and Kevin Knotts. *Happy Birthday to Me*. Illustrated by Soo Jeong. New York: Grosset & Dunlap, 2008. 112 p. (Amy Hodgepodge)

In this sequel to *All Mixed Up!* Amy looks forward to celebrating her birthday with her new friends as well as with her family. Maya, Jesse, Pia, and Lola accept her invitation to her tenth birthday sleepover where Amy plans to have a Japanese tea ceremony and do origami. Amy's spirits wane when she fears her family is planning to move to California. She is really upset when her four friends decide to go to an Amber Skye concert instead of her party. When Lola's brother Cole discovers that Amy has not invited other guests, he texts the concertgoers, and the four girls leave the concert to go to Amy's house. It is then that Amy discovers what true friends they are and the advisability of telling her problems and her fears to her family. This book points out the mixed heritages of Amy and most of her friends.
African-Puerto Rican-American
Primary, Intermediate; Fiction

Wayans, Kim, and Kevin Knotts. *Lost and Found*. Illustrated by Soo Jeong. New York: Grosset & Dunlap, 2008. 112 p. (Amy Hodgepodge)
Amy Hodgepodge persuades her parents to let her go on the fourth grade two-and-a-half day wilderness trip. However, she doesn't feel as pleased about it when she is placed in a group without her friends, but with Jennifer and Rory who don't like her. Further, she falls in the mud during the obstacle course, goes overboard with Jennifer in their canoe, and is embarrassed that she doesn't know what s'mores are. However, Amy is supported by Lola, Jesse, Maya, and Pia with whom she shares a tent. Together they enjoy tricking Cole, Rusty, and two other boys. Then when she, Jennifer, Rory, and two others get lost in the woods, Amy uses her compass to lead them back to camp—and receives the Best Camper award. In this third book in the series, Amy's mixed heritage is noted. Readers of the first book, *All Mixed Up!*, will be aware of the mixed heritages of five of her friends.
African-Puerto Rican-American
Primary, Intermediate; Fiction

Wayans, Kim, and Kevin Knotts. *Playing Games*. Illustrated by Soo Jeong. New York: Grosset & Dunlap, 2008. 112 p. (Amy Hodgepodge)
When Evelyn, the star player of the Comets girls' basketball team, injures her arm, Amy Hodgepodge reluctantly agrees to take her place so that the team will have the required eight players. Amy has neither played basketball nor is she familiar with the game. She is a terrible player, and her mistake causes the team to lose to the worst team in the league. Amy tries to fake a twisted ankle so she can be on the bench, but even that fails and she decides to quit. However, after confessing her problem to Rusty, he offers to coach her, with Amy, in return, helping him sing harmony in the friends' fourth grade music class performance. Unaware of the fact that Amy has improved, her teammates don't pass her the ball. It is not until the end of an important game that Amy demonstrates her secret talent as a three-point shooter. Amy's mixed heritage is noted in this fourth book in the series. Readers of the first book, *All Mixed Up!*, will be familiar with the mixed heritages of most of her friends.
African-Puerto Rican-American
Primary, Intermediate; Fiction

Wayans, Kim, and Kevin Knotts. *The Secret's Out*. Illustrated by Soo Jeong. New York: Grosset & Dunlap, 2009. 112 p. (Amy Hodgepodge)

Amy, Lola, Jesse, Pia, and Maya decide to enter as a group in their school's competitive annual spring art show. Amy comes up with the idea of tracing their body outlines on a large poster board and then painting and decorating them. The girls would stand behind holes that would show their faces. With the exception of Pia, the others are enthused about Amy's plan. Indeed, Pia's personality seems to have changed. She has become distracted, negative, and rude. Finally, she confides to Amy, with Amy's promise not to tell, that she fears that, since her father and stepmother are going to have a baby, her father won't pay attention to her. When Amy accidentally reveals Pia's secret to Lola, there are unforeseen consequences. Lola tells Jesse, and Jesse lets the secret out to classmates. The friends become so angry at each other that their Best Friends art display is jeopardized. It is not until they practice forgiveness that they restore their friendship—and their project ties for fourth grade first place. In this fifth book in the series, Amy's mixed heritage is noted, and series readers will be aware of the mixed heritages of most of her friends.
African-Puerto Rican-American
Primary, Intermediate; Fiction

Woodson, Jacqueline. *Miracle's Boys*. New York: G. P. Putnam's Sons, 2000. 144 p.

This story, which occurs during one weekend, tells of three orphaned brothers who still suffer from deaths they feel they could have prevented. Twenty-two-year-old Ty´ree, who has given up a college opportunity to be his brothers' legal guardian, wishes that twelve years ago he had not alerted his father to a drowning woman and dog so that his father would not have died a hero's death from hypothermia. Twelve-year-old Lafayette, the book's narrator, agonizes that when he was nine he could have saved his mother Milagro by getting help earlier when she was in insulin shock. Fifteen year-old Charlie regrets that he wasn't there when his parents died and that an injured dog he helped did not live. Ty´ree and Lafayette are very close, but Charlie, who seems to have changed into a different person, is headed for trouble. At the story's conclusion all three of Milagro's boys stand together as a family.
African-American/Puerto Rican
Older; Fiction

St. Kitts and Nevisian-American

Hamilton, Virginia. *Junius Over Far*. New York: Harper & Row Publishers, 1985. 288 p.

Fourteen-year-old American, Junius Rawlings, has grown up very close to his grandfather Jackabo and speaks with a Caribbean accent and lilt. When Jackabo, feeling that he is a burden, returns to his tiny island, he lives on the old rundown Rawlings plantation with Burtie Rawlings, its elderly white owner with whom Jackabo has a contentious relationship. When Burtie disappears, Jackabo, who is forgetful and disoriented, writes Junius' family that Burtie was taken by pirates and he himself was accosted by them. Junius and his father Damius, who has rejected his island past, fly down to check on Jackabo. The mystery is solved, Jackabo agrees to go back to the States, Damius comes to enjoy the island, and the black Rawlings finally are accorded their due.

African-St. Kitts and Nevisian/African-American
Older; Fiction

St. Lucian-American

Porte, Barbara Ann. *Something Terrible Happened: A Novel*. New York: Orchard Books, 1994. 224 p.

When Gillian is ten, her mother, who is black, gets AIDS, and nothing is ever the same for Gillian and her family. Affected in both body and mind, her mother takes Gillian from New York City to Florida where they end up homeless. The two return to New York City where Gillian's grandmother tends to her daughter and sends Gillian to live with her late white father's brother and his family in Oak Ridge, Tennessee. Filled with resentment, worry, and loneliness, Gillian hates her life in that white community and, after her mother's death, runs wild. Things improve both for Gillian's grandmother as she takes up running and graduate work and for Gillian when she learns of the difficult pasts of a "cousin" who had been adopted from the Philippines and of her Uncle Henry.
European-American/St. Lucian-Trinidadian-American
Older; Fiction

Trinidadian and Tobagonian-American

Trinidadian-American

Porte, Barbara Ann. *Something Terrible Happened: A Novel*. New York: Orchard Books, 1994. 224 p.

When Gillian is ten, her mother, who is black, gets AIDS, and nothing is ever the same for Gillian and her family. Affected in both body and mind, her mother takes Gillian from New York City to Florida where they end up homeless. The two return to New York City where Gillian's grandmother tends to her daughter and sends Gillian to live with her late white father's brother and his family in Oak Ridge, Tennessee. Filled with resentment, worry, and loneliness, Gillian hates her life in that white community and, after her mother's death, runs wild. Things improve both for Gillian's grandmother as she takes up running and graduate work and for Gillian when she learns of the difficult pasts of a "cousin" who had been adopted from the Philippines and of her Uncle Henry.
European-American/St. Lucian-Trinidadian-American
Older; Fiction

Virgin Islander-American

Hausherr, Rosmarie. *Celebrating Families*. New York: Scholastic Press, 1997. 32 p.

Among the families celebrated in this book are Jahsee's, whose father is from the Virgin Islands and whose mother is Norwegian-American, and Alexandra's, who was adopted from Brazil by two European-American mothers. The book is illustrated with photographs.
African-Virgin Islander/Norwegian-American
Primary, Intermediate; Nonfiction

Virgin Islander of the United States-American

Skurzynski, Gloria, and Alane Ferguson. *Escape from Fear*. Washington, D.C.: National Geographic Society, 2002. 160 p. (Mysteries in Our National Parks)

When the Landon family visits St. John Island in the Virgin Islands, they meet thirteen-year-old Forrest, the adopted son of a wealthy American diplomat and his wife. Forrest has run away from his Denver home to find his birthmother and to save her from danger. He manages to locate her and, with the Landon children, watches as she aids illegal aliens who have fled from poverty-stricken Haiti on a boat involved in poaching endangered hawksbill turtles.

European-American/African-Virgin Islander of the United States

Intermediate, Older; Fiction

Crucian-American

See   Schomburg, Arthur Alfonso

D. Asian

Canaanite

Chaldean-Canaanite

See   Ishmael

Egyptian-Canaanite

See   Ishmael

Chinese

Doyle, Brian. *Spud Sweetgrass*. Toronto: Groundwood Books, 1996. 144 p.

Spud Sweetgrass, who has been kicked out of his Ottawa school, spends his time both selling french-fries while playing Beethoven at a chipwagon and hanging out with his friends, Dink the Thinker and Connie Pan, who is Vietnamese and Chinese. Spud goes with Connie and some E.S.L. students to Westboro Beach where they play an exciting game of volleyball without a ball and a net and he discovers that the Ottawa River seems to be polluted with chip grease. Suspecting the uncouth Dumper Stubbs, who changes the grease in the chipwagon, Spud catches him in the act of pouring grease into a sewer, but is unable to prove it. Thanks to the support of his friends, the Department of Physical Environment, and an Aboriginal medicine man, Spud establishes Dumper's guilt.
Vietnamese-Chinese/Chinese
Older; Fiction

Vietnamese-Chinese

Doyle, Brian. *Spud Sweetgrass*. Toronto: Groundwood Books, 1996. 144 p.

Spud Sweetgrass, who has been kicked out of his Ottawa school, spends his time both selling french-fries while playing Beethoven at a chipwagon and hanging out with his friends, Dink the Thinker and Connie Pan, who is Vietnamese and Chinese. Spud goes with Connie and some E.S.L. students to Westboro Beach where they play an exciting game of volleyball without a ball and a net and he discovers that the Ottawa River seems to be polluted with chip grease. Suspecting the uncouth Dumper Stubbs, who changes the grease in the chipwagon, Spud catches him in the act of pouring grease into a sewer, but is unable to prove it. Thanks to the support of his friends, the Department of Physical Environment, and an Aboriginal medicine man, Spud establishes Dumper's guilt.
Vietnamese-Chinese/Chinese
Older; Fiction

Hong Konger

Chinese-Hong Konger

See   O'Hearn, Claudine Chiawei

Irish-American-Hong Konger

See   O'Hearn, Claudine Chiawei

Indian

Banerjee, Anjali. *Maya Running*. New York: Wendy Lamb Books, 2005. 224 p.

Maya, who was born in Calcutta, has lived in Manitoba, Canada, since infancy and does not want her family to move to California. Furthermore, she does not like her braces, hates being called "nigger," and is embarrassed that she cannot speak Bengali. Also, she has a crush on fourteen-year-old Jamie. Maya persuades her parents to let her cousin Pinky visit from India, but Pinky turns out to be a well-developed beauty who is truly Indian and who captivates Jamie. Unhappy, Maya tells her problems to Pinky's statue of Ganesh, the Hindu god with an elephant head. Plied with Jelly Bellies, Ganesh grants Maya's wishes: that her family not move to California, that she knows Bengali, that she be perceived as Indian by Jamie and an Indian family, that Jamie always be close to her, and that she'll be shapely and beautiful. Maya soon realizes the foolishness of her wishes when her parents with blank eyes do everything she asks and lose their identities, Jamie is so love-struck that he even spends nights standing outside her window, Pinky is distressed and returns to India, and no one can remember what Maya was like earlier. Throughout the rest of the story Maya seeks to get their old life back, but cannot get Ganesh to undo her wishes even when she travels to India with her father and steals the same Ganesh statue. At last, Maya discovers that there are better things to wish for and what she, not Ganesh, must do.

Indian/English-Indian

Intermediate, Older; Fiction

English-Indian

Banerjee, Anjali. *Maya Running*. New York: Wendy Lamb Books, 2005. 224 p.

Maya, who was born in Calcutta, has lived in Manitoba, Canada, since infancy and does not want her family to move to California. Furthermore, she does not like her braces, hates being called "nigger," and is embarrassed that she cannot speak Bengali. Also, she has a crush on fourteen-year-old Jamie. Maya persuades her parents to let her cousin Pinky visit from India, but Pinky turns out to be a well-developed beauty who is truly Indian and who captivates Jamie. Unhappy, Maya tells her problems to Pinky's statue of Ganesh, the Hindu god with an elephant head. Plied with Jelly Bellies, Ganesh grants Maya's wishes: that her family not move to California, that she knows Bengali, that she be perceived as Indian by Jamie and an Indian family, that Jamie always be close to her, and that

she'll be shapely and beautiful. Maya soon realizes the foolishness of her wishes when her parents with blank eyes do everything she asks and lose their identities, Jamie is so love-struck that he even spends nights standing outside her window, Pinky is distressed and returns to India, and no one can remember what Maya was like earlier. Throughout the rest of the story Maya seeks to get their old life back, but cannot get Ganesh to undo her wishes even when she travels to India with her father and steals the same Ganesh statue. At last, Maya discovers that there are better things to wish for and what she, not Ganesh, must do.
Indian/English-Indian
Intermediate, Older; Fiction

Indonesian

African-American-Indonesian

Kurtz, Jane. *Jakarta Missing*. New York: Greenwillow Books, 2001. 272 p.

Twelve-year-old Dakar has just moved with her parents from Kenya to a small town in North Dakota and greatly misses her older, adopted sister Jakarta, who has remained behind. Shy, bookish, imaginative, and a worrier, Dakar wants most of all for her family to be together. However, when Jakarta does join the family, she resents having to leave Kenya. Then, as Jakarta starts to adjust to her new school, their mother leaves to be with her injured great-aunt, and their father, who constantly places humanitarian work ahead of the family, leaves to care for earthquake victims in Guatemala. In the concluding chapters Jakarta becomes a basketball star, Dakar learns about balancing safety and risk, and the family reaches a decision on its future.
African-American and Japanese/Iranian
Intermediate, Older; Fiction

Iranian-Indonesian

Kurtz, Jane. *Jakarta Missing*. New York: Greenwillow Books, 2001. 272 p.

Twelve-year-old Dakar has just moved with her parents from Kenya to a small town in North Dakota and greatly misses her older, adopted sister Jakarta, who has remained behind. Shy, bookish, imaginative, and a worrier, Dakar wants most of all for her family to be together. However, when Jakarta does join the family, she resents having to leave Kenya. Then, as Jakarta starts to adjust to her new school, their mother leaves to be with her injured great-aunt, and their father, who constantly places humanitarian work ahead of the family, leaves to care for earthquake victims in Guatemala. In the concluding chapters Jakarta becomes a basketball star, Dakar learns about balancing safety and risk, and the family reaches a decision on its future.
African-American and Japanese/Iranian
Intermediate, Older; Fiction

Japanese-Indonesian

Kurtz, Jane. *Jakarta Missing*. New York: Greenwillow Books, 2001. 272 p.

Twelve-year-old Dakar has just moved with her parents from Kenya to a small town in North Dakota and greatly misses her older, adopted sister Jakarta, who has remained behind. Shy, bookish, imaginative, and a worrier, Dakar wants most of all for her family to be together. However, when Jakarta does join the family, she resents having to leave Kenya. Then, as Jakarta starts to adjust to her new school, their mother leaves to be with her injured great-aunt, and their father, who constantly places humanitarian work ahead of the family, leaves to care for earthquake victims in Guatemala. In the concluding chapters Jakarta becomes a basketball star, Dakar learns about balancing safety and risk, and the family reaches a decision on its future.
African-American and Japanese/Iranian
Intermediate, Older; Fiction

Japanese

Thompson, Holly. *The Wakame Gatherers*. Illustrated by Kazumi Wilds. Walnut Creek, Calif.: Shen's Books, 2007. 32 p.

When Gram, Nanami's Maine grandmother, visits Japan, she joins Nanami and her Japanese grandmother Baachan in going into the surf to gather wakame seaweed. As they work, the women remember how their countries were enemies when they were young and tell Nanami to protect the peace. Upon her return home Gram finds wakame in a store and invites Baachan to join in the family's Maine summer vacation. This picture book includes information about wakame and also some wakame recipes.
Japanese/European-American
Primary, Intermediate; Fiction

European-American-Japanese

Thompson, Holly. *The Wakame Gatherers*. Illustrated by Kazumi Wilds. Walnut Creek, Calif.: Shen's Books, 2007. 32 p.

When Gram, Nanami's Maine grandmother, visits Japan, she joins Nanami and her Japanese grandmother Baachan in going into the surf to gather wakame seaweed. As they work, the women remember how their countries were enemies when they were young and tell Nanami to protect the peace. Upon her return home Gram finds wakame in a store and invites Baachan to join in the family's Maine summer vacation. This picture book includes information about wakame and also some wakame recipes.
Japanese/European-American
Primary, Intermediate; Fiction

Jordanian

See   Abdullah II bin Al Hussein, King of Jordan

English-Jordanian

See   Abdullah II bin Al Hussein, King of Jordan

Lebanese

Harris, Rosemary. *Zed*. Boston: Faber and Faber, 1984. 192 p.

Fifteen-year-old Zed is asked by his house master to write up the time when, as an eight-year-old, he, together with his father, Uncle Omar, and others, was held captive in a London building by the Free Army of United Arabia. As Zed writes, he relives those terrible four days: the terrorists, guns, grenades, discomforts, and overwhelming dread. Through the experience Zed comes to appreciate the kindness and bravery of Uncle Omar, who was Saudi-Turkish, and Arabi, one of the terrorists. Both were killed by gunshots, while Zed's English father, a self-centered coward, survived. After writing the manuscript, Zed arranges a meeting between Omar and Arabi's sons. This novel is for teenagers.
Saudi-Turkish-Lebanese and Muslim/Lebanese and Christian Maronite
Older; Fiction

American-Lebanese

See   Reeves, Keanu

Chinese-Lebanese

See   Reeves, Keanu

English-Lebanese

See   Reeves, Keanu

Hawaiian-Lebanese

See   Reeves, Keanu

Irish-Lebanese

See   Reeves, Keanu

Portuguese-Lebanese

See   Reeves, Keanu

Saudi-Lebanese

Harris, Rosemary. *Zed*. Boston: Faber and Faber, 1984. 192 p.

Fifteen-year-old Zed is asked by his house master to write up the time when, as an eight-year-old, he, together with his father, Uncle Omar, and others, was held captive in a London building by the Free Army of United Arabia. As Zed writes, he relives those terrible four days: the terrorists, guns, grenades, discomforts, and overwhelming dread. Through the experience Zed comes to appreciate the kindness and bravery of Uncle Omar, who was Saudi-Turkish, and Arabi, one of the terrorists. Both were killed by gunshots, while Zed's English father, a self-centered coward, survived. After writing the manuscript, Zed arranges a meeting between Omar and Arabi's sons. This novel is for teenagers. Saudi-Turkish-Lebanese and Muslim/Lebanese and Christian Maronite
Older; Fiction

Turkish-Lebanese

Harris, Rosemary. *Zed*. Boston: Faber and Faber, 1984. 192 p.

Fifteen-year-old Zed is asked by his house master to write up the time when, as an eight-year-old, he, together with his father, Uncle Omar, and others, was held captive in a London building by the Free Army of United Arabia. As Zed writes, he relives those terrible four days: the terrorists, guns, grenades, discomforts, and overwhelming dread. Through the experience Zed comes to appreciate the kindness and bravery of Uncle Omar, who was Saudi-Turkish, and Arabi, one of the terrorists. Both were killed by gunshots, while Zed's English father, a self-centered coward, survived. After writing the manuscript, Zed arranges a meeting between Omar and Arabi's sons. This novel is for teenagers. Saudi-Turkish-Lebanese and Muslim/Lebanese and Christian Maronite
Older; Fiction

South Korean

Wilkinson, Sook, and Nancy Fox, eds. *After the Morning Calm: Reflections of Korean Adoptees*. Bloomfield Hills, Mich.: Sunrise Ventures, 2002. 192 p.

In this book nine men and seventeen women present their experiences and feelings about being adopted from South Korea. One went to live with a Dutch family, another was adopted by Norwegians, and the remainder became the children of American parents. Their ages at adoption ranged from infancy to teenager. One suffered in Korea because he was the son of a Korean woman and a white American soldier. Another was the subject of her mother Marjorie Ann Waybill's fictional book. All were succeeding as adults. Their writings describe the impact of looking different from their peers, the difficulties of reconciling two cultures, and the effects of visiting South Korea. The book contains photographs and an appended resource section.

European-American/South Korean
Older; Nonfiction

European-American-South Korean

Wilkinson, Sook, and Nancy Fox, eds. *After the Morning Calm: Reflections of Korean Adoptees.* Bloomfield Hills, Mich.: Sunrise Ventures, 2002. 192 p.

In this book nine men and seventeen women present their experiences and feelings about being adopted from South Korea. One went to live with a Dutch family, another was adopted by Norwegians, and the remainder became the children of American parents. Their ages at adoption ranged from infancy to teenager. One suffered in Korea because he was the son of a Korean woman and a white American soldier. Another was the subject of her mother Marjorie Ann Waybill's fictional book. All were succeeding as adults. Their writings describe the impact of looking different from their peers, the difficulties of reconciling two cultures, and the effects of visiting South Korea. The book contains photographs and an appended resource section.

European-American/South Korean,
Older; Nonfiction

Thai

Richardson, Judith Benét. *First Came the Owl.* New York: Bantam Doubleday Dell Books for Young Readers, 1998. 160 p. (A Yearling Book)

Having recently returned from a trip to her native Thailand, Nita's mother becomes depressed and is hospitalized. Nita's father leaves to go out on a Coast Guard boat and she has to stay at her friend Anne's house. This story tells how eleven-year-old Nita's report on Thailand, her playing Snow White in a class play, the snowy owl who comes to her Massachusetts beach, and the Roots Committee composed of Nita, Anne, and a Coast Guard officer whose Thai wife has died all work together to help reunite Nita's family.

European-American/Thai
Intermediate; Fiction

European-American-Thai

Richardson, Judith Benét. *First Came the Owl.* New York: Bantam Doubleday Dell Books for Young Readers, 1998. 160 p. (A Yearling Book)

Having recently returned from a trip to her native Thailand, Nita's mother becomes depressed and is hospitalized. Nita's father leaves to go out on a Coast Guard boat and she has to stay at her friend Anne's house. This story tells how eleven-year-old Nita's report on Thailand, her playing Snow White in a class play, the snowy owl who comes to her Massachusetts beach, and the Roots Committee composed of Nita, Anne, and a Coast Guard officer whose Thai wife has died all work together to help reunite Nita's family.

European-American/Thai
Intermediate; Ficton

Turkish

Skrypuch, Marsha Forchuk. *Daughter of War: A Novel*. Brighton, Mass.: Fitzhugh & Whiteside, 2008. 224 p.

This novel is set during the Armenian Genocide in Turkey during World War I. It centers on Armenian teenagers Mariam and Marta Hovsepian and Kevork Adomian. Orphaned because of the 1909 Adana Massacre, they were placed in an orphanage run by German missionaries in Maresh, Turkey. When the Turks decided to relocate Armenians, Mariam, the older sister, was taken to a slave auction where she was bought by a Turkish man who had fallen in love with her. She is returned to the orphanage for her safety when the man's mother has another Armenian woman's neck wrung. Marta and Kevork, who were betrothed, were marched into the desert. Marta was saved by a Turkish woman whose husband made her one of his wives and raped her. Pregnant Marta is returned to the orphanage where she has a baby girl, Pauline. Kevork was rescued by Arabs in Syria. Disguised as an Arab, he works as a shoemaker and then accepts the dangerous job of a courier bringing money to starving Armenians who had been deported to the Syrian Desert. Becoming ill with typhus, he recovers under the care of a German missionary in one of the deportation camps. The book tells of the horrible fate of the Armenians and some of those who secretly helped them. It concludes with Kevork's reunion with Marta at the Maresh orphanage, now run by American missionaries.
Turkish/Armenian-Turkish
Older; Fiction

Armenian-Turkish

Skrypuch, Marsha Forchuk. *Daughter of War: A Novel*. Brighton, Mass.: Fitzhugh & Whiteside, 2008. 224 p.

This novel is set during the Armenian Genocide in Turkey during World War I. It centers on Armenian teenagers Mariam and Marta Hovsepian and Kevork Adomian. Orphaned because of the 1909 Adana Massacre, they were placed in an orphanage run by German missionaries in Maresh, Turkey. When the Turks decided to relocate Armenians, Mariam, the older sister, was taken to a slave auction where she was bought by a Turkish man who had fallen in love with her. She is returned to the orphanage for her safety when the man's mother has another Armenian woman's neck wrung. Marta and Kevork, who were betrothed, were marched into the desert. Marta was saved by a Turkish woman whose husband made her one of his wives and raped her. Pregnant Marta is returned to the orphanage where she has a baby girl, Pauline. Kevork was rescued by Arabs in Syria. Disguised as an Arab, he works as a shoemaker and then accepts the dangerous job of a courier bringing money to starving Armenians who had been deported to the Syrian Desert. Becoming ill with typhus, he recovers under the care of a German missionary in one of the deportation camps. The book tells of the horrible fate of the Armenians and some of those who secretly helped them. It concludes with Kevork's reunion with Marta at the Maresh orphanage, now run by American missionaries.

Turkish/Armenian-Turkish
Older; Fiction

Vietnamese

See   Steiner, Matthew Ray

Garland, Sherry. *Song of the Buffalo Boy*. San Diego: Harcourt Brace & Company, 1992. 288 p.

Seventeen-year-old Loi lives with her mother in a Vietnamese village where she is generally scorned and rejected because she is a "half-breed" whose American soldier father belonged to the hated army that was an enemy of the Viet Cong and caused genetic abnormalities by spraying Vietnamese land. Loi longs to know her American father and is in love with Khai, a Vietnamese buffalo boy. When her relatives force her to become engaged to a cruel man, Khai and Loi fake her drowning and Loi escapes to Ho Chi Minh City where Khai is to join her. Sleeping for weeks in a park across from the Foreign Office with Joe, a boy about twelve-years-old who longs to go to America, Loi suffers from hunger and poverty. Her opportunity to emigrate comes just when Khai finds her. Since he has decided he does not want to go to the United States, Loi makes the difficult decision to remain in Vietnam with him and send Joe in her stead.
European-American/Vietnamese
Older; Fiction

Skurzynski, Gloria, and Alane Ferguson. *Rage of Fire*. Washington, D.C.: National Geographic Society, 2001. 160 p. (Mysteries in Our National Parks)

When the Landon family visits Hawaii Volcanoes National Park, the parents, Steven and Olivia, take in Danny, a nine-year-old Vietnamese boy, for emergency foster care. He is to fly back with them later to Jackson Hole, Wyoming, to meet and live with his American grandfather, who had been a soldier during the Vietnam War. When Danny and the Landon children, Jack and Ashley, take a hike, they are chased by a woman who resembles Pele, the queen of the sacred fire of Hawaiian lore. Terrified, the three of them slide down into Kilauea Iki Crater where they encounter steam vents, an earthquake, and thick mist. They then pass through Thurston Lava Tube where there is an aftershock and the lights go off. That evening after watching an erupting volcano, the children discover the truth about the mysterious woman.
Vietnamese/Vietnamese and European-American
Intermediate; Fiction

European-Vietnamese

English-Vietnamese

Dixon, Paige. *Promises To Keep*. New York: Atheneum, 1974. 176 p.

When his deceased uncle's son, fourteen-year-old Lon, moves from Vietnam to his grandmother's house next door, Charles worries that Lon will undermine his efforts to gain acceptance. Seventeen-year-old Charles suffers from his family's high status in the New Hampshire town which bears its name as well as from his tall ungainly height and severe acne. However, as Charles comes to know Lon, who is the target of the town's bigotry and who believes in peace, Charles learns to stand up for Lon and his own plans.

European-American/English-French-Vietnamese

Older; Fiction

French-Vietnamese

Dixon, Paige. *Promises To Keep*. New York: Atheneum, 1974. 176 p.

When his deceased uncle's son, fourteen-year-old Lon, moves from Vietnam to his grandmother's house next door, Charles worries that Lon will undermine his efforts to gain acceptance. Seventeen-year-old Charles suffers from his family's high status in the New Hampshire town which bears its name as well as from his tall ungainly height and severe acne. However, as Charles comes to know Lon, who is the target of the town's bigotry and who believes in peace, Charles learns to stand up for Lon and his own plans.

European-American/English-French-Vietnamese

Older; Fiction

European-American-Vietnamese

See   Steiner, Matthew Ray

Dixon, Paige. *Promises To Keep*. New York: Atheneum, 1974. 176 p.

When his deceased uncle's son, fourteen-year-old Lon, moves from Vietnam to his grandmother's house next door, Charles worries that Lon will undermine his efforts to gain acceptance. Seventeen-year-old Charles suffers from his family's high status in the New Hampshire town which bears its name as well as from his tall ungainly height and severe acne. However, as Charles comes to know Lon, who is the target of the town's bigotry and who believes in peace, Charles learns to stand up for Lon and his own plans.

European-American/English-French-Vietnamese

Older; Fiction

Garland, Sherry. *Song of the Buffalo Boy*. San Diego: Harcourt Brace & Company, 1992. 288 p.

Seventeen-year-old Loi lives with her mother in a Vietnamese village where she is generally scorned and rejected because she is a "half-breed" whose American soldier father belonged to the hated army that was an enemy of the Viet Cong and caused genetic abnormalities by spraying Vietnamese land. Loi longs to know her American father and is in love with Khai, a Vietnamese buffalo boy. When her relatives force her to become engaged to a cruel man, Khai and Loi fake her drowning and Loi escapes to Ho Chi Minh City where Khai is to join her. Sleeping for weeks in a park across from the Foreign Office with Joe, a boy about twelve-years-old who longs to go to America, Loi suffers from hunger and poverty. Her opportunity to emigrate comes just when Khai

finds her. Since he has decided he does not want to go to the United States, Loi makes the difficult decision to remain in Vietnam with him and send Joe in her stead.
European-American/Vietnamese
Older; Fiction

Skurzynski, Gloria, and Alane Ferguson. *Rage of Fire*. Washington, D.C.: National Geographic Society, 2001. 160 p. (Mysteries in Our National Parks)
   When the Landon family visits Hawaii Volcanoes National Park, the parents, Steven and Olivia, take in Danny, a nine-year-old Vietnamese boy, for emergency foster care. He is to fly back with them later to Jackson Hole, Wyoming, to meet and live with his American grandfather, who had been a soldier during the Vietnam War. When Danny and the Landon children, Jack and Ashley, take a hike, they are chased by a woman who resembles Pele, the queen of the sacred fire of Hawaiian lore. Terrified, the three of them slide down into Kilauea Iki Crater where they encounter steam vents, an earthquake, and thick mist. They then pass through Thurston Lava Tube where there is an aftershock and the lights go off. That evening after watching an erupting volcano, the children discover the truth about the mysterious woman.
Vietnamese/Vietnamese and European-American
Intermediate; Fiction

E. Canadian

Aboriginal Canadian. See Native Canadian

African-Canadian

South African-Canadian

Craig, Colleen. *Afrika*. Plattsburgh, N.Y.: Tundra Books of Northern New York, 2008. 240 p.

Kim's mother Riana moved to Canada when she was pregnant with Kim and the only information she will give Kim about her father is that he is South African. When she is thirteen, Kim and her mother travel to South Africa where Riana, a journalist, covers the proceedings of the Truth and Reconciliation Commission. Throughout their stay Riana becomes increasingly distraught both because of the horrific stories of abuse under apartheid which she must report and because of the attitudes of her Afrikaner family. Kim learns much about South Africa: the beauty of the Karoo, the terrible suffering which existed, the racial attitudes which still abound, and the reason for her mother's family's behavior. She becomes friends with Themba, a black classmate and the son of the family's servant. Together they try to find the identity of Kim's father. Kim finally meets her father, who is coloured, and during the commission hearings Themba sees the policeman who murdered his father when Themba was six.
Coloured-South African/Afrikaner-South African
Older; Fiction

American-Canadian

African-American-Canadian

Bell, William. *Zack*. New York: Simon & Schuster Books for Young Readers, 1999. 192 p.

Although Zack is close to his father's parents, who are Romanian-Canadian Jewish, his mother, who is black, refuses to say anything about her family. Resentful that his parents have moved from Toronto to the small town of Fergus, Ontario, Zack does poorly in high school until he is assigned a local history project. Investigating the objects he had dug up from his yard, Zack is inspired by the story of the African former slave who had lived there and then, unbeknownst to his parents, travels to Natchez to find his black grandfather. Zack discovers that it was his grandfather with his hatred of whites, not his mother, who has kept him from his black relatives. In this story Zack learns not only about his heritage, but also about the power of courage and the far-reaching effects of one's actions.
Romanian-Canadian Jewish/African-American-Canadian
Older; Fiction

Asian–Canadian

Japanese-Canadian

Okimoto, Jean Davies. *The Eclipse of Moonbeam Dawson*. New York: Tom Doherty Associates, 1998. 192 p.

Fifteen-year-old Moonbeam knows that he no longer wants to live with his hippie-activist mother. Taking a job at a nearby resort in British Columbia, he befriends Gloria, who is of European-Japanese-Canadian heritage, and falls for Michelle, a rich pretty hotel guest. By the end of the story, Moonbeam has recognized Michelle's falseness and decided both to change his name to Reid, the last name of a half-Haida sculptor, and to look up his late Haida father's family.
European-Canadian/Japanese-Canadian
Older; Fiction

Tamaki, Mariko. *Skim*. Illustrated by Jillian Tamaki. Toronto: Groundwood Books, 2008. 144 p.

This graphic novel for high schoolers presents the life of unpopular biracial Kimberly (Skim) Keiko Cameron, a sixteen-year-old tenth grader who, with her best friend Lisa, is learning how to be a Wiccan. It is a year (1993) in which her parents are separated; a classmate, Katie, experiences the suicide of a probably-gay boy with whom she has broken up; Katie falls off a roof and breaks her arms; a group of popular girls form a club to celebrate life; and Lisa falls in love with her female English/drama teacher, who subsequently leaves the school. The book details Skim's deepening depression until she decides that the tarot cards mean change, bleaches her hair, and gets a new best friend: Katie.
European-Canadian/Asian-Canadian
Older; Fiction

European-Canadian

Levin, Betty. *Brother Moose*. New York: Greenwillow Books, 1990. 224 p.

When Nell, an orphan from England, is sent in the 1870s to live with a couple in Canada's Maritime Provinces, she discovers that her prospective mother, Mrs. Fowler, has moved to Maine to have a baby. Next Nell is kidnapped by robbers, escapes, and travels with her fellow orphan Louisa, an Indian named Joe Pennowit, and his twelve year old grandson to Maine. However, because Joe mistakenly thinks he has killed one of the men who kidnapped Nell, the four leave the road to escape the robbers and the police. On their difficult journey they go by wagon, by sleigh, and by an abandoned train car, which is pulled by their horse and a moose they have tamed. Nell finally reaches Mrs. Fowler, but her adoption hopes take a surprising turn.
European-Canadian or European-American/Canadian Micmac or American Passamaquoddy or Penobscot
Older; Fiction

Okimoto, Jean Davies. *The Eclipse of Moonbeam Dawson*. New York: Tom Doherty Associates, 1998. 192 p.

Fifteen-year-old Moonbeam knows that he no longer wants to live with his hippie-activist mother. Taking a job at a nearby resort in British Columbia, he befriends Gloria, who is of European-Japanese-Canadian heritage, and falls for Michelle, a rich pretty hotel guest. By the end of the story, Moonbeam has recognized Michelle's falseness and decided both to change his name to Reid, the last name of a half-Haida sculptor, and to look up his late Haida father's family.
Haida/European-American
Older; Fiction

Slipperjack, Ruby. *Little Voice*. Illustrated by Sherry Farrell Racette. Regina, Saskatchewan: Coteau Books, 2002. 256 p. (In the Same Boat)
This story describes Canadian Ray's life from the summer of 1978 when she is ten to the summer of 1982. Terribly unhappy since the death of her non-Native father two years earlier and harassed by her schoolmates, Ray seldom speaks. When her mother marries Dave (who is Mohawk and Ojibwa), Ray feels as if she doesn't belong. It is only when she is with her Ojibwa mother's mother during four summers and the winter of 1981-82 that she is truly happy. There, Ray lives in her grandmother's cabin in an Ojibwa community, but they are often traveling by canoe and camping. Ray watches her grandmother kill the bear which is tearing apart their tent and enjoys the baby bear adopted by a trapper friend, the puppy which he gives her grandmother, and the orphan seagull which she tends. Finally, Ray learns that she can stay permanently with her grandmother and that, like her, she will become a medicine woman.
European-Canadian/Ojibwa
Intermediate, Older; Fiction

Tamaki, Mariko. *Skim*. Illustrated by Jillian Tamaki. Toronto: Groundwood Books, 2008. 144 p.
This graphic novel for high schoolers presents the life of unpopular biracial Kimberly (Skim) Keiko Cameron, a sixteen-year-old tenth grader who, with her best friend Lisa, is learning how to be a Wiccan. It is a year (1993) in which her parents are separated; a classmate, Katie, experiences the suicide of a probably-gay boy with whom she has broken up; Katie falls off a roof and breaks her arms; a group of popular girls form a club to celebrate life; and Lisa falls in love with her female English/drama teacher, who subsequently leaves the school. The book details Skim's deepening depression until she decides that the tarot cards mean change, bleaches her hair, and gets a new best friend: Katie.
European-Canadian/Asian-Canadian
Older; Fiction

English-Canadian

Mercredi, Morningstar. *Fort Chipewyan Homecoming: A Journey to Native Canada*. Photographs by Darren McNally. Minneapolis: Lerner Publications Company, 1997. 48 p. (We Are Still Here, Native Americans Today)
Color photographs and text record the author and her twelve-year-old son Matthew's visit to Fort Chipewyan in Alberta, Canada, where she grew up. During the week Matthew sees his relatives and

learns of his Chipewyan, Cree, and Métis heritage. He accompanies a Chipewyan fisherman as he sets and pulls in a fishing net and smokes fish. He also helps make bannock (bread), receives a pair of beaded moccasins, and attends Treaty Days where he dances the drum dance.
English-Irish-Scottish-Canadian/Cree, Chipewyan, Métis, and Scottish-Canadian
Intermediate; Nonfiction

Robinson, Margaret A. *A Woman of Her Tribe*. New York: Charles Scribner's Sons, 1990. 144 p.

Annette has grown up in her father's Nootka village on Vancouver Island. He had died in Vietnam when she was a baby. When Annette is fifteen, she receives a scholarship to St. John's Academy and with her English mother moves to Victoria. Annette is terribly homesick, missing Granmaw, her friends and her Nootka life there and finding it difficult to adjust to her new school. She doesn't like the fast pace and the prejudice of a couple classmates, but, on the other hand, enjoys her anthropology and art classes and makes a close friend, Katie. Annette can't wait to return to her Nootka home for Christmas vacation. She discovers she is no longer as close to two of her friends, but works hard to pass the long ritual running test that makes her a Nootka woman. Then Annette must decide whether she will remain in her Nootka village or return to Victoria.
Nootka/English
Older; Fiction

Trottier, Maxine. *Under a Shooting Star*. New York: Stoddart Kids, 2002. 224 p. (The Circle of Silver Chronicles)

A sequel to *A Circle of Silver* and *By the Standing Stone*, this book is set in the border area of Canada and the United States during the War of 1812. Fifteen-year-old Canadian Edward Wolf MacNeil (the son of English Jamie and Sarah, the half-sister of Owela) is escorting two American girls to their home in Sandusky, Ohio, on his way to his Uncle John MacNeil's Canadian home on Pêche Island. When the merchant ship on which they are traveling sinks during a storm on Lake Erie, the three manage to reach South Bass Island. There they meet Paukeesaa, Tecumseh's son, who takes them to John MacNeil's empty house where they befriend the great-grandson of Marie Roy and Pierre LaButte (who is also named Pierre LaButte), and Edward reads the journal of Mack, John MacNeil's ward. This story tells of Edward and the girls' stay at Fort Amhertsburg where Edward helps build the English ship *Detroit*, of their involuntary involvement in the Battle of Lake Erie, and of John MacNeil's safe return.
English/Scottish-Canadian, Oneida, and Miami
Older; Fiction

Walters, Eric. *War of the Eagles*. Custer, Wash.: Orca Book Publishers, 1998. 224 p.

This book is set in and near Prince Rupert, British Columbia, in the time preceding and following the Japanese attacks on Pearl Harbor and Hong Kong. Fourteen-year-old Jed is staying with his mother and grandmother in a Tsimshian village while his English father is a fighter pilot in Europe. His best friend Tadashi Fukushima, who was born in Canada, lives in a neighboring village of Japanese immigrants and Japanese-Canadians. Jed, who loves to hunt, gets a job providing food for the nearby army camp and helping his mother, who is the camp's cook. He is also responsible for tending to an injured

bald eagle. The story traces the increasingly hostile treatment of Tadashi, who has to leave his job working with Jeb at the army camp and who, together with the others in his village, is declared an enemy alien and forced to leave his home. The night before Tadashi departs, he and Jed free the eagle so that it won't have to live in captivity in a zoo, and after Tadashi's departure, Jed, with the help of a soldier friend, saves the Fukushima family's possessions which are to be confiscated.
English/Haida and Tsimshian
Older; Fiction

French Canadian

See   Hruska, Shelly
       LaButte, Pierre (1796-   ?)
       McLoughlin, Jean-Baptiste (John)
       Roy, Marie

Noël, Michel. *Good For Nothing*. Translated from French by Shelley Tanaka. Toronto: Douglas & McIntyre, 2004. 328 p. (A Groundwood Book)
    Teenager Nipishish, a Métis whose parents have died, returns to his Algonquin reserve in Quebec Province after being mistreated at a residential school for Indians. When life on the reserve worsens because of governmental policy, Nipishish welcomes the opportunity to live with a white foster family in Mont-Laurier. There he is imprisoned when he loses his temper while trying to receive his paycheck. Nipishish feels he is good for nothing, a feeling reinforced when his white heritage makes it difficult for him to marry his Indian girlfriend. Things change when he is reunited with his Algonquin "family." He becomes a leader in their fight against logging in the reserve and, discovering that his father was probably secretly murdered for his advocacy of Indian rights, successfully enlists a lawyer to pursue the case.
Métis (Anishinabe/French Canadian)
Older; Fiction

Sommerdorf, Norma. *Red River Girl*. New York: Holiday House, 2006. 240 p.
    In her 1846-1848 journal, Josette, a Canadian Métis girl, records her experiences from the time of her thirteenth birthday when she lives in St. Eustache and is mourning the death of her Ojibwa mother. Her father, who has been a voyageur, decides to take Josette and her two younger brothers to visit their Ojibwa grandmother and then go on a buffalo hunt in what is now northern Minnesota. Josette dreams of someday going to school in Montreal. Thus, she is very upset with her father when he decides to become a teamster on a cart train bound for St. Paul and to have the family remain there even though it doesn't have a school. As time passes, Josette makes friends, has a beau, enjoys being a helper to the new schoolteacher, and goes with her on a visit to Galena, Illinois, and St. Louis. In the story a Dakota woman who helps out at the buffalo hunt has a Métis husband.
French-Canadian and Native Canadian/Ojibwa (Métis)
Intermediate, Older; Fiction

Trottier, Maxine. *By the Standing Stone*. New York: Stoddart Kids, 2001. 256 p. (The Circle of Silver Chronicles)

   This sequel to *A Circle of Silver* is set in 1773. John MacNeil's thirteen-year-old brother Jamie and his fifteen-year-old ward Mack (Charlotte) are kidnapped from a beach near Fort Niagara. John, Samuel (the younger brother of Marie Roy), and Owela (an Oneida whose Scottish-Miami stepfather is the son of Wallace Doig) set off to rescue them. This story recounts Jamie and Mack's journey to Boston as captives and after their release with Owela, their participation in the Boston Tea Party, their reunion in Boston with John and Samuel, the winter they all spend in Owela's village, their return to John's home on Pêche Island, and Mack's final acceptance of Owela's love.
French/Miami
Older; Fiction

Irish-Canadian

See   Caldwell, Billy
      McLoughlin, Jean-Baptiste (John)

Doyle, Brian. *Spud Sweetgrass*. Toronto: Groundwood Books, 1996. 144 p.

   Spud Sweetgrass, who has been kicked out of his Ottawa school, spends his time both selling french-fries while playing Beethoven at a chipwagon and hanging out with his friends, Dink the Thinker and Connie Pan, who is Vietnamese and Chinese. Spud goes with Connie and some E.S.L. students to Westboro Beach where they play an exciting game of volleyball without a ball and a net and he discovers that the Ottawa River seems to be polluted with chip grease. Suspecting the uncouth Dumper Stubbs, who changes the grease in the chipwagon, Spud catches him in the act of pouring grease into a sewer, but is unable to prove it. Thanks to the support of his friends, the Department of Physical Environment, and an Aboriginal medicine man, Spud establishes Dumper's guilt.
Aboriginal-Canadian/Irish-other-Canadian
Older; Fiction

Mercredi, Morningstar. *Fort Chipewyan Homecoming: A Journey to Native Canada*. Photographs by Darren McNally. Minneapolis: Lerner Publications Company, 1997. 48 p. (We Are Still Here, Native Americans Today)

   Color photographs and text record the author and her twelve-year-old son Matthew's visit to Fort Chipewyan in Alberta, Canada, where she grew up. During the week Matthew sees his relatives and learns of his Chipewyan, Cree, and Métis heritage. He accompanies a Chipewyan fisherman as he sets and pulls in a fishing net and smokes fish. He also helps make bannock (bread), receives a pair of beaded moccasins, and attends Treaty Days where he dances the drum dance.
English-Irish-Scottish-Canadian/Cree, Chipewyan, Métis, and Scottish-Canadian
Intermediate; Nonfiction

Romanian-Canadian

Bell, William. *Zack*. New York: Simon & Schuster Books for Young Readers, 1999. 192 p.

Although Zack is close to his father's parents, who are Romanian-Canadian Jewish, his mother, who is black, refuses to say anything about her family. Resentful that his parents have moved from Toronto to the small town of Fergus, Ontario, Zack does poorly in high school until he is assigned a local history project. Investigating the objects he had dug up from his yard, Zack is inspired by the story of the African former slave who had lived there and then, unbeknownst to his parents, travels to Natchez to find his black grandfather. Zack discovers that it was his grandfather with his hatred of whites, not his mother, who has kept him from his black relatives. In this story Zack learns not only about his heritage, but also about the power of courage and the far-reaching effects of one's actions.
Romanian-Canadian Jewish/African-American-Canadian
Older; Fiction

Scottish-Canadian

See   McLoughlin, Jean-Baptiste (John)

Mercredi, Morningstar. *Fort Chipewyan Homecoming: A Journey to Native Canada*. Photographs by Darren McNally. Minneapolis: Lerner Publications Company, 1997. 48 p. (We Are Still Here, Native Americans Today)

Color photographs and text record the author and her twelve-year-old son Matthew's visit to Fort Chipewyan in Alberta, Canada, where she grew up. During the week Matthew sees his relatives and learns of his Chipewyan, Cree, and Métis heritage. He accompanies a Chipewyan fisherman as he sets and pulls in a fishing net and smokes fish. He also helps make bannock (bread), receives a pair of beaded moccasins, and attends Treaty Days where he dances the drum dance.
English-Irish-Scottish-Canadian/Cree, Chipewyan, Métis, and Scottish-Canadian
Intermediate; Nonfiction

Trottier, Maxine. *By the Standing Stone*. New York: Stoddart Kids, 2001. 256 p. (The Circle of Silver Chronicles)

This sequel to *A Circle of Silver* is set in 1773. John MacNeil's thirteen-year-old brother Jamie and his fifteen-year-old ward Mack (Charlotte) are kidnapped from a beach near Fort Niagara. John, Samuel (the younger brother of Marie Roy), and Owela (an Oneida whose Scottish-Miami stepfather is the son of Wallace Doig) set off to rescue them. This story recounts Jamie and Mack's journey to Boston as captives and after their release with Owela, their participation in the Boston Tea Party, their reunion in Boston with John and Samuel, the winter they all spend in Owela's village, their return to John's home on Pêche Island, and Mack's final acceptance of Owela's love.
Scottish/Miami
Older; Fiction

Trottier, Maxine. *Under a Shooting Star*. New York: Stoddart Kids, 2002. 224 p. (The Circle of Silver Chronicles)

A sequel to *A Circle of Silver* and *By the Standing Stone*, this book is set in the border area of Canada and the United States during the War of 1812. Fifteen-year-old Canadian Edward Wolf MacNeil (the son of English Jamie and Sarah, the half-sister of Owela) is escorting two American girls to their home in Sandusky, Ohio, on his way to his Uncle John MacNeil's Canadian home on Pêche Island. When the merchant ship on which they are traveling sinks during a storm on Lake Erie, the three manage to reach South Bass Island. There they meet Paukeesaa, Tecumseh's son, who takes them to John MacNeil's empty house where they befriend the great-grandson of Marie Roy and Pierre LaButte (who is also named Pierre LaButte), and Edward reads the journal of Mack, John MacNeil's ward. This story tells of Edward and the girls' stay at Fort Amhertsburg where Edward helps build the English ship *Detroit*, of their involuntary involvement in the Battle of Lake Erie, and of John MacNeil's safe return.
English/Scottish-Canadian, Oneida, and Miami
Older; Fiction

Jewish-Canadian

Bell, William. *Zack*. New York: Simon & Schuster Books for Young Readers, 1999. 192 p.

Although Zack is close to his father's parents, who are Romanian-Canadian Jewish, his mother, who is black, refuses to say anything about her family. Resentful that his parents have moved from Toronto to the small town of Fergus, Ontario, Zack does poorly in high school until he is assigned a local history project. Investigating the objects he had dug up from his yard, Zack is inspired by the story of the African former slave who had lived there and then, unbeknownst to his parents, travels to Natchez to find his black grandfather. Zack discovers that it was his grandfather with his hatred of whites, not his mother, who has kept him from his black relatives. In this story Zack learns not only about his heritage, but also about the power of courage and the far-reaching effects of one's actions.
Romanian-Canadian Jewish/African-American Canadian
Older; Fiction

Little, Jean. *Kate*. New York: Harper & Row, Publishers, 1971. 176 p.

This sequel to *Look Through My Window* focuses on Emily's best friend Kate. Everything changes for Kate and her close relationship with Emily when she discovers that Sheila, a new girl in her Ontario class whom she doesn't particularly like, and Susannah, an eight-year-old whom she immediately adores, are sisters, are Jewish, and are the daughters of one of her father's childhood friends. Kate meets her aunt, her cousin, and her grandfather for the first time; becomes familiar with and proud of her Jewishness; and, learning from the estrangement which caused her father years of suffering, makes up with Emily.
European-Canadian Jewish/European-Canadian non-Jewish
Intermediate, Older; Fiction

Little, Jean. *Look Through My Window*. Illustrated by Joan Sandin. New York: Harper & Row, Publishers, 1970. 272 p.

When her aunt is hospitalized with tuberculosis and her father is transferred to a different city in Ontario, only child Emily's parents buy a large house and take in her four rambunctious cousins, aged three to seven. This story relates Emily's adventures helping look after the children, learning to appreciate the elderly cantankerous next-door neighbor, experiencing the unexpected arrival of Sophie, a seventeen-year-old Belgian girl, and rescuing the cat Wilhelmina Shakespeare. Most of all, the book is about Emily's finally meeting Kate, a kindred poetry-writer, their friendship, and their acceptance of Emily's being Presbyterian and Kate part-Jewish. This is the first book about Emily and Kate.
European-Canadian Jewish/European-Canadian non-Jewish
Intermediate; Fiction

Native Canadian

Doyle, Brian. *Spud Sweetgrass*. Toronto: Groundwood Books, 1996. 144 p.

Spud Sweetgrass, who has been kicked out of his Ottawa school, spends his time both selling french-fries while playing Beethoven at a chipwagon and hanging out with his friends, Dink the Thinker and Connie Pan, who is Vietnamese and Chinese. Spud goes with Connie and some E.S.L. students to Westboro Beach where they play an exciting game of volleyball without a ball and a net and he discovers that the Ottawa River seems to be polluted with chip grease. Suspecting the uncouth Dumper Stubbs, who changes the grease in the chipwagon, Spud catches him in the act of pouring grease into a sewer, but is unable to prove it. Thanks to the support of his friends, the Department of Physical Environment, and an Aboriginal medicine man, Spud establishes Dumper's guilt.
Aboriginal-Canadian/Irish-other-Canadian
Older; Fiction

Little, Jean. *Willow and Twig*. Toronto: Viking, 2000. 240 p.

Ten-year-old Willow, who is Native Canadian, and her four-year-old brother Twig, a child of mixed race, have been repeatedly abandoned by their drug-addicted single mother. Willow has become the surrogate mother for her brother who is deaf, has disturbing tantrums, and appears retarded. When their latest caretaker becomes ill, the two of them go from Vancouver to live with their grandmother, their great-uncle, and their great-aunt in rural Ontario. Although afraid that they will not be accepted, Willow experiences her family's love, goes to school for the first time, makes a friend, and learns to be less possessive of Twig, who receives help for his deafness.
Jamaican or Trinidadian/Native Canadian
Intermediate, Older; Fiction

Sommerdorf, Norma. *Red River Girl*. New York: Holiday House, 2006. 240 p.

In her 1846-1848 journal, Josette, a Canadian Métis girl, records her experiences from the time of her thirteenth birthday when she lives in St. Eustache and is mourning the death of her Ojibwa mother. Her father, who has been a voyageur, decides to take Josette and her two younger brothers to visit their Ojibwa grandmother and then go on a buffalo hunt in what is now northern Minnesota. Josette dreams

of someday going to school in Montreal. Thus, she is very upset with her father when he decides to become a teamster on a cart train bound for St. Paul and to have the family remain there even though it doesn't have a school. As time passes, Josette makes friends, has a beau, enjoys being a helper to the new schoolteacher, and goes with her on a visit to Galena, Illinois, and St. Louis. In the story a Dakota woman who helps out at the buffalo hunt has a Métis husband.
French-Canadian and Native Canadian/Ojibwa (Métis)
Intermediate, Older; Fiction

Anishinabe. See Ojibwa

Chippewa. See Ojibwa

Chipewyan

Mercredi, Morningstar. *Fort Chipewyan Homecoming: A Journey to Native Canada*. Photographs by Darren McNally. Minneapolis: Lerner Publications Company, 1997. 48 p. (We Are Still Here, Native Americans Today)
   Color photographs and text record the author and her twelve-year-old son Matthew's visit to Fort Chipewyan in Alberta, Canada, where she grew up. During the week Matthew sees his relatives and learns of his Chipewyan, Cree, and Métis heritage. He accompanies a Chipewyan fisherman as he sets and pulls in a fishing net and smokes fish. He also helps make bannock (bread), receives a pair of beaded moccasins, and attends Treaty Days where he dances the drum dance.
English-Irish-Scottish-Canadian/Cree, Chipewyan, Métis, and Scottish-Canadian
Intermediate; Nonfiction

Cree

Mercredi, Morningstar. *Fort Chipewyan Homecoming: A Journey to Native Canada*. Photographs by Darren McNally. Minneapolis: Lerner Publications Company, 1997. 48 p. (We Are Still Here, Native Americans Today)
   Color photographs and text record the author and her twelve-year-old son Matthew's visit to Fort Chipewyan in Alberta, Canada, where she grew up. During the week Matthew sees his relatives and learns of his Chipewyan, Cree, and Métis heritage. He accompanies a Chipewyan fisherman as he sets and pulls in a fishing net and smokes fish. He also helps make bannock (bread), receives a pair of beaded moccasins, and attends Treaty Days where he dances the drum dance.
English-Irish-Scottish-Canadian/Cree, Chipewyan, Métis, and Scottish-Canadian
Intermediate; Nonfiction

Haida

Walters, Eric. *War of the Eagles*. Custer, Wash.: Orca Book Publishers, 1998. 224 p.
   This book is set in and near Prince Rupert, British Columbia, in the time preceding and following

the Japanese attacks on Pearl Harbor and Hong Kong. Fourteen-year-old Jed is staying with his mother and grandmother in a Tsimshian village while his English father is a fighter pilot in Europe. His best friend Tadashi Fukushima, who was born in Canada, lives in a neighboring village of Japanese immigrants and Japanese-Canadians. Jed, who loves to hunt, gets a job providing food for the nearby army camp and helping his mother, who is the camp's cook. He is also responsible for tending to an injured bald eagle. The story traces the increasingly hostile treatment of Tadashi, who has to leave his job working with Jeb at the army camp and who, together with the others in his village, is declared an enemy alien and forced to leave his home. The night before Tadashi departs, he and Jed free the eagle so that it won't have to live in captivity in a zoo, and after Tadashi's departure, Jed, with the help of a soldier friend, saves the Fukushima family's possessions which are to be confiscated.
English/Haida and Tsimshian
Older; Fiction

Métis. See also individual heritages

See   Hruska, Shelly

Mercredi, Morningstar. *Fort Chipewyan Homecoming: A Journey to Native Canada*. Photographs by Darren McNally. Minneapolis: Lerner Publications Company, 1997. 48 p. (We Are Still Here, Native Americans Today)
    Color photographs and text record the author and her twelve-year-old son Matthew's visit to Fort Chipewyan in Alberta, Canada, where she grew up. During the week Matthew sees his relatives and learns of his Chipewyan, Cree, and Métis heritage. He accompanies a Chipewyan fisherman as he sets and pulls in a fishing net and smokes fish. He also helps make bannock (bread), receives a pair of beaded moccasins, and attends Treaty Days where he dances the drum dance.
English-Irish-Scottish-Canadian/Cree, Chipewyan, Métis, and Scottish-Canadian
Intermediate; Nonfiction

Noël, Michel. *Good For Nothing*. Translated from French by Shelley Tanaka. Toronto: Douglas & McIntyre, 2004. 328 p. (A Groundwood Book)
    Teenager Nipishish, a Métis whose parents have died, returns to his Algonquin reserve in Quebec Province after being mistreated at a residential school for Indians. When life on the reserve worsens because of governmental policy, Nipishish welcomes the opportunity to live with a white foster family in Mont-Laurier. There he is imprisoned when he loses his temper while trying to receive his paycheck. Nipishish feels he is good for nothing, a feeling reinforced when his white heritage makes it difficult for him to marry his Indian girlfriend. Things change when he is reunited with his Algonquin "family." He becomes a leader in their fight against logging in the reserve and, discovering that his father was probably secretly murdered for his advocacy of Indian rights, successfully enlists a lawyer to pursue the case.
Métis (Anishinabe/French Canadian)
Older; Fiction

Pendziwol, Jean E. *The Red Sash*. Illustrated by Nicolas Debon. Toronto: Greenwood Book/House of Anansi Press (Distributed by Publishers Group West), 2005. 36 p.

In this picture book a Métis boy and his sister go with a boy from Fort William, a fur trading post, to the Traverse Islands to trap hares. There they help a gentleman whose canoe is damaged by paddling him to Fort William. It is then that the boy sights his father, a voyaguer, who has been gone all winter as a fur trader guide—and that his father gives him the coveted red sash of the voyaguers. This picture book is set in Canada in the early 1800s.
Métis Canadian
Primary, Intermediate; Fiction

Sommerdorf, Norma. *Red River Girl*. New York: Holiday House, 2006. 240 p.

In her 1846-1848 journal, Josette, a Canadian Métis girl, records her experiences from the time of her thirteenth birthday when she lives in St. Eustache and is mourning the death of her Ojibwa mother. Her father, who has been a voyageur, decides to take Josette and her two younger brothers to visit their Ojibwa grandmother and then go on a buffalo hunt in what is now northern Minnesota. Josette dreams of someday going to school in Montreal. Thus, she is very upset with her father when he decides to become a teamster on a cart train bound for St. Paul and to have the family remain there even though it doesn't have a school. As time passes, Josette makes friends, has a beau, enjoys being a helper to the new schoolteacher, and goes with her on a visit to Galena, Illinois, and St. Louis. In the story a Dakota woman who helps out at the buffalo hunt has a Métis husband.
French-Canadian and Native Canadian/Ojibwa (Métis)
Intermediate, Older; Fiction

Miami

See LaButte, Pierre (1796- ?)
Roy, Marie

Trottier, Maxine. *By the Standing Stone*. New York: Stoddart Kids, 2001. 256 p. (The Circle of Silver Chronicles)

This sequel to *A Circle of Silver* is set in 1773. John MacNeil's thirteen-year-old brother Jamie and his fifteen-year-old ward Mack (Charlotte) are kidnapped from a beach near Fort Niagara. John, Samuel (the younger brother of Marie Roy), and Owela (an Oneida whose Scottish-Miami stepfather is the son of Wallace Doig) set off to rescue them. This story recounts Jamie and Mack's journey to Boston as captives and after their release with Owela, their participation in the Boston Tea Party, their reunion in Boston with John and Samuel, the winter they all spend in Owela's village, their return to John's home on Pêche Island, and Mack's final acceptance of Owela's love.
French/Miami; Scottish /Miami
Older; Fiction

Trottier, Maxine. *Under a Shooting Star*. New York: Stoddart Kids, 2002. 224 p. (The Circle of Silver Chronicles)

A sequel to *A Circle of Silver* and *By the Standing Stone*, this book is set in the border area of Canada and the United States during the War of 1812. Fifteen-year-old Canadian Edward Wolf MacNeil (the son of English Jamie and Sarah, the half-sister of Owela) is escorting two American girls to their home in Sandusky, Ohio, on his way to his Uncle John MacNeil's Canadian home on Pêche Island. When the merchant ship on which they are traveling sinks during a storm on Lake Erie, the three manage to reach South Bass Island. There they meet Paukeesaa, Tecumseh's son, who takes them to John MacNeil's empty house where they befriend the great-grandson of Marie Roy and Pierre LaButte (who is also named Pierre LaButte), and Edward reads the journal of Mack, John MacNeil's ward. This story tells of Edward and the girls' stay at Fort Amhertsburg where Edward helps build the English ship *Detroit*, of their involuntary involvement in the Battle of Lake Erie, and of John MacNeil's safe return.
English/Scottish-Canadian, Oneida, and Miami
Older; Fiction

Micmac

Levin, Betty. *Brother Moose*. New York: Greenwillow Books, 1990. 224 p.
When Nell, an orphan from England, is sent in the 1870s to live with a couple in Canada's Maritime Provinces, she discovers that her prospective mother, Mrs. Fowler, has moved to Maine to have a baby. Next Nell is kidnapped by robbers, escapes, and travels with her fellow orphan Louisa, an Indian named Joe Pennowit, and his twelve year old grandson to Maine. However, because Joe mistakenly thinks he has killed one of the men who kidnapped Nell, the four leave the road to escape the robbers and the police. On their difficult journey they go by wagon, by sleigh, and by an abandoned train car, which is pulled by their horse and a moose they have tamed. Nell finally reaches Mrs. Fowler, but her adoption hopes take a surprising turn.
European-Canadian or European-American/Canadian Micmac or American Passamaquoddy or Penobscot
Older; Fiction

Mohawk

See   Caldwell, Billy?

Slipperjack, Ruby. *Little Voice*. Illustrated by Sherry Farrell Racette. Regina, Saskatchewan: Coteau Books, 2002. 256 p. (In the Same Boat)
This story describes Canadian Ray's life from the summer of 1978 when she is ten to the summer of 1982. Terribly unhappy since the death of her non-Native father two years earlier and harassed by her schoolmates, Ray seldom speaks. When her mother marries Dave (who is Mohawk and Ojibwa), Ray feels as if she doesn't belong. It is only when she is with her Ojibwa mother's mother during four summers and the winter of 1981-82 that she is truly happy. There, Ray lives in her grandmother's cabin in an Ojibwa community, but they are often traveling by canoe and camping. Ray watches her

grandmother kill the bear which is tearing apart their tent and enjoys the baby bear adopted by a trapper friend, the puppy which he gives her grandmother, and the orphan seagull which she tends. Finally, Ray learns that she can stay permanently with her grandmother and that, like her, she will become a medicine woman.
Mohawk/Ojibwa
Intermediate, Older; Fiction

Nootka

Robinson, Margaret A. *A Woman of Her Tribe*. New York: Charles Scribner's Sons, 1990. 144 p.

Annette has grown up in her father's Nootka village on Vancouver Island. He had died in Vietnam when she was a baby. When Annette is fifteen, she receives a scholarship to St. John's Academy and with her English mother moves to Victoria. Annette is terribly homesick, missing Granmaw, her friends and her Nootka life there and finding it difficult to adjust to her new school. She doesn't like the fast pace and the prejudice of a couple classmates, but, on the other hand, enjoys her anthropology and art classes and makes a close friend, Katie. Annette can't wait to return to her Nootka home for Christmas vacation. She discovers she is no longer as close to two of her friends, but works hard to pass the long ritual running test that makes her a Nootka woman. Then Annette must decide whether she will remain in her Nootka village or return to Victoria.
Nootka/English
Older; Fiction

Ojibwa

See   McLoughlin, Jean-Baptiste (John)

Noël, Michel. *Good For Nothing*. Translated from French by Shelley Tanaka. Toronto: Douglas & McIntyre, 2004. 328 p. (A Groundwood Book)

Teenager Nipishish, a Métis whose parents have died, returns to his Algonquin reserve in Quebec Province after being mistreated at a residential school for Indians. When life on the reserve worsens because of governmental policy, Nipishish welcomes the opportunity to live with a white foster family in Mont-Laurier. There he is imprisoned when he loses his temper while trying to receive his paycheck. Nipishish feels he is good for nothing, a feeling reinforced when his white heritage makes it difficult for him to marry his Indian girlfriend. Things change when he is reunited with his Algonquin "family." He becomes a leader in their fight against logging in the reserve and, discovering that his father was probably secretly murdered for his advocacy of Indian rights, successfully enlists a lawyer to pursue the case.
Métis (Anishinabe/French Canadian)
Older; Fiction

Slipperjack, Ruby. *Little Voice*. Illustrated by Sherry Farrell Racette. Regina, Saskatchewan: Coteau Books, 2002. 256 p. (In the Same Boat)

This story describes Canadian Ray's life from the summer of 1978 when she is ten to the summer of 1982. Terribly unhappy since the death of her non-Native father two years earlier and harassed by her schoolmates, Ray seldom speaks. When her mother marries Dave (who is Mohawk and Ojibwa), Ray feels as if she doesn't belong. It is only when she is with her Ojibwa mother's mother during four summers and the winter of 1981-82 that she is truly happy. There, Ray lives in her grandmother's cabin in an Ojibwa community, but they are often traveling by canoe and camping, Ray watches her grandmother kill the bear which is tearing apart their tent and enjoys the baby bear adopted by a trapper friend, the puppy which he gives her grandmother, and the orphan seagull which she tends. Finally, Ray learns that she can stay permanently with her grandmother and that, like her, she will become a medicine woman.
European-Canadian/Ojibwa; Mohawk/Ojibwa
Intermediate, Older; Fiction

Sommerdorf, Norma. *Red River Girl*. New York: Holiday House, 2006. 240 p.
In her 1846-1848 journal, Josette, a Canadian Métis girl, records her experiences from the time of her thirteenth birthday when she lives in St. Eustache and is mourning the death of her Ojibwa mother. Her father, who has been a voyageur, decides to take Josette and her two younger brothers to visit their Ojibwa grandmother and then go on a buffalo hunt in what is now northern Minnesota. Josette dreams of someday going to school in Montreal. Thus, she is very upset with her father when he decides to become a teamster on a cart train bound for St. Paul and to have the family remain there even though it doesn't have a school. As time passes, Josette makes friends, has a beau, enjoys being a helper to the new schoolteacher, and goes with her on a visit to Galena, Illinois, and St. Louis. In the story a Dakota woman who helps out at the buffalo hunt has a Métis husband.
French-Canadian and Native Canadian/Ojibwa (Métis)
Intermediate, Older; Fiction

Oneida

Trottier, Maxine. *Under a Shooting Star*. New York: Stoddart Kids, 2002. 224 p. (The Circle of Silver Chronicles)
A sequel to *A Circle of Silver* and *By the Standing Stone*, this book is set in the border area of Canada and the United States during the War of 1812. Fifteen-year-old Canadian Edward Wolf MacNeil (the son of English Jamie and Sarah, the half-sister of Owela) is escorting two American girls to their home in Sandusky, Ohio, on his way to his Uncle John MacNeil's Canadian home on Pêche Island. When the merchant ship on which they are traveling sinks during a storm on Lake Erie, the three manage to reach South Bass Island. There they meet Paukeesaa, Tecumseh's son, who takes them to John MacNeil's empty house where they befriend the great-grandson of Marie Roy and Pierre LaButte (who is also named Pierre LaButte), and Edward reads the journal of Mack, John MacNeil's ward. This story tells of Edward and the girls' stay at Fort Amhertsburg where Edward helps build the English ship *Detroit*, of their involuntary involvement in the Battle of Lake Erie, and of John MacNeil's safe return.

English/Scottish-Canadian, Oneida, and Miami
Older; Fiction

Potawatomi

See   Caldwell, Billy?

Tsimshian

Walters, Eric. *War of the Eagles*. Custer, Wash.: Orca Book Publishers, 1998. 224 p.

This book is set in and near Prince Rupert, British Columbia, in the time preceding and following the Japanese attacks on Pearl Harbor and Hong Kong. Fourteen-year-old Jed is staying with his mother and grandmother in a Tsimshian village while his English father is a fighter pilot in Europe. His best friend Tadashi Fukushima, who was born in Canada, lives in a neighboring village of Japanese immigrants and Japanese-Canadians. Jed, who loves to hunt, gets a job providing food for the nearby army camp and helping his mother, who is the camp's cook. He is also responsible for tending to an injured bald eagle. The story traces the increasingly hostile treatment of Tadashi, who has to leave his job working with Jeb at the army camp and who, together with the others in his village, is declared an enemy alien and forced to leave his home. The night before Tadashi departs, he and Jed free the eagle so that it won't have to live in captivity in a zoo, and after Tadashi's departure, Jed, with the help of a soldier friend, saves the Fukushima family's possessions which are to be confiscated.

English/Haida and Tsimshian
Older; Fiction

West Indian-Canadian

Jamaican-Canadian

Little, Jean. *Willow and Twig*. Toronto: Viking, 2000. 240 p.

Ten-year-old Willow, who is Native Canadian, and her four-year-old brother Twig, a child of mixed race, have been repeatedly abandoned by their drug-addicted single mother. Willow has become the surrogate mother for her brother who is deaf, has disturbing tantrums, and appears retarded. When their latest caretaker becomes ill, the two of them go from Vancouver to live with their grandmother, their great-uncle, and their great-aunt in rural Ontario. Although afraid that they will not be accepted, Willow experiences her family's love, goes to school for the first time, makes a friend, and learns to be less possessive of Twig, who receives help for his deafness.

Jamaican or Trinidadian/Native Canadian
Intermediate, Older; Fiction

Trinidadian and Tobagonian-Canadian

Trinidadian-Canadian

Little, Jean. *Willow and Twig*. Toronto: Viking, 2000. 240 p.

Ten-year-old Willow, who is Native Canadian, and her four-year-old brother Twig, a child of mixed race, have been repeatedly abandoned by their drug-addicted single mother. Willow has become the surrogate mother for her brother who is deaf, has disturbing tantrums, and appears retarded. When their latest caretaker becomes ill, the two of them go from Vancouver to live with their grandmother, their great-uncle, and their great-aunt in rural Ontario. Although afraid that they will not be accepted, Willow experiences her family's love, goes to school for the first time, makes a friend, and learns to be less possessive of Twig, who receives help for his deafness.
Jamaican or Trinidadian/Native Canadian
Intermediate, Older; Fiction

F. Central American

Guatemalan

Mayan

Cameron, Ann. *Colibrí*. New York: Frances Foster Books, 2003. 240 p.

    Kidnapped at the age of four from her Mayan parents, Rosa (whose nickname had been Colibrí) spends the next eight years with "Uncle," her kidnapper. With Rosa too old to be sold for adoption, Uncle has kept her with him because of a fortune-teller's prediction that she will bring him a treasure. Together they travel from town to town in Guatemala as Uncle, pretending to be deaf, blind, lame, or dumb, begs for their living. It is when Uncle and a friend try to include her in a plan to steal a valuable church statue that Rosa gets up her courage and reports the plot to the church priest. Although she then happily lives with a kind woman she met earlier, Rosa almost loses her life when Uncle escapes from prison.

Spanish-Guatemalan and Mayan

Intermediate, Older; Fiction

Spanish-Guatemalan

Cameron, Ann. *Colibrí*. New York: Frances Foster Books, 2003. 240 p.

    Kidnapped at the age of four from her Mayan parents, Rosa (whose nickname had been Colibrí) spends the next eight years with "Uncle," her kidnapper. With Rosa too old to be sold for adoption, Uncle has kept her with him because of a fortune-teller's prediction that she will bring him a treasure. Together they travel from town to town in Guatemala as Uncle, pretending to be deaf, blind, lame, or dumb, begs for their living. It is when Uncle and a friend try to include her in a plan to steal a valuable church statue that Rosa gets up her courage and reports the plot to the church priest. Although she then happily lives with a kind woman she met earlier, Rosa almost loses her life when Uncle escapes from prison.

Spanish-Guatemalan and Mayan

Intermediate, Older; Fiction

Honduran

Mayan

Schwartz, Perry. *Carolyn's Story: A Book about an Adopted Girl*. Photographs by author. Minneapolis: Lerner Publications Company, 1996. 40 p.

    Colorful photographs and text present the adoption of the author's daughter from Honduras, her return with her adoptive parents two years later to adopt the baby who became her brother, her activities

as a nine-year-old, and her feelings about adoption. The book contains information about adoption, a glossary, a reading list, and a resource list.
Spanish-Honduran and Mayan
Intermediate; Nonfiction

Spanish-Honduran

Schwartz, Perry. *Carolyn's Story: A Book about an Adopted Girl*. Photographs by author. Minneapolis: Lerner Publications Company, 1996. 40 p.

    Colorful photographs and text present the adoption of the author's daughter from Honduras, her return with her adoptive parents two years later to adopt the baby who became her brother, her activities as a nine-year-old, and her feelings about adoption. The book contains information about adoption, a glossary, a reading list, and a resource list.
Spanish-Honduran and Mayan
Intermediate; Nonfiction

Panamanian

American-Panamanian

See   Blades. Rubén

Colombian-Panamanian

See   Blades. Rubén?

Cuban-Panamanian

See   Blades. Rubén

Spanish-Panamanian

See   Blades. Rubén

St. Lucian-Panamanian

See   Blades. Rubén

G. European

Belgian

Mandelbaum, Pili. *You Be Me, I'll Be You*. Brooklyn: Kane/Miller Book Publishers, 1990. 36 p.

When little Anna, who is of mixed race, complains to her white father that she wants to have his skin color, he combines coffee, like her mother, and milk, like him, to make coffee-milk, which is like Anna. When Anna then complains about her hair, he suggests trading heads. With his face covered with coffee grounds and his hair braided and Anna's face covered with flour and topped by her father's hat, the two go out to meet the startled mother. The book was first published in Belgium.
Belgian/African-Belgian
Pre-K, Primary; Fiction

African-Belgian

Mandelbaum, Pili. *You Be Me, I'll Be You*. Brooklyn: Kane/Miller Book Publishers, 1990. 36 p.

When little Anna, who is of mixed race, complains to her white father that she wants to have his skin color, he combines coffee, like her mother, and milk, like him, to make coffee-milk, which is like Anna. When Anna then complains about her hair, he suggests trading heads. With his face covered with coffee grounds and his hair braided and Anna's face covered with flour and topped by her father's hat, the two go out to meet the startled mother. The book was first published in Belgium.
Belgian/African-Belgian
Pre-K, Primary; Fiction

English

See   Gladwell, Malcolm
       Welsh, Zoë

Benjamin, Floella. *My Two Grannies*. Illustrated by Margaret Chamberlain. London: Frances Lincoln Children's Books, 2008. 28 p.

In this picture book, when Alvina's parents go on holiday, she is left in the care of her granny from Trinidad and her English granny. The two grandmothers can't agree on anything until Alvina suggests that they be in charge on alternating days. Then everything works out well, and the grannies come to appreciate each other.
English/Trinidadian
Pre-K, Primary; Fiction

Blackman, Malorie. *Checkmate*. London: Doubleday, 2005. 512 p.

The sequel to *Naughts & Crosses* and *Knife Edge*, this book, which is apparently set in an alternate England, presents the first sixteen years in the life of Callie Rose, the daughter of Callum, a Naught

Liberation Militia member who was hung, and Sephy, who comes from a prominent family of the oppressive Crosses. Callum's brother Jude decides to seek revenge for his brother's death by alienating Callie Rose from her mother and through deception recruiting her to join the Liberation Militia and blow up her Cross grandfather. The book describes his apparently successful mission to corrupt Callie Rose; Sephy's problems and her efforts to keep Callie Rose safe; Jude's mother's dilemma as to whether to protect her son or her granddaughter; Callie Rose's difficulties growing up as a child of mixed race amidst family secrets; and the day of reckoning.
English/African-English
Older; Fiction

Blackman, Malorie. *Knife Edge*. New York: Simon & Schuster Books for Young Readers, 2007. 368 p.

This book is the sequel to *Naughts & Crosses*, a book for the oldest teenagers set in an apparently alternate England where black Crosses oppress white Naughts. Stephy, the eighteen-year-old Cross daughter of the Deputy Prime Minister, is pregnant with the baby of Callum, a Naught whom she loves, but who has been hanged for being part of the Naught's Liberation Militia group that had kidnapped her. Blaming Stephy for the death of his brother, Jude is determined to destroy her and shoots, although not fatally, Stephy's sister. Stephy has her baby, Callie Rose, and regales Callie with stories about her father Callum. However, when Stephy receives a hateful letter Callum had written her from prison, she starts calling her baby Rose and becomes almost indifferent to her. Jude, who hates Crosses, finds himself falling in love with a Cross woman so he kills her. Throughout this story Stephy encounters racism, but her life becomes even more tragic when, for the sake of Callum and Jude's mother, she provides a false alibi for Jude and an innocent man is murdered. There is a breath-taking denouement.
English/African-English
Older; Fiction

Brooks, Kevin. *The Road of the Dead*. New York: The Chicken House, 2006. 348 p.

When their older sister Rachel is raped and strangled on a lonely moor in Devon, seventeen-year-old Cole, a rash troublemaker, and fourteen-year-old Kevin, who is thoughtful and psychic, travel from their London home to bring her body back for burial. The two find themselves in the midst of a hostile community where they are constantly endangered as they try to discover who killed Rachel and why the murderer is now dead. This book for high schooolers is one of suspense and violence, of psychic visions and bigotry towards gypsies, and of the bonding of the brothers.
Romani-English/English
Older; Fiction

Broome, Errol. *Gracie and the Emperor*. Toronto: Annick Press (Distributed by Firefly Books), 2005. 128 p.

In 1815 when Napoleon is exiled on the isolated British island of St. Helena, eleven-year-old Gracie, who has heard terrible things about him, is ordered to make his bed and leaves behind an angry note. Fired, she goes to work at The Briars where Napoleon stays until his permanent quarters

are ready. Although Gracie never talks to Napoleon, she comes to think better of him and they have important interactions. Napoleon secures her more convenient working hours and improves her relationship with her father, while Gracie sends Napoleon seeds for a garden. In 1821 when Napoleon's exile is ended by his death, so too is Gracie's as she fulfills her dream of leaving St. Helena and going to England.
English/Chinese-St. Helenian
Intermediate; Fiction

Cadnum, Michael. *The King's Arrow*. New York: Viking, 2008. 224 p.
This book of historical fiction is set in 1100 in England where there is tension among the Normans and between them and the conquered English. Affront is easily taken, and reprisals are swift and severe. Eighteen-year-old Simon, who is half-Norman and half-English, is invited to serve the Norman count, Walter Tirel, in a deer hunt together with, among others, King William II and Roland Monfort, the cruel royal marshal who detests Tirel. In the course of the hunt, Tirel's arrow kills the king, either by accident or because it was intended for Monfort. Simon, Tirel, and Tirel's herald flee from Monfort's forces, first by land and then by freighter where they encounter Monfort on a fast craft that intercepts them. Then, thanks to the new king, Henry, something surprising happens.
Norman-English/English
Older; Fiction

Garland, Sarah. *Billy and Belle*. New York: Reinhardt Books in association with Viking, 1992. 28 p.
When Billy and Belle's mother goes to the hospital to have a baby, little Belle accompanies Billy to school. It's pet day so Belle captures a classroom spider to be her pet. Wanting to count its legs for a picture she is making, Belle slips out to the playground to look for it and in the process releases all the other pets. The illustrations in this picture book show that the children's father is African-English and the mother Caucasian.
African-English/English
Pre-K, Primary; Fiction

Godden, Rumer. *Fu-dog*. Illustrated by Valerie Littlewood. New York: Viking, 1990. 64 p.
Seven-year-old Li-la loves the tiny satin Fu-dog that she receives from her Chinese great-uncle. Wanting to meet Great Uncle, Li-la and her brother Malcolm, unbeknownst to their parents, take the train from their home in Devon to London where they manage to locate their great-uncle's restaurant. Li-la is delighted with Great Uncle's Chinese garden, Malcolm is injured trying to rescue Fu-dog from being trampled in a Chinese New Year celebration, and Li-la's lost Fu-dog is replaced by a real Fu, a Pekingese puppy.
English/Chinese-English
Primary, Intermediate; Fiction

Kaye, Geraldine. *Comfort Herself*. Illustrated by Jennifer Northway. London: André Deutsch, 1984. 160 p.
Just after Comfort turns eleven, her mother is run over by a London bus. Comfort wants to go live

with her long-absent father in Ghana, but he cannot be contacted. Although initially reluctant to live with her mother's parents in Kent, Comfort comes to accept their ways and makes a best friend. Then, with her father located, she travels to Accra, Ghana, to stay with him and his new wife. Not welcomed by her stepmother, she is sent to her Ghanaian grandmother where she adapts to the life of a Ghanaian village girl. Finally, knowing that she has no chance for schooling and that she is regarded as her grandmother's property, Comfort realizes that she is her own person and returns to Kent on the day of her twelfth birthday.
Ghanaian (Ga)/English
Intermediate, Older; Fiction

Pullman, Philip. *The Broken Bridge*. New York: Alfred A. Knopf, 1992. 224 p.

Sixteen-year-old Ginny, who is very close to her English father, has been told that her Haitian artist mother died from hepatitis years earlier. When she discovers to her horror that she has a Caucasian half-brother who is coming to Wales to live with them, all her wonderings about her past emerge. Unable to get any information from her father, Ginny searches for the truth, a search that takes her to her grandparents in Chester, an art gallery in Liverpool, and the house of the dreaded Joe Chicago. Finally, Ginny not only learns about her family and early life, but also of how lucky she is. Andy, one of Ginny's friends whose parents were African, has been adopted by a white English couple.
English/African-Haitian
Older; Fiction

Roy, Jacqueline. *Soul Daddy*. San Diego: Gulliver Books, 1992. 240 p.

Fifteen-year-old identical twins Hannah and Rosie's lives change dramatically when their white mother tells them that their black father, whom they had never known, has a fourteen-year-old daughter, Nicola, and that both of them are moving into their Surrey home. Nicola initially feels isolated and homesick for London. Rosie, who has been the weaker twin, becomes friends with Nicola and starts to stand on her own. It is Hannah who has the worst time: she resents her father for having left them and dreads the possibility of his leaving again. Further, she is jealous of the more mature Nicola, hurt that Rosie no longer follows her lead, angry at her mother, and so upset when she is asked by her father to keep his secret that she runs away to London.
African-English/English
Older; Fiction

Saksena, Kate. *Hang On In There, Shelley*. New York: Bloomsbury Children's Books, 2003. 224 p.

On her fourteenth birthday Shelley decides that during the next year she will write reports on her life to Ziggy, the leader of a band whose albums, posters, and magazines she treasures. The book is written in the form of her letters, and each chapter is prefaced with a selection from the pop star's songs. Shelley has a difficult life. Her mother is an alcoholic who often disappears, suffers periods of depression, emotionally and physically abuses Shelley and her sensitive eight-year-old brother Jake, and causes Jake to be lost overnight in London. Shelley spends much of her time caring for Jake; she is tormented at her new girls school by a trio of bullies, who even frame her for possessing drugs; and one of her grandmothers has a stroke. On the plus side Shelley is supported by a caring father, extended

family, two new friends, her first boyfriend, and Ziggy, who sends her postcards. At the end of the book Ziggy writes Shelley a letter, proclaiming her a star.
African-English/ English
Older; Fiction

Stainer, M. L. *The Lyon's Crown*. Illustrated by James Melvin. Circleville, N.Y.: Chicken Soup Press, 2004. 176 p. (The Lyon Saga)

In this final book of *The Lyon Saga*, smallpox has come to Croatan Island and killed many residents, including Jess's Croatan husband Akaiyan and her English mother. Jess sends her three children away to Jamestown as Robert Ashbury, who has long loved her, has offered to provide sanctuary for them. Now in their early twenties and of mixed Croatan-English blood, the three must pretend to be English, adapt to English ways, and endure hostility towards "savages" from Virginian residents who have suffered Indian attacks. Suzanne/Oohah-ne falls in love with and marries Robert Ashbury's stepson, and William/Caun-reha adapts to life in Jamestown and Henrico, where they move. However, George/Wauh-kuaene suffers in the English environment until Jess comes to take him back to Croatan Island. This book tells of John Rolfe's work in cultivating tobacco for the English market, of his love for Pocahontas, who comes to Henrico, and of her acceptance of Christianity.
Croatan/English
Older; Fiction

Stainer, M. L. *The Lyon's Throne*. Illustrated by James Melvin. Circleville, N.Y.: Chicken Soup Press, 1999. 168 p. (The Lyon Saga)

In this sequel to *The Lyon's Pride*, English Jess, her Croatan husband Akaiyan, their baby Oohahn-ne/Suzanne, Spanish Enrique, his Croatan wife Te-lah-tai, and other Croatan Indians are captured by pirates. When the pirate ship is sunk by an English vessel, they are all taken to England where their freedom is bought by John White, who had been the governor of the Lost Colony. This book tells of Jess's successful efforts to have Queen Elizabeth I free Enrique, who is imprisoned in the Tower of London, and send the group back to Croatan Island. During the story Jess gives birth to a baby, Caun-reha/William, when she is in the Queen's quarters, Te-lah-tai has a baby, and Jess rejects an Englishman, Robert Ashbury, who falls in love with her. Robert gives her a magnificent white mare, and, upon their return, Jess has a third baby, Wauh kuaene/George.
Croatan/English
Older; Fiction

African-English

See   Gladwell, Malcolm

Blackman, Malorie. *Checkmate*. London: Doubleday, 2005. 512 p.

The sequel to *Naughts & Crosses* and *Knife Edge*, this book, which is apparently set in an alternate England, presents the first sixteen years in the life of Callie Rose, the daughter of Callum, a Naught Liberation Militia member who was hung, and Sephy, who comes from a prominent family of

the oppressive Crosses. Callum's brother Jude decides to seek revenge for his brother's death by alienating Callie Rose from her mother and through deception recruiting her to join the Liberation Militia and blow up her Cross grandfather. The book describes his apparently successful mission to corrupt Callie Rose; Sephy's problems and her efforts to keep Callie Rose safe; Jude's mother's dilemma as to whether to protect her son or her granddaughter; Callie Rose's difficulties growing up as a child of mixed race amidst family secrets; and the day of reckoning.
English/African-English
Older; Fiction

Blackman, Malorie. *Knife Edge*. New York: Simon & Schuster Books for Young Readers, 2007. 368 p.

This book is the sequel to *Naughts & Crosses*, a book for the oldest teenagers set in an apparently alternate England where black Crosses oppress white Naughts. Stephy, the eighteen-year-old Cross daughter of the Deputy Prime Minister, is pregnant with the baby of Callum, a Naught whom she loves, but who has been hanged for being part of the Naught's Liberation Militia group that had kidnapped her. Blaming Stephy for the death of his brother, Jude is determined to destroy her and shoots, although not fatally, Stephy's sister. Stephy has her baby, Callie Rose, and regales Callie with stories about her father Callum. However, when Stephy receives a hateful letter Callum had written her from prison, she starts calling her baby Rose and becomes almost indifferent to her. Jude, who hates Crosses, finds himself falling in love with a Cross woman so he kills her. Throughout this story Stephy encounters racism, but her life becomes even more tragic when, for the sake of Callum and Jude's mother, she provides a false alibi for Jude and an innocent man is murdered. There is a breath-taking denouement.
English/African-English
Older; Fiction

Garland, Sarah. *Billy and Belle*. New York: Reinhardt Books in association with Viking, 1992. 28 p.

When Billy and Belle's mother goes to the hospital to have a baby, little Belle accompanies Billy to school. It's pet day so Belle captures a classroom spider to be her pet. Wanting to count its legs for a picture she is making, Belle slips out to the playground to look for it and in the process releases all the other pets. The illustrations in this picture book show that the children's father is African-English and the mother Caucasian.
African-English/English
Pre-K, Primary; Fiction

Pullman, Philip. *The Broken Bridge*. New York: Alfred A. Knopf, 1992. 224 p.

Sixteen-year-old Ginny, who is very close to her English father, has been told that her Haitian artist mother died from hepatitis years earlier. When she discovers to her horror that she has a Caucasian half-brother who is coming to Wales to live with them, all her wonderings about her past emerge. Unable to get any information from her father, Ginny searches for the truth, a search that takes her to her grandparents in Chester, an art gallery in Liverpool, and the house of the dreaded Joe Chicago. Finally, Ginny not only learns about her family and early life, but also of how lucky she is. Andy, one of Ginny's friends whose parents were African, has been adopted by a white English couple.

English/African-Haitian
Older; Fiction

Roy, Jacqueline. *Soul Daddy*. San Diego: Gulliver Books, 1992. 240 p.

Fifteen-year-old identical twins Hannah and Rosie's lives change dramatically when their white mother tells them that their black father, whom they had never known, has a fourteen-year-old daughter, Nicola, and that both of them are moving into their Surrey home. Nicola initially feels isolated and homesick for London. Rosie, who has been the weaker twin, becomes friends with Nicola and starts to stand on her own. It is Hannah who has the worst time: she resents her father for having left them and dreads the possibility of his leaving again. Further, she is jealous of the more mature Nicola, hurt that Rosie no longer follows her lead, angry at her mother, and so upset when she is asked by her father to keep his secret that she runs away to London.
African-English/English; African-English/African-French
Older; Fiction

Saksena, Kate. *Hang On In There, Shelley*. New York: Bloomsbury Children's Books, 2003. 224 p.

On her fourteenth birthday Shelley decides that during the next year she will write reports on her life to Ziggy, the leader of a band whose albums, posters, and magazines she treasures. The book is written in the form of her letters, and each chapter is prefaced with a selection from the pop star's songs. Shelley has a difficult life. Her mother is an alcoholic who often disappears, suffers periods of depression, emotionally and physically abuses Shelley and her sensitive eight-year-old brother Jake, and causes Jake to be lost overnight in London. Shelley spends much of her time caring for Jake; she is tormented at her new girls school by a trio of bullies, who even frame her for possessing drugs; and one of her grandmothers has a stroke. On the plus side Shelley is supported by a caring father, extended family, two new friends, her first boyfriend, and Ziggy, who sends her postcards. At the end of the book Ziggy writes Shelley a letter, proclaiming her a star.
African-English/ English
Older; Fiction

Ghanaian (Ga)-English

Kaye, Geraldine. *Comfort Herself*. Illustrated by Jennifer Northway. London: André Deutsch, 1984. 160 p.

Just after Comfort turns eleven, her mother is run over by a London bus. Comfort wants to go live with her long-absent father in Ghana, but he cannot be contacted. Although initially reluctant to live with her mother's parents in Kent, Comfort comes to accept their ways and makes a best friend. Then, with her father located, she travels to Accra, Ghana, to stay with him and his new wife. Not welcomed by her stepmother, she is sent to her Ghanaian grandmother where she adapts to the life of a Ghanaian village girl. Finally, knowing that she has no chance for schooling and that she is regarded as her grandmother's property, Comfort realizes that she is her own person and returns to Kent on the day of her twelfth birthday.

Ghanian (Ga)/English
Intermediate, Older; Fiction

American-English

See   McCartney, Stella Nina

Harris, Rosemary. *Zed*. Boston: Faber and Faber, 1984. 192 p.

Fifteen-year-old Zed is asked by his house master to write up the time when, as an eight-year-old, he, together with his father, Uncle Omar, and others, was held captive in a London building by the Free Army of United Arabia. As Zed writes. he relives those terrible four days: the terrorists, guns, the grenade, discomforts, and overwhelming dread. Through the experience Zed comes to appreciate the kindness and bravery of Uncle Omar, who was Saudi-Turkish, and Arabi, one of the terrorists. Both were killed by gunshots, while Zed's English father, a self-centered coward, survived. After writing the manuscript, Zed arranges a meeting between Omar and Arabi's sons. This novel is for teenagers.

American-Jewish-English and Catholic/Lebanese and Christian Maronite
Older; Fiction

Croatan-English

Stainer, M. L. *The Lyon's Crown*. Illustrated by James Melvin. Circleville, N.Y.: Chicken Soup Press, 2004. 176 p. (The Lyon Saga)

In this final book of *The Lyon Saga*, smallpox has come to Croatan Island and killed many residents, including Jess's Croatan husband Akaiyan and her English mother. Jess sends her three children away to Jamestown as Robert Ashbury, who has long loved her, has offered to provide sanctuary for them. Now in their early twenties and of mixed Croatan-English blood, the three must pretend to be English, adapt to English ways, and endure hostility towards "savages" from Virginian residents who have suffered Indian attacks. Suzanne/Oohah-ne falls in love with and marries Robert Ashbury's stepson, and William/Caun-reha adapts to life in Jamestown and Henrico, where they move. However, George/Wauh-kuaene suffers in the English environment until Jess comes to take him back to Croatan Island. This book tells of John Rolfe's work in cultivating tobacco for the English market, of his love for Pocahontas, who comes to Henrico, and of her acceptance of Christianity.

Croatan/English
Older; Fiction

Stainer, M. L. *The Lyon's Throne*. Illustrated by James Melvin. Circleville, N.Y.: Chicken Soup Press, 1999. 168 p. (The Lyon Saga)

In this sequel to *The Lyon's Pride*, English Jess, her Croatan husband Akaiyan, their baby Oohahn-ne/Suzanne, Spanish Enrique, his Croatan wife Te-lah-tai, and other Croatan Indians are captured by pirates. When the pirate ship is sunk by an English vessel, they are all taken to England where

their freedom is bought by John White, who had been the governor of the Lost Colony. This book tells of Jess's successful efforts to have Queen Elizabeth I free Enrique, who is imprisoned in the Tower of London, and send the group back to Croatan Island. During the story Jess gives birth to a baby Caun-reha/William, when she is in the Queen's quarters, Te-lah-tai has a baby, and Jess rejects an Englishman, Robert Ashbury, who falls in love with her. Robert gives her a magnificent white mare, and, upon their return, Jess has a third baby, Wauh-kuaene/George.
Croatan/English; Spanish/Croatan
Older; Fiction

Asian-English

Chinese-English

Broome, Errol. *Gracie and the Emperor*. Toronto: Annick Press (Distributed by Firefly Books), 2005. 128 p.
    In 1815 when Napoleon is exiled on the isolated British island of St. Helena, eleven-year-old Gracie, who has heard terrible things about him, is ordered to make his bed and leaves behind an angry note. Fired, she goes to work at The Briars where Napoleon stays until his permanent quarters are ready. Although Gracie never talks to Napoleon, she comes to think better of him and they have important interactions. Napoleon secures her more convenient working hours and improves her relationship with her father, while Gracie sends Napoleon seeds for a garden. In 1821 when Napoleon's exile is ended by his death, so too is Gracie's as she fulfills her dream of leaving St. Helena and going to England.
English/Chinese-St. Helenian
Intermediate; Fiction

Godden, Rumer. *Fu-dog*. Illustrated by Valerie Littlewood. New York: Viking, 1990. 64 p.
    Seven-year-old Li-la loves the tiny satin Fu-dog that she receives from her Chinese great-uncle. Wanting to meet Great Uncle, Li-la and her brother Malcolm, unbeknownst to their parents, take the train from their home in Devon to London where they manage to locate their great-uncle's restaurant. Li-la is delighted with Great Uncle's Chinese garden, Malcolm is injured trying to rescue Fu-dog from being trampled in a Chinese New Year celebration, and Li-la's lost Fu-dog is replaced by a real Fu, a Pekingese puppy.
English/Chinese-English
Primary, Intermediate; Fiction

Lebanese-English

Harris, Rosemary. *Zed*. Boston: Faber and Faber, 1984. 192 p.
    Fifteen-year-old Zed is asked by his house master to write up the time when, as an eight-year-old, he, together with his father, Uncle Omar, and others, was held captive in a London building by the Free Army of United Arabia. As Zed writes. he relives those terrible four days: the terrorists, guns, grenades,

discomforts, and overwhelming dread. Through the experience Zed comes to appreciate the kindness and bravery of Uncle Omar, who was Saudi-Turkish, and Arabi, one of the terrorists. Both were killed by gunshots, while Zed's English father, a self-centered coward, survived. After writing the manuscript, Zed arranges a meeting between Omar and Arabi's sons. This novel is for teenagers.
American-Jewish-English and Catholic/Lebanese and Christian Maronite
Older; Fiction

European-English

Eastern European-English

Peacock, Shane. *Death in the Air: The Boy Sherlock Holmes, His Second Case.* Plattsburgh, N.Y.: Tundra Books of Northern New York, 2008. 264 p. (The Boy Sherlock Holmes)
In this second book in the series, thirteen-year-old Sherlock Holmes has left home and gets a room and a job with Sigerson Bell, an elderly apothecary. Holmes' second case literally arrives at his feet when the famed trapeze artist Mercure plunges to the floor during a performance at London's Crystal Palace. Sherlock immediately realizes that it was not an accident and resolves to solve the case. When he discovers that it was the dreaded Brixton Gang that both caused Mercure's fall and robbed the palace vault, he decides to secure their capture. In the face of dangers and with the help of Bell and another trapeze artist, he succeeds, but once again is denied both recognition of his achievement and the award, which was to save Bell and himself from eviction and further his education.
Eastern European-English Jewish/French-English non-Jewish
Older; Fiction

Peacock, Shane. *Eye of the Crow: The Boy Sherlock Holmes, His First Case.* Plattsburgh, N.Y.: Tundra Books of Northern New York, 2007. 264 p. (The Boy Sherlock Holmes)
This is the first in a series about young Sherlock Holmes, the son of Jewish Eastern European-English Wilber and French-English Rose, who is from a high-class family. When Rose married Wilber, her parents disowned her and made sure that Wilber, a teacher in training at the University College of London, not only could not teach there, but also would not be able to get any jobs befitting his talents. Sherlock lives with his much-loved parents in a London flat and is often taunted as a half-Jew. In 1867 after thirteen-year-old Sherlock reads of the murder of a beautiful young woman in a London slum, he goes to the murder site and is arrested by the police as an accomplice to the alleged Arab murderer. Through ingenuity Sherlock manages to escape from the jail and then seek the actual murderer. Helped by the older boy Malefactor and his gang of boy criminals, by his only friend Irene, and by his mother, Sherlock prowls the streets of London at night and encounters many dangers. Although Scotland Yard takes full credit for solving the crime, it is Sherlock who discovers the truth. However, in doing so Irene is severely injured and Rose dies of poisoning. Sherlock resolves never again to form emotional attachments, but to devote his deductive powers solely to seeking justice.
Eastern European-English Jewish/French-English non-Jewish
Older; Fiction

Peacock, Shane. *The Secret Fiend: The Boy Sherlock Holmes, His 4th Case*. Plattsburgh, N.Y.: Tundra Books of Northern New York, 2010. 256 p. (The Boy Sherlock Holmes)

In 1868 when he has just turned fourteen, Sherlock Holmes' childhood friend Beatrice and her companion Louise are attacked on Westminster Bridge by what Beatrice thinks looks like the fictional Spring Heeled Jack. Sherlock seeks to protect Beatrice and rid London of the fiend, who is increasingly terrorizing the city. Discarding his initial suspicion that the Jack might be Sigerson Bell, his elderly employer, Sherlock focuses on Crew, the criminal Malefactor's lieutenant. Despite encounters with the Jack and a Jack imposter, Sherlock continues to pursue his mission. Then, falsely implicated as the Jack's accomplice, Sherlock plans to leave London. The story ends with the surprising discovery of the identities of the fiend and his accomplices, Sherlock and Bell's fight with the Jack, and encouraging advice given to Sherlock by Prime Minister Benjamin Disraeli, who is Jewish.
Eastern European-English Jewish/French-English non-Jewish
Older; Fiction

Peacock, Shane. *Vanishing Girl: The Boy Sherlock Holmes, His 3rd Case*. Plattsburgh, N.Y.: Tundra Books of Northern New York, 2009. 320 p. (The Boy Sherlock Holmes)

Sherlock Holmes apparently fails in his attempt to solve the case of kidnapped fourteen-year-old Victoria Rathbone when, after thinking he has found her in the supposedly-haunted Grimwood Hall in St. Neots, she is found by Scotland Yard elsewhere. Then, in this third book of the series, the wealthy Rathbone family is robbed and, shortly thereafter, Victoria is again kidnapped. In addition, the fate of Paul, a five-year-old boy with rapidly progressing blindness, depends on quickly solving the complicated case. Still living with the apothecary Sigerson Bell, Sherlock makes daring entrances into the Rathbone residence and Grimwood Hall and uses his observational skills, his ingenuity, and his newly-acquired fighting skills to keep ahead of Malefactor's criminal gang and his Scotland Yard nemesis, Inspector Lestrade. When Sherlock finally succeeds in finding the culprits and the real, not the disguised, Victoria, he heeds Bell's advice and lets Scotland Yard take the credit. Further, while Sherlock is solving the case, Bell, who feels he can now cure Paul, is removing him from the London workhouse where he had been placed.
Eastern European-English Jewish/French-English non-Jewish
Older; Fiction

French-English

Peacock, Shane. *Death in the Air: The Boy Sherlock Holmes, His Second Case*. Plattsburgh, N.Y.: Tundra Books of Northern New York, 2008. 264 p. (The Boy Sherlock Holmes)

In this second book in the series, thirteen-year-old Sherlock Holmes has left home and gets a room and a job with Sigerson Bell, an elderly apothecary. Holmes' second case literally arrives at his feet when the famed trapeze artist Mercure plunges to the floor during a performance at London's Crystal Palace. Sherlock immediately realizes that it was not an accident and resolves to solve the case. When he discovers that it was the dreaded Brixton Gang that both caused Mercure's fall and robbed the palace vault, he decides to secure their capture. In the face of dangers and with the help of Bell and another trapeze artist, he succeeds, but once again is denied both recognition of his achievement and the award,

which was to save Bell and himself from eviction and further his education.
Eastern European-English Jewish/French-English non-Jewish
Older; Fiction

Peacock, Shane. *Eye of the Crow: The Boy Sherlock Holmes, His First Case*. Plattsburgh, N.Y.: Tundra Books of Northern New York, 2007. 264 p. (The Boy Sherlock Holmes)

This is the first in a series about young Sherlock Holmes, the son of Jewish Eastern European-English Wilber, and French-English Rose, who is from a high-class family. When Rose married Wilber, her parents disowned her and made sure that Wilber, a teacher in training at the University College of London, not only could not teach there, but also would not be able to get any jobs befitting his talents. Sherlock lives with his much-loved parents in a London flat and is often taunted as a half-Jew. In 1867 after thirteen-year-old Sherlock reads of the murder of a beautiful young woman in a London slum, he goes to the murder site and is arrested by the police as an accomplice to the alleged Arab murderer. Through ingenuity Sherlock manages to escape from the jail and then seek the actual murderer. Helped by the older boy Malefactor and his gang of boy criminals, by his only friend Irene, and by his mother, Sherlock prowls the streets of London at night and encounters many dangers. Although Scotland Yard takes full credit for solving the crime, it is Sherlock who discovers the truth. However, in doing so Irene is severely injured and Rose dies of poisoning. Sherlock resolves never again to form emotional attachments, but to devote his deductive powers solely to seeking justice.
Eastern European-English Jewish/French-English non-Jewish
Older; Fiction

Peacock, Shane. *The Secret Fiend: The Boy Sherlock Holmes, His 4th Case*. Plattsburgh, N.Y.: Tundra Books of Northern New York, 2010. 256 p. (The Boy Sherlock Holmes)

In 1868 when he has just turned fourteen, Sherlock Holmes' childhood friend Beatrice and her companion Louise are attacked on Westminster Bridge by what Beatrice thinks looks like the fictional Spring Heeled Jack. Sherlock seeks to protect Beatrice and rid London of the fiend, who is increasingly terrorizing the city. Discarding his initial suspicion that the Jack might be Sigerson Bell, his elderly employer, Sherlock focuses on Crew, the criminal Malefactor's lieutenant. Despite encounters with the Jack and a Jack imposter, Sherlock continues to pursue his mission. Then, falsely implicated as the Jack's accomplice, Sherlock plans to leave London. The story ends with the surprising discovery of the identities of the fiend and his accomplices, Sherlock and Bell's fight with the Jack, and encouraging advice given to Sherlock by Prime Minister Benjamin Disraeli, who is Jewish.
Eastern European-English Jewish/French-English non-Jewish
Older; Fiction

Peacock, Shane. *Vanishing Girl: The Boy Sherlock Holmes, His 3rd Case*. Plattsburgh, N.Y.: Tundra Books of Northern New York, 2009. 320 p. (The Boy Sherlock Holmes)

Sherlock Holmes apparently fails in his attempt to solve the case of kidnapped fourteen-year-old Victoria Rathbone when, after thinking he has found her in the supposedly-haunted Grimwood Hall in St. Neots, she is found by Scotland Yard elsewhere. Then, in this third book of the series, the wealthy Rathbone family is robbed and, shortly thereafter, Victoria is again kidnapped. In addition, the

fate of Paul, a five-year-old boy with rapidly progressing blindness, depends on quickly solving the complicated case. Still living with the apothecary Sigerson Bell, Sherlock makes daring entrances into the Rathbone residence and Grimwood Hall and uses his observational skills, his ingenuity, and his newly-acquired fighting skills to keep ahead of Malefactor's criminal gang and his Scotland Yard nemesis, Inspector Lestrade. When Sherlock finally succeeds in finding the culprits and the real, not the disguised, Victoria, he heeds Bell's advice and lets Scotland Yard take the credit. Further, while Sherlock is solving the case, Bell, who feels he can now cure Paul, is removing him from the London workhouse where he had been placed.
Eastern European-English Jewish/French-English non-Jewish
Older; Fiction

Roy, Jacqueline. *Soul Daddy*. San Diego: Gulliver Books, 1992. 240 p.
Fifteen-year-old identical twins Hannah and Rosie's lives change dramatically when their white mother tells them that their black father, whom they had never known, has a fourteen-year-old daughter, Nicola, and that both of them are moving into their Surrey home. Nicola initially feels isolated and homesick for London. Rosie who has been the weaker twin, becomes friends with Nicola and starts to stand on her own. It is Hannah who has the worst time: she resents her father for having left them and dreads the possibility of his leaving again. Further, she is jealous of the more mature Nicola, hurt that Rosie no longer follows her lead, angry at her mother, and so upset when she is asked by her father to keep his secret that she runs away to London.
African-English/African-French
Older; Fiction

Greek-English

Bawden, Nina. *The Outside Child*. New York: Lothrop, Lee & Shepard Books, 1989. 240 p.
When thirteen-year-old Jane discovers that she has a half sister and a half brother whom she has never met, she and her best friend Plato set out to find them—and discover why she has been excluded from her father's family. Plato is Welsh-Greek and is the title character of Bawden's *The Real Plato Jones*.
Welsh/Greek
Intermediate, Older; Fiction

Bawden, Nina. *The Real Plato Jones*. New York: Clarion Books, 1993. 176 p.
Welsh on his father's side and Greek on his mother's, thirteen-year-old Plato has a hard time knowing where he belongs. He feels Greek when he is in Wales and England and Welsh when he is in Greece. Visiting Greece for his grandfather's funeral, Plato discovers that although his Welsh grandfather is a renowned hero, his mother's father is regarded by many of his Greek neighbors as a traitor. During the ensuing months Plato comes to a better understanding of heroism and of himself. He is no longer torn apart, but proud of both of his heritages.
Welsh/Greek
Intermediate, Older; Fiction

Irish-English

See   McCartney, Stella Nina

Norman-English

Cadnum, Michael. *The King's Arrow*. New York: Viking, 2008. 224 p.

This book of historical fiction is set in 1100 in England where there is tension among the Normans and between them and the conquered English. Affront is easily taken, and reprisals are swift and severe. Eighteen-year-old Simon, who is half-Norman and half-English, is invited to serve the Norman count, Walter Tirel, in a deer hunt together with, among others, King William II and Roland Monfort, the cruel royal marshal who detests Tirel. In the course of the hunt, Tirel's arrow kills the king, either by accident or because it was intended for Monfort. Simon, Tirel, and Tirel's herald flee from Monfort's forces, first by land and then by freighter where they encounter Monfort on a fast craft that intercepts them. Then, thanks to the new king, Henry, something surprising happens.
Norman-English/English
Older; Fiction

Romani-English

Brooks, Kevin. *The Road of the Dead*. New York: The Chicken House, 2006. 348 p.

When their older sister Rachel is raped and strangled on a lonely moor in Devon, seventeen-year-old Cole, a rash troublemaker, and fourteen-year-old Kevin, who is thoughtful and psychic, travel from their London home to bring her body back for burial. The two find themselves in the midst of a hostile community where they are constantly endangered as they try to discover who killed Rachel and why the murderer is now dead. This book for high schooolers is one of suspense and violence, of psychic visions and bigotry towards gypsies, and of the bonding of the brothers.
Romani-English/English
Older; Fiction

Scottish-English

See   Gladwell, Malcolm

Spanish-English

Stainer, M. L. *The Lyon's Throne*. Illustrated by James Melvin. Circleville, NY: Chicken Soup Press, 1999. 168 p. (The Lyon Saga)

In this sequel to *The Lyon's Pride*, English Jess, her Croatan husband Akaiyan, their baby Oohahn-ne/Suzanne, Spanish Enrique, his Croatan wife Te-lah-tai, and other Croatan Indians are captured by pirates. When the pirate ship is sunk by an English vessel, they are all taken to England where their freedom is bought by John White, who had been the governor of the Lost Colony. This book tells

of Jess's successful efforts to have Queen Elizabeth I free Enrique, who is imprisoned in the Tower of London, and send the group back to Croatan Island. During the story Jess gives birth to a baby, Caun-reha/William, when she is in the Queen's quarters, Te-lah-tai has a baby, and Jess rejects an Englishman Robert Ashbury, who falls in love with her. Robert gives her a magnificent white mare, and, upon their return, Jess has a third baby, Wauh-kuaene/George.
Spanish/Croatan
Older; Fiction

St. Helenian-English

Broome, Errol. *Gracie and the Emperor*. Toronto: Annick Press (Distributed by Firefly Books), 2005. 128 p.

In 1815 when Napoleon is exiled on the isolated British island of St. Helena, eleven-year-old Gracie, who has heard terrible things about him, is ordered to make his bed and leaves behind an angry note. Fired, she goes to work at The Briars where Napoleon stays until his permanent quarters are ready. Although Gracie never talks to Napoleon, she comes to think better of him and they have important interactions. Napoleon secures her more convenient working hours and improves her relationship with her father, while Gracie sends Napoleon seeds for a garden. In 1821 when Napoleon's exile is ended by his death, so too is Gracie's as she fulfills her dream of leaving St. Helena and going to England.
English/Chinese-St. Helenian
Intermediate; Fiction

Welsh-English

Bawden, Nina. *The Outside Child*. New York: Lothrop, Lee & Shepard Books, 1989. 240 p.

When thirteen-year-old Jane discovers that she has a half sister and a half brother whom she has never met, she and her best friend Plato set out to find them—and discover why she has been excluded from her father's family. Plato is Welsh-Greek and is the title character of Bawden's *The Real Plato Jones*.
Welsh/Greek
Intermediate, Older; Fiction

Bawden, Nina. *The Real Plato Jones*. New York: Clarion Books, 1993. 176 p.

Welsh on his father's side and Greek on his mother's, thirteen-year-old Plato has a hard time knowing where he belongs. He feels Greek when he is in Wales and England and Welsh when he is in Greece. Visiting Greece for his grandfather's funeral, Plato discovers that although his Welsh grandfather is a renowned hero, his mother's father is regarded by many of his Greek neighbors as a traitor. During the ensuing months Plato comes to a better understanding of heroism and of himself. He is no longer torn apart, but proud of both of his heritages.
Welsh/Greek
Intermediate, Older; Fiction

Jewish-English

See   Gladwell, Malcolm
         McCartney, Stella Nina

Harris, Rosemary. *Zed*. Boston: Faber and Faber, 1984. 192 p.

Fifteen-year-old Zed is asked by his house master to write up the time when, as an eight-year-old, he, together with his father, Uncle Omar, and others, was held captive in a London building by the Free Army of United Arabia. As Zed writes. he relives those terrible four days: the terrorists, guns, the grenade, discomforts, and overwhelming dread. Through the experience Zed comes to appreciate the kindness and bravery of Uncle Omar, who was Saudi-Turkish, and Arabi, one of the terrorists. Both were killed by gunshots, while Zed's English father, a self-centered coward, survived. After writing the manuscript, Zed arranges a meeting between Omar and Arabi's sons. This novel is for teenagers.
American-Jewish-English and Catholic/Lebanese and Christian Maronite
Older; Fiction

Peacock, Shane. *Death in the Air: The Boy Sherlock Holmes, His Second Case*. Plattsburgh, N.Y.: Tundra Books of Northern New York, 2008. 264 p. (The Boy Sherlock Holmes)

In this second book in the series, thirteen-year-old Sherlock Holmes has left home and gets a room and a job with Sigerson Bell, an elderly apothecary. Holmes' second case literally arrives at his feet when the famed trapeze artist Mercure plunges to the floor during a performance at London's Crystal Palace. Sherlock immediately realizes that it was not an accident and resolves to solve the case. When he discovers that it was the dreaded Brixton Gang that both caused Mercure's fall and robbed the palace vault, he decides to secure their capture. In the face of dangers and with the help of Bell and another trapeze artist, he succeeds, but once again is denied both recognition of his achievement and the award, which was to save Bell and himself from eviction and further his education.
Eastern European-English Jewish/French-English non-Jewish
Older; Fiction

Peacock, Shane. *Eye of the Crow: The Boy Sherlock Holmes, His First Case*. Plattsburgh, N.Y.: Tundra Books of Northern New York, 2007. 264 p. (The Boy Sherlock Holmes)

This is the first in a series about young Sherlock Holmes, the son of Jewish Eastern European-English Wilber and French-English Rose, who is from a high-class family. When Rose married Wilber, her parents disowned her and made sure that Wilber, a teacher in training at the University College of London, not only could not teach there, but also would not be able to get any jobs befitting his talents. Sherlock lives with his much-loved parents in a London flat and is often taunted as a half-Jew. In 1867 after thirteen-year-old Sherlock reads of the murder of a beautiful young woman in a London slum, he goes to the murder site and is arrested by the police as an accomplice to the alleged Arab murderer. Through ingenuity Sherlock manages to escape from the jail and then seek the actual murderer. Helped by the older boy Malefactor and his gang of boy criminals, by his only friend Irene, and by his mother, Sherlock prowls the streets of London at night and encounters many dangers. Although Scotland

Yard takes full credit for solving the crime, it is Sherlock who discovers the truth. However, in doing so Irene is severely injured and Rose dies of poisoning. Sherlock resolves never again to form emotional attachments, but to devote his deductive powers solely to seeking justice.
Eastern-European-English Jewish/French-English non-Jewish
Older; Fiction

Peacock, Shane. *The Secret Fiend: The Boy Sherlock Holmes, His 4th Case*. Plattsburgh, N.Y.: Tundra Books of Northern New York, 2010. 256 p. (The Boy Sherlock Holmes)
    In 1868 when he has just turned fourteen, Sherlock Holmes' childhood friend Beatrice and her companion Louise are attacked on Westminster Bridge by what Beatrice thinks looks like the fictional Spring Heeled Jack. Sherlock seeks to protect Beatrice and rid London of the fiend, who is increasingly terrorizing the city. Discarding his initial suspicion that the Jack might be Sigerson Bell, his elderly employer, Sherlock focuses on Crew, the criminal Malefactor's lieutenant. Despite encounters with the Jack and a Jack imposter, Sherlock continues to pursue his mission. Then, falsely implicated as the Jack's accomplice, Sherlock plans to leave London. The story ends with the surprising discovery of the identities of the fiend and his accomplices, Sherlock and Bell's fight with the Jack, and encouraging advice given to Sherlock by Prime Minister Benjamin Disraeli, who is Jewish.
Eastern European-English Jewish/French-English non-Jewish
Older; Fiction

Peacock, Shane. *Vanishing Girl: The Boy Sherlock Holmes, His 3rd Case*. Plattsburgh, N.Y.: Tundra Books of Northern New York, 2009. 320 p. (The Boy Sherlock Holmes)
    Sherlock Holmes apparently fails in his attempt to solve the case of kidnapped fourteen-year-old Victoria Rathbone when, after thinking he has found her in the supposedly-haunted Grimwood Hall in St. Neots, she is found by Scotland Yard elsewhere. Then, in this third book of the series, the wealthy Rathbone family is robbed and, shortly thereafter, Victoria is again kidnapped. In addition, the fate of Paul, a five-year-old boy with rapidly progressing blindness, depends on quickly solving the complicated case. Still living with the apothecary Sigerson Bell, Sherlock makes daring entrances into the Rathbone residence and Grimwood Hall and uses his observational skills, his ingenuity, and his newly-acquired fighting skills to keep ahead of Malefactor's criminal gang and his Scotland Yard nemesis, Inspector Lestrade. When Sherlock finally succeeds in finding the culprits and the real, not the disguised, Victoria, he heeds Bell's advice and lets Scotland Yard take the credit. Further, while Sherlock is solving the case, Bell, who feels he can now cure Paul, is removing him from the London workhouse where he had been placed.
Eastern European-English Jewish/French-English non-Jewish
Older; Fiction

West Indian-English

Haitian-English

Pullman, Philip. *The Broken Bridge*. New York: Alfred A. Knopf, 1992. 224 p.

Sixteen-year-old Ginny, who is very close to her English father, has been told that her Haitian artist mother died from hepatitis years earlier. When she discovers to her horror that she has a Caucasian half-brother who is coming to Wales to live with them, all her wonderings about her past emerge. Unable to get any information from her father, Ginny searches for the truth, a search that takes her to her grandparents in Chester, an art gallery in Liverpool, and the house of the dreaded Joe Chicago. Finally, Ginny not only learns about her family and early life, but also of how lucky she is. Andy, one of Ginny's friends whose parents were African, has been adopted by a white English couple.
English/African-Haitian
Older; Fiction

Jamaican-English

See   Gladwell, Maxwell
          Welsh, Zoë

Trinidadian-English

Benjamin, Floella. *My Two Grannies*. Illustrated by Margaret Chamberlain. London: Frances Lincoln Children's Books, 2008. 28 p.

In this picture book, when Alvina's parents go on holiday, she is left in the care of her granny from Trinidad and her English granny. The two grandmothers can't agree on anything until Alvina suggests that they be in charge on alternating days. Then everything works out well, and the grannies come to appreciate each other.
English/Trinidadian
Pre-K, Primary; Fiction

French

Klein, Norma. *Bizou: A Novel*. New York: The Viking Press, 1983. 144 p.

Thirteen-year-old Bizou, whose deceased father was French and whose mother is African-American, is temporarily abandoned by her mother when the two of them travel from France to visit the United States which her mother had left years before. Entrusted to Nicholas, a man they met on the plane, Bizou travels with him to Vermont and Washington, D.C. before they locate a friend of Bizou's mother in Pennsylvania. It is there that Bizou discovers that she has a half-brother, meets her grandfather, and is reunited with her mother.
French and Jewish/African-American
Older; Fiction

Modiano, Patrick. *Catherine Certitude*. Translated from French by William Rodarmor. Illustrated by Jean-Jacques Sempé. Boston: David R. Godine, 2001. 64 p.

This is the unusual story of the little girl, Catherine Certitude, and her father, who like to take off their glasses so that they can be removed from the real world and enter their own dream worlds. Set in Paris, the book abounds with unresolved questions: the father's actual business, the nature of the difficulty from which his business partner has extricated him, the lack of a listing of the residence where he and Catherine attend a party, the real reasons Catherine's mother went back to the United States, and why Catherine's ballet teacher has assumed a new identity. Within its mysterious overtones, the story presents the warm relationship of Catherine and her father.
French/European-American
Intermediate, Older; Fiction

Ringgold, Faith. *Bonjour, Lonnie*. Illustrated by author. New York: Hyperion Books for Children, 1996. 32 p.

Thanks to a Love Bird that flies into Lonnie's window one night, he discovers his family background. During World War I his paternal grandfather was an African-American soldier in France. There he met and married Lonnie's French grandmother and became an opera singer. Their son (Lonnie's father) married a Jewish French woman. During World War II he died fighting for France and, after Lonnie's mother gave him to a friend for his safety, she became a victim of the Nazis. Subsequently, Lonnie was taken to the United States where he was adopted by an African-American couple, Aunt Connie and Uncle Bates. This picture book is a companion book to *Dinner at Aunt Connie's House*.
African-American-French and non-Jewish/French and Jewish
Primary; Fiction

Ringgold, Faith. *Dinner at Aunt Connie's House*. Illustrated by author. New York: Hyperion Books for Children, 1993. 32 p.

This picture book is based on the artist-author's "The Dinner Quilt," a painted story quilt, which has been exhibited in museums. When African-American Melody visits her Aunt Connie, she meets her aunt's adopted son, Lonnie, a black boy with red hair and green eyes. Before the family dinner, they go into the attic where they see Aunt Connie's portraits of twelve famous African-American women, paintings that speak to the children about their subjects' accomplishments. Lonnie's heritage is revealed in a companion book, *Bonjour, Lonnie*.
African-American-French and non-Jewish/French and Jewish
Primary; Fiction

American-French

African-American-French

Klein, Norma. *Bizou: A Novel*. New York: The Viking Press, 1983. 144 p.

Thirteen-year-old Bizou, whose deceased father was French and whose mother is African-American, is temporarily abandoned by her mother when the two of them travel from France to visit the United States which her mother had left years before. Entrusted to Nicholas, a man they met on the

plane, Bizou travels with him to Vermont and Washington, D.C., before they locate a friend of Bizou's mother in Pennsylvania. It is there that Bizou discovers that she has a half-brother, meets her grandfather, and is reunited with her mother.
French and Jewish/African-American
Older; Fiction

Ringgold, Faith. *Bonjour, Lonnie*. Illustrated by author. New York: Hyperion Books for Children, 1996. 32 p.

Thanks to a Love Bird that flies into Lonnie's window one night, he discovers his family background. During World War I his paternal grandfather was an African-American soldier in France. There he met and married Lonnie's French grandmother and became an opera singer. Their son (Lonnie's father) married a Jewish French woman. During World War II he died fighting for France and, after Lonnie's mother gave him to a friend for his safety, she became a victim of the Nazis. Subsequently, Lonnie was taken to the United States where he was adopted by an African-American couple, Aunt Connie and Uncle Bates. This picture book is a companion book to *Dinner at Aunt Connie's House*.
African-American-French and non-Jewish/French and Jewish
Primary; Fiction

Ringgold, Faith. *Dinner at Aunt Connie's House*. Illustrated by author. New York: Hyperion Books for Children, 1993. 32 p.

This picture book is based on the artist-author's "The Dinner Quilt," a painted story quilt, which has been exhibited in museums. When African-American Melody visits her Aunt Connie, she meets her aunt's adopted son, Lonnie, a black boy with red hair and green eyes. Before the family dinner, they go into the attic where they see Aunt Connie's portraits of twelve famous African-American women, paintings that speak to the children about their subjects' accomplishments. Lonnie's heritage is revealed in a companion book, *Bonjour, Lonnie*.
African-American-French and non-Jewish/French and Jewish
Primary; Fiction

European-American-French

Modiano, Patrick. *Catherine Certitude*. Translated from French by William Rodarmor. Illustrated by Jean-Jacques Sempé. Boston: David R. Godine, 2001. 64 p.

This is the unusual story of the little girl, Catherine Certitude, and her father, who like to take off their glasses so that they can be removed from the real world and enter their own dream worlds. Set in Paris, the book abounds with unresolved questions: the father's actual business, the nature of the difficulty from which his business partner has extricated him, the lack of a listing of the residence where he and Catherine attend a party, the real reasons Catherine's mother went back to the United States, and why Catherine's ballet teacher has assumed a new identity. Within its mysterious overtones, the story presents the warm relationship of Catherine and her father.
French/European-American
Intermediate, Older; Fiction

Jewish-French

Klein, Norma. *Bizou: A Novel*. New York: The Viking Press, 1983. 144 p.

Thirteen-year-old Bizou, whose deceased father was French and whose mother is African-American, is temporarily abandoned by her mother when the two of them travel from France to visit the United States which her mother had left years before. Entrusted to Nicholas, a man they met on the plane, Bizou travels with him to Vermont and Washington, D.C., before they locate a friend of Bizou's mother in Pennsylvania. It is there that Bizou discovers that she has a half-brother, meets her grandfather, and is reunited with her mother.
French and Jewish/African-American
Older; Fiction

Ringgold, Faith. *Bonjour, Lonnie*. Illustrated by author. New York: Hyperion Books for Children, 1996. 32 p.

Thanks to a Love Bird that flies into Lonnie's window one night, he discovers his family background. During World War I his paternal grandfather was an African-American soldier in France. There he met and married Lonnie's French grandmother and became an opera singer. Their son (Lonnie's father) married a Jewish French woman. During World War II he died fighting for France and, after Lonnie's mother gave him to a friend for his safety, she became a victim of the Nazis. Subsequently, Lonnie was taken to the United States where he was adopted by an African-American couple, Aunt Connie and Uncle Bates. This picture book is a companion book to *Dinner at Aunt Connie's House*.
African-American-French and non-Jewish/French and Jewish
Primary; Fiction

Ringgold, Faith. *Dinner at Aunt Connie's House*. Illustrated by author. New York: Hyperion Books for Children, 1993. 32 p.

This picture book is based on the artist-author's "The Dinner Quilt," a painted story quilt, which has been exhibited in museums. When African-American Melody visits her Aunt Connie, she meets her aunt's adopted son, Lonnie, a black boy with red hair and green eyes. Before the family dinner, they go into the attic where they see Aunt Connie's portraits of twelve famous African-American women, paintings that speak to the children about their subjects' accomplishments. Lonnie's heritage is revealed in a companion book, *Bonjour, Lonnie*.
African-American-French and non-Jewish/French and Jewish
Primary; Fiction

German

Bunting, Eve. *Spying on Miss Müller*. New York: Clarion Books, 1995, 192 p.

With the advent of World War II, Miss Müller, a well-liked half-German teacher and dorm mistress in a Belfast boarding school, becomes the "enemy" and the target of students' hostility. Jessie and three other girls suspect that Miss Müller is a spy sending signals to the Germans and decide to

trail her. Their plan becomes ominous when a Polish Jewish girl, who wants to harm Miss Müller, is determined to join them. The story ends with the revelation of Miss Müller's secret and Jessie's revelation of hers.
German/Northern Irish
Intermediate, Older; Fiction

Chotjewitz, David. *Daniel Half Human: And the Good Nazi*. Translated from German by Doris Orgel. New York: Atheneum Books for Young Readers, 2004. 304 p. (A Richard Jackson Book)

In 1933 thirteen-year-old best friends David and Armin paint swastikas on a courtyard wall in a Communist district of Hamburg, Germany. This moving, distressing novel traces the ensuing lives of the two boys. Disdaining Jews, Daniel experiences shock and changing emotions as he discovers and tries to cope with his mother's Jewish heritage. Armin strives to become a Nazi leader, yet keep his friendship with Daniel and have a Jewish girlfriend. The book details the downfall of Daniel's prominent family amidst the tightening of Nazi power and its increasing persecution of Jews. Daniel and his parents emigrate from Germany in July 1939. Returning in 1945 as a member of the American military on loan to the Royal British Army, Daniel must make a decision as to the fate of Armin, who has served in the notorious SS.
German and Protestant/Jewish-German and Protestant
Older; Fiction

Rahlens, Holly-Jane. *Prince William, Maximilian Minsky, and Me*. Cambridge, Mass.: Candlewick Press, 2005. 320 p.

Nelly, who is thirteen and brainy, suddenly has a major crush on England's Prince William. Although she is unathletic, she decides to try out for her Berlin school's basketball team since it will be playing in England. The story relates how she persuades Max, a seemingly weird American-German boy, to be her basketball tutor, how she resents her Jewish-American mother who insists that she have a bat mitzvah, how she discovers that her adored German father is having an affair with Max's mother, and how Prince William is displaced as her love.
German and non-Jewish/Polish-Russian-Jewish-American; European-American/Jewish-German
Older; Fiction

American-German

European-American-German

Rahlens, Holly-Jane. *Prince William, Maximilian Minsky, and Me*. Cambridge, Mass: Candlewick Press, 2005. 320 p.

Nelly, who is thirteen and brainy, suddenly has a major crush on England's Prince William. Although she is unathletic, she decides to try out for her Berlin school's basketball team since it will be playing in England. The story relates how she persuades Max, a seemingly weird American-German boy, to be her basketball tutor, how she resents her Jewish-American mother who insists that she have a bat mitzvah, how she discovers that her adored German father is having an affair with Max's

mother, and how Prince William is displaced as her love.
European-American/Jewish-German
Older; Fiction

European-German

Northern Irish-German

Bunting, Eve. *Spying on Miss Müller*. New York: Clarion Books, 1995, 192 p.

With the advent of World War II, Miss Müller, a well-liked half-German teacher and dorm mistress in a Belfast boarding school, becomes the "enemy" and the target of students' hostility. Jessie and three other girls suspect that Miss Müller is a spy sending signals to the Germans and decide to trail her. Their plan becomes ominous when a Polish Jewish girl, who wants to harm Miss Müller, is determined to join them. The story ends with the revelation of Miss Müller's secret and Jessie's revelation of hers.
German/Northern Irish
Intermediate, Older; Fiction

Polish-German

Rahlens, Holly-Jane. *Prince William, Maximilian Minsky, and Me*. Cambridge, Mass.: Candlewick Press, 2005. 320 p.

Nelly, who is thirteen and brainy, suddenly has a major crush on England's Prince William. Although she is unathletic, she decides to try out for her Berlin school's basketball team since it will be playing in England. The story relates how she persuades Max, a seemingly weird American-German boy, to be her basketball tutor, how she resents her Jewish-American mother who insists that she have a bat mitzvah, how she discovers that her adored German father is having an affair with Max's mother, and how Prince William is displaced as her love.
German and non-Jewish/Polish-Russian-Jewish-American
Older; Fiction

Russian-German

Rahlens, Holly-Jane. *Prince William, Maximilian Minsky, and Me*. Cambridge, Mass.: Candlewick Press, 2005. 320 p.

Nelly, who is thirteen and brainy, suddenly has a major crush on England's Prince William. Although she is unathletic, she decides to try out for her Berlin school's basketball team since it will be playing in England. The story relates how she persuades Max, a seemingly weird American-German boy, to be her basketball tutor, how she resents her Jewish-American mother who insists that she have a bat mitzvah, how she discovers that her adored German father is having an affair with Max's mother, and how Prince William is displaced as her love.

German and non-Jewish/Polish-Russian-Jewish-American
Older; Fiction

Jewish-German

Chotjewitz, David. *Daniel Half Human: And the Good Nazi*. Translated from German by Doris Orgel. New York: Atheneum Books for Young Readers, 2004. 304 p. (A Richard Jackson Book)

In 1933 thirteen-year-old best friends David and Armin paint swastikas on a courtyard wall in a Communist district of Hamburg, Germany. This moving, distressing novel traces the ensuing lives of the two boys. Disdaining Jews, Daniel experiences shock and changing emotions as he discovers and tries to cope with his mother's Jewish heritage. Armin strives to become a Nazi leader, yet keep his friendship with Daniel and have a Jewish girlfriend. The book details the downfall of Daniel's prominent family amidst the tightening of Nazi power and its increasing persecution of Jews. Daniel and his parents emigrate from Germany in July 1939. Returning in 1945 as a member of the American military on loan to the Royal British Army, Daniel must make a decision as to the fate of Armin, who has served in the notorious SS.
German and Protestant/Jewish-German and Protestant
Older; Fiction

Gehrts, Barbara. *Don't Say a Word*. Translated from German by Elizabeth D. Crawford. New York: Margaret K. McElderry Books, 1986. 176 p.

This book presents, with only a few changes and the use of fictional names, the moving account of the author's adolescence in Germany during World War II. As part of a close extended Christian family which hated Hitler, she endured the death on the Russian front of a cousin whom she loved, the death of her brother from an ear infection which the military ignored, and the execution of her father, a colonel in the Luftwaffe, for "undermining the war effort." Her friend who was half-Jewish committed suicide together with the other members of her family when a gallows was set up in front of their home.
German Jewish and German non-Jewish
Older; Nonfiction

Nichols, Joan Kane. *All But the Right Folks*. Owings Mills, Md.: Stemmer House Publishers, 1985. 112 p.

Danny doesn't realize he is half white until he meets his grandmother Helga and goes to spend the summer with her in New York City. Suffering from asthma, bed-wetting, and teasing at his San Francisco school, Danny enjoys New York as he bikes with his grandmother; befriends Thelma Jean, her little brother Willy, and Charlayne; and starts learning karate from Charlayne's older sister. However, his new friends, two of whom are of mixed heritage, reject him because he lied that Helga was his nanny. Further, he worries that his deceased mother was a druggie like his Uncle Billy; his father insists that Danny is black and is not proud of him; and he discovers that Helga has lied to him. Everything improves when Danny uses his karate mental and kicking skills to escape kidnappers, and

he decides that he is a bridge between black and white.
German non-Jewish/German Jewish
Intermediate; Fiction

Rahlens, Holly-Jane. *Prince William, Maximilian Minsky, and Me*. Cambridge, Mass.: Candlewick Press, 2005. 320 p.

    Nelly, who is thirteen and brainy, suddenly has a major crush on England's Prince William. Although she is unathletic, she decides to try out for her Berlin school's basketball team since it will be playing in England. The story relates how she persuades Max, a seemingly weird American-German boy, to be her basketball tutor, how she resents her Jewish-American mother who insists that she have a bat mitzvah, how she discovers that her adored German father is having an affair with Max's mother, and how Prince William is displaced as her love.
German and non-Jewish/Polish-Russian-Jewish-American; European-American/Jewish-German
Older; Fiction

Watts, Irene N. *Finding Sophie*. Plattsburgh, N.Y.: Tundra Books of Northern New York, 2002. 144 p.

    This book, which is a sequel to and contains excerpts from *Good-bye Marianne* and *Remember Me*, relates what happened to seven-year-old Sophie whose mother placed her on the 1938 *Kindertransport* train in Berlin and told eleven-year-old Marianne to look after her. Sophie went to live with "Aunt Em," a friend of her parents, and loves being with her as well as life in England. Now, turning fourteen-years-old, Sophie hopes that after the war she will not have to return to Germany and the parents she barely remembers. By chance she and Marianne are reunited, and Sophie participates in the May 1945 celebration of Germany's defeat. Shortly thereafter she receives a letter from her father containing both the happy news that he has survived the Dachau Concentration Camp and the sorrowful news that her mother was killed in an air raid. Sophie's concerns about her future are happily resolved when she remains with Aunt Em and her father comes to live nearby.
German and Jewish/German and Christian
Intermediate, Older; Fiction

Hungarian

Ibbotson, Eva. *The Star of Kazan*. Illustrated by Kevin Hawkes. New York: Dutton Children's Books, 2004. 416 p.

    Celebrating the Vienna of the early 1900s and especially its Lippizaner stallions, this book tells how, as a foundling, Annika had been taken in by two Viennese women who are servants in the house of three professors. Raised in a warm family atmosphere by the five of them, with two best friends, and a close relationship with an elderly neighbor, Annika leads a happy life, but dreams that her mother will someday arrive. What happens next involves the trunk with its "fake" jewels which the old woman leaves to Annika, the discovery by her "mother" of the truth about the jewels, Annika's restricted life as an aristocrat in a moated house in Germany, her friendship with the stable boy whose mother was a gypsy, and the extraordinary actions on her behalf by those who love her.

Hungarian/Hungarian Romani
Intermediate, Older; Fiction

Romani-Hungarian

Ibbotson, Eva. *The Star of Kazan*. Illustrated by Kevin Hawkes. New York: Dutton Children's Books, 2004. 416 p.

Celebrating the Vienna of the early 1900s and especially its Lippizaner stallions, this book tells how, as a foundling, Annika had been taken in by two Viennese women who are servants in the house of three professors. Raised in a warm family atmosphere by the five of them, with two best friends, and a close relationship with an elderly neighbor, Annika leads a happy life, but dreams that her mother will someday arrive. What happens next involves the trunk with its "fake" jewels which the old woman leaves to Annika, the discovery by her "mother" of the truth about the jewels, Annika's restricted life as an aristocrat in a moated house in Germany, her friendship with the stable boy whose mother was a gypsy, and the extraordinary actions on her behalf by those who love her.
Hungarian/Hungarian Romani
Intermediate, Older; Fiction

Irish

Quinn, John. *Duck and Swan*. Dublin: Poolbeg, 1993. 160 p.

When twelve-year-old Emer comes back from a field trip to Dublin, she discovers a black boy under the broken bus seat in front of her. She keeps his existence a secret as he hides in a school bicycle shed, in a chapel, and with a welcoming older couple, Granny Flynn and her blind husband Tom, who teaches him the Irish sport of hurling. The boy, who is known as Duck, has run away from an institution for troubled children where he was placed after his father returned to his native Nigeria and his Irish mother was jailed for selling drugs. Duck finally emerges from hiding to join a hurling team and, despite racial animosity, is finally accepted by Emer's classmates and the community.
Nigerian/Irish
Older; Fiction

Raphael, Marie. *A Boy from Ireland: A Novel*. New York: Persea Books, 2007. 224 p.

When his Irish mother dies, fourteen-year-old Liam and his older sister must move across Ireland to Connemara to stay with his mother's brother. Living in 1901 in a country which had suffered from English persecution, Liam's uncle hates the children and Liam's schoolmates bully him because of his English blood. Liam and his sister accompany their uncle, their uncle's friend, and the friend's son Colin, one of Liam's tormentors, on a trip to New York City's Hell's Kitchen. Liam is determined to find his English father who had left the family when he was little. When Colin secures letters that reveal Liam's father's whereabouts, he uses them to blackmail Liam, including getting him to snatch a purse and ride a dangerous horse. There are unexpected consequences of Liam's actions, but he finally learns to live in the present, not in his unrealistic dream.

English/Irish
Older; Fiction

English-Irish

Raphael, Marie. *A Boy from Ireland: A Novel*. New York: Persea Books, 2007. 224 p.

When his Irish mother dies, fourteen-year-old Liam and his older sister must move across Ireland to Connemara to stay with his mother's brother. Living in 1901 in a country which had suffered from English persecution, Liam's uncle hates the children and Liam's schoolmates bully him because of his English blood. Liam and his sister accompany their uncle, their uncle's friend, and the friend's son Colin, one of Liam's tormentors, on a trip to New York City's Hell's Kitchen. Liam is determined to find his English father who had left the family when he was little. When Colin secures letters that reveal Liam's father's whereabouts, he uses them to blackmail Liam, including getting him to snatch a purse and ride a dangerous horse. There are unexpected consequences of Liam's actions, but he finally learns to live in the present, not in his unrealistic dream.
English/Irish
Older; Fiction

Nigerian-Irish

Quinn, John. *Duck and Swan*. Dublin: Poolbeg, 1993. 160 p.

When twelve-year-old Emer comes back from a field trip to Dublin, she discovers a black boy under the broken bus seat in front of her. She keeps his existence a secret as he hides in a school bicycle shed, in a chapel, and with a welcoming older couple, Granny Flynn and her blind husband Tom, who teaches him the Irish sport of hurling. The boy, who is known as Duck, has run away from an institution for troubled children where he was placed after his father returned to his native Nigeria and his Irish mother was jailed for selling drugs. Duck finally emerges from hiding to join a hurling team and, despite racial animosity, is finally accepted by Emer's classmates and the community.
Nigerian/Irish
Older; Fiction

Italian

German-Italian

Easton, Kelly. *White Magic: Spells to Hold You: A Novel*. New York: Wendy Lamb Books, 2007. 208 p.

This is the story of three high school sophomore friends: Yvonne, whose half-German, half-gypsy father had stolen her from her gypsy mother in Italy when she was six and who practices witchcraft; Karen, who is boy-crazy and has low self-esteem; and Chrissie, who misses her Vermont home and her deceased father and hates both being in California and her mother's having a boyfriend. All their lives change as Chrissie joins Yvonne and Karen in their coven; Karen has a terrible sexual experience and then almost drowns; Chrissie's mother gets married; and Yvonne's mother suddenly appears.

German and Romani/Romani
Older; Fiction

Romani-Italian

Easton, Kelly. *White Magic: Spells to Hold You: A Novel*. New York: Wendy Lamb Books, 2007. 208 p.

This is the story of three high school sophomore friends: Yvonne, whose half-German, half-gypsy father had stolen her from her gypsy mother in Italy when she was six and who practices witchcraft; Karen, who is boy-crazy and has low self-esteem; and Chrissie, who misses her Vermont home and her deceased father and hates both being in California and her mother's having a boyfriend. All their lives change as Chrissie joins Yvonne and Karen in their coven; Karen has a terrible sexual experience and then almost drowns; Chrissie's mother gets married; and Yvonne's mother suddenly appears.
German and Romani/Romani
Older; Fiction

Polish

Scott, Elaine. *Secrets of the Cirque Medrano: A Novel*. Watertown, Mass.: Charlesbridge, 2008. 216 p.

In 1904 after her mother dies, fourteen-year-old Brigitte leaves her Warsaw home to go to live with her Parisian aunt and uncle and work in their Café Dominique. There she endures the unpleasantness of Henri, a young Russian coworker, and often serves Russian Monsieur Pavlov and Pablo Picasso. Brigitte is bored with her life and longs to be at the nearby Cirque Medrano where she befriends a young acrobat-trapeze artist, Paco, and his sister. However, she gets more excitement than she bargained for when, spying on Monsieur Pavlov, she is trapped inside the headquarters of the Russian secret police and then, with Paco, enters Picasso's studio to prevent Henri from destroying Picasso's masterpiece, "Family of Saltimbanques." It is then that Brigitte realizes that the café has become her home.
Polish/French
Older; Fiction

French-Polish

Scott, Elaine. *Secrets of the Cirque Medrano: A Novel*. Watertown, Mass.: Charlesbridge, 2008. 216 p.

In 1904 after her mother dies, fourteen-year-old Brigitte leaves her Warsaw home to go to live with her Parisian aunt and uncle and work in their Café Dominique. There she endures the unpleasantness of Henri, a young Russian coworker, and often serves Russian Monsieur Pavlov and Pablo Picasso. Brigitte is bored with her life and longs to be at the nearby Cirque Medrano where she befriends a young acrobat-trapeze artist, Paco, and his sister. However, she gets more excitement than she bargained for when, spying on Monsieur Pavlov, she is trapped inside the headquarters of the Russian secret police and then, with Paco, enters Picasso's studio to prevent Henri from destroying Picasso's masterpiece, "Family of Saltimbanques." It is then that Brigitte realizes that the café has become her home.

Polish/French
Older; Fiction

Jewish-Polish

Orlev, Uri. *The Man from the Other Side*. Translated from Hebrew by Hillel Halkin. Boston: Houghton Mifflin Company, 1991. 192 p.

During the German occupation of Poland during World War II, fourteen-year-old Marek joins other boys in robbing a Jew who had escaped from the Warsaw ghetto. When his mother finds out she tells Marek that he had sentenced the Jew to death and reveals that Marek's father, who died when he was four, was a Jew. Consumed with guilt, Marek discovers Pan Jozek, an escaped Jew, and manages to get him into a safe hiding place. When Pan Jozek wants to return to join the Jews in their ghetto uprising, Marek, who has accompanied his stepfather through the sewers of Warsaw when he smuggled food into the Jewish ghetto, guides Pan Jozek through the underground tunnels. Marek is stuck in the ghetto when part of the tunnel collapses from an explosion and joins the Jews in fighting the Germans. He is rescued by his much-resented stepfather and finally agrees to be adopted as his son.
Jewish-Polish/Polish and Catholic
Older; Fiction

Scandinavian

Viking

Foreman, Michael, and Richard Seaver. *The Boy Who Sailed with Columbus*. Illustrated by Michael Foreman. New York: Arcade Publishing, 1992. 72 p.

An orphan, twelve-year-old Leif sails as a ship's boy on Christopher Columbus's first voyage to the West Indies. His admiration for Columbus changes when Leif sees that Columbus is taking some of the island natives back to Spain. As a punishment for a mistake he had made, Leif is left behind with some of Columbus's crew on one of the islands. There he is kidnapped by Arawak, who attack the island fort. Leif then serves as the eyes for a wise blind Secotan healer who was with the Arawak and travels with him among different tribes. Becoming the medicine man's successor, Leif, who is half Viking, marries a Secotan. As a grandfather in the Secotan village [which was probably in present day North Carolina on or near Roanoke Island], Leif sees approaching European ships and leads the Secotan villagers westward to avoid possible capture.
Viking/other
Intermediate; Fiction

Spanish

See   de Pareja, Juan

African-Spanish

See de Pareja, Juan

H. Mexican

See   Ronstadt, Federico (Fred) Jose María

De la Peña, Matt. *Mexican Whiteboy*. New York: Delacorte Press, 2008. 256 p.

    Sixteen-year-old Danny chooses to spend his summer vacation with his Mexican-American father's family in National City, California, so that he can then fly to Ensenada, Mexico, and find his father. Since his father left his San Diego family three years earlier, Danny has been heartbroken to the extent that he seldom speaks, not wanting to use his mother's English. His goal is to please his father by becoming a great pitcher. He has exceptional talent, but is plagued by his lack of control. During the eventful summer Danny makes an unlikely best friend, Uno, who initially punched Danny. Uno needs to make money so that he can move away from his Mexican-American mother and step-father and live with his black father. Through hours of practice with Uno, Danny works on his pitching skills and discovers how to keep the ball in the strike zone when people are watching. Together Uno and Danny successfully hustle the area's best hitters, thereby earning money for Uno. Although he cannot speak Spanish and she cannot speak English, Danny falls in love with Liberty, who is newly arrived from Mexico and has a white father. Further, Danny finally finds out the truth about his father and comes to accept himself.
European-American/Mexican
Older; Fiction

American-Mexican

European-American-Mexican

De la Peña, Matt. *Mexican Whiteboy*. New York: Delacorte Press, 2008. 256 p.

    Sixteen-year-old Danny chooses to spend his summer vacation with his Mexican-American father's family in National City, California, so that he can then fly to Ensenada, Mexico, and find his father. Since his father left his San Diego family three years earlier, Danny has been heartbroken to the extent that he seldom speaks, not wanting to use his mother's English. His goal is to please his father by becoming a great pitcher. He has exceptional talent, but is plagued by his lack of control. During the eventful summer Danny makes an unlikely best friend, Uno, who initially punched Danny. Uno needs to make money so that he can move away from his Mexican-American mother and step-father and live with his black father. Through hours of practice with Uno, Danny works on his pitching skills and discovers how to keep the ball in the strike zone when people are watching. Together Uno and Danny successfully hustle the area's best hitters, thereby earning money for Uno. Although he cannot speak Spanish and she cannot speak English, Danny falls in love with Liberty, who is newly arrived from Mexico and has a white father. Further, Danny finally finds out the truth about his father and comes to accept himself.
European-American/Mexican
Older; Fiction

Asian-Mexican

Lebanese-Mexican

See   Hayek-Jiménez, Salma Valgarma

European-Mexican

German-Mexican

See   Ronstadt, Federico (Fred) Jose María

Spanish-Mexican

See   Hayek-Jiménez, Salma Valgarma

Merino, José María. *The Gold of Dreams*. Translated by Helen Lane. New York: Farrar, Straus and Giroux, 1994. 224 p. (A Sunburst Book)
   Living in a village near Mexico City in the sixteenth century, Miguel is the son of a Spanish Conquistador father who disappeared years ago and a Native Mexican mother. When he is fifteen, Miguel goes with his Spanish godfather on a mission to find the kingdom of Queen Yupaha and bring back its gold. During the long and difficult journey Miguel witnesses the cruelties of both the Spaniards and the Indians, engages in battle, is captured by Indians, finds his father, and learns that the reported gold of Queen Yupaha is a myth. Miguel makes close friends, including an Indian boy, who having earlier been captured by the Spaniards and taken to Spain, now finds it difficult to fit into either culture.
Spanish and Catholic/Native Mexican and non-Christian
Older; Fiction

Native Mexican

Merino, José María. *The Gold of Dreams*. Translated by Helen Lane. New York: Farrar, Straus and Giroux, 1994. 224 p. (A Sunburst Book)
   Living in a village near Mexico City in the sixteenth century, Miguel is the son of a Spanish Conquistador father who disappeared years ago and a Native Mexican mother. When he is fifteen, Miguel goes with his Spanish godfather on a mission to find the kingdom of Queen Yupaha and bring back its gold. During the long and difficult journey Miguel witnesses the cruelties of both the Spaniards and the Indians, engages in battle, is captured by Indians, finds his father, and learns that the reported gold of Queen Yupaha is a myth. Miguel makes close friends, including an Indian boy, who having earlier been captured by the Spaniards and taken to Spain, now finds it difficult to fit into either culture.
Spanish and Catholic/Native Mexican and non-Christian
Older; Fiction

I. Oceanian

Australian

Aboriginal Australian

Hill, Anthony. *The Burnt Stick*. Illustrated by Mark Sofilas. Boston: Houghton Mifflin Company, 1995. 64 p.

John Jagamarra's mother tries in vain to save him from being taken to a distant mission where, with other mixed race children, he will be raised by whites. Twice she fools the authorities by darkening his light brown skin with a burnt stick. However, the authorities catch on to her deception and remove John, who is not yet five-years-old. John never forgets his mother and Aboriginal life, and, as a grown man, reclaims his Aboriginal heritage.
European-Australian/Aboriginal-Australian
Intermediate; Fiction

Asian-Australian

Chinese-Australian

Murray, Kirsty. *The Secret Life of Maeve Lee Kwong*. Crows Nest, Australia: Allen & Unwin, 2006. 264 p. (Children of the Wind)

Thirteen-year-old Maeve's life turns upside down when her mother dies in an automobile accident. Unable to live with her baby half-brother and her stepfather because he has not adopted her, she stays with her mother's traditional Chinese parents and at her school's boarding house. It is with the support of her two best friends, a caring teacher who tells her of secret lives, a boy with whom she dances in *Seussmania*, and then her entire family that Maeve goes on a school trip to Ireland where she finds and meets her father, who was unaware of her existence.
Irish/Chinese-Australian
Intermediate, Older; Fiction

Indian-Australian

Clarke, Judith. *Kalpana's Dream*. Asheville, N.C.: Front Street, 2005. 168 p.

Tied together by the dreaded essay "Who Am I" which Ms. Dallimore assigns her English class, this novel is one of dreams and of finding one's true self. Katie discovers that whoever she is, she doesn't hate her pesky little sister. Her friend Neema meets the boy whom she keeps associating with sheep and shepherd, comes to treasure her Indian great-grandmother Kalpana, and realizes her own worth as Nirmolini, her Indian name. Kalpana, traveling alone to Australia, forces herself to speak English and fulfils her dream of skimming quickly over the ground (by skateboard) and of seeing her late husband's face (when Neema smiles). In conclusion, the rumor about Ms. Dallimore is true. She

is the Bride of Dracula.
Australian/Indian
Older; Fiction

European-Australian

Clarke, Judith. *Kalpana's Dream*. Asheville, N.C.: Front Street, 2005. 168 p.

Tied together by the dreaded essay "Who Am I" which Ms. Dallimore assigns her English class, this novel is one of dreams and of finding one's true self. Katie discovers that whoever she is, she doesn't hate her pesky little sister. Her friend Neema meets the boy whom she keeps associating with sheep and shepherd, comes to treasure her Indian great-grandmother Kalpana, and realizes her own worth as Nirmolini, her Indian name. Kalpana, traveling alone to Australia, forces herself to speak English and fulfils her dream of skimming quickly over the ground (by skateboard) and of seeing her late husband's face (when Neema smiles). In conclusion, the rumor about Ms. Dallimore is true. She is the Bride of Dracula.
Australian/Indian
Older; Fiction

Hill, Anthony. *The Burnt Stick*. Illustrated by Mark Sofilas. Boston: Houghton Mifflin Company, 1995. 64 p.

John Jagamarra's mother tries in vain to save him from being taken to a distant mission where, with other mixed race children, he will be raised by whites. Twice she fools the authorities by darkening his light brown skin with a burnt stick. However, the authorities catch on to her deception and remove John, who is not yet five-years-old. John never forgets his mother and Aboriginal life, and, as a grown man, reclaims his Aboriginal heritage.
European-Australian/Aboriginal-Australian
Intermediate; Fiction

Irish-Australian

Murray, Kirsty. *The Secret Life of Maeve Lee Kwong*. Crows Nest, Australia: Allen & Unwin, 2006. 264 p. (Children of the Wind)

Thirteen-year-old Maeve's life turns upside down when her mother dies in an automobile accident. Unable to live with her baby half-brother and her stepfather because he has not adopted her, she stays with her mother's traditional Chinese parents and at her school's boarding house. It is with the support of her two best friends, a caring teacher who tells her of secret lives, a boy with whom she dances in *Seussmania*, and then her entire family that Maeve goes on a school trip to Ireland where she finds and meets her father, who was unaware of her existence.
Irish/Chinese-Australian
Intermediate, Older; Fiction

New Zealander

European-New Zealander

Savage, Deborah. *A Stranger Calls Me Home*. Boston: Houghton Mifflin Company, 1992. 240 p.

A portrait of Paul's great-great-grandfather showing his hand on a partially opened box of bones with a carved Maori taniwha (a spiritually powerful force) on the lid affects the interconnected lives of three New Zealand teenagers: Paul, whose father is New Zealander and mother American; Simon, who has learned that his real father is Maori and who lives with his Irish mother and Italian-New Zealander stepfather; and Fiona, a white New Zealander who has been largely raised by a Maori woman and who discovers that she is Paul's cousin. The three new friends try to come to grips with their pasts and with the underlying issue of whether the Maori should be able to take back the sacred land which had been taken from them by Paul and Fiona's ancestor, the land that is lonely Fiona's "place."

European-New Zealander/European-American
Older; Fiction

Irish-New Zealander

Savage, Deborah. *A Stranger Calls Me Home*. Boston: Houghton Mifflin Company, 1992. 240 p.

A portrait of Paul's great-great-grandfather showing his hand on a partially opened box of bones with a carved Maori taniwha (a spiritually powerful force) on the lid affects the interconnected lives of three New Zealand teenagers: Paul, whose father is New Zealander and mother American; Simon, who has learned that his real father is Maori and who lives with his Irish mother and Italian-New Zealander stepfather; and Fiona, a white New Zealander who has been largely raised by a Maori woman and who discovers that she is Paul's cousin. The three new friends try to come to grips with their pasts and with the underlying issue of whether the Maori should be able to take back the sacred land which had been taken from them by Paul and Fiona's ancestor, the land that is lonely Fiona's "place."

Maori New Zealander/Irish
Older; Fiction

European-American-New Zealander

Savage, Deborah. *A Stranger Calls Me Home*. Boston: Houghton Mifflin Company, 1992. 240 p.

A portrait of Paul's great-great-grandfather showing his hand on a partially opened box of bones with a carved Maori taniwha (a spiritually powerful force) on the lid affects the interconnected lives of three New Zealand teenagers: Paul, whose father is New Zealander and mother American; Simon, who has learned that his real father is Maori and who lives with his Irish mother and Italian-New Zealander stepfather; and Fiona, a white New Zealander who has been largely raised by a Maori woman and who discovers that she is Paul's cousin. The three new friends try to come to grips with their pasts and with the underlying issue of whether the Maori should be able to take back the sacred land which had been taken from them by Paul and Fiona's ancestor, the land that is lonely Fiona's "place."

European-New Zealander/European-American
Older; Fiction

Maori-New Zealander

Savage, Deborah. *A Stranger Calls Me Home*. Boston: Houghton Mifflin Company, 1992. 240 p.

A portrait of Paul's great-great-grandfather showing his hand on a partially opened box of bones with a carved Maori taniwha (a spiritually powerful force) on the lid affects the interconnected lives of three New Zealand teenagers: Paul, whose father is New Zealander and mother American; Simon, who has learned that his real father is Maori and who lives with his Irish mother and Italian-New Zealander stepfather; and Fiona, a white New Zealander who has been largely raised by a Maori woman and who discovers that she is Paul's cousin. The three new friends try to come to grips with their pasts and with the underlying issue of whether the Maori should be able to take back the sacred land which had been taken from them by Paul and Fiona's ancestor, the land that is lonely Fiona's "place."
Maori-New Zealander/Irish
Older; Fiction

Pitcairner

English-Pitcairner

Rinaldi, Ann. *Mutiny's Daughter*. New York: HarperTrophy, 2005. 224 p.

In this book of historical fiction, Mary is the daughter of Fletcher Christian, who took over the HMS Bounty in the famous mutiny of 1789. Born three years later on Pitcairn Island, Mary is brought by him at the age of five to his family's Isle of Man home. Wanted by the authorities, Fletcher disappears and Mary lives as the daughter of his brother Charles. Sent to a boarding school in London at age fourteen, Mary must protect the secret of her identity and longs to see her father. She is blackmailed by one of the girls who uncovers her secret and helped by a twelve-year-old street boy, who also discovers the truth. By the end of the story, Mary learns who of the people she has met is, in fact, her father.
English/Tahitian
Intermediate, Older; Fiction

Tahitian-Pitcairner

Rinaldi, Ann. *Mutiny's Daughter*. New York: HarperTrophy, 2005. 224 p.

In this book of historical fiction, Mary is the daughter of Fletcher Christian, who took over the HMS Bounty in the famous mutiny of 1789. Born three years later on Pitcairn Island, Mary is brought by him at the age of five to his family's Isle of Man home. Wanted by the authorities, Fletcher disappears and Mary lives as the daughter of his brother Charles. Sent to a boarding school in London at age fourteen, Mary must protect the secret of her identity and longs to see her father. She is blackmailed by one of the girls who uncovers her secret and helped by a twelve-year-old street boy, who also discovers the truth. By the end of the story, Mary learns who of the people she has met is, in fact, her father.

English/Tahitian

Intermediate, Older; Fiction

J. South American

Argentine

European-Argentine

English-Argentine

See   Borges, Jorge Luis

Portuguese-Argentine

See   Borges, Jorge Luis

Spanish-Argentine

See   Borges, Jorge Luis

Uruguayan-Argentine

See   Borges, Jorge Luis

Brazilian

Allende, Isabel. *City of the Beasts*. Translated from the Spanish by Margaret Sayers Peden. New York: HarperCollins Publishers, 2002. 416 p.

    Fifteen-year-old Alex, his intrepid grandmother, twelve-year-old Nadia, who is Canadian-Brazilian, and her father are part of an expedition seeking the Beast, the Yeti-like creature rumored to live in the Amazon jungle along the Brazilian-Venezuelan border. In this story of adventure and the spiritual world, Alex and Nadia discover their totemic animals, are kidnapped by Indians of the Stone Age, travel to the mountain of the gods, see the Beasts, go on individual quests, and help prevent the Indians from being injected with the measles virus and being exploited by the modern world. Although Nadia is also in the sequels, *Kingdom of the Golden Dragon* and *Forest of the Pygmies*, she is referred to as Brazilian with no mention of her mixed heritage.

Brazilian/Canadian

Older; Fiction

Canadian-Brazilian

Allende, Isabel. *City of the Beasts*. Translated from the Spanish by Margaret Sayers Peden. New York: HarperCollins Publishers, 2002. 416 p.

Fifteen-year-old Alex, his intrepid grandmother, twelve-year-old Nadia, who is Canadian-Brazilian, and her father are part of an expedition seeking the Beast, the Yeti-like creature rumored to live in the Amazon jungle along the Brazilian-Venezuelan border. In this story of adventure and the spiritual world, Alex and Nadia discover their totemic animals, are kidnapped by Indians of the Stone Age, travel to the mountain of the gods, see the Beasts, go on individual quests, and help prevent the Indians from being injected with the measles virus and being exploited by the modern world. Although Nadia is also in the sequels, *Kingdom of the Golden Dragon* and *Forest of the Pygmies*, she is referred to as Brazilian with no mention of her mixed heritage.
Brazilian/Canadian
Older; Fiction

English-Brazilian

Ibbotson, Eva. *Journey to the River Sea*. Illustrated by Kevin Hawkes. New York: Dutton Children's Books, 2001. 304 p.

When in 1910 Maia, an orphan, is sent from London to live with her dreadful English relatives in Brazil, she meets two boys: Clovis, a homesick English actor in a traveling company, and Finn, whose Brazilian Indian mother died during his birth and whose naturalist English father has just died. When agents of Finn's grandfather arrive to take him to England, Finn, who loves the Amazon, hides at his father's hut. Then, with Maia's help, Clovis pretends to be Finn and is taken to Finn's grandfather's estate. All seems well as Finn, Maia, Maia's governess, and an older museum curator from Manaus, Brazil, enjoy going by boat deep into the Amazon rainforest, but events take several unexpected turns.
English/Native Brazilian
Intermediate, Older; Fiction

Native Brazilian

Ibbotson, Eva. *Journey to the River Sea*. Illustrated by Kevin Hawkes. New York: Dutton Children's Books, 2001. 304 p.

When in 1910 Maia, an orphan, is sent from London to live with her dreadful English relatives in Brazil, she meets two boys: Clovis, a homesick English actor in a traveling company, and Finn, whose Brazilian Indian mother died during his birth and whose naturalist English father has just died. When agents of Finn's grandfather arrive to take him to England, Finn, who loves the Amazon, hides at his father's hut. Then, with Maia's help, Clovis pretends to be Finn and is taken to Finn's grandfather's estate. All seems well as Finn, Maia, Maia's governess, and an older museum curator from Manaus, Brazil, enjoy going by boat deep into the Amazon rainforest, but events take several unexpected turns.
English/Native Brazilian
Intermediate, Older; Fiction

Surinamese

African-Surinamese

See   Matzeliger, Jan Ernst

Dutch-Surinamese

See   Matzeliger, Jan Ernst

K. West Indian

Haitian

African-Haitian

See   Du Sable, Jean Baptiste Pointe

Forrester, Sandra. *Dust from Old Bones*. New York: Morrow Junior Books, 1999. 176 p.
This story is set in the stratified society of the New Orleans of 1838. Thirteen-year-old Simone, who is a person of color, struggles with the probability that her pretty cousin Claire-Marie will go to quadroon balls and be chosen by a Creole "protector" [as his mistress]. She envies the life of Madelon, her aunt who lives in France where she is not faced with racial discrimination. Nevertheless, Simone comes to realize that her restricted life as a person of color is much better than that of black slaves, who if lucky enough to be freed had to leave New Orleans. Simone's admiration for Madelon, who comes to visit, disappears when she betrays not only Simone, but also the two slaves she was committed to free. It is Simone who leads the slaves through a swamp to a safe house.
African-Creole-Haitian
Older; Fiction

Beninese-Haitian

Vaught, Susan. *Stormwitch*. New York: Bloomsbury, 2005. 208 p.
In 1969 sixteen-year-old Ruba, who has come from Haiti, finds it hard to adjust to life with her African-American grandmother in Pas Christian, Mississippi. Believing herself the last of the Dahomean Amazon women, Ruba practices voodoo, whereas her grandmother is a Baptist who faced danger in the 1964 Freedom Summer and advocates push, not shove for black rights. Ruba feels that she was responsible for the death of her Haitian grandmother during a hurricane there. Together with her grandmother, two other relatives, and two neighbors, Ruba is captured by the son of a Ku Klux Klan Grand Wizard during Hurricane Camille. During the destructive hurricane Ruba bests Zashar, the evil stormwitch, and everyone is saved.
African-American/Dahomean
Older; Fiction

Dahomean-Haitian. See Beninese-Haitian

American-Haitian

African-American-Haitian

Vaught, Susan. *Stormwitch*. New York: Bloomsbury, 2005. 208 p.
In 1969 sixteen-year-old Ruba, who has come from Haiti, finds it hard to adjust to life with her

African-American grandmother in Pas Christian, Mississippi. Believing herself the last of the Dahomean Amazon women, Ruba practices voodoo, whereas her grandmother is a Baptist who faced danger in the 1964 Freedom Summer and advocates push, not shove for black rights. Ruba feels that she was responsible for the death of her Haitian grandmother during a hurricane there. Together with her grandmother, two other relatives, and two neighbors, Ruba is captured by the son of a Ku Klux Klan Grand Wizard during Hurricane Camille. During the destructive hurricane Ruba bests Zashar, the evil stormwitch, and everyone is saved.
African-American/Dahomean-Haitian
Older; Fiction

Creole-Haitian

Forrester, Sandra. *Dust from Old Bones*. New York: Morrow Junior Books, 1999. 176 p.
This story is set in the stratified society of the New Orleans of 1838. Thirteen-year-old Simone, who is a person of color, struggles with the probability that her pretty cousin Claire-Marie will go to quadroon balls and be chosen by a Creole "protector" [as his mistress]. She envies the life of Madelon, her aunt who lives in France where she is not faced with racial discrimination. Nevertheless, Simone comes to realize that her restricted life as a person of color is much better than that of black slaves, who if lucky enough to be freed had to leave New Orleans. Simone's admiration for Madelon, who comes to visit, disappears when she betrays not only Simone, but also the two slaves she was committed to free. It is Simone who leads the slaves through a swamp to a safe house.
African-Creole-Haitian
Older; Fiction

European-Haitian

French-Haitian

See   Du Sable, Jean Baptiste Pointe

Jamaican

African-Jamaican

See   Marley, Nesta Robert (Bob)
       McCallum, Shara
       Russwurm, John Brown

Landau, Elaine. *Interracial Dating and Marriage*. New York: Julian Messner, 1993. 112 p.
This book's introduction presents two detailed histories of interracial marriage: the first of African-American intermarriage with Caucasians and the second of intermarrages involving Japanese-Americans. In both cases the introduction describes factors, including governmental actions

and societal attitudes, which affected the frequency of these marriages. The bulk of the book presents interviews with ten teenagers and five adults or adult couples who describe their views of and/or experiences with interracial dating and marriage. Seven of the teens interviewed came to the United States from other countries; two of the teens are interracial. Two of the adult interviews are with interracial couples; another contains advice from a minister. A resource list and an index are included.
African-Jamaican/African-Chinese-Jamaican
Older; Nonfiction

American-Jamaican

European-American-Jamaican

See   Russworm, John Brown

Asian-Jamaican

Chinese-Jamaican

Landau, Elaine. *Interracial Dating and Marriage*. New York: Julian Messner, 1993. 112 p.

This book's introduction presents two detailed histories of interracial marriage: the first of African-American intermarriage with Caucasians and the second of intermarrages involving Japanese-Americans. In both cases the introduction describes factors, including governmental actions and societal attitudes, which affected the frequency of these marriages. The bulk of the book presents interviews with ten teenagers and five adults or adult couples who describe their views of and/or experiences with interracial dating and marriage. Seven of the teens interviewed came to the United States from other countries; two of the teens are interracial. Two of the adult interviews are with interracial couples; another contains advice from a minister. A resource list and an index are included.
African-Jamaican/African-Chinese-Jamaican
Older; Nonfiction

Indian-Jamaican

See   McCallum, Shara

European-Jamaican

English-Jamaican

See   Marley, Nesta Robert (Bob)
       McCallum, Shara

Portuguese-Jamaican

See   McCallum, Shara

Scottish-Jamaican

See   McCallum, Shara

Jewish-Jamaican

See   McCallum, Shara

South American-Jamaican

Venezuelan-Jamaican

See   McCallum, Shara

Trinidadian and Tobagonian

Trinidadian

African-Trinidadian

Singer, Marilyn, ed. *Face Relations: 11 Stories about Seeing beyond Color*. New York: Simon & Schuster Books for Young Readers, 2004. 240 p.

In "Gold" by Marina Budhos fifteen-year-old Jemma, who has moved from Trinidad to New Jersey, goes out with Jared and comes to realize that they are going too far in their relatiionship. Then, when Jared apologizes to her mother, Jemma recognizes how good he is and that for them, as for her parents, differences in heritage do not matter.
African-Indian-Trinidadian/African-Trinidadian
Older; Fiction

Indian-Trinidadian

Singer, Marilyn, ed. *Face Relations: 11 Stories about Seeing beyond Color*. New York: Simon & Schuster Books for Young Readers, 2004. 240 p.

In "Gold" by Marina Budhos fifteen-year-old Jemma, who has moved from Trinidad to New Jersey, goes out with Jared and comes to realize that they are going too far in their relatiionship. Then, when Jared apologizes to her mother, Jemma recognizes how good he is and that for them, as for her parents, differences in heritage do not matter.

African-Indian-Trinidadian/African-Trinidadian
Older; Fiction

III. Persons of Mixed Religious Heritage

Introduction

Books about individual persons of mixed religious heritage are covered in this chapter. Books about persons who are Jewish are included here as well as in the chapter "Persons of Mixed Racial and/or Ethnic Heritage." This chapter includes books involving organized religions, but not all differing religious beliefs. For instance, the mixed religious heritage of a person whose Navajo father holds beliefs different from those of his/her Hopi mother is not included. The "General" chapter covers books that provide a more overall discussion.

Each category first lists the names of persons covered in the "Biography" chapter and cross-references these names to that chapter. Book listings follow these name listings.

The chapter is organized alphabetically by religion with, in some cases, subcategories, e.g.:

Christian
Protestant
Methodist

The heritage designation for each book reads:

Religious heritage from father/Religious heritage from mother
e.g., Jewish/Christian or
Jewish and Christian (if the side of the family is not known)

The order in which the heritages are listed is immaterial.

References

Agnostic

See   McCartney, James Paul
       McCartney, Stella Nina

Atheist

Weinheimer, Beckie. *Converting Kate*. New York: Viking 2007. 320 p.

Kate's mother is a devout member of the fictitious ultraconservative Church of the Holy Divine, which homeschools its children until the age of fourteen and then sends them to public schools where

their mission is to proselytize other students. When her dogmatic mother had not been able to convert Kate's father, whom Kate adored, she divorced him. When Kate's father had died suddenly the previous year, her mother did not hold a service for him. Kate had been so upset that she rode her bike for miles to retrieve and hide his ashes. After Kate's refusal to leave her room, her mother finally allowed her to have her father's books, but she was not to read them. This story begins when fifteen-year-old Kate has moved from Phoenix to Maine with her mother, who is running her great-aunt's bed and breakfast, and it details Kate's efforts to establish her own religious identity. She defies her mother by going lobster trapping with schoolmate Will and his grandfather, reading *To Kill a Mockingbird* (which causes her mother to remove her father's books), and attending a different church where she becomes active in its youth group and befriends its minister, Pastor Browning. Constantly condemned by her mother, Kate is supported by her Aunt Katherine, an environmentalist fellow cross-country member who believes in homosexual rights, and Pastor Browning. The story concludes with Kate and Aunt Katherine spreading Kate's father's ashes, the firing of Pastor Browning because he is gay, Kate's discovery that it is good to have things in common with a boyfriend, her recognition of her mother's love, and her appreciation of seeing "through a glass, darkly."
European-American and atheist/European-American and Christian
Older; Fiction

Wittlinger, Ellen. *Blind Faith*. New York: Simon & Schuster Books for Young Readers, 2006. 288 p.
    This book tells of the experiences of two families, each dealing with the death of a much loved family member. When fifteen-year-old Liz's grandmother Bunny dies, her mother Christine is devastated for they had an extremely close relationship in contrast to the indifference Christine has always shown Liz. Christine starts going to a Spiritualist Church where she believes Bunny communicates with her, and in the process she causes a rift with Liz's atheist father. Meanwhile sixteen-year-old Nathan, his young sister, and his dying mother Lily move in with Lily's crabby mother from whom she has been estranged. The story focuses on the evolving relationship between Liz and Nathan: their grief, the anger Nathan holds towards living with his grandmother, Liz's resentment towards her mother, and their questionings of religious beliefs. At the conclusion, there is reconciliation in both families.
Atheist/Presbyterian, Spiritualist
Older; Fiction

Buddhist

See   Woods, Tiger

Easton, Kelly. *Hiroshima Dreams*. New York: Dutton Children's Books, 2007. 208 p.
    When Lin's Japanese grandmother comes to visit, she immediately recognizes five-year-old Lin as a kindred spirit. Lin is so shy that she barely speaks, but is able to sense what is about to happen. Lin becomes very close to her Obaachan, who teaches her about Japan, shows how her how to meditate, imparts wisdom, and tells Lin that she too has precognition. As the years pass and with Obaachan's support, Lin plays her cello in an orchestra, makes a best friend in her new school, and uses

her vision to help police locate a missing boy. When Obaachan dies from leukemia, the result of being a fifteen-year-old in Hiroshima when the atomic bomb was dropped, Lin is devastated. Then, the boy she has been attracted to since kindergarten becomes her boyfriend and Lin accepts her gift of vision. Irish-American Catholic/Japanese Buddhist, Shinto, and Catholic
Older; Fiction

Werlin, Nancy. *Black Mirror: A Novel*. New York: Dial Books, 2001. 256 p.

In this book for older teenagers sixteen-year-old Frances is a loner and so upset by her mixed race appearance that for years she has not been able to look at herself in the mirror. When her brother Daniel commits suicide by an overdose of heroin, Frances is shocked and feels guilty that she had no longer been close to him. When she considers joining Unity Service, the preparatory school charitable institution in which Daniel was so active, she experiences conflicting emotions and encounters negative reactions from its members. Discovering that something strange is going on at Unity, Frances, with the help of a man who has mild developmental disabilities, finds out the terrible truth about Unity and the death of her brother.
European-American and Jewish/Japanese-American and Buddhist
Older; Fiction

Christian

Baskin, Nora Raleigh. *The Truth about My Bat Mitzvah*. New York: Simon & Schuster Books for Young Readers, 2008. 144 p.

Twelve-year-old Caroline's father is Christian and her mother is non-practicing Jewish. Caroline has never thought about being Jewish until her grandmother's death and receiving the Star of David necklace her grandmother had wanted her to have. She keeps the necklace a secret, learns about being Jewish from her best friend Rachel who is about to have a bat mitzvah celebration, and discovers that her great-grandparents, who came from a non-practicing Jewish German-American family, had objected to her grandfather's marriage to her Russian Jewish immigrant grandmother. Also, initially her grandparents had not been happy about her mother's marrying a non-Jew. Caroline comes to realize that she wants to be Jewish and that she doesn't need a bat mitzvah party to be a bat mitzvah.
European-American Christian/German-Russian-American Jewish
Intermediate; Fiction

Blume, Judy. *Are You There God? It's Me, Margaret*. Scarsdale, N.Y.: Bradbury Press, 1970. 156 p.

When eleven-year-old Margaret moves to New Jersey, she joins a club with three other girls and together they puzzle about growing up: bras, menstruation, and kissing boys. Margaret, whose Jewish father and Christian mother don't practice any religion, also spends time on her school project to determine which religion she should be. After attending Jewish and Protestant services, briefly visiting a Catholic confessional, and being with her Jewish grandmother and Christian grandparents, Margaret concludes that she is not ready to decide, but she does learn that you shouldn't always believe what people tell you.

Jewish/Christian
Intermediate; Fiction

Cohen, Deborah Bodin. *Papa Jethro*. Illustrated by Jane Dippold. Minneapolis: Kar-Ben Publishing, 2007. 32 p.

When Rachel wonders why her grandfather is Christian and she is Jewish, he tells her a story about Moses' son Gershom, who was Jewish, and his Midianite grandfather Jethro, whose daughter Zipporah was Moses' wife.
Christian and Jewish
Pre-K, Primary; Fiction

Howe, James. *Kaddish for Grandpa in Jesus' Name Amen*. Illustrated by Catherine Stock. New York: Atheneum Books for Young Readers, 2004. 32 p.

When her much loved Christian grandfather dies, five-year-old Emily, who is Jewish, remembers him at a Christian funeral, at a Jewish ceremony in her home, and, in her own way, by touching his glasses case each night at bedtime.
Christian and Jewish/Jewish
Pre-K, Primary; Fiction

Kuklin, Susan. *Families*. Photographs by author. New York: Hyperion Books for Children, 2006. 40 p.

Text and color photographs present interviews with American children, who talk about their families. Their families include seven families with children of mixed race, ethnicity, or religion, with one also including a child adopted from Sierra Leone. In an eighth family a child has been adopted from China. In a ninth family an adopted American child is of a race different from that of one of her fathers.
Christian/Jewish
Primary, Intermediate; Nonfiction

McCaughrean, Geraldine. *The Pirate's Son*. New York: Scholastic Press, 1998. 304 p.

In 1719 fourteen-year-old Nathan is expelled from his English school when the school discovers that he is a pauper. The newly-orphaned Nathan, who has long been fascinated with pirates, and his "mousy" thirteen-year-old sister Maud go off to Madagascar with Nathan's older schoolmate Tamo, whose late father was a notorious pirate. There Tamo, who despised his father, learns that his Malagasy mother has married another pirate and feels compelled to take up piracy. Nathan, steeped in his parson father's Christianity, cannot accept the lifestyle and beliefs of the Malagasies. It is Maud who releases Tamo from his pirate fate, expels the pirates from the village, and thrives in her new environment.
English and Christian/Malagasy and non-Christian
Older; Fiction

Older, Effin. *My Two Grandmothers*. Illustrated by Nancy Hayashi. San Diego: Harcourt, 2000. 32 p.

In this picture book Lily loves visiting her two grandmothers and enjoys each of their traditions,

including Hanukkah and Christmas. Deciding that they should be able to try each other's special food and activities, she invites them to her first traditional grandmothers' party.
Jewish and Christian
Pre-K, Primary; Fiction

Rosenberg, Maxine B. *Living in Two Worlds*. Photographs by George Ancona. New York: Lothrop, Lee & Shepard Books, 1986. 48 p.

This book explains how races evolved and how many children have a greater resemblance to one of their parents. It discusses the teasing and unwanted questions biracial children face and points to the benefits of living in two cultures. The book's text and black-and-white photographs focus on five children: Toah, who is African-European-American; Megan, who is African-European-American and Cherokee; Jesse, who is Chinese-European American; and Shashi and Anil, who are Indian-European-American.
European-American and Jewish/Chinese-American and Christian
Intermediate; Nonfiction

Watts, Irene N. *Finding Sophie*. Plattsburgh, N.Y.: Tundra Books of Northern New York, 2002. 144 p.

This book, which is a sequel to and contains excerpts from *Good-bye Marianne* and *Remember Me*, relates what happened to seven-year-old Sophie whose mother placed her on the 1938 *Kindertransport* train in Berlin and told eleven-year-old Marianne to look after her. Sophie went to live with "Aunt Em," a friend of her parents, and loves being with her as well as life in England. Now, turning fourteen-years-old, Sophie hopes that after the war she will not have to return to Germany and the parents she barely remembers. By chance she and Marianne are reunited, and Sophie participates in the May 1945 celebration of Germany's defeat. Shortly thereafter she receives a letter from her father containing both the happy news that he has survived the Dachau Concentration Camp and the sorrowful news that her mother was killed in an air raid. Sophie's concerns about her future are happily resolved when she remains with Aunt Em and her father comes to live nearby.
German and Jewish/German and Christian
Intermediate, Older; Fiction

Weinheimer, Beckie. *Converting Kate*. New York: Viking 2007. 320 p.

Kate's mother is a devout member of the fictitious ultraconservative Church of the Holy Divine, which homeschools its children until the age of fourteen and then sends them to public schools where their mission is to proselytize other students. When her dogmatic mother had not been able to convert Kate's father, whom Kate adored, she divorced him. When Kate's father had died suddenly the previous year, her mother did not hold a service for him. Kate had been so upset that she rode her bike for miles to retrieve and hide his ashes. After Kate's refusal to leave her room, her mother finally allowed her to have her father's books, but she was not to read them. This story begins when fifteen-year-old Kate has moved from Phoenix to Maine with her mother, who is running her great-aunt's bed and breakfast, and it details Kate's efforts to establish her own religious identity. She defies her mother by going lobster trapping with schoolmate Will and his grandfather, reading *To Kill a Mockingbird* (which

causes her mother to remove her father's books), and attending a different church where she becomes active in its youth group and befriends its minister, Pastor Browning. Constantly condemned by her mother, Kate is supported by her Aunt Katherine, an environmentalist fellow cross-country member who believes in homosexual rights, and Pastor Browning. The story concludes with Kate and Aunt Katherine spreading Kate's father's ashes, the firing of Pastor Browning because he is gay, Kate's discovery that it is good to have things in common with a boyfriend, her recognition of her mother's love, and her appreciation of seeing "through a glass, darkly."
European-American and atheist/European-American and Christian
Older; Fiction

Anglican

Church of England

See   McCartney, James Paul
        McCartney, Stella Nina

Episcopalian

Cooper, Ilene. *Sam I Am*. New York: Scholastic Press, 2004. 256 p.
    The celebration of Hanukkah-Christmas at Sam's house is a disaster with bad feelings between Sam's Jewish father and Episcopal mother that are exacerbated by the arguing of their grandmothers. Because of this bad experience and studying the Holocaust as a school assignment, twelve-year-old Sam questions who he is, why there are so many religions, why religions fight, and why God allows bad things to occur. Finally, with the help of his family and through recognizing that his first "crush" is not what she seems, Sam begins to find answers to his questions. Both he and his family come to recognize that they can be Jewish and Christian.
European-American and Jewish/European-American and Episcopal
Intermediate, Older; Fiction

Catholic

See   Goldman, Francisco
        Grace, Princess of Monaco
        Kidd, Jason Frederick
        McCartney, James Paul
        McCartney, Stella Nina
        Williams, William Carlos

Amado, Elisa. *Cousins*. Illustrated by Luis Garay. Toronto: Groundwood Books, 2004. 32 p.
    A little girl, who lives with her Latin-American father and her maternal grandmother, is jealous of her Catholic cousin, who will celebrate her first communion and carry the pretty rosary that is at her

paternal grandmother's house. Stealing the rosary, she feels terribly guilty and on her own goes to the Catholic church to confess.
Latin-American and Catholic/European-American and non-Catholic
Pre-K, Primary; Fiction

Bode, Janet. *Different Worlds: Interracial and Cross-Cultural Dating*. New York: Franklin Watts, 1989. 128 p.

Based primarily on interviews with six teenage couples who are dating interracially and/or cross-culturally, this book is written for and about teens. It looks at the history of prejudice and racism; discusses negative reactions of parents, relatives, and classmates; examines why adolescents make their dating choices; and mentions some positive aspects of interracial dating. Although it does not cover the topics of interracial marriage and families, four of the twelve teens interviewed are of mixed race or heritage: African-American/European-American; Protestant English-American/Catholic Irish-American; Cuban/Puerto Rican; and Mexican-Spanish-American. A bibliography, a listing of resource organizations, and an index are included.
English-American Protestant/Irish-American Catholic
Older; Nonfiction

Brown, Don. *The Notorious Izzy Fink*. New Milford, Conn.: Roaring Brook Press, 2006. 160 p. (A Deborah Brodie Book)

New York City's Lower East Side of the 1890s comes alive in this book about the thirteen-year-olds Sam Glodsky, who is Irish-Russian-American, and Izzy Fink, who twice double-crosses Sam. It is a story of boys eeking out a living—hawking newspapers, cleaning a stable, grabbing coal that has fallen off a coal wagon—; of the teenage gangs of Irish, Jewish, Italians, and pickpockets; of a gangster; of corrupt police; of Tammany; and of the threat of cholera. Amazingly, in the end it is Sam's father who emerges from his depression and comes to Sam's rescue.
Russian and Jewish/Irish and Catholic
Intermediate, Older; Fiction

Easton, Kelly. *Hiroshima Dreams*. New York: Dutton Children's Books, 2007. 208 p.

When Lin's Japanese grandmother comes to visit, she immediately recognizes five-year-old Lin as a kindred spirit. Lin is so shy that she barely speaks, but is able to sense what is about to happen. Lin becomes very close to her Obaachan, who teaches her about Japan, shows how her how to meditate, imparts wisdom, and tells Lin that she too has precognition. As the years pass and with Obaachan's support, Lin plays her cello in an orchestra, makes a best friend in her new school, and uses her vision to help police locate a missing boy. When Obaachan dies from leukemia, the result of being a fifteen-year-old in Hiroshima when the atomic bomb was dropped, Lin is devastated. Then, the boy she has been attracted to since kindergarten becomes her boyfriend and Lin accepts her gift of vision.
Irish-American Catholic/Japanese Buddhist, Shinto, and Catholic
Older; Fiction

Ernst, Kathleen. *Highland Fling*. Chicago: Cricket Books, 2006. 224 p.

Exceedingly upset by her Polish-American father who had an extramarital affair, by moving from Wisconsin to North Carolina with her divorced mother and younger sister, and by the immersion of her mother and sister in everything to do with the Scottish MacDonald clan, fifteen-year-old Tanya reluctantly goes with them to the Highland Games. Longing to become an independent filmmaker, Tanya decides to make a documentary revealing the nostalgic pretense of the Highland Games. However, after meeting a young bagpiper from Puerto Rico who has Scottish heritage, his grandmother, and a Highland Games woman athlete whose mixed heritage does not include Scottish forebears, Tanya decides to make a different documentary and to have a talk with her father.
Polish-American and Catholic/Scottish-American and Presbyterian
Older; Fiction

Harris, Rosemary. *Zed*. Boston: Faber and Faber, 1984. 192 p.

Fifteen-year-old Zed is asked by his house master to write up the time when, as an eight-year-old, he, together with his father, Uncle Omar, and others, was held captive in a London building by the Free Army of United Arabia. As Zed writes. he relives those terrible four days: the terrorists, guns, grenades, discomforts, and overwhelming dread. Through the experience Zed comes to appreciate the kindness and bravery of Uncle Omar, who was Saudi-Turkish, and Arabi, one of the terrorists. Both were killed by gunshots, while Zed's English father, a self-centered coward, survived. After writing the manuscript, Zed arranges a meeting between Omar and Arabi's sons. This novel is for teenagers.
American-Jewish-English and Catholic/Lebanese and Christian Maronite
Older; Fiction

Holm, Jennifer L. *Penny from Heaven*. New York: Random House, 2006. 288 p.

During the eventful summer of 1953 Penny spends time with both sides of her divided family: her mother and maternal grandparents and her late Italian father's mother, siblings, and relatives. Abetted by her cousin Freddie, Penny sneaks into her Italian grandmother's room to find out the color of her underwear, digs in the yard for treasure, and disobeys her mother by going to the beach. She gets a black eye, goes to a Dodgers game for her twelfth birthday, misbehaves to discourage her mother's Irish-American suitor, and, when her arm is caught in a clothes wringer, spends weeks in the hospital. It is there that she comes to accept her soon-to-be stepfather and discovers that her father had been imprisoned during World War II because, as an Italian "enemy alien," he had a radio. Penny also manages to ease the hostilities between the two branches of her family.
Italian and Catholic/European-American and Methodist
Intermediate, Older; Fiction

Lamba, Marie. *What I Meant*. New York: Random House, 2007. 320 p.

Ever since her father's sister-in law has moved in, there has been a change in fifteen-year-old Sang's family. Her widowed Indian aunt Chachi is a complaining, critical kleptomaniac who steals food and money and blames the thefts on Sang. In the meantime Sang is head over heels in love with her class-mate Jason and is upset that her parents will not allow her to date until she is sixteen. When her mother catches Sang in the lie that she was at an ice skating rink with her best friend Gina, her parents don't

believe her allegations about Chachi. Her mother even takes her to a doctor since she believes Sang is bulimic. To make matters worse, for an unknown reason Gina turns against Sang. The situation comes to a climax when Sang sneaks off to Philadelphia to see a concert with Jason and his friend Gary. She sees Gina alone in another train car, and, when Gina leaves the train toting a large backpack, Sang realizes that she is running away. Getting off the train Sang follows Gina through the dark city streets and then calls Gina's mother as to her whereabouts. Robbed of her money and return ticket, Sang goes back to the train station where Gary is searching for her. Sang comes to realize that Gina and Jason are no longer her friends, but that she has other supportive classmates. Further, when Sang stands up to Chachi, who is about to reveal a damaging secret about her mother, Sang's parents and her visiting Indian uncle believe her and Chachi is made to leave.
Indian and Sikh/Italian-American and Catholic
Older; Fiction

Merino, José María. *The Gold of Dreams*. Translated by Helen Lane. New York: Farrar, Straus and Giroux, 1994. 224 p. (A Sunburst Book)
    Living in a village near Mexico City in the sixteenth century, Miguel is the son of a Spanish Conquistador father who disappeared years ago and a Native Mexican mother. When he is fifteen, Miguel goes with his Spanish godfather on a mission to find the kingdom of Queen Yupaha and bring back its gold. During the long and difficult journey Miguel witnesses the cruelties of both the Spaniards and the Indians, engages in battle, is captured by Indians, finds his father, and learns that the reported gold of Queen Yupaha is a myth. Miguel makes close friends, including an Indian boy, who having earlier been captured by the Spaniards and taken to Spain, now finds it difficult to fit into either culture.
Spanish and Catholic/Native Mexican and non-Christian
Older; Fiction

Meyer, Carolyn. *Jubilee Journey*. San Diego: Gulliver Books, 1997. 288 p.
    In this sequel to *White Lilacs*, it is 1996 and eighty-seven-year-old Rose Lee has invited her thirteen-year-old great-granddaughter Emily Rose and her family to attend the Freedomtown Juneteenth Diamond Jubilee. Growing up in Connecticut, Emily Rose has always regarded herself as a "double" as her father is French-American and her mother is African-American. However, she and her brothers Steven and Robbie have no idea what it means to be black in Dillon, Texas. They quickly learn of the attitudes of some whites when Steven is set up and abused and of the closeness and pride of the African-American community. In this story Rose Lee reveals what has happened to her and her family during the past seventy-five years. Emily Rose gets a new friend who thinks she should be just black and decides to remain in Denton to learn more about being black so she can better understand herself. Alicia, Rose Lee's best friend in Connecticut, has a Nigerian father and an English mother.
French-American and Catholic/African-European-American, Seminole, and Baptist
Intermediate, Older; Fiction

Orlev, Uri. *The Man from the Other Side*. Translated from Hebrew by Hillel Halkin. Boston: Houghton Mifflin Company, 1991. 192 p.

During the German occupation of Poland during World War II, fourteen-year-old Marek joins other boys in robbing a Jew who had escaped from the Warsaw ghetto. When his mother finds out she tells Marek that he had sentenced the Jew to death and reveals that Marek's father, who died when he was four, was a Jew. Consumed with guilt, Marek discovers Pan Jozek, an escaped Jew, and manages to get him into a safe hiding place. When Pan Jozek wants to return to join the Jews in their ghetto uprising, Marek, who has accompanied his stepfather through the sewers of Warsaw when he smuggled food into the Jewish ghetto, guides Pan Jozek through the underground tunnels. Marek is stuck in the ghetto when part of the tunnel collapses from an explosion and joins the Jews in fighting the Germans. He is rescued by his much-resented stepfather and finally agrees to be adopted as his son.
Jewish-Polish/Polish and Catholic
Older; Fiction

Ostow, Micol. *Emily Goldberg Learns to Salsa*. New York: Razorbill, 2006. 212 p.
Emily with her family flies from New York to Puerto Rico for the funeral of the grandmother she had never met. As Emily's mother is stressed out by returning to her Puerto Rican family, Emily stays behind in Puerto Rico to help her. Emily has trouble adjusting to her newfound family and especially to Lucy, a cousin who dislikes her. By the end of the stay Emily has come to appreciate Puerto Rico, she and Lucy are friends, and the two discover that Emily's mother had not returned to Puerto Rico by choice, but because, by marrying a Jewish man, she was cut off by the grandmother.
European-Jewish-American/Puerto Rican and Catholic
Older; Fiction

Viglucci, Patricia Costa. *Sun Dance at Turtle Rock*. Rochester, N.Y.: Stone Pine Books, 1996. 136 p.
Twelve-year-old Cody, whose white father had died in a car accident six years earlier, goes to spend the summer with his paternal grandfather Zachariah, who had objected to the marriage of his father to his African-American mother. Cody is treated lovingly by his aunt, uncle, and their toddler son and spends much of the time exploring the town and the surrounding Allegheny Mountains with their daughter Jem. However, although his grandfather shows warmth towards Cody's cousins, he treats Cody coldly because of his race and is especially upset that Cody may be adopted by his black stepfather and take his stepfather's name. The last straw for Cody comes when Zachariah takes the side of a bigoted neighbor boy instead of his. Cody realizes that he is like the Plains Indians who in a Sun Dance had tortured themselves to prove themselves worthy, in Cody's case of his father's father. Cody plans to leave until he saves Jem from a bear. Then Zachariah expresses his love for Cody, and Cody decides that, although it will take time for his grandfather to change, he will stay for the rest of the summer.
European-American Catholic/African-American Baptist
Intermediate; Fiction

Wyeth, Sharon Dennis. *The World of Daughter McGuire*. New York: Delacorte Press, 1994. 176 p.
Eleven-year-old Daughter's parents have separated, and she, her two younger brothers, and her mother have moved into a house next to her mother's parents. Daughter, whose deceased grandfather was Irish-American Catholic and whose other grandparents are Russian Jewish, African-American, and

Italian-American, is called a "zebra" by a schoolmate and wishes that she was not all mixed-up. She is further concerned that the differences between her mother and father in careers and lifestyles will result in divorce. In this story Daughter learns to be proud of her heritages and is relieved when her parents decide to try to stay together despite their differences.
Irish-American Catholic and Russian-American Jewish/African-Italian-American
Intermediate; Fiction

Church of England. See Anglican

Episcopalian. See Anglican

Jehovah's Witness

See   Jackson, Michael Joseph

Maronite

Harris, Rosemary. *Zed*. Boston: Faber and Faber, 1984. 192 p.
Fifteen-year-old Zed is asked by his house master to write up the time when, as an eight-year-old, he, together with his father, Uncle Omar, and others, was held captive in a London building by the Free Army of United Arabia. As Zed writes, he relives those terrible four days: the terrorists, guns, grenades, discomforts, and overwhelming dread. Through the experience Zed comes to appreciate the kindness and bravery of Uncle Omar, who was Saudi-Turkish, and Arabi, one of the terrorists. Both were killed by gunshots, while Zed's English father, a self-centered coward, survived. After writing the manuscript, Zed arranges a meeting between Omar and Arabi's sons. This novel is for teenagers.
American-Jewish-English and Catholic/Lebanese and Christian Maronite; Saudi-Turkish-Lebanese and Muslim/Lebanese and Christian Maronite
Older; Fiction

Mormon

See   Farmanfarmaian, Roxane

Protestant

See   Woods, Tiger

Adoff, Arnold. *All the Colors of the Race*. Illustrated by John Steptoe. New York: Lothrop, Lee & Shepard Books, 1982. 56 p.
Poems celebrate a girl who is Polish, German, Russian, and Jewish on her father's side and African-American and Protestant on her mother's. She looks forward to the time when we will cease

looking at colors and *love* all colors of the human race.
Polish-German-Russian-American Jewish/African-American Protestant
Intermediate, Older; Fiction

Bode, Janet. *Different Worlds: Interracial and Cross-Cultural Dating*. New York: Franklin Watts, 1989. 128 p.

Based primarily on interviews with six teenage couples who are dating interracially and/or cross-culturally, this book is written for and about teens. It looks at the history of prejudice and racism; discusses negative reactions of parents, relatives, and classmates; examines why adolescents make their dating choices; and mentions some positive aspects of interracial dating. Although it does not cover the topics of interracial marriage and families, four of the twelve teens interviewed are of mixed race or heritage: African-American/European-American; Protestant English-American/Catholic Irish-American; Cuban/Puerto Rican; and Mexican-Spanish-American. A bibliography, a listing of resource organizations, and an index are included.
English-American Protestant/Irish-American Catholic
Older; Nonfiction

Chotjewitz, David. *Daniel Half Human: And the Good Nazi*. Translated from German by Doris Orgel. New York: Atheneum Books for Young Readers, 2004. 304 p. (A Richard Jackson Book)

In 1933 thirteen-year-old best friends David and Armin paint swastikas on a courtyard wall in a Communist district of Hamburg, Germany. This moving, distressing novel traces the ensuing lives of the two boys. Disdaining Jews, Daniel experiences shock and changing emotions as he discovers and tries to cope with his mother's Jewish heritage. Armin strives to become a Nazi leader, yet keep his friendship with Daniel and have a Jewish girlfriend. The book details the downfall of Daniel's prominent family amidst the tightening of Nazi power and its increasing persecution of Jews. Daniel and his parents emigrate from Germany in July 1939. Returning in 1945 as a member of the American military on loan to the Royal British Army, Daniel must make a decision as to the fate of Armin, who has served in the notorious SS.
German and Protestant/Jewish-German and Protestant
Older; Fiction

Danziger, Paula. *It's an Aardvark-Eat-Turtle World*. New York: Delacorte Press, 1985. 144 p.

When fourteen-year-old Rosie's mother and Rosie's best friend Phoebe's father move in together, Rosie is pleased that the four of them will form a family. However, when Phoebe gets upset with Rosie's mother and also with Rosie because she spends time with Jason, her first boyfriend, and when Phoebe decides to move out and live with her mother, Rosie discovers that family relationships are not easy. She also suffers from the hateful remark of a man who objects to mixed race Rosie and Canadian Jason being together. At the story's end Phoebe decides to work things out and come back and Rosie spends a happy Christmas Eve with both Jason and Phoebe.
African-American Protestant/European-American Jewish
Intermediate, Older; Fiction

Baptist

See   Jackson, Michael Joseph
         Kidd, Jason Frederick
         McBride, James

Meyer, Carolyn. *Jubilee Journey*. San Diego: Gulliver Books, 1997. 288 p.

In this sequel to *White Lilacs*, it is 1996 and eighty-seven-year-old Rose Lee has invited her thirteen-year-old great-granddaughter Emily Rose and her family to attend the Freedomtown Juneteenth Diamond Jubilee. Growing up in Connecticut, Emily Rose has always regarded herself as a "double" as her father is French-American and her mother is African-American. However, she and her brothers Steven and Robbie have no idea what it means to be black in Dillon, Texas. They quickly learn of the attitudes of some whites when Steven is set up and abused and of the closeness and pride of the African-American community. In this story Rose Lee reveals what has happened to her and her family during the past seventy-five years. Emily Rose gets a new friend who thinks she should be just black and decides to remain in Denton to learn more about being black so she can better understand herself. Alicia, Rose Lee's best friend in Connecticut, has a Nigerian father and an English mother.
French-American and Catholic/African-European-American, Seminole, and Baptist
Intermediate, Older; Fiction

Viglucci, Patricia Costa. *Sun Dance at Turtle Rock*. Rochester, N.Y.: Stone Pine Books, 1996. 136 p.

Twelve-year-old Cody, whose white father had died in a car accident six years earlier, goes to spend the summer with his paternal grandfather Zachariah, who had objected to the marriage of his father to his African-American mother. Cody is treated lovingly by his aunt, uncle, and their toddler son and spends much of the time exploring the town and the surrounding Allegheny Mountains with their daughter Jem. However, although his grandfather shows warmth towards Cody's cousins, he treats Cody coldly because of his race and is especially upset that Cody may be adopted by his black stepfather and take his stepfather's name. The last straw for Cody comes when Zachariah takes the side of a bigoted neighbor boy instead of his. Cody realizes that he is like the Plains Indians who in a Sun Dance had tortured themselves to prove themselves worthy, in Cody's case of his father's father. Cody plans to leave until he saves Jem from a bear. Then Zachariah expresses his love for Cody, and Cody decides that, although it will take time for his grandfather to change, he will stay for the rest of the summer.
European-American Catholic/African-American Baptist
Intermediate; Fiction

Hutterite

Stucky, Naomi R. *Sara's Summer*. Scottsdale, Pa.: Herald Press, 1990. 144 p.

Recently orphaned, fifteen-year-old Sara goes to spend the summer in Manitoba with her father's Hutterite family whom she has never met. There she is fondly welcomed and fully participates in the

life of the contained community. Sara experiences both the Hutterite traditions, rituals, and rules which govern even the most minute aspects of their lives and the isolation of the community's residents, both physically and because of the absence of telephones, radio, and television. Sara learns that her musician father left the Hutterites because they did not permit musical instruments. Faced with the difficult decision as to whether to leave her new family at the end of the summer, Sara chooses to return to Toronto to pursue her education and have the options to determine her own future.
European-Canadian Hutterite/European-American non-Hutterite
Intermediate, Older; Fiction

Lutheran

See   Grace, Princess of Monaco

Erlbach, Arlene. *The Families Book: True Stories about Real Kids and the People They Live With and Love*. Photographs by Stephen J. Carrera. Illustrated by Lisa Wagner. Minneapolis: Free Spirit Publishing, 1996. 120 p.

In a section of this book children tell about their families, that include a family in which the father is Lutheran and the mother Jewish; a family in which the father is African-American and the mother Caucasian; a family with four children in which Caucasian parents have adopted a biracial American girl and a boy from Romania; and a family with Caucasian parents and eleven children, six of whom were adopted from Korea.
Lutheran/Jewish
Intermediate; Nonfiction

Methodist

Hausman, Gerald. *Night Flight*. New York: Philomel Books, 1996. 144 p.

Set in the summer of 1957, this is the story of two twelve-year-old boys: Max, who is incredibly cruel and controlling, and Jeff, who always tries to please him. When the boys' dogs as well as many others are poisoned, Max, whose father had been a Nazi, decides that Jews, whom he hates, are the culprits. Jeff, who had previously ignored his own Jewish heritage, struggles with Max's extreme views and actions, but, egged on by Max, shoots a dart into a Jewish family's front door. Jeff finally comes to realize what Max is—and what he himself can be.
Hungarian-Jewish/Dutch-English-Scottish-American and Iroquois and Methodist
Older; Fiction

Holm, Jennifer L. *Penny from Heaven*. New York: Random House, 2006. 288 p.

During the eventful summer of 1953 Penny spends time with both sides of her divided family: her mother and maternal grandparents and her late Italian father's mother, siblings, and relatives. Abetted by her cousin Freddie, Penny sneaks into her Italian grandmother's room to find out the color of her underwear, digs in the yard for treasure, and disobeys her mother by going to the beach. She gets a black eye, goes to a Dodgers game for her twelfth birthday, misbehaves to discourage her mother's

Irish-American suitor, and, when her arm is caught in a clothes wringer, spends weeks in the hospital. It is there that she comes to accept her soon-to-be stepfather and discovers that her father had been imprisoned during World War II because, as an Italian "enemy alien," he had a radio. Penny also manages to ease the hostilities between the two branches of her family.
Italian and Catholic/European-American and Methodist
Intermediate, Older; Fiction

Presbyterian

Ernst, Kathleen. *Highland Fling*. Chicago: Cricket Books, 2006. 224 p.
Exceedingly upset by her Polish-American father who had an extramarital affair, by moving from Wisconsin to North Carolina with her divorced mother and younger sister, and by the immersion of her mother and sister in everything to do with the Scottish MacDonald clan, fifteen-year-old Tanya reluctantly goes with them to the Highland Games. Longing to become an independent filmmaker, Tanya decides to make a documentary revealing the nostalgic pretense of the Highland Games. However, after meeting a young bagpiper from Puerto Rico who has Scottish heritage, his grandmother, and a Highland Games woman athlete whose mixed heritage does not include Scottish forebears, Tanya decides to make a different documentary and to have a talk with her father.
Polish-American and Catholic/Scottish-American and Presbyterian
Older; Fiction

Wittlinger, Ellen. *Blind Faith*. New York: Simon & Schuster Books for Young Readers, 2006. 288 p.
This book tells of the experiences of two families, each dealing with the death of a much loved family member. When fifteen-year-old Liz's grandmother Bunny dies, her mother Christine is devastated for they had an extremely close relationship in contrast to the indifference Christine has always shown Liz. Christine starts going to a Spiritualist Church where she believes Bunny communicates with her, and in the process she causes a rift with Liz's atheist father. Meanwhile sixteen-year-old Nathan, his young sister, and his dying mother Lily move in with Lily's crabby mother from whom she has been estranged. The story focuses on the evolving relationship between Liz and Nathan: their grief, the anger Nathan holds towards living with his grandmother, Liz's resentment towards her mother, and their questionings of religious beliefs. At the conclusion, there is reconciliation in both families.
Atheist/Presbyterian, Spiritualist
Older; Fiction

Shaker

Hickman, Janet. *Susannah*. New York: Greenwillow Books, 1998. 144 p.
It is 1810 and thirteen-year-old Susannah's mother has died. Against Susannah's wishes, her father takes her with him to live in the Shaker community near Lebanon, Ohio. There she rarely is able to speak to her father and is unhappy with Shaker life and beliefs, especially the separation of Shaker children from their parents. When her father finally gives her permission to leave and live with

a great-aunt, Susannah finds that she cannot leave the little girl Mary, who longs for her non-Shaker mother and has become attached to Susannah. Staying to be a surrogate mother to Mary, Susannah is not able to give her enough attention. Susannah finally runs away with Mary to Lebanon where she discovers her great-aunt has died and gives the money her great-aunt had left for her to Mary and her mother so that they may escape from the area.
Shaker/Non-Shaker
Intermediate, Older; Fiction

Unitarian

See   Williams, William Carlos

Jewish

See   Cardozo, Francis Lewis
        Espinel, Luisa
        Gladwell, Malcolm
        Goldman, Francisco
        Hughes, James Mercer Langston
        McBride, James
        McCallum, Shara
        McCartney, Stella Nina
        Mehta, Nina
        Ronstadt, Linda
        Smalls, Robert
        Williams, William Carlos

Adoff, Arnold. *All the Colors of the Race*. Illustrated by John Steptoe. New York: Lothrop, Lee & Shepard Books, 1982. 56 p.

   Poems celebrate a girl who is Polish, German, Russian, and Jewish on her father's side and African-American and Protestant on her mother's. She looks forward to the time when we will cease *looking* at colors and *love* all colors of the human race.
Polish-German-Russian-American Jewish/African-American Protestant
Intermediate, Older; Fiction

Baskin, Nora Raleigh. *The Truth about My Bat Mitzvah*. New York: Simon & Schuster Books for Young Readers, 2008. 144 p.

   Twelve-year-old Caroline's father is Christian and her mother is non-practicing Jewish. Caroline has never thought about being Jewish until her grandmother's death and receiving the Star of David necklace her grandmother had wanted her to have. She keeps the necklace a secret, learns about being Jewish from her best friend Rachel who is about to have a bat mitzvah celebration, and discovers that

her great-grandparents, who came from a non-practicing Jewish German-American family, had objected to her grandfather's marriage to her Russian Jewish immigrant grandmother. Also, initially her grandparents had not been happy about her mother's marrying a non-Jew. Caroline comes to realize that she wants to be Jewish and that she doesn't need a bat mitzvah party to be a bat mitzvah.
European-American Christian/German-Russian-American Jewish
Intermediate; Fiction

Bell, William. *Zack*. New York: Simon & Schuster Books for Young Readers, 1999. 192 p.
    Although Zack is close to his father's parents, who are Romanian-Canadian Jewish, his mother, who is black, refuses to say anything about her family. Resentful that his parents have moved from Toronto to the small town of Fergus, Ontario, Zack does poorly in high school until he is assigned a local history project. Investigating the objects he had dug up from his yard, Zack is inspired by the story of the African former slave who had lived there and then, unbeknownst to his parents, travels to Natchez to find his black grandfather. Zack discovers that it was his grandfather with his hatred of whites, not his mother, who has kept him from his black relatives. In this story Zack learns not only about his heritage, but also about the power of courage and the far-reaching effects of one's actions.
Romanian-Canadian Jewish/African-American-Canadian
Older; Fiction

Blume, Judy. *Are You There God? It's Me, Margaret*. Scarsdale, N.Y.: Bradbury Press, 1970. 156 p.
    When eleven-year-old Margaret moves to New Jersey, she joins a club with three other girls and together they puzzle about growing up: bras, menstruation, and kissing boys. Margaret, whose Jewish father and Christian mother don't practice any religion, also spends time on her school project to determine which religion she should be. After attending Jewish and Protestant services, briefly visiting a Catholic confessional, and being with her Jewish grandmother and Christian grandparents, Margaret concludes that she is not ready to decide, but she does learn that you shouldn't always believe what people tell you.
Jewish/Christian
Intermediate; Fiction

Brown, Don. *The Notorious Izzy Fink*. New Milford, Conn.: Roaring Brook Press, 2006. 160 p. (A Deborah Brodie Book)
    New York City's Lower East Side of the 1890s comes alive in this book about the thirteen-year-olds Sam Glodsky, who is Irish-Russian-American, and Izzy Fink, who twice double-crosses Sam. It is a story of boys eeking out a living—hawking newspapers, cleaning a stable, grabbing coal that has fallen off a coal wagon—; of the teenage gangs of Irish, Jewish, Italians, and pickpockets; of a gangster; of corrupt police; of Tammany; and of the threat of cholera. Amazingly, in the end it is Sam's father who emerges from his depression and comes to Sam's rescue.
Russian and Jewish/Irish and Catholic
Intermediate, Older; Fiction

Chotjewitz, David. *Daniel Half Human: And the Good Nazi*. Translated from German by Doris Orgel. New York: Atheneum Books for Young Readers, 2004. 304 p. (A Richard Jackson Book)

In 1933 thirteen-year-old best friends David and Armin paint swastikas on a courtyard wall in a Communist district of Hamburg, Germany. This moving, distressing novel traces the ensuing lives of the two boys. Disdaining Jews, Daniel experiences shock and changing emotions as he discovers and tries to cope with his mother's Jewish heritage. Armin strives to become a Nazi leader, yet keep his friendship with Daniel and have a Jewish girlfriend. The book details the downfall of Daniel's prominent family amidst the tightening of Nazi power and its increasing persecution of Jews. Daniel and his parents emigrate from Germany in July 1939. Returning in 1945 as a member of the American military on loan to the Royal British Army, Daniel must make a decision as to the fate of Armin, who has served in the notorious SS.
German and Protestant/Jewish-German and Protestant
Older; Fiction

Cohen, Deborah Bodin. *Papa Jethro*. Illustrated by Jane Dippold. Minneapolis: Kar-Ben Publishing, 2007. 32 p.

When Rachel wonders why her grandfather is Christian and she is Jewish, he tells her a story about Moses' son Gershom, who was Jewish, and his Midianite grandfather Jethro, whose daughter Zipporah was Moses' wife.
Christian and Jewish
Pre-K, Primary; Fiction

Cooper, Ilene. *Sam I Am*. New York: Scholastic Press, 2004. 256 p.

The celebration of Hanukkah-Christmas at Sam's house is a disaster with bad feelings between Sam's Jewish father and Episcopal mother that are exacerbated by the arguing of their grandmothers. Because of this bad experience and studying the Holocaust as a school assignment, twelve-year-old Sam questions who he is, why there are so many religions, why religions fight, and why God allows bad things to occur. Finally, with the help of his family and through recognizing that his first "crush" is not what she seems, Sam begins to find answers to his questions. Both he and his family come to recognize that they can be Jewish and Christian.
Jewish and European-American/Episcopal and European-American
Intermediate, Older; Fiction

Danziger, Paula. *It's an Aardvark-Eat-Turtle World*. New York: Delacorte Press, 1985. 144 p.

When fourteen-year-old Rosie's mother and Rosie's best friend Phoebe's father move in together, Rosie is pleased that the four of them will form a family. However, when Phoebe gets upset with Rosie's mother and also with Rosie because she spends time with Jason, her first boyfriend, and when Phoebe decides to move out and live with her mother, Rosie discovers that family relationships are not easy. She also suffers from the hateful remark of a man who objects to mixed race Rosie and Canadian Jason being together. At the story's end Phoebe decides to work things out and come back and Rosie spends a happy Christmas Eve with both Jason and Phoebe.

African-American Protestant/European-American Jewish
Intermediate, Older; Fiction

Elkeles, Simone. *How to Ruin a Summer Vacation*. Woodbury, Minn.: Flux, 2006. 240 p.

Sixteen-year-old Amy's parents never married, and her Israeli father, now an American resident, has been largely absent from her life. When Amy has to go with him to Israel to meet his family, that knows nothing about her existence, she is angry with her father, resentful about changing her summer vacation plans, and fearful about the safety of being in Israel. Overreactive Amy immediately likes her Israeli grandmother and her little Israeli cousin, but has to endure the hostility of the cousin with whom she rooms and eighteen-year-old Avi. She is constantly doing something wrong in their presence. It is not until the last part of her trip that Amy comes to appreciate her Israeli heritage, learns that her father had been rebuffed in his efforts to be with her, and falls in love with Avi.
German-Israeli Jewish/European-American non-Jewish
Older; Fiction

Erlbach, Arlene. *The Families Book: True Stories about Real Kids and the People They Live With and Love*. Photographs by Stephen J. Carrera. Illustrated by Lisa Wagner. Minneapolis: Free Spirit Publishing, 1996. 120 p.

In a section of this book children tell about their families, that include a family in which the father is Lutheran and the mother Jewish; a family in which the father is African-American and the mother Caucasian; a family with four children in which Caucasian parents have adopted a biracial American girl and a boy from Romania; and a family with Caucasian parents and eleven children, six of whom were adopted from Korea.
Lutheran/Jewish
Intermediate; Nonfiction

Freeman, Martha. *The Trouble with Babies*. Illustrated by Cat Bowman Smith. New York: Holiday House, 2002. 128 p.

When nine-year-old Holly moves into her new house, she meets her interesting neighbors, including Annie, who thinks her month-old sister is yucky, and Xavier, who has invented a de-yuckification device. The de-yuckification box produces surprising results, Annie realizes she likes her sister, and Holly discovers that she too is going to become a big sister. Annie and her baby sister have a Chinese father and a mother who is Polish-American and Jewish.
Chinese/Polish American and Jewish
Intermediate; Fiction

García, Cristina. *I Wanna Be Your Shoebox*. New York: Simon & Schuster Books for Young Readers, 2008. 208 p.

Eighth-grader Zumi loves surfing, her baby cousin adopted from Guatemala, and playing clarinet in her middle school orchestra—and even spearheads the orchestra's money-raising punk-reggae concert to save it from being eliminated. However, most of all she treasures her cancer-ridden grandfather and the story of his life which he tells her before dying.

Japanese-Russian-American Jewish/Guatemalan-Cuban
Older; Fiction

Gehrts, Barbara. *Don't Say a Word*. Translated from German by Elizabeth D. Crawford. New York: Margaret K. McElderry Books, 1986. 176 p.

This book presents, with only a few changes and the use of fictional names, the moving account of the author's adolescence in Germany during World War II. As part of a close extended Christian family which hated Hitler, she endured the death on the Russian front of a cousin whom she loved, the death of her brother from an ear infection which the military ignored, and the execution of her father, a colonel in the Luftwaffe, for "undermining the war effort." Her friend who was half-Jewish committed suicide together with the other members of her family when a gallows was set up in front of their home.
German Jewish and German non-Jewish
Older; Nonfiction

Harris, Rosemary. *Zed*. Boston: Faber and Faber, 1984. 192 p.

Fifteen-year-old Zed is asked by his house master to write up the time when, as an eight-year-old, he, together with his father, Uncle Omar, and others, was held captive in a London building by the Free Army of United Arabia. As Zed writes, he relives those terrible four days: the terrorists, guns, grenades, discomforts, and overwhelming dread. Through the experience Zed comes to appreciate the kindness and bravery of Uncle Omar, who was Saudi-Turkish, and Arabi, one of the terrorists. Both were killed by gunshots, while Zed's English father, a self-centered coward, survived. After writing the manuscript, Zed arranges a meeting between Omar and Arabi's sons. This novel is for teenagers.
American-Jewish-English and Catholic/Lebanese and Christian Maronite
Older; Fiction

Hausman, Gerald. *Night Flight*. New York: Philomel Books, 1996. 144 p.

Set in the summer of 1957, this is the story of two twelve-year-old boys: Max, who is incredibly cruel and controlling, and Jeff, who always tries to please him. When the boys' dogs as well as many others are poisoned, Max, whose father had been a Nazi, decides that Jews, whom he hates, are the culprits. Jeff, who had previously ignored his own Jewish heritage, struggles with Max's extreme views and actions, but, egged on by Max, shoots a dart into a Jewish family's front door. Jeff finally comes to realize what Max is—and what he himself can be.
Hungarian-Jewish/Dutch-English-Scottish-American and Iroquois and Methodist
Older; Fiction

Herron, Carolivia. *Always an Olivia: A Remarkable Family History*. Illustrated by Jeremy Tugeau. Minneapolis: Kar-Ben Publishing, 2007. 32 p.

In this picture book Carol Olivia's great-grandmother tells her about her Jewish ancestors, who were banished from Spain and Portugal and finally moved to Italy. One of their descendents and her future husband escaped from pirates and traveled by ship to Georgia. Their descendents intermarried with the Geechees (Gullahs) of Sea Island.

Gullah-Italian-Spanish-American Jewish
Primary, Intermediate; Fiction

Howe, James. *Kaddish for Grandpa in Jesus' Name Amen*. Illustrated by Catherine Stock. New York: Atheneum Books for Young Readers, 2004. 32 p.

When her much loved Christian grandfather dies, five-year-old Emily, who is Jewish, remembers him at a Christian funeral, at a Jewish ceremony in her home, and, in her own way, by touching his glasses case each night at bedtime.
Christian and Jewish/Jewish
Pre-K, Primary; Fiction

Klein, Norma. *Bizou: A Novel*. New York: The Viking Press, 1983. 144 p.

Thirteen-year-old Bizou, whose deceased father was French and whose mother is African-American, is temporarily abandoned by her mother when the two of them travel from France to visit the United States which her mother had left years before. Entrusted to Nicholas, a man they met on the plane, Bizou travels with him to Vermont and Washington, D.C., before they locate a friend of Bizou's mother in Pennsylvania. It is there that Bizou discovers that she has a half-brother, meets her grandfather, and is reunited with her mother.
French and Jewish/African-American
Older; Fiction

Kuklin, Susan. *Families*. Photographs by author. New York: Hyperion Books for Children, 2006. 40 p.

Text and color photographs present interviews with American children, who talk about their families. Their families include seven families with children of mixed race, ethnicity, or religion, with one also including a child adopted from Sierra Leone. In an eighth family a child has been adopted from China. In a ninth family an adopted American child is of a race different from that of one of her fathers.
German-Jewish-American and Mescalero Apache/African-American; Christian/Jewish
Primary, Intermediate; Nonfiction

Little, Jean. *Kate*. New York: Harper & Row, Publishers, 1971. 176 p.

This sequel to *Look Through My Window* focuses on Emily's best friend Kate. Everything changes for Kate and her close relationship with Emily when she discovers that Sheila, a new girl in her Ontario class whom she doesn't particularly like, and Susannah, an eight-year-old whom she immediately adores, are sisters, are Jewish, and are the daughters of one of her father's childhood friends. Kate meets her aunt, her cousin, and her grandfather for the first time; becomes familiar with and proud of her Jewishness; and, learning from the estrangement which caused her father years of suffering, makes up with Emily.
European-Canadian Jewish/European-Canadian non-Jewish
Intermediate, Older; Fiction

Little, Jean. *Look Through My Window*. Illustrated by Joan Sandin. New York: Harper & Row, Publishers, 1970. 272 p.

When her aunt is hospitalized with tuberculosis and her father is transferred to a different city in Ontario, only child Emily's parents buy a large house and take in her four rambunctious cousins, aged three to seven. This story relates Emily's adventures helping look after the children, learning to appreciate the elderly cantankerous next-door neighbor, experiencing the unexpected arrival of Sophie, a seventeen-year-old Belgian girl, and rescuing the cat Wilhelmina Shakespeare. Most of all, the book is about Emily's finally meeting Kate, a kindred poetry-writer, their friendship, and their acceptance of Emily's being Presbyterian and Kate part-Jewish. This is the first book about Emily and Kate.
European-Canadian Jewish/European-Canadian non-Jewish
Intermediate; Fiction

Murphy, Rita. *Black Angels*. New York: Delacorte Press, 2001. 176 p.

It is 1961 and Freedom Riders are on the way to a small Georgia town. Sophie, the Jenkins family's maid whom eleven-year-old Celli adores, is an outspoken African-American in the conservative Southern town. Celli finds it difficult to grasp the meaning of the civil rights movement and to cope with the sudden discovery that the grandmother she had never met is black. During the summer Celli becomes less concerned with the negative effects Sophie's actions have on her life and helps free Sophie from jail and save a friend who is Jewish and African-American.
European-American and Jewish/African-American
Intermediate, Older; Fiction

Nichols, Joan Kane. *All But the Right Folks*. Owings Mills, Md.: Stemmer House Publishers, 1985. 112 p.

Danny doesn't realize he is half white until he meets his grandmother Helga and goes to spend the summer with her in New York City. Suffering from asthma, bed-wetting, and teasing at his San Francisco school, Danny enjoys New York as he bikes with his grandmother; befriends Thelma Jean, her little brother Willy, and Charlayne; and starts learning karate from Charlayne's older sister. However, his new friends, two of whom are of mixed heritage, reject him because he lied that Helga was his nanny. Further, he worries that his deceased mother was a druggie like his Uncle Billy; his father insists that Danny is black and is not proud of him; and he discovers that Helga has lied to him. Everything improves when Danny uses his karate mental and kicking skills to escape kidnappers, and he decides that he is a bridge between black and white.
German non-Jewish/German Jewish
Intermediate; Fiction

Older, Effin. *My Two Grandmothers*. Illustrated by Nancy Hayashi. San Diego: Harcourt, 2000. 32 p.

In this picture book Lily loves visiting her two grandmothers and enjoys each of their traditions, including Hanukkah and Christmas. Deciding that they should be able to try each other's special food and activities, she invites them to her first traditional grandmothers' party.
Jewish and Christian
Pre-K, Primary; Fiction

Olivas, Daniel A. *Benjamin and the Word/Benjamín y la palabra*. Illustrated by Don Dyen. Spanish translation by Gabriele Baeze Ventura. Houston: Piñata Books, 2005. 32 p.

In this bilingual picture book, Benjamin is terribly upset when his friend James calls him a derogatory word. Benjamin's Mexican-American father points out that Benjamin looks like him and his Russian-American mother and that people sometimes use mean words to hurt the feelings of those who are different. Benjamin's father also helps Benjamin see that James was angry because Benjamin had beaten him at handball. When Benjamin gets to school, James apologizes and agrees never again to use mean words, and the boys resume their friendship.
Mexican-American/Russian-American and Jewish
Primary; Fiction

Orlev, Uri. *The Man from the Other Side*. Translated from Hebrew by Hillel Halkin. Boston: Houghton Mifflin Company, 1991. 192 p.

During the German occupation of Poland during World War II, fourteen-year-old Marek joins other boys in robbing a Jew who had escaped from the Warsaw ghetto. When his mother finds out she tells Marek that he had sentenced the Jew to death and reveals that Marek's father, who died when he was four, was a Jew. Consumed with guilt, Marek discovers Pan Jozek, an escaped Jew, and manages to get him into a safe hiding place. When Pan Jozek wants to return to join the Jews in their ghetto uprising, Marek, who has accompanied his stepfather through the sewers of Warsaw when he smuggled food into the Jewish ghetto, guides Pan Jozek through the underground tunnels. Marek is stuck in the ghetto when part of the tunnel collapses from an explosion and joins the Jews in fighting the Germans. He is rescued by his much-resented stepfather and finally agrees to be adopted as his son.
Jewish-Polish/Polish and Catholic
Older; Fiction

Ostow, Micol. *Emily Goldberg Learns to Salsa*. New York: Razorbill, 2006. 212 p.

Emily with her family flies from New York to Puerto Rico for the funeral of the grandmother she had never met. As Emily's mother is stressed out by returning to her Puerto Rican family, Emily stays behind in Puerto Rico to help her. Emily has trouble adjusting to her newfound family and especially to Lucy, a cousin who dislikes her. By the end of the stay Emily has come to appreciate Puerto Rico, she and Lucy are friends, and the two discover that Emily's mother had not returned to Puerto Rico by choice, but because, by marrying a Jewish man, she was cut off by the grandmother.
European-Jewish-American/Puerto Rican and Catholic
Older; Fiction

Peacock, Shane. *Death in the Air: The Boy Sherlock Holmes, His Second Case*. Plattsburgh, N.Y.: Tundra Books of Northern New York, 2008. 264 p. (The Boy Sherlock Holmes)

In this second book in the series, thirteen-year-old Sherlock Holmes has left home and gets a room and a job with Sigerson Bell, an elderly apothecary. Holmes' second case literally arrives at his feet when the famed trapeze artist Mercure plunges to the floor during a performance at London's Crystal Palace. Sherlock immediately realizes that it was not an accident and resolves to solve the case. When he discovers that it was the dreaded Brixton Gang that both caused Mercure's fall and robbed the palace

vault, he decides to secure their capture. In the face of dangers and with the help of Bell and another trapeze artist, he succeeds, but once again is denied both recognition of his achievement and the award, which was to save Bell and himself from eviction and further his education.
Eastern European-English Jewish/French-English non-Jewish
Older; Fiction

Peacock, Shane. *Eye of the Crow: The Boy Sherlock Holmes, His First Case.* Plattsburgh, N.Y.: Tundra Books of Northern New York, 2007. 264 p. (The Boy Sherlock Holmes)
This is the first in a series about young Sherlock Holmes, the son of Jewish Eastern European-English Wilber and French-English Rose, who is from a high-class family. When Rose married Wilber, her parents disowned her and made sure that Wilber, a teacher in training at the University College of London, not only could not teach there, but also would not be able to get any jobs befitting his talents. Sherlock lives with his much-loved parents in a London flat and is often taunted as a half-Jew. In 1867 after thirteen-year-old Sherlock reads of the murder of a beautiful young woman in a London slum, he goes to the murder site and is arrested by the police as an accomplice to the alleged Arab murderer. Through ingenuity Sherlock manages to escape from the jail and then seek the actual murderer. Helped by the older boy Malefactor and his gang of boy criminals, by his only friend Irene, and by his mother, Sherlock prowls the streets of London at night and encounters many dangers. Although Scotland Yard takes full credit for solving the crime, it is Sherlock who discovers the truth. However, in doing so Irene is severely injured and Rose dies of poisoning. Sherlock resolves never again to form emotional attachments, but to devote his deductive powers solely to seeking justice.
Eastern European-English Jewish/French-English non-Jewish
Older; Fiction

Peacock, Shane. *The Secret Fiend: The Boy Sherlock Holmes, His 4th Case.* Plattsburgh, N.Y.: Tundra Books of Northern New York, 2010. 256 p. (The Boy Sherlock Holmes)
In 1868 when he has just turned fourteen, Sherlock Holmes' childhood friend Beatrice and her companion Louise are attacked on Westminster Bridge by what Beatrice thinks looks like the fictional Spring Heeled Jack. Sherlock seeks to protect Beatrice and rid London of the fiend, who is increasingly terrorizing the city. Discarding his initial suspicion that the Jack might be Sigerson Bell, his elderly employer, Sherlock focuses on Crew, the criminal Malefactor's lieutenant. Despite encounters with the Jack and a Jack imposter, Sherlock continues to pursue his mission. Then, falsely implicated as the Jack's accomplice, Sherlock plans to leave London. The story ends with the surprising discovery of the identities of the fiend and his accomplices, Sherlock and Bell's fight with the Jack, and encouraging advice given to Sherlock by Prime Minister Benjamin Disraeli, who is Jewish.
Eastern European-English Jewish/French-English non-Jewish
Older; Fiction

Peacock, Shane. *Vanishing Girl: The Boy Sherlock Holmes, His 3rd Case.* Plattsburgh, N.Y.: Tundra Books of Northern New York, 2009. 320 p. (The Boy Sherlock Holmes)
Sherlock Holmes apparently fails in his attempt to solve the case of kidnapped fourteen-year-old Victoria Rathbone when, after thinding he has found her in the supposedly-haunted Grimwood Hall

in St. Neots, she is found by Scotland Yard elsewhere. Then, in this third book of the series, the wealthy Rathbone family is robbed and, shortly thereafter, Victoria is again kidnapped. In addition, the fate of Paul, a five-year-old boy with rapidly progressing blindness, depends on quickly solving the complicated case. Still living with the apothecary Sigerson Bell, Sherlock makes daring entrances into the Rathbone residence and Grimwood Hall and uses his observational skills, his ingenuity, and his newly-acquired fighting skills to keep ahead of Malefactor's criminal gang and his Scotland Yard nemesis, Inspector Lestrade. When Sherlock finally succeeds in finding the culprits and the real, not the disguised, Victoria, he heeds Bell's advice and lets Scotland Yard take the credit. Further, while Sherlock is solving the case, Bell, who feels he can now cure Paul, is removing him from the London workhouse where he had been placed.
Eastern European-English Jewish/French-English non-Jewish
Older; Fiction

Rahlens, Holly-Jane. *Prince William, Maximilian Minsky, and Me*. Cambridge, Mass.: Candlewick Press, 2005. 320 p.

Nelly, who is thirteen and brainy, suddenly has a major crush on England's Prince William. Although she is unathletic, she decides to try out for her Berlin school's basketball team since it will be playing in England. The story relates how she persuades Max, a seemingly weird American-German boy, to be her basketball tutor, how she resents her Jewish-American mother who insists that she have a bat mitzvah, how she discovers that her adored German father is having an affair with Max's mother, and how Prince William is displaced as her love.
German and non-Jewish/Polish-Russian-Jewish-American; European-American/ Jewish-German
Older; Fiction

Ringgold, Faith. *Bonjour, Lonnie*. Illustrated by author. New York: Hyperion Books for Children, 1996. 32 p.

Thanks to a Love Bird that flies into Lonnie's window one night, he discovers his family background. During World War I his paternal grandfather was an African-American soldier in France. There he met and married Lonnie's French grandmother and became an opera singer. Their son (Lonnie's father) married a Jewish French woman. During World War II he died fighting for France and, after Lonnie's mother gave him to a friend for his safety, she became a victim of the Nazis. Subsequently, Lonnie was taken to the United States where he was adopted by an African-American couple, Aunt Connie and Uncle Bates. This picture book is a companion book to *Dinner at Aunt Connie's House*.
African-American-French and non-Jewish/French and Jewish
Primary; Fiction

Ringgold, Faith. *Dinner at Aunt Connie's House*. Illustrated by author. New York: Hyperion Books for Children, 1993. 32 p.

This picture book is based on the artist-author's "The Dinner Quilt," a painted story quilt, which has been exhibited in museums. When African-American Melody visits her Aunt Connie, she meets her aunt's adopted son, Lonnie, a black boy with red hair and green eyes. Before the family dinner, they

go into the attic where they see Aunt Connie's portraits of twelve famous African-American women, paintings that speak to the children about their subjects' accomplishments. Lonnie's heritage is revealed in a companion book, *Bonjour, Lonnie.*
African-American-French and non-Jewish/French and Jewish
Primary; Fiction

Rosenberg, Maxine B. *Living in Two Worlds.* Photographs by George Ancona. New York: Lothrop, Lee & Shepard Books, 1986. 48 p.

This book explains how races evolved and how many children have a greater resemblance to one of their parents. It discusses the teasing and unwanted questions biracial children face and points to the benefits of living in two cultures. The book's text and black-and-white photographs focus on five children: Toah, who is African-European-American; Megan, who is African-European-American and Cherokee; Jesse, who is Chinese-European-American; and Shashi and Anil, who are Indian-European-American.
European-American and Jewish/Chinese-American and Christian
Intermediate; Nonfiction

Schwartz, Ellen. *Stealing Home.* Plattsburgh, N.Y.: Tundra Books of Northern New York, 2006. 224 p.

When ten-year-old Joey's mother dies, he is sent to live with her estranged family: his disapproving grandfather, his loving aunt, and his cousin, a girl who loves baseball as much as he does. Set in 1947, this is a story about the racial prejudice facing biracial Joey, first in his native Bronx by African-American boys who won't let him play baseball and then in Brooklyn where white boys won't let him play ball and where a woman insults him and his deceased mother. It relates how Joey's new friends and his aunt finally stand up for him against the bigots, how Joey and his grandfather come to understand and accept each other, and how, home at last, Joey changes his allegiance from the Bronx Bombers to Jackie Robinson and the Brooklyn Dodgers.
African-American and non-Jewish/European-American and Jewish
Intermediate; Fiction

Watts, Irene N. *Finding Sophie.* Plattsburgh, N.Y.: Tundra Books of Northern New York, 2002. 144 p.

This book, which is a sequel to and contains excerpts from *Good-bye Marianne* and *Remember Me,* relates what happened to seven-year-old Sophie whose mother placed her on the 1938 *Kindertransport* train in Berlin and told eleven-year-old Marianne to look after her. Sophie went to live with "Aunt Em" a friend of her parents, and loves being with her as well as life in England. Now, turning fourteen-years-old, Sophie hopes that after the war she will not have to return to Germany and the parents she barely remembers. By chance she and Marianne are reunited, and Sophie participates in the May 1945 celebration of Germany's defeat. Shortly thereafter she receives a letter from her father containing both the happy news that he has survived the Dachau Concentration Camp and the sorrowful news that her mother was killed in an air raid. Sophie's concerns about her future are happily resolved when she remains with Aunt Em and her father comes to live nearby.
German and Jewish/German and Christian
Intermediate, Older; Fiction

Werlin, Nancy. *Black Mirror: A Novel*. New York: Dial Books, 2001. 256 p.

In this book for older teenagers sixteen-year-old Frances is a loner and so upset by her mixed race appearance that for years she has not been able to look at herself in the mirror. When her brother Daniel commits suicide by an overdose of heroin, Frances is shocked and feels guilty that she had no longer been close to him. When she considers joining Unity Service, the preparatory school charitable institution in which Daniel was so active, she experiences conflicting emotions and encounters negative reactions from its members. Discovering that something strange is going on at Unity, Frances, with the help of a man who is mildly retarded, finds out the terrible truth about Unity and the death of her brother.

European-American and Jewish/Japanese-American and Buddhist

Older; Fiction

Wing, Natasha. *Jalapeño Bagels*. Illustrated by Robert Casilla. New York: Atheneum Books for Young Readers, 1996. 24 p.

Pablo helps his parents at their Mexican-Jewish-American bakery and decides that he will take jalapeño bagels to his class International Day as they, like him are a mixture of two cultures. This picture book includes recipes for chango bars and jalapeño bagels as well as a glossary of Spanish and Yiddish words.

European-American and Jewish/Mexican-American

Pre-K, Primary; Fiction

Wyeth, Sharon Dennis. *The World of Daughter McGuire*. New York: Delacorte Press, 1994. 176 p.

Eleven-year-old Daughter's parents have separated, and she, her two younger brothers, and her mother have moved into a house next to her mother's parents. Daughter, whose deceased grandfather was Irish-American Catholic and whose other grandparents are Russian Jewish, African-American, and Italian-American, is called a "zebra" by a schoolmate and wishes that she was not all mixed-up. She is further concerned that the differences between her mother and father in careers and lifestyles will result in divorce. In this story Daughter learns to be proud of her heritages and is relieved when her parents decide to try to stay together despite their differences.

Irish-American Catholic and Russian-American Jewish/African-Italian-American

Intermediate; Fiction

Muslim

See   Farmanfarmaian, Roxane

Harris, Rosemary. *Zed*. Boston: Faber and Faber, 1984. 192 p.

Fifteen-year-old Zed is asked by his house master to write up the time when, as an eight-year-old, he, together with his father, Uncle Omar, and others, was held captive in a London building by the Free Army of United Arabia. As Zed writes, he relives those terrible four days: the terrorists, guns, grenades, discomforts, and overwhelming dread. Through the experience Zed comes to appreciate the kindness and bravery of Uncle Omar, who was Saudi-Turkish, and Arabi, one of the terrorists. Both

were killed by gunshots, while Zed's English father, a self-centered coward, survived. After writing the manuscript, Zed arranges a meeting between Omar and Arabi's sons. This novel is for teenagers.
Saudi-Turkish-Lebanese and Muslim/Lebanese and Christian Maronite
Older; Fiction

Rastafari

See   McCallum, Shara

Shinto

Easton, Kelly. *Hiroshima Dreams*. New York: Dutton Children's Books, 2007. 208 p.
When Lin's Japanese grandmother comes to visit, she immediately recognizes five-year-old Lin as a kindred spirit. Lin is so shy that she barely speaks, but is able to sense what is about to happen. Lin becomes very close to her Obaachan, who teaches her about Japan, shows how her how to meditate, imparts wisdom, and tells Lin that she too has precognition. As the years pass and with Obaachan's support, Lin plays her cello in an orchestra, makes a best friend in her new school, and uses her vision to help police locate a missing boy. When Obaachan dies from leukemia, the result of being a fifteen-year-old in Hiroshima when the atomic bomb was dropped, Lin is devastated. Then, the boy she has been attracted to since kindergarten becomes her boyfriend and Lin accepts her gift of vision.
Irish-American Catholic/Japanese Buddhist, Shinto, and Catholic
Older; Fiction

Sikh

Lamba, Marie. *What I Meant*. New York: Random House, 2007. 320 p.
Ever since her father's sister-in law has moved in, there has been a change in fifteen-year-old Sang's family. Her widowed Indian aunt Chachi is a complaining, critical kleptomaniac who steals food and money and blames the thefts on Sang. In the meantime Sang is head over heels in love with her classmate Jason and is upset that her parents will not allow her to date until she is sixteen. When her mother catches Sang in the lie that she was at an ice skating rink with her best friend Gina, her parents don't believe her allegations about Chachi. Her mother even takes her to a doctor since she believes Sang is bulimic. To make matters worse, for an unknown reason Gina turns against Sang. The situation comes to a climax when Sang sneaks off to Philadelphia to see a concert with Jason and his friend Gary. She sees Gina alone in another train car, and, when Gina leaves the train toting a large backpack, Sang realizes that she is running away. Getting off the train Sang follows Gina through the dark city streets and then calls Gina's mother as to her whereabouts. Robbed of her money and return ticket, Sang goes back to the train station where Gary is searching for her. Sang comes to realize that Gina and Jason are no longer her friends, but that she has other supportive classmates. Further, when Sang stands up to Chachi, who is about to reveal a damaging secret about her mother, Sang's parents and her visiting Indian uncle believe her and Chachi is made to leave.

Indian and Sikh/Italian-American and Catholic
Older; Fiction

Spiritualist

Wittlinger, Ellen. *Blind Faith*. New York: Simon & Schuster Books for Young Readers, 2006. 288 p.

This book tells of the experiences of two families, each dealing with the death of a much loved family member. When fifteen-year-old Liz's grandmother Bunny dies, her mother Christine is devastated for they had an extremely close relationship in contrast to the indifference Christine has always shown Liz. Christine starts going to a Spiritualist Church where she believes Bunny communicates with her, and in the process she causes a rift with Liz's atheist father. Meanwhile sixteen-year-old Nathan, his young sister, and his dying mother Lily move in with Lily's crabby mother from whom she has been estranged. The story focuses on the evolving relationship between Liz and Nathan: their grief, the anger Nathan holds towards living with his grandmother, Liz's resentment towards her mother, and their questionings of religious beliefs. At the conclusion, there is reconciliation in both families.

Atheist/Presbyterian, Spiritualist
Older; Fiction

IV. Couples of Mixed Heritage

Introduction

This chapter covers books presenting specific couples of mixed heritage. Books providing a more overall discussion can be found in the "General" chapter.

This chapter is divided into two sections.

The first section, Couples Listings, provides information on persons covered in the "Biography" chapter who are or have been spouses of or in long-term relationships with persons of a different heritage. Couples are included only if the names of both parties are available. If there is no section on a woman in the "Biography" chapter, she is listed only under her name at the time of her marriage.

The heritage designation for each book reads:

Man's name (Heritage)—Woman's name (Heritage)

e.g., Lennon, John Winston (English)—Ono, Yoko (Japanese)

The listings next cross-reference these persons to the "Biography" chapter.

The second part of the chapter, References, presents, in alphabetical order, books which include couples of mixed heritage who do not have children of mixed heritage or whose children of mixed heritage are adopted. Those books are included in the "Individuals of Mixed Racial and/or Ethnic Heritage" or "Individuals of Mixed Religious Heritage" chapters. The heritage designation in this section is:

Heritage of man and Heritage of woman

e.g., Portuguese and Catholic man and Mozambican and Shona woman

The order in which the heritages are listed is immaterial.

Couples Listing

Abdul, Paula (Canadian and Syrian Jewish)—Estévez, Emilio (Irish-Spanish-European-American)
See   Abdul, Paula
       Estévez, Emilio

Abdullah II bin Al Hussein, King of Jordan (English-Jordanian)—Rania Al Yasin (Palestinian-Kuwaiti)

See   Abdullah II bin Al Hussein, King of Jordan
         Rania Al Abdullah, Queen of Jordan

Adoff, Arnold (Russian-American and Jewish)—Hamilton, Virginia Esther (African-American, Cherokee, and Potawatomi)
See   Adoff, Arnold
         Hamilton, Virginia

Allison, Lori Anne (European-American)—Depp, John (Johnny) Christopher II (German-Irish-American and Cherokee)
See   Depp, John (Johnny) Christopher II

Anderson, Alpharita Constantia (Rita) (African-Jamaican)—Marley, Nesta Robert (Bob) (African-English-Jamaican)
See   Marley, Nesta Robert (Bob)

Arosen, Francois Xavier (Canadian Mohawk)—Williams, Eunice (English Puritan)
See   Williams, Eunice

Aubry, Gabriel (French Canadian)—Berry, Halle Maria (African-American and English)
See   Berry, Halle Maria

Babbit(t), Elizabeth (European-American)—Haynes, Lemuel (African-European-American)
See   Haynes, Lemuel

Baez, Joan Chandos (Mexican and Scottish)—Harris, David Victor (European-American)
See   Baez, Joan Chandos

Balanchine, George (Georgian)—Danilova, Alexandra (Choura) (Russian)
See   Balanchine, George

Balanchine, George (Georgian)—Geva, Tamara (Russian and Swedish)
See   Balanchine, George

Balanchine, George (Georgian)—Le Clerq, Tanaquil (French and European-American)
See   Balanchine, George

Balanchine, George (Georgian)—Tallchief, Maria (Scottish-Irish-American and Osage)
See   Balanchine, George
         Tallchief, Maria

Balanchine, George (Georgian)—Zorina, Vera (German)
See   Balanchine, George

Bannaky (Banneky) (African, probably Senegalese)—Banneky (Bannaky), Molly Welsh (Walsh) (English)
See   Banneky (Bannaky), Molly Welsh (Walsh)

Banneky (Bannaky), Molly Welsh (Walsh) (English)—Bannaky (Banneky) (African, probably Senegalese)
See   Banneky (Bannaky), Molly Welsh (Walsh)

Benét, Eric (African-American)—Berry, Halle Maria (African-American and English)
See   Berry, Halle Maria

Bent, Charles (European-American)—Jaramillo, Maria Ignacia (Mexican)
See   Bent, Charles

Bent, William (European-American)—Harvey, Adalina (European-American and Blackfoot)
See   Bent, William

Bent, William (European-American)—Mis-stan-stur (Owl Woman) (Cheyenne)
See   Bent, William

Bent, William (European-American)—Yellow Woman (Cheyenne)
See   Bent, William

Berry, Halle Maria (African-American and English)—Aubry, Gabriel (French Canadian)
See   Berry, Halle Maria

Berry, Halle Maria (African-American and English)—Benét, Eric (African-American)
See   Berry, Halle Maria

Berry, Halle Maria (African-American and English)—Justice, David (African-American)
See   Berry, Halle Maria

Beyoncé (African-Creole-American)—Carter, Shawn Corey (Jay-Z) (African-American)
See   Beyoncé

Bibb, Henry (African-European-American)—Malinda (African-European-American)
See   Bibb, Henry

Bibb, Henry (African-European-American)—Miles, Mary (African-American)
See   Bibb, Henry

Blades, Rubén (St. Lucian-Colombian?-Panamanian and American-Spanish-Cuban)—Lebenzon, Lisa (European-American)
See   Blades, Rubén

Blaise, Clark (European-American)—Mukherjee, Bharati (Indian)
See   Mukherjee, Bharati

Blake, Betty (European-American)—Rogers, William (Will) Penn Adair (English-American or Scottish-Irish-American, Dutch-Irish-Welsh-American, and Cherokee)
See   Rogers, William (Will) Penn Adair

Bosomworth, Mary Musgrove Matthews (English or Scottish-Irish and Creek)—Bosomworth, Thomas (English)
See   Bosomworth, Mary Musgrove Matthews

Bosomworth, Thomas (English)— Matthews, Mary Musgrove (English or Scottish-Irish and Creek)
See   Bosomworth, Mary Musgrove Matthews

Bowie, David (English)—Iman (Somali)
See   Bowie, David

Bracco, Lorraine (English-Italian-American)—Olmos, Edward James (Mexican and Mexican-American)
See   Olmos, Edward James

Brant, Joseph (Mohawk)—Christine (Oneida)
See   Brant, Joseph

Brant, Joseph (Mohawk)—Croghan, Catherine Adonwentishon (British or Irish and Mohawk)
See   Brant, Joseph

Brant, Joseph (Mohawk)—Susanna(h) (Oneida)
See   Brant, Joseph

Brant, Molly (Mohawk)—Johnson, William (1715-1774) (Irish)
See   Brant, Molly
        Johnson, William (1715-1774)

Burton, Henry S. (European-American Protestant)—Ruiz, María Amparo (Mexican Catholic)
See   Ruiz de Burton, María Amparo

Cameron, Lucille (European-American)—Johnson, John (Jack) Arthur (African-American)
See   Johnson, John (Jack) Arthur

Cannon, Poppy (European American)—White, Walter Francis (African-European-American)
See   White, Walter Francis

Carey, Mariah (African-Irish-Venezuelan-American)—Mottola, Tommy (Italian-American and Jewish)
See   Carey, Mariah

Carlquist, Doris (Swedish-American)—Halaby, Najeeb Elias (Syrian and European-American)
See   Halaby, Najeeb Elias

Carson, Christopher (Kit) Houston (European-American)—Jaramillo, Josefa Maria (Mexican)
See   Carson, Christopher (Kit) Houston

Carson, Christopher (Kit) Houston (European-American)—Making-Out-Road (Cheyenne)
See   Carson, Christopher (Kit) Houston

Carson, Christopher (Kit) Houston (European-American)—Waanibe (Arapaho)
See   Carson, Christopher (Kit) Houston

Carter, Shawn Corey (Jay-Z) (African-American)—Knowles, Beyoncé Giselle (African-Creole-American)
See   Beyoncé

Cary, Mary Ann Shadd (African-Dominican Republican-German-American)—Cary, Thomas F. (African-Canadian)
See   Cary, Mary Ann Shadd

Cary, Thomas F. (African-Canadian)—Cary, Mary Ann Shadd (African-Dominican Republican-German-American)
See   Cary, Mary Ann Shadd

Charbonneau, Toussaint (French Canadian)—Sacagawea ((Lemhi Shoshone)
See   Charbonneau, Toussaint
      Sacagawea

Christine (Oneida)— Brant, Joseph (Mohawk)
See   Brant, Joseph

Chung, Constance (Connie) Yu-Hwa (Chinese-American)—Povich, Maurice (Maury) Richard (Jewish and Lithuanian-European-American)
See   Chung, Constance (Connie) Yu-Hwa

Croghan, Catherine Adonwentishon (British or Irish and Mohawk)—Brant, Joseph (Mohawk)
See   Brant, Joseph

Cuffe, Paul (Ashanti and Gayhead Wampanoag or Pequot)—Pequit, Alice (Wampanoag or Pequot)
See   Cuffe, Paul

Dandridge, Dorothy (African-English-Jamaican-Native Mexican-Spanish-American)—Denison, Jack (European-American)
See   Dandridge, Dorothy

Dandridge, Dorothy (African-English-Jamaican-Native Mexican-Spanish-American)—Nicholas, Harold (African-American)
See   Dandridge, Dorothy

Danilova, Alexandra (Choura) (Russian)—Balanchine, George (Georgian)
See   Balanchine, George

Davidson, Olivia A. (African-European-American)—Washington, Booker T. (African-European-American)
See   Washington, Booker Taliaferro
        Washington, Olivia A. Davidson

Dean, Carl (European-American)—Parton, Dolly Rebecca (European-Scottish-Irish-American and Cherokee)
See   Parton, Dolly Rebecca

Denison, Jack (European-American)—Dandridge, Dorothy (African-English-Jamaican-Native Mexican-Spanish-American)
See   Dandridge, Dorothy

Depp, John (Johnny) Christopher II (German-Irish-American and Cherokee)—Allison, Lori Anne (European-American)
See   Depp, John (Johnny) Christopher II

Depp, John (Johnny) Christopher II (German-Irish-American and Cherokee)—Paradis, Vanessa (French)
See   Depp, John (Johnny) Christopher II

Dorris, Michael (Modoc and French-English-Irish-Swiss-American)—Erdrich, Louise (German-American, French Canadian, and Turtle Mountain Chippewa)
See   Dorris, Michael
        Erdrich, Louise

Douglass, Frederick (African-European-American)—Murray, Anna (African-American)
See   Douglass, Frederick

Douglass, Frederick (African-European-American)—Pitts, Helen (European-American)
See   Douglass, Frederick

Dove, Rita (African-American)—Viebahn, Fred (German)
See   Dove, Rita

Du Bois, William Edward Burghardt (W. E. B.) (African-Bahamian-French Huguenot-American-Haitian and African-Dutch)—Gomer, Nina (African-American)
See   Du Bois, William Edward Burghardt (W. E. B.)

Du Bois, William Edward Burghardt (W. E. B.) (African-Bahamian-French Huguenot-American-Haitian and African-Dutch)—Graham, Shirley (African-American)
See   Du Bois, William Edward Burghardt (W. E. B.)

Du Sable, Jean Baptiste Pointe (French and African)—Kihihawa (Catherine) (Potawatomi)
See   Du Sable, Jean Baptiste Pointe

Duryea, Etta Terry (European-American)— Johnson, John (Jack) Arthur (African-American)
See   Johnson, John (Jack) Arthur

Early, Jordan Winston (African-American)—Early, Sarah Jane Woodson (African-English-Welsh?-American)
See   Early, Sarah Jane Woodson

Early, Sarah Jane Woodson (African-English-Welsh?-American)—Early, Jordan Winston (African-American)
See   Early, Sarah Jane Woodson

Eastman, Linda Louise (Russian-American Jewish)—McCartney, James Paul (English agnostic, Church of England, and Catholic)
See   McCartney, James Paul

Erdrich, Louise (German-American, French Canadian, and Turtle Mountain Chippewa)—Dorris, Michael (Modoc and French-English-Irish-Swiss-American)
See   Dorris, Michael
        Erdrich, Louise

Estévez, Emilio (Irish-Spanish-European-American)— Abdul, Paula (Canadian and Syrian Jewish)
See   Abdul, Paula
        Estévez, Emilio

Estevez, Ramón Antonio Gerardo (Irish and Spanish)—Templeton, Janet (European-American)
See   Sheen, Martin

Farragut, David Glasgow (Spanish [Minorcan] and European-American)—Loyall, Virginia Dorcas (European-American)
See   Farragut, David Glasgow

Farragut, David Glasgow (Spanish [Minorcan] and European-American)—Marchant (or Merchant), Susan Connie (European-American)
See   Farragut, David Glasgow

Flavin, Barbara (European-American)—Richardson, William (Bill) Blaine III (European-American-Mexican-Nicaraguan and Spanish-Mexican)
See   Richardson, William (Bill) Blaine III

Garcia, Dany (Cuban-American)—Johnson, Dwayne Douglass (The Rock) (African-Canadian and Samoan)
See   Johnson, Dwayne Douglass (The Rock)

Gellar, Sarah Michelle (European-American and Jewish)—Prinze, Freddie James, Jr. (Hungarian and European-Puerto Rican-American)
See   Prinze, Freddie James, Jr.

Gentry, Tiana Rogers (European-American and Cherokee)—Houston, Samuel (Scottish-Irish-American)
See   Houston, Samuel

Geva, Tamara (Russian and Swedish)—Balanchine, George (Georgian)
See   Balanchine, George

Gomer, Nina (African-American)—Du Bois, William Edward Burghardt (W. E. B.) (African-Bahamian-French Huguenot-American-Haitian and African-Dutch)
See   Du Bois, William Edward Burghardt (W. E. B.)

Gonzàles, Lucia (Lucy) (probably African-American, Creek and Mexican)—Parsons, Albert (European-American)
See   Parsons, Lucia (Lucy) Gonzàles

Grace, Princess of Monaco (German-Irish-American)—Rainier III, Prince of Monaco (Monocan)
See   Grace, Princess of Monaco
        Rainier III, Prince of Monaco

Graham, Shirley (African-American)—Du Bois, William Edward Burghardt (W. E. B.) (African-Bahamian-French Huguenot-American-Haitian and African-Dutch)
See   Du Bois, William Edward Burghardt (W. E. B.)

Halaby, Lisa Najeeb (European-Swedish-Syrian-American)—Hussein bin Talal, King of Jordan (Jordanian)
See   Hussein bin Talal, King of Jordan
        Noor Al Hussein, Queen of Jordan

Halaby, Najeeb Elias (Syrian and European-American)—Carlquist, Doris (Swedish-American)
See   Halaby, Najeeb Elias

Hamilton, Virginia Esther (African-American, Cherokee, and Potawatomi)—Adoff, Arnold (Russian-American and Jewish)
See   Adoff, Arnold
        Hamilton, Virginia

Harris, David Victor (European-American)—Baez, Joan Chandos (Mexican and Scottish)
See   Baez, Joan Chandos

Harvey, Adalina (European-American and Blackfoot)—Bent, William (European-American)
See   Bent, William

Hasek, Mary Anne (European-American)—Morgan, Garrett Augustus (African-European-American and Native American)
See   Morgan, Garrett Augustus

Hayek-Jiménez, Salma Valgarma (Lebanese-Spanish-Mexican)—Pinault, François-Henri (French)
See   Hayek-Jiménez, Salma Valgarma

Haynes, Lemuel (African-European-American)—Babbit(t), Elizabeth (European-American)
See   Haynes, Lemuel

Hayton, Lennie (European-American)—Horne, Lena (African-European-American and Native American)
See   Horne, Lena

Hemings, Sally (English and African-English-American)—Jefferson, Thomas (English and Welsh-American)
See   Hemings, Sally
        Jefferson, Thomas

Herman, Florence (German)—Williams, William Carlos (English and Dutch-French-Spanish-Puerto Rican, Jewish, Catholic, and Unitarian)
See   Williams, William Carlos

Hiokatoo (Seneca)—Jemison, Mary (Irish-American or Scottish-Irish-American)
See   Jemison, Mary

Horne, Lena (African-European-American and Native American)—Hayton, Lennie (European-American)
See   Horne, Lena

Houston, Samuel (Scottish-Irish-American)—Gentry, Tiana Rogers (European-American and Cherokee)
See   Houston, Samuel

Hussein bin Talal, King of Jordan (Jordanian)—Halaby, Lisa Najeeb (European-Swedish-Syrian-American)

See   Hussein bin Talal, King of Jordan
       Noor Al Hussein, Queen of Jordan

Iman (Somali)—Bowie, David (English)
See   Bowie, David

Jackson, Michael Joseph (African-American, Baptist, and Jehovah's Witness)—Presley, Lisa Marie (English-French-Norwegian-Scottish-Irish-American and Cherokee)
See   Jackson, Michael Joseph

Jackson, Michael Joseph (African-American, Baptist, and Jehovah's Witness)—Rowe, Deborah (European-American)
See   Jackson, Michael Joseph

Jacobs, Harriet Ann (African-European-American)—Sawyer, Samuel (European-American)
See   Jacobs, Harriet Ann

Jaramillo, Josepha Maria (Mexican)—Carson, Christopher (Kit) Houston (European-American)
See   Carson, Christopher (Kit) Houston

Jaramillo, Maria Ignacia (Mexican)—Bent, Charles (European-American)
See   Bent, Charles

Jay-Z (African-American)—Beyoncé (African-Creole-American)
See   Beyoncé

Jefferson, Thomas (English and Welsh-American)—Hemings, Sally (English and African-English-American)
See   Hemings, Sally
       Jefferson, Thomas

Jemison, Mary (Irish-American or Scottish-Irish-American)—Hiokatoo (Seneca)
See   Jemison, Mary

Jemison, Mary (Irish-American or Scottish-Irish-American)—Sheninjee (Delaware)
See   Jemison, Mary

Jen, Gish (Chinese-American)—O'Connor, David (Irish-American)
See   Jen, Gish

Jenny (Shoshone)—Leigh, Richard (Beaver Dick) (English)
See   Leigh, Richard (Beaver Dick)

Jerk Meat (Comanche)—Sacagawea (Lemhi Shoshone)?
See   Sacagawea

Jeter, Mildred Delores (African-American and Rappahannock)—Loving, Richard Perry (European-American)
See   Loving, Mildred Delores Jeter

Johnson, Alice (African-European-American and Jewish)—Williams, Daniel Hale (African-European-American and Native American)
See   Williams, Daniel Hale

Johnson, Dwayne Douglass (The Rock) (African-Canadian and Samoan)—Garcia, Dany (Cuban-American)
See   Johnson, Dwayne Douglass (The Rock)

Johnson, John (Jack) Arthur (African-American)—Cameron, Lucille (European-American)
See   Johnson, John (Jack) Arthur

Johnson, John (Jack) Arthur (African-American)—Duryea, Etta Terry (European-American)
See   Johnson, John (Jack) Arthur

Johnson, William (1715-1774) (Irish)—Brant, Molly (Mohawk)
See   Brant, Molly
       Johnson, William (1715-1774)

Johnson, William (late 1700s-1800s) (English)—Nancy (Cheyenne)
See   Johnson, William (late 1700s-1800s)

Justice, David (African-American)—Berry, Halle Maria (African-American and English)
See   Berry, Halle Maria

Keel, Kaija (European-American)— Olmos, Edward James (Mexican and Mexican-American)
See   Olmos, Edward James

Keller, Maria (Romanian-American)—Montezuma, Carlos (Yavapai)
See   Montezuma, Carlos

Kelly, Grace (German-Irish-American)—Rainier III, Prince of Monaco (Monocan)
See   Grace, Princess of Monaco
       Rainier III, Prince of Monaco

Kihihawa (Catherine) (Potawatomi)—Du Sable, Jean Baptiste Pointe (French and African)
See   Du Sable, Jean Baptiste Pointe

Knowles, Beyoncé Giselle (African-Creole-American)—Carter, Shawn Corey (Jay-Z) (African-American)
See   Beyoncé

Kocoum (Patawomeke)—Pocahontas (Powhatan)?
See   Pocahontas

LaButte, Pierre (1698-1774) (French)—Roy, Marie (French and Miami)
See   LaButte, Pierre (1698-1774)
       Roy, Marie

LaFlesche, Susan (European-French-American, Iowa, Omaha?, Oto?, and Ponca?)—Picotte, Henry (French-American and Sioux)
See   Picotte, Susan LaFlesche

LaFlesche, Susette (European-French-American, Iowa, Omaha?, Oto?, and Ponca?)—Tibbles, Thomas Henry (European-American)
See   Tibbles, Susette LaFlesche

Lamp, Virginia Bess (European-American)—Thomas, Clarence (African-American)
See   Thomas, Clarence

Le Clerq, Tanaquil (French and European-American)— Balanchine, George (Georgian)
See   Balanchine, George

Lebenzon, Lisa (European-American)—Blades, Rubén (St. Lucian-Colombian?-Panamanian and American-Spanish-Cuban)
See   Blades, Rubén

Leigh, Richard (Beaver Dick) (English)—Jenny (Shoshone)
See   Leigh, Richard (Beaver Dick)

Leigh, Richard (Beaver Dick) (English)—Tadpole, Sue (Bannock)
See   Leigh, Richard (Beaver Dick)

Lennon, John Winston (English)—Ono, Yoko (Japanese)
See   Lennon, John Winston

Leventhal, Melvyn Rosenman (European-American and Jewish)—Walker, Alice Malsenior (African-American and Cherokee)
See   Walker, Alice Malsenior

Levin, Sara (European-American Jewish)— Ronstadt, Federico (Fred) José María (German and Mexican)
See   Ronstadt, Federico (Fred) José María

Loving, Mildred Delores Jeter (Rappahannock and African-American)—Loving. Richard Perry (European-American)
See   Loving, Mildred Delores Jeter

Loving, Richard Perry (European-American)—Jeter, Mildred Delores (Rappahannock and African-American)
See   Loving, Richard Perry

Loyall, Virginia Dorcas (European-American)—Farragut, David Glasgow (Spanish [Minorcan] and European-American)
See   Farragut, David Glasgow

MacKay, Marguerite Waddens (French Canadian Chippewa)—McLoughlin, Jean Baptiste (John) (Irish-Scottish-French Canadian)
See   McLoughlin, Jean Baptiste (John)

Making-Out-Road (Cheyenne)—Carson, Christopher (Kit) Houston (European-American)
See   Carson, Christopher (Kit) Houston

Malcolm X (African-American and African-Scottish-Grenadian)—Sanders, Betty Dean (Betty X) (African-American)
See   Malcolm X

Malinda (African-European-American)—Bibb, Henry (African-European-American)
See   Bibb, Henry

Marchant (or Merchant), Susan Connie (European-American)—Farragut, David Glasgow (Spanish [Minorcan] and European-American)
See   Farragut, David Glasgow

Marley, Nesta Robert (Bob) (African-English-Jamaican)—Anderson, Alpharita Constantia (Rita) (African-Jamaican)
See   Marley, Nesta Robert (Bob)

Mary (Coosaponakeesa) (English or Scottish-Irish and Creek)—Musgrove, John (English and Creek)
See   Bosomworth, Mary Musgrove Matthews

Matthews, Jacob (English)—Musgrove, Mary (English or Scottish-Irish and Creek)
See   Bosomworth, Mary Musgrove Matthews

Matthews, Mary Musgrove (English or Scottish-Irish and Creek)—Bosomworth, Thomas (English)
See   Bosomworth, Mary Musgrove Matthews

McCartney, James Paul (English agnostic, Church of England, and Catholic)—Eastman, Linda Louise (Russian-American Jewish)
See   McCartney, James Paul

McCauley, Rosa Louise (African-European-Scottish-Irish-American and Native American)—Parks, Raymond (African-European-American)
See   Parks, Rosa Louise McCauley

McLoughlin, Jean Baptiste (John) (Irish-Scottish-French Canadian—MacKay, Marguerite Waddens (French Canadian Chippewa)
See   McLoughlin, Jean Baptiste (John)

Meeks, Joseph (Joe) Lafayette (European-American)—Virginia (Nez Percé)
See   Meeks, Joseph (Joe) Lafayette

Miles, Mary (African-American)— Bibb, Henry (African-European-American)
See   Bibb, Henry

Miller, Iva Margaret (European-American and Cherokee)—Thorpe, James (Jim) Francis (Irish-French Canadian-American, Kickapoo, Potawatomi, and Sac and Fox)
See   Thorpe, James (Jim) Francis

Mis-stan-stur (Owl Woman) (Cheyenne)—Bent, William (European-American)
See   Bent, William

Mitchell, Maggie Dalena (Lena) (African-Irish-American)—Walker, Armstead (African-American)
See   Walker, Maggie Dalena (Lena) Mitchell

Montezuma, Carlos (Yavapai)— Keller, Maria (Romanian-American)
See   Montezuma, Carlos

Morgan, Garrett Augustus (African-European-American and Native American)—Hasek, Mary Anne (European-American)
See   Morgan, Garrett Augustus

Moses (Hebrew-Egyptian)—Zipporah (Midianite)
See   Moses

Mottola, Tommy (Italian-American and Jewish)—Carey, Mariah (African-Irish-Venezuelan-American)
See   Carey, Mariah

Mukherjee, Bharati (Indian)—Blaise, Clark (European-American)
See   Mukherjee, Bharati

Mura, David (Japanese-American and Episcopalian)—Sencer, Susan (European-Jewish-American and Protestant)
See   Mura, David

Murray, Anna (African-American)—Douglass, Frederick (African-European-American)
See   Douglass, Frederick

Murray, Margaret James (African-Irish-American)—Washington, Booker T. (African-European-American)
See   Washington, Booker Taliaferro
        Washington, Margaret James Murray

Musgrove, John (English and Creek)—Mary (Coosaponakeesa) (English or Scottish-Irish and Creek)
See   Bosomworth, Mary Musgrove Matthews

Musgrove, Mary (English or Scottish-Irish and Creek)—Matthews, Jacob (English)
See   Bosomworth, Mary Musgrove Matthews

Nacona, Peta (Comanche)—Parker, Cynthia Ann (Scottish-Irish-American)
See   Parker, Cynthia Ann

Nadal, Lymari (Puerto Rican)— Olmos, Edward James (Mexican and Mexican-American)
See   Olmos, Edward James

Nancy (Cheyenne)—Johnson, William (late 1700s-1800s) (English)
See   Johnson, William (late 1700s-1800s)

Nicholas, Harold (African-American)—Dandridge, Dorothy (African-English-Jamaican-Native Mexican-Spanish-American)
 See   Dandridge, Dorothy

Noor Al Hussein, Queen of Jordan (European-Swedish-Syrian-American)—Hussein bin Talal, King of Jordan (Jordanian)
See   Hussein bin Talal, King of Jordan
       Noor Al Hussein, Queen of Jordan

Nordegren, Elin Maria Pernilla (Swedish)— Woods, Tiger (African-Chinese-American, Native American Protestant and Chinese-Dutch-Thai Buddhist)
See   Woods, Tiger

Obama, Barack (Kenyan, English-Irish-Scottish-American, and Cherokee?)—Robinson, Michelle LaVaughn (African-American)
See   Obama, Barack
       Obama, Michelle LaVaughn Robinson

Obama, Michelle LaVaughn Robinson (African-American)—Obama, Barack (Kenyan, English-Irish-Scottish-American, and Cherokee?)
See   Obama, Barack
       Obama, Michelle LaVaughn Robinson

O'Connor, David (Irish-American)—Jen, Gish (Chinese-American)
See   Jen, Gish

Olmos, Edward James (Mexican and Mexican-American)—Bracco, Lorraine (English-Italian-American)
See   Olmos, Edward James

Olmos, Edward James (Mexican and Mexican-American)—Keel, Kaija (European-American)
See   Olmos, Edward James

Olmos, Edward James (Mexican and Mexican-American)—Nadal, Lymari (Puerto Rican)
See   Olmos, Edward James

Ono, Yoko (Japanese)—Lennon, John Winston (English)
See   Lennon, John Winston

Paradis, Vanessa (French)—Depp, John (Johnny) Christopher II (German-Irish-American and Cherokee)
See   Depp, John (Johnny) Christopher II

Parker, Cynthia Ann (Scottish-Irish-American)—Nacona, Peta (Comanche)
See   Parker, Cynthia Ann

Parks, Raymond (African-European-American)—McCauley, Rosa Louise (African-European-Scottish-Irish-American and Native American)
See   Parks, Rosa Louise McCauley

Parks, Rosa Louise McCauley (African-European-Scottish-Irish-American and Native American)—Parks, Raymond (African-European-American)
See   Parks, Rosa Louise McCauley

Parsons, Albert (European-American)— Gonzàles, Lucia (Lucy) (probably African-American, Creek and Mexican)
See   Parsons, Lucia (Lucy) Gonzàles

Parsons, Lucia (Lucy) Gonzàles (probably African-American, Creek and Mexican)—Parsons, Albert (European-American)
See   Parsons, Lucia (Lucy) Gonzàles

Parton, Dolly Rebecca (European-Scottish-Irish-American and Cherokee)—Dean, Carl (European-American)
See   Parton, Dolly Rebecca

Pequit, Alice (Wampanoag or Pequot)—Cuffe, Paul (Ashanti and Gayhead Wampanoag or Pequot)
See   Cuffe, Paul

Picotte, Henry (French-American and Sioux)—LaFlesche, Susan (European-French-American, Iowa, Omaha?, Oto?, and Ponca?)
See   Picotte, Susan LaFlesche

Picotte, Susan LaFlesche (European-French-American, Iowa, Omaha?, Oto?, and Ponca?)—Picotte, Henry (French-American and Sioux)
See   Picotte, Susan LaFlesche

Pinault, François-Henri (French)—Hayek-Jiménez, Salma Valgarma (Lebanese-Spanish-Mexican)
See   Hayek-Jiménez, Salma Valgarma

Pitts, Helen (European-American)—Douglass, Frederick (African-European-American)
See   Douglass, Frederick

Pocahontas (Powhatan)—Kocoum (Patawomeke)
See   Pocahontas

Pocahontas (Powhatan)—Rolfe, John (English)
See   Pocahontas
        Rolfe, John

Povich, Maurice (Maury) Richard (Lithuanian-European-American and Jewish)—Chung, Constance (Connie) Yu-Hwa (Chinese-American)
See   Chung, Constance (Connie) Yu-Hwa

Powell, Gladys (African-American)—White, Walter Francis (African-European-American)
See   White, Walter Francis

Poythress, Jane (English)—Rolfe, Thomas (English and Powhatan)
See   Rolfe, Thomas

Presley, Lisa Marie (English-French-Norwegian-Scottish-Irish-American and Cherokee)—Jackson, Michael Joseph (African-American, Baptist, and Jehovah's Witness)
See   Jackson, Michael Joseph

Prinze, Freddie James, Jr. (Hungarian and European-Puerto Rican-American)—Gellar, Sarah Michelle (European-American and Jewish)
See   Prinze, Freddie James, Jr.

Rainier III, Prince of Monaco (Monocan)—Kelly, Grace (German-Irish-American)
See   Grace, Princess of Monaco
        Rainier III, Prince of Monaco

Rania Al Abdullah, Queen of Jordan (Palestinian-Kuwaiti)—Abdullah II bin Al Hussein, King of Jordan (English-Jordanian)

See   Abdullah II bin Al Hussein, King of Jordan
          Rania Al Abdullah, Queen of Jordan

Rania Al Yasin (Palestinian-Kuwaiti)—Abdullah II bin Al Hussein, King of Jordan (English-Jordanian)
See   Abdullah II bin Al Hussein, King of Jordan
          Rania Al Abdullah, Queen of Jordan

Richardson, William (Bill) Blaine III (European-American-Mexican-Nicaraguan and Spanish-Mexican)—Flavin, Barbara (European-American)
See   Richardson, William (Bill) Blaine III

Robinson, Michelle LaVaughn (African-American)—Obama, Barack (Kenyan, English-Irish-Scottish-American, and Cherokee?)
See   Obama, Barack
          Obama, Michelle LaVaughn Robinson

Rogers, William (Will) Penn Adair (English-American or Scottish-Irish-American, Dutch-Irish Welsh-American, and Cherokee)—Blake, Betty (European-American)
See   Rogers, William (Will) Penn Adair

Rolfe, John (English)—Pocahontas (Powhatan)
See   Pocahontas
          Rolfe, John

Rolfe, Thomas (English and Powhatan)—Poythress, Jane (English)
See   Rolfe, Thomas

Rolfe, Thomas (English and Powhatan)—Washington, Elizabeth (English)
See   Rolfe, Thomas

Ronstadt, Federico (Fred) José María (German and Mexican)—Levin, Sara (European-American Jewish)
See   Ronstadt, Federico (Fred) José María

Ross, Catherine (Narragansett)—Stanton, Moses (African-American)
See   Stanton, Catherine Ross
          Stanton, Moses

Rowe, Deborah (European-American)—Jackson, Michael Joseph (African-American, Baptist, and Jehovah's Witness)
See   Jackson, Michael Joseph

Roy, Marie (French and Miami)—LaButte, Pierre (1698-1774) (French)
See   LaButte, Pierre (1698-1774)
        Roy, Marie

Ruiz, María Amparo (Mexican and Catholic)—Burton, Henry S. (European-American and Protestant)
See   Ruiz de Burton, María Amparo

Ruiz de Burton, María Amparo (Mexican and Catholic)—Burton, Henry S. (European-American and Protestant)
See   Ruiz de Burton, María Amparo

Sacagawea (Lemhi Shoshone)—Charbonneau, Toussaint (French Canadian)
See   Charbonneau, Toussaint
        Sacagawea

Sacagawea (Lemhi Shoshone)—Jerk Meat (Comanche)?
See   Sacagawea

Sanders, Betty Dean (Betty X) (African-American)—Malcolm X (African-American and African-Scottish-Grenadian)
See   Malcolm X

Sawyer, Samuel (European-American)—Jacobs, Harriet Ann (African-European-American)
See   Jacobs, Harriet Ann

Schwarzenegger, Arnold (Austrian)—Shriver, Maria (Irish-German-American)
See   Schwarzenegger, Arnold
        Shriver, Maria

Sencer, Susan (European-Jewish-American and Protestant)—Mura, David (Japanese-American and Episcopalian)
See   Mura, David

Shadd, Mary Ann (African-Dominican Republic-German-American)—Cary, Thomas F. (African-Canadian)
See   Cary, Mary Ann Shadd

Sheninjee (Delaware)—Jemison, Mary (Irish-American or Scottish-Irish-American)
See   Jemison, Mary

Sheen, Martin (Irish and Spanish)—Templeton, Janet (European-American)
See   Sheen, Martin

Shriver, Maria (Irish-German-American)—Schwarzenegger, Arnold (Austrian)
See   Schwarzenegger, Arnold
        Shriver, Maria

Smith, Fannie Norton (African-American and Shawnee)—Washington, Booker T. (African-European-American)
See   Washington, Booker Taliaferro
        Washington, Fannie Norton Smith

Stanton, Catherine Ross (Narragansett)—Stanton, Moses (African-American)
See   Stanton, Catherine Ross
        Stanton, Moses

Stanton, Moses (African-American)—Ross, Catherine (Narragansett)
See   Stanton, Catherine Ross
        Stanton, Moses

Susanna(h) (Oneida)—Brant, Joseph (Mohawk)
See   Brant, Joseph

Tadpole, Sue (Bannock)—Leigh, Richard (Beaver Dick) (English)
See   Leigh, Richard (Beaver Dick)

Tallchief, Maria (Scottish-Irish-American and Osage)—Balanchine, George (Georgian)
See   Balanchine, George
        Tallchief, Maria

Templeton, Janet (European-American)—Sheen, Martin (Irish and Spanish)
See   Sheen, Martin

Thomas, Clarence (African-American)—Lamp, Virginia Bess (European-American)
See   Thomas, Clarence

Thorpe, James (Jim) Francis (Irish-French Canadian-American, Kickapoo, Potawatomi, and Sac and Fox)—Miller, Iva Margaret (European-American and Cherokee)
See   Thorpe, James (Jim) Francis

Tibbles, Susette LaFlesche (European-French-American, Iowa, Omaha?, Oto?, and Ponca?)—Tibbles, Thomas Henry (European-American)
See   Tibbles, Susette LaFlesche

Tibbles, Thomas Henry (European-American)—LaFlesche, Susette (European-French-American, Iowa, Omaha?, Oto?, and Ponca?)
See   Tibbles, Susette LaFlesche

Turner, Izear (Ike) Luster (African-American)—Turner, Tina (African-American, Cherokee, and Navajo)
See   Turner, Tina

Turner, Tina (African-American, Cherokee, and Navajo)—Turner, Izear (Ike) Luster (African-American)
See   Turner, Tina

Viebahn, Fred (German)—Dove, Rita (African-American)
See   Dove, Rita

Virginia (Nez Percé)— Meeks, Joseph (Joe) Lafayette (European-American)
See   Meeks, Joseph (Joe) Lafayette

Waanibe (Arapaho)—Carson, Christopher (Kit) Houston (European-American)
See   Carson, Christopher (Kit) Houston

Walker, Alice Malsenior (African-American and Cherokee)—Leventhal, Melvyn Rosenman (European-American and Jewish)
See   Walker, Alice Malsenior

Walker, Armstead (African-American)—Mitchell, Maggie Dalena (Lena) (African-Irish-American)
See   Walker, Maggie Dalena (Lena) Mitchell

Walker, Maggie Dalena (Lena) Mitchell (African-Irish-American)—Walker, Armstead (African-American)
See   Walker, Maggie Dalena (Lena) Mitchell

Washington, Booker Taliaferro (African-European-American)—Davidson, Olivia A. (African-European-American)
See   Washington, Booker Taliaferro
         Washington, Olivia A. Davidson

Washington, Booker Taliaferro (African-European-American)—Murray, Margaret James (African-Irish-American)
See   Washington, Booker Taliaferro
       Washington, Margaret James Murray

Washington, Booker Taliaferro (African-European-American)—Smith, Fannie Norton (African-American and Shawnee)
See   Washington, Booker Taliaferro
       Washington, Fannie Norton Smith

Washington, Elizabeth (English)—Rolfe, Thomas (English and Powhatan)
See   Rolfe, Thomas

Washington, Fannie Norton Smith (African-American and Shawnee)—Washington, Booker T. (African-European-American)
See   Washington, Booker Taliaferro
       Washington, Fannie Norton Smith

Washington, Margaret James Murray (African-Irish-American)—Washington, Booker T. (African-European-American)
See   Washington, Booker Taliaferro
       Washington, Margaret James Murray

Washington, Olivia A. Davidson (African-European-American)—Washington, Booker T. (African-European-American)
See   Washington, Booker Taliaferro
       Washington, Olivia A. Davidson

White, Walter Francis (African-European-American)—Cannon, Poppy (European-American)
See   White, Walter Francis

White, Walter Francis (African-European-American)—Powell, Gladys (African-American)
See   White, Walter Francis

Williams, Daniel Hale (African-European-American and Native American)—Johnson, Alice (African-European-American and Jewish)
See   Williams, Daniel Hale

Williams, Eunice (English Puritan)—Arosen, Francois Xavier (Canadian Mohawk)
See   Williams, Eunice

Williams, William Carlos (English and Dutch-French-Spanish-Puerto Rican, Jewish, Catholic, and Unitarian)—Herman, Florence (German)
See   Williams, William Carlos

Woods, Tiger (African-Chinese-American, Native American Protestant and Chinese-Dutch-Thai Buddhist)—Nordegren, Elin Maria Pernilla (Swedish)
See   Woods, Tiger

Woodson, Sarah Jane (African-English-Welsh?-American)—Early, Jordan Winston (African-American)
See   Early, Sarah Jane Woodson

Yellow Woman (Cheyenne)—Bent, William (European-American)
See   Bent, William

Zipporah (Midianite)—Moses (Hebrew-Egyptian)
See   Moses

Zorina, Vera (German)—Balanchine, George (Georgian)
See   Balanchine, George

References

Alderman, Bruce, editor. *Interracial Relationships*. Farmington Hills, Mich.: Greenhaven Press, 2007. 112 p. (Social Issues Firsthand)
    In a narrative reproduced from www.about.com, Tracey Sanford Crim describes how the racial hatred she learned as an African-American child changed when she met the white man who became her best friend and then her husband.
European-American man and African-American woman
Older; Nonfiction

Alvarez, Julia. *Finding Miracles*. New York: Alfred A. Knopf, 2004. 272 p.
    Fifteen-year-old Milly was adopted as an infant from an unnamed Latin-American country when her Jewish father and her Mormon mother were there in the Peace Corps. Milly prefers to keep her adoption a secret and not think about it. However, when Pablo, who is from the same country, comes to her Vermont high school, Milly's outlook gradually changes. Through his friendship and a visit to her birth country with him and his parents, Milly comes to an increased understanding and appreciation of herself and her American family.

European-American Jewish man and European-American Mormon woman
Older; Fiction

Banks, Lynne Reid. *One More River*. New York: Avon Books, 1993. 256 p.

Fourteen-year-old Lesley hates leaving her comfortable life in Saskatoon, Saskatchewan, Canada, and moving to the kibbutz in Israel where she and her Orthodox Jewish parents emigrate. Before leaving she makes contact with her much older brother, whom her father had exiled from the family when he married a Catholic. During the ensuing year Lesley's letters to her brother help her to adjust to life in the kibbutz; she secretly crosses the Jordan River to befriend a Jordanian boy and his donkey; and she experiences the 1967 Six Day War. This book confronts the issues of war versus peace, Jew versus Arab, Jewishness as a religion or a people, and family reconciliation.
Canadian Catholic Jewish man and Canadian Catholic woman
Older; Fiction

Creel, Ann Howard. *Call Me the Canyon: A Love Story*. Weston, Conn.: Brown Barn Books, 2006. 224 p.

This novel takes place durng the turn of the twentieth century in the Glen Canyon area of Utah and Arizona. Fifteen-year-old Madolen, whose Navajo mother had died years before, leaves her father to live with a Mormon family from whom she can learn to read. She becomes close to the family, especially to its daughter Claire, who becomes her steadfast friend, but is forced by the mother to leave after Claire's little brother Gabriel dies accidentally while under the girls' care. Madolen lives alone in a cabin as she supports herself by gathering gold dust and searches in vain for a gold-filled canyon she remembers from her childhood. Madolen then guides Wallis, a wealthy and educated young man, to places where he can pursue his interests in the area's ancient history. Madolen's love for Wallis is not returned until almost the end of the story when they decide to get married. However, realizing his reluctance to introduce a woman of Navajo blood to his Eastern family, Madolen leaves him and later marries Yiska, the Navajo whom she had previously disliked.
Navajo man and European-American and Navajo woman
Older; Fiction

DeFelice, Cynthia. *Bringing Ezra Back*. New York: Farrar Straus Giroux, 2006. 160 p.

In this sequel to *Weasel*, Nathan and his family discover that their friend Ezra, who had left to be with his late wife's Shawnee family, is instead being displayed as a tongueless white Indian in a Pennsylvania traveling show. Twelve-year-old Nathan sets out with a peddler to find Ezra. In the process, Nathan learns much about people: how they can be combinations of good and bad and how you can learn to read them. He finds Ezra and, with the help of the show's "freaks," frees him. Then Nathan not only brings Ezra back to Ohio, but also pulls him out of his deep depression.
European-American man and Shawnee woman
Intermediate, Older; Fiction

DeFelice, Cynthia. *Weasel*. New York: Atheneum Books for Young Readers, 1990. 128 p.

In 1839 eleven-year-old Nathan and nine-year-old Molly wait six days for their father to return from what was to be several hours of hunting. A stranger, Ezra, takes them to his Shawnee-type shelter where he is tending their injured father, who had been caught in a trap. His gun had been taken by Weasel, a cruel former government Indian fighter who now kills animals and people for pleasure. Weasel had earlier removed Ezra's tongue and killed his Shawnee wife and unborn baby. When Nathan returns to his cabin to tend the animals, he discovers that Weasel has been there, killing the pig and chickens and stealing the family's horse and mule. On the way back to Ezra's, Nathan is captured by Weasel. Nathan escapes and, seeking revenge, wants to kill him, but then discovers how best to remove Weasel from his tormented thoughts.

European-American man and Shawnee woman

Intermediate, Older; Fiction

Farmer, Nancy. *A Girl Named Disaster*. New York: Orchard Books, 1996. 320 p. (A Richard Jackson Book)

Set in about 1981 in Mozambique and Zimbabwe, this is the story of the girl Nhamo whose mother had been killed by a leopard and whose father had fled from Mozambique after he killed a man. Despite the efforts of her beloved grandmother and of a Portuguese-Mozambican couple, a spirit medium commands that Nhamo be married as payment to the cruel brother of the man her father had killed. Escaping, Nhamo undertakes the lonely journey from Mozambique to Zimbabwe to find her father. Resourceful and imaginative, Nhamo spends countless hours rowing a small boat against the current; encounters Shona spirits; takes comfort in talking to her "mother," the woman depicted in a magazine margarine advertisement; stays among baboons; and reaches a Zimbabwean scientific research center where she comes to feel at home and is exorcised from a curse by Vapostori Christians. She discovers her father is dead, lives as an unwelcome guest with his wealthy relatives, learns from her sympathetic great-grandfather about her parents, and is able to spend summers working at the research center. Throughout the book Nhamo is a teller of southeastern African stories.

Portuguese and Catholic man and Mozambican and Shona woman

Older; Fiction

Foreman, Michael, and Richard Seaver. *The Boy Who Sailed with Columbus*. Illustrated by Michael Foreman. New York: Arcade Publishing, 1992. 72 p.

An orphan, twelve-year-old Leif sails as a ship's boy on Christopher Columbus's first voyage to the West Indies. His admiration for Columbus changes when Leif sees that Columbus is taking some of the island natives back to Spain. As a punishment for a mistake he had made, Leif is left behind with some of Columbus's crew on one of the islands. There he is kidnapped by Arawak, who attack the island fort. Leif then serves as the eyes for a wise blind Secotan healer who was with the Arawak and travels with him among different tribes. Becoming the medicine man's successor, Leif, who is half-Viking, marries a Secotan. As a grandfather in the Secotan village [which was probably in present day North Carolina on or near Roanoke Island], Leif sees approaching European ships and leads the Secotan villagers westward to avoid possible capture.

Viking-other man and Secotan woman

Intermediate; Fiction

Forrester, Sandra. *Dust from Old Bones*. New York: Morrow Junior Books, 1999. 176 p.

    This story is set in the stratified society of the New Orleans of 1838. Thirteen-year-old Simone, who is a person of color, struggles with the probability that her pretty cousin Claire-Marie will go to quadroon balls and be chosen by a Creole "protector" [as his mistress]. She envies the life of Madelon, her aunt who lives in France where she is not faced with racial discrimination. Nevertheless, Simone comes to realize that her restricted life as a person of color is much better than that of black slaves, who if lucky enough to be freed had to leave New Orleans. Simone's admiration for Madelon, who comes to visit, disappears when she betrays not only Simone, but also the two slaves she was committed to free. It is Simone who leads the slaves through a swamp to a safe house.

French man and African-Creole-Haitian woman

Older; Fiction

George, Jean Craighead. *Julie's Wolf Pack*. Illustrated by Wendell Minor. New York: HarperCollins Publishers, 1997. 208 p.

    This sequel to *Julie* is devoted almost entirely to the story of Julie's Avalik River wolf pack. It traces its activities through four years during which Kapu asserts himself as its Alpha (leader); the wolf Ice Blink spreads rabies on the tundra; Silver has two more puppies; Kapu is trapped for a medical study; Silver dies; Kapu's daughter Sweet Fur Amy becomes the new Alpha; and, released, Kapu joins his mate Aaka. There is little about Julie and her human family. However, her little half brother Amaroq bonds with one of Silver's wolf pups, which becomes a sled dog leader for Kapugen. At the book's end Julie and Peter marry and are hired to live on the tundra and study the wolves.

Russian Eskimo man and American Eskimo woman

Intermediate, Older; Fiction

George, Jean Craighead. *Water Sky*. New York: Harper & Row, 1987. 220 p.

    Teenage Lincoln travels to Barrow, Alaska, to stay with his father's elderly Eskimo friend Vincent Ologak and to find his Uncle Jack, who had taught Lincoln how to sail. Uncle Jack had not been heard from in the two years since he left for Barrow to stop the Eskimo from killing the endangered bowhead whale. When Lincoln arrives in Alaska, he discovers that one of his great-great-grandmothers was an Eskimo and that the whales killed by the Eskimo are not causing the bowhead whale to become extinct, but are essential for their survival. Lincoln spends his time at Vincent's whale camp looking for the whale Nukik, which Vincent believes is to come to Lincoln to be killed. Lincoln learns that the man called Musk Ox is really Uncle Jack, who has changed his belief about the whales and married an Eskimo. The whale does come to Lincoln, but he cannot make himself kill it. It is killed by another boy on the umiaq; Vincent dies happily after learning Nukik has been killed; and the grateful people of Barrow are filled with the spirit of tolerance and sharing. Filled with information about the Eskimo culture and whaling, this story describes the hostility some Eskimos showed towards whites, Lincoln's wanting to be accepted as an Eskimo, the recognition he is given, and his realization that he will always be an outsider.

European-American man and American Iñupiat Eskimo woman

Older; Fiction

Headley, Justina Chen. *Nothing but the Truth (and a few white lies)*. Boston: Little, Brown and Company, 2006. 256 p.

Fifteen-year-old Patty Ho is tormented by a schoolmate, is lectured to and overprotected by her Taiwanese mother, and believes she is a misfit. When her mother sends her to California to spend a month attending Stanford University's math camp, she experiences a new world: a daring roommate who shows her how to climb buildings, an understanding camp teaching assistant, and her first kiss, from a boy who subsequently breaks her heart. She also meets Auntie Lu and Uncle Vic, her aunt's African-American significant other; learns the truth about her father; and comes to appreciate both her mother and her own hapa (half Asian, half white) self.
African-American man and Taiwanese woman
Older; Fiction

Kudlinski, Kathleen V. *My Lady Pocahontas: A Novel*. Tarrytown, N.Y.: Marshall Cavendish, 2006. 288 p.

This story of Pocahontas' life is written from the viewpoint of her fictional friend Neetah. Appamatuck Neetah is adopted by Powhatan to be Pocahontas' guardian. Together the two girls spy on the newly arrived Jamestown colonists. They befriend three boys, Samuel, Thomas, and Henry, who come to stay with the Powhatans. Pocahontas has a vision in which she, Neetah, John Smith, and a baby of much importance appear. Believing from the vision that she will marry John Smith, she betrays her father and warns Smith of a plot to kill him. As Smith shows no inclination to marry her, Pocahontas returns depressed to her Pamunkey village. When the three boys try to escape, Samuel is killed, Thomas is captured, and Pocahontas leads Henry and Neetah to refuge with the Patawomeke. There both Pocahontas and Neetah marry Patawomekes, but they are blamed for a deadly measles outbreak, are imprisoned by the colonists, and are taken to Jamestown. Later brought to Henrico, Pocahontas becomes a Christian, takes a new name Rebecca, falls in love with John Rolfe, and, fulfilling her vision, has a son Thomas. Neetah accompanies Pocahontas, John, and Thomas to England where both she and Pocahantas die before returning home. An afterword, an author's note, and a source list are appended.
Patawomeke man and Powhatan (Appamattuck) woman
Older; Fiction

Landau, Elaine. *Interracial Dating and Marriage*. New York: Julian Messner, 1993. 112 p.

This book's introduction presents two detailed histories of interracial marriage: the first of African-American intermarriage with Caucasians and the second of intermarriages involving Japanese-Americans. In both cases the introduction describes factors, including governmental actions and societal attitudes, which affected the frequency of these marriages. The bulk of the book presents interviews with ten teenagers and five adults or adult couples who describe their views of and/or experiences with interracial dating and marriage. Seven of the teens interviewed came to the United States from other countries; three of the teens are interracial. Two of the adult interviews are with interracial couples; another contains advice from a minister. A resource list and an index are included.

Iranian Muslim man and European-American Christian woman; African-Jamaican man and African-American woman
Older; Nonfiction

Levin, Beatrice. *John Hawk: White Man, Black Man, Indian Chief.* Austin: Eakin Press, 1988. 192 p.

This is the fictional story of John White, the son of a Georgia plantation owner and a slave mother, who becomes the lifelong friend of Osceola. The two meet as boys and, at Osceola's urging, John runs away to live with the Seminoles. He takes a new name, John Hawk, marries a Seminole woman, befriends a man who is Spanish and African-American, and becomes a Seminole chief. With Osceola he experiences the betrayals and tragedies preceding and during the Second Seminole War. A bibliography is included.
African-European-American man and Seminole woman
Older; Fiction

Little, Mimi Otey. *Yoshiko and the Foreigner.* Illustrated by author. New York: Frances Foster Books, 1996. 36 p.

Yoshiko overcomes her reluctance to speak to a foreigner, an American Air Force officer who is lost in Tokyo. She secretly continues to see him and then, thanks to his honoring of the Japanese culture, receives her parents' blessing to marry him. This picture book is based on the author's family history.
European-American man and Japanese woman
Pre-K, Primary; Fiction

Machado, Ana Maria. *Nina Bonita.* Illustrated by Rosana Faría. Translated from Spanish by Elena Iribarren. Brooklyn, N.Y.: Kane/Miller Book Publishers, 1996. 28 p.

A white rabbit, who admires Nina Bonita's blackness, wants to have a daughter as black as she is. However, when he asks her how she got to be so dark, she doesn't know and gives ridiculous answers. Trying out her answers, the rabbit doesn't turn black, but learns that Nina's grandmother is black. The white rabbit then marries a black rabbit and they have bunnies of different shades. Nina becomes the godmother of the bunny who is black. The book's setting is not identified, but it was first published in Venezuela.
Pre-K, Primary; Fiction

McKissack, Patricia C. *Run Away Home.* New York: Scholastic Press, 1997. 176 p.

In 1888 Sky, a fifteen-year-old Chiricahua Apache boy, escapes from a train of Apache prisoners and hides on the farm of twelve-year-old Sarah Jane Crossman, her African-American father, and her mother, who is of African-Scottish-Irish and Seminole heritage. George Wrattan, an Army scout and interpreter, allows the Crossmans to keep Sky with them until he recovers from his swamp fever. In the meantime boll weevils destroy the family's cotton crop, night riders come to their farm, and Sarah Jane's father, who is skilled as a carpenter, gets an order from Booker T. Washington to build desks

for nearby Tuskegee Institute. Sky becomes healthy, but Wrattan, whose wife is Apache, gives permission for him to remain on the farm.
English-French-Swedish-American man and Apache woman
Intermediate, Older; Fiction

Moonshower, Candie. *The Legend of Zoey: A Novel*. New York: Delacorte Press, 2006. 224 p.

This story is based on the legend of the 1811 and 1812 New Madrid Earthquakes that alleges they resulted from the curse placed by a Choctaw chief on the Chickasaw chief Reelfoot who defied him by marrying his daughter Laughing Eyes. When thirteen-year-old Zoey goes on a school field trip to Reelfoot Lake in western Tennessee she is swept away in a drainage ditch during an electrical storm and finds herself back in 1811 with a thirteen-year-old girl Prudence and her mother. Journals written by Zoey and Prudence tell of their difficult journey as they try to reach safety from the earthquakes. They learn of each other's lives, hopes, and worries; become friends; and spend time with Reelfoot and Laughing Eyes, whom Zoey discovers are her ancestors. There are surprises awaiting Zoey when she returns to the present day.
Chickasaw man and Choctaw woman
Intermediate, Older; Fiction

Morpurgo, Michael. *The Amazing Story of Adolphus Tips*. New York: Scholastic Press, 2006. 144 p.

In 1943 when she was twelve years old, Lily and her family have to move from their home in Slapton Sands, Devon, England, because American soldiers need land, including the village, to practice for their D-day landing in Normandy. Lily befriends Adie and Harry, two African-American soldiers, who help search for her missing cat, Tips, and warn her not to continue crawling under the barbed wire to look for him. Harry is killed in a German E-boat attack, and Lily falls in love with eighteen-year-old Adie. More than sixty years later Lily surprises her family by traveling to Atlanta and marrying Adie.
African-American man and English woman
Intermediate, Older; Fiction

Murray, Millie. *Cairo Hughes*. London: Livewire Books, 1996. 144 p.

Sixteen-year-old Cairo, who is black, grows up in a caring adoptive white family, but yearns to be around people of her own color. When she and a black classmate, Diane, become friends, Cairo spends much of her free time with Diane and her family: having her hair plaited, eating soul food, and, in general, being introduced to the black culture. However, Cairo is torn between her love for her adoptive family and her black identity and is especially upset when she cannot experience her family's grief upon the death of the intolerant white grandmother who never accepted her. Cairo finally decides that when she turns eighteen, she will search for her birthmother so that she can better understand herself. In this story, which is set in London, Cairo's favorite uncle is married to a French woman.
English man and French woman
Older; Fiction

Myers, Anna. *Rosie's Tiger*. New York: Walker and Company, 1994. 128 p.

It is 1952 in Oklahoma, and sixth-grader Rosie, whose mother is dead, can't wait for her big brother to come home safely from Korea. However, when he returns with a Korean wife and her little boy, Rosie is terribly jealous. Although she is impressed by their kindness, she recruits her best friend to use her magical power to send them back to Korea. The story reaches its climax when the little boy falls down a cistern and Rosie realizes she must rescue him.
European-American man and Korean woman
Intermediate, Older; Fiction

Polacco, Patricia. *In Our Mothers' House*. Illustrated by author. New York: Philomel Books, 2009. 48 p.

In this story an African-American woman relates how she, her Asian-American brother Will, and her red-haired sister Millie were adopted by their two mothers. The large paintings and the text reveal the happy times they had in their Berkeley, California, home with their mothers, their extended family, and their (with one exception) supportive neighbors. At their mothers' instigation, the neighbors helped build a tree house in their backyard and held a block party complete with an international food court and games in each front yard. As the years pass, the children go off to pursue careers, to marry in the garden of their mothers' house, to bury their mothers, and to continue to gather in the house, now owned by Will and his family. A picture shows that the narrator's husband is European-American.
European-American man and African-American woman
Pre-K, Primary; Fiction

Richardson, Judith Benét. *First Came the Owl*. New York: Bantam Doubleday Dell Books for Young Readers, 1998. 160 p. (A Yearling Book)

Having recently returned from a trip to her native Thailand, Nita's mother becomes depressed and is hospitalized. Nita's father leaves to go out on a Coast Guard boat and she has to stay at her friend Anne's house. This story tells how eleven-year-old Nita's report on Thailand, her playing Snow White in a class play, the snowy owl who comes to her Massachusetts beach, and the Roots Committee composed of Nita, Anne, and a Coast Guard officer whose Thai wife has died all work together to help reunite Nita's family.
European-American man and Thai woman
Intermediate; Fiction

Rinn, Miriam. *The Saturday Secret*. Illustrated by Spark. Los Angeles: Alef Design Group, 1998. 160 p.

Jason, whose father has died, is angry that his stepfather David insists on his wearing a kippah (skullcap), keeping kosher, and observing Shabbat (the Jewish Sabbath)—and that his mother goes along with all the restrictive rules. Loving baseball, Jason lies to and defies his parents by playing in two Saturday baseball games. It is only when David stands up against prejudice and abuse and drives him to the hospital on the Shabbat that Jason accepts him as his father.
European-American Orthodox Jewish man and European-American non-Orthodox Jewish woman
Intermediate; Fiction

Rosenberg, Maxine B. *Being Adopted*. Photographs by George Ancona. New York: Lothrop, Lee & Shepard Books, 1984. 48 p.

Illustrated with black-and-white photographs, this book features three children. Seven-year-old Rebecca, whose birth father is African-American and birth mother European-American and Cheyenne, is the adopted daughter of an African-American father and a European-American mother. Ten-year-old Andrei was adopted from India by European-American parents, and Karin, the author's eight-year-old daughter, was adopted from Korea by her European-American parents. The book covers some of the questions and fears of younger adopted children: being afraid when they come to their adoptive families, wondering whether they caused their parents to give them up, fearing their adoptive parents will give them up, dreaming and wondering about their birth parents, and not looking like other members of their families. It also affirms that adopted children are just as much family members as are biological children.
African-American man and European-American woman
Primary, Intermediate; Nonfiction

Sauerwein, Leigh. *The Way Home*. Illustrated by Miles Hyman. New York: Farrar, Straus & Giroux, 1994. 128 p.

This book contains six stories, including "Storm Warning" and "The Dress." "Storm Warning" is set in Nebraska in 1989. When Jonathan, the Indian who is Joe's best friend, saves the twelve-year-old boy during a tornado, Joe realizes that Jonathan is his father. "The Dress," which is set in 1876, tells of Laura's first visit to her Aunt Ella. Laura learns that when Ella was young, she was captured by Cheyenne. She married a Cheyenne warrior and they had three children. However, Ella was the only survivor when soldiers attacked the Cheyenne village, and she was returned to her white family, who continue to ostracize her.
Cheyenne man and European-American woman
Intermediate; Fiction

Singer, Marilyn, ed. *Face Relations: 11 Stories About Seeing Beyond Color*. New York: Simon & Schuster Books for Young Readers, 2004. 240 p.

In "Hum" by Naomi Shihab Nye, Palestinian Sami and his parents have moved to Texas from Bethlehem to escape the violence there. Initially accepted, they find life increasingly difficult because of the animosity towards Arabs following September 11. It is a blind widower, whose wife had been African-American, and his humming dog who finally bring them happiness.
European-American man and African-American woman
Older; Fiction

Smith, Cynthia Leitich. *Indian Shoes*. Illustrated by Jim Madsen. New York: HarperCollins Publishers, 2002. 80 p.

This book tells of the close relationship between Ray and his Grampa Halfmoon, who live together in Chicago. For instance, Ray cleverly bargains to get a pair of Seminole moccasins for his homesick grandfather and together they attend a Cubs game, celebrate Christmas with the neighborhood pets, solve the problem of missing pants when Ray serves as wedding ring bearer for their Choctaw

friend and her Polish-Menominee groom, and, visiting their relatives in Oklahoma, go fishing and catch more than fish.
Polish-American and Menominee man and Choctaw woman
Primary, Intermediate; Fiction

Sommerdorf, Norma. *Red River Girl*. New York: Holiday House, 2006. 240 p.

In her 1846-1848 journal, Josette, a Canadian Métis girl, records her experiences from the time of her thirteenth birthday when she lives in St. Eustache and is mourning the death of her Ojibwa mother. Her father, who has been a voyageur, decides to take Josette and her two younger brothers to visit their Ojibwa grandmother and then go on a buffalo hunt in what is now northern Minnesota. Josette dreams of someday going to school in Montreal. Thus, she is very upset with her father when he decides to become a teamster on a cart train bound for St. Paul and to have the family remain there even though it doesn't have a school. As time passes, Josette makes friends, has a beau, enjoys being a helper to the new schoolteacher, and goes with her on a visit to Galena, Illinois, and St. Louis. In the story a Dakota woman who helps out at the buffalo hunt has a Métis husband.
Métis man and Dakota woman
Intermediate, Older; Fiction

Spooner, Michael. *Last Child*. New York: Henry Holt and Company, 2005. 240 p.

Set in 1837 in the midst of a smallpox epidemic in what is now North Dakota, Rosalie is more comfortable helping her Scottish father, who is the bookkeeper at Fort Clark, than in being with her Mandan mother. Because of her superior attitude, she has only her father and her grandmother Muskrat Woman as friends. When Rosalie goes with her father to keep a log of the buffalo robes which have fallen from the capsized boat of the French trapper Bedeaux, they are attacked by Dakota and she is kidnapped by those responsible for the attack: a Mandan who is under the influence of whiskey and a scoundrel who has deliberately brought smallpox to the area and wants revenge on her father. Rosalie manages to escape and to make a bull boat with which she saves Bedeaux and returns to the Mandan village. There, with the assistance of her former husband Bedeaux, Muskrat Woman isolates Rosalie, inoculates her with the virus of a Mandan recovering from smallpox, holds the ceremony which makes her a woman, and helps her in resolving the conflict between her Mandan and Scottish identities. Antoine Garreau, who serves as interpreter for Fort Clark's managing officer, is a minor character in this novel.
French man and Mandan woman and then Hidatsa woman
Older; Fiction

Stainer, M. L. *The Lyon's Crown*. Illustrated by James Melvin. Circleville, N.Y.: Chicken Soup Press, 2004. 176 p. (The Lyon Saga)

In this final book of *The Lyon Saga*, smallpox has come to Croatan Island and killed many residents, including Jess's Croatan husband Akaiyan and her English mother. Jess sends her three children away to Jamestown as Robert Ashbury, who has long loved her, has offered to provide sanctuary for them. Now in their early twenties and of mixed Croatan-English blood, the three must pretend to be English, adapt to English ways, and endure hostility towards "savages" from Virginian residents

who have suffered Indian attacks. Suzanne/Oohah-ne falls in love with and marries Robert Ashbury's stepson, and William/Caun-reha adapts to life in Jamestown and Henrico, where they move. However, George/Wauh-kuaene suffers in the English environment until Jess comes to take him back to Croatan Island. This book tells of John Rolfe's work in cultivating tobacco for the English market and of his love for Pocahontas, who comes to Henrico and accepts Christianity.
English man and English-American and Croatan woman
Older; Fiction

Stainer, M. L. *The Lyon's Pride*. Illustrated by James Melvin. Circleville, N.Y.: Chicken Soup Press, 1998. 176 p. (The Lyon Saga)

The sequel to *The Lyon's Roar* and *The Lyon's Cub*, this book is part of *The Lyon Saga*, which relates a story of Jess Archarde and some of the other English settlers of the Lost Colony, who believing to be abandoned by their governor John White, move from Roanoke Island to live with the nearby Croatan Indians. In this book Jess helps lead some of the colonists who are leaving Croatan Island; marries Akaiyan, a Croatan; helps raise wolf cubs; has a baby, Oohahn-ne/Suzanne; mourns the death of her father; celebrates the marriage of Enrique, a former Spanish soldier, to a Croatan woman; and, again pregnant, hides when a pirate ship lands at Croatan Island.
Spanish man and Croatan woman
Older; Fiction

Trottier, Maxine. *A Circle of Silver*. New York: Stoddart Kids, 1999. 224 p. (The Circle of Silver Chronicles)

Set in 1760 this first book in *The Circle of Silver Chronicles* relates the story of thirteen-year-old John MacNeil, who leaves his English home to spend two years with his father, Captain James MacNeil, traveling to and then returning from the British Fort Detroit. It tells of the growing enmity of the Indians living near Fort Detroit who are poorly treated by the British, of John's being appointed King George III's artist in Canada, of John's love of Canada, of his friendship with the Ottawa Natka and Wallace Doig whose Miami wife had died, of his encounter with Pontiac, and of his closeness to Marie Roy, the French-Canadian Miami girl whom he adores, and to Pierre La Butte, the interpreter for the British and then merchant who becomes Marie Roy's husband.
Scottish man and Miami woman
Older: Fiction

Trottier, Maxine. *Under a Shooting Star*. New York: Stoddart Kids, 2002. 224 p. (The Circle of Silver Chronicles)

A sequel to *A Circle of Silver* and *By the Standing Stone,* this book is set in the border area of Canada and the United States during the War of 1812. Fifteen-year-old Canadian Edward Wolf MacNeil (the son of English Jamie and Oneida Sarah, the half-sister of Owela) is escorting two American girls to their home in Sandusky, Ohio, on his way to his Uncle John MacNeil's Canadian home on Pêche Island. When the merchant ship on which they are traveling sinks during a storm on Lake Erie, the three manage to reach South Bass Island. There they meet Paukeesaa, Tecumseh's son, who takes them to John MacNeil's empty house where they befriend the great-grandson of Marie Roy

and Pierre LaButte (who is also named Pierre LaButte), and Edward reads the journal of Mack, John MacNeil's ward. This story tells of Edward and the girls' stay at Fort Amhertsburg where Edward helps build the English ship Detroit, of their involuntary involvement in the Battle of Lake Erie, and of John MacNeil's safe return.
Oneida man and English woman
Older; Fiction

Williams, Garth. *The Rabbits' Wedding*. Illustrated by author. New York: Harper & Brothers, 1958. 36 p.

Featuring large illustrations, this picture book tells how the little black rabbit's wish that he could always be with the little white rabbit comes true when they are wed. Published in 1958, this book created controversy because of its depiction of a black-white marriage.
Pre-K; Fiction

Wittlinger, Ellen. *Hard Love*. New York: Aladdin Paperbacks, 2001. 240 p.

Sixteen-year-old John hasn't gotten over his egotistical father's leaving him and his mother when he was ten nor the way since then that his mother has shut him out emotionally, even shying away from touching him. Feeling himself an emotionless loner, John leaves a zine, a short homemade magazine with his own writing, at the Tower Records zine exchange center. He is impressed by a zine written by Marisol, a lesbian Puerto Rican-American with adoptive Cuban and European-American parents, and he contacts her. They share each other's writings and feelings about their families, and John falls in love. It is at a zine writers conference on Cape Cod that Marisol, although telling John (whom she calls Gio) that he is her best friend, leaves him for a group of lesbian women. It is there too that John discovers that his mother and stepfather-to-be care for him and that he is ready to socialize. Gio also appears in the book *Love & Lies: Marisol's Story*.
Cuban man and European-American woman
Older; Fiction

Wittlinger, Ellen. *Love & Lies: Marisol's Story*. New York: Simon & Schuster Books for Young Readers, 2008. 256 p.

This book for the oldest readers is the sequel to *Hard Love*. Eighteen-year-old Marisol decides to take a year off to write a novel before attending Stanford University. To earn money she works at a Harvard Square coffee shop where she meets Lee, a shy homesick girl from Indiana, who left there after telling her parents she was gay. When Marisol attends a novel writing course at the Cambridge Center for Adult Education, she discovers that her friend Gio (John) is also taking the course and that it is being taught by an amazingly beautiful woman, Olivia Frost. Marisol, who is a lesbian, falls in love with Olivia, and the two make love. Ignoring the negative opinion of Gio, Marisol fails to realize how Olivia is dominating her. Her lie to Olivia that Lee is Gio's girlfriend upsets Lee so much that she flies back to Indiana. Finally, Marisol realizes that Olivia is a fraud: she did not graduate from Harvard, she is not writing a novel, she quotes others' sayings as her own, and Marisol is unimportant to her. In this story the novel which Marisol is writing is based on her unknown Puerto Rican birthmother. Readers of *Hard Love* will be aware of the mixed heritages of Marisol's adoptive parents.

Cuban man and European-American woman
Older; Fiction

V. Families Including a Child of the Same Nationality, But a Different Heritage

Introduction

The great majority of books in this chapter cover families of mixed heritage created when children are adopted domestically, a parent remarries, or, due to parental death or other circumstances, new caregiver situations (including orphanages) occur. In some instances, the books tell of slave or abducted children who must live with adults of a different heritage. The chapter does not include books in which children go to live with a grandparent. The "General" chapter provides a more overall discussion.

Each category in this chapter first lists the names of actual persons covered in the "Biography" chapter and cross-references these names to that chapter. Book listings follow these name listings.

The listings are categorized by the nation in which the family resides at the time of the adoption. For instance, if a Greek adult residing in the United States cares for an American child, the book would be listed under United States.

This chapter is organized alphabetically into the following major categories: Africa, Asia, Canada, Central America, Europe, Mexico, Oceania, and United States. Within these categories there are often subcategories of either individual nations or the heritage of the adult caregiver, e.g., Asian-American.

The heritage designation for each book reads:

Identity of adult(s) followed by identity of child(ren)

e.g., Mohican of European-American

The order in which the heritages are listed is immaterial.

References

Africa

Egypt

See   Moses

South Africa

Jones, Toecky. *Skindeep*. New York: Harper & Row Publishers, 1986. 256 p.

Set in apartheid South Africa, this novel for older teenagers tells of the love affair of blond eighteen-year-old Rhonda and nineteen-year-old Dave, who is coloured, but passing for white. Their dating has its ups and downs as Dave is afraid of its long-term consequences. When by chance he encounters his birthmother, who had given him to a Jewish family to raise when he was seven, he finally reveals his identity to Rhonda. Initially shocked, she then tries, despite her family's objections, to get back together with Dave, but he refuses. Rhonda, who had wanted to go to England, decides to remain in South Africa and work against apartheid.

German Jewish and European-South African Jewish of Coloured-South African
Older; Fiction

Asia

Indonesia

Lewis, Richard. *The Flame Tree*. New York: Simon & Schuster Books for Young Readers, 2004. 288 p.

Set in September 2001, this novel for the oldest children is one of life in an American missionary compound and in a Javanese town, of Christian and Muslim beliefs, of the symbolism of crows and a flame tree, and of terrorism and forgiveness. When an anti-American fundamentalist becomes imam of the mosque across the street from the compound where twelve-year-old Isaac lives, his whole life changes. His Muslim friend, Ismail, turns against him, Muslims attack the compound, and Isaac is captured. During his two week captivity Isaac is cared for by a Muslim woman and an Islamic scholar who tries to convert him, but is abused by extremist Muslims who forcibly circumcise him. It is the leader of an Islamic organization who frees Isaac and through whom Isaac and his mother experience Allah/God.

Indonesian Muslims of European-American Christian
Older: Fiction

Turkey

Skrypuch, Marsha Forchuk. *Daughter of War: A Novel*. Brighton, Mass.: Fitzhugh & Whiteside, 2008. 224 p.

This novel is set during the Armenian Genocide in Turkey during World War I. It centers on the Armenian teenagers Mariam and Marta Hovsepian and Kevork Adomian. Orphaned because of the 1909 Adana Massacre, they were placed in an orphanage run by German missionaries in Maresh, Turkey. When the Turks decided to relocate Armenians, Mariam, the older sister, was taken to a slave auction where she was bought by a Turkish man who had fallen in love with her. She is returned to the orphanage for her safety when the man's mother has another Armenian woman's throat wrung. Marta and Kevork, who were betrothed, were marched into the desert. Marta was saved by a Turkish

woman whose husband made her one of his wives and raped her. Pregnant Marta is returned to the orphanage where she has a baby girl, Pauline. Kevork was rescued by Arabs in Syria. Disguised as an Arab, he works as a shoemaker and then accepts the dangerous job of a courier bringing money to starving Armenians who had been deported to the Syrian Desert. Becoming ill with typhus, he recovers under the care of a German missionary in one of the deportation camps. The book tells of the horrible fate of the Armenians and some of those who secretly helped them. It concludes with Kevork's reunion with Marta at the Maresh orphanage, now run by American missionaries.
Turkish of Armenian-Turkish; German of Armenian-Turkish; American of Armenian-Turkish
Older; Fiction

Canada

Noël, Michel. *Good For Nothing*. Translated from French by Shelley Tanaka. Toronto: Douglas & McIntyre, 2004. 328 p. (A Groundwood Book)
Teenager Nipishish, a Métis whose parents have died, returns to his Algonquin reserve in Quebec Province after being mistreated at a residential school for Indians. When life on the reserve worsens because of governmental policy, Nipishish welcomes the opportunity to live with a white foster family in Mont-Laurier. There he is imprisoned when he loses his temper while trying to receive his paycheck. Nipishish feels he is good for nothing, a feeling reinforced when his white heritage makes it difficult for him to marry his Indian girlfriend. Things change when he is reunited with his Algonquin "family." He becomes a leader in their fight against logging in the reserve and, discovering that his father was probably secretly murdered for his advocacy of Indian rights, successfully enlists a lawyer to pursue the case.
French Canadian of Métis (Anishinabe/French Canadian)
Older; Fiction

Olsen, Sylvia. *White Girl*. Winlaw, British Columbia: Sono Nis Press (Distributed by Orca Book Publishers), 2004. 240 p.
When fifteen-year-old Josie's mother marries an Indian, the two of them move into his home on the reserve. Josie has a terrible time adjusting: missing her friends in the city, feeling out-of-place and rejected in her new surroundings, not fully trusting her new Indian girlfriend, and being taunted and then threatened for being "Blondie." This story for teenagers tells how Josie comes to accept her new life, how the reserve opens up her perspectives, and how her stepfather comes to terms with what had long ago happened to his sister.
Native Canadian and European-Canadian of European-Canadian
Older; Fiction

Slipperjack, Ruby. *Little Voice*. Illustrated by Sherry Farrell Racette. Regina, Saskatchewan: Coteau Books, 2002. 256 p. (In the Same Boat)
This story describes Canadian Ray's life from the summer of 1978 when she is ten to the summer of 1982. Terribly unhappy since the death of her non-Native father two years earlier and harassed by her schoolmates, Ray seldom speaks. When her mother marries Dave (who is Mohawk and Ojibwa),

Ray feels as if she doesn't belong. It is only when she is with her Ojibwa mother's mother during four summers and the winter of 1981-82 that she is truly happy. There, Ray lives in her grandmother's cabin in an Ojibwa community, but they are often traveling by canoe and camping. Ray watches her grandmother kill the bear which is tearing apart their tent and enjoys the baby bear adopted by a trapper friend, the puppy which he gives her grandmother, and the orphan seagull which she tends. Finally, Ray learns that she can stay permanently with her grandmother and that, like her, she will become a medicine woman.

Mohawk and Ojibwa of European-Canadian and Ojibwa; English-Canadian and Ojibwa of Mohawk and Ojibwa

Intermediate, Older; Fiction

Trottier, Maxine. *By the Standing Stone*. New York: Stoddart Kids, 2001. 256 p. (The Circle of Silver Chronicles)

This sequel to *A Circle of Silver* is set in 1773. John MacNeil's thirteen-year-old brother Jamie and his fifteen-year-old ward Mack (Charlotte) are kidnapped from a beach near Fort Niagara. John, Samuel (the younger brother of Marie Roy), and Owela (an Oneida whose Scottish-Miami stepfather is the son of Wallace Doig) set off to rescue them. This story recounts Jamie and Mack's journey to Boston as captives and after their release with Owela, their participation in the Boston Tea Party, their reunion in Boston with John and Samuel, the winter they all spend in Owela's village, their return to John's home on Pêche Island, and Mack's final acceptance of Owela's love.

Scottish-Canadian Miami and Oneida of Oneida

Older; Fiction

Central America

Guatemala

Cameron, Ann. *Colibrí*. New York: Frances Foster Books, 2003. 240 p.

Kidnapped at the age of four from her Mayan parents, Rosa (whose nickname had been Colibrí) spends the next eight years with "Uncle," her kidnapper. With Rosa too old to be sold for adoption, Uncle has kept her with him because of a fortune-teller's prediction that she will bring him a treasure. Together they travel from town to town in Guatemala as Uncle, pretending to be deaf, blind, lame, or dumb, begs for their living. It is when Uncle and a friend try to include her in a plan to steal a valuable church statue that Rosa gets up her courage and reports the plot to the church priest. Although she then happily lives with a kind woman she met earlier, Rosa almost loses her life when Uncle escapes from prison.

Spanish-Guatemalan and Mayan of Mayan

Intermediate, Older; Fiction

Europe

England

Murray, Millie. *Cairo Hughes*. London: Livewire Books, 1996. 144 p.

Sixteen-year-old Cairo, who is black, grows up in a caring adoptive white family, but yearns to be around people of her own color. When she and a black classmate, Diane, become friends, Cairo spends much of her free time with Diane and her family: having her hair plaited, eating soul food, and, in general, being introduced to the black culture. However, Cairo is torn between her love for her adoptive family and her black identity and is especially upset when she cannot experience her family's grief upon the death of the intolerant white grandmother who never accepted her. Cairo finally decides that when she turns eighteen, she will search for her birthmother so that she can better understand herself. In this story, which is set in London, Cairo's favorite uncle is married to a French woman.

English of African-English

Older; Fiction

Pullman, Philip. *The Broken Bridge*. New York: Alfred A. Knopf, 1992. 224 p.

Sixteen-year-old Ginny, who is very close to her English father, has been told that her Haitian artist mother died from hepatitis years earlier. When she discovers to her horror that she has a Caucasian half-brother who is coming to Wales to live with them, all her wonderings about her past emerge. Unable to get any information from her father, Ginny searches for the truth, a search that takes her to her grandparents in Chester, an art gallery in Liverpool, and the house of the dreaded Joe Chicago. Finally, Ginny not only learns about her family and early life, but also of how lucky she is. Andy, one of Ginny's friends whose parents were African, has been adopted by a white English couple.

English of Ethiopian-English

Older; Fiction

France

See   Millman, Isaac

Ireland

Quinn, John. *Duck and Swan*. Dublin: Poolbeg, 1993. 160 p.

When twelve-year-old Emer comes back from a field trip to Dublin, she discovers a black boy under the broken bus seat in front of her. She keeps his existence a secret as he hides in a school bicycle shed, in a chapel, and with a welcoming older couple, Granny Flynn and her blind husband Tom, who teaches him the Irish sport of hurling. The boy, who is known as Duck, has run away from an institution for troubled children where he was placed after his father returned to his native Nigeria and his Irish mother was jailed for selling drugs. Duck finally emerges from hiding to join a hurling team and, despite racial animosity, is finally accepted by Emer's classmates and the community.

Irish of Nigerian-Irish
Older; Fiction

Netherlands

Adler, David A. *Hiding from the Nazis*. Illustrated by Karen Ritz. New York: Holiday House, 1997. 32 p.

    This picture book tells the true story of Lore Baer and her Jewish family. When the Nazis come to Amsterdam where the Baers are refugees from Germany, Lore's grandfather is arrested. For her safety her parents send four-year-old Lore away for two years and she goes to live with a Dutch Christian farm family. Feeling rejected by her parents, she comes to regard that family as her own and at first does not want to go back to her parents. This book provides information on the Holocaust.
Dutch Christian of Dutch Jewish
Primary, Intermediate; Nonfiction

Oppenheim, Shulamith Levey. *The Lily Cupboard*. Illustrated by Ronald Himler. New York: HarperCollins Publishers, 1992. 32 p. (A Charlotte Zolotow Book)

    This picture book is set during the German occupation of the Netherlands in World War II. Miriam is sent by her Jewish parents to live with a non-Jewish family in the country where she will be safer. When German soldiers come to search the farmhouse, little Miriam not only hides successfully in a cupboard, but also protects the rabbit whom she has named after her father.
Dutch non-Jewish of Dutch Jewish
Primary; Fiction

Propp, Vera W. *When the Soldiers Were Gone*. New York: G. P. Putman's Sons, 1999. 112 p.

    Based on a true experience, this book tells the story of Henk, a Jewish boy who was hidden during the German occupation of the Netherlands by the Staals, a Dutch Christian farm family. Unaware that the Staals are not really his family, Henk is shocked and upset when, after the war, his parents come to bring him home. Henk learns that his name is Benjamin, that he has an adopted baby brother, that he is Jewish, and that his parents suffered during the war and greatly missed him. Living in a city and for the first time going to school, Henk no longer has to fear soldiers, gets to visit with the Staals, and, finally remembering his past, accepts his parents.
Dutch Christian of Dutch Jewish
Intermediate; Fiction

Poland

See   Lobel, Anita

Wolf, Joan M. *Someone Named Eva*. New York: Clarion Books, 2007. 208 p.

    This fictional story is based on events which took place in Lidice, Czechoslovakia, in June 1942. At that time eleven-year-old Milada and her family are removed from their home by Nazi soldiers.

Her father and fifteen-year-old brother are taken to an unknown destination, while Milada, her grandmother, her mother, and her baby sister stay with other women and children in a school. There Milada, with her blond hair and light-colored eyes, is chosen to be an Aryan child and future German wife and mother who will help save the world from Jews. She goes to a Polish training center where she must speak only German, is taught Nazi values, must constantly salute "Heil Hitler," befriends a Polish girl, is given the name Eva, and struggles to keep her Czech identity. After almost two years, Eva is adopted by a German family whose father is the commander of the Nazi Ravensbrück women's camp. Eva becomes close to her new sister, but longs for her own family. After the war she is reunited with her mother. Her father and brother had been shot, her grandmother had died in a concentration camp, and her little sister had not been located.

German of Polish
Older; Fiction

Slovakia

Winter, Kathryn. *Katarína: A Novel*. New York: Farrar Straus Giroux, 1998. 272 p.

This story, which is based on some of the author's experiences, tells of Katarína from the time she was almost eight until her approaching tenth birthday. She lives with her beloved aunt and her uncle, who are nonobservant Jews, and comes to love the Catholic religion which the maid Anka teaches her. Because of the persecution of Jews by Slovakia's German puppet government, Katarína loses contact with her best friend, hides in a barn for four months with her aunt and uncle, and is left with a peasant family, which believes she is Catholic. After the villagers discover she is Jewish, Katarína is hidden in the family's storage room until this becomes too dangerous for her benefactors. Katarína then wanders the countryside until she finds Anka, who takes her to a Lutheran orphanage. Throughout, Katarína dreams of being reunited with her family, but when at war's end she is returned to her village, she finds that only her teacher has survived.

Catholic Slovak of Jewish Slovak; Lutheran Slovak of Jewish Slovak
Intermediate, Older; Fiction

Spain

See   de Pareja, Juan

Mexico

Jennings, Patrick. *Faith and the Electric Dogs*. Decorations by author. New York: Scholastic, 1996. 144 p.

The narrator—and author—of this fanciful tale is Edison. A mutt from San Cristóbal de las Casas, Mexico, he asserts that it is true. Edison is taken in by Faith, a ten-year-old homesick American girl whose mother has married a Mexican and who hates Mexico because she can't speak Spanish and is teased. With help from a craftsman, Faith builds a rocket powered by pig fat and jalapeño peppers and sets off with Edison for San Francisco. Unfortunately, the rocket goes down in a storm. The two of them end up on an island in the Pacific Ocean, which is deserted except for four mutts and a seventy-year-old man who had come down on the island when he was ten after the balloon he was taking to return from Mexico to England was pierced by a seagull. The story concludes with Faith and Edison's return to Mexico, her happiness there, and an explanation of how Edison became a writer. Definitions of the many Spanish and Bowwow (canine) words used in the text are provided in the margins and also in a glossary.

Mexican and German-Scottish-Irish-American of German-Italian-Scottish-Irish-American
Intermediate; Fiction

Jennings, Patrick. *Faith and the Rocket Cat*. Decorations by author. New York: Scholastic Press, 1998. 240 p.

In this sequel to *Faith and the Electric Dogs*, Edison the mutt relates another fantastic story. When Faith, her mother, and her stepfather move to San Francisco, Faith wants to impress classmate Alex and Edison wishes to befriend Daphne, a whippet show dog, by taking them for a ride in Faith's rocket. Faith, Edison, Alex, Daphne—and Faith's mother—crash-land in Death Valley where they encounter coyotes and find Faith's late father's cat. All ends well in this story in which words presented in Bowwow and Arf (dog languages), Mew (cat language), Spanish, French, Italian, Chinese, Latin, and Turkish are defined both in the margins and in a glossary.

Mexican and German-Scottish-Irish-American of German-Italian-Scottish-Irish-American
Intermediate; Fiction

Merino, José María. *The Gold of Dreams*. Translated by Helen Lane. New York: Farrar, Straus and Giroux, 1994. 224 p. (A Sunburst Book)

Living in a village near Mexico City in the sixteenth century, Miguel is the son of a Spanish Conquistador father who disappeared years ago and a Native Mexican mother. When he is fifteen, Miguel goes with his Spanish godfather on a mission to find the kingdom of Queen Yupaha and bring back its gold. During the long and difficult journey Miguel witnesses the cruelties of both the Spaniards and the Indians, engages in battle, is captured by Indians, finds his father, and learns that the reported gold of Queen Yupaha is a myth. Miguel makes close friends, including an Indian boy, who having earlier been captured by the Spaniards and taken to Spain, now finds it difficult to fit into either culture.

Spanish of Native Mexican
Older; Fiction

Oceania

Australia

Hill, Anthony. *The Burnt Stick*. Illustrated by Mark Sofilas. Boston: Houghton Mifflin Company, 1995. 64 p.

John Jagamarra's mother tries in vain to save him from being taken to a distant mission where, with other mixed race children, he will be raised by whites. Twice she fools the authorities by darkening his light brown skin with a burnt stick. However, the authorities catch on to her deception and remove John, who is not yet five-years-old. John never forgets his mother and Aboriginal life, and, as a grown man, reclaims his Aboriginal heritage.

European-Australian of Aboriginal-European-Australian

Intermediate; Fiction

Murray, Kirsty. *The Secret Life of Maeve Lee Kwong*. Crows Nest, Australia: Allen & Unwin, 2006. 264 p. (Children of the Wind)

Thirteen-year-old Maeve's life turns upside down when her mother dies in an automobile accident. Unable to live with her baby half-brother and her stepfather because he has not adopted her, she stays with her mother's traditional Chinese parents and at her school's boarding house. It is with the support of her two best friends, a caring teacher who tells her of secret lives, a boy with whom she dances in Seussmania, and then her entire family that Maeve goes on a school trip to Ireland where she finds and meets her father, who was unaware of her existence.

European-Australian and Chinese-Australian of Chinese-Australian and Irish

Intermediate, Older; Fiction

New Zealand

Savage, Deborah. *A Stranger Calls Me Home*. Boston: Houghton Mifflin Company, 1992. 240 p.

A portrait of Paul's great-great-grandfather showing his hand on a partially opened box of bones with a carved Maori taniwha (a spiritually powerful force) on the lid affects the interconnected lives of three New Zealand teenagers: Paul, whose father is New Zealander and mother American; Simon, who has learned that his real father is Maori and who lives with his Irish mother and Italian-New Zealander stepfather; and Fiona, a white New Zealander, who has been largely raised by a Maori woman and who discovers that she is Paul's cousin. The three new friends try to come to grips with their pasts and with the underlying issue of whether the Maori should be able to take back the sacred land which had been taken from them by Paul and Fiona's ancestor, the land that is lonely Fiona's "place."

Italian-New Zealander and Irish of Maori New Zealander and Irish; Maori New Zealander of European-New Zealander

Older; Fiction

United States

African-American Adults

Becker, John T., and Stanli K. Becker, eds. *All Blood Is Red . . . All Shadows Are Dark!* Illustrated by J. Howard Noel. Cleveland: Seven Shadows Press, 1984. 168 p.

John T. (Tom) Becker, who is Irish-German-American, and his wife, Stanli K. Becker, who is African-American, have five young children. Of the four who are adopted one is biracial. All seven family members are responsible for individual sections of this book, which recounts their personal and family experiences as a multiracial family. Teaching their children to be aware of and proud of their individual differences, the editors present information on the history of racial classification in the United States and advocate their belief that race is and should be regarded as an "absurdity."
African-American and German-Irish-American of African-European-American and of African-American
Intermediate, Older; Nonfiction

Grimes, Nikki. *Dark Sons*. New York: Jump at the Sun, 2005. 224 p.

Written in verse, this book intertwines the often parallel stories of the teen-aged boys, Ishmael, the son of Abraham and the maid-servant Hagar, and Sam, the American son of African-American parents. Although their lives are separated by centuries, both grow up with strong bonds with their fathers and experience rejection and confusion when their fathers abandon their mothers and focus their attention on sons they father with other women. In Ishmael's case, because of Sarah's antagonism, Abraham sends Ishmael and Hagar away. In Sam's case, his father, new wife, and baby son move across the country. At the end of the book Sam reads the story of Ishmael and imagines that, as kindred brothers, he too will be able to carry on his own life.
African-American and Italian-American of African-American
Older; Fiction

Johnston, Tony. *Angel City*. Illustrated by Carole Byard. New York: Philomel Books, 2006. 40 p.

In a poor and crime-ridden barrio of Los Angeles, Joseph, an elderly black man, finds a newborn Mexican-American boy in a dumpster and wonders where there is love in Angel City. Taking the baby to his room, Joseph tends to him and names him Juan. This picture book's text and paintings present Juan's growing up and his introduction by Joseph to the cultures of Mexico, Africa, and Georgia, Joseph's home state. When he is six, Juan makes a best friend, Chucho. When Juan is nine, Chucho is shot and killed. Where is the love in Angel City? It is in the love between this father and son.
African-American of Mexican-American
Primary, Intermediate; Fiction

Kuklin, Susan. *Families*. Photographs by author. New York: Hyperion Books for Children, 2006. 40 p.

Text and color photographs present interviews with American children, who talk about their families. Their families include seven families with children of mixed race, ethnicity, or religion, with one also including a child adopted from Sierra Leone. In an eighth family a child has been adopted from China. In a ninth family an adopted American child is of a race different from that of one of her fathers.
African-American and European-American of African-American
Primary, Intermediate; Nonfiction

Lewin, Michael Z. *Cutting Loose*. New York: Henry Holt and Company, 1999. 528 p.

Set in the nineteenth century, this is the story of Jackie's search for Teddy Zeph, who has murdered

Jackie's best friend, Nance. The text alternates between the present and the past, starting with the story of Jackie's grandmother Claudette at the time she was orphaned. There are parallels among the characters' lives. Claudette is sold at a pauper auction, Jackie's father Matthew is sold by his New York City baseball team to a team in St. Louis, and Jackie goes to live with a new family that chooses her when she is displayed by the Children's Aid Society. Claudette murders her lover's father, and Matthew and Nance are murdered. Claudette disguises herself as a man to escape capture, and Jackie disguises herself as a man to pursue a baseball career. Both Jackie and her father play baseball in England as well as in the United States. Nance performs for Buffalo Bill's Wild West Show, and Jackie and Teddy Zeph perform on the stage in London. Further, Claudette's father is French, Teddy's mother is Spanish, and Nance, whose mother is African-American, passes as white.
African-American of French and European-American
Older; Fiction

McKissack, Patricia C. *Run Away Home*. New York: Scholastic Press, 1997. 176 p.
In 1888 Sky, a fifteen-year-old Chiricahua Apache boy, escapes from a train of Apache prisoners and hides on the farm of twelve-year-old Sarah Jane Crossman, her African-American father, and her mother, who is of African-Scottish-Irish and Seminole heritage. George Wrattan, an Army scout and interpreter, allows the Crossmans to keep Sky with them until he recovers from his swamp fever. In the meantime boll weevils destroy the family's cotton crop, night riders come to their farm, and Sarah Jane's father, who is skilled as a carpenter, gets an order from Booker T. Washington to build desks for nearby Tuskegee Institute. Sky becomes healthy, but Wrattan, whose wife is Apache, gives permission for him to remain on the farm.
African-American and African-Scottish-Irish-American and Seminole of Chiricahua Apache
Intermediate, Older; Fiction

Naylor, Phyllis Reynolds. *Sang Spell*. New York: Aladdin Paperbacks, 2000. 224 p.
Hitchhiking from Massachusetts to Dallas to live with his aunt because his mother has died, teenager Josh is mugged and left on a road in Appalachia where he is picked up by a Melungeon, who takes him to Canara, an isolated primitive community. Everything is strange and illogical there, and Josh becomes increasingly frustrated in his efforts to escape. The road he takes ends up at the exact place he started. Trying to swim towards a river's opposite shore takes him only a short distance, and a roadside restaurant and a school appear and disappear at regular intervals. Josh discovers that his father was probably Melungeon and befriends a girl whose father was stoned to death when his efforts to escape accidentally caused fatalities Finally, with new insights and the realization that he must keep Canara's secrets, Josh is able to get away. [The Melungeon people are of mixed race living primarily in the central Appalachians. There is controversy as to their origin and their heritage, but they are often regarded as tri-racial: European-American, African-American, and Native American. In this novel they are identified as Portuguese who over time became mixed with a number of other peoples.]
Portuguese (Melungeon)-American of Irish-Portuguese (Melungeon)-American
Older, Fiction

Park, Hee Jung, creator. *Hotel Africa Volume 2*. Translated from Korean by Jihae Hong. Los Angeles: Tokyopop, 2008. 264 p.

In this continuation of volume one, little Elvis meets more hotel guests: Dominique, his mother's inconsiderate and demanding high school classmate who returns from the city and gets together with a classmate who has long loved her; a seventeen-year-old boy and a fifteen-year-old girl who say they are siblings, but are really lovers; Hillie, an old dog who dies after his master dies, but not before Elvis has come to love him; and an African-American friend of his mother who confesses she had loved Tran before he became Elvis' father. She was devastated after he died until she found Lionel, a blind white boy whom she cares for. The book also tells how Elvis ironed his hair to make it straight and it ended up in an Afro. As adults, Elvis' friend Ed tells how he discovered he was gay when he fell in love with Ian, who died of a drug overdose, and Elvis gets a puppy, whom he names Hillie.
African-American of European-American
Older; Fiction

Peck, Robert Newton. *Extra Innings*. New York: Harper Trophy, 2003. 224 p.

Sixteen-year-old Tate is the sole survivor of a private plane crash that kills his parents, his older sister, and his grandparents. With his leg so injured that he can hardly walk, let alone fulfill his dream of being a major league pitcher, and his spirit crushed, Tate goes to live with his eighty-two-year-old great-grandfather Abbott and his seventy-year-old great aunt Vidalia. Vidalia tells Tate how as an African-American baby she was left in the bus of the Ethiopia's Clowns' traveling baseball club and how, until she was adopted at age ten by Abbott and his wife, she was raised by the team and especially by its pitcher and catcher. In the "extra inning" allotted them, Abbott and Vidalia realize that they have the opportunity to raise Tate—to restore his life and give him a reason for living.
European-American and African-American of European-American
Older; Fiction

Porte, Barbara Ann. *I Only Made Up the Roses*. New York: Greenwillow Boooks, 1987. 128 p.

Seventeen-year-old Cydra, who is white, describes her earlier longing for her "real" father, the love and support of her African-American stepfather, and the experiences, tragedies, memories, dreams, and closeness of her immediate and extended family.
African-American and Native American and European-American of European-American
Older; Fiction

Rosenberg, Maxine B. *Being Adopted*. Photographs by George Ancona. New York: Lothrop, Lee & Shepard Books, 1984. 48 p.

Illustrated with black-and-white photographs, this book features three children. Seven-year-old Rebecca, whose birthfather is African-American and birthmother European-American and Cheyenne, is the adopted daughter of an African-American father and a European-American mother. Ten-year-old Andrei was adopted from India by European-American parents, and Karin, the author's eight-year-old daughter, was adopted from Korea by her European-American parents. The book covers some of the questions and fears of younger adopted children: being afraid when they come to their adoptive families, wondering whether they caused their parents to give them up, fearing their adoptive

parents will give them up, dreaming and wondering about their birthparents, and not looking like other members of their families. It also affirms that adopted children are just as much family members as are biological children.
African-American and European-American of African-European-American and Cheyenne
Primary, Intermediate; Nonfiction

Viglucci, Patricia Costa. *Sun Dance at Turtle Rock*. Rochester, N.Y.: Stone Pine Books, 1996. 136 p.

Twelve-year-old Cody, whose white father had died in a car accident six years earlier, goes to spend the summer with his paternal grandfather Zachariah, who had objected to the marriage of his father to his African-American mother. Cody is treated lovingly by his aunt, uncle, and their toddler son and spends much of the time exploring the town and the surrounding Allegheny Mountains with their daughter Jem. However, although his grandfather shows warmth towards Cody's cousins, he treats Cody coldly because of his race and is especially upset that Cody may be adopted by his black stepfather and take his stepfather's name. The last straw for Cody comes when Zachariah takes the side of a bigoted neighbor boy instead of his. Cody realizes that he is like the Plains Indians who in a Sun Dance had tortured themselves to prove themselves worthy, in Cody's case of his father's father. Cody plans to leave until he saves Jem from a bear. Then Zachariah expresses his love for Cody, and Cody decides that, although it will take time for his grandfather to change, he will stay for the rest of the summer.
African-American of African-European-American
Intermediate; Fiction

Asian-American Adults

See   Hanks, Thomas (Tom) J.

Banish, Roslyn with Jennifer Jordan-Wong. *A Forever Family*. Photographs by author. New York: HarperCollins, 1992. 48 p.

Numerous photographs and a brief text, written with second grader Jennifer Jordan-Wong as the narrator, explain how she was adopted and show her with her family, extended family, and schoolmates. After living with an African-American foster family, whom she still visits, she became the daughter of Susan, who is European-American, and Ron, who is Chinese-American. The book does not specify Jennifer's racial identity although she appears to be a child of color.
Chinese-American and European-American of probably child of color
Pre-K, Primary; Nonfiction

Gregory, Kristiana. *Orphan Runaways*. New York: Scholastic Press, 1998. 160 p.

In 1878, having recently been orphaned by an influenza epidemic, twelve-year-old Danny and his six-year-old brother Judd escape from an abusive orphanage and travel from San Francisco to find their uncle in a rowdy California mining town. They are looked after by a hotel owner who cares for orphan children until, after several months, the boys' uncle locates them. However, Danny, influenced by the prejudice of his new friends and the community, rejects his kind uncle because of his Chinese-American girlfriend whom he later marries. Danny finally overcomes his prejudice and with Judd becomes part of

his uncle's family.
Chinese-American and European-American of Irish-European-American
Intermediate; Fiction

Canadian-American Adults

See   Lasky, Marven

Highwater, Jamake. *I Wear the Morning Star*. New York: Harper & Row, Publishers, 1986. 160 p.
(The Ghost Horse Cycle)
     This third book in *The Ghost Horse Cycle* for the oldest readers tells the story of Sitko and his
miserable boyhood. Sitko is placed in a boarding school where he is mistreated by the adults and
scorned by the other children. His alcoholic father, Jamie Ghost Horse, realizing that Sitko deserves
a better life, allows Alexander, his former friend and now the lover of his ex-wife Jemina, to adopt
Sitko, and Sitko goes to live with Alexander, Jemina, and his grandmother Amana in the San Fernando
Valley. Not able to figure out his past and deeply confused about his identity, Sitko continues a life
filled with unhappiness, mitigated only by his friendship with a farm boy, his school's art club, and
his painting. At the end of the book, Jamie shoots Jemina and Alexander, killing her and wounding
Alexander. Jamie perishes in a truck crash, Sitko's older brother loses his life in a plane crash, the eld-
erly Amana dies, and Sitko, the only one remaining, preserves his Blood (Blackfoot) past through his
paintings.
Greek, French Canadian-American, and Blackfoot (Blood) of African-French Canadian-American,
Blackfoot (Blood), and Cherokee
Older; Fiction

European Adults

See   Montezuma, Carlos

Highwater, Jamake. *I Wear the Morning Star*. New York: Harper & Row, Publishers, 1986. 160 p.
(The Ghost Horse Cycle)
     This third book in *The Ghost Horse Cycle* for the oldest readers tells the story of Sitko and his
miserable boyhood. Sitko is placed in a boarding school where he is mistreated by the adults and
scorned by the other children. His alcoholic father, Jamie Ghost Horse, realizing that Sitko deserves
a better life, allows Alexander, his former friend and now the lover of his ex-wife Jemina, to adopt
Sitko, and Sitko goes to live with Alexander, Jemina, and his grandmother Amana in the San Fernando
Valley. Not able to figure out his past and deeply confused about his identity, Sitko continues a life
filled with unhappiness, mitigated only by his friendship with a farm boy, his school's art club, and
his painting. At the end of the book, Jamie shoots Jemina and Alexander, killing her and wounding
Alexander. Jamie perishes in a truck crash, Sitko's older brother loses his life in a plane crash, the elderly Amana dies, and Sitko, the only one remaining, preserves his Blood (Blackfoot) past through his
paintings.

Greek, French Canadian-American, and Blackfoot (Blood) of African-French Canadian-American, Blackfoot (Blood), and Cherokee
Older; Fiction

Patron, Susan. *The Higher Power of Lucky*. Illustrated by Matt Phelan. New York: Atheneum Books for Young Readers, 2006. 144 p. (A Richard Jackson Book)
Ten-year-old Lucky lives in Hard Pan, California (population 43), which consists of trailers, sheds, shacks, and the Found Object Wind Chime Museum and Visitor Center where she has a job cleaning up the trash after meetings of various anonymous groups (e.g., alcoholics, smokers). She has a survival backpack filled with objects needed for studying insects and scorpions, a best friend who spends his time tying knots, and a dog named HMS Beagle after Darwin's ship. Most of all, Lucky wants to find the Higher Power talked about by recovering addicts, which will tell her how to keep her guardian Brigitte from returning to her native France. To prevent Brigitte's leaving, Lucky runs away in a dust storm into the Mojave Desert.
French of European-American
Intermediate; Fiction

Rees, Celia. *Sorceress*. Cambridge, Mass.: Candlewick Press, 2003. 352 p.
Agnes, an eighteen-year-old Mohawk college student, decides to help a researcher who is trying to learn the fate of Mary Newbury, an English girl forced to flee from her Puritan settlement because she was accused of practicing witchcraft. Agnes feels a strange connection to Mary, who may be the medicine woman whose story has been carried down in her family. Visiting her aunt on her Mohawk reservation, Agnes is transported back to the 1600s where she experiences Mary's life. Mary marries Jaybird, a Pennacook Indian, and bears two children: a daughter, who is murdered as a child by the English, and a son, Black Fox, who becomes a warrior. Mary saves Ephraim, an eleven-year-old white boy injured in an Indian attack, and raises him as her son. When she, Black Fox, and Ephraim visit Mount Royale to trade furs, Mary is captured by a Frenchman and then rescued by her two sons. Fleeing from their pursuers, they end up living in a Mohawk village where Mary is able to stem a smallpox epidemic. The author relates Mary's earlier story in the book *Witch Child*.
English and Pennacook (Pentucket) of European-American
Older; Fiction

Resau, Laura. *Red Glass*. New York: Delacorte Press, 2007. 304 p.
This novel details the transformation of Sophie from Sophie la Delicada (the Delicate whose life is restricted by allergies, worries, and fears) into Sophie la Fuerte (the Strong, who undertakes and completes a very dangerous journey). Sixteen-year-old Sophie lives in Tucson with her English mother, her Mexican stepfather, and her great-aunt Dika, a Bosnian refugee. Then the family takes in five-year-old Pablo whose parents have died as his family tried to escape from Mexico. A year later, so that Pablo can see his relatives and decide where he wants to live, Sophie, Pablo, and Dika join Dika's boyfriend Mr. Lorenzo and his son Ángel, who are bound, via Mexico, for Guatemala to see whether Flor Blanca, their wife and mother, respectively, is alive and to find her jewels. The group spends a week in Pablo's Oaxaca village where Sophie and Ángel express their feelings for each other. Mr. Lorenzo and

Ángel then go on to Guatemala, but are unable to return as Ángel is savagely attacked and their passports and money stolen. With Dika injured from a fall, Sophie travels by herself to Guatemala, a trip which is not at all safe, especially for a white girl. In Guatemala Ángel shares a hospital room with one of his attackers, Flor Blanca's fate is revealed, and Ángel decides whether to remain in Guatemala. Likewise, in Mexico Pablo decides whether he will stay there.
Mexican and English of English-European-American
Older; Fiction

Tenny, Dixie. *Call the Darkness Down*. New York: Atheneum, 1984. 204 p. (A Margaret K. McElderry Book)
Although for years Morfa has heard tales of Wales from Gwenfair, her Welsh mother, Gwenfair has refused to say anything about her parents and why she left her beloved Wales. When Morfa spends her freshman year at a Welsh college, she immediately becomes immersed in Welsh life: having Welsh friends, learning the Welsh language, and experiencing Welsh culture. She also has scary moments with a strange man in a dark coat and, pushed off a castle wall, narrowly escapes death. In this suspenseful story of the forces of light and dark, of mystical powers, and of spells, Morfa finally discovers the terrible truth about her family and must save her life from her murderous grandmother.
English-European-American and Welsh of Welsh-American
Older; Fiction

Wosmek, Frances. *A Brown Bird Singing*. Illustrated by Ted Lewin. New York: Beech Tree Paperback Books, 1986. 128 p.
Years ago, after her mother had died from a fever, Anego's Chippewa father Hamigeesek had left her to stay with the Veselka family. The only Indian in her northern Minnesota community, Anego sometimes thinks about the brown bird she once held and gets a warm supportive feeling. Anego passes fourth grade, raises an orphaned fawn and grieves when a hunter shoots it, joins in the excitement of the family's getting a car, and, after thinking she is not needed when a baby brother is born, helps save his life and realizes how much she cares for him. Anego is very close to her Irish Ma, sister Sheila, and Austrian-American Pa, who is her best friend, and she dreads the time that the hardly-remembered Hamigeesek will take her from them. However, when he does come, Hamigeesek kindly assures Anego that she can remain with the Veselkas and, by having her hold a brown bird, brings back her memories of her Chippewa mother.
Austrian-American and Irish of Chippewa
Intermediate; Fiction

European-American Adults

See   Anderson, Ross
        Cole, Lynette
        Culberson, Sarah
        Farragut, David Glasgow
        Hanks, Thomas (Tom) J.

Haynes, Lemuel
Jacobs, Harriet Ann
Limber, Jim
Malcolm X
O'Brien, Daniel (Dan) Dion
Silkwood, Priscilla
Williams, Mary Harris

Anderson, Laurie Halse. *Chains*. New York: Simon & Schuster Books for Young Readers, 2008. 320 p. (Seeds of America)

This book of historical fiction is set in New York City in 1776 and 1777, where first the Patriots and then the British army and their Tory allies are in control. Although promised their freedom in Rhode Island upon the death of their mistress, Isabel and her five-year old sister are sold to the Locktons, a Tory family in New York City. The book chronicles the hardships endured by Isabel as she suffers the continuing abuse of Mrs. Lockton; is devastated when her vulnerable little sister is taken away to be sold; gives the Patriots information about a plot to kill George Washington, but is not rewarded with her freedom; likewise cannot secure her freedom from the British; is branded with an I for "Insolence"on her cheek; and brings food to the prison where Patriot captives including her only friend, the slave Curzon, live in inhumane conditions. Isabel finally escapes with Curzon to New Jersey.
English-American (Loyalist) of African-American
Older; Fiction

Angel, Ann. *Real for Sure Sister*. Illustrated by Joanne Bowring. Fort Wayne, Ind.: Perspectives Press, 1988. 72 p.

Nine-year-old Amanda is adopted as are her brothers Nicky and Joey, who is Mexican Indian. Although she adores her little brothers, she has conflicting feelings about Stevi, the biracial (black/white) baby her family is planning to adopt. Amanda initially wants another brother, not a sister, and then tries to ignore Stevi in case the adoption doesn't go through. She shares her concern with her parents, who are white, and with her best friend, who has been adopted from Korea. It is a happy day when Amanda's entire family goes to court and Stevi becomes her real sister.
European-American of African-European-American
Primary; Fiction

Banish, Roslyn with Jennifer Jordan-Wong. *A Forever Family*. Photographs by author. New York: HarperCollins, 1992. 48 p.

Numerous photographs and a brief text, written with second grader Jennifer Jordan-Wong as the narrator, explain how she was adopted and show her with her family, extended family, and school-mates. After living with an African-American foster family, whom she still visits, she became the daughter of Susan, who is European-American, and Ron, who is Chinese-American. The book does not specify Jennifer's racial identity although she appears to be a child of color.

European-American and Chinese-American of probably child of color
Pre-K, Primary; Nonfiction

Banks, Sara H. *Remember My Name*. Illustrated by Birgitta Saflund. Niwot, Colo.: Roberts Rinehart Publishers, 1993. 128 p.

When her parents die, eleven-year-old Annie, who is half Cherokee and half Scottish-American, leaves her Cherokee grandmother to live with her Cherokee uncle and his wife in New Echota. She attends school and becomes best friends with Righteous Cry, a black girl about her age who is a slave. When in 1838 the Cherokees are forced to leave to travel westward in the Trail of Tears, Annie's uncle sends her and Righteous (now freed) to travel, almost all the way by themselves, back to Annie's mountain home.
European-American and Cherokee of Scottish-American and Cherokee
Intermediate; Fiction

Becker, John T., and Stanli K. Becker, eds. *All Blood Is Red . . . All Shadows Are Dark!* Illustrated by J. Howard Noel. Cleveland: Seven Shadows Press, 1984. 168 p.

John T. (Tom) Becker, who is Irish-German-American, and his wife, Stanli K. Becker, who is African-American, have five young children. Of the four who are adopted one is biracial. All seven family members are responsible for individual sections of this book, which recounts their personal and family experiences as a multiracial family. Teaching their children to be aware of and proud of their individual differences, the editors present information on the history of racial classification in the United States and advocate their belief that race is and should be regarded as an "absurdity."
German-Irish-American and African-American of African-European-American and of African-American
Intermediate, Older; Nonfiction

Brashares, Ann. *Forever in Blue: The Fourth Summer of the Sisterhood*. New York: Delacorte Press, 2007. 400 p. (Sisterhood of the Traveling Pants)

This fourth book of the series takes place after Carmen, Lena, Tibby, and Bridget's freshman year in college. Carmen's year at Williams College has been a disaster. She finds herself ungrounded with her mother, stepfather, and baby brother moving into a new house, discovers that she has no idea how to make friends, and feels invisible. Her only college friend, aspiring actress Julia, has persuaded Carmen to spend the summer with her at a theater festival in Vermont where Carmen will be on a stage crew. When the casting director persuades Carmen to audition, Carmen, who has never acted, is amazed to discover that she is the only apprentice chosen for a role in the theater's major production. Julia becomes hostile to Carmen and, then, pretending to be helpful, teaches Carmen how to read her role in meter. The professional actors are dismayed that Carmen now sounds like a robot. Carmen finally realizes that Julia takes pleasure in her failures, and she once again immerses herself in her role. Lena, who had been crushed when her Greek boyfriend Kostas married a Greek woman whom he had impregnated, is enrolled in a painting class in Providence, Rhode Island. There she is impressed with classmate Leo, an outstanding artist who is equally engrossed in painting. Getting to know him and his artistic African-American mother, Lena has her first sexual experience with him. Tibby, who has been going with Bailey's friend Brian, also loses her virginity. However, she becomes

distressed that she may be pregnant and, after discovering that she isn't, breaks up with Brian. She then gives Lena's younger sister Effie an okay to go out with him. With Bridget's boyfriend Eric away for the summer in Mexico, she goes to Turkey for an archaeological dig. There she discovers that she loves digging and falls for an archaeology professor until she sees his wife and children. At the book's conclusion Tibby is reunited with Brian, Bridget is reunited with Eric, and Lena, Tibby, and Bridget go to Vermont to attend Carmen's successful opening night. Then the four friends fly to Greece to search for the Traveling Pants, which Effie has accidentally lost, Lena and Kostas meet, and the four friends realize that they have moved beyond the Pants. The mixed heritages of Carmen, Bridget, and Eric should be familiar to readers of *The Sisterhood of the Traveling Pants*.
European-American of European-Puerto Rican-American
Older; Fiction

Brashares, Ann. *Girls in Pants: The Third Summer of the Sisterhood*. New York: Delacorte Press, 2005. 352 p. (Sisterhood of the Traveling Pants)

Bridget, Lena, Tibby, and Carmen graduate from high school at the beginning of this third book in the series, which details the four seventeen-year-olds' lives during the summer before college. Lena, who is still getting over Kostas, enjoys her summer drawing class. Defying and lying to her father, she continues to attend after he has forbidden her to continue because of the nude models. When he discovers her deceit, he announces that he will not pay for her going to the Rhode Island School of Design. Heeding the suggestion of the class teacher, Lena embarks on an art portfolio project that just may win her a scholarship to the RISD. Tibby has conflicting feelings when Brian asks her to the senior party, but is devastated when, because she has left her window open, her three-year-old sister tries to climb the nearby apple tree and, falling, has a fractured skull and broken bones. Finding it difficult to have her new stepfather David living in her house and upset by the news that she will become a sister, Carmen considers going to the nearby University of Maryland rather than Williams College so that she can be closer to home. She hates her job taking care of Valia, Lena's grandmother, who has become very disagreeable because she is homesick for her native Greece. Carmen also worries that Win, the boy she likes, has the false impression that she is a good person. Bridget spends her summer coaching at a soccer camp in Pennsylvania where she is surprised to discover that one of the coaches is Eric with whom she had a relationship two summers earlier in California. Still strongly drawn to him, but trying to be more sensible, she and Eric become friends and he nurses her through an illness. It is an eventful summer as Carmen and Win frantically drive to Downington, Pennsylvania, to bring David back to Bethesda for his son's early birth and Carmen discovers that she loves her baby brother and wants to go to Williams. Valia is happy that she can return to Greece, and Lena receives the RSID scholarship and her father's approval. Tibby overcomes her feelings of unworthiness by climbing out of her window and down the apple tree and being Carmen's mother's successful, albeit unorthodox, birth coach. It is then that she is able to get back together with Brian. And, Eric tells Bridget that he has broken up with his girlfriend, and they profess how much they care for each other. Readers of the initial book in this series will be aware of the mixed heritages of Carmen, Bridget, and Eric.
European-American of European-Puerto Rican-American
Older; Fiction

Brashares, Ann. *The Second Summer of the Sisterhood*. New York: Delacorte Press, 2003. 384 p. (Sisterhood of the Traveling Pants)

This second book of the series describes Carmen, Lena, Bridget, and Tibby's experiences during the summer before their seventeenth birthdays. Once again, the pants are passed among them, but they no longer fit Bridget, who has been so down because of her earlier sexual relationship with Eric, that she has gained weight, given up soccer, and dyed her pretty blonde hair. Using a fake name, Bridget travels to Alabama where she gets a job cleaning her grandmother Greta's attic and finds mementos of her deceased mother. As the summer progresses Bridget gets back in shape, is able to wear the pants, confesses her identity to Greta and to her long ago best friend Billy, coaches and then stars for Billy's soccer team, and realizes that Greta is like a mother to her. Tibby goes to a film program at a college in Virginia. Befriending two shallow classmates, she produces a highly embarrassing film about her mother and is excruciated when her mother comes to the viewing. Upset by the damage she has done to her relationships with her mother and Brian, a friend of hers and Bailey's, she redeems herself by making a moving film about Bailey, who died from cancer. Both Carmen and Lena also experience strained relationships with their mothers. Carmen is jealous of her mother's romance with David, sabotages it, and then manages to restore it. Lena pesters her mother about the man Eugene in her mother's past and regrets that she has broken off with Kostas. When Kostas visits her, she discovers that he really is in love with her. However, going to Greece for her beloved grandfather's funeral, Lena finds out that Kostas has had to marry a Greek woman whom he impregnated. Fortunately, she learns about Eugene from her mother and is attracted to Carmen's stepbrother Paul. The story ends when the girls' mothers, who had not been close since Bridget's mother's death, resume their friendship. The mixed heritages of Carmen, Bridget, and Eric were revealed in *The Sisterhood of the Traveling Pants*.
European-American of European-Puerto Rican-American
Older; Fiction

Brashares, Ann. *The Sisterhood of the Traveling Pants*. New York: Delacorte Press, 2001. 304 p. (Sisterhood of the Traveling Pants)

In this initial book of the series, four girls who are almost sixteen discover that a pair of blue jeans that Carmen had purchased at a thrift shop somehow fits all of them. Close friends their entire lives, the girls establish a Sisterhood in which they will pass the pants among each other as they separate during their summer vacation. Bridget, an athlete whose father is Dutch and whose mother had committed suicide, goes to a soccer camp in Baja, California, where she shines as a player. She is strongly attracted to camp coach Eric whose mother is Mexican, loses her virginity to him, and then becomes confused and upset. Carmen, who had been looking forward to a vacation with her divorced father in South Carolina, is shocked to learn that he is engaged and is living with his fiancée and her two children. Ignored and treated like an outsider because of her Puerto Rican appearance, Carmen finally becomes so frustrated and angry that she throws a rock through the house window and runs away back to Bethesda, Maryland. Lena, a beautiful introverted girl, goes with her sister to stay in Greece with her grandparents. Enjoying painting the lovely scenery, she inadvertently leads her grandparents to believe she has been raped by Kostas, a family friend, and causes a fight between their grandfathers. Tibby, who remains at home, gets a tedious job at a drugstore and becomes friends with

Bailey, a twelve-year-old girl who has leukemia and with whom she films a movie. The pants seem to have no positive effect on the girls' experiences until the end of the summer. Then Lena gets the courage to apologize to Kostas and tell him she loves him; Carmen gets the courage to go to her father's wedding after telling him that she is mad at him; Tibby gets the courage to visit Bailey in the hospital when she is dying; and Bridget receives the support she needs from the pants (and Lena who brings them to her).
European-American of European-Puerto Rican-American
Older; Fiction

Bruchac, Joseph. *Hidden Roots*. New York: Scholastic Press, 2004. 144 p.
It is 1954 and eleven-year-old Sonny lives with his mother and his father, who is often angry and physically abusive. Sonny enjoys the company of an older friend "Uncle" Louie, a man who had worked for his mother's parents when she was a child and from whom he learns much about the Adirondack area of New York State where they live. Sonny wonders about the many subjects he is not allowed to discuss and questions that remain unanswered: why he should be afraid of being "crept up on," what bad things happened in Vermont, and why his father doesn't want Uncle Louis around. It is only after he and Uncle Louis learn from the Jewish school librarian that as a child her parents had sent her from Germany to England for safety, that Uncle Louis tells Sonny the truth. Uncle Louis is his grandfather, who, like his late wife, had been sterilized during the Vermont Eugenics Project because they were Indians and who had fled Vermont so that Sonny's mother would not be taken away. It was because Sonny's family wanted to protect him from being treated like an Indian that they had kept his identity a secret, but it is when the secret is revealed to Sonny that his father, who is also part-Indian, is released from his anger and shame.
European-American of French Canadian-American, Abenaki and Mohican
Intermediate, Older; Fiction

Bunin, Catherine, and Sherry Bunin. *Is That Your Sister? A True Story of Adoption*. New York: Pantheon Books, 1976. 44 p.
Narrator six-year-old Catherine Bunin, who appears to be at least partial African-American, explains how she answers the questions children ask her about adoption and, in the process, presents the story of her adoption and that of her African-American four- year-old sister. The book includes numerous family photographs of the two girls, their two brothers, their father, and their mother Sherry Bunin.
European-American of African-American
Primary; Nonfiction

Cannon, A. E. *The Shadow Brothers*. New York: Delacorte Press, 1990. 192 p.
During their junior year of high school, there are changes in both Marcus and his foster brother Henry. Marcus stops being the shadow brother and comes into his own, and Henry struggles with his neglected Navaho heritage. The two come to realize that whatever their future paths, they are always brothers.
European-American and European-American Mormon of Navajo
Older; Fiction

Creel, Ann Howard. *Call Me the Canyon: A Love Story*. Weston, Conn.: Brown Barn Books, 2006. 224 p.

This novel takes place during the turn of the twentieth century in the Glen Canyon area of Utah and Arizona. Fifteen-year-old Madolen, whose Navajo mother had died years before, leaves her father to live with a Mormon family from whom she can learn to read. She becomes close to the family, especially to its daughter Claire, who becomes her steadfast friend, but is forced by the mother to leave after Claire's little brother Gabriel dies accidentally while under the girls' care. Madolen lives alone in a cabin as she supports herself by gathering gold dust and searches in vain for a gold-filled canyon she remembers from her childhood. Madolen then guides Wallis, a wealthy and educated young man, to places where he can pursue his interests in the area's ancient history. Madolen's love for Wallis is not returned until almost the end of the story when they decide to get married. However, realizing his reluctance to introduce a woman of Navajo blood to his Eastern family, Madolen leaves him and later marries Yiska, the Navajo whom she had previously disliked.
European-American Mormon of European-American and Navajo
Older; Fiction

Crutcher, Chris. *Whale Talk*. New York: Dell Laurel-Leaf, 2002. 224 p.

This novel tells of T. J. Jones, an adopted seventeen-year-old of mixed race who in his senior year of high school organizes a swimming team of boys regarded as misfits by their classmates and the school and who are, except for T. J., mediocre swimmers. The story focuses on T. J.'s efforts to have his teammates rewarded for their Herculean efforts by receiving athletic letters. The book shows how the boys come to share their backgrounds and feelings and to become part of a cohesive group in which each feels valued and accepted. Thanks primarily to his father, T. J. learns to control his own rage.
European-American of African-Japanese-Norwegian-Swiss-American
Older; Fiction

Dadey, Debbie. *Cherokee Sister*. New York: Delacorte Press, 2000. 128 p.

Twelve-year-old Allie, who is Scottish-American, and Leaf, who is Cherokee, are best friends. This story takes place in 1838 in Georgia when the Cherokees are forced to leave their homes and travel westward in the Trail of Tears. Allie, who is trying on Leaf's new dress, is mistaken for a Cherokee and seized together with Leaf, her grandmother, and others by American soldiers. Leaf's brother is killed when the army first comes, her grandmother dies from a wound, the large Cherokee village to which they are taken is destroyed, and there is much suffering. Thanks to the beads Allie has pulled off the Indian dress, her father finds her and, with the army captain's okay, rescues both Allie and Leaf, his two "daughters."
Scottish-American of Cherokee
Intermediate; Fiction

Erlbach, Arlene. *The Families Book: True Stories about Real Kids and the People They Live With and Love*. Photographs by Stephen J. Carrera. Illustrated by Lisa Wagner. Minneapolis: Free Spirit Publishing, 1996. 120 p.

In a section of this book children tell about their families, that include a family in which the father is Lutheran and the mother Jewish; a family in which the father is African-American and the mother Caucasian; a family with four children in which Caucasian parents have adopted a biracial American girl and a boy from Romania; and a family with Caucasian parents and eleven children, six of whom were adopted from Korea.
European-American of African-European-American
Intermediate; Nonfiction

Erskine, Kathryn. *Quaking*. New York: Philomel Books, 2007. 240 p.

In this novel for the oldest readers, fourteen-year-old Matt goes to live with a Quaker couple, Sam and Jessica. This is the latest in a series of home placements for Matt, who as a small child lived in terror of her abusive father and could not save her mother from dying. Matt copes by running away from difficult situations, avoids relationships, and is upset when someone is nice to her because she thinks it can't last. At school Matt is frightened by a bully and hates an authoritarian, warmongering teacher, while at home she comes to realize that Sam is not the fool she presumed him to be, but the brave, intelligent leader of the local Quaker peace movement. With the unconditional love and support of Sam and Jessica, Matt finally realizes her own strength.
European-American Quaker of European-American non-Quaker
Older; Fiction

Friedrich, Molly. *You're Not My REAL Mother!* Illustrated by Christy Hale. Boston: Little, Brown and Company, 2004. 32 p.

In this picture book when a little girl questions whether her adoptive mother is her real mother since they do not look alike, her mother tells of things she does for her as a real mother—and then the girl adds some more.
European-American of non-European-American
Pre-K, Primary; Fiction

Gaeddert, LouAnn. *Hope*. New York: Aladdin Paperbacks, 1997. 176 p.

Set in 1851, this is the story of twelve-year-old Hope and her nine-year-old brother John whose father is in California searching for gold and whose mother has just died. They are taken by their uncle to Hancock Shaker Village near Pittsfield, Massachusetts, where they are separated since Shakers live apart by gender with virtually no contact between them. This book describes in detail the practices, rules, and loving nature of the Shakers. John, who suffers from asthma, thrives with the Shakers, becomes healthy, and enjoys working with wood. Hope, although appreciating the Shakers' kindnesses, chafes under their restrictions and the conformity in beliefs that is demanded by them. When the children's father finally is able to learn where they are, John, who cannot remember him, decides to remain with the Shakers while Hope leaves to join her father in California.
European-American Shaker of European-American non-Shaker
Intermediate, Older; Fiction

George, Jean Craighead. *Julie*. Illustrated by Wendell Minor. New York: HarperCollins Publishers, 1994. 240 p.

In this sequel to *Julie of the Wolves*, Julie, who is now fourteen, is living in Kangik with her father Kapugen and his new wife Ellen. Trapped with Ellen in a blizzard, Julie comes to accept her white stepmother. However, Julie knows that Kapugen was the one who killed her adoptive wolf father Amaroq and will kill his son Kapu and the new wolf pack in order to protect his herd of musk ox that sustains the Alaskan village's economy. Journeying to find the wolf pack, Julie manages to lead it away from the village to a place where the wolves can feed on moose. Kapugen and Ellen name their new baby boy Amaroq; Julie falls in love with Peter, an Eskimo from Siberia; and when the wolves come back, Kapugen finally returns to his Eskimo ways and spares them.
European-American and Eskimo of Eskimo
Intermediate, Older; Fiction

George, Jean Craighead. *Julie of the Wolves*. Illustrated by John Schoenherr. New York: Harper Trophy, 1974. 176 p.

When her "husband" in an arranged child marriage tries to rape her, thirteen-year-old Julie, who is an Eskimo, runs away from Barrow, Alaska, to catch a ship at Point Hope that will take her to live with her San Francisco pen pal. Lost and starving on the tundra, she observes a nearby wolf pack and learns how to communicate with them. She is adopted by Amaroq, its leader, and grows to love Amaroq, the spiritual father wolf Nails, the mother wolf Silver, and the wolf puppies. Julie is devastated when hunters shooting from an airplane kill Amaroq and wound her favorite pup Kapu. Julie discovers that her father Kapugen, whom she had thought dead, is living in nearby Kangik. Going to him, she finds out that he has a white wife and an airplane for hunting. After running away again, Julie realizes that the old Eskimo times are gone and she must return to Kapugen.
European-American and Eskimo of Eskimo
Intermediate, Older; Fiction

George, Jean Craighead. *Julie's Wolf Pack*. Illustrated by Wendell Minor. New York: HarperCollins Publishers, 1997. 208 p.

This sequel to *Julie* is devoted almost entirely to the story of Julie's Avalik River wolf pack. It traces its activities through four years during which Kapu asserts himself as its Alpha (leader); the wolf Ice Blink spreads rabies on the tundra; Silver has two more puppies; Kapu is trapped for a medical study; Silver dies; Kapu's daughter Sweet Fur Amy becomes the new Alpha; and, released, Kapu joins his mate Aaka. There is little about Julie and her human family. However, her little half-brother Amaroq bonds with one of Silver's wolf pups which becomes a sled dog leader for Kapugen. At the book's end Julie and Peter marry and are hired to live on the tundra and study the wolves.
European-American and Eskimo of Eskimo
Intermediate, Older; Fiction

Gregory, Kristiana. *Orphan Runaways*. New York: Scholastic Press, 1998. 160 p.

In 1878, having recently been orphaned by an influenza epidemic, twelve-year-old Danny and his six-year-old brother Judd escape from an abusive orphanage and travel from San Francisco to find their

uncle in a rowdy California mining town. They are looked after by a hotel owner who cares for orphan children until, after several months, the boys' uncle locates them. However, Danny, influenced by the prejudice of his new friends and the community, rejects his kind uncle because of his Chinese-American girlfriend whom he later marries. Danny finally overcomes his prejudice and with Judd becomes part of his uncle's family.
European-American and Chinese-American of Irish-European-American
Intermediate; Fiction

Grimes, Nikki. *Dark Sons*. New York: Jump at the Sun, 2005. 224 p.

Written in verse, this book intertwines the often parallel stories of the teen-aged boys, Ishmael, the son of Abraham and the maid-servant Hagar, and Sam, the American son of African-American parents. Although their lives are separated by centuries, both grow up with strong bonds with their fathers and experience rejection and confusion when their fathers abandon their mothers and focus their attention on sons they father with other women. In Ishmael's case, because of Sarah's antagonism, Abraham sends Ishmael and Hagar away. In Sam's case, his father, new wife, and baby son move across the country. At the end of the book Sam reads the story of Ishmael and imagines that, as kindred brothers, he too will be able to carry on his own life.
Italian-American and African-American of African-American
Older; Fiction

Hickman, Janet. *Susannah*. New York: Greenwillow Books, 1998. 144 p.

It is 1810 and thirteen-year-old Susannah's mother has died. Against Susannah's wishes, her father takes her with him to live in the Shaker community near Lebanon, Ohio. There she rarely is able to speak to her father and is unhappy with Shaker life and beliefs, especially the separation of Shaker children from their parents. When her father finally gives her permission to leave and live with a great-aunt, Susannah finds that she cannot leave the little girl Mary, who longs for her non-Shaker mother and has become attached to Susannah. Staying to be a surrogate mother to Mary, Susannah is not able to give her enough attention. Susannah finally runs away with Mary to Lebanon where she discovers her great-aunt has died and gives the money her great-aunt had left for her to Mary and her mother so that they may escape from the area.
European-American Shaker of European-American non-Shaker
Intermediate, Older; Fiction

Holland, Isabelle. *The Journey Home*. New York: Scholastic, 1990. 224 p.

Pursuant to their mother's wishes, at her death twelve-year-old Maggie and seven-year-old Annie travel with the Children's Aid Society from their New York City slum to rural Kansas. There they are taken in by a Baptist farm couple. Missing their mother, the girls have a difficult adjustment, made harder by harassment because they are poor Irish Catholics. Maggie, who takes seriously her obligation to care for spirited Annie, finally realizes that her new mother can share that responsibility—and that with her recently-acquired reading skills, she has come to like her Kansas home.
European (non-Irish)-American Baptist of Irish Catholic
Intermediate, Older; Fiction

Holland, Isabelle. *The Promised Land*. New York: Scholastic, 1996. 160 p.

This sequel to *The Journey Home* takes place three years later when Maggie is fifteen and Annie ten. Michael, their Irish uncle, visits for the purpose of taking them back to New York City where they can practice their Catholic faith. Although Maggie loves Kansas and the couple who cares for, but has not legally adopted them, she is somewhat torn because of the anti-Irish Catholic sentiments she encounters and because she feels rejected by the boy whom she likes. Fortunately, Michael decides not to pursue his claim on the girls and both of them happily remain with their Midwestern family.
European (non-Irish)-American Baptist of Irish Catholic
Intermediate, Older; Fiction

Holm, Jennifer L. *Penny from Heaven*. New York: Random House, 2006. 288 p.

During the eventful summer of 1953 Penny spends time with both sides of her divided family: her mother and maternal grandparents and her late Italian father's mother, siblings, and relatives. Abetted by her cousin Freddie, Penny sneaks into her Italian grandmother's room to find out the color of her underwear, digs in the yard for treasure, and disobeys her mother by going to the beach. She gets a black eye, goes to a Dodgers game for her twelfth birthday, misbehaves to discourage her mother's Irish-American suitor, and, when her arm is caught in a clothes wringer, spends weeks in the hospital. It is there that she comes to accept her soon-to-be stepfather and discovers that her father had been imprisoned during World War II because, as an Italian "enemy alien," he had a radio. Penny also manages to ease the hostilities between the two branches of her family.
Irish-American and European-American of European-Italian-American, Catholic, and Methodist
Intermediate, Older; Fiction

Irwin, Hadley. *Kim/Kimi*. New York: Margaret K. McElderry Books, 1987. 208 p.

Sixteen-year-old Kim's Japanese-American father died before her birth and she enjoys living with her European-American mother and stepfather in Iowa. However, she is upset about others regarding her as Japanese and associating her with World War II Japan. Into teen romance novels which always have perfect endings for their heroines and in the habit of running away from problems, Kim "runs" off to Sacramento to try to find her father's family, which had disowned him. There she learns of the terrible Japanese-American concentration camps of World War II and of their effects on those imprisoned—and she meets her grandmother and her aunt.
European-American and Irish-American of Irish-Japanese-American
Older; Fiction

Jennings, Patrick. *Faith and the Electric Dogs*. Decorations by author. New York: Scholastic, 1996. 144 p.

The narrator—and author—of this fanciful tale is Edison. A mutt from San Cristóbal de las Casas, Mexico, he asserts that it is true. Edison is taken in by Faith, a ten-year-old homesick American girl whose mother has married a Mexican and who hates Mexico because she can't speak Spanish and is teased. With help from a craftsman, Faith builds a rocket powered by pig fat and jalapeño peppers and sets off with Edison for San Francisco. Unfortunately, the rocket goes down in a storm. The two of them end up on an island in the Pacific Ocean, which is deserted except for four mutts and a seventy-

year-old man who had come down on the island when he was ten after the balloon he was taking to return from Mexico to England was pierced by a seagull. The story concludes with Faith and Edison's return to Mexico, her happiness there, and an explanation of how Edison became a writer. Definitions of the many Spanish and Bowwow (canine) words used in the text are provided in the margins and also in a glossary.
German-Scottish-Irish-American and Mexican of German-Italian-Scottish-Irish-American
Intermediate; Fiction

Jennings, Patrick. *Faith and the Rocket Cat*. Decorations by author. New York: Scholastic Press, 1998. 240 p.

In this sequel to *Faith and the Electric Dogs*, Edison the mutt relates another fantastic story. When Faith, her mother, and her stepfather move to San Francisco, Faith wants to impress classmate Alex and Edison wishes to befriend Daphne, a whippet show dog, by taking them for a ride in Faith's rocket. Faith, Edison, Alex, Daphne—and Faith's mother—crash-land in Death Valley where they encounter coyotes and find Faith's late father's cat. All ends well in this story in which words presented in Bowwow and Arf (dog languages), Mew (cat language), Spanish, French, Italian, Chinese, Latin, and Turkish are defined both in the margins and in a glossary.
German-Scottish-Irish-American and Mexican of German-Italian-Scottish-Irish-American
Intermediate; Fiction

Koller, Jackie French. *A Place to Call Home*. New York: Atheneum Books for Young Readers, 1995. 208 p.

Fifteen-year-old Anna struggles to take care of her five-year-old sister and baby brother when their alcoholic abusive mother abandons them. Soon Anna discovers that their mother has committed suicide. Realizing that no one will want to adopt all three of them since the little ones are Caucasian and she is much older and of mixed race, Anna keeps her mother's disappearance a secret. Then, disguised as a boy, Anna takes the bus from Connecticut to Mississippi in hopes that her mother's parents will look after them. There she learns why her mother left. Her grandparents disapproved of her mother's relationship with a black man, and, after Anna was born, her police chief grandfather probably murdered her father. Anna finally realizes that she cannot care for her siblings and, with the help of a wise boyfriend, agrees to the adoption. Surprisingly Anna too will be adopted: by the older couple who runs the neighborhood convenience store.
European (probably Greek)-American of African-European-American
Older; Fiction

Krementz, Jill. *How It Feels To Be Adopted*. Photographs by author. New York: Alfred A. Knopf, 1982. 120 p.

Black-and-white photographs accompany the author's interviews with nineteen children who talk about being adopted: how they feel about it, their knowledge of and feelings about their birthparents and whether they want to meet them, their experiences as adopted children, and for five of them, what it is like to be part of a mixed race family. One of these children, who is African-American, has been adopted by an African-American father, but has adopted brothers who are of different ethnicities.

European-American of African-American; Greek-American and Puerto Rican of Puerto Rican-American; European-American of Chickasaw, Choctaw, and Seminole
Intermediate, Older; Nonfiction

Kroll, Virginia. *Beginnings: How Families Come to Be*. Illustrated by Stacey Schuett. Morton Grove, Ill.: Albert Whitman & Company, 1994. 32 p.

In this look at six American families, one family includes a little girl adopted as a baby from Korea by a father of color and a European-American mother and another family in which a girl of color, who had been in foster homes, is adopted by a European-American couple.
European-American of child of color
Pre-K, Primary; Fiction

Kuklin, Susan. *Families*. Photographs by author. New York: Hyperion Books for Children, 2006. 40 p.

Text and color photographs present interviews with American children, who talk about their families. Their families include seven families with children of mixed race, ethnicity, or religion, with one also including a child adopted from Sierra Leone. In an eighth family a child has been adopted from China. In a ninth family an adopted American child is of a race different from that of one of her fathers.
European-American and African-American of African-American
Primary, Intermediate; Nonfiction

Lisle, Janet Taylor. *The Crying Rocks*. New York: Atheneum Books for Young Readers, 2003. 208 p. (A Richard Jackson Book)

Thirteen-year-old Joelle, who was adopted at the age of five by Vern and Aunt Mary Louise, does not look like anyone she knows in Rhode Island. She is upset by what she is told of her past: of being thrown out of a Chicago apartment window by her mother, being put in an orphanage there, traveling by freight train to Connecticut, and then being cared for by an old woman while living in a wooden crate near a railway depot. Joelle is befriended by an adoring eight-year-old girl who is European- and Japanese-American and by a classmate Carlos, who is of mixed heritage. Together Joelle and Carlos learn of the early Narragansett Indians and explore the wooded area, including the Crying Rocks, where they lived. Carlos learns the truth about the accident at the Crying Rocks where his older brother died and Joelle learns the truth about her background. Vern is her real father, her mother was Narragansett, and both her mother and twin sister died in Chicago.
Irish American and European-American of Irish-American and Narragansett
Intermediate, Older; Fiction

Little, Kimberley Griffiths. *The Last Snake Runner*. New York: Alfred A. Knopf, 2002. 208 p.

In this sequel to *Enchanted Runner*, Kendall, now fourteen, has just returned from the Acoma Pueblo where he has become a full member of the Acoma, his late mother's people. Very upset when he learns that his father has married a woman descended from the Spanish conquistadors who in 1599 destroyed the Acoma Pueblo, Kendall has his brother take him back to Acoma. There, in a mesa near

the pueblo, he is transported back to the sixteenth century where he experiences life in the ancient Snake Clan and participates in the last Acoma Snake dance. Although Kendall is unable to save the pueblo from the conquistadors, he brings hope that the Acoma will survive.
European-American and Spanish-Mexican-American of European-American and Acoman
Older; Fiction

MacGregor, Rob. *Prophecy Rock*. New York: Laurel-Leaf Books, 1995. 208 p.

When teenager Will goes to spend the summer with his father, who is chief of police on the Hopi reservation, he becomes involved in the investigation of two murders. It first appears that the murderer is a preacher, a Hopi who now condemns the Hopis and their prophecies. Suspicion then turns to whoever believes himself to be Pahana, the Elder White Brother, who is the expected Hopi savior. However, who is that person: the mixed race hospital worker, the white doctor, or the ethnologist, who is also white? As Will helps in solving this mystery, he falls for a Hopi girl, travels about the Arizona reservation, and learns of the Hopi culture.
European-American of European and Hopi
Older; Fiction

McClain, Lee. *My Alternate Life*. New York: Smooch, 2004. 188 p.

At age fifteen Trinity B. Jones is sent from foster care in Pittsburgh to live with a well-off rural family. Tracy wants instead to be reunited with her birthmother who had left her at Saint Helen's Home for Girls when she was eight. Thanks to the amazing computer game her social worker gives her, Trinity is able to observe and hear her mother, who has married a wealthy man and craves media attention. Tracy focuses her efforts on becoming reunited with her mother. To that end, she tries to get the cruel sex-crazy boy, who will probably become the Fall King, to invite her to the Fall Dance so that she will become the Fall Queen and win her mother's acclaim. However, that project ends when he almost rapes her. Trinity also gets her foster mother to let the Fall Dance be a benefit for Saint Helen's and, using a classmate's name, invites her birthmother to be dance sponsor. At the dance, Trinity realizes which family is best for her.
European-American of African-European American
Older; Fiction

McKissack, Patricia C. *Run Away Home*. New York: Scholastic Press, 1997. 176 p.

In 1888 Sky, a fifteen-year-old Chiricahua Apache boy, escapes from a train of Apache prisoners and hides on the farm of twelve-year-old Sarah Jane Crossman, her African-American father, and her mother, who is of African-Scottish-Irish and Seminole heritage. George Wrattan, an Army scout and interpreter, allows the Crossmans to keep Sky with them until he recovers from his swamp fever. In the meantime boll weevils destroy the family's cotton crop, night riders come to their farm, and Sarah Jane's father, who is skilled as a carpenter, gets an order from Booker T. Washington to build desks for nearby Tuskegee Institute. Sky becomes healthy, but Wrattan, whose wife is Apache, gives permission for him to remain on the farm.
African-American and African-Scottish-Irish-American and Seminole of Chiricahua Apache
Intermediate, Older; Fiction

Meyer, Carolyn. *Denny's Tapes*. New York: Margaret K. McElderry Books, 1987. 224 p.

Almost-eighteen-year old Denny, the son of an African-American father and a white mother, and sixteen-year-old Stephanie, the daughter of his white stepfather, fall in love. When his stepfather discovers them together, he orders Denny to leave the house. This story for high school readers is about Denny's journey from Pennsylvania to San Francisco to find his father and on the way to meet his two grandmothers. Although Denny doesn't get together with his musician father who has left for a couple months for a gig in Houston, his trip turns out to be a memorable one. In Chicago he meets his African-American grandmother, who is highly cultivated and had objected to his parents' marriage because of his mother's lower social status. In Nebraska, he meets his mother's mother, who had objected to the marriage because of his father's race and believes Africans-Americans have lower intelligence. However, Denny comes to care for both his grandmothers. His Chicago grandmother spends time teaching him about black history, including about her friend Langston Hughes, and shows him how to develop his natural talent on the piano. Denny discovers that his Nebraska grandmother is largely imprisoned in bed by her cruel daughter-in-law, is full of love for him, and greatly appreciates his organ playing. In Chicago Denny also has a romantic relationship with a beautiful twenty-four-year-old African-American woman and in Colorado is rescued by a cowgirl from a pair of tourists who object to what they wrongly assume is an interracial relationship. When he gets to San Francisco, Denny realizes that he has learned a lot about himself, that he wants to become a musician, and that he is going to wait for his father.
European-American and Swedish-American of African-Swedish-American
Older; Fiction

Naylor, Phyllis Reynolds. *Sang Spell*. New York: Aladdin Paperbacks, 2000. 224 p.

Hitchhiking from Massachusetts to Dallas to live with his aunt because his mother has died, teenager Josh is mugged and left on a road in Appalachia where he is picked up by a Melungeon, who takes him to Canara, an isolated primitive community. Everything is strange and illogical there, and Josh becomes increasingly frustrated in his efforts to escape. The road he takes ends up at the exact place he started. Trying to swim towards a river's opposite shore takes him only a short distance, and a roadside restaurant and a school appear and disappear at regular intervals. Josh discovers that his father was probably Melungeon and befriends a girl whose father was stoned to death when his efforts to escape accidentally caused fatalities Finally, with new insights and the realization that he must keep Canara's secrets, Josh is able to get away. [The Melungeon people are of mixed race living primarily in the central Appalachians. There is controversy as to their origin and their heritage, but they are often regarded as tri-racial: European-American, African-American, and Native American. In this novel they are identified as Portuguese who over time became mixed with a number of other peoples.]
Portuguese (Melungeon)-American of Irish-Portuguese (Melungeon)-American
Older, Fiction

Neufeld, John. *Edgar Allan*. New York: New American Library, 1969. 128 p. (A Signet Book)

With twelve-year-old Michael as the narrator, this is the disturbing story of a white family in California who take a little black boy, Edgar Allan, into their family for a trial period before adopting him. Michael's fourteen-year-old sister, Mary Nell, and a number of church people and townspeople

object to Edgar Allan's presence, and a cross is burned on the family's lawn. Caving in to the pressure, Robert, Michael's minister father, returns Edgar Allan to the adoption agency. Michael and the rest of the family, including Mary Nell, struggle to make peace with Robert, who deeply regrets his mistake.
European-American of African-American
Intermediate, Older; Fiction

Nickman, Steven L. *The Adoption Experience: Stories and Commentaries*. New York: Julian Messner, 1985. 192 p.

This book includes two stories, with accompanying commentaries, about interracial adoption. In "The Ghosts in the Box" a boy who has been adopted from Vietnam after his parents have been killed during the Vietnam War struggles to accept his adoptive parents and American life, especially the celebration of the Fourth of July. In "Hormones Have No Color" the Jewish adoptive father of an African-American teenager struggles with his feelings when the boy makes friends in a neighboring black community.
European-Jewish-American of African-American
Older; Fiction

Okimoto, Jean Davies. *Molly by Any Other Name*. New York: Scholastic, 1990. 288 p.

When she is seventeen-years-old, Molly, who knows only that she is Asian-American, learns at school about an adoptee search organization. Excited, but scared, she agonizes over whether to learn more about her birthmother and perhaps meet her. As her search proceeds, the novel explores the reactions of Molly, her father, her mother, her birthmother, and her birthmother's husband and young son.
European-American of Japanese-Canadian
Older; Fiction

Okimoto, Jean Davies. *Talent Night*. New York: Scholastic, 1995. 176 p.

When seventeen-year-old Rodney and his nineteen-year-old sister Suzanne learn that their great-uncle Hideki, whom they have never met, might give them each $10,000 if they have kept their Japanese heritage, Rodney works on mastering karate kicks, Suzanne tries out Japanese flower arranging, and they both learn about haiku poetry and Japanese cooking. They discover when Uncle Hideki visits that he is not worth impressing since he is unbearably traditional and insults Rodney's half-African-American girlfriend. However, they become closer to their Japanese heritage by learning from their mother about the prejudice she endured as a Japanese-American during the 1940s. Molly from *Molly by Any Other Name* appears very briefly in this book.
European-American of Japanese-Canadian
Older; Fiction

Peck, Robert Newton. *Extra Innings*. New York: Harper Trophy, 2003. 224 p.

Sixteen-year-old Tate is the sole survivor of a private plane crash that kills his parents, his older sister, and his grandparents. With his leg so injured that he can hardly walk, let alone fulfill his dream of being a major league pitcher, and his spirit crushed, Tate goes to live with his eighty-two-year-old

great-grandfather Abbott and his seventy-year-old great aunt Vidalia. Vidalia tells Tate how as an African-American baby she was left in the bus of the Ethiopia's Clowns' traveling baseball club and how, until she was adopted at age ten by Abbott and his wife, she was raised by the team and especially by its pitcher and catcher. In the "extra inning" allotted them, Abbott and Vidalia realize that they have the opportunity to raise Tate—to restore his life and give him a reason for living.
European-American of African-American; European-American and African-American of European-American
Older; Fiction

Polacco, Patricia. *In Our Mothers' House*. Illustrated by author. New York: Philomel Books, 2009. 48 p.

In this story an African-American woman relates how she, her Asian-American brother Will, and her red-haired sister Millie were adopted by their two mothers. The large paintings and the text reveal the happy times they had in their Berkeley, California, home with their mothers, their extended family, and their (with one exception) supportive neighbors. At their mothers' instigation, the neighbors helped build a tree house in their backyard and held a block party complete with an international food court and games in each front yard. As the years pass, the children go off to pursue careers, to marry in the garden of their mothers' house, to bury their mothers, and to continue to gather in the house, now owned by Will and his family. A picture shows that the narrator's husband is European-American.
Italian-American and European-American of African-American; Italian-American and European-American of Asian-American
Pre-K, Primary; Fiction

Porte, Barbara Ann. *I Only Made Up the Roses*. New York: Greenwillow Boooks, 1987. 128 p.

Seventeen-year-old Cydra, who is white, describes her earlier longing for her "real" father, the love and support of her African-American stepfather, and the experiences, tragedies, memories, dreams, and closeness of her immediate and extended family.
African-American and Native American and European-American of European-American
Older; Fiction

Porte, Barbara Ann. *Something Terrible Happened: A Novel*. New York: Orchard Books, 1994. 224 p.

When she is ten, Gillian's African-American mother gets AIDS, and nothing is ever the same for Gillian and her family. Affected in both body and mind, her mother takes Gillian from New York City to Florida where they end up homeless. The two return to New York City where Gillian's grandmother tends to her daughter and sends Gillian to live with her late white father's brother and his family in Oak Ridge, Tennessee. Filled with resentment, worry, and loneliness, Gillian hates her life in that white community and, after her mother's death, runs wild. Things improve both for Gillian's grandmother as she takes up running and graduate work and for Gillian when she learns of the difficult pasts of a "cousin" who had been adopted from the Philippines and of her Uncle Henry.
European-American of European-St. Lucian-Trinidadian-American; European-American of Filipino
Older; Fiction

Powell, Neva. *The Long Crossing*. Illustrated by Eugene Powell. New York: Avocet Press, 1998. 128 p.

Leading a horse-drawn sleigh carrying logs from a lumber camp, young Johnny makes a perilous trip through a blizzard and cracking ice across Lake Michigan to a railroad siding. As he travels, he recalls his life from the time his mother died and he went to live with an old man and his cruel wife, who refused to let his Indian father see him. As a nine-year-old Johnny began doing a man's farm work and he continued to do so when, after the old couple died, he went to live in the house of the old woman's kind niece and her husband. While living there, he experienced his first automobile ride, saw an aeroplane, and was given a bike. As Johnny safely completes his dangerous journey, he proudly acclaims his Indian heritage.
European-American of European-American and Native American
Intermediate, Older; Fiction

Ray, Mary Lyn. *Shaker Boy*. Illustrated by Jeanette Winter. San Diego: Browndeer Press, 1994. 48 p.

When Caleb is six, his mother takes him to live in the Shaker village in Canterbury, New Hampshire. This picture book's paintings, text, and songs present Caleb experiencing Shaker life as he grows up to become deacon of the apple orchard. An author's note provides further information about the Shakers.
European-American Shaker of European-American non-Shaker
Primary; Fiction

Reinhardt, Dana. *A Brief Chapter in My Impossible Life*. New York: Wendy Lamb Books, 2006. 240 p.

In this novel for high school readers, sixteen-year-old narrator Simone is happy living with her parents and younger brother and doesn't want to know about her birthmother. However, at her parents urging, she finally calls Rivka who has asked to meet her and then spends the night at Rivka's house. When Rivka was a pregnant Hasidic Jewish teenager, she decided to give her baby to Simone's mother, who was representing the Jews in an ACLU law case. Simone, whose parents are atheists and who joins the Atheist Student Alliance, learns about Judaism from Rivka. When Simone finds out that Rivka is dying from ovarian cancer, she and her parents, with the help of her newly-acquired first boyfriend, put on a Passover seder for Rivka in their home.
European-American atheist of Russian-American Hasidic Jewish
Older; Fiction

Rinaldi, Ann. *Broken Days*. New York: Scholastic, 1995. 288 p. (The Quilt Trilogy)

This sequel to *A Stitch in Time* is set immediately preceding and during the War of 1812. Fourteen-year-old Ebie Chelmsford is the narrator of this book which continues the story of the Chelmsford family. The daughter of Cabot, who is often away at sea, and of a mother who deserted them, Ebie lives with her Aunt Hannah, who is loved by both Richard Lander, a sea captain, and Louis Gaudineer, an Indian agent. Ebie's Aunt Thankful, who has lived with the Shawnee, dies and at her request, her half-Shawnee daughter, fourteen-year-old Walking Breeze, comes to Salem to live with her Aunt Hannah. Resentful of her intrusion, Ebie steals Thankful's family quilt, the only proof of Walking Breeze's identity. She places it in a bundle for Georgie, the half-Shawnee woman earlier

known as Night Song, who, filled with anger at the whites, has become a disturbed recluse. As the story evolves, Louis is killed in the massacre at Fort Dearborn, Georgie becomes a Quaker, Hannah and Richard marry, and Ebie finally comes to her senses and helps restore her family by getting Thankful's quilt to Hannah.
European-American of Shawnee and European-American
Older; Fiction

Rinaldi, Ann. *Cast Two Shadows: The American Revolution in the South*. San Diego: Gulliver Books, 1998. 288 p. (Great Episodes)

Set in 1780 in South Carolina, this story is narrated by fourteen-year-old Caroline, the daughter of a white father and a mixed race slave. Looking white, Caroline is raised by her white family: her Loyalist stepmother, her imprisoned rebel father, her older half-brother Johnny who is fighting with the Loyalists, and her older half-sister Georgia Ann who is dining with Lord Rawdon, the British colonel who has commandeered their plantation and confines Caroline, Georgia Ann, and her stepmother in an upstairs chamber. Because of the extreme cruelty of the British, Caroline decides to be a rebel. She cleverly convinces Rawdon to let her go with her Negro grandmother Miz Melindy to bring home Johnny, who is injured and, unbeknownst to Rawdon, has become a rebel. On the journey, Caroline bonds with Miz Melindy and learns the truth about her mother. Upon her return, she and her stepmother escape from Rawdon and his British troops.
European-American of Angolan-European-American
Older; Fiction

Rinaldi, Ann. *Come Juneteenth*. New York: Harcourt, 2007. 256 p.

Although President Lincoln delivered his Emancipation Proclamation in January 1863, Texas plantation owners kept their slaves unaware of their freedom until General Gordon Granger issued the Emancipation Proclamation for Texas on June 19, 1865, a day later celebrated as Juneteenth. This historical novel relates the effects of the owners' secret on one Texas family and of the secret which young teenager Luli has promised to keep. It tells of the relationship between Luli and her almost-sister Sis Goose, who is half-white and half-black and is very much a part of the plantation family, of the bond between Luli and her adult brother Gabe, and of Gabe's love for Sis Goose. The story ends tragically when, in an attempt to take Sis Goose away from a Yankee colonel, Luli shoots her. Other characters in the novel are a little African-American boy who has nowhere to go and a Kickapoo boy whose mother Gabe has killed during the war.
European-Americans of African-European-American; European-American of African-American; European-American of Kickapoo
Older; Fiction

Rinaldi, Ann. *A Stitch in Time*. New York: Scholastic, 1994. 320 p. (The Quilt Trilogy)

In this first book of a trilogy about the Chelmsford family of Salem, Massachusetts, the narrator is Hannah, the oldest sister who strives to keep her family together as symbolized by the quilt she and her sisters are making that includes fabric from those whom the family trusts. In the eventful period from 1788 to 1791, Nathaniel Chelmsford, their cruel father, goes on to a trip to Ohio Territory. He is

accompanied by his elder son Lawrence and his headstrong youngest daughter Thankful. Thankful is kidnapped by the Shawnee and decides to remain with them. Abby, the fifteen-year-old sister, elopes with Nate Videau, a Southern ship captain, and together they survive a shipwreck in the Caribbean. Cabot, the youngest sibling whose mother died during his childbirth, discovers that Nathaniel is not his father. Hannah, who with Cabot remains at their Salem home, saves her father's cotton mill, becomes betrothed to Richard Lander, who takes his ship on a secret trade route to Sumatra, and agrees to raise Night Song, the half-Shawnee baby of Louis Gaudineer, the man to whom she was earlier betrothed. Sequels to this book are *Broken Days* and *The Blue Door*.
European-American of European-American and Shawnee
Older; Fiction

Rinn, Miriam. *The Saturday Secret*. Illustrated by Spark. Los Angeles: Alef Design Group, 1998. 160 p.

Jason, whose father has died, is angry that his stepfather David insists on his wearing a kippah (skullcap), keeping kosher, and observing Shabbat (the Jewish Sabbath)—and that his mother goes along with all the restrictive rules. Loving baseball, Jason lies to and defies his parents by playing in two Saturday baseball games. It is only when David stands up against prejudice and abuse and drives him to the hospital on the Shabbat that Jason accepts him as his father.
European-American Orthodox Jewish and European-American non-Orthodox Jewish of European-American non-Orthodox Jewish
Intermediate; Fiction

Rosenberg, Maxine B. *Being Adopted*. Photographs by George Ancona. New York: Lothrop, Lee & Shepard Books, 1984. 48 p.

Illustrated with black-and-white photographs, this book features three children. Seven-year-old Rebecca, whose birthfather is African-American and birthmother European-American and Cheyenne, is the adopted daughter of an African-American father and a European-American mother. Ten-year-old Andrei was adopted from India by European-American parents, and Karin, the author's eight-year-old daughter, was adopted from Korea by her European-American parents. The book covers some of the questions and fears of younger adopted children: being afraid when they come to their adoptive families, wondering whether they caused their parents to give them up, fearing their adoptive parents will give them up, dreaming and wondering about their birthparents, and not looking like other members of their families. It also affirms that adopted children are just as much family members as are biological children.
African-American and European-American of African-European-American and Cheyenne
Primary, Intermediate; Nonfiction

Rosenberg, Maxine B. *Growing Up Adopted*. Afterword by Lois Ruskai Melina. New York: Bradbury Press, 1989. 128 p.

In this book eight children and six adults relate their experiences and thoughts about growing up as adopted children. The four children who were adopted by parents of a different race, in each case European-American, are Josh, adopted as was a little sister from Colombia; Amy, who was adopted from Ecuador; Mark, who was adopted from Korea; and Shakine, an African-American boy who was born with spinal bifida in the United States and lives in a family of seven children, four of whom are adopted and of ethnicities other than their adoptive parents. Three of the adults are of a different race than their European-American parents. Chris was adopted from France as was her brother, Sam was adopted from Korea and has an adopted sister of mixed race and two non-adopted brothers, and Jamie, an African-European-American, has two sisters who are not adopted and four adopted siblings of mixed race.

European-American of African-European-American; European-American of African-American

Intermediate, Older; Nonfiction

Skurzynski, Gloria, and Alane Ferguson. *Escape from Fear*. Washington, D.C.: National Geographic Society, 2002. 160 p. (Mysteries in Our National Parks)

When the Landon family visits St. John Island in the Virgin Islands, they meet thirteen-year-old Forrest, the adopted son of a wealthy American diplomat and his wife. Forrest has run away from his Denver home to find his birthmother and to save her from danger. He manages to locate her and, with the Landon children, watches as she aids illegal aliens who have fled from poverty-stricken Haiti on a boat involved in poaching endangered hawksbill turtles.

European-American of European-American and African-Virgin Islander of the United States

Intermediate, Older; Fiction

Skurzynski, Gloria, and Alane Ferguson. *Ghost Horses*. Washington, D.C.: National Geographic Society, 2000. 160 p. (Mysteries in Our National Parks)

When Jack and Ashley Landon's parents take in a Shoshone brother and sister, Ethan, twelve, and Summer, ten, as emergency foster care children, blond Jack immediately senses the dislike which Ethan has for whites. Traveling together to visit Zion National Park and the nearby area, Jack unfairly blames Ethan for the rocks which fall down the canyon walls towards them and for Ashley's almost being trampled by a wild white mustang, "a ghost horse." Ethan is pleased with the bad luck that the Landons are experiencing which he attributes to the Ghost Dance that Jack and Ashley danced. Steven, the Landons' father, takes Jack and Ethan for a hike in the Zion Narrows to help them work out their enmity, while Olivia, the Landons' mother, takes Ashley and Summer to revisit the mustangs. In an eventful finish Ethan saves Jack during a flash flood, Jack suffers hypothermia during which he may have seen Ethan and Summer's deceased parents, and Summer gives Olivia the clue that solves the problem of the ghost horses' strange behavior. In this book the Landons' heritage is identified, a factor which is relevant as Ethan's animosity is directed towards Jack who looks like his Norwegian-American father, whereas Ashley resembles her Italian-American mother.

Norwegian-American and other and Italian-American of Shoshone

Intermediate, Older; Fiction

Smith, Greg Leitich. *Ninjas, Piranhas, and Galileo*. New York: Little, Brown and Company, 2003. 192 p.

This is the story of three seventh grade friends and the school science fair they enter. Honoria tries to teach her piranha to prefer bananas to meat. Elias seeks to confirm (à la Galileo) his much older brother's science fair finding that plants grow faster when exposed to chamber music. Shohei assists Elias by doing the same experiment at his house. The results are disastrous for Elias. He finds no diference in plant

growth; Soshei, thinking he has messed up, fakes his results to show a difference; and Elias ends up with a bad grade. Elias compounds the situation by sneaking into the school's atrium garden and substituting its baroque CD with a *Puff, the Magic Dragon* one. Caught, Elias is brought up before the student court where Honoria is his counsel. The friends' relationship is complicated because Elias knows that Honoria likes Shohei and Shohei knows that Elias likes Honoria. Further, Shohei's adoptive Irish-American parents are trying to immerse him in Japanese culture since he is Japanese-American, a process which causes his five-year-old non-adopted brother to pretend he is a ninja. Finally, Shoshei gets his parents to stop by dying his hair green and acting like he is Irish.
Irish-American of Japanese-American
Intermediate, Older; Fiction

Springer, Nancy. *The Boy on a Black Horse*. New York: Atheneum, 1994. 176 p.
Gray, whose parents and brother have died in a boating accident, lives with her Aunt Liana, who is depressed after the death of her husband and two children in the same accident. Gray befriends a new classmate, a fifteen-year-old gypsy boy Chav, who rides a black stallion, takes care of his younger brother and sister, and lives in a silo. Chav feels worthless and is filled with anger at himself and non-gypsies. When his sister becomes ill with chicken pox, Gray takes Chav and his siblings to her house where Liana finds purpose in caring for them. However, hating to be penned up in the house, falsely accused of vandalism, and about to lose his beloved stallion, Chav sets off with a gun to kill himself and those attending a homecoming game. Thanks to Gray, disaster is averted. Chav and his brother, who witnessed their father murdering their mother, receive the support they need, and Gray is finally able to speak about her family's accident.
European-American of European-Romani-American
Older; Fiction

Tenny, Dixie. *Call the Darkness Down*. New York: Atheneum, 1984. 204 p. (A Margaret K. McElderry Book)
Although for years Morfa has heard tales of Wales from Gwenfair, her Welsh mother, Gwenfair has refused to say anything about her parents and why she left her beloved Wales. When Morfa spends her freshman year at a Welsh college, she immediately becomes immersed in Welsh life: having Welsh friends, learning the Welsh language, and experiencing Welsh culture. She also has scary moments with a strange man in a dark coat and, pushed off a castle wall, narrowly escapes death. In this suspenseful story of the forces of light and dark, of mystical powers, and of spells, Morfa finally discovers the terrible truth about her family and must save her life from her murderous grandmother.
English-European-American and Welsh of Welsh-American
Older; Fiction

Terris, Susan. *Whirling Rainbows*. Garden City, N.Y.: Doubleday & Company, 1974. 168 p.
Thirteen-year-old Leah, who was adopted in infancy by a Jewish couple, wants to find her Indian roots when she goes to a Wisconsin summer camp. One disaster seems to follow another as she is mocked for being "Indian" and blamed, often unjustly, for misdeeds. However, although she does not find the Indian relics she is seeking, Leah learns much during the summer: that she has been trying to

be close to the wrong cousin, that she has become an accomplished canoeist, that she has displayed leadership on a hazardous camping trip, and that she is no longer concerned about being adopted.
European-American Jewish of Polish-American and Chippewa
Older; Fiction

Viglucci, Pat Costa. *Cassandra Robbins, Esq.* Madison: Square One Publishers, 1987. 190 p.
Adopted as a baby by white parents, seventeen-year-old Cassandra, who is of mixed race, feels that being the family's only girl is of more significance than being its only brown member. However, when her brother brings Josh, his African-American college roommate, home for the summer, Cassandra experiences mixed feelings about her identity. She is especially jealous when Josh is with a white girl. She finds that the white boy with whom she goes to a concert is surprisingly nice, but that his mother is a bigot, and she encounters hostility from two black girls. By the end of the summer Cassandra has learned a lot about herself and the complexities of love.
European-American and Italian-American of African-European-American
Older; Fiction

Williams, Mary E., ed. *Adoption.* Farmington Hills, Mich.: Greenhaven Press, 2006. 232 p.
In a chapter "Transracial Adoption Should Be Encouraged," Arlene Istar Lev, who is Jewish, tells how she and her lesbian partner adopted their African-American and biracial sons.
European-American Jewish of African-American; European-American Jewish of African-Irish-American
Older; Nonfiction

Wittlinger, Ellen. *Hard Love.* New York: Aladdin Paperbacks, 2001. 240 p.
Sixteen-year-old John hasn't gotten over his egotistical father's leaving him and his mother when he was ten nor the way since then that his mother has shut him out emotionally, even shying away from touching him. Feeling himself an emotionless loner, using the name Giovani, John leaves a zine, a short homemade magazine with his own writing, at the Tower Records zine exchange center. He is impressed by a zine written by Marisol, a lesbian Puerto Rican-American with adoptive Cuban and European-American parents, and he contacts her. They share each other's writings and feelings about their families, and John falls in love. It is at a zine writers conference on Cape Cod that Marisol, although telling John (whom she calls Geo) that he is her best friend, leaves him for a group of lesbian women. It is there too that John discovers that his mother and stepfather-to-be care for him and that he is ready to socialize. Gio also appears in the book *Love & Lies: Marisol's Story.*
Cuban and European-American of Puerto Rican-American
Older; Fiction

Wittlinger, Ellen. *Love & Lies: Marisol's Story.* New York: Simon & Schuster Books for Young Readers, 2008. 256 p.
This book for the oldest readers is the sequel to *Hard Love.* Eighteen-year-old Marisol decides to take a year off to write a novel before attending Stanford University. To earn money she works at a Harvard Square coffee shop where she meets Lee, a shy homesick girl from Indiana, who left there

after telling her parents she was gay. When Marisol attends a novel writing course at the Cambridge Center for Adult Education, she discovers that her friend Gio (John) is also taking the course and that it is being taught by an amazingly beautiful woman, Olivia Frost. Marisol, who is a lesbian, falls in love with Olivia, and the two make love. Ignoring the negative opinion of Gio, Marisol fails to realize how Olivia is dominating her. Her lie to Olivia that Lee is Gio's girlfriend upsets Lee so much that she flies back to Indiana. Finally, Marisol realizes that Olivia is a fraud: she did not graduate from Harvard, she is not writing a novel, she quotes others' sayings as her own, and Marisol is unimportant to her. In this story the novel which Marisol is writing is based on her unknown Puerto Rican birthmother. Readers of *Hard Love* will be aware of the mixed heritages of Marisol's adoptive parents.

Cuban and European-American of Puerto Rican-American
Older; Fiction

Wosmek, Frances. *A Brown Bird Singing*. Illustrated by Ted Lewin. New York: Beech Tree Paperback Books, 1986. 128 p.

Years ago, after her mother had died from a fever, Anego's Chippewa father Hamigeesek had left her to stay with the Veselka family. The only Indian in her northern Minnesota community, Anego sometimes thinks about the brown bird she once held and gets a warm supportive feeling. Anego passes fourth grade, raises an orphaned fawn and grieves when a hunter shoots it, joins in the excitement of the family getting a car, and, after thinking she is not needed when a baby brother is born, helps save his life and realizes how much she cares for him. Anego is very close to her Irish Ma, sister Sheila, and Austrian-American Pa, who is her best friend, and she dreads the time that the hardly-remembered Hamigeesek will take her from them. However, when he does come, Hamigeesek kindly assures Anego that she can remain with the Veselkas and, by having her hold a brown bird, brings back her memories of her Chippewa mother.

Austrian-American and Irish of Chippewa
Intermediate; Fiction

Wright, Bil. *When the Black Girl Sings*. New York: Simon & Schuster Books for Young Readers, 2008. 272 p.

Fourteen-year-old Lahni is going through a difficult time. Her white adoptive parents are getting a divorce, she is being stalked by a strange high school boy, and, as the only black girl in her private school, she feels out of place. When her music teacher urges her to enter a competition for her middle school's best vocalist award, Lahni is reluctant to do so. However, her life changes when she and her mother start attending a church where she is deeply moved by the music played by its African-American organist Marcus and the gospel singing of Carietta, a black choir member. Lahni joins the church choir, and with the encouragement of Marcus, Carietta, her music teacher, her best friend, and her mother, she not only wins the competition, but while singing "His Eye Is on the Sparrow" realizes that God's eye has been and is on her, Lahni, a black girl.

European-American of African-American
Older; Fiction

Wright, Susan Kimmel. *The Secret of the Old Graveyard*. Scottdale, Pa.: Herald Press, 1993. 184 p.

At the same time that thirteen-year-old Nellie's parents are notified they are to go to Colombia to adopt the baby they've wanted, strange things start to happen at her family farm's old graveyard. This story tells of Nellie's worry about her parents traveling to Colombia, of her concerns as to how a baby will affect her already offbeat family, of her exciting detective work with her friend Peggy to find whoever has vandalized the cemetery, and of her discoveries that the boy she has a crush on is adopted, is of mixed heritage—and likes her.

German-American of English-French-Irish-American

Intermediate, Older; Fiction

Mexican Adults

Resau, Laura. *Red Glass*. New York: Delacorte Press, 2007. 304 p.

This novel details the transformation of Sophie from Sophie la Delicada (the Delicate whose life is restricted by allergies, worries, and fears) into Sophie la Fuerte (the Strong, who undertakes and completes a very dangerous journey). Sixteen-year-old Sophie lives in Tucson with her English mother, her Mexican stepfather, and her great-aunt Dika, a Bosnian refugee. Then the family takes in five-year-old Pablo whose parents have died as his family tried to escape from Mexico. A year later, so that Pablo can see his relatives and decide where he wants to live, Sophie, Pablo, and Dika join Dika's boyfriend Mr. Lorenzo and his son Ángel, who are bound, via Mexico, for Guatemala to see whether Flor Blanca, their wife and mother, respectively, is alive and to find her jewels. The group spends a week in Pablo's Oaxaca village where Sophie and Ángel express their feelings for each other. Mr. Lorenzo and Ángel then go on to Guatemala, but are unable to return as Ángel is savagely attacked and their passports and money stolen. With Dika injured from a fall, Sophie travels by herself to Guatemala, a trip which is not at all safe, especially for a white girl. In Guatemala Ángel shares a hospital room with one of his attackers, Flor Blanca's fate is revealed, and Ángel decides whether to remain in Guatemala. Likewise, in Mexico Pablo decides whether he will stay there.

Mexican and English of English-European-American

Older; Fiction

Mexican-American Adults

De la Peña, Matt. *Mexican Whiteboy*. New York: Delacorte Press, 2008. 256 p.

Sixteen-year-old Danny chooses to spend his summer vacation with his Mexican-American father's family in National City, California, so that he can then fly to Ensenda, Mexico, and find his father. Since his father left his San Diego family three years earlier, Danny has been heartbroken to the extent that he seldom speaks, not wanting to use his mother's English. His goal is to please his father by becoming a great pitcher. He has exceptional talent, but is plagued by his lack of control. During the eventful summer Danny makes an unlikely best friend, Uno, who initially punched Danny. Uno needs to make money so that he can move away from his Mexican-American mother and stepfather and live with his black father. Through hours of practice with Uno, Danny works on his pitching skills and discovers how to keep the ball in the strike zone when people are watching. Together

Uno and Danny successfully hustle the area's best hitters, thereby earning money for Uno. Although he cannot speak Spanish and she cannot speak English, Danny falls in love with Liberty, who is newly arrived from Mexico and has a white father. Further, Danny finally finds out the truth about his father and comes to accept himself.
Mexican-American of African-Mexican-American
Older; Fiction

Little, Kimberley Griffiths. *The Last Snake Runner*. New York: Alfred A. Knopf, 2002. 208 p.

In this sequel to *Enchanted Runner*, Kendall, now fourteen, has just returned from the Acoma Pueblo where he has become a full member of the Acoma, his late mother's people. Very upset when he learns that his father has married a woman descended from the Spanish conquistadors who in 1599 destroyed the Acoma Pueblo, Kendall has his brother take him back to Acoma. There, in a mesa near the pueblo, he is transported back to the sixteenth century where he experiences life in the ancient Snake Clan and participates in the last Acoma Snake dance. Although Kendall is unable to save the pueblo from the conquistadors, he brings hope that the Acoma will survive.
European-American and Spanish-Mexican-American of European-American and Acoman
Older; Fiction

Native American Adults

See   Campbell, Mary
        Dare, Virginia
        Fairchild, Olive Oatman
        Houston, Samuel
        Jemison, Mary
        Parker, Cynthia Ann
        Sacagawea
        Silkwood, Priscilla
        Tanner, John

Banks, Sara H. *Remember My Name*. Illustrated by Birgitta Saflund. Niwot, Colo.: Roberts Rinehart Publishers, 1993. 128 p.

When her parents die, eleven-year-old Annie, who is half Cherokee and half Scottish-American, leaves her Cherokee grandmother to live with her Cherokee uncle and his wife in New Echota. She attends school and becomes best friends with Righteous Cry, a black girl about her age who is a slave. When the Cherokees are forced to leave to travel westward in the Trail of Tears, Annie's uncle sends her and Righteous (now freed) to travel, almost all the way by themselves, back to Annie's mountain home.
Cherokee and European-American of Scottish-American and Cherokee
Intermediate; Fiction

Curry, Jane Louise. *Dark Shade*. New York: Margaret K. McElderry Books, 1998. 176 p.

Independently Kip and Maggie are able to climb through a newly-formed spring to enter the world

of the 1758 French and Indian War where British forces are cutting a road through the Pennsylvania forest to reach the French-controlled Fort Dusquesne and where the Lenape (Delaware) have a village near the road. Maggie saves the life of Robert Mackenzie, a lost Scottish Redcoat, and Kip is going to be adopted into a Lenape family until Maggie finds him. Afraid that their actions are changing the course of history, Kip and Maggie learn that they have altered and then restored it and that they are distant cousins, both descendents of Robert Mackenzie and his Lenape wife, Shawanaken. Corn Tassel, a minor character in this novel, is a British woman who has been adopted by the Lenape.
Delaware of English
Older; Fiction

Durrant, Lynda. *Echohawk*. New York: Clarion Books, 1996. 192 p.

After describing how, in 1738, little Jonathan Starr was kidnapped by Mohicans from his Hudson River home, this book tells the story of Jonathan, now twelve-year-old Echohawk, whose beloved Mohican mother has died and who is very close to his Mohican father Glickihigan and his seven-year old brother Bamaineo. Echohawk becomes a deer hunter, goes on his Vision Quest, and with Bamaineo is taken by Glickihigan to learn English at an English town based on the Village of Saratoga (now Schuylerville, New York). The two boys run off when Echohawk learns that their teacher intends to take him to Boston. Realizing that Echohawk needs to discover the past he is starting to remember, Glickihigan takes him to his childhood home. After burying the bones of Echohawk's birth family, the three set off to the Ohio River to escape the encroachment and sicknesses of the English.
Mohican of European-American
Intermediate, Older; Fiction

Durrant, Lynda. *Turtle Clan Journey*. New York: Clarion Books, 1999. 192 p.

In this sequel to *Echohawk*, Echohawk, his brother Bamaineo, and their father Glickihigan set off on a journey to the place where the Monongahela and Allegheny Rivers meet the Ohio River. They soon discover that the governor of New York is offering ransoms for the return of white captives, such as Echohawk. Echohawk meets Red Fox, a boy adopted by Munsee, and then both of them are captured by British soldiers. Echohawk is taken to Albany to live with his birth aunt, who is nice to him, but oblivious of his wanting to be with his Mohican family. When she decides to send him to school in Boston, Echohawk runs away and joins his father and brother in resuming their tiring and dangerous trek. All three are captured by two Mohawks who want Echohawk for the ransom and Bamaineo for adoption into an Onondaga family. In escaping and finally reaching their destination, Echohawk comes to feel that, regardless of culture, everyone is the same.
Mohican of European-American; Munsee of European-American
Intermediate, Older; Fiction

Finley, Mary Peace. *Meadow Lark*. Palmer Lake, Colo.: Filter Press, 2003. 208 p.

This book covers the same time period as the two earlier books in the trilogy, *Soaring Eagle* and *White Grizzly*, but tells the story of thirteen-year-old Teresita, Julio's Mexican sister who had to stay behind when Julio and their father left for Bent's Fort. Fearing from a vision that something has happened to them, Teresita, who is working for Charles and Maria Ignacia Bent, joins a wagon train bound

for Bent's Fort. After looking after her goats and surviving a wagon ride down perilous Raton Pass, Teresita arrives at Bent's Fort only to learn that her father is dead and Julio has gone on to Bent's Farm. Then, persuading a Mexican couple to hire her and taking Silent Walker, whom she has befriended, along as a goatherder, Teresita joins a wagon train that will pass by Bent's Farm. She is kidnapped by Kiowa and escapes by floating down the Arkansas River in a log drum. Silent Walker meets some Kiowa from whom she had been kidnapped as a child, and both she and Teresita are reunited with Julio at Bent's Farm. It is in this book that readers learn that Silent Walker, a character in the earlier books, is Kiowa, not Cheyenne.
Cheyenne of European-American; Cheyenne of Kiowa
Intermediate, Older; Fiction

Finley, Mary Peace. *Soaring Eagle*. New York: Simon & Schuster Books for Young Readers, 1993. 176 p.
    Young Julio, who has green eyes, blond hair, and light skin, feels that he is different from the rest of his Mexican family. In 1845 when his father heads back from Taos to Bent's Fort where he works, Julio decides to go with him and, hopefully, discover who he is. Early in the journey his father is killed by Jicarilla Apache. Trying to catch up to a wagon train, Julio and his dog continue on. Injured by a wolf, ill, and blinded by glaring snow, Julio is found by Cheyenne, who nurse him back to health and adopt him as a Cheyenne, Soaring Eagle. While seeking his vision, Julio remembers the song his birthmother had sung to him and his name, Billy. Uncertain whether to live as a Cheyenne, he is shocked by the death of his Indian friend and by a Cheyenne victory celebration—and decides to proceed to Bent's Fort where someone should know who Billy is. This is the first of three books about Julio and his family.
Cheyenne of European-American
Intermediate, Older; Fiction

Finley, Mary Peace. *White Grizzly*. Palmer Lake, Colo.: Filter Press, 2000. 224 p.
    In this sequel to *Soaring Eagle* Julio finds out at Bent's Fort that his birth name is William Allen Forester and that his grandfather might still be in Independence, Missouri, where he had decided to wait ten years for word of his missing family. Worried that the ten years have passed, Julio sets off with William Bent and his wagon train on the long perilous journey to Independence. Working as a sheepherder with his dog and an African-American blacksmith, Julio is almost killed by a grizzly bear and by two wanted outlaws; again sees Silent Walker, the young Cheyenne woman whom he has come to care for; is captured by Pawnee; and is reunited in Independence with his grandfather, who was about to leave. Still uncertain whether his allegiances are to the Mexicans, the Americans, or the Cheyenne, Julio and his grandfather spend the winter at Bent's Farm near Independence. The book includes information about William Bent and about Bent Fort's importance as a trading post.
Cheyenne of European-American
Intermediate, Older; Fiction

George, Jean Craighead. *Julie*. Illustrated by Wendell Minor. New York: HarperCollins Publishers, 1994. 240 p.

In this sequel to *Julie of the Wolves*, Julie, who is now fourteen, is living in Kangik with her father Kapugen and his new wife Ellen. Trapped with Ellen in a blizzard, Julie comes to accept her white stepmother. However, Julie knows that Kapugen was the one who killed her adoptive wolf father Amaroq and will kill his son Kapu and the new wolf pack in order to protect his herd of musk ox that sustains the Alaskan village's economy. Journeying to find the wolf pack, Julie manages to lead it away from the village to a place where the wolves can feed on moose. Kapugen and Ellen name their new baby boy Amaroq; Julie falls in love with Peter, an Eskimo from Siberia; and when the wolves come back, Kapugen finally returns to his Eskimo ways and spares them.
Eskimo and European-American of Eskimo
Intermediate, Older; Fiction

George, Jean Craighead. *Julie of the Wolves*. Illustrated by John Schoenherr. New York: Harper Trophy, 1974. 176 p.

When her "husband" in an arranged child marriage tries to rape her, thirteen-year-old Julie, who is an Eskimo, runs away from Barrow, Alaska, to catch a ship at Point Hope that will take her to live with her San Francisco pen pal. Lost and starving on the tundra, she observes a nearby wolf pack and learns how to communicate with them. She is adopted by Amaroq, its leader, and grows to love Amaroq, the spirtual father wolf Nails, the mother wolf Silver, and the wolf puppies. Julie is devastated when hunters shooting from an airplane kill Amoroq and wound her favorite pup Kapu. Julie discovers that her father Kapugen, whom she had thought dead, is living in nearby Kangik. Going to him, she finds out that he has a white wife and an airplane for hunting. After running away again, Julie realizes that the old Eskimo times are gone and she must return to Kapugen.
Eskimo and European-American of Eskimo
Intermediate, Older; Fiction

George, Jean Craighead. *Julie's Wolf Pack*. Illustrated by Wendell Minor. New York: HarperCollins Publishers, 1997. 208 p.

This sequel to *Julie* is devoted almost entirely to the story of Julie's Avalik River wolf pack. It traces its activities through four years during which Kapu asserts himself as its Alpha (leader); the wolf Ice Blink spreads rabies on the tundra; Silver has two more puppies; Kapu is trapped for a medical study; Silver dies; Kapu's daughter Sweet Fur Amy becomes the new Alpha; and, released, Kapu joins his mate Aaka. There is little about Julie and her human family. However, her little half-brother Amaroq bonds with one of Silver's wolf pups which becomes a sled dog leader for Kapugen. At the book's end Julie and Peter marry and are hired to live on the tundra and study the wolves.
Eskimo and European-American of Eskimo
Intermediate, Older; Fiction

Highwater, Jamake. *I Wear the Morning Star*. New York: Harper & Row, Publishers, 1986. 160 p. (The Ghost Horse Cycle)

This third book in *The Ghost Horse Cycle* for the oldest readers tells the story of Sitko and his miserable boyhood. Sitko is placed in a boarding school where he is mistreated by the adults and scorned by the other children. His alcoholic father, Jamie Ghost Horse, realizing that Sitko deserves

a better life, allows Alexander, his former friend and now the lover of his ex-wife Jemina, to adopt Sitko, and Sitko goes to live with Alexander, Jemina, and his grandmother Amana in the San Fernando Valley. Not able to figure out his past and deeply confused about his identity, Sitko continues a life filled with unhappiness, mitigated only by his friendship with a farm boy, his school's art club, and his painting. At the end of the book, Jamie shoots Jemina and Alexander, killing her and wounding Alexander. Jamie perishes in a truck crash, Sitko's older brother loses his life in a plane crash, the elderly Amana dies, and Sitko, the only one remaining, preserves his Blood (Blackfoot) past through his paintings.
Greek, French Canadian-American, and Blackfoot (Blood) of African-French Canadian-American, Blackfoot (Blood), and Cherokee
Older; Fiction

Hotze, Sollace. *A Circle Unbroken*. New York: Clarion Books, 1988. 208 p.

When she was ten, Rachel Porter was kidnapped by renegade Sioux, who treated her badly. However, the Oglala Sioux who bought her from them, made her part of a loving family and Rachel (now Kata Wi) was happy with her new life. This book opens seven years later in 1845 with the re-kidnapping of Rachel by men hired by her father to bring her from the prairie near the Black Hills to her birth family in St. Joseph, Missouri. In this story Rachel rejoices in being reunited with her sister and her Aunt Sarah and in her close friendship with her little brother, her father's new wife, and the man Peter. However, she finds it unbearably difficult to readjust to life in the white world. When Peter and her sister marry and move away and her Aunt Sarah dies, Rachel leaves St. Joseph to return to her Sioux family and especially to White Hawk, the man she loves.
Dakota of European-American
Older; Fiction

Kretzer-Malvehy, Terry. *Passage to Little Bighorn*. Flagstaff, Ariz.: Rising Moon, 1999. 232 p.

Fifteen-year-old Dakota is discouraged because his Irish-American father has remarried and left the family, his Lakota mother has just returned from a two year treatment of depression, and he has been living with his father's father. When he visits the Little Bighorn Battlefield, Dakota finds himself swept back to 1876 where he becomes the "chosen relative" of wise and kind Sitting Bull. He experiences Lakota life: going on a buffalo hunt, counting coup by capturing two Crow horses, surviving a grizzly bear attack, receiving a Lakota name, becoming friends with a boy who is European-American and Lakota, falling for a daughter of Sitting Bull, meeting his great-great-great grandmother and great-great grandfather, and witnessing the terrible battles of the Rosebud and the Little Bighorn. It is with the Lakota that Dakota learns how he should live, and he decides to return to his real family.
Lakota (Hunkpapa) of European-American and Lakota
Older; Fiction

Kudlinski, Kathleen V. *My Lady Pocahontas: A Novel*. Tarrytown, N.Y.: Marshall Cavendish, 2006. 288 p.

This story of Pocahontas' life is written from the viewpoint of her fictional friend Neetah. Appamatuck Neetah is adopted by Powhatan to be Pocahontas' guardian. Together the two girls spy on the newly arrived Jamestown colonists. They befriend three boys, Samuel, Thomas, and Henry, who come to stay with the Powhatans. Pocahontas has a vision in which she, Neetah, John Smith, and a baby of much importance appear. Believing from the vision that she will marry John Smith, she betrays her father and warns Smith of a plot to kill him. As Smith shows no inclination to marry her, Pocahontas returns depressed to her Pamunkey village. When the three boys try to escape, Samuel is killed, Thomas is captured, and Pocahontas leads Henry and Neetah to refuge with the Patawomeke. There both Pocahontas and Neetah marry Patawomekes, but they are blamed for a deadly measles outbreak, are imprisoned by the colonists, and are taken to Jamestown. Later brought to Henrico, Pocahontas becomes a Christian, takes a new name, Rebecca, falls in love with John Rolfe, and, fulfilling her vision, has a son Thomas. Neetah accompanies Pocahontas, John, and Thomas to England where both she and Pocahantas die before returning home. An afterword, an author's note, and a source list are appended.

Powhatan (Pamunkey) of Powhatan (Appamattuck)

Older; Fiction

Levin, Beatrice. *John Hawk: White Man, Black Man, Indian Chief*. Austin: Eakin Press, 1988. 192 p.

This is the fictional story of John White, the son of a Georgia plantation owner and a slave mother, who becomes the lifelong friend of Osceola. The two meet as boys and, at Osceola's urging, John runs away to live with the Seminoles. He takes a new name, John Hawk, marries a Seminole woman, befriends a man who is Spanish-American and African-American, and becomes a Seminole chief. With Osceola he experiences the betrayals and tragedies preceding and during the Second Seminole War. A bibliography is included.

Seminole of African-European-American

Older; Fiction

McKissack, Patricia C. *Run Away Home*. New York: Scholastic Press, 1997. 176 p.

In 1888 Sky, a fifteen-year-old Chiricahua Apache boy, escapes from a train of Apache prisoners and hides on the farm of twelve-year-old Sarah Jane Crossman, her African-American father, and her mother, who is of African-Scottish-Irish and Seminole heritage. George Wrattan, an Army scout and interpreter, allows the Crossmans to keep Sky with them until he recovers from his swamp fever. In the meantime boll weevils destroy the family's cotton crop, night riders come to their farm, and Sarah Jane's father, who is skilled as a carpenter, gets an order from Booker T. Washington to build desks for nearby Tuskegee Institute. Sky becomes healthy, but Wrattan, whose wife is Apache, gives permission for him to remain on the farm.

African-American and African-Scottish-Irish-American and Seminole of Chiricahua Apache

Intermediate, Older; Fiction

Moore, Robin. *Maggie among the Seneca*. New York: J. B. Lippincott, 1990. 112 p.

Sixteen-year-old Maggie, who is Irish, is kidnapped in 1778 by the Seneca and taken from central Pennsylvania to the Seneca village on the Genesee River. Staying at first with two Seneca women,

Maggie then goes to live with Frenchgirl, who, kidnapped at an early age, is French and English, but now regards herself as Seneca. Maggie agrees to marry Frenchgirl's brother so she can go on a hunting trip to the Allegheny River and escape from there to her aunt's. However, when Maggie's husband dies, she stays to tend his burial scaffold. Maggie has a baby, survives the destruction of the village by the colonial army, and then goes to live with her aunt. The book is the sequel to *The Bread Sister of Sinking Creek*.
Seneca of Irish-American; Seneca of French-English-American
Intermediate, Older; Fiction

Naylor, Phyllis Reynolds. *Sang Spell*. New York: Aladdin Paperbacks, 2000. 224 p.

Hitchhiking from Massachusetts to Dallas to live with his aunt because his mother has died, teenager Josh is mugged and left on a road in Appalachia where he is picked up by a Melungeon, who takes him to Canara, an isolated primitive community. Everything is strange and illogical there, and Josh becomes increasingly frustrated in his efforts to escape. The road he takes ends up at the exact place he started. Trying to swim towards a river's opposite shore takes him only a short distance, and a roadside restaurant and a school appear and disappear at regular intervals. Josh discovers that his father was probably Melungeon and befriends a girl whose father was stoned to death when his efforts to escape accidentally caused fatalities Finally, with new insights and the realization that he must keep Canara's secrets, Josh is able to get away. [The Melungeon people are of mixed race living primarily in the central Appalachians. There is controversy as to their origin and their heritage, but they are often regarded as tri-racial: European-American, African-American, and Native American. In this novel they are identified as Portuguese who over time became mixed with a number of other peoples.]
Portuguese (Melungeon)-American of Irish-Portuguese (Melungeon)-American
Older, Fiction

Osborne, Mary Pope. *Standing in the Light: The Captive Diary of Catharine Carey Logan, Delaware Valley, Pennsylvania, 1763*. New York: Scholastic, 1998. 192 p. (Dear America)

In her journal, Catharine, a fictional Quaker girl about thirteen years old, describes how she and her brother Thomas were kidnapped and adopted by Lenape (Delaware Indians). Catharine relates her anger and disgust at the Indians, her successful effort to be reunited with Thomas, her growing appreciation of the Delaware, her falling in love with Snow Hunter (who had also been kidnapped), her despair when the English attack the Delaware and recapture her and Thomas, and her Quaker father's appraisal that in accepting others she has seen God's truth. The story is accompanied by historical information on the Quakers and the Lenape.
Delaware of English Quaker
Intermediate, Older; Fiction

Porte, Barbara Ann. *I Only Made Up the Roses*. New York: Greenwillow Boooks, 1987. 128 p.

Seventeen-year-old Cydra, who is white, describes her earlier longing for her "real" father, the love and support of her African-American stepfather, and the experiences, tragedies, memories, dreams, and closeness of her immediate and extended family.

African-American and Native American and European-American of European-American
Older; Fiction

Pryor, Bonnie. *Thomas in Danger*. Illustrated by Bert Dodson. New York: Morrow Junior Books, 1999. 176 p. (American Adventures)
When, in his mother's inn, Thomas spots a customer whom he recognizes as a Tory, he is kidnapped and taken north in a wagon train filled with war supplies for the Tories. Falling ill, Thomas is given by his captors to Joseph Brant, who takes him to a Mohawk village where he becomes the adopted son of an Indian woman whose sons have died. There Thomas is befriended by an Indian boy, kills a bear, and discovers why the Iroquois have sided with the British in the Revolutionary War. However, he hates the scalps taken by the Indians and constantly thinks of escape. When found by the Continental army, Thomas is happy that he will soon be reunited with his family, but sorrowful for his Mohawk friends who have been driven away from their village and their sustenance. This book is the sequel to *Thomas*.
Mohawk of European-American
Intermediate; Fiction

Rees, Celia. *Sorceress*. Cambridge, Mass.: Candlewick Press, 2003. 352 p.
Agnes, an eighteen-year-old Mohawk college student, decides to help a researcher who is trying to learn the fate of an English girl Mary Newbury, forced to flee from her Puritan settlement because she was accused of practicing witchcraft. Agnes feels a strange connection to Mary, who may be the medicine woman whose story has been carried down in her family. Visiting her aunt on her Mohawk reservation, Agnes is transported back to the 1600s where she experiences Mary's life. Mary marries Jaybird, a Pennacook Indian, and bears two children: a daughter, who is murdered as a child by the English, and a son, Black Fox, who becomes a warrior. Mary saves Ephraim, an eleven-year-old white boy injured in an Indian attack, and raises him as her son. When she, Black Fox, and Ephraim visit Mount Royale to trade furs, Mary is captured by a Frenchman and then rescued by her two sons. Fleeing from their pursuers, they end up living in a Mohawk village where Mary is able to stem a smallpox epidemic. The author relates Mary's earlier story in the book *Witch Child*.
English and Pennacook (Pentucket) of European-American
Older; Fiction

Rinaldi, Ann. *A Stitch in Time*. New York: Scholastic, 1994. 320 p. (The Quilt Trilogy)
In this first book of a trilogy about the Chelmsford family of Salem, Massachusetts, the narrator is Hannah, the oldest sister who strives to keep her family together as symbolized by the quilt she and her sisters are making that includes fabric from those whom the family trusts. In the eventful period from 1788 to 1791, Nathaniel Chelmsford, their cruel father, goes on to a trip to Ohio Territory. He is accompanied by his elder son Lawrence and his headstrong youngest daughter Thankful. Thankful is kidnapped by the Shawnee and decides to remain with them. Abby, the fifteen-year-old sister, elopes with Nate Videau, a Southern ship captain, and together they survive a shipwreck in the Caribbean. Cabot, the youngest sibling whose mother died during his childbirth, discovers that Nathaniel is not his father. Hannah, who with Cabot remains at their Salem home, saves her father's cotton mill, becomes

betrothed to Richard Lander, who takes his ship on a secret trade route to Sumatra, and agrees to raise Night Song, the half-Shawnee baby of Louis Gaudineer, the man to whom she was earlier betrothed. Sequels to this book are *Broken Days* and *The Blue Door*.
Shawnee of European-American
Older; Fiction

Sauerwein, Leigh. *The Way Home*. Illustrated by Miles Hyman. New York: Farrar, Straus & Giroux, 1994. 128 p.
This book contains six stories, including "Storm Warning" and "The Dress." "Storm Warning" is set in Nebraska in 1989. When Jonathan, the Indian who is Joe's best friend, saves the twelve-year-old boy during a tornado, Joe realizes that Jonathan is his father. "The Dress," which is set in 1876, tells of Laura's first visit to her Aunt Ella. Laura learns that when Ella was young, she was captured by Cheyenne. She married a Cheyenne warrior and they had three children. However, Ella was the only survivor when soldiers attacked the Cheyenne village, and she was returned to her white family, who continue to ostracize her.
Cheyenne of European-American
Intermediate; Fiction

Urban, Betsy. *Waiting for Deliverance*. New York: Orchard Books, 2000. 192 p.
This book is set in 1793 in western New York where there is tension between the Americans and the Seneca, who supported the British during the Revolutionary War. Fourteen-year-old orphan Livy, who is terrified of Indians, is sold at pauper's auction to Gideon, who was raised by Senecas and educated by Anglican Canadians, and whose Seneca brother Rising Hawk often stays with him and his wife. When Livy is sent to a Seneca village to help its women learn how to spin, she is suddenly accused of being a witch. After escaping with Rising Hawk, with whom she is often at odds, Livy discovers that she is in love with him. In this story Rising Hawk has a French ancestor.
Seneca of European-American
Older; Fiction

West Indian Adults

Wittlinger, Ellen. *Hard Love*. New York: Aladdin Paperbacks, 2001. 240 p.
Sixteen-year-old John hasn't gotten over his egotistical father's leaving him and his mother when he was ten nor the way since then that his mother has shut him out emotionally, even shying away from touching him. Feeling himself an emotionless loner, using the name Giovani, John leaves a zine, a short homemade magazine with his own writing, at the Tower Records zine exchange center. He is impressed by a zine written by Marisol, a lesbian Puerto Rican-American with adoptive Cuban and European-American parents, and he contacts her. They share each other's writings and feelings about their families, and John falls in love. It is at a zine writers conference on Cape Cod that Marisol, although telling John (whom she calls Gio) that he is her best friend, leaves him for a group of lesbian women. It is there too that John discovers that his mother and stepfather-to-be care for him and that he is ready to socialize. Gio also appears in the book *Love & Lies: Marisol's story*.

Cuban and European-American of Puerto Rican-American
Older; Fiction

Wittlinger, Ellen. *Love & Lies: Marisol's Story*. New York: Simon & Schuster Books for Young Readers, 2008. 256 p.

This book for the oldest readers is the sequel to *Hard Love*. Eighteen-year-old Marisol decides to take a year off to write a novel before attending Stanford University. To earn money she works at a Harvard Square coffee shop where she meets Lee, a shy homesick girl from Indiana, who left there after telling her parents she was gay. When Marisol attends a novel writing course at the Cambridge Center for Adult Education, she discovers that her friend Gio (John) is also taking the course and that it is being taught by an amazingly beautiful woman, Olivia Frost. Marisol, who is a lesbian, falls in love with Olivia, and the two make love. Ignoring the negative opinion of Gio, Marisol fails to realize how Olivia is dominating her. Her lie to Olivia that Lee is Gio's girlfriend upsets Lee so much that she flies back to Indiana. Finally, Marisol realizes that Olivia is a fraud: she did not graduate from Harvard, she is not writing a novel, she quotes others' sayings as her own, and Marisol is unimportant to her. In this story the novel which Marisol is writing is based on her unknown Puerto Rican birthmother. Readers of *Hard Love* will be aware of the mixed heritages of Marisol's adoptive parents.
Cuban and European-American of Puerto Rican-American
Older; Fiction

West Indian-American Adults

Krementz, Jill. *How It Feels To Be Adopted*. Photographs by author. New York: Alfred A. Knopf, 1982. 120 p.

Black-and-white photographs accompany the author's interviews with nineteen children who talk about being adopted: how they feel about it, their knowledge of and feelings about their birthparents and whether they want to meet them, their experiences as adopted children, and, for five of them, what it is like to be part of a mixed race family. One of these children, who is African-American, has been adopted by an African-American father, but has adopted brothers who are of different ethnicities.
Puerto Rican-American and Greek-American of Puerto Rican-American
Intermediate, Older; Nonfiction

VI. Families Including a Child of a Different Nationality

Introduction

Most of the books included in this chapter cover specific families of mixed heritage created when children are adopted from another country. In some instances, the books tell of slave or abducted children or children cared for in orphanages. The "General" chapter contains books discussing the topic of international adoptions.

The names of persons covered in the "Biography" chapter are listed first in each category and cross-referenced to that chapter. Book listings follow these listings.

The listings are categorized by the nation in which the adult adopter or caretaker resides.

This chapter is organized alphabetically into the following major categories: Unspecified Countries of Origin and Destination, Unspecified Countries of Destination, Africa, Asia, Canada, Europe, Mexico, Oceania, and United States. Within these categories there are usually subcategories of individual nations. There are then subcategories of the countries from which the child has come:

    e.g., England

        From Guatemala

The heritage designation for each book reads:

    Identity of adult(s) or

    Identity of adult(s) followed by identity of child(ren) of mixed or more specific heritage

    e.g., English or

        English of Mayan Guatemalan

The order in which the heritages are listed is immaterial.

References

Unspecified Countries of Origin and Destination

Karvoskaia, Natacha, and Zidrou. *Dounia*. Illustrated by Natacha Karvoskaia. Brooklyn: Kane/Miller Book Publishers, 1995. 28 p.

This picture book presents a tiny girl of color's arrival in a different country where she is met by her Caucasian prospective parents. She is afraid to speak or touch anything in her new house, but feels that the next day she will be able to do so. The countries of origin and destination and the ethnicities

of the little girl and the parents are not specified.
Pre-K; Fiction

Layne, Steven L. *Over Land and Sea: A Story of International Adoption*. Illustrated by Jan Bower. Gretna, La.: Pelican Publishing Company, 2005. 32 p.

Paintings of babies and young children of different ethnicities distinguish this picture book on international adoption. It does not mention the birthparents of the adopted children, the cultures from which they have come, nor the locations of their adoptive families, but states that they have come home.
Pre-K; Fiction

McCutcheon, John. *Happy Adoption Day!* Illustrated by Julie Paschkis. Boston: Little, Brown and Company, 1996. 28 p.

John McCutcheon is the writer of both the lyrics and the music of the song, "Happy Adoption Day!" It can be sung to celebrate any adoption, but the colorful illustrations accompanying the lyrics depict a Caucasian couple who travel by plane to bring home an Asian boy.
Pre-K, Primary; Fiction

Zisk, Mary. *The Best Single Mom in the World: How I Was Adopted*. Illustrated by author. Morton Grove, Ill.: Albert Whitman & Company, 2001. 32 p.

Full-page color pictures illustrate the story of a single woman who adopts a baby girl from abroad.
Pre-K, Primary; Fiction

Unspecified Countries of Destination

From China

Dorow, Sara. *When You Were Born in China: A Memory Book for Children Adopted from China*. Photographs by Stephen Wunrow. St. Paul: Yeong & Yeong Book Company, 1997. 48 p.

Filled with numerous photographs, this book for children adopted from China describes the country of China, explains its population rule, and tells of orphanages, foster families, baby photographs and health reports, the arrival of adoptive parents from other countries, time spent by the new families seeing China, and departures for the babies' new homes.
Primary, Intermediate; Nonfiction

Lin, Grace. *The Red Thread: An Adoption Fairy Tale*. Illustrated by author. Morton Grove, Ill.: Albert Whitman & Company, 2007. 32 p.

In this picture book fairy tale, which is based on a Chinese belief, the king and queen have pains in their hearts which no one can cure. A peddler shows them the red threads being pulled from their hearts and then joined together. Heeding his advice, they follow the thread across land and sea until in a distant kingdom they discover the baby girl who is destined to be their daughter.
Pre-K, Primary; Fiction

Mother Bridge of Love, text provider. *Motherbridge of Love*. Illustrated by Josée Masse. Cambridge, Mass.: Barefoot Books, 2007. 36 p.

This picture book presents a poem submitted anonymously to the Mother Bridge of Love charity and accompanying double-page color illustrations. It celebrates the two women shaping the life of a small girl adopted from China: her birthmother and her Caucasian adoptive mother.
Pre-K, Primary; Fiction

Oelschlager, Vanita. *Made in China: A Story of Adoption*. Illustrated by Kristin Blackwood. Akron, Ohio: Vanita Books, 2008. 36 p.

In this picture book featuring large vibrant illustrations, a little girl is upset when her older sister teases that she, like their toys and clothes, is labeled "Made in China." Her father explains how, unlike a toy, she was made in China with love and is loved forever by her new parents.
Pre-K, Primary; Fiction

Africa

Ethiopia

From Sudan

Williams, Mary. *Brothers in Hope: The Story of the Lost Boys of Sudan*. Illustrated by R. Gregory Christie. New York: Lee & Low Books, 2005. 40 p.

This story of Garang is based on the experiences of approximately 30,000 Lost Boys of Sudan, who were forced to leave Sudan in the mid-1980s because of the war there. Becoming the leader of a group and responsible for a five-year-old boy, Garang suffers with the others from hunger and thirst as they walk to a refugee camp in Ethiopia. There Tom, an American, helps them get food and shelter, and they go to school. However, when fighting comes to Ethiopia, they must go to a refugee camp in Kenya. Garang relates his experiences to Tom, who has come to the camp, but leaves to share Garang's story with others. When Tom returns to Kenya, he enables Garang, now twenty-one, and other Lost Boys of Sudan to go to the United States.
American and international relief workers
Intermediate; Fiction

Kenya

From Sudan

Williams, Mary. *Brothers in Hope: The Story of the Lost Boys of Sudan*. Illustrated by R. Gregory Christie. New York: Lee & Low Books, 2005. 40 p.

This story of Garang is based on the experiences of approximately 30,000 Lost Boys of Sudan, who were forced to leave Sudan in the mid-1980s because of the war there. Becoming the leader of a

group and responsible for a five-year-old boy, Garang suffers with the others from hunger and thirst as they walk to a refugee camp in Ethiopia. There Tom, an American, helps them get food and shelter, and they go to school. However, when fighting comes to Ethiopia, they must go to a refugee camp in Kenya. Garang relates his experiences to Tom, who has come to the camp, but leaves to share Garang's story with others. When Tom returns to Kenya, he enables Garang, now twenty-one, and other Lost Boys of Sudan to go to the United States.
American and international relief workers
Intermediate; Fiction

South Africa

From Poland

See   Lehrman, Devorah

Asia

Indonesia

From United States

See   Obama, Barack

Japan

From England

Morpurgo, Michael. *Kensuke's Kingdom*. New York: Scholastic Press, 2003. 176 p.

In 1987 after Michael's parents lose their jobs, his father buys a yacht for their family's home so that, after months of training, they can sail around the world. The three of them with their dog, Stella, spend time visiting such places as Brazil, South Africa, and Australia, but on the eve of his twelfth birthday Michael and Stella are swept overboard and end up on the beach of a tiny island in the Pacific Ocean. There they meet an old Japanese man, Kensuke, who has been on the island with its gibbons and orangutans since his ship beached there during World War II. Although Kensuke provides the two castaways with food and water, he initially resents their presence and even tramples down the fire Michael has built to alert rescuers. When Michael is paralyzed by the stings of a large jellyfish, Kensuke, a doctor, nurses him back to life and Michael learns that Kensuke had earlier rescued him and Stella from the ocean. Kensuke and Michael become close friends, painting shells and fishing together and finally sharing the stories of their lives. Michael learns that Kensuke believes his wife and son were killed by the atomic bombing of Nagasaki and that hunters had earlier come to the island shooting gibbons. When the hunters return, Kensuke and Michael manage to save the orangutans by

hiding them in Kensuke's cave. When Michael's parents finally find him, Kensuke has decided to remain on the island with his orangutan family and instructs Michael to tell no one of his presence for ten years. Japanese
Intermediate, Older; Fiction

Syria

From Turkey

Skrypuch, Marsha Forchuk. *Daughter of War: A Novel*. Brighton, Mass.: Fitzhugh & Whiteside, 2008. 224 p.

This novel is set during the Armenian Genocide in Turkey during World War I. It centers on the Armenian teenagers Mariam and Marta Hovsepian and Kevork Adomian, all of whom were orphaned because of the 1909 Adana Massacre and lived in an orphanage run by German missionaries in Maresh, Turkey. When the Turks decided to relocate Armenians, Mariam, the older sister, was taken to a slave auction where she was bought by a Turkish man who had fallen in love with her. She is returned to the orphanage for her safety when the man's mother has another Armenian woman's throat wrung. Marta and Kevork, who were betrothed, were marched into the desert. Marta was saved by a Turkish woman whose husband made her one of his wives and raped her. Pregnant Marta is returned to the orphanage where she has a baby girl, Pauline. Kevork was rescued by Arabs in Syria. Disguised as an Arab, he works as a shoemaker and then accepts the dangerous job of a courier bringing money to starving Armenians who had been deported to the Syrian Desert. Becoming ill with typhus, he recovers under the care of a German missionary in one of the deportation camps. The book tells of the horrible fate of the Armenians and some of those who secretly helped them. It concludes with Kevork's reunion with Marta at the Maresh orphanage, now run by American missionaries.
Arab-Syrian of Armenian-Turkish; German of Armenian-Turkish
Older; Fiction

Canada

From Belgium

Little, Jean. *Look Through My Window*. Illustrated by Joan Sandin. New York: Harper & Row, Publishers, 1970. 272 p.

When her aunt is hospitalized with tuberculosis and her father is transferred to a different city in Ontario, only child Emily's parents buy a large house and take in her four rambunctious cousins, aged three to seven. This story relates Emily's adventures helping look after the children, learning to appreciate the elderly cantankerous next-door neighbor, experiencing the unexpected arrival of Sophie, a seventeen-year-old Belgian girl, and rescuing the cat Wilhelmina Shakespeare. Most of all, the book is about Emily's finally meeting Kate, a kindred poetry-writer, their friendship, and their acceptance of Emily's being Presbyterian and Kate part-Jewish. This is the first book about Emily and Kate.

European-Canadian
Intermediate; Fiction

From China

Okimoto, Jean Davies, and Elaine M. Aoki. *The White Swan Express: A Story about Adoption.*
Illustrated by Meilo So. New York: Clarion Books, 2002. 32 p.

From Miami; Toronto; Minnetonka, Minnesota; and Vashon Island, Washington, prospective parents fly to China where they meet to travel to Guangzhou to receive their respective new daughters. They welcome their baby girls, travel back to their homes, and exchange cards during the holidays and at the Lunar New Year. In this picture book, the text includes some Mandarin phrases and an afterword elaborates upon the process of adopting Chinese children.
Asian-Canadian
Pre-K, Primary; Fiction

Ye, Ting-xing with William Bell. *Throwaway Daughter.* Scarborough, Ontario: Doubleday Canada, 2003. 240 p.

This is the fictional story of Grace Dong-mei Margaret Parker, who was adopted from an orphanage in Yangzhou, China, in 1981 and of her life with her parents and older sister in Ontario, Canada. After years of resisting her mother's advice to learn about her Chinese culture, Grace takes courses in Mandarin and learns to love it. She continues to be angry at her birthmother who gave her away, but in 1999 decides to go to China to take a course at a business college in Shanghai and search for her birthfamily. This book is also the story of Grace's Chinese grandfather Chen Da-li, who had been the party secretary in his village, worshipped Chairman Mao who redistributed land to the peasants, and longs for a grandson. It is the story of her father Loyal, who approves of Mao's successor Deng Xiaoping's economic reforms, seeks to make money, and who, after Dong-mei is born, pretends she is born dead and buried in the vegetable garden. It is the story of her mother Chun-mei, whose landlord family had been deprived of its land and given low status under Chairman Mao's policies and who, because of the Communist's family planning rules, worries about the fate of the baby she is carrying should it be a girl. When Dong-mei is born, Chun-mei saves her by running away from the village to take her to the Yangzhou Orphanage. She returns to the orphanage a year later and is told there is no knowledge of the baby. Chun-mei temporarily goes mad and, divorced by Loyal, goes to live with her brothers. The story concludes with Grace Dong-mei's finding her birthfamily.
European-Canadian
Older; Fiction

From England

Levin, Betty. *Brother Moose.* New York: Greenwillow Books, 1990. 224 p.

When Nell, an orphan from England, is sent in the 1870s to live with a couple in Canada's Maritime Provinces, she discovers that her prospective mother, Mrs. Fowler, has moved to Maine to have a baby. Next Nell is kidnapped by robbers, escapes, and travels with her fellow orphan Louisa,

an Indian named Joe Pennowit, and his twelve year old grandson to Maine. However, because Joe mistakenly thinks he has killed one of the men who kidnapped Nell, the four leave the road to escape the robbers and the police. On their difficult journey they travel by wagon, by sleigh, and by an abandoned train car, which is pulled by their horse and a moose they have tamed. Nell finally reaches Mrs. Fowler, but her adoption hopes take a surprising turn.
Canadian Micmac or American Passamaquoddy or Penobscot
Older; Fiction

From Turkey

Skrypuch, Marsha Forchuk. *Aram's Choice*. Illustrated by Muriel Wood. Brighton, Mass.: Fitzhenry & Whiteside, 2006. 84 p. (New Beginnings)
　　Although works of fiction, this book and its sequel, *Call Me Aram*, are based on the experiences of the Georgetown Boys in the 1920s. It is June 1923 and Armenians twelve-year-old Aram and his grandmother have escaped from the genocide in Turkey to the island of Corfu, Greece. There Aram lives in an orphanage run by foreign missionaries. Now he must make the decision as to whether to go with other boys to live in an orphanage in Georgetown, Canada. Hating to leave his destitute grandmother, but urged by her to go so he will be safe from the Turks, Aram chooses to leave and, like the others, is given a Canadian quarter by the orphanage head. This book details his journey: the cargo ship ride to Marseilles, the train ride to Paris during which his young friend Mgerdich is injured when he falls out of a window, the train trip to Cherbourg, the voyage on an elegant steamship to Quebec, and the train trip to Montreal. There, after learning that their accompanying Armenian teacher will have to return to danger in Corfu, Aram persuades the other boys to pool their quarters so that their teacher may go to Ottawa to plead his case. After two more train rides, the boys arrive in Georgetown where Aram realizes he has made the right choice.
European-Canadian of Armenian-Turkish
Intermediate; Fiction

Skrypuch, Marsha Forchuk. *Call Me Aram*. Illustrated by Muriel Wood. Brighton, Mass.: Fitzhenry & Whiteside, 2009. 88 p. (New Beginnings)
　　This sequel to *Aram's Choice* describes the experiences of Aram Davidian at the Armenian Relief Association of Canada's boys farm in Georgetown, Ontario, Canada, and is based on the Armenian Georgetown Boys' actual experiences. Aram is exposed to many new things at the farm: porridge (which he dislikes), cornflakes, cameras, and showers and is treated kindly by the minister and his wife who are in charge. However, they cannot understand Armenian and call him by a new name, David Adams. Aram worries about his grandmother, who remains in Corfu, Greece, and about his younger friend Mgerdich, left behind in a Paris hospital after falling out of a train window. In the story Aram is helped by three Armenian adults, learns that his grandmother is well and working at his old orphanage, is thrilled when Mgerdich arrives at the farm, and, with the other boys, persuades the minister and his wife to call them, not by the names of their Canadian benefactors, but by their own names.
European-Canadian of Armenian-Turkish
Intermediate; Fiction

From United States

See   Williams, Eunice

Cooney, Caroline B. *The Ransom of Mercy Carter*. New York: Delacorte Press, 2001. 256 p.

Twenty-nine of the children (under age twenty) captured in the February 1704 Canadian Indian and French attack on Deerfield, Massachusetts, did not return. This novel tells the story of eleven-year-old Mercy Carter, who was one of the captives refusing to be ransomed, but about whom little is known. It describes the arduous trip upon which she was taken to the Mohawk village of Kahnawake on the St. Lawrence River and of her becoming part of a Mohawk family. It describes her experiences and those of other Deerfield captives who were taken in by the Indians and the French. Mercy not only was thrust into the drastically different lifestyle of the Mohawks and the Catholic religion, a far cry from her Puritan upbringing, but also had to live with those who had murdered members of her family and community. This story details her conflicting feelings as she becomes more assimilated into Indian life. In May 1705 when Mercy has the chance to be ransomed and return home, she chooses to remain in Kahnawake.
Mohawk
Older; Fiction

Urban, Betsy. *Waiting for Deliverance*. New York: Orchard Books, 2000. 192 p.

This book is set in 1793 in western New York where there is tension between the Americans and the Seneca, who supported the British during the Revolutionary War. Fourteen-year-old orphan Livy, who is terrified of Indians, is sold at pauper's auction to Gideon, who was raised by Senecas and educated by Anglican Canadians, and whose Seneca brother Rising Hawk often stays with him and his wife. When Livy is sent to a Seneca village to help its women learn how to spin, she is suddenly accused of being a witch. After escaping with Rising Hawk, with whom she is often at odds, Livy discovers that she is in love with him. In this story Rising Hawk has a French ancestor.
Canadian Anglican of Seneca-adopted European-American non-Christian
Older; Fiction

Europe

From Russia

Bell, Julia. *Dirty Work*. New York: Walker & Company, 2008. 192 p.

This is a disturbing story of modern-day child slavery. Fifteen-year-old Oksana's mother had died when she was eight. She lived in poverty in Russia with her father and little brother, for whom she was responsible, until at the age of fourteen she was kidnapped and sold in Italy as a sex slave. Oksana suffers unimaginable horrors and is then taken to England where she hopes she can free herself and join Adik, a childhood friend from whom she had received a postcard with a London return address. Seeking a second girl to replace the girl who had gotten away and committed suicide, Oksana's new owner, who is from Chechnya, kidnaps Hope, the very innocent fourteen-year-old daughter of a wealthy and prominent English family. The story describes their experiences during the several terrifying days until they escape. Hope returns to her worrying family, and Oksana manages to find Adik.

Chechen

Older; Fiction

England

From Eritrea

Bradman, Tony, ed. *Give Me Shelter: Stories about Children Who Seek Asylum*. London: Frances Lincoln Children's Books (Distributed by Publishers Group West), 2007. 224 p.

In the story "Only Up From Here" by Sulaiman Addonia, in the late 1980s Kareem is sent away by his Eritrean mother to escape from Ethiopian bomber planes. Arriving in London, he is given asylum-seeker status, but is placed in an adult accommodation because he had been told to lie about his age. When Kareem returns to the refugee charity organization, he reveals that he is only thirteen and is placed in a children's house for asylum-seekers.

English

Older; Fiction

From Eritrea and Ethiopia

Zephaniah, Benjamin. *Refugee Boy*. New York: Bloomsbury Children's Books, 2001. 304 p.

Alem was born in the town of Badme, which was claimed by both Eritrea and Ethiopia. When Alem and his parents lived in Ethiopia, soldiers forced them to leave because Alem's mother was Eritrean and when they moved to Eritrea, soldiers demanded that they leave because of his Ethiopian father. Fourteen-year-old Alem and his father go to England, supposedly on holiday, but when Alem wakes up in their hotel he discovers that his father has left him so that he can grow up in safety. The Refugee Council places Alem in a children's home, but he runs away after one night because of the intolerable environment. He is then placed with Irish foster parents, the Fitzgeralds. Alem likes the kind and supportive Fitzgerald family, his English school, and his new friends. This story details the process which Alem must follow to gain political asylum, the murder of his mother near the Eritrean-Ethiopian border, his father's arriving in England, the denial of their asylum request which means that they will have to return to life-threatening Ethiopia, the campaign waged by Alem's schoolmates on their behalf, and finally the killing of Alem's father outside the London headquarters of the East African Solidarity Trust, an organization advocating unity and peace which his parents had helped found.

Irish

Older; Fiction

From Ethiopia

Bradman, Tony, ed. *Give Me Shelter: Stories about Children Who Seek Asylum*. London: Frances Lincoln Children's Books (Distributed by Publishers Group West), 2007. 224 p.

In the story "Give Me Shelter" by Solomon Gebremedhin, twelve-year-old Danny and two thirteen-year-old friends manage to get from their Ethiopian homes to Sudan to avoid being conscripted as soldiers. Falsely accused of stealing from his Sudan employer, Danny escapes from jail and travels to England. There he lives in a children's home and then a foster home, but is still uncertain as to whether he can stay.
English
Older; Fiction

From Germany

See   Drucker, Olga Levy

Bruchac, Joseph. *Hidden Roots*. New York: Scholastic Press, 2004. 144 p.

It is 1954 and eleven-year-old Sonny lives with his mother and his father, who is often angry and physically abusive. Sonny enjoys the company of an older friend "Uncle" Louie, a man who had worked for his mother's parents when she was a child and from whom he learns much about the Adirondack area of New York State where they live. Sonny wonders about the many subjects he is not allowed to discuss and questions that remain unanswered: why he should be afraid of being "crept up on," what bad things happened in Vermont, and why his father doesn't want Uncle Louis around. It is only after he and Uncle Louis learn from the Jewish school librarian that her parents had sent her as a child from Germany to England for safety, that Uncle Louis tells Sonny the truth. Uncle Louis is his grandfather, who, like his late wife, had been sterilized during the Vermont Eugenics Project because they were Indians and who had fled Vermont so that Sonny's mother would not be taken away. It was because Sonny's family wanted to protect him from being treated like an Indian that they had kept his identity a secret, but it is when the secret is revealed to Sonny that his father, who is also part Indian, is released from his anger and shame.
English of German Jewish
Intermediate, Older; Fiction

Watts, Irene N. *Finding Sophie*. Plattsburgh, N.Y.: Tundra Books of Northern New York, 2002. 144 p.

This book, which is a sequel to and contains excerpts from *Good-bye Marianne* and *Remember Me*, relates what happened to seven-year-old Sophie whose mother placed her on the 1938 Kindertransport train in Berlin and told eleven-year-old Marianne to look after her. Sophie went to live with "Aunt Em," a friend of her parents, and loves being with her as well as life in England. Now, turning fourteen-years-old, Sophie hopes that after the war she will not have to return to Germany and the parents she barely remembers. By chance she and Marianne are reunited, and Sophie participates in the May 1945 celebration of Germany's defeat. Shortly thereafter she receives a letter from her father containing both the happy news that he has survived the Dachau Concentration Camp and the sorrowful news that her mother was killed in an air raid. Sophie's concerns about her future are happily resolved when she remains with Aunt Em and her father comes to live nearby.

English Quaker of German Jewish and Christian

Intermediate, Older; Fiction

Watts, Irene N. *Remember Me*. Plattsburgh, N.Y.: Tundra Books of Northern New York, 2000. 192 p.

Remember Me contains excerpts from and is the sequel to *Good-bye Marianne*, which concludes with eleven-year-old Marianne's departure trip from Berlin in December 1938 as part of the Kindertransport which rescued Jewish children from the horrors of Nazi Germany by sending them to England. This book describes Marianne's homesickness as she is placed with a London couple who had expected an older girl and treat her with coldness. As war with England becomes imminent, Marianne and her schoolmates are part of the September 1, 1939 evacuation of London children to the country. They end up in Wales where Marianne is placed with a grieving couple who change her name and try to make her into their dead daughter. Fortunately, her mother is finally able to get to Great Britain.

English Christian of German Jewish

Intermediate, Older; Fiction

From Guatemala

Guillain, Adam. *Bella Balistica and the African Safari*. Chicago: Milet Publishing, 2006. 240 p. (Bella Balistica Adventure Novels)

This is the third book in the *Bella Balistica* series. When Quetzal, the bird who is Bella's twin, tells twelve-year-old Bella that her Guatemalan father wants her to join him in Ethiopia, she disregards Quetzal's instruction to wait for him and takes off by herself from her adoptive English home. On her journey she encounters the evil Askar Karpov, who, like Bella, has the mystical power to turn himself into his animal twin, in this case a terrifying vulture. Karpov is a director of the Corporation, a worldwide offshoot of the early Knights Templar, that seeks world power and is against global warming prevention and fair trade practices. Bella finally reaches her father in a village on Lake Tana in Ethiopia and joins in the amazing meeting he has organized of humans, animals, and birds from every corner of the earth who are united in opposition to the cruelness and greed of the Corporation. The ensuing battle between the two forces has an unexpected outcome.

English of Mayan Guatemalan

Older; Fiction

Guillain, Adam. *Bella Balistica and the Forgotten Kingdom*. Chicago: Milet Publishing, 2009. 192 p. (Bella Balistica Adventure Novels)

Twelve-year-old Bella Balistica disobeys her Guatemalan father and, taking the form of a quetzal bird, flies off to New York City to see him after learning that Orom Hunter, the chairman of the evil Corporation, has purchased three stone tablets from the British Museum. He is returning them to Mount Nemrud, Turkey, where through them and after locating Antiochos' tomb within Mount

Nemrud, he can unleash and gain the fearsome powers of the ancient Kingdom of Kommagene. Unfortunately, because of her trip, Bella has unwittingly blown her father's cover at the Corporation, and Hunter, entering Bella's London attic, steals her father's diagram showing Antiochos' tomb. Joined by Quetzal, the bird that is her twin, Bella flies to Turkey where, with the help of a thrush, a cat, a lizard, the young woman journalist Muna, and the thirteen-year-old javelin thrower Herak, Hunter, in the form of the monster Syeku, is destroyed. However, this is not before Syeku has killed Bella's father and most probably Quetzal. This is the fourth book in the *Bella Balistica* series.
English of Mayan Guatemalan
 Older; Fiction

Guillain, Adam. *Bella Balistica and the Indian Summer*. Illustrated by Rachel Goslin. London: Milet Publishing, 2005. 272 p. (Bella Balistica Adventure Novels)

In this second book in the *Bella Balistica* series, eleven-year-old Bella goes with her adoptive English mother and her mother's boyfriend Bruce to Delhi, India. Bella not only dislikes Bruce, but increasingly realizes that he is in league with Diva Devaki, the famous Indian acrobat and illusionist. Diva, the owner of the Mumbai Circus, uses homeless children as enforced child labor, murders animals for their skins, and is determined to secure Bella's powerful pendant. In this adventure story Bella, who sometimes turns into a quetzal bird, escapes from Diva, saves a Bengal tiger, discovers that Bruce is under Diva's spell, recruits homeless children to take fund-raising photographs of their lives, and encounters her Guatemalan father.
English of Mayan Guatemalan
Older; Fiction

Guillain, Adam. *Bella Balistica and the Temple of Tikal*. Illustrated by Rachel Goslin. London: Milet Publishing, 2004. 288 p. (Bella Balistica Adventure Novels)

This is the first in a series about Bella Balistica for older children. Bella lives with her adoptive English mother, who assisted in Bella's birth in Guatemala and adopted her shortly thereafter when her birthmother died from an infection. Eleven-year-old Bella enjoys being with her best friend Charlie, but is tormented by schoolmate Eugene Briggs and his gang and by the fearsome new school head teacher, a cohort of Eugene's father who locks up exotic animals and loots artifacts from Guatemala. In this adventure story a quetzal bird, Bella's animal twin, arrives in her attic and persuades her to accompany him to Guatemala to save the Temple of Tikal and to keep its Itzamna Emerald from being taken by Eugene's father. It turns out that Bella is Itzamna's descendent and, when wearing her birthmother's pendant, she can heal, fly, talk with animals, and exercise other mystical powers. In Guatemala Bella learns much about her native country, befriends Guatemalan children, and faces continuing dangers, especially from Mr. Briggs.
English of Mayan Guatemalan
Older; Fiction

Guillain, Adam. *Bella's Brazilian Football*. Illustrated by Elke Steiner. Chicago: Milet Publishing, 2007. 32 p. (Bella Balistica Picture Books)

In this *Bella Balistica* picture book, Guatemalan Bella tells her friend Charlie that their football (soccer) team needs new clothes, new boots, and a new ball so they can play better. Flying with her animal twin Quetzal from London to Brazil, which has won five World Cups, Bella learns from playing with Rio de Janeiro's barefoot street children that it is teamwork and skills that win games.
English of Mayan Guatemalan
Primary, Intermediate; Fiction

Guillain, Adam. *Bella's Chocolate Surprise*. Illustrated by Elke Steiner. Chicago: Milet Publishing, 2007. 32 p. (Bella Balistica Picture Books)
Guatemalan Bella and her animal twin Quetzal fly from her London home to Ghana so Bella can discover where chocolate comes from. In this picture book Bella helps Ghanaian children with the cacao harvest and learns how important fair trade chocolate is to their community.
English of Mayan Guatemalan
Primary, Intermediate; Fiction

From Iraq

Bradman, Tony, ed. *Give Me Shelter: Stories about Children Who Seek Asylum*. London: Frances Lincoln Children's Books (Distributed by Publishers Group West), 2007. 224 p.
In the story "Samir Hakkim's Healthy Eating Diary" by Miriam Halahmy, in 2002 when his family is arrested during Saddam Hussein's regime, ten-year-old Samir is sent from Baghdad to England as a refugee. After living in a children's home, he is sent to a foster home where he is unhappy and goes to a school where he has only one friend whose family also befriends him. Then Samir's aunt arrives from Iraq with news that at least his older brother is alive.
English
Older; Fiction

From Italy (Emilia-Romagna)

Welsh, T. K. *Resurrection Men*. New York: Dutton's Children's Books, 2007. 224 p.
When in 1830 twelve-year-old Victor's parents are killed, he is hired in Genoa as a merchant ship cabin boy. However, when Victor falls off the rigging and shatters his leg, he is tossed overboard since he is no longer of use. Ending up on a beach in Portsmouth, England, Victor is tended by an old man, who makes him a crutch. Unable to keep him after four months, the old man sells Victor to two men who call themselves undertakers and take him to London in a casket on top of a corpse. Victor's experiences there include joining a group of children who secure their living by begging for their master, watching the "undertakers" steal and sell a body after a funeral, going to live with a doctor who operates on his leg and cares for him, discovering that the blind girl whom he loves is being sexually abused, watching a surgeon dissect the body of a close friend, and then discovering that the surgeon is capturing children and infecting them with cholera. The identity of the story's narrator is revealed at the end of this book, which is for older teenagers.

English
Older; Fiction

From Nigeria?

See   Bonetta, Sarah Forbes-Egbado

From Spain

Arthur, Ruth M. *Requiem for a Princess*. Illustrated by Margery Gill. New York: Atheneum, 1967. 200 p.

When Willow is told by a schoolmate that she is adopted, she becomes depressed, feels estranged from her parents, and cannot work up the nerve to broach the subject with them. Ill, she goes for an extended stay at a guesthouse in Cornwall that has been in the Tresilian family for generations. There she becomes intrigued by Issable de Calverados, the girl in a portrait. As a child Issable, who was Spanish, somehow turned up in Cornwall where she was adopted by the Tresilians and, according to a memorial stone, probably died of drowning in 1602. Feeling a kinship with Issable because she also was adopted, Willow restores her Spanish garden, finds the medallion which she is pictured wearing, and, as she becomes increasingly involved with Issable, has dreams in which she experiences her life. When Willow finally discovers Issable's fate, she is able to accept her own parents and realize how much she is indebted to them.

English
Older; Fiction

From Tanzania

Doherty, Berlie. *The Girl Who Saw Lions*. New York: Roaring Brook Press, 2008. 256 p. (A Neal Porter Book)

In alternating chapters this book relates the stories of Rosa, the thirteen-year-old daughter of a Tanzanian father and an English mother who lives with her mother in Sheffield, England, and Abela, a nine-year-old Tanzanian whose parents both die of AIDS. Rosa, who loves taking ice skating lessons with her mother, initially feels rejected when her mum wants to adopt a little girl and then hurt when the four-year-old Tanzanian boy whom she comes to love cannot be adopted because his father shows up. Abela is sent for sale to London by her unscrupulous uncle, is kept captive in the apartment of his naïve white bride, runs away to a nearby school, and goes to live with a Nigerian foster family. When Abela is given resident status, she becomes Rosa's little sister.

English; Nigerian
Intermediate, Older; Fiction

From Vietnam

Anderson, Rachel. *The War Orphan*. Oxford, England: Oxford University Press, 1984. 264 p.

Ha, a boy who has been traumatized by the fighting in Vietnam and has regressed into infancy,

comes to live in Simon's home on a trial adoption basis. Simon, the narrator, becomes driven to relive Ha's Vietnam experiences and, in doing so, becomes terrified and repulsed by Ha. In this disturbing, but moving story, Simon and Ha finally become true brothers, sharing the story of Ha's past. This book provides a vivid picture of childhood in war-torn Vietnam.
English
Older; Fiction

France

From Vietnam

Mosher, Richard. *Zazoo: A Novel*. New York: Clarion Books, 2001. 256 p.

Set in France, this is a story of young love and abiding love, of growing up and growing old, of separation and reconciliation, of evil and good—and of the poem about the gray cat who lives by the canal. When sixteen-year-old Marius bikes along the towpath next to the canal where thirteen-year-old Zazoo is out in her boat, everything changes: for her, for the elderly Grand-Pierre who adopted her from Vietnam, for the village pharmacist, for Marius, and for his grandmother.
French
Older; Fiction

Germany

From Austria

Ibbotson, Eva. *The Star of Kazan*. Illustrated by Kevin Hawkes. New York: Dutton Children's Books, 2004. 416 p.

Celebrating the Vienna of the early 1900s and especially its Lippizaner stallions, this book tells how, as a foundling, Annika had been taken in by two Viennese women who are servants in the house of three professors. Raised in a warm family atmosphere by the five of them, with two best friends, and a close relationship with an elderly neighbor, Annika leads a happy life, but dreams that her mother will someday arrive. What happens next involves the trunk with its "fake" jewels which the old woman leaves to Annika, the discovery by her "mother" of the truth about the jewels, Annika's restricted life as an aristocrat in a moated house in Germany, her friendship with the stable boy whose mother was a gypsy, and the extraordinary actions on her behalf by those who love her.
German
Intermediate, Older; Fiction

From Czech Republic

Wolf, Joan M. *Someone Named Eva*. New York: Clarion Books, 2007. 208 p.

This fictional story is based on events which took place in Lidice, Czechoslovakia, in June 1942. At that time eleven-year-old Milada and her family are removed from their home by Nazi soldiers.

Her father and fifteen-year-old brother are taken to an unknown destination, while Milada, her grand-mother, her mother, and her baby sister stay with other women and children in a school. There Milada, with her blond hair and light-colored eyes, is chosen to be an Aryan child and future German wife and mother who will help save the world from Jews. She goes to a Polish training center where she must speak only German, is taught Nazi values, must constantly salute "Heil Hitler," befriends a Polish girl, is given the name Eva, and struggles to keep her Czech identity. After almost two years, Eva is adopted by a German family whose father is the commander of the Nazi Ravensbrück women's camp. Eva becomes close to her new sister, but longs for her own family. After the war she is reunited with her mother. Her father and brother had been shot, her grandmother had died in a concentration camp, and her little sister had not been located.
German
Older; Fiction

From Poland

Matas, Carol. *In My Enemy's House*. New York: Simon & Schuster Books for Young Readers, 1999. 176 p.

In 1941 when the Nazis occupy Poland, fifteen-year-old Marisa's family members are either taken by the Germans or go into hiding. Because Marisa does not look Jewish with her blond hair and blue eyes, she hides her Jewish identity and escapes Poland by going with other Poles to work as servants in Germany. In her first job Marisa is physically abused by her employer, but it is even more difficult for her when she takes care of the children in a prominent German family. Although the family treats her kindly, the children play a game of getting rid of Jews and she is informed that Jews are not even human. At the end of the story, Marisa finally realizes that others cannot take away the love in one's heart.
German Christian of Polish Jewish
Older; Fiction

From Rwanda

See   Umubyeyi, Jeanne d'Arc

Greece

From Turkey

Skrypuch, Marsha Forchuk. *Aram's Choice*. Illustrated by Muriel Wood. Brighton, Mass.: Fitzhenry & Whiteside, 2006. 84 p. (New Beginnings)

Although works of fiction, this book and its sequel, *Call Me Aram*, are based on the experiences of the Georgetown Boys in the 1920s. It is June 1923 and Armenians twelve-year-old Aram and his grandmother have escaped from the genocide in Turkey to the island of Corfu, Greece. There Aram lives in an orphanage run by foreign missionaries. Now he must make the decision as to whether to go with other boys to live in an orphanage in Georgetown, Canada. Hating to leave his destitute grand-mother, but urged by her to go so he will be safe from the Turks, Aram chooses to leave and, like the others, is given a Canadian quarter by the orphanage head. This book details his journey: the cargo ship ride to Marseilles, the train ride to Paris during which his young friend Mgerdich is injured when he falls out of a window, the train trip to Cherbourg, the voyage on an elegant steamship to Quebec, and the train trip to Montreal. There, after learning that their accompanying Armenian teacher will have to return to danger in Corfu, Aram persuades the other boys to pool their quarters so that their teacher may go to Ottawa to plead his case. After two more train rides, the boys arrive in Georgetown where Aram realizes he has made the right choice.

British, Canadian, or American of Armenian-Turkish

Intermediate; Fiction

Italy

From Russia

Bell, Julia. *Dirty Work*. New York: Walker & Company, 2008. 192 p.

This is a disturbing story of modern-day child slavery. Fifteen-year-old Oksana's mother had died when she was eight. She lived in poverty in Russia with her father and little brother, for whom she was responsible, until at the age of fourteen she was kidnapped and sold in Italy as a sex slave. Oksana suffers unimaginable horrors and is then taken to England where she hopes she can free herself and join Adik, a childhood friend from whom she had received a postcard with a London return address. Seeking a second girl to replace the girl who had gotten away and committed suicide, Oksana's new owner, who is from Chechnya, kidnaps Hope, the very innocent fourteen-year-old daughter of a wealthy and prominent English family. The story describes their experiences during the several terri-fying days until they escape. Hope returns to her worrying family, and Oksana manages to find Adik.

Italian

Older; Fiction

Netherlands

From South Korea

Wilkinson, Sook, and Nancy Fox, eds. *After the Morning Calm: Reflections of Korean Adoptees*. Bloomfield Hills, Mich.: Sunrise Ventures, 2002. 192 p.

In this book nine men and seventeen women present their experiences and feelings about being adopted from South Korea. One went to live with a Dutch family, another was adopted by Norwegians, and the remainder became the children of American parents. Their ages at adoption ranged from infancy to teenager. One suffered in Korea because he was the son of a Korean woman and a white American soldier. Another was the subject of her mother Marjorie Ann Waybill's fiction-al book. All were succeeding as adults. Their writings describe the impact of looking different from their peers, the difficulties of reconciling two cultures, and the effects of visiting South Korea. The

book contains photographs and an appended resource section.
Dutch
Older; Nonfiction

Norway

From South Korea

Wilkinson, Sook, and Nancy Fox, eds. *After the Morning Calm: Reflections of Korean Adoptees.* Bloomfield Hills, Mich.: Sunrise Ventures, 2002. 192 p.

In this book nine men and seventeen women present their experiences and feelings about being adopted from South Korea. One went to live with a Dutch family, another was adopted by Norwegians, and the remainder became the children of American parents. Their ages at adoption ranged from infancy to teenager. One suffered in Korea because he was the son of a Korean woman and a white American soldier. Another was the subject of her mother Marjorie Ann Waybill's fictional book. All were succeeding as adults. Their writings describe the impact of looking different from their peers, the difficulties of reconciling two cultures, and the effects of visiting South Korea. The book contains photographs and an appended resource section.
Norwegian
Older; Nonfiction

Scotland

From Austria

Metzger, Lois. *Missing Girls*. New York: Viking, 1999. 192 p.

Since the death of her mother four years earlier in 1963, thirteen-year-old Carrie has felt empty inside and upset that she cannot remember more of her mother. Moving in with her Jewish Austrian grandmother, Carrie is ashamed of her grandmother's immigrant ways and is attracted to the mother of a classmate who seems very American. Carrie dreads the upcoming visit of Angus, the Scotsman who looked after her refugee mother during World War II, as she fears he will find her fat and not beautiful. Carrie tries to find out how to be awake inside her dreams, but when Angus visits she discovers that she was really trying to be awake when she was awake. Carrie also learns that she is just like her mother at the age of thirteen.
Scottish Christian of Austrian Jewish
Intermediate, Older; Fiction

Sweden

From Poland

See   Lobel, Anita

Wales

From Germany

Watts, Irene N. *Remember Me*. Plattsburgh, N.Y.: Tundra Books of Northern New York, 2000. 192 p.

Remember Me contains excerpts from and is the sequel to *Good-bye Marianne*, which concludes with eleven-year-old Marianne's departure trip from Berlin in December 1938 as part of the *Kindertransport* which rescued Jewish children from the horrors of Nazi Germany by sending them to England. This book describes Marianne's homesickness as she is placed with a London couple who had expected an older girl and treat her with coldness. As war with England becomes imminent, Marianne and her schoolmates are part of the September 1, 1939 evacuation of London children to the country. They end up in Wales where Marianne is placed with a grieving couple who change her name and try to make her into their dead daughter. Fortunately, her mother is finally able to get to Great Britain.
Welsh Baptist of German Jewish
Intermediate, Older; Fiction

Mexico

From United States

Finley, Mary Peace. *Meadow Lark*. Palmer Lake, Colo.: Filter Press, 2003. 208 p.

This book covers the same time period as the two earlier books in the trilogy, *Soaring Eagle* and *White Grizzly*, but tells the story of thirteen-year-old Teresita, Julio's Mexican sister who had to stay behind when Julio and their father left for Bent's Fort. Fearing from a vision that something has happened to them, Teresita, who is working for Charles and Maria Ignacia Bent, joins a wagon train bound for Bent's Fort. After looking after her goats and surviving a wagon ride down perilous Raton Pass, Teresita arrives at Bent's Fort only to learn that her father is dead and Julio has gone on to Bent's Farm. Then, persuading a Mexican couple to hire her and taking Silent Walker, whom she has befriended, along as a goatherder, Teresita joins a wagon train that will pass by Bent's Farm. She is kidnapped by Kiowa and escapes by floating down the Arkansas River in a log drum. Silent Walker meets some Kiowa from whom she had been kidnapped as a child, and both she and Teresita are reunited with Julio at Bent's Farm. It is in this book that readers learn that Silent Walker, a character in the earlier books, is Kiowa, not Cheyenne.
Mexican
Intermediate, Older; Fiction

Finley, Mary Peace. *Soaring Eagle*. New York: Simon & Schuster Books for Young Readers, 1993. 176 p.

Young Julio, who has green eyes, blond hair, and light skin, feels that he is different from the rest of his Mexican family. In 1845 when his father heads back from Taos to Bent's Fort where he works, Julio decides to go with him and, hopefully, discover who he is. Early in the journey his father is killed by Jicarilla Apache. Trying to catch up to a wagon train, Julio and his dog continue on. Injured by a wolf, ill, and blinded by glaring snow, Julio is found by Cheyenne, who nurse him back to health and adopt him as a Cheyenne, Soaring Eagle. While seeking his vision, Julio remembers the song his birthmother had sung to him and his name, Billy. Uncertain whether to live as a Cheyenne, he is shocked by the death of his Indian friend and by a Cheyenne victory celebration—and decides to proceed to Bent's Fort where someone should know who Billy is. This is the first of three books about Julio and his family.
Mexican
Intermediate, Older; Fiction

Finley, Mary Peace. *White Grizzly*. Palmer Lake, Colo.: Filter Press, 2000. 224 p.

In this sequel to *Soaring Eagle* Julio finds out at Bent's Fort that his birth name is William Allen Forester and that his grandfather might still be in Independence, Missouri, where he had decided to wait ten years for word of his missing family. Worried that the ten years have passed, Julio sets off with William Bent and his wagon train on the long perilous journey to Independence. Working as a sheepherder with his dog and an African-American blacksmith, Julio is almost killed by a grizzly bear and by two wanted outlaws; again sees Silent Walker, the young Cheyenne woman whom he has come to care for; is captured by Pawnee; and is reunited in Independence with his grandfather, who was about to leave. Still uncertain whether his allegiances are to the Mexicans, the Americans, or the Cheyenne, Julio and his grandfather spend the winter at Bent's Farm near Independence. The book includes information about William Bent and about Bent Fort's importance as a trading post.
Mexican
Intermediate, Older; Fiction

Oceania

Australia

From Vietnam

Bradman, Tony, ed. *Give Me Shelter: Stories about Children Who Seek Asylum*. London: Frances Lincoln Children's Books (Distributed by Publishers Group West), 2007. 224 p.

Ten-year-old Huy's escape from South Vietnam in 1977 and time in a Malaysian refugee camp are described in the story "Little Fish" by Kim Kitson. Then, living with a foster family in Sydney, he receives a letter telling him that his family is on its way to Australia.

Australian
Older; Fiction

United States

Buzzeo, Toni. *The Sea Chest*. Illustrated by Mary GrandPré. New York: Dial Books for Young Readers, 2002. 32 p.

As a little girl waits for her parents to bring her new sister from a country across the Atlantic, her great-great-aunt tells how, as a girl, she too received a sister from the Atlantic, a baby washed up in a sea chest on the rocks of her Maine lighthouse from a sunken schooner. It was this baby who became the little girl's great-grandmother.
European-American
Primary, Intermediate; Fiction

Caseley, Judith. *Sisters*. Illustrated by author. New York: Greenwillow Books, 2004. 32 p.

Alternating chapters present the experiences of Melissa and her new sister Kika, who has just been adopted from a non-English speaking country.
European-American
Pre-K, Primary; Fiction

Petertyl, Mary E. *Seeds of Love: For Brothers and Sisters of International Adoption*. Illustrated by Jill Chamber. Grand Rapids, Mich.: Folio One Publishing, 1997. 32 p.

In this picture book Carly learns that when her parents go abroad to adopt a baby sister, they will be gone a long time. To make the separation easier, Carly's mother gives her both stickers to mark off each day until their return date and seeds, which when watered, should sprout at about that same time. Her mother also reassures Carly that her grandmother will know how to care for her. All works out as planned, and at the end of the story Carly greets not only her parents, but also her new baby sister.
European-American
Pre-K, Primary; Fiction

From Africa

From Cape Verde

Lyons, Mary E. *Letters from a Slave Boy: The Story of Joseph Jacobs*. New York: Atheneum Books for Young Readers, 2007. 208 p.

This book of historical fiction is a companion book to *Letters from a Slave Girl*, which tells the story of Harriet Jacobs. It presents her son Joseph's narrative of his life from the age of nine until his departure to mine gold in Australia in about 1852. Growing up in Edenton, North Carolina, with his great-grandmother and sister, he is unaware that his mother Harriet, who is an escaped slave, is hiding in the house and that he is the son of a white neighbor, Samuel Sawyer. In 1843 Joseph leaves for

Boston where he briefly attends the abusive Smith School and then becomes a printer's apprentice. Running away to New Bedford, he works on the docks and goes off for almost three years on a whaling ship. On board the ship he encounters a sailor from the Cape Verde Islands who has been looked after since boyhood by the ship's Quaker captain. Joseph next goes to California to mine for gold with his Uncle John, until the two set off for Australia where they will be free. Joseph struggles with the treatment he receives as a slave, his feelings about the Irish boy who works on the ship with him and dies, the decision as to whether he should pass as white, and the terrible worry that he and his mother will be captured by slave hunters. The book includes some information on Joseph's later life.
European-American Quaker of Portuguese-African-Cape Verdean
Older; Fiction

From Sierra Leone

Kuklin, Susan. *Families*. Photographs by author. New York: Hyperion Books for Children, 2006. 40 p.
    Text and color photographs present interviews with American children, who talk about their families. Their families include seven families with children of mixed race, ethnicity, or religion, with one also including a child adopted from Sierra Leone. In an eighth family a child has been adopted from China. In a ninth family an adopted American child is of a race different from that of one of her fathers.
English-German-American and Ecuadorian
Primary, Intermediate; Nonfiction

From West Africa

See   Smith, Venture

From Asia

Carlson, Nancy. *My Family Is Forever*. Illustrated by author. New York: Viking, 2004. 32 p.
    In this picture book a little girl tells of her adoption from Asia and of the love she feels in her family.
European-American
Pre-K, Primary; Fiction

Gabel, Susan. *Where the Sun Kisses the Sea*. Illustrated by Joanne Bowring. Indianapolis, Ind.: Perspectives Press, 1989. 32 p.
    A little Asian boy likes being cared for and having many playmates in the large house next to the sea where they all live, but misses the parents he can't remember. Flying to the United States, he still sees the sun, now kissing the earth instead of the sea, and is greeted by new parents who hold him as he has wanted parents to do.
European-American
Pre-K, Primary; Fiction

Turner, Ann. *Through Moon and Stars and Night Skies*. Illustrated by James Graham Hale. New York: Harper & Row, Publishers, 1990. 32 p. (A Charlotte Zolotow Book)

In this picture book story a little boy tells of the photos he was sent of his future family and house, of his long airplane flight, and of the fear and comforting he experienced during his first night in his new home.

European-American

Pre-K, Primary; Fiction

From Cambodia

Jenness, Aylette. *Families: A Celebration of Diversity, Commitment, and Love*. Photographs by author. Boston: Houghton Mifflin Company, 1990. 48 p.

In this look at seventeen families, Nhor, who is Cambodian, describes life with his foster father in California.

European-American

Intermediate, Older; Nonfiction

From China

Capone, Deb. *Dumplings Are Delicious*. Illustrated by Stan Jaskiel. Montauk, N.Y.: As Simple As That, 2005. 28 p.

Five-year-old Rain, who is adopted from China, loves to help her mother make jiaozi, Chinese dumplings. When she goes to school she discovers there are dumplings from many countries. But, whether they are ravioli from Italy, quenelles from France, pirozhki from Russia, or paranthas from India, they are all different, all dumplings, and all delicious.

European-American

Pre-K, Primary; Fiction

Capone, Deb. *Tooth Fairy Tales*. Illustrated by Stan Jaskiel. Montauk, N.Y.: As Simple As That, 2005. 32 p.

When five-year-old Rain loses her first tooth, she gets a quarter from the Tooth Fairy. She then discovers the different things that happen to lost teeth in Guatemala, in some African countries, in Russia, in India, and in her native China and that, whatever happens to them, they are always replaced by new teeth.

European-American

Pre-K, Primary; Fiction

Capone, Deb, and Craig Sherman. *Families Are Forever*. Illustrated by John McCoy. Montauk, N.Y.: As Simple As That, 2003. 36 p.

Rain has heard from her mother how as a baby she was adopted from China. With her stuffed hippo, who had been her mother's childhood friend, she relates her adoption story as depicted in pictures she has drawn.

European-American
Pre-K, Primary; Fiction

Coste, Marion. *Finding Joy*. Illustrated by Yong Chen. Honesdale, Pa.: Boyds Mills Press, 2006. 32 p.

Large double-page pictures illustrate this story of a Chinese baby whose family could not keep her because she was a girl and of the American family who had both room and a need for her.
European-American
Pre-K, Primary; Fiction

Cummings, Mary. *Three Names of Me*. Illustrated by Lin Wang. Morton Grove, Ill.: Albert Whitman & Company, 2006. 40 p.

A young girl adopted from China tells of the unremembered name she received as a baby from her mother, the name given her at a Chinese orphanage, and her American name. She presents scrapbook pages about her life and her likes.
European-American
Primary, Intermediate; Fiction

D'Antonio, Nancy. *Our Baby from China: An Adoption Story*. Morton Grove, Ill.: Albert Whitman & Company, 1997. 24 p.

Photographs record Nancy D'Antonio and her husband Gerald Lee Farnham's trip to China where, after seeing some of the country, they went to Ningbo to meet Ariela Xiangwei, the baby whom they adopted. The three of them went sightseeing, met other American parents and their adopted babies, and flew back to the United States where Ariela became part of her new extended family.
European-American
Pre-K, Primary; Nonfiction

Fry, Ying Ying, and Amy Klatzkin. *Kids Like Me in China*. Photographs by Brian Boyd, Terry M. Fry, and Ying Ying Fry. St. Paul: Yeong & Yeong Book Company, 2001. 48 p.

Numerous color photographs illustrate this presentation of eight-year-old Ying Ying Fry's trip with her parents to Changsha in Hunan Province, China, the province in which she was born. Every day for two weeks she visits the orphanage where she lived as a baby and even meets the caregiver who had looked after her. Ying Ying also visits and becomes acquainted with the children at a primary school and spends time enjoying the sights and restaurants of Changsha. She wonders about her birthfamily and what it would have been like to have grown up in the orphanage.
European-American
Primary, Intermediate; Nonfiction

Haugen, David M. and Matthew J. Box, eds. *Adoption*. Detroit: Greenhaven Press, 2006. 112 p. (Social Issues Firsthand)

In this book one narrative by Laurie Landry tells of the process she and her husband followed to adopt a baby from China and another gives an account by seventeen-year-old Thai, Tanawan Free,

explaining how it was not until high school that he came to accept his looking different from his Caucasian adoptive parents and classmates.
European-American
Older; Nonfiction

Kuklin, Susan. *Families*. Photographs by author. New York: Hyperion Books for Children, 2006. 40 p.

Text and color photographs present interviews with American children, who talk about their families. Their families include seven families with children of mixed race, ethnicity, or religion, with one also including a child adopted from Sierra Leone. In an eighth family a child has been adopted from China. In a ninth family an adopted American child is of a race different from that of one of her fathers.
European-American
Primary, Intermediate; Nonfiction

Lewis, Rose. *I Love You Like Crazy Cakes*. Illustrated by Jane Dyer. Boston: Little, Brown and Company, 2000. 32 p.

Watercolor paintings and text present a woman's trip to China to adopt a baby girl, their flight back together, and the baby's first day and night in her new home. This story of the mother's love is based on the author's own experience.
European-American
Pre-K, Primary; Fiction

Marsden, Carolyn, and Virginia Shin-Mui Loh. *The Jade Dragon*. Cambridge, Mass.: Candlewick Press, 2006. 176 p.
Second grader Ginny, whose parents are Chinese immigrants, longs to have Stephanie, the Chinese girl who has just come to her school, as a best friend. However, Stephanie, who has been adopted from China, has been brought up as an American girl and, despite her adoptive mother's wishes, wants nothing to do with anything Chinese. On the other hand, Ginny grows up in a home where everything is Chinese. Ginny constantly tries to please Stephanie and even secretly loans her the jade dragon which her parents have had carved in honor of Ginny's birth year. The two girls share their feelings about being Chinese and come to value their identities.
European-American
Primary, Intermediate; Fiction

McMahon, Patricia, and Conor Clarke McCarthy. *Just Add One Chinese Sister*. Illustrated by Karen A. Jerome. Honesdale, Pa.: Boyds Mills Press, 2005. 32 p.

Watercolor paintings enhance this story of the adoption of a little girl from Kunming, China. The text by Patricia McMahon, Claire's mother, is accompanied by the journal entries of her brother Conor. It describes the family's preparation for the adoption, their trip to China, their time in China with Claire, and their life together in the United States. The book presents Claire's initial fear as well as the feelings of her older brother.

European-American
Pre-K, Primary, Intermediate; Nonfiction

Molnar-Fenton, Stephan. *An Mei's Strange and Wondrous Journey*. Illustrated by Vivienne Flesher. New York: DK Publishing, 1998. 32 p. (A DK Ink Book)

This story, based on the experiences of the author's daughter An Mei, is illustrated with large colorful paintings. Assuming that even a newborn is aware of what's happening, the book is told from An Mei's standpoint. It traces her life from her birth on a train in China to her sixth birthday with her adoptive family in her American home.
European-American
Pre-K, Primary; Fiction

Okimoto, Jean Davies, and Elaine M. Aoki. *The White Swan Express: A Story about Adoption*. Illustrated by Meilo So. New York: Clarion Books, 2002. 32 p.

From Miami; Toronto; Minnetonka, Minnesota; and Vashon Island, Washington, prospective parents fly to China where they meet to travel to Guangzhou to receive their respective new daughters. They welcome their baby girls, travel back to their homes, and exchange cards during the holidays and at the Lunar New Year. In this picture book, the text includes some Mandarin phrases and an afterword elaborates upon the process of adopting Chinese children.
European-American; European-American and Christian; European-American and Jewish
Pre-K, Primary; Fiction

Peacock, Carol Antoinette. *Mommy Far, Mommy Near: An Adoption Story*. Illustrated by Shawn Costello Brownell. Morton Grove, Ill.: Albert Whitman & Company, 2000. 32 p.

A young girl, who was adopted from China as a baby, has many questions about her other mother and being adopted. She plays at adopting her doll and stuffed animals, knows that her little sister and the family dog are also adopted, feels sad when she sees a Chinese woman and her daughter, and throughout the story is comforted and supported by her adoptive mother.
European-American
Pre-K, Primary; Fiction

Rodowsky, Colby. *Ben and the Sudden Too-Big Family*. New York: Farrar Straus Giroux, 2007. 128 p.

When Ben is ten years old, his life begins to change. First, his widowed father Mitch marries Casey, who with her cat moves into their house. Ben likes both of them, so this change is okay. Next, the family adopts a baby girl from China. Ben enjoys going to China with his parents and, although having a little sister causes some adjustments, overall this is fine with Ben. However, when Ben must give up soccer camp to go on a trip with Casey's twenty-six family members, this is too much. Ben doesn't like the noise and activities of so many people and especially suffers from being corralled by an elderly complaining relative, who keeps him from being with the other boys. However, by the end of the trip Ben acknowledges that he is glad he came.
European-American
Intermediate; Fiction

Sonnenblick, Jordan. *Zen and the Art of Faking*. New York: Scholastic Press, 2007. 272 p.

San Lee, who is adopted from China, moves to yet another town after his father is finally arrested and imprisoned for fraud. San has to decide what identity he should assume in his new school. By circumstance and then through research and deception, he convinces his eighth-grade classmates that he is a Zen master. When San's lie is exposed, schoolmates turn against him, but he learns the real meaning of Zen.
European-American
Older; Fiction

Stoeke, Janet Morgan. *Waiting for May*. Illustrated by author. New York: Dutton Children's Books, 2005. 32 p.

In this picture book a young boy participates in the preparations for adopting a baby sister from China: talking to a social worker, getting fingerprinted, being in a family photo, having a shot, helping choose the baby's name, looking at her picture on the computer screen, and going with his parents on the long flight to China. Baby May cries and cries when she gets to their hotel room, but finally, entranced by the turtle buttons on the boy's shirt, wants to be with him—and the long wait is over.
European-American
Pre-K, Primary; Fiction

Thomas, Eliza. *The Red Blanket*. Illustrated by Joe Cepeda. New York: Scholastic Press, 2004. 32 p.

In this picture book a single woman, elated that she can adopt a baby girl from China, buys what the baby will need, including a red blanket. In her hotel room in China it is the comforting red blanket that stops the baby's crying. As the little girl grows older, the blanket is her treasured companion.
European-American
Pre-K, Primary; Fiction

Williams, Laura E. *Slant*. Minneapolis: Milkweed Editions, 2008. 168 p.

Thirteen-year-old Lauren and her five-year-old Chinese sister live with their adoptive English professor father in Connecticut. Their mother had died three years earlier. Lauren hates being called derogatory names by two classmates and even called "Slant" by Sean, the boy she has a crush on. She feels she can stop the abuse and be much happier by having surgery to change the shape of her Korean eyes. When Lauren discovers that her mother had committed suicide and that corrective surgery on her nose when she was thirteen had not stopped her depression, she decides against the surgery. Lauren discovers that she can stand up for herself, and she even gets Sean as a boyfriend.
English-European-American
Intermediate, Older; Fiction

Young, Ed. *My Mei Mei*. Illustrated by author. New York: Philomel Books, 2006. 36 p.

In this picture book story, which is based on the author's family, Antonia, who has been adopted from China, loves to play big sister. However, when at the age of three, she gets a little sister from China, Antonia is disappointed because the baby can't do anything. As they both grow older, Antonia comes to love being a real big sister.

Chinese and Italian
Pre-K, Primary; Fiction

From India

Krishnaswami, Uma. *Bringing Asha Home*. Illustrated by Jamel Akib. New York: Lee & Low Books, 2006. 32 p.

As Arun endures a seemingly endless wait for his new baby sister Asha to come from India, he continues to fold paper airplanes, using some of them as a mobile for her room, others to demonstrate his father flying to India and returning home with Asha, and a special decorated one to be given to Asha in India. When Asha arrives at the airport, thanks to her caregivers in India, she gives Arun a rakhi bracelet, the bracelet given by sisters to brothers on the Rakhi Indian holiday.

Indian and European-American
Pre-K, Primary; Fiction

Perkins, Mitali. *Monsoon Summer*. New York: Laurel-Leaf Books, 2004. 272 p.

Fifteen-year-old Jazz and her family go to Pune, India, for the summer so that her Indian mother can set up a clinic for pregnant women at the orphanage from which she was adopted. Jazz hates to leave Steve, her best friend and business partner whom she secretly loves. She also feels that because of a disastrous earlier experience she is unable to help others and should not volunteer at the orphanage. During the summer things change. Jazz's introverted father finds he enjoys teaching computer skills to the orphan's nuns, her ten-year-old brother temporarily gives up being a "bug" guy to become a "soccer" guy, and Jazz comes to realize that she is not only big, but beautiful, that she has a unique way of helping one of the orphans, and that she should tell Steve of her true feelings.

Nordic-American
Older; Fiction

Rosenberg, Maxine B. *Being Adopted*. Photographs by George Ancona. New York: Lothrop, Lee & Shepard Books, 1984. 48 p.

Illustrated with black-and-white photographs, this book features three children. Seven-year-old Rebecca, whose birthfather is African-American and birthmother European-American and Cheyenne, is the adopted daughter of an African-American father and a European-American mother. Ten-year-old Andrei was adopted from India by European-American parents, and Karin, the author's eight-year-old daughter, was adopted from Korea by her European-American parents. The book covers some of the questions and fears of younger adopted children: being afraid when they come to their adoptive families, wondering whether they caused their parents to give them up, fearing their adoptive parents will give them up, dreaming and wondering about their birthparents, and not looking like other members of their families. It also affirms that adopted children are just as much family members as are biological children.

European-American
Primary, Intermediate; Nonfiction

From Indonesia

Kurtz, Jane. *Jakarta Missing*. New York: Greenwillow Books, 2001. 272 p.

Twelve-year-old Dakar has just moved with her parents from Kenya to a small town in North Dakota and greatly misses her older, adopted sister Jakarta, who has remained behind. Shy, bookish, imaginative, and a worrier, Dakar wants most of all for her family to be together. However, when Jakarta does join the family, she resents having to leave Kenya. Then, as Jakarta starts to adjust to her new school, their mother leaves to be with her injured great-aunt, and their father, who constantly places humanitarian work ahead of the family, leaves to care for earthquake victims in Guatemala. In the concluding chapters Jakarta becomes a basketball star, Dakar learns about balancing safety and risk, and the family reaches a decision on its future.
European-American of African-American-Iranian-Japanese-Indonesian
Intermediate, Older; Fiction

From Japan

See   Nakahama, Manjiro

Say, Allen. *Allison*. Illustrated by author. Boston: Houghton Mifflin Company, 1997. 32 p.

When Allison, who has been adopted from Japan, realizes that her adoptive parents aren't her "real parents," she is so upset with them that she damages their treasured possessions. Then Allison realizes that the stray cat outside her window has no parents. She feels good when her parents agree to adopt the cat as part of their family.
European-American
Pre-K, Primary; Fiction

Singer, Marilyn, ed. *Face Relations: 11 Stories About Seeing Beyond Color*. New York: Simon & Schuster Books for Young Readers, 2004. 240 p.

The story "Black and White" by Kyoko Mori tells of Asako, a high school junior who lived in Japan until she was eight and then moved to Wisconsin to her stepfather's dairy farm. Asako joins two high school friends in an act of Halloween vandalism and it is she who is caught because the victim, elderly Mr. Hansen, recognizes her. Upset that she doesn't fit in because she is different, Asako comes to realize that however Mr. Hansen recognized her, she owes him an apology.
European-American and Japanese
Older; Fiction

From Pakistan

Perkins, Mitali. *First Daughter: Extreme American Makeover*. New York: Dutton Children's Books, 2007. 288 p.

This is the first book about sixteen-year-old Sameera (Sparrow) Righton, who was adopted from Pakistan at age three, who loves to blog to the twenty-nine friends who are on her personal website, and whose father is running for United States president. When Sparrow finishes the term at her Belgian school, she is immediately taken over by a fashion stylist, a hair and makeup expert, and a campaign communications specialist who want to convert her into Sammy, a giggly hip "American" girl who has an official website that is written for her. Sparrow sticks by her original plans to spend her vacation at her grandparents' farm in Ohio where she enjoys being home with them, her aunt, her uncle, her best friend and cousin Miranda, and the Labrador Jingle. She learns to work the milking machines and earns her driver's license. All this changes when reporters "invade" the farm, thereby creating increased stress on her grandmother who is recovering from a heart attack. Sparrow joins the campaign, but manages to sneak out of a Washington, D.C. hotel disguised as a Muslim woman to meet new friends who belong to the South Asian Republican Students' Association and starts her own new website which is available to the public.

European-American

Older; Fiction

Perkins, Mitali. *First Daughter: White House Rules*. New York: Dutton Children's Books, 2008. 224 p.

In this sequel to *First Daughter: Extreme American Makeover*, sixteen-year-old Sameera, her adoptive parents, and her visiting seventeen-year-old cousin Miranda have just moved into the White House. Placed in the midst of the perks and the restrictions of the White House, the girls manage to pursue their own lives. Together they endure home schooling, decorate rooms in the family quarters, and promote a romance between their mother's office manager and a Secret Service agent. Miranda earns money by baking family-recipe cookies, produces a movie about life in the White House, and befriends a Senator's son. Sameera continues blogging on her website, keeps up contact with Mariam, the Pakistani girl she had met during the campaign, and is able to meet her SARSA (South Asian Republican Students' Association) friends by wearing a burka to escape from her Secret Service agents. Together she and her mother manage to make an incognito visit to Mariam's public school, which Sameera then decides to attend. Throughout the story Sameera dreams of being with Bobby, one of the SARSA college students. They are separated because of his Hindu family's fear that his dating a Pakistani girl of Muslim birth will upset his ill grandfather in India. Bobby goes with his parents to India to be near his grandfather, who, before he dies, gives Bobby his blessing to court Sameera.

European-American

Older; Fiction

From Philippines

Porte, Barbara Ann. *Something Terrible Happened: A Novel*. New York: Orchard Books, 1994. 224 p.

When Gillian is ten, her mother, who is black, gets AIDS, and nothing is ever the same for Gillian and her family. Affected in both body and mind, her mother takes Gillian from New York City to Florida where they end up homeless. The two return to New York City where Gillian's grandmother tends to her daughter and sends Gillian to live with her late white father's brother and his family in Oak Ridge, Tennessee. Filled with resentment, worry, and loneliness, Gillian hates her life in that white

community and, after her mother's death, runs wild. Things improve both for Gillian's grandmother as she takes up running and graduate work and for Gillian when she learns of the difficult pasts of a "cousin" who had been adopted from the Philippines and of her Uncle Henry.
American
Older; Fiction

From Russia

George, Jean Craighead. *Julie*. Illustrated by Wendell Minor. New York: HarperCollins Publishers, 1994. 240 p.

In this sequel to *Julie of the Wolves*, Julie, who is now fourteen, is living in Kangik with her father Kapugen and his new wife Ellen. Trapped with Ellen in a blizzard, Julie comes to accept her white stepmother. However, Julie knows that Kapugen was the one who killed her adoptive wolf father Amaroq and will kill his son Kapu and the new wolf pack in order to protect his herd of musk ox that sustains the Alaskan village's economy. Journeying to find the wolf pack, Julie manages to lead it away from the village to a place where the wolves can feed on moose. Kapugen and Ellen name their new baby boy Amaroq; Julie falls in love with Peter, an Eskimo from Siberia; and when the wolves come back, Kapugen finally returns to his Eskimo ways and spares them.
American Eskimo of Russian Eskimo
Intermediate, Older; Fiction

From South Korea

See   Cho, Stephanie
       Dawson, Toby
       Robinson, Catherine (Katy) Jeanne
       Yung, Kim So

Adler, C. S. *Youn Hee & Me*. San Diego: Harcourt Brace & Company, 1995. 192 p.

When it is discovered that Caitlin's adopted younger brother Simon has an older sister still living in Korea, Caitlin welcomes her mother's decision to adopt her. However, the going is rough. Youn Hee feels uncomfortable in her new surroundings, regards Simon as her property, and feels Caitlin is a bad influence on him. Caitlin is jealous of Youn Hee's attention to Simon and upset that Youn Hee rejects her. Then, on Caitlin's twelfth birthday, Youn Hee gives her the best gift: she calls Caitlin her sister.
European-American
Intermediate; Fiction

Angel, Ann. *Real for Sure Sister*. Illustrated by Joanne Bowring. Fort Wayne, Ind.: Perspectives Press, 1988. 72 p.

Nine-year-old Amanda is adopted as are her brothers Nicky and Joey, who is Mexican Indian. Although she adores her little brothers, she has conflicting feelings about Stevi, the biracial (black/white)

baby her family is planning to adopt. Amanda initially wants another brother, not a sister, and then tries to ignore Stevi in case the adoption doesn't go through. She shares her concern with her parents, who are white, and with her best friend, who has been adopted from Korea. It is a happy day when Amanda's entire family goes to court, and Stevi becomes her real sister.
European-American
Primary; Fiction

Boyd, Brian. *When You Were Born in Korea: A Memory Book for Children Adopted from Korea.* Photographs by Stephen Wunrow. St. Paul: Yeong & Yeong Book Company, 1993. 48 p.

Text and photographs show the process that brings Korean children to their adoptive American parents. It tells of birthmothers, birthmother's homes, baby's homes, foster homes, and adoption agencies and emphasizes the many people who care for and about the children: birthparents, nurses, social workers, foster parents, doctors, trip escorts, and Traveler's Aid Society volunteers.
European-American
Primary, Intermediate; Nonfiction

Bunting, Eve. *Jin Woo.* Illustrated by Chris P. Soentpiet. New York: Clarion Books, 2001. 32 p.

Davey, who is adopted, has reservations when his parents adopt a baby from Korea—until his mother reads him a letter "the baby" has written to him.
European-American
Pre-K, Primary; Fiction

Czech, Jan M. *An American Face.* Illustrated by Frances Clancy. Washington, D.C.: Child and Family Press, 2000. 32 p.

Jessie, who is adopted from Korea, wonders what kind of American face he will get when he becomes an American citizen. He discovers that Americans have all kinds of faces and that he will keep his own.
European-American
Pre-K, Primary; Fiction

Czech, Jan M. *The Coffee Can Kid.* Illustrated by Maurie J. Manning. Washington, D.C.: Child & Family Press, 2002. 24 p.

Six-year-old Annie loves to hold the blue coffee can and hear her father tell the story about her early life: about how she was born faraway to a mother too young and poor to care for her; about being taken by her mother to a baby home for adoption; and about the coffee can that contains her baby picture taken on that day. The coffee can also holds the letter her birthmother wrote that tells Annie of her continuing love.
European-American
Pre-K, Primary; Fiction

Erlbach, Arlene. *The Families Book: True Stories about Real Kids and the People They Live With and Love.* Photographs by Stephen J. Carrera. Illustrated by Lisa Wagner. Minneapolis: Free Spirit Publishing, 1996. 120 p.

In a section of this book, children tell about their families, that include a family in which the father is Lutheran and the mother Jewish; a family in which the father is African-American and the mother Caucasian; a family with four children in which Caucasian parents have adopted a biracial American girl and a boy from Romania; and a family with Caucasian parents and eleven children, six of whom were adopted from Korea.
European-American
Intermediate; Nonfiction

Fisher, Iris L. *Katie-Bo: An Adoption Story*. Illustrated by Miriam Schaer. New York: Adama Books, 1988. 56 p.

Full-page color paintings illustrate this story of two brothers who wait for their new baby sister to arrive from Korea, welcome her, and go with their family to a judge for the formal adoption.
European-American
Pre-K, Primary; Fiction

Girard, Linda Walvoord. *We Adopted You, Benjamin Koo*. Illustrated by Linda Shute. Niles, Ill.: Albert Whitman & Company, 1989. 32 p.

Based on the experiences of Benjamin Koo Andrews, this book tells of his adoption from Korea as an infant, the difficult time he had in second grade when he finally realized what his adoption meant and wanted to find his birthmother, the adoption of his three-year-old sister from Brazil when he was eight, the teasing by some children when he is nine, and, throughout, the support of his insightful parents.
European-American
Primary, Intermediate; Nonfiction

Gravelle, Karen, and Susan Fischer. *Where Are My Birth Parents? A Guide for Teenage Adoptees*. New York: Walker and Company, 1993. 144 p.

This book includes the account of a teenager who went to Korea with her adoptive mother to search for her birthmother. It tells of the problems she had had because she was different, of the reactions of her adoptive parents to her search, of the disappointments she suffered when a number of Korean women did not turn out to be her mother, and of her increased closeness to her adoptive mother.
European-American Jewish
Older; Nonfiction

Hautman, Pete, and Mary Logue. *Doppelganger*. New York: G. P. Putnam's Sons, 2008. 176 p. (The Bloodwater Mysteries)

This third book in *The Bloodwater Mysteries* series begins when thirteen-year-old Brian's picture appears in the Bloodwater, Minnesota newspaper for winning a paper-airplane design contest. At the same time high school reporter Roni discovers a picture on the Internet of abducted Bryce Doblemun whose age-progressed photo looks like Brian and who was also adopted from Korea. Roni and Brian try to figure out whether Brian was kidnapped from his first adoptive home, where Bryce Doblemun is now, and why strangers are so interested in Brian. The two friends encounter real dangers, but finally

discover that "Bryce Doblemun" is Brian's twin brother who, with their birthmother, must continue to remain missing.
European-American
Intermediate, Older; Fiction

Hautman, Pete, and Mary Logue. *Skullduggery*. New York: G. P. Putnam's Sons, 2007. 192 p. (The Bloodwater Mysteries)

In this book, the second in *The Bloodwater Mysteries* series, high school reporter Roni and Korean freshman Brian find an injured archaeological professor, Andrew Dart, in a cave on Indian Bluff. Dr. Dart is an opponent of the bluff's being turned into a condo development. Roni and Brian use their investigative skills to discover whether the bluff was really an Indian burial ground, who attacked Dr. Dart, and who trapped them in the cave. Their suspect list includes condo developer Fred Bloodwater and his son Eric, who have moved with the rest of their family into Bloodwater House, and Dr. Dart's ex-fiancée, but, as the young detectives discover, the guilty party is none of the above.
European-American
Intermediate, Older; Fiction

Hautman, Pete, and Mary Logue. *Snatched*. New York: G. P. Putnam's Sons, 2006. 208 p. (The Bloodwater Mysteries)

This is the first in a series of mysteries set in the fictional town of Bloodwater, Minnesota. Roni, a pushy reporter for her high school newspaper, meets Brian, a thirteen-year-old freshman who has been adopted from South Korea and sometimes disrupts the school with his science experiments. The unlikely pair decides to investigate the beating and subsequent abduction of a schoolmate, who lives in Bloodwater House which is rumored to be under a curse. Despite being grounded by their parents, they manage to pursue clues, but even they are surprised by what really happened.
European-American
Intermediate, Older; Fiction

Kent, Rose. *Kimchi & Calamari*. New York: HarperCollins Publishers, 2007. 240 p.

Everything seems to take a turn for the worse when eighth grader Joseph Calderaro is assigned a paper about his heritage. Adopted from Pusan, Korea, as an infant, fourteen-year-old Joseph is part of a loving Italian family that regards him as being Italian. Knowing virtually nothing about his birthparents, Joseph writes his essay about a Korean Olympics marathon gold medal winner whom he claims was his grandfather. Unfortunately, Joseph's essay is chosen to be an entrant in a national essay contest. Joseph must confess his lie to his parents and teacher; the girl whom he has a crush on rejects him; and he is greatly disappointed when, after thinking he had found his birthmother on the Internet, he learns he is mistaken. Fortunately, Joseph realizes that the girl he jokes around with is the girl he likes; she agrees to go with him to the Farewell Formal; and not only do his parents decide to help him with his adoption search, but also he and his father will travel with a group of adoptees to Pusan. Joseph even gets an A on his essay rewrite in which he describes himself as an ethnic sandwich.
Italian-American
Intermediate, Older; Fiction

Kraus, Joanna Halpert. *Tall Boy's Journey*. Illustrated by Karen Ritz. Minneapolis: Carolrhoda Books, 1992. 48 p.

When Kim Moo Yong is in the third grade, his grandmother dies. Since he is an orphan, he is sent from Korea to live with a couple in the United States. Kim Moo Yong is dismayed and scared by what he encounters: a teddy bear, strange food, hot water for bathing, a room where he is to sleep by himself, staring photographs, the absence of spirit posts, and no protection from the tigers which might come down from the mountains. With the help of a Korean man who works with his adoptive father and a neighbor boy who takes him tobogganing, Kim Moo Yong begins to feels better.
European-American
Primary, Intermediate; Fiction

Kroll, Virginia. *Beginnings: How Families Come to Be*. Illustrated by Stacey Schuett. Morton Grove, Ill.: Albert Whitman & Company, 1994. 32 p.

In this look at six American families, one family includes a little girl adopted as a baby from Korea by a father of color and a European-American mother and another family in which a girl of color, who had been in foster homes, is adopted by a European-American couple.
Of color and European-American
Pre-K, Primary; Fiction

Lee, Marie G. *If It Hadn't Been for Yoon Jun*. Boston: Houghton Mifflin Company, 1993. 144 p.

Adopted as a baby, seventh grader Alice hates her Korean looks and background. Wanting to be just American like everyone else, she is upset when Yoon Jun, a chubby Korean immigrant, joins her class and when her father wants her to befriend him. However, after being paired with Yoon Jun for an International Day project, Alice comes to appreciate both Yoon Jun and her Korean heritage.
Norwegian-American
Intermediate; Fiction

Pellegrini, Nina. *Families Are Different*. Illustrated by author. New York: Holiday House, 1991. 32 p.

In this picture book six-year-old Nico, who was adopted from Korea as a baby, is concerned because she does not look like her white parents. When her mother points out that there are different kinds of families, Nico observes for herself that this is true.
European-American
Pre-K, Primary; Fiction

Rosenberg, Maxine B. *Being Adopted*. Photographs by George Ancona. New York: Lothrop, Lee & Shepard Books, 1984. 48 p.

Illustrated with black-and-white photographs, this book features three children. Seven-year-old Rebecca, whose birthfather is African-American and birthmother European-American and Cheyenne, is the adopted daughter of an African-American father and a European-American mother. Ten-year-old Andrei was adopted from India by European-American parents, and Karin, the author's eight-year-old daughter, was adopted from Korea by her European-American parents. The book covers some of the questions and fears of younger adopted children: being afraid when they come to their adoptive families, wondering whether they caused their parents to give them up, fearing their adoptive parents will give them up, dreaming and wondering about their birthparents, and not looking like other members of their families. It also affirms that adopted children are just as much family members as are biological children.

European-American

Primary, Intermediate; Nonfiction

Rosenberg, Maxine B. *Growing Up Adopted*. Afterword by Lois Ruskai Melina. New York: Bradbury Press, 1989. 128 p.

In this book eight children and six adults relate their experiences and thoughts about growing up as adopted children. The four children who were adopted by parents of a different race, in each case European-American, are Josh, adopted as was a little sister from Colombia; Amy, who was adopted from Ecuador; Mark, who was adopted from Korea; and Shakine, an African-American boy who was born with spinal bifida in the United States and lives in a family of seven children, four of whom are adopted and of ethnicities other than their adoptive parents. Three of the adults are of a different race than their European-American parents. Chris was adopted from France as was her brother, Sam was adopted from Korea and has an adopted sister of mixed race and two non-adopted brothers, and Jamie, an African-European-American, has two sisters who are not adopted and four adopted siblings of mixed race.

European-American

Intermediate, Older; Nonfiction

Sobol, Harriet Langsam. *We Don't Look Like Our Mom and Dad*. Photographs by Patricia Agre. New York: Coward-McCann, 1984. 32 p.

Black-and-white photographs illustrate this look at the Levin family: Mr. and Mrs. Levin and their sons, eleven-year-old Joshua and ten-year-old Eric, who were adopted from Korea. The book describes the boys' activities, the day they became American citizens, and their questioning about their appearances, their birthmothers, and the reasons they were adopted.

European-American

Primary, Intermediate; Nonfiction

Taylor, Theodore. *Tuck Triumphant*. New York: Avon Books, 1992. 160 p.

Fourteen-year-old Helen and her family are shocked to discover that Chok-Do, the six-year-old boy they are adopting from Korea, is profoundly deaf and cannot speak. The challenge Chok-Do poses becomes increasingly apparently as he likes to wander off, once walking three miles along a Los Angeles street before being found by the police and another time hiding in a storm pipe until Helen and the family's blind Labrador, Tuck, rescue him as a thunderstorm strikes. The family has several options such as putting Chok-Do in an orphanage, having him adopted by a Korean family, or enrolling him in a boarding school for deaf children. After a harrowing experience in a Colorado national forest where Tuck saves both Chok-Do and Helen from drowning, Helen's mother decides to take a two-year leave from her job in order to teach Chok-Do sign language. This book is a sequel to *The Trouble with Tuck*.

European-American
Intermediate, Older; Fiction

Waybill, Marjorie Ann. *Chinese Eyes*. Illustrated by Pauline Cutrell. Scottdale, Pa.: Herald Press, 1974. 40 p.

First-grader Becky, who has been adopted from Korea, is upset when a third-grade boy calls her "Chinese Eyes." When she gets home, her mother tells her about Chinese children and the beauty of their eyes—and of hers.
European-American
Pre-K, Primary; Fiction

Wilkinson, Sook, and Nancy Fox, eds. *After the Morning Calm: Reflections of Korean Adoptees*. Bloomfield Hills, Mich.: Sunrise Ventures, 2002. 192 p.

In this book nine men and seventeen women present their experiences and feelings about being adopted from South Korea. One went to live with a Dutch family, another was adopted by Norwegians, and the remainder became the children of American parents. Their ages at adoption ranged from infancy to teenager. One suffered in Korea because he was the son of a Korean woman and a white American soldier. Another was the subject of her mother Marjorie Ann Waybill's fictional book. All were succeeding as adults. Their writings describe the impact of looking different from their peers, the difficulties of reconciling two cultures, and the effects of visiting South Korea. The book contains photographs and an appended resource section.
American of South Korean; American of European-American-South Korean
Older; Nonfiction

Williams, Laura E. *Slant*. Minneapolis: Milkweed Editions, 2008. 168 p.

Thirteen-year-old Lauren and her five-year old Chinese sister live with their adoptive English professor father in Connecticut. Their mother had died three years earlier. Lauren hates being called derogatory names by two classmates and even called "Slant" by Sean, the boy she has a crush on. She feels she can stop the abuse and be much happier by having surgery to change the shape of her Korean eyes. When Lauren discovers that her mother had committed suicide and that corrective surgery on her nose when she was thirteen had not stopped her depression, she decides against the surgery. Lauren discovers that she can stand up for herself, and she even gets Sean as a boyfriend.
English-European-American
Intermediate, Older; Fiction

From Thailand

Haugen, David M. and Matthew J. Box, eds. *Adoption*. Detroit: Greenhaven Press, 2006. 112 p. (Social Issues Firsthand)

In this book one narrative by Laurie Landry tells of the process she and her husband followed to adopt a baby from China and another gives an account by seventeen-year-old Thai, Tanawan Free,

explaining how it was not until high school that he came to accept his looking different from his Caucasian adoptive parents and classmates.
European-American
Older; Nonfiction

From Vietnam

See   Steiner, Matthew Ray

Cross, Gilbert B. *Mystery at Loon Lake*. New York: Aladdin Books, 1986. 144 p.
Twelve-year-old Jeff, his twelve-year-old adopted brother Nguyen, and their new friend Jenny explore an underground tunnel and try to get proof that it is being used to smuggle pre-Columbian art from New Hampshire to Canada. In the process they are trapped in a dilapidated dormitory, almost struck by a boulder that is pushed down a cliff, saved from poisoning by a raccoon, and captured by the smugglers. Fortunately, all ends well.
European-American
Intermediate, Older; Fiction

Nickman, Steven L. *The Adoption Experience: Stories and Commentaries*. New York: Julian Messner, 1985. 192 p.
This book includes two stories, with accompanying commentaries, about interracial adoption. In "The Ghosts in the Box" a boy who has been adopted from Vietnam after his parents have been killed during the Vietnam War struggles to accept his adoptive parents and American life, especially the celebration of the Fourth of July. In "Hormones Have No Color" the Jewish adoptive father of an African-American teenager struggles with his feelings when the boy makes friends in a neighboring black community.
European-American
Older; Fiction

Pettit, Jayne. *My Name Is San Ho*. New York: Scholastic, 1992. 160 p.
This is a story of the Vietnamese boy San Ho. It tells of his early years during the Vietnam War: of the spreading by the government and the Americans of the napalm that destroys his village's crops, of the death of the soldier father he never knew, of the air attacks with their artillery fire, and of the Viet Cong who raid his village and murder his teacher. To keep him safer, San Ho's mother takes him at age nine to Saigon to live with a friend, but in Saigon there are air raids and refugees and San Ho greatly misses his mother. As a twelve year old, San Ho, together with other Vietnamese children, takes the long flight to Philadelphia where he is reunited with his mother and meets her new husband, an American marine. San Ho has a very difficult time adjusting to the different life of Americans, to the English language, and to his stepfather. Thanks to friends and his teacher, San Ho never forgets Vietnam, but comes to feel that America is his home.
European-American and Vietnamese
Intermediate; Fiction

Sugarman, Brynn Olenberg. *Rebecca's Journey Home*. Illustrated by Michelle Shapiro. Minneapolis: Kar-Ben Publishing, 2006. 32 p.

As Jacob and Gabriel eagerly await and then welcome a baby sister from Vietnam, they learn that she is many things: Le Thi Hong (Vietnamese), Rebecca Rose (American), and Rivka Shoshanah (Jewish)— and will be more things as she pursues her interests.
European-American Jewish
Pre-K, Primary; Fiction

From Canada

See   Sainte-Marie, Beverly (Buffy)

From Central America

From El Salvador

Rosen, Michael J. *Bonesy and Isabel*. Illustrated by James Ransome. San Diego: Harcourt Brace & Company, 1995. 36 p.

When Spanish-speaking Isabel comes from El Salvador to live in the farmhouse on Sunbury Road, she enters a place where, regardless of their language, the birds, the horses, the cats, and the nine stray dogs who had been abandoned recognize that the English-speaking man and woman who live there care about them. Isabel becomes especially close to Bonesy, the twelve-year-old Labrador retriever. When after three weeks he dies, Isabel discovers that there is no need for a shared language to express grief and caring.
European-American
Primary, Intermediate; Fiction

From Guatemala

Alderman, Bruce, ed. *Interracial Relationships*. Farmington Hills, Mich.: Greenhaven Press, 2007. 112 p. (Social Issues Firsthand)

In a narrative reproduced from Pacific Citizen, writer Stewart David Ikeda tells how the adoption of a Guatemalan baby by his Caucasian uncle and Japanese-American aunt prompted him to think about his Japanese-American culture and about the possible culturally mixed identity of all Americans.
European-American and Japanese-American
Older; Nonfiction

García, Cristina. *I Wanna Be Your Shoebox*. New York: Simon & Schuster Books for Young Readers, 2008. 208 p.

Eighth-grader Zumi loves surfing, her baby cousin adopted from Guatemala, and playing clarinet in her middle school orchestra—and even spearheads the orchestra's money-raising punk-reggae concert

to save it from being eliminated. However, most of all she treasures her cancer-ridden grandfather and the story of his life which he tells her before dying.
Guatemalan-Cuban
Older; Fiction

Katz, Karen. *The Colors of Us*. Illustrated by author. New York: Henry Holt and Company, 1999. 28 p.

Seven-year-old Lena, who has been adopted from Guatemala, paints pictures of her friends, who are of all shades of brown, such as chocolate brown and butterscotch.
European-American
Pre-K, Primary; Fiction

Katz, Karen. *Over the Moon: An Adoption Tale*. Illustrated by author. New York: Henry Holt and Company, 1997. 28 p.

This picture book presents in its text and illustrations the anticipation an American couple feels waiting for their daughter to be born and the joy, after flying to a distant country, of becoming her parents. The author's note and the jacket of the sequel, *The Colors of Us*, reveal that the book is about their daughter Lena, who was adopted from Guatemala.
European-American
Pre-K, Primary; Fiction

From Honduras

Schwartz, Perry. *Carolyn's Story: A Book about an Adopted Girl*. Photographs by author. Minneapolis: Lerner Publications Company, 1996. 40 p.

Colorful photographs and text present the adoption of the author's daughter from Honduras, her return with her adoptive parents two years later to adopt the baby who became her brother, her activities as a nine-year-old, and her feelings about adoption. The book contains information about adoption, a glossary, a reading list, and a resource list.
European-American of Spanish-Honduran and Mayan
Intermediate; Nonfiction

From Europe

From Croatia

Atinsky, Steve. *Trophy Kid or How I Was Adopted by the Rich and Famous*. New York: Delacorte Press, 2008. 192 p.

When he was three, shortly after his father was reported dead, Joe's mother and sister were killed in the fighting in Dubrovnik, Croatia, an event recorded and broadcast worldwide. Joe became the object of a bidding war and was finally awarded for adoption at the price of $3.2 million to the newly-married famous actress Greta Powell and the movie-celebrity, human-rights crusader, and potential

Senate candidate Robert Francis. Since then Joe's life has been scripted to reflect his gratitude to his adoptive parents and enhance their reputations. Now thirteen, Joe is asked, together with a ghost-writer Tom Dolan, to write his obviously complimentary autobiography. In Tom, Joe finds a friend to whom he can express his true feelings about life with Greta and Robert, his grief about losing his family, and his feeling that Robert and Greta are keeping him from learning about his father, who might be alive. Thanks to Tom, the family goes to Croatia where Robert's attitude changes, and Joe visits his mother and sister's graves, learns that his father was killed, and comes to accept his adoptive family.
European-American
Intermediate, Older; Fiction

From England

See   Collier, Samuel
       Savage, Thomas
       Spelman, Henry

Fitz-Gibbon, Sally. *Lizzie's Storm*. Illustrated by Muriel Wood. Allston, Mass.: Fitzhenry & Whiteside, 2004. 68 p. (New Beginnings)

   Illustrated with color paintings, this book tells of Lizzie, who comes from London to live in North Dakota with her aunt's family because her parents have been killed in a car accident. Lizzie has a difficult time adjusting to the hardships of 1931 farm life on the prairie: the lack of conveniences such as indoor plumbing, the constant chores, and the silence of her relatives. She is further upset by her tenth birthday being forgotten and by the frightening dust storm outside. However, feeling that her aunt needs her help, Lizzie fastens one end of a rope to the house door and, holding onto the rope, braves the storm to rescue her injured aunt. Lizzie realizes then that her new family loves her. A glossary, a reading list, and an index are appended.
European-American and English
Intermediate; Fiction

Levin, Betty. *Brother Moose*. New York: Greenwillow Books, 1990. 224 p.

   When Nell, an orphan from England, is sent in the 1870s to live with a couple in Canada's Maritime Provinces, she discovers that her prospective mother, Mrs. Fowler, has moved to Maine to have a baby. Next Nell is kidnapped by robbers, escapes, and travels with her fellow orphan Louisa, an Indian named Joe Pennowit, and his twelve year old grandson to Maine. However, because Joe mistakenly thinks he has killed one of the men who kidnapped Nell, the four leave the road to escape the robbers and the police. On their difficult journey they travel by wagon, by sleigh, and by an abandoned train car, which is pulled by their horse and a moose they have tamed. Nell finally reaches Mrs. Fowler, but her adoption hopes take a surprising turn.
American Passamaquoddy or Penobscot or Canadian-Micmac; European-American
Older; Fiction

From France

Ringgold, Faith. *Bonjour, Lonnie*. Illustrated by author. New York: Hyperion Books for Children, 1996. 32 p.

Thanks to a Love Bird that flies into Lonnie's window one night, he discovers his family background. During World War I his paternal grandfather was an African-American soldier in France. There he met and married Lonnie's French grandmother and became an opera singer. Their son (Lonnie's father) married a Jewish French woman. During World War II he died fighting for France and, after Lonnie's mother gave him to a friend for his safety, she became a victim of the Nazis. Subsequently, Lonnie was taken to the United States where he was adopted by an African-American couple, Aunt Connie and Uncle Bates. This picture book is a companion book to *Dinner at Aunt Connie's House*.
African-American of Jewish and non-Jewish African-American-French
Primary; Fiction

Ringgold, Faith. *Dinner at Aunt Connie's House*. Illustrated by author. New York: Hyperion Books for Children, 1993. 32 p.

This picture book is based on the artist-author's "The Dinner Quilt", a painted story quilt, which has been exhibited in museums. When African-American Melody visits her Aunt Connie, she meets her aunt's adopted son, Lonnie, a black boy with red hair and green eyes. Before the family dinner, they go into the attic where they see Aunt Connie's portraits of twelve famous African-American women, paintings that speak to the children about their subjects' accomplishments. Lonnie's heritage is revealed in a companion book, *Bonjour, Lonnie*.
African-American of Jewish and non-Jewish African-American-French
Primary; Fiction

Rosenberg, Maxine B. *Growing Up Adopted*. Afterword by Lois Ruskai Melina. New York: Bradbury Press, 1989. 128 p.

In this book eight children and six adults relate their experiences and thoughts about growing up as adopted children. The four children who were adopted by parents of a different race, in each case European-American, are Josh, adopted as was a little sister from Colombia; Amy, who was adopted from Ecuador; Mark, who was adopted from Korea; and Shakine, an African-American boy who was born with spinal bifida in the United States and lives in a family of seven children, four of whom are adopted and of ethnicities other than their adoptive parents. Three of the adults are of a different race than their European-American parents. Chris was adopted from France as was her brother, Sam was adopted from Korea and has an adopted sister of mixed race and two non-adopted brothers, and Jamie, an African-European-American, has two sisters who are not adopted and four adopted siblings of mixed race.
European-American
Intermediate, Older; Nonfiction

From Germany

Griffis, Molly Levite. *The Feester Filibuster*. Austin: Eakin Press, 2002. 244 p.

It is in this sequel to *The Rachel Resistance* that fifth grader Simon Green makes his appearance. He tells his classmates that he was adopted as an infant and doesn't know his birth date [although in the sequel, *Simon Says*, it turns out this is the past he has been told to say and has even come to believe]. Simon achieves a truce between his classmates, John Alan Feester and Rachel Dalton. The three friends, who live in Oklahoma, experience World War II with its rationing, defense plants, Japanese detention camps, war stamps, newspaper collecting, and friends and family members (including Simon's father) serving in the military. A glossary is included.
German and German-American of Jewish Polish-German
Intermediate; Fiction

Griffis, Molly Levite. *Simon Says*. Austin: Eakin Press, 2004. 272 p.

This book, which is a sequel to *The Feester Filibuster*, is set during World War II. When eleven-year-old Simon Green, who is Jewish, sees a postcard from his birthfather, he is haunted by the thought of really being Simon Singer who was sent from Germany to the United States at age six to escape the horrors of Nazi Germany. The memories he had been able to dismiss reapppear, and he is terrified that the Nazis are coming after him. Simon and his friends Rachel Dalton and Kenneth Stumbling Bear set out to determine who is drawing swastikas at their playground meeting place and outside a Jewish man's store, but discover it is Kenneth's four-year-old brother who is duplicating a Kiowa sacred symbol. Simon finally discusses his past with his new mother; his new father returns with a Purple Heart from the Pacific; Simon learns that his birthparents and grandmother have died; and he is reunited with his older sister.
German and German-American of Jewish Polish-German
Intermediate; Fiction

From Romania

Erlbach, Arlene. *The Families Book: True Stories about Real Kids and the People They Live With and Love*. Photographs by Stephen J. Carrera. Illustrated by Lisa Wagner. Minneapolis: Free Spirit Publishing, 1996. 120 p.

In a section of his book, children tell about their families, which include a family in which the father is Lutheran and the mother Jewish; a family in which the father is African-American and the mother Caucasian; a family with four children in which Caucasian parents have adopted a biracial American girl and a boy from Romania; and a family with Caucasian parents and eleven children, six of whom were adopted from Korea.
European-American
Intermediate; Nonfiction

From Spain

Foreman, Michael, and Richard Seaver. *The Boy Who Sailed with Columbus*. Illustrated by Michael Foreman. New York: Arcade Publishing, 1992. 72 p.

An orphan, twelve-year-old Leif sails as a ship's boy on Christopher Columbus's first voyage to the West Indies. His admiration for Columbus changes when Leif sees that Columbus is taking some of the island natives back to Spain. As a punishment for a mistake he had made, Leif is left behind with some of Columbus's crew on one of the islands. There he is kidnapped by Arawak, who attack the island fort. Leif then serves as the eyes for a wise blind Secotan healer who was with the Arawak and travels with him among different tribes. Becoming the medicine man's successor, Leif, who is half Viking, marries a Secotan. As a grandfather in the Secotan village [which was probably in present day North Carolina on or near Roanoke Island], Leif sees approaching European ships and leads the Secotan villagers westward to avoid possible capture.
Secotan of half-Viking
Intermediate; Fiction

From Latin America. See also From Central America, From Mexico, From South America

Alvarez, Julia. *Finding Miracles*. New York: Alfred A. Knopf, 2004. 272 p.

Fifteen-year-old Milly was adopted as an infant from an unnamed Latin-American country when her Jewish father and her Mormon mother were there in the Peace Corps. Milly prefers to keep her adoption a secret and not think about it. However, when Pablo, who is from the same country, comes to her Vermont high school, Milly's outlook gradually changes. Through his friendship and a visit to her birth country with him and his parents, Milly comes to an increased understanding and appreciation of herself and her American family.
European-American Jewish and European-American Mormon
Older; Fiction

From Mexico

Angel, Ann. *Real for Sure Sister*. Illustrated by Joanne Bowring. Fort Wayne, Ind.: Perspectives Press, 1988. 72 p.

Nine-year-old Amanda is adopted as are her brothers Nicky and Joey, who is Mexican Indian. Although she adores her little brothers, she has conflicting feelings about Stevi, the biracial (black/white) baby her family is planning to adopt. Amanda initially wants another brother, not a sister, and then tries to ignore Stevi in case the adoption doesn't go through. She shares her concern with her parents, who are white, and with her best friend, who has been adopted from Korea. It is a happy day when Amanda's entire family goes to court and Stevi becomes her real sister.
European-American
Primary; Fiction

Resau, Laura. *Red Glass*. New York: Delacorte Press, 2007. 304 p.

This novel details the transformation of Sophie from Sophie la Delicada (the Delicate whose life is restricted by allergies, worries, and fears) into Sophie la Fuerte (the Strong, who undertakes and completes a very dangerous journey). Sixteen-year-old Sophie lives in Tucson with her English mother, her Mexican stepfather, and her great-aunt Dika, a Bosnian refugee. Then the family takes in five-year-old Pablo whose parents have died as his family tried to escape from Mexico. A year later, so that Pablo can see his relatives and decide where he wants to live, Sophie, Pablo, and Dika join Dika's boyfriend Mr. Lorenzo and his son Ángel, who are bound, via Mexico, for Guatemala to see whether Flor Blanca, their wife and mother, respectively, is alive and to find her jewels. The group spends a week in Pablo's Oaxaca village where Sophie and Ángel express their feelings for each other. Mr. Lorenzo and Ángel then go on to Guatemala, but are unable to return as Ángel is savagely attacked and their passports and money stolen. With Dika injured from a fall, Sophie travels by herself to Guatemala, a trip which is not at all safe, especially for a white girl. In Guatemala Ángel shares a hospital room with one of his attackers, Flor Blanca's fate is revealed, and Ángel decides whether to remain in Guatemala. Likewise, in Mexico Pablo decides whether he will stay there.
Mexican and English
Older; Fiction

Schreck, Karen Halvorsen. *Lucy's Family Tree*. Illustrated by Stephen Gassler III. Gardiner, Maine: Tilbury House Publishers, 2007. 40 p.

Because she has been adopted from Mexico, Lucy doesn't want to do a class family tree assignment. Accepting her parents' challenge to find three families that are the same, she fails at first when she encounters families with a stay-at-home father, a stepfather, and a child who has died as well as a family which is Jewish. However, Lucy finally comes up with three families that are the same: all have adopted Mexican children. Then, with her parents' help, Lucy creates her own unique Tree of Life.
European-American
Intermediate; Fiction

From South America

From Brazil

Girard, Linda Walvoord. *We Adopted You, Benjamin Koo*. Illustrated by Linda Shute. Niles, Ill.: Albert Whitman & Company, 1989. 32 p.

Based on the experiences of Benjamin Koo Andrews, this book tells of his adoption from Korea as an infant, the difficult time he had in second grade when he finally realized what his adoption meant and wanted to find his birthmother, the adoption of his three-year-old sister from Brazil when he was eight, the teasing by some children when he is nine, and, throughout, the support of his insightful parents.
European-American
Primary, Intermediate; Nonfiction

Hausherr, Rosmarie. *Celebrating Families*. New York: Scholastic Press, 1997. 32 p.

Among the families celebrated in this book are Jahsee's, whose father is from the Virgin Islands and whose mother is Norwegian-American, and Alexandra's, who was adopted from Brazil by two European-American mothers. The book is illustrated with photographs.
European-American
Primary, Intermediate; Nonfiction

Miner, Chalise. *Rain Forest Girl: More Than an Adoption Story*. Photographs by Phil Miner. Childs, Md.: Mitchell Lane Publishers, 1998. 48 p.

Photographs and text describe Diana's adoption as she experienced it. Seven-year-old Diana and her newborn sister were removed from their home in the Brazilian jungle as their grandmother and mother were not able to care for them. Diana lived in a Brazilian convent before she was adopted by American parents and went with them to her new home in Kansas City. At first everything was strange to Diana, but she felt better when she became friends with a Portuguese-speaking girl, whose parents were American and Brazilian. Now as a teenager, Diana still keeps in touch with her Brazilian friends.
European-American
Intermediate; Nonfiction

From Colombia

Rosenberg, Maxine B. *Growing Up Adopted*. Afterword by Lois Ruskai Melina. New York: Bradbury Press, 1989. 128 p.

In this book eight children and six adults relate their experiences and thoughts about growing up as adopted children. The four children who were adopted by parents of a different race, in each case European-American, are Josh, adopted as was a little sister from Colombia; Amy, who was adopted from Ecuador; Mark, who was adopted from Korea; and Shakine, an African-American boy who was born with spinal bifida in the United States and lives in a family of seven children, four of whom are adopted and of ethnicities other than their adoptive parents. Three of the adults are of a different race than their European-American parents. Chris was adopted from France as was her brother, Sam was adopted from Korea and has an adopted sister of mixed race and two non-adopted brothers. and Jamie, an African-European-American, has two sisters who are not adopted and four adopted siblings of mixed race.
European-American
Intermediate, Older; Nonfiction

Wright, Susan Kimmel. *The Secret of the Old Graveyard*. Scottdale, Pa.: Herald Press, 1993. 184 p.

At the same time that thirteen-year-old Nellie's parents are notified they are to go to Colombia to adopt the baby they've wanted, strange things start to happen at her family farm's old graveyard. This story tells of Nellie's worry about her parents traveling to Colombia, of her concerns as to how a baby will affect her already offbeat family, of her exciting detective work with her friend Peggy to find whoever has vandalized the cemetery, and of her discoveries that the boy she has a crush on is adopted—and likes her.

German-American
Intermediate, Older; Fiction

From Ecuador

Rosenberg, Maxine B. *Growing Up Adopted.* Afterword by Lois Ruskai Melina. New York: Bradbury Press, 1989. 128 p.

In this book eight children and six adults relate their experiences and thoughts about growing up as adopted children. The four children who were adopted by parents of a different race, in each case European-American, are Josh, adopted as was a little sister from Colombia; Amy, who was adopted from Ecuador; Mark, who was adopted from Korea; and Shakine, an African-American boy who was born with spinal bifida in the United States and lives in a family of seven children, four of whom are adopted and of ethnicities other than their adoptive parents. Three of the adults are of a different race than their European-American parents. Chris was adopted from France as was her brother, Sam was adopted from Korea and has an adopted sister of mixed race and two non-adopted brothers, and Jamie, an African-European-American, has two sisters who are not adopted and four adopted siblings of mixed race.
European-American
Intermediate, Older; Nonfiction

VII. Biographies

Introduction

This chapter covers books about actual persons, both living and dead. Each person in this chapter has been cross-referenced from one or more of the previous five chapters: "Persons of Mixed Racial and/or Ethnic Heritage;" "Persons of Mixed Religious Heritage;" "Couples of Mixed Heritage;" "Families Including a Child of the Same Nationality, But a Different Heritage;" and "Families Including a Child of a Different Nationality."

The term biography is used broadly to include not only nonfictional accounts of a person's life, but also fictional life stories and books of nonfiction and fiction in which the person appears. Further, the books do not have to mention the mixed heritage of the person or his/her family to be included.

Persons are listed under the name by which they are generally known.

Each person's heritage is identified preceding the annotated book listings about that person. The term "by" refers to the identity of caregivers. The term "to" refers to a civil, religious, or common law marriage or a longterm relationship with a person of a different heritage whose name is known. Partners are included if they are mentioned in a referenced book or if a woman's name indicates her marriage. The designation for each person reads:

Name (Date of birth-Date of death) Country of birth

Heritage from father/Heritage from mother or Heritage of parents (if parents are of the same heritage), by Identity of caretaker(s), to Heritage of partner

e.g., Haynes, Lemuel (1753-1833) (United States)

    African-American/European-American, by European-American, to European-American

        or

    Rolfe, John (1585-1622) England

    English, to Powhattan

The order in which the heritages are listed is immaterial.

References

Abdul, Paula (1962-   ) United States
Syrian Jewish/Canadian Jewish, to Irish-Spanish-European-American

Ford, M. Thomas. *Paula Abdul: Straight Up*. New York: Dillon Press, 1992. 72 p. (Taking Part Books)
    Color photographs accompany this detailed description of Paula Abdul's childhood and career

through her receiving a star on the Hollywood Walk of Fame in December 1991. The book includes a discography and video collection insert and an index.
Intermediate, Older; Nonfiction

Hamilton, Sue L. *Paula Abdul: Choreographer, Dancer, Singer*. Edina, Minn: Abdo & Daughters, 1990. 32 p. (Reaching for the Stars)
A text that includes numerous quotations from Paula Abdul and black-and-white photographs present the entertainer's personal life and career through the 1980s.
Intermediate; Nonfiction

Press, Skip. *Charlie Sheen, Emilio Estevez, & Martin Sheen*. Parsippany, N.J.: Crestwood House, 1996. 48 p. (Star Families)
This look at the Sheen family provides biographical information on Martin Sheen and his sons Emilio Estévez and Charlie Sheen: their acting careers, their personal lives, and their interest in social justice. Photographs, a glossary, and an index are included.
Intermediate, Older; Nonfiction

Zannos, Susan. *Paula Abdul*. Childs, Md.: Mitchell Lane Publishers, 1998. 32 p. (A Real-Life Reader Biography)
This biography of Paula Abdul tells of her early love of dancing and sports and traces her successful career as a choreographer, dancer, singer, and actress. It discusses her struggle with bulimia, covers her brief marriage to Emilio Estévez, and includes black-and-white photographs, a discography, a chronology, and an index.
Intermediate, Older; Nonfiction

Abdullah II bin Al Hussein, King of Jordan (1962-   ) Jordan
Jordanian/English, to Palestinian-Kuwaiti

Darraj, Susan Muaddi. *Queen Noor*. Philadelphia: Chelsea House Publishers, 2003. 128 p. (Women in Politics)
Photographs, a chronology, chapter notes, a bibliography, a resource list, and an index are included in this comprehensive biography of Queen Noor, stepmother of King Abdullah of Jordan. Placing her life within the context of Jordanian society, world events, and her husband King Hussein's policies, the book highlights her many humanitarian works and the sometimes controversial role she played as Queen.
Older; Nonfiction

Raatma, Lucia. *Queen Noor: American-Born Queen of Jordan*. Minneapolis: Compass Point Books, 2006. 112 p. (Signature Lives)
This biography tells of Queen Noor's childhood in the United States, her marriage to King Hussein of Jordan, her role as Queen, her struggles to be accepted by the peoples of Jordan, and her humanitarian work. There is extensive background information on the Middle East's history, politics,

and culture and on the policies which King Hussein pursued in trying to bring peace to the region. The book includes photographs, informational inserts, chapter notes, a timeline, a glossary, a resource list, a bibliography, and an index.
Older; Nonfiction

Adoff, Arnold (1935-   ) United States
Jewish Russian-American, to African-American, Cherokee, and Potawatomi

Mangal, Mélina. *Virginia Hamilton*. Bear, Del.: Mitchell Lane Publishers, 2002. 32 p. (A Real-Life Reader Biography)
　　This biography of Virginia Hamilton tells of her marriage to the author Arnold Adoff, of their family, and of his serving as her literary agent.
Intermediate; Nonfiction

Aguilera, Christina (1980-   ) United States
Ecuadorian/Irish-American

Granados, Christine. *Christina Aguilera*. Bear, Del.: Mitchell Lane Publishers, 2001. 32 p. (A Real-Life Reader Biography)
　　Illustrated with photographs, this biography of Christina Aguilera relates how she sang to her stuffed animals using a baton as a microphone at the age of two, was a Star Search contestant at age eight, and two years later sang the national anthem at professional sports games. She suffered during her early years from her parents' unhappy marriage and divorce and from the jealous behavior of schoolmates. At the age of twelve Christina became a Mouseketeer on The New Mickey Mouse Club and found it both enjoyable and a good learning experience. In 1998 she sang "Reflections" for the movie *Mulan* and signed a recording contract with RCA. In 2000 she won a Grammy for Best New Artist. This book contains a chronology and an index.
Intermediate; Nonfiction

Ahyoka (1815?-?) United States
Cherokee and European-American/Cherokee

Fitterer, C. Ann. *Sequoyah: Native American Scholar*. Chanhassen, Minn.: The Child's World, 2003. 32 p. (Spirit of America)
　　This biography of Sequoyah also tells of the work of his daughter Ahyoka.
Primary, Intermediate; Nonfiction

Oppenheim, Joanne. *Sequoyah: Cherokee Hero*. Illustrated by Bert Dodson. Mahwah, N.J.: Troll Associates, 1979. 48 p.
　　Sequoyah's childhood, his work on the syllabary, and the role played by his daughter Ahyoka are described in this fictionalized account of his life.
Primary; Fiction

Roop, Peter, and Connie Roop. *Ahyoka and the Talking Leaves*. Illustrated by Yoshi Miyake. New York: Lothrop, Lee & Shepard Books, 1992. 64 p.

This fictionalized story of Ahyoka, Sequoyah's young daughter, tells how she tried to help him draw pictures for the words of the Cherokee language; joined him when her mother Utiya burned his drawings and forced him to leave; and, after the cabin where she and Sequoyah lived was destroyed by an angry medicine man, accompanied Sequoyah on his travels westward. In this story it is Ahyoka who comes up with the idea of writing symbols for Cherokee sounds. The book includes an epilogue and a bibliography.
Primary; Fiction

Alba, Jessica Marie (1981-   ) United States
Mexican-American/Danish-French Canadian-American

Rivera, Ursula. *Jessica Alba*. New York: Children's Press, 2002. 48 p. (Celebrity Bios)

This description of the career of Jessica Alba, the leading actress in the television series *Dark Angel*, tells of her earlier movie and television roles. It includes color photography, a timeline, a glossary, a fact sheet, resource listings, and an index.
Intermediate; Nonfiction

Alexie, Sherman J., Jr. (1966-   ) United States
Coeur d'Alene/Spokane

Rappaport, Doreen. *We Are the Many: A Picture Book of American Indians*. Illustrated by Cornelius Van Wright and Ying-Hwa Hu. New York: HarperCollins Publishers, 2002. 32 p.

An illustrated vignette about the writer, Sherman Alexie, includes poetry he wrote about the athletes of a Navajo reservation high school in Arizona. The commentary mentions his screenplay, *Smoke Signals*, set on the Spokane Indian Reservation in Wellpinit, Washington, where he was born.
Primary, Intermediate; Nonfiction

Anderson, Ross (1971 or 1972-   ) United States
Cheyenne-Arapaho and Mescalero Apache, by European-American

Schilling, Vincent. *Native Athletes in Action!* Summertown, Tenn.: 7th Generation, 2007. 128 p. (Native Trailblazers)

A biographical chapter tells of Ross Anderson's competitive ski racing from the age of six and his professional speed skiing achievements, including winning a bronze medal in the 2005 World Cup Championships and setting a United States record in 2006.
Intermediate, Older; Nonfiction

Attucks, Crispus (1723?-1770) United States
African-American/probably Natick

Altman, Susan. *Extraordinary African-Americans: From Colonial to Contemporary Times*. Rev. ed. New York: Children's Press, 2001. 288 p. (Extraordinary People)

This book's summary of Crispus Attucks' life reports that he spent twenty years as a sailor and was killed when he incited an angry crowd of colonists in what became known as the Boston Massacre.

Intermediate, Older; Nonfiction

Dramer, Kim. *Native Americans and Black Americans*. Philadelphia: Chelsea House Publishers, 1997. 96 p. (Indians of North America)

This book not only describes Crispus Attucks' role in the Boston Massacre, but also states that his ancestor John Attucks was one of the Natick Indians, who were converted to Christianity and became known as Praying Indians. When the Puritans confined the Praying Indians to an island in Boston Harbor, John Attucks escaped and was hung by the Puritans as an alleged spy.

Older; Nonfiction

Haskins, Jim. *One More River To Cross: The Stories of Twelve Black Americans*. New York: Scholastic, 1992. 224 p.

The chapter on Crispus Attucks reports that there is little information about him prior to March 5, 1770, other than that he escaped slavery twenty years earlier. It focuses on Attucks' role as probable instigator of the Boston crowd's confrontation with British soldiers that provoked the Boston Massacre. Attucks was the first American to be killed that evening and the first to die for the colonies' freedom.

Intermediate, Older; Nonfiction

Kranz, Rachel C. *The Biographical Dictionary of Black Americans*. New York: Facts on File, 1992. 192 p.

An account of Crispus Attucks tells of his role in the Boston Massacre and in the subsequent trial of the British soldiers and of how he has been commemorated.

Intermediate, Older; Nonfiction

Masoff, Joy. *The African American Story: The Events That Shaped Our Nation . . . and the People Who Changed Our Lives*. Waccabuc, N.Y.: Five Ponds Press, 2007. 96 p.

This history of African-Americans includes a paragraph about and a picture of Crispus Attucks.

Older; Nonfiction

McKissack, Patricia C., and Frederick L. McKissack. *Black Hands, White Sails: The Story of African-American Whalers*. New York: Scholastic Press, 1999. 176 p.

This book includes information on Crispus Attucks, who was on leave from a whaling ship at the time of the Boston Massacre. It describes his actions in the confrontation and states that it was Samuel Adams who described the incident as a massacre and publicized it in a pamphlet.

Older; Nonfiction

Baez, Joan Chandos (1941-   ) United States
Mexican/Scottish, to European-American

Alegre, Cèsar. *Extraordinary Hispanic Americans*. New York: Children's Press, 2007. 288 p. (Extraordinary People)
    A chapter in this book details Joan Baez' career as a folk singer who has used her musical talent to promote political causes.
Older; Nonfiction

Heller, Jeffrey. *Joan Baez: Singer with a Cause*. Chicago: Children's Press, 1991. 112 p. (People of Distinction)
    A timeline placing Joan Baez' career in the context of world events, chapter notes, photographs, a listing of her recordings and publications, and an index complement this biography of the folk singer, who throughout her career has adamantly—and often controversially—advocated the cause of world peace.
Older; Nonfiction

Balanchine, George (born Gyorgy [different spellings] Melitonovich Balanchivadze) (1904-1983) Russia
Georgian, to Russian/Swedish, to Russian, to German, to Scottish-Irish-American and Osage, to French and European-American

Kristy, Davida. *George Balanchine: American Ballet Master*. Minneapolis: Lerner Publications Company, 1996. 128 p.
    This detailed account of the personal life and career of choreographer George Balanchine tells how he came to love music and ballet, of his leaving Russia, of the creation of the School of American Ballet and the New York City Ballet, of his choreographic style, of the ballets he choreographed, and of his four marriages and a common-law marriage to ballerinas. Photographs, source notes, a bibliography, and an index complete the biography.
Older; Nonfiction

Ballard, Louis (1931-2007) United States
Cherokee/Quapaw

Avery, Susan, and Linda Skinner. *Extraordinary American Indians*. Chicago: Children's Press, 1992. 272 p.
    As a child Louis Ballard composed songs that drew upon his exposure to Quapaw music. He went on to study music of other tribes and to write compositions that melded Western music with Native American music and often included Native American instruments. Among his compositions mentioned in this section are the ballets *Koshare* and *The Four Moons* and the orchestral work *Incident at Wounded Knee*.
Older; Nonfiction

Banneker, Benjamin (1731-1806) United States
Guinean/African (probably Senegalese)-English-American

Altman, Susan. *Extraordinary African-Americans: From Colonial to Contemporary Times*. Rev. ed. New York: Children's Press, 2001. 288 p. (Extraordinary People)
   This book contains a biographical chapter summarizing Benjamin Banneker's work as an astronomer, inventor, mathematician, and surveyor.
Intermediate, Older; Nonfiction

Blue, Rose, and Corinne J. Naden. *Benjamin Banneker: Mathematician and Stargazer*. Brookfield, Conn.: The Millbrook Press, 2001. 48 p.
   Taught initially by his grandmother Molly Welsh Banneky, Benjamin Banneker attended a Quaker school for four winters. At the age of about twenty-one, by observing a pocket watch, he built a chiming wooden clock that kept perfect time for more than half a century. Interested in mathematics and astronomy and especially in developing ephemerides, tables showing the daily positions of celestial bodies, Banneker published yearly almanacs from 1792 through 1797. He also worked on the team that surveyed land for the District of Columbia. This biography includes information on ways in which his accomplishments have been remembered, pictures, a chronology, a resource list, and an index.
Intermediate; Nonfiction

Conley, Kevin. *Benjamin Banneker: Scientist and Mathematician*. Philadelphia: Chelsea House Publishers, 1989. 112 p. (Black Americans of Achievement)
   This comprehensive biography of Benjamin Banneker tells of his family background, his childhood on the family's tobacco farm, his early adult life, and the changes which occurred at the age of forty when the Ellicotts became his neighbors. It was with their assistance that he learned surveying and astronomy, published his first almanac, and served on the surveying team that laid out the boundaries of the District of Columbia. The book includes illustrations, a chronology, a reading list, and an index.
Older; Nonfiction

Cox, Clinton. *African American Teachers*. New York: John Wiley & Sons, 2000. 176 p. (Black Stars)
   A section on Benjamin Banneker describes how, though not a teacher in the traditional sense, Banneker taught others through his writings.
Older; Nonfiction

Ferris, Jeri. *What Are You Figuring Now?: A Story about Benjamin Banneker*. Illustrated by Amy Johnson. Minneapolis: Carolrhoda Books, 1988. 64 p. (A Carolrhoda Creative Minds Book)
   This illustrated chapter book tells of Benjamin Banneker's love of mathematical puzzles, of his wooden clock, of his life as a farmer, of his becoming an astronomer, of his work in surveying the District of Columbia, and of his almanacs.
Primary, Intermediate; Fiction

Haber, Louis. *Black Pioneers of Science and Invention*. San Diego: Harcourt Brace & Company, 1992. 288 p. (An Odyssey Book)

Quotations from Benjamin Banneker's 1791 letter to Thomas Jefferson, Jefferson's letter in reply, the preface to Banneker's 1796 almanac, and Banneker's plan for a Federal Department of Peace are features of this book's biographical chapter on the mathematician and astronomer. A bibliography, photographs, and an index are included.
Older; Nonfiction

Hayden, Robert C. *Seven Black American Scientists*. Reading, Mass.: Addison Wesley, 1970. 176 p.

This book's biographical chapter on Benjamin Banneker focuses on his almanacs. It includes the letter written by James McHenry urging the publication of Banneker's first almanac.
Older; Nonfiction

Kranz, Rachel C. *The Biographical Dictionary of Black Americans*. New York: Facts on File, 1992. 192 p.

A biographical account of Benjamin Banneker points out how he used his self-taught skills in astronomy and mathematics to calculate and publish ephemerides and to participate in surveying land for the District of Columbia.
Intermediate, Older; Nonfiction

Masoff, Joy. *The African American Story: The Events That Shaped Our Nation . . . and the People Who Changed Our Lives*. Waccabuc, N.Y.: Five Ponds Press, 2007. 96 p.

This history of African-Americans includes a paragraph about and a picture of Benjamin Banneker.
Older; Nonfiction

Maupin, Melissa. *Benjamin Banneker*. Chanhassen, Minn.: The Child's World, 1999. 40 p.

Illustrations, a glossary defining italicized words in the text, a copy of one of Benjamin Banneker's mathematical puzzles, a timeline, and a resource list add to this biography. It includes information on his grandparents (the Bannakys) and on the possibility that Banneker was able to duplicate the plans for the capital city which the architect Pierre L'Enfante made and then took back to France with him. The book contains an index.
Intermediate; Nonfiction

Nash, Gary B. *Forbidden Love: The Secret History of Mixed-Race America*. New York: Henry Holt and Company, 1999. 224 p.

The book describes how Benjamin Banneker sent a copy of his almanac to Thomas Jefferson in an effort to show him that African-Americans were not of inferior intelligence.
Older; Nonfiction

Patterson, Lillie. *Benjamin Banneker: Genius of Early America*. Illustrated by David Scott Brown. Nashville: Abingdon Press, 1978. 144 p.

Molly Bannaky tells young Benjamin Banneker about her life in this biography, which includes fictionalized dialogue. It describes in detail his friendship with George Ellicott, his help in laying out the District of Columbia and the city of Washington, and the preparation of his first almanac, which included not only an ephemeris, but also a tide table for Chesapeake Bay and weather predictions.
Intermediate, Older; Fiction

Pinkney, Andrea Davis. *Dear Benjamin Banneker*. Illustrated by Brian Pinkney. San Diego: Gulliver Books, 1994. 32 p.

Illustrated with large hand-colored oil scratchboard renderings, this book focuses on Benjamin Banneker's first almanac and on his correspondence with Secretary of State Thomas Jefferson that pointed out the discrepancy between Jefferson's profession of the equality of man in the Declaration of Independence and his owning of slaves.
Primary, Intermediate; Nonfiction

Potter, Joan, and Constance Claytor. *African Americans Who Were First*. New York: Cobblehill Books, 1997. 128 p.

A page on Benjamin Banneker acclaims his building of a clock, his first almanac, and his surveying of the District of Columbia.
Intermediate, Older; Nonfiction

Sullivan, Otha Richard. *African American Inventors*. New York: John Wiley & Sons, 1998. 176 p. (Black Stars)

Information on Benjamin Banneker's grandparents is presented in this book's chapter that describes his life and accomplishments. Pictures, text inserts, and references are included.
Older; Nonfiction

Banneky (Bannaky), Molly Welsh (Walsh) (c.1666-post 1731) England
English, to African, probably Senegalese

Maupin, Melissa. *Benjamin Banneker*. Chanhassen, Minn.: The Child's World, 1999. 40 p.

Illustrations, a glossary defining italicized words in the text, a copy of one of Benjamin Banneker's mathematical puzzles, a timeline, and a resource list add to this biography. It includes information on his grandparents (the Bannakys) and on the possibility that Banneker was able to duplicate the plans for the capital city which the architect Pierre L'Enfante made and then took back to France with him. The book contains an index.
Intermediate; Nonfiction

McGill, Alice. *Molly Bannaky*. Illustrated by Chris K. Soentpiet. Boston: Houghton Mifflin Company, 1999. 32 p.

Large double-page colored paintings illustrate this story of Molly Walsh Bannaky, who was sentenced in England in 1683 to become an indentured servant in the American colonies. Freed after seven years, she bought Bannaky, an African slave, to help her tend the Maryland farm she had staked

out. They fell in love, she freed him, and, in violation of the law, they were married. Molly later taught her grandson Benjamin Banneker to read and write.
Pre-K, Primary; Nonfiction

Patterson, Lillie. *Benjamin Banneker: Genius of Early America*. Illustrated by David Scott Brown. Nashville: Abingdon Press, 1978. 144 p.
   Molly Bannaky tells young Benjamin Banneker about her life in this biography, which includes fictionalized dialogue. It describes in detail his friendship with George Ellicott, his help in laying out the District of Columbia and the city of Washington, and the preparation of his first almanac, which included not only an ephemeris, but also a tide table for Chesapeake Bay and weather predictions.
Intermediate, Older; Fiction

Sullivan, Otha Richard. *African American Inventors*. New York: John Wiley & Sons, 1998. 176 p. (Black Stars)
   Information on Benjamin Banneker's grandparents is presented in this book's chapter that describes his life and accomplishments. Pictures, text inserts, and references are included.
Older; Nonfiction

Beckwourth (Beckwith), James (Jim) Pierson (c. 1800-1866) United States
English/African-European-American

Altman, Susan. *Extraordinary African-Americans: From Colonial to Contemporary Times*. Rev ed. New York: Children's Press, 2001. 288 p. (Extraordinary People)
   This book's summary of James Beckwourth's life relates a legend about his death at a Crow farewell feast.
Intermediate, Older; Nonfiction

Dolan, Sean. *James Beckwourth: Frontiersman*. Philadelphia: Chelsea House Publishers, 1992. 120 p. (Black Americans of Achievement)
   Photographs, a chronology, a reading list, and an index add to this comprehensive biography of James Beckwourth. The book states that is difficult to determine the true details of the life of this skilled raconteur, who dictated his life story for an 1856 memoir. However, Beckwourth is known as a generous thief, a friend and a killer of Indians, and an adventurer. He spent years in the Rocky Mountains as a fur trapper; established trading posts; worked as a guide and messenger; lived with the Crow Indians; was forced to serve as a guide in the Sand Creek, Colorado massacre of Cheyenne and Arapaho Indians; and discovered the Beckwourth Pass.
Older; Nonfiction

Dramer, Kim. *Native Americans and Black Americans*. Philadelphia: Chelsea House Publishers, 1997. 96 p. (Indians of North America)
   James Beckwourth's relationship with the Crow is emphasized in this book's survey of his life.
Older; Nonfiction

Glass, Andrew. *Mountain Men: True Grit and Tall Tales*. Illustrated by author. New York: Doubleday Books for Young Readers, 2001. 48 p.
This book includes a tale of Jim Beckwourth as a Crow warrior.
Intermediate; Fiction

Gregson, Susan R. *James Beckwourth: Mountaineer, Scout, and Pioneer*. Minneapolis: Compass Point Books, 2005. 112 p. (Signature Lives)
Highlighting his role in the Sand Creek Massacre which turned his Cheyenne friends against him, this detailed biography of James Beckwourth tells of his childhood, his trapping for the Rocky Mountain Fur Company and the American Fur Company, his storytelling, his life with the Crows as a war chief and horse-stealer, his participation in the Second Seminole War and the Bear Flag Rebellion, his trading posts, and his discovery of Beckwourth Pass. It includes photographs, informational insets, a chronology of Beckwourth's life and of world events, a glossary, source notes, a bibliography, a resource listing, and an index.
Intermediate, Older; Nonfiction

Katz, William Loren. *Black Indians: A Hidden Heritage*. New York: Atheneum, 1986. 208 p.
The section on Jim Beckwourth tells of his fur trapping, his love of fighting, and his important discovery of what is now called Beckwourth Pass in the Sierra Nevada Mountains.
Intermediate, Older; Nonfiction

Kranz, Rachel C. *The Biographical Dictionary of Black Americans*. New York: Facts on File, 1992. 192 p.
The summary of Jim Beckwourth's life mentions his living with the Blackfoot and the Crow, his soldiering, his work as a guide, and his establishment of trading posts at what are now Taos, New Mexico, and Los Angeles.
Intermediate, Older; Nonfiction

Monceaux, Morgan, and Ruth Katcher. *My Heroes, My People: African Americans and Native Americans in the West*. Illustrated by Morgan Monceaux. New York: Frances Foster Books, 1999. 64 p.
A full-page portrait of Jim Beckwourth accompanies a short account of his career.
Intermediate, Older; Nonfiction

Schlissel, Lillian. *Black Frontiers: A History of African American Heroes in the Old West*. New York: Simon & Schuster Books for Young Readers, 1995. 80 p.
A section on Jim Beckwourth presents his varied careers and his relationships with Indians whom he both lived with and fought against.
Intermediate, Older; Nonfiction

Bent, Charles (1799-1847) United States
European-American, to Mexican

Finley, Mary Peace. *Meadow Lark*. Palmer Lake, Colo.: Filter Pres, 2003. 208 p.

This book covers the same time period as the two earlier books in the trilogy, *Soaring Eagle* and *White Grizzly*, but tells the story of thirteen-year-old Teresita, Julio's Mexican sister who had to stay behind when Julio and their father left for Bent's Fort. Fearing from a vision that something has happened to them, Teresita, who is working for Charles and Maria Ignacia Bent, joins a wagon train bound for Bent's Fort. After looking after her goats and surviving a wagon ride down perilous Raton Pass, Teresita arrives at Bent's Fort only to learn that her father is dead and Julio has gone on to Bent's Farm. Then persuading a Mexican couple to hire her and taking Silent Walker, whom she has befriended, along as a goatherder, Teresita joins a wagon train that will pass by Bent's Farm. She is kidnapped by Kiowa and escapes by floating down the Arkansas River in a log drum. Silent Walker meets some Kiowa from whom she had been kidnapped as a child, and both she and Teresita are reunited with Julio at Bent's Farm. It is in this book that readers learn that Silent Walker, a character in the earlier books, is Kiowa, not Cheyenne.
Intermediate, Older; Fiction

Bent, William (1809-1869) United States
European-American, to Cheyenne, to Cheyenne, to European-American and Blackfoot

Finley, Mary Peace. *Little Fox's Secret: The Mystery of Bent's Fort*. Illustrated by Martha Jane Spurlock. Palmer Lake, Colo.: Filter Press, 1999. 72 p.

This is the fictionalized account of the destruction of Bent's Fort in 1849. When Gray Owl of the Cheyenne has a vision that Bent's Fort will be destroyed, he warns William Bent and then, directing eleven-year-old Little Fox to destroy it, leaves him outside the fort. Little Fox thinks that he could blow it up with the gunpowder in the munitions room, but he does not want to harm his friends, William Bent and his son Robert. Bent's wife Yellow Woman returns early from a tribal council and confirms Gray Owl's vision of the spread of disease (cholera). When all the occupants of the fort leave it unoccupied, Little Fox goes into the fort to blow it up. Discovered by William Bent, he helps Bent spread the gunpowder and, promising to keep Bent's role a secret, watches him blow it up. In reality, it is unknown how Bent's Fort was destroyed, but most historians feel that since Bent did not want his trading post turned into a fort to be used against the Indians and Mexicans and to further the spread of cholera, he blew up his own fort. This book includes a glossary as well as information on the restored Bent's Old Fort and the trading post which Bent built later.
Intermediate; Fiction

Finley, Mary Peace. *White Grizzly*. Palmer Lake, Colo.: Filter Press, 2000. 224 p.

In this sequel to *Soaring Eagle* Julio finds out at Bent's Fort that his birth name is William Allen Forester and that his grandfather might still be in Independence, Missouri, where he had decided to wait for ten years for word of his missing family. Worried that the ten years have passed, Julio sets off with William Bent and his wagon train on the long perilous journey to Independence. Working as a sheepherder with his dog and an African-American blacksmith, Julio is almost killed by a grizzly bear and by two wanted outlaws; again sees Silent Walker, the young Cheyenne woman whom he has come to care for; is captured by Pawnee; and is reunited in Independence with his grandfather, who

was about to leave. Still uncertain whether his allegiances are to the Mexicans, the Americans, or the Cheyenne, Julio and his grandfather spend the winter at Bent's Farm near Independence. The book includes information about William Bent and about Bent's Fort's importance as a trading post.
Intermediate, Older: Fiction

Gregson, Susan R. *James Beckwourth: Mountaineer, Scout, and Pioneer*. Minneapolis: Compass Point Books, 2005. 112 p. (Signature Lives)
This biography of James Beckwourth tells of the experiences of William Bent and his three sons in the Sand Creek Massacre and mentions that Beckwourth briefly worked for the Bents.
Intermediate, Older; Nonfiction

Berry, Halle Maria (1966-   ) United States
African-American/ English, to African-American, to African-American, to French-Canadian

Banting, Erinn. *Halle Berry*. New York: Weigl Publishers, 2005. 24 p. (Great African-American Women)
Information on becoming an actor, making a movie, Hollywood, Ohio, racism, and diabetes; directions for making a flip book; and a suggestion for a research project are included in the text of this short biography of Halle Berry. The text is supplemented by color photographs, a list of Berry's movies, a timeline, a glossary of bolded text words, a resource list, and an index.
Primary, Intermediate; Nonfiction

Cruz, Bárbara C. *Multiethnic Teens and Cultural Identity: A Hot Issue*. Berkeley Heights, N.J.: Enslow Publishers, 2001. 64 p.
A page on Halle Berry tells of her childhood and of her views on her identity.
Older; Nonfiction

Gogerly, Liz. *Halle Berry*. Chicago: Raintree, 2005. 48 p. (Star Files)
In this book's biography of Halle Berry the pages are divided into sections of text, sidebars, color photographs, and, at the bottom, definitions of bolded text words. A filmography, a television show listing, a resource list, a glossary, and an index are appended.
Intermediate, Older; Nonfiction

Hinds, Maureen J. *Halle Berry*. Broomall, Pa.: Mason Crest Publishers, 2009. 64 p. (Overcoming Adversity: Sharing the American Dream)
The difficulties Halle Berry had in getting roles because of her race and beauty, her production and acting in the TV film *Introducing Dorothy Dandridge*, the ups and downs of her personal life, and her career successes are chronicled in this biography. Color photographs, a section of pages elaborating upon the text, a glossary, chapter notes, a chronology, a list of accomplishments and awards, a resource listing, and an index add to the content.
Intermediate, Older; Nonfiction

Masoff, Joy. *The African American Story: The Events That Shaped Our Nation . . . and the People Who Changed Our Lives*. Waccabuc, N.Y.: Five Ponds Press, 2007. 96 p.

This history of African-Americans includes a paragraph about and two pictures of Halle Berry.
Older; Nonfiction

Naden, Corinne J., and Rose Blue. *Halle Berry*. Philadelphia: Chelsea House Publishers, 2001. 104 p. (Black Americans of Achievement)

The text of this detailed biography of Halle Berry includes related information on interracial marriage; domestic violence; the effects on children of an abusive, alcoholic, and abandoning parent (Berry's father); and black actresses, including Dorothy Dandridge, who made progress towards overcoming Hollywood's racial prejudice. The book includes black-and-white photographs, a chronology, a filmography, a reading list, and an index.
Older; Nonfiction

Sapet, Kerrily. *Halle Berry: Academy Award-Winning Actress*. Broomall, Pa.: Mason Crest Publishers, 2010. 64 p. (Transcending Race in America, Biographies of Biracial Achievers)

Covering Halle Berry's life into 2009, this biography tells of the variety of her movie roles, of her personal life, and of the impact of being biracial. Color photographs, quotations printed in differing ink colors, informational inserts, a glossary defining bolded text words, a chronology, an award listing, a filmography, a resource section, and an index complement the text.
Older; Nonfiction

Schuman, Michael A. *Halle Berry: "Beauty Is Not Just Physical."* Berkeley Heights, N.J.: Enslow Publishers, 2006. 112 p. (African-American Biography Library)

This biography of Halle Berry gives extensive information on her childhood, her successes in beauty pageants, her work as a model, and her acting career. Color photographs, a chronology, chapter notes, a filmography, resource listings, and an index are additional features.
Intermediate, Older; Nonfiction

Beyoncé (born Beyoncé Giselle Knowles) (1981-) United States
African-American/Creole-American, to African-American

Bednar, Chuck. *Beyoncé: Singer-Songwriter, Actress, and Record Producer*. Broomall, Pa.: Mason Crest Publishers, 2010. 64 p. (Transcending Race in America: Biographies of Biracial Achievers)

This detailed biography of Beyoncé tells of her mixed race, her childhood, her performances and recordings as part of the group Destiny's Child, her solo albums, and her movie roles. It concludes with the year 2009, during which she received the Outstanding Female Artist award at the NAACP Image Awards, performed at one of President Barack Obama's inaugural balls, and her film *Obsessed* was released. The book includes color photographs, informational inserts, numerous quotations, a glossary defining bolded text words, a chronology, an accomplishments and awards listing, a resource list, and an index.
Older; Nonfiction

Dylan, Penelope. *Beyoncé*. New York: The Rosen Publishing Group, 2007. 48 p. (Contemporary Musicians and Their Music)

This book emphasizes Beyoncé's musical career from being part of a girls' singing group as a youngster through winning five 2004 Grammy Awards. Color photographs, a timeline, a discography, a glossary, resource listings, a bibliography, and an index complete the book.
Intermediate, Older; Nonfiction

Tracy, Kathleen. *Beyoncé*. Hockessin, Del.: Mitchell Lane Publishers, 2005. 32 p. (A Blue Banner Biography)

Banners inserted in the text highlight the major points in this account of Beyoncé's singing, songwriting, and acting careers. The biography contains color photographs, a chronology, a resource list, a discography, a filmography, and an index.
Intermediate; Nonfiction

Waters, Rosa. *Beyoncé*. Broomall, Pa.: Mason Crest Publishers, 2007. 64 p. (Hip-Hop)

Emphasizing the importance of Beyoncé's relationships with her family, members of Destiny's Child, and Jay-Z, this account of her life features numerous quotations, color photographs, a glossary defining bolded text words, a listing of her accomplishments and awards, a chronology, a resource list, and an index.
Intermediate, Older; Nonfiction

Bibb, Henry (1815-1854) United States
European-American/African-European-American, to African-European-American, to African-American

Cooper, Afua. *My Name Is Henry Bibb: A Story of Slavery and Freedom*. Tonawanda, N.Y.: KCP Fiction, 2009. 160 p.

This is a novel about Henry Bibb's childhood. A slave on a Kentucky plantation, Henry was hired out at age nine to be the personal servant of a woman who kicked and beat him. Henry was subsequently hired out to a merchant and his wife in Shelbyville, who were even meaner, and he was next returned to the plantation. The situation became worse there when his master brought his bride home as she detested Henry's mother, who had been her new husband's mistress, and her children. Resenting the woman's cruel treatment, Henry began destroying property and unsuccessfully ran away. He was next hired out to be valet to a Louisville judge where, in the judge's courtroom, Henry constantly observed the severe penalties meted out to slaves. At the age of fifteen, after the judge discovered he was learning to read, he was once more sent back home where he was put to work in the tobacco fields. During his time there he married a slave from a neighboring plantation and had a daughter. Then, like the Ibo's in the story his mother told, Henry "walked on water" across the Ohio River to freedom.
Intermediate, Older; Fiction

Ferris, Jeri Chase. *Demanding Justice: A Story about Mary Ann Shadd Cary*. Illustrated by Kimanne Smith. Minneapolis: Carolrhoda Books, 2003. 64 p. (A Creative Minds Biography)

This biography of Mary Ann Shadd Cary stresses her determination that fugitive slaves should have equal rights with whites and her belief that they could demonstrate this entitlement through their self-reliance. During her life she not only taught in both the United States and Canada, but also became the first black woman to publish a weekly newspaper (the *Provincial Freeman*) and to enter a law school (Howard University Law School) where she earned a law degree. The book tells of her disputes with Henry Bibb, her writings, her speeches, and her recruitment work for the Union army. Intermediate; Nonfiction

Katz, William Loren. *Black Pioneers: An Untold Story*. New York: Atheneum Books for Young Readers, 1999. 208 p.

This book's section on Henry Bibb describes how, after numerous failed attempts, he escaped from slavery and thereafter lectured against slavery and wrote an autobiography detailing his experiences as a slave. Fearing capture after passage of the 1850 Fugitive Slave Law, Bibb moved to Canada where he published the newspaper *Voice of the Fugitive* and urged African-Americans to emigrate to Canada.
Older; Nonfiction

Turner, Glennette Tilley. *Follow in Their Footsteps*. Illustrated with Photographs. New York: Puffin Books, 1999. 192 p.

The biographical chapter on Mary Ann Shadd Cary, who was a newspaper editor in Canada, tells of her disagreements with Henry Bibb and his second wife Mary.
Intermediate, Older; Fiction, Nonfiction

Blades, Rubén (born Rubén Blades Bellido de Luna) (1948-) Panama
St. Lucian-Colombian?-Panamanian /American-Spanish-Cuban, to European-American

Alegre, Cèsar. *Extraordinary Hispanic Americans*. New York: Children's Press, 2007. 288 p. (Extraordinary People)

A chapter in this book describes Rubén Blades' career as a singer and songwriter, especially of salsa, as a movie actor, and as Panamanian Minister of Tourism.
Older; Nonfiction

Cruz, Bárbara C. *Rubén Blades: Salsa Singer and Social Activist*. Springfield, N.J.: Enslow Publishers, 1997. 128 p. (Hispanic Biographies)

This detailed biography of Rubén Blades tells of the Panama Canal Zone riot in 1964 that triggered his love of Latin music, his gaining a law degree from the University of Panama and a masters degree in international law from Harvard University, his writing and performance of salsa music with a social concern and as urban music, his acting roles in movies and on television, and his 1994 candidacy for the presidency of Panama. Photographs; a chronology; chapter notes; a reading list; a listing of sound recordings, films, and TV programs; and an index are included.
Older; Nonfiction

Marton, Betty A. *Rubén Blades*. Philadelphia: Chelsea House Publishers, 1992. 112 p. (Hispanics of Achievement)

Complemented by photographs, a selected discography and filmography, a chronology, a reading list, and an index, this extensive biography of Rubén Blades includes words from some of his songs and covers his personal life and career prior to his campaign to be president of Panama.
Older; Nonfiction

Bonetta, Sarah Forbes (1843?-1880) Nigeria
Egbado (Nigerian?), by British

Myers, Walter Dean. *At Her Majesty's Request: An African Princess in Victorian England*. New York: Scholastic Press, 1999. 160 p.

This biography relates the remarkable life story of Sarah Forbes Bonetta. Born an Egbado of royal blood in what is probably now Nigeria, she was kidnapped as a little girl by Dahomians who killed her parents. Two years later the English Commander Frederick Forbes saved her from being sacrificed by the Dahomian king by having her given as a gift to Queen Victoria. Sarah became a protégée of Queen Victoria's. Her expenses were paid by Queen Victoria; she became a friend of the Queen's children; she often visited Queen Victoria; Queen Victoria gave her presents and determined where she was to live; and the Queen became her older daughter's godmother. Sarah initially lived with the Forbes' family, but Commander Forbes died soon thereafter. For four years she attended a girls' school in Freetown, Sierra Leone, and then, at the age of twelve, became part of the family of Reverend James Frederick Schoen and his wife Elizabeth who lived in Gillingham, England. Sarah reluctantly married, lived in Sierra Leone and Nigeria, and died of tuberculosis in Madeira. This book includes a bibliography.
Intermediate, Older; Nonfiction

Bonga, George (1802-1880) United States
African-American/Chippewa

Katz, William Loren. *Black Indians: A Hidden Heritage*. New York: Atheneum, 1986. 208 p.

The book gives a brief account of the fur trapper George Bonga, who negotiated a treaty between the United States and the Chippewa Nation.
Intermediate, Older; Nonfiction

Katz, William Loren. *Black Pioneers: An Untold Story*. New York: Atheneum Books for Young Readers, 1999. 208 p.

This book's account of the Bonga family points out that George Bonga worked as a fur trapper for the Hudson's Bay Company and then independently as a fur trader. He served the Michigan territorial governor as an interpreter and a treaty negotiator with the Chippewa.
Older; Nonfiction

Monceaux, Morgan, and Ruth Katcher. *My Heroes, My People: African Americans and Native Americans in the West*. Illustrated by Morgan Monceaux. New York: Frances Foster Books, 1999. 64 p.

George Bonga was part of a family of successful traders, according to this book's brief description of the Bongas. A portrait of George and his brother Stephen accompany the account.
Intermediate, Older; Nonfiction

Bonnin, Gertrude Simmons; also Zitkala-sa (1876-1938) United States
European-American/Yankton Dakota

Avery, Susan, and Linda Skinner. *Extraordinary American Indians*. Chicago: Children's Press, 1992. 272 p.

One section of the book describes the life of Gertrude Simmons Bonnin. Advocate of an intertribal reform movement, Gertrude Simmons Bonnin spent her childhood on both the Yankton Reservation in South Dakota and at a school for Indians in Indiana. After attending Earlham College, Bonnin worked as a teacher, a musician, and an author. In 1916 she became secretary of the Society of American Indians. She later founded and was president of the National Council of American Indians and promoted reform of the Federal government's Indian policy.
Older; Nonfiction

Borges, Jorge Luis (1899-1986) Argentina
Spanish-Portuguese-English-Argentine/Spanish-Portuguese?-Urugauyan-Argentine

Lennon, Adrian. *Jorge Luis Borges*. Philadelphia: Chelsea House Publishers, 1992. 112 p. (Hispanics of Achievement)

This biography of Jorge Luis Borges provides a detailed account of both the life and the literary works of the Argentine writer. Growing up in Buenos Aires, Borges was introduced to philosophy and books by his father and spoke not only Spanish, but also English, thanks to his paternal grandmother. The advent of World War I in 1914 extended a family vacation in Europe to an almost seven year stay. Borges returned to Argentina at the age of twenty-one. He wrote essays, short stories (for which he received worldwide recognition), and poetry (which he was able to continue after he became blind). Borges served as director of Argentina's National Library; won, together with Samuel Beckett, the 1961 International Publishers Prize; and traveled extensively in his later years. The book includes photographs, a chronology, a reading list, and an index.
Older; Nonfiction

Bosomworth, Mary Musgrove Matthews (also Coosaponakeesa) (c. 1700-c. 1765) United States
English or Scottish-Irish/Creek, to English/Creek, to English, to English

Nash, Gary B. *Forbidden Love: The Secret History of Mixed-Race America*. New York: Henry Holt and Company, 1999. 224 p.

This book reports that when Coosaponakeesa was married to John Musgrove, they set up a trading post and Mary served as James Oglethorpe's interpreter and negotiator between the British and the Creek/Yamacraw. Upon Musgrove's death she married Jacob Matthews and influenced the Creek to side with the British in their conflict with the Spanish. By then a major landowner, Mary married Thomas Bosomworth, who was an Anglican minister.
Older; Nonfiction

Bowie, David (born David Robert Jones) (1947-   ) England
English, to Somali

Forget, Thomas. *David Bowie*. New York: Rosen Central, 2002. 112 p. (Rock & Roll Hall of Famers)
     This biography of the rock and roll star David Bowie tells of his early career struggles, his introduction of innovative musical blends and stage personae, and his marriage to the Somali supermodel Iman. Captioned photographs, informational inserts, a discography, a filmography, a glossary, a resource section, and an index complement the text.
Older; Nonfiction

Brant, Joseph (also Thayendanegea) (1742-1807) United States
Mohawk, to Oneida, to Oneida, to British or Irish and Mohawk

Nash, Gary B. *Forbidden Love: The Secret History of Mixed-Race America*. New York: Henry Holt and Company, 1999. 224 p.
     As pointed out in this book, Joseph Brant supported the British in both the French and Indian War and the Revolutionary War. A Mohawk chief, he translated the Anglican prayer book and the Gospel of Mark into Mohawk.
Older; Nonfiction

Pryor, Bonnie. *Thomas in Danger*. Illustrated by Bert Dodson. New York: Morrow Junior Books, 1999. 176 p. (American Adventures)
     When, in his mother's inn, Thomas spots a customer whom he recognizes as a Tory, he is kidnapped and taken north in a wagon train filled with war supplies for the Tories. Falling ill, Thomas is given by his captors to Joseph Brant, who takes him to a Mohawk village where he becomes the adopted son of an Indian woman whose sons have died. There Thomas is befriended by an Indian boy, kills a bear, and discovers why the Iroquois have sided with the British in the Revolutionary War. However, he hates the scalps taken by the Indians and constantly thinks of escape. When found by the Continental army, Thomas is happy that he will soon be reunited with his family, but sorrowful for his Mohawk friends who have been driven away from their village and their sustenance. This book is the sequel to *Thomas*.
Intermediate; Fiction

Brant, Molly (also Degonwadonti, Konwatsitsienni) (c. 1736-1796) or (c. 1735-c. 1795) United States
Mohawk, to Irish

Nash, Gary B. *Forbidden Love: The Secret History of Mixed-Race America*. New York: Henry Holt and Company, 1999. 224 p

This book stresses the important role which Molly Brant played as the wife of Sir William Johnson in getting the Iroquois Confederacy to support the British in the French and Indian War. It also contains information on their children.
Older; Nonfiction

Rappaport, Doreen. *We Are the Many: A Picture Book of American Indians*. Illustrated by Cornelius Van Wright and Ying-Hwa Hu. New York: HarperCollins Publishers, 2002. 32 p.

This book contains an illustrated vignette of Molly Brant as she wonders who is at her door: American colonists who will arrest her or British soldiers friendly to her because of the support she and her late husband (Sir William Johnson) have given them in the Revolutionary War.
Primary, Intermediate; Nonfiction

Brown, Anne Wiggins (1912-2009) United States
African-American/African-Scottish-Irish-American and Cherokee

Cruz, Bárbara C. *Multiethnic Teens and Cultural Identity: A Hot Issue*. Berkeley Heights, N.J.: Enslow Publishers, 2001. 64 p.

A page on the opera singer, Anne Wiggins Brown describes her mixed heritage and relates how, although she was the original Bess in *Porgy and Bess*, she was denied the right to sing at the Metropolitan Opera and moved to Norway because of the racial discrimination she encountered.
Older; Nonfiction

Brown, Eve (19??-   ) United States
African-French-American and Native American

Stanford, Eleanor, ed. *Interracial America: Opposing Viewpoints*. Farmington Hills, Mich.: Greenhaven Press, 2006. 208 p. (Opposing Viewpoints)

In an opinion piece titled "The Multiracial Classification Is Necessary" Eve Brown, who is African-American, French-American and Native American, explains her decision to identify herself as multiracial as opposed to black.
Older; Nonfiction

Bruchac, Joseph (1942-   ) United States
Slovak-American/English-American and Abenaki

Bruchac, Joseph. *Bowman's Store: A Journey to Myself*. New York: Dial Books, 1997. 320 p.

Joseph Bruchac, author and professional teller of Native American tales of the Adirondacks, was raised near Saratoga Springs, New York, by his maternal grandparents. This memoir of his childhood tells of his father's abuse and of the constant support and incredible outpouring of love which his grandparents gave him. Although Joseph's grandfather never acknowledged nor spoke of his Abenaki

heritage and his relatives were not permitted to visit, he imbued in Joseph the love of nature and animals and the values and ways of the Abenaki. Stories of the Abenaki, Seneca, Ojibway, and Mohawk nations introduce a number of the chapters that relate Joseph's childhood experiences growing up in the 1940s and 1950s.
Older; Nonfiction

Parker-Rock, Michelle. *Joseph Bruchac: An Author Kids Love*. Berkeley Heights, N.J.: Enslow Elementary, 2009. 48 p. (Authors Kids Love)

This biography of Joseph Bruchac tells of his heritage; his childhood love of nature and writing, reading, and listening to stories; and the influence of his grandfather, who kept his Abenaki identity hidden because of prejudice. The book covers his undergraduate time at Cornell University, his graduate work at Syracuse University, his three years with his wife Carol in Ghana, and his storytelling and writing career. Listings of Bruchac's books and an index are included.
Intermediate; Nonfiction

Caldwell, Billy (also Sagaunash) (1780-1841) Canada
Irish /Canadian Mohawk or Canadian Potawatomi

Alder, Elizabeth. *Crossing the Panther's Path*. New York: Farrar Straus Giroux, 2002. 240 p.

This book is based on the life of Billy Caldwell and his close relationship with Tecumseh, the Shawnee chief. Tecumseh, as leader of warriors from a number of Indian nations and in alliance with the British army in Canada, sought to reclaim the lands which the Americans took from the Indians. Billy, who is Irish-Mohawk, serves as soldier, interpreter, and then captain in the British Indian Department in the War of 1812. This story tells of the battles of Tippecanoe, Chicago, Detroit, the River Raisin, and the Thames River; of Billy's courageous actions; of his love of a European-American and Ojibwa woman; and of his decision to forgo fighting and help the Indians through peaceful means.
Older; Fiction

Campbell, Ben Nighthorse (1933-   ) United States
Northern Cheyenne and other/Portuguese

Allen, Paula Gunn, and Patricia Clark Smith. *As Long as the Rivers Flow: The Stories of Nine Native Americans*. New York: Scholastic Press, 1996. 336 p.

The chapter on Ben Nighthorse Campbell describes his childhood with his alcoholic father and his mother, who was seriously ill with tuberculosis; his expertise in judo: studying judo in Korea and Japan, winning a gold medal at the 1963 Pan-American games, being a member the 1964 American Olympic judo team, and teaching judo; his innovative Indian jewelry business; his raising of quarter horses; and his time as a state legislator, United States Congressman, and first-term United States Senator.
Intermediate, Older; Nonfiction

Henry, Christopher. *Ben Nighthorse Campbell: Cheyenne Chief and U.S. Senator*. Philadelphia: Chelsea House Publishers, 1994. 104 p. (North American Indians of Achievement)

This biography of Ben Nighthorse Campbell provides extensive coverage of his life through his 1992 election to the United States Senate. It details Campbell's positions and work during his six years as a congressman and presents historical information on the Cheyenne. The book includes photographs, a chronology, a reading list, and an index.

Older; Nonfiction

Campbell, Mary (1747-1801) United States
Scottish-American, by Delaware

Durrant, Lynda. *The Beaded Moccasins: The Story of Mary Campbell*. New York: Dell Yearling, 2000. 192 p.

This story, based on the life of Mary Campbell, tells how as a twelve-year-old she was kidnapped from her home in what is now Snyder County, Pennsylvania, by Delaware Indians. She was taken to a Delaware village in western Pennsylvania and then moved with the residents of that village to a cave in present day Cuyahoga Falls, Ohio. Mary was kidnapped to replace a sachem's granddaughter who had died. As the story's narrator, Mary relates her experiences and feelings as she develops strength as a person and changes so that she realizes that, although she greatly misses her family, she is now loved and a part of her new family, with a new name, Woman-Who-Saved-the-Corn. In reality, Mary Campbell was reunited with her Campbell family in 1765 when, under a treaty with the British, white Indian captives were returned.

Intermediate, Older; Fiction

Campeche, José (1752-1809?) Puerto Rico
African-Puerto Rican/Spanish (Canary Islands)

Alegre, Cèsar. *Extraordinary Hispanic Americans*. New York: Children's Press, 2007. 288 p. (Extraordinary People)

A biographical chapter on José Campeche describes his work as a painter of religious subjects and his native Puerto Rico.

Older; Nonfiction

Cardozo, Francis Lewis (1837-1903) United States
European-Jewish-American/African-American and Native American

Cox, Clinton. *African American Teachers*. New York: John Wiley & Sons, 2000. 176 p. (Black Stars)

This book's biographical section on Francis Lewis Cardozo describes how, after studying in Glasgow, Edinburgh, and London and serving as pastor of a Congregational church in New Haven, he returned to his native Charleston. There he established Avery Institute, a school that provided both basic and advanced courses for black children. Cardozo was also the principal of schools in Washington, D.C.,

and served as South Carolina's secretary of state. As chairman of a state committee on education, he was instrumental in establishing South Carolina's public school system.
Older; Nonfiction

Carey, Mariah (1970—   ) United States
African-Venezuelan-American/Irish-American, to Italian-American Jewish

Cole, Melanie. *Mariah Carey*. Childs, Md.: Mitchell Lane Publishers, 1997. 32 p. (A Real-Life Reader Biography)

This biography of Mariah Carey reports that her mother was a mezzo-soprano for the Metropolitan Opera and that Mariah displayed remarkable singing talent at an early age. Determined to become a singer, she wrote songs and lyrics as a schoolgirl and as an adult composed and produced her own songs. Discovered in New York City by Tommy Mottola, a record executive whom she later married, Mariah recorded a number of best-selling albums and singles and in 1997 was placed in charge of Crave, a new record label. The book includes photographs, a discography, a chronology, and an index.
Intermediate; Nonfiction

Cruz, Bárbara C. *Multiethnic Teens and Cultural Identity: A Hot Issue*. Berkeley Heights, N.J.: Enslow Publishers, 2001. 64 p.

A page on Mariah Carey tells how the singer identifies with her mixed heritage and how, growing up, she and her family suffered from racial prejudice.
Older; Nonfiction

Jeter, Derek with Jack Curry. *The Life You Imagine: Life Lessons for Achieving Your Dreams*. New York: Crown Publishers, 2000. 304 p.

In this book Derek Jeter points out that Mariah Carey has fulfilled her ambitious dream of becoming a top singer through her continuing hard work and that she is under constant media scrutiny.
Older; Nonfiction

McDonald, Janet. *Off-Color*. New York: Frances Foster Books, 2007. 176 p.

Fifteen-year-old Cameron, who believes that her father is Italian, loves hanging out with her three best friends and doesn't take school seriously. Then her mother loses her job in a nail salon and gets one at lower wages in the owner's other salon in an African-American section of Brooklyn. Cameron and her mother must move into the projects, but, thanks to the school guidance counselor Mr. Siciliano, she is able to remain at her old high school. When Cameron discovers from an old photo that her father is black, she is shocked and blames her mother for not having told her about him and for his not being there for her. Cameron, her mother, her friends, her mother's coworkers, her multi-cultures class, and Mr. Siciliano spend time talking about race, about being biracial, about Mariah Carey, and about Malcolm X who Cameron hears in class was propelled to become a black national-ist because of his white-appearing mother. Cameron learns that one of her mother's coworkers is Korean and Irish, that Mr. Siciliano is half black, and that many celebrities are of mixed race. At her

Sweet Sixteen party, Cameron enjoys her old best friends and new friends from the projects and even meets the boy who becomes her boyfriend.
Older; Fiction

Parker, Judy. *Mariah Carey*. New York: Children's Press, 2001. 48 p. (Celebrity Bios, High Interest Books)
Covering Mariah Carey's life to 2001, this biography focuses on her career, especially her albums. Color photographs, a timeline, a glossary, a fact sheet, a resource listing, and an index are included.
Intermediate, Older; Nonfiction

Wellman, Sam. *Mariah Carey*. Philadelphia: Chelsea House Publishers, 1999. 64 p. (Galaxy of Superstars)
A comprehensive biography of Mariah Carey, this book describes her childhood: its difficulties and the support she received from her mother and music. It tells of the Columbia Records party at which she was discovered, her quick emergence as a recording superstar, her live concerts, her marriage to and divorce from Tommy Mottola, and her performance in the 1998 "Divas Live" concert. The book includes color photographs; a chronology; a listing of Mariah's albums, number-one singles, videos, movies, and awards; a reading list; and an index.
Older; Nonfiction

Carson, Adaline (Adeline) (1837-1861) United States
European-American/Arapaho

Osborne, Mary Pope. *Adaline Falling Star*. New York: Scholastic Press, 2000. 176 p.
In this fictionalized story of Adaline Carson, her Arapaho mother dies of a fever when Adaline is about eleven. Her father, Kit Carson, leaves her with his cousin in St. Louis when he goes off to join Frémont's expedition. However, instead of enrolling Adaline in school the cousin makes her work as a servant and treats her poorly as a half-breed. As narrated by Adaline, she decides to remain mute. Only her promise to her father that she will wait for his return keeps her from leaving. When she discovers that Kit Carson has not returned with John Frémont, Adaline and a stray dog who befriends her set off along the Mississippi and Missouri Rivers for Bent's Fort. Given the chance to ride westward on a steamboat, Adaline rejects the dog and then discovers that being with the one you love is most important. At the end Adaline is reunited with both the dog and her father.
Intermediate; Fiction

Carson, Christopher (Kit) Houston (1809-1868) United States
European-American, to Arapaho, to Cheyenne, to Mexican

Boraas, Tracey. *Kit Carson: Mountain Man*. Mankato, Minn.: Bridgestone Books, 2003. 48 p. (Let Freedom Ring)
Joining a wagon train to Santa Fe to escape from an apprenticeship with Missouri saddlemakers, young Kit Carson was finally able to become part of a trapping party and worked as a fur trapper and

hunter for some thirteen years. Carson then served as a guide for John Frémont's three western expeditions, aided General Stephan Kearney's army during the Mexican War, fought as a lieutenant colonel for the North in the Civil War, and became commanding general at Fort Garland, Colorado. He knew a number of Indian languages and served as an Indian agent, but forced Apache and Navajo onto reservations. His wife Josepha raised his daughter Adaline, whose Arapaho mother had died, and the couple had other children. Photographs, a timeline, a glossary, an index, and lists of reading resources, places of interest, and internet sites are included in this book.
Intermediate; Nonfiction

Glass, Andrew. *Mountain Men: True Grit and Tall Tales*. Illustrated by author. New York: Doubleday Books for Young Readers, 2001. 48 p.
This book includes a tale of Kit Carson's confrontation with a bully at a Green River Valley rendezvous.
Intermediate; Fiction

Glass, Andrew. *A Right Fine Life: Kit Carson on the Santa Fe Trail*. Illustrated by author. New York: Holiday House, 1997. 44 p.
This picture book tells a tall tale of how a prairie fire and stampeding buffalo caused young Kit Carson to be separated from a wagon train and of the fleas, fire ants, and Indian girl he encountered. The book includes historical sections on the Santa Fe Trail and Kit Carson.
Primary, Intermediate; Fiction

Gleiter, Jan, and Kathleen Thompson. *Kit Carson*. Illustrated by Rick Whipple. Austin: Raintree Steck-Vaughn Publishers, 1995. 32 p. (First Biographies)
Kit Carson's life from his moving to Missouri as a toddler to his role as a government messenger to the Utes is covered in this picture book. Part of a series which is based on both facts and legends, it shows him as a boy hunting and fishing with Daniel Boone.
Primary; Fiction

Osborne, Mary Pope. *Adaline Falling Star*. New York: Scholastic Press, 2000. 176 p.
In this fictionalized story of Adaline Carson, her Arapaho mother dies of a fever when Adaline is about eleven. Her father, Kit Carson, leaves her with his cousin in St. Louis when he goes off to join Frémont's expedition. However, instead of enrolling Adaline in school the cousin makes her work as a servant and treats her poorly as a half-breed. As narrated by Adaline, she decides to remain mute. Only her promise to her father that she will wait for his return keeps her from leaving. When she discovers that Kit Carson has not returned with John Frémont, Adaline and a stray dog who befriends her set off along the Mississippi and Missouri Rivers for Bent's Fort. Given the chance to ride westward on a steamboat, Adaline rejects the dog and then discovers that being with the one you love is most important. At the end Adaline is reunited with both the dog and her father.
Intermediate; Fiction

Cary, Mary Ann Shadd (1823-1893) United States
African-Dominican Republican-German-American/African-American, to African-Canadian

Ferris, Jeri Chase. *Demanding Justice: A Story about Mary Ann Shadd Cary*. Illustrated by Kimanne Smith. Minneapolis: Carolrhoda Books, 2003. 64 p. (A Creative Minds Biography)

This biography of Mary Ann Shadd Cary stresses her determination that fugitive slaves should have equal rights with whites and her belief that they could demonstrate this entitlement through their self-reliance. During her life she not only taught in both the United States and Canada, but also became the first black woman to publish a weekly newspaper (the *Provincial Freeman*) and to enter a law school (Howard University Law School) where she earned a law degree. The book tells of her disputes with Henry Bibb, her writings, her speeches, and her recruitment work for the Union army.
Intermediate; Nonfiction

Potter, Joan, and Constance Claytor. *African Americans Who Were First*. New York: Cobblehill Books, 1997. 128 p.

A photograph of Mary Ann Shadd Cary accompanies a page summary of her life, which points out that she was the first African-American woman to publish a newspaper in North America and the second African-African woman to receive a law degree in the United States.
Intermediate, Older; Nonfiction

Turner, Glennette Tilley. *Follow in Their Footsteps*. Illustrated with Photographs. New York: Puffin Books, 1999. 192 p.

A chapter on Mary Ann Shadd tells of her childhood and her careers as a teacher, a principal, a newspaper editor in Canada, a founder of the Colored Women's Progressive Franchise Association, and a lawyer. It includes a skit telling of her family's relationship to John Brown and of her nephew Alfred Shadd.
Intermediate, Older; Nonfiction, Fiction

Charbonneau, Jean Baptiste (Pomp) (1805-1866) United States
French Canadian/Shoshone

Bruchac, Joseph. *Sacajawea: The Story of Bird Woman and the Lewis and Clark Expedition*. San Diego: Harcourt/Silver Whistle, 2000. 208 p.

When Jean Baptiste (Pomp) Charbonneau was a young boy, he and his parents visited his adopted uncle Captain William Clark in St. Louis. In this novel Pomp relays the story of his mother and the Lewis and Clark Expedition as it was told to him then through alternating chapters narrated by Sacajawea and Clark. Clark's accounts are preceded by excerpts from his journal and Sacajawea's by traditional tales of the Native Americans encountered during the expedition. In addition to presenting a detailed picture of the Lewis and Clark Expedition from two vantage points, the book includes information on what happened later to the members of the expedition.
Older; Fiction

Collard, Sneed B. III. *Sacagawea: Brave Shoshone Girl*. New York: Benchmark, 2007. 48 p. (American Heroes)

Pages of color reproductions face pages of text in this presentation of Sacagawea's life. A postscript, a chronology, a glossary, a pronunciation guide, a resource section, and an index are appended.
Intermediate; Fiction

Crosby, Michael T. *Sacagawea: Shoshone Explorer*. Stockton, N.J.: OTTN Publishing, 2008. 144 p. (Shapers of America)

Color photographs, maps, informational inserts, a detailed chronology, a glossary, chapter notes, resource lists, and an index combine to provide a well-rounded portrayal of Sacajawea's life. The book tells of the contributions to the Lewis and Clark Expedition made by Toussaint Charbonneau, Pierre Cruzatte, George Drouillard, and François Labiche and presents biographical information on Jean Baptiste (Pomp) Charbonneau.
Older; Nonfiction

Farnsworth, Frances Joyce. *Winged Mocassins: The Story of Sacajawea*. Illustrated by Lorence F. Bjorklund. Englewood Cliffs, N.J.: Responsive Environments Corp., 1954. 190 p.

This fictionalized story of Sacajawea tells of Pomp as a baby on the Lewis and Clark Expedition, of his schooling in St. Louis, of his going to Europe, of his becoming a guide and an interpreter, and of his feeling of not belonging.
Intermediate, Older; Fiction

Frazier, Neta Lohnes. *Sacagawea: The Girl Nobody Knows*. New York: David McKay Company, 1967. 192 p.

This biography of Sacagawea presents the Lewis and Clark Expedition as an important drama placed within the context of American history, with its climax the amazing reunion of Sacagawea with her brother, the Shoshone chief Cameahwait. It quotes from the journals written on the expedition and contains information on their publication. There is also an extensive examination of the later lives of Sacajawea, of Touissant Charbonneau and of Jean Baptiste (Pomp) Charbonneau, who became guide, trader, and interpreter for Kit Carson, Jim Bridger, and others. The book includes a bibliography and an index.
Older; Nonfiction

Murphy, Claire Rudolph. *I Am Sacajawea, I Am York: Our Journey West with Lewis and Clark*. Illustrated by Higgins Bond. New York: Walker & Company, 2005. 32 p.

Text and double-page illustrations present the Lewis and Clark expedition's journey to the Pacific Ocean as seen through the eyes of Sacagawea and York. An afterword, book and website lists, and a pronunciations note are appended.
Primary, Intermediate; Nonfiction

Roop, Peter, and Connie Roop. *Girl of the Shining Mountains: Sacagawea's Story*. New York: Hyperion Books for Children, 1999. 192 p.

As Sacagawea, Charbonneau, and their young son Pomp travel in a flatboat to St. Louis so Pomp can receive the education which Captain Cook has promised, Sacagawea tells the story of her journey to the Pacific Ocean and back and of her earlier life. Her narrative is interspersed with Pomp's questions and her responses. She relates how she had planned to remain with the Shoshone once she was reunited with them in the Shining Mountains (the Rockies), but decided instead to continue with Lewis and Clark when she discovered that her father and sisters were dead and that the Shoshone were suffering from hunger. There is a favorable portrayal of "Papa," Pomp's father Toussaint Charbonneau. Intermediate, Older; Fiction

Seymour, Flora Warren. *Sacagawea: American Pathfinder*. Illustrated by Robert Doremus. New York: Aladdin Paperbacks, 1991. 192 p. (Childhood of Famous Americans)

Sacagawea's childhood with the Shoshone is the focus of this fictionalized biography. It tells of keeping her baby brother from drowning, of her learning to ride a horse, of her making a basket and a dress, of the Sun Dance in which her older brother and other young men had to cut themselves, of her kindness to her grandmother, and of her desires to have a horse and to see white men and the huge salt lake beyond the rivers. After telling of Sacagawea's capture by Minnetaree and her purchase by Toussaint Charbonneau, the story moves on to an account of her return to the Shoshone as part of the Lewis and Clark expedition and a description of the important role she played in its success. Intermediate; Fiction

Williams, Mark London. *Trail of Bones*. Cambridge, Mass.: Candlewick Press, 2005. 320 p. (Danger Boy)

This book is part of a science fiction series in which Eli, an American boy, Thea, a girl from ancient Alexandria, and Clyne, a talking dinosaur, travel in time through the Fifth Dimension. In this story they end up in 1804 where Eli becomes part of the Lewis and Clark Corps of Discovery. Going with the expedition from St. Louis to the Mandan village, he encounters Pierre Cruzatte as well as Sacagawea and Toussaint Charbonneau and witnesses the birth of their son Pomp. Thea is also transported close to St. Louis where both she and Eli meet Thomas Jefferson and Sally Hemings, who have secretly traveled there for the start of Lewis and Clark's trip. However, Thea is mistaken for a runaway slave and is taken back to Monticello. Clyne lands in the wild near the Mandans. At the tale's conclusion all three are together in New Orleans where they once again go into the Fifth Dimension. Intermediate, Older; Fiction

Charbonneau, Toussaint (c. 1758 or 1767-1843) Canada
French Canadian, to Shoshone

Bruchac, Joseph. *Sacajawea: The Story of Bird Woman and the Lewis and Clark Expedition*. San Diego: Harcourt/Silver Whistle, 2000. 208 p.

This story contains extensive references to Toussaint Charbonneau, both as to his character and as to his role as interpreter on the expedition. Older; Fiction

Collard, Sneed B. III. *Sacagawea: Brave Shoshone Girl*. New York: Benchmark, 2007. 48 p. (American Heroes)

Pages of color reproductions face pages of text in this presentation of Sacagawea's life. A postscript, a chronology, a glossary, a pronunciation guide, a resource section, and an index are appended.
Intermediate; Fiction

Crosby, Michael T. *Sacagawea: Shoshone Explorer*. Stockton, N.J.: OTTN Publishing, 2008. 144 p. (Shapers of America)

Color photographs, maps, informational inserts, a detailed chronology, a glossary, chapter notes, resource lists, and an index combine to provide a well-rounded portrayal of Sacajawea's life. The book tells of the contributions to the Lewis and Clark Expedition made by Toussaint Charbonneau, Pierre Cruzatte, George Drouillard, and François Labiche and presents biographical information on Jean Baptiste (Pomp) Charbonneau.
Older; Nonfiction

Farnsworth, Frances Joyce. *Winged Moccasins: The Story of Sacajawea*. Illustrated by Lorence F. Bjorklund. Englewood Cliffs, N.J.: Responsive Environments Corp., 1954. 190 p.

Charbonneau is portrayed very negatively in this story's description of his life before, during, and after the Lewis and Clark Expedition.
Intermediate, Older; Fiction

Frazier, Neta Lohnes. *Sacagawea: The Girl Nobody Knows*. New York: David McKay Company, 1967. 192 p.

This biography of Sacagawea presents the Lewis and Clark Expedition as an important drama placed within the context of American history, with its climax the amazing reunion of Sacagawea with her brother, the Shoshone chief Cameahwait. It quotes from the journals written on the expedition and contains information on their publication. There is also an extensive examination of the later lives of Sacajawea, of Touissaint Charbonneau, and of Jean Baptiste (Pomp) Charbonneau, who became guide, trader, and interpreter for Kit Carson, Jim Bridger, and others. The book includes a bibliography and an index.
Older; Nonfiction

Murphy, Claire Rudolph. *I Am Sacajawea, I Am York: Our Journey West with Lewis and Clark*. Illustrated by Higgins Bond. New York: Walker & Company, 2005. 32 p.

Text and double-page illustrations present the Lewis and Clark expedition's journey to the Pacific Ocean as seen through the eyes of Sacagawea and York. An afterword, book and website lists, and a pronunciations note are appended.
Primary, Intermediate; Nonfiction

O'Dell, Scott. *Streams to the River, River to the Sea: A Novel of Sacagawea*. Boston: Houghton Mifflin Company, 1986. 208 p.

This story relates that Sacagawea was kidnapped twice; that she escaped the second time and survived by herself for a while on an island; that she was won in a game of chance by Charbonneau, whom she despised; that she fell in love with Captain Clark, but came to realize that she could not be his wife; and that Captain Lewis gave her his huge dog Scannon (or Seaman).
Older; Fiction

Roop, Peter, and Connie Roop. *Girl of the Shining Mountains: Sacagawea's Story*. New York: Hyperion Books for Children, 1999. 192 p.
As Sacagawea, Charbonneau, and their young son Pomp travel in a flatboat to St. Louis so Pomp can receive the education which Captain Cook has promised, Sacagawea tells the story of her journey to the Pacific Ocean and back and of her earlier life. Her narrative is interspersed with Pomp's questions and her responses. She relates how she had planned to remain with the Shoshone once she was reunited with them in the Shining Mountains (the Rockies), but decided instead to continue with Lewis and Clark when she discovered that her father and sisters were dead and that the Shoshone were suffering from hunger. There is a favorable portrayal of "Papa," Pomp's father Toussaint Charbonneau.
Intermediate, Older; Fiction

Roop, Peter, and Connie Roop, eds. *Off the Map: The Journals of Lewis and Clark*. Illustrated by Tim Tanner. New York: Walker and Company, 1993. 48 p.
Excerpts from Lewis and Clark's journals cover the commencement of their expedition's journey on May 13, 1804 to its departure on March 23, 1806 from Fort Clatsop for the return trip. The book includes journal entries referring to George Drouillard, Toussaint Charbonneau, and Sacagawea. A prologue presents the expedition's background and the June 20, 1803 letter from President Jefferson to Meriwether Lewis. An epilogue describes the homeward journey and the later lives of members of the Corps of Discovery.
Intermediate, Older; Nonfiction

Seymour, Flora Warren. *Sacagawea: American Pathfinder*. Illustrated by Robert Doremus. New York: Aladdin Paperbacks, 1991. 192 p. (Childhood of Famous Americans)
Sacagawea's childhood with the Shoshone is the focus of this fictionalized biography. It tells of keeping her baby brother from drowning, of her learning to ride a horse, of her making a basket and a dress, of the Sun Dance in which her older brother and other young men had to cut themselves, of her kindness to her grandmother, and of her desires to have a horse and to see white men and the huge salt lake beyond the rivers. After telling of Sacagawea's capture by Minnetaree and her purchase by Toussaint Charbonneau, the story moves on to an account of her return to the Shoshone as part of the Lewis and Clark expedition and a description of the important role she played in its success.
Intermediate; Fiction

Williams, Mark London. *Trail of Bones*. Cambridge, Mass.: Candlewick Press, 2005. 320 p. (Danger Boy)
This book is part of a science fiction series in which Eli, an American boy, Thea, a girl from ancient Alexandria, and Clyne, a talking dinosaur, travel in time through the Fifth Dimension. In this

story they end up in 1804 where Eli becomes part of the Lewis and Clark Corps of Discovery. Going with the expedition from St. Louis to the Mandan village, he encounters Pierre Cruzatte as well as Sacagawea and Toussaint Charbonneau and witnesses the birth of their son Pomp. Thea is also transported close to St. Louis where both she and Eli meet Thomas Jefferson and Sally Hemings, who have secretly traveled there for the start of Lewis and Clark's trip. However, Thea is mistaken for a runaway slave and is taken back to Monticello. Clyne lands in the wild near the Mandans. At the tale's conclusion all three are together in New Orleans where they once again go into the Fifth Dimension. Intermediate, Older; Fiction

Chau, Jen (1970s?-   ) United States
Chinese-American and European-American Jewish

Alderman, Bruce, editor. *Interracial Relationships*. Farmington Hills, Mich.: Greenhaven Press, 2007. 112 p. (Social Issues Firsthand)
    In a narrative reproduced from *New/Demographic* Jen Chau relates how, growing up, she didn't tell her parents of her experiences as a mixed race child. As founder of Swirl, Inc., an organization serving the mixed race community, she urges parents to initiate open discussions of race with their mixed race children.
Older; Nonfiction

Chisholm, Jesse (1805 or 1806-1868) United States
Scottish-American/Cherokee

Basel, Roberta. *Sequoyah: Inventor of Written Cherokee*. Minneapolis: Compass Point Books, 2007. 112 p. (Signature Lives)
    This biography of Sequoyah reports that Jesse Chisholm went to search for Sequoyah after he failed to return from his Mexican trip, reported his death to the Cherokee Nation, and fulfilled Sequoyah's mission of bringing a group of Cherokee north out of Mexico.
Older; Nonfiction

Sanford, William R. *The Chisholm Trail in American History*. Berkeley Heights, N.J.: Enslow Publishers, 2000. 112 p. (In American History)
    This book on the Chisholm Trail, which contains a picture of Jesse Chisholm, tells how he worked for the United States government to make trails in Indian Territory, had three trading posts in what is now Oklahoma, remained neutral in the Civil War, and traded with the Apaches, Kiowa, and Comanche. The route Chisholm used to trade with the Kiowa was later used to drive cattle north to the railroad shipping town of Abilene, Kansas, and was named after him.
Intermediate; Nonfiction

Santella, Andrew. *The Chisholm Trail*. New York: Children's Press, 1997. 32 p. (Cornerstones of Freedom)
    This book briefly mentions Jesse Chisholm and the trading wagon he drove on the trail between

Wichita, Kansas, and the Washita River. The trail later became part of the Chisholm Trail.
Primary, Intermediate; Nonfiction

Cho, Stephanie (19??-   ) South Korea
South Korean, by European-American

Stanford, Eleanor, ed. *Interracial America: Opposing Viewpoints*. Farmington Hills, Mich.: Greenhaven Press, 2006. 208 p. (Opposing Viewpoints)
    In Stephanie Cho and Kim So Yung's opinion piece "Transracial Adoption Should be Discouraged" the authors describe how their negative experiences as Korean children adopted by whites caused them to found Transracial Abductees, an organization assisting those adoptees in assimilating into communities of color.
Older; Nonfiction

Chung, Constance (Connie) Yu-Hwa ((1946-   ) United States
Chinese-American non-Jewish, to Lithuanian-European-American Jewish

Malone, Mary. *Connie Chung: Broadcast Journalist*. Hillside, N.J.: Enslow Publishers, 1992. 128 p. (Contemporary Women Series)
    This in-depth biography of Connie Chung places her life and career within the context of events occurring in the broadcasting industry and the political world. It describes her childhood; her start as a copygirl for a Washington, D.C. television station; her coverage for CBS of George McGovern's 1972 presidential campaign, the Watergate scandal, and Nelson Rockefeller's vice-presidential confirmation; her job as local news anchor at a Los Angeles television station; and her later work as a television anchor at NBC and CBS. The book tells of her demanding work ethic, her learning to be aggressive and to develop sources, and her marriage to Maury Povich. Photographs, a chronology, a reading list, and an index are included.
Older; Nonfiction

Coker, Daniel (1780-1846) United States
African-American/European-American

Cox, Clinton. *African American Teachers*. New York: John Wiley & Sons, 2000. 176 p. (Black Stars)
    A biographical chapter describes how Daniel Coker, who was born a slave, became a Methodist minister who argued against slavery, helped found the African Methodist Episcopal Church, and built a church in Freetown, Sierra Leone. He also taught for fourteen years at the African School in Baltimore.
Older; Nonfiction

Cole, Lynette (1978-   ) United States
European-Puerto Rican-American, by European-American

Slade, Suzanne Buckingham. *Adopted: The Ultimate Teen Guide*. Illustrated by Christopher Papile, Mary Sandage, and Odelia Witt. Photographs by Chris Washburn. Lanham, Md.: The Scarecrow Press, 2007. 272 p. (It Happened to Me, No. 20)

As reported in one of this book's chapters, Lynette Cole's adoptive parents had to move to another state because Michigan would not allow their adoption of a child who was part Puerto Rican. In 2000 she was crowned Miss Tennessee and then Miss USA. She has worked with the Congressional Coalition on Adoption.
Older; Nonfiction

Coleman, Elizabeth (Bessie) (1892-, 1893-, or 1896-1926) United States
African-American, Cherokee and/or Choctaw/African-American

Borden, Louise, and Mary Kay Kroeger. *Fly High! The Story of Bessie Coleman*. Illustrated by Teresa Flavin. New York: Margaret K. McElderry Books, 2001. 40 p.

Color paintings illustrate this story of the life of aviatrix Bessie Coleman, who became "somebody" and told black children that they could too.
Intermediate; Nonfiction

Brager, Bruce L. *Bessie Coleman*. Illustrated by Ron Mazellan. New York: Scholastic, 2002. 16 p.
This illustrated book presents a factual account of Bessie Coleman's life.
Intermediate; Nonfiction

Braun, Eric. *Bessie Coleman*. Mankato, Minn.: Capstone Press, 2006. 24 p. (First Biographies)
An introduction to Bessie Coleman for beginning readers, this book includes text, a timeline, a glossary, a reading list, photographs, and an index.
Pre-K, Primary; Nonfiction

Briggs, Carole S. *At the Controls: Women in Aviation*. Minneapolis: Lerner Publications Company, 1991. 72 p.
A chapter on barnstormers and ferry pilots includes a photograph and several paragraphs on Bessie Coleman.
Intermediate, Older; Nonfiction

Fisher, Lillian M. *Brave Bessie Flying Free*. Dallas: Hendrick-Long Publishing Co., 1995. 88 p.
Photographs, a postscript, a listing of books about airplanes, a glossary, a poem entitled "Bessie's Song," the words of the chorus of "Come Josephine in My Flying Machine," and an index are included in this biography of Bessie Coleman.
Intermediate, Older; Nonfiction

Grimes, Nikki. *Talkin' About Bessie: The Story of Aviator Elizabeth Coleman*. Illustrated by E. B. Lewis. New York: Orchard Books, 2002. 48 p.
Each double-page spread in this fictional biography, which is based on fact, presents a different

period in Bessie Coleman's life: a page of imaginary monologue by a family member, an acquaintance, or an observer faces a full-page painting depicting Bessie Coleman during that period.
Intermediate, Older; Fiction

Hart, Philip S. *Bessie Coleman*. Minneapolis: Lerner Publications Company, 2005. 112 p. (Just the Facts Biographies)
    Informational inserts and chapter section headings distinguish this account of Bessie Coleman's life. It also contains photographs, a timeline, a glossary, a bibliography, a resource section, and an index.
Intermediate, Older; Nonfiction

Hart, Philip S. *Up in the Air: The Story of Bessie Coleman*. Minneapolis: Carolrhoda Books, 1996. 80 p.
    This comprehensive biography of Bessie Coleman emphasizes her desire to establish a flight school for African-Americans and relates how, after her death, the Bessie Coleman Aero Club was founded in Los Angeles. Photographs, notes, a bibliography, and an index complement the text.
Intermediate, Older; Nonfiction

Haskins, Jim. *Black Eagles: African-Americans in Aviation*. New York: Scholastic, 1995. 208 p.
    A chapter in this book discusses how Bessie Coleman had to go to Europe to receive pilot training, how she continually struggled to receive financing, and how she promoted her career. It includes photographs.
Intermediate, Older; Nonfiction

Johnson, Dolores. *She Dared To Fly: Bessie Coleman*. New York: Benchmark Books, 1997. 48 p. (Benchmark Biographies)
    Large black-and-white photographs are features of this biography of Bessie Coleman, which also includes a glossary, a reading list, and an index.
Primary, Intermediate; Nonfiction

Johnson, LaVerne C. *Bessie Coleman*. Illustrated by Craig Rex Perry. Chicago: Empak Enterprises, 1992. 32 p. (The Empak Heritage Kids)
    In this graphic story two fictional African children magically travel through time and space to present Bessie Coleman to young children.
Pre-K, Primary; Fiction

Jones, Stanley P. *African-American Aviators: Bessie Coleman, William J. Powell, James Herman Banning, Benjamin O. Davis Jr., General Daniel James Jr.* Mankato, Minn.: Capstone High/Low Books, 1998. 48 p. (Capstone Short Biographies)
    With photographs and a brief text, a chapter in this book presents an introduction to Bessie Coleman.
Primary; Nonfiction

Joseph, Lynn. *Fly, Bessie, Fly*. Illustrated by Yvonne Buchanan. New York: Simon & Schuster Books for Young Readers, 1998. 32 p.

Full-page watercolor paintings illustrate this story of Bessie Coleman's fulfillment of her dream to fly. An author's note is appended.
Pre-K, Primary; Fiction

Lindbergh, Reeve. *Nobody Owns the Sky: The Story of "Brave Bessie" Coleman*. Illustrated by Pamela Paparone. Cambridge, Mass.: Candlewick Press, 1996. 24 p.

In this picture book about Bessie Coleman, a poem by the author, who is the daughter of Charles Lindbergh, is accompanied by large colorful paintings.
Pre-K, Primary; Fiction

McLoone, Margo. *Women Explorers of the Air: Harriet Quimby, Bessie Coleman, Amelia Earhardt, Beryl Markham, Jacqueline Cochran*. Mankato, Minn.: Capstone Books, 2000. 48 p.

Photographs and text present a summary of Bessie Coleman's life in one of this book's chapters.
Primary; Nonfiction

Plantz, Connie. *Bessie Coleman: First Black Woman Pilot*. Berkeley Heights, N.J.: Enslow Publishers, 2001. 128 p. (African-American Biographies)

This extensive biography places Bessie Coleman's life within the context of the periods and places where she lived and describes her legacy. Photographs, chapter notes, a chronology, a reading list, internet addresses, and an index are included.
Older; Nonfiction

Potter, Joan, and Constance Claytor. *African Americans Who Were First*. New York: Cobblehill Books, 1997. 128 p.

A page description of Bessie Coleman's career, accompanied by a photograph, acclaims her as the first African-American woman to receive a pilot's license.
Intermediate, Older; Nonfiction

Rappaport, Doreen. *Living Dangerously: American Women Who Risked Their Lives for Adventure*. New York: HarperCollins Publishers, 1991. 128 p.

A story in this book tells of Bessie Coleman's flying exhibition in her hometown of Waxahachie, Texas.
Intermediate; Fiction

Robbins, Trina. *Bessie Coleman: Daring Stunt Pilot*. Illustrated by Ken Steacy. Mankato, Minn.: Capstone, 2007. 32 p. (Graphic Biographies)

This graphic presentation of Bessie Coleman includes fictional dialogue, direct quotations with sources, appended information, a glossary, a reading list, a bibliography, and an index.
Intermediate, Older; Fiction

Turner, Glennette Tilley. *Follow in Their Footsteps*. Illustrated with Photographs. New York: Puffin Books, 1999. 192 p.

A biographical chapter on the pilot Bessie Coleman tells how she received an international pilot's license, became a barnstormer, and was killed in an airplane crash at an air show in Jacksonville, Florida. It includes a skit about her flying exhibition in Illinois in 1922.
Intermediate, Older; Fiction, Nonfiction

Walker, Sally M. *Bessie Coleman: Daring to Fly*. Illustrated by Janice Lee Porter. Minneapolis: Carolrhoda Books, 2003. 48 p. (On My Own Biography)

Emphasizing Bessie Coleman's venturesomeness and determination, this easy-to-read biography covers her life from childhood through her recovery from a plane crash in California. It includes an afterword and a chronology.
Pre-K, Primary; Nonfiction

Yount, Lisa. *Women Aviators*. New York: Facts on File, 1995. 160 p. (American Profiles)

This book's chapter on Bessie Coleman, which includes two photographs, a chronology, and a reading list, recounts her life and its inspiration to African-Americans.
Older; Nonfiction

Collier, Samuel (1595?-1622) England
English, by Warraskoyack

Carbone, Elisa. *Blood on the River: James Town, 1607*. New York: Viking, 2006. 256 p.

Londoner Samuel Collier is the narrator of this novel, which chronicles his life from 1606 when he was chosen at age eleven to go to Virginia as John Smith's page to 1610 when he was safely living in Point Comfort, Virginia, with the Laydon family. It details the discomforts of the voyage, the experiences of the passengers in the West Indies, and the struggles of the colonists in Jamestown. Samuel observes firsthand the selfishness and foolishness of the gentlemen who lived in Jamestown and their hostility towards John Smith. In Virginia, Samuel learned the values of working cooperatively and of channeling his anger and enjoyed the months he spent living with the Warraskoyack Indians. After Smith had gone back to England, and realizing that Jamestown was in peril, Samuel saved Ann Laydon and her baby by kidnapping the baby. The book mentions Thomas Savage and how Thomas spent time with the Pamunkey. It also contains an afterword.
Intermediate, Older; Fiction

Karwoski, Gail Langer. *Surviving Jamestown: The Adventures of Young Sam Collier*. Illustrated by Paul Casale. Atlanta: Peachtree Publishers, 2001. 208 p.

This fictionalized biography of Sam Collier covers his life as John Smith's page from their trip to Virginia aboard the *Susan Constant* to Smith's return to England when Sam's service to him ended. It tells of the severe illness which Smith, Sam, and others suffered in Jamestown in 1607; of the animosity of the gentlemen towards Smith, who was of a lower social class and a strict taskmaster; of Sam's

closeness to Smith; of his relationships with the settlement's three other English boys; and of his time with the Warraskoyack Indians,
Intermediate, Older; Fiction

Ransom, Candice. *Sam Collier and the Founding of Jamestown*. Illustrated by Matthew Archambault. Minneapolis: Millbrook Press, 2006. 48 p.
(On My Own History)

This fictionalized story of Sam Collier, John Smith's page, presents the twelve-year-old's 1607 experiences in Jamestown following the colonists' April landing. The early reader tells of the difficulties the settlers experienced and of both the hostility and the friendship of Indians they encountered. An afterword gives no mention of Collier's spending time with the Indians.
Pre-K, Primary; Fiction

Crawford, Goldsby (also Cherokee Bill) (1876-1896) United States
African-European-American and Cherokee and possibly Sioux or Mexican

Monceaux, Morgan, and Ruth Katcher. *My Heroes, My People: African Americans and Native Americans in the West*. Illustrated by Morgan Monceaux. New York: Frances Foster Books, 1999. 64 p.

Remembered as part of the history of the West, Crawford Goldsby (Cherokee Bill) was a notorious robber and murderer until he was executed at the age of twenty. The book's brief presentation includes his portrait.
Intermediate, Older; Nonfiction

Cruzatte, Pierre (?-?) United States
French/Omaha

Crosby, Michael T. *Sacagawea: Shoshone Explorer*. Stockton, N.J.: OTTN Publishing, 2008. 144 p.
(Shapers of America)

Color photographs, maps, informational inserts, a detailed chronology, a glossary, chapter notes, resource lists, and an index combine to provide a well-rounded portrayal of Sacajawea's life. The book tells of the contributions to the Lewis and Clark Expedition made by Toussaint Charbonneau, Pierre Cruzatte, George Drouillard, and François Labiche and presents biographical information on Jean Baptiste (Pomp) Charbonneau.
Older; Nonfiction

Myers, Laurie. *Lewis and Clark and Me. A Dog's Tale*. Illustrated by Michael Dooling. New York: Henry Holt and Company, 2002. 80 p.

Seaman, a Newfoundland, describes his purchase by Meriwether Lewis and his adventures on the Lewis and Clark expedition: catching numerous swimming squirrels, being mistaken for a bear by Shawnee Indians, feeling jealous of a buffalo calf, almost losing his life to a wounded beaver, saving men from a charging buffalo, being briefly stolen by Clatsop Indians, and, above all, treasuring his relationship with Lewis. Seaman's account mentions George Drouillard, Sacagawea, and Pierre

Cruzatte. The book features full- and double-page paintings, a map, an introduction, an afterword, and a source list.

Intermediate; Fiction

Williams, Mark London. *Trail of Bones*. Cambridge, Mass.: Candlewick Press, 2005. 320 p. (Danger Boy)

This book is part of a science fiction series in which Eli, an American boy, Thea, a girl from ancient Alexandria, and Clyne, a talking dinosaur, travel in time through the Fifth Dimension. In this story they end up in 1804 where Eli becomes part of the Lewis and Clark Corps of Discovery. Going with the expedition from St. Louis to the Mandan village, he encounters Pierre Cruzatte as well as Sacagawea and Toussaint Charbonneau and witnesses the birth of their son Pomp. Thea is also transported close to St. Louis where both she and Eli meet Thomas Jefferson and Sally Hemings, who have secretly traveled there for the start of Lewis and Clark's trip. However, Thea is mistaken for a runaway slave and is taken back to Monticello. Clyne lands in the wild near the Mandans. At the tale's conclusion all three are together in New Orleans where they once again go into the Fifth Dimension.

Intermediate, Older; Fiction

Wolf, Allan. *New Found Land: Lewis and Clark's Voyage of Discovery, A Novel*. Cambridge, Mass.: Candlewick Press, 2004. 512 p.

Although he had only one eye, Pierre Cruzatte served as river pilot on the Lewis and Clark Expedition and also raised the spirits of the Corps of Discovery with his fiddle playing. He is one of the narrators of this detailed story of the expedition. Speaking in prose and poetry and expressing their individual perspectives and feelings, often with a sense of humor, the narrators cover the period from the June 1803 request of President Thomas Jefferson to Meriwether Lewis to lead the expedition to July 1819, ten years after Lewis's death. The novel contains maps, a glossary, resources, and additional information on the expedition, including what later happened to each narrator.

Older; Fiction

Cuffe, Paul (1759-1817) United States
Ashanti/Gay Head Wampanoag or Pequot, to Wampanoag or Pequot

Diamond, Arthur. *Paul Cuffe: Merchant and Abolitionist*. Philadelphia: Chelsea House Publishers, 1989. 112 p. (Black Americans of Achievement)

This detailed biography of the merchant Paul Cuffe tells of the development of his shipping company, which included a shipyard and engaged in trans-Atlantic as well as coastal trading. It describes his efforts to establish a trading relationship with Sierra Leone, to set up a home there for American freed slaves, to develop Sierra Leone's economy, and to stop the slave trade.

Intermediate, Older; Nonfiction

Greenfield, Eloise. *How They Got Over: African Americans and the Call of the Sea*. Illustrated by Jan Spivey Gilchrist. New York: Amistad, 2003. 128 p.

A biographical chapter on Paul Cufffe emphasizes his connection to the sea: his learning about boats as a boy, his sailing on cargo ships, and his successful shipping business.
Intermediate; Nonfiction

Harbison, David. *Reaching for Freedom: Paul Cuffe, Norbert Rillieux, Iva Aldridge, James McCune Smith*. New York: Scholastic Book Services, 1972. 128 p. (Firebird Biographies)
Illustrated with photographs, five chapters in this book present a biography of Paul Cuffe that focuses on his shipping career and his efforts to persuade free blacks to emigrate to Sierra Leone.
Intermediate, Older; Nonfiction

Katz, William Loren, and Paula A. Franklin. *Proudly Red and Black: Stories of African and Native Americans*. New York: Atheneum, 1993. 96 p.
The chapter on Paul Cuffe emphasizes his background, his protest against Massachusetts' taxation without representation of men of color, and his work towards establishing an African-American colony in Sierra Leone.
Intermediate, Older; Nonficton

Kranz, Rachel C. *The Biographical Dictionary of Black Americans*. New York: Facts on File, 1992. 192 p.
Paul Cuffe's support of the rights of black people, his desire to bring Christianity to Sierra Leone, and his efforts to settle American blacks in that African country are highlighted in a section on the successful shipping company owner.
Intermediate, Older; Nonfiction

McKissack, Patricia C., and Frederick L. McKissack. *Black Hands, White Sails: The Story of African-American Whalers*. New York: Scholastic Press, 1999. 176 p.
A section on Paul Cuffe tells of the development of his shipping business, of his whaling voyages to Africa, of his advocacy of returning blacks to Africa, and of the careers at sea of his two sons, a son-in-law, and a nephew.
Older; Nonfiction

Nash, Gary B. *Forbidden Love: The Secret History of Mixed-Race America*. New York: Henry Holt and Company, 1999. 224 p.
This book's profile of Paul Cuffe emphasizes that he was a man of three cultures. He adopted the African name of his father rather the English name of his father's slave owner and worked towards setting up a refuge for African-Americans in Africa. He married Alice Pequit, who was Wampanoag or Pequot, and joined in business with an Indian brother-in-law. He became a Quaker, dressed as a Quaker, and is buried in a Quaker cemetery.
Older; Nonfiction

Culberson, Sarah (1976-   ) United States
Sierra Leonean/European-American, by European-American

Slade, Suzanne Buckingham. *Adopted: The Ultimate Teen Guide*. Illustrated by Christopher Papile, Mary Sandage, and Odelia Witt. Photographs by Chris Washburn. Lanham, Md.: The Scarecrow Press, 2007. 272 p. (It Happened to Me, No. 20)

An informational insert in this book tells how Sarah Culberson, who grew up in her adoptive European-American family in Morgantown, West Virginia, discovered as a young adult that she was the daughter of a Mende chief in Sierra Leone. After visiting him she helped with a foundation bearing his name that raises funds to help African people.
Older; Nonfiction

Dandridge, Dorothy (1922-1965) United States
English-African-American/Jamaican-Spanish-Native Mexican-American, to African-American, to European-American

Schoell, William. *Heartbreaker: The Dorothy Dandridge Story*. Greensboro, N.C.: Avisson Press, 2002. 128 p. (Avisson Young Adult Series)

This biography of the singer-actress Dorothy Dandridge tells how her entertainer mother arranged tours where young Dorothy and her sister Vivian performed as the Wonder Kids. It describes in detail the movies in which Dandridge appeared, the career difficulties she encountered because of her mixed race, her nomination for a Best Actress Oscar for her role in *Carmen Jones*, her two unfortunate marriages, her severely developmentally-disabled daughter, her later problems financially and as a Hollywood has-been, and her tragic death. The book includes a filmography, a bibliography, and an index.
Older; Nonfiction

Dare, Virginia (1587-?) United States
English-American, by Croatan (legend)

Hooks, William H. *The Legend of White Doe*. Illustrated by Dennis Nolan. New York: Macmillan Publishing Company, 1988. 48 p.

Virginia Dare was the first child born of English parents in America. However, when the English returned to her Roanoke Island birthplace three years later, the entire colony had disappeared. This book relates the legend in which Virginia was adopted by a Croatan woman, who lived on Croatan Island. She fell in love with a young Croatan, but when they had to run away to be married, Virginia, now known as Ulalee, was changed into a white deer.
Intermediate; Fiction

Dawson, Toby (born Kim Bong-seok) (1978-   ) South Korea
South Korean, by European-American

Slade, Suzanne Buckingham. *Adopted: The Ultimate Teen Guide*. Illustrated by Christopher Papile, Mary Sandage, and Odelia Witt. Photographs by Chris Washburn. Lanham, Md.: The Scarecrow Press, 2007. 272 p. (It Happened to Me, No. 20)

An informational insert in this book describes how Toby Dawson was lost while with his mother at a Busan, South Korea market, put in an orphanage in Seoul, and adopted by ski instructors from Vail, Colorado. In the 2006 Olympics in Torino, Italy, he won the bronze medal in the men's mogul event. After the Olympics he was reunited with his birthfather, who had looked for him. Dawson has worked at the Korean heritage camp which he attended as a boy.
Older; Nonfiction

de Pareja, Juan (c.1610-1670) Spain
Spanish/African-Spanish, by Portuguese-Spanish

Borton de Treviño, Elizabeth. *I, Juan de Pareja*. New York: Bell Books, 1965. 192 p.
This book of historical fiction traces the life of Juan de Pareja, assistant to the painter Diego Velázquez and a painter in his own right. After the death of his mistress in Seville, Pareja, her orphan slave, was sent in the care of a cruel gypsy to the Madrid home of her nephew, Velázquez. There he worked for Velázquez, who was a court painter for King Philip IV, and became friends with Velázquez's apprentice Bartolomé Esteban Murillo. Pareja longed to paint, but a Spanish law prohibited slaves from engaging in the arts. After guiltily painting in secret, Parejo was freed by Velázquez when his secret was revealed.
Older; Fiction

Deloria, Ella Cara (also Anpetu Waste Win, Beautiful Day) (1889-1971) United States
French-American and Dakota/Dakota and Irish-American

Avery, Susan, and Linda Skinner. *Extraordinary American Indians*. Chicago: Children's Press, 1992. 272 p.
As reported in a section on the Deloria family, Ella Deloria, a Columbia University graduate, spent most of her working life researching and writing about the Dakota culture and language. A noted linguist and anthropologist, she also wrote a novel, *Waterlily*.
Older; Nonfiction

Deloria, Philip Samuel (Sam) (19?-   ) United States
French- and Irish-American and Dakota/European-American?

Avery, Susan, and Linda Skinner. *Extraordinary American Indians*. Chicago: Children's Press, 1992. 272 p.
Included in the section on the Delorias is Sam Deloria, a son of Vine Deloria, Sr. A lawyer, he became director of the University of New Mexico Law School's American Indian Law Center and Secretary General of the World Council of Indigenous Peoples.
Older; Nonfiction

Deloria, Vine, Jr. (1933-2005) United States
French- and Irish-American and Dakota/European-American?

Avery, Susan, and Linda Skinner. *Extraordinary American Indians*. Chicago: Children's Press, 1992. 272 p.

As related in the biographical section on the Delorias, Vine Deloria, Jr., a son of Vine Deloria, Sr., graduated from the University of Colorado Law School, served as executive director of the National Council of American Indians, became a professor of political science, and wrote, among other books, *Custer Died for Your Sins: An Indian Manifesto*.
Older; Nonfiction

Deloria, Vine, Sr. (1901-1990) United States
French-American and Dakota/Dakota and Irish-American

Avery, Susan, and Linda Skinner. *Extraordinary American Indians*. Chicago: Children's Press, 1992. 272 p.

The book's section on the Delorias reports that Vine was a cousin of Ella Deloria, but other sources state that he was her brother and his background is listed here as the same as hers. Like his father he became an Episcopal priest. He not only served as a minister on Indian reservations in South Dakota and in Denison, Iowa, but also became General Secretary for Indian Work at the national headquarters of the Episcopal Church.
Older; Nonfiction

dePaola, Tomie (1934-   ) United States
Italian-American/Irish-American

Braun, Eric. *Tomie dePaola*. Mankato, Minn.: Capstone Press, 2005. 24 p. (First Biographies)

This early reader introduction to children's book author and illustrator Tomie dePaola features a large print text, a timeline, photographs, a glossary, a resource list, and an index.
Pre-K, Primary; Nonfiction

dePaola, Tomie, *The Art Lesson*. Illustrated by author. New York: G. P. Putnam's Sons, 1989. 32 p.

In this picture book art-loving Tommy (Tomie dePaola) is in first grade and finally has an art teacher. When the class is told that they can have only one piece of paper, must copy what the teacher has drawn, and can use only the eight crayons which the school provides, Tommy refuses to draw. The art teacher and the classroom teacher agree that after he has completed the assignment he may have a second piece of paper to make a picture using the sixty-four crayons he has received for his birthday. Tommy then makes his own picture and has continued to make them.
Pre-K, Primary; Fiction

dePaola, Tomie. *The Baby Sister*. Illustrated by author. New York: G. P. Putnam' Sons, 1996. 32 p.

Tomie (called Tommy in this book) awaits the birth of his baby sibling: hoping it will be a sister, painting pictures for the baby's room, initially not wanting his Italian grandmother Nana Fall-River to care for him—and then happily holding his new sister Maureen.
Pre-K, Primary; Fiction

dePaola, Tomie. *Christmas Remembered*. Illustrated by author. New York: G. P. Putnam's Sons, 2006. 96 p

Tomie dePaola presents his memories of Christmases that he spent as a boy in Meriden, Connecticut, as a young man at Benedictine monasteries in Connecticut and in Vermont, and later in Vermont, San Francisco, New York City, Santa Fe, and New Hampshire.
Intermediate, Older; Nonfiction

dePaola, Tomie. *Here We All Are*. Illustrated by author. New York: G. P. Putnam's Sons, 2000. 80 p. (A 26 Fairmount Avenue Book)

In this sequel to *26 Fairmount Avenue*, Tomie dePaola, now living in his new house, licks the bedpost of his maple bed to see if it tastes like maple syrup, steals the show in his kindergarten class play, makes a valentine mailbox for the kindergarten-first grade valentine party, and gets his long-awaited baby sister with the red ribbon in her hair.
Pre-K, Primary; Fiction

dePaola, Tomie. *I'm Still Scared*. Illustrated by author. New York: G.P. Putnam's Sons, 2006. 96 p. (A 26 Fairmount Avenue Book)

During December 1941 second grader Tomie experiences many changes in his life: the country going to war, his uncle joining the army, his father taking a nighttime war job, being called an enemy because of his Italian heritage, air raid drills, blackout curtains, and a newsreel of the bombing of London. It's all scary, especially when adults whisper to each other, but won't tell children what's going on. Tomie's parents and grandfather make it better by giving explanations, but at the end of the year, Tomie is still scared. This is the sixth *26 Fairmount Avenue Book*.
Primary; Fiction

dePaola, Tomie. *Nana Upstairs & Nana Downstairs*. Illustrated by author. New York: G. P. Putnam's Sons, 1988. 32 p.

This picture book tells of four-year-old Tommy's (Tomie dePaola's) Sunday visits with his grandmother Nana Downstairs and his ninety-four year-old great-grandmother Nana Upstairs. Tommy and Nana Upstairs are the best of friends, but one morning Tommy learns that she has died.
Pre-K, Primary; Fiction

dePaola, Tomie. *On My Way*. Illustrated by author. New York: G. P. Putnam's Sons, 2001. 80 p. (A 26 Fairmount Avenue Book)

In this third book of the *26 Fairmount Avenue* series, Tomie is frightened when his newborn sister Maureen gets pneumonia, recalls going to the 1939 New York World's Fair earlier in his kindergarten year, gets a slippery blacktop driveway at his house, learns how to play forfeits, celebrates the Fourth of July, goes to two beaches, and starts first grade. Eager to learn to read, he sneaks his reading book home, learns to read the entire book over the weekend, and gets his much-wanted library card.
Pre-K, Primary; Fiction

dePaola, Tomie. *Things Will Never Be the Same*. Illustrated by author. New York: G. P. Putnam's Sons, 2003. 80 p. (A 26 Fairmount Avenue Book)

This fifth *26 Fairmount Avenue Book* presents Tomie's experiences in 1941, both through text and pages of his diary. Tomie enjoys sledding, watching the movie Fantasia, and being a pirate in his dance school's spring recital. In July he can't go swimming or to the movies because of a polio threat, but in August he goes to an amusement park. Tomie starts second grade in September. On December 7 he learns of the Japanese attack on Pearl Harbor, and, although he's not sure what it means, he hears his mother say that "things will never be the same."
Primary; Fiction

dePaola, Tomie. *Tom*. Illustrated by author. New York: G. P. Putnam's Sons, 1993. 32 p.

Based on Tomie dePaola's life, this picture book shows how he loved being with his Irish-American grandfather. One time he planted a chicken head from his grandparents' grocery store in the garden and another time he turned two chicken feet into hands that scared his schoolmates and a teacher.
Pre-K, Primary; Fiction

dePaola, Tomie. *26 Fairmount Avenue*. Illustrated by author. New York: G. P. Putnam's Sons, 1999. 64 p. (A 26 Fairmount Avenue Book)

This is the first in a series of autobiographical chapter books about Tomie dePaola's childhood. It tells of Tomie as a four- and five-year-old during the period his family's new house at 26 Fairmount Avenue is being built and describes the 1938 hurricane which hits Meriden, Connecticut. Tomie's experiences include his mistaking laxatives for chocolates, yelling out during the movie *Snow White and the Seven Dwarfs* because the film isn't true to the book, decorating the plasterboard of the new house with drawings of his family, walking out of kindergarten because the teacher won't teach him how to read, and finally moving into his new home.
Pre-K, Primary; Fiction

dePaola, Tomie. *What a Year*. Illustrated by author. New York: G. P. Putnam's Sons, 2002. 80 p. (A 26 Fairmount Avenue Book)

Celebrations are an important part of Tomie's first grade year. He celebrates his September birthday at school, at home, and at his grandparents; trick-or-treats with his brother as Snow White and the Wicked Witch; enjoys seeing the movie *Pinocchio* the day after Thanksgiving; has an important role in his class Christmas play; receives a Junior Flexible Flyer sled from Santa Claus; and stays up on New Years Eve. He also suffers through a bad case of chickenpox. This is the fourth *26 Fairmount Avenue Book*.
Primary; Fiction

dePaola, Tomie. *Why?* Illustrated by author. New York: G. P. Putnam's Sons, 2007. 96 p. (A 26 Fairmont Avenue Book)

As a second grader in early 1942, Tomie dePaola helps in his grandparents' grocery store, hates penmanship, loses his first baby tooth, and loves learning how to make valentines. However, with the

beginning of World War II he also learns about shortages and rationing and experiences the death of his beloved cousin Blackie whose bomber is shot down in Europe. This book is the seventh in the *26 Fairmont Avenue* series.
Primary, Intermediate; Fiction

Woods, Mae. *Tomie dePaola*. Edina, Minn.: ABDO Publishing Company, 2000. 24 p. (Children's Authors)
Photographs, a glossary of bolded words in the text, website and address information, and an index accompany this look at Tomie dePaola.
Primary, Intermediate; Nonfiction

Depp, John (Johnny) Christopher II (1963-   ) United States
German-Irish-American and Cherokee, to European-American, to French

Bingham, Jane. *Johnny Depp*. Chicago: Raintree, 2006. 48 p. (Star Files)
This book provides information on Johnny Depp's personal and professional life and tells of his Cherokee heritage. Its pages include text, color photographs, inserts often giving information on persons mentioned in the text, and definitions of bolded words. A reading list; listings of Depp's films, music videos and albums; a glossary; and an index are appended.
Intermediate, Older; Nonfiction

Hawes, Esma. *Johnny Depp*. Philadelphia: Chelsea House Publishers, 1998. 48 p. (Superstars of Film)
Johnny Depp's career through 1996 is described in depth in this biography, which features color photographs and contains a filmography and an index.
Older; Nonfiction

Higgins, Kara. *Johnny Depp*. Farmington Hills, Mich.: Lucent Books, 2004. 96 p. (People in the News)
This comprehensive biography of Johnny Depp covers his early ambition to be a rock star, his emergence as a movie character actor and director, his movie roles, his romances, the downtimes in his personal life, and the beneficial effects of fatherhood. It includes photographs, a chronology, chapter notes, a listing of consulted works, a reading list, and an index.
Older; Nonfiction

Thomas, William David. *Johnny Depp*. Milwaukee: Garth Stevens Publishing, 2007. 32 p. (Today's Superstars: Entertainment)
This biography of Johnny Depp tells how the nonconformist actor likes to play different, sometimes unusual, characters. It traces his personal life and describes his movie and television roles. Color photographs, informational inserts, a timeline, a glossary, a resource list, and an index are included.
Intermediate; Nonfiction

Tracy, Kathleen. *Johnny Depp*. Hockessin, Del.: Mitchell Lane Publishers, 2008. 32 p. (Blue Banner Biography)

A number of quotations from Johnny Depp are included in this biography, which also features color photographs, a chronology, a filmography, a source list, a resource list, and an index.
Intermediate, Older; Nonfiction

Dockstader, Frederick J. (1919-1998) United States
Oneida and Navajo

Avery, Susan, and Linda Skinner. *Extraordinary American Indians*. Chicago: Children's Press, 1992. 272 p.
   A section on the anthropologist Frederick J. Dockstader relates that he lived most of his childhood on Navajo and Hopi reservations and received advanced degrees from Arizona State College and Western Reserve University. He was a renowned silversmith, wrote books on Native American art, and for some twenty years served as director of the Museum of the American Indian, Heye Foundation, in New York City as well as a commissioner of the U. S. Interior Department's Indian Arts and Crafts Board.
Older; Nonfiction

Dorris, Michael (1945-1997) United States
Modoc and English-French American/Irish-Swiss-American, to Turtle Mountain Chippewa, German-American, and French Canadian

Allen, Paula Gunn, and Patricia Clark Smith. *As Long as the Rivers Flow: The Stories of Nine Native Americans*. New York: Scholastic Press, 1996. 336 p.
   The chapter on Louise Erdrich tells of her husband, Michael Dorris: his professorship at Dartmouth College, his writing with Erdrich, and his book *The Broken Cord* about their adopted Sioux son who had Fetal Alcohol Syndrome.
Intermediate, Older; Nonfiction

Avery, Susan, and Linda Skinner. *Extraordinary American Indians*. Chicago: Children's Press, 1992. 272 p.
   A section on Louise Erdrich and Michael Dorris stresses their mutual assistance in writing books about Native Americans.
Older; Nonficton

Douglass, Frederick (born Frederick Augustus Washington Bailey) (1817 or 1818-1895) United States
European-American/African-American, to African-American, to European-American

Adler, David A. *A Picture Book of Frederick Douglass*. Illustrated by Samuel Byrd. New York: Holiday House, 1993. 32 p.
   Colored illustrations complement the text of this book, which covers a number of events in the life

of Frederick Douglass. A chronology is appended.
Pre-K, Primary; Nonfiction

Altman, Susan. *Extraordinary African-Americans: From Colonial to Contemporary Times*. Rev. ed. New York: Children's Press, 2001. 288 p. (Extraordinary People)

A chapter in this book provides a brief biography of Frederick Douglass that states that he is sometimes called the father of the civil rights movement.
Intermediate, Older; Nonfiction

Banta, Melissa. *Frederick Douglass*. New York: Chelsea Juniors, 1993. 80 p. (Junior World Biographies)

This biography presents Frederick Douglass's life within the context of the periods in which he lived: the slavery of the South where he was born, the abolitionist movement in the North, the Civil War, and the Reconstruction. It tells of the cruelties he endured as a child and the important roles he played, after his escape to the North, as an abolitionist and an advocate of equal rights. The book includes photographs, a chronology, a glossary, a reading list, and an index.
Intermediate; Nonficton

Becker, Helaine. *Frederick Douglass*. Woodbridge, Conn.: Blackbirch Press, 2001. 104 p. (The Civil War)

Born Frederick Augustus Washington Bailey, Frederick Douglass was the son of a white man, probably the master of the Maryland farm where he was born, and a slave mother, from whom he was largely separated while very young. He suffered severely during his childhood, where he was at one point rented out to a cruel slave breaker. However, when he was about seven, he was sent for a time to the Hugh Auld family in Baltimore, where initially Mrs. Auld began teaching him to read. When she stopped, he traded bread for lessons with poor white boys and later, living with a different master, taught other slaves to read. Sent back to the Aulds, he was hired out as a shop caulker. In 1838 Frederick escaped from Baltimore and traveled to New Bedford, Massachusetts, where for protection from slave catchers he changed his name to Frederick Douglass. This book not only covers Douglass's early life, but also gives a detailed account of Douglass's accomplishments with focus on his lecturing, autobiography, newspaper, and advocacy of the Thirteenth, Fourteenth, and Fifteenth Amendments. It includes photographs, inserts with additional information, a glossary, a resource list, and an index.
Intermediate, Older; Nonfiction

Burchard, Peter. *Frederick Douglass: For the Great Family of Man*. New York: Atheneum Books for Young Readers, 2003. 240 p.

Photographs, a map, chapter notes, a bibliography, and an index are features of this comprehensive biography of Frederick Douglass. Highlighting the speech Douglass made in Nantucket in 1841, the book includes coverage of his living in Lynn, Massachusetts, and Rochester, New York; his meeting the Irish patriot Daniel O'Connell; his lecturing in Ireland and Great Britain; the purchase of his freedom by English antislavery friends; his support of women's rights; his increasingly strained relationships with

William Lloyd Garrison and with his wife Anna; his son Lewis's Civil War service; his affair with Ottille Assing; and his marriage to Helen Pitts.
Older; Nonfiction

Denenberg, Dennis, and Lorraine Roscoe. *50 American Heroes Every Kid Should Meet*. Brookfield, Conn.: The Millbrook Press, 2001. 128 p.
A double-page spread focuses on the importance of learning to read in Frederick Douglass's life and urges young readers to help other learn to read. Photographs, a quotation, and a reference are included.
Intermediate, Older; Nonfiction

Garrison, Mary. *Slaves Who Dared: The Stories of Ten African-American Heroes*. Shippensburg, Pa.: White Mane Kids, 2002. 152 p.
This illustrated account of Frederick Douglass emphasizes the hardships of his childhood and his work in recruiting black soldiers and promoting their equal treatment.
Intermediate, Older; Nonfiction

Girard, Linda Walvoord. *Young Frederick Douglass: The Slave Who Learned to Read*. Illustrated by Colin Bootman. Morton Grove, Ill.: Albert Whitman & Company, 1994. 40 p.
Numerous color paintings illustrate this story of Frederick Douglass's life from about the age of eight when Sophia Auld started to teach him to read through his escape from Baltimore. It emphasizes his determination and ingenuity in learning to read and write. A summary of Douglass's work as a free man is appended.
Primary, Intermediate; Nonfiction

Kranz, Rachel C. *The Biographical Dictionary of Black Americans*. New York: Facts on File, 1992. 192 p.
The importance of Frederick Douglass's autobiography, *Narrative of the Life of Frederick Douglass*; his efforts to promote black voting rights, self-improvement, and equality as well as to abolish slavery; and his later marriage to a white woman, Helen Pitts, are covered in this book's biographical account.
Intermediate, Older; Nonfiction

Lilley, Stephen R. *Fighters against American Slavery*. San Diego: Lucent Books, 1999. 128 p. (History Makers)
This book's detailed biography of Frederick Douglass includes coverage of his relationship with the abolitionist William Lloyd Garrison, his own work as an abolitionist lecturer and publisher, and his appointments as marshal and recorder of deeds for the District of Columbia and as United States consul general to Haiti.
Older; Nonfiction

Masoff, Joy. *The African American Story: The Events That Shaped Our Nation . . . and the People Who Changed Our Lives*. Waccabuc, N.Y.: Five Ponds Press, 2007. 96 p.

This history of African-Americans includes a paragraph about and a picture of Frederick Douglass.
Older; Nonfiction

McKissack, Patricia C., and Frederick L. McKissack. *Black Hands, White Sails: The Story of African-American Whalers.* New York: Scholastic Press, 1999. 176 p.
A section of this book describes how Frederick Douglass, who worked as a caulker on whaling ships, became a leader in the abolitionist movement.
Older; Nonfiction

McLoone, Margo. *Frederick Douglass: A Photo-Illustrated Biography.* Mankato, Minn.: Bridgestone Books, 1997. 24 p.
Full-page photographs, two quotations from Frederick Douglass, a chronology, a glossary, a resource list, and an index are featured in this introductory biography.
Primary; Nonfiction

Miller, William. *Frederick Douglass: The Last Day of Slavery.* Illustrated by Cedric Lucas. New York: Lee & Low Books, 1995. 32 p.
Large paintings illustrate this picture book biography of Frederick Douglass which covers his early life up to his daring to fight back against a slave breaker.
Primary; Nonfiction

Nash, Gary B. *Forbidden Love: The Secret History of Mixed-Race America.* Illustrated by author. New York: Henry Holt and Company, 1999. 224 p.
This book reports that Frederick Douglass was criticized, even by family members, when he married a white woman, Helen Pitts.
Older; Nonfiction

Patterson, Lillie. *Frederick Douglass: Freedom Fighter.* Illustrated by Gray Morrow and Daniel Mark Duffy. New York: Chelsea Juniors, 1991. 80 p. (A Discovery Biography)
This illustrated fictionalized biography traces Frederick Douglass's life from his living as a slave with his grandmother in a cabin on an Eastern Shore of Maryland plantation to his living as "The Sage of Anacostia" in a large home in the District of Columbia.
Primary, Intermediate; Fiction

Russell, Sharman Apt. *Frederick Douglass: Abolitionist Editor.* Legacy ed. Philadelphia: Chelsea House Publishers, 2005. 112 p. (Black Americans of Achievement)
Quotations from Frederick Douglass, informational inserts, pictures, a chronology, and a resource list add to this comprehensive biography of the slave who became an African-American leader and spokesman. An index is included.
Older; Nonfiction

Schomp, Virginia. *Frederick Douglass: He Fought for Freedom*. New York: Benchmark Books, 1997. 48 p. (Benchmark Biographies)
Based on his writings, this biography of Frederick Douglass includes numerous photographs, including those of his family; a glossary; a resource list; and an index.
Intermediate; Nonfiction

Schraff, Anne. *Frederick Douglass: Speaking Out Against Slavery*. Berkeley Heights, N.J.: Enslow Publishers, 2002. 128 p. (African-American Biographies)
Photographs, chapter notes, a chronology, a reading list, a listing of internet addresses, and an index complement this detailed biography of Frederick Douglass, which covers his childhood experiences as a slave and his continuing efforts and successes in promoting equality and justice for blacks.
Intermediate, Older; Nonfiction

Weidt, Maryann N. *Voice of Freedom: A Story about Frederick Douglass*. Illustrated by Jeni Reeves. Minneapolis: Carolrhoda Books, 2001. 64 p. (A Creative Minds Biography)
Illustrated with drawings, this book provides a survey of Frederick Douglass's life that includes coverage of his advocacy of women's rights and the importance of his lecturing and three autobiographies. A bibliography and a list of websites are appended and there is an index.
Intermediate; Nonfiction

Welch, Catherine A. *Frederick Douglass*. Illustrated by Tim Parlin. Minneapolis: Lerner Publications Company, 2003. 48 p. (History Maker Bios)
Photographs and illustrations enhance this biography of Frederick Douglass. A section on his violin playing, a timeline, a resource list, a bibliography, and an index are appended.
Primary, Intermediate; Nonfiction

Dove, Rita (1952-   ) United States
African-American, to German

Kimmel, Elizabeth Cody. *Ladies First: 40 Daring American Women Who Were Second to None*. Washington, D.C.: National Geographic, 2006. 192 p.
This book's profile of Rita Dove describes her childhood love of books and writing, her selection as a Presidential Scholar and a Fulbright scholar, her marriage to the writer Fred Viebahn, her writing career, and her appointment as Poet Laureate of the United States.
Intermediate, Older; Nonfiction

Potter, Joan, and Constance Claytor. *African Americans Who Were First*. New York: Cobblehill Books, 1997. 128 p.
A photograph of Rita Dove accompanies a page summary of the life of the first African-American to serve as poet laureate of the United States.
Intermediate, Older; Nonfiction

Drouillard, George (c 1775 –1810) United States
French Canadian/Shawnee

Bruchac, Joseph. *Sacajawea: The Story of Bird Woman and the Lewis and Clark Expedition.* San Diego: Harcourt/Silver Whistle, 2000. 208 p.

This story of Sacajawea describes the important roles as hunter and interpreter that George Drouillard played on the Lewis and Clark Expedition.
Older; Fiction

Crosby, Michael T. *Sacagawea: Shoshone Explorer.* Stockton, N.J.: OTTN Publishing, 2008. 144 p. (Shapers of America)

Color photographs, maps, informational inserts, a detailed chronology, a glossary, chapter notes, resource lists, and an index combine to provide a well-rounded portrayal of Sacajawea's life. The book tells of the contributions to the Lewis and Clark Expedition made by Toussaint Charbonneau, Pierre Cruzatte, George Drouillard, and François Labiche and presents biographical information on Jean Baptiste (Pomp) Charbonneau.
Older; Nonfiction

Frazier, Neta Lohnes. *Sacagawea: The Girl Nobody Knows.* New York: David McKay Company, 1967. 192 p.

This book includes information on George Drouillard whom it refers to as George Drewyer, which is how his name was reported in the journals of both Clark and Lewis.
Older; Nonfiction

Myers, Laurie. *Lewis and Clark and Me. A Dog's Tale.* Illustrated by Michael Dooling. New York: Henry Holt and Company, 2002. 80 p.

Seaman, a Newfoundland. describes his purchase by Meriwether Lewis and his adventures on the Lewis and Clark expedition: catching numerous swimming squirrels, being mistaken for a bear by Shawnee Indians, feeling jealous of a buffalo calf, almost losing his life to a wounded beaver, saving men from a charging buffalo, being briefly stolen by Clatsop Indians, and, above all, treasuring his relationship with Lewis. Seaman's account mentions George Drouillard, Sacagawea, and Pierre Cruzatte. The book features full- and double-page paintings, a map, an introduction, an afterword, and a source list.
Intermediate; Fiction

O'Dell, Scott. *Streams to the River, River to the Sea: A Novel of Sacagawea.* Boston: Houghton Mifflin Company, 1986. 208 p.

George Drouillard is regarded as an important member of the Corps of Discovery in this novel about Sacagawea.
Older; Fiction

Roop, Peter, and Connie Roop. *Girl of the Shining Mountains: Sacagawea's Story.* New York: Hyperion Books for Children, 1999. 192 p.

Sacagawea's account to Pomp of her experiences on the Lewis and Clark Expedition frequently mentions George Drouillard.
Intermediate, Older; Fiction

Roop, Peter, and Connie Roop, eds. *Off the Map: The Journals of Lewis and Clark*. Illustrated by Tim Tanner. New York: Walker and Company, 1993. 48 p.

Excerpts from Lewis and Clark's journals cover the commencement of their expedition's journey on May 13, 1804 to its departure on March 23, 1806 from Fort Clatsop for the return trip. The book includes journal entries referring to George Drouillard, Toussaint Charbonneau, and Sacagawea. A prologue presents the expedition's background and the June 20, 1803 letter from President Jefferson to Meriwether Lewis. An epilogue describes the homeward journey and the later lives of members of the Corps of Discovery.
Intermediate, Older; Nonfiction

Wolf, Allan. *New Found Land: Lewis and Clark's Voyage of Discovery, A Novel*. Cambridge, Mass.: Candlewick Press, 2004. 512 p.

Fourteen members of the Corps of Discovery, including Sacagawea, George Drouillard, Pierre Cruzatte, and Oolum (the Newfoundland dog Seaman), narrate this detailed story of the Lewis and Clark Expedition. Speaking in prose and poetry and expressing their individual perspectives and feelings, often with a sense of humor, the narrators cover the period from the June 1803 request of President Thomas Jefferson to Meriwether Lewis to lead the expedition to 1819, ten years after Lewis's death. The novel contains maps, a glossary, resources, and additional information on the expedition, including what later happened to each narrator.
Older; Fiction

Drucker, Olga Levy (1927-   ) Germany
Jewish German, by British

Drucker, Olga Levy. *Kindertransport*. New York: Henry Holt and Company, 1992. 160 p.

Olga Levy Drucker's autobiographical account covers the years from 1933 to 1945. It tells how the life of her German non-practicing Jewish family changed when Hitler assumed power and there followed increasing hatred, restrictions, and abuse of Jews. Olga has to leave her school and go to a Jewish school. She is shunned by former friends, and her father is arrested and temporarily placed in the Dachau concentration camp. At age eleven, Olga is sent for safety from Stuttgart to England as part of Kindertransport, a program sponsored by the Jewish Refugee Committee. Separated from her parents for the next six years, she is placed in a succession of foster families and a boarding school. Well-meaning, but often insensitive foster parents and siblings make her life difficult. In England, even though she is Jewish, she is taken to Anglican, Quaker and Baptist churches. Despite the difficulties Olga experiences some happy moments. When Olga is sixteen, she leaves school and works as a nanny's helper in a loving English family. Then, finally, she is able to rejoin her parents, who have managed to escape to New York City.
Intermediate, Older; Fiction

Du Bois, William Edward Burghardt (W. E. B.) (1868-1963) United States
African-Bahamian-French Huguenot-American-Haitian/African-Dutch American, to African-American, to African-American

Bednar, Chuck. *Rosa Parks: Civil Rights Activist*. Broomall, Pa.: Mason Crest Publishers, 2010. 64 p. (Transcending Race in America: Biographies of Biracial Achievers)
   This biography of Rosa Parks points out the important role W. E .B. DuBois played as a protest leader for black rights.
Older; Nonfiction

Cryan-Hicks, Kathryn T. *W. E. B. Du Bois: Crusader for Peace*. Illustrated by David H. Huckins. Lowell, Mass.: Discovery Enterprises. 1991. 48 p.
   Full-page color paintings alternate with pages of text in this biography of W. E. B. Du Bois. It tells of his education at Fisk University, Harvard University, and in Berlin; the book *The Souls of Black Folks* and the magazine *Crisis*, which were among his many publications; his important roles in the Niagra Movement, the NAACP, Pan African Congresses, and the Peace Information Center; the criminal suit placed against him by the Federal government; his support of socialism; and his work in Ghana on the *Encyclopedia Africana*.
Intermediate, Older; Nonfiction

McDaniel, Melissa. *W. E. B. Du Bois: Scholar and Civil Rights Activist*. New York: Franklin Watts, 1999. 96 p. (A Book Report Biography)
   W. E. B. Du Bois' educational achievements; his scholarly studies of African-Americans, including his book *The Philadelphia Negro*; his disputes with Booker T. Washington, Marcus Garvey, and Walter Francis White; his friendship with John Hope; his advocacy of world peace; and his renouncing of his United States citizenship are covered in this biography. It includes photographs, a chronology, a source note, resource listings, and an index.
Older; Nonfiction

Stafford, Mark, and John Davenport. *W. E. B. Du Bois: Scholar and Activist*. Legacy ed. Philadelphia: Chelsea House Publishers, 2004. 128 p. (Black Americans of Achievement)
   This comprehensive biography of W. E. B. Du Bois provides insights on the economic and social status of African-Americans during his lifetime, tells of his numerous publications, and focuses on his Talented Tenth theory, his contentious vying with Booker T. Washington and Washington's Tuskegee machine, his global perspective, and his increasing radicalism. Photographs, informational inserts, a list of Du Bois writings, a chronology, a reading list, and an index complete the work.
Older; Nonfiction

Troy, Don. *W. E. B. Du Bois*. Mankato, Minn.: The Child's World, 1998. 40 p. (Journey to Freedom)
   Photographs with descriptive captions, a glossary defining italicized text words, a timeline, and an index are features of this biography of W. E. B. Du Bois.
Intermediate, Older; Nonfiction

Du Sable, Jean Baptiste Pointe (c.1745-1818) Haiti
French/African, to Potawatomi

Altman, Susan. *Extraordinary African-Americans: From Colonial to Contemporary Times*. Rev. ed. New York: Children's Press, 2001. 288 p. (Extraordinary People)
    This book's biography of Jean Baptiste Pointe Du Sable provides information on his trading post at what is now Chicago and points to the problems his French background caused him.
Intermediate, Older; Nonfiction

Katz, William Loren. *Black Indians: A Hidden Heritage*. New York: Atheneum, 1986. 208 p.
    An account of Jean Baptiste Pointe Du Sable tells of the fur trapper's French paintings and of his fur trading post, which became the city of Chicago.
Intermediate, Older; Nonfiction

Katz, William Loren. *Black Pioneers: An Untold Story*. New York: Atheneum Books for Young Readers, 1999. 208 p.
    A section in this book on Jean Baptiste Pointe Du Sable relates how the young Haitian came to settle on the Chicago River during the Revolutionary War where, because of his French background, he initially was regarded with distrust and even arrested by the British, who subsequently appointed him manager of one of their settlements. The book describes the impressive trading post of Du Sable and his Potawatomi wife, Catherine, and tells of his fur trading with the Indians. The Du Sables became Catholics and moved from Chicago to St. Charles, Missouri. There is a Du Sable Museum in Chicago.
Older; Nonfiction

Kranz, Rachel C. *The Biographical Dictionary of Black Americans*. New York: Facts on File, 1992. 192 p.
    As reported in one of this book's sections, Jean Baptiste Pointe Du Sable not only founded Chicago, but also served briefly as a British spy, lived for a while with the Peoria and Potawatomi Indians, one of whom he married, and served under a territorial governor as liaison officer with the Indians.
Intermediate, Older; Nonfiction

Duwali (also Bowles; The Bowl) (c. 1756-1839) United States
Scottish/Cherokee

Gregson, Susan R. *Sam Houston: Texas Hero*. Minneapolis: Compass Point Books, 2006. 112 p. (Signature Lives)
    This book reports that Chief Bowles promised his friend Sam Houston that the Cherokee would not side with Mexico in the Texans' war for independence. Later, when Mirabeau Lamar became president of the Republic of Texas, he sought to remove the Cherokee from Texas and in an ensuing battle his soldiers shot elderly Chief Bowles in the back.
Older; Nonfiction

Early, Sarah Jane Woodson (1825-1907) United States
African-English-Welsh?-American/African-American, to African-American

Katz, William Loren. *Black Pioneers: An Untold Story*. New York: Atheneum Books for Young Readers, 1999. 208 p.

This book's presentation of the Woodson family points out that Sarah Woodson Early's father was Thomas Woodson, who was probably the son of Thomas Jefferson and Sally Hemings. Growing up in a family active in the AME (African Methodist Episcopal) Church, Sarah graduated in 1856 from Oberlin College, taught in AME schools, and become the first African-American woman to have full college faculty status when she taught at Wilberforce College. After her marriage to AME minister Jordan Winston Early, she continued to teach, was principal of several schools, lectured for the Prohibition Party, and was head of the Women's Christian Temperance Union's Colored Division. Her brother was Lewis Woodson.
Older; Nonfiction

Lanier, Shannon, and Jane Feldman. *Jefferson's Children: The Story of One American Family*. Photographs by Jane Feldman. Introduction by Lucian K. Truscott IV. Historical Essays by Annette Gordon-Reed and Beverley Gray. New York: Random House, 2000. 144 p.

This book features interviews of descendants of Thomas Jefferson, who speak of their family histories and their personal experiences. It contains information on Sarah Jane Woodson Early and on her father, Thomas Woodson.
Older; Nonfiction

Erdrich, Louise (1954-) United States
German-American/Turtle Mountain Chippewa and French Canadian, to Modoc and French-English-Irish-Swiss-American

Allen, Paula Gunn, and Patricia Clark Smith. *As Long as the Rivers Flow: The Stories of Nine Native Americans*. New York: Scholastic Press, 1996. 336 p.

Loving the Chippewa and Bible stories she heard and the stories she read, Louise Erdrich at an early age began writing little "books." The chapter on her life describes her teenage years, her times at Dartmouth College, her marriage to and writing collaboration with Michael Dorris, and the novels she wrote.
Intermediate, Older; Nonfiction

Avery, Susan, and Linda Skinner. *Extraordinary American Indians*. Chicago: Children's Press, 1992. 272 p.

A section on Louise Erdrich and Michael Dorris stresses their mutual assistance in writing books about Native Americans.
Older; Nonfiction

Espinel, Luisa (born Luisa Ronstadt) (1892-1963) United States
German-Mexican/European-American Jewish

Alegre, Cèsar. *Extraordinary Hispanic Americans*. New York: Children's Press, 2007. 288 p. (Extraordinary People)
    Luisa Ronstadt's career as a performer and publisher of Hispanic folk music is described in a biographical section that includes information on her father Fred Ronstadt and her niece Linda Ronstadt.
Older; Nonfiction

Estévez, Emilio (1962   ) United States
Irish-Spanish-American/European-American, to Canadian and Syrian Jewish

Hargrove, Jim. *Martin Sheen: Actor and Activist*. Chicago: Children's Press, 1991. 128 p. (People of Distinction Biographies)
    This comprehensive biography of Martin Sheen is based largely on his 1990 interview with the author. It covers Sheen's childhood, his career, his family, including his sons Emilio and Charlie, and his political activism. The book includes a listing of Sheen's stage, film, and television appearances, an annual chronology of his life and world events from 1940 through 1991, black-and-white photographs, and an index.
Older; Nonfiction

Press, Skip. *Charlie Sheen, Emilio Estevez, & Martin Sheen*. Parsippany, N.J.: Crestwood House, 1996. 48 p. (Star Families)
    This look at the Sheen family provides biographical information on Martin Sheen and his sons Emilio Estévez and Charlie Sheen: their acting careers, their personal lives, and their interest in social justice. Photographs, a glossary, and an index are included.
Intermediate, Older; Nonfiction

Zannos, Susan. *Paula Abdul*. Childs, Md.: Mitchell Lane Publishers, 1998. 32 p. (A Real-Life Reader Biography)
    This biography of Paula Abdul tells of her early love of dancing and sports and traces her successful career as a choreographer, dancer, singer, and actress. It discusses her struggle with bulimia, covers her brief marriage to Emilio Estévez, and includes black-and-white photographs, a discography, a chronology, and an index.
Intermediate, Older; Nonfiction

Fairchild, Olive Oatman (1838?-1903) United States
European-American, by Apache (or Yavapai), by Mohave

Rau, Margaret. *The Ordeal of Olive Oatman: A True Story of the American West.* Greensboro, N.C.; Morgan Reynolds, 1997. 112 p.

As reported in this biography, when in 1851 Olive Oatman's family set out in a lone wagon to go from an Arizona Pima village to Fort Yuma, it was attacked by Apache Indians. They kidnapped Olive and her younger sister, Mary Ann, and killed her parents and all her siblings except her brother Lorenzo, who miraculously lived. The two girls survived the brutal treatment they received as Apache slaves and were sold one year later to be slaves of the Mohave. Protected by the chief and treated with kindness by his wife and daughter, they again suffered from hostility and from starvation, which contributed to Mary Ann's death. In 1856 Olive was released by the Mohave and reunited with Lorenzo, whom she had thought dead. The book includes a bibliography and an index.
Older; Nonfiction

Farmanfarmaian, Roxane (19??   ) United States
Iranian and Muslim/European-American and Mormon

O'Hearn, Claudine Chiawei, editor. *Half and Half: Writers on Growing Up Biracial and Bicultural.* New York: Pantheon Books, 1998. 288 p.

In one chapter the writer Roxane Farmanfarmaian explains the similarities of Iran and Utah, describes her difficulties in feeling she belonged in either the United States or Iran, and relates how she came to identify herself with Iran, a country to which she cannot return.
Older; Nonfiction

Farragut, David Glasgow (born James Glasgow Farragut) (1801-1870) United States
Spanish (Minorcan)/European-American, by European-American, to European-American, to European-American

Adelson, Bruce. *David Farragut: Union Admiral.* Philadelphia: Chelsea House Publishers, 2002. 80 p. (Famous Figures of the Civil War Era)

This biography of David Farragut traces his career from becoming a U.S. Navy midshipman at age nine to being the Navy's only full admiral. Placing Farragut's experiences within the context of his times, the book also includes photographs, a glossary that defines bolded words in the text, a chronology of Farragut's life, a Civil War timeline, a reading list, and an index.
Intermediate; Nonfiction

Alegre, Cèsar. *Extraordinary Hispanic Americans.* New York: Children's Press, 2007. 288 p. (Extraordinary People)

A biographical chapter on David Glasgow Farragut emphasizes his naval victories at New Orleans and Mobile Bay, Alabama, during the Civil War.
Older; Nonfiction

Foster, Leila Merrell. *David Glasgow Farragut: Courageous Navy Commander.* Chicago: Children's Press, 1991. 112 p. (People of Distinction)

Detailed descriptions of David Farragut's family background, childhood, service in the War of 1812 under Captain David Porter, experiences in the period preceding the Civil War, and Civil War naval successes are accompanied by photographs, a glossary, a chronology, and an index.
Older; Nonfiction

Gleiter, Jan, and Kathleen Thompson. *David Farragut*. Illustrated by Frances Balistreri. Milwaukee: Raintree Publishers, 1989. 32 p. (Raintree Hispanic Stories)
    Text and a glossary in both English and Spanish distinguish this illustrated biography of David Farragut.
Intermediate; Nonfiction

Latham, Jean Lee. *Anchors Aweigh: The Story of David Glasgow Farragut*. Illustrated by Eros Keith. New York: Harper & Row, Publishers, 1968. 288 p.
    This fictionalized presentation of David Farragut focuses on his fifteen years as a midshipman, his marriages to Susan Marchant and Virginia Loyall, and his Civil War capture of New Orleans, blockade of the Red River, and victory at Mobile Bay.
Intermediate, Older; Fiction

Latham, Jean Lee. *David Glasgow Farragut: Our First Admiral*. Illustrated by Paul Frame. Champaign, Ill.: Garrard Publishing Company, 1967. 80 p. (A Discovery Book)
    Illustrated with full-page pictures, this book tells a fictionalized story of David Farragut's life.
Intermediate; Fiction

Rodriguez, Robert, and Tamra Orr, contributing writers. *Great Hispanic-Americans*. Lincolnwood, Ill.: Publications International, 2005. 128 p.
    According to a biographical section of this book, after James Farrragut's mother died, his father George Farragut gave him for adoption to naval officer David Porter. James Farragut changed his first name to David in his adoptive father's honor.
Older; Nonfiction

Roop, Peter, and Connie Roop. *Take Command, Captain Farragut*. Illustrated by Michael McCurdy. New York: Atheneum Books for Young Readers, 2002. 48 p.
    This book describes David Farragut's life as a midshipman aboard the frigate Essex preceding and during the War of 1812. It is presented in the form of a long letter to his father which twelve-year-old Farragut could have written in 1814 when he was imprisoned by the English in Valparaiso, Chile. Illustrated with scratchboard drawings, the book includes a glossary of nautical terms, a bibliography, and an author's note about Farragut.
Intermediate; Fiction

Shorto, Russell. *David Farragut and the Great Naval Blockade*. Englewood Cliffs, N.J.: Silver Burdett Press, 1991. 136 p. (The History of the Civil War)
    In this book a comprehensive biography of David Farragut is combined with a presentation of

American history during the first seventy years of the nineteenth century. Photographs, maps, timelines of the Civil War and of Farragut's life, a source list, a reading list, and an index supplement the text. Older; Nonfiction

Stein, R. Conrad. *David Farragut: First Admiral of the U.S. Navy*. Chanhassen, Minn.: The Child's World, 2005. 40 p.

David Farragut's naval battles during the Civil War are emphasized in this biography, which also features photographs of ships, text inserts, a glossary defining bolded text words, a timeline, and an index.
Intermediate; Nonfiction

Garreau, Antoine (1800s) United States
French and Arikara

Spooner, Michael. *Last Child*. New York: Henry Holt and Company, 2005. 240 p.

Set in 1837 in the midst of a smallpox epidemic in what is now North Dakota, Rosalie is more comfortable helping her Scottish father, who is the bookkeeper at Fort Clark, than in being with her Mandan mother. Because of her superior attitude, she has only her father and her grandmother Muskrat Woman as friends. When Rosalie goes with her father to keep a log of the buffalo robes which have fallen from the capsized boat of the French trapper Bedeaux, they are attacked by Dakota and she is kidnapped by those responsible for the attack: a Mandan who is under the influence of whiskey and a scoundrel who has deliberately brought smallpox to the area and wants revenge on her father. Rosalie manages to escape and to make a bull boat with which she saves Bedeaux and returns to the Mandan village. There, with the assistance of her former husband Bedeaux, Muskrat Woman isolates Rosalie, inoculates her with the virus of a Mandan recovering from smallpox, holds the ceremony which makes her a woman, and helps her in resolving the conflict between her Mandan and Scottish identities. Antoine Garreau, who served as interpreter for Fort Clark's managing officer, is a minor character in this novel.
Older; Fiction

Gladwell, Malcolm (1963-   ) England
English/African-Jewish-Scottish-Jamaican

O'Hearn, Claudine Chiawei, editor. *Half and Half: Writers on Growing Up Biracial and Bicultural*. New York: Pantheon Books, 1998. 288 p.

In one chapter the journalist Malcolm Gladwell describes his English father's obliviousness to differences, his Jamaican mother's discernment when differences are unimportant, and his own ambivalent feelings as a member of a third category.
Older; Nonfiction

Goldman, Francisco (1954-   ) United States
European-Jewish-American/Mayan-Spanish-Guatemalan and Catholic

O'Hearn, Claudine Chiawei, editor. *Half and Half: Writers on Growing Up Biracial and Bicultural.* New York: Pantheon Books, 1998. 288 p.

In a chapter by the Jewish and Guatemalan-American writer Francisco Goldman, he describes the extreme bigotry he encountered in Madrid, Spain, where he was continually mistaken as a Moor. Older; Nonfiction

Grace, Princess of Monaco (born Grace Patricia Kelly) (1929-1982) United States
Irish-American Catholic/German-American Lutheran, to Monacan

O'Shei, Tim. *Princess Grace of Monaco.* Mankato, Minn.: Capstone Press, 2009. 32 p. (Snap Books, Queens and Princesses)

Photographs, text, bolded words defined at page bottoms and in a glossary, and a resource section present Princess Grace's childhood, acting career, and life as Princess of Monaco. An index is included. Intermediate; Nonfiction

Surcouf, Elizabeth Gillen. *Grace Kelly, American Princess.* Minneapolis: Lerner Publications Company, 1992. 64 p.

A foreword by Frank Sinatra and numerous photographs are included in this biography of Grace Kelly, which describes her childhood; her career on the stage, on television, and in movies; her wedding celebration; and her extensive philanthropic accomplishments as Princess Grace of Monaco. Intermediate; Nonfiction

Halaby, Najeeb Elias (1915-2003) United States
Syrian/European-American, to Swedish-American

Darraj, Susan Muaddi. *Queen Noor.* Philadelphia: Chelsea House Publishers, 2003. 128 p. (Women in Politics)

This biography of Najeeb Halaby's daughter contains extensive information on his career. Older; Nonfiction

Raatma, Lucia. *Queen Noor: American-Born Queen of Jordan.* Minneapolis: Compass Point Books, 2006. 112 p. (Signature Lives)

This book discusses Queen Noor's relationship with her father, Najeeb Halaby, and points out that he flew as a test pilot, served as director of the Federal Aviation Administration, became chief executive officer of Pan American World Airways, and founded Arab Air Services. Older; Nonfiction

Haley, Alexander (Alex) Murray Palmer (1921-1992) United States
African-Irish-American/African-American

Gonzales, Doreen. *Alex Haley: Author of Roots.* Hillside, N.J.: Enslow Publishers, 1994. 128 p. (People to Know)

The son of a college professor father and a pianist mother, Alex Haley, as a child, heard stories of his ancestors and relatives at his maternal grandmother's home. He served in the United States Coast Guard from 1939 to 1959 where he achieved the position of Chief Journalist. He then struggled to earn his living as a writer. He published *The Autobiography of Malcolm X* in 1965, and, after years of research and writing, published *Roots: The Saga of an American Family* in 1976. Highly successful, *Roots* aired as a television miniseries in 1977. This biography discusses the controversy raised as to the accuracy and originality of *Roots* as well as the positive impact it had on race relations and African-Americans' interest in learning their families' genealogies. Following *Roots*' publication, Haley lectured extensively and wrote *A Different Kind of Christmas* and the unfinished book *Queen*. Photographs, a chronology, chapter notes, a reading list, and an index are included in this presentation of Haley's life.
Older; Nonfiction

Greenfield, Eloise. *How They Got Over: African-Americans and the Call of the Sea*. Illustrated by Jan Spivey Gilchrist. New York: Amistad, 2003. 128 p.
A section on Alex Haley points out how his writing of letters for himself and fellow Coast Guard crew members launched his writing career as chief journalist for the Coast Guard and as a noted author.
Intermediate; Nonfiction

Masoff, Joy. *The African American Story: The Events That Shaped Our Nation . . . and the People Who Changed Our Lives*. Waccabuc, N.Y.: Five Ponds Press, 2007. 96 p.
This history of African-Americans includes a paragraph about and a picture of Alex Haley.
Older; Nonfiction

Otfinoski, Steven. *Great Black Writers*. New York: Facts On File, 1994. 128 p. (American Profiles)
A biographical section on Alex Haley includes two excerpts from *Roots*, photographs, a chronology, and a reading list.
Older; Nonfiction

Shirley, David, and Heather Lehr Wagner. *Alex Haley: Author*. Philadelphia: Chelsea House Publishers, 2005. 120 p. (Black Americans of Achievement Legacy Edition)
This extensive biography of Alex Haley includes photographs, a chronology, a list of his written works, a reading list, a list of websites, and an index. Covering both his personal and professional life in detail, this biography points out that his Playboy interview of Miles Davis led to a new type of magazine interview, that his viewing of the Rosetta Stone extended the scope of the manuscript which became *Roots*, and that he felt an obligation toward those readers and viewers who were affected by *Roots*.
Older; Nonfiction

Turner, Glennette Tilley. *Follow in Their Footsteps*. Illustrated with Photographs. New York: Puffin Books, 1999. 192 p.

A skit about the family stories told on his grandmother's porch accompanies this book's biography of Alex Haley.
Intermediate, Older; Fiction, Nonfiction

Williams, Sylvia B. *Alex Haley*. Edina, Minn.: Abdo & Dughters, 1996. 32 p. (I Have a Dream)
This book relates how *Roots* traced the story of Alex Haley's ancestors from Kinte, his great-great-great-great-grandfather, and includes a *Roots* genealogy. Photographs, a glossary, a bibliography, and an index add to this survey of Haley's life.
Intermediate; Nonfiction

Hamilton, Virginia Esther (1936-2002) United States
African-American/African-American, Cherokee, and Potawatomi, to Russian-American Jewish

Mangal, Mélina. *Virginia Hamilton*. Bear, Del.: Mitchell Lane Publishers, 2002. 32 p. (A Real-Life Reader Biography)
This biography of Virginia Hamilton, an acclaimed author of children's books, describes her childhood near Yellow Springs, Ohio, and how, after living in New York City and southern France, she returned to Yellow Springs with her husband, Arnold Adoff, and their two children. It tells of the diversity of the numerous (37) books she wrote, of the awards (including the Hans Christian Andersen Award) that she won, and of how she characterized a great deal of her writing, which incorporates history, as "liberation literature." The book includes photographs, a chronology, a list of Hamilton's books, and an index.
Intermediate; Nonfiction

Hanks, Thomas (Tom) J. (1956-   ) United States
European-American, by European-American and Chinese-American

Isle, Mick. *Tom Hanks and Colin Hanks*. New York: The Rosen Publishing Group, 2005. 48 p. (Famous Families)
The acting careers of Tom and Colin Hanks and their father-son relationship are described in this book, which includes captioned photographs, text inserts, a timeline, a filmography, a glossary, a resource list, a bibliography, and an index.
Older; Nonfiction

Kramer, Barbara. *Tom Hanks: Superstar*. Berkeley Heights, N.J.: Enslow Publishers, 2001. 112 p. (People to Know)
Tom Hanks' career and the movies in which he acted are covered in detail in this biography. It tells of the many times he moved during his childhood and of his father's marriage to Frances Wong, Hanks' second stepmother. Photographs, a chronology, a filmography, chapter notes, a resource list, and index complement the text.
Older; Nonfiction

McAvoy, Jim. *Tom Hanks*. Philadelphia: Chelsea House Publishers, 1999. 64 p. (Galaxy of Superstars)

Color photographs distinguish this biography of Tom Hanks, which also includes a chronology, a filmography, a list of honors, a reading list, and an index.
Older; Nonfiction

Parish, James Robert. *Tom Hanks: Actor*. New York: Ferguson, 2004. 128 p. (Ferguson Career Biographies)

This extensive biography of Tom Hanks includes coverage of his childhood. In addition to photographs, a timeline, and a resource list, the book contains sections on working as an actor and as a producer.
Older; Nonfiction

Wallner, Rosemary. *Tom Hanks: Academy Award-Winning Actor*. Edina, Minn.: Abdo & Daughters, 1994. 32 p. (Reaching for the Stars)

This biography traces Tom Hanks' life by describing the movies in which he acted, including *Splash*, which launched his popularity; *Big*, for which he received an Academy Award nomination; and *Philadelphia*, where his performance earned him the Best Actor Oscar. Photographs and a listing of Hanks' television shows and movies are included.
Intermediate; Nonfiction

Wheeler, Jill C. *Tom Hanks*. Edina, Minn.: ABDO Publishing Company, 2001. 64 p. (Star Tracks)

Numerous color photographs of Tom Hanks are featured in this chronicle of his career through the filming of *Cast Away*. It includes a list of websites, a glossary, and an index.
Intermediate, Older; Nonfiction

Harjo, Joy (1951-   ) United States
Muskogee/French-American and Cherokee

Avery, Susan, and Linda Skinner. *Extraordinary American Indians*. Chicago: Children's Press, 1992. 272 p.

Holding a graduate degree in creative writing, Joy Harjo became a poet. Her poems embrace the themes of nature, the spiritual, remembering, and being a Native American woman. One of them, "Remember," is reprinted in this book's section on Harjo. Harjo also worked as a screenwriter and a professor at the University of New Mexico.
Older; Nonfiction

Harris, Betty Wright (1940-   ) United States
Cherokee/Kenyan

Sullivan, Otha Richard. *African American Women Scientists and Inventors*. New York: John Wiley & Sons, 2001. 160 p. (Black Stars)

A section of this book on Betty Wright Harris tells how she grew up in a hard-working farm family, received a Ph.D. in chemistry from the University of New Mexico, as a chemist with the Los Alamos National Laboratory invented a way to test for explosives, and has worked on weapons site cleanup. A photograph of Dr. Harris is included.
Older; Nonfiction

Hayek-Jiménez, Salma Valgarma (1966-   ) Mexico
Lebanese-Mexican/Spanish-Mexican, to French

Menard, Valerie. *Salma Hayek*. Childs, Md.: Mitchell Lane Publishers, 1999. 32 p. (A Real-Life Reader Biography)
   This biography of the Mexican actress, Salma Hayek, tells of her childhood, her attending a Louisiana boarding school, her popularity on Mexican telenovelas (soap operas), her moving to Hollywood and being in the movie *Desperado*, her depiction of the Mexican painter Frida Kahlo in the movie *Frida*, and her setting up her own production company. The book includes black-and-white photographs, text-highlighting sidebars, a chronology, a listing of Hayek's movies, and an index.
Intermediate; Nonfiction

Sapet, Kerrily. *Salma Hayek: Actress, Director, and Producer*. Broomall, Pa.: Mason Crest Publishers, 2009. 64 p. (Transcending Race in America, Biographies of Biracial Achievers)
   Pointing out that Salma Hayek was co-executive producer of the *Ugly Betty* television series, this book provides extensive coverage of her life, her multifaceted film career, her charitable work, and her support of Hispanic actresses. The text includes color photographs, informational inserts, and numerous quotations. A chronology, a listing of Hayek's accomplishments and awards, a glossary defining bolded text words, a resource list, and an index complete the biography.
Older; Nonfiction

Scott, Kieran. *Salma Hayek*. Philadelphia: Chelsea House Publishers, 2001. 64 p. (Latinos in the Limelight)
   Accompanied by color photographs and highlighting her work in promoting Latinos in the film industry, this biography of Salma Hayek presents a detailed account of her life, career, and goals. A chronology, a listing of her accomplishments, a reading list, and an index are appended.
Older; Nonfiction

Wine, Bill. *Salma Hayek*. Philadelphia: Mason Crest Publishers, 2009. 64 p. (Overcoming Adversity: Sharing the American Dream)
   Pages of information on such topics as the Academy Awards, the ALMA Awards, the Golden Globe Awards, Diego Rivera, Robert Rodriguez, and the paparazzi add to this biography of Salma Hayek. It contains color photographs, chapter notes, a glossary, a chronology, an accomplishments and awards listing, a resource list, and an index.
Intermediate, Older; Nonfiction

Haynes, Lemuel (1753-1833) United States
African-American/European-American, by European-American, to European-American

Nash, Gary B. *Forbidden Love: The Secret History of Mixed-Race America*. Illustrated by author. New York: Henry Holt and Company, 1999. 224 p.

   This book's profile of Lemuel Haynes points out that he was adopted when he was a baby by a European-American farm couple. He was their indentured servant, but was able to attend school. At the end of Haynes' indenture he served as a minuteman in the Battle of Lexington. He became a Congregational minister, preached to white congregations, and married a white schoolteacher, Elizabeth Babbit(t).
Older; Nonfiction

Healy, James Augustine (1830-1900) United States
Irish/African-European-American

Cox, Clinton. *African American Teachers*. New York: John Wiley & Sons, 2000. 176 p. (Black Stars)

   This book's biographical section on Patrick Francis Healy contains an insert noting that his brother, James Augustine Healy, served as a Catholic bishop in Maine and New Hampshire and was called "the children's bishop."
Older; Nonfiction

Kranz, Rachel C. *The Biographical Dictionary of Black Americans*. New York: Facts on File, 1992. 192 p.

   A biographical account of James Augustine Healy details his accomplishments as a Catholic priest and bishop. He became pastor of the largest church in Boston and deputy to the Boston bishop. Healy then served for twenty-five years as the bishop of Portland, Maine, where he was known for his work in founding children's homes and in being an advocate for children and the poor. In addition, Healy played a role in the establishment of Washington, D.C.'s Catholic University of America.
Intermediate, Older; Nonfiction

Healy, Michael (1839-1904) United States
Irish/African-European-American

Nash, Gary B. *Forbidden Love: The Secret History of Mixed-Race America*. New York: Henry Holt and Company, 1999. 224 p.

   This book highlights the career of Michael Healy, the younger brother of James Augustine and Patrick Francis Healy. Progressing from a teenage cabin boy, he became an officer in the U. S. Revenue Service and then commanded an icebreaker in the Arctic where he achieved legendary status as "Hell Roaring Mike."
Older; Nonfiction

Healy, Patrick Francis (1834-1910) United States
Irish/African-European-American

Cox, Clinton. *African American Teachers*. New York: John Wiley & Sons, 2000. 176 p. (Black Stars)
   This book provides a brief biography of Patrick Francis Healy, brother of James Augustine Healy and Michael Healy. Patrick Francis Healy graduated from Holy Cross College, earned a doctorate in philosophy, was ordained a Jesuit priest, and become president of Georgetown College, which he transformed into a major university. The impressive building he built there is named Healy Hall in his honor.
Older; Nonfiction

Hemings, Beverly (1798-?) United States
English-Welsh-American?/African-English-American

Rinaldi, Ann. *Wolf by the Ears*. New York: Scholastic, 1991. 272 p.
   This novel focuses on Harriet Hemings' agonizingly difficult decision to leave Monticello when she turns twenty-one—and, when doing so, to pass as white. The daughter of Sally Hemings and probably Thomas Jefferson (although her mother never reveals her father's identity), Harriet loves Monticello, her life there, and Jefferson, who is a kind master to her and the other slaves. It is after she is attacked by a drunken man who has married one of Jefferson's granddaughters that Harriet realizes she cannot remain at Monticello. Supportive Thomas Mann Randolph, Jefferson's son-in-law, convinces Harriet that she must pass and arranges for her both a teaching position in Washington and betrothal to a white man. It is he, who, unlike Jefferson, pushes for the abolition of slavery in Virginia. In this novel the decision as to whether to leave also faces Harriet's brother Beverly, who unrealistically hopes that Jefferson will get him into his university. The novel also mentions Tom, Harriet's oldest brother, who had run away some years earlier, and her little brothers Madison and Eston.
Older; Fiction

Hemings, Harriet (1801-?) United States
English-Welsh-American?/African-English-American

Rinaldi, Ann. *Wolf by the Ears*. New York: Scholastic, 1991. 272 p.
   This novel focuses on Harriet Hemings' agonizingly difficult decision to leave Monticello when she turns twenty-one—and, when doing so, to pass as white. The daughter of Sally Hemings and probably Thomas Jefferson (although her mother never reveals her father's identity), Harriet loves Monticello, her life there, and Jefferson, who is a kind master to her and the other slaves. It is after she is attacked by a drunken man who has married one of Jefferson's granddaughters that Harriet realizes she cannot remain at Monticello. Supportive Thomas Mann Randolph, Jefferson's son-in-law, convinces Harriet that she must pass and arranges for her both a teaching position in Washington and betrothal to a white man. It is he, who, unlike Jefferson, pushes for the abolition of slavery in Virginia.

In this novel the decision as to whether to leave also faces Harriet's brother Beverly, who unrealistically hopes that Jefferson will get him into his university. The novel also mentions Tom, Harriet's oldest brother, who had run away some years earlier, and her little brothers Madison and Eston.
Older; Fiction

Hemings, John (1775 or 1776-1830+) United States
English or Irish/African-English-American

Bober, Natalie S. *Thomas Jefferson: Draftsman of a Nation*. Charlottesville, Va.: University of Virginia Press, 2007. 376 p.

This book tells of John Hemings, the half brother of Sally Hemings. A slave of Jefferson's, who became a master carpenter, he did decorative woodworking at Monticello, carried out repair work at Jefferson's Poplar Forest house, crafted furniture, including a writing desk Jefferson gave to his granddaughter Ellen, and made Jefferson's coffin.
Older; Nonfiction

Hemings, Sally (1773-1835) United States
English/African-English-American, probably to English and Welsh-American

Bober, Natalie S. *Thomas Jefferson: Draftsman of a Nation*. Charlottesville, Va.: University of Virginia Press, 2007. 376 p.

This detailed and insightful presentation of Thomas Jefferson's life for high school students places it within its historical context and chronicles his work, his ideas, and his personal life. It describes the import of his father, James Maury, William Small, George Wythe, and Francis Fauquier on his early development; his passion for books, learning, architecture, and gardening; his abilities as a writer, but not as a speaker; and his love of his family. It covers the process through which the colonies came to declare their separation from England, Jefferson's writing of the Declaration of Independence, his work with Wythe to rewrite Virginia's laws, his failure as governor to prevent the British from invading Virginia, his years in Paris, his disagreements as Secretary of State with Alexander Hamilton, his vice presidency, his presidency, his pleasure in his grandchildren, his friendship with John Adams, and his founding of the University of Virginia. The book explores Jefferson's relationship with Sally Hemings and his conflicting views and actions with respect to slavery. It emphasizes Jefferson's love from boyhood of "Tom's Mountain" on which he buried his friend Dabney Carr, his wife, and his children, built Monticello, and spent as much time as possible. The book includes photographs, a chronology, a family tree, an author's note, chapter notes, a bibliography, and an index.
Older; Nonfiction

Kranz, Rachel C. *The Biographical Dictionary of Black Americans*. New York: Facts on File, 1992. 192 p.

This biographical account of Sally Hemings reports that there were rumors before the 1804 election of her probable affair with Thomas Jefferson and that earlier she returned from France only when

Jefferson agreed to free all her children upon their maturity.
Intermediate, Older; Nonfiction

Lanier, Shannon, and Jane Feldman. *Jefferson's Children: The Story of One American Family.* Photographs by Jane Feldman. Introduction by Lucian K. Truscott IV. Historical Essays by Annette Gordon-Reed and Beverley Gray. New York: Random House, 2000. 144 p.

After attending the May 1999 Monticello reunion of descendants of Thomas Jefferson, Sidney Lanier, who is a descendant of Madison Hemings, teamed up with photographer Jane Feldman to interview descendants of Thomas Jefferson and his wife, Martha Wayles Jefferson, and of Thomas Woodson, Madison Hemings, and Eston Hemings, those three of Jefferson and Sally Hemings' children whose lines can be traced. The resulting book contains a variety of individual and family interviews and photographs that reveal the family histories of the interviewees as well as their personal experiences and opinions. There is talk about whether the Hemings family members are indeed descendants of Jefferson's and should be allowed in the family graveyard, which is controlled by the Monticello Association. The bulk of the book consists of Hemings family interviews that tell what it means to be of mixed race; how some family members have passed as white; of some not being personally accepted because they look black or, on the other hand, look white; and of the Hemings' many achievements throughout the generations. Both Jeffersons and Hemings talk of family, of the importance of learning of their past, and of the hope for many that members of this family can eventually become one.
Older; Nonfiction

Rinaldi, Ann. *Wolf by the Ears.* New York: Scholastic, 1991. 272 p.

This novel focuses on Harriet Hemings' agonizingly difficult decision to leave Monticello when she turns twenty-one—and, when doing so, to pass as white. The daughter of Sally Hemings and probably Thomas Jefferson (although her mother never reveals her father's identity), Harriet loves Monticello, her life there, and Jefferson, who is a kind master to her and the other slaves. It is after she is attacked by a drunken man who has married one of Jefferson's granddaughters that Harriet realizes she cannot remain at Monticello. Supportive Thomas Mann Randolph, Jefferson's son-in-law, convinces Harriet that she must pass and arranges for her both a teaching position in Washington and betrothal to a white man. It is he, who, unlike Jefferson, pushes for the abolition of slavery in Virginia. In this novel the decision as to whether to leave also faces Harriet's brother Beverly, who unrealistically hopes that Jefferson will get him into his university. The novel also mentions Tom, Harriet's oldest brother, who had run away some years earlier, and her little brothers Madison and Eston.
Older; Fiction

Ruffin, Frances E. *Sally Hemings.* New York: Rosen Publishing Group/PowerKids Press, 2002. 24 p. (American Legends)

As related in this biography, Sally Hemings was born as a slave on the John Wayles plantation in Cumberland County, Maryland. When Wayles' daughter Martha Wayles (Skelton) married Thomas Jefferson, Sally moved to Monticello with her mother, who became the Monticello housekeeper. Sally was a half sister of Martha Jefferson. Martha died when Sally was about nine, and, when Sally was

fourteen, she took one of Jefferson's daughters to France where Jefferson was the American minister. It was probably in France that Sally and Thomas Jefferson began a relationship. Sally had seven children, three of whom died early. Jefferson was the father of at least one and perhaps all of these children. This biography includes a glossary and an index.
Primary, Intermediate; Nonfiction

Williams, Mark London. *Trail of Bones*. Cambridge, Mass.: Candlewick Press, 2005. 320 p. (Danger Boy)
   This book is part of a science fiction series in which Eli, an American boy, Thea, a girl from ancient Alexandria, and Clyne, a talking dinosaur, travel in time through the Fifth Dimension. In this story they end up in 1804 where Eli becomes part of the Lewis and Clark Corps of Discovery. Going with the expedition from St. Louis to the Mandan village, he encounters Pierre Cruzatte as well as Sacagawea and Toussaint Charbonneau and witnesses the birth of their son Pomp. Thea is also transported close to St. Louis where both she and Eli meet Thomas Jefferson and Sally Hemings, who have secretly traveled there for the start of Lewis and Clark's trip. However, Thea is mistaken for a runaway slave and is taken back to Monticello. Clyne lands in the wild near the Mandans. At the tale's conclusion all three are together in New Orleans where they once again go into the Fifth Dimension.
Intermediate, Older; Fiction

Hinojosa-Smith, Rolando (1929-   ) United States
Mexican-American/European-American

Alegre, Cèsar. *Extraordinary Hispanic Americans*. New York: Children's Press, 2007. 288 p. (Extraordinary People)
   Rolando Hinjosa-Smith's career as a Hispanic novelist and a university professor is described in one of this book's biographical chapters.
Older; Nonfiction

Rodriguez, Robert, and Tamra Orr, contributing writers. *Great Hispanic-Americans*. Lincolnwood, Ill.: Publications International, 2005. 128 p.
   One section of this book relates how the writer Rolando Hinojosa-Smith grew up in South Texas in a family that loved to read and raised him in both the Anglo and Mexican cultures. The interaction of these cultures in that region are presented in his Klail City Death Trap novels, one of which won the 1976 Casa de las Américas award.
Older; Nonfiction

Hodges, Ben (1856-1929) United States
African-American/Mexican

Monceaux, Morgan, and Ruth Katcher. *My Heroes, My People: African Americans and Native Americans in the West*. Illustrated by Morgan Monceaux. New York: Frances Foster Books, 1999. 64 p.

According to the section on Ben Hodges, the Dodge City, Kansas cowboy was noted for his swindling schemes. A portrait of Hodges accompanies the brief description.
Intermediate, Older; Nonfiction

Hope, John (1868-1936) United States
Scottish/African-American

Becker, John T., and Stanli K. Becker, eds. *All Blood Is Red . . . All Shadows Are Dark!* Illustrated by J. Howard Noel. Cleveland: Seven Shadows Press, 1984. 168 p.
The editors of this book became friends with the son of John Hope. They relate that despite his Caucasian appearance John Hope chose to live as an African-American. He served as president of Morehouse College and Atlanta University.
Intermediate, Older; Nonfiction

Cox, Clinton. *African American Teachers*. New York: John Wiley & Sons, 2000. 176 p. (Black Stars)
As pointed out in this book's biography of John Hope, after graduating from Brown University, Hope taught at Roger Williams University in Nashville and became president of what is now called Morehouse College. He founded Atlanta University by drawing together Morehouse and other black colleges and developed it into a first-class university by attracting top teachers and establishing graduate schools. Standing up against Booker T. Washington's acceptance of black inequality, Hope believed that blacks should have the opportunity for higher education.
Older; Nonfiction

McDaniel, Melissa. *W. E. B. Du Bois: Scholar and Civil Rights Activist*. New York: Franklin Watts, 1999. 96 p. (A Book Report Biography)
W. E. B. Du Bois' educational achievements; his scholarly studies of African-Americans, including his book *The Philadelphia Negro*; his disputes with Booker T. Washington, Marcus Garvey, and Walter Francis White; his friendship with John Hope; his advocacy of world peace; and his renouncing of his United States citizenship are covered in this biography. It includes photographs, a chronology, a source note, resource listings, and an index.
Older; Nonfiction

Horne, Lena (1917-2010) United States
African-European-American and Native American/African-American, to European-American

Nash, Gary B. *Forbidden Love: The Secret History of Mixed-Race America*. Illustrated by author. New York: Henry Holt and Company, 1999. 224 p.
According to this book the 1947 marriage of the popular Lena Horne to Lennie Hayton shocked the nation. A photograph of the couple is included.
Older; Nonfiction

Palmer, Leslie. *Lena Horne: Entertainer*. Philadelphia: Chelsea House Publishers, 1989. 128 p. (Black Americans of Achievement)

Lena Horne's personal life and career are presented in detail in this biography. During her childhood she was shuttled between her grandparents—her grandfather, who exposed her to the arts, and her grandmother, who was active in the NAACP—and her itinerant actress mother. At the age of sixteen she left school to join the chorus line at Harlem's Cottton Club. Horne's career embraced club solo acts, movies, Broadway theater, records, television, and her touring show *Lena Horne: the Lady and Her Music*. She married a white man, the arranger-composer Lennie Hayton, and became a civil rights advocate. The book contains photographs, a chronology, a list of some of Horne's record albums, a reading list, and an index.
Older; Nonfiction

Horse, John (also Cohia, Cowaya) (1812?-1882) United States
Seminole/African-American, to Seminole

Dramer, Kim. *Native Americans and Black Americans*. Philadelphia: Chelsea House Publishers, 1997. 96 p. (Indians of North America)

According to this book's account, in 1870 John Horse brought a group of black Seminoles back to the United States from Mexico and founded settlements near Fort Duncan and Fort Clark. A number of the black Seminoles became part of the United States army where they served as scouts and captured outlaws. However, because of the hostility of some white Texans and of the Federal government's broken promise of food and land, Horse led the black Seminoles back to Mexico in 1882.
Older; Nonfiction

Katz, William Loren. *Black Indians: A Hidden Heritage*. New York: Atheneum, 1986. 208 p.

The book's historical account of black Seminoles includes many references to the role of John Horse.
Intermediate, Older; Nonfiction

Katz, William Loren, and Paula A. Franklin. *Proudly Red and Black: Stories of African and Native Americans*. New York: Atheneum, 1993. 96 p.

John Horse fought for the Seminole Indians of Florida in the Second Seminole War and later, having moved with Seminoles to Indian Territory, unsuccessfully sought to defend them from the Creeks. As the chapter on the black Seminole leader relates, he then led a group of black Seminoles to Mexico where they settled and served as border guards.
Intermediate, Older; Nonfiction

Monceaux, Morgan, and Ruth Katcher. *My Heroes, My People: African Americans and Native Americans in the West*. Illustrated by Morgan Monceaux. New York: Frances Foster Books, 1999. 64 p.

This book states that John Horse farmed in Mexico and patrolled for the Mexican government. It includes a full-page portrait of House and his Seminole wife.
Intermediate, Older; Nonfiction

Schlissel, Lillian. *Black Frontiers: A History of African American Heroes in the Old West*. New York: Simon & Schuster Books for Young Readers, 1995. 80 p.

According to this book, John Horse, together with Snake Warrior, led the United States Army's Seminole Negro Indian Scouts in patrolling in the Southwest and he requested the government to honor its promise of land for the Seminoles.
Intermediate, Older; Nonfiction

Houston, Samuel (also Colonneh, the Raven) (1793-1863) United States
Scottish-Irish-American, by Cherokee, to European-American and Cherokee

Alter, Judy. *Sam Houston: A Leader for Texas*. New York: Children's Press, 1998. 48 p. (Community Builders)

Sites commemorating Sam Houston are featured in this survey of his life. The book includes informational inserts, photographs, a timeline, a resource section, and an index.
Primary, Intermediate; Nonfiction

Alter, Judy. *Sam Houston Is My Hero*. Fort Worth: TCU Press, 2003. 144 p. (A Chaparrel Book for Young Readers)

This book of historical fiction is based on an incident in the life of Catherine Jennings. After her father is killed at the Alamo, twelve-year-old Cat runs away from her home near Bastrop, Texas, to recruit soldiers for Sam Houston's army. On her adventurous horseback ride she encounters different reactions at the cabins she visits and eventually ends up with the Texan army. Continuing to believe in Houston despite his retreat from Santa Anna's army, Cat's faith is finally justified when Houston wins the Battle of San Jacinto.
Intermediate, Older; Fiction

Boraas, Tracey. *Sam Houston: Soldier and Statesman*. Mankato, Minn.: Bridgestone Books, 2003. 48 p. (Let Freedom Ring)

This look at Sam Houston tells of his close relationship with Andrew Jackson and points out his flaws as well as his strengths. Photographs, a timeline, a glossary, a reading list, information about internet sites and places of interest, and an index supplement this biography.
Intermediate; Nonfiction

Caravantes, Peggy. *An American in Texas: The Story of Sam Houston*. Greensboro, N.C.: Morgan Reynolds Publishing, 2003. 144 p. (Founders of the Republic)

Sam Houston's life, including his relationships with the Cherokee, receives extensive coverage in this biography. Photographs, a timeline, a source list, a bibliography, and an index complement the text.
Older; Nonfiction

Fritz, Jean. *Make Way for Sam Houston*. Illustrated by Elise Primavera. New York, G. P. Putnam's Sons, 1986. 112 p.

Sam Houston's personality emerges in this detailed and sometimes humorous biography, which includes full-page drawings, page notes, a bibliography, and an index.
Intermediate, Older; Nonfiction

Gregson, Susan R. *Sam Houston: Texas Hero*. Minneapolis: Compass Point Books, 2006. 112 p. (Signature Lives)
A timeline showing events occurring in the world and in Sam Houston's life, photographs, informational inserts, a glossary, source notes, a resource list, and an index are included in this detailed biography.
Older; Nonfiction

Harkins, Susan Sales, and William H. Harkins. *Sam Houston*. Hockessin, Del.: Mitchell Lane Publishers, 2006. 32 p. (A Robbie Reader/What's So Great About...?)
Sam Houston's life story is presented in this chapter book, which includes captioned photographs, a glossary of bolded text words, a chronology, a resource list, and an index.
Primary, Intermediate; Nonfiction

Kiely Miller, Barbara. *Sam Houston*. Pleasantville, N.Y.: Weekly Reader Publishing, 2008. 24 p. (Great Americans)
Captioned photographs, a glossary, a resource list, and an index accompany this introductory biography of Sam Houston.
Primary; Nonfiction

Nash, Gary B. *Forbidden Love: The Secret History of Mixed-Race America*. New York: Henry Holt and Company, 1999. 224 p.
This book discusses the close relationship of Sam Houston and the Cherokee. Running away from Tennessee when he was sixteen, Houston was adopted by the Cherokee chief Ooleteka [or Oolooteka] (John Jolly) and renamed Colloneh (the Raven). Although he left the Cherokee three years later, Houston's Tennessee militia regiment fought together with the Cherokee and the Creek in the Battle of Horseshoe Bend during the War of 1812, and he tried to get the best possible outcome for the Cherokee when they were made to move westward. Resigning from his governorship of Tennessee, Houston lived with the Western Cherokee for three years during which time he tried to protect their interests and married Tiana Rogers Gentry, whose father was a white trader and whose mother was part Cherokee. One of Gentry's uncles was Ooleteka. Houston dreamed of making an Anglo-Indian republic in Mexico's Territory of Texas and after he became president of the independent Republic of Texas worked towards guaranteeing the Cherokee a large homeland within the republic.
Older; Nonfiction

Sanford, William R., and Carl R. Green. *Sam Houston: Texas Hero*. Springfield, N.J.: Enslow Publishers, 1996. 48 p. (Legendary Heroes of the Wild West)
This biography covers Sam Houston's personal life and his varied career as a general and a statesman. It includes photographs, chapter notes, a glossary, a reading list, and an index.
Intermediate, Older; Nonfiction

Trumbauer, Lisa. *Sam Houston*. Mankato, Minn.: Capstone Press, 2004. 24 p. (First Biographies)

    Photographs, a timeline, a glossary, a resource listing, and an index are included in this introduction to Sam Houston for early readers.

Pre-K, Primary; Nonfiction

Woodward, Walter M. *Sam Houston: For Texas and the Union*. New York: PowerPlus Books, 2003. 112 p. (The Library of American Lives and Times)

    This detailed biography of Sam Houston emphasizes his efforts as a Southerner to preserve the Union. It includes photographs with accompanying descriptions, a timeline, a glossary, a resource list, a bibliography, and an index.

Older; Nonfiction

Hruska, Shelly (c.1980-) Canada

Métis

Schilling, Vincent. *Native Athletes in Action!* Summertown, Tenn.: 7th Generation, 2007. 128 p. (Native Trailblazers)

    A biographical chapter describes how Shelly Hruska started playing ringette, a competitive team sport played on ice, at the age of five and progressed to being a player on Team Canada which won the World Ringette Championships in 2002 and 2004.

Intermediate, Older; Nonfiction

Hughes, James Mercer Langston (1902-1967) United States

African-Jewish-Scottish-American/Cherokee and African-English-French-American

Altman, Susan. *Extraordinary African-Americans: From Colonial to Contemporary Times*. Rev. ed. New York: Children's Press, 2001. 288 p. (Extraordinary People)

    A brief biographical chapter on Langston Hughes includes his poem "Mother to Son" and notes that, although he wrote in a number of genres, he is generally thought of as a poet.

Intermediate, Older; Nonfiction

Berry, S. L. *Langston Hughes*. Mankato, Minn.: Creative Education, 1994. 48 p. (Voices in Poetry)

    Against a background of photographs and large American and foreign postage stamps, chronological sections presenting Langston Hughes' life are interspersed with his poems. The book includes a selected list of Hughes' works and an index.

Intermediate, Older; Nonfiction

Burleigh, Robert. *Langston's Train Ride*. Illustrated by Leonard Jenkins. New York: Orchard Books, 2004. 32 p.

    This colorful picture book presents Langston Hughes at the time of the publication of his first poetry book as he recalls the poem he wrote as an eighteen-year-old riding the train from Ohio to visit his father, who lived in Mexico. As the train crossed the Mississippi River aglow in a golden sunset,

Hughes, thinking of earlier Negroes and their rivers, composed "The Negro Speaks of Rivers" and realized he was a poet. Biographical information on Hughes is provided in an afterword.
Primary, Intermediate; Nonfiction

Cooper, Floyd. *Coming Home: From the Life of Langston Hughes*. Illustrated by author. New York: Philomel Books, 1994. 32 p.

Large paintings and text tell of Langston Hughes' lonely childhood and his longing for a real "home." It describes his living with his elderly grandmother, who told him of her first husband who had died in John Brown's raid at Harpers Ferry and of his great uncle John Mercer Langston, who had become a Congressman. Hughes spent time with his father, his mother, and family friends. As an adult he discovered his real home, his African-American people. An author's note provides further information on Hughes.
Primary, Intermediate; Nonfiction

Cruz, Bárbara C. *Multiethnic Teens and Cultural Identity: A Hot Issue*. Berkeley Heights, N.J.: Enslow Publishers, 2001. 64 p.

A page on Langston Hughes describes the mixed ancestry of the Poet Laureate of the Harlem Renaissance.
Older; Nonfiction

Denenberg, Dennis, and Lorraine Roscoe. *50 American Heroes Every Kid Should Meet*. Brookfield, Conn.: The Millbrook Press, 2001. 128 p.

A double-page spread focuses on Langston Hughes' decision to become a poet and suggests that the book's readers write poems. Photographs, a quotation, and references are included.
Intermediate, Older; Nonfiction

Faber, Doris, and Harold Faber. *Great Lives: American Literature*. New York: Atheneum Books for Young Readers, 1995. 320 p. (Great Lives)

Langston Hughes' varied experiences and works are chronicled in this book's profile of the African-American writer.
Older; Nonfiction

Greenfield, Eloise. *How They Got Over: African Americans and the Call of the Sea*. Illustrated by Jan Spivey Gilchrist. New York: Amistad, 2003. 128 p.

A vignette on Langston Hughes relates that as a young man he worked as a ship mess boy and that his first autobiography is entitled *The Big Sea*.
Intermediate; Nonfiction

Hardy, P. Stephen, and Sheila Jackson Hardy. *Extraordinary People of the Harlem Renaissance*. New York: Children's Press, 2000. 288 p. (Extraordinary People)

This book's chapter on the poet Langston Hughes provides a summary of his life, including his role as part of the Harlem Renaissance. It points out that there is now a Langston Hughes Community

Library and Cultural Center in New York City.
Older; Nonfiction

Haugen, Brenda. *Langston Hughes: The Voice of Harlem*. Minneapolis: Compass Point Books, 2005. 112 p. (Signature Lives)

Quoting extensively from Langston Hughes' autobiography, *The Big Sea*, this biography describes the hardships of his childhood and his experiences as a world traveler, war reporter, newspaper columnist, poet, novelist, and playwright. The book includes photographs, informational inserts, a chronology of Hughes' life and world events, a bibliography, source notes, a resource listing, a glossary, and an index.
Intermediate, Older; Nonfiction

Hill, Christine M. *Langston Hughes: Poet of the Harlem Renaissance*. Berkeley Heights, N.J.: Enslow Publishers, 1997. 128 p. (African-American Biographies)

This biography of Langston Hughes traces the highlights and low points in his personal life and writing career. It tells of his childhood; his experiences at Columbia University and Lincoln University; his writing of poetry, plays, stories, children's books, and an autobiography; his creation of the fictional character "Simple;" his appearance before Senator Joseph McCarthy's subcommittee; and the recognition given his works. Photographs, chapter notes, a chronology, a reading list, and an index are included.
Older; Nonfiction

Hopkins, Lee Bennett, selector. *Lives: Poems about Famous Americans*. Illustrated by Leslie Staub. New York: HarperCollins Publishers, 1999. 36 p.

Langston Hughes is commemorated in this book by Hopkins' poem "Dreamer," a full-page color painting, and a biographical note.
Intermediate; Fiction

Kranz, Rachel C. *The Biographical Dictionary of Black Americans*. New York: Facts on File, 1992. 192 p.

This book's informative account of Langston Hughes covers both his life and his works.
Intermediate, Older; Nonfiction

Leach, Laurie F. *Langston Hughes: A Biography*. Westport, Conn.: Greenwood Press, 2004. 200 p. (Greenwood Biographies)

This biography of Langston Hughes is written for high school students. It provides a comprehensive account of his life, which includes a detailed description of the controversy between Hughes and Zora Neale Hurston over the authorship of the play *Mule Bone*. An extensive chronology, a bibliography, photographs, and an index are included.
Older; Nonfiction

Lewis, J. Patrick. *Freedom Like Sunlight: Praisesongs for Black Americans*. Illustrated by John Thompson. Mankato, Minn.: Creative Editons, 2000. 40 p.

This poetry book that celebrates African-Americans includes "Because My Mouth Is Wide with Laughter," a poem presenting Langston Hughes in each of the four seasons.
Intermediate, Older; Fiction

Masoff, Joy. *The African American Story: The Events That Shaped Our Nation . . . and the People Who Changed Our Lives*. Waccabuc, N.Y.: Five Ponds Press, 2007. 96 p.
This history of African-Americans includes a quotation from, a paragraph about, and a picture of Langston Hughes.
Older; Nonfiction

Medina, Tony. *Love to Langston*. Illustrated by R. Gregory Christie. New York: Lee & Low Books, 2002. 36 p.
In this illustrated picture book, the author, who is a poet, presents fourteen poems that provide a biographical introduction to Langston Hughes. Notes at the end of the book elaborate upon each poem.
Intermediate; Nonfiction

Meltzer, Milton. *Langston Hughes: An Illustrated Edition*. Illustrated by Stephen Alcorn. Brookfield, Conn.: Millbrook Press, 1997. 240 p.
Enriched by its distinctive illustrations, this biography provides a detailed look at Langston Hughes' life and notes those of his works which feature the theme of mixed parentage. It is written by a friend and collaborator of Hughes and includes a postscript, a list of Hughes' works, a bibliography, and an index.
Older; Nonfiction

Meyer, Carolyn. *Denny's Tapes*. New York: Margaret K. McElderry Books, 1987. 224 p.
Almost eighteen-year old Denny, the son of an African-American father and a white mother, and sixteen-year-old Stephanie, the daughter of his white stepfather, fall in love. When his stepfather discovers them together, he orders Denny to leave the house. This story for high school readers is about Denny's journey from Pennsylvania to San Francisco to find his father and on the way to meet his two grandmothers. Although Denny doesn't get together with his musician father who has left for a couple months for a gig in Houston, his trip turns out to be a memorable one. In Chicago he meets his African-American grandmother, who is highly cultivated and had objected to his parents' marriage because of his mother's lower social status. In Nebraska, he meets his mother's mother, who had objected to the marriage because of his father's race and believes Africans-Americans have lower intelligence. However, Denny comes to care for both his grandmothers. His Chicago grandmother spends time teaching him about black history, including about her friend Langston Hughes, and shows him how to develop his natural talent on the piano. Denny discovers that his Nebraska grandmother is largely imprisoned in bed by her cruel daughter-in-law, is full of love for him, and greatly appreciates his organ playing. In Chicago Denny also has a romantic relationship with a beautiful twenty-four-year-old African-American woman and in Colorado is rescued by a cowgirl from a pair of tourists who object to what they wrongly assume is an interracial relationship. When he gets to San

Francisco, Denny realizes that he has learned a lot about himself, that he wants to become a musician, and that he is going to wait for his father.
Older; Fiction

Osofsky, Audrey. *Free to Dream: The Making of a Poet: Langston Hughes*. New York: Lothrop, Lee & Shepard Books, 1996. 112 p.

This biography of Langston Hughes incorporates his poetry into the text. It shows how, despite the many hardships he endured throughout his life, he held on to his dreams. The author has set the words of a Hughes' poem to music in an appended song, "Hold Fast to Dreams." This book contains photographs and prints, chapter notes, a bibliography, and an index.
Older; Nonfiction

Otfinoski, Steven. *Great Black Writers*. New York: Facts On File, 1994. 128 p. (American Profiles)

This book's section on Langston Hughes includes a biography, three of his poems, an excerpt from his 1965 *Simple* collection, photographs, a chronology, and a reading list.
Older; Nonfiction

Perdomo, Willie. *Visiting Langston*. Illustrated by Bryan Collier. New York: Henry Holt and Company, 2000. 32 p.

In this picture book a young poet writes in verse of her visit to Langston Hughes's house in Harlem.
Primary; Fiction

Rhynes, Martha E. *I, Too, Sing America: The Story of Langston Hughes*. Greensboro, N.C.: Morgan Reynolds Publishers, 2002. 144 p. (World Writers)

Photographs, a timeline, quotation sources, a glossary, a list of major works, a bibliography, a listing of websites, and an index add to this detailed biography of Langston Hughes, which includes information on his evolving political views.
Older; Nonfiction

Rummel, Jack. *Langston Hughes: Poet*. Philadelphia: Chelsea House Publishers, 1988. 112 p. (Black Americans of Achievement)

This book provides a comprehensive biography of Langston Hughes, the African-American author whose writing in both content and style was about his people: their circumstances, their speech, their music, and their experiences. It includes a chronology of Hughes' life, photographs, a reading list, and an index.
Older; Nonfiction

Shull, Jodie A. *Langston Hughes: "Life Makes Poems."* Berkeley Heights, N.J.: Enslow Publishers, 2006. 128 p. (African-American Biography Library)

The book's subtitle was the title used by Langston Hughes in poetic presentations of his life story. This biography tells of the numerous works in which Hughes used the written word to express the

experiences, sorrows, and dreams of African-Americans. It includes photographs, informational inserts, a chronology, chapter notes, a resource list, and an index.
Older; Nonfiction

Strickland, Michael R. *African-American Poets*. Springfield, N.J.: Enslow Publishers, 1996. 112 p. (Collective Biographies)
    Langston Hughes' writings are featured in this book's biographical chapter, which notes how he used jazz rhythms in his poetry and wrote about ordinary African-Americans.
Older; Nonfiction

Turner, Glennette Tilley. *Follow in Their Footsteps*. Illustrated with photographs. New York: Puffin Books, 1999. 192 p.
    A chapter on Charlemae Rollins, distinguished children's librarian, includes a skit in which Langston Hughes tells of his life to children who grow up to pursue noted careers.
Intermediate, Older; Fiction, Nonfiction

Walker, Alice. *Langston Hughes: American Poet*. Illustrated by Catherine Deeter. Rev. ed. New York: Amistad, 2002. 44 p.
    Paintings illustrate this biography of Langston Hughes, which concentrates on his earlier years and includes two of his poems. In an author's note Alice Walker describes her contacts with Hughes and her desire through writing this book to introduce children to the man and his writings.
Primary, Intermediate; Nonfiction

Wallace, Maurice. *Langston Hughes: The Harlem Renaissance*. New York: Marshall Cavendish/ Benchmark, 2007. 144 p. (Writers and Their Works)
    This book includes a biography of Langston Hughes; a detailed description of his books *The Weary Blues*, *Fine Clothes to the Jew*, and *Not Without Laughter* and his play *Mule Bone*; a chapter on the Harlem Renaissance; a listing of his works; chapter notes; a filmography; a bibliography; a chronology; a resource list; and an index.
Older; Nonfiction

Hussein bin Talal, King of Jordan (1935-1999) Jordan
Jordanian, to European-Syrian-Swedish-American

Darraj, Susan Muaddi. *Queen Noor*. Philadelphia: Chelsea House Publishers, 2003. 128 p. (Women in Politics)
    Photographs, a chronology, chapter notes, a bibliography, a resource list, and an index are included in this comprehensive biography of Queen Noor. Placing her life within the context of Jordanian society, world events, and her husband King Hussein's policies, the book highlights her many humanitarian works and the sometimes controversial role she played as Queen.
Older; Nonfiction

Raatma, Lucia. *Queen Noor: American-Born Queen of Jordan*. Minneapolis: Compass Point Books, 2006. 112 p. (Signature Lives)

This biography tells of Queen Noor's childhood in the United States, her marriage to King Hussein of Jordan, her role as Queen, her struggles to be accepted by the peoples of Jordan, and her humanitarian work. There is extensive background information on the Middle East's history, politics, and culture and on the policies which King Hussein pursued in trying to bring peace to the region. The book includes photographs, informational inserts, chapter notes, a timeline, a glossary, a resource list, a bibliography, and an index.
Older; Nonfiction

Ikeda, Stewart David (19??-   ) United States
Japanese-American/European-American

Alderman, Bruce, editor. *Interracial Relationships*. Farmington Hills, Mich.: Greenhaven Press, 2007. 112 p. (Social Issues Firsthand)

In a narrative reproduced from *Pacific Citizen*, writer Stewart David Ikeda tells how the adoption of a Guatemalan baby by his Caucasian uncle and Japanese-American aunt prompted him to think about his Japanese-American culture and about the possible culturally mixed identity of all Americans.
Older; Nonfiction

Ishmael (?-?) Canaan
Chaldean/Egyptian

Grimes, Nikki. *Dark Sons*. New York: Jump at the Sun, 2005. 224 p.

Written in verse, this book intertwines the often parallel stories of the teen-aged boys, Ishmael, the son of Abraham and the maid-servant Hagar, and Sam, the American son of African-American parents. Although their lives are separated by centuries, both grow up with strong bonds with their fathers and experience rejection and confusion when their fathers abandon their mothers and focus their attention on sons they father with other women. In Ishmael's case, because of Sarah's antagonism, Abraham sends Ishmael and Hagar away. In Sam's case, his father, new wife, and baby son move across the country. At the end of the book Sam reads the story of Ishmael and imagines that, as kindred brothers, he too will be able to carry on his own life.
Older; Fiction

Jackson, Michael Joseph (1958-2009) United States
African-American Baptist/African-American Jehovah's Witness, to English-French-Norwegian-Scottish-Irish-American and Cherokee, to European-American

George, Nelson. *The Michael Jackson Story*. New York: Dell Publishing Co., 1984. 192 p.

Drawing some of its material from interviews with Michael Jackson's family members and others associated with them, this biography covers his life into the early 1980s and contains a section of

black-and-white photographs, a discography, and listings of Jackson's awards and favorite books and vocalists.
Older; Nonfiction

Graves, Karen Marie. *Michael Jackson*. San Diego, Calif.: Lucent Books, 2001. 112 p.
This biography of Michael Jackson provides detailed coverage of his career and of the impact of his family and professional life on his increasing loneliness and eccentricity. Black-and-white photographs, chapter notes, a chronology, a reading list, a bibliography, and an index complete the work.
Older; Nonfiction

Halliburton, Warren J. *The Picture Life of Michael Jackson*. New York: Franklin Watts, 1984. 48 p.
Numerous black-and-white full-page photographs are featured in this introductory biography of Michael Jackson.
Primary, Intermediate; Nonfiction

Haskins, James. *About Michael Jackson*. Hillside, N.J.: Enslow Publishers, 1985. 96 p.
Michael Jackson's early performing, the role of Motown and Berry Gordy in developing the Jackson Five, their dissatisfaction with Motown that caused all but Jermaine going to Epic Records (CBS), Michael's playing the Scarecrow in the movie *The Wiz*, his role in integrating MTV, and his winning eight Grammy awards in 1984 are among the topics covered in this book. Noting Jackson's love of fantasy, yet astuteness as a businessman, this biography includes black-and-white photographs, a discography, and an index.
Intermediate, Older; Nonfiction

Krohn, Katherine. *Michael Jackson: Ultimate Music Legend*. Minneapolis, Minn.: Lerner Publications Company, 2010. 48 p. (Gateway Biographies)
Text, photographs, a chronology, source notes, a bibliography, a resource list, and an index combine to provide a biography of Michael Jackson that covers not only his life, but also his memorial service and the posthumous release of the film *Michael Jackson's This Is It*.
Intermediate; Nonfiction

Mabery, D. L. *This Is Michael Jackson*. Minneapolis: Lerner Publications Company, 1984. 48 p.
Color and black-and-white photographs complement the text in this introduction to Michael Jackson's career and to his home in Encino, California. A listing of Jackson's records and awards and an index are appended.
Intermediate; Nonfiction

Matthews, Gordon. *Michael Jackson*. New York: Wanderer Books, 1984. 64 p.
This up-close look at Michael Jackson and his musical career features a section of photographs from the 1984 Grammy Awards, answers to questions fans might ask him, and a discography.
Intermediate; Nonfiction

Nicholson, Lois P. *Michael Jackson: Entertainer*. Philadelphia: Chelsea House Publishers, 1994. 104 p. (Black Americans of Achievement)

This biography of Michael Jackson provides a comprehensive account of his personal life and career and includes a description of Neverland. Black-and-white photographs, a chronology, a reading list, and an index are included.
Older; Nonfiction

Overbey, Theresa. *Michael Jackson*. Hockessin, Del.: Mitchell Lane Publishers, 2003. 32 p. (A Blue Banner Biography)

The text of this biography of Michael Jackson is accompanied by color photographs, a chronology, a discography, a videography, an award list, a reading list, and an index.
Intermediate; Nonfiction

Pratt, Mary K. *Michael Jackson: King of Pop*. Edina, Minn.: ABDO Publishing Company, 2010. 112 p. (Lives Cut Short)

Michael Jackson's musical successes and the controversies surrounding his later years and his death are chronicled in this biography. Informational inserts, including one describing his professional relationship with Paul McCartney, photographs, a timeline, a fact list, chapter source notes, a glossary, a resource list, and an index are included.
Intermediate, Older; Nonfiction

Rubenstein, Bruce. *Michael Jackson's Magic*. Mankato, Minn.: Creative Education, 1984. 32 p. (Rock'n Pop Stars)

Michael Jackson's on-stage dynamic performing is contrasted with his off-stage introverted childlike personality in this biography, which includes black-and-white photographs.
Intermediate; Nonfiction

Wallner, Rosemary. *Michael Jackson: Music's Living Legend*. Edina, Minn.: Abdo & Daughters, 1991. 32 p. (Reaching for the Stars)

A text divided into chronological sections and full-page black-and-white photographs present Michael Jackson's life story in this introduction to the versatile musician.
Intermediate; Nonfiction

Jacobs, Harriet Ann (1813-1897) United States
African-European-American/African-European-American, by European-American, to European-American

Lyons, Mary E. *Letters from a Slave Boy: The Story of Joseph Jacobs*. New York: Atheneum Books for Young Readers, 2007. 208 p.

This book of historical fiction is a companion book to *Letters from a Slave Girl*, which tells the story of Harriet Jacobs. It presents her son Joseph's narrative of his life from the age of nine until his departure to mine gold in Australia in about 1852. Growing up in Edenton, North Carolina, with his

great-grandmother and sister, he is unaware that his mother, who is an escaped slave, is hiding in the house and that he is the son of a white neighbor, Samuel Sawyer. In 1843 Joseph leaves for Boston where he briefly attends the abusive Smith School and then becomes a printer's apprentice. Running away to New Bedford, he works on the docks and goes off for almost three years on a whaling ship. On board the ship he encounters a sailor from the Cape Verde Islands who has been looked after since boyhood by the ship's Quaker captain. Joseph next goes to California to mine for gold with his Uncle John, until the two set off for Australia where they will be free. Joseph struggles with the treatment he receives as a slave, his feelings about the Irish boy who works on the ship with him and dies, the decision as to whether he should pass as white, and the terrible worry that he and his mother will be captured by slave hunters. The book includes some information on Joseph's later life.
Older; Fiction

Lyons, Mary E. *Letters from a Slave Girl: The Story of Harriet Jacobs*. New York: Charles Scribner's Sons, 1992. 160 p.

This fictionalized biography of Harriet Jacobs is based on her autobiography. After her mother's death when Harriet was six, her mistress was kind to her and taught her to read, but did not free her. Instead, upon her death, she left eleven-year-old Harriet to her cruel niece Maria and Maria's husband, Dr. James Norcom, who soon subjected Harriet to continuing sexual harassment. Knowing that she would be forced to have sexual relationships with the doctor, she gave herself to Samuel Sawyer, a white resident of Edenton, North Carolina, with whom she bore two children, Joseph and Louisa. When she was twenty-one, Harriet decided to escape from the Norcoms, hide, and trick Dr. Norcom into believing she had gone north so he would sell Joseph and Louisa and Samuel Sawyer could buy them. This plan worked to an extent, but although she escaped, Dr. Norcom was deceived, and Samuel bought the children, Harriet suffered through almost seven years hiding in her grandmother's tiny garret and the children were not freed. Harriet faced danger even after she escaped to the north because of the Fugitive Slave Law of 1850. After 1852, when Harriet was finally freed, she wrote her autobiography, which advanced the causes of antislavery, and did relief work with needy blacks. This book tells of the support Harriet received from family members, of the horrors to which they were subjected, and of what happened to each of them.
Older; Fiction

Jacobs, Joseph (1829-1863?) United States
European-American/African-European-American

Lyons, Mary E. *Letters from a Slave Boy: The Story of Joseph Jacobs*. New York: Atheneum Books for Young Readers, 2007. 208 p.

This book of historical fiction is a companion book to *Letters from a Slave Girl*, which tells the story of Harriet Jacobs. It presents her son Joseph's narrative of his life from the age of nine until his departure to mine gold in Australia in about 1852. Growing up in Edenton, North Carolina, with his great-grandmother and sister, he is unaware that his mother Harriet, who is an escaped slave, is hiding in the house and that he is the son of a white neighbor, Samuel Sawyer. In 1843 Joseph leaves for Boston where he briefly attends the abusive Smith School and then becomes a printer's apprentice.

Running away to New Bedford, he works on the docks and goes off for almost three years on a whaling ship. On board the ship he encounters a sailor from the Cape Verde Islands who has been looked after since boyhood by the ship's Quaker captain. Joseph next goes to California to mine for gold with his Uncle John, until the two set off for Australia where they will be free. Joseph struggles with the treatment he receives as a slave, his feelings about the Irish boy who works on the ship with him and dies, the decision as to whether he should pass as white, and the terrible worry that he and his mother will be captured by slave hunters. The book includes some information on Joseph's later life.
Older; Fiction

Lyons, Mary E. *Letters from a Slave Girl: The Story of Harriet Jacobs*. New York: Charles Scribner's Sons, 1992. 160 p.

This fictionalized biography of Harriet Jacobs is based on her autobiography. After her mother's death when Harriet was six, her mistress was kind to her and taught her to read, but did not free her. Instead, upon her death, she left eleven-year-old Harriet to her cruel niece Maria and Maria's husband, Dr. James Norcom, who soon subjected Harriet to continuing sexual harassment. Knowing that she would be forced to have sexual relationships with the doctor, she gave herself to Samuel Sawyer, a white resident of Edenton, North Carolina, with whom she bore two children, Joseph and Louisa. When she was twenty-one, Harriet decided to escape from the Norcoms, hide, and trick Dr. Norcom into believing she had gone north so he would sell Joseph and Louisa and Samuel Sawyer could buy them. This plan worked to an extent, but although she escaped, Dr. Norcom was deceived, and Samuel bought the children, Harriet suffered through almost seven years hiding in her grandmother's tiny garret and the children were not freed. Harriet faced danger even after she escaped to the north because of the Fugitive Slave Law of 1850. After 1852, when Harriet was finally freed, she wrote her autobiography, which advanced the causes of antislavery, and did relief work with needy blacks. This book tells of the support Harriet received from family members, of the horrors to which they were subjected, and of what happened to each of them.
Older; Fiction

Jefferson, Thomas (1743-1826) United States
Welsh-American/English, probably to English and African-English-American

Aldridge, Rebecca. *Thomas Jefferson*. Mankato, Minn.: Bridgestone Books, 2002. 48 p. (Let Freedom Ring)

This survey of Thomas Jefferson's life is presented through short sections, inserts, and illustrations. It covers his achievements such as the Declaration of Independence, the Statute of Virginia for Religious Freedom, the Louisiana Purchase, Monticello, and the University of Virginia and discusses the question of a relationship with his slave Sally Hemings. A timeline, glossary, resource section, and index are appended.
Intermediate; Nonfiction

Armstrong, Jennifer. *Thomas Jefferson: Letters from a Philadelphia Bookworm*. Delray Beach, Fla.: Winslow Press, 2001. 128 p. (Dear Mr. President)

Correspondence between fictional Amelia Hornsby, an inquisitive and independent-minded girl, and President Thomas Jefferson provides an informative and interesting account of Jefferson's presidency, the Lewis and Clark expedition, Monticello, and Philadelphia and Pittsburgh in the early 1800s. The letters and accompanying illustrations are followed by biographical information on Jefferson, which contains one sentence on evidence of an affair with Sally Hemings; a timeline; a resource list that includes subjects located on the publisher's website; and an index.
Intermediate, Older; Fiction

Bober, Natalie S. *Thomas Jefferson: Draftsman of a Nation.* Charlottesville, Va.: University of Virginia Press, 2007. 376 p.

This detailed and insightful presentation of Thomas Jefferson's life for high school students places it within its historical context and chronicles his work, his ideas, and his personal life. It describes the import of his father, James Maury, William Small, George Wythe, and Francis Fauquier on his early development; his passion for books, learning, architecture, and gardening; his abilities as a writer, but not as a speaker; and his love of his family. It covers the process through which the colonies came to declare their separation from England, Jefferson's writing of the Declaration of Independence, his work with Wythe to rewrite Virginia's laws, his failure as governor to prevent the British from invading Virginia, his years in Paris, his disagreements as Secretary of State with Alexander Hamilton, his vice presidency, his presidency, his pleasure in his grandchildren, his friendship with John Adams, and his founding of the University of Virginia. The book explores Jefferson's relationship with Sally Hemings and his conflicting views and actions with respect to slavery. It emphasizes Jefferson's love from boyhood of "Tom's Mountain" on which he buried his friend Dabney Carr, his wife, and his children, built Monticello, and spent as much time as possible. The book includes photographs, a chronology, a family tree, an author's note, chapter notes, a bibliography, and an index.
Older; Nonfiction

Ferris, Jeri Chase. *Thomas Jefferson: Father of Liberty.* Minneapolis: Carolrhoda Books, 1998. 112 p.

The importance of Thomas Jefferson's writings—his notebooks, his letters, his garden book, his farm book, *A Manual of Parliamentary Practice*, *Notes on the State of Virginia*, the Declaration of Independence, and the Statute of Virginia for Religious Freedom—is highlighted in this detailed biography. The book includes photographs, notes, a bibliography, and an index.
Intermediate, Older; Nonfiction

Greene, Carol. *Thomas Jefferson: Author, Inventor, President.* Chicago: Children's Press, 1991. 48 p. (A Rookie Biography)

This introductory biography of Thomas Jefferson is illustrated with photographs and includes a chronology and an index.
Primary; Nonfiction

Harness, Cheryl. *Thomas Jefferson.* Illustrated by author. Washington, D.C.: National Geographic Society, 2004. 44 p.

Numerous detailed colorful paintings distinguish this biography of Thomas Jefferson. Among these are maps and layouts showing American, British, and French troop movements and victories during the Revolutionary War, the routes of the Lewis and Clark Expedition, the interior and exterior of Monticello, and the world as it was during Jefferson's presidency. A chronology of world events during his presidential years is also included. The book notes that evidence suggests the birth of six children to Jefferson and Sally Hemings.
Primary, Intermediate; Nonfiction

Kukla, Amy, and Joe Kukla. *Thomas Jefferson: Life, Liberty, and the Pursuit of Happiness*. New York: PowerPlus Books, 2005. 112 p. (The Library of American Lives and Times)
This biography of Thomas Jefferson covers such topics as the Jefferson Bible, the manner in which Virginia's 1774 committee of correspondence was formed, the three parts of the Declaration of Independence, the Federalists and the Republicans, the Alien and Sedition Acts, and the negotiation of the Louisiana Purchase. The book points out that Sally Hemings may have been an aunt of Jefferson's daughters Martha and Maria and includes an 1804 cartoon depicting the rumored relationship between Hemings and Jefferson. Numerous photographs, a timeline, a glossary, a bibliography, a resource section, and an index are included.
Intermediate, Older; Nonfiction

Lanier, Shannon, and Jane Feldman. *Jefferson's Children: The Story of One American Family*. Photographs by Jane Feldman. Introduction by Lucian K. Truscott IV. Historical Essays by Annette Gordon-Reed and Beverley Gray. New York: Random House, 2000. 144 p.
After attending the May 1999 Monticello reunion of descendants of Thomas Jefferson, Sidney Lanier, who is a descendant of Madison Hemings, teamed up with photographer Jane Feldman to interview descendants of Thomas Jefferson and his wife, Martha Wayles Jefferson, and of Thomas Woodson, Madison Hemings, and Eston Hemings, those three of Jefferson and Sally Hemings' children whose lines can be traced. The resulting book contains a variety of individual and family interviews and photographs that reveal the family histories of the interviewees as well as their personal experiences and opinions. There is talk about whether the Hemings family members are indeed descendants of Jefferson's and should be allowed in the family graveyard, which is controlled by the Monticello Association. The bulk of the book consists of Hemings family interviews that tell what it means to be of mixed race; how some family members have passed as white; of some not being personally accepted because they look black or, on the other hand, look white; and of the Hemings' many achievements throughout the generations. Both Jeffersons and Hemings talk of family, of the importance of learning of their past, and of the hope for many that members of this family can eventually become one.
Older; Nonfiction

Leslie, Tonya. *Thomas Jefferson: A Life of Patriotism*. Illustrated by Tina Walski. Minneapolis: Bellwether Media, 2008. 24 p. (Blastoff! Readers. People of Character)
This illustrated introduction to Thomas Jefferson for beginning readers focuses on his writing of the Declaration of Independence. It includes a glossary defining bolded text words, a resource list, and

an index.
Primary, Intermediate; Nonfiction

Nash, Gary B. *Forbidden Love: The Secret History of Mixed-Race America*. New York: Henry Holt and Company, 1999. 224 p.

This book points to the discrepancy between Thomas Jefferson's desire to remove white mothers of mulatto children from Virginia while being the father of at least one of Sally Hemings' children.
Older; Nonfiction

Pinkney, Andrea Davis. *Dear Benjamin Banneker*. Illustrated by Brian Pinkney. San Diego: Gulliver Books, 1994. 32 p.

Illustrated with large hand-colored oil scratchboard renderings, this book focuses on Benjamin Banneker's first almanac and on his correspondence with Secretary of State Thomas Jefferson that pointed out the discrepancy between Jefferson's profession of the equality of man in the Declaration of Independence and his owning of slaves.
Primary, Intermediate; Nonfiction

Rinaldi, Ann. *Wolf by the Ears*. New York: Scholastic, 1991. 272 p.

This novel focuses on Harriet Hemings' agonizingly difficult decision to leave Monticello when she turns twenty-one—and, when doing so, to pass as white. The daughter of Sally Hemings and probably Thomas Jefferson (although her mother never reveals her father's identity), Harriet loves Monticello, her life there, and Jefferson, who is a kind master to her and the other slaves. It is after she is attacked by a drunken man who has married one of Jefferson's granddaughters that Harriet realizes she cannot remain at Monticello. Supportive Thomas Mann Randolph, Jefferson's son-in-law, convinces Harriet that she must pass and arranges for her both a teaching position in Washington and betrothal to a white man. It is he, who, unlike Jefferson, pushes for the abolition of slavery in Virginia. In this novel the decision as to whether to leave also faces Harriet's brother Beverly, who unrealistically hopes that Jefferson will get him into his university. The novel also mentions Tom, Harriet's oldest brother, who had run away some years earlier, and her little brothers Madison and Eston.
Older; Fiction

Roberts, Russell. *The Life and Times of Thomas Jefferson*. Hockessin, Del.: Mitchell Lane Publishers, 2007. 48 p. (Profiles in American History)

Text, informational pages, photographs, chapter notes, chronologies of Thomas Jefferson's life and times, a resource list, a glossary, and an index present an account of the third President.
Intermediate, Older; Nonfiction

Ruffin, Frances E. *Sally Hemings*. New York: Rosen Publishing Group/PowerKids Press, 2002. 24 p. (American Legends)

As related in this biography, Sally Hemings was born as a slave on the John Wayles plantation in Cumberland County, Maryland. When Wayles' daughter Martha Wayles (Skelton) married Thomas Jefferson, Sally moved to Monticello with her mother, who became the Monticello housekeeper. Sally

was a half-sister of Martha Jefferson. Martha died when Sally was about nine, and, when Sally was fourteen, she took one of Jefferson's daughters to France where Jefferson was the American minister. It was probably in France that Sally and Thomas Jefferson began a relationship. Sally had seven children, three of whom died early. Jefferson was the father of at least one and perhaps all of these children. This biography includes a glossary and an index.
Primary, Intermediate; Nonfiction

Severance, John B. *Thomas Jefferson: Architect of Democracy*. New York: Clarion Books, 1998. 192 p.
This biography provides a comprehensive account of Thomas Jefferson's life and views and of the period in which he lived. It includes a section of quotations from Jefferson, illustrations, a bibliography, and an index.
Older; Nonfiction

Usel, T. M. *Thomas Jefferson: A Photo-Illustrated Biography*. Mankato, Minn.: Bridgestone Books, 1996. 24 p.
Full-page photographs and pages of text alternate in this biography of Thomas Jefferson, which includes an excerpt from a letter which Jefferson wrote to his oldest daughter, a chronology, a glossary, a resource list, and an index.
Primary; Nonfiction

Whitelaw, Nancy. *Thomas Jefferson: Philosopher and President*. Greensboro, N.C.: Morgan Reynolds Publishers, 2001. 144 p.
This in-depth presentation of Thomas Jefferson's life focuses on his philosophies, which were largely rooted in the Enlightenment's belief in human reason; the political world of his time; and the intricacies of his remarkable career. A timeline, sources, a bibliography, illustrations, and an index are included.
Older; Nonfiction

Williams, Mark London. *Trail of Bones*. Cambridge, Mass.: Candlewick Press, 2005. 320 p. (Danger Boy)
This book is part of a science fiction series in which Eli, an American boy, Thea, a girl from ancient Alexandria, and Clyne, a talking dinosaur, travel in time through the Fifth Dimension. In this story they end up in 1804 where Eli becomes part of the Lewis and Clark Corps of Discovery. Going with the expedition from St. Louis to the Mandan village, he encounters Pierre Cruzatte as well as Sacagawea and Toussaint Charbonneau and witnesses the birth of their son Pomp. Thea is also transported close to St. Louis where both she and Eli meet Thomas Jefferson and Sally Hemings, who have secretly traveled there for the start of Lewis and Clark's trip. However, Thea is mistaken for a runaway slave and is taken back to Monticello. Clyne lands in the wild near the Mandans. At the tale's conclusion all three are together in New Orleans where they once again go into the Fifth Dimension.
Intermediate, Older; Fiction

Jemison, Mary (also Dehgewanus) (1742 or 1743-1833) United States
Irish-American or Scottish-Irish-American, by Seneca, to Delaware, to Seneca

Dickinson, Alice. *Taken by the Indians: True Tales of Captivity*. New York: Franklin Watts, 1976. 144 p.

The account in this book of Mary Jemison's life is based on the story that she told at the age of eighty to James Seaver, and it includes extensive quotations from his report. The book describes Jemison's life from the time of her capture at the age of fifteen and relates that shortly after her capture she knew that her parents and three of her siblings had been killed. It tells of her being adopted as the sister of two kind Seneca sisters, her two marriages to Indian men, her son John's killing of his two brothers and subsequent murder, and of her living at the Gardow Flats on the Genessee River in New York.
Older; Nonfiction

Lenski, Lois. *Indian Captive: The Story of Mary Jemison*. Illustrated by author. New York: Frederick A. Stokes Company, 1941. 296 p.

This is a fictionalized story of Mary Jemison's experiences as a child captive. It relates she continues to yearn for her family when she is kidnapped by Indians and Frenchmen from her home in southern Pennsylvania and taken to live with the Delaware, first near present day Steubenville, Ohio, and then to the Seneca's settlement near what is now Cuylerville, New York. Twelve-year-old Mary is adopted by two sisters (one kind, one cross) to take the place of their brother who had died. She is nursed to health by Earth Mother, understood by wise Shagbark, and befriended by the children Beaver Girl and Little Turtle as well as by a white captive young man who successfully escapes. After she learns her parents and three of her siblings have been murdered, she must decide whether she wants to be sold to the British. She chooses to remain with the Seneca.
Intermediate, Older; Fiction

Roop, Connie, and Peter Roop, editors. *The Diary of Mary Jemison, Captured by the Indians*. Illustrated by Laszlo Kubinyi. New York: Benchmark Books, 2001. 64 p. (In My Own Words)

This book tells Mary Jemison's story by using selected passages taken from her oral account to James Seaver. It covers her life from her capture at age twelve through her decision to remain with the Seneca. An epilogue summarizes her later years. The passages are edited for young readers, and definitions of some of the words are included next to the text. The book contains a glossary, a resource section, and an index and is illustrated with full-page color paintings.
Intermediate, Older; Nonfiction

Seaver, James E. *Captured by Indians: The Life of Mary Jemison*. Edited by Karen Zeinert. North Haven, Conn. Linnet Books, 1995. 128 p.

Seaver's narrative of his interview with Mary Jemison has been edited to remove his comments about the Indians and the account of Mary's second husband, which was taken from another source and is included separately in this book. The book retains much of the original text (a glossary is appended) and, based on the views of historians, changes the date of her capture from 1755 to 1758, thereby making her about fifteen, not twelve years of age. It has a timeline, which presents among other dates the date of her adoption by two Seneca sisters; her marriage to Sheninjee, a Delaware; his death; her marriage to Hiokatoo, a Seneca; and the birth dates of her eight children. This comprehensive

biography includes Seaver's introduction, background information, boxed-in additional information, photographs, an editor's note, an afterword, a bibliography, and a resource section.
Older; Nonfiction

Jen, Gish (born Lillian Jen) (1955-   ) United States
Chinese-American, to Irish-American

Alderman, Bruce, editor. *Interracial Relationships*. Farmington Hills, Mich.: Greenhaven Press, 2007. 112 p. (Social Issues Firsthand)
O'Hearn, Claudine Chiawei, editor. *Half and Half: Writers on Growing Up Biracial and Bicultural*. New York: Pantheon Books, 1998. 288 p.
   In a narrative included in both books, the writer Gish Jen tells of her four-year-old son's attending Chinese-culture school and notes how in the United States certain ethnicities are perceived as trumping others, i.e., persons who are Chinese-Irish-American are regarded as Asian and persons who are African-European-American are regarded as black.
Older; Nonfiction

Jeter, Derek Sanderson (1974-   ) United States
African-American/Irish-American

Donovan, Sandy. *Derek Jeter*. Minneapolis: Lerner Sports, 2004. 32 p. (Amazing Athletes)
   This biography of Derek Jeter concentrates on his baseball career through his becoming New York Yankees team captain in 2003. It includes a section on Jeter's Turn 2 Foundation, a glossary of words highlighted in the text, a chronology of his baseball accomplishments, a resource list, color photographs, and an index. A photograph of his parents shows that is father is African-American and his mother European-American.
Primary, Intermediate; Nonfiction

January, Brendan. *Derek Jeter: Shortstop Sensation*. New York: Children's Press, 2000. 48 p. (Sports Stars)
   Containing Derek Jeter's batting statistics for the years 1995 through 1999, this book describes his professional baseball career in the minors and with the New York Yankees. It tells of the positive influence of his parents, but does not mention that he is of mixed race. A chronology and color photographs are included.
Intermediate; Nonfiction

Jeter, Derek, with Jack Curry. *The Life You Imagine: Life Lessons for Achieving Your Dreams*. New York: Crown Publishers, 2000. 304 p.
   In this book Derek Jeter sets forth ten lessons to follow to achieve your dreams. He draws these lessons from his own life experiences and from the many truths he has learned from his parents, his teammates, and other ballplayers. In one chapter Jeter describes what it was like growing up as a biracial child and how he and his family responded to the situations they encountered.
Older; Nonfiction

Marcovitz, Hal. *Derek Jeter*. Broomall, Pa.: Mason Crest Publishers, 2009. 64 p. (Modern Role Models)

This account of Derek Jeter's career features one-page elaborations of eight topics referred to in the text. Color photographs with descriptive captions, quotations printed in different ink colors, bolded words defined in a glossary, a chronology, a listing of Jeter's accomplishments and awards, a resource section, page notes, and an index complement the text.

Intermediate, Older; Nonfiction

Stout, Glenn. *On the Field with . . . Derek Jeter*. New York: Little, Brown, and Company, 2000. 128 p. (Matt Christopher Sports Bio Bookshelf)

Focusing on Derek Jeter's baseball career, this biography provides a detailed account of his baseball playing as a young boy and a teenager, his struggles in the rookie league, his later successes in the minor leagues, and his development as an outstanding New York Yankees shortstop. It gives game coverage of the Yankees playoff games from 1996 through 1999 and of their World Series games in 1996, 1998, and 1999. Photographs, a chronology of Jeter's accomplishments, and tables of his batting and fielding statistics from 1995 through 1999 are included.

Intermediate, Older; Nonfiction

Torres, John Albert. *Derek Jeter*. Hockessin, Del.: Mitchell Lane Publishers, 2005. 32 p. (A Blue Banner Biography)

Derek Jeter's childhood, his experiences in the minor leagues, and his charitable work are among the areas covered in this look at the New York Yankees shortstop. It includes his major league statistics through the 2004 season, a chronology, color photographs, and an index.

Intermediate; Nonfiction

Johnson, Dwayne Douglass (also The Rock) (1972-   ) United States
African-Canadian/Samoan, to Cuban-American

Gorman, Jacqueline Laks. *Dwayne "The Rock" Johnson*. Pleasantville, N.Y.: Gareth Stevens Publishing, 2008. 32 p. (Today's Superstars, Entertainment)

Inserts on professional wrestling, the University of Miami football team, Dwayne Johnson's crowning as a Samoan high chief, and facts about Johnson; color photographs; a timeline; a glossary; a resource list; and an index are features of this biography of the wrestler/actor.

Intermediate; Nonfiction

Kjelle, Marylou Morano. *Dwayne "The Rock" Johnson*. Hockessin, Del.: Mitchell Lane Publishers, 2009. 32 p. (A Robbie Reader)

This biography of Dwayne Johnson points out that his father, his mother's father, and other Samoan relatives wrestled professionally. A graduate of the University of Miami where he played on its football team, Johnson has become famous as a professional wrestler and more recently as a movie actor. The book includes color photography, a glossary defining bolded text words, a chronology, a filmography, a resource list, and an index.

Primary; Nonfiction

Johnson, John (Jack) Arthur (1878-1946) United States
African-American, to European-American, to European-American

Nash, Gary B. *Forbidden Love: The Secret History of Mixed-Race America*. Illustrated by author. New York: Henry Holt and Company, 1999. 224 p.

As pointed out in this book, Jack Johnson, the champion heavyweight boxer, achieved notoriety when he married Etta Terry Duryea, a white woman, and, upon her death, Lucille Cameron, who was also white. Older; Nonfiction

Johnson, William (1715-1774) Ireland
Irish, to Mohawk

Bland, Celia. *Pontiac: Ottawa Rebel*. Philadelphia: Chelsea House Publishers, 1994. 112 p. (North American Indians of Achievement)

This biography of Pontiac reports that, in contrast to French fur traders, Sir William Johnson was the only British trader to seek an alliance with the Indians. He secured the support of the Iroquois confederation, was British superintendent of Indian affairs for the Northern colonies, and his home was a meeting place for British officers and Indian leaders. The book includes pictures of Johnson and of the certificate he gave to loyal Indian chiefs. Older; Nonfiction

Lenski, Lois. *Indian Captive: The Story of Mary Jemison*. Illustrated by author. New York: Frederick A. Stokes Company, 1941. 296 p.

This story of Mary Jemison refers several times to Sir William Johnson: his taking of Fort Niagara from the French, his marrying a Mohawk woman (Molly Brant), and his efforts to persuade the Iroquois to join with the British against the French in the French and Indian War. Intermediate, Older; Fiction

Nash, Gary B. *Forbidden Love: The Secret History of Mixed-Race America*. New York: Henry Holt and Company, 1999. 224 p.

This book points out that William Johnson, who was born in Ireland, became very close to the Mohawks, living and trading with them, marrying a Mohawk, Molly Brant, and negotiating for the British with the Iroquois nations. Older; Nonfiction

Johnson, William (late 1700s-1800s) England
English, to Cheyenne

Lampman, Evelyn Sibley. *Half-Breed*. Illustrated by Ann Grifalconi. Garden City, N.Y.: Doubleday & Company, 1967. 264 p.

Twelve-year-old Hardy leaves his Crow mother because she is marrying a man of the same clan and travels by himself to Oregon to find the white father who had left when he was six. Reaching his

father's cabin with the help of Dr. John McLoughlin [later known as "Father of Oregon"] and his half Chippewa wife Marguerite and marshal Joe Meeks and his Cheyenne wife Virginia, Hardy discovers that his father has left to go to California to mine gold. Hardy decides to await his father and is aided during his stay by *Old Ironsides* veteran Bill Johnson and his Cheyenne wife Nancy on whose land the cabin is located. To Hardy's surprise his father's sister Rhody arrives from the East and stays with Hardy. Hardy is very upset by her white ways, especially her making him perform squaw's chores and burning his medicine bag. He also suffers from the poor treatment he receives in Portland because he is part Indian. After Hardy's father returns and then leaves, Hardy decides to go back to live with the Crow. However, after his father again returns and then decides to leave, Hardy realizes that the responsible thing to do is to remain with Aunt Rhody who is his family.
Intermediate, Older; Fiction

Jones, John (1817-1879) United States
German-American/African-American

Katz, William Loren. *Black Pioneers: An Untold Story*. New York: Atheneum Books for Young Readers, 1999. 208 p.

A section of this book details the accomplishments of John Jones, who became a successful businessman in Chicago, led the effort leading to repeal of the Illinois Black Laws, and, with his election to the Cook County Board of Commissioners, became the first person of color to hold elective office in the West.
Older; Nonfiction

Keys, Alicia (born Alicia Augello Cook) (1981-   ) United States
African-American/Irish-Italian-American

Bankston, John. *Alicia Keys*. Hockessin, Del.: Mitchell Lane Publishers, 2004. 32 p. (A Blue Banner Biography)

This biography of Alicia Keys tells of her exposure to the arts as a child in Clinton (Hell's Kitchen), New York City, her graduation at age sixteen as valedictorian from the Professional Performing Arts School in Harlem, the time she spent producing her first album, her refusal to accept Columbia Records' demands to alter it, the role of Clive Davis in getting Keys on the *Tonight Show* and *Oprah Winfrey* before releasing the album under his J Records label, the album's immediate success, and the awards Keys has received. The book includes color photographs, fact inserts, a discography, a chronology, a resource list, and an index.
Intermediate, Older; Nonfiction

Brown, Terrell. *Alicia Keys*. Broomall, Pa.: Mason Crest Publishers, 2007. 64 p. (Hip-Hop)

Alicia Keys' piano instruction in the Suzuki method when she was young; her childhood enjoyment of classical, pop, and hip-hop music; the development of her own musical style; the impacts of her manager Jeff Robinson, record executive Clive Davis, and producer Kerry "Krucial" Brothers on her career; her success as a songwriter and singer; and her charity work, especially in fighting AIDS,

are emphasized in this biography. It features color photographs; bolded text words defined in a glossary; a chronology; resource information; listings of Keys' albums, singles, books, television appearances, films, videos and awards; and an index.
Intermediate, Older; Nonfiction

Horn, Geoffrey M. *Alicia Keys*. Milwaukee: Gareth Stevens Publishing, 2006. 32 p. (Today's Superstars, Entertainment)
A text accompanied by color photographs, fact files, and informational paragraphs; a timeline; a glossary; a resource list; and an index present Alicia Keys' musical career.
Intermediate; Nonfiction

Kidd, Jason Frederick (1973-   ) United States
African-American Baptist/Irish-American Catholic

Finkel, Jon. *Jason Kidd*. Los Angeles: TOKYOPOP, 2005. 96 p. (Greatest Stars of the NBA)
This graphic presentation of Jason Kidd's basketball career is filled with photographs of Kidd in action with accompanying commentary by fictional announcers Lil' Hops and T-Minus. The book covers Kidd's skills and his greatest moments and contains a timeline, playing statistics, and comments about Kidd by NBA coaches and players.
Intermediate, Older; Fiction, Nonfiction

Gray, Valerie A. *Jason Kidd: Star Guard*. Berkeley Heights, N.J.: Enslow Publishers, 2000. 104 p. (Sports Reports)
Jason Kidd's basketball playing at St. Joseph of Notre Dame High School in Alameda, California, and at the University of California at Berkeley and his professional career with the Dallas Mavericks and the Phoenix Suns are detailed in this book. It includes game descriptions, photographs, fact inserts, chapter notes, career statistics, and an index.
Older; Nonfiction

James, Brant. *Jason Kidd*. Philadelphia: Chelsea House Publishers, 1997. 64 p. (Basketball Legends)
Playing statistics, a chronology, photographs, a reading list, and an index add to this examination of Jason Kidd's basketball career through his 1995-96 season with the Dallas Mavericks.
Intermediate, Older; Nonfiction

Moore, David. *The Jason Kidd Story*. New York: Scholastic, 1997. 80 p. (Fast Breaks)
Full-page black-and-white photographs and a section of full-page color photographs highlight this biographical look at Jason Kidd's childhood and his basketball successes.
Intermediate, Older; Nonfiction

Rappoport, Ken. *Jason Kidd: Leader on the Court*. Berkeley Heights, N.J.: Enslow Publishers, 2004. 104 p.
Presenting Jason Kidd's career into his 2003-04 NBA season with the New Jersey Nets, this biography

features accounts of the point guard's highlight games, coverage of his participation in the 2000 Olympics, black-and-white photographs, quotations, chapter notes, career statistics, internet addresses, and an index.
Older; Nonfiction

Thornley, Stew. *Super Sports Star Jason Kidd*. Berkeley Heights, N.J.: Enslow Publishers, 2002. 48 p. (Super Sports Star)
 Jason Kidd is introduced in this biography, which concludes with his being traded to the New Jersey Nets. It includes color photographs, Kidd's NBA statistics, a glossary, a resource list, and an index.
Intermediate; Nonfiction

Torres, John Albert. *Sports Great Jason Kidd*. Springfield, N.J.: Enslow Publishers, 1998. 64 p. (Sports Great Books)
 This biography of Jason Kidd chronicles his development into a superstar point guard and contains photographs, career statistics, and an index.
Intermediate, Older; Nonfiction

Labiche, François (?-1828) United States
French/Omaha

Crosby, Michael T. *Sacagawea: Shoshone Explorer*. Stockton, N.J.: OTTN Publishing, 2008. 144 p. (Shapers of America)
 Color photographs, maps, informational inserts, a detailed chronology, a glossary, chapter notes, resource lists, and an index combine to provide a well-rounded portrayal of Sacajawea's life. The book presents biographical information on Jean Baptiste (Pomp) Charbonneau and tells of the contributions to the Lewis and Clark Expedition made by Toussaint Charbonneau, Pierre Cruzatte, George Drouillard, and François Labiche, who served as a boatman and interpreter.
Older; Nonfiction

LaButte, Pierre (1698-1774) France
French, to French and Miami

Trottier, Maxine. *A Circle of Silver*. New York: Stoddart Kids, 1999. 224 p. (The Circle of Silver Chronicles)
 Set in 1760 this first book in *The Circle of Silver Chronicles* relates the story of thirteen-year-old John MacNeil, who leaves his English home to spend two years with his father, Captain James MacNeil, traveling to and then returning from the British Fort Detroit. It tells of the growing enmity of the Indians living near Fort Detroit who are poorly treated by the British, of John's being appointed King George III's artist in Canada, of John's love of Canada, of his friendship with the Ottawa Natka and Wallace Doig whose Miami wife had died, of his encounter with Pontiac, and of his closeness

to Marie Roy, the French-Canadian Miami girl whom he adores, and to Pierre La Butte, the interpreter for the British and then merchant who becomes Marie Roy's husband.
Older; Fiction

LaButte, Pierre (1796-?) Canada
French-Canadian and Miami/French Canadian

Trottier, Maxine. *Under a Shooting Star*. New York: Stoddart Kids, 2002. 224 p. (The Circle of Silver Chronicles)

A sequel to *A Circle of Silver* and *By the Standing Stone*, this book is set in the border area of Canada and the United States during the War of 1812. Fifteen-year-old Canadian Edward Wolf MacNeil (the son of English Jamie and Oneida Sarah, the half-sister of Owela) is escorting two American girls to their home in Sandusky, Ohio, on his way to his Uncle John MacNeil's Canadian home on Pêche Island. When the merchant ship on which they are traveling sinks during a storm on Lake Erie, the three manage to reach South Bass Island. There they meet Paukeesaa, Tecumseh's son, who takes them to John MacNeil's empty house where they befriend the great-grandson of Marie Roy and Pierre LaButte (who is also named Pierre LaButte), and Edward reads the journal of Mack, John MacNeil's ward. This story tells of Edward and the girls' stay at Fort Amhertsburg where Edward helps build the English ship *Detroit*, of their involuntary involvement in the Battle of Lake Erie, and of John MacNeil's safe return.
Older; Fiction

LaFlesche, Francis (Frank) (1857-1932) United States
French-American and Omaha or Ponca/European-American, Omaha?, Oto?, and Iowa

Avery, Susan, and Linda Skinner. *Extraordinary American Indians*. Chicago: Children's Press, 1992. 272 p.

As reported in a section on siblings Francis LaFlesche, Susan LaFlesche Picotte, and Susette LaFlesche Tibbles, their father was Ponca and French in his ancestry although he became an Omaha chief. Growing up on the Omaha reservation, Frank LaFlesche became a lawyer and an anthropologist. He did research on the Omaha and the Osage and wrote the memoir, *The Middle Five*.
Older; Nonfiction

Langston, John Mercer (1829-1897) United States
European-American/African-American and Native American00

Katz, William Loren. *Black Pioneers: An Untold Story*. New York: Atheneum Books for Young Readers, 1999. 208 p.

As pointed out in this book, John Mercer Langston was a graduate of Oberlin College where he also earned a master's degree. During the Civil War he recruited African-American soldiers, advocated civil rights in his Cincinnati newspaper *Colored Citizen*, and founded the Ohio Equal Rights

League.
Older; Nonfiction

Katz, William Loren, and Paula A. Franklin. *Proudly Red and Black: Stories of African and Native Americans*. New York: Atheneum, 1993. 96 p.

The chapter on Edmonia Lewis tells of her lawyer, John Mercer Langston, who later served as dean of the law department at Howard University and as a member of Congress.
Intermediate, Older; Nonfiction

Wolfe, Rinna Evelyn. *Edmonia Lewis: Wildfire in Marble*. Parsippany, N.J.: Dillon Press, 1998. 128 p. (A People in Focus Book)

This book describes John Mercer Langston's defense of Edmonia Lewis in her trial for poisoning and mentions his career and his recruitment of African-American soldiers for the North during the Civil War.
Older; Nonfiction

Lasky, Marven (1907-1998) United States
Jewish Russian-American, by French-Canadian-American

Lasky, Kathryn. *Marven of the Great North Woods*. Illustrated by Kevin Hawkes. San Diego: Harcourt Brace & Company, 1997. 48 p.

This picture book relates how in 1918 ten-year-old Marven Lasky, the son of Russian Jewish immigrants, was sent to a logging camp near Bemidji, Minnesota, to escape an influenza epidemic in Duluth. There he lived amidst French-Canadian lumberjacks. Keeping the camp's books and managing to eat kosher, he became the special friend of one of the lumberjacks. Marven returned to his family four months later.
Primary, Intermediate; Fiction

Lehrman, Devorah (1908 or 1909-between 1968 & 1979) Poland
Polish Jewish, by South African Jewish

Wulf, Linda Press. *The Night of the Burning: Devorah's Story*. New York: Farrar Straus Giroux, 2006. 224 p.

This novel is based on the life of the author's mother-in-law from 1915 when Devorah is living in the Polish village of Domachevo with her close Jewish family. The story tells of her uncle's being conscripted by the Czar's army and dying of poisonous gas, of the death of her ill, starving father, of her mother's death from typhoid, and of the terrible night in 1920 when her aunt is stabbed to death during the Cossack and Christian burning of Domachevo. Devorah is taken with her younger sister to an orphanage in Pinsk where they are selected by Isaac Ochberg to be among the two hundred Jewish orphans to be rescued and brought to South Africa. They travel via London to Cape Town where they live in an orphanage until they adopted by different families. Throughout her experiences Devorah is a sad orphan, striving to keep alive the memories of her family and its Jewish beliefs. Finally, she recognizes that she

must start anew and that she is happy living with her adoptive family.
Older; Fiction

Leigh, Richard (also Beaver Dick) (?-1899) England
English, to Shoshone, to Bannock

Gregory, Kristiana. *Jenny of the Tetons*. San Diego: Gulliver Books, 1989. 128 p.

This book of historical fiction is based on the lives of Richard "Beaver Dick" Leigh, who served as a guide for the 1872 Hayden Survey, and his Shoshone wife Jenny. Members of the survey expedition recognized their services by giving their names to three lakes in the Tetons: Leigh Lake, Jenny Lake and Beaver Dick Lake (now String Lake). In the story a fictional fifteen-year girl, Carrie, whose parents had been killed when Indians attacked their wagon train, comes to live with the Leigh family and finally to accept it as her own. Carrie experiences life in a cabin near present day Rexburg, Idaho, and summer camping with the Leighs in the Tetons. Jenny and the Leigh family's five children die from smallpox in 1876. Carrie marries and is reunited with one of her younger brothers who had been kidnapped by the Blackfeet.
Intermediate, Older; Fiction

Lennon, John Winston (1940-1980) England
English, to Japanese

Bradman, Tony. *John Lennon*. Illustrated by Karen Heywood. London: Hamish Hamilton, 1985. 64 p. (Profiles)

Illustrated with black-and-white drawings, this book tells the story of John Lennon's life and of the people and events that shaped it. A list of Lennon's recordings is appended.
Intermediate, Older; Nonfiction

Conord, Bruce W. *John Lennon*. Philadelphia: Chelsea House Publishers, 1994. 128 p. (Pop Culture Legends)

This biography covers both Lennon's music career and his emotional problems. It describes his childhood in Liverpool living with his aunt and uncle; his early career; the astounding success of the Beatles; their breakup; his relationship with Yoko Ono; his suffering from parental abandonment and the deaths of relatives and close friends; his use of drugs, alcohol, transcendental meditation, and scream therapy; his post-Beatle years; and his murder. The book includes photographs, a discography, a reading list, a chronology, and an index.
Older; Nonfiction

Corbin, Carole Lynn. *John Lennon*. New York: Franklin Watts, 1982. 128 p. (An Impact Biography)

John Lennon's life and music are detailed in this biography, which contains photographs, a chronology, and an index.
Older; Nonfiction

Dowswell, Paul. *John Lennon: An Unauthorized Biography*. Chicago: Heinemann Library, 2001. 56 p. (Heinemann Profiles)

Numerous quotations by and about John Lennon; a look at his legacy; a glossary defining bolded words in the text; photographs; a listing of Lennon's records, films, and books; a reading list; and an index add to this life story of the famous rock musician.
Intermediate; Nonfiction

Duggleby, John. *Revolution: The Story of John Lennon*. Greensboro, N.C.: Morgan Reynolds Publishing, 2007. 176 p. (Modern Music Masters)

This comprehensive biography of John Lennon covers such topics as the tragedies of his childhood, the importance of Beatles' manager Brian Epstein, Beatlemania, Lennon's relationships with Cynthia Powell and Yoko Ono, the change in Lennon's public image, his activism for world peace, and the aftermath of his murder. Photographs, a timeline, chapter notes, a bibliography, a website listing, and an index complete the book.
Older; Nonfiction

Glassman, Bruce. *John Lennon & Paul McCartney: Their Magic and Their Music*. Woodbridge, Conn.: Blackbirch Press, 1995. 112 p. (Partners)

Although differing in background, temperament, musical strengths, and compositional content, Liverpool natives John Lennon and Paul McCartney collaborated to produce world-acclaimed popular music. This book describes how the two met, their closeness, their contributions to the Beatles' success, the development of their music, their later hostility towards each other, their solo careers, and the impact of the Beatles. Photographs, a reading list, a bibliography, a chronology, and an index are included.
Intermediate, Older; Nonfiction

Gogerly, Liz. *John Lennon: Voice of a Generation*. Austin, N.Y.: Raintree Steck-Vaughn Publishers, 2003. 48 p. (Famous Lives)

Color and black-and-white photographs, quotation inserts, a glossary, a chronology, a reading list, and an index are features of this life story of John Lennon.
Intermediate; Nonfiction

Hamilton, Sue L. *The Killing of a Rock Legend: John Lennon*. Bloomington, Minn.: Abdo & Daughters, 1989. 32 p. (Days of Tragedy)

Focusing on John Lennon's murder, this book traces his life and the life of his killer, Mark David Chapman. It includes full-page photographs and a source list.
Intermediate; Nonfiction

Kallen, Stuart A. *John Lennon*. San Diego: Lucent Books, 2001. 112 p. (The Importance Of)

Featuring lengthy quotations from commentaries relating to John Lennon and the Beatles, this book places Lennon's life within the context of the times in which he lived and emphasizes the impact which he made. Chapter notes, an annotated reading list and bibliography, and an index add to this

extensive biography, which notes that Lennon's interracial relationship with Yoko Ono was the cause of controversy.
Older; Nonfiction

Leigh, Vanora. *John Lennon*. Illustrated by Richard Hook. New York: The Bookwright Press, 1986. 32 p. (Great Lives)
　　Numerous paintings and photographs complement the text in this biography of John Lennon, which also contains a chronology, a glossary, a reading list, and an index.
Intermediate; Nonfiction

Partridge, Elizabeth. *John Lennon: All I Want Is the Truth: A Photographic Biography*. New York: Viking, 2005. 240 p.
　　This coffee-table book is characterized by numerous black-and-white photographs and a comprehensive biography of John Lennon that includes detailed coverage of Paul McCartney and Yoko Ono. Chapter notes, a bibliography, a reading list, and an index complete the book.
Older; Nonfiction

Rappaport, Doreen. *John's Secret Dreams: The Life of John Lennon*. Illustrated by Bryan Collier. New York: Hyperion Books for Children, 2004. 40 p.
　　Prose, creative paintings, and lyrics from his songs combine to present John Lennon's life story, his feelings, and his dreams. A chronology, a discography, a bibliography, and a reading list are appended.
Intermediate, Older; Nonfiction

Santrey, Laurence. *John Lennon: Young Rock Star*. Illustrated by Ellen Beier. Mahwah, N.J.: Troll Associates, 1990. 48 p.
　　John Lennon's childhood and teenage years are described in this book, which is illustrated with black-and-white drawings.
Primary, Intermediate; Nonfiction

White, Michael. *John Lennon*. Watford, England: Exley Publications, 1992. 64 p. (The World's Great Composers)
　　Presented in short sections of text accompanied by descriptions of its numerous photographs, this extensive biography points out the changes which occurred in John Lennon and his music, examines the success of the Beatles and the critical role played by Brian Epstein, and notes the impact of Lennon's life and message.
Older; Nonfiction

Wootton, Richard. *John Lennon*. New York: Random House, 1985. 128 p.
　　Containing numerous black-and-white photographs, this book presents a detailed narrative of John Lennon's life and the Beatles. An index is included.
Older; Nonfiction

Wright, David K. *John Lennon: The Beatles and Beyond.* Springfield, N.J.: Enslow Publishers, 1996. 112 p. (People To Know)

Photographs, a chronology, a discography, chapter notes, a reading list, and an index supplement this presentation of John Lennon's childhood, his career, and his relationships with the other Beatles and Yoko Ono.
Older; Nonfiction

Lewis, Mary Edmonia (also Wildfire) (1844?-1890? or 1911?) United States
African-American/Chippewa and African-American

Hardy, P. Stephen, and Sheila Jackson Hardy. *Extraordinary People of the Harlem Renaissance.* New York: Children's Press, 2000. 288 p. (Extraordinary People)

A biographical section on Edmonia Lewis points out how she brought realism to the then prevalent neoclassical style of sculpture.
Older; Nonfiction

Katz, William Loren. *Black Indians: A Hidden Heritage.* New York: Atheneum, 1986. 208 p.

This book's account of Edmonia Lewis summarizes her life and tells how her sculptures were acclaimed in both the United States and Europe.
Intermediate, Older; Nonfiction

Katz, William Loren, and Paula A. Franklin. *Proudly Red and Black: Stories of African and Native Americans.* New York: Atheneum, 1993. 96 p.

The chapter describing Edmonia Lewis relates how she lived for three years with the Chippewa as a child and attended Oberlin College. After learning to sculpt in Boston, she pursued her career as a sculptor in Rome. Lewis employed the neoclassical style of sculpture, and her subjects were often based on her African-American and Native American heritages.
Intermediate, Older; Nonfiction

Kranz, Rachel C. *The Biographical Dictionary of Black Americans.* New York: Facts on File, 1992. 192 p.

This book provides an account of Edmonia Lewis's life as well as information on her sculpturing.
Intermediate, Older; Nonfiction

Monceaux, Morgan, and Ruth Katcher. *My Heroes, My People: African Americans and Native Americans in the West.* Illustrated by Morgan Monceaux. New York: Frances Foster Books, 1999. 64 p.

A paragraph on Edmonia Lewis and her portrait are included in this book's presentation of people of color.
Intermediate, Older; Nonfiction

Nash, Gary B. *Forbidden Love: The Secret History of Mixed-Race America.* Illustrated by author. New York: Henry Holt and Company, 1999. 224 p.

This book's profile of Edmonia Lewis provides a summary of her life and her career as a sculptress. Older; Nonfiction

Potter, Joan, and Constance Claytor. *African Americans Who Were First*. New York: Cobblehill Books, 1997. 128 p.

A photograph of Edmonia Lewis accompanies a brief summary of her life that recognizes her as the first professional African-American sculptor.
Intermediate, Older; Nonfiction

Turner, Glennette Tilley. *Follow in Their Footsteps*. Illustrated with Photographs. New York: Puffin Books, 1999. 192 p.

A chapter in this book includes a detailed biography of Edmonia Lewis and a skit in which a family discovers a bust of Frederick Douglass which she sculpted.
Intermediate, Older; Fiction, Nonfiction

Wolfe, Rinna Evelyn. *Edmonia Lewis: Wildfire in Marble*. Parsippany, N.J.: Dillon Press, 1998. 128 p. (A People in Focus Book)

This is a scholarly biography of Edmonia Lewis that includes photographs, notes, a bibliography, an index, and a list of the sculptures mentioned. It tells of her early life, her experiences at Oberlin College where she was accused (but not brought to trial) of poisoning two housemates, of her initial work sculpting in Boston, and especially of her career as a sculptress in Rome. The book tells of specific sculptures, such as those of Abraham Lincoln, Henry Wadsworth Longfellow, Hiawatha, and Cleopatra and where they were sold, exhibited, and, in some cases, rediscovered after being lost.
Older; Nonfiction

Limber, Jim (or Davis, Jim Limber) (mid-1800s-?) United States
African-American or African-European-American, by European-American

Pittman, Rickey. *Jim Limber Davis: A Black Orphan in the Confederate White House*. Illustrated by Judith Hierstein. Gretna, La.: Pelican Publishing Company, 2007. 32 p.

According to this picture book, little African-American Jim Limber was rescued from a cruel guardian by Varina Davis, was registered as free by her husband Confederacy President Jefferson Davis, and was put under the guardianship of Jefferson and Varina Davis. Jim enjoyed playing with the Davis children, but was kidnapped by Union soldiers and then publicly displayed under the false accusation that he had been beaten by Jefferson Davis.
Primary; Fiction

Little, Frank (1879-1917) United States
European-American/Cherokee

Avery, Susan, and Linda Skinner. *Extraordinary American Indians*. Chicago: Children's Press, 1992. 272 p.

A section on Frank Little reports that, initially a metal miner, he became a union organizer for the Industrial Workers of the World, a union that sought to unite largely unskilled workers regardless of trade into one union and that advocated worker ownership of factories and mines. The pacifist son of a Quaker father, Little participated in nonviolent strikes and was disliked by many because of his "revolutionary" ideas and his pacifism during wartime. He was lynched in 1917.
Older; Nonfiction

Lobel, Anita (1934-   ) Poland
Jewish Polish, by Catholic Polish, by Lutheran Swedish

Lobel, Anita. *No Pretty Pictures: A Child of War*. New York: Greenwillow Books, 1998. 208 p.
In this autobiographical account, children's book author and illustrator Anita Lobel writes of her life as a Polish Jew from the ages of five through sixteen: from her father's leaving the family because of the Nazi occupation of Kraków to her emigration to the United States with her family. The book tells of the amazing devotion of her beloved Polish Catholic nanny, who looked after Anita and her younger brother as they escaped the Germans by first staying in a Polish village with Anita's father's relatives and, when that became too dangerous, by hiding in a village where her nanny's mother had lived and in a Benedictine convent. When the convent was raided, the siblings were captured. They were imprisoned first in Kraków and then at the Plaszów concentration camp. They were forced to walk from that camp to Auschwitz where they were taken in a train boxcar to Ravensbrück concentration camp. Released at the end of war, Anita and her brother were diagnosed with tuberculous and sent to a Lutheran sanatorium in Sweden. Anita loved her almost two years there, but, after recovering her health, she was sent to live in a Swedish shelter for Polish refugee children. She was finally reunited with her parents and lived in Stockholm before going to the United States. The book includes photographs.
Intermediate, Older; Nonfiction

Loving, Mildred Delores Jeter (1939-2008) United States
African-American and Rappahannock, to European-American

Alonso, Karen. *Loving v. Virginia: Interracial Marriage*. Berkeley Heights, N.J.: Enslow Publishers, 2000. 112 p. (Landmark Supreme Court Cases)
Including information on Richard and Mildred Loving's marriage, the history of Virginia laws against racial intermarriage, and the "Jim Crow Laws" in the South, this book provides an in-depth look at the Lovings' case contesting the constitutionality of Virginia's anti-miscegenation law. It covers the rulings by the Virginia trial court and the Supreme Court of Appeals of Virginia, United States Supreme Court precedents, the cases presented by the opposing sides, the Supreme Court's June 12, 1967 unanimous decision that Virginia's law was unconstitutional, and the Court's opinion. The book includes photographs, discussion questions, chapter notes, a glossary, a resource list, and an index.
Older; Nonfiction

Robson, David. *Soledad O'Brien: Television Journalist.* Broomall, Pa.: Mason Crest Publishers, 2009. 64 p. (Transcending Race in America: Biographies of Biracial Achievers)

This biography of Soledad O'Brien contains a photograph of and information on the interracial couple Richard Loving and Mildred Jeter Loving, who were married in Washington, D.C. in 1958 and returned to Virginia, their state of residence. They were criminally charged with miscegenation in Virginia. The 1967 Supreme Court decision in Loving v. Virginia ruled that the state law banning interracial marriage was unconstitutional.
Older; Nonfiction

Loving, Richard Perry (1933-1975) United States
European-American, to African-American Rappahannock

Alonso, Karen. *Loving v. Virginia: Interracial Marriage.* Berkeley Heights, N.J.: Enslow Publishers, 2000. 112 p. (Landmark Supreme Court Cases)

Including information on Richard and Mildred Loving's marriage, the history of Virginia laws against racial intermarriage, and the "Jim Crow Laws" in the South, this book provides an in-depth look at the Lovings' case contesting the constitutionality of Virginia's anti-miscegenation law. It covers the rulings by the Virginia trial court and the Supreme Court of Appeals of Virginia, United States Supreme Court precedents, the cases presented by the opposing sides, the Supreme Court's June 12, 1967 unanimous decision that Virginia's law was unconstitutional, and the Court's opinion. The book includes photographs, discussion questions, chapter notes, a glossary, a resource list, and an index.
Older; Nonfiction

Robson, David. *Soledad O'Brien: Television Journalist.* Broomall, Pa.: Mason Crest Publishers, 2009. 64 p. (Transcending Race in America: Biographies of Biracial Achievers)

This biography of Soledad O'Brien contains a photograph of and information on the interracial couple Richard Loving and Mildred Jeter Loving, who were married in Washington, D.C. in 1958 and returned to Virginia, their state of residence. They were criminally charged with miscegenation in Virginia. The 1967 Supreme Court decision in Loving v. Virginia ruled that the state law banning interracial marriage was unconstitutional.
Older; Nonfiction

Lynn, Loretta Webb (1935-   ) United States
European-American and Cherokee/Irish-American and Cherokee

Krishef, Robert K. *Loretta Lynn.* Minneapolis: Lerner Publications Company, 1978. 64 p. (Country Music Library)

This biography of Loretta Lynn tells of her growing up in a large family in a log cabin in Kentucky, of her meeting her husband Oliver Vanetta (Mooney) Lynn, Jr. at a pie social when she was thirteen, of his recognition of her singing talent and promotion of her career, and of her rise to and life as the Queen of Country Music. The book is illustratred with numerous black-and-white photographs

and has a list of some of Loretta Lynn's recordings and an index.
Intermediate, Older; Nonfiction

Malcolm X (also El-Hajj Malik El Shabazz, Malik Shabazz) (born Malcolm Little) (1925-1965)
United States
African-American/African-Scottish-Grenadian, by European-American, to African-American

Adoff, Arnold. *Malcolm X*. Illustrated by John Wilson. New York: Thomas Y. Crowell Company, 1970. 48 p. (Crowell Biographies)
    The illustrations add to this introductory biography of Malcolm X, which traces his life through the racial violence his family experienced; his removal from his home at age twelve; his stealing; his time in the Norfolk Prison Colony where he spent hours reading and corresponding with Elijah Muhammad, leader of the Muslim Nation of Islam; his changing his name to Malcolm X; his becoming a spokesman for the Nation of Islam; his marriage to Betty X; his pilgrimage to Mecca; his leaving the Nation of Islam to establish the more embracing Organization of Afro-American Unity; and his assassination.
Primary, Intermediate; Nonfiction

Benson, Michael. *Malcolm X*. Minneapolis: Lerner Publications Company, 2002. 112 p. (Biography)
    This detailed biography of Malcolm X emphasizes his changing relationship with the Black Muslim Nation of Islam, his beliefs as they differed from Martin Luther King, Jr.'s, and his assassination. It contains sections on the early civil rights movement, Elijah Muhammad, Martin Luther King, Jr., Muhammad Ali, and Louis Farrakhan and covers Betty X's later life. The book includes photographs, source notes, a bibliography, and an index.
Older; Nonfiction

Brown, Kevin. *Malcolm X: His Life and Legacy*. Brookfield, Conn.: The Millbrook Press, 1995. 112 p.
    Presenting his evolution from Malcolm Little to Rhythm Red, Detroit Red, Satan, Malcolm X, and El-Hajj Malik El Shabazz, this book analyzes Malcolm X's life and beliefs within the context of the broader civil rights movement. Large photographs, sidebars containing quotations from Malcolm X, a chronology, a bibliography, source notes, and an index complete this perceptive biography.
Older; Nonfiction

Collins, David R. *Black Rage: Malcolm X*. New York: Dillon Press, 1992. 104 p. (A People in Focus Book)
    Extensive coverage of Malcolm X's childhood and youth and of his assassination characterizes this biography. It takes note of his lighter skin and reddish-brown hair, which made him different within his family, and of his living as a junior high student in a detention home operated by a white couple. The book includes a section of photographs, a bibliography, and an index.
Intermediate, Older; Nonfiction

Crushshon, Theresa. *Malcolm X*. Chanhassen, Minn.: The Child's World, 2002. 40 p. (Journey to Freedom, The African American Library)

Photographs with accompanying information on more than half of the pages, a glossary defining and giving examples for bolded text words, a timeline, a resource list, and an index are features of this biography of Malcolm X.
Intermediate; Nonfiction

Cwiklik, Robert. *Malcolm X and Black Pride*. Brookfield, Conn.: The Millbrook Press, 1991. 32 p. (Gateway Civil Rights)

Pages on Islam and on Marcus Garvey, whom Malcolm X's father supported, and photographs of Malcolm's grave and the Audubon Ballroom in Harlem where Malcolm had been assassinated are features of this biography of the controversial advocate of black pride. A timeline, a resource list, and an index are included.
Intermediate; Nonfiction

Davies, Mark. *Malcolm X: Another Side of the Movement*. Illustrated by Glenn Wolff. Englewood Cliffs, N.J.: Silver Burdett Press, 1990. 136 p. (The History of the Civil Rights Movement)

This comprehensive biography of Malcolm X focuses on his willingness to learn and change as he progressed through the different stages of his life. Quotations from Malcolm X, photographs, drawings, a timeline, a reading list, a list of sources, and an index augment the text.
Older; Nonfiction

Davis, Lucile. *Malcolm X: A Photo-Illustrated Biography*. Mankato, Minn.: Bridgestone Books, 1998. (Read and Discover)

Full-page photographs alternating with pages of text, quotations from Malcolm X, a timeline, a glossary, and a resource list provide an introduction to Malcolm X for young children. An index is included.
Primary; Nonfiction

Diamond, Arthur. *Malcolm X: A Voice for Black America*. Hillside, N.J.: Enslow Publishers, 1994. 128 p. (People To Know)

Extensive discussion of the Nation of Islam—its beliefs and Malcolm X's evolving involvement—is a feature of this biography, which contains photographs, a chronology, chapter notes, a reading list, and an index.
Older; Nonfiction

Downing, David. *Malcolm X*. Chicago: Heinemann Library, 2002. 64 p. (Leading Lives)

A section on important people living during Malcolm X's lifetime, photographs of cities in which he lived and worked, and a chapter on his legacy are among the features of this biography. It also contains informational inserts, a glossary defining bolded text words, a timeline, a reading list, and an index.
Intermediate, Older; Nonfiction

Draper, Allison Stark. *The Assassination of Malcolm X*. New York: The Rosen Publishing Group, 2002. 64 p. (The Library of Political Assassinations)

In addition to covering the assassination of Malcolm X and its aftermath, this book presents a biography of the African-American leader, two timelines, photographs, a glossary, resource lists, and an index.
Intermediate, Older; Nonfiction

Gormley, Beatrice. *Malcolm X: A Revolutionary Voice*. New York: Sterling, 2008. 128 p. (Sterling Biographies)

Text, informational inserts that add context, chapter-heading quotations, photographs, a glossary for bolded text words, and a timeline provide an account of Malcolm X's life. The book includes a bibliography and an index.
Older; Nonfiction

Grimes, Nikki. *Malcolm X: A Force for Change*. New York: Fawcett Columbine, 1992. 192 p. (Great Lives)

This biography provides extensive coverage both of Malcolm X's childhood and youth and of his life and work as a Muslim. Several photographs are included.
Older; Nonfiction

Helfer, Andrew. *Malcolm X: A Graphic Biography*. Illustrated by Randy DuBurke. New York: Hill and Wang, 2006. 116 p. (A Novel Graphic)

Black-and-white art combines with detailed text, including conversations, to make this graphic biography of Malcolm X a well-balanced portrayal. Photographs and a reading list are appended.
Older; Fiction

Keller, Kristin Thoennes. *Malcolm X: Force for Change*. Mankato, Minn.: Capstone Press, 2006. 32 p. (Fact Finders Biographies)

Fact and quotation inserts, a page of facts about Malcolm X, and a timeline showing events in American history and Malcolm X's life distinguish this introduction to the spokesman for African-Americans. Photographs, a glossary of bolded words, a resource list, and an index also supplement the text.
Primary, Intermediate; Nonfiction

Masoff, Joy. *The African American Story: The Events That Shaped Our Nation . . . and the People Who Changed Our Lives*. Waccabuc, N.Y.: Five Ponds Press, 2007. 96 p.

This history of African-Americans includes a quotation from, a paragraph about, and a picture of Malcolm X.
Older; Nonfiction

McDonald, Janet. *Off-Color*. New York: Frances Foster Books, 2007. 176 p.

Fifteen-year-old Cameron, who believes that her father is Italian, loves hanging out with her three best

friends and doesn't take school seriously. Then her mother loses her job in a nail salon and gets one at lower wages in the owner's other salon in an African-American section of Brooklyn. Cameron and her mother must move into the projects, but, thanks to the school guidance counselor Mr. Siciliano, she is able to remain at her old high school. When Cameron discovers from an old photo that her father is black, she is shocked and blames her mother for not having told her about him and for his not being there for her. Cameron, her mother, her friends, her mother's coworkers, her multicultures class, and Mr. Siciliano spend time talking about race, about being biracial, about Mariah Carey, and about Malcolm X who Cameron hears in class was propelled to become a black nationalist because of his white-appearing mother. Cameron learns that one of her mother's coworkers is Korean and Irish, that Mr. Siciliano is half black, and that many celebrities are of mixed race. At her Sweet Sixteen party, Cameron enjoys her old best friends and new friends from the projects and even meets the boy who becomes her boyfriend.
Older; Fiction

Mis, Melody S. *Meet Malcolm X*. New York: PowerKids Press, 2008. 24 p. (Civil Rights Leaders)
    This introduction to Malcolm X features large font, facing pages of text and photographs, a glossary defining bolded words, and an index.
Primary; Nonfiction

Myers, Walter Dean. *Malcolm X: A Fire Burning Brightly*. New York: HarperCollins Publishers, 2000. 32 p.
    In this picture book, color paintings, text, and a chronology that includes quotations from Malcolm X survey the life of the powerful black leader of the 1950s and 1960s.
Primary, Intermediate; Nonfiction

Myers, Walter Dean. *Malcolm X: By Any Means Necessary: A Biography*. New York: Scholastic, 1993. 224 p.
    Descriptions of the settings in which Malcolm X lived and worked, events occurring during his lifetime, and the country's divergent racial attitudes flesh out this biography. It includes chapters on Malcolm X's father, the Nation of Islam, Martin Luther King, Jr., and the March on Washington as well as photographs, a chronology, a bibliography, and an index.
Older; Nonfiction

Rummel, Jack. *Malcolm X: Militant Black Leader*. Philadelphia: Chelsea House Publishers, 1989. 112 p. (Black Americans of Achievement)
    This straightforward account of Malcolm X's life is accompanied by photographs, a chronology, a reading list, and an index.
Older; Nonfiction

Sagan, Miriam. *Malcolm X*. San Diego: Lucent Books, 1997. 96 p. (Mysterious Deaths)
    Following a biographical introduction to Malcolm X, this book presents a thorough examination of his assassination from his murder at Harlem's Audubon Ballroom through the New York City

police investigation, the trial, the conviction of Talmadge Hayer, Norman Butler, and Thomas Johnson, and Qubilah Shabazz's possible attempt years later to hire an assassin to kill Louis Farrakhan whom she believed responsible for her father's murder. The book explores the questions of involvement by the Nation of Islam, the CIA, the FBI, and drug lords and concludes that members of the Nation of Islam murdered Malcolm X. It reports that it is still unclear as to who ordered the assassination and whether Butler and Johnson were innocent. Photographs, informational inserts, a reading list, a bibliography, and an index are included.
Older; Nonfiction

Shirley, David. *Malcolm X.* Philadelphia: Chelsea Juniors, 1994. 80 p. (Junior World Biographies)
    The changes in Malcolm X's life and views are chronicled in this biography, which contains photographs, a glossary of italicized text words, a chronology, a reading list, and an index.
Intermediate, Older; Nonfiction

Slater, Jack. *Malcolm X.* Chicago: Children's Press, 1993. 32 p. (Cornerstones of Freedom)
    Photographs and text, supplemented by an index, survey the life of Malcolm X.
Intermediate; Nonfiction

Stine, Megan. *The Story of Malcolm X, Civil Rights Leader.* Milwaukee: Gareth Stevens Publishing, 1995. 112 p. (Famous Lives)
    A chronology providing a summary of Malcolm X's life accompanies a detailed biographical text, a section of photographs, a resource list, and an index.
Intermediate, Older; Nonfiction

Turner, Glennette Tilley. *Follow in Their Footsteps.* Illustrated with Photographs. New York: Puffin Books, 1999. 192 p.
    A skit relating to his study of the dictionary accompanies a detailed biography of Malcolm X.
Intermediate, Older; Fiction, Nonfiction

Mankiller, Wilma Pearl (1945-2010) United States
Cherokee/Dutch-Irish-American

Allen, Paula Gunn, and Patricia Clark Smith. *As Long as the Rivers Flow: The Stories of Nine Native Americans.* New York: Scholastic Press, 1996. 336 p.
    Wilma Mankiller's life prior to becoming deputy chief of the Cherokee Nation is the focus of this book's biographical chapter. It provides detailed information on her early years in Oklahoma; the difficulties of moving to San Francisco, including the importance of the San Francisco American Indian Center; and the impact on her future of the 1969 Native American occupation of Alcatraz.
Intermediate, Older; Nonfiction

Avery, Susan, and Linda Skinner. *Extraordinary American Indians.* Chicago: Children's Press, 1992. 272 p.

Wilma Mankiller's life story and the beliefs which underlie her work for the Cherokee Nation are described in one of this book's sections.
Older; Nonfiction

Kimmel, Elizabeth Cody: *Ladies First: 40 Daring American Women Who Were Second to None.* Washington, D.C.: National Geographic, 2006. 192 p.
A full-page photograph of Wilma Mankiller accompanies this profile of the first female Principal Chief of the Cherokee Nation.
Intermediate, Older; Nonfiction

Lazo, Caroline. *Wilma Mankiller.* New York: Dillon Press, 1994. 64 p. (Peacemakers)
Illustrated with photographs, this biography features Wilma Mankiller's accomplishments as Principal Chief of the Cherokee Nation and includes many quotations from Mankiller.
Intermediate, Older; Nonfiction

Lowery, Linda. *Wilma Mankiller.* Illustrated by Janice Lee Porter. Minneapolis: Carolrhoda Books, 1996. 56 p. (Carolrhoda On My Own Book)
This easy-to-read story with its brightly colored illustrations tells of the sadness ten-year-old Wilma Mankiller felt when she had to leave her native Oklahoma to move to San Francisco and of how she thought about the earlier Cherokees who had to leave their homes and journey westward in the Trail of Tears. She returned to Oklahoma years later and then, despite prejudice against women, became deputy chief and then chief of the Cherokee Nation.
Primary; Nonfiction

Rand, Jacki Thompson. *Wilma Mankiller.* Illustrated by Wayne Anthony Still. Austin: Steck-Vaughn, 1993. 32 p. (American Indian Stories)
This picture book biography of Wilma Mankiller summarizes her life from her early childhood in Oklahoma to her struggles as an older child in California, her serious health problems, and her continuing work to improve the lives of the Cherokees. It tells how as the Cherokee Nation's principal chief she continues in the tradition of earlier Cherokee clan mothers.
Primary, Intermediate; Nonfiction

Rappaport, Doreen. *We Are the Many: A Picture Book of American Indians.* Illustrated by Cornelius Van Wright and Ying-Hwa Hu. New York: HarperCollins Publishers, 2002. 32 p.
Wilma Mankiller is shown helping dig a water pipeline in the painting that accompanies a brief description of the projects she undertook for the Cherokee Nation.
Primary, Intermediate; Nonfiction

Schwarz, Melissa. *Wilma Mankiller: Principal Chief of the Cherokees.* Philadelphia: Chelsea House Publishers, 1994. 112 p. (North American Indians of Achievement)
This book intertwines the life story of Wilma Mankiller with the history of the Cherokees. A comprehensive biography, it describes her early life and her roles as the Cherokee's economic-stimulus

coordinator, program development specialist, director of its community development department, deputy chief, and principal chief. It tells how she dealt with the Cherokee issues of the views of mixed bloods versus full bloods, business development versus social services, the traditional Cherokee versus the European-American role of women, and the question of cooperation with the state and Federal governments. The book includes photographs, a reading list, a chronology, and an index.
Older; Nonfiction

Sneve, Virginia Driving Hawk. *The Cherokees*. Illustrated by Ronald Himler. New York: Holiday House, 1996. 32 p. (A First Americans Book)
   This history of the Cherokees includes three quotations from Wilma Mankiller.
Intermediate; Nonfiction

Yannuzzi, Della A. *Wilma Mankiller: Leader of the Cherokee Nation*. Hillside, N.J.: Enslow Publishers, 1994. 104 p. (People To Know)
   Wilma Mankiller's belief that Cherokees, working together, can help themselves guided her work as deputy chief and then principal chief of the Cherokee Nation. In addition to describing Mankiller's early life, this book provides an in-depth look at her work for the Cherokee Nation: the obstacles she faced both as a woman and from poor health, her work schedule, and her achievements. It is illustrated with photographs.
Intermediate, Older; Nonfiction

Marley, Nesta Robert (Bob) (1945-1981) Jamaica
English-Jamaican/African-Jamaican, to African-Jamaican

Dolan, Sean. *Bob Marley*. Philadelphia: Chelsea House Publishers, 1996. 120 p. (Black Americans of Achievement)
   This comprehensive biography describes the development of Bob Marley's musical talents from being surrounded by music as a young child in Nine Miles, Jamaica, to becoming a world-renowned reggae songwriter and performer. Moving as a boy to the Trench Town slum section of Kingston, he benefited from the tutelage of Joe Higgs, and the group, the Wailers, was formed. The book tells how Marley and the other Wailers became Rastafarians, chronicles their musical successes, and tells of Marley's impact on Jamaica's contentious politics. Black-and-white photographs, a discography, a chronology, a reading list, and an index are included.
Older; Nonfiction

Gilfoyle, Millie. *Bob Marley*. Philadelphia: Chelsea House Publishers, 2000. 48 p. (They Died Too Young)
   Color photographs illustrate this detailed account of Bob Marley's life. The book contains a chronology and an index.
Intermediate, Older; Nonfiction

Jeffrey, Gary. *Bob Marley: The Life of a Musical Legend*. Illustrated by Terry Riley. New York: The Rosen Publishing Group, 2007. 48 p. (Graphic Biographies)

This graphic presentation of Bob Marley's musical career tells of the social consciousness of his lyrics and the role he played in defusing Jamaica's volatile political situation. A who's who section, a discography, a glossary, a resource list, and an index complete the book.
Intermediate; Nonfiction

Marley, Cedella, and Gerald Hausman. *The Boy from Nine Miles: The Early Life of Bob Marley*. Illustrated by Mariah Fox. Charlottesville, Va.: Hampton Roads Publishing Company, 2002. 64 p.

Full- and double-page colorful paintings illustrate this book's story of Bob Marley's experiences as a young child: enjoying life with his mother and grandparents in the country village of Nine Miles, Jamaica, as a five-year-old being deposited by his father with an elderly ill Kingston woman whom he had to care for, and, after a year, being found by his mother, who took him back to Nine Miles. Co-written by Marley's daughter Cedella, this fictionalized biography has an afterword, a glossary of italicized text words, a chronology, and a discography.
Primary, Intermediate; Fiction

Medina, Tony. *I and I, Bob Marley*. Illustrated by Jesse Joshua Watson. New York: Lee & Low Books, 2009. 40 p.

This picture book biography of Bob Marley features not only large paintings and accompanying verses, but also a section of notes that, by elaborating upon the preceding double-page presentations, is in itself a biography.
Primary, Intermediate; Fiction

Miller, Calvin Craig. *Reggae Poet: The Story of Bob Marley*. Greensboro, N.C.: Morgan Reynolds Publishing, 2008. 128 p. (Modern Music Masters)

This biography provides an in-depth look at Bob Marley's personal and professional life. It also presents posthumous information on members of his family as well as on the Wailers, albums that were released, and honors he received. Photographs, a timeline, source notes, a bibliography, a website listing, and an index complement the text.
Older; Nonfiction

Moskowitz, David. *Bob Marley: A Biography*. Westport, Conn.: Greenwood Press, 2007. 148 p. (Greenwood Biographies)

Written for high school students, this exhaustive biographical account provides detailed information about Bob Marley's life; his individual recordings, tours, musicians, and entourage members; his message; his posthumous releases; and up-to-date information on the careers of his numerous children. A discography, bibliography, and index are included.
Older: Nonfiction

Waters, Rosa. *Bob Marley and the Wailers*. Broomall, Pa.: Mason Crest Publishers, 2008. 64 p. (Popular Rock Superstars of Yesterday and Today)

Numerous quotations are included in this look at Bob Marley's career, his Rastafari beliefs, and his legacy. The book contains color photographs; a glossary of bolded text words; a chronology; a resource list; an album, video, and awards listing; and an index.
Older; Nonfiction

Martínez, Rubén (1962-   ) United States
Native Mexican-American and Spanish-Mexican-American/Salvadoran

O'Hearn, Claudine Chiawei, editor. *Half and Half: Writers on Growing Up Biracial and Bicultural.* New York: Pantheon Books, 1998. 288 p.
In a chapter by the writer Rubén Martínez, he tells of growing up in Hollywood where he identified with the whites in films and in life. As an older teenager he rejected whiteness to be Latino, and then, although still feeling the tensions, became mestizo, being at home with all cultures.
Older; Nonfiction

Mason, Bridget (Biddy) (1818-1891) United States
African-American and Choctaw, Seminole, and other, to European-American

Pinkney Andrea Davis. *Let It Shine: Stories of Black Women Freedom Fighters.* Illustrated by Stephen Alcorn. San Diego: Gulliver Books, 2000. 120 p.
According to a section of this book, Biddy Mason, who was born a slave in Mississippi, had several masters, including Robert Marion Smith, who fathered her three children. Becoming a Mormon, Smith moved his family and possessions to free-state California where Biddy, with the help of those familiar with California's law, successfully petitioned for freedom for herself and other Smith slaves. Taking work as a nurse and midwife, Biddy used her savings to buy first her own house and then property where she built rental houses for black families. She also donated land for businesses, a school, and the Los Angeles First African Methodist Episcopal Church.
Intermediate; Nonfiction

Schlissel, Lillian. *Black Frontiers: A History of African American Heroes in the Old West.* New York: Simon & Schuster Books for Young Readers, 1995. 80 p.
A section on Biddy Mason describes her successful suit to be declared a free woman, her business foresight in accumulating real estate, and her philanthropic generosity to the Los Angeles black community.
Intermediate, Older; Nonfiction

Matzeliger, Jan Ernst (1852-1859) Suriname
Dutch/African-Surinamese

Haber, Louis. *Black Pioneers of Science and Invention.* San Diego: Harcourt Brace & Company, 1992. 288 p. (An Odyssey Book)

A chapter in this book relates how Jan E. Matzeliger, after being a machine shop apprentice and a cobbler apprentice, took a job in a shoe manufacturing company in Lynn, Massachusetts. Working at night on his own, he invented a shoe lasting machine that replaced hand lasting and revolutionized the shoe industry. A bibliography, photographs, and an index are included.
Older; Nonfiction

Hudson, Wade. *Five Notable Inventors.* Illustrated by Ron Garnet. New York: Scholastic, 1995. 48 p. (Great Black Heroes, Hello Reader!—Level 4)
Jan Ernst Matzeliger's development of his shoe-lasting machine is described in a biographical chapter in this book. Color illustrations complement the text.
Primary; Nonfiction

Mitchell, Barbara. *Shoes for Everyone: A Story about Jan Matzeliger.* Illustrated by Hetty Mitchell. Minneapolis: Carolrhoda Books, 1986. 64 p. (A Carolrhoda Creative Minds Book)
Full-page drawings illustrate this detailed biography of Jan Ernst Matzeliger, which contains an author's note and an afterword.
Intermediate; Nonfiction

Sims, Doris J. *Shoes Got Soles: Jan Ernest Matzeliger Inventor.* Illustrated by Rodel A. Santiago. Designed by Chuck Johnson. Los Angeles: Children's Cultu-Lit Book Company, 1994. 32 p.
Facing pages of text and color paintings provide an introduction to Jan Ernst Matzeliger and his shoe-lasting machine.
Pre-K, Primary; Nonfiction

Sullivan, Otha Richard. *African American Inventors.* New York: John Wiley & Sons, 1998. 176 p. (Black Stars)
A biographical chapter on Jan E. Matzeliger describes his persistence in developing a shoe lasting machine and the unexpected benefit to the North Congregational Church in Lynn, Massachusetts, of accepting him, a black man, as a member. Pictures, text inserts, and references are included.
Older; Nonfiction

McBride, James (1957-   ) United States
African-American and Baptist/Jewish-Russian-Polish and Baptist

O'Hearn, Claudine Chiawei, editor. *Half and Half: Writers on Growing Up Biracial and Bicultural.* New York: Pantheon Books, 1998. 288 p.
In one of this book's chapters the writer and musician James McBride writes about his African-American father who died before he was born, his Jewish mother, and his African-American stepfather; about his questions and feelings about his identity; and about his insight that because of his parents' love, he likes himself.
Older; Nonfiction

McCallum, Shara (19??-   ) Jamaica
African-English-Indian-Scottish-Jamaican, Jewish, and Rastafari/African-English-Portuguese-Venezuelan-Jamaican and Jewish

Stanford, Eleanor, ed. *Interracial America: Opposing Viewpoints*. Farmington Hills, Mich.: Greenhaven Press, 2006. 208 p. (Opposing Viewpoints)
    In the opinion piece "Biracial Identity Can Be a Source of Conflict," the poet Shara McCallum describes the conflict she sometimes feels because she is of mixed race.
Older; Nonfiction

McCartney, James Paul (1942-   ) England
Irish-English Church of England then agnostic/Irish-English Catholic, to Russian-American Jewish, to English

Boyes, Kate. *Paul McCartney*. San Diego: Lucent Books, 2004. 112 p. (The Importance Of)
    Many interesting facts about Paul McCartney and the Beatles are presented in this comprehensive biography of the rock musician. It describes the importance of the Beatles' December 27, 1960, Liverpool performance, the recording of "Love Me Do," and the album *Sgt. Pepper's Lonely Hearts Club Band*. It tells of McCartney's abstract painting, filmmaking, *Liverpool Oratorio*, and charitable work. Photographs, a timeline, informational inserts, chapter notes, a bibliography, a resource section, and an index complete the book.
Older; Nonfiction

Dowswell, Paul. *Paul McCartney: An Unauthorized Biography*. Chicago: Heinemann Library, 2001. 56 p. (Heinemann Profiles)
    Paul McCartney's Liverpool childhood, his songwriting collaboration with John Lennon, his falling out and then reconciliation with Lennon, his marriage to Linda Eastman, his musical group Wings, and his later activities are among the topics covered in this biography. It contains informational inserts, photographs, a glossary of bolded text words, a listing of McCartney's films and records, and an index.
Intermediate; Nonfiction

Gelfand, M. Howard. *Paul McCartney*. Mankato, Minn.: Creative Education, 1983. 32 p. (Rock'n PopStars)
    Written when Paul McCartney was experiencing success with his band Wings, this biography is tailored for a young audience and illustrated with full-page black-and-white photographs.
Primary, Intermediate; Nonfiction

Glassman, Bruce. *John Lennon & Paul McCartney: Their Magic and Their Music*. Woodbridge, Conn. Blackbirch Press, 1995. 112 p. (Partners)
    Although differing in background, temperament, musical strengths, and compositional content, Liverpool natives John Lennon and Paul McCartney collaborated to produce world-acclaimed popular

music. This book describes how the two met, their closeness, their contributions to the Beatles' success, the development of their music, their later hostility towards each other, their solo careers, and the impact of the Beatles. Photographs, a reading list, a bibliography, a chronology, and an index are included.
Intermediate, Older; Nonfiction

Pratt, Mary K. *Michael Jackson: King of Pop*. Edina, Minn.: ABDO Publishing Company, 2010. 112 p. (Lives Cut Short)
Michael Jackson's musical successes and the controversies surrounding his later years and his death are chronicled in this biography. Informational inserts, including one describing his professional relationship with Paul McCartney, photographs, a timeline, a fact list, chapter source notes, a glossary, a resource list, and an index are included.
Intermediate, Older; Nonfiction

Ungs, Tim. *Paul McCartney and Stella McCartney*. New York: The Rosen Publishing Group, 2005. 48 p. (Famous Families)
This joint biography tells of the unaffectedness of the family life of Stella McCartney's childhood, of her development into a noted fashion designer, and of her father Paul McCartney's Beatles and post-Beatles career. It includes a timeline, a glossary, a reading list, and an index.
Intermediate; Nonfiction

McCartney, Stella Nina (1971-   ) England
Irish-English Church of England, agnostic, Catholic/Russian-American Jewish

Ungs, Tim. *Paul McCartney and Stella McCartney*. New York: The Rosen Publishing Group, 2005. 48 p. (Famous Families)
This joint biography tells of the unaffectedness of the family life of Stella McCartney's childhood, of her development into a noted fashion designer, and of her father Paul McCartney's Beatles and post-Beatles career. It includes a timeline, a glossary, a reading list, and an index.
Intermediate; Nonfiction

McLoughlin, Jean-Baptiste (John) (1784-1857) Canada
Irish-Scottish-French Canadian, to French-Canadian Chippewa

Lampman, Evelyn Sibley. *Half-Breed*. Illustrated by Ann Grifalconi. Garden City, N.Y.: Doubleday & Company, 1967. 264 p.
Twelve-year-old Hardy leaves his Crow mother because she is marrying a man of the same clan and travels by himself to Oregon to find the white father who had left when he was six. Reaching his father's cabin with the help of Dr. John McLoughlin [later known as "Father of Oregon"] and his half Chippewa wife Marguerite and marshal Joe Meeks and his Cheyenne wife Virginia, Hardy discovers that his father has left to go to California to mine gold. Hardy decides to await his father and is aided during his stay by *Old Ironsides* veteran Bill Johnson and his Cheyenne wife Nancy on whose land

the cabin is located. To Hardy's surprise his father's sister Rhody arrives from the East and stays with Hardy. Hardy is very upset by her white ways, especially her making him perform squaw's chores and burning his medicine bag. He also suffers from the poor treatment he receives in Portland because he is part Indian. After Hardy's father returns and then leaves, Hardy decides to go back to live with the Crow. However, after his father again returns and then decides to leave, Hardy realizes that the responsible thing to do is to remain with Aunt Rhody who is his family.
Intermediate, Older; Fiction

Meeks, Joseph (Joe) Lafayette (1810-1875) United States
European-American, to Nez Percé

Lampman, Evelyn Sibley. *Half-Breed*. Illustrated by Ann Grifalconi. Garden City, N.Y.: Doubleday & Company, 1967. 264 p.
    Twelve-year-old Hardy leaves his Crow mother because she is marrying a man of the same clan and travels by himself to Oregon to find the white father who had left when he was six. Reaching his father's cabin with the help of Dr. John McLoughlin [later known as "Father of Oregon"] and his half Chippewa wife Marguerite and marshal Joe Meeks and his Cheyenne wife Virginia, Hardy discovers that his father has left to go to California to mine gold. Hardy decides to await his father and is aided during his stay by *Old Ironsides* veteran Bill Johnson and his Cheyenne wife Nancy on whose land the cabin is located. To Hardy's surprise his father's sister Rhody arrives from the East and stays with Hardy. Hardy is very upset by her white ways, especially her making him perform squaw's chores and burning his medicine bag. He also suffers from the poor treatment he receives in Portland because he is part Indian. After Hardy's father returns and then leaves, Hardy decides to go back to live with the Crow. However, after his father again returns and then decides to leave, Hardy realizes that the responsible thing to do is to remain with Aunt Rhody who is his family.
Intermediate, Older; Fiction

Mehta, Nina (19??-) United States
Indian/Austrian-English-Jewish Russian-American

O'Hearn, Claudine Chiawei, editor. *Half and Half: Writers on Growing Up Biracial and Bicultural*. New York: Pantheon Books, 1998. 288 p.
    In one chapter the writer Nina Mehta writes about her childhood life in Bombay and New Jersey and of interviewing her paternal grandmother to gain knowledge and insight into her grandmother's life and her belief in Jainism.
Older; Nonfiction

Millman, Isaac (born Isaac Sztrymfman) (1933-) France
Polish-French and Jewish, by Belgian and Catholic

Millman, Isaac. *Hidden Child*. Illustrated by author. New York: Frances Foster Books, 2005. 80 p.
    Photographs and composite paintings complement the text in this autobiographical account of

Isaac Millman's boyhood experiences hiding as a Jew during the German's occupation of northern France. After his father is arrested, Isaac hides with his mother for several days in Paris and then the two of them try to escape to the free French zone. Captured, his mother bribes a guard to take him to a nearby hospital which tends to Jewish children who pretend to be ill. From there, now using the non-Jewish French name Jean, Isaac stays for two months with a cruel French couple and then, thanks to the help of a Jewish woman, spends the rest of the war years with a kind and poor Christian Belgian woman who treats him like a son. After the war, Isaac lives in a home for Jewish children in Le Mans and then in 1948 travels to the United States where he is adopted by the Millmans. Both of Isaac's parents die at Auschwitz.
Intermediate, Older; Nonfiction

Momaday, Navarre Scott (1934-   ) United States
Kiowa/European-American and Cherokee

Avery, Susan, and Linda Skinner. *Extraordinary American Indians*. Chicago: Children's Press, 1992. 272 p.

Scott Momaday has pursued the same careers as his parents: teacher (both), artist (father), and writer (mother). Inspired by the stories he heard as a child at his Kiowa grandparents' home, he received a Ph.D. in English literature from Stanford University where, as well as at other universities, he became a professor. He wrote the Pulitzer prize-winning *House Made of Dawn*. Two autobiographical works, *The Way to Rainy Mountain* and *The Names*, are also mentioned in this book's section on Momaday.
Older; Nonfiction

Montezuma, Carlos (born Wassaja) (1866-1923) United States
Yavapai, by Puma, by Italian, to Romanian-American

Capaldi, Gina, adapter. *A Boy Named Beckoning: The True Story of Dr. Carlos Montezuma, Native American Hero*. Illustrated by adapter. Minneapolis: Carolrhoda Books, 2008. 32 p.

Double-page paintings and sidebars with period photographs add to this life story of Wassaja, who at the age of five was captured by Pima from his Yavapai homeland in Arizona and then sold to Carlo Gentile, a traveling Italian photographer. Gentile renamed the boy Carlos Montezuma and treated him as a son. Montezuma graduated from the University of Illinois at age seventeen and later from the Chicago Medical College at Northwestern University. He worked as a physician and a professor. Opposed to the Office of Indian Affairs' treatment of reservation Indians, Montezuma lobbied extensively for rights and opportunities for Native Americans. An author's note and a bibliography complete the biography.
Primary, Intermediate; Nonfiction

Morgan, Garrett Augustus (1877-1963) United States
African-European-American/ African-American and Native American, to European-American

Amram, Fred M. B. *African-American Inventors: Lonnie Johnson, Frederick McKinley Jones, Marjorie Stewart Joyner, Elijah McCoy, Garrett Augustus Morgan*. Mankato, Minn.: Capstone Press, 1996. 48 p. (Capstone Short Biographies)

Four photographs from the U. S. Patent Office accompany text that relates how Garrett Augustus Morgan wore the gas mask he invented to save men trapped in a tunnel explosion and that describes in detail the workings of his traffic signal.

Intermediate; Nonfiction

Haber, Louis. *Black Pioneers of Science and Invention*. San Diego: Harcourt Brace & Company, 1992. 288 p. (An Odyssey Book)

A chapter in this book describes in detail Garrett A. Morgan's inventions of a human hair straightener, a safety hood (gas mask), and a traffic light signal system. A bibliography, photographs, and an index are included.

Older; Nonfiction

Hudson, Wade. *Five Notable Inventors*. Illustrated by Ron Garnet. New York: Scholastic, 1995. 48 p. (Great Black Heroes, Hello Reader!—Level 4)

The bravery of Garrett Morgan and his brother Frank in getting men out of a smoke- and natural gas-filled tunnel is highlighted in one of this book's chapters. This illustrated account tells how Garrett Morgan invented not only the gas mask the brothers wore, but also a hair straightener and a traffic signal.

Primary; Nonfiction

Jackson, Garnet Nelson. *Garrett Morgan, Inventor*. Illustrated by Thomas Hudson. Cleveland: Modern Curricula Press, 1992. 28 p. (Beginning Biographies)

Garrett Morgan is introduced in this easy reader's rhyming text, colored-pencil pictures, and glossary.

Pre-K, Primary; Nonfiction

Murphy, Patricia J. *Garrett Morgan: Inventor of the Traffic Light and Gas Mask*. Berkeley Heights, N.J.: Enslow Publishers, 2004. 32 p. (Famous Inventors)

This biography of Garrett Morgan describes his inventing an improved sewing machine belt, a hair straightener, a safety hood (gas mask), a traffic safety system, an electric hair curling comb, and ashtray safety pellets. It also tells of his publication of a newspaper for African-Americans. Photographs, a timeline, a glossary, a resource section, and an index complete the book.

Primary, Intermediate; Nonfiction

Oluonye, Mary N. *Garrett Augustus Morgan: Businessman, Inventor, Good Citizen*. Bloomington, Ind.: AuthorHouse, 2008. 68 p.

Photographs; listings of Garrett Morgan's patents, awards, and honors; a resource section; a bibliography; and an index accompany this biography, which places Morgan's life and inventions within the context of his times and tells of his heritage and of the opposition of both families to his marriage

to Mary Anne Hasek, who was white.
Intermediate; Nonfiction

Sullivan, Otha Richard. *African American Inventors*. New York: John Wiley & Sons, 1998. 176 p. (Black Stars)

This biographical chapter on Garrett A. Morgan focuses on his inventions and includes an insert describing the 1916 success of his safety hood in enabling the rescue of men trapped in a fire in a tunnel below Lake Erie.
Older; Nonfiction

Moses (? B.C.-? B.C.) Egypt
Hebrew-Egyptian, by Egyptians, to Midianite

Cohen, Deborah Bodin. *Papa Jethro*. Illustrated by Jane Dippold. Minneapolis: Kar-Ben Publishing, 2007. 32 p.

When Rachel wonders why her grandfather is Christian and she is Jewish, he tells her a story about Moses' son Gershom, who was Jewish, and his Midianite grandfather Jethro whose daughter Zipporah was Moses' wife.
Pre-K, Primary; Fiction

Lester, Julius. *Pharaoh's Daughter: A Novel of Ancient Egypt*. New York: Harper Trophy, 2000. 192 p.

This is a fictional story of Moses' sister Almah, who befriended the Pharaoh's daughter Bythia and became an Egyptian priestess; of Bythia, who raised Moses and came to accept the Hebrews' faith; of Pharaoh Ramses II, who regarded Moses as his grandson; and of young Moses who, confused as to whether he was Hebrew or Egyptian, killed an Egyptian and fled to Midian.
Older; Fiction

Mukherjee, Bharati (1940-   ) India
Indian, to European-American

O'Hearn, Claudine Chiawei, editor. *Half and Half: Writers on Growing Up Biracial and Bicultural*. New York: Pantheon Books, 1998. 288 p.

In one of this book's chapters Bharati Mukherjee tells how she chose to marry an American and thereby to be part of the United States, not accepting all of America's lifestyle nor regarding it with contempt, but instead being "resilient and compassionate in the face of change."
Older; Nonfiction

Mura, David (1952-   ) United States
Japanese-American and Episcopalian, to European-Jewish-American and Protestant

O'Hearn, Claudine Chiawei, editor. *Half and Half: Writers on Growing Up Biracial and Bicultural*. New York: Pantheon Books, 1998. 288 p.

In a chapter by the poet David Mura he writes about his eight-year-old daughter: of her experiences as a child of mixed race and culture and of how he and his wife teach her of her heritage.
Older; Nonfiction

Nakahama, Manjiro (1827-1898) Japan
Japanese, by European-American

McCully, Emily Arnold. *Manjiro: The Boy Who Risked His Life for Two Countries*. Illustrated by author. New York: Farrar Straus Giroux, 2008. 40 p.

Large watercolor paintings illustrate this story of Manjiro Nakahama, a fourteen-year-old fisherman who in 1841 was shipwrecked with the four other crew members on Torishima Island in the Pacific Ocean. They were picked up months later by an American whaling ship, Befriended by its captain, William Whitfield, Manjiro chose to go with him to Massachusetts rather than get off in Honolulu with the other castaways. Manjiro lived with the Whitfield family, studied navigation, and earned money working on a ship and in the California gold rush. Then, buying his own little whaleboat, Manjiro brought it aboard a ship which took him and two of his fellow castaways, who joined him in Honolulu, to Japan's Ryukyu Islands. During extensive questioning upon his return, Manjiro told the Japanese about American inventions, such as the railroad and steamship, assured them of the United States' peaceful intentions and desire for trade, and was reunited with his mother. An author's note explains how Manjiro helped end Japan's centuries-old self-imposed isolation from the rest of the world and paved the way for the 1854 American-Japan peace treaty. Manjiro became a samurai and a member of the first Japanese diplomatic delegation to the West.
Primary, Intermediate; Nonfiction

Noguchi, Isamu (1904-1988) United States
Japanese/Irish-American

Leathers, Noel L. *The Japanese in America*. Rev. ed. Minneapolis: Lerner Publications Company, 1991. 64 p. (The In America Series)

This book includes a paragraph summarizing Isamu Noguchi's accomplishments as a sculptor as well as a photograph of Noguchi with one of his acclaimed works.
Intermediate, Older; Nonfiction

Tobias, Tobi. *Isamu Noguchi: The Life of a Sculptor*. New York: Thomas Y. Crowell Company, 1974. 48 p. (A Biography for Young People)

This biography of Isamu Noguchi tells how as the son of a Japanese father, who left the family when he was little, and an American mother, who sent him away from Japan to the United States for schooling when he was thirteen, Noguchi often felt different and alone, caring mainly about his work. The book explains how he used many different materials in his sculptures, which were not realistic, but intended to evoke feelings. Noguchi's talent and creativity attained important recognition in 1946 when his sculptures were shown at the Museum of Modern Art in New York City. Later he designed items for people's homes as well as playgrounds and gardens. This book is illustrated with numerous

photographs of Noguchi's works.
Intermediate, Older; Nonfiction

Noor Al Hussein, Queen of Jordan (born Lisa Najeeb Halaby) (1951-   ) United States
European-Syrian-American/Swedish-American, to Jordanian

Darraj, Susan Muaddi. *Queen Noor*. Philadelphia: Chelsea House Publishers, 2003. 128 p. (Women in Politics)
    Photographs, a chronology, chapter notes, a bibliography, a resource list, and an index are included in this comprehensive biography of Queen Noor. Placing her life within the context of Jordanian society, world events, and her husband King Hussein's policies, the book highlights her many humanitarian works and the sometimes controversial role she played as Queen.
Older; Nonfiction

Raatma, Lucia. *Queen Noor: American-Born Queen of Jordan*. Minneapolis: Compass Point Books, 2006. 112 p. (Signature Lives)
    This biography tells of Queen Noor's childhood in the United States, her marriage to King Hussein of Jordan, her role as Queen, her struggles to be accepted by the people of Jordan, and her humanitarian work. There is extensive background information on the Middle East's history, politics, and culture and on the policies which King Hussein pursued in trying to bring peace to the region. The book includes photographs, informational inserts, chapter notes, a timeline, a glossary, a resource list, a bibliography, and an index.
Older; Nonfiction

Nye, Naomi Shihab (1952-   ) United States
Palestinian/European-American

Nye, Naomi Shihab. *19 Varieties of Gazelle: Poems of the Middle East*. New York: Greenwillow Books, 2002. 160 p.
    A number of these poems about the Middle East, its peoples, and its suffering are based on the lifestyles and experiences of the author's extended Palestinian family.
Older; Fiction

Obama, Barack (born Barack Hussein Obama, Jr.) (1961-   ) United States
Kenyan/English-Irish-Scottish-American and Cherokee?, by English-Irish-Scottish-American and Indonesian, to African-American

Abramson, Jill. *Obama: The Historic Journey*. New York: The New York Times/Callaway, 2009. 96 p.
    The author of this biography of Barack Obama has drawn upon articles published in *The New York Times*. Numerous photographs, a family tree, a summary of Obama and John McCain's views on important issues, a map showing red and blue states in the 2008 election, facts about Obama, and

quotations from him are features of this distinctive portrayal of Obama's life through his presidential inauguration.
Intermediate, Older; Nonfiction

Brill, Marlene Targ. *Barack Obama: President for a New Era*. Rev. ed. of *Barack Obama: Working to Make a Difference*. Minneapolis: Lerner Publications Company, 2009. 48 p. (Gateway Biographies)
  This biography of Barack Obama tells of his birth in Honolulu to a father from Kenya and a mother from Kansas. His father left the family when Barack, called Barry as a child, was very young. Obama lived as a six-to-ten-year-old in Jakarta, Indonesia, with his mother, his Indonesian stepfather, and their baby. Moving back to Honolulu where he lived some of the time with his maternal grandparents and for a period with his mother and half-sister, Obama spent seven years attending a preparatory school where he played basketball. He attended Occidental College in Los Angeles for two years, graduated from Columbia University in New York City, and, after working in Chicago as a community organizer, went to Harvard Law School where he was elected president of the *Harvard Law Review*. Following graduation he married Michelle Robinson, a fellow lawyer; worked as a civil rights lawyer in Chicago; wrote an autobiography; served for seven years in the Illinois Senate; gave the keynote address at the 2004 Democratic National Convention; was elected to the United States Senate; and became the forty-fourth President of the United States. This biography includes photographs, informational inserts, a reading list, a chronology, and an index.
Intermediate, Older; Nonfiction

Davis, William Michael. *Barack Obama: The Politics of Hope*. Stockton, N.J.: OTTN Publishing, 2008. 168 p. (Shapers of America)
  Illustrated with color photographs, this in-depth biography of Barack Obama includes inserts of quotations by and about Obama, a chronology, chapter notes, a reading list, internet resources, and an index.
Older; Nonfiction

Falk, Laine. *Meet President Barack Obama*. New York: Children's Press, 2009. 24 p. (Scholastic News Nonfiction Readers)
  Full-page photographs and an early-reader text introduce Barack Obama in this biographical summary that includes a resource list and an index.
Pre-K, Primary; Nonfiction

Gilchrist, Jan Spivey. *Obama: The Day the World Danced: A Family Heirloom*. Graphic Design by William Kelvin Gilchrist. Flossmoor, Ill.: Pegasus Books for Children, 2009. 32 p.
  On November 4, 2008, Breyna and Emily stay up late in Breyna's house to make family heirloom books and to watch history being made as their fellow Chicagoan Barack Obama is elected the first African-American President. They dance with Breyna's parents and grandparents and with the children shown on television in Obama's father's Kenya, his mother's Kansas, his and his grandmother's Hawaii, his old school in Indonesia, and countries throughout the world.
Pre-K, Primary; Fiction

Grimes, Nikki. *Barack Obama: Son of Promise, Child of Hope*. Illustrated by Bryan Collier. New York: Simon & Schuster Books for Young Readers, 2008. 40 p.

Featuring large watercolor and collage pictures, this introduction to Barack Obama is presented as the story of his life as told by an African-American single mother in response to the questions and comments of her young son. A family tree including Obama's Kenyan family, a chronology, and bibliographic references are appended.
Pre-K, Primary, Intermediate; Nonfiction

Hopkinson, Deborah. *First Family*. Illustrated by AG Ford. New York: Katherine Tegan Books, 2010. 32 p.

This picture book introduces the White House and the Obama family's life there. It shows the White House museum rooms, Oval Office, private quarters, Rose Garden playground, Kitchen Garden, and President's Park and provides a look at the President and First Lady's work, Marian Robinson's role as First Grandmother, and Malia, Sasha, and dog Bo's activities.
Pre-K, Primary; Nonfiction

Katirgis, Jane. *Celebrating President Barack Obama in Pictures*. Berkeley Heights, N..J.: Enslow Publishers, 2009. 32 p. (The Obama Family Photo Album)

Barack Obama's life, including his early activities as President, is portrayed in color photographs and accompanying text. Resource listings and an index are included.
Pre-K, Primary, Intermediate; Nonfiction

Katirgis, Jane. *Celebrating the Inauguration of Barack Obama in Pictures*. Berkeley Heights, N.J.: Enslow Publishers, 2009. 32 p. (The Obama Family Photo Album)

The train ride from Philadelphia to Washington, D.C., the opening celebration, the National Day of Service, the swearing-in ceremony, the inaugural address, the President's lunch with Congress, the inaugural parade, and the inaugural balls are commemorated in this photographic depiction of Barack Obama's 2009 inauguration. A resource list and an index accompany the text.
PreK, Primary, Intermediate; Nonfiction

Katirgis, Jane. *Celebrating the Obama Family in Pictures*. Berkeley Heights, N.J.: Enslow Publishers, 2010. 32 p. (The Obama Family Photo Album)

Color photographs and descriptive text introduce the Obamas: Barack, Michelle, Malia, Sasha, and their dog Bo. The book includes resource listings and an index.
Pre-K, Primary, Intermediate; Nonfiction

Masoff, Joy. *The African American Story: The Events That Shaped Our Nation . . . and the People Who Changed Our Lives*. Waccabuc, N.Y.: Five Ponds Press, 2007. 96 p.

This history of African-Americans includes two quotations from, a paragraph about, and a picture of Barack Obama.
Older; Nonfiction

Mendell, David. *Obama: A Promise of Change*. Adapted by Sarah L. Thomson. New York: Amistad/ Collins, 2008. 192 p.

This book is adapted from Mendell's *Obama: From Promise to Power*, a biography for adults. It provides extensive coverage of Barack Obama's 2002 Chicago speech taking a stand against starting a war with Iraq, his 2004 campaign for the Senate, his 2004 keynote address to the Democratic National Convention, and his 2006 trip as a Senator to Africa. Photographs and chapter notes are included.
Older; Nonfiction

Thomas, Garen. *Yes We Can: A Biography of President Barack Obama*. New York: Feiwel & Friends, 2008. 256 p.

Full pages of black-and-white photographs and quotations by Barack Obama precede the chapters in this comprehensive portrayal of Obama through his election as President. It describes the impact of his father's absence, his relationships with his family members, his community organizing, his two trips to Kenya, his accomplishments in the Illinois legislature and the United States Senate, and his presidential campaign. A bibliography and an index complete the book.
Older; Nonfiction

Weatherford, Carole Boston. *First Pooch: The Obamas Pick a Pet*. Illustrated by Amy Bates. Tarrytown, N.Y.: Marshall Cavendish Children, 2009. 32 p.

Colorful paintings illustrate this picture book that tells how Barack Obama promised his daughters Malia and Sasha they would get a dog when his presidential campaign was over. After waiting for twenty-two months they finally were able to choose their dog, a dog who would have to perform such duties as meeting the presidential helicopter and negotiating treats. Would it be of the same breed as an earlier president's dog? Would it be a shelter dog? What name would it have? This book describes how the family selected Bo, a Portuguese water dog, to be First Pooch. It includes information about other presidential pets.
Pre-K, Primary; Fiction

Wheeler, Jill C. *Barack Obama*. Edina, Minn.: ABDO Publishing Company, 2009. 40 p. (The United States Presidents)

A timeline, a glossary defining bolded text words, color photographs, and an index supplement the text in this account of Barack Obama's life. Information on the office of the president, the Presidential Succession Act of 1947, presidential benefits, and the terms of the preceding forty-three Presidents is appended.
Primary, Intermediate; Nonfiction

Winter, Jonah. *Barack*. Illustrated by AG Ford. New York: Collins, 2008. 32 p.

Concentrating on his early years, this picture book relates how Barack Obama wondered who he was until he discovered the answer in a Chicago church and went on to become a presidential candidate. An author's note is included.
Pre-K, Primary; Nonfiction

Obama, Michelle LaVaughn Robinson (1964-   ) United States
African-American, to Kenyan, English-Irish-Scottish-American, and Cherokee?

Brill, Marlene Targ. *Michelle Obama: From Chicago's South Side to the White House*. Minneapolis: Lerner Publications Company, 2009. 48 p. (Gateway Biographies)
   Michelle Obama's life through her early days as First Lady is chronicled in this biography. It contains photographs, informational inserts, a chronology, a glossary, source notes, a selected bibliography, a reading list, and an index.
Intermediate, Older; Nonfiction

Brophy, David Bergen. *Michelle Obama: Meet the First Lady*. New York: Collins, 2009. 128 p.
   This biography of Michelle Obama presents her growing up on Chicago's South Side, her experiences at Princeton University and Harvard Law School, and her work at Sidley Austin (a Chicago law firm), the Chicago mayor's office, Public Allies (a nonprofit national service organization), the University of Chicago, and the University of Chicago Medical Center where she was vice president of community and external affairs. It relates how she met Barack Obama, tells of her family, and provides extensive coverage of her campaigning for his presidency. A glossary, a section on national political conventions, and chapter notes are included.
Intermediate, Older; Nonfiction

Hopkinson, Deborah. *First Family*. Illustrated by AG Ford. New York: Katherine Tegan Books, 2010. 32 p.
   This picture book introduces the White House and the Obama family's life there. It shows the White House museum rooms, Oval Office, private quarters, Rose Garden playground, Kitchen Garden, and President's Park and provides a look at the President and First Lady's work, Marian Robinson's role as First Grandmother, and Malia, Sasha, and dog Bo's activities.
Pre-K, Primary; Nonfiction

Hopkinson, Deborah. *Michelle*. Illustrated by AG Ford. New York: Katherine Tegen Books, 2009. 32 p.
   Large color paintings are featured in this picture book, which traces Michelle Obama's life from her childhood to her becoming First Lady. An author's note provides a biographical summary.
Primary, Intermediate; Nonfiction

Katirgis, Jane. *Celebrating First Lady Michelle Obama in Pictures*. Berkeley Heights, N.J.: Enslow Publishers, 2009. 32 p. (The Obama Family Photo Album)
   Numerous color photographs and accompanying text provide a biographical presentation of Michelle Obama. Resource listings and an index complete the book.
Pre-K, Primary, Intermediate; Nonfiction

Katirgis, Jane. *Celebrating the Obama Family in Pictures*. Berkeley Heights, N.J.: Enslow Publishers, 2010. 32 p. (The Obama Family Photo Album)

Color photographs and descriptive text introduce the Obamas: Barack, Michelle, Malia, Sasha, and their dog Bo. The book includes resource listings and an index.
Pre-K, Primary, Intermediate; Nonfiction

Weatherford, Carole Boston. *First Pooch: The Obamas Pick a Pet*. Illustrated by Amy Bates. Tarrytown, N.Y.: Marshall Cavendish Children, 2009. 32 p.
Colorful paintings illustrate this picture book that tells how Barack Obama promised his daughters Malia and Sasha they would get a dog when his presidential campaign was over. After waiting for twenty-two months they finally were able to choose their dog, a dog who would have to perform such duties as meeting the presidential helicopter and negotiating treats. Would it be of the same breed as an earlier president's dog? Would it be a shelter dog? What name would it have? This book describes how the family selected Bo, a Portuguese water dog, to be First Pooch. It includes information about other presidential pets.
Pre-K, Primary; Fiction

O'Brien, Daniel (Dan) Dion (1966-) United States
African-American/Finnish, by European-American

Gutman, Bill. *Dan O'Brien*. Austin: Raintree Steck-Vaughn Publishers, 1998. 48 p. (Overcoming the Odds)
This biography of decathlete Dan O'Brien tells of his struggles—undiagnosed ADHD (attention deficit hyperactivity disorder), losing eligibility in college because of academic problems, unexpected failure to make the 1992 Olympics team—; of his supportive coaches; and of his successes: setting a world decathlon record in 1992 in Talence, France, and winning the gold medal in the 1996 Olympics. Photographs, decathlon record listings, a reading list, and an index supplement the text.
Older; Nonfiction

O'Brien, Maria de la Soledad Teresa (Soledad) (1966-) United States
Irish-Australian/African-Cuban

Robson, David. *Soledad O'Brien: Television Journalist*. Broomall, Pa.: Mason Crest Publishers, 2009. 64 p. (Transcending Race in America: Biographies of Biracial Achievers)
This biography provides an in-depth look at Soledad O'Brien's television career. It tells of her scientific college courses that helped her secure jobs co-hosting *The Know Zone* and hosting *The Site*, her co-anchoring *Weekend Today* with David Bloom until his tragic death in Iraq, her co-hosting *American Morning* with Bill Hemmer and then Miles O'Brien, and her documentaries, including *Black in America* and *Black in America 2*. Color photographs, informational inserts, a glossary defining bolded text words, a chronology, a listing of accomplishments and awards, a resource list, and an index add to the presentation.
Older; Nonfiction

O'Hearn, Claudine Chiawei (1971-   ) Hong Kong
Irish-American/Chinese

O'Hearn, Claudine Chiawei, ed. *Half and Half: Writers on Growing Up Biracial and Bicultural*. New York: Pantheon Books, 1998. 288 p.

The editor of this book talks about her life as a biracial woman, who looks more Caucasian than Chinese. Having spent most of her childhood abroad, in the United States she sometimes plays the role of an American and sometimes of a foreigner, not really being of either group.
Older; Nonfiction

Ohno, Apolo Anton (1982-   ) United States
Japanese/European-American

Aldridge, Rebecca. *Apolo Anton Ohno*. New York: Chelsea House Publishers, 2009. 128 p. (Asian-Americans of Achievement)

This biography of Apolo Anton Ohno provides extensive coverage of his childhood, his short-track speed-skating career through 2008, and his experiences on *Dancing with the Stars*. The book's informational inserts cover such topics as short-track speed skating, Japanese immigrants in the United States, and Ohno's heroes, inspirations, trademark, career highlights, and induction into the Asian Hall of Fame. Color photographs, a chronology, a timeline, a glossary, a bibliography, a resource list, and an index complement the text.
Older; Nonfiction

Lang, Thomas. *Going for the Gold: Apolo Anton Ohno, Skating on the Edge*. New York: Avon Books, 2002. 128 p.

A section of color photographs, listings of short-track speed-skating Olympic medals and Apolo Ohno's championships and medals, and a fact sheet about Ohno are contained in this presentation of his life through the 2002 Olympics.
Intermediate; Nonfiction

Layden, Joe. *All About Apolo!* New York: Aladdin Paperbacks, 2002, 32 p.

The glossy pages of this biography of Apolo Ohno are filled with color photographs, many courtesy of Ohno. The account culminates with his accomplishments at the 2002 Winter Olympics.
Primary, Intermediate, Older; Nonfiction

Ohno, Apolo Anton with Nancy Ann Richardson. *A Journey: The Autobiography of Apolo Anton Ohno*. New York: Simon & Schuster Books for Young Readers, 2002. 160 p.

This autobiography of Apolo Ohno covers the first twenty years of his life. It not only provides his descriptions of his short-track skating career, but also his thoughts, strategies, and feelings as it progressed. In the book Ohno tells of his rebellion against his father's sending him to Lake Placid; his failure to qualify in the 1998 Olympic trials; his debilitating back injury; the allegation that he had

conspired to ensure Shani Davis's winning the 1,000 meters at the 2002 Olympic Trials; the support he received from his father, Pat Wentland, Dave Cresswell, and others; and his many race successes, including winning gold and silver medals in the 2002 Winter Olympics.
Older; Nonfiction

Olmos, Edward James (1947-) United States
Mexican/Mexican-American, to European-American, to English-Italian-American, to Puerto Rican

Alegre, Cèsar. *Extraordinary Hispanic Americans*. New York: Children's Press, 2007. 288 p. (Extraordinary People)
The career of Edward James Olmos as a television, movie, and stage actor and his interest in social issues is described in a biographical chapter.
Older; Nonfiction

Carrillo, Louis. *Edward James Olmos*. Austin: Raintree Steck-Vaught Publishers, 1997. 48 p. (Contemporary Hispanic Americans)
This biography of Edward James Olmos tells of his childhood devotion to baseball and music, of his decision to become an actor, of the importance of the musical *Zoot Suit* in launching his stardom, of his decision to make an innovative use of English and Spanish in the movie *The Ballad of Gregorio Cortez*, and of his portrayal of the teacher Jaime Escalante in *Stand and Deliver*. The book describes the movies in which Olmos acted and his public service work. Photographs, a chronology, a glossary, a bibliography, and an index are included.
Older; Nonfiction

Martinez, Elizabeth Coonrod. *Edward James Olmos: Mexican-American Actor*. Brookfield, Conn.: The Millbrook Press, 1994. 32 p. (Hispanic Heritage)
Photographs complement this account of the actor Edward James Olmos, which emphasizes his choice of roles depicting Latinos of integrity. The book includes a chronology, reading lists, and an index.
Intermediate; Nonfiction

Osceola (also Asiyahola) (c.1804-1838) United States
European-American (father or stepfather) or Creek/European-American and upper Muskogee Creek

Jumper, Moses, and Ben Sonder. *Osceola: Patriot and Warrior*. Illustrated by Patrick Soper. Austin: Raintree Steck-Vaughn, 1993. 88 p. (Stories of America)
This book relates the story of Osceola and the Second Seminole War. It tells of his efforts to keep the Seminoles in Florida, of the free and runaway African-Americans who lived with and were allies of the Seminoles, and of the betrayals of the United States government. The book contains an introduction, an epilogue, illustrations, and chapter notes.
Intermediate; Nonfiction

Koestler-Grack, Rachel A. *Osceola, 1804-1838*. Mankato, Minn.: Blue Earth Books, 2003. 32 p. (American Indian Biographies)

Directions for making and playing a Creek ballgame and for baking pumpkin bread cake, a map, a chronology, a glossary, a resource list, and an index are included in this illustrated biography of Osceola. It states that there is disagreement as to whether his father was the white trader William Powell and describes his childhood as well as his adult life as a Seminole warrior.
Intermediate; Nonfiction

Levin, Beatrice. *John Hawk: White Man, Black Man, Indian Chief*. Austin: Eakin Press, 1988. 192 p.

This is the fictional story of John White, the son of a Georgia plantation owner and a slave mother, who becomes the lifelong friend of Osceola. The two meet as boys and, at Osceola's urging, John runs away to live with the Seminoles. He takes a new name, John Hawk, marries a Seminole woman, befriends a man who is Spanish and African-American, and becomes a Seminole chief. With Osceola he experiences the betrayals and tragedies preceding and during the Second Seminole War. A bibliography is included.
Older; Fiction

Oppenheim, Joanne. *Osceola: Seminole Warrior*. Illustrated by Bill Ternay. Mahwah, N.J.: Troll Associates, 1979. 48 p.

Fictionalized dialogue is included in this illustrated biography of Osceola.
Primary, Intermediate; Fiction

Rappaport, Doreen. *We Are the Many: A Picture Book of American Indians*. Illustrated by Cornelius Van Wright and Ying-Hwa Hu. New York: HarperCollins Publishers, 2002. 32 p.

The painting of a battle scene during the Second Seminole War illustrates this vignette on Osceola, who led the Seminole's fight against American soldiers in Florida.
Primary, Intermediate; Nonfiction

Parker, Cynthia Ann (also Naduah, She Who Carries Herself With Dignity and Grace) (c.1826-c.1870) United States
Scottish-Irish-American, by Comanche, to Comanche

Meyer, Carolyn. *Where the Broken Heart Still Beats: The Story of Cynthia Ann Parker*. San Diego: Gulliver Books, 1992. 208 p.

This fascinating and tragic story begins in 1861 when Cynthia Ann Parker, who had been captured as a nine-year-old by the Comanche, was recaptured with her baby daughter by Texas Rangers and returned to her relatives. The chapters alternate between fictional journal entries by twelve-year-old Lucy Parker, as she tries to understand her cousin's behavior, and those presenting Naduah's feelings as she longs to return to her Comanche husband, Peta Nacona, and her sons, Pecos and Quanah, the soon-to-be Comanche leader.
Intermediate, Older; Fiction

Parker, Quanah, (also Quanah, Fragrant) (c.1845-1911) United States
Comanche/Scottish-Irish-American

Freedman, Russell. *Indian Chiefs*. New York: Holiday House, 1987.
    Illustrated with photographs, the chapter on Quanah Parker summarizes the life of the renowned Comanche chief. The son of Peta Nacona, a Comanche leader, and Cynthia Ann Parker, who had been kidnapped by the Comanche as a child, Quanah became family-less as a teenager when his mother and baby sister were captured by the Texas Rangers and his father and brother soon died. He led the Kwahadi (Quahadi), the band of Comanche most resistant to the efforts of the United States cavalry to settle them on a reservation. After the Comanche were finally defeated, not by troops, but by the slaughter of the buffalo on which they depended, Quanah became a successful cattle rancher, a spokesman for the Comanche, and a friend of Theodore Roosevelt.
Intermediate, Older; Nonfiction

Hilts, Len. *Quanah Parker*. San Diego: Harcourt Brace Jovanovich, 1987. 192 p. (An Odyssey/Great Episodes Book)
    This story of Quanah Parker's life, which is fictionalized and presented primarily from his standpoint, includes coverage of the individual battles which the Comanche fought.
Intermediate, Older; Fiction

Marrin, Albert. *Plains Warrior: Chief Quanah Parker and the Comanches*. New York: Atheneum Books for Young Readers, 1996. 208 p.
    Photographs and extensive notes are included in this biography, which describes Quanah Parker's life in terms of the context in which he lived. The book provides a detailed look at Comanche living: the importance of the horse and the buffalo to their existence; their treatment of white captives; their relationships with other tribes, the Comancheros, the Texans, and the Americans; their warfare; their beliefs; and their life on the Fort Sill reservation.
Older; Nonfiction

May, Julian. *Quanah: Leader of the Comanche*. Illustrated by Phero Thomas. Mankato, Minn.: Creative Educational Society. 1973. 40 p.
    This fictionalized biography of Quanah Parker is illustrated with sketches and focuses on Quanah's boyhood.
Intermediate; Fiction

Sanford, William R. *Quanah Parker: Comanche Warrior*. Hillsdale, N.J.: Enslow Publishers, 1994. 48 p. (Native American Leaders of the Wild West)
    Quanah Parker's roles as a Comanche leader, both as a warrior and later as the tribe's peaceful advocate, are presented in this book, which is illustrated with photographs.
Intermediate; Nonfiction

Zemlicka, Shannon. *Quanah Parker*. Illustrated by Tim Parlin. Minneapolis: Lerner Publications Company, 2004. 48 p. (History Maker Bios)

This biography of Quanah Parker describes his feats as a Comanche warrior and, after the Comanche were removed to a reservation, his efforts to protect their interests and the peyote religion. The book presents information on the reunions of Quanah's Comanche descendants and the descendants of his European-American mother's family. A timeline, a bibliography, a resource listing, and an index are also included.
Primary, Intermediate; Nonfiction

Parks, Rosa Louise McCauley (1913-2005) United States
African-American and Native American/African-European-Scottish-Irish-American, to African-European-American

Adler, David A. *A Picture Book of Rosa Parks*. Illustrated by Robert Casilla. New York: Holiday House, 1993. 32 p.

Color paintings and text combine to present a biography of Rosa Parks, who has been called the "Mother of the Civil Rights Movement." A chronology is appended.
Pre-K, Primary; Nonfiction

Bednar, Chuck. *Rosa Parks: Civil Rights Activist*. Broomall, Pa.: Mason Crest Publishers, 2010. 64 p. (Transcending Race in America: Biographies of Biracial Achievers)

Rosa Parks' contributions to equal justice are placed within the history of civil rights in this book which covers her life, funeral, and legacy. It includes photographs, highlighted quotations, informational inserts, bolded text words defined in a glossary, a chronology, a listing of accomplishments and awards, a resource list, and an index.
Older; Nonfiction

Giovanni, Nikki. *Rosa*. Illustrated by Bryan Collier. New York: Henry Holt and Company, 2005. 32 p.

Large double pages, each featuring a painting and a sidebar, and a foldout four-page spread at the conclusion tell the story of Rosa Parks' courageous refusal to give up her bus seat and of the likewise courageous response of Montgomery's black community.
Primary, Intermediate; Nonfiction

Greenfield, Eloise. *Rosa Parks*. Illustrated by Gil Ashby. New York: HarperCollins Publishers, 1995. 64 p.

Illustrated with drawings, this introduction to Rosa Parks culminates with her sitting wherever she chose on a Montgomery, Alabama bus following the Supreme Court's decision that ended the successful lengthy bus boycott.
Primary; Nonfiction

Hull, Mary with additional text by Gloria Blakely and Dale Evva Gelfand. *Rosa Parks: Civil Rights Leader*. Legacy ed. New York: Chelsea House Publishers, 2007. 128 p. (Black Americans of Achievement)

Informational sections on such topics as the NAACP, the Ku Klux Klan, the Browder v. Gayle case, and John Conyers; black-and-white photographs; a chronology; a resource list; and an index complement this detailed biography of Rosa Parks.
Older; Nonfiction

Mara, Wil. *Rosa Parks*. New York: Children's Press, 2003. 32 p. (Rookie Biographies)

A brief text, photographs, and pictures depicting text words introduce Rosa Parks and the difference she made. The book contains an index.
Pre-K, Primary; Nonfiction

Parks, Rosa with Jim Haskins. *Rosa Parks: My Story*. New York: Dial Books, 1992. 200 p.

In this autobiography Rosa Parks describes her family's heritage and her growing up in Alabama: suffering from chronic tonsillitis, attending Pine Level's inferior school, chopping and picking cotton, encountering prejudice, experiencing her family's fear of the Klan, and, on the positive side, being taken fishing by an elderly white woman and attending the Montgomery Industrial School for Girls. It tells of her marriage to Raymond Parks and her work for the NAACP. Parks recounts an earlier experience with a segregated Montgomery bus and explains why she was riding that particular bus and refused to give up her seat. She gives detailed accounts of what happened to her after her arrest, of the bus boycott, and of the legal outcome. Her book also covers her moving to Detroit and her work for Congressman John Conyers. Photographs and an index are included.
Intermediate, Older; Nonfiction

Pingry, Patricia A. *The Story of Rosa Parks*. Illustrated by Steven Walker. Nashville, Tenn.: Candy Cane Press, 2007. 24 p.

This board book, which features oil paintings, presents a brief biographical look at Rosa Parks.
Pre-K; Nonfiction

Pinkney, Andrea Davis. *Boycott Blues: How Rosa Parks Inspired a Nation*. Illustrated by Brian Pinkney. New York: Amistad, 2008. 40 p.

Within a setting of blues music, this picture book's text and paintings show how the people of Montgomery, Alabama, kept on walking until Jim Crow was defeated and the segregation of their city's buses ended.
Pre-K, Primary; Fiction

Ringgold, Faith. *If a Bus Could Talk: The Story of Rosa Parks*. Illustrated by author. New York: Simon & Schuster Books for Young Readers, 1999. 32 p.

In this picture book, when a little girl gets on a bus to go to school, she discovers it is a driverless talking bus that once a year honors Rosa Parks on her birthday. The bus tells the girl of Rosa Parks' life, including her refusal to give up her seat and the resulting bus boycott. Then when Rosa

gets on the bus, the girl and the other passengers, including Dr. Martin Luther King, Jr., civil rights leader E.D. Nixon, and Rosa's husband, celebrate Rosa's birthday.
Pre-K, Primary, Intermediate; Fiction

Roop, Peter, and Connie Roop. *Take a Stand, Rosa Parks!* New York: Scholastic, 2005. 64 p. (Before I Made History: a Scholastic Chapter Book Biography)
 This beginning chapter book focuses on Rosa Parks' early years and explains how, learning from her grandfather to stand up for her rights, she would not give up her bus seat for a white rider.
Primary, Intermediate; Nonfiction

Schraff, Anne. *Rosa Parks: "Tired of Giving In."* Berkeley Heights, N.J.: Enslow Publishers, 2005. 128 p. (African-American Biography Library)
 Highlighting Rosas Parks' determination to vote by taking the Alabama literacy test until she was granted passage, this book details her continuing work to advance civil rights. It includes coverage of her later years when she founded the Rosa and Raymond Parks Institute for Self-Development, wrote three books, and received the Congressional Medal of Honor. The biography contains photographs, a chronology, chapter notes, and an index.
Intermediate, Older; Nonfiction

Wilson, Camilla. *Rosa Parks: From the Back of the Bus to the Front of a Movement.* New York: Scholastic, 2001. 80 p.
 Setting Rosa Parks' life within the broader context of race relations in the South, this biography includes a section of black-and-white photographs and a source list.
Intermediate; Nonfiction

Parsons, Lucia (Lucy) González (1853-1942) United States
African-American, Creek, and Mexican, to European-American

Nash, Gary B. *Forbidden Love: The Secret History of Mixed-Race America.* New York: Henry Holt and Company, 1999. 224 p.
 This book reports that Lucy González Parsons and her European-American husband Albert Parsons became members of the Socialist Labor Party and were radical labor activists. After Albert Parsons was executed because of a bomb thrown during Chicago's Haymarket Riot, Lucy continued her activist speaking and writing.
Older; Nonfiction

Parton, Dolly Rebecca (1946-   ) United States
Scottish-Irish-American/European-American and Cherokee, to European-American

Keely, Scott. *Dolly Parton.* Mankato, Minn.: Creative Education, 1979. 32 p. (Rock'n PopStars)
 Photographs and a number of quotations from Dolly Parton are featured in this biography, which traces the country music star's life from her song composing as a five-year-old to her 1997 album

Here You Come Again.
Intermediate; Nonfiction

Parton, Dolly. *Coat of Many Colors.* Illustrated by Judith Sutton. New York: Harper Collins Publishers, 1994. 32 p. (A Byron Preiss Book)
　　Color paintings illustrate Dolly Parton's song "Coat of Many Colors." The song tells of Dolly's childhood experience when, because of her family's poverty, her mother had to make her new coat out of rags. After learning about Joseph's coat of many colors, Dolly proudly wore her coat to school, only to be ridiculed by her schoolmates, who could not understand that the coat was made of love.
Pre-K, Primary; Fiction

Saunders, Susan. *Dolly Parton: Country Goin' to Town.* Illustrated by Rodney Pate. New York: Puffin Books, 1986. 64 p. (Women of Our Time)
　　This biography of Dolly Parton tells of her life through the early 1980s. It describes her childhood: being part of a large poor family in the Great Smoky Mountains of Tennessee, loving to sing, and dreaming of singing at the Grand Ole Opry. Dolly sang regularly on a Knoxville radio station at the age of ten, signed a songwriting contract at age fourteen, and released a record with Mercury Records when she was sixteen. Traveling to Nashville at age eighteen, she met her future husband Carl Dean when she first arrived. Dolly was female vocalist on Porter Wagoner's television show from 1967 to 1974 when she left to extend her singing repertoire beyond country-and-western. She started an acting career with the movie *Nine to Five.*
Intermediate; Nonfiction

Payne, Andrew Hartley (1907-1977) United States
European-American and Cherokee

Griffis, Molly Levite. *The Great American Bunion Derby.* Researched by Jim Ross. Austin: Eakin Press, 2003. 96 p.
　　In 1927 Andy Payne, who had won mile races for his Oklahoma high school. saw a poster advertising the First Annual International Trans-Continental Foot Race, which was to be run from Los Angeles to New York City and had a first place prize of $25,000. When Andy was unable to raise money for the entry fee and deposit, his father took out a loan for the race that began in March 1928. This book tells of Andy's running of that race: his training, his bout with tonsillitis, the overwhelming support he received running in Oklahoma, his friendships with his competitors, and his triumphant entry into Madison Square Garden. This story includes some fictional dialogue.
Intermediate, Older; Fiction, Nonfiction

Peake, Mary Smith Kelsey (1823-1862) United States
European/African-European-American

Cox, Clinton. *African American Teachers.* New York: John Wiley & Sons, 2000. 176 p. (Black Stars)
　　This book's brief biography of Mary Smith Kelsey Peake tells how she taught African-American

children and adults, first in a secret school in her Hampton, Virginia home and then by establishing the first black school sponsored by the American Missionary Association.
Older; Nonfiction

Pelotte, Donald (1945-2010) United States
Abenaki/French Canadian descent

Avery, Susan, and Linda Skinner. *Extraordinary American Indians*. Chicago: Children's Press, 1992. 272 p.

The section on Donald Pelotte relates that he was raised in Maine by his mother, who was a Catholic. Becoming a Catholic priest with a Ph.D. in theology, Pelotte became the first Native American bishop. With a diocese that included New Mexico and Arizona, he worked on the daunting task of connecting Catholicism with Native American beliefs and culture.
Older; Nonfiction

Pickett, Bill (1870-1932) United States
African-European-American and Cherokee/African-European-American, Native American, and Mexican

Katz, William Loren. *Black Indians: A Hidden Heritage*. New York: Atheneum, 1986. 208 p.

A section on Bill Pickett relates how he created and performed the rodeo act of bulldogging and was in two silent movies.
Intermediate, Older; Nonfiction

Katz, William Loren, and Paula A. Franklin. *Proudly Red and Black: Stories of African and Native Americans*. New York: Atheneum, 1993. 96 p.

The chapter on Bill Pickett tells how, with his unusual rodeo act, he starred in the 101 Ranch Wild West Show, which performed in the United States, South America, and England.
Intermediate, Older; Nonfiction

Monceaux, Morgan, and Ruth Katcher. *My Heroes, My People: African Americans and Native Americans in the West*. Illustrated by Morgan Monceaux. New York: Frances Foster Books, 1999. 64 p.

A full-page portrait accompanies a brief description of Bill Pickett and his bulldogging.
Intermediate, Older; Nonfiction

Pinkney, Andrea D. *Bill Pickett: Rodeo-Ridin' Cowboy*. Illustrated by Brian Pinkney. San Diego: Gulliver Books, 1996. 32 p.

Illustrated with scratchboard pictures colored in oil paint, this book tells a tale of the young boy Bill Pickett holding down a roped calf with his teeth in imitation of a bulldog he had seen. Pickett later performed his bulldogging act at rodeos in the West and then, moving with his family to the large 101 Ranch in Oklahoma, worked there as a cowhand and as a performer in the ranch's traveling Wild West show.
Pre-K, Primary; Nonfiction

Potter, Joan, and Constance Claytor. *African Americans Who Were First*. New York: Cobblehill Books, 1997. 128 p.

A page summary presents the career of Bill Pickett, who was the first African-American to be in the Rodeo Cowboy Hall of Fame. A photograph of Pickett is included.
Intermediate, Older; Nonfiction

Schlissel, Lillian. *Black Frontiers: A History of African American Heroes in the Old West*. New York: Simon & Schuster Books for Young Readers, 1995. 80 p.

The 101 Wild West Show and Bill Pickett's trick of biting steers' lips in order to throw them are featured in one of this book's sections.
Intermediate, Older; Nonfiction

Picotte, Susan LaFlesche (1865-1915) United States
French-American and Omaha or Ponca/European-American, Omaha?, Oto?, and Iowa, to French-American and Sioux

Avery, Susan, and Linda Skinner. *Extraordinary American Indians*. Chicago: Children's Press, 1992. 272 p.

As reported in a section on siblings Francis LaFlesche, Susan LaFlesche Picotte, and Susette LaFlesche Tibbles, their father was Ponca and French in his ancestry although he became an Omaha chief. Susan LaFlesche Picotte graduated from the Women's Medical College of Pennsylvania. As the first female Native American doctor, she provided health care to the Omaha and worked for the prohibition of the sale of alcohol on their reservation.
Older; Nonfiction

Ferris, Jeri. *Native American Doctor: The Story of Susan LaFlesche Picotte*. Minneapolis: Carolrhoda Books, 1991. 88 p.

Photographs illustrate this biography of Susan LaFlesche Picotte, who sought to become the Omaha's bridge from their earlier life of buffalo hunting, tipis, and earth lodges to the life of farming and wooden houses. The book describes in detail Susan's education at the Omaha Agency school on the reservation, the Elizabeth Institute for Young Ladies in Elizabeth, New Jersey, the Hampton Institute in Hampton, Virginia, and the Women's Medical College of Pennsylvania. It tells how Susan served as the doctor for the entire Omaha reservation, was the first Native American missionary, fought against alcoholism, and assumed the role of unofficial leader of the Omaha.
Intermediate, Older; Nonfiction

Ketchum, Liza. *Into a New Country: Eight Remarkable Women of the West*. Boston: Little, Brown and Company, 2000. 144 p.

A chapter on Susan LaFlesche Picotte emphasizes her experiences at Hampton Institute and the Women's Medical College of Pennsylvania and her devotion to improving the health of the Omaha, who found it difficult to adjust to reservation life.
Intermediate, Older; Nonfiction

Rappaport, Doreen. *We Are the Many: A Picture Book of American Indians*. Illustrated by Cornelius Van Wright and Ying-Hwa Hu. New York: HarperCollins Publishers, 2002. 32 p.

Susan LaFlesche Picotte is depicted riding a horse through a snowstorm to treat an ill child in the painting which accompanies a brief written sketch of her work.
Primary, Intermediate; Nonfiction

Pocahontas (also Matoaka, Rebecca) (c. 1595-1617) United States
Powhatan [Pamunkey], to Patawomeke, to English

Accorsi, William. *My Name Is Pocahontas*. Illustrated by author. New York: Holiday House, 1992. 32 p.

This picture book biographical tale is written with Pocahontas as the narrator and shows her often accompanied by a younger brother Hokamo and his dog. Pocahontas saves John's Smith life and befriends him; is captured by the colonists; marries John Rolfe, thereby bringing peace between the English and the Indians; gives birth to a son Thomas (whom she calls Hoko after her brother); and travels with her family to London where she again sees John Smith. The book has a glossary.
Pre-K, Primary; Fiction

Adams, Colleen. *The True Story of Pocahontas*. New York: The Rosen Publishing Group, 2009. 24 p. (What Really Happened?)

This introductory biography focuses on still unestablished details of Pocahontas' life. It features a large font, photographs, a glossary defining bolded text words, and an index.
Primary, Intermediate; Nonfiction

Benjamin, Anne. *Young Pocahontas: Indian Princess*. Illustrated by Christine Powers. Mahwah, N.J.: Troll Associates, 1992. 32 p. (A Troll First-Start Biography)

This biography, which is an illustrated easy reader, stresses how Pocahontas helped Jamestown by saving John Smith's life and bringing the colonists food. It tells of her marrying John Rolfe and dying before she could return to Virginia from London.
Pre-K, Primary; Nonfiction

Bruchac, Joseph. *Pocahontas*. Orlando, Fla.: Harcourt/Silver Whistle, 2003. 192 p.

In this novel, John Smith and Pocahontas present in alternating chapters their accounts of what happened in 1607, the year in which, accused of mutiny, Smith was restrained aboard ship even after its arrival in Virginia on April 26 and not completely released from confinement until June 10. He tells of the continuing dissension among the colonists, of their terrible sufferings from hunger and illness, of the friendly and hostile Indians they encountered, and of his exploration of the Chickahominy River. Eleven-year-old Pocahontas, the curious favored daughter of the chief of the Powhatan, describes, often including Powhatan words, what she heard from her people of the inconsistencies, foolishness, and cowardice of the colonists, with the exception of the Little Red-Haired Warrior. In late December she and that warrior, John Smith, finally met when, carrying out the plan of her father, she rushed forth to the stones of justice and, embracing him, claimed him as her uncle. Each chapter in this book is introduced by an English quotation from that period or a Powhatan story. The book

includes glossaries of early seventeenth-century English and Powhatan words as well as resource notes, and a bibliography.
Older; Fiction

d'Aulaire, Ingri, and Edgar Parin d'Aulaire. *Pocahontas*. (Illustrated by authors) Garden City, N.J.: Doubleday & Company, 1946. 48 p.

Large double-page and full-page lithographs, in both color and black-and-white, distinguish this story of Pocahontas. It presents her playfulness as a child, her closeness to John Smith, her bringing corn to Jamestown, and her stay in London. It also shows Powhatan receiving gifts sent by the king of England.
Primary, Intermediate; Nonfiction

Edwards, Judith. *Jamestown, John Smith, and Pocahontas in American History*. Berkeley Heights, N.J.: Enslow Publishers, 2002. 128 p. (In American History)

Pocahontas's role in Jamestown history is noted in this book which provides extensive coverage of the settlement from its founding in 1607 to its destruction by the end of the century. The book includes photographs, a chronology, chapter notes, and an index.
Older; Nonfiction

Fritz, Jean. *The Double Life of Pocahontas*. Illustrated by Ed Young. New York: G. P. Putnam's Sons, 1983. 96 p.

This story of Pocahontas emphasizes the two cultures in which she lived. After becoming what she regarded as a sister to John Smith, Pocahontas spent her time bridging the worlds of the Indians and the Jamestown colonists and having divided loyalties. After Smith left, she spent four years with no contact with the colonists. This changed when she was kidnapped and taken to Henrico. When Powhatan did not trade for her, she converted to Christianity and married John Rolfe. In England, however, she probably worried about the English intent to take away the Indians' religion by converting them to Christianity. This book, which provides a detailed history of Jamestown, includes a map, notes, a bibliography, and an index.
Intermediate, Older; Nonfiction

Fritz, Jean. *Who's Saying What in Jamestown, Thomas Savage?* Illustrated by Sally Wern Comport. New York: G. P. Putnam's Sons, 2007. 64 p.

This book of historical fiction presents a biography of Thomas Savage, who served as a cabin boy on the first supply ship sent to Jamestown that arrived in January 1608. Realizing the need for interpreters with the Indians, Christopher Newport, the ship's captain, assigned young Thomas to go live with the Powhatan Indians so he could learn the language. There he befriended Pocahontas, delivered messages between the colonists and the Indians, and came to know another English boy, Henry Spelman, who had arrived on one of the third supply ships in April 1609 and whom John Smith sent to Powhatan to become an interpreter. In 1613 Savage was sent as an interpreter for Captain Samuel Argall to the Eastern Shore where he became a friend of the Accawmacke's king, Debedeavon, who gave him land where he built a house and raised a family. As a boy Henry ran away to the Patawomekes

where he happily settled and continued to be an interpreter for the colonists.
Intermediate; Fiction

Gleiter, Jan, and Kathleen Thompson. Retold by Edith Vann. *Pocahontas*. Illustrated by Deborah L. Chabrian. Austin: Raintree-Steck Vaughn Publishers, 1995. 32 p. (First Biographies)
   This story shows Pocahontas befriending the Jamestown settlers and John Smith before she saves his life. (A note in the chronology reports that the incident may not be true.) The text is imprinted on double-page color illustrations.
Primary, Intermediate; Nonfiction

Gosda, Randy T. *Pocahontas*. Edina, Minn.: Buddy Books, ABDO Publishing Company, 2002. 32 p. (First Biographies)
   Large print, simple sentences, labeled pictures, a chronology, a glossary, websites, and an index are features of this biography of Pocahontas. It states that the story of Pocahontas saving John Smith's life is a legend that may or may not be true.
Primary; Nonfiction

Gourse, Leslie. *Pocahontas*. Illustrated by Meryl Henderson. New York: Aladdin Paperbacks, 1996. 176 p. (Childhood of Famous Americans)
   Pocahontas's life from her first seeing the English after their arrival in Powhatan's land to her death in England is covered in this fictionalized biography. It emphasizes her close relationship to her father and to John Smith and tells of her son Thomas Rolfe's moving to Jamestown when he was a young man.
Intermediate; Fiction

Greene, Carol. *Pocahontas: Daughter of a Chief*. (Illustrated by Steven Dobson) Chicago: Children's Press, 1988. 48 p. (A Rookie Biography)
   This biography of Pocahontas includes dialogue and statements about her thoughts. It is illustrated with photographs of drawings and paintings and has a chronology and an index.
Primary, Intermediate; Fiction

Holler, Anne. *Pocahontas: Powhatan Peacemaker*. Philadelphia: Chelsea House Publishers, 1993. 104 p. (North American Indians of Achievement)
   Background information on the Powhatan and English colonization is provided in this book, which gives a detailed account of Pocahontas's life and of Jamestown and includes photographs, a chronology, a reading list, and an index.
Older; Nonfiction

Iannone, Catherine. *Pocahontas*. Philadelphia: Chelsea Juniors, 1996. 80 p. (Junior World Biographies, A Junior Native Americans of Achievement Book)
   In this biography of Pocahontas and history of Jamestown, words from the glossary are italicized

in the text. Photographs, a reading list, a chronology, and an index are also included.
Intermediate; Nonfiction

Krull, Kathleen. *Pocahontas: Princess of the New World*. Illustrated by David Diaz. New York: Walker & Company, 2007. 32 p.

Full-page color pictures decorate the life story of Pocahontas. An author's note and a source list are included in this picture book.
Primary; Nonfiction

Kudlinski, Kathleen V. *My Lady Pocahontas: A Novel*. Tarrytown, N.Y.: Marshall Cavendish, 2006. 288 p.

This story of Pocahontas' life is written from the viewpoint of her fictional friend Neetah. Appamatuck Neetah is adopted by Powhatan to be Pocahontas' guardian. Together the two girls spy on the newly arrived Jamestown colonists. They befriend three boys, Samuel, Thomas, and Henry, who come to stay with the Powhatans. Pocahontas has a vision in which she, Neetah, John Smith, and a baby of much importance appear. Believing from the vision that she will marry John Smith, she betrays her father and warns Smith of a plot to kill him. As Smith shows no inclination to marry her, Pocahontas returns depressed to her Pamunkey village. When the three boys try to escape, Samuel is killed, Thomas is captured, and Pocahontas leads Henry and Neetah to refuge with the Patawomeke. There both Pocahontas and Neetah marry Patawomekes, but they are blamed for a deadly measles out-break, are imprisoned by the colonists, and are taken to Jamestown. Later brought to Henrico, Pocahontas becomes a Christian, takes a new name Rebecca, falls in love with John Rolfe, and, ful-filling her vision, has a son Thomas. Neetah accompanies Pocahontas, John, and Thomas to England where both she and Pocahantas die before returning home. An afterword, an author's note, and a source list are appended.
Older; Fiction

McLeese, Don. *Pocahontas*. Vero Beach, Fla.: Rourke Publishing, 2003. 32 p. (Native American Legends)

Captioned photographs, informational inserts, a resource list, a timeline, a glossary, information about the descendants of the Powhatan, and an index are features of this biography of Pocahontas. It points out that Matoaka was her real name and discusses whether or not she saved John Smith's life.
Primary, Intermediate; Nonfiction

Monceaux, Morgan, and Ruth Katcher. *My Heroes, My People: African Americans and Native Americans in the West*. Illustrated by Morgan Monceaux. New York: Frances Foster Books, 1999. 64 p.

A portrait of Pocahontas accompanies a brief description of her life.
Intermediate, Older; Nonfiction

Nash, Gary B. *Forbidden Love: The Secret History of Mixed-Race America*. New York: Henry Holt and Company, 1999. 224 p.

This book asserts that the saving of John Smith from execution by Pocahontas was planned by

Powhatan and that Pocahontas thereafter provided her father with information about the Jamestown colony. In its detailed discussion of the marriage of John Rolfe and Pocahontas it points out that sentiments opposing such unions were based on the difference of culture and religion, not of race.
Older; Nonfiction

O'Dell, Scott. *The Serpent Never Sleeps: A Novel of Jamestown and Pocahontas*. Reprint edition. New York: Fawcett Juniper, Ballantine Books, 1989. 192 p.

This fictional story tells of young Serena Lynn, the book's narrator, who leaves England to follow Anthony Foxcroft, the man she loves who is bound for Jamestown to escape murder charges. Their vessel is shipwrecked in Bermuda and then Anthony dies when a longboat he is in breaks apart. Serena finally gets to Jamestown, but can't wait to return to England. This changes, however, when she meets Pocahontas and assists Captain Argall in her capture. Serena befriends Pocahontas and marries a colonist two months before the marriage of John Rolfe and Pocahontas.
Older; Fiction

Penner, Lucille Recht. *The True Story of Pocahontas*. Illustrated by Pamela Johnson. New York: Random House, 1994. 48 p. (Step into Reading, A Step 2 Book)

An illustrated easy reader, this book traces Pocahontas's life story. It tells how she saves John Smith's life, secures the release of seven Powhatan captives, is tricked into becoming a prisoner of the colonists, marries John Rolfe, and, with him and their baby son, goes to live in England.
Pre-K, Primary; Nonfiction

Raatma, Lucia. *Pocahontas*. Minneapolis: Compass Point Books, 2002. 32 p. (Compass Point Early Biographies)

In this biography of Pocahontas words bolded in the text are defined in a glossary. The book also includes a chronology, a resource page, and an index. It questions whether Pocahontas saved John Smith's life and reports that Pocahontas did not want to return to Jamestown.
Primary, Intermediate; Nonfiction

Roop, Connie, and Peter Roop. *Tales of Famous Americans*. Illustrated by Charlie Powell. New York: Scholastic Reference, 2007. 112 p.

Illustrated with a photograph of the James River and small color pictures including one of Thomas Rolfe, a chapter in this book gives an account of Pocahontas' life.
Intermediate; Nonfiction

Sonneborn, Liz. *Pocahontas: 1595-1617*. Mankato, Minn.: Blue Earth Books, 2003. 32 p.

This biography of Pocahontas includes information about Powhatan life, a map of the Powhatan Confederacy, directions for making Powhatan pottery and Indian pumpkin pudding, photographs, a chronology, a glossary, a resource list, and an index.
Primary; Nonfiction

Stainer, M. L. *The Lyon's Crown*. Illustrated by James Melvin. Circleville, N.Y.: Chicken Soup Press, 2004. 176 p. (The Lyon Saga)

In this final book of *The Lyon Saga*, smallpox has come to Croatan Island and killed many residents, including Jess's Croatan husband Akaiyan and her English mother. Jess sends her three children away to Jamestown as Robert Ashbury, who has long loved her, has offered to provide sanctuary for them. Now in their early twenties and of mixed Croatan-English blood, the three must pretend to be English, adapt to English ways, and endure hostility towards "savages" from Virginian residents who have suffered Indian attacks. Suzanne/Oohah-ne falls in love with and marries Robert Ashbury's stepson, and William/Caun-reha adapts to life in Jamestown and Henrico, where they move. However, George/Wauh-kuaene suffers in the English environment until Jess comes to take him back to Croatan Island. This book tells of John Rolfe's work in cultivating tobacco for the English market and of his love for Pocahontas, who comes to Henrico and accepts Christianity.
Older; Fiction

Sullivan, George. *Pocahontas*. New York: Scholastic Reference, 2002. 128 p. (In Their Own Words)

The book points to the primary sources of information on Pocahontas as John Smith's books and reports and a book by William Strachey, the Jamestown historian, and notes that information on Pocahontas is more limited after John Smith left Virginia in 1609. It provides not only a detailed biography of Pocahontas, but also extensive information about John Smith, Jamestown, and the relationships between the Powhatan and the colonists. The biography reports that Pocahontas married Kocoum, possibly a Patawomeke, and had been separated from him at the time of her kidnapping. The book also contains information on historical sites of interest in Jamestown, Henrico, and the Pamunkey Reservation.
Intermediate, Older; Nonfiction

Zemlicka, Shannon. *Pocahontas*. Illustrated by Jeni Reeves. Minneapolis: Carolrhoda Books, 2002. 48 p. (On My Own Biography)

This biography of Pocahontas points out that it is difficult to establish the truth about some aspects of her life. For instance, it is unknown whether she really saved John Smith's life when he was captured, whether she was in love with John Rolfe, and whether she abandoned her earlier beliefs for Christianity. The book describes her warning to John Smith that his life was in danger, her transfer as a captive from Jamestown to Henrico where she was taught English and learned about Christianity, and her move from London to Brentford, England. It includes a chronology and a selected bibliography.
Primary, Intermediate; Nonfiction

Pontiac (c.1720-1769) United States
Ottawa/Chippewa

Avery, Susan, and Linda Skinner. *Extraordinary American Indians*. Chicago: Children's Press, 1992. 272 p.

One section tells of the Ottawa chief Pontiac, who also headed a loose confederacy of Ottawa,

Chippewa, and Potawatomi. Hoping to have the support of the French, he led local tribes in a campaign to expel the British from the area south of the Great Lakes. Although he met with some success, his siege of Fort Detroit ultimately failed, and the French ended up making peace with the British. Pontiac signed a peace treaty with the British in 1766 that ended the fighting.
Older; Nonfiction

Bland, Celia. *Pontiac: Ottawa Rebel*. Philadelphia: Chelsea House Publishers, 1994. 112 p. (North American Indians of Achievement)
Set in historical context, this biography reports that little is known of Pontiac's childhood, but tells how he developed an amazing alliance of Native American nations of the Great Lakes region, one which also promoted attacks against colonists by Indians of the Middle Atlantic. It contains detailed accounts of the alliance's lengthy siege of Detroit, the forts captured, the battles fought, and the strategies Pontiac employed in fighting against the British in the French and Indian War. The book includes pictures, a chronology, a reading list, and index.
Older; Nonfiction

Trottier, Maxine. *A Circle of Silver*. New York: Stoddart Kids, 1999. 224 p. (The Circle of Silver Chronicles)
Set in 1760 this first book in *The Circle of Silver Chronicles* relates the story of thirteen-year-old John MacNeil, who leaves his English home to spend two years with his father, Captain James MacNeil, traveling to and then returning from the British Fort Detroit. It tells of the growing enmity of the Indians living near Fort Detroit who are poorly treated by the British, of John's being appointed King George III's artist in Canada, of John's love of Canada, of his friendship with the Ottawa Natka and Wallace Doig whose Miami wife had died, of his encounter with Pontiac, and of his closeness to Marie Roy, the French Canadian Miami girl whom he adores and to Pierre La Butte, the interpreter for the British and then merchant who becomes Marie Roy's husband.
Older; Fiction

Prinze, Freddie James, Jr. (1976   ) United States
Hungarian and Puerto Rican-American/European-American, to European-American Jewish

Abrams, Lea. *Freddie Prinze, Jr.* Philadelphia: Chelsea House Publishers, 2001. 64 p. (Latinos in the Limelight)
This biography of Freddie Prinze, Jr. points out the impact on his life of his actor father's suicide when he was a baby and of his childhood pretending to be superheroes. It details his acting career, including the importance of the movies, *To Gillian on Her 37th Birthday*, *I Know What You Did Last Summer*, and *She's All That*. Color photographs, a chronology, a reading list, an accomplishments listing, and an index are included.
Older; Nonfiction

Catalano, Grace. *Freddie Prinze, Jr.: He's All That, An Unauthorized Biography*. New York: Laurel-Leaf Books, 1999. 144 p.

Descriptions of Freddie Prinze, Jr.'s films, both in the text and in a filmography, facts about Prinze, quotations from him, and color photographs are features of this life story of the popular actor. Intermediate, Older; Nonfiction

Lee, Sally. *Freddie Prinze, Jr.: From Shy Guy to Movie Star*. Berkeley Heights, N.J.: Enslow Publishers, 2008. 128 p. (Latino Biography Library)

Chronicling Freddie Prinze, Jr.'s life into 2007, this book covers not only his acting career, but also his stage acting, scriptwriting, and producing. Color photographs, inserts on such topics as independent films and the employment of Latinos in television, a listing of Prinze's career accomplishments, a chronology, chapter notes, a resource list, and an index complete the book. Intermediate, Older; Nonfiction

McCracken, Kristen. *Freddie Prinze, Jr.* New York: Children's Press, 2001. 48 p. (Celebrity Bios)

In this introductory biography of Freddie Prinze, Jr., photographs, quotations, a timeline, a fact sheet, a glossary, source lists, and an index supplement the text. Intermediate; Nonfiction

Wilson, Wayne. *Freddie Prinze, Jr.* Bear, Del.: Mitchell Lane Publishers, 2000. 32 p. (A Real-Life Reader Biography)

This book on Freddie Prinze, Jr. emphasizes the effect his father's suicide and legacy has played in his life. It includes black-and-white photographs, summary sidebars, a filmography, a chronology, and an index. Intermediate; Nonfiction

Rainier III, Prince of Monaco (1923-2005) Monaco
Monacan, to German-Irish-American

Surcouf, Elizabeth Gillen. *Grace Kelly, American Princess*. Minneapolis: Lerner Publications Company, 1992. 64 p.

A foreword by Frank Sinatra and numerous photographs are included in this biography of Grace Kelly, which describes her childhood; her career on the stage, on television, and in movies; her wedding celebration; and her extensive philanthropic accomplishments as Princess Grace of Monaco. Intermediate; Nonfiction

Rania Al Abdullah, Queen of Jordan (born Rania Al Yasin) (1970-   ) Kuwait
Palestinian-Kuwaiti, to English-Jordanian

Darraj, Susan Muaddi. *Queen Noor*. Philadelphia: Chelsea House Publishers, 2003. 128 p. (Women in Politics)

This biography of Queen Noor includes a section on Queen Rania, wife of King Abdullah II of Jordan. Older; Nonfiction

Englar, Mary. *Queen Rania of Jordan*. Mankato, Minn.: Capstone Press, 2009. 32 p. (Queens and Princesses)

Color photographs enhance this biography of Queen Rania which tells of her childhood in Kuwait, her marriage to King (then Prince) Abdullah, her family life, and her charitable work, especially in helping women and children. Bolded words defined both at page bottoms and in a glossary, resource lists, and an index complete the book.
Intermediate; Nonfiction

Tait, Leia. *Queen Rania al-Abdullah*. New York: Weigl Publishers, 2008. 24 p. (Remarkable People)

Queen Rania's work as a humanitarian is the focus of this biography. Featuring numerous color photographs and text inserts, the book presents quotations from Queen Rania, describes her achievements, and provides information on Jordan. It includes a timeline, a glossary of bolded text words, website resources, and an index.
Intermediate; Nonfiction

Reeves, Keanu (1969-   ) Lebanon
Chinese-Hawaiian-Irish-Portuguese-American/English

Burke, Bronwen. *Keanu Reeves*. New York: Dell Publishing, 1992. 48 p. (Who's Hot!)

Written in an informal style and illustrated with black-and-white photographs, this pocket-sized book provides young fans with an up-close biography of Keanu Reeves.
Older; Nonfiction

Holt, Julia. *Keanu Reeves*. Lincolnwood, Ill.: Jamestown Publishers, 1998. 32 p. (Livewire Real Lives)

Black-and-white photographs illustrate this portrayal of Keanu Reeves, which points out the ordinariness and the differentness of his personal life and traces his acting career.
Intermediate, Older; Nonfiction

Membery, York. *Keanu Reeves*. Philadelphia: Chelsea House Publishers, 1998. 48 p. (Superstars of Film)

This biography of Keanu Reeves provides detailed coverage of his acting career and the films in which he performed. Color photographs, a filmography, and an index complete the book.
Older; Nonfiction

Richardson, William (Bill) Blaine III (1947-   ) United States
European-American-Mexican-Nicaraguan/Spanish-Mexican, to European-American

Alegre, Cèsar. *Extraordinary Hispanic Americans*. New York: Children's Press, 2007. 288 p. (Extraordinary People)

A biographical chapter traces Bill Richardson's career from Congressman, U.S. Ambassador to the United Nations, and U.S. Secretary of Energy to Governor of New Mexico.
Older; Nonfiction

Rice, Liz. *Bill Richardson*. Philadelphia: Mason Crest Publishers, 2009. 64 p. (Overcoming Adversity: Sharing the American Dream)

   Photographs, text notes directing readers to appended pages with related information, chapter notes, a glossary, a chronology, a listing of accomplishments and awards, a resource list, and an index add to this detailed presentation of Bill Richardson's childhood, education, and career achievements.
Older; Nonfiction

Rillieux, Norbert (1806-1894) United States
French/African-European-American

Haber, Louis. *Black Pioneers of Science and Invention*. San Diego: Harcourt Brace & Company, 1992. 288 p. (An Odyssey Book)

   The son of a prominent plantation owner who invented a steam-operated cotton baling press, Norbert Rillieux was sent to Paris for his education. He developed the theory of multiple-effect evaporation there and continued working on an evaporator in New Orleans. However, after encountering prejudice, including rejection of his plan for preventing yellow fever, he returned to Paris. This book's chapter on Rillieux provides a detailed description (including excerpts from his patents) of his invention of a vacuum pan evaporator upon which the sugar industry is based. A bibliography, photographs, and an index are included.
Older; Nonfiction

Harbison, David. *Reaching for Freedom: Paul Cuffe, Norbert Rillieux, Iva Aldridge, James McCune Smith*. New York: Scholastic Book Services, 1972. 128 p. (Firebird Biographies)

   Illustrated with photographs, four chapters in this book tell of the history of sugar, of Norbert Rillieux's invention of the multiple-effect evaporator to produce higher quality and less expensive sugar, of his astuteness as a businessman, and of his study of Egyptian hieroglyphics.
Intermediate, Older; Nonfiction

Sims, Doris J. *Sugar Makes Sweet: Norbert Rillieux Inventor*. Illustrated by Rodel A. Santiago. Designed by Chuck Johnson. Los Angeles: Children's Cultu-Lit Book Company, 1994. 32 p.

   Facing pages of paintings and brief text tell how Norbert Rillieux, who remembered how hard Southern slaves worked to produce thick dark sugar, invented a way to refine sugar without its turning brown.
Pre-K, Primary; Nonfiction

Sullivan, Otha Richard. *African American Inventors*. New York: John Wiley & Sons, 1998. 176 p. (Black Stars)

   Photographs and text inserts add to this book's biographical chapter on Norbert Rillieux.
Older; Nonfiction

Robinson, Catherine (Katy) Jeanne (born Kim Ji-yun) (1970?-   ) South Korea
South Korean, by European-American

Slade, Suzanne Buckingham. *Adopted: The Ultimate Teen Guide*. Illustrated by Christopher Papile, Mary Sandage, and Odelia Witt. Photographs by Chris Washburn. Lanham, Md.: The Scarecrow Press, 2007. 272 p. (It Happened to Me, No. 20)

Katy Robinson was adopted at the age of seven by a couple from Salt Lake City. As an adult she returned to her native South Korea where she located some members of her birth family. She is the author of *A Single Square Picture*, which describes her experiences.
Older; Nonfiction

Rogers, Will, Jr. (born William Vann Rogers) (1911-1993) United States
English-American or Scottish-Irish-American, Dutch-Irish-Welsh-American, and Cherokee/European-American

Avery, Susan, and Linda Skinner. *Extraordinary American Indians*. Chicago: Children's Press, 1992. 272 p.

The section on Will Rogers also tells of his son, Will Rogers, Jr., who became a newspaper publisher, movie actor, and U. S. Congressman.
Older; Nonfiction

Rogers, William (Will) Penn Adair (1879-1935) United States
English-American or Scottish-Irish-American, Irish-American, and Cherokee/Dutch-Welsh-American and Cherokee, to European-American

Allen, Paula Gunn, and Patricia Clark Smith. *As Long as the Rivers Flow: The Stories of Nine Native Americans*. New York: Scholastic Press, 1996. 336 p.

The chapter on Will Rogers, the renowned humorist, covers his family background, his childhood, and his life as a cowboy, a roper in Wild West and vaudeville shows, a Ziegfried Follies performer, a movie and radio actor, and a newspaper columnist. Named after a Cherokee chief, Rogers grew up in Indian Territory, experienced the drastic reduction of his father's cattle ranch by the Curtis Act, and performed as "The Cherokee Kid."
Intermediate, Older; Nonfiction

Avery, Susan, and Linda Skinner. *Extraordinary American Indians*. Chicago: Children's Press, 1992. 272 p.

The biographical section on Will Rogers emphasizes his humorous commentaries on news items, which endeared him to stage and radio audiences and to the readers of his books and newspaper column. He was the father of Will Rogers, Jr., who became a U.S. Congressman.
Older; Nonfiction

Bennett, Cathereen L. *Will Rogers: Quotable Cowboy*. Minneapolis: Runestone Press, 1995. 96 p.

Numerous photographs and sidebars with Rogers' quotations enhance this biography of Will Rogers that includes information on his family life as well as on his multifaceted career.
Intermediate, Older; Nonfiction

Donovan, Sandy. *Will Rogers: Cowboy, Comedian, and Commentator*. Minneapolis: Compass Point Books, 2007. 112 p. (Signature Lives)

This comprehensive biography of Will Rogers tells of his childhood love of lariat throwing, his excelling in elocution at Willie Halsell College, and his discovery of the appeal of making fun of himself, all of which contributed to his later success. The book contains photographs, informational inserts, source notes, a glossary, a timeline, a family facts list, a bibliography, a resource list, and an index.
Older; Nonfiction

Keating, Frank. *Will Rogers: An American Legend*. Illustrated by Mike Wimmer. San Diego: Silver Whistle, Harcourt, 2002. 32 p.

In this book a full-page painting illustrates each page of text, which has a few lines about Will Rogers and a quotation of one of his sayings. The book is not written as a bibliographic account.
Primary; Nonfiction

Sonneborn, Liz. *Will Rogers: Cherokee Entertainer*. Philadelphia: Chelsea House Publishers, 1993. 112 p. (North American Indians of Achievement)

This detailed and informative biography of Will Rogers includes numerous photographs, a chronology, references, and an index.
Older; Nonfiction

Rolfe, John (1585-1622) England
English, to Powhatan

Fritz, Jean. *The Double Life of Pocahontas*. Illustrated by Ed Young. New York: G. P. Putnam's Sons, 1983. 96 p.

In this biography of Pocahontas, John Rolfe, a devout Christian, is depicted as caring for Pocahontas, but not understanding her feelings as an Indian.
Intermediate, Older; Nonfiction

Gourse, Leslie. *Pocahontas*. Illustrated by Meryl Henderson. New York: Aladdin Paperbacks, 1996. 176 p. (Childhood of Famous Americans)

Pocahontas's life from her first seeing the English after their arrival in Powhatan's land to her death in England is covered in this fictionalized biography. It emphasizes her close relationship to her father and to John Smith and tells of her son Thomas Rolfe's moving to Jamestown when he was a young man.
Intermediate; Fiction

Holler, Anne. *Pocahontas: Powhatan Peacemaker*. New York: Chelsea House Publishers, 1993. 104 p. (North American Indians of Achievement)

John Rolfe's tobacco planting, his love for Pocahontas, and their life together after their marriage are described in this biography of Pocahontas.
Older; Nonfiction

Nash, Gary B. *Forbidden Love: The Secret History of Mixed-Race America*. New York: Henry Holt and Company, 1999. 224 p.

This book asserts that the saving of John Smith from execution by Pocahontas was planned by Powhatan and that Pocahontas thereafter provided her father with information about the Jamestown colony. In its detailed discussion of the marriage of John Rolfe and Pocahontas it points out that sentiments opposing such unions were based on the difference of culture and religion, not of race.
Older; Nonfiction

Stainer, M. L. *The Lyon's Crown*. Illustrated by James Melvin. Circleville, N.Y.: Chicken Soup Press, 2004. 176 p. (The Lyon Saga)

In this final book of *The Lyon Saga*, smallpox has come to Croatan Island and killed many residents, including Jess's Croatan husband Akaiyan and her English mother. Jess sends her three children away to Jamestown as Robert Ashbury, who has long loved her, has offered to provide sanctuary for them. Now in their early twenties and of mixed Croatan-English blood, the three must pretend to be English, adapt to English ways, and endure hostility towards "savages" from Virginian residents who have suffered Indian attacks. Suzanne/Oohah-ne falls in love with and marries Robert Ashbury's stepson, and William/Caun-reha adapts to life in Jamestown and Henrico, where they move. However, George/Wauh-kuaene suffers in the English environment until Jess comes to take him back to Croatan Island. This book tells of John Rolfe's work in cultivating tobacco for the English market and of his love for Pocahontas, who comes to Henrico and accepts Christianity.
Older; Fiction

Sullivan, George. *Pocahontas*. New York: Scholastic Reference, 2002. 128 p. (In Their Own Words)

This book describes John Rolfe's teaching of Pocahontas at Henrico, their marrying, their moving to London and Brentford, and his return alone to Virginia. It notes the importance of his experimenting with different types of tobacco growing.
Intermediate, Older; Nonfiction

Rolfe, Thomas (1615-c. 1675) United States
English/Powhatan, to English, to English

Gourse, Leslie. *Pocahontas*. Illustrated by Meryl Henderson. New York: Aladdin Paperbacks, 1996. 176 p. (Childhood of Famous Americans)

Pocahontas's life from her first seeing the English after their arrival in Powhatan's land to her death in England is covered in this fictionalized biography. It emphasizes her close relationship to her father and to John Smith and tells of her son Thomas Rolfe's moving to Jamestown when he was a young man.
Intermediate; Fiction

Sullivan, George. *Pocahontas*. New York: Scholastic Reference, 2002. 128 p. (In Their Own Words)

This biography of Pocahontas tells of Thomas Rolfe's going to London with his parents when he was a baby, remaining there because of illness when his father went back to Virginia, being raised by

Rolfe's brother, returning to Virginia as a young man, growing tobacco on land left to him by Powhatan, and marrying Jane Poythress, an Englishwoman.
Intermediate, Older; Nonfiction

Ronstadt, Federico (Fred) José María ((1868-1954) Mexico
German/Mexican, to European-American Jewish

Alegre, Cèsar. *Extraordinary Hispanic Americans*. New York: Children's Press, 2007. 288 p. (Extraordinary People)
A chapter on the Ronstadt family describes how, in Tucson, Fred Ronstadt founded the Club Filarmónico orchestra and had a successful business.
Older; Nonfiction

Ronstadt, Linda (1946-   ) United States
European-German-Mexican-American Jewish/Dutch-English-German-American

Alegre, Cèsar. *Extraordinary Hispanic Americans*. New York: Children's Press, 2007. 288 p. (Extraordinary People)
This book's section on the Ronstadts provides biographical information on top vocalist Linda Ronstadt, the granddaughter of Fred Ronstadt and the niece of Luisa Ronstadt.
Older; Nonfiction

Amdur, Melissa. *Linda Ronstadt*. Philadelphia: Chelsea House Publishers, 1993. 112 p. (Hispanics of Achievement)
Linda Ronstadt's personal life and career are covered in detail in this biography. It describes the impact of being born into a musical family, the effects of her shyness and insecurity, her albums and her live performances, and her versatility in singing country, pop, rock, opera, pre-1950's songs, and Mexican mariachi. Photographs, a chronology, a selected discography, a reading list, and an index are included.
Older; Nonfiction

Fissinger, Laura. *Linda Ronstadt*. Mankato, Minn.: Creative Education, 1983. 32 p. (Rock'n PopStars)
Single- and double-page black-and-white photographs complement this introductory biography of Linda Ronstadt, which relates how she fulfilled her childhood dream of a singing career.
Primary, Intermediate; Nonfiction

Rose, Edward (c. 1780-c. 1833) United States
European-American/Cherokee and African-American

Dolan, Sean. *James Beckwourth: Frontiersman*. Philadelphia: Chelsea House Publishers, 1992. 120 p. (Black Americans of Achievement)
This biography of James Beckwourth points out that Edward Rose participated in the 1822-1823 Ashley-Henry Rocky Mountain fur trapping expeditions, spoke numerous Indian languages, and was

an outstanding woodsman who was greatly admired by the Crow Indians.
Older; Nonfiction

Katz, William Loren. *Black Indians: A Hidden Heritage*. New York: Atheneum, 1986. 208 p.
The book's brief account of the frontiersman Edward Rose emphasizes his rapport with Native Americans and his knowledge of their languages.
Intermediate, Older; Nonfiction

Katz, William Loren, and Paula A. Franklin. *Proudly Red and Black: Stories of African and Native Americans*. New York: Atheneum, 1993. 96 p.
The chapter on Edward Rose tells how, after joining a company that went to the Bighorn to establish a trading post, he went to live with the Crow. Rose worked as a fur trader and trapper and served as a guide and interpreter for fur-trading expeditions.
Intermediate, Older; Nonfiction

Ross, John (1790-1866) United States
Scottish/Scottish and Cherokee

Banks, Sara H. *Remember My Name*. Illustrated by Birgitta Saflund. Niwot, Colo.: Roberts Rinehart Publishers, 1993. 128 p.
In this story the girl Annie visits Chief John Ross in his home. The book includes information about Ross's activities as Cherokee chief during the period when the Cherokee Nation was forced to move westward.
Intermediate; Fiction

Basel, Roberta. *Sequoyah: Inventor of Written Cherokee*. Minneapolis: Compass Point Books, 2007. 112 p. (Signature Lives)
This biography of Sequoyah includes the text of the note written by John Ross which accompanied the 1825 Cherokee National Council's medal given to Sequoyah, a picture of John Ross, and information on the Ross Party.
Older; Nonfiction

Caravantes, Peggy. *An American in Texas: The Story of Sam Houston*. Greensboro, N.C.: Morgan Reynolds Publishing, 2003. 144 p. (Founders of the Republic)
According to this biography of Sam Houston, John Ross's division of the Cherokee into smaller groups reduced their fatalities on the Trail of Tears.
Older; Nonfiction

Cwiklik, Robert. *Sequoyah and the Cherokee Alphabet*. Introduction by Alvin M. Josephy, Jr. Illustrated by T. Lewis. Englewood Cliffs, N.J.: Silver Burdett Press, 1989. 144 p. (Alvin Josephy's Biography Series of American Indians)

In this fictionalized biography of Sequoyah, John Ross is depicted as initially disparaging of Sequoyah's syllabary, but later realizing the great impact it would have. The book also mentions Ross's efforts to keep the Cherokee from being removed from their eastern lands.
Intermediate, Older; Fiction

Fitterer, C. Ann. *Sequoyah: Native American Scholar*. Chanhassen, Minn.: The Child's World, 2003. 32 p. (Spirit of America)
This biography of Sequoyah tells of Ross's friendship with Sequoyah and of his explaining to Sequoyah how English was written and then read.
Primary, Intermediate; Nonfiction

Klausner, Janet. *Sequoyah's Gift: A Portrait of the Cherokee Leader*. Afterword by Duane H. King. New York: HarperCollins Publishers, 1993. 128 p.
The efforts of the Cherokee's principal chief John Ross to prevent the forced removal of the Cherokee Nation from the southeastern United States are described in this book.
Intermediate, Older; Nonfiction

Schwarz, Melissa. *Wilma Mankiller: Principal Chief of the Cherokees*. Philadelphia: Chelsea House Publishers, 1994. 112 p. (North American Indians of Achievement)
This biography of Wilma Mankiller points out that under John Ross's leadership as the first Principal Chief of the Cherokee Nation a democratic constitution was adopted and that, to save Cherokees from starving, he finally agreed to their moving west.
Older; Nonfiction

Shumate, Jane. *Sequoyah: Inventor of the Cherokee Alphabet*. Philadelphia: Chelsea House Publishers, 1994. 112 p. (North American Indians of Achievement)
This biography of Sequoyah tells how John Ross worked towards assimilation of the eastern Cherokees with the white culture through the establishment of New Echota, how he opposed the Treaty of New Echota signed by other Cherokees who agreed to be removed to the West, and how, after the Trail of Tears, he sought to set up the eastern Cherokee government structure in the Cherokee western territory.
Older; Nonfiction

Sneve, Virginia Driving Hawk. *The Cherokees*. Illustrated by Ronald Himler. New York: Holiday House, 1996. 32 p. (A First Americans Book)
An illustration of John Ross and information on the Ross Party is included in this history of the Cherokees.
Intermediate; Nonfiction

Roy, Marie (1710-1732) Canada
French/Miami, to French

Trottier, Maxine. *A Circle of Silver*. New York: Stoddart Kids, 1999. 224 p. (The Circle of Silver Chronicles)

Set in 1760 this first book in *The Circle of Silver Chronicles* relates the story of thirteen-year-old John MacNeil, who leaves his English home to spend two years with his father, Captain James MacNeil, traveling to and then returning from the British Fort Detroit. It tells of the growing enmity of the Indians living near Fort Detroit who are poorly treated by the British, of John's being appointed King George III's artist in Canada, of John's love of Canada, of his friendship with the Ottawa Natka and Wallace Doig whose Miami wife had died, of his encounter with Pontiac, and of his closeness to Marie Roy, the French-Canadian Miami girl whom he adores, and to Pierre La Butte, the interpreter for the British and then merchant who becomes Marie Roy's husband.
Older; Fiction

Ruiz de Burton, María Amparo (1832-1895) Mexico
Mexican Catholic, to European-American Protestant

Alegre, Cèsar. *Extraordinary Hispanic Americans*. New York: Children's Press, 2007. 288 p. (Extraordinary People)

A biographical chapter on María Amparo Ruiz de Burton tells of her two novels and her marriage to Henry S. Burton, an American military officer.
Older; Nonfiction

Russwurm, John Brown (1799-1851) Jamaica
European-American/African-Jamaican

Nash, Gary B. *Forbidden Love: The Secret History of Mixed-Race America*. New York: Henry Holt and Company, 1999. 224 p.

As pointed out in this book, John Brown Russwurm, who was one of the earliest black American college graduates (Bowdoin College, 1826), became an editor of the first African-American newspaper, *Freedom's Journal*, and then moved to Liberia where he played an important leadership role.
Older; Nonfiction

Sacagawea (c.1788-1812 or 1884) United States
Lemhi Shoshone, by Hidatsa, to French Canadian, to Comanche?

Adler, David A. *A Picture Book of Sacagawea*. Illustrated by Dan Brown. New York: Holiday House, 2000. 32 p.

This picture book relates how Sacagawea was kidnapped by Hidatsa (Minnetaree) Indians at the age of ten or eleven, was sold to (or won in a gambling game by) the trader Toussaint Charbonneau to be his second wife, and had their baby two months before going on the Lewis and Clark Expedition. It describes her role during the expedition, mentions how she may have died in 1812 or lived until 1884, and includes a list of dates and a bibliography.
Primary; Nonfiction

Alter, Judy. *Sacagawea: Native American Interpreter*. Chanhassen, Minn.: The Child's World, 2002, 32 p. (Spirit of America)

This biography of Sacagawea contains sections on the different spellings of her name, the honors she was accorded in the early 1900s, and the differing accounts of her later life. It is illustrated with photographs and includes a timeline, a glossary, a guide to additional information, and an index. Intermediate; Nonfiction

Armstrong, Jennifer. *Thomas Jefferson: Letters from a Philadelphia Bookworm*. Delray Beach, Fla.: Winslow Press, 2001. 128 p. (Dear Mr. President)

Correspondence between fictional Amelia Hornsby, an inquisitive and independent-minded girl, and President Thomas Jefferson provides an informative and interesting account of Jefferson's presidency, the Lewis and Clark expedition, Monticello, and Philadelphia and Pittsburgh in the early 1800s. Amelia is particularly curious about Sacagawea. The letters and accompanying illustrations are followed by biographical information on Jefferson, which contains one sentence on evidence of an affair with Sally Hemings; a timeline; a resource list that includes subjects located on the publisher's website; and an index. Intermediate, Older; Fiction

Brown, Marion Marsh. *Sacagawea: Indian Interpreter to Lewis and Clark*. Chicago: Children's Press, 1988. 120 p.

This book covers Sacagawea's life from her kidnapping to her return to the Hidatsa villages in August 1806. Most of the narrative is based on the Lewis and Clark journals and emphasizes Sacagawea's importance in interpreting with the Shoshones and securing horses from them, in finding food for the expedition, and, by her presence and that of her baby, in showing other Indians that the expedition was peaceful. The story includes fictionalized dialogue and descriptions of Sacagawea's feelings. A list of events occurring during each year of Sacagawea's life (1787-1812) is appended. Intermediate, Older; Fiction

Bruchac, Joseph. *Sacajawea: The Story of Bird Woman and the Lewis and Clark Expedition*. San Diego: Harcourt/Silver Whistle, 2000. 208 p.

When Jean Baptiste (Pomp) Charbonneau was a young boy, he and his parents visited his adopted uncle Captain William Clark in St. Louis. In this novel Pomp relays the story of his mother and the Lewis and Clark Expedition as it was told to him then through alternating chapters narrated by Sacajawea and Clark. Clark's accounts are preceded by excerpts from his journal and Sacajawea's by traditional tales of the Native Americans encountered during the expedition. In addition to presenting a detailed picture of the Lewis and Clark Expedition from two vantage points, the book includes information on what happened later to the members of the expedition. Older; Fiction

Collard, Sneed B. III. *Sacagawea: Brave Shoshone Girl*. New York: Benchmark, 2007. 48 p. (American Heroes)

Pages of color reproductions face pages of text in this presentation of Sacagawea's life. A postscript, a chronology, a glossary, a pronunciation guide, a resource section, and an index are appended.
Intermediate; Fiction

Cosson, M.J. *Sacagawea: Indian Guide.* Illustrated by Reed Sprunger. Edina, Minn.: Magic Wagon, 2009. 32 p. (Beginner Biographies)
Alternating pages of text and color paintings, a fact list, a timeline, a glossary, a resource list, and an index present an introduction to Sacagawea.
Primary; Nonfiction

Crosby, Michael T. *Sacagawea: Shoshone Explorer.* Stockton, N.J.: OTTN Publishing, 2008. 144 p. (Shapers of America)
Color photographs, maps, informational inserts, a detailed chronology, a glossary, chapter notes, resource lists, and an index combine to provide a well-rounded portrayal of Sacajawea's life. The book tells of the contributions to the Lewis and Clark Expedition made by Toussaint Charbonneau, Pierre Cruzatte, George Drouillard, and François Labiche and presents biographical information on Jean Baptiste (Pomp) Charbonneau.
Older; Nonfiction

Dramer, Kim. *Native Americans and Black Americans.* Philadelphia: Chelsea House Publishers, 1997. 96 p. (Indians of North America)
This book points out Sacajawea's importance to the Lewis and Clark Expedition.
Older; Nonfiction

Farnsworth, Frances Joyce. *Winged Moccasins: The Story of Sacajawea.* Illustrated by Lorence F. Bjorklund. Englewood Cliffs, N.J.: Responsive Environments Corp., 1954. 190 p.
This fictionalized story of Sacajawea tells of her constant longing to be like wild geese and go somewhere faraway. It tells of her kidnapping, her becoming Charbonneau's squaw, her experiences with the Lewis and Clark Expedition, her time in St. Louis, her marriage to Jerk Meat of the Comanche, her return to the Shoshones, her reuniting with Pomp, and her moving to the Shoshone Indian Reservation in Wyoming.
Intermediate, Older; Fiction

Feinstein, Stephen. *Read about Sacagawea.* Berkeley Heights, N.J.: Enslow Publishers, 2004. 24 p. (I Like Biographies!)
Color illustrations, a glossary, a timeline, a resource list, and an index are included in this introductory biography of Sacagawea.
Primary; Nonfiction

Frazier, Neta Lohnes. *Sacagawea: The Girl Nobody Knows.* New York: David McKay Company, 1967. 192 p.
This biography of Sacagawea presents the Lewis and Clark Expedition as an important drama

placed within the context of American history, with its climax the amazing reunion of Sacagawea with her brother, the Shoshone chief Cameahwait. It quotes from the journals written on the expedition and contains information on their publication. There is also an extensive examination of the later lives of Sacajawea, of Touissaint Charbonneau, and of Jean Baptiste (Pomp) Charbonneau, who became guide, trader, and interpreter for Kit Carson, Jim Bridger, and others. The book includes a bibliography and an index.
Older; Nonfiction

Hopkins, Lee Bennett, selector. *Lives: Poems about Famous Americans*. Illustrated by Leslie Staub. New York: HarperCollins Publishers, 1999. 36 p.

This poetry collection includes the poem "A Song for Sacagawea" by Jane Yolen as well as a portrait and a brief biographical note.
Intermediate; Fiction

Kimmel, Elizabeth Cody: *Ladies First: 40 Daring American Women Who Were Second to None*. Washington, D.C.: National Geographic, 2006. 192 p.

This book's biographical section on Sacagawea highlights how, although she was a Native American woman, she was given a vote on the Corps of Discovery's decision as to where to make its winter camp.
Intermediate, Older; Nonfiction

Lourie, Peter. *On the Trail of Sacagawea*. Photographs by author. Honesdale, Pa.: Boyds Mills Press, 2001. 48 p.

One summer the author, together with his wife and their two children, followed the trail of Sacajawea and the Lewis and Clark Expedition from the reconstructed Fort Mandan in North Dakota to the reconstructed Fort Clatsop in Oregon. Both the book's text and photographs tie together the Lewis and Clark's Expedition's experiences and the Louries' present day trip. On the way the Louries visited Indian reservations to gain Native American perspectives on the expedition's journey.
Intermediate; Nonfiction

Milton, Joyce. *Sacajawea: Her True Story*. Illustrated by Shelly Hehenberger. New York: Grosset & Dunlap, 2001. 48 p. (All Aboard Reading)

Sacajawea's life story from her kidnapping to her death—either in 1812 or much later—is presented through a text for beginning readers and color illustrations.
Pre-K, Primary; Nonfiction

Murphy, Claire Rudolph. *I Am Sacajawea, I Am York: Our Journey West with Lewis and Clark*. Illustrated by Higgins Bond. New York: Walker & Company, 2005. 32 p.

Text and double-page illustrations present the Lewis and Clark expedition's journey to the Pacific Ocean as seen through the eyes of Sacagawea and York. An afterword, book and website lists, and a pronunciations note are appended.
Primary, Intermediate; Nonfiction

Myers, Laurie. *Lewis and Clark and Me. A Dog's Tale*. Illustrated by Michael Dooling. New York: Henry Holt and Company, 2002. 80 p

Seaman, a Newfoundland. describes his purchase by Meriwether Lewis and his adventures on the Lewis and Clark expedition: catching numerous swimming squirrels, being mistaken for a bear by Shawnee Indians, feeling jealous of a buffalo calf, almost losing his life to a wounded beaver, saving men from a charging buffalo, being briefly stolen by Clatsop Indians, and, above all, treasuring his relationship with Lewis. Seaman's account mentions George Drouillard, Sacagawea, and Pierre Cruzatte. The book features full- and double-page paintings, a map, an introduction, an afterword, and a source list.
Intermediate; Fiction

O'Dell, Scott. *Streams to the River, River to the Sea: A Novel of Sacagawea*. Boston: Houghton Mifflin Company, 1986. 208 p.

This story relates that Sacagawea was kidnapped twice; that she escaped the second time and survived by herself for a while on an island; that she was won in a game of chance by Charbonneau, whom she despised; that she fell in love with Captain Clark, but came to realize that she could not be his wife; and that Captain Lewis gave her his huge dog Scannon (or Seaman).
Older; Fiction

Raphael, Elaine, and Don Bolognese. *Sacajawea: The Journey West*. Illustrated by authors. New York: Cartwheel Books: Scholastic, 1994. 32 p. (Drawing America)

Starting with the young Sacajawea's riding a pony with her brother Cameahwait and ending with her reunion with him during the Lewis and Clark Expedition, this book features double-page color pictures and guides for drawing Sacajawea, a Shoshone pinto, and other subjects associated with the expedition.
Primary; Fiction

Roop, Peter, and Connie Roop. *Girl of the Shining Mountains: Sacagawea's Story*. New York: Hyperion Books for Children, 1999. 192 p.

As Sacagawea, Charbonneau, and their young son Pomp travel in a flatboat to St. Louis so Pomp can receive the education which Captain Cook has promised, Sacagawea tells the story of her journey to the Pacific Ocean and back and of her earlier life. Her narrative is interspersed with Pomp's questions and her responses. She relates how she had planned to remain with the Shoshone once she was reunited with them in the Shining Mountains (the Rockies), but decided instead to continue with Lewis and Clark when she discovered that her father and sisters were dead and that the Shoshone were suffering from hunger. There is a favorable portrayal of "Papa," Pomp's father Toussaint Charbonneau.
Intermediate, Older; Fiction

Roop, Peter, and Connie Roop, eds. *Off the Map: The Journals of Lewis and Clark*. Illustrated by Tim Tanner. New York: Walker and Company, 1993. 48 p.

Excerpts from Lewis and Clark's journals cover the commencement of their expedition's journey

on May 13, 1804 to its departure on March 23, 1806 from Fort Clatsop for the return trip. The book includes journal entries referring to George Drouillard, Toussaint Charbonneau, and Sacagawea. A prologue presents the expedition's background and the June 20, 1803 letter from President Jefferson to Meriwether Lewis. An epilogue describes the homeward journey and the later lives of members of the Corps of Discovery.
Intermediate, Older; Nonfiction

Rowland, Della. *The Story of Sacajawea, Guide to Lewis and Clark.* Illustrated by Richard Leonard. New York: Yearling/Dell Publishing, 1989. 96 p.
This biography of Sacajawea includes information on the Shoshoni and the Minnetaree and on the background of the Corps of Discovery (the Lewis and Clark party).
Intermediate, Older; Nonfiction

Seymour, Flora Warren. *Sacagawea: American Pathfinder.* Illustrated by Robert Doremus. New York: Aladdin Paperbacks, 1991. 192 p. (Childhood of Famous Americans)
Sacagawea's childhood with the Shoshone is the focus of this fictionalized biography. It tells of keeping her baby brother from drowning, of her learning to ride a horse, of her making a basket and a dress, of the Sun Dance in which her older brother and other young men had to cut themselves, of her kindness to her grandmother, and of her desires to have a horse and to see white men and the huge salt lake beyond the rivers. After telling of Sacagawea's capture by Minnetaree and her purchase by Toussaint Charbonneau, the story moves on to an account of her return to the Shoshone as part of the Lewis and Clark expedition and a description of the important role she played in its success.
Intermediate; Fiction

St. George, Judith. *Sacagawea.* New York: G. P. Putnam's Sons, 1997. 128 p.
Factual, except for its assumptions of Sacagawea's feelings, this biography provides a detailed account of her time with the Corps of Discovery. A bibliography and an index are included.
Intermediate; Fiction

White, Alana L. *Sacagawea: Westward with Lewis and Clark.* Springfield, N.J.: Enslow Publishers, 1997. 128 p. (Native American Biographies)
Illustrations including reproductions of several Karl Bodmer paintings, a chronology, chapter notes, a glossary, a reading list, an index, and a text divided into short titled sections are features of this biography of Sacagawea.
Intermediate, Older; Nonfiction

Williams, Mark London. *Trail of Bones.* Cambridge, Mass.: Candlewick Press, 2005. 320 p. (Danger Boy)
This book is part of a science fiction series in which Eli, an American boy, Thea, a girl from ancient Alexandria, and Clyne, a talking dinosaur, travel in time through the Fifth Dimension. In this story they end up in 1804 where Eli becomes part of the Lewis and Clark Corps of Discovery. Going with the expedition from St. Louis to the Mandan village, he encounters Pierre Cruzatte as well as

Sacagawea and Toussaint Charbonneau and witnesses the birth of their son Pomp. Thea is also transported close to St. Louis where both she and Eli meet Thomas Jefferson and Sally Hemings, who have secretly traveled there for the start of Lewis and Clark's trip. However, Thea is mistaken for a runaway slave and is taken back to Monticello. Clyne lands in the wild near the Mandans. At the tale's conclusion all three are together in New Orleans where they once again go into the Fifth Dimension.
Intermediate, Older; Fiction

Witteman, Barbara. *Sacagawea: A Photo-Illustrated Biography*. Mankato, Minn.: Bridgestone Books/ Capstone Press, 2002. 24 p.
   This biography of Sacagawea's life features a full-page photograph facing each page of text, a chronology, a glossary, references to further information, and an index.
Primary, Intermediate; Nonfiction

Wolf, Allan. *New Found Land: Lewis and Clark's Voyage of Discovery, A Novel*. Cambridge, Mass.: Candlewick Press, 2004. 512 p.
   Fourteen members of the Corps of Discovery, including Sacagawea, George Drouillard, Pierre Cruzatte, and Oolum (the Newfoundland dog Seaman), narrate this detailed story of the Lewis and Clark Expedition. Speaking in prose and poetry and expressing their individual perspectives and feelings, often with a sense of humor, the narrators cover the period from the June 1803 request of President Thomas Jefferson to Meriwether Lewis to lead the expedition to 1819, ten years after Lewis's death. The novel contains maps, a glossary, resources, and additional information on the expedition, including what later happened to each narrator.
Older; Fiction

Sainte-Marie, Beverly (Buffy) (1942-   ) Canada
Canadian Cree, by Micmac and European-American

Avery, Susan, and Linda Skinner. *Extraordinary American Indians*. Chicago: Children's Press, 1992. 272 p.
   Orphaned as an infant, Buffy Sainte-Marie, a Cree from Saskatchewan, Canada, was adopted by parents who were part Micmac. Raised in Maine and Massachusetts, she became a world-famous singer and songwriter. Through her lectures and songs she worked as an activist, seeking to improve the lives of Native Americans.
Older; Nonfiction

Savage, Thomas (1590s?-1600s)
English, by Powhatan (Pamunkey)

Carbone, Elisa. *Blood on the River: James Town, 1607*. New York: Viking, 2006. 256 p.
   Londoner Samuel Collier is the narrator of this novel, which chronicles his life from 1606 when he was chosen at age eleven to go to Virginia as John Smith's page to 1610 when he was safely living in Point Comfort, Virginia, with the Laydon family. It details the discomforts of the voyage, the

experiences of the passengers in the West Indies, and the struggles of the colonists in Jamestown. Samuel observes firsthand the selfishness and foolishness of the gentlemen who lived in Jamestown and their hostility towards John Smith. In Virginia Samuel learned the values of working cooperatively and of channeling his anger and enjoyed the months he spent living with the Warraskoyack Indians. After Smith had gone back to England and realizing that Jamestown was in peril, Samuel saved Ann Laydon and her baby by kidnapping the baby. The book mentions Thomas Savage and how Thomas spent time with the Pamunkey. It also contains an afterword.
Intermediate, Older; Fiction

Fritz, Jean. *Who's Saying What in Jamestown, Thomas Savage?* Illustrated by Sally Wern Comport. New York: G. P. Putnam's Sons, 2007. 64 p.

This book of historical fiction presents a biography of Thomas Savage, who served as a cabin boy on the first supply ship sent to Jamestown that arrived in January 1608. Realizing the need for interpreters with the Indians, Christopher Newport, the ship's captain, assigned young Thomas to go live with the Powhatan Indians so he could learn the language. There he befriended Pocahontas, delivered messages between the colonists and the Indians, and came to know another English boy, Henry Spelman who had arrived on one of the third supply ships in April 1609 and whom John Smith sent to Powhatan to become an interpreter. In 1613 Savage was sent as an interpreter for Captain Samuel Argall to the Eastern Shore where he became a friend of the Accawmacke's king, Debedeavon, who gave him land where he built a house and raised a family. As a boy Henry ran away to the Patawomekes where he happily settled and continued to be an interpreter for the colonists.
Intermediate; Fiction

Kudlinski, Kathleen V. *My Lady Pocahontas: A Novel*. Tarrytown, N.Y.: Marshall Cavendish, 2006. 288 p.

This story of Pocahontas' life is written from the viewpoint of her fictional friend Neetah. Appamatuck Neetah is adopted by Powhatan to be Pocahontas' guardian. Together the two girls spy on the newly arrived Jamestown colonists. They befriend three boys, Samuel, Thomas, and Henry, who come to stay with the Powhatans. Pocahontas has a vision in which she, Neetah, John Smith, and a baby of much importance appear. Believing from the vision that she will marry John Smith, she betrays her father and warns Smith of a plot to kill him. As Smith shows no inclination to marry her, Pocahontas returns depressed to her Pamunkey village. When the three boys try to escape, Samuel is killed, Thomas is captured, and Pocahontas leads Henry and Neetah to refuge with the Patawomeke. There both Pocahontas and Neetah marry Patawomekes, but they are blamed for a deadly measles outbreak, are imprisoned by the colonists, and are taken to Jamestown. Later brought to Henrico, Pocahontas becomes a Christian, takes a new name Rebecca, falls in love with John Rolfe, and, fulfilling her vision, has a son Thomas. Neetah accompanies Pocahontas, John, and Thomas to England where both she and Pocahantas die before returning home. An afterword, an author's note, and a source list are appended.
Older; Fiction

Schomburg Arthur Alfonso (1874-1938) United States
German/African-Crucian

Alegre, Cèsar. *Extraordinary Hispanic Americans*. New York: Children's Press, 2007. 288 p. (Extraordinary People)
 Arthur Schomburg's advocacy of Cuba and Puerto Rico's independence from Spain, his co-founding of the Negro Society for Historical Research, and his extensive collection of items of black history are covered in a biographical chapter on the bibliophile and art collector.
Older; Nonfiction

Rodriguez, Robert, and Tamra Orr, contributing writers. *Great Hispanic-Americans*. Lincolnwood, Ill.: Publications International, 2005. 128 p.
 A section relates how Arthur Alfonso Schomburg, who was born in Puerto Rico, determined in the fifth grade that he would show his teacher that black people do have an important history and heroes. Becoming an archivist, he gathered materials for his Schomburg Collection of Negro Literature and History. Selling it to the New York Public Library, he then served as its curator.
Older; Nonfiction

Schwarzenegger, Arnold (1947-   ) Austria
Austrian, to Irish-German-American

Doherty, Craig A., and Katherine M. Doherty. *Arnold Schwarzenegger: Larger Than Life*. New York: Walker and Company, 1993. 128 p.
 This comprehensive biography tells of Arnold Schwarzenegger's childhood dream to be like South African bodybuilder and movie actor Reg Park and of how he fulfilled this dream. It tells of his involvement with the Special Olympics and provides extensive coverage of his bodybuilding strategies and competitions and of the movies in which he acted. The book traces Maria Shriver's career from her first job at a Philadelphia television station to her "First Person with Maria Shriver" specials. Photographs, chronological listings of Arnold Schwarzenegger's bodybuilding titles and movies, source notes, a reading list, and an index complete the book.
Older; Nonfiction

Hamilton, Sue L. *Arnold Schwarzenegger: No. 1 Movie Star in the World*. Edina, Minn.: ABDO & Daughters, 1992. 32 p. (Reaching for the Stars)
 Black-and-white photographs accompany this survey of Arnold Schwarzenegger's bodybuilding and movie careers.
Older; Nonfiction

Meeks, Christopher. *Arnold Schwarzenegger: Hard Work Brought Success*. Illustrated by Teri Rider. Vero Beach, Fla.: The Rourke Corporation, 1993. 24 p. (Reaching Your Goal)
 Arnold Schwarzenegger is introduced to young children through this book's text and color paintings.
Primary; Nonfiction

North, Jack. *Arnold Schwarzenegger*. New York: Dillon Press, 1994. 64 p. (Taking Part)

Arnold Schwarzenegger's pre-1976 life as a bodybuilder and his continuing support of the sport is emphasized in this biography which also tells of his childhood, his movie acting, and his advocacy of physical fitness. Color photographs and an index are included.
Intermediate, Older; Nonfiction

Watson, B. S. *Arnold Schwarzenegger*. Chicago: Kidsbooks, 1993. 64 p.

This detailed biography of Arnold Schwarzenegger describes his childhood, his bodybuilding career, and his movie career through his performance in the 1993 film, *The Last Action Hero*. It includes black-and-white photographs, a trivia information section, and a quiz on the book's contents.
Older; Nonfiction

Seattle (also Seathl, Sealth) (c.1786 or 1778-1866) United States
Suquamish/Duwamish

Avery, Susan, and Linda Skinner. *Extraordinary American Indians*. Chicago: Children's Press, 1992. 272 p.

Seathl, chief of the Suquamish and then of a larger confederation which included the Duwamish, fought against other Indian tribes, but became a friend of the French missionaries and the first white settlers, who in 1851 established a trading post and in 1852 changed its name to Seattle. Despite later problems between white settlers and Native Americans, Seathl was an advocate of peace. His oratorical skills are reflected in his 1854 speech to the governor of the Washington Territory, part of which is printed in this section.
Older; Nonfiction

See, Lisa (1955-   ) United States
Chinese-European-American/European-American

O'Hearn, Claudine Chiawei, editor. *Half and Half: Writers on Growing Up Biracial and Bicultural*. New York: Pantheon Books, 1998. 288 p.

Although she looks white and is only one-eighth Chinese, the writer Lisa See explains that because of her ties to her Chinese family, she is Chinese in her heart.
Older; Nonfiction

Senna, Danzy (1970-   ) United States
African-Mexican-American/Irish-American

O'Hearn, Claudine Chiawei, editor. *Half and Half: Writers on Growing Up Biracial and Bicultural*. New York: Pantheon Books, 1998. 288 p.

In a chapter written by the novelist Danzy Senna, she tells how, because of the black power movement, she was taught to identify herself as black. She describes a tongue-in-cheek situation in which

the year 2000 is the year of the mulatto.
Older; Nonfiction

Sequoyah (also George Gist, George Guess, George Guest) (c.1773, 1778?-1843) United States
European-American/Cherokee

Avery, Susan, and Linda Skinner. *Extraordinary American Indians*. Chicago: Children's Press, 1992. 272 p.
 A section on Sequoyah relates how, raised by his Cherokee mother, he became a silversmith and was a U.S. Army soldier in the Creek War. Fascinated by the writing of European-Americans, he spent years developing a Cherokee syllabary that enabled the Cherokees to write and read their language and to communicate with each other, especially after many Cherokees were forced to move westward.
Older; Nonfiction

Basel, Roberta. *Sequoyah: Inventor of Written Cherokee*. Minneapolis: Compass Point Books, 2007. 112 p. (Signature Lives)
 A detailed text, informational inserts, photographs, a glossary, a timeline presenting events in Sequoyah's life and world events, a fact list, source notes, a bibliography, a resource list, and an index distinguish this biography.
Older; Nonfiction

Cwiklik, Robert. *Sequoyah and the Cherokee Alphabet*. Introduction by Alvin M. Josephy, Jr. Illustrated by T. Lewis. Englewood Cliffs, N.J.: Silver Burdett Press, 1989. 144 p. (Alvin Josephy's Biography Series of American Indians)
 In this fictionalized biography of Sequoyah, George Gist is assumed to be his father and as a teen Sequoyah buys a book from a white hunter. Sequoyah suffers an illness that results in his lame leg; he has only one wife, Sally, Ahyoka's mother; and he perseveres in developing his Cherokee syllabary. This book contains a map showing the locations of various Native American peoples.
Intermediate, Older; Fiction

Fitterer, C. Ann. *Sequoyah: Native American Scholar*. Chanhassen, Minn.: The Child's World, 2003. 32 p. (Spirit of America)
 Sequoyah's mixed heritage, his work as a silversmith and blacksmith, his friendship with John Ross, and his development and teaching of a Cherokee syllabary are covered in this biography. It also tells of the work of his daughter Ahyoka and of the Cherokees and includes a timeline, a glossary, and a resource list.
Primary, Intermediate; Nonfiction

Klausner, Janet. *Sequoyah's Gift: A Portrait of the Cherokee Leader*. Afterword by Duane H. King. New York: HarperCollins Publishers, 1993. 128 p.
 This biography of Sequoyah describes the Cherokee life which he would have experienced as a child; the destruction of his town Tah-skee-gee in 1776; his work as a trader, silversmith, and blacksmth;

his struggles and final success in developing Cherokee "talking leaves;" and his journey to find Cherokees in Mexico. The book provides information on the syllabary and the ways in which it was used. Photographs, a map, a resource list, a list of places to visit, and an index are included.
Intermediate, Older; Nonfiction

Oppenheim, Joanne. *Sequoyah: Cherokee Hero*. Illustrated by Bert Dodson. Mahwah, N.J.: Troll Associates, 1979. 48 p.
Sequoyah's childhood, his work on the syllabary, and the role played by his daughter Ahyoka are described in this fictionalized account of his life.
Primary; Fiction

Roop, Peter, and Connie Roop. *Ahyoka and the Talking Leaves*. Illustrated by Yoshi Miyake. New York: Lothrop, Lee & Shepard Books, 1992. 64 p.
This fictionalized story of Ahyoka, Sequoyah's young daughter, tells how she tried to help him draw pictures for the words of the Cherokee language; joined him when her mother Utiya burned his drawings and forced him to leave; and, after the cabin where she and Sequoyah lived was destroyed by an angry medicine man, accompanied Sequoyah on his travels westward. In this story it is Ahyoka who comes up with the idea of writing symbols for Cherokee sounds. The book includes an epilogue and a bibliography.
Primary; Fiction

Rumford, James. *Sequoyah: The Cherokee Man Who Gave His People Writing*. Illustrated by author. Translated into Cherokee by Anna Sixkiller Huckaby. Boston: Houghton Mifflin Company, 2004. 32 p.
A father tells how the tall sequoia trees are named for Sequoyah, a Cherokee who stood tall as a leader. Written in English and Cherokee, this picture book describes how Sequoyah tried to provide a written Cherokee language by drawing a symbol for each word, but abandoned that effort after his cabin was burned down. He then came up with a syllabary, a writing system which has proved invaluable to the Cherokee Nation.
Primary, Intermediate; Nonfiction

Shumate, Jane. *Sequoyah: Inventor of the Cherokee Alphabet*. Philadelphia: Chelsea House Publishers, 1994. 112 p. (North American Indians of Achievement)
This comprehensive biography of Sequoyah presents his life as part of the complex history of the Cherokees: their facing land encroachment, treaty violations, assimilation, and removal by the whites and the disagreements which existed among them as to their best courses of action. The book relates how Sequoyah sought to preserve the Cherokee culture by developing a Cherokee syllabary, which provided a means of communication among the Cherokees and made possible the publication of the bilingual tribal newspaper, the *Cherokee Phoenix*. Serving as temporary president of the Cherokee Nation West, Sequoyah worked with the eastern Cherokee emigrants to come up with an Act of Union. This book contains a chronology, reading list, and pictures.
Older; Nonfiction

Sneve, Virginia Driving Hawk. *The Cherokees*. Illustrated by Ronald Himler. New York: Holiday House, 1996. 32 p. (A First Americans Book)

A quotation from Sequoyah, his picture, and a mention of his work are included in this history of the Cherokees.

Intermediate; Nonfiction

Waxman, Laura Hamilton. *Sequoyah*. Illustrated by Tim Parlin. Minneapolis: Lerner Publishing Company, 2004. 48 p. (History Maker Bios)

This biography of Sequoyah features informational inserts, photographs, color illustrations, a list of places and an event honoring Sequoyah, a timeline, a reading list, a bibliography, a website listing, and an index.

Intermediate; Nonfiction

Sheen, Charlie (born Carlos Irwin Estévez) (1965-   ) United States
Irish-Spanish-American/European-American

Hargrove, Jim. *Martin Sheen: Actor and Activist*. Chicago: Children's Press, 1991. 128 p. (People of Distinction Biographies)

This comprehensive biography of Martin Sheen is based largely on his 1990 interview with the author. It covers Sheen's childhood, his career, his family, including his sons Emilio and Charlie, and his political activism. The book includes a listing of Sheen's stage, film, and television appearances, an annual chronology of his life and world events from 1940 through 1991, black-and-white photographs, and an index.

Older; Nonfiction

Press, Skip. *Charlie Sheen, Emilio Estevez, & Martin Sheen*. Parsippany, N.J.: Crestwood House, 1996. 48 p. (Star Families)

This look at the Sheen family provides biographical information on Martin Sheen and his sons Emilio Estévez and Charlie Sheen: their acting careers, their personal lives, and their interest in social justice. Photographs, a glossary, and an index are included.

Intermediate, Older; Nonfiction

Sheen, Martin (born Ramón Antonio Gerardo Estévez) (1940-   ) United States
Spanish/Irish, to European-American

Alegre, Cèsar. *Extraordinary Hispanic Americans*. New York: Children's Press, 2007. 288 p. (Extraordinary People)

A biographical chapter on Martin Sheen emphasizes his advocacy of peace and social justice.

Older; Nonfiction

Hargrove, Jim. *Martin Sheen: Actor and Activist*. Chicago: Children's Press, 1991. 128 p. (People of Distinction Biographies)

This comprehensive biography of Martin Sheen is based largely on his 1990 interview with the author. It covers Sheen's childhood, his career, his family, including his sons Emilio and Charlie, and his political activism. The book includes a listing of Sheen's stage, film, and television appearances, an annual chronology of his life and world events from 1940 through 1991, black-and-white photographs, and an index.
Older; Nonfiction

Press, Skip. *Charlie Sheen, Emilio Estevez, & Martin Sheen.* Parsippany, N.J.: Crestwood House, 1996. 48 p. (Star Families)
This look at the Sheen family provides biographical information on Martin Sheen and his sons Emilio Estévez and Charlie Sheen: their acting careers, their personal lives, and their interest in social justice. Photographs, a glossary, and an index are included.
Intermediate, Older; Nonfiction

Rodriguez, Robert, and Tamra Orr, contributing writers. *Great Hispanic-Americans.* Lincolnwood, Ill.: Publications International, 2005. 128 p.
A section relates how the actor Ramón Estévez assumed the stage name Martin Sheen so that his acting would not be restricted to ethnic roles. He has starred in movies and on television, including his portrayal of President Josiah Bartlett in *The West Wing*, and has promoted his beliefs through political activism.
Older; Nonfiction

Shriver, Maria (1955-   ) United States
German-American/Irish-American, to Austrian

Doherty, Craig A., and Katherine M. Doherty. *Arnold Schwarzenegger: Larger Than Life.* New York: Walker and Company, 1993. 128 p.
This comprehensive biography tells of Arnold Schwarzenegger's childhood dream to be like South African bodybuilder and movie actor Reg Park and of how he fulfilled this dream. It tells of his involvement with the Special Olympics and provides extensive coverage of his bodybuilding strategies and competitions and of the movies in which he acted. The book traces Maria Shriver's career from her first job at a Philadelphia television station to her "First Person with Maria Shriver" specials. Photographs, chronological listings of Arnold Schwarzenegger's bodybuilding titles and movies, source notes, a reading list, and an index complete the book.
Older; Nonfiction

Watson, B. S. *Arnold Schwarzenegger.* Chicago: Kidsbooks, 1993. 64 p.
This detailed biography of Arnold Schwarzenegger describes his childhood, his bodybuilding career, and his movie career through his performance in the 1993 film, *The Last Action Hero*. It includes black-and-white photographs, a trivia information section, and a quiz on the book's contents.
Older; Nonfiction

Silkwood, Priscilla (born Priscilla) (c.1824-1892) United States
African-American, by Cherokee, by European-American

Broyles, Anne. *Priscilla and the Hollyhocks*. Illustrated by Anna Alter. Watertown, Mass.: Charlesbridge, 2008. 32 p.

This picture book relates that, when Priscilla was very young, her mother was sold from her plantation. Priscilla worked as a house slave until her master's death and she was sold to a Cherokee family. As the Cherokee passed through Jonesboro, Illinois, on the Trail of Tears, Priscilla saw Basil Silkwood, the white man who had been sympathetic to her when he visited her Southern plantation. He bought Priscilla's freedom from the Cherokee and then adopted her as one of his and his wife's sixteen children. Priscilla had brought with her seeds originating from the hollyhocks her mother had planted years earlier and their flowers are now called Priscilla's hollyhocks.
Primary; Fiction

Smalls, Robert (1839-1915) United States
European-American and Jewish/African-American

Cooper, Michael L. *From Slave to Civil War Hero: The Life and Times of Robert Smalls*. New York: Lodestar Books, 1994. 80 p. (A Rainbow Biography)

More than half of this biography of Robert Smalls covers his accomplishments following his 1862 capture of the Confederate ship *Planter* for the Union Navy. Photographs and contemporary drawings, a glossary, a chronology, and an index add to this detailed account, which places Smalls' life within the context of his times.
Intermediate, Older; Nonfiction

Garrison, Mary. *Slaves Who Dared: The Stories of Ten African-American Heroes*. Shippensburg, Pa.: White Mane Kids, 2002. 152 p.

A chapter in this book details twenty-three-year-old Robert Smalls' daring capture of the Confederate steamboat on which he was wheelman. He not only brought the boat with its four guns to the Union forces, but also provided valuable information on the location of Confederate torpedoes and the military vulnerability of Charleston. Smalls later became a Union ship pilot and then captain (the first black man to do so in the United States) and served as a South Carolina state legislator and a United States congressman.
Intermediate, Older; Nonfiction

Greenfield, Eloise. *How They Got Over: African-Americans and the Call of the Sea*. Illustrated by Jan Spivey Gilchrist. New York: Amistad, 2003. 124 p.

As related in a one of this book's chapters, when he was about twelve-years-old, the slave Robert Smalls was sent to Charleston, South Carolina, where he at some point started working jobs associated with the sea: stevedore, sailmaker and rigger, and then wheelman (pilot) of the Confederate ship *Planter*. The story tells of Smalls' amazing conveyance of the *Planter* to the Union Navy and of his

subsequent achievements.
Intermediate; Nonfiction

Halfman, Janet. *Seven Miles to Freedom: The Robert Smalls Story*. Illustrated by Duane Smith. New York: Lee & Low Books, 2008. 40 p.

After describing Robert Smalls' early life, this book's text and large color paintings present his daring stealing of the Confederate steamer *Planter* and delivery of the ship with its cannons, its crew members, and their families to the blockading Union fleet. An afterword detailing Smalls' later life and a bibliography complete the book.
Primary, Intermediate; Nonfiction

Kranz, Rachel C. *The Biographical Dictionary of Black Americans*. New York: Facts on File, 1992. 192 p.

Robert Smalls was born a slave in South Carolina although his father was Jewish and a free man. This account tells of his heroism during the Civil War, his political career, and his serving as a customs collector in Beaufort, South Carolina.
Intermediate, Older; Nonfiction

Masoff, Joy. *The African American Story: The Events That Shaped Our Nation . . . and the People Who Changed Our Lives*. Waccabuc, N.Y.: Five Ponds Press, 2007. 96 p.

This history of African-Americans includes a paragraph about and a picture of Robert Smalls.
Older; Nonfiction

McKissack, Patricia C., and Frederick L. McKissack. *Black Hands, White Sails: The Story of African-American Whalers*. New York: Scholastic Press, 1999. 176 p.

This book mentions that Robert Smalls commandeered a Confederate gunboat out of Charleston and gave it to the Union navy. It includes illustrations of the boat and of Smalls.
Older; Nonfiction

Rappaport, Doreen. *Freedom Ship*. Illustrated by Curtis James. New York: Jump at the Sun, 2006. 36 p.

Illustrated with large colorful paintings, this picture book is set in Charleston, South Carolina, on May 13, 1862. On that night young Samuel, his mother, and other families secretly board the Confederate ship *Planter* where Samuel's father is a crew member and Robert Smalls is the wheelman. With the ship's captain and officers absent, Smalls assumes command. Flying the Confederate flag, the ship successfully passes Fort Sumter and Fort Moultrie and then, with Samuel's bedsheet hoisted as a sign of surrender, reaches the Union's warships. The Union forces take possession of the Confederate ship with its cannons and ammunition, and Samuel and his family receive their freedom. The book includes a historical note, a reading list, and a listing of web sites.
Primary, Intermediate; Fiction

Smith, Nolle (1889-1982) United States
European-American/ African-American and Choctaw

Katz, William Loren. *Black Women of the Old West.* New York: Atheneum Books for Young Readers, 1995. 96 p.

This book's description of Melissa Boulware Smith, whose father was Choctaw and mother an African-American, relates that she married Silas Smith, a Caucasian former Army scout. They moved from Missouri to Wyoming where they owned ranches in Chugwater and near Casper. Their son, Nolle, was elected to the Hawaiian territorial legislature in a district with few African-Americans.

Intermediate, Older; Nonfiction

Smith, Venture (born Broteer Furro) (c.1729-1805) West Africa

West African, by European-American

Nelson, Marilyn. *The Freedom Business, Including a Narrative of the Life & Adventures of Venture, a Native of Africa.* Illustrated by Deborah Dancy. Honesdale, Pa.: Wordsong, 2008. 72 p.

The verso pages of this book reproduce a 1798 autobiographical narrative by the African slave Venture, while the recto pages present poems written by Marilyn Nelson relating to Venture's experiences. At the age of six Broteer was kidnapped from his West African home by slave traders. He was bought on the ship taking him to America by the vessel's steward, who renamed him Venture. Venture lived on Fisher's Island where he spent his early years carding wool and performing other tasks within his master's house, and where he later suffered abuse from his master's son. During his life Venture was cheated and was sold three times, but he managed to purchase his freedom when he was thirty-six years old. He thereafter purchased the freedom of his wife and three children and owned a farm and boats.

Older; Nonfiction

Spelman, Henry (1595-1623) England

English, by Powhatan (Pamunkey), by Patawomeke

Fritz, Jean. *Who's Saying What in Jamestown, Thomas Savage?* Illustrated by Sally Wern Comport. New York: G. P. Putnam's Sons, 2007. 64 p.

This book of historical fiction presents a biography of Thomas Savage, who served as a cabin boy on the first supply ship sent to Jamestown that arrived in January 1608. Realizing the need for interpreters with the Indians, Christopher Newport, the ship's captain, assigned young Thomas to go live with the Powhatan Indians so he could learn the language. There he befriended Pocahontas, delivered messages between the colonists and the Indians, and came to know another English boy, Henry Spelman who had arrived on one of the third supply ships in April 1609 and whom John Smith sent to Powhatan to become an interpreter. In 1613 Savage was sent as an interpreter for Captain Samuel Argall to the Eastern Shore where he became a friend of the Accawmacke's king, Debedeavon, who gave him land where he built a house and raised a family. As a boy Henry ran away to the Patawomekes where he happily settled and continued to be an interpreter for the colonists.

Intermediate; Fiction

Kudlinski, Kathleen V. *My Lady Pocahontas: A Novel*. Tarrytown, N.Y.: Marshall Cavendish, 2006. 288 p.

This story of Pocahontas' life is written from the viewpoint of her fictional friend Neetah. Appamatuck Neetah is adopted by Powhatan to be Pocahontas' guardian. Together the two girls spy on the newly arrived Jamestown colonists. They befriend three boys, Samuel, Thomas, and Henry, who come to stay with the Powhatans. Pocahontas has a vision in which she, Neetah, John Smith, and a baby of much importance appear. Believing from the vision that she will marry John Smith, she betrays her father and warns Smith of a plot to kill him. As Smith shows no inclination to marry her, Pocahontas returns depressed to her Pamunkey village. When the three boys try to escape, Samuel is killed, Thomas is captured, and Pocahontas leads Henry and Neetah to refuge with the Patawomeke. There both Pocahontas and Neetah marry Patawomekes, but they are blamed for a deadly measles outbreak, are imprisoned by the colonists, and are taken to Jamestown. Later brought to Henrico, Pocahontas becomes a Christian, takes a new name Rebecca, falls in love with John Rolfe, and, fulfilling her vision, has a son Thomas. Neetah accompanies Pocahontas, John, and Thomas to England where both she and Pocahantas die before returning home. An afterword, an author's note, and a source list are appended.
Older; Fiction

Stanton, Catherine Ross (1810-1904) United States
Narragansett, to African-American

Katz, William Loren. *Black Pioneers: An Untold Story*. New York: Atheneum Books for Young Readers, 1999. 208 p.

According to this book, in the mid 1800s Moses and Catherine Stanton founded Stantonville (now Chilton), Wisconsin, and established an Underground Railroad station there.
Older; Nonfiction

Stanton, Moses (?-1862) United States
African-American, to Narragansett

Katz, William Loren. *Black Pioneers: An Untold Story*. New York: Atheneum Books for Young Readers, 1999. 208 p.

According to this book, in the mid 1800s Moses and Catherine Stanton founded Stantonville (now Chilton), Wisconsin, and established an Underground Railroad station there.
Older; Nonfiction

Steiner, Matthew Ray (born Hoang Van Long) (1966-   ) Vietnam
European-American/Vietnamese Buddhist, by European-American Mennonite

Warren, Andrea. *Escape from Saigon: How a Vietnam War Orphan Became an American Boy*. New York: Melanie Kroupa Books, 2004. 128 p.

This book presents the early life of Matt Steiner (known as Long) within the context of the Vietnam

War and its devastating effects upon the people of Vietnam. Long's American father had left the family by the time he was two, and Long and his mother lived both in Saigon and his mother's village. When Long was six, his mother committed suicide. His grandmother then moved with him to Saigon where she held several jobs, but found it difficult to care for him. On Long's seventh birthday his grandmother took him to the Holt Center, an orphanage primarily populated by Amerasian children where he stayed until leaving in April 1975 as part of Operation Babylift. As Saigon was about to fall to the North Vietnamese and one day after the crash of the first "orphan" plane bound for the United States, Ray flew together with sixty adults and 408 other orphans on a Pan American Airlines 747 jumbo jet to meet his adoptive family in Chicago. Although he greatly missed his grandmother, Long, now Matt, happily adjusted to his new parents and three older brothers and to life in West Liberty, Ohio. At the age of twenty-nine Matt Steiner, who was about to start his medical practice, visited his native Vietnam. The book includes photographs, an afterword, resource recommendations, sources, and an index.
Intermediate, Older; Nonfiction

Stewart, John (1786-1823) United States
African-American and Native American

Katz, William Loren. *Black Pioneers: An Untold Story*. New York: Atheneum Books for Young Readers, 1999. 208 p.
    This book describes how John Stewart preached to the Wyandot in Ohio and thereby became the first Methodist missionary to Native Americans.
Older; Nonfiction

Tallchief, Maria (also Wa-Xth-Tohuba, Woman of Two Worlds) (born Elizabeth Marie Tall Chief) (1925-   ) United States
Osage/Scottish-Irish-American, to Georgian

Allen, Paula Gunn, and Patricia Clark Smith. *As Long as the Rivers Flow: The Stories of Nine Native Americans*. New York: Scholastic Press, 1996. 336 p.
    The chapter on Maria Tallchief shows how her path to becoming a prima ballerina started in her early childhood when she and her sister Marjorie studied and performed piano and dance. When Maria was seven, the family moved to Beverly Hills to develop their talents. The book details Maria's tutelage by the renowned choreographers Bronislawa Nijinska and George Balanchine, her five year marriage to Balanchine, and her performances with the Ballet Russe de Monte Carlo and the New York City Ballet.
Intermediate, Older; Nonfiction

Avery, Susan, and Linda Skinner. *Extraordinary American Indians*. Chicago: Children's Press, 1992. 272 p.
    A section on Maria Tallchief presents a brief, but informative, account of her life and the impact of her dancing.
Older; Nonfiction

Gridley, Marion E. *Maria Tallchief: The Story of an American Indian*. Minneapolis: Dillon Press, 1973. 80 p.

This biography, which is illustrated with photographs, provides a detailed account of Maria Tallchief's career—and of the hard work and frustrations she encountered in becoming a ballerina. Intermediate, Older; Nonfiction

Kimmel, Elizabeth Cody: *Ladies First: 40 Daring American Women Who Were Second to None*. Washington, D.C.: National Geographic, 2006. 192 p.

Maria Tallchief's ballet career is summarized in one of this book's profiles. Intermediate, Older; Nonfiction

Rappaport, Doreen. *We Are the Many: A Picture Book of American Indians*. Illustrated by Cornelius Van Wright and Ying-Hwa Hu. New York: HarperCollins Publishers, 2002. 32 p.

A painting and accompanying text present Maria Tallchief dancing as Clara in *The Nutcracker* ballet. Primary, Intermediate; Nonfiction

Stux, Erica. *Eight Who Made a Difference: Pioneer Women in the Arts*. Greensboro, N.C.: Avisson Press, 1999. 128 p. (Avisson Young Adult Series)

A profile of Maria Tallchief covers her career and her personal life. Older; Nonfiction

Tallchief, Maria with Rosemary Wells. *Tallchief: America's Prima Ballerina*. Illustrated by Gary Kelley. New York: Viking, 1999. 32 p.

Full- and double-page paintings add to this memoir of Maria Tallchief's childhood in Oklahoma and California. She tells of her innate love of music and dance, of studying piano and ballet, and of how, when at the age of twelve she had to choose between them, she decided to pursue ballet because it embraced music and dance. Pre-K, Primary; Nonfiction

Tobias, Tobi. *Maria Tallchief*. Illustrated by Michael Hampshire. New York: Thomas Y. Crowell Company, 1970. 40 p. (A Crowell Biography)

This illustrated biography of Maria Tallchief touches on her dance performances as a five-year-old, her early ballet training, and her work as a ballerina for George Balanchine. Primary; Nonficton

Tallchief, Marjorie Louise (born Marjorie Louise Tall Chief) (1927-   ) United States
Osage/Scottish-Irish-American

Allen, Paula Gunn, and Patricia Clark Smith. *As Long as the Rivers Flow: The Stories of Nine Native Americans*. New York: Scholastic Press, 1996. 336 p.

Marjorie Tallchief grew up performing with her older sister Maria when they were very young and, like her sister, studied under the ballerina Bronislawa Nijinska. The chapter on Maria Tallchief tells of Marjorie's dancing with the Los Angeles Light Opera Company, the American Ballet Theater,

and European dance companies.
Intermediate, Older; Nonfiction

Tanner, John (1778 or 1779-1846?) United States
European-American, by Ottawa and Ojibway

Dickinson, Alice. *Taken by the Indians: True Tales of Captivity*. New York: Franklin Watts, 1976. 144 p.

A chapter on John Tanner, which is based on his narrative, relates how he was kidnapped at the age of ten from his home situated where the Great Miami River meets the Ohio River. He was taken somewhere past Detroit to become the son of an Indian woman whose son had died. After about two years he was sold to an Ottawa woman whose husband was an Ojibwa. Becoming a hunter and beaver trapper, Tanner spent most of his life in the area of the Great Lakes and the Canadian Assiniboine and Red Rivers. A man with a sometimes violent temper, he returned for a while to his siblings, but found it difficult to fit in anywhere.
Older; Nonfiction

Te Ata (born Mary Frances Thompson) (1895 or 1897-1995) United States
Chickasaw/European-American and Osage

Avery, Susan, and Linda Skinner. *Extraordinary American Indians*. Chicago: Children's Press, 1992. 272 p.

The section on Te Ata relates that she learned about her Native American heritage from her parents, graduated from the Oklahoma College for Women, and attended Carnegie Institute of Technology's Theater School. She became renowned as a Chickasaw storyteller. Incorporating dance, song, and drama, Te Ata interpreted Native American folklore for audiences in both the United States and Europe.
Older; Nonfiction

Thomas, Clarence (1948-   ) United States
African-American, to European-American

Collins, David R. *Clarence Thomas: Fighter with Words*. Illustrated by Rosalie M. Shepherd. Gretna, La.: Pelican Publishing Company, 2003. 32 p.

Illustrated with full-and double-page paintings, this picture book traces Clarence Thomas's life from the poverty of Pin Point, Georgia, to his confirmation as Associate Justice of the United States Supreme Court.
Primary; Nonfiction

Deegan, Paul J. *Clarence Thomas*. Edina, Minn.: Abdo & Daughters, 1992. 40 p. (United States Supreme Court Library)

This biography of Clarence Thomas tells how, born a Baptist, he went to live at age seven with his Catholic grandfather and attended Catholic schools, including Immaculate Conception Seminary

and Holy Cross College. It discusses his opposition to affirmative action as chairman of the Equal Employment Opportunity Commission, his appointments by President George H. W. Bush to the Washington, D.C. appellate court and to the Supreme Court, his Senate confirmation hearings, the sexual harassment allegation of Anita Hill, and his marriage to Virginia Lamp, who is white. Emphasizing Thomas's remarkable achievements, the book includes photographs, a glossary, and an index.
Intermediate, Older; Nonfiction

Halliburton, Warren J. *Clarence Thomas: Supreme Court Justice*. Hillside, N.J.: Enslow Publishers, 1993. 104 p. (People To Know)
   Chapters on the workings of the Supreme Court and the racial history of Savannah, where Clarence Thomas spent much of his childhood, add to the text of this biography, which also includes photographs, a chronology, a reading list, and an index.
Older; Nonfiction

Macht, Norman. *Clarence Thomas*. Philadelphia: Chelsea House Publishers, 1995. 120 p. (Black Americans of Achievement)
   This comprehensive biography of Clarence Thomas emphasizes the roles which his grandfather and his educational experiences played in shaping his conservative views. It presents his early career, his Supreme Court confirmation ordeal, and his work as an associate justice. Photographs, a chronology, a reading list, and an index complete the book.
Older; Nonfiction

Thompson, Beverly Yuen (19??-   ) United States
European-American/Chinese

Haugen, David M., editor. *Interracial Relationships*. Farmington Hills, Mich.: Thomson, 2006. 104 p. (At Issue)
   In one of this book's articles, author Beverly Yuen Thompson tells of her resistance, even as a two-year-old, to speaking Chinese, of her parents' interracial marriage, of her encounters with racism, and of the benefits of her learning and writing about mixed race issues.
Older: Nonfiction

Thorpe, James (Jim) Francis (also Wa-tho-huk, Bright Path) (1888-1953) United States
Sac and Fox and Irish-American/Potawatomi, Kickapoo, and French Canadian-American, to European-American and Cherokee

Allen, Paula Gunn, and Patricia Clark Smith. *As Long as the Rivers Flow: The Stories of Nine Native Americans*. New York: Scholastic Press, 1996. 336 p.
   The biographical chapter on Jim Thorpe covers the death of his twin brother and his relationship with his father; Indian schools he attended and often left, including Carlisle Indian Industrial School where he become a track and football star; his baseball playing; the gold medals he won in the pentathlon

and decathlon at the 1912 Olympics; the stripping of his medals; and his later life.
Intermediate, Older; Nonfiction

Avery, Susan, and Linda Skinner. *Extraordinary American Indians*. Chicago: Children's Press, 1992. 272 p.
     Illustrated with photographs, a section on Jim Thorpe tells of his life and accomplishments.
Older; Nonfiction

Bernotas, Bob. *Jim Thorpe: Sac and Fox Athlete*. Philadelphia: Chelsea House Publishers, 1992. 112 p. (North American Indians of Achievement)
     This comprehensive biography of Jim Thorpe includes photographs, a chronology, a reading list, and an index.
Older; Nonfiction

Brown, Don. *Bright Path: Young Jim Thorpe*. New Milford, Conn.: Roaring Brook Press, 2006. 40 p.
     Large paintings add to this presentation of Jim Thorpe's life through his 1912 winning of the Olympic gold medals in the pentathlon and the decathlon. A detailed biographical account and a bibliographic note are appended.
Pre-K, Primary; Nonfiction

Bruchac, Joseph. *Jim Thorpe: Original All-American*. New York: Dial Books, 2006. 288 p.
     Written in the form of an autobiography, this novel is based, to the best of the author's research, on Jim Thorpe's actual experiences. It covers the years from his attending the Sac and Fox Indian Agency School through his years at Carlisle Indian Industrial School, which he left after being stripped of his Olympic medals because he had been paid to play baseball. The book concentrates on Thorpe's time at Carlisle. It provides detailed coverage of the football games in which he played and tells of his marriage to Iva Margaret Miller. An author's note provides information on Thorpe's later life and the lives of some of his teammates.
Older; Fiction

Bruchac, Joseph. *Jim Thorpe's Bright Path*. Illustrated by S. D. Nelson. New York: Lee & Low Books, 2004. 40 p.
     Double-page paintings provide the background for this picture book's story of Jim Thorpe (Bright Path). It covers his childhood and youth: his time at home with his twin brother Charlie, Charlie's death when they were at an Indian Agency boarding school, his time at Haskell Institute, and the day he showed Pop Warner at Carlisle Indian Industrial School that he could indeed play football. An author's note and a chronology continue the story of Thorpe's amazing athletic accomplishments.
Primary, Intermediate; Nonfiction

Lipsyte, Robert. *Jim Thorpe: 20th Century Jock*. New York: HarperCollins Publishers, 1993. 112 p.
     This book places the story of Jim Thorpe's life within the context of the prevailing attitudes toward Indians and emphasizes his football and track experiences under Glenn "Pop" Warner at

Carlisle Indian Industrial School. It is illustrated with photographs.
Intermediate, Older; Nonfiction

Rappaport, Doreen. *We Are the Many: A Picture Book of American Indians*. Illustrated by Cornelius Van Wright and Ying-Hwa Hu. New York: HarperCollins Publishers, 2002. 32 p.
A brief description of Jim Thorpe's Olympic experiences is accompanied by a painting of his crossing the finish line in the pentathlon's 1,500 meter race.
Primary, Intermediate; Nonfiction

Rivinus, Edward F. *Jim Thorpe*. Illustrated by Bob Masheris. Milwaukee: Raintree Publishers, 1990. (American Indian Stories)
This picture book biography of Jim Thorpe focuses on his athletic feats as a college and professional football player, a semi-pro and professional baseball player, and a double gold medal winner at the 1912 Olympics.
Primary, Intermediate; Nonficton

Schilling, Vincent. *Native Athletes in Action!* Summertown, Tenn.: 7th Generation, 2007. 128 p. (Native Trailblazers)
Interesting facts about Jim Thorpe are bolded in the text of this book's biographical chapter on the great athlete. Photographs are included.
Intermediate, Older; Nonfiction

Uschan, Michael V. *Male Olympic Champions*. San Diego: Lucent Books, 2000. 128 p.
The extensive use of statistics and quotations distinguish this book's chapter on Jim Thorpe. Its biographical account, illustrated with photographs, includes details about his life after the 1912 Olympics.
Intermediate, Older; Nonfiction

Tibbles, Susette LaFlesche (also Inshtatheumba, Bright Eyes) (1854-1903) United States
French-American and Omaha or Ponca/European-American, Omaha?, Oto?, and Iowa, to European-American

Avery, Susan, and Linda Skinner. *Extraordinary American Indians*. Chicago: Children's Press, 1992. 272 p.
As stated in a section on siblings Francis LaFlesche, Susan LaFlesche Picotte, and Susette LaFlesche Tibbles, their father was Ponca and French in his ancestry although he became an Omaha chief. Although raised on the Omaha reservation, Susette became concerned about the suffering of the Ponca, when they were forced to move from Nebraska to Indian Territory, and she worked for the release of an imprisoned group of Ponca who had tried to return to Nebraska. Susette then became a public lecturer, going on tours to promote reform of government Indian policies. She was also a writer and an illustrator.
Older; Nonfiction

Ketchum, Liza. *Into a New Country: Eight Remarkable Women of the West*. Boston: Little, Brown and Company, 2000. 144 p.

The chapter on Susette LaFlesche Tibbles relates how she lived during a time of crisis for the Omaha when the buffalo on which they depended were being destroyed. Susette was raised first in the traditional tribal way and then, because of her father's views, in the way of the whites. After attending a Presbyterian mission school and the Elizabeth Institute for Young Ladies in New Jersey, she returned to her reservation where she became a teacher. Upset by the plight of the Ponca who had been sent to Indian Territory, Susette joined their chief, Standing Bear, on an eastern tour where they lectured for Indian rights. As a writer, speaker, and illustrator, she continued to educate whites on the Omaha's life and plight.
Intermediate, Older; Nonfiction

Tinker, Clarence Leonard (1887-1942) United States
European-American, Acadian-French-American, and Osage/German-English-American

Avery, Susan, and Linda Skinner. *Extraordinary American Indians*. Chicago: Children's Press, 1992. 272 p.

Although only one-eighth Osage, Major General Clarence L. Tinker was the son of the publisher of an Osage newspaper and attended an Osage school and the Haskell Institute for Indians. As related in one of the book's sections, he became a military pilot and rose to the rank of major general in the U. S. Army Air Corps. Tinker was responsible for reorganizing the Air Corps in Hawaii following its decimation at Pearl Harbor and for preparing it for the Battle of Midway. Dying during that victorious battle, he was posthumously awarded the Distinguished Service Medal.
Older; Nonfiction

Tsang, Lori (19??-   ) United States
Chinese-American/Chinese-Jamaican

O'Hearn, Claudine Chiawei, editor. *Half and Half: Writers on Growing Up Biracial and Bicultural*. New York: Pantheon Books, 1998. 288 p.

In an essay by the poet Lori Tsang, she writes of her family: of her father who chose to remain in the United States and her aunt who returned to China, of the Chinese-Jamaican side of her family, and of being Asian-American.
Older; Nonfiction

Turner, Tina (born Anna Mae Bullock) (1939-   ) United States
African-American/African-American, Cherokee, and Navajo, to African-American

Busnar, Gene. *The Picture Life of Tina Turner*. New York: Franklin Watts, 1987. 64 p.

This biography of Tina Turner describes her childhood and highlights her career. It tells of Ike and Tina Turner's performances, recordings, and marriage; of Tina's breaking up their relationship in 1976; of her taking the next eight years to pay off their tour debts; and of her emerging as a star in her

own right in 1984. The book contains photographs, an index, and listings both of Ike and Tina Turner albums and singles and of Tina Turner's albums, singles, videos, and films.
Intermediate, Older; Nonfiction

Hasday, Judy L. *Tina Turner: Entertainer*. Philadelphia: Chelsea House Publishers, 1999. 104 p. (Black Americans of Achievement)
Highlighting Tina Turner's winning of three Grammy Awards in 1985, this comprehensive biography includes photographs, a chronology, a bibliography, a discography, and an index. It provides a detailed account of Tina Turner's childhood spent shuttling among her parents and relatives; her meeting Ike Turner at age sixteen; her performances with the Kings of Rhythm and the Ike and Tina Turner Revue; the years of abuse she suffered before leaving Ike; her acceptance of Nichiren Shoshu Buddhism; and her career successes during the 1980s and 1990s.
Older; Nonfiction

Umubyeyi, Jeanne d'Arc (1986-   ) Rwanda
Tutsi-Rwandan, by German

Jansen, Hanna. *Over a Thousand Hills I Walk with You*. Translated from German by Elizabeth D. Crawford. Minneapolis: Carolrhoda Books, 2006. 344 p.
When she was eight-years-old, Jeanne d'Arc Umubyeyi's parents, brother, and sister were murdered by Hutus in the 1994 genocide in Rwanda. The only survivor in her Tutsi family, Jeanne was brought to Germany and became part of the author's family when she was ten. This novel by her adoptive mother is based on Jeanne's experiences from the age of six until she remembered that she had an aunt in Germany who might get her out of Rwanda. It tells in detail of Jeanne's secure life with her well-off teacher parents that ended abruptly with the genocide when she witnessed the killing of her mother and brother, sought to survive in the midst of a continuing nightmare, and, after she was safe with the Rebels, withdrew into herself and stopped speaking. The author's comments precede each chapter. A timeline and glossary are appended.
Older; Fiction

Walker, Alice Malsenior (1944-   ) United States
African-American/African-American and Cherokee, to European-American Jewish

Altman, Susan. *Extraordinary African-Americans: From Colonial to Contemporary Times*. Rev. ed. New York: Children's Press, 2001. 288 p. (Extraordinary People)
A biographical sketch of Alice Walker notes a number of the books she has written, including the award-winning *The Color Purple*.
Intermediate, Older; Nonfiction

Gentry, Tony. *Alice Walker: Author*. Philadelphia: Chelsea House Publishers, 1998. 112 p. (Black Americans of Achievement)
This comprehensive biography of Alice Walker tells of the accident that destroyed the vision in her

right eye, the impact that watching Martin Luther King, Jr. on television had on her activism in the civil rights movement, her college years, her promotion of the previously unrecognized works of women and African-American writers, her family life, her writing, the acclaim she received from the book and later the movie *The Color Purple*, and her promotion of the rights of all living things. Photographs, a list of Walker's books, a chronology, a reading list, and an index are included.
Older; Nonfiction

Kramer, Barbara. *Alice Walker: Author of The Color Purple*. Berkeley Heights, N.J.: Enslow Publishers, 1995. 128 p. (People to Know)
Extensive discussion of Alice Walker's works—her novels, stories, essays, and poems—is included in this biography, which notes her interest in Native American culture. The book points out that Walker is an optimist, believing in one's ability to change, and that her writing tackles thought-provoking issues. It contains photographs, a chronology, chapter notes, a reading list, and an index.
Older; Nonfiction

Kranz, Rachel C. *The Biographical Dictionary of Black Americans*. New York: Facts on File, 1992. 192 p.
A biographical account of Alice Walker provides an overview of her works and notes the controversial features of her best-known book, *The Color Purple*.
Intermediate, Older; Nonfiction

Lazo, Caroline. *Alice Walker: Freedom Writer*. Minneapolis: Lerner Publications Company, 2000. 112 p.
Photographs, source notes, a bibliography, and an index add to this detailed biography of Alice Walker, which highlights the love of flowers and their symbolism which has permeated her life and her writings and also her continued activism on behalf of women of color.
Older; Nonfiction

Masoff, Joy. *The African American Story: The Events That Shaped Our Nation . . . and the People Who Changed Our Lives*. Waccabuc, N.Y.: Five Ponds Press, 2007. 96 p.
This history of African-Americans includes a paragraph about and a picture of Alice Walker.
Older; Nonfiction

Rennert, Richard, ed. *Female Writers*. Philadelphia: Chelsea House Publishers, 1994. 64 p. (Profiles of Great Black Americans)
A chapter on Alice Walker chronicles her life, her writings, and her social activism.
Older; Nonfiction

Wilkinson, Brenda. *African American Women Writers*. New York: John Wiley & Sons, 2000. 176 p. (Black Stars)
This book's profile of Alice Walker emphasizes the influence of her native South on her writing and her opposition to injustice, especially towards women. The text lists the awards she has won as

well as the books she has written.
Older; Nonfiction

Walker, Maggie Dalena (Lena) Mitchell (1864, 1865, or 1867-1934) United States
Irish/African-American, to African-American

Branch, Muriel Miller, and Dorothy Marie Rice. *Pennies to Dollars: The Story of Maggie Lena Walker*. North Haven, Conn.: Linnet Books, 1997. 112 p. (Revised and rewritten edition of Branch and Rice's *A Biography of Maggie Lena Walker*, 1984)
   This biography of Maggie Lena Walker details her many contributions to the African-American residents of her native Richmond, Virginia. Joining the African-American fraternal Independent Order of the Sons and Daughters of St. Luke at the age of fourteen, she became the driving force behind the establishment of its juvenile branch which she served as grand deputy matron. In 1899 Walker became grand secretary of the fraternal order and in that capacity expanded it into a business enterprise, which included a newspaper, clothing store, educational loan fund, and insurance business. In 1903 she founded and then served as president of the St. Luke Penny Savings Bank, which after a merger continued to exist as the Consolidated Bank and Trust Company. The book includes photographs and an index.
Older; Nonfiction

Masoff, Joy. *The African American Story: The Events That Shaped Our Nation . . . and the People Who Changed Our Lives*. Waccabuc, N.Y.: Five Ponds Press, 2007. 96 p.
   This history of African-Americans includes a paragraph about and a picture of Maggie Lena Walker.
Older; Nonfiction

Ransom, Candice. *Maggie L. Walker: Pioneering Banker and Community Leader*. Minneapolis: Twenty-First Century Books, 2009. 112 p.
   This comprehensive biography of Maggie L. Walker describes her childhood, her many accomplishments, the impact of her son's shooting of her husband, and her work to promote the business careers of black women. Photographs, a timeline, source notes, a bibliography, a resource list, and an index complete the book.
Intermediate, Older; Nonfiction

Wamba, Philippe (1971-2002) United States
Zairian (now Democratic Republic of the Congo)/African-American

O'Hearn, Claudine Chiawei, editor. *Half and Half: Writers on Growing Up Biracial and Bicultural*. New York: Pantheon Books, 1998. 288 p.
   Philippe Wamba writes about spending the first eight years of his life in the United States, where most of his playmates were white and he enjoyed the food, music, and family gatherings of the separate worlds of his Zairian father and his African-American mother. For the next eight years he lived

in Tanzania where he experienced another culture and another language and then returned for schooling in the United States, where he fit in with neither the African nor African-American students. However, he now appreciates his freedom to be of different homes and countries.
Older; Nonfiction

Washakie (c. 1802-1900) United States
Flathead/Shoshone

Farnsworth, Frances Joyce. *Winged Moccasins: the Story of Sacajawea*. Illustrated by Lorence F. Bjorklund. Englewood Cliffs, N.J.: Responsive Environments Corp., 1954. 190 p.
This story tells of Shoshone Chief Washakie, who sought and secured the creation of the Shoshone Indian Reservation in Wyoming.
Intermediate, Older; Fiction

Washington, Booker Taliaferro (1856-1915) United States
European-American/African-American, to African-American and Shawnee, to African-European-American, to African-Irish-American

Altman, Susan. *Extraordinary African-Americans: From Colonial to Contemporary Times*. Rev. ed. New York: Children's Press, 2001. 288 p. (Extraordinary People)
This book's brief biography of Booker T. Washington emphasizes his role as an educator and notes his advocacy of the economic advancement of African-Americans.
Intermediate, Older; Nonfiction

Amper, Thomas. *Booker T. Washington*. Illustrated by Jeni Reeves. Minneapolis: Carolrhoda Books, 1998. 48 p. (Carolrhoda On My Own Books)
This chapter book tells of Booker T. Washington's childhood from the age of seven when he wanted to go to school to the age of sixteen when he journeyed 500 miles to Hampton Institute where, thanks to the meticulousness he had learned earlier as a servant, he was admitted as a student. The book includes color illustrations, an afterword, and a chronology.
Pre-K, Primary; Nonfiction

Bradby, Marie. *More Than Anything Else*. Illustrated by Chris K. Soentpiet. New York: Orchard Books, 1995. 32 p.
As a nine-year-old shoveling salt at a saltworks, Booker T. Washington yearns to learn to read. His mother gives him an alphabet book which he puzzles over, but it is not until he finds the man who can read a newspaper that he learns the sounds of the letters and sees his name, Booker, written on the ground.
Pre-K, Primary; Nonfiction

Braun, Eric. *Booker T. Washington: Great American Educator*. Illustrated by Cynthia Martin. Mankato: Minn.: Capstone Press, 2006. 32 p. (Graphic Library, Graphic Biographies)

This biography of Booker T. Washington is presented in a graphic novel format and includes fictionalized dialogue. It presents an overview of Washington's life, including the opposition from many African-Americans which he faced during his later years and his secret support of equal rights. Additional biographical facts, a list of internet sites, a glossary, a reading list, a bibliography, and an index are included.
Primary, Intermediate; Fiction

Cox, Clinton. *African American Teachers*. New York: John Wiley & Sons, 2000. 176 p. (Black Stars)
A biographical summary in this book emphasizes Booker T. Washington's work as an educator and discusses the contradictions between the view he expressed in his Atlanta Compromise speech that blacks should accept segregation and his less-publicized efforts to end it.
Older; Nonfiction

Frost, Helen. *Let's Meet Booker T. Washington*. Philadelphia: Chelsea Clubhouse, 2004. 32 p. (Let's Meet Biographies)
Photographs, highlighted words which are defined in a glossary, a chronology, a section on Tuskegee University, a resource list, and an index are features of this introductory biography of Booker T. Washington.
Primary; Nonfiction

Garrison, Mary. *Slaves Who Dared: The Stories of Ten African-American Heroes*. Shippensburg, Pa.: White Mane Kids, 2002. 152 p.
The son of an unknown white father and a slave mother, Booker T. Washington and his family were freed by the Emancipation Proclamation when he was a boy. This book's account relates how, despite having to work in a salt furnace and a coal mine, he managed to take lessons from a schoolteacher. At age sixteen he traveled to Hampton Institute where, earning tuition money as a janitor, he graduated with honors. Then, at the age of twenty-five he became principal of a new school for blacks which he developed into the renowned Tuskegee Institute.
Intermediate, Older; Nonfiction

Gleiter, Jan, and Kathleen Thompson. *Booker T. Washington*. Illustrated by Rick Whipple. Milwaukee: Raintree Children's Books, 1988. 32 p.
Colored pictures illustrate this biography of Booker T. Washington, which covers his childhood, his attendance at Hampton Institute, and his success at Tuskegee Institute.
Primary; Nonfiction

Gosda, Randy T. *Booker T. Washington*. Edina, Minn.: Buddy Books, 2002. 32 p.
Numerous captioned photographs, including those of his childhood home, add to this biography of Booker T. Washington. A chronology, a glossary, information on web sites, and an index are appended.
Pre-K, Primary; Nonfiction

Kranz, Rachel C. *The Biographical Dictionary of Black Americans*. New York: Facts on File, 1992. 192 p.

This account of Booker T. Washington emphasizes the political influence he had after founding Tuskegee Institute and the controversial view he held stressing the importance of black's economic development through industrial education as opposed to their advancement through promoting social and political equality.

Intermediate, Older; Nonfiction

Masoff, Joy. *The African American Story: The Events That Shaped Our Nation . . . and the People Who Changed Our Lives*. Waccabuc, N.Y.: Five Ponds Press, 2007. 96 p.

This history of African-Americans includes a paragraph about and a picture of Booker T. Washington.

Older; Nonfiction

McDaniel, Melissa. *W. E. B. Du Bois: Scholar and Civil Rights Activist*. New York: Franklin Watts, 1999. 96 p. (A Book Report Biography)

W. E. B. Du Bois' educational achievements; his scholarly studies of African-Americans, including his book *The Philadelphia Negro*; his disputes with Booker T. Washington, Marcus Garvey, and Walter Francis White; his friendship with John Hope; his advocacy of world peace; and his renouncing of his United States citizenship are covered in this biography. It includes photographs, a chronology, a source note, resource listings, and an index.

Older; Nonfiction

McKissack. Patricia. *Run Away Home*. New York: Scholastic Press, 1997. 176 p.

In 1888 Sky, a fifteen-year-old Chiricahua Apache boy, escapes from a train of Apache prisoners and hides on the farm of twelve-year-old Sarah Jane Crossman, her African-American father, and her mother, who is of African-Scottish-Irish and Seminole heritage. George Wrattan, an Army scout and interpreter, allows the Crossmans to keep Sky with them until he recovers from his swamp fever. In the meantime boll weevils destroy the family's cotton crop, night riders come to their farm, and Sarah Jane's father, who is skilled as a carpenter, gets an order from Booker T. Washington to build desks for nearby Tuskegee Institute. Sky becomes healthy, but Wrattan, whose wife is Apache, gives permission for him to remain on the farm.

Intermediate, Older; Fiction

McKissack, Patricia, and Frederick McKissack. *Booker T. Washington: Leader and Educator*. Illustrated by Michael Bryant. Springfield, N.J.: Enslow Publishers, 1992. 32 p. (Great African Americans Series)

This biography of Booker T. Washington for younger children discusses his work at Tuskegee Institute and points out that he founded the National Negro Business League and wrote an autobiography.

Primary; Nonfiction

McLoone, Margo. *Booker T. Washington: A Photo-Illustrated Biography*. Mankato, Minn.: Bridgestone Books, 1997. 24 p.

Booker T. Washington's hiring of George Washington Carver as a Tuskegee Institute teacher, his family, and his Atlanta Compromise speech are mentioned in this introductory biography. It includes three quotations from Washington, a chronology, a glossary, a resource list, and an index.
Primary; Nonfiction

Neyland, James. *Booker T. Washington: Educator*. Los Angeles: Melrose Square Publishing Company, 1992. 192 p. (Black Americans Series)

Illustrated with drawings and photographs, this biography provides an extensive coverage of Booker T. Washington's childhood, including the possible identity of his father; of his successes at Hampton Institute and Tuskegee Institute; of his siblings, wives, and children; of his relationships with United States presidents; of his increasingly controversial views; and of his later years. It contains an index.
Older; Nonfiction

Nicholson, Lois P. *Booker T. Washington*. New York: Chelsea Juniors, 1997. 88 p. (Junior World Biographies, A Junior Black Americans of Achievement Book)

This biography of Booker T. Washington reports that, in contrast to many other slave owners, the master of the farm where he lived as a young child was not cruel, that at Hampton Institute he taught Kiowa and Cheyenne Indians as well as blacks, that most of the buildings at Tuskegee were built by students, and that later a number of white philanthropists contributed to Tuskegee. The book stresses the priority which Washington placed on learning a trade rather than academics and on accommodating with whites rather than being a racial activist. Photographs, a reading list, a chronology, a glossary, and an index are included in the book.
Intermediate; Nonfiction

Potter, Joan, and Constance Claytor. *African Americans Who Were First*. New York: Cobblehill Books, 1997. 128 p.

A brief summary of Booker T. Washington's life points out that he was the first African-American to be pictured on a postage stamp.
Intermediate, Older; Nonfiction

Roberts, Jack L. *Booker T. Washington: Educator and Leader*. Brookfield, Conn.: The Millbrook Press, 1995. 32 p. (Gateway Civil Rights)

Photographs illustrate this biography of Booker T. Washington, which shows how he came to succeed Frederick Douglass as the spokesman for African-Americans and later in his life, because of his "separate but equal" racial views, lost this role to W. E. B. Du Bois. The book includes inserts on Du Bois and George Washington Carver as well as a chronology, a reading list, and an index.
Primary, Intermediate; Nonfiction

Schroeder, Alan. *Booker T. Washington: Educator*. Philadelphia: Chelsea House Publishers, 1992. 144 p. (Black Americans of Achievement)

A discussion of Booker T. Washington's 1895 speech in Atlanta, Georgia, is highlighted in this comprehensive biography of the African-American educator. It includes coverage of the effect that General Samuel Chapman Armstrong, head of Hampton Institute, had on Washington's educational approach; extensive discussion of his development of Tuskegee Institute; the high regard he had attained by 1901 as evidenced by his dinner with President Theodore Roosevelt in the White House; the growing opposition to his accommodationist policies within the black community; his lecturing and fundraising; and the demanding work schedule which he followed throughout his adult life. The book includes photographs, a chronology, a reading list, and an index.
Older; Nonfiction

Troy, Don. *Booker T. Washington*. Chanhassen, Minn.: The Child's World, 1999. 40 p.

Numerous photographs are included in this biography of Booker T. Washington, which surveys his life and critiques his Atlanta Compromise. A chronology, a glossary, a resource list, and an index are appended.
Intermediate; Nonfiction

Washington, Fannie Norton Smith (1858-1884) United States
African-American and Shawnee/African-American, to African-European-American

Neyland, James. *Booker T. Washington: Educator*. Los Angeles: Melrose Square Publishing Company, 1992. 192 p. (Black Americans Series)

This Booker T. Washington biography reports that Fannie Norton Smith Washington, his childhood friend and first wife, graduated from Hampton Institute, worked on developing the domestic services department at Tuskegee Institute, gave birth to their daughter Portia, and died less than two years after their marriage.
Older; Nonfiction

Washington, Margaret James Murray (1865-1925) United States
Irish/African-American, to African-European-American

Neyland, James. *Booker T. Washington: Educator*. Los Angeles: Melrose Square Publishing Company, 1992. 192 p. (Black Americans Series)

According to this biography of Booker T. Washington, Margaret James Murray Washington was a teacher and principal at Tuskegee Institute, became his third wife in 1892, and accompanied him on the European trip where they had tea with Queen Victoria and Susan B. Anthony.
Older; Nonfiction

Washington, Olivia A. Davidson (1854-1889) United States
African-American and European-American, to African-European-American

Neyland, James. *Booker T. Washington: Educator*. Los Angeles: Melrose Square Publishing Company, 1992. 192 p. (Black Americans Series)

This biography of Booker T. Washington tells of the valuable work which Olivia A. Davidson Washington performed in the early years of Tuskegee Institute, of her 1886 marriage to Washington, of the birth of their two sons, and of her death in 1899.
Older; Nonfiction

Watie, Stand (1806-1871) United States
Cherokee/European-American and Cherokee

Nash, Gary B. *Forbidden Love: The Secret History of Mixed-Race America*. Illustrated by author. New York: Henry Holt and Company, 1999. 224 p.

This book points out that Stand Watie, a Cherokee chief, became a Confederate general leading Indian soldiers during the Civil War.
Older; Nonfiction

Weatherford, William (also Red Eagle) (1781-1824) United States
Scottish/Creek and other

Gregson, Susan R. *Sam Houston: Texas Hero*. Minneapolis: Compass Point Books, 2006. 112 p. (Signature Lives)

This book reports that when Andrew Jackson's American forces defeated the Creek Red Sticks at Horseshoe Bend, Alabama, their leader Chief Red Eagle was not present. After the battle he secured the release of the captured Creek women and children.
Older; Nonfiction

Welsh, Zoë (1968-   ) England
Jamaican/English

Alderman, Bruce, editor. *Interracial Relationships*. Farmington Hills, Mich.: Greenhaven Press, 2007. 112 p. (Social Issues Firsthand)

In this narrative reproduced from *People in Harmony*, television producer Zoë Welsh, who was raised by her English mother and grandmother, describes how her trip to Jamaica as a thirty-six-year-old changed her life. No longer confused as to who she is, she feels part of a new extended family and a new land—and is happy to be her mixed race self.
Older; Nonfiction

West, W. Richard, Jr. (1943-   ) United States
Cheyenne/European-American

Avery, Susan, and Linda Skinner. *Extraordinary American Indians*. Chicago: Children's Press, 1992. 272 p.

A section on W. Richard West, Jr. and his father, a famous Cheyenne artist, tells how the younger West graduated from Stanford University School of Law and represented Native American groups in his law practice. He then, as its director, became responsible for establishing the Smithsonian Institution's National Museum of the American Indian.
Older; Nonfiction

White, George Henry (1852-1918) United States
African-Irish-American and Native American

Katz, William Loren, and Paula A. Franklin. *Proudly Red and Black: Stories of African and Native Americans*. New York: Atheneum, 1993. 96 p.

A graduate of Howard University and a lawyer, George Henry White served in the North Carolina House of Representatives and Senate before being elected to the United States Congress. Despite the increasing power of racist Southern politicians and the extension of segregation, he was a spokesman for African-Americans and even introduced anti-lynching legislation.
Intermediate, Older; Nonfiction

White, Walter Francis (1893-1955) United States
European-American and African-American, to African-American, to European-American

Becker, John T., and Stanli K. Becker, eds. *All Blood Is Red . . . All Shadows Are Dark!* Illustrated by J. Howard Noel. Cleveland: Seven Shadows Press, 1984. 168 p.

This books tells of Walter Francis White, who, although he was blond, blue-eyed, and fair-skinned and only a small part African-American, identified himself as an African-American. He served as executive secretary of the NAACP (National Association for the Advancement of Colored People) in the 1930s and 1940s and wrote an autobiography, *A Man Called White*, which attacked the belief that there are separate races.
Intermediate, Older; Nonfiction

Fraser, Jane. *Walter White: Civil Rights Leader*. Philadelphia: Chelsea House Publishers, 1991. 112 p. (Black Americans of Achievement)

This detailed biography of Walter Francis White includes photographs, a chronology, a reading list, and an index. It describes his youth, but concentrates on his work and achievements as assistant secretary and then executive secretary of the NAACP. During his tenure there he worked tirelessly to end lynching, race riots, and discrimination against black military personnel. White also wrote two novels, an autobiography, and books on the history of lynching and the migration of blacks to the north.
Older; Nonfiction

Kranz, Rachel C. *The Biographical Dictionary of Black Americans*. New York: Facts on File, 1992. 192 p.

A biographical account of Walter Francis White tells of his accomplishments with the NAACP, his emphasis on using the courts to further black rights, his disagreements with W. E. B. Du Bois and

Ralphe Bunche, and his writings.
Intermediate, Older; Nonfiction

McDaniel, Melissa. *W. E. B. Du Bois: Scholar and Civil Rights Activist*. New York: Franklin Watts, 1999. 96 p. (A Book Report Biography)

W. E. B. Du Bois' educational achievements; his scholarly studies of African-Americans, including his book *The Philadelphia Negro*; his disputes with Booker T. Washington, Marcus Garvey, and Walter Francis White; his friendship with John Hope; his advocacy of world peace; and his renouncing of his United States citizenship are covered in this biography. It includes photographs, a chronology, a source note, resource listings, and an index.
Older; Nonfiction

Nash, Gary B. *Forbidden Love: The Secret History of Mixed-Race America*. New York: Henry Holt and Company, 1999. 224 p.

This book reports that there was much criticism when Walter White of the NAACP married Poppy Cannon, a white businesswoman and journalist.
Older; Nonfiction

Williams, Daniel Hale (1856-1931) United States
African-European-American and Native American, to African-European-American Jewish

Haber, Louis. *Black Pioneers of Science and Invention*. San Diego: Harcourt Brace & Company, 1992. 288 p. (An Odyssey Book)

This book's biographical chapter on Daniel Hale Williams details his medical career from his apprenticeship to a Janesville, Wisconsin physician through, among other accomplishments, his founding of the first American interracial hospital and his performing the first successful chest cavity surgery. It places his achievements within the context of the medical advances of his times and tells of the continued enmity of a doctor whose job application he had rejected and of his relationship with Booker T. Washington. A bibliography, photographs, and an index are included.
Older; Nonfiction

Hayden, Robert C. *Seven Black American Scientists*. Reading, Mass.: Addison Wesley, 1970. 176 p.

Daniel Hale Williams' 1893 sewing of a wound in a man's heart pericardium is described in detail in a chapter of this book, which also tells how Williams developed his surgical skills when working as a barber.
Older; Nonfiction

Kaye, Judith. *The Life of Daniel Hale Wiliams*. New York: Twenty-First Century Books, 1993. 80 p. (Pioneers in Health and Medicine)

This biography of Daniel Hale Williams covers in detail his childhood, his medical career, his surgeries, and the positive impact which he made on the careers of African-American physicians and nurses and on the care of African-American patients. The book includes photographs, a reading list,

and an index.
Older; Nonfiction

Meriwether, Louise. *The Heart Man: Dr. Daniel Hale Williams*. Illustrated by Floyd Sowell. Englewood Cliffs, N.J.: Prentice-Hall, 1972. 32 p.

Daniel Hale Williams is introduced in this illustrated biography, which includes three photographs of the surgeon.
Pre-K, Primary; Nonfiction

Patterson, Lillie. *Sure Hands, Strong Heart: The Life of Daniel Hale Williams*. Illustrated by David Scott Brown. Nashville: Abingdon, 1981. 160 p.

Accompanied by drawings and a list of selected readings, this fictionalized biography of Daniel Hale Williams provides extensive coverage of his life, including the the years after he left Freedmen's Hospital.
Older; Fiction

Potter, Joan, and Constance Claytor. *African Americans Who Were First*. New York: Cobblehill Books, 1997. 128 p.

A photograph of Daniel Hale Williams accompanies a page summary of the life of the doctor who performed the first successful open-heart surgery.
Intermediate, Older; Nonfiction

Sullivan, Otha Richard. *African American Inventors*. New York: John Wiley & Sons, 1998. 176 p. (Black Stars)

This biographical chapter on Daniel Hale Williams tells of the importance of his practicing antiseptic surgery. It includes a photograph and a text insert.
Older; Nonfiction

Yount, Lisa. *Black Scientists*. New York: Facts on File, 1991. 128 p. (American Profiles)

A chapter on Daniel Hale Williams relates how he graduated from Chicago Medical College, established the nation's first interracial hospital and first training school for black nurses (Chicago's Provident Hospital and Training School), was the chief surgeon at Washington, D.C.'s hospital for blacks (Freedmen's Hospital), worked with others to found the National Medical Association for black physicians, and was associate attending surgeon at Chicago's St. Luke's Hospital. The account describes Williams performing the first successful heart surgery and a difficult spleen operation. It includes photographs, a chronology, and a reading list.
Older; Nonfiction

Williams, Eunice (1696-1785) United States
English-American Puritan, by Canadian Mohawk and Catholic, to Canadian Mohawk

Nash, Gary B. *Forbidden Love: The Secret History of Mixed-Race America*. New York: Henry Holt and Company, 1999. 224 p.

As related in this book young Eunice Williams was kidnapped together with her family during the 1704 French and Indian raid on Deerfield, Massachusetts. She was the only family member to remain with the Mohawk in their Canadian village. Eunice converted to Catholicism and married a Mohawk. Although in future years the two of them visited her Deerfield family, they continued to live with the Mohawk and Eunice remained a Mohawk.
Older; Nonfiction

Williams, Mary Harris (c.1817 or 1819—?) United States
African-European-Native-West Indian/? and non-Quaker, by European-American Quaker

Rinaldi, Ann. *The Education of Mary: A Little Miss of Color, 1832*. New York: Jump at the Sun, 2000. 256 p.

Prudence Crandall's private boarding school in Canterbury, Connecticut, was converted into a school for African-Americans and Mary Harris was one of the students. Supported by William Lloyd Garrison, editor of *The Liberator*, it was opposed by citizens of Canterbury, who, with one exception, refused to sell goods to the school and some of whom engaged in violence against it. Prudence Crandall was even jailed. After Crandall's marriage, the school was closed. Placed within this historical context, this novel tells of Mary Harris, a confidante of Crandall's, who observes the tensions occurring among the students, with one faction favoring use of the school as a vehicle to support the abolitionists and to advance their vanity. Fearing what is to come, Mary struggles to determine what is right. In the end it is Mary who takes action to disband the school, which she no longer regards favorably. Further, it is Mary who comes to the rescue of a passenger (or passengers) on the Underground Railroad. The story also tells of Mary's sister, Celinda, who, passing as white, gets a job at a Lowell, Massachusetts cotton mill and tries to improve the terrible working conditions of the girls employed there.
Older; Fiction

Williams, William Carlos (1883-1963) United States
English Unitarian/Dutch-French-Spanish-Puerto Rican Jewish and Catholic, to German

Alegre, Cèsar. *Extraordinary Hispanic Americans*. New York: Children's Press, 2007. 288 p. (Extraordinary People)

A biographical chapter on the poet William Carlos Williams tells of his poems about typical Americans, his writing in a variety of genres, and his winning the Pulitzer prize.
Older; Nonfiction

Baldwin, Neil. *To All Gentleness: William Carlos Williams, The Doctor-Poet*. New York: Atheneum, 1984. 256 p.

This comprehensive biography of William Carlos Williams, for the oldest readers, provides detailed coverage of his medical career, the development of his poetry, and his personal life and feelings. It quotes extensively from his poems and stresses his frustrations in being both a doctor and a lover of poetry, his commitment to writing about his own locale, and the impact of his writer and artist

friends. The book includes photographs, source notes, a bibliography, a listing of quoted poems, and an index.
Older: Nonfiction

Berry, S. L. *William Carlos Williams*. Illustrated by Yan Nascimbene. Mankato, Minn.: Creative Education, 2002. 48 p. (Voices in Poetry)

Photograph-illustrated biographical text interspersed with painting-illustrated poems by William Carlos Williams present a portrait of the poet who was influenced by the voices of the patients he tended as their doctor. It tells of the impact of his friend Ezra Pound, of his lengthy poem "Paterson," and of his development of the poetic variable foot. A listing of Williams' selected works and an index complete the book.
Older; Fiction, Nonfiction

Bryant, Jen. *A River of Words: The Story of William Carlos Williams*. Illustrated by Melissa Sweet. Grand Rapids, Mich.: Eerdmans Books for Young Readers, 2008. 32 p.

This picture book biography of William Carlos Williams features collage illustrations; a parallel chronology of events in his life, world events, and poetry publication dates; and appended additional information on his life, a reading list, and a sampling of his poetry.
Primary, Intermediate; Nonfiction

Rodriguez, Robert, and Tamra Orr, contributing writers. *Great Hispanic-Americans*. Lincolnwood, Ill.: Publications International, 2005. 128 p.

As pointed out in one of this book's sections, William Carlos Williams was born in Rutherford, New Jersey, in a family speaking several languages, and he was sent to boarding schools in Europe. He pursued the dual careers of physician and poet. His poetry, often written in free verse, embodied American speech.
Older; Nonfiction

Wong, Janet S. (1962-   ) United States
Chinese/South Korean

Wong, Janet S. *A Suitcase of Seaweed and Other Poems*. Illustrated by author. New York: Margaret K. McElderry Books, 1996. 48 p.

Janet S. Wong's poetry is presented in three sections–Korean poems, Chinese poems, and American poems–and draws upon her childhood experiences as an American girl with a Chinese father and a Korean mother.
Intermediate, Older; Fiction

Woods, Tiger (born Eldrick Woods) (1975-   ) United States
African-Chinese-American, Native American Protestant/Chinese-Dutch-Thai Buddhist, to Swedish

Altman, Susan. *Extraordinary African-Americans: From Colonial to Contemporary Times*. Rev. ed. New York: Children's Press, 2001. 288 p. (Extraordinary People)

This book contains a biographical sketch of Tiger Woods that notes how his success has encouraged minority children to take up golf.
Intermediate, Older; Nonfiction

Boyd, Aaron. *Tiger Woods*. Greensboro, N.C.: Morgan Reynolds, 1997. 64 p.
This biography of Tiger Woods covers primarily his amateur career. It tells of his natural talent as a toddler and his winning his Optimist Junior World Championship age divisions six times, the U. S. Junior Amateur Championship three times, and the U. S. Amateur Championship three times. It describes the racial discrimination he faced, his parents' emphasis on education, his play on the Stanford University golf team, his turning professional, and his being the youngest golfer to win the Masters Tournament. The book contains black-and-white photographs, a glossary of golf terms, and an index.
Intermediate, Older; Nonfiction

Collins, David R. *Tiger Woods: Golf Superstar*. Illustrated by Larry Nolte. Gretna, La.: Pelican Publishing Company, 1999. 32 p.
Brightly colored illustrations are featured in this picture book which emphasizes Tiger Wood's childhood golfing experiences. It concludes with his win at the 1997 Masters Tournament.
Primary; Nonfiction

Collins, David R. *Tiger Woods, Golfing Champion*. Illustrated by Larry Nolte. Gretna, La.: Pelican Publishing Company, 1999. 104 p.
This detailed biography focuses on Tiger Woods' personal life as well as on his golf game and tournament playing. It covers his career through his winning the 1999 Buick Invitational. Illustrated with drawings of Woods, the book includes a history of golf, a glossary, a bibliography, and an index.
Intermediate, Older; Nonfiction

Cruz, Bárbara C. *Multiethnic Teens and Cultural Identity: A Hot Issue*. Berkeley Heights, N.J.: Enslow Publishers, 2001. 64 p.
A page on Tiger Woods tells of his identifying himself as Cabilinasian in recognition of his mixed ethnic heritage.
Older; Nonfiction

Dougherty, Terri. *Tiger Woods*. Edina, Minn.: ABDO Publishing Company, 1999. 32 p. (Jam Session)
A number of quotations are included in this brief biography, which concludes with Tiger Woods winning of the 1998 BellSouth Classic. The book contains color photographs, a profile, a chronology, a list of awards and honors, a glossary, and an index.
Intermediate; Nonfiction

Durbin, William. *Tiger Woods*. Philadelphia: Chelsea House Publishers, 1998. 64 p. (Golf Legends)
This book, which covers Tiger Woods' career through 1997, presents statistics comparing Woods with Nicklaus and Palmer. Black-and-white photographs, a reading list, a chronology, and an index

are also included.
Older; Nonfiction

Feinstein, Stephen. *Read about Tiger Woods*. Berkeley Heights, N.J.: Enslow Elementary, 2005. 24 p. (I Like Biographies!)
　　Pages of text and photographs alternate in this brief biography of Tiger Woods, which emphasizes his childhood golfing experiences. It includes a glossary, a timeline, a list of resources, and an index.
Pre-K, Primary; Nonfiction

Gutman, Bill. *Tiger Woods: A Biography*. New York: Pocket Books, 1997. 144 p. (An Archway Paperback)
　　This biography of Tiger Woods focuses on his family and his professional tournament play through the 1997 Masters. It tells of the five African-American PGA tour golfers who preceded him, discusses why his drives are so long, and contains a section of color photographs.
Intermediate, Older; Nonfiction

Kramer, S. A. *Tiger Woods: Golfing to Greatness*. New York: Random House, 1997. 128 p.
　　Detailed information about the tournaments in which Tiger Woods played is provided in this book, which also stresses his role as a man of color. It contains a section of color photographs.
Intermediate; Nonfiction

Lace, William W. *Tiger Woods: Star Golfer*. Berkeley Heights, N.J.: Enslow Publishers, 1999. 104 p. (Sports Reports)
　　Golf facts and black-and-white photographs are interspersed throughout the text of this detailed look at Tiger Woods' life and tournament play. The book includes tournament statistics through 1998, notes, addresses, and an index.
Intermediate, Older; Nonfiction

Masoff, Joy. *The African American Story: The Events That Shaped Our Nation . . . and the People Who Changed Our Lives*. Waccabuc, N.Y.: Five Ponds Press, 2007. 96 p.
　　This history of African-Americans includes a paragraph about and a picture of Tiger Woods.
Older; Nonfiction

Nash, Gary B. *Forbidden Love: The Secret History of Mixed-Race America*. Illustrated by author. New York: Henry Holt and Company, 1999. 224 p.
　　This book's profile of Tiger Woods stresses how he refuses to be identified by only one of his racial heritages.
Older; Nonfiction

Rambeck, Richard. *Tiger Woods*. Chanhassen, Minn.: Child's World, 1998. 24 p. (Sports Superstars Series)

A short biography of Tiger Woods, this book touches on several of his amateur wins and his 1996 play as a professional golfer. It includes full-page color photographs.
Intermediate; Nonfiction

Savage, Jeff. *Tiger Woods: King of the Course*. Minneapolis: Lerner Publications Company, 1998. 64 p.
Numerous color photographs show Tiger Woods as a golfer from the age of eleven months to adulthood. A list of career highlights, a glossary, a source list, and an index are also included in this biography.
Intermediate; Nonfiction

Sirimarco, Elizabeth. *Tiger Woods*. Mankato, Minn.: Capstone Books, 2001. 48 p. (Sports Heroes)
This book summarizes Tiger Woods' golf career through the 2000 Pebble Beach Pro-Am. It includes color photographs, a glossary, resources, a chronology, addresses, websites, and an index.
Intermediate; Nonfiction

Teague, Allison L. *Prince of the Fairway: The Tiger Woods Story*. Greensboro, N.C.: Avisson Press, 1997. 112 p. (Avisson Young Adult Series)
Notes, a detailed chronology, a bibliography, a glossary, and an index are featured in this biography, which includes discussion of the implications of Tiger Woods' success at such a young age and as a person of color. It provides information on his parents and on his play on the American team that won the Eisenhower Trophy and covers the many milestones of his career.
Older; Nonficton

Woodson, Lewis (1806-1878) United States
African-English-Welsh?-American/African-American

Katz, William Loren. *Black Pioneers: An Untold Story*. New York: Atheneum Books for Young Readers, 1999. 208 p.
As described in this book's section on the Woodson family, Lewis Woodson was the brother of Sarah Woodson Early, the son of Thomas Woodson, and probably the grandson of Thomas Jefferson and Sally Hemings. He was a Methodist minister, furthered the development of African-American schools and churches, and was a trustee of what became Wilberforce College.
Older; Nonfiction

Lanier, Shannon, and Jane Feldman. *Jefferson's Children: The Story of One American Family*. Photographs by Jane Feldman. Introduction by Lucian K. Truscott IV. Historical Essays by Annette Gordon-Reed and Beverley Gray. New York: Random House, 2000. 144 p.
This book features interviews of descendants of Thomas Jefferson, who speak of their family histories and their personal experiences. It includes a picture of Lewis Woodson, information on his father, Thomas Woodson, and an interview with Byron Woodson, one of Lewis's descendants.
Older; Nonfiction

Yung, Kim So (19??-   ) South Korea
South Korean, by European-American

Stanford, Eleanor, ed. *Interracial America: Opposing Viewpoints*. Farmington Hills, Mich.: Green-haven Press, 2006. 208 p. (Opposing Viewpoints)

In Stephanie Cho and Kim So Yung's opinion piece "Transracial Adoption Should be Discouraged," the authors describe how their negative experiences as Korean children adopted by whites caused them to found Transracial Abductees, an organization assisting those adoptees in assimilating into communities of color.

Older; Nonfiction

Selected References

Publications

Asian American Curriculum Project, Inc. *Asian American Books for All Ages: 2003 AACP Catalog.* San Mateo, CA: AACP, Inc., 2002. 62 p.

Book Links 8 (September 1998)—19 (June 2010).

The Horn Book Magazine 60 (February 1984)—86 (July/August 2010).

Hoxie, Frederick E., editor. *Encyclopedia of North American Indians.* Boston: Houghton Mifflin Company, 1996. 768 p.

Johansen, Bruce E., and Donald A. Grinde, Jr. *The Encyclopedia of Native American Biography: Six Hundred Life Stories of Important People, from Powhatan to Wilma Mankiller.* New York: Da Capo Press, 1998. 480 p.

Kranz, Rachel C. *The Biographical Dictionary of Black Americans.* New York: Facts on File, 1991. 192 p.

Nakazawa, Donna Jackson. *Does Anybody Else Look like Me? A Parent's Guide to Raising Multiracial Children.* Cambridge, MA: Perseus Publishing, 2003. 240 p.

Reynolds, Nancy Thalia. *Mixed Heritage in Young Adult Literature.* Lanham, MD: The Scarecrow Press, 2009. 272 p. (Scarecrow Studies in Young Adult Literature, No. 32)

School Library Journal 30 (January 1984)—44 (October 1988); 44 (December 1988)— 56 (July 2010).

Skipping Stones: A Multicultural Children's Magazine 10 (September-October 1998)—11 (March-April 1999).

Waldman, Carl. *Encyclopedia of Native American Tribes.* Rev. ed. Illustrated by Molly Brown. New York: Checkmark Books, 1999. 336 p.

Websites

Amazon, www.amazon.com

Wikipedia, the free encyclopedia, www.wikipedia.org

Author/Editor Index

Abrams, Lea, 687

Abramson, Jill, 665-666

Accorsi, William, 681

Ada, Alma Flor, 107, 228, 236

Adams, Colleen, 681

Addonia, Sulaiman, 505

Adelson, Bruce, 600

Adler, C. S., 527

Adler, David A., 452, 589-590, 675, 697

Adoff, Arnold, 32-33, 108, 181, 202, 205, 218, 391-392, 396, 648

Adoff, Jaime, 33-34, 72, 108, 165, 248

Agard, John, 6

Alder, Elizabeth, 109, 254, 564

Alderman, Bruce, 6, 434, 535, 574, 623, 633, 730

Aldridge, Rebecca, 627, 671

Alegre, Cèsar, 549, 559, 565, 599, 600, 612, 672, 689, 694, 697, 705, 709, 734

Allen, Paula Gunn, 564, 589, 598, 652, 691, 715-719

Allende, Isabel, 373-374

Alonso, Karen, 646-647

Alter, Judy, 615, 698

Altman, Susan, 548, 550, 553, 590, 597, 617, 722, 725, 735-736

Alvarez, Julia, 434-435, 540

Amado, Elisa, 109, 225, 386-387

Amdur, Melissa, 694

Amper, Thomas, 725

Amram, Fred M. B., 662

Anderson, Laurie Halse, 463

Anderson, Rachel, 510-511

Angel, Ann, 34, 109, 463, 527-528, 540

Aoki, Elaine M., 502, 522

Applegate, Stan, 109-110, 256

Armstrong, Jennifer, 627-628, 698

Arthur, Ruth M., 510

Atinsky, Steve, 536-537

Avery, Susan, 7, 549, 561, 584-585, 589, 598, 606, 639, 645-646, 652-653, 661, 679-680, 686-687, 691, 703, 706-707, 715, 717, 719-721, 730-731

Baldwin, Neil, 734-735

Title Index

Person Index

Subject Index